MOON BOOKS®

BAJA

© KAT KALAMARAS

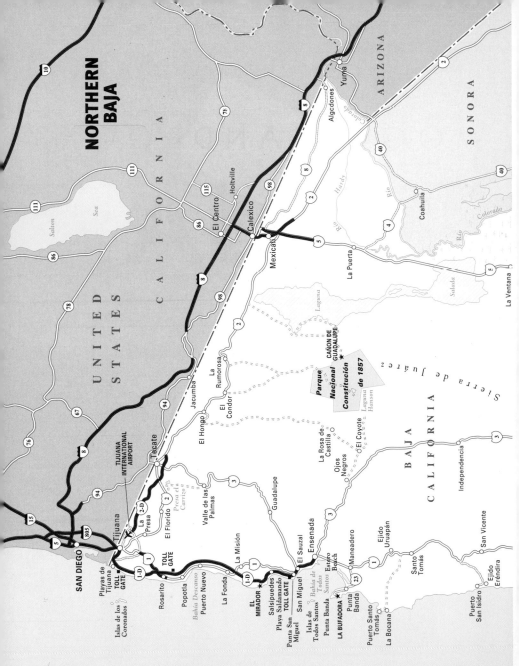

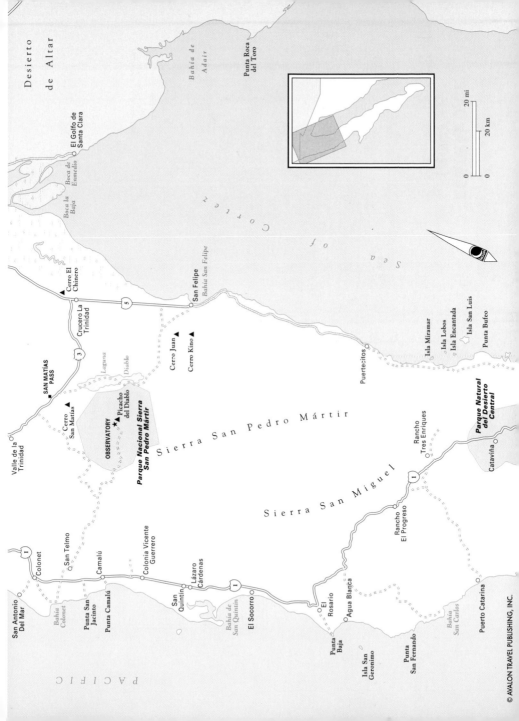

© AVALON TRAVEL PUBLISHING, INC.

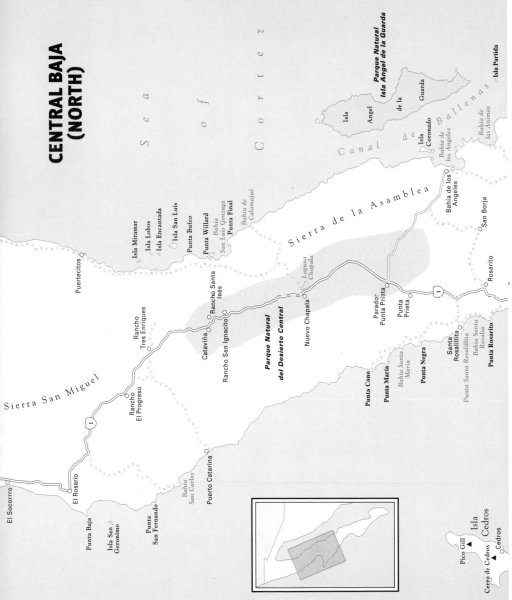

CENTRAL BAJA (NORTH)

S e a   o f   C o r t e z

Parque Natural
Isla Angel de la Guarda

Isla Partida

Isla
Angel
de la
Guarda

Isla
Coronado

Bahía de
las Ánimas

C a n a l   d e   B a l l e n a s

Bahía de
los Ángeles

Bahía de los
Ángeles

Sierra de la Asamblea

San Borja

Puertecitos

Isla Miramar
Isla Lobos
Isla Encantada
Isla San Luis
Punta Bufeo
Punta Willard
*Bahía
San Luis Gonzaga*
Punta Final

*Bahía de
Calamajué*

Rosarito

Laguna
Chapala

Parador
Punta Prieta

Punta
Prieta

Rancho
Tres Enriques

Rancho Santa
Inés

Cataviña

Rancho San Ignacito

*Parque Natural
del Desierto Central*

Nuevo Chapala

Santa
Rosalilita

*Bahía Santa
Rosalía*

Punta Rosarito

Sierra San Miguel

Rancho
El Progreso

Punta Cono

Punta María

*Bahía Santa
María*

Punta Negra

Punta Santa Rosalilita

El Socorro

El Rosario

Punta Baja

Isla San
Gerónimo

Punta
San Fernando

*Bahía
San Carlos*

Puerto Catarina

Pico Gill

Isla
Cedros

Cerro de Cedros   Cedros

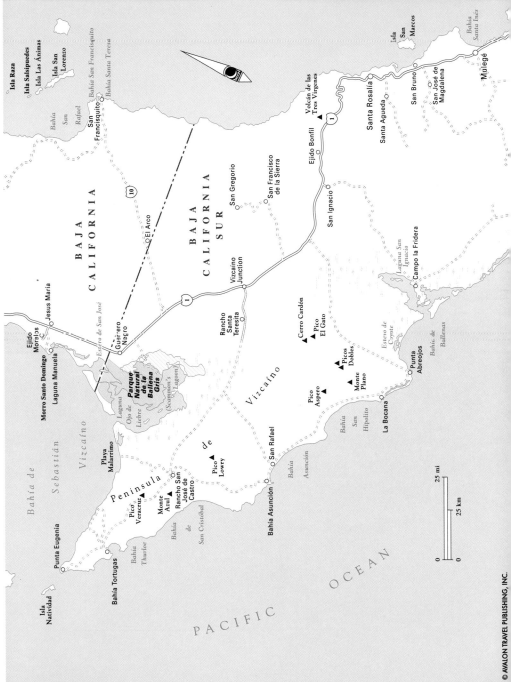

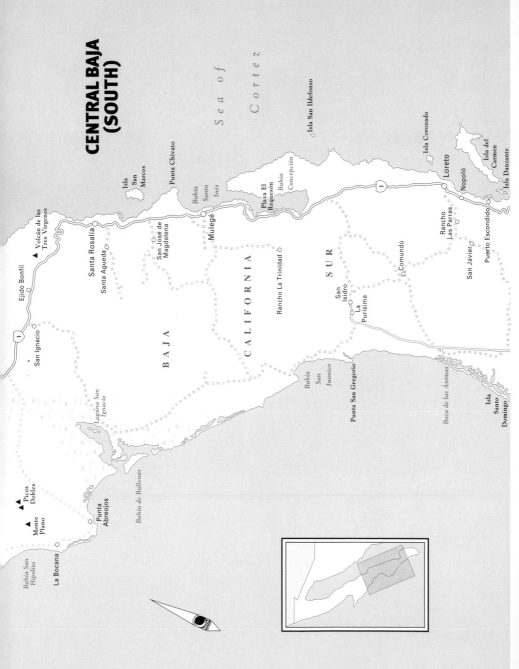

CENTRAL BAJA (SOUTH)

Sea of Cortez

Isla San Ildefonso

Isla Coronado

Loreto

Isla del Carmen

Nopoló

Isla Danzante

Punta Chivato

Isla San Marcos

Bahía Santa Inés

Playa El Requesón

Bahía Concepción

1

Santa Rosalía

San José de Magdalena

Mulegé

Rancho Las Parras

Santa Agueda

San Javier

Puerto Escondido

▲ Volcán de las Tres Vírgenes

Ejido Bonfil

Comundú

B A J A

C A L I F O R N I A

S U R

Rancho La Trinidad

San Ignacio

1

San Isidro

La Purísima

Laguna San Ignacio

Bahía San Juanico

Punta San Gregorio

Boca de las Ánimas

Isla Santo Domingo

▲ ▲ Picos Dobles

▲ Monte Plano

Punta Abreojos

Bahía de Ballenas

Bahía San Hipólito

La Bocana

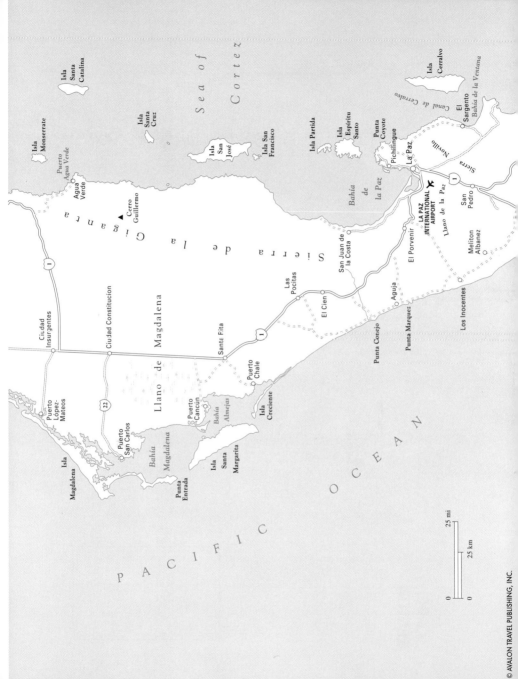

Sea of Cortez

Isla Santa Catalina

Isla Monserrate

Isla Santa Cruz

Isla Cerralvo

Bahía de la Ventana

Canal de Cerralvo

Puerto Agua Verde

Agua Verde

Cerro Guillermo

Isla San José

Isla San Francisco

Isla Partida

Isla Espíritu Santo

Punta Coyote

El Sargento

Sierra de la Giganta

Bahía de la Paz

Pichilingue

La Paz

Novillo

Sierra

San Juan de la Costa

El Porvenir

LA PAZ INTERNATIONAL AIRPORT

Llano de la Paz

San Pedro

Ciudad Insurgentes

Ciudad Constitucion

Llano de Magdalena

Santa Fita

Las Pocitas

El Cien

Aguja

Meliton Albañez

Los Inocentes

Puerto López-Mateos

Puerto Chale

Punta Conejo

Punta Marquez

Isla Magdalena

Puerto San Carlos

Puerto Cancun

Bahía Almejas

Bahía Magdalena

Isla Creciente

Isla Santa Margarita

Punta Entrada

PACIFIC OCEAN

25 mi

25 km

© AVALON TRAVEL PUBLISHING, INC.

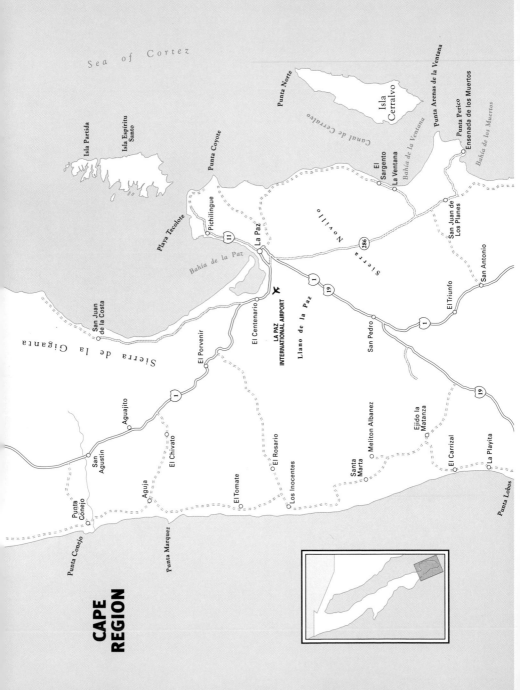

Sea of Cortez

Isla Cerralvo

Punta Norte

Canal de Cerralvo

Punta Arenas de la Ventana

Punta Perico
Ensenada de los Muertos

Bahía de la Ventana

Bahía de los Muertos

Isla Partida

Isla Espíritu Santo

El Sargento
La Ventana

San Juan de Los Planes

San Antonio

Punta Coyote

Playa Tecolote

Pichilingue

Sierra Novillo

286

El Triunfo

1

San Juan de la Costa

Bahía de la Paz

El Centenario

LA PAZ INTERNATIONAL AIRPORT

Llano de la Paz

1

19

San Pedro

El Porvenir

Sierra de la Giganta

1

San Agustín

Aguajito

El Chivato

El Rosario

Santa Marta

Meliton Albanez

Ejido la Matanza

19

El Carrizal

La Playita

Punta Conejo

Aguja

El Tomate

Los Inocentes

Punta Lobos

Punta Marquez

CAPE REGION

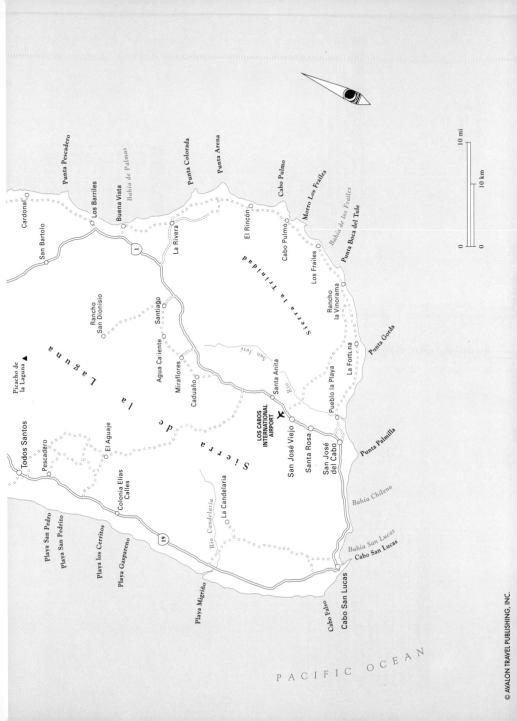

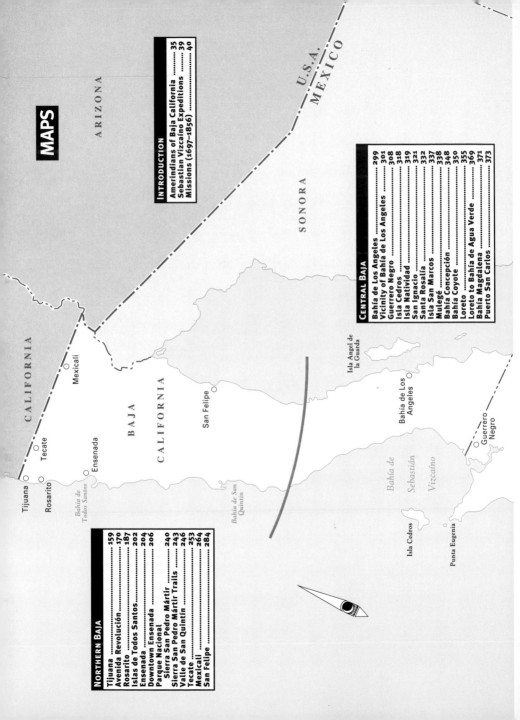

MAPS

ARIZONA

CALIFORNIA

U.S.A.

MEXICO

SONORA

BAJA CALIFORNIA

Tijuana

Rosarito

Tecate

Mexicali

Ensenada

Bahía de Todos Santos

Bahía de San Quintín

San Felipe

Isla Angel de la Guarda

Bahía de Los Angeles

Bahía de Sebastián Vizcaíno

Isla Cedros

Punta Eugenia

Guerrero Negro

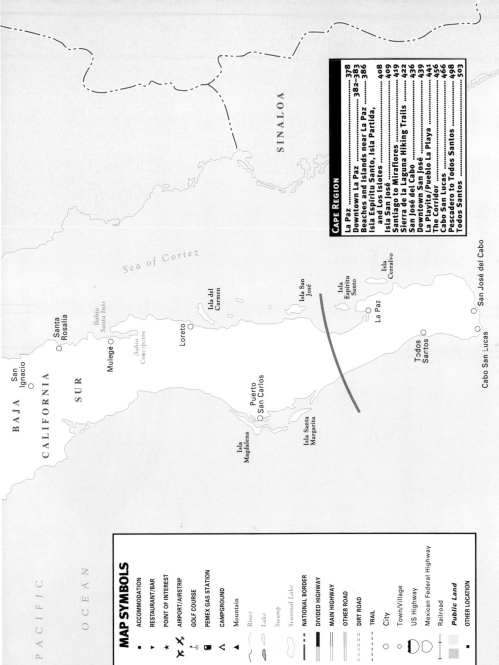

MAP SYMBOLS

- ● ACCOMMODATION
- ► RESTAURANT/BAR
- ★ POINT OF INTEREST
- ✈ AIRPORT/AIRSTRIP
- ⛳ GOLF COURSE
- ⛽ PEMEX GAS STATION
- ⛺ CAMPGROUND
- ▲ Mountain

River
Lake
Swamp
Seasonal Lake

- ▬▬ NATIONAL BORDER
- ▬▬ DIVIDED HIGHWAY
- ▬▬ MAIN HIGHWAY
- ═══ OTHER ROAD
- ▬▬▬ DIRT ROAD
- ----- TRAIL
- ○ City
- ○ Town/Village
- US Highway
- Mexican Federal Highway
- ┼ Railroad
- *Public Land*
- ■ OTHER LOCATION

© AVALON TRAVEL PUBLISHING, INC.

PACIFIC OCEAN

BAJA CALIFORNIA SUR

San Ignacio
Santa Rosalía
Bahía Santa Inés
Mulegé
Bahía Concepción
Loreto
Isla del Carmen
Puerto San Carlos
Isla Magdalena
Isla Santa Margarita

Sea of Cortez

SINALOA

Isla San José
Isla Espíritu Santo
Isla Cerralvo
La Paz
Todos Santos
San José del Cabo
Cabo San Lucas

MOON HANDBOOKS®

BAJA

SIXTH EDITION

JOE CUMMINGS

AVALON
TRAVEL

Contents

© KAT KALAMARAS

Introduction

Mexico's slender frontier peninsula is a blend of contrasts: parched deserts and lush groves of mangoes, shiny skyscrapers and shady cabanas, freshwater lagoons and saltwater bays, 12-dollar margaritas and 30-cent cervezas. Mix in sunny skies and friendly bajacalifornianos and you have all the ingredients for a perfect getaway.

On the Road

Whether you're snorkeling or sailing, shopping or dining, RVing or staying at a resort, understanding your options and surroundings is essential. From crossing the border to ordering fish tacos, here are all the details you'll need to set your trip in motion.

Northern Baja ... 158

The northern municipalities are infamous for their bustling border culture, robust nightlife, and never-ending string of beachfront hotels. Step beyond the tourist circuit and you'll discover some true gems: Tijuana's college-town ambience, Ensenada's renowned wineries, Bahía de San Quintín's empty beaches, Cañon de Guadalupe's turquoise-hued hot springs, and many more.

Central Baja ... 295

A landscape of towering cacti, jutting bays, palm oases, and temperate waters, central Baja attracts road warriors and outdoors enthusiasts. Take a whale-watching tour, hike in canyons dotted with ancient rock-art murals, kayak to deserted islands, sample fresh pescado—then return to your palapa to watch the sun set slowly at day's end.

Cape Region

*Cabo San Lucas is the epitome of resort luxury,
with upscale villas hemming sparkling waters.
The rest of the region promises more diverse
offerings: world-class fishing and scuba diving
in the bay of La Paz, gallery-hopping in Todos
Santos, pottery shopping in La Candelaria,
and picnicking in the arid-tropical meadows
of Sierra de la Laguna.*

ABOUT THE AUTHOR
Joe Cummings

Joe Cummings was born in New Orleans and raised in Texas, California, France, and Washington, D.C. A good portion of his childhood was spent in San Antonio, Texas, and a weekend family trip to Nuevo Laredo, Mexico, brought him face to face with his first *taco al carbon* in the 1960s. Following the smell of fresh corn tortillas southward, he made his first solo trip to Mexico in 1973 and has been stuck on the Tortilla Trail ever since.

Joe's affinity for Mexican border culture prompted him to take an epic road trip down Baja's Transpeninsular Highway in 1991 to research and write the first edition of *Moon Handbooks Baja,* followed a few years later by *Moon Handbooks Cabo.* Joe has traveled hundreds of thousands of miles in Mexico by burro, Volkswagen, and four-wheel-drive, and built a house near the beach in Baja's Cape Region.

In addition to writing Moon Handbooks to Baja, Cabo, Mexico, Mexico City, and Northern Mexico, Joe has penned numerous other guidebooks, phrasebooks, and atlases for countries around the world. As a restless freelance journalist, Joe also finds himself contributing to the likes of *Ambassador, Bangkok Post, BBC Holidays, Car & Travel, The Guardian, The Independent on Sunday, Los Angeles Times, The Nation, Outside Magazine, San Francisco Chronicle, South China Morning Post,* and the *Wall Street Journal* on occasion. He has twice received the Lowell Thomas Travel Journalism Gold Award, and twice been a finalist in London's Thomas Cook Guidebook of the Year awards. In 2001 the government of Mexico awarded him the *Pluma de Plata* (Silver Quill) for outstanding foreign journalism on Mexico.

The very air here is miraculous,
and outlines of reality change with the moment.

John Steinbeck,
The Log from the Sea of Cortez

Introduction

The first maps of Baja California, drawn by 16th-century Spanish explorers, depicted it not as a peninsula but as an island. Lured by tales of gold cities and a kingdom of warrior women, the conquistadors were among the first in a long line of seekers who have approached Baja's shores with a sense of mystery. Though the maps have long since been corrected, explorers continue to tramp the peninsula with dreams of finding Shangri-La in a hidden canyon or secluded cove.

Scattered along Baja's natural and artificial borders are outward concessions to the modern world—including Mexico's fifth-largest city—as well as sufficient recreational opportunities to

satisfy the most hedonistic refugees from that same world. This is one Baja: a peninsula wedged between one of the world's wealthiest and most technologically advanced countries and one struggling to develop with dignity.

But another Baja remains an island, in spite of 21st-century mapping. For four centuries, this Baja has stubbornly resisted the efforts of conquistadors, missionaries, miners, developers, and tourist boards to bring "civilization" into its rugged interior. The fortunate few who make it to the cultural and geographic heart of the peninsula will find it belongs to an era long ago lost to most of North America.

© KAT KALAMARAS

Between these seeming polar opposites the visitor can pick and choose from a broad spectrum of travel experiences. Whether it's stretching out on a beach towel, margarita in hand, at the edge of the Sea of Cortez, or hoisting a backpack and hiking deep into the sierras, whether it's perusing the art galleries of Todos Santos or wandering the neon-bathed bars of Tijuana, Baja offers something for just about every proclivity.

Standing physically and culturally apart from the rest of Mexico—the former territories achieved Mexican statehood only during the last half century—Baja California and Baja California Sur represent a side of the country largely unfamiliar to foreigners and mainland Mexicans alike. Often dubbed "the other Mexico," the thousand-kilometer peninsula is in some ways more sophisticated, and in other ways more untamed, than the mainland. If your mental picture of Mexico conjures up Aztec temple ruins and grand Spanish baroque cathedrals, you're in for a surprise—you won't find these anywhere in Baja. Most of the architecture visible today in Baja was created only within the last 200 years.

Bajacaliforniano culture likewise stands apart from that of mainland Mexico. Although the cuisine, regional literature, and social patterns of the peninsula share much in common with Mexico as a whole, the visitor will notice myriad small differences. Whether it's the way they fashion rustic furniture from *palo de arco* or the way they fillet halibut for a fish taco, *bajacalifornianos* are proud of the many ways in which they don't conform to the rest of Mexico.

Being the two least-populated states in Mexico, Baja California and Baja California Sur have largely escaped the relatively heavier pressures on the natural environment that occur in more densely populated regions of the mainland. Thus opportunities for the enjoyment of one's natural surroundings and for outdoor recreation are, by comparison, greatly enhanced. Baja tends to attract more of a physically active, nature- and sports-loving crowd than the mainland. Fishing, surfing, scuba diving, hiking, camping, birding,

whale-watching, and off-highway exploration top the list.

Cultural draws begin with historic Spanish missions—some little more than rustic adobe ruins, others fully restored and functioning as places of worship—strung out along the peninsula from top to bottom. The rare ochre-and-black cave paintings of Central Baja lead travelers yet further into the past. Reaching the caves via horse-and-burro caravans adds an element of adventure and heightened anticipation to such journeys.

Back in the present, Baja's magical desert light and sense of seclusion has attracted artists from all over the country and beyond. In Tijuana, Rosarito, Ensenada, La Paz, and Todos Santos in particular, you'll find a thriving arts scene. Even the most remote locations feature beer-can folk art.

Mexican food fanatics can lose themselves in Baja's unique culinary palette, ranging from the famous clam cocktails sold from humble carts along Baja's city streets to the Mexico City–style *alta cocina* menus of Tijuana and Cabo San Lucas. In yet another way in which Baja stands out from the rest of Mexico is in the fame of its wineries. While Mexico at large is identified with beer and tequila, Baja California has carved out a niche for itself in the highly competitive world of fine wines.

Although this "forgotten peninsula" every year gains more development and better facilities, much of it remains a true frontier with an attendant frontier ethos. If you run out of gas or need help fixing a tire, don't be surprised to find a seemingly impoverished fisherman or rancher coming to your aid and then politely refusing a fistful of pesos in return, declaring sincerely, "Out here we are all brothers."

The further and deeper you explore the peninsula, the farther you get from Baja's border cities and main highways, the closer you'll come to the "real" Baja of remote villages, fish camps, empty beaches, and rugged islands. We hope that, together with courtesy and common sense, this guide will go a long way toward getting you safely to wherever you want to go. Then, as many of us have found, the biggest danger is you may not want to come back.

The Land

BIRTH OF A PENINSULA

Baja California is the world's fourth-longest peninsula after the Kamchatka, Malay, and Antarctic, but its landmass wasn't always scissored from the rest of Mexico. At one time its entire length was attached to a broad tropical plain along Mexico's Pacific coast; about two-thirds of the area lay beneath the ocean. The 23-ton duck-billed hadrosaur roamed the region (its fossilized bones have been found near El Rosario), as did the mammoth, bison, hyracotherium (a small, primitive horse), and camel. The peninsula's eventual divergence from the mainland came about as a result of the continual shifting of massive sections of the earth's surface, a process known as plate tectonics.

Like much of coastal California to the north, Baja California is part of the North Pacific Plate, while the rest of the North American continent belongs to the North American Plate. The boundary line between these two plates is the San Andreas Fault, which extends northward through the center of Mexico's Sea of Cortez and into California, where it parallels the coast on a southeast-northwest axis before veering off into the Pacific Ocean near San Francisco. The North Pacific and North American Plates have shifted along this gap for millions of years, with the Pacific Plate moving in a northwesterly direction at a current rate of about 2–5 cm (1–2 inches) a year.

This movement eventually tore basins in the earth's crust that allowed the Sea of Cortez to form, thus separating the land area west of the fault zone from land to the east. At one time the Sea of Cortez extended as far north as Palm Springs, California; the sea would have continued moving northward at a gradual pace had it not met with the Colorado River. Silting in the Colorado River delta reversed the northward movement of the basins, holding the northern limit of the Sea of Cortez at a point well below what is now the United States–Mexico border. Cut off by delta sedimentation, California's Salton Sea is a remnant of the northernmost extension of the Sea of Cortez.

As the peninsula moved slowly northwestward (257 km from the mainland by the time the Sea of Cortez became a stable feature—about five million years ago), the coastal plains tipped toward the west, creating a series of fault-block mountain ranges that now form one of Baja California's most outstanding topographic features. Volcanism further contributed to the peninsular and island geography, as seen in the massive lava flows east of San Ignacio (where the Tres Vírgenes volcanoes erupted as recently as 1746), the basaltic geology south of Bahía de los Ángeles, the various cinder cones near San Quintín, and the volcanic islands of Isla Raza, Isla Guadalupe, and Isla San Luis. At Laguna de los Volcanes in northeastern Baja, boiling mud pits and steam vents are the most visible signs of recent volcanic activity.

A third topographical contributor, sedimentation, has created the salient features of Baja's larger valleys and southwestern coastal plains. Prehistoric Mexican rivers, cut off from their mainland sources upon the creation of the Sea of Cortez, deposited sediments west of Mexicali to form the vast Laguna Salada. The fertile Valle de Mexicali, like California's Imperial Valley, holds silt from the Colorado River—much of it composed of earth and rock once contained in the Grand Canyon. The low coastal plain that forms the western portion of the Vizcaíno Desert region features sedimentary deposits up to 16 km (10 miles) thick, a combination of sierra river deposits and material left over from the period 15 million years ago when this area lay beneath the Pacific Ocean.

GEOGRAPHY

Size and Area

Baja California extends 1,300 km (806 miles) from the United States–Mexico border to the peninsula's southernmost tip—a hundred miles longer than Italy and twice the length of Florida. If the coastline could be straightened,

MAJOR BAJA CALIFORNIA MOUNTAIN RANGES

Range	Highest Peak	Summit Elevation
Sierra de San Pedro Mártir	Picacho del Diablo	3,095 meters (10,154 feet)
Sierra de la Laguna	Picacho de la Laguna	2,161 meters (7,090 feet)
Sierra de San Francisco	Pico Santa Monica	2,104 meters (6,904 feet)
Sierra San Borja	Pico Echeverría	1,907 meters (6,258 feet)
Sierra Juárez	Cerro Torre Blanco	1,800 meters (5,904 feet)
Sierra de la Giganta	Cerro La Giganta	1,765 meters (5,792 feet)
Sierra de la Asamblea	Cerro Dos Picachos	1,658 meters (5,438 feet)
Sierra de Guadalupe	Monte Thetis	1,640 meters (5,380 feet)

it would span a distance equivalent to that between Tijuana and Juneau, Alaska. Its widest girth, measured across land only, is at the 193-km (120-mile) border. Measuring across land and water to include Bahía de Sebastián Vizcaíno, the widest point is about 230 km (143 miles), from Punta Eugenio on the west coast to Punta San Francisquito on the east. The peninsula reaches its narrowest point at a section 161 km (100 miles) above the southern tip, where it's only 45 km (28 miles) between the Pacific Ocean and Bahía de la Paz.

The total land area of the states of Baja California (or Baja California Norte) and Baja California Sur is about 144,000 square km (55,600 square miles)—add another 2,460 square km (950 square miles) for the dozens of islands and islets nearby. The coastline created by the Pacific Ocean, the Sea of Cortez, and the dozens of bays, lagoons, coves, and inlets totals about 4,800 shore km (3,000 miles).

Mountain Ranges

Baja's most striking geographical feature is the spine of mountain ranges, or sierras, that run down its center from northwest to southeast. For the most part, Baja's sierras are a continuation of a mountain system that stretches southward from Alaska's Aleutian Islands to the spectacular rock formations at Cabo San Lucas. The peninsula holds 23 named ranges in all; most are of fault-block origin, but a scattered few are volcanic.

Because of the way the underground fault

blocks tipped to create these sierras, the mountains tend to slope gradually toward the west and fall off dramatically toward the east (the Cape Region's Sierra de la Laguna is the one major exception). Like California's Sierra Nevada, Baja's high sierras typically feature granitic peaks topped by conifer forests. The eastern escarpment, facing the Sea of Cortez, is dissected by stream-eroded canyons and usually dry arroyos.

Baja's four most substantial mountain ranges are the **Sierra Juárez** and **Sierra de San Pedro Mártir** in the north, the volcanic **Sierra de la Giganta** in the upper south, and the **Sierra de la Laguna** in the center of the southern Cape. Baja's highest peak, **Picacho del Diablo** (3,095 meters/10,154 feet), lies in the Sierra de San Pedro Mártir; during the winter its snowcapped peak can be seen from the Mexican mainland 225 km (140 miles) away.

Deserts

About 65 percent of Baja California's total land area can be classified as desert; these portions receive an average of less than 25 cm (10 inches) of rain per year. From a botanical perspective, Baja's desert lands belong to the Sonoran Desert, which extends across northwestern Mexico into parts of southeastern California and southern Arizona. However, Baja's portion supports so many endemic plant species that it probably deserves a classification all its own.

Any visitor who has previously traveled in the Sonoran Desert areas of Northern Mexico, southeastern California, or southern Arizona will note many subtle differences in Baja. Because of the peninsula's numerous sierras and its location between two large bodies of water, aridity varies considerably along the peninsula. As a result, Baja's deserts can be divided into four subregions, each distinguished by its own unique geography and dominant flora.

San Felipe Desert: This southwestern extension of California's Colorado Desert is wedged between the eastern escarpment of the northern sierras and the coastal plains of the Sea of Cortez. The peninsula's driest desert, it averages only five cm (two inches) of rainfall a year. Most of the topography is a mixture of salt flats, rocky plains, sand dunes, arroyos, and extinct volcanic craters.

The Valle de Mexicali is part of the San Felipe Desert, but it is made productive by an irrigation system fed by the Colorado River. The large Isla Ángel de la Guarda and nearby islands also belong to this region. The dominant plant species throughout the sparsely vegetated area are bursage (*huizapol*) and creosote bush (*hediondilla*), along with a variety of succulents and hardy trees.

Gulf Coast Desert: This narrow subregion stretches along the Sea of Cortez from just below Bahía de los Ángeles to the tip of the peninsula near San José del Cabo. On average, the elevation is substantially higher here (with peaks up to 1,500 meters) than in the San Felipe Desert to the north, and the terrain is marked by several broken sierras of granitic and volcanic rock. These sierras contain numerous arroyos and a few perennial streams that allow for pockets of subsistence farming. The underground stream at Mulegé supports intensive cultivation in the surrounding valley.

The southern reaches of the Gulf Coast Desert receive a bit of extra precipitation from the occasional tropical storm that blows in from the south. As a result of the added moisture and elevation, many more trees and flowering cacti are found here than in the San Felipe Desert, including *torote,* palo blanco, paloverde, *palo adán,* and *palo de arco.* Sea of Cortez islands to the east feature similar terrain, although the endemic vegetation varies from island to island.

Vizcaíno Desert: After a worldwide search for the perfect desert habitat, the designers of **Biosphere II,** an ecological research laboratory in Arizona, modeled their dome's desert biome on the Vizcaíno Desert. Baja's largest desert area, this subregion lies along the Pacific coast from a point just north of El Rosario to the Magdalena Plains some 1,000 km (600 miles) south. Its eastern boundary is the eastern escarpment of the central sierras. This positioning places it just out of reach of the northwestern rains, so important to coastal California and northwestern Baja, as well as the southern tropical storms that bring water to the Cape Region and lower Gulf Coast Desert. In 1988 a large portion of the Vizcaíno Desert was declared a Biosphere Reserve under the United Nations' Man and the Biosphere program.

In spite of the lack of measurable precipitation, desert plants proliferate here. The entire region is sparsely populated because of the lack of dependable water sources, but the desert vegetation, especially yucca, thrives on night and morning fog from the Pacific Ocean. The whimsical-looking *cirio* (called "boojum tree" by many Californians) is another dominant succulent in the Vizcaíno Desert; toward the Pacific coast it's often draped with ball moss. Other common species here include agave, mesquite, cholla, prickly pear, and *pitahaya.*

The major coastal feature in this subregion is Laguna Ojo de Liebre, also called Scammon's Lagoon, one of several bays favored by wintering gray whales. The most substantial inland water source is the Río San Ignacio, which flows westward from a large date palm oasis in the heart of the peninsula into the open desert near the coast.

Magdalena Plains (Llano Magdalena): Beginning below the Vizcaíno Desert and bounded by the Pacific coast on the west and by the central and southern sierras on the east, the Magdalena Plains extend southward until they come to an abrupt halt at the northwestern escarpment of the Sierra de la Laguna. The main feature of the Pacific side is Bahía Magdalena, Baja's largest bay, which is sheltered by the huge, L-shaped Isla Magdalena to the northwest and the equally large Isla Santa Margarita to the southwest. The Canal

Gaviota connects Bahía Magdalena with Bahía Almejas to the immediate south. Other saltwater bays and lagoons along the Pacific coast include Bahía de Ballenas and Laguna San Ignacio; all are used as calving areas by migrating whales.

Other coastal features include mangrove swamps, dunes, and small sandbar islands. The only inland waterway of note is the Río La Purísima, which drops westward from the Sierra de la Giganta to Punta San Gregorio on the Pacific coast. Large underground aquifers in the vicinity of Ciudad Constitución support intensive area agriculture. The aquifer is becoming increasingly saline, however, as fresh water is pumped out faster than it's replenished. Arroyos on the west side of the Sierra de la Giganta supply water to the area when rainfall is sufficient.

Cactus varieties are abundant throughout the Magdalena Plains. Stands of date palm, paloverde, *torote,* mesquite, and palo blanco line the riverine corridors and upland arroyos.

The Vizcaíno Desert and the Magdalena Plains are sometimes referred to as one entity, the **Central Desert.**

Californian Region

Most of northwestern Baja California features the same topography, climate, and ecosystems as southwestern California. These conditions extend almost as far south as El Rosario, near the Pacific coast, and eastward to the eastern escarpment of the Sierra Juárez and Sierra de San Pedro Mártir. Within this region are four subregions, for the most part defined by changes in elevation from the coast to the highest mountain peaks in the center of the peninsula.

Conifer Forests: This subregion begins at an elevation of about 1,500 meters (5,000 feet) in the Sierra Juárez and from about 2,400 meters (8,000 feet) in the Sierra de San Pedro Mártir. The granitic substrata of these fault-block mountains becomes more apparent the higher you go, as rocky ledges poke through soil and sediment accumulated over the eons. Abundant precipitation supports lush forests and meadows along the flats, ridges, and plateaus of both ranges. In winter, snow is the most common source of moisture in the higher elevations; peaks are often snowcapped.

Dominant trees in the Sierra Juárez include the canyon live oak, juniper, piñon pine, and Jeffrey pine. The forests of the Sierra de San Pedro Mártir also feature incense cedar, white fir, and sugar pine, and at least three tree types not found in either the Sierra Juárez or San Diego County, California: quaking aspen, lodgepole pine, and the endemic San Pedro Mártir cypress. Along the streams and meadows at slightly lower elevations are manzanita, Indian paintbrush, hedgehog cactus, snowberry, and other flowering plants.

Pine-Juniper-Oak Woodlands: On the intermediate slopes of the two sierras, at elevations of about 900–1,500 meters (3,000–5,000 feet), are stands of pine, oak, and juniper. The lower southern reaches of the Sierra de San Pedro Mártir offer a Darwinian salad of conifer, chaparral, and desert species, mixing pines and juniper with blue fan palm, Mojave yucca, palmita, sagebrush, sand verbena, and barrel cactus.

Chaparral: At just below 900 meters on either side of the mountain ranges, the woodlands give way to chaparral, a dense shrub community that supports sagebrush, scrub oak, wild lilac, manzanita, coast live oak, chaparral ash, and other hardy species with deep-branching root systems. Interspersed with the chaparral are boulders of varying size; some of the larger are used as billboards by *bajacalifornianos,* who paint them with political slogans, declarations of love, and religious messages.

Palm Canyons: These lie at chaparral elevation on the eastern slopes, but because of abundant water year-round they feature unique terrain. Eroded by mountain streams that terminate in the San Felipe Desert, these canyons and steep-walled arroyos shelter picturesque groves of California fan palm and endemic blue fan palm. Volcanic activity on the peninsula's eastern side has resulted in underground geothermal reservoirs; hot springs are found in some of the canyons.

Coastal Sage Scrub: On the Sea of Cortez side of the northern mountain ranges, the chaparral subregion gives way to the arid San Felipe Desert. On the Pacific side, chaparral fades into the rolling hills of the coastal plains. The terrain is rocky, with a blend of chaparral vegetation and the low-lying shrubs that dominate the coastal sage-scrub biome. Common species include chamiso, barrel cactus, agave, ash, cholla, flat-top buckwheat, hedgehog cactus, jimsonweed, margarita, buckeye, jojoba, saltbush, and a variety of grasses.

Cape Region

In many ways, Baja California's Cape Region has the most distinctive geography on the peninsula. The Sierra de la Laguna, in the center of the Cape, runs north to south rather than northwest to southeast. And unlike other ranges in the southern half of the peninsula, it's granitic rather than volcanic. Yet in contrast to the granitic, fault-block ranges of northern Baja, it tips eastward so that its steepest slopes face west. It's also more lushly vegetated than the northern sierras. Arroyos on the eastern slopes of the Sierra de la Laguna are filled with water much of the year, enabling this area to support fruit and vegetable farming.

The entire region receives substantially more rainfall than any other part of Baja, save the Californian Region in the northwest. Most of the rain falls in the highland areas, however, leaving the coastal lowlands fairly dry for beachgoing tourists. About a fourth of the Cape Region falls below the Tropic of Cancer; the combination of dry coastal areas, moist uplands, and tropical latitudes has created two unique subregions.

Cape Oak–Piñon Woodlands: The Sierra de la Laguna has been called an "island in the sky" because of its remarkable isolation from the Central Desert to the north and the Gulf Coast Desert to the east. The peaks receive up to 100 cm (40 inches) of annual rainfall; extensive stands of Mexican piñon pine, *madroño,* and *palmita* grow at higher elevations. Oaks are also found on the higher slopes of the Sierra de la Giganta to the north, which also falls within the Cape Region.

Cape Arid Tropical Forest: The coastal areas of the Cape Region as well as the lower slopes of the region's sierras share characteristics typical of both tropical and arid biomes, hence the seemingly oxymoronic term "arid tropical forest." Like tropical forests worldwide, the lower Cape forests hold trees, shrubs, and undergrowth of varying heights that create a canopied effect. Mixed with this tangled growth is a profusion of succulents more associated with arid climes, including the *cardón-barbón,* a shorter cousin of the towering *cardón* found throughout Baja's deserts.

Much of the vegetation in the Cape Arid Tropical Forest is normally associated with the tropical thornforests of coastal Colima and Guerrero on the Mexican mainland. Prominent marker plants unique to the Cape subregion include the native Tlaco palm, wild fig *(zalate), mauto,* and the alleged aphrodisiac herb damiana.

Coastal Wetlands Region

Wetland pockets exist in numerous spots along the peninsular coast; they lie in shallow areas along bays and lagoons and aren't limited to any particular longitude or latitude. In Baja, these wetlands usually consist of saltmarshes (which contain high concentrations of salt-tolerant plants such as cordgrass, eelgrass, saltwort, and salt cedar) or mangrove *(mangle)* communities containing one or more of the five species common in Baja—black mangrove, white mangrove, red mangrove, buttonwood mangrove, and sweet mangrove. Within any given wetland, salinity, temperature, and wetness can vary considerably;

red mangrove

BOB RACE

BAJA ISLAND-HOPPING

Visitors intent on setting foot on the delicate islands of the Sea of Cortez should heed the recommendations proffered by Conservation International Mexico, as follows:

- Check your equipment and provisions thoroughly before landing to avoid the introduction of rats, mice, insects, or seeds from other islands or from the mainland. Check your shoes and cuffs.
- Don't bring cats, dogs, or any other animals to the islands.
- Don't take plants, flowers, shells, rocks, or animals from the island.
- The animals and plants that live on the islands are not used to human presence. Keep this in mind during your visit.
- Keep a minimum distance of 45 meters (150 feet) from all sea bird and sea lion colonies, and keep at least 300 meters (1,000 feet) away from pelicans during their nesting period (April–May).
- Don't cut cacti or shrubs. Don't gather wood; plants take a long time to grow on these arid islands. Dry trunks are the home of many small animals. If you need to cook, take your own stove, and avoid making fires.
- Don't make new walking paths. Don't remove stones or dig holes; you will cause erosion.

- Human waste and toilet paper take a long time to decompose on the islands. Go to the bathroom in the water and burn your toilet paper very carefully, or use smooth stones . . . be creative.
- Don't camp on the island unless you are familiar with low-impact techniques. Conservation International Mexico can provide you with that information.
- Help keep the islands clean. Don't throw or leave garbage on the islands or in the sea. Help even more by bringing back any garbage you find.
- To camp or even land for any activity on the islands of the Sea of Cortez you need a permit from the Secretaria de Medio Ambiente y Recursos Naturales (SEMARNAT). To obtain a permit, contact Instituto Nacional de Ecología, Dirección de Aprovechamiento Ecológico, Periférico 5000, Col. Insurgentes Cuicuilco, C.P. 04530, Delegación Coyoacán México D.F. 01049, México, www.ine.gob.mx.

For more information, contact Conservation International Mexico, Calle Miramar 59-A, Col. Miramar, Guaymas, Son. 85450, México, tel. 622/221-0194, fax 622/221-2030, ci-guaymas@conservation.org, www.ci-mexico.org.mx.

hence, an extensive variety of plants and animals can adapt to wetland areas. Because of this environmental variation, saltmarshes and mangrove wetlands support the highest biomass concentrations on the planet. For most visitors, the main attraction of the wetlands is the abundance of waterfowl.

Areas with substantial wetlands include Bahía San Quintín (saltmarshes), Laguna Ojo de Liebre (saltwater estuarine marshes), Laguna San Ignacio (saltmarshes, mangrove forests), Bahía Magdalena (saltmarshes, mangrove forests), Bahía de la Paz (mangrove forests), Río Mulegé (mixed saltwater/freshwater estuarine marshes), Estero San Bruno (mangrove forests), Bahía de los Ángeles (saltmarshes, some mangrove), and Bahía San Luis Gonzaga (saltmarshes).

Islands

More than a hundred islands and islets surround the Baja peninsula, with the great preponderance on the Sea of Cortez side. Accounting for over half of Mexico's island territory, the Sea of Cortez islands comprise one of the most ecologically intact archipelagos in the world. Many of the them were created as the peninsula broke away from mainland Mexico and hence are "land-bridge" or "continental" islands rather than true oceanic islands. Because of their low elevation, these islands don't snag much of the rain that moves up from the south in summer. As a result, they're arid, although the larger islands harbor a number of endemic plant and animal species. Among the largest of these islands are Isla Ángel de la Guarda, Isla Espíritu Santo, and

Isla Cerralvo. The smaller Isla San Luis and Isla Raza are of volcanic origin. Isla Raza is one of the most important bird rookeries in Mexico and has been a national reserve since 1964.

On the Pacific side, Baja's islands tend to feature semimoist Californian Region climates on their northwestern (windward) shores and desert conditions on their southeastern (leeward) shores. Isla Guadalupe, about 250 km (155 miles) west of the Pacific coast, is one of the few islands of volcanic (therefore, oceanic) origin. It's rarely visited by cruising boats because of its steep (up to 450 meters) shores but is an important habitat for the endemic Guadalupe fur seal and northern elephant seal, as well as various species of endemic pine, cypress, and palm.

Other Pacific islands of note are the Islas de Todos Santos, just 16 km (10 miles) southwest of Ensenada. These twin isles are well known among surfers for having the highest surf—up to nine meters (30 feet) high in winter—on the entire North American west coast. The state of Baja California has five inhabited islands, while Baja California Sur counts six. The most populated are Isla San Marcos in the Sea of Cortez—where gypsum mining and fishing support a population of around 590—and Isla Cedros, north of the Vizcaíno Peninsula in the Pacific, where a transshipment port for salt from the huge Guerrero evaporative saltworks employs many of the island's nearly 3,000 inhabitants.

THE SEA OF CORTEZ

The Sea of Cortez was apparently named by Spanish sea captain Francisco de Ulloa after he sailed the entire perimeter of this body of water in 1539 and 1540 at the command of the most famous of all Spanish conquistadors, Hernán Cortés. Four years previously Cortés had himself sailed the sea in an aborted attempt to colonize the peninsula. The name Mar de Cortés henceforth appeared intermittently on maps of the region, alternating with Mar Vermejo (Vermillion Sea, in reference to the color reflected from huge numbers of pelagic crabs) until the Mexican government officially renamed it the Gulf of California (Golfo de California) early in the 20th century. Sailors, writers, and other assorted romantics, however, have continued to call it by its older name.

The sea is roughly 1,125 km (700 miles) long, with an average width of 150 km (93 miles). Oceanographers have divided it into four regions based on the prominent characteristics—depth, bottom contours, and marine productivity—of each zone. The northern quarter of the gulf, between the Colorado River delta and the Midriff Islands, is shallow in relation to the zones farther south because of silt deposited by the Colorado River. The silt has also rounded the bottom contours. The tidal range in this zone is up to 10 vertical meters (33 vertical feet), and the seawater is highly saline due to evaporation. Before the damming of the Colorado River, the bore created when the seaward river currents met the incoming tide was powerful enough to sink ships.

The next zone farther south encompasses the Midriff Islands, where basins reach depths of 820 meters (2,700 feet) and strong currents bring nutrients up from the bottom while aerating the water. This leads to an unusually high level of biological productivity, otherwise known as "good fishin'."

From the Midriff Islands to La Paz, basin depth doubles, silting is minimal, and water temperatures begin decreasing dramatically.

The final sea zone below La Paz is oceanic, with trenches and submarine canyons over 3,650 meters (12,000 feet) deep. Around the tip of the Cape, the Sea of Cortez meets the Pacific Ocean and their respective currents battle, producing some wicked riptides. This means that although the tip of the Cape is the warmest area on the peninsula during the winter months, beach swimming can be treacherous.

Of the 25 named islands in the Sea of Cortez, the largest is Isla Tiburón (Shark Island), a geological remnant of the mainland with an area of around 1,000 square km (386 square miles). Because of their isolation, the Cortez islands feature a high number of endemic natural species; at least half of the 120 cactus varieties found on the islands are endemic.

The Sea of Cortez is biologically the richest body of water on the planet, supporting over

900 species of marine vertebrates and over 2,000 invertebrates at last count. The reported number rises with the publication of each new marine study. Scripps Institution of Oceanography in San Diego, California, has pronounced the Cortez "one of the most productive and diverse marine nurseries on Earth," while at the same time recognizing that greedy commercial interests may be devastating the natural balance in the Cortez through overfishing.

Climate

In satellite photographs of the North American continent snapped a hundred miles above the earth, Baja California invariably jumps off the plate. The rest of the continent north and east may be obscured by whorls of clouds while the shores, plains, and mountains of Baja are carved into the photographic image, remarkably clear. According to truth-in-travel magazine *Condé Nast Traveler,* Baja California is the best dollar value per hour of sunshine for any North American area west of Denver; the chances of a day without rain in the winter are 95 percent in Baja, beating out Hawaii's 84 percent and Florida's 87 percent.

How does Baja California get so much sunshine? The simple answer is that it's almost out of reach of the major weather systems that influence climate in western North America. Northwesterly storms from Eurasia and the Arctic bring rain and snow to the American Northwest and Midwest all winter long, while tropical storms roll across the South Pacific from Asia, dumping loads of rainfall along the lower Mexican coast and Central America in summer.

Baja is only slightly affected by the outer edges of these systems. Anchored between the warm, fish-filled waters of the Sea of Cortez and the heaving Pacific Ocean, bisected by plains and cordilleras, the peninsula's isolated ecosystems range in climate from Mediterranean to desert to tropical. In some areas, overlapping microclimates defy classification, combining elements of semiarid, arid, subtropical, and tropical climes.

HOT AND COLD

Three variables influence temperatures at any given Baja California location: elevation, latitude, and longitude. In plain talk, that means the higher you climb, the cooler it gets; the farther south you go, the warmer it gets; and it's usually cooler on the Pacific side of the peninsula and warmer on the Sea of Cortez side.

Pacific Coast

Because of prevailing ocean currents, the Pacific coast shows the least overall variation in temperature, staying relatively cool year-round. From March to July, the California Current flows southward along the coast, bringing cooler temperatures from the north that moderate seasonal atmospheric warming, while in December and January the coast is warmed by the northward movement of the Davidson Current. These seasonal currents stabilize the air temperatures so that Ensenada, for example, averages 12°C (54°F) in January and 20°C (68°F) in August, a range of only 8°C (14°F). Along much of the central Pacific coast during the summer, the cool air brought by the California Current meets warm air from the interior of the peninsula, resulting in fog masses that can sweep as far inland as 32 km (20 miles).

In winter, the southern Pacific coast from Bahía Magdalena to Cabo San Lucas usually enjoys the warmest temperatures of any coastal region on the peninsula because of its relative protection from cool northern winds.

Sea of Cortez

The Sea of Cortez has its own set of currents—sometimes lumped together as the Gulf Current—that are fed by tropical waters of the South Pacific. The waters travel counterclockwise north along the mainland's upper Pacific coast and then south along the peninsular coast. As a result, the Sea of Cortez enjoys an average annual surface temperature of 24°C (75°F), significantly warmer than the Pacific's 18°C (64°F). The high rate of evaporation at the north end of the sea also contributes to warmer air temperatures; this combination of warm air and water temperatures means the Sea of Cortez can be classified as tropical over its entire length.

Temperature differences between winter and summer, however, are more extreme than along the Pacific coast. The weather along the Cortez coast is mild and sunny all winter long with average January temperatures ranging from 13°C (55°F) in San Felipe to 18°C (64°F) in Loreto. Summer temperatures leap up the thermometer. In August, average temperatures are 28°C (82°F) in San Felipe and 31°C (88°F) in Loreto, although daily high figures in the summer, at either locale, can easily reach 38°C (100°F) or more. La Paz is usually warmer than San Felipe but cooler than Loreto.

Winters on the Sea of Cortez coast can be cooler than you might suspect, due to the coastline's relatively open exposure to northeastern winds. In Mulegé and Loreto, for example, it's not unusual for nighttime temperatures in January and February to drop as low as 14°C (57°F). At the same time, the Pacific coastline directly opposite may be as much as 5°C (10°F) warmer, especially along the southern Pacific coast. Cabo San Lucas has the warmest overall winter temperatures of any coastal location in Baja.

Chubascos, Coromuels, Cordonazos

Monthly average wind velocities for Baja California as a whole are moderate. From mid-May to mid-November, however, tropical storms from the south or east, known as *chubascos,* can bring high winds and rain to the coasts of the Cape Region. Although they usually blow over quickly, local mythology has it that if a *chubasco* lasts more than three hours, it will last a day; if it lasts more than a day, it will last three days; and if more than three days, it'll be a five-day blow.

Occasionally these storms escalate into hurricanes, which are much less frequent here than in the Gulf of Mexico and the Caribbean. In 1997 two such storms passed near the west coast of Baja, neither doing much damage (that same year the Gulf of Mexico saw around a dozen hurricanes), and in 2001 a hurricane hit the Cape,

causing some flood damage. Back in 1993 a *chubasco* caused major damage and loss of life along the Sea of Cortez coast between Cabo San Lucas and San José del Cabo (the area of the Cape Region most exposed to tropical storms).

Another Sea of Cortez weather pattern is the *cordonazo,* a small but fierce summer storm that originates locally and is usually spent within a few hours. A more welcome weather phenomenon is the *coromuel* of Bahía de la Paz, a stiff afternoon breeze that blows from offshore during the hot summer and early fall months. This wind was named for English Lord Protector Oliver Cromwell, identified with English pirates who took advantage of the wind's regular occurrence for the plunder of ships trapped in the bay.

WET AND DRY

The Land of Little Rain, as Baja has been called, isn't unique in its aridity, since most of the earth's desert areas are found between 15° and 30° latitude either north or south of the equator; Baja is positioned roughly between 23° N and 31° N. Global convection currents in the atmosphere create a more or less permanent high-pressure shield over these zones, insulating them from the low-pressure fronts that bring rain clouds.

Only about two-thirds of Baja California can be classified as true desert (less than 25 cm—10 inches—of annual precipitation), and even the driest areas receive occasional rain. In the peninsula's Central Desert this may be as little as 2.5 cm (one inch) a year, while in the interior of the Cape Region's Sierra de la Laguna annual rainfall may approach 100 cm (40 inches). Since mountain peaks trap rain clouds, Baja's higher elevations invariably receive more rain than the low-lying coastal zones.

Variation in rainfall also occurs on a seasonal basis. For the northwestern peninsula, the wettest months are December–April (with about 7.5 cm—three inches—per month in Ensenada, more in the mountains), while in the Cape Region rain usually arrives August–November (an average of 5.8 cm, or 2.3 inches, in September for Cabo San Lucas and La Paz). The central peninsula, including both coasts, is relatively dry all year long, receiving only brief spurts of rain from the north in the winter or from the south in the late summer and early fall.

The driest coastal area in all of Baja lies along the northwestern shores of the Sea of Cortez. San Felipe records an average annual precipitation of only five cm, with no measurable rainfall most months. At the other extreme, the peaks of the Sierra de San Pedro Mártir are often covered with a one-meter snowpack during the winter.

TRAVEL SEASONS

Northwestern Baja

The area encompassing Tijuana, Tecate, Rosarito, and Ensenada lies within the Californian Region and is affected by the mild Pacific climate. Hence it's fairly comfortable year-round, very much like California's San Diego County. Although rain is almost never heavy or frequent, even in the winter months, you can usually avoid all rain by planning visits for anytime from May to October. The beaches between Rosarito and Ensenada are warmest July–September, when they're most visited by southern Californians. To get away from the crowds and enjoy low-season prices, visit between October and April. December to February can be a bit chilly and cloudy, so if maximum sunshine is your objective, head farther south.

High Sierras

For those who like to travel light, the summer months are best for mountain hiking; even in July everything above 1,500 meters (5,000 feet) will feel like spring. From mid-October to mid-April, come prepared for winter camping for hikes at similar elevations.

To appreciate the beauty of spring flowers, the best hiking season is just after the end of the rainy seasons. For the northern ranges, i.e., Sierra Juárez and San Pedro Mártir, this means April and May. For the Sierra de la Laguna in the Cape Region, October or early November is best. The Cape's rainy season occurs from late summer to early fall.

> *Although rain is almost never heavy or frequent, even in the winter months, you can usually avoid all rain by planning visits from May to October.*

Deserts

Inland desert explorations should be absolutely avoided May–October, when daytime temperatures are fierce. The remaining cooler months are usually fine, although in the Central Desert, January daytime temperatures may be a bit on the cool side in areas exposed to high coastal winds or at higher elevations. The San Felipe and Gulf Coast Deserts are usually warm and comfortable throughout the winter. Keep in mind, however, that desert nights can be cold at any time of year.

Sea of Cortez Coast

Along Baja's Sea of Cortez coast, temperatures are moderate October through mid-June. High tourist season is November–March, even though for most people the north coast is too cool for swimming during these months. Days and nights grow progressively warmer as you move south, so that water sports are enjoyable from Loreto down, even in the winter.

From mid-June through September, the entire coast can be uncomfortably hot; the fishing, however, is usually very good during these months, and out on the sea it's usually breezy. But if you don't fish, forget it. One of the best times to visit the Sea of Cortez coast is April to mid-June, when the weather is balmy and few tourists are about.

Cape Region

The flat end of the peninsula from San José del Cabo to Cabo San Lucas is warm year-round. Pacific influences generally moderate the heat July–September, while the tropic waters of the Gulf Current make this stretch the warmest coastal zone on the peninsula during winter months. Except for the occasional *chubasco* in late summer, the climate seems darn near perfect here, which is why "Los Cabos" has become such a popular vacation destination. Cabo San Lucas receives about 45 percent of its measurable annual rainfall—a total of 15–18 cm (6–7 inches) a year—in September, so if there's a month to avoid for weather reasons, that's the one.

August and September may also be uncomfortably warm for visitors from northern California, the northwestern United States, or Canada, though for many U.S. residents it's no worse than summers back home. Todos Santos over on the West Cape's Pacific coastline is considerably cooler than Cabo San Lucas in the summer, and Cabo San Lucas is usually cooler than San José del Cabo or La Paz.

The two months when you're least likely to have Los Cabos beaches to yourself are December and January, when large numbers of North Americans come here seeking respite from rainstorms and blizzards.

Flora

A thorough examination of all the plants and creatures of interest in Baja California would take volumes. The following sections cover only a few of either the most remarkable or most common forms of Baja plant life. The complex interconnecting ecosystems of the peninsula and its islands hold a high number of unique species and remain relatively unexplored by biologists. Several botanists, marine biologists, zoologists, and paleontologists have undertaken solo research in the area, but only in the last five years has the first interdisciplinary team, sponsored by a Canadian university, begun studying the region.

In many ways, these researchers are heir to the Spanish fortune-seeker tradition of nearly five centuries ago. As George Lindsay, director of the California Academy of Sciences, has said, "For the scientist, Baja California is a treasure chest, just barely opened." Botanists estimate that over 4,000 varieties of plants make Baja California their home. The most complete reference available on Baja vegetation, Dr. Ira L. Wiggins's *Flora of Baja California,* lists 2,958 species among 155 families and 884 genera. Another good source of information is Norman C. Roberts's *Baja California Plant Field Guide,* which covers over 550 notable species and provides excellent photos of about half of these.

CACTI

Many visitors find the desert plants of Baja the most exciting simply because they're often the most exotic-appearing forms of life in the region. Like Alice in *Through the Looking Glass,* they find that the farther they travel into the interior, the "curiouser and curiouser" the land-scape becomes. The seemingly bizarre appearance of many succulents is due to the evolutionary gymnastics they've had to perform to adapt themselves to an environment where water is scarce.

Around 120 species of cactus have been identified on the peninsula and its surrounding islands, more than anywhere else on the planet. Almost three-fourths are unique to Baja.

barrel cactus

© JOE CUMMINGS

Cardón

One of the most common cacti throughout Baja is the towering *cardón (Pachycereus pringlei)*, the world's tallest species of cactus. Individuals can reach as high as 18 meters (60 feet) or more and weigh 12 tons, not counting the root system, which can spread up to 50 meters (165 feet) in diameter. More commonly they top out at 7–9 meters (23–30 feet). The giant, pale-green trunks feature 11–17 vertical ribs and may measure one meter thick. Some live over 400 years.

The *cardón* is often confused with the smaller saguaro cactus of Sonora and Arizona; one major difference is that the branches of the *cardón* tend to be more vertical than those of the saguaro.

The *cardón* is near-endemic to Baja California, found throughout the peninsula—except in the Californian Region—and islands, and also along the coast of Sonora. The hardwood cores of *cardón* columns have been used by *bajacalifornianos* for centuries as building beams and fence posts. Among Baja residents, a *cardón* forest is called a *cardonal.* The state of Baja California Norte sent a 13-meter (43-foot) *cardón* as a gift to the recent Seville World Fair.

Biznaga

Another extremely common and highly visible cactus is the *biznaga* or barrel cactus (genus *Ferocactus*). There are at least 15 species in Baja, most endemic. The cactus's English name refers to its shape, which is short and squat like a barrel. Most common varieties reach about waist-high. One variety, however, *Ferocactus diguettii*, easily reaches four meters (13 feet) in height and a meter (three feet) in diameter. It grows only on a few Sea of Cortez islands, sporting red-tinged spines and, in spring, gorgeous yellow to red flowers.

The indigenous Amerindians of Baja reportedly used hollowed-out *biznagas* as Dutch ovens, inserting food into the cavity along with heated stones, then sealing off the cactus till the food was cooked. The sturdy, curved spines also served as fishhooks on native fishing expeditions.

Pitahaya

Among Baja's original populations, another important cactus was the *pitahaya dulce,* known among Anglos as organ pipe cactus. It has slender, vertical ribs that grow in clusters, and its spiny, orange-size fruit contains a sweet, juicy, pleasant-tasting pulp the color of red watermelon. According to accounts of Spanish missionaries, the Pericú Amerindians based their yearly calendar on the harvest of the ripe fruit in late summer and early fall. During this season, the Amerindians engaged in a veritable fruit orgy, gorging themselves on the pulp until they fell asleep, then waking to begin eating again. The early Spanish explorers took the fruit along on long sea journeys—its vitamin C content helped to prevent scurvy.

The *pitahaya dulce* is commonly found on the peninsula south of the Sierra de San Borja and on several Sea of Cortez islands. A similar species, *pitahaya agria* (*agria* means sour in Spanish; *dulce* is sweet), branches more densely and lower to the ground, hence its English name, galloping cactus. It grows throughout the peninsula and on most Sea of Cortez islands. The fruit of the *pitahaya agria* is similar in appearance to that of the *pitahaya dulce,* but, as implied by the Spanish name, it's less sweet, more acidic. Both types of *pitahaya* fruit remain popular among Baja residents and travelers; the sweet ones ripen in July.

Opuntia

Another cactus variety well represented throughout Baja is the genus *Opuntia*, which includes all types known as **cholla,** as well as the **nopal,** or prickly pear. Chollas are a bane to Baja hikers because they're so prolific and densely covered with spines. A typical branch looks somewhat like braided or twisted rope. The cholla historically has had few domestic uses, although a tea made from the roots of the fuzzy-looking **teddy-bear cholla** (also called "jumping cholla" for its propensity to cling to the legs of hikers), found along the east coast of the peninsula, is reportedly used by the Seri Amerindians as a diuretic.

In contrast, the much-loved prickly pear has broad, flat stems and branches and a sparser distribution of spines. In Northern Mexico and Baja its fleshy pads are a dietary staple. The most highly prized parts of the nopal are the young stem shoots, called *nopalitos,* and the ripe fruits, dubbed *tuna.* The flavor of the pads is a bit bland, like a cross between bell pepper and okra. The fruit, on the other hand, is juicy and sweet, available in season in many Baja markets. If you want to taste it in the wild, remove the *tunas* carefully, cut them lengthwise with a sharp knife, and scoop out the insides with a spoon. Nine species of nopal are found in Baja, including the endemic *tuna tapona* found south of Loreto.

AGAVES

Nineteen species of the sizable agave family grow in Baja; 11 are native. All have long, spine-edged leaves, as well as flowers that bloom on tall stalks.

Yucca

One of the most common and striking desert plants is the yucca, which appears in several varieties throughout Baja. The largest is the **tree yucca,** called *datilillo* or "little date" for its resemblance to a date palm. *Datilillos* grow in clusters 3–7 meters (10–23 feet) tall, their daggerlike blades supported by long woody trunks. This endemic is found throughout the desert plains and chaparral subregions of the peninsula—just about anywhere except in the mountains. The best place to view it in numbers is on the Pacific side of the Vizcaíno Desert, where it's the dominant plant.

Yuccas are extremely useful plants for rural *bajacalifornianos.* The fruit and flowers are edible (a candy called *colache* is made from the cooked flower buds), the roots can be boiled to make soap or leather softener, and the tough leaf fibers are used to make cordage, sandals, baskets, and mats. In some parts of central Baja you may see fences made from packed-together *datilillo* stalks, which often take root and produce a living fence.

Maguey

Also common in Baja are the many varieties of maguey, or century plant. The maguey has broad, closely clustered leaves that grow at ground level without a visible trunk. In most species, the plant flowers only once in its lifetime, sending up a tall, slender stalk after maturation—typically at 5–20 years, depending on variety and locale.

Early Anglo settlers in the southwestern United States spread the myth that magueys bloomed only once in a hundred years, hence the fanciful name "century plant."

The maguey was an important food source for certain aboriginal populations, who harvested the plant just before it bloomed (when it's full of concentrated nutrients). Trimmed of its leaves, the heart of the plant was baked in an underground pit for 1–3 days, then eaten or stored. Some ranchers still prepare it in this manner. As with *datilillo,* the leaf fibers are used as cordage for weaving various household goods.

Sotol

Sotol is similar to yucca, but its leaves are narrower and softer. Some sotols produce long flower stalks like those of the century plant, though the flower buds occur along the stalk's entire length instead of only at the top.

One spectacular variety of sotol in Baja is the endemic *Nolina beldingii,* sometimes called *palmita* because of its resemblance to a small palm tree. *Palmitas,* which can reach seven meters (23 feet) in height, grow clusters of thick leaves branching from their short, woody trunks. They're most commonly found at higher elevations in the Cape Region; isolated stands also exist in mountain areas northwest of Mulegé, north of Bahía de los Ángeles, and on Volcán Las Tres Vírgenes.

FOUQUIERIACEAE
Cirio

The Fouquieria family of succulents contains what many travelers consider to be the plant most symbolic of Baja—the *cirio,* or "boojum tree." Most naturalists describe the *cirio* by likening it to an inverted carrot, since the plant's tall stalk is thickest near the ground and very gradually tapers along its height until it reaches a skinny point at the top. The Spanish name *cirio* (candle) seems far more evocative when one compares the plant to the slender wax tapers typically found on mission altars. In times of abundant rain, the *cirio* even puts forth at its tip a golden bloom resembling a flaring candle flame.

© JOE CUMMINGS

cirio

tant from the "tourist shores" of northwestern Baja, Loreto, and Los Cabos.

Because of its uniqueness, some botanists award the *cirio* with its own genus, *Idria,* within the Fouquieria family, so the Latin name can appear as either *Fouquieria columnaris* or *Idria columnaris.* Like all plants in this family, the white-barked *cirio* sprouts tiny leaves over the entire plant surface when there's sufficient rainfall. During long periods of dry weather, the leaves drop off to conserve the internal water supply.

Ocotillo and Palo Adán

Much more common throughout Baja's desert lands are two other members of the Fouquieria family, the **ocotillo** and *palo adán* (Adam's tree). The ocotillo features long, whiplike branches that radiate directly from the ground in a shape comparable to an exploding shell. In the southwestern United States, it's sometimes known as a "coachwhip." As with the *cirio,* tiny leaves come and go on ocotillo stems according to changing weather conditions. After a good rainfall, a mature (two meters or more) plant puts forth droopy red blossoms at the end of each branch.

Ocotillo grows profusely in all the desert regions of Baja north of the 28th parallel and as far northeast as New Mexico and Texas, occasionally appearing as far south as Bahía Concepción. A rare endemic species, *Fouquieria burragei (ocotillo de flor),* is distinguished by its salmon-pink flowers and grows between Bahía Concepción and La Paz and on a few Sea of Cortez islands. Rancheros use ocotillo branches for fencing, shade ramadas, and as bracing in adobe construction.

At about the point on the peninsula where ocotillo begins fading, its cousin the *palo adán* begins making an appearance. Looking like a larger ocotillo, the Adam's tree has considerably thicker branches radiating from a short, woody trunk. The leaves, when present, are slightly larger than the ocotillo's, while the flowers are smaller. In the Bahía de los Ángeles area, ocotillo and Adam's tree often grow side by side. The latter is also popular as a fencing material and makes excellent firewood when dry.

In height, the *cirio* is second only to Baja's *cardón* cactus, with mature plants extending 12–15 meters (40–50 feet) high from a base 30 cm (12 inches) or so in diameter. Since a *cirio* on average grows only three cm a year (or a foot every 10 years), a 15-meter individual is around 500 years old.

The whimsical name "boojum" was bestowed ad hoc upon the *cirio* by Arizona botanist Godfrey Sykes during a 1922 expedition to Baja. Sykes had apparently been reading Lewis Carroll's *Hunting of the Snark,* a tale that mentioned an imaginary boojum without describing it except to say it inhabited "distant shores." In this sense Sykes's spontaneous epithet was indeed descriptive since the *cirio* grows only in a relatively narrow, 320-km-wide band between the 30th and 27th parallels on the Baja peninsula; the exception is a small *cirio* colony near La Libertad in Sonora, at the same latitude. Although the *cirio* is abundant within this area, the area itself is dis-

TREES

Palms

Seven varieties of palm grow wild in Baja California; four are native to the peninsula and islands while three are introduced species. Palms are important to the local economy of the peninsula's southern half, where they're most common. The long, straight trunks are used as roof beams, the leaves are used in basketry and for roof and wall thatching, and the fruits provide nutrition.

Among the most handsome Baja palm trees is the endemic **blue fan palm** or *palma azul,* which reaches up to 24 meters (79 feet) tall and sports bluish, fan-shaped leaves at its crown. The 4.5-meter (15-foot) flower stalks, which usually appear February–March, often extend well below the shag, or thatch of dead leaves below the crown. The blue fan palm typically grows in the canyons and arroyos of the Sierra Juárez and in similar locales as far south as San Ignacio.

Another native variety, the **Tlaco palm** (also called "taco palm," *palma palmía,* and *palma colorado*), is common in the canyons and arroyos of the Cape Region sierras below Loreto. The smooth, slender trunks, crowned by stiff, fan-shaped leaves, stand up to 20 meters (65 feet) tall. Its durable trunks have long been valued for house construction in Baja California Sur's Cape Region. A closely related species, the **Guadalupe Island palm,** is native to Isla Guadalupe; its self-shedding trunk leaves little or no shag, which has made the tree popular as a cultivated palm.

Baja's tallest palm variety is the endemic **Mexican fan palm** (also Baja California fan palm, skyduster, or *palma blanca*), which reaches heights of 27–30 meters (90–100 feet). As the name implies, its leaves are fan-shaped. Although it's not as durable as the Tlaco palm, the long trunk makes the tree useful for local construction. The fan palm's native habitats include the Sierra de la Giganta and Isla Ángel de la Guarda, but it has also spread west of Cataviña and reached southern California as an ornamental import. More common in the northern peninsula is the similar, nonendemic **California fan palm,** which is a bit shorter than its Mexican cousin.

Two palm varieties were imported to Baja for their fruit value. The **date palm** was introduced to Baja by Jesuit missionaries and is now common near former mission sites, including Loreto, Comondú, Mulegé, San Ignacio, and San José del Cabo. The tree typically reaches 15–20 meters (50–65 feet) tall at maturity; its oblong fruit grows beneath feather-shaped leaves in large clusters, turning from pale yellow to dark brown as it ripens. Baja dates are eaten locally and shipped to mainland Mexico but are generally not considered of high enough quality for export. The 30-meter (100-foot), feather-leafed **coconut palm** commonly grows along coastal areas of the Cape Region as far north as Mulegé and is an important local food source.

Elephant Trees

At least two different species from completely different plant families have received the name "elephant tree." The first, which some Baja experts claim is the only "true" elephant tree, is the sumac family's *Pachycormus discolor,* called either *copalquín* or *torote blanco.* The English name refers to the thick, gray, gnarled-looking trunks and branches. Travelers to East Africa may note a resemblance to the baobab tree.

The papery bark of the elephant tree continually peels off in sheets to reveal the dark green, spongy inner trunk. Drought-deciduous leaves form on the branches when rainfall is sufficient; between May and September small pink flowers may bloom for a few weeks, casting a pink glow over the whole. This endemic species is often seen in the same central desert areas that feature *cirios.* It's particularly prolific in volcanic soils and lava flows.

The second elephant tree, very similar in appearance to the *Pachycormus* but belonging to the torchwood family, is the *Bursera odorata.* Like the other elephant tree, the *Bursera* has thick, gnarled trunks and branches; the thin bark also peels off in papery sheets. The inner trunk is yellow, however, rather than dark green. This one grows south of Bahía Concepción and on the Mexican mainland only. The Spanish name for the tree is the same as for the "true" elephant tree, *torote blanco.* A close relative, the *torote colorado* (another *Bursera*), has a reddish bark. It's found throughout

elephant tree

the deserts of Baja and on many Sea of Cortez islands, as well as in California's Anza-Borrego Desert (in the United States).

Conifers

The high sierras of Baja support a surprising number and variety of conifers, including species of cypress, cedar, juniper, fir, and pine. Among the most interesting, because of its relative confinement to the Baja region, is the **Tecate cypress,** found on the western slopes of the Sierra Juárez and in the Valle San Vicente, as well as in southern California as far north as Orange County. Likewise, the **San Pedro Mártir cypress** is confined to the eastern escarpment of the Sierra de San Pedro Mártir, the **Cedros Island pine** is found only on Isla Cedros, and the **Guadalupe Island pine** grows only on Isla Guadalupe.

Other, more common conifer varieties found at higher elevations include incense cedar, Mormon tea, white fir, piñon pine, Jeffrey pine, sugar pine, bishop pine, and lodgepole pine.

Oaks

Varieties of oak *(encino)* abound along the Pacific slopes of the northern sierras and in the canyons, arroyos, and meadows of the two Cape Region sierras. Of the many species found in Baja, four are endemic: the **cape oak,** found in the canyons and arroyos of the Cape Region sierras; **black oak,** confined to the lower slopes of the Cape Region; **Cedros Island oak,** on Isla Cedros and from San Vicente south to Sierra San Borja; and **peninsular oak,** on the lower slopes of the northern and central sierras. Other common oaks are coast live oak, canyon live oak, white oak, scrub oak, mesa blue oak, and Palmer oak.

Mimosas

This subfamily of the Leguminosae or pea family includes dozens of genera common to arid and semiarid zones worldwide. Characterized by linear seedpods and double rows of tiny leaves, common mimosa varieties in Baja include the **mesquite** and various endemic kinds of **acacia.**

Amerindians have long used the trunk, roots, leaves, beans, and bark of the mesquite tree for a variety of purposes, from lumber to medicine. Ground mesquite leaves mixed with water form a balm for sore eyes, a remedy still used by *cu-*

randeros (healers) in rural Mexico today. Chewing the leaves relieves toothache. And mesquite gum has been used as a balm for wounds, a ceramic glue, dye, and digestive.

Mesquite beans are a good source of nutrition—a ripe bean pod, growing as long as 23 cm (nine inches), contains roughly 30 percent glucose and is high in protein. Many animals and birds savor the beans; horses will eat them until they're sick. Rural Mexicans grind the dried pods into a flour, with which they make bread and a kind of beer. The Seri Amerindians, who live along the Sonoran coast of the Sea of Cortez, have separate names for eight different stages of the bean pod's development.

One of the prettiest endemic mimosas is the **palo blanco,** which has a tall, slender trunk with silver-white bark and a feathery crown that produces small, white, fragrant blossoms March–May. This tree is found the length of the peninsula although it's most easily seen in the Sierra de la Giganta and in the vicinity of Loreto.

Wild Figs

Three types of wild fig trees *(zalates),* one endemic, are common in peninsular Baja. Most are found in rocky areas of the Cape Region. In the village of Pueblo La Playa, east of San José del Cabo, stands a venerable collection of *zalates* of impressive stature.

Cottonwoods and Willows

Various cottonwoods *(alamos)* and willows *(sauces)* grow at higher elevations throughout the peninsula. The *huerivo* or *güeribo (Populus brandegeei)* is a beautiful endemic cottonwood found in the canyons and arroyos of the Cape Region sierras. Its tall, straight trunk reaches heights of 30 meters and is a highly valued source of lumber for building construction and furniture-making.

An unlikely Baja find is the **quaking aspen,** which grows in high mountain meadows of the Sierra de San Pedro Mártir and nowhere else in Baja. The name derives from the fluttering of the small leaves as they turn yellow in the fall and shimmer against the white bark of the tree. In Spanish this tree is called *alamillo* or "little cottonwood."

HERBS

Most herbs—those shrubs with culinary, medicinal, or religious value—thrive in arid climates, and in Baja California they grow in some abundance. To get an idea of the variety, visit any peninsula *botánica* (herb shop) and ask to see *yerbas indígenas.* Most likely your query will turn up the following herbs, plus a dozen others.

One of the most common plants in northern Baja is **Great Basin sagebrush,** named for the area of the western United States where it's a dominant species. In Baja it's called *chamizo blanco* and is found in chaparral and piñon-juniper zones throughout the foothills of the northern sierras. Despite its name, the bluish evergreen shrub isn't a true sage but a member of the mayweed tribe. Like sage, however, its leaves are sometimes used by Mexican herbalists in medicinal teas.

True sages or *salvia* belong to the mint family and are readily identified by the savory aroma of their crushed leaves. **White sage** proliferates on rocky hillsides from southern California to as far south as Punta Prieta. The grayish-green shrub grows up to three meters tall and between March and July produces pale lavender flowers along its stalks. Several varieties of white sage are endemic to the peninsula and islands. Sage tea will mitigate the symptoms of a sore throat; the crushed leaves are also used to flavor cooked meats.

The much sought-after *chia* is a species of sage that grows only in the desert areas of Baja, Sonora, and the southwestern United States. The plant produces sizable rose-colored flowers and 2.5-cm-wide (one-inch) nutlets containing seeds valued for their stimulant properties.

Another psychoactive plant found in Baja is **datura** or **jimsonweed** *(toloache).* A member of the potato family—a group that also includes nightshade and tobacco—jimsonweed produces large, fragrant, trumpet-shaped flowers that open in the evening and close by noon the following day. According to one folk remedy, the flowers will relieve insomnia if placed beside the pillow at night. All parts of the plant are considered toxic; in certain Yaqui Amerindian ceremonies, the seeds are eaten for their hallucinatory effect. Datura grows in abundance on rocky and sandy soils below 800 meters (2,600 feet) throughout the peninsula and on some Sea of Cortez islands.

More docile but also widespread in dry, lower elevations is the **creosote bush** *(gobernadora),* also found in the deserts of Northern Mexico, Utah, and Texas. This venerable shrub originated near the lower Colorado River and has been around at least 17,000 years, cloning itself in rings that widen with time. It's a fairly inconspicuous plant, with sparse evergreen branches that reach a maximum height of about 3.5 meters (11 feet). The English name derives from the creosote-like odor the shrub exudes after rainfall. Dubbed "the smell of the desert" by admirers, this redolence is caused by the reaction of rainwater with a resin on the plant's outer skin. In periods of drought the resin protects the plant from dehydration.

The indigenous peoples of Baja California and Northern Mexico have known about the medicinal properties of *gobernadora* for ages. A tea made from the leaves relieves indigestion, coughs, and colds; a root tea is used to treat ulcers; a root poultice eases arthritis. Rancheros wash their feet in a root solution to prevent foot odor. Pharmacologists are now experimenting with several different chemical components of the plant shown to possess analgesic,

diuretic, antihistaminic, expectorant, and antibacterial properties.

The homely **oregano** plant belongs to the same botanical family (Verbenaceae) as the creosote bush. The crushed leaves of this herb are used mainly in Mexico as a flavoring for stews and tomato sauces; oregano tea is also used by some women to relieve menstrual pain. The small evergreen shrub is found on Isla Magdalena, along the peninsula near Bahía Magdalena, and on many Sea of Cortez islands.

Probably the most well-known herb native to Baja is **damiana** *(Turnera diffusa),* a small shrub with bright, five-petaled yellow or golden flowers. The plant's aphrodisiac properties are its main claim to fame; these are often derided as nonsense by self-appointed Baja analysts. But according to botanist Norman C. Roberts, damiana "stimulates the genito-urinary tract and is used in the treatment of sexual problems such as impotence, frigidity, sterility, and sexual exhaustion." Other benefits ascribed to the herb include use as a sedative and diuretic.

Damiana grows most commonly in rocky areas of the Cape Region but is also found as far away as Sonora, Texas, and in the West Indies. The two most common ways of ingesting the herb are in sweetened tea made from the leaves or in a liqueur containing damiana extract. In resort areas a "Baja margarita" substitutes damiana liqueur for triple sec.

Fauna

LAND MAMMALS

Had Charles Darwin happened to explore the peninsula and islands of Baja California instead of Ecuador's Galapagos Islands, he might well have arrived at the same conclusions about evolution. Baja's unique environment—an arid-to-tropical slice of mountains and plains isolated between two large bodies of water—has led to superlative endemism, or what one naturalist called "a nice degree of freakishness," among its plant and animal species.

Of the hundred or so species of mammals found in Baja California, around 28 are endemic.

Carnivores

One of the most widespread carnivores on the peninsula as well as on some Sea of Cortez islands is the **coyote,** which seems to adapt itself equally well to mountain, desert, and coastal terrain. Anyone venturing into the interior of the peninsula is virtually guaranteed to spot at least one. In some areas they don't seem particularly afraid of humans, although they always maintain a distance of at least 15 meters (50 feet) between themselves and larger mammals. A coyote will sometimes fish for crab, placing a furry tail in the water, waiting for a crab to grab on, then, with a flick of the tail, tossing the crab onto the beach. Before the crustacean can recover from the shock, the coyote is enjoying a fine crab feast.

Rarely sighted is the **mountain lion**—also called cougar, panther, or puma—which, like all cats, is mostly nocturnal. These beautiful creatures occasionally attack humans, so those hiking in the sierras should avoid hiking at night. If you do meet up with a lion, wildlife experts suggest you convince the beast you are not prey and may be dangerous yourself. Don't run from the animal, as this is an invitation to chase. Instead, shout, wave your hands, and, if the lion acts aggressively, throw stones at it. If you're carrying a backpack, raise it above your shoulders so that you appear larger. One or more of these actions is virtually guaranteed to frighten the lion away. If not, grab the biggest, heaviest stick you can find and fight it out to avoid becoming cat food.

Smaller, less intimidating carnivores commonly encountered in Baja include the kit fox, gray fox, northern fox, ringtail, bobcat, lynx, skunk, raccoon, and badger. Although there haven't been any recent sightings, the **gray wolf** may still exist in small numbers in the central sierras. Until the middle of this century the gray wolf was fairly common in Baja, but farmers and ranchers made an unfortunate tradition of killing them on sight.

Ungulates

One of the largest hoofed beasts still roaming wild in Baja is the **mule deer,** of which there is an endemic peninsular variety. Mule deer are most commonly seen on mountain slopes below 1,500 meters (5,000 feet). Lesser numbers of **white-tailed deer** inhabit higher elevations. Deer are a popular source of meat for ranchers living in the sierras, who also use deerskin to make soft, home-made boots called *teguas.*

At one time herds of **desert bighorn sheep** *(borrego cimarrón)* lived throughout the peninsular deserts. Big-game hunting in the 1920s and '30s as well as overgrazing of domestic livestock reduced their numbers to an estimated 4,500–7,500 individuals. An adult ram measures 81–124 cm (32–48 inches) high at the shoulder and may weigh around 73 kg (160 pounds).

BOB RACE

desert bighorn sheep

Rams rut in summer, the only time dominant rams mingle with ewes; the rest of the year they roam only with other rams. During mating season, butting matches between bighorn rams are common.

The elegant but endangered **peninsular pronghorn** *(berrendo),* often mistakenly referred to as an antelope, was once found from San Felipe south to Bahía Magdalena. Until recently it was thought that less than 100 pronghorns were hanging on in the Vizcaíno Desert, but recent aerial surveys have concluded there are around 200 *berrendo,* all of which are under the official protection of the Mexican government. Like many life forms on the Vizcaíno Peninsula, pronghorns draw moisture from dew left behind by Pacific fogs. The penalties for killing a pronghorn include a large fine plus three years in prison.

In the central Baja sierras roam a smattering of wild horses and many wild cattle. Every five years or so local vaqueros gather in the El Arco area to round up wild, unbranded cattle.

Rabbits

At least four varieties of rabbit hop around Baja: the brush rabbit, desert cottontail, black-tailed jackrabbit, and the rare, endemic black jackrabbit. Each is especially adapted to its particular

THE BURRO

Long-eared, slow-plodding, dim-witted, the quintessential beast of burden: This is the city person's image of *Equus asinus*. But to rural Mexicans the donkey, or *burro*, is a beast of strength and surefootedness. Compared to its taller, more graceful-appearing cousin the horse, the burro is a far more useful animal in mountainous or arid domains. On slopes, rocky surfaces, and sand the burro moves with great agility while balancing any load—whether human or inanimate. Standing only about a meter high at the shoulder, burros can also cover greater distances than horses on less water and food; they actually seem to prefer rough forage such as dead cactus or thorny paloverde over nutrient-rich—and, in Baja, scarce—grasses.

Although a burro's coloring may vary from light to dark brown, its withers are almost always marked with a cross of darker hair. Mexican mythology explains this cross as a symbol of divine protection—the burro's reward for carrying Mary and the infant Christ from Egypt to the Holy Land. The burro's legendary stubbornness can often be attributed to mistreatment by its owner; an animal well cared for is usually quite loyal.

Wild burros roam the peninsula's interior, particularly in the area between the Sierra de la Asamblea and Sierra San Borja. Ranchers, or *campesinos*, occasionally capture a wild burro for domestic use—they're fairly easy to tame. The wild male burro, or "jack," is considered the best stud for producing a mule, so ranchers occasionally turn mares loose to breed with them. Mules produced from such a union are especially hardy.

Mountain trekkers occasionally hire burros or mules as pack animals in Baja's sierras. For long forays, it's sometimes cheaper to purchase a burro rather than pay a daily hire rate; prices range from around US$40 for a poor animal to around US$80 for an exemplary burro—if you can find a rancher willing to sell one. If the price doesn't include an *aparejo* (or *burriqueta*), a saddlelike wooden frame for carrying cargo, you'll have to buy one or have one made. The best are made from the wood of the *zacate* (wild fig) tree and sheathed in hand-tooled leather. If possible, have a veterinarian inspect the animal for diseases before agreeing on a purchase.

© JOE CUMMINGS

habitat. The long, upright ears of the **black-tailed jackrabbit,** for example, enable it to hear sounds from a long distance, a necessity for an animal that is prey for practically every larger animal in Baja. The more delicate ears of the **desert cottontail** act as radiators on hot desert days, allowing it to release excess body heat into the air.

The **black jackrabbit** *(Lepus insularis)* is found only on Isla Espíritu Santo. Zoologists haven't yet been able to explain why the fur of this rabbit is mostly black, or why a cinnamon-red coloring appears along the ears and underparts.

Rodents

The Californian Region and the sierras of Baja support a wide variety of common and not-so-common rodents—the white-tailed antelope squirrel, marsh rice rat, Botta's pocket gopher, and piñon mouse, to name a few. What may surprise some travelers is how many varieties manage to survive in the desert. Among these are the desert pocket mouse, cactus mouse, desert wood rat, and five endemic species of kangaroo rat.

The **kangaroo rat,** which you may see hopping in front of your headlights at night—its long tail acts as a powerful spring—is built so it doesn't need to drink water, ever. It derives moisture from seeds, from the air deep inside its burrows where the relative humidity is 30–50 percent, and from condensation in its nasal passages (its nostrils are much cooler than the rest of its body). The creature's efficient kidneys excrete uric acid in a concentrated paste, rather than in liquid form. Because its body is so full of moisture, it's prized quarry for larger desert mammals and birds of prey. Backcountry rancheros occasionally trap kangaroo rats for fiesta food.

GRAY WHALES

The marine mammal usually of most interest to Baja travelers is the gray whale, which migrates some 19,300 km (12,000 miles) a year between its feeding grounds above the Arctic Circle and its calving grounds in the Pacific lagoons of southern Baja California. The gray is the easiest of the whales to view since it frequents shallow coastal waters.

Physiology and Behavior

The *Eschrichtius robustus,* or gray whale, often called the California gray whale, reaches 10–15 meters (35–50 feet) in length at maturity (the average length is 13 meters (43 feet) for males, slightly longer for females) and weighs 20–40 tons. Its skin is almost black at birth, but mottling caused by barnacles and barnacle scars imparts an overall gray tone to the portion of the animal exposed when it breathes. Bite scars on flukes and flippers from orca (killer whale) attacks are common—at least 20 percent of all grays are attacked at one time or another. Most survive; juveniles are the most common fatalities.

Unlike many other whale species that feed on plankton, the gray whale feeds mainly on amphipods, small crustaceans that live on the ocean floor. To get at them, the gray dives to the bottom, scoops water and sand into its mouth cavity, then expels the water through its baleen (a whalebone "sieve" in the mouth), filtering out the amphipods. In spite of an esophagus that's only about 10 cm (four inches) wide, one whale can ingest up to a ton of food per day.

Although gray whales may engage in mating behavior at any point along their migration route, females conceive only while at the north end, in the vicinity of the Bering Strait, and give birth at or near the southern end, in Baja's Pacific lagoons. In a remarkable display of tribal rhythm, 90 percent of all gray whale conceptions take place within three weeks of December 5. Hence it's incorrect to say the whales "breed" in Baja lagoons, since the females cannot conceive at that point in the calendar. The female grays give birth after a gestation period of about 13 months, by which time the whales have arrived at the lagoons or are well on their way.

The females usually calve in water 3–15 meters (10–50 feet) deep, which is remarkably shallow considering newborn grays are four to five meters long (13–16 feet) and weigh up to 1.5 tons. Following birth, the newborns are exercised and fattened up so they'll be strong enough for the migration north. A female gray has recessed nipples on her underside, but the calf doesn't actually suck the milk from the mammaries like other mammals; instead the calf takes the nipple in its

WHALE-WATCHING

The gray whale is the most common subject of whale-watching expeditions. While other whales tend to frequent deeper parts of the ocean, the gray swims mostly in coastal shallows and seeks out lagoons for calving. Also, because it's a bottom feeder, the gray tolerates areas so shallow its abdomen rests on the sea bottom, a position no other large whale can accomplish; most whales would suffocate in such a position. This means large grays are often seen very close to shore.

A visit to a gray calving lagoon can be exciting. Sometimes whales seem to be everywhere you look—"spouting" (clearing their blowholes with pneumatic blasts that send vapor spumes high into the air), "breaching" (leaping out of the sea and arching through the air), "spyhopping" (poking their heads, eyes, and mouths vertically out of the water, possibly to peek at the nonaquatic world), "tail lobbing" (slapping their flukes on the water surface), or just floating by, sleeping on the tide. At other times the whales are relatively inactive. Choppy water seems to occasion more activity.

You can spot grays almost anywhere along Baja's peninsular coast, from Punta Banda near Ensenada right around to the Sea of Cortez. However the best places to see them up close and in large numbers are three protected bays in Baja California Sur: Laguna Ojo de Liebre (Scammon's Lagoon) near Guerrero Negro; Laguna San Ignacio, southwest of San Ignacio; and Bahía Magdalena or adjacent Bahía Almejas, southwest of Ciudad Constitución. Of these three areas, Laguna San Ignacio seems to attract the greatest number of "friendlies," gray whales that actively approach whale-watching boats for human contact.

Although whales can be seen in Baja waters from the beginning of January through the end of March, February is when they're generally present in greatest numbers. At any given lagoon, you can view whales from three vantage points: shore, air, and water. Viewing from shore is sometimes frustrating, since even the closest whales frolic at least 100 meters away; also, since the closest whales usually lie in the shallowest water, they're less likely to perform their more exciting maneuvers, like spyhopping or breaching. Distance is also a problem from the air, since you can't approach too closely without endangering the whale's life as well as the lives of those in the plane. And, of course, to consider whale-watching from the air you must either own a small plane, know someone who does, or charter one.

The optimum way to experience the gray whale, then, is from the water. Any boat entering an area where whales are protected—including all three of the bays mentioned above—during calving season must possess a special whale-watching permit issued by the Mexican government on a year-to-year basis. Ordinarily permits are issued only to boat owners with registered whale-watching concessions and academic researchers from approved institutions.

The least expensive whale-watching trips are those you arrange on your own from the shores of the lagoons. During the season, licensed Mexican boatmen linger with their *pangas* (skiffs) at approved launching points in each lagoon. All you have to do is drive out there, park your vehicle, and pay the going price, which varies with the distance the boats must travel to reach the whales and the number of hours you stay out.

In Guerrero Negro and San Ignacio, a couple of local hotels arrange excursions that include round-trip ground transportation to the lagoons. Prices are usually reasonable; the per-person rate usually goes down the more people you have in your party. Next up in price are trips arranged in major tourist towns like Ensenada, Mulegé, Loreto, La Paz, and Cabo San Lucas. The problem with locally hired whale-watching tours is that the guides are often not very knowledgeable about the whales or can't speak enough English to communicate the knowledge they do possess to non-Spanish-speakers.

Some whale-watchers prefer the convenience and expertise of whale-watching cruises sponsored by scientific or environmental organizations. This sort of trip costs a great deal more than arranging one on your own, but you'll enjoy the advantage of having every contingency planned in advance and will receive the commentary of experienced naturalists. Some organizations in the United States that operate Baja whale-watching expeditions are:

American Cetacean Society
P.O. Box 1391
San Pedro, CA 90733-1391
tel. 310/548-6279
info@acsonline.org
www.acsonline.org

Baja Discovery
P.O. Box 152527
San Diego, CA 92195
tel. 619/262-0700, 800/829-2252
bajadis@aol.com
www.bajadiscovery.com

Baja Expeditions
2625 Garnet Ave.
San Diego, CA 92109
tel. 858/581-3311 or 800/843-6967
travel@bajaex.com
www.bajaex.com

Natural Habitat Adventures
2945 Center Green Court, Suite H
Boulder, CO 80301
tel. 303/449-3711, 800/543-8917
info@nathab.com
www.nathab.com

Oceanic Society Expeditions
Fort Mason Center, Bldg. E
San Francisco, CA 94123
tel. 800/326-7491
www.oceanic-society.org

Pacific SeaFari Tours
2803 Emerson St.
San Diego, CA 92106
tel. 619/226-8224
hmmail@hmlanding.com
www.hmlanding.com/seafari.htm

Searcher Natural History Tours
2838 Garrison St.
San Diego, CA 92106
tel. 619/226-2403
searcher@bajawhale.com

Sven-Olof Lindblad's Special Expeditions
720 Fifth Ave.
New York, NY 10019
tel. 800/397-3348 outside New York, or 212/765-7740 in New York
www.expeditions.com

Most of the foregoing also operate programs in the Sea of Cortez that focus on other marine mammals, including dolphins and humpback, finback, and blue whales.

mouth, and, after a watertight seal has formed, the mother discharges a stream of milk into the calf's throat.

Since whale milk is about 800 percent richer in fat than human milk, the calves gain weight rapidly. By the time the return migration begins, roughly three months after birth, the young whales average six meters (20 feet) long and weigh about 2.5 tons.

Migration

At one time the gray whale swam the Atlantic Ocean, Baltic Sea, and North Sea as well as the Pacific. It was wiped out by Dutch, British, and American whalers in the North Atlantic by the beginning of the 19th century and now survives only in the Arctic-Pacific corridor. In the 1930s, its numbers were estimated at just 250 worldwide. After passage of the U.S. Marine Mammal Protection Act of 1972, grays rebounded and now number around 21,000. They spend their summers feeding in the Bering, Chukchi, and Beaufort Seas in the vicinity of Alaska and Siberia, where the long Arctic days result in highly productive marine growth.

The gray's primary feeding grounds lie in the Chirikof Basin, where they begin their annual migration south in mid- to late fall. Swimming at an average of four knots, the whales cover the 9,600-km (6,000-mile) journey to the southern Baja lagoons in about two months. Traveling in pods of three or four whales, they typically rest for a few hours each night. When there's a full moon, they swim all night.

On their way southward the grays follow the North American shoreline closely, taking the outside coast of major islands. Like many two-legged mammals, gray whales prefer to spend their winters south of the border, and by early January they begin arriving at protected bays and lagoons on the Pacific side of Baja, primarily Laguna Ojo de Liebre, Laguna San Ignacio, and Bahía Magdalena. The grays used to winter farther north in California's San Diego Bay, but heavy sea traffic now forces them to stay south.

During the grays' winter sojourn in Baja, the females calve and nurse their young in the interiors of the lagoons, while the males tend to loiter at or near the lagoon entrances. Since female grays are fertile every other year, each available female—those not calving or nursing—has an average of two suitors at each lagoon entry at any given time. When not actively mating, males watch their rivals coupling or seek out other females. Fighting for access to a female is not a known whale behavior.

Calving season runs December–April, but because of individual differences in pacing, some whales begin migrating north as early as February while others may linger in the lagoons until June. The entire 19,000-km (12,000-mile) migration, the longest of any mammal on the planet, occurs within a period of seven to eight months. Apparently, adult whales don't eat during this interval.

The Rise and Fall of Pacific Whaling

The Amerindians of Alta and Baja California as well as the Inuit of Alaska were known to hunt whales for tribal consumption. But whaling as an industry didn't begin along the Pacific coast until the 19th century, when American whaleboats from New England and Hawaii began cruising Pacific waters in significant numbers. At first gray whales were left alone; because they're fiercely defensive when under attack, grays are very difficult to kill using traditional harpooning techniques. Often they would destroy attacking whaleboats.

The gray's destiny was altered in 1857 when Boston whaler Charles Melville Scammon followed a pod into Baja's Laguna Ojo de Liebre. Taking advantage of the local geography, Scammon figured out how to bomb the trapped whales with explosive harpoons while his whaleboats remained safely anchored in the shallows, where larger whales couldn't reach them. Scores of whalers followed his example, and within less than 20 years an estimated 10,000 gray whales had been killed.

The slaughter quickened in the 20th century with the introduction of factory boats, which meant whales could be processed on site. By the 1930s the estimated number of grays was down to 250 from a pre-1850s population of 25,000. International fishing agreements signed in 1937 and 1946 forbade the killing of gray whales, but American whalers didn't comply until the U.S.

government enacted the Marine Mammal Protection Act of 1972, by which time the gray whale was thought to be extinct. The animal's remarkable comeback over the last 30 years has been one of the greatest successes of the environmental movement.

In an ironic historical footnote, whaler Charles Melville Scammon later became a naturalist of some note, and his book, *The Marine Mammals of the Northwestern Coast of North America,* is considered a classic of amateur zoology. It remains one of the most important reference works on whales and the whaling industry.

OTHER MARINE MAMMALS

Cetaceans

The protected lagoons of Baja California's Pacific coast and the warm waters of the Sea of Cortez are practically made for whales and dolphins. Twenty-five species of cetaceans—about a third of all world species—frequent Baja waters, from the **blue whale,** the largest mammal on earth, to the **common dolphin** *(Delphinus delphis),* which is sometimes seen in the Sea of Cortez in pods as large as 10,000.

In addition to the gray whale (discussed at length earlier), whale species known to visit Baja or make it their year-round habitat include minke, fin, Sei, Bryde's, humpback, goose-beaked, sperm, dwarf sperm, false killer, killer, and pilot. Commonly seen dolphins include the Pacific white-sided, bottle-nosed, spotted, Risso's, spinner, and striped. The **vaquita,** a rare type of harbor porpoise, is endemic to the northern Sea of Cortez.

Seals and Sea Lions

Various seals and sea lions flourish along Baja's coasts, including two species, the **elephant seal** (or sea elephant) and the **Guadalupe fur seal,** that have only recently come back from the brink of extinction. Both are native to the volcanic Isla Guadalupe and were heavily hunted in the 19th century, the elephant seal for its oil and the Guadalupe fur seal for its furry skin.

The elephant seal is the largest seal on the planet. Males reach five meters (16 feet) or more

and weigh up to two tons, while females are typically around three meters and about half a ton. The male's thick, flexible proboscis resembles a bobbed elephant's trunk. To scare off rivals in breeding season (December–February), the male places the tip of his trunk into his mouth and blows, producing a roaring snort. If the rival doesn't flee, a bloody fight ensues until one bull surrenders.

Lumbering on land but amazingly graceful in water, elephant seals can dive 1,490 meters (4,900 feet) below the sea's surface—deeper than any other seal—to feed on squid, their favorite source of nourishment.

When the seal-hunting era began in the early 19th century, the elephant seal's range extended all the way north to California's Point Reyes, near San Francisco. By 1911 seal hunters had wiped out every elephant seal in California waters and reduced the elephant's numbers on Isla Guadalupe to 125. After the Mexican government enacted a ban on seal hunting in 1922, the seals began repopulating Isla Guadalupe and nearby islands. The current population is estimated at around 80,000, most living on Pacific islands of Baja California. The elephant seal is gradually working its way back up the California coast as well.

The smaller Guadalupe fur seal had a more difficult time recovering from the seal-hunting era. It was believed to be extinct by the end of the 19th century, but in 1926 a small herd of around 60 living on Isla Guadalupe was discovered by American angler William Clover. Clover captured a pair of the seals and sold them to the San Diego Zoo, but, following a quarrel with the zoo's director, he returned to the island and attempted to kill and skin the entire remaining population. After selling the skins in Panama he met his demise in a barroom brawl. Fortunately he missed some of the seals in his massacre, and the current population on the island is estimated at around 500.

California sea lions, or *lobos marinas,* number some 145,000, 62 percent of which live in the Sea of Cortez—principally around the islands of San Esteban, San Jorge, Ángel de la Guarda, San Pedro Mártir, and Espíritu Santo.

FISH

The seas surrounding Baja California contain an amazing variety of marinelife. In the Sea of Cortez alone, around 900 varieties of fish have been identified. Marine biologists estimate around 3,000 species, including invertebrates, between the Golfo de Santa Clara at the north end of the sea and the southern tip of Cabo San Lucas. This would make the area the richest sea, or gulf, in the world. The wide spectrum of aquatic environments along both coasts is largely responsible for this abundance and has led to Baja's reputation as a mecca for seafood aficionados and fishing and diving enthusiasts.

About 90 percent of all known Baja fish varieties are found close to the shores of the peninsula or its satellite islands. The Midriff Islands area in the center of the Sea of Cortez is especially rich— tidal surges aerate the water and stir up nutrients, supporting a thick food chain from plankton to fish to birds and sea lions. The Cortez, in fact, has acted as a giant fish trap, collecting an assortment of marine species over thousands of years from the nearby Pacific, the more distant equatorial zones of South America, and even the Caribbean, through a water link that once existed between the two seas.

A brief guide to Baja's fish is provided below. Habitats are described as being onshore, inshore, or offshore. Onshore fish frequent the edge of the tidal zone and can be caught by casting from shore; inshore fish inhabit shallow waters accessible by small boat; and offshore fish lurk in the deep waters of the open Pacific or the southern Sea of Cortez. (Also see Sports and Recreation in the On the Road chapter.)

Billfish

Baja is the world capital of sailfish and marlin fishing; serious saltwater anglers from across the globe make the pilgrimage to La Paz or Cabo San Lucas in hopes of landing a swordfish, sailfish, or striped, blue, or black marlin. The sailfish and striped marlin are generally the most acrobatic, but all billfish are strong fighters. They inhabit a wide range of offshore waters in the Pacific and in the Sea of Cortez south of Bahía Magdalena and the Midriff Islands; the swordfish is found mostly on the Pacific side.

Corvinas and Croakers

About 30 species in Baja belong to this group of small- to medium-size fish that make croaking sounds. Among the largest is the **totuava,** formerly one of the most famous game fish in the upper Sea of Cortez. Overfishing has led to a scarcity of these silvery 35- to 250-pounders (15–115 kg), and it's now illegal to take or possess them in Mexico. The totuava is reportedly one of best tasting of all game fish; others in this category, found inshore to onshore in a variety of coastal waters, include white seabass, Gulf corvina, orangemouth corvina, California corvina, yellowfin croaker, and spotfin croaker.

Jack

Popular jacks include yellowtail (one of the most popular fish for use in *tacos de pescado*), Pacific amberjack, various pompanos, jack crevalle, and the strong-fighting roosterfish, named for its tall dorsal comb. These fish are most prevalent in inshore to onshore areas in the Sea of Cortez and in the Pacific south of Magdalena.

Dorado, Mackerel, and Tuna

Among the more sought-after food fish, found offshore to inshore throughout parts of both seas, are: dorado, sometimes called dolphinfish (though it isn't related to mammalian dolphins or porpoises) or mahimahi (its Hawaiian name); sierra, especially good in ceviche; the knife-shaped wahoo, one of the fastest of all fish, reaching speeds of 50 knots; Pacific bonito; and three kinds of tuna—the bluefin, albacore, and highly prized yellowfin. Yellowfins can weigh up to 180 kg (400 pounds) and are among the best-tasting of all tunas.

Bass

Seabass are an inshore fish; different species dominate different Baja waters, and all commonly find their way into Mexican seafood restaurants. The larger bass are *garropa* (groupers), the smaller *cabrilla*. Popular varieties are the leopard grouper, found in the Sea of Cortez near San Felipe; the gulf grouper, which weighs up to 90 kg (200 pounds) and inhabits waters off San Felipe to the Midriff Islands; giant seabass, ranging from San Quintín to above the Midriff Islands; spotted cabrilla, Isla Cedros to the upper Sea of Cortez; flag cabrilla, lower Sea of Cortez; kelp bass, northwest Pacific coast; and spotted sand bass, Pacific coast north of Magdalena and the upper Sea of Cortez.

Bottomfish

These smaller (13 kg or less—under 29 pounds) bottom-feeding fish favor the inshore Pacific above Magdalena and include the lingcod, sculpin, and rockfish.

Surf Fish

Most of the 25 or so species of surf fish weigh less than two kg and are found along the Pacific coast, since there's no surf to speak of in the Sea of Cortez. Popular catches among gringos—this isn't a popular fish with Mexican anglers—are barred surfperch, rubberlip surfperch, and sargo. The sargo also frequents the upper Sea of Cortez coast.

Flatfish

These include flounder and halibut, usually called *lenguado* in Spanish. The most common variety on the Pacific side is California halibut; on the gulf side it's Cortez halibut. Both make good eating and are often used in tourist areas for *tacos de pescado*.

Snapper

Generally found south of Magdalena and round the Cape as far north as the upper Sea of Cortez, locally popular snappers include red snapper, yellow snapper, barred pargo, and dog snapper. All snappers are called *pargo* in Spanish, except for the red snapper, which is *huachinango*. All are common food fish.

Sharks, Rays, and Squid

Of the more than 60 species of sharks found in Baja waters, some are rare and most stay clear of humans. The more common species are found offshore to inshore from Magdalena to the Midriff, and include the smooth hammerhead, common thresher, bonito (mako), sand, blue,

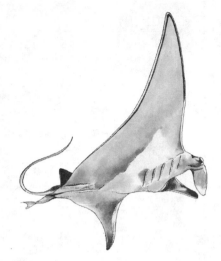

manta ray

blacktip, and the whale shark, the world's largest fish, which reaches 18 meters (59 feet) and 3,600 kg (almost four tons). Shark-fishing is an important activity in Baja, supplying much of the seafood eaten locally. Hammerhead, thresher, bonito, and leopard shark fillets are all very tasty.

Rays are common in warmer offshore-to-inshore waters throughout Baja. Many varieties have barbed tail spines that can inflict a painful wound. Contrary to myth, the barb is not actually venomous, although a ray "sting" can be extremely painful and easily becomes infected. Experienced beachgoers perform the "stingray shuffle" when walking on sandy bottoms: if you bump into a ray resting on the bottom, it will usually swim away; if you step on one, it's likely to give you a flick of the barb.

Common smaller rays found inshore include the butterfly ray and the aptly named shovelnose guitarfish, a ray with a thick tail and a flat head. Two species of rays—the mobula and the huge Pacific manta ray—are sometimes called "devilfish" because of their hornlike pectoral fins. The Pacific manta possesses a "wingspan" of up to seven meters (23 feet) and can weigh nearly two tons. Pacific mantas have become rare due to overfishing. Another fairly large ray, the bat ray, is sometimes

ENDANGERED SEA

Novelist John Steinbeck, in his 1941 account of a scientific marine expedition into the Sea of Cortez accompanying marine biologist Ed Ricketts, described how he watched six Japanese shrimpers—weighing at least 600 tons each—purse-dredge the sea bottom, killing hundreds of tons of fish that were merely discarded after each dredging. One of his reactions: "Why the Mexican government should have permitted the complete destruction of a valuable food supply is one of those mysteries which have their ramifications possibly back in pockets it is not well to look into."

In 1996, the *Sacramento Bee* published a multipage report by Pulitzer Prize–winning writer Tom Knudson, exposing corruption among fishing interests and the state governments on all sides of the Cortez. The evidence presented in the report is clear: overfishing by greedy commercial interests is devastating the natural balance in the Sea of Cortez. Reading this report is virtually guaranteed to put you off eating seafood for a while.

According to the report, primary culprits include gillnetters, purse seiners, spear-fishermen, and shrimp trawlers. The latter drag huge, cone-shaped, fixed nets over the ocean bottom, ripping up the seafloor; for every pound of shrimp harvested they destroy 10 pounds of other sea life. Asian long-liners were a problem in the 1960s through the '80s, but their presence in the Sea of Cortez has diminished drastically; in fact long-liners hardly ever enter the Sea of Cortez anymore, instead staying just outside international limits in the Pacific.

Two species native to the northern Sea of Cortez, **totuava** and **vaquita dolphin,** are of particular concern. Gillnetting for the totuava (yielding 70–100 tons annually) has severely threatened the vaquita, which is now thought to be the world's most endangered marine mammal. The current vaquita population is estimated at only 200–500 individuals. Mexican laws passed in 1993 included a ban on the use of gillnets in the upper Sea of Cortez, yet their current use is not uncommon.

Most of the species taken commercially from the Sea of Cortez are sold primarily in the United States, Canada, Korea, and Japan. In addition to the vaquita and totuava, those disappearing fast include the sea cucumber, bay scallop, sardine, shrimp, turtle, marlin, grouper, yellowfin tuna,

confused with the manta, though it doesn't have the characteristic pectoral fins. A friendly manta will allow scuba divers to hitch rides by hanging on to the base of the pectorals, although most divemasters now discourage such activity.

Squids of various species and sizes, most under 30 cm (one foot) in length, are found throughout the Pacific Ocean and Sea of Cortez. In deeper Pacific waters off the west coast glides the enormous Humboldt squid, which reaches lengths of 4.5 meters (15 feet) and may weigh as much as 150 kg (330 pounds). In the Cape Region, squid (*calamar* in Spanish) is popularly eaten in *cocteles* or used as sportfishing bait.

Elongated Fish

These varieties share the characteristics of long,

slender bodies and beaklike jaws. The sharp-toothed California barracuda swims in the Pacific from the border down to Cabo San Lucas, while a smaller, more edible variety is found in the Sea of Cortez. In spite of their somewhat frightful appearance, barracudas rarely attack humans.

The silvery flying fish can be seen leaping above offshore waters throughout the Pacific and lower Sea of Cortez. It is not generally considered a food fish. The most edible of the elongated fish is probably the acrobatic Mexican needlefish, or *agujón,* which reaches two meters (6.5 feet) in length and has green bones.

Shellfish

Baja's shores abound with deep-water and shallow-water shellfish species, including around 75

yellowtail, manta and other rays, and sharks. The Pacific manta has been virtually wiped out by gillnetting, while porpoises, dolphins, and sea lions face a similar fate. An estimated 17 major species have declined 60–90 percent over the last decade alone.

Sportfishing is not a problem except when anglers go over their limits, which isn't uncommon. The federal limit on taking dorado, for example, is three per angler, but it's not unusual to see Americans and Canadians coming back from a day's fishing with catches of over 10 times the limit—and bragging about it. Many foreigners practice spearfishing in Baja, which is a federal crime in Mexico if done in conjunction with scuba gear. There's no sport to scuba spearfishing, which can only be likened to shooting ducks in a barrel.

To protect the Cortez ecosystem from coastal industries and overfishing, the Mexican government has asked the United Nations to bestow International Biosphere Reserve status upon the northern Sea of Cortez and its surrounding shores. With such status, the area would become eligible for various kinds of U.N. and international conservation funds.

Whether or not the request is granted, the government is taking further steps to upgrade protection for the sea, which is finally being recognized as one of Mexico's greatest natural assets. A 9,580-square-kilometer (3,700-square-mile) Mexican biosphere reserve has been established in the northern Sea of Cortez; within a core zone of 1,650 square kilometers (636 square miles), reaching from San Felipe to Golfo de Santa Clara, all sportfishing, commercial fishing, and oil drilling are banned. The remaining area is a buffer zone in which "sanitary fishing" (meaning no shrimp trawling) is permitted under strict regulations.

Unfortunately, Mexican government resources for enforcing the country's many fine-sounding laws are hopelessly inadequate. The PESCA (Mexico Department of Fisheries) inspector in Loreto, for example, is paid less than half the wage of an average Mexican factory worker—and isn't even supplied with a boat or car, nor telephone, paper, electric lights, or even gas money for use with his own car.

The only way the situation will improve and things will change is with international, i.e., U.N., involvement. One can only hope that intervention is soon enough and strong enough to preserve Mexico's great marine resources.

---

varieties of clams, oysters, mussels, scallops, and shrimp, many of which have disappeared from coastal California, United States. Baja's most famous shellfish is undoubtedly the spiny lobster, which appears on virtually every *mariscos* menu on the peninsula.

BIRDS

Hosting around 300 known species of birds (one of the highest concentrations in North America), the peninsula and islands of Baja California provide undisturbed avian habitat par excellence. Ornithological research is incomplete, however, and reference materials are difficult to come by; one of the most up-to-date works available is Ernest Preston Edwards's *The Birds of Mexico*

and Adjacent Areas, published in 1998 (see Suggested Reading).

Coastal and Pelagic Species

The vast majority of Baja's native and migrating species are either coastal or open-sea (pelagic) birds. The Sea of Cortez islands are particularly rich in bird life; the Mexican government has designated 49 of the Midriff Islands as wildlife refuges to protect the many rare and endangered species there. The most famous of these islands among birders is Isla San Pedro Mártir, home to the rare and clownish **blue-footed booby** and its more common cousins, the **brown booby** and the **masked booby.**

Isla de Raza, a tiny guano-covered Midriff island of only 100 hectares (250 acres), is another birding mecca. Every April this island is the site of territorial "wars" between **Heermann's gulls** and **elegant terns.**

Common throughout the coastal areas of southern Baja is the **magnificent frigate,** called *tijera* (scissors) in Mexico because of its scissors-shaped tail. In spite of their seafood diet, frigates can't swim or even submerge their heads to catch fish—instead they glide high in the air on boomerang-shaped wings, swooping down to steal fish from other birds, especially slow-witted boobies.

Among the more commonly seen birds along the Sea of Cortez coast is the **brown pelican,** which in global terms is not so common. The pelican species go back 30 million years; pale-ontologists use the modern pelican as a model for creating visual representations of the pteranodon, an extinct flying reptile with an eight-meter wingspan. Brown pelicans, the only truly marine species among the world's seven pelican species, dive 10–30 meters (30–100 feet) underwater to catch fish. Other pelicans only dip their beaks beneath the surface and tend to frequent inland waterways rather than marine habitats. Browns have disappeared almost entirely from the U.S. shores of the Gulf of Mexico and are declining in the coastal islands of California—apparently due to the pesticide content of the Pacific Ocean. Baja's Cortez and Pacific coasts are among the last habitats where the brown pelican thrives.

Another noteworthy bird along the coast is the **fisher eagle,** which, as its name implies, catches and eats fish. The fisher eagle is also occasionally seen along freshwater rivers and around the Pacific lagoons.

Other coastal birds of Baja include two species of cormorant, the long-billed curlew, four species of egret, four species of grebe, 10 species of gull, three species of heron, the belted kingbird, two species of ibis, three species of loon, the osprey, the American oystercatcher, six species of plover, six species of sandpiper, the tundra swan, and seven species of tern.

Certain fish-eating birds are usually seen only by boaters since they tend to fly over open ocean. These pelagics include two species of albatross, the black-legged kittiwake, the red phalarope, three species of shearwater, the surf scoter, the south polar skua, five species of storm petrel, the black tern, and the red-billed tropic bird.

Estuarine and Inland Species

Another group of waterfowl in Baja frequents only freshwater ponds, *tinajas* (springs), lakes, streams, and marshes. These birds include two species of bittern, the American coot, two species of duck, the snow goose, the northern harrier, six species of heron, the white-faced ibis, the common moorhen, two species of rail, five species of sandpiper, the lesser scaup, the shoveler, the common snipe, the sora, the roseate spoonbill, the wood stork, three species of teal, the northern waterthrush, and the American wigeon. Some of these birds are native; others only winter over.

In Baja's sierras dwell the golden eagle, the western flycatcher, the lesser goldfinch, the black-headed grosbeak, the red-tailed hawk, two species of hummingbird, the pheasant, the yellow-eyed junco, the white-breasted nuthatch, the mountain plover, four species of vireo, eight species of warbler, the acorn woodpecker, and the canyon wren.

Common in the desert and other open country are three species of falcon (peregrine, prairie, and Cooper's), three species of flycatcher, six species of hawk, the black-fronted hummingbird, the American kestrel, the merlin, two species of owl, the greater roadrunner, eight species of sparrow, two species of thrasher, the vernon, the turkey vulture, the ladder-backed woodpecker, and the cactus wren.

Once very common throughout Baja California, the **California condor** (*Gymnogyps californianus*) is now a very endangered species, with just over 150 individuals alive in the world. Weighing up to 11 kg (24 pounds), with a wingspan of nearly 3.6 meters (12 feet), California condors are the largest North American bird, and the second largest bird in the world after the Andean condor of South America. Captive breeding at zoos in Los Angeles and San Diego has met limited success, but subsequent release programs in the Grand Canyon and southern California have not been successful. A group of U.S. and Mexican scientists has plans to try releasing condors in Baja's Sierra de San Pedro Mártir, in hopes that the more limited human presence will permit the bird to survive in the wild.

REPTILES AND AMPHIBIANS

Among the slippery, slimy, scaly, crawly things that live in Baja California are around 30 species of lizards, including two endemics; five species of frogs and toads; six turtles; and around 35 different kinds of snakes, including the endemic rattleless rattlesnake.

Lizards

One four-legged reptilian of note is the **chuckwalla,** which is found on certain islands in the Sea of Cortez; it sometimes grows to nearly a meter in length. The chuckwalla drinks fresh water when available, storing it in sacs that gurgle when it walks; when a freshwater source is not available, the lizard imbibes saltwater, which it processes through a sort of internal desalinator. Another good-sized Baja lizard is the **desert iguana,** found throughout the Gulf Coast Desert and possibly farther north. Larger iguanas are sometimes eaten in ranchero stews and are said to taste better than chicken. The **coast horned lizard,** similar to the horny toad of the American Southwest, is another Baja endemic.

Turtles

Of the six turtle varieties present in Baja, five are sea turtles: the leatherback, green, hawksbill, western ridley, and loggerhead. The **loggerhead** migrates back and forth between the Japanese island of Kyushu and the Sea of Cortez, a distance of 10,460 km (6,500 miles). Because their eggs, meat, and shells are highly valued among coastal Mexican populations, all sea turtles are on the endangered species list. The Mexican government has declared turtle hunting and turtle egg collecting illegal; the devastation of the turtles has slowed considerably but hasn't yet stopped. *Bajacalifornianos* say they're upholding the laws while anglers along the mainland coast of the Sea of Cortez still take sea turtles.

The main culprit has apparently been Japan, which is the world's largest importer of sea turtles—including the endangered ridley and hawksbill. The Japanese use the turtles for meat, turtle leather, and turtle-shell fashion accessories. In 1991, the Japanese government announced a ban on the importation of sea turtles, so perhaps the Sea of Cortez populations will eventually make a comeback.

Snakes

The rocky desert lands and chaparrals of Baja are perfect snake country. The bad news is that about half the known species are venomous; the good news is they rarely come into contact with humans. Scorpion stings far outnumber snakebites in Baja.

Harmless species include the western blind snake, rosy boa, Baja California rat snake, spotted leaf-nosed snake, western patch-nosed snake, bull snake, coachwhip, king snake, Baja sand snake, and California lyre snake.

The venomous kinds fall into two categories, one of which contains only a single snake species, the **yellow-bellied sea snake.** Sea snakes usually flee the vicinity when they sense human presence, but as a general precaution don't grab anything in the water that looks like a floating stick—that's how sea snakes deceive their prey.

The other venomous category comprises the rattlesnakes, of which there are supposedly 18 species stretched out along Baja California. The most common species is the near-endemic **Baja California rattler,** whose range includes the lower three-fourths of the peninsula. Look for scaly mounds over the eyes if you care to make an identification. The **red diamondback** frequents the northern deserts and chaparral and is also fairly common. The most dangerous of Baja rattlers is the **Western diamondback;** it's the largest and therefore has the greatest potential to deliver fatal or near-fatal doses of venom. Fortunately, the diamondback is mostly confined to the canyons of the northern sierras.

All other rattlesnakes in Baja are more a nuisance than an actual threat since they overwhelmingly tend toward the injection of nonfatal doses of venom. For Graham Mackintosh, the Briton who hiked almost the entire perimeter of the Baja peninsula and wrote a book about his experiences *(Into A Desert Place)*, rattlesnake became a welcome part of his desert diet.

The only rattler fully endemic to Baja is also the strangest. The **rattleless rattlesnake** *(Crotalus catalinensis)* was first discovered in 1952 on Isla Santa Catalina, a small mountainous Sea of Cortez island south of Loreto. Fortunately, Santa Catalina is the only habitat for this snake; its lack of a warning signal might otherwise keep most of us away from the peninsular deserts forever.

The general all-inclusive Spanish term for snake is *serpiente;* a nonvenomous snake is referred to as *culebra,* the venomous sort *víbora.* A rattlesnake is *un serpiente de cascabel* or simply *un cascabel.* For tips on how to avoid snakebite, see the sidebar Snakebite Prevention and Treatment in the On the Road chapter. An encouraging factoid: According to Spanish records, no missionary ever died of snakebite during the 300-year period of Spanish colonization of the New World.

History

PRE-CORTESIAN HISTORY

Because Baja California lacks spectacular archaeological remains, such as the Mayan and Aztec ruins in the southern reaches of mainland Mexico, it has largely been ignored by archaeologists. It is highly likely, however, that the Baja California peninsula was inhabited by human populations well before the rest of Mexico. Baja was the logical termination for the coastal migration route followed by Asian groups who crossed the Bering Strait land bridge between Asia and North America beginning around 50,000 B.C.

San Dieguito and La Jolla Cultures

The earliest known Baja inhabitants were members of the San Dieguito culture who migrated south into northern Baja approximately 7,000 years ago. Evidence of their presence in California dates back 9,000 years. The San Dieguito people spent much of the year wandering in small migratory bands of 15–20, guided by freshwater sources and the availability of game. Their simple economy was based on hunting, fishing, and the gathering of edible wild plants. Archaeological remains include circles of stones, stone tools—choppers, raspers, knives, spear points, axe heads, mortars *(metates)*—and simple pottery.

Evidence suggests the San Dieguitos coexisted, at least for a time, with the Jollanos (or La Jolla culture), about whom little is known except that they lived by gathering fish and shellfish, seeds, roots, and wild vegetables.

The Yumanos

The San Dieguito culture either developed into or was superseded by that of the Yumanos, whose archaeological signature of rock paintings and petroglyphs indicates their presence on the peninsula around 2,500 years ago. The Yumanos made use of more-sophisticated hunting equipment as well as fishing nets; they also seem to have developed ceramics well before their counterparts in the American Southwest. Upon the arrival of the Spanish in the 16th century, some Yumano groups were practicing cultivation in the Río Colorado floodplains of northern Baja. These groups included the Cucapá, Tipai, Paipai (or Pa'ipai), Kumyai, and Kiliwa.

Like many of the less aggressive Amerindians throughout Mexico and Mesoamerica, the Yumano tribes didn't last very long after missionization. Those who weren't killed by European-borne diseases or executed for rebelling against the padres were assimilated. All that is left of the Yumano culture today is scattered galleries of petroglyphs and rock paintings.

A Yumano rock painting near La Rumorosa depicts a winter solstice celebration, suggesting a rudimentary knowledge of astronomy. One of the figures in the painting, a 30-cm (12-inch) red human caricature that may represent a shaman, catches light only on December 21, for about 20 minutes beginning at sunrise.

The Cochimís and Guaycuras

Amerindian groups living in the central and southern reaches of the peninsula when the Spanish arrived were apparently much less advanced technologically than the Yumanos. Because of the lack of archaeological research in these areas, the only record we have of these cultures consists of Spanish accounts, which were undoubtedly biased in light of their mission to subordinate the peoples of the New World. Mission histories are full of lurid tales of Amerindian customs, many probably written to convince the Spanish crown of the desperate need to convert the natives. Nevertheless, the Amerindians of central and southern Baja appear to have been among the more "primitive" of the tribes encountered by the Spanish in Mexico or Mesoamerica. In modern archaeological terms, they hadn't progressed beyond the Paleolithic epoch (the early Stone Age).

According to these accounts, the Cochimís inhabited the central peninsula and Comonú while Guaycuras—divided into the Pericú, Huchiti, and Guaicura tribes—occupied the Cape Region. One fringe anthropological view has suggested a portion of the Guaycura tribes may have descended from Tahitian seafarers who were blown off course on their way to Hawaii. Whatever their place of origin, they spent most of their daylight hours searching for food; the men hunted small game or gathered shellfish while the women gathered fruit, seeds, and roots. If game was scarce, the people subsisted on insects and would even eat dried animal skins, including, according to reports, the leather boots of the conquistadors.

The southern Amerindians generally lived in the open and sought shelter only in the severest weather. Men wore little or no clothing, while women wore leather or yucca-fiber thongs around the waist with woven grasses or twigs suspended from the front and animal skins in the back. These garments were sometimes painted with bright colors. The tips of arrows and spears were generally of sharpened hardwood only, though chipped stone points were occasionally used. The Guaycuras also used

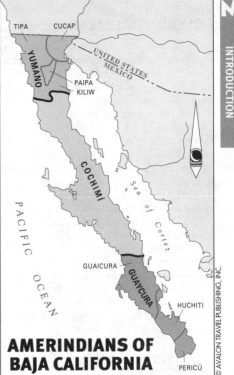

AMERINDIANS OF BAJA CALIFORNIA

© AVALON TRAVEL PUBLISHING, INC.

reed blowguns. The most important time of year among these Amerindians was when the fruit of the *pitahaya* cactus ripened; the fruit was then so abundant the Amerindians allegedly abandoned all activities save sleeping and eating.

Neither the Guaycuras nor the Cochimís apparently left behind any artwork. This has been attributed to their harsh living environment; they had little time or energy for artistic pursuits. However, in the inland areas of the peninsula once inhabited by the Guaycura and Cochimí tribes, numerous spectacular rock-art sites have been discovered. The Cochimís told the Spanish this rock art was created by a race of giants who'd preceded them. Almost nothing is known about this lost Amerindian culture, a people Baja rock-art expert Harry Crosby has dubbed "the Painters."

THE SPANISH CONQUEST OF MEXICO

Following 700 years of conflict with the Moors over control of the Iberian peninsula, Spain in the 15th century emerged as the most powerful nation in Europe. Convinced that a Roman Catholic God was destined to rule the world with Spain as His emissary, the Spanish monarchy sent Christopher Columbus in search of a new route to the Far East. His mission was to establish contact with a mythical "Great Khan" to develop an alternate trade route with the Orient, since Arabs controlled the overland route through the Middle East. Along the way as many pagans as possible would be converted to Christianity. Once the Arab trade monopoly was broken, the Holy Land would be returned to Christian control.

Columbus's landing in the West Indies in 1492 was followed by Pope Alexander VI's historic 1493 decree, which gave the Spanish rights to any new land discovered west of the Azores, as long as the Spanish made "God's name known there." Hence, the Spanish conquest of the New World started as a roundabout extension of the Holy Crusades.

A succession of Spanish expeditions into the Caribbean and Gulf of Mexico rapidly achieved the conquest of Mexico and Central America. Conquistador Hernán Cortés subdued the Valley of Mexico Aztecs in three years (1519–21), and the allegiance—or decimation—of other Aztecs and Mayans followed quickly.

Early Explorations

When the Spanish conquistadors came to the western edge of mainland Mexico and looked beyond toward the landforms they could see above the sea, they concluded that Baja California was a huge island and that the as-yet-unnamed Sea of Cortez led to the Atlantic. The idea of a northwest passage to the Atlantic persisted for years, even among seasoned explorers like Cabrillo, Drake, and Vizcaíno. Cortés himself directed four voyages from the mainland to the island of La California, although he accompanied only the third. The history of these early expeditions exposes the enmity and extreme sense of competition among those conquistadors supposedly working toward a common cause.

The first voyage, launched in 1532, never made it to the peninsula. The ships were captured in the Sea of Cortez by Nuño de Guzmán, an archrival of Cortés operating farther north in Mexico. The next year a second expedition, under Captain Diego Becerra of the *Concepción,* suffered a mutiny in which the captain was killed. Basque pilot Fortún Jiménez took charge, and the ship landed in Bahía de la Paz in early 1534. Thus the first European visitors to reach Baja California, a group of mutineers, arrived there just 42 years after Columbus touched down in the West Indies and nearly a century before the Pilgrims landed at Plymouth Rock.

Before they had much of a chance to explore, Jiménez and 22 of his crew were killed by Amerindians while filling their water casks at a spring. The survivors managed to sail the *Concepción* back to the mainland, where most were promptly captured by Guzmán. One of the escapees managed to reach Cortés with tales of rich caches of black pearls on a huge island with "cliffs and headlands and rocky coasts," as in the California of popular myth.

Cortés, inspired by these stories, organized and led a third expedition, partially financed by his own personal wealth. His party consisted of three ships and a group of 500 Spanish colonists that included women and children. They landed at the northeast end of Bahía de la Paz—which Cortés named Santa Cruz—in May of 1535, the same year New Spain was officially established. Although Cortés apparently found pearls in abundance, his attempt to colonize the peninsula lasted only two years, by which time disease, hostile Amerindians, and *chubascos* had driven the colonists back to the mainland.

The fourth attempt by Cortés to establish a Spanish foothold on Baja was led by the highly competent Captain Francisco de Ulloa, who'd accompanied Cortés on the failed Santa Cruz expedition. Cortés stayed behind on this one, hoping Ulloa's expedition would be able to find a more hospitable Baja beachhead. Ulloa set sail from Acapulco with two ships in July 1539, and over the next eight months he managed to explore the entire perimeter of the Sea of Cortez, reaching the mouth of the Río Colorado and rounding the Cape along the Pacific coast as far north as Isla Cedros.

Upon reaching Isla Cedros, Ulloa reportedly sent one ship back to Acapulco for supplies; it isn't known for certain what happened to the other vessel. According to some historical accounts, Ulloa found his way back to the mainland and was murdered by one of his own crew near Guadalajara; other accounts say he disappeared north of Isla Cedros. At any rate, his written report of the voyage—which indicated Baja was not an island but a peninsula—didn't surface until a hundred years later. His biggest contribution to the geography of the times was the naming of the Mar de Cortés, now the Sea of Cortez or Gulf of California.

After squandering most of his wealth in futile attempts to explore Baja, Cortés was recalled to Spain in 1541, never to return to Mexican shores. In his place, Spain dispatched experienced Portuguese navigator Juan Rodríguez Cabrillo in 1542 with orders to explore the Pacific coast. Starting from the southern tip of the peninsula, his expedition made it as far north as the Oregon coast and mapped several major bays along the way, including those of San Diego and Monterey. Cabrillo himself never made it past California's Santa Barbara Islands, where he died following a mysterious fall.

Manila Galleons and Privateers

On the other side of the globe, events were unfolding that would influence Baja California's history for the next 250 years. Although Portuguese navigator Ferdinand Magellan reached the Philippines in 1521, it wasn't until 1565 that López de Legaspi defeated the archipelago's native defenders. Immediately thereafter, Esteban Rodríguez and Padre Andrés de Urdaneta pioneered a ship route from Manila to the New World that took advantage of the 14,500-km (9,000-mile) Japanese Current across the northern Pacific, thus establishing a trade connection between the Orient and New Spain.

The ships making the annual round-trip voyages between Manila and Acapulco beginning in 1566 came to be called "Manila galleons." The lengthy sea journey was very difficult, however, because of the lack of fresh water during the final weeks of the five- to seven-month eastward crossing. This provided further impetus for establishing some sort of settlement in Baja where ships could put in for water and supplies.

A Baja California landfall became even more desirable when in 1572 the Manila galleons started carrying shipments of gold, silks, and spices to New Spain. Laden with Asian exports, these ships were so heavy they became easy prey for faster pirate vessels. By 1580, England's Sir Francis Drake had entered the Pacific via the Straits of Magellan and circumnavigated the globe, thus ending Spanish dominion over the seas. Drake plundered Spanish ships with regularity, and as news of the treasure-laden ships spread, other English as well as Dutch privateers were lured into the Pacific.

Their raids on Spanish ships became an embarrassment to the crown and a drain on Spanish wealth, so the Spaniards were forced to seek out harbors in Baja's Cape Region where they could hide. Since the first land sighting on the

Manila galleon

INTRODUCTION

NAMING CALIFORNIA

The name "California," as applied to what was originally thought to be an island northwest of Mexico, made its first appearance in the diary of a seaman on the 1539–40 Francisco de Ulloa expedition. The term began appearing on maps shortly thereafter, though its derivation was never explained. Until the late 18th century, there were two competing suppositions. One theory said that the oppressive heat of the peninsula led the Spanish to call the place Calida Fornax, Latin for "Hot Furnace," and that "California" was a corrupted version of this phrase. Another theory claimed the name derived from a mixture of the Spanish *cala,* or "little bay," and the Latin *fornix,* meaning "arch," and that it referred to the arch at Bahía San Lucas. This didn't make much sense either since Bahía San Lucas wasn't a favored harbor in the early days of peninsular exploration.

The true origin of the name wasn't discovered until 1862, when American Edward Everett Hale came across the word in a four-part Spanish novel, *Las Sergas de Esplandián (The Adventures of Esplandián),* written by Garcia Ordoñez de Montalvo and first published in 1510. In the fourth tale of this extremely popular 16th-century novel, the fictional California was:

> . . . . *an island on the right hand of the Indies very near the terrestrial Paradise, peopled by black women among whom there was not a single man. They had beautiful, robust bodies, spirited courage and great strength. Their island was the most impregnable in the world with its cliffs and headlands and rocky coasts. Their weapons were all of gold . . . because in all the island there was no metal except gold.*

In the tale the warrior women are known as Amazons—a name later bestowed upon South America's most famous river—and the island's name is a compound of Califia, their queen (from the Greek *kalli,* or "beautiful"), and *ornix,* the Greek word for "bird"—a reference to the 500 griffins that supported the Amazons in battles. In the novel the Amazons were pagan allies of a Persian king, so the story dovetailed well with the con-

quistadors' promise to the Vatican to convert the heathen hordes away from "the Great Khan."

Since this novel was widely read during the years of the Spanish conquest of Mexico, the California myth probably joined other gold-tinged stories circulating among the conquistadors. Captain Gonzalo de Sandoval, for example, reported to Cortés that in 1523 he had heard a tale from the "lords of the Cihuatá region, who insist on the existence of an island inhabited entirely by women, with not one man, and that at certain times men from the mainland go there, with whom the women lie, and those who fall pregnant, if they bear girls, these are kept, and if boys, are cast out, and this place is ten days from this province, and many of them have been there and have seen this; they say also that the island is rich in pearls and gold."

At first the name California was applied to all lands west of the Colorado River; the distinction between Baja (Lower) and Alta (Upper) California wasn't made until the late 18th century. For the next hundred years or so, if you said "California," it was understood that you meant Baja California, since this was where the first California missions were established. Even after California became a U.S. state in 1850, the "Alta" persisted—in the 1880s, San Franciscans were still publishing a newspaper called the *Daily Alta Californian.*

Today, whenever you get a quorum of Baja aficionados around a table of *cervezas,* you have the raw material for a name debate. Are the peninsula and islands properly called "Baja California" or is just "Baja" okay? What about "the Baja"—which seems to be particularly popular among Canadians, perhaps because they relate it to "the Yukon"? *Bajacalifornianos* (the preferred term for residents of Baja California) often pretend to be rankled at the abbreviated form, yet you may occasionally catch them using it themselves.

The official names of the two Mexican states separated by the peninsula's 28th parallel are "Baja California" (BC) and "Baja California Sur" (BCS), but many *bajacalifornianos* refer to the northern state as "Baja California Norte" (BCN) to distinguish it from the southern state. In this book, the latter practice will be followed so as not to confuse the northern state with the whole peninsula.

east Pacific leg of the Manila–Acapulco voyage was below the peninsula's midpoint, the Cape Region was the logical choice for a landing. Following much experimentation, Bahía San Lucas and Bahía de la Paz became the two harbors most frequently used.

Eventually, however, the keen privateers figured out how to trap Spanish ships in the very bays their crews sought for protection. Thomas Cavendish plundered the Manila galleon *Santa Ana* at Cabo San Lucas in 1587, and so many ships were captured in Bahía de la Paz that the landfall there, originally called Santa Cruz by Cortés, eventually earned the name Pichilingue, a Spanish mispronunciation of Vlissingen, the provenance of most of the Dutch pirates.

Pirating continued off the Baja coast throughout the entire 250-year history of the Manila–Acapulco voyages. One of the more celebrated English privateers in later years was Woodes Rogers, who arrived in the Pacific in 1709 and captured the Manila galleon *Encarnación* off Cabo San Lucas. On his way to Baja California that same year Rogers rescued Alexander Selkirk, a sailor marooned on an island off the coast of Chile for four years. Selkirk served as shipmaster on Rogers's vessel and later became the inspiration for Daniel Defoe's 1719 novel *Robinson Crusoe*.

Further Exploration and Colonization Attempts

As the Spaniards' need for a permanent settlement in California grew more dire, coastal explorations were resumed after a hiatus of over 50 years. Cabrillo was succeeded by merchant-turned-admiral Sebastián Vizcaíno, who in 1596 landed at the same bay on the southeast coast chosen by his predecessors, Jiménez and Cortés. This time, however, the natives were friendly (perhaps because it was *pitahaya* fruit season when they arrived) and Vizcaíno named the site La Paz (Peace). After loading up on *pitahaya* fruit—effective for preventing scurvy—and pearls, Vizcaíno continued north along the Sea of Cortez coast, stopping to gather more pearls before returning to the mainland.

In 1602 Vizcaíno commanded a second, more ambitious expedition that sailed along the Pa-

cific coast to near present-day Mendocino, California. His names for various points and bays along the coasts of both Californias superseded most of those bestowed by Cabrillo and Cortés.

Upon his return Vizcaíno told his superiors that the Monterey Bay area of California was well suited to colonization. However, because he was no longer in favor with New Spain's fickle viceroys, no one paid much attention to his findings and he was reassigned to an obscure Sinaloa port. The cartographer for the voyage, Gerónimo Martínez, was beheaded for forgery, although his maps of the California coast and Baja remained the best available for over 200 years.

This neglect of California's potential enabled an Englishman to put first claim to the territory. Sir Francis Drake, who landed at what is now Drake's Bay in northern California during his 1578–80 voyage, christened the land New Albion on behalf of the English crown. Like the Spanish maps of the time, his maps depicted California and Baja as an island.

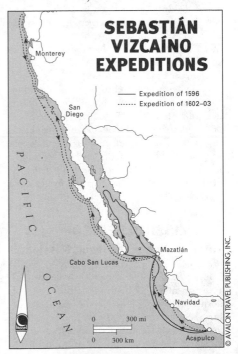

SEBASTIÁN VIZCAÍNO EXPEDITIONS

—— Expedition of 1596
······ Expedition of 1602–03

Monterey

San Diego

PACIFIC OCEAN

Mazatlán

Cabo San Lucas

Navidad

Acapulco

0   300 mi

0   300 km

For a time Spain left both Californias unexplored. In 1615 Captain Juan de Iturbi obtained the first official concession for peninsular pearl diving, but no land settlement was established. After two of his ships were captured by Dutch privateers off Cabo San Lucas, de Iturbi sailed his remaining vessel northward in the Sea of Cortez as far as the 28th parallel, harvesting pearls along the way. Because of dwindling provisions, the expedition was forced to turn back to the mainland after only a few months.

The peninsula remained unconquered by the Spanish for another 80 years. In 1683, Spain's Royal Council for the Indies authorized an expedition under Admiral Isidor Atondo y Antillón and Padre Eusebio Francisco Kino, which managed to occupy an area of La Paz for three and a months before being driven back to the mainland by dwindling provisions and hostile natives. After two months of rest and provisioning on the mainland, they crossed the Sea of Cortez again, this time establishing a mission and presidio just above the 26th parallel at a place they named San Bruno. Supported by a friendly Amerindian population, the mission lasted 19 months. Lack of water and food—they had to rely on supply ships from the mainland—forced Kino and Atondo back to the mainland.

Kino never returned to Baja California but later became famous for his missionary efforts in northwestern Mexico and Arizona, where he is said to have converted thousands of Amerindians to Roman Catholicism. In 1701 he accompanied an expedition from the northwest of Sonora to the mouth of the Río Colorado that confirmed Ulloa's claim that Baja California was a peninsula. He died in Sonora in 1711.

THE MISSION PERIOD
The Founding of the Jesuit Missions
Padre Juan María Salvatierra finally succeeded in giving Spain and the church what they wanted: a permanent Spanish settlement on the Baja California peninsula. Backed by the mainland missionary system, a 30,000-peso annual subsidy from the Royal Council of the Indies, and a contingent of Spanish soldiers, Salvatierra landed in

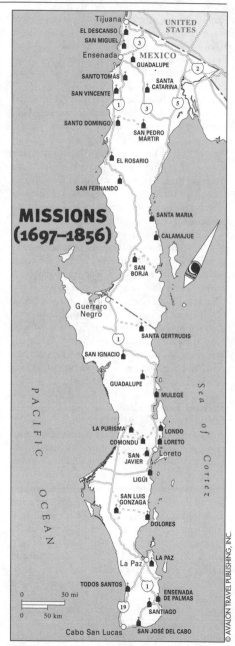

MISSIONS (1697–1856)

San Bruno in October 1697, located a better water source 24 km south of the original presidio, and proceeded to establish the mother of all California missions, Nuestra Señora de Loreto.

The founding of the Loreto mission initiated what Baja historians usually call the Jesuit missionary period, lasting 1697–1767. During this interval, the Jesuits established 20 missions, stretching from the southern tip of the peninsula to near present-day Cataviña in central Baja. That wasn't a spectacular accomplishment compared with the progress of mainland colonization, but Baja was a much more difficult area to colonize. It had taken 167 years from the time the first Spaniard had set foot on the shore until the first successful settlement was established on Baja California soil.

The Spanish mission system basically worked like this: the padres, always in the company of armed escorts, approached groups of natives and offered them the protection of the church and the Spanish crown in return for a willingness to undergo religious instruction. Those natives who agreed were congregated at a suitable spot and directed to build a mission. The mission in turn became a refuge for the Amerindians and a place for them to learn European farming techniques and other trades, as well as Catholic ways. Once pacification was complete, the mission became a secularized church community *(pueblo),* and the missionaries moved on to new areas.

The system worked well with the docile Amerindians of Central Mexico but was often unsuccessful among the nomadic, fiercely independent Amerindians of Northern Mexico and Baja. Elsewhere in Mexico and Latin America, the norm was to secularize after 10 years; in Baja, the Spanish church never voluntarily secularized its missions.

Amateur historians like to say Baja was missionized by the cross, not the sword. This was actually no more true in Baja than it was on the mainland. The military presence here was indeed less, but only because the Jesuits were given greater administrative power in Baja and had to finance themselves, and their militia, through church funds. The conversion techniques were the same: natives who obeyed the padres were rewarded with land and protection, those who re-belled were punished, and those who organized rebellions were executed. Apologists claim the padres never endorsed violence, but if this were true, they wouldn't have brought along the militia in the first place.

Of the 21 principal Jesuit padres who missionized Baja, only four came from Spain. The other 17 hailed from Italy, Germany, Honduras, Bohemia, Austria, and France. Unlike their counterparts on the mainland, who managed to publish 11 grammars analyzing the Uto–Aztecan languages of northwestern Mexico, none of these Jesuit priests ever published a text describing any of the Baja languages.

A contemporary report of the founding of Misión San Juan Bautista describes how Padres Salvatierra and Pedro de Ugarte approached the natives of Liguí in 1703:

The two Padres, the soldier who accompanied them, and two Christian Indians were given a real fright by a large band of Indians who fired a shower of arrows toward them, but after the soldier . . . discharged his musket into the air the Indians threw down their weapons and prostrated themselves on the earth, presently sitting up to await the coming of the Padres. Through an interpreter, Padre Salvatierra explained to them the purpose of their visit and distributed among them some small gifts, expressing the hope that Padre Pedro de Ugarte might return later and be welcomed by them. Before leaving they brought 48 Indian children for baptism.

Amerindian Revolts, Disease, and the Decline of the Jesuits

Several times during the Jesuit period, groups of Amerindians revolted against missionization. The most significant rebellion occurred in 1734–36 among the Pericú of the southern peninsula. Apparently the revolt was triggered by Padre Nicolás Tamaral's injunction against polygamy—long a practice among the Pericú and Guaicura, tribes in which women outnumbered men. The punishment of a Pericú

INTRODUCTION

© JOE CUMMINGS

Spanish crest, Misión San Ignacio

shaman under the injunction doubled the perceived assault on native culture, and a group of disaffected Amerindians organized themselves against the entire mission structure.

In October 1734, the Pericú attacked and burned the missions at Santiago and San José del Cabo, killing Padre Tamaral and his counterpart at Santiago; they also set fire to the mission in La Paz although the padre there escaped unharmed and was able to send to the mainland for assistance. In Todos Santos, the rebels killed 49 Amerindian inhabitants who tried to defend their pueblo. The provincial governor of Sinaloa, after receiving letters from Loreto describing the uprising, dispatched a ship from the mainland with 60 Yaqui warriors and a number of Spanish soldiers. The troops marched from mission to mission, meeting little resistance from the poorly equipped Pericú.

Unrest among the Pericú continued for another two years, a situation that led to the founding of a large garrison at San José del Cabo. As a further precaution, the garrisons at every mis-

sion in the south were expanded by 10 soldiers each. Besides reinforcing the missions, this increased military presence encouraged Manila galleons to make Cabo San Lucas a regular stop on their return voyages from the Orient.

In the years to follow, epidemics of smallpox and measles—diseases borne by Europeans for which Amerindians had no natural immunity—devastated the Amerindian population. In 1738, Padre Jacobo Baegert of Misión San Luis Gonzaga estimated Baja California's Amerindian population at about 50,000. In three outbreaks of smallpox in 1742, 1744, and 1748, an estimated 42,000 Amerindians—84 percent of the native population—perished. Gathering the natives into mission settlements only hastened their demise, intensifying the spread of contagions. A significant number of Amerindians also lost their lives in continued rebellions against the padres. The La Paz mission was abandoned in 1748; by 1767, only one member of the entire Huchiti branch of the Guaycura nation survived.

As the southern Amerindians died out, the missionaries moved quickly northward, seeking new sheep for their flocks. The last four missions established by the Jesuits—Santa Gertrudis (1752), San Borja (1762), Calamajué (1766), and Santa María (1767)—were scattered widely in northern Baja in an obvious push toward California.

In 1767, King Charles III ordered the expulsion of the Jesuit Order from all Spanish dominions, including Baja California. Accounts of the expulsion disagree as to the reasons behind his action. According to crown representatives, the Jesuits were too power-hungry and would no longer be held accountable for their actions. The Jesuits themselves claimed persecution because they'd dared criticize corruption among the nobility and royalty of Europe. Whatever the reason, in 1768 the 16 Jesuit padres of Baja found themselves herded onto a ship bound for the mainland port of San Blas, where the same ship received a contingent of Franciscan padres sent to replace them.

The Franciscans and Dominicans

The 14 Franciscan padres who arrived in Loreto in 1768 included Padre Junípero Serra, often dubbed the Father of California. That title really belongs to Italian Padre Salvatierra, who established the first mission in Baja California 72 years prior to Serra's arrival at San Diego.

To counter the flow of non-Spanish Europeans toward California—the English across the south and middle of today's United States, the French across Canada, and the Russians south from Alaska along the coast—Serra was under orders to establish missions and presidios as quickly as possible in a northward direction.

Serra and the Franciscans only established one mission in Baja before moving on to California. This was San Fernando Velicatá, founded in 1769 about 64 km southeast of today's El Rosario. The Velicatá mission was primarily used as a staging area for expeditions to California. There were two initial expeditions, one by sea from La Paz and one by land from Velicatá; both would rendezvous in San Diego Bay. Padre Serra accompanied the land expedition, led by Captain Gaspár de Portolá, and established California's first mission at San Diego, the first in a chain of 20 missions that stretched along the upper California coast as far as Sonoma, north of San Francisco.

The ambitious Serra, realizing that the arid, underpopulated peninsula did not offer the empire-building potential of California, sent to Mexico City a proposal that the administration of the Baja California missions be released to the Dominican Order, who'd been clamoring for a place in California/Baja missionary action. The viceroy approved Serra's request in 1772, and the first Dominican priests arrived on the peninsula in 1773 under the direction of Padre Vicente Mora.

The first new Dominican mission, Nuestra Señora del Rosario Viñaraco, was founded in the valley now known as Arroyo del Rosario in 1774. Eight more missions and one visiting chapel were established by the Dominicans between 1774 and 1834, all north of El Rosario. The northernmost was Misión El Descanso, located between modern-day Ensenada and Rosarito and built on the edge of Arroyo del Descanso, the official boundary line separating the respective domains of the Dominican order to the south and the Franciscan order to the north. This boundary also served to separate the New Spain provinces of Alta and Baja California, as officially designated in 1777. The current border between Baja California and the U.S. state of California was created by the Treaty of Hidalgo at the end of the Mexican-American War in 1848.

By the end of the 18th century it was clear that Spain and the church could no longer afford to support the Baja missions. The peninsula's Amerindian population had dwindled to less than 5,000 by 1800, and without an abundance of free native labor, maintaining a colony wasn't an easy task. The California missions to the north seemed much more promising—water was more available and the Amerindian labor force was more docile and plentiful. The growing unrest in Mexico placed the peninsula even lower on Spain's list of priorities.

INDEPENDENCE FROM SPAIN

The Catholic Church in Mexico had amassed huge amounts of wealth by the beginning of the 19th century and had become a lender to the colony's growing entrepreneurial class. At the other end of the economic spectrum, the increasing numbers of mestizos—Mexican-born residents of mixed Spanish and Amerindian ancestry—were denied land ownership and other rights and were generally treated as second-class citizens.

Fearing the church was becoming too powerful, King Charles III of Spain decreed in 1804 that all church funds be turned over to the royal coffers. As padres all over Mexico were forced to comply with the decree, calling back large sums of money lent out to entrepreneurs, economic chaos ensued. Mexicans blamed their economic and social problems on Spain's remote rule; when Napoleon invaded Spain in 1808, limiting authority to Spanish loyalists in Mexico City, the disaffected clergy began planning a revolt.

Mexico's struggle for independence from Spain began on September 16, 1810, a date celebrated annually as Día de la Independencia or Mexican Independence Day. Padre Miguel Hidalgo y Costilla issued a call for independence today known as the Grito de Dolores (Dolores Cry) from the mainland city of Dolores, Guanajuato. Although the rebels who gathered around Hidalgo soon captured Zacatecas, Valladolid, and San Luis Potosí, Mexico wasn't completely free of Spanish rule for another 11 years. When Hidalgo was captured and executed by loyalists, another padre took his place, and the fighting continued until Mexico City acceded to the demands of the rebels in 1821.

The 1821 Plan de Iguala treaty between Spain and Mexico guaranteed three political underpinnings of the new regime: the religious dominance of the Catholic Church, a constitutional monarchy, and equal rights for mestizos as well as Mexican-born Spaniards. Former viceroy Agustín de Iturbide was appointed emperor of the new republic, but his reign only lasted two years before he was overthrown by another junta that established a short-lived federal republic called Los Estados Unidos de México—the United States of Mexico—in 1824.

Over the next six years the Mexican republic endured two more coups; it wasn't until 1829 that all Spanish troops were expelled from Mexico. In 1832 all non-Dominican missions in Baja were secularized and converted to parish churches. The Dominican missions of the northern peninsula were allowed to remain because they were considered the only outposts of civilization north of La Paz and Loreto and as such were important links with prospering Alta California. Another change in policy involved the encouragement of Anglo-American immigration to the northeastern Mexican state of Coahuila y Texas—a policy that would have profound implications later on.

The Mexican-American War

In 1833 Antonio López de Santa Anna, a megalomaniac general in charge of enforcing the expulsion of Spanish troops, seized power and revoked the Constitution of 1824, thus initiating a series of events that eventually led to a war with the United States and the resultant loss of huge amounts of territory. During the first 30 years of Mexican independence, Mexico changed governments 50 times; Santa Anna—who called himself the Napoleon of the West—headed 11 of these regimes.

Mexican citizens everywhere were angry at the revocation of their republican constitution by a self-appointed dictator. But none were more frustrated than the Anglo-American immigrants who had voluntarily abandoned their U.S. citizenship to take Mexican citizenship under the Constitution of 1824 and live in the northern half of Coahuila y Texas. In 1836 the "Texicans" declared an independent Republic of Texas, fought and lost San Antonio's famous Battle of the Alamo, then routed Santa Anna's defending troops in San Jacinto, Texas.

Defeated and captured, Santa Anna signed the Velasco Agreement, which guaranteed Texas independence and recognized the Rio Grande as the border between Mexico and the new Texan republic. There matters lay until the United States granted statehood to the near-bankrupt republic in 1845. Santa Anna's government refused to recognize the Velasco Agreement, claiming Texas only extended as far south as the Nueces River, about 160 km north of the Rio Grande at the widest gap. When the U.S. Army moved into the area south of the Nueces, Santa Anna retaliated by sending troops across the Rio Grande, thus initiating the Mexican-American War.

After a series of skirmishes along the Rio Grande, U.S. president James Polk ordered the army to invade Mexico. In Baja California, Mexican and American forces engaged at Santo Tomás, Mulegé, La Paz, and San José del Cabo. Mexico City finally fell to U.S. troops in March 1847, and Santa Anna signed the Treaty of Guadalupe Hidalgo in 1848. In the treaty, Mexico conceded not only the Rio Grande area of Texas but part of New Mexico and all of California for a payment of US$25 million and the cancellation of all Mexican debt.

In retrospect, it is likely the annexation of Texas was part of a U.S. plan to provoke Mexico into declaring war so the United States could gain more of the Southwest. The war so damaged Mexico's already weakened economy that in 1853 Santa Anna sold Arizona and southern New Mexico to the United States for another US$10 million. During that same year, American freebooter William Walker sailed to La Paz and declared himself President of Lower California. He and his mercenary troops fled upon hearing that Mexican forces were on the way. He was later tried—and acquitted—in the United States for violation of neutrality laws. Walker was executed after a similar escapade in Nicaragua two years later.

For the Mexican population, already strongly dissatisfied with Santa Anna, these losses of territory became the final straw; in 1855 Santa Anna was overthrown by populist Benito Juárez.

Depopulation of the Peninsula, Civil War, and Reform

The second half of the 19th century was even more turbulent for Mexico than the first. At the end of the Mexican-American War, the California Gold Rush of 1849 lured many Mexicans and Amerindians away from the peninsula to seek their fortunes in California, reducing Baja's already scant population even further and transforming it into a haven for bandits, pirates, and an assortment of other outlaws and misfits. Only six Dominican padres remained on the peninsula by the 1880s.

BOB RACE

Benito Juárez

Meanwhile, back on the mainland, a civil war (called the War of Reform in Mexico) erupted in 1858 following the removal of Santa Anna; self-appointed governments in Mexico City and Veracruz vied for national authority. Once again, church wealth was the principal issue. The liberals, under Zapotec lawyer Benito Juárez, had promulgated a new constitution in 1857 and passed a law further restricting the financial powers of the church; all church property save for church buildings themselves had to be sold or otherwise relinquished. A reactionary opposition group took control of Mexico City, and fighting continued until 1861, when the liberals won and Juárez was elected president.

Juárez immediately had to deal with the 1862 French invasion of Mexico, which came in response to Mexico's nonpayment of debts to France. Napoleon III's first invading force was defeated at Puebla near the Gulf of Mexico coast, but the following year the French captured the city and continued onward to take Mexico City, where they installed Austrian Ferdinand Maximilian as emperor of Mexico. Under U.S. pressure, the French gradually withdrew from Mexico, and Juárez was back in power by 1867.

Over the next four years Juárez initiated many economic and educational reforms. Upon his death in 1872, political opponent Porfirio Díaz took over and continued reforms begun by Juárez, albeit in a more authoritarian manner. Díaz and/or his cronies ruled for the next 28 years, suspending political freedoms but modernizing the country's education and transportation systems.

Foreign Investment in Baja California

In Baja, Díaz and the "Porfiriato" encouraged foreign investment on a large scale, and in the 1880s vast land tracts were sold to American or European mining, farming, manufacturing, and railway concessions. All but the mining concessions met failure within a few years, mainly because the investors weren't prepared to deal with the peninsula's demanding climate and lack of transportation. A Connecticut company invested US$5 million as a down payment on US$16 million for extensive land holdings in Ensenada and San Quintín. There it planned to develop farmlands, railways, and seaports. When the first wheat crop succumbed to lack of rain, the company sold out to a similar English development syndicate, which also failed.

Mineral excavation in late-19th-century Baja enjoyed a boom—gold, silver, copper, and gypsum were the main finds, along with graphite, mercury, nickel, and sulfur. One of the most successful mining endeavors was that of Compañía del Boleo, a French mining syndicate in Santa Rosalía that for many years was the largest copper-mining and smelting operation in Mexico.

THE 20TH CENTURY

The Mexican Revolution

By the early 20th century, it was obvious that the gap between rich and poor was increasing, caused by the extreme procapitalist policies of the Díaz regime and the lack of a political voice for workers and peasants. In response to the situation, a liberal opposition group, using Texas as a base, formed in exile, organizing strikes throughout the country. This forced Díaz to announce an election in 1910; his opponent was Francisco Madero, a liberal from Coahuila. As it became clear that Madero was garnering mass support, Díaz imprisoned him on trumped-up charges.

Upon his release, Madero fled to Texas and began organizing the overthrow of the Díaz government. The rebels, with the assistance of colorful bandit-turned-revolutionary Pancho Villa and peasant-hero Emiliano Zapata, managed to gain control of the Northern Mexico states of Sonora and Chihuahua. Unable to contain the revolution, Díaz resigned in May 1910, and Madero was elected president. His one-time allies, however, broke into several factions—the Zapatistas, Reyistas, Vasquistas, and Felicistas, named for the leaders of each movement—and Madero was executed in 1913. Baja California had its own faction, the Magonistas, who briefly held Tijuana in 1911.

For the next six years the various factions played musical chairs with national leadership; Mexico remained extremely unstable until rev-olutionary leader Venustiano Carranza emerged as president. Carranza held a historic convention that resulted in the Constitution of 1917, the current Mexican constitution. This document established the *ejido* program to return lands traditionally cultivated by the Amerindian peasantry, but taken away by rich ranch and plantation owners under Díaz, to local communities throughout Mexico. Three years later opponent Álvaro Obregón and his supporters overthrew Carranza.

Obregón managed to hang onto the office for four years, establishing important educational reforms; he was followed in 1924 by Plutarco Elías Calles. Calles instituted wide-reaching agrarian reforms, including the redistribution of three million hectares of land. He also participated in the establishment of the National Revolutionary Party (PNR), the forerunner of the Institutional Revolutionary Party (PRI), which remained Mexico's dominant party until the National Action Party (PAN) won the presidency in 2000.

U.S. Prohibition

In the same year that Obregón took power in Mexico City, the U.S. government amended its own constitution to make the consumption, manufacture, and sale of alcoholic beverages a federal offense. This proved to be a disastrous experiment for the United States, ushering in an era of organized crime, but was a boon to Baja California development. Americans began rushing across the border to buy booze from the restaurants, cantinas, and liquor stores of Northern Mexico.

Border towns added casinos and brothels to the assortment of liquor venues and became so prosperous that the municipal leadership was able to lobby successfully for the division of Baja California into northern and southern territories. On the negative side, Tijuana and Mexicali became renowned as world sleaze capitals. Their reputations persisted long after Prohibition ended in 1933 and the Mexican government outlawed gambling—prostitution remained legal—in 1938. The cities wisely channeled much of their unexpected revenue into manufacturing, agriculture, and other non-tourist-related development.

Nationalist Reforms and World War II

The year 1938 proved a turning point in modern Mexican history as PNR candidate Lázaro Cárdenas ascended to the presidency. Cárdenas, a mestizo with Tarascan Amerindian heritage, instituted the most sweeping social reforms of any national leader to date, effecting significant changes in education, labor, agriculture, and commerce.

His land reforms included the redistribution of 18.6 million hectares (46 million acres) among newly created *ejidos*—a legacy that is as hot a topic for debate today as it was then. Foreign-owned oil interests were expropriated, and a national oil company, Petróleos Mexicanos (Pemex), was established. Even though foreign investors were compensated for expropriations at fair market value (under a treaty signed by both the United States and Mexico), these reforms frightened off foreign investors for many years, and it has been only very recently that Mexico has reattracted foreign capital. Cárdenas also reorganized the PNR as the Mexican Revolution Party (PRM—Partido de la Revolución Mexicana), which soon changed its name to the Institutional Revolutionary Party (PRI—Partido Revolucionario Institucional).

Between the Cárdenas period and the 2000 presidential election, Mexican political history was characterized by comparatively subtle shifts. Mexican leadership succession also had stabilized, a process often referred to as the oxymoronic "institutionalization of the revolution" (meaning the PRI had won every national election in that period).

During World War II, Mexican troops fought in the Pacific on the Allied side. The Mexican economy grew with the increased demand for materials and labor in the United States; the scarcity of imported goods in Mexico forced the nation to increase domestic production. In 1942 the United States instituted the Bracero Program, which permitted Mexicans to work north of the border for short periods of time; the program lasted until 1962 and had a profound effect on urban development along the United States–Mexico border.

Baja Statehood and the Transpeninsular Highway

After the war Mexico continued to industrialize, and the economy remained relatively stable under one PRI president after another. In 1952, the Territory of (Northern) Baja California was declared Mexico's 29th state as its population moved past the 80,000 required for statehood. Northern Baja was, in fact, better off economically than most of the rest of the country. The boomtowns of Tijuana and Mexicali were servicing a fast-growing border economy, and Valle de Mexicali farming competed well with California's Imperial Valley. In 1958 it was determined that Baja was second only to Mexico City in the number of automobiles per capita.

Throughout the 1960s, most of Baja south of Ensenada remained benevolently neglected, which led travel writers of the time to employ the famous catchphrase, "the forgotten peninsula." The population of the Territory of Southern Baja California was stagnating, perhaps even decreasing; except for La Paz, it was limited to tiny collections of hardy souls here and there who scratched for cash as rancheros or *pescadores* (fishermen). Even La Paz was just a step above a sleepy backwater port, although its status as a duty-free port was beginning to attract a steady trickle of mainland Mexicans.

By the 1970s, it was obvious that southern Baja wasn't going to catch up with northern Baja unless transportation between the south, north, and mainland improved. Travel between Tijuana and La Paz took up to 10 days via rough dirt tracks. Construction of the Transpeninsular Highway (Mexico 1) was finally completed in 1973, connecting Tijuana with Cabo San Lucas for the first time. In less than a year, the population of Baja California Sur passed the 80,000 mark, and the territory became Mexico's 30th state.

The 1,700-km-long (1,054-mile-long) Transpeninsular Highway has greatly contributed to the modernization of one of Mexico's last frontiers. Fishing and agricultural cooperatives can now transport their products to the border or to the ports of Santa Rosalía, Guerrero Negro, and La Paz. The highway has brought Americans, Canadians, and Europeans deep into the peninsula in greater numbers than ever before, and the revenue from their visits provides another means of livelihood for the people of Baja.

Another boost to peninsular political and economic development came along in the 1980s when former president Miguel de la Madrid proclaimed a new era of modernization and plupartyism—equivalent in word if not in deed to Gorbachev's perestroika/glasnost proclamation. Already-modernizing Baja California Norte, partial stronghold of the PAN (Partido Acción Nacional, the nation's conservative opposition party) particularly benefited from a relaxation of PRI's hold. The era of optimism was extended by Mexican president Carlos Salinas de Gortari, who was a strong supporter of the much-debated North American Free Trade Agreement (NAFTA); see Government and Economy, later, for more information on the treaty.

The Crisis of 1994–95

Although the Mexican economy went for a rollercoaster ride in the 1970s and early '80s when the government nationalized banks and devalued the peso, things brightened considerably in the late '80s and early '90s under Salinas's market modernization. Then in 1994 everything seemed to go awry on the mainland.

On January 1, 1994, the day NAFTA took effect, a group of several hundred armed Lacandón Amerindians under the leadership of a masked, pipe-smoking mestizo who dubbed himself "Subcommandante Marcos" dramatically seized four towns in the state of Chiapas in a series of well-coordinated attacks. The group retreated swiftly in the face of overwhelming Mexican armed force but not before 145 people were killed in armed skirmishes. The Zapatista National Liberation Army (EZLN), as the guerrilla group called itself, was not only protesting NAFTA—which the EZLN believed would have negative effects on the rural southern Mexican economy—but was also airing traditional grievances regarding fraudulent regional elections and land seizure from Lacandón peasants.

While the EZLN and Mexican government were negotiating in Chiapas, another event un-

folded to create even more difficulties for the Salinas government. Luis Donaldo Colosio, the PRI's prime presidential candidate groomed to take Salinas's place, was shot to death by a factory worker while campaigning in Tijuana on March 23, 1994. In the ensuing federal investigation the deputy attorney general, Mario Ruiz Massieu, and Salinas's brother, Raúl, were implicated in the suspected assassination plot.

Meanwhile, Colosio's campaign manager, Yale University graduate Ernesto Zedillo, was elected to the presidency in an August 1994 election widely considered the cleanest in Mexico's history. The decisive PRI victory was little cause for optimism, however; Mexico City politics unraveled further when investigators uncovered a trail of corruption that threatened to implicate Mexico's former wunderkind, Carlos Salinas. To avoid testifying against his own brother—or perhaps to protect himself—Carlos fled the country (Salinas now resides in Dublin, Ireland).

Raúl Salinas was subsequently found to have amassed a US$24 million fortune through illicit means. In May 1994, the government seized 117 kg of cocaine base during a raid on a ranch in Quintana Roo owned by a PRI senator, and around the same time a senior Ministry of Tourism official involved in deciding whether to legalize gambling casinos was arrested and charged with illegal enrichment.

By the end of 1994 the events in Chiapas, the Colosio assassination, and glimpses into high-level Mexican corruption had resulted in an extreme loss of investor confidence in Mexico, leading in turn to a stock sell-off and a domestic run on the U.S. dollar. To protect draining reserves, Mexico City responded by allowing the peso to float, sending the currency into a deflationary tailspin at the beginning of 1995.

Over the months of January and February 1995 the peso dropped from an exchange rate of N$3 per U.S. dollar to around N$8. The worst recession the country had seen in 60 years ensued. The Clinton administration, along with the International Monetary Fund (IMF), bailed out the government with loans to pay off international debt, but Mexicans of all economic classes—especially those involved with international business—suffered heavy losses and a substantial drop in standard of living.

In Baja California Norte, home base for the notorious Arellano Félix drug cartel, seven federal agents and a state prosecutor involved in antinarcotics efforts were assassinated in 1996. Such assassinations may be seen as a tribute to the integrity of the agents, for whom the only real choice when confronting powerful *narcotraficantes* may be to accept bribes or be assassinated.

INTO THE 21ST CENTURY

In his first state-of-the-nation address, President Zedillo acknowledged that corruption was deeply rooted in Mexican institutions and in the general social conduct of the nation. He confirmed the determination of his administration to confront official corruption and to encourage the creation of a new culture of respect for law, beginning with the behavior of public officials. Zedillo also signed the Organization of American States (OAS) Corruption Convention, which was ratified unanimously by the Mexican Senate. Whether any of this will make a difference is difficult to tell; virtually every president who has taken office in Mexico during the last 25 years has vowed to fight corruption. Antonio Lozano Gracia, Mexico's first attorney general ever appointed from an opposition party, dismissed more than 1,250 officials for incompetence or corruption and completely revamped hiring, training, and internal accountability.

Shortly thereafter the attorney general himself was forced to resign for alleged corruption. Once again mass firings of state and local police took place, this time for dereliction of duty. Often these positions were taken over by military officers, who are presumed to be less corruptible than civilian law-enforcement agents. In Baja California all 87 *judiciales* or federal agents involved in narcotics interdiction were replaced by members of the Mexican military in 1996. Mexico's increasing militarization is itself cause for concern, as there is no evidence whatsoever that members of the military, with less training in law enforcement than their police counterparts, will be any less corrupt than the police. The army general put in charge of the national counternarcotics effort quickly succumbed to cartel bribes and was forced to resign that same year. Most observers agree they have only so far seen gradual success at the lower levels of government and law enforcement.

Baja, because of its ties to the U.S. economy and access to the U.S. dollar, weathered "the crisis" much better than most parts of Mexico. By 2000 most sectors of the Mexican economy showed signs of recovery, though foreign investor confidence remained shaky as scandals in law enforcement, the military, and the drug arena continued to surface on an almost weekly basis. Many observers, both Mexican and international, now see the rosy Salinas years as an elaborate setup of smoke and mirrors that masked the overvaluation of the peso, corruption, and other economic and political ills that had just begun to be addressed by the sober Zedillo administration. In Baja, people just shake their heads and blame it all on the *chilangos* (Mexico City residents).

Most *bajacalifornianos* are facing the new millennium with the same self-reliance and flexibility that have enabled them to cope with the two political systems, two economies, and singular isolation that have helped forge their unique destiny.

Government and Economy

POLITICAL BOUNDARIES

The 28th parallel divides the peninsula into two states, officially named Baja California (abbreviated BC) above the parallel and Baja California Sur (BCS) below. Unofficially, the northern state is often called Baja California Norte (BCN); a debate continually simmers as to whether or not to make this version official. In this book, BCN is used so as not to confuse the northern state with the whole peninsula.

Mexicali is BCN's state capital, which governs five *municipios* that are similar to U.S. counties: Tijuana, Rosarito, Ensenada, Mexicali, and Tecate. Besides its southern border with BCS, BCN shares a northern border with the United States and an eastern border, formed above the Sea of Cortez by the Colorado River, with the Mexican state of Sonora.

Baja California Sur is likewise divided into five *municipios:* La Paz, Cabo San Lucas, Mulegé, Loreto, and Comondú. La Paz is the state capital.

POLITICAL SYSTEM

As Mexican states, BCN and BCS are part of Mexico's federal system (Estados Unidos Mexicanos, or United Mexican States), which allows for some degree of autonomous rule by state governors and their legislatures. Both states are considered among the nation's most socially progressive. Over half of Mexico's orphanages, for example, are in Baja. In 1989, BCN became the first state in Mexico to vote in an opposition party when citizens elected a PAN (Partido Acción Nacional or National Action Party) state government—most other states in Mexico have been ruled by the PRI (Partido Revolucionario Institucional) since the Mexican Revolution. PAN is usually described as a conservative party because it favors private over government ownership, yet in the context of Mexican politics it's more reform-minded than PRI. As elsewhere in the world, political labels and their meanings shift with time. Baja California has tended to

follow the example of other wealthier northern Mexican states by keeping PAN administrations in office.

Meanwhile, the residents of Baja California Sur most recently voted in a leftist coalition party consisting of the PRD (Partido Revolucionario Democrático or Democratic Revolutionary Party) and the PT (Partido Trabajadores or Workers Party). Many were surprised to see that the state containing Baja's most extensive resort area (Los Cabos) elected a PRD/PT candidate. However, these parties are very well organized in southern Baja, whose residents are generally more agrarian and poorer than their neighbors to the immediate north.

PAN and PRD/PT victories in BCN and BCS are considered by some as watersheds in Mexican political affairs, which have been notorious for election fraud since adopting the republican system in 1917. Hard-boiled cynics insist all high political offices are part of a ruling dynasty extending outward from the presidency in Mexico City; even municipal mayors in Mexico are called *el presidente,* and the local seat of government is the *palacio municipal.* Wags point out other symbolic evidence—the president wears an imperial sash and sits upon a throne when making official proclamations—and note that political candidates endorsed by the incumbents always win succeeding elections.

The PRI won every presidential election, held every six years, for over 70 years until the 2000 runoff installed, for the first time in Mexican history, an opposition president. Vicente Fox, former Guanajuato state governor and candidate for the Alliance of Change (an alliance between PAN and the Green Ecologist Party of Mexico), landed an astounding 42.5 percent of the vote, with PRI candidate Francisco Labastida next at 36.1 percent and PRD candidate Cuauhtémoc Cárdenas trailing at 16.6 percent. The Alliance also took the two governorships of Guanajuato and Morelos, nearly half the seats in the 500-person Chamber of Deputies, and 53 seats in the 128-person Senate. The coalition even seized a majority in Mexico City's legislative assembly and the head offices for five of Mexico City's 16 delegations, formerly seen as a last bastion of the center-left.

Fox immediately surprised many observers by appointing a left-of-center academic, Jorge Castaneda, as Minister of Foreign Affairs. Although Castaneda had been an early opponent of NAFTA, he has since reversed his position on the trade treaty.

Whether Fox's administration can live up to the dreams of its supporters, observers agree that if nothing else a degree of election reform has finally been achieved in Mexico, and the republic has established itself as a pluralistic democracy—at least for the time being.

The *presidentes municipales* appoint city *delegados* to represent federal power at the local level; smaller communities may have *subdelegados*. These *delegados* and *subdelegados* are the highest authority within their jurisdictions and are part of a chain of command that reaches back to the president of Mexico.

At the national level, the bicameral Congreso de la Unión (National Congress) is divided into a 128-seat Camara de Senadores (Senate) and 500-seat Camara de Diputados (Chamber of Deputies). Elections for congressional positions are held every three years.

INCOME AND EMPLOYMENT

Agriculture, fishing, and tourism are Baja's main revenue-earners, followed by manufacturing and services in the border area. Per-capita income figures for BCN and BCS are well above the Mexican national average and second within the nation only to that of Mexico's D.F. (Distrito Federal) and neighboring states in the Valle de México. Both states of Baja register the lowest unemployment in the country; of the new jobs created in Mexico these days, more are on the peninsula than in any other part of the country.

Most large-scale farming is centered in the Río Colorado delta (Valle de Mexicali), Valle de Guadalupe, Valle de San Quintín, and the Plano de Magdalena surrounding Ciudad Constitución. Fishing boats work both coasts, but the Sea of Cortez produces the largest catch, and La Paz is the main fishing center. Tourism is for the most part concentrated in Tijuana, Rosarito-Ensenada, Mulegé-Loreto, La Paz, and Los Cabos (San José del Cabo and Cabo San Lucas).

Despite NAFTA, the stars of the manufacturing sector remain the *maquiladoras,* or in-bond industries, which combine third-world labor costs with first-world capital and management. These are predominantly located in special export-processing zones in the Tijuana area, although nearby Tecate and Mexicali also feature industrial parks. While wages at the *maquiladoras* are far below comparable wages in the United States, on average they're about twice Mexico's current minimum daily wage of US$5 a day and in many cases up to four times higher.

Border Economy

The border is also the focus of a mostly undocumented shadow economy supported by both legal and illegal migrant Mexican labor in the United States. Mexican labor migration has become so integrated into the regional economy that it is now considered largely responsible for the competitive and stable pricing of U.S. consumer goods.

That Mexican labor is essential to U.S. production is also indicated by the cyclical nature of immigration statistics relative to upturns and downturns in the U.S. economy. Intertwined with the shadow economy, Baja's border economy tends to move with the U.S. economic tide.

Ejidos

One of the unique features of the Mexican economy is the *ejido* institution, which has its roots in the Spanish *reconquista* (when Spanish Christians retook the Iberian Peninsula from the Moors during the late 15th century). The Spanish crown honored Spanish nobles who had fought in the conflict by granting them land tracts confiscated from the Moors. In Nueva España the Spanish monarchy continued the tradition by offering communal land to conquistadors in return for dominating the Amerindian inhabitants. In his reforms of 1863 and 1867, Benito Juárez, Mexico's first president, converted church and *ejido* lands into individually owned plots in Mexico's first attempt to give peasants land rights.

Following the Mexican Revolution the *ejido* concept became a way of restoring lands that had been taken (usually legally purchased) from peasants by rich *hacendados* (big ranchers and plantation owners) during Spanish colonization and early Mexican independence. Considered a mainstay of PRI policy, nowadays in Mexico an *ejido* is a land tract held in common by a peasant community. It usually includes not only cultivated fields but also school properties, urban zones, water and forest resources, and any other facilities or resources either native to the land or produced by collective efforts. *Ejidos* are granted to *ejidatarios* by the government without rents or fees of any kind. They were originally nontransferable, nonattachable, and inalienable, i.e., *ejido* lands couldn't be sold, used as loan collateral, or taken away by local, regional, or national legal bodies.

According to Mexican law, *ejidos* are considered neither state property nor private property but are entities of the "social interest sector." How they are used is solely the concern of the peasant communities that hold them, but around 95 percent of them are "individual" *ejidos* in which the common holdings are divided into individual plots and cultivated by individual *ejidatarios* and their families. The remaining five percent are "collective" *ejidos* that pool all land resources for collective production. The number and total acreage of Mexico's *ejidos* is not well documented, but by 1970 they were estimated to encompass around 46 percent of national farmlands. According to every survey ever conducted nationwide, *ejido* lands are the least productive of all agricultural lands in Mexico.

Various bits of *ejido* legislation enacted since the Revolution have alternately strengthened and weakened the program. In the 1980s laws were passed that allowed *ejidatarios* to lease their lands to neighboring private estates for agricultural or livestock purposes. In the 1990s the government established regulations that now permit the sale of *ejido* lands. Thus for the first time ever individuals living in *ejidos* have property rights.

Has the *ejido* program been successful? On the one hand, it has kept hereditary lands in the hands of peasant communities who have worked them for hundreds of years—without them, many *ejidatarios* would probably become landless migrant workers. On the other hand, because *ejido* production is notoriously low (as are fixed prices for agricultural products), the need for cash to survive in Mexico's cash economy has forced many *ejidatarios* to work as laborers on private neighboring lands. As a result, it has been estimated that *ejidatarios* are among the poorest and most exploited of Mexico's rural workers.

The selling of *ejido* lands, as is now permitted, may gradually erode the *ejido* system, although it will certainly enrich many *ejidatarios* in the short term. Without the opportunity to buy, sell, and trade their lands, however, *ejidatarios* live entirely without true ownership rights, and their lands remain the Mexican equivalent of U.S. Amerindian reservations.

RECENT ECONOMIC CONDITIONS

On a macroeconomic level, Baja finds itself caught between two economic systems. Because it's so isolated from the rest of Mexico, the regional economy tends to be American-influenced yet subject to the same economic vicissitudes as the rest of the country, most notably a weak currency and high inflation. Although the country's current-account balance rose from a deficit of US$6.2 billion in 1982 to a surplus of US$4 billion in 1987, the inflation rate that same year hit 146 percent. Because of its regional ties to the United States, particularly California, the Baja economy weathered this period better than many areas of Mexico. A similar phenomenon occurred during the 1994–95 period, when a negative balance reappeared.

During the Salinas and Zedillo administrations the nation moved closer to United States–style growth-led economics, thus lessening the schizoid nature of Baja's regional economy. One of the biggest steps taken by the federal government was the reprivatizing of the national banking system, the telephone system, and several other state industries (Pemex is the major exception). Still, the eight largest employers in Mexico are government agencies connected with education, social security, Pemex, or defense. Despite overall budget deficits, government social spending continues to increase.

Led by exports, construction, and manufacturing, the country's gross national product (GNP) managed to grow 5.1 percent in 1996, and in 1997 Mexico repaid the final US$3.5 billion of its US$13.5 billion emergency loan package from the U.S. government, three years ahead of schedule. A portion of the IMF loan was also repaid ahead of schedule.

On a microeconomic level, the national minimum wage hovers at US$5 per day, attractive to foreign manufacturers looking for cheap labor but just barely enough for survival in today's Mexico.

The political and economic crisis that ensued during 1994–95 was largely stabilized by PRI president Ernesto Zedillo. Vicente Fox's ascension to the presidency kept the economy relatively stable, although the global recession of 2001–02 has put the brakes on the Mexican economy as well. Some optimistic economists predict that if Mexico continues its current economic reforms, and world markets recover from the global recession, it may become Latin America's fastest-growing economy by the year 2005. Growth in Baja will probably be slower, however, since much of the current and projected growth is in areas of Mexico that are "catching up" with the north.

The People and Culture

The people of Baja California are in many ways a breed apart from their compatriots on the mainland. As Mexico's last frontier, the peninsula continues to attract residents seeking something they haven't been able to find elsewhere, whether it's the rugged, independent life of the interior deserts and sierras, the tropical ambience of La Paz or Cabo San Lucas, or the promising multicultural world in Tijuana and Mexicali, where California and Baja California meet.

For the rest of Mexico, Baja California occupies a place in the national psyche somewhat analogous to that of Hawaii for many Americans. It's seen as a place that's part of the nation yet almost out of reach—an exotic destination that most of the population will never have an opportunity to see. Hence, mainlanders typically regard *bajacalifornianos* as somehow different from themselves.

POPULATION

The current population of the entire peninsula is approximately 2.5 million, about 85 percent of whom live above the 28th parallel in Baja California Norte. Well over half the people on the peninsula live in Mexicali and Tijuana, with an additional 13 percent in Ensenada. Obviously, most of the peninsula is sparsely populated— the average density, even if these and all other Baja cities are included in the estimate, is only 1.5 persons per square km (about four persons per square mile). Outside the three most populated cities it's less than one person per 26 square km (one body per 10 square miles).

Mexico's population growth rate is currently estimated at 1.9 percent per annum, relatively low for a developing country. The average for Baja California is probably somewhat higher than the national average because of immigration. Baja California Sur is Mexico's least populated state.

ORIGINS

Bajacalifornianos (sometimes called *bajacalifornios*) are an unusually varied lot. Elsewhere in Mexico, the average citizen is a mix of Spanish and Amerindian bloodlines. In Baja, the mix is typically more complicated, mainly because the peninsula remained a frontier much longer than most of the mainland, attracting people who arrived in the New World long after the Spanish colonized the Mexican mainland. It was 167 years after the conquest of Mexico before the Spanish were able to maintain a permanent settlement on the peninsula; by this time, tales of the

Californias were on the tongues of adventurers throughout the world.

By the end of the 19th century the peninsula had become a favorite spot for sea-weary sailors to jump ship. The eastern shores of the peninsula were placid, and there was little chance deserters would be rounded up and incarcerated by local militia, who were scarce then and remain so today. Most of the ex-sailors who retired to Baja in this manner were English, but during World War I a few Germans and other Europeans came ashore. Their ship captains might have considered them cowardly deserters, but survival in Baja in the 19th and early 20th centuries was possible only for the brave, hardy, and resourceful.

Other immigrants who pioneered the Baja frontier included Chinese workers who came via the Mexican mainland and eventually flourished in the Mexicali area, Russian viticulturists who settled the Valle de Guadalupe, French miners in Santa Rosalía and Mulegé, and Mexican intellectuals and dissidents fleeing political oppression on the mainland and gravitating toward La Paz, Ensenada, and Tijuana. Many of these newcomers intermarried, and their descendants have greatly contributed to the peninsula's multicultural spirit.

Since in a very real sense much of Baja is still a frontier area—with more immigrants wandering in year by year—Baja's demographics have yet to solidify into recognizable pie-graph proportions. About two percent of the residents aren't even Mexican citizens; many are American, Canadian, or European retirees, and a lesser number are gringos who've simply dropped out of the rat race. With the current relaxation of investment and trade laws, a growing number of foreigners are also setting up businesses on the peninsula.

Bajacalifornianos

If there's a personality trait common to all true *bajacalifornianos,* it's a do-or-die spirit that says, "I belong here because my family was tough

> *If there's a personality trait common to all true* **bajacalifornianos,** *it's this do-or-die spirit: "I belong here because my family was tough enough to survive in Baja back when this was the toughest place in Mexico to survive."*

enough to survive in Baja back when this was the toughest place in Mexico to survive." While opinions vary, the popular definition of a "true" *bajacaliforniano* is someone whose forebears came to and stayed on the peninsula sometime before World War II.

A self-adopted nickname for *bajacalifornianos,* particularly popular in northern Baja, is *cachanilla* (sometimes spelled *cachanía*), the name of a hardy desert plant (arrowweed) that produces rose-colored flowers under even the harshest conditions.

Bajacalifornianos love to rant about how the peninsula was neglected by the mainland for centuries, how they cultivated Baja for themselves, without any help from Mexico City. Now that the Transpeninsular Highway is complete and the economic infrastructure is expanding, the *bajacalifornianos* complain that weak mainlanders are coming to harvest the fruits of Baja's development. A special scorn is reserved for *chilangos,* a derogatory term used by *bajacalifornianos* for Mexico City politicians or businesspeople who come to Baja and tell the *cachanillas* how to run things.

Amerindians

Of the estimated 50,000 Amerindians who inhabited the peninsula when the Spanish established their first Baja mission of any duration in 1697, at least 80 percent were wiped out by disease or colonial violence within 100 years. None of the Guaycura tribes of the south—Guaicura, Pericú, Huchiti—survived the Spanish occupation, but small numbers of the central and northern Cochimí and Yumano tribes still reside in the valleys and sierras of BCN.

According to Mexico's most recent census (1995), the Paipai (Pa'ipai, or "Clever People") are the largest surviving native tribe, numbering around 300; most are concentrated in the vicinity of Santa Catarina and San Isidoro. About 165 Kumyai live in Valle de Guadalupe and Juntas de Neji, 200 Cochimí in Valle Ojos Ne-

seminomadic existence dependent on hunting, gathering, and fishing; in winter they live in semi-subterranean shelters and in summer under thatched-roof ramadas. The Kiliwa of the northern Sierra de San Pedro Mártir also maintain a hunter-gatherer culture. The Cucapá and the Kiliwa together comprise the last surviving cultures of this kind left along the entire North American Pacific coast. Most other groups may marry along tribal lines but in most other respects appear to lead the sedentary existence of the average rural Mexican peasant.

Outnumbering the Amerindians native to Baja are the thousands of Amerindians from Sonora, Oaxaca, and Chiapas who've come to Baja to work as migrant laborers, mirroring the transmigration of mestizo laborers north into the United States. Most numerous in the Valle de San Quintín, they're also commonly found in the Ensenada and Ciudad Constitución areas. Migrant Amerindians unable to find agricultural jobs are often seen hawking blankets and other handicrafts on the streets of the tourist districts in Tijuana, Ensenada, and Cabo San Lucas.

© JOE CUMMINGS

bajacaliforniano, Tijuana

gros and San Antonio Necua, 200 Kiliwa (Quilihua) in Ejido Tribu Quilihua, and about 200 Cucapá in Cucapá El Mayor in the Río Colorado delta.

The Mexican government has set aside tracts of BCN land for each tribe; the Paipai, for example, own 160,000 acres from the Alamo plain eastward. For the most part, Baja's native tribespeople work on small ranches and farms; the livestock trade in particular has been a primary source of income ever since the Amerindians acquired horses, burros, cattle, goats, and sheep from Spanish missionaries. It is not known how many *indígenas* preserve tribal traditions, since, as in the American Southwest, many customs and ceremonies have gone underground due to a deep and understandable suspicion of outsiders. The Cucapá, who call themselves Koi'Pat (Those Who Come and Go), appear to live the most traditional lifestyle of the Yumano groups, preferring a

LANGUAGE

As in the rest of Mexico, Spanish is the primary language in Baja California. English is widely spoken by merchants, hotel staff, and travel agents in Tijuana, Mexicali, Ensenada, Loreto, La Paz, San José del Cabo, and Cabo San Lucas. Even in these cities, however, you can't count on finding English-speaking Mexicans outside the tourist districts. Hence it's incumbent upon the non-Spanish-speaking visitor to learn at least enough Spanish to cope with everyday transactions. Knowing a little Spanish will not only mitigate communication problems, it will also bring you more respect among the local Mexicans, who quite naturally resent foreign visitors who expect Mexicans to abandon their mother tongue whenever a gringo approaches. A popular sign seen in tourist restaurants reads "We promise not to laugh at your broken Spanish if you won't laugh at our broken English." Out of courtesy, you should at least attempt to communicate in Spanish whenever possible.

The type of Spanish spoken in Mexico is usually referred to as Latin-American Spanish, in contrast to the Castilian Spanish spoken in Spain. Still, the Spanish here differs significantly from that of even other Spanish-speaking countries in the Western Hemisphere. In Baja California especially, many Anglicisms have crept into the language. For example, the common Latin-American Spanish term for "car" is *coche*, but in Baja you'll more often hear *carro*. Signs at automotive stores may read *"auto partes"* rather than *"refacciones"*; *"yonke"* or *"yunque"* (junk) is also commonly seen, and refers to new and used auto parts rather than junked cars.

Dictionaries and Phrasebooks

The Glossary and Spanish Phrasebook at the back of this book will get you started on a basic vocabulary in *español*. For further study, you'll want a dictionary and a larger phrasebook. One of the best portable dictionaries for the Spanish student is the paperback *University of Chicago Spanish-English, English-Spanish Dictionary*, which emphasizes New World usages and contains useful sections on grammar and pronunciation. If even this small volume is too large for your backpack, the *Collins Gem Dictionary: Spanish-English, English-Spanish* comes in a tiny 4-by-3.5-by-1-inch edition with a sturdy plastic cover and more than 40,000 entries.

Berlitz's *Latin-American Spanish for Travellers* is a small phrasebook divided by topics and situations (e.g., grammar, hotel, eating out, post office). Not all the phrases and terms it contains are used in Baja, but it's better than nothing.

One of the best references for off-the-road adventurers is Burleson and Riskind's *Backcountry Mexico: A Traveler's Guide and Phrase Book* (University of Texas Press). Although it's rather bulky for carrying in a backpack and is oriented toward travel in northern mainland Mexico, it contains many words and phrases of value to Baja hikers and campers.

Advanced Spanish students can improve their command of idiomatic Spanish with Frances de Talavera Berger's *¡Mierda!* (Plume, New York). Subtitled *The Real Spanish You Were Never Taught in School,* the book's copious *vulgarismos* or slang expressions have a decidedly scatological slant and should probably be aired in public only after practice with a trusted native speaker.

Language Schools in Baja

Those who plan to spend an extended period of time in Baja should seriously consider enrolling in an intensive Spanish course. Night classes at an adult community school or summer university courses are a fine introduction, but the most time- and cost-effective study programs are those that immerse you in the language and culture of the country. Mainland Mexico holds several Spanish language schools, but if Baja is your travel focus, it would be prudent to investigate schools on the peninsula. At the moment only two cities offer regularly scheduled instruction: Ensenada and La Paz.

Ensenada has three well-established schools, the **Colegio de Idiomas de Baja California** (Baja California Language College), the **International Spanish Institute of Ensenada,** and the **Center of Languages and Latin American Studies,** while La Paz offers the relatively new **Centro de Idiomas, Cultura y Comunicación (CICC)** and **Se Habla . . . La Paz**—see the Ensenada and La Paz sections for more information.

Another option is the long-running Spanish conversation course offered by the Glendale Community College Baja California Field Studies Program. This course is held for 15 days in late June at the GCC's rustic field studies center in Bahía de los Ángeles. Students sleep on cots in the center itself. The course fee of US$685 includes round-trip transportation between GCC and Bahía de los Ángeles, dormitory-style accommodations, and meals. For further information, contact Dr. José Mercadé, Glendale Community College, 1500 N. Verdugo Rd., Glendale, CA 91208, tel. 818/240-1000, ext. 5515, baja@glendale.cc.ca.us.

RELIGION

The original inhabitants of Mexico were indoctrinated in the ways of Roman Catholicism by Spanish missionaries between the 16th and 19th centuries. That Catholicism is now the majority religion in Mexico (around 90 percent) is an amazing achievement considering that it was laid over a vast variety of native belief systems in existence for perhaps thousands of years, and considering that the Mexicans eventually forcefully expelled the Spanish.

Mexican Catholics tend to be devout practitioners of their faith. Mexican Catholicism, however, has its own variations that distinguish the religion from its European predecessors. Some of these variations can be traced to preexisting Amerindian spiritual traditions that were absorbed by the Catholic faith and are localized according to tribe.

One variation common to all of Mexican Catholicism is the Virgin of Guadalupe cult, which began in 1531 when a dark-skinned Virgin Mary appeared before Amerindian peasant Juan Diego (1474–1548) in a series of three visions at Tepeyac, near Mexico City—which was, coincidentally, a sacred Aztec site dedicated to the goddess Tonantzin. According to legend, in the third vision the Virgin commanded Diego to gather roses and present them to the local bishop, requesting that a church be built in her honor. When the devout Diego unfolded his rose-filled cloak on December 12, 1531, both he and the bishop beheld an image of the dark-skinned Virgin imprinted on the garment. This was deemed a miracle, and church construction commenced at once. The Vatican beatified Juan Diego in 1990 and is considering full canonization, which would add the peasant to the Catholic pantheon of saints.

Today, many Mexican churches are named for Our Lady of Guadalupe, who has become so fused with Mexican identity that the slogan *¡Viva Guadalupe!* is commonly used at political rallies. The affectionate Mexican nickname for Guadalupe is La Morenita, "Little Darkling." She has become, as Mexican-American cultural commentator Richard Rodriguez puts it, the "official private flag of Mexico," and symbolizes one way in which Catholicism has been absorbed by indigenous cultures rather than vice versa. The official feast day for Guadalupe, December 12, is fervently celebrated throughout the country.

At one time the entire peninsula was under the ecclesiastical jurisdiction of the Guadalajara diocese; now there are regional dioceses centered in Tijuana, Mexicali, and La Paz. Since Baja has fewer churches per capita than the mainland, a church *(iglesia)* will sometimes hold as many as 18 masses a day. In southern Baja it isn't uncommon for a parish priest to hail from abroad—usually Italy—since native priests are in short supply on the peninsula.

Roadside Religion

Along Baja's roadways you'll occasionally see small roadside crosses (sometimes in clusters) or shrines. Often placed at fatal accident sites, each cross marks a soul's point of departure from this world. Larger shrines containing Christ or Virgin figures are erected to confer blessings or protection on passing motorists. These can vary from simple enclosures made of vegetable-oil cans to elaborate sculptural designs.

roadside shrine

© JOE CUMMINGS

In the brush beside the track there was a little heap of light, and as we came closer to it we saw a rough wooden cross lighted indirectly. The cross-arm was bound to the staff with a thong, and the whole cross seemed to glow, alone in the darkness. When we came close we saw that a kerosene can stood on the ground and that in it was a candle which threw its feeble light upward on the cross. And our companion told us how a man had come from a fishing boat, sick and weak and tired. He tried to get home, but at this spot he fell down and died. And his family put the little cross and the candle there to mark the place. And eventually they would put up a stronger cross. It seems good to mark and to remember for a little while the place where a man died. This is his one whole lonely act in all his life. In every other thing, even in his birth, he is bound close to others, but the moment of his dying is his own.

John Steinbeck, The Log from the Sea of Cortez

CONDUCT AND CUSTOMS

Time and Appointments

Of the many stereotypes about Mexican culture, the one about the Mexican sense of time being highly flexible is probably the most accurate. The whys and wherefores are too numerous and complex for the context of this book; read Octavio Paz's *The Labyrinth of Solitude* for a glimpse of an explanation. However, it's important to realize that the so-called *mañana* attitude is a generalization; in many cases Mexican individuals are punctual—especially when it comes to doing business with Americans. Furthermore, *bajacalifornianos,* it is said, tend to be more punctual than their mainland counterparts.

If you make an appointment with a *bajacaliforniano* for dinner, a party, or some other social engagement, you should figure the actual meeting time will occur two hours later than verbally scheduled. As with business engagements, if the person involved has dealt frequently with Americans, this might not always be the case. Also, Mexicans will typically accept an invitation rather than say no, even if they don't plan to attend the scheduled event. This is because, within the Mexican social context, it is usually worse to refuse an invitation than to not show up. To avoid disappointment, prepare yourself for any of these scenarios.

When hiring a fishing boat or any sort of guide in Baja, you can expect a modicum of punctuality—most Mexicans in the tourist industry have adapted themselves to the expectations of gringo tourists. Again, note the difference between business and social appointments.

Siesta

The stereotypical afternoon siesta, when everyone goes off to sleep for a couple of hours, is fast becoming history throughout Mexico. Nevertheless, a vestige of the siesta lingers in the hours kept by offices and small businesses, which are typically closed 2–4 P.M. or 3–5 P.M. The first hour is reserved for *comida,* the midday meal, while the second hour is for relaxing or taking care of personal business. This long lunch hour is usually offset by longer evening hours; most Mexican offices and businesses stay open until 7–8 P.M.

No matter what hours are posted for small businesses, the actual opening and closing times may vary with the whims of the proprietors. This is also true for tourist information offices. Banks, on the other hand, usually follow their posted hours to the minute.

Meal Times

If you'll be meeting Mexican acquaintances for meals, whether at a restaurant or in their homes, be aware that customary eating times differ from those north of the border.

The first meal of the day, *desayuno* (breakfast), is usually taken at about the same time as the average American breakfast, say 6–8 A.M. Around 11 A.M., another breakfast/early lunch called *almuerzo* is sometimes eaten; on weekdays it's light, on weekends and holidays it may be more substantial. Around 2 or 3 P.M. comes the *comida,* the largest meal of the day. In small towns, workers often go home for this meal, not returning to the workplace until around 4 or 5 P.M.

mariachis, Ensenada

After work, at anywhere from around 8 to 10 P.M., *la cena,* the final meal of the day, is eaten. *Cenas* are usually as light and informal as *desayunos,* so it's not often that guests are invited to a home for this meal. On weekends and holidays, the *cena* can become a grander occasion.

Terms of Address

Mexicans frequently use titles of respect when addressing one another. At a minimum, *señor* will do for men, *señora* for married women, and *señorita* for unmarried women or girls. When in doubt about a woman's marital status, *señorita* can be used.

Professional titles can also be used for variety and to show additional respect. *Maestro* (master) or *maestra* (mistress) are common and can be used to address skilled workers (cobblers, auto mechanics, seamstresses, etc.) and any teacher except those at secondary schools and colleges or universities (who are *profesores*).

College graduates are *licenciado* (men) or *licenciada* (women), while doctors are *doctor* or *doctora.* Some other professional titles include *arquitecto* (architect), *abogado* (attorney), *ingeniero* (engineer), and *químico* (chemist).

Body Language

Mexicans tend to use their arms and hands a lot during verbal communication. Learning to "read" the more common gestures can greatly enhance your comprehension of everyday conversations, even when you don't understand every word being spoken.

One of the more confusing gestures for Americans is the way Mexicans beckon to other persons by holding the hand out, palm down, and waving in a downward motion. This looks similar to a farewell gesture in the United States and Canada but means "come here" in Mexico. Holding the palm upward and crooking the fingers toward the body, the typical American gesture for "come here," is a vaguely obscene gesture in Mexico.

Extending the thumb and forefinger from a closed hand and holding them about a half-inch apart means "a little bit" in America but in Mexico usually means "just a moment" or "wait a minute," and is often accompanied by the utterance *"momentito"* or *"poquito."*

The wagging of an upright forefinger means "no" or "don't do that." This is a good gesture to use when children hanging around at stoplights or gasoline pumps begin wiping your windshield

WHAT'S A GRINGO?

The Latin-American Spanish word "gringo," reportedly a corruption of the Spanish word *griego* or "Greek," has different meanings in different parts of Latin America. In Argentina and Uruguay, for example, it is used to refer to anyone of Italian descent. In Mexico and Central America, it's almost always reserved for persons of northern European descent, especially Canadians and Americans. In Cabo Pulmo, I once heard a naive, newly arrived white Canadian archaeologist comment that it would be easy for him to carry out his research in Baja because he wasn't a gringo. (Sorry, pal, but you're a gringo, too.) In spite of everyday linguistic evidence to the contrary, many non-Spanish-speakers insist that only Americans are gringos. The Mexicans, however, have a more precise epithet for Americans: *yanquis* or "Yankees."

Is "gringo" a derogatory term? It can certainly be used that way. Most of the time, however, it's simply an unconscious racial identification of neutral value. Educated Mexicans tend not to use it; instead they typically say *norteamericano* or *americano* for Americans. Some Mexicans insist on the former, even though the term is a slight to Canadians and Mexicans, who, after all, are North Americans, too. *Canadiense* is used for Canadians, *alemán* for Germans, and so forth. A more precise term for U.S. citizens is *estadounidense*.

between the sexes and among children and adults. Mexican males who are friends will sometimes greet one another with an *abrazo* (embrace), and urban women may kiss one another on the left cheek. Foreigners should stick to the handshake until they establish more intimate relationships with *bajacalifornianos*. Handshakes are also used upon parting.

Dress

Compared to their mainland counterparts, who tend to be more conservative, *bajacalifornianos* are relatively tolerant about the way visitors dress. Nonetheless, invisible lines exist that, out of respect for Mexican custom, shouldn't be crossed.

Number one is that beachwear is not considered suitable dress for town visits. Rosarito, Cabo San Lucas, and San Felipe are the most obvious exceptions to this general rule since during peak tourist seasons visitors outnumber residents in these towns, so the locals are used to gringo immodesty. In Ensenada, however, beachwear will result in indignant stares if you wander far from the Avenida López Mateos tourist strip. In La Paz and other Baja towns, you're disrespecting local custom if you wear a bathing suit anywhere other than the beaches.

Upon entering a church or chapel in Baja, men are expected to remove their hats. Many Mexican males will also remove their hats when passing in front of a church. More tradition-minded *bajacaliforniano* women will cover their heads when inside a church, but younger women usually don't and foreign females aren't expected to. Shorts, sleeveless shirts/blouses, sandals, and bare feet are considered improper dress (for both men and women) in churches, even for brief sightseeing visits.

and you don't want them to. Don't overdo it, though—they only need to see a few seconds of the wagging finger—otherwise you'll look out of control.

Mexicans commonly greet one another with handshakes, which are used universally, including

On the Road

Baja offers a unique doorway into a world of adventure that will appeal in different ways to different kinds of visitors. Foodies can delve into a broad range of eating experiences, from roadside *tacos de carne asada* stands to upscale Pacific Rim fusion emporiums. History and culture buffs can busy themselves with Baja's mission churches, frequent festivals, historical museums, and differing local customs. Sporting types will find their choices especially challenging, with world-class sea kayaking, deep-sea fishing, hiking and camping, and mountain-climbing just a few of the possibilities.

Travel in Baja can be magical or frustrating depending on what your expectations are and how much you plan to meet those expectations. If you intend to navigate the entire length and breadth of the peninsula in your own vehicle, for example, you need to be very well prepared in advance. By the same token a quick fly-in trip to Cabo San Lucas or Loreto requires much less planning.

©KAT KALAMARAS

Sports and Recreation

Baja California's major attractions largely fall under this heading—from trekking in the Sierra de San Pedro Mártir to scuba diving off Cabo Pulmo. An added bonus is that, for the most part, you can enjoy Baja outdoor recreation at little or no cost. User demand is low, and when fees are involved they're usually reasonable.

HIKING AND BACKPACKING

National Parks, Natural Areas, and Wildlife Preserves

Baja has two national parks (Parque Nacional Sierra San Pedro Mártir and Parque Nacional Constitución de 1857), three natural parks (Parque Natural del Desierto Central de Baja California, Parque Natural Isla Ángel de la Guarda, and Parque Natural de la Ballena Gris), two wildlife sanctuaries (Isla Guadalupe and the Midriff Islands), two underwater marine parks (Arrecife Pulmo and Bahía Cabo San Lucas), and one regular marine park (Bahía de Loreto). At the two national parks, public facilities are few and rudimentary; in the other government-protected areas they're virtually nonexistent. These public lands are described in detail in later sections of this guidebook. In 1975 the islands of the Sea of Cortez were declared a Zona de Reserva y Refugio de Aves Migratorias y de la Fauna Silvestre (Migratory Bird Reserve and Wildlife Refuge), a status somewhat strengthened in 1995 with the formation of the Secretaría de Medio Ambiente y Recursos Naturales (SEMARNAT, the Secretariat of the Environment and Natural Resources).

In addition, Baja boasts one UNESCO Biosphere Reserve, the Desierto del Vizcaíno.

Trails

Hiking trails are plentiful in the northern sierras, from wide, 150-year-old paths created by Amerindians or shepherds to smaller, more recent trails worn by hikers. In the smaller central sierras, which are more arid, trails are scarce—it's a good idea to scout an area first and ask questions locally about the best way to get from point A to point B. Although it's sometimes tempting to venture off established trails, that's a good way to get lost; you might also contribute to the destruction of delicate ecosystems. Light trails that don't seem to go anywhere may be cattle or coyote trails that connect surface water sources.

Maps

Topographic maps, which chart trails and elevation differentials, are essential for extended hiking and backpacking. **Map Link,** 30 S. La Patera Lane #5, Santa Barbara, CA 93117, tel. 805/692-6777 or 800/962-1394, fax 805/692-6787 or 800/627-7768, custserv @maplink.com, www.maplink.com; **Map Centre,** 3191 Sports Arena Blvd., Ste. F, San Diego, CA 92110, tel. 619/291-3830 or 888/849-6277, fax 619/291-3840, maps@mapworld.com, www.mapcentre.com; and **Treaty Oak,** P.O. Box 50295, Austin, TX 78763-0295, 512/326-4141, fax 512/443-0973, maps@treatyoak.com, www .treatyoak.com, carry a complete line of Baja topo maps in three scales (1:1,000,000, 1:250,000, and 1:50,000), sold separately according to region. The maps cost around US$12 each. All three stores will mail out a Baja map list on request. You can also check out their inventory online.

These same topographic maps are also available in Baja from any **Instituto Nacional de Estadística, Geografía e Informática** (INEGI) office for US$4 per sheet. Some topos may be out of print, in which case you can usually obtain a photocopy of archival prints from an INEGI office for US$6. These maps show not only trails and contour lines, but also villages not normally marked on other maps. In Mexico they're mostly used by the military, surveyors, miners, and *narcotraficantes.*

Although you won't need a great deal of Spanish to read the INEGI maps, you might need to know the following translations for the map legend:

- *brecha*—gravel road
- *vereda*—path
- *terracería transitable en todo tiempo*—all-weather dirt road
- *terracería transitable en tiempo de secas*—dirt road passable only in dry weather
- *carretera pavimentada*—paved highway
- *carretera de más de dos carriles, caseta de pago*—toll highway of more than two lanes

INEGI has three offices in Baja where maps are distributed: in Mexicali at the Palacio Federal, 3rd floor, Centro Cívico, 686/557-3914 or 686/556-0932; in Tijuana at Avenida Revolución 1041, Col. Centro, 664/638-7938; and in La Paz at Plaza Cuatro Molinos, Calle Altamirano 2790, Col. Centro, 612/123-1545 or 612/122-4146. INEGI has a website at www.inegi.gob.mx.

The easy-to-read, well-printed *Baja California Almanac,* basically a collection of scaled-down and simplified INEGI maps, sells for US$24.95 and is available via mail/telephone/email from Map Link, Map Centre, and Treaty Oak, or directly from Baja Almanac Publishing, 30 E. Charleston Blvd. #5-52, Las Vegas, NV 89142-100, www.baja-almanac.com.

What to Bring

For a hike of a day or less, all you need is sturdy footwear (light, high-topped hiking boots are preferable to sneakers in rocky terrain) and whatever food or water you plan to consume for the day. Count on at least two liters of water per person for chaparral or lower sierra hiking, more if the weather is hot.

Longer hikes obviously require more preparation and equipment. Whether in the desert or the mountains, bring clothing that allows you to remain comfortable at both ends of the temperature spectrum; throughout the peninsula days tend to be warm, nights chilly. A light sleeping bag, for temperatures down to -4°C/25°F in the high sierras, and a backpacking tent with plenty of ventilation for camping at lower elevations are necessities for coping with potentially harsh environments.

Good hiking boots are essential. Thick lug soles with steel shanks are preferable, as they pro-vide protection from sharp rocks and desert plants. Bring along a first-aid kit that includes an elastic bandage for sprains, snakebite treatment, as well as a pair of tweezers for removing thorns and cactus spines. Also pack a flashlight, compass, waterproof matches, knife, extra batteries, foul-weather gear, and a signal device (mirror or whistle). A handy addition, if you're hiking near Baja's shoreline, is a telescoping fishing rod with light tackle, as surf fish are usually plentiful.

Always carry plenty of water: a minimum of five liters per person per full day of walking during hot weather, two liters in winter. Although springs and *tinajas* exist in the sierras, the water level varies considerably, and you shouldn't count on finding water sources along the way. If you need drinking water from one of these sources, always boil it first for at least 10 minutes or treat it with iodine or a water filter designed to remove impurities. Bring enough food for the duration of your hike (count on about 1.5 pounds of dry

© JOE CUMMINGS

camping is easy in Baja

ON THE ROAD

food per person per day), plus an extra one or two days' worth. One to three nestable pans will suffice for up to six hikers, along with a spoon, small plastic bowl, and cup for each person.

Camping Tips

In addition to all the usual rules for choosing campsites, don't camp beneath coconut palms (a falling coconut could knock down your tent or fracture your skull) or in arroyos (danger of flash floods).

Open fires are permitted just about anywhere in Baja except within city limits. Even in the desert, fuel is plentiful, as dried ocotillo and cactus skeletons make excellent fuels. Imitate the locals and keep your fires small. Never leave hot coals or ashes behind; smother with sand—or water, if you can spare it—till cool to the touch.

Pack out all trash that won't burn, including cigarette butts; they take 10–12 years to decompose. Bury human waste six inches down, and don't use soap in streams or springs.

Desert Hiking

For hikes in Baja's desert lands, special precautions are appropriate. Water is the most important concern; desert hiking requires at least five liters of water per day per person. Some people recommend at least eight liters per day for hikes that span the midday hours. On extended excursions of more than a night or two, the weight of anything beyond eight liters—water weighs about one kilogram per liter—is prohibitive; you'll need to learn in advance where to obtain water from reliable local sources. While hiking, keep your mouth closed and breathe through your nose to keep the mouth and throat from drying out. This will keep you cooler, as the nasal cavities are designed to moderate outside air temperature as air passes into your lungs.

Sun protection is especially essential in the desert. Wear long-sleeved clothing in light, reflective colors (white is best), sunglasses, a wide-brimmed hat, and sunscreen. Between 11 A.M. and 3 P.M., it's best to take shelter from the sun, especially during the hotter months. Most of Baja's deserts offer plenty of shade in the form of

mesquite trees, overhanging cliffs, or leaning boulders. But it's also a good idea to carry your own shade—a light, opaque tarp. A poncho can double as tarp and rain protection; yes, it does occasionally rain in the desert. The Desierto del Vizcaíno is the most barren of the peninsular deserts, but also the coolest because of the tendency for fog to form when the hot desert air meets cool Pacific breezes.

Anyone contemplating an extended desert hike for the first time might consider reading at least one of the books on desert travel listed in this tome's Suggested Reading section. These contain important information on desert survival topics, from how to test the edibility of plants to making your own water with an improvised solar still.

Organized Trips

Very few outfitters have attempted to lead hiking or backpacking trips in Baja. **Baja Motion Tours,** 41 E. 12th St., Suite C, National City, CA 91950, 800/511-4848, fax 619/474-7166, www .mexicotravelnet.com, offers a few interesting land-only itineraries in northern Baja at reasonable prices. They cater mostly to large groups; custom tours are available.

FISHING

Baja's reputation as one of the world's best sportfishing regions is well deserved. Nowhere else will you find as many varieties of fish in an area as compact and accessible as the waters of Baja. Although it's most famous for acrobatic billfish—marlin, sailfish, and swordfish—and other deep-sea fishing, Baja also offers opportunities for surf casters, small-boaters, and sport divers, as well as folks who don't yet know a rod from a reel.

Onshore Fishing

Most accessible to travelers, since it doesn't require a boat, is onshore or surf fishing, which you can enjoy anywhere along the coast where you can get a line into the water. In Baja, Prohibido Pescar (Fishing Prohibited) signs are vary rare.

Surf fishing is best along the Pacific coast between El Rosario and Bahía Magdalena, and on the Sea of Cortez between San José del Cabo

FISH TRANSLATORS

Mexican guides who lead sportfishing trips often use the local terms for game fish; when they don't, the English terms they use aren't always correct. This works the other way around, too—many gringos use incorrect Spanish names for Baja fish, which can cause confusion when asking about local fishing conditions. Here is a key to some of the most common translations:

albacore tuna—*albacora*
barracuda—*picuda*
black seabass—*mero prieto*
bluefin tuna—*atún de aleta azul*
blue marlin—*marlín azul*
dolphinfish (mahimahi)—*dorado*
grouper (generic)—*garropa*
halibut—*lenguado*
hammerhead shark—*cornuda*
jack crevalle—*toro*
ladyfish—*sabalo*
mackerel—*sierra, makerela*
manta ray—*manta*
marbled scorpionfish—*cabezón*
octopus—*pulpo*

Pacific amberjack—*pez fuerte*
perch (generic)—*mojarra*
pompano—*palometa*
puffer (generic)—*bolete*
red snapper—*huachinango*
roosterfish—*papagallo, pez gallo*
sailfish—*pez vela*
seabass (cabrilla)—*cabrilla*
shark (generic)—*tiburón*
small shark—*cazón*
squid—*calamar*
stingray (generic)—*raya*
striped marlin—*marlín rayado*
swordfish—*pez espada*
triggerfish—*cochi*
wahoo—*sierra wahoo, peto*
whale shark—*pez sapo*
white seabass—*corvina blanca*
yellowfin tuna—*atún de aleta, amarilla*
yellowtail—*jurel*

Pez is the generic word for fish. Once fish has been caught and is ready for cooking (or has been cooked), it's called *pescado*.

and La Paz, but fish can be taken just about anywhere along Baja's 4,800-km (3,000-mile) shoreline. Common onshore fish include surfperch, *cabezón,* sand bass, ladyfish, halibut, corvina, opaleye, leopard shark, triggerfish, and croakers. Submarine canyons along the shore of the East Cape can yield onshore catches of roosterfish, California yellowtail, and yellowfin tuna for anglers using the right tackle; shore-caught dorado (dolphinfish) and even marlin are not unknown. All of these except the marlin are considered excellent food fish, and even the marlin is edible when smoked.

One fish commonly caught onshore, the puffer, is *not* a good food fish; the meat is toxic to humans and can cause poisoning. The two puffer species common to Baja are easily identified, as their bodies expand like balloons when they're disturbed. Further identifiers: The bullseye puffer features a brownish body with black spots; depending on its stage of maturity, the golden puffer is either all golden or a dark purple-black with white spots and white fin trim. In Mexico, this fish is called *bolete*.

Inshore Fishing

Anyone with access to a small boat, either a skiff trailered in or a rented *panga* (an open fiberglass skiff that's usually 5–6 meters long and powered by a 40–60 hp outboard motor), can enjoy inshore fishing at depths of around 50–100 meters (165–330 feet). Common inshore catches include many of the surf fishes mentioned above, plus various kinds of groupers, seabass, bonito shark, sculpin (scorpionfish), barracuda, rockfish, lingcod, sierra, pompano, amberjack, red

ON THE ROAD

© JOE CUMMINGS

and yellow snapper, pargo, and cabrilla. Cabrilla, however, must be released when caught.

Larger game fish occasionally taken inshore are the bluefin and yellowfin tuna, yellowtail, dorado, jack crevalle, and roosterfish. Again, all fish mentioned make good eating.

Offshore Fishing

The bigger game fish are found in deeper waters—over 200 meters (650 feet)—and require bigger tackle and more technique, including specialized trolling methods prescribed for each type of fish. Larger boats—fishing cruisers—are usually necessary simply because of the distance from shore to the fishing area. In the Cape Region, however, you can reach depths of over 200 meters less than 1.5 km (one mile) offshore. These areas are accessible by skiff or *panga,* though strong seasonal currents are sometimes a problem, requiring a larger outboard motor. Contrary to the popular image of Cabo San Lucas sportfishing, it isn't necessary

to use a boat equipped with fighting chairs to catch the big ones, although it's undoubtedly more comfortable.

Because of the special tackle and techniques involved in offshore fishing, many Baja visitors hire local fishing guides, who usually provide boats and tackle, to transport them to offshore fishing grounds. A sometimes less expensive alternative involves signing up for fishing cruises, which take groups of tourist anglers out on big powerboats.

Most offshore anglers go after striped, blue, or black marlin, sailfish, swordfish, wahoo, dorado, roosterfish, yellowtail, and tuna. These fish are large, powerful fighters, requiring skill in handling rod and line. The billfish are the most acrobatic, performing high leaps and pirouettes when hooked; wahoo and roosterfish will also "greyhound," performing a series of long, low jumps while swimming rapidly in one direction.

Of the billfish, only the swordfish is considered good eating. The rest are traditionally regarded as trophy fish, meant to be stuffed and mounted in the den or living room. To their credit, an increasing number of anglers these days release billfish after catch; many outfitters discourage or even forbid the taking of these beautiful creatures unless the fish has been badly damaged in the fight.

The wahoo, dorado, roosterfish, yellowtail, and various tunas all make excellent eating.

Fishing Seasons

Baja presents a complex set of fishing conditions that vary from month to month and year to year. Fish are biting somewhere in Baja waters year-round, but water temperature, ocean currents, weather patterns, fish migrations, and other variables mean you usually won't find the same type of fish in the same spot in, say, December as in July. An unusually dry year in the American Southwest, for example, lessens the outflow of nutrients from the Colorado River into the Sea of Cortez, diminishing the store of plankton and other small marine creatures at the bottom of the Cortez food chain. This in turn affects populations of larger fish, from seabass to whale sharks.

BOB RACE

blue marlin

erally spend Dec.–Apr. at the Cape, moving up toward Bahía Magdalena and the southern Cortez in the warmer months.

If your trip occurs between December and April, head for the Cape; from May to November you can angle anywhere along a horseshoe-shaped loop extending from Bahía Magdalena on the Pacific side to Mulegé on the Cortez. You can, if you wish, fish farther north on both coasts, especially in the summer, but if sportfishing is your reason for traveling to Baja, you're more likely to be satisfied by heading to the other areas.

As a final caveat, remember that an unusually warm winter means better fishing all over Baja; likewise a particularly cold winter forces many fish far south, making even Cabo San Lucas, the "fisherman's paradise," less productive.

Because of the numerous variables, all the fishing calendars can serve only as guidelines. But some calendars are more accurate than others. The best is the set devised by the late Tom Miller in his *Angler's Guide to Baja California,* which divides the Baja coast into 10 fishing zones, with a calendar for each zone. Even with detailed calendars in hand, it's wise to seek the counsel of local fishing guides or other anglers on the scene before investing time and money in trying to catch a particular fish in a particular area.

A few generalizations are possible. The greatest variety and number of game fish swim the widest range of Baja waters from April through October, when the water temperatures are relatively warm. In winter, many species migrate south and are available only off the Cape. Fortunately for winter anglers farther north, exceptions abound. The widely distributed California yellowtail, for example, is present year-round, migrating up and down the Sea of Cortez—La Paz and the East Cape in winter, central to northern Cortez in summer—as well as the lower Pacific coast. Barred perch and rock cod are present year-round on the northern Pacific coast. Sierra peak season is winter, when they're found in abundance near Bahía Magdalena. Wahoo gen-

Tackle

Although bait and tackle are available at shops in Ensenada, San Felipe, Loreto, Mulegé, La Paz, and Cabo San Lucas, supplies are variable, and you can't count on finding exactly what you want. Therefore, you ought to have your gear assembled before arriving in Baja.

A full fishing kit containing tackle for every conceivable Baja sportfishing possibility would probably weigh in excess of 70 kg. Seasoned Baja anglers claim you can get by in just about any situation with four basic rigs: two trolling rods with appropriate reels and 50- to 80-pound-test monofilament line for offshore fishing; one medium-duty eight- or nine-foot rod and spinner with 30-pound mono for surf casting and onshore fishing; and a six-foot light spinning rig loaded with four- to eight-pound line for bait fishing, freshwater fishing, or light surf casting. Two trolling rigs are recommended because these are the rods used against fish most likely to yank your outfit into the sea; it's always best to have a spare.

No matter how many rods you bring into Mexico, you're legally permitted to fish with only one at a time. Electric reels are permitted for use by handicapped persons only.

Bait

What a fish will take at any given moment is highly variable, hence the properly equipped an-

ON THE ROAD

gler comes prepared with an array of natural and artificial bait. Live or frozen bait—including everything from squid to mackerel to clams—is usually available near the more frequented fishing areas; you can also catch your own bait easily with a light rig. A cooler is necessary for keeping bait fresh; hired boats will usually supply them. Among the vast selection of artificial lures available, the most reliable seem to be those perennials that imitate live bait, such as spoons, leadheads, candybars, swimmers, and, for offshore fishing, trolling heads. Bring along a few of each in different colors and sizes. You can purchase a few highly specialized lures, such as marlin heads and wahoo specials, in Loreto and Cabo San Lucas.

Tide Tables

Serious onshore-inshore anglers should bring along a set of current tide tables so they can decide what time to wake up in the morning.

Fishing Licenses

The red tape surrounding fishing in Mexico is minimal. The basic requirement is that anyone over 16 who intends to fish must possess a Mexican fishing license; technically, this includes all persons aboard boats equipped with fishing tackle, whether they plan to fish or not. This is important to remember for anyone going along on fishing trips as a spectator.

A single license is valid for all types of fishing, anywhere in Mexico, and is issued for periods of one day, one week, one month, or one year. A license is usually included in the price of sportfishing cruises, but not necessarily on *panga* trips—if you don't have a license, be sure to ask if one is provided before embarking on a guided trip. The cost of a Mexican license has risen steadily over the last few years but remains less expensive than most fishing licenses in the United States or Canada. Last time we checked the cost was US$21.20 for a week, US$30.40 for a month, and US$39.50 for an annual license.

Fishing licenses are available from a number of sources, including tackle shops and Mexican insurance companies near the United States–Mexico border. They can be obtained by mail from the **Mexico Department of Fisheries (PESCA)**, 2550 Fifth Ave., Suite 101, San Diego, CA 92103-6622, 619/233-6956, fax 619/233-0344, or from California branches of the **American Automobile Association (AAA)** and **Discover Baja Travel Club**, 3089 Clairemont Dr., San Diego, CA 92117, 619/275-1836 or 800/727-BAJA, ask@discoverbaja.com, www.discoverbaja.com.

Mexican Regulations

The general daily bag limit is 10 fish per person, including no more than five of any one

---

WORLD'S FISHING RECORDS SET IN BAJA

The nonprofit International Game Fish Association (IGFA) tracks world records set for each species of game fish according to weight, weight/test ratio (fish weight to line test), place where the catch was made, and other significant record details. World-record catches achieved by Baja anglers for specific line classes include those for the following fish: Pacific blue marlin, striped marlin, Pacific sailfish, swordfish, roosterfish, dolphinfish (dorado), gulf grouper, California yellowtail, Pacific bonito, bigeye trevally, spotted cabrilla, spearfish, giant seabass, white seabass, California halibut, Pacific jack crevalle, black skipjack, yellowfin tuna, Pacific bigeye tuna, and chub mackerel.

At one time or another, Baja anglers have held all-tackle records—highest weight of any fish species regardless of line test—for gulf grouper, olive grouper, roosterfish, Pacific amberjack, white seabass, spotted cabrilla, rainbow runner, black skipjack, yellowfin tuna, Pacific jack crevalle, chub mackerel, and California yellowtail.

For information on IGFA membership and record entries, write to IGFA, 3000 E. Las Olas Blvd., Fort Lauderdale, FL 33316, or visit www.igfa.org. Membership includes the bimonthly *International Angler* newsletter and a copy of the IGFA's annual *World Record Game Fishes Book*, which contains a list of all current fishing records. IGFA members are also eligible for discounts on fishing charters offered by several sportfishing outfitters in Cabo San Lucas.

species. Certain fish varieties are further protected as follows (per-day limits): one full-grown marlin, sailfish, or swordfish; two dorado, roosterfish, halibut, tarpon, or shark. Extended sportfishing by boat is limited to three consecutive days if the daily bag limit is reached each of the three days.

Bag limits are the same for free divers as for rod-and-reelers. Only handheld spears and band-powered spearguns—no gas guns or powerheads—are permitted, and no tanks or compressors may be used. A further weight limitation permits no more than 25 kg (55 pounds) of fish in a day's catch of five specimens, or one specimen of unlimited weight. Gillnets, purse nets, and every other kind of net except for handling nets are prohibited for use by nonresident aliens, as are traps, explosives, and poisons.

The taking of shellfish—clams, oysters, abalone, shrimp, and lobster—by nonresident aliens is officially prohibited. However, taking a reasonable amount—no more than can be eaten in a meal or two—is customarily permitted. This regulation is in place to protect Mexican fishing unions; even buying shellfish from local sources is prohibited unless you purchase from a public market or *cooperativa*. Obtain a receipt in case of inspection.

Totuava, sea turtles, and cabrilla are protected species that cannot be taken by anyone. Nor can any fish be caught for "ornamental purposes" (i.e., for aquarium use). Mexican fishing regulations are subject to change; check with the Mexico Department of Fisheries for the latest version before embarking on a fishing expedition.

Two areas off limits to all fishing are Bahía Cabo San Lucas harbor and Pulmo Reef, the only official fish sanctuaries along the peninsular coast. Many other areas probably ought to be protected for educational and recreational purposes, since the government-regulated bag limits help to preserve fish species but not fish habitats. Fishing, boating, diving, and other aquatic activities can wreak havoc on lagoons and delicate reef systems; use special care when traversing these areas. Never drop an anchor or a fishing line on a coral reef; such contact can cause irreversible damage to reef systems.

U.S. Customs and California State Regulations

Once you've obeyed Mexican fishing regulations and bagged a load of fish, you still have to conform to U.S. Customs regulations if you wish to enter the United States with your catch. Fortunately, U.S. regulations conform with Mexican bag limits, so whatever you've legally caught south of the border can be transported north.

The U.S. state of California further requires anyone transporting fish into the state to present a completed California Declaration of Entry form, available at the border or at any international airport in California. To facilitate identification of the transported fish, some part of each fish—head, tail, or skin—must be left intact. In other words, you can't just show up at the customs station with a cooler full of anonymous fish fillets. You may also be asked to show a valid Mexican fishing license or a PESCA form confirming legal purchase of fish or shellfish. For more information, contact the California Department of Fish and Game, 1416 9th St., Sacramento, CA 95814, 916/445-0411, fax 916/653-1856, www.dfg.ca.gov.

HUNTING

The Mexican government allows licensed hunting in season, as regulated by the Secretaría de Medio Ambiente y Recursos Naturales (SEMARNAT). Hunting has long been popular in Baja among foreigners and Mexicans alike but is for the most part restricted to various species of rabbit, quail, dove, pheasant, and waterfowl (ducks, widgeons, and geese). White-tailed deer and mule deer are also hunted, but permits are limited in number and quite expensive by international standards. Occasionally the government sponsors a special hunt (in southern Baja only) for the rare desert bighorn sheep *(borrego cimarrón);* bighorn permits cost a rich US$30,000 and aren't usually issued to foreigners. Early in the 20th century bighorn hunting by foreigners nearly wiped out the entire population.

Permits come in six types: Type I, waterfowl; Type II, doves; Type III, other birds; Type IV, small mammals; Type V, limited; and Type VI, special. Hunting regulations, which include bag limits (size and number), are strictly enforced. Signs that say Prohibido Cazar mean Hunting Prohibited. To apply directly to the Mexican government for a permit, contact **SEMARNAT,** Av. Francisco I. Madero #537, Col. Centro, Mexicali, BCN, 686/551-8700; or in La Paz at Calle Ocampo 1045 between Rubio and Ortiz de Domínguez, 612/122-4414. The offices are open Mon.– Fri. 9 A.M.– 2 P.M. You can also check SEMARNAT's website at www.semarnat.gob.mx or email contactodgeia@semarnat.gob.mx.

In addition to the SEMARNAT hunting permit, foreign hunters need a consular certificate, special visa, and military gun permit. You can obtain the consular certificate from any Mexican consulate upon presentation of a letter from your local law enforcement agency verifying you have no criminal record. This certificate is also necessary for obtaining the military gun permit, issued by the army garrison in Tijuana or Mexicali. Proof of U.S. citizenship is required, plus eight passport-sized pictures for each gun permit and hunting license. The hunting license costs about US$450 and includes the gun permit. Once you possess the consular certificate, gun permit, and hunting permit, you can bring your guns across the border, where you'll receive a special hunter's visa. A maximum of two rifles per hunter is allowed, along with 50 American cartridges per gun. With the proper hunting permit, additional shells may be purchased in Mexico through the specially licensed sporting goods dealers. Only .22-caliber bullets or 12-, 16-, 20-, and 40-gauge shotgun cartridges are legally available. *Do not attempt to bring either guns or ammo into Mexico without a permit; penalties for either offense are severe.*

A newer regulation requires that all foreign hunters be accompanied by a licensed Mexican hunting guide. If this whole process sounds daunting (it is actually very time-consuming, even if you speak perfect Spanish), you'd be much better off arranging the guide and all the necessary paperwork through a U.S. broker or Mexican hunting outfitter; a list of outfitters can be requested from any Mexican consulate. This costs considerably more than applying directly through SE-

MARNAT because you have to pay either membership dues or a surcharge, but the procedure is guaranteed to be much smoother and quicker.

BOATING

Recreational boating along Baja's peninsular and island coastlines has been popular since the 1950s. In the days before the Transpeninsular Highway, it was one of the safest, if slowest, ways of traveling from California to the southern peninsula. Despite recent improvements in highway travel, interest in navigating Baja waters has only increased. The main difference now is that smaller vessels can be trailered or cartopped down the peninsula, saving days and weeks that might otherwise be spent just reaching your cruising destination.

An extremely wide range of pleasure boats plies Baja waters, from sea kayaks to huge motor yachts. The most heavily navigated areas lie along the northwest coast between San Diego and Ensenada and in the Cabo San Lucas to La Paz corridor, but even these waters are relatively uncrowded compared to the marinas and bays of California. Cabo San Lucas, the most popular southern Baja harbor, checks in only around 2,000 foreign-owned vessels per year, an average of less than six arrivals per day.

The Pacific vs. the Sea of Cortez

Although some visitors circumnavigate the entire Baja peninsula, most boaters select one area for cruising and transport their crafts to that area by land. Because of the relative safety of Sea of Cortez boating, it's the most popular coast, particularly for smaller craft—kayaks, skiffs, and motor- or sail-powered vessels under 10 meters (35 feet). Cortez waters are relatively calm most of the time; late summer and early fall are the exceptions, when *chubascos* or hurricanes can whip up sizable and sometimes treacherous swells. The Pacific coast is prone to high winds and challenging swells throughout the year.

The major difference between the two coasts is the number of available, safe anchorages. The Pacific side offers about 30 anchorages along the peninsula as well as island shorelines that provide protection when northwest winds prevail; this number is reduced to approximately 12 anchorages during prevailing southwesterlies, common July–Sept. Over on the Cortez side lie more than 60 protected anchorages— roughly 35 along the peninsula and 30 more on islands just off the coast. The Sea of Cortez offers not only safer waters but a wider selection of places to drop anchor.

Open-ocean Pacific sailing is not for the novice and shouldn't be attempted along Baja's Pacific coast without plenty of prior experience. The relative absence of assistance and boat-repair facilities makes Pacific boating south of Ensenada an especially risky venture.

If they wish, boaters may navigate from ports in California, British Columbia, or Alaska to the Ensenada marina and then arrange for overland transportation of their boats on hired trailers from Ensenada to San Felipe on the Cortez side. Contact the **Ensenada tourist office,** Blvd. Costero at Calle Las Rocas, Ensenada, BCN, 646/172-3022, for details on this service.

> *The Sea of Cortez offers not only safer waters but a wider selection of places to drop anchor than the Pacific. For these reasons, it's the most popular coast for smaller craft.*

Cartopping

The most popular boats for short-range cruising, fishing, and diving are those that can be transported on top of a car, RV, or truck—aluminum skiffs in the four- to five-meter (12- to 15-foot) range. This type of boat can be launched just about anywhere; larger, trailered boats are restricted to boat launches with trailer access. The most appropriate outboard motor size for a boat this size is 15–20 hp; larger motors are generally too heavy to carry separately from the boat, a necessity for cartopping.

If you decide to transport a skiff or sea kayak on top of your vehicle, be sure to use a sturdy, reliable rack or loader with a bow line to the front bumper and plenty of tie-downs. The rough road surfaces typical of even Baja's best highways can make it difficult to keep a boat in place; crosswinds are also a problem in many areas. Frequent load checks are necessary. If you're shopping around for a rack, the type that bolts to

the vehicle roof will hold up better than the kind that clamps to the roof gutters or door edges.

Inflatables

Rigid inflatable boats (RIBs), such as those manufactured by Achilles or Zodiac, are also well suited to Baja travel as they allow easy, stable beach landings. You can carry them on top or even in the cargo area of a large car or truck and inflate them with a foot pump or compressor as needed. A small 24-hp outboard motor is the best source of power. Inquire at **Pacific Marine Supply,** 4114 Napier, San Diego, CA 92110, 619/275-0508, fax 619/275-0903, www.pacmarinesupply.com, for the latest gear.

NavTec Expeditions, 321 N. Main St., Moab, UT 84532, 800/833-1278, www.navtec.com, organizes guided RIB trips in the Sea of Cortez along the coast of Baja California Sur for US$2,000 pp for seven nights/eight days. NavTec also offers three-day trips from Loreto to offshore islands for US$595 pp.

Trailering

Larger boats that require trailering because of their weight, and which then must be floated from the trailer at a launch site, are much less versatile than cartop boats. On the entire peninsula fewer than 20 launches—five or six on the Pacific side, the remainder on the Sea of Cortez—offer trailer access. Another disadvantage to boat trailering is that Baja road conditions make towing a slow, unpleasant task. On the other hand, if one of these spots happens to be your destination and you plan to stay awhile, the added cruising range of a larger vessel might be worthwhile.

Ocean Cruising

The typical ocean cruiser on Baja's Pacific side is a 12- to 24-meter (40- to 80-foot) powerboat; on the Cortez side, 10- to 18-meter (35- to 60-foot) sailboats are popular. Properly equipped and crewed, these boats can navigate long distances and serve as homes away from home.

ON THE ROAD

Smaller motor-powered vessels are usually prevented from ocean cruising simply because of the lack of available fueling stations—their smaller fuel capacities greatly diminish cruising range. Sailboats smaller than nine meters (30 feet) have a similar problem because of the lack of storage space for food and water.

If you want to try your hand at ocean cruising, contact **Cortez Yacht Charters,** 3609 Hartzel Dr., Spring Valley, CA 91977, 619/469-4255, fax 619/461-9303, cortezcharters@sbcglobal.net, www.cortezcharters.com, or **Baja SeaFaris,** 933 Márquez de León, La Paz, 612/125-9765, information@bajaseafaris.com, www.bajaseafaris.com.

Charts

The best nautical charts for Baja waters are those compiled by the U.S. government. They come in two series: the Coastal Series, which covers the entire Pacific and Cortez coastlines in three large charts (numbers 21008, 21014, and 21017) with a scale of around 1:650,000 each; and the Golfo de California Series, which offers much more detailed maps—in scales from 1:30,000 for La Paz to 1:290,610 for the entire Cape Region—of selected areas along the Cortez coast and around the Cape. Both series are based on nautical surveys conducted between 1873 and 1901, so many of the place-names are out of date.

You can purchase these charts individually from the **Defense Mapping Agency** (DMA), Washington, DC 20315-0010, 301/227-2000. Two of the Coastal Series are out of print, however, and others may eventually drop from sight as well. A much better and less expensive source of these charts is *Charlie's Charts: The Western Coast of Mexico (Including Baja),* which is a compilation of all U.S. nautical charts from San Diego to Guatemala, including those currently unavailable from the DMA. The charts have been extensively updated from the DMA originals, with more recent markings for anchorages, boat ramps, hazards, and fishing and diving spots. The spiral-bound volume, 7th edition, is available from **Charles E. Wood,** Box 1244, Station A, Surrey, BC, Canada V3W 1G0. It's also available in many California marine supply stores and from www.amazon.com.

Waterproof, tear-resistant, double-sided plastic charts published by **Fish-n-Map,** 8535 W. 79th Ave., Arvada, CO 80005, 303/421-5994, fax 303/420-0843, www.fishnmap.com, are available in four sheets: Sea of Cortez North Chart (San Felipe to Mulegé, with inset maps of Bahía de los Ángeles, Las Islas Encantadas, Bahía San Francisquito, Puerto Refugio, and Guaymas); Sea of Cortez South Chart (Loreto to Cabo San Lucas, with inset maps of Loreto south to Bahía Agua Verde, Bahía de la Paz, Isla Espíritu Santo, and Cabo San Lucas); the Baja California Chart North Pacific (Tijuana to Bahía Tortugas, with inset maps of the Coronado Islands, San Quintín area, Isla San Benito, and Isla Guadalupe); and Baja California Chart South Pacific (Punta Eugenia to Cabo San Lucas). Each of these measures 60 by 90 cm (24 by 36 inches), or 10 by 22.5 cm (four by nine inches) folded, costs US$7, and is available wherever Baja maps are sold.

Gerry Cruising Charts, P.O. Box 976, Patagonia, AZ 85624, 520/394-2393, www.gerrycruise.com, produces 15 navigation charts for the entire Sea of Cortez (including the mainland Mexico side), plus a packet of charts for the Pacific side of Baja, costing US$17–30 depending on the number of charts per packet. Gerry Cunningham, who compiled these charts, also wrote *The Complete Guide to the Sea of Cortez,* which comes in three volumes and costs US$20–30 per volume or US$75 for the whole set. Also available on CD-ROM for US$95, the set contains 360 color photos.

Tide Tables

Tide tables are published annually; to cover the entire Baja coastline, you'll need two sets: one that pertains to the Pacific tides and one for the Sea of Cortez tides. Either or both are available from **Map Link,** 30 S. La Patera Lane #5, Santa Barbara, CA 93117, tel. 805/692-6777 or 800/962-1394, fax 805/692-6787 or 800/627-7768, custserv@maplink.com, www.maplink.com; **Gerry Cruising Charts** (see previous mention); or marine supply stores. You can also order Sea of Cortez tide tables from the **University of Arizona** Printing and Graphics Services, 102 West Stadium, Tucson, AZ 85721, 520/621-2571, fax 520/621-6478.

Boat Permits

Any nonresident foreigner operating a boat in Mexican waters who intends to fish from that boat is required to carry a Mexican boat permit as well as a fishing permit. Even if you transport a boat to Baja with no fishing tackle and no plans to fish, it's a good idea to obtain a boat permit; first, because you might change your mind when you see all the fish everyone else is pulling in, and second, because you never know when you might end up carrying a passenger with fishing tackle. *All* boats used for fishing require a permit, whether cartopped, trailered, carried inside a motor vehicle, or sailed on the open seas.

Permits are available by mail from the Mexico Department of Fisheries, 2550 Fifth Ave., Suite 101, San Diego, CA 92103-6622, 619/233-6956, fax 619/233-0344, or from the Discover Baja Travel Club, 3089 Claremont Dr., San Diego, CA 92117, tel. 619/275-1836 or 800/727-BAJA, ask@discoverbaja.com, www.discoverbaja.com. A

© JOE CUMMINGS

the calm waters of Bahía Agua Verde

boat permit is valid for 12 months; fees vary according to the length of the craft.

Temporary Import Permits

These aren't necessary for Baja but are required if you plan to take a boat to mainland Mexico, whether by land or water. You can obtain the permit from offices in La Paz or Santa Rosalía or from a Registro Federal de Vehículos office in Tijuana, Mexicali, Ensenada, or La Paz.

Port Check-Ins

If you launch a boat at a Mexican port, specifically within the jurisdiction of a captain of the port (COTP), you must comply with official check-in procedures. This simply involves reporting to the COTP office and completing some forms. The only time it's a hassle is when the captain isn't present; you may have to wait around a few hours. Some ports charge filing fees of up to US$15.

Anytime you enter another COTP's jurisdiction, you're required to check in. Checking out is not required except when you leave the port of origin—i.e., the port at which you first launched. Currently, COTPs in Baja are found at Ensenada, Guerrero Negro, Bahía Magdalena (San Carlos), Cabo San Lucas, San José del Cabo, La Paz, Puerto Escondido, Loreto, Mulegé, Santa Rosalía, Bahía de los Ángeles, and San Felipe.

Fuel, Parts, and Repairs

At present only seven permanent marinas offer fuel year-round: one each in Ensenada, Cabo San Lucas, Puerto Escondido, and Santa Rosalía, and three in La Paz. Elsewhere you must count on your own reserves or try your luck at canneries, boatyards, and fish camps, where prices will probably exceed official Pemex rates. At places other than marinas you'll often have to go ashore and haul your own fuel back to the boat; come prepared with as many extra fuel containers as you can manage.

Obtaining marine supplies and repairs in Baja is more challenging than finding fuel. Ensenada, Cabo San Lucas, and La Paz are the best locales for both—there's usually someone around who can work minor miracles. To a limited extent, parts—

but not necessarily competent repair work—are also available for established-brand outboard motors in San Felipe, Santa Rosalía, Loreto, and Mulegé. As with all other motorized conveyances in Baja, it's best to bring along plenty of spare parts, especially props, filters, water pumps, shear pins, hoses, and belts. Don't forget to bring at least one life jacket per person—statistics show that in 80 percent of all boating fatalities, the victims weren't wearing them.

Water-Makers

Ocean cruisers might consider equipping their boats with desalinators. **Waterlog Yacht Water-makers,** Waterlog International Ltd., 1 Hartham Rd., London, N7 9, England, waterlogsupport@ aol.com, www.yachtwatermaker.com, produces a line of water-powered reverse-osmosis desalinators that produce 4–7 liters (5–12 pints) of drinking water per hour from seawater depending on the model. A 12-volt clip-on motor is available for use while at anchor.

Emergencies

The U.S. Coast Guard monitors VHF radio channel 16 and can pick up transmissions from as far south as Ensenada. Elsewhere along the Baja coastline, this channel is monitored by Mexican agencies (including the Mexican Navy and all COTPs), ferry vessels, and commercial ships.

Citizens-band (CB) radio is commonly used as a substitute for a telephone system in the peninsula's remote areas; it's also heavily used by RVers, the Green Angels, CB clubs, and other boaters, and is a quick way to get attention. As in the United States and Canada, channel 9 is the most used, but channels 1, 3, 4, 7, and 10 are also monitored. Special radio permits for foreign visitors are no longer required for CB radios with a transmission power of five watts or less.

SEA KAYAKING

Kayaking is one of the best ways to experience coastal Baja. Coves, inlets, water caves, and beaches inaccessible to skiffs or four-wheel-drive vehicles are easily approached in a kayak, especially on the Sea of Cortez. The Cortez is truly a world-class kayaking environment, as more and more kayakers discover each year. It's also an excellent place to learn sea kayaking skills, because seas are generally calm compared to the Pacific side.

© JOE CUMMINGS

open-cockpit kayaking in Bahía Concepción

The most popular kayaking areas on the Cortez coast lie between Mulegé and Loreto and between Puerto Escondido and La Paz. Bahía Concepción, protected by land on three sides, is a favorite among novice kayakers. Bahía de los Ángeles, with its many islets and islands, is good for kayakers of all levels, though the strong channel currents require some caution.

Wherever you go in the Sea of Cortez, the Gulf Current, which runs counterclockwise around the Cortez, favors trips planned in a north-south direction, with pickup arranged at the south end. A few intrepid, experienced kayakers have completed voyages across the currents from Bahía de los Ángeles to the Mexican mainland by using the "Stepping Stones" route from island to island. Seri Amerindians once followed the same route in reed canoes. Extended Cortez trips are fairly easy when the weather's good, since campsites are available at a huge selection of beaches and coves. If you bring along some light fishing gear, you'll never go without food.

Kayaking on the Pacific side is for the experienced paddler only. Punta Banda, an inlet-scalloped cape near Ensenada, is the most popular Pacific Baja kayaking area because of its proximity to San Diego. Bahía Magdalena, a large, protected bay in southern Baja, also attracts many kayakers with more time; whale-watching is a big attraction here. Gray whales sometimes use their enormous tails to toss kayaks around, however, so your first Magdalena Bay outing in whale season should be in the company of someone who understands whale behavior. Rule one: Never paddle directly toward a nearby whale; instead, run parallel to the whale's course. Also, never paddle between a cow and her calf.

Elsewhere on the Pacific coast, high surf and strong currents require equal quantities of strength and expertise. Finding a beach campsite isn't too difficult, but reaching it through the surf might be.

Types of Kayaks

Sea-touring kayaks come in four basic types, each with several variations. All fall in the 4.2- to 6.4-meter (14- to 21-foot) range necessary for extended paddling. The traditional closed-cockpit,

hardshell boat comes in single (one-person) and double (two-person) models and is made of either molded polyethylene plastic or fiberglass. A "glass" boat is lighter and faster; a polyethylene boat, though heavier and slower, holds up on Baja's rocky beaches much better. This type of kayak is easily cartopped, but a sturdy, secure rack is necessary on Baja's rough roads. Touring models can carry up to 115 kg (250 pounds) of gear in built-in hatches, an attribute that makes them a good choice for extended overnight kayaking. Because of the sealed cockpits, they're also very good in the colder waters of the Pacific and the northern Cortez.

Folding kayaks are much easier to transport and are popular among kayakers who fly to their destinations or who want to keep boats inside their vehicles rather than on top. The disadvantages are that a folding kayak costs more and is a bit slower because of a wider beam, up to 86 cm (34 inches) compared with a 60-cm (24-inch) beam on a hardshell boat. The hull is usually hypalon, a synthetic rubber, stretched over aluminum tubing—assembly and disassembly is not as easy as the sales representative claims. For carrying convenience, however, it can't be beat. The wider beam also means the craft will carry up to twice the payload of a hardshell.

Gaining popularity in recent years, especially in Baja, are open-cockpit kayaks. The advantage to these is that the paddler sits on top of the deck rather than underneath it, which makes it much easier to exit and thus somewhat safer overall. Like the closed-cockpit variety, some models feature hatched stowage compartments that carry up to 115 kg. Open-cockpit kayaks are easier to paddle and more stable than traditional kayaks; just about anyone can paddle one with little or no practice. An open-cockpit model is also a bit slower because of a wider beam and higher center of gravity. An open-cockpit kayak costs several hundred dollars less than the closed-deck version, making it the ideal kayak for the Baja visitor for whom kayaking is just one among several recreational activities; it also makes an excellent dive station for short scuba or free diving trips. A few models, such as the Aquaterra Kahuna or Scupper Scrambler, are designed specifically to carry scuba gear. As with other hardshell kayaks, they're easily cartopped.

Inflatables are the lightest of the touring kayaks, which makes them even easier to transport than folding kayaks. However, inflation requires an air compressor or electric air pump because the craft's rigidity depends on air pressure of 2–4 pounds per square inch. Like the folding kayak, an inflatable's main advantage is ease of storage and transport.

Accessories

Paddle styles are very much a matter of personal choice; as a general rule, Aleuts or asymmetrical paddles are useful on the windy Pacific side, traditional shapes on the Cortez. Whatever you bring, bring a spare. Other essentials include a paddle leash, a 15-meter (50-foot) parachute-cord towline, a waterproof flashlight, and, in winter, a wetsuit. A detachable two-wheel cart or "skate" for the stern is helpful for transporting a kayak short distances on land; you can easily store it in one of the hatches.

Foot-controlled rudders are not necessary for Sea of Cortez kayaking for much of the year because winds and currents are usually moderate. The exception is Nov.–Mar. when wind and swells are up. Parts and service for a broken rudder are virtually nonexistent. On the Pacific side, or if you're going to attempt a cross-Cortez route to the mainland, a foot-controlled rudder is a good idea. Bring spare parts.

If you can manage the extra weight, include a kayak sail rig to give your arms a rest during a good breeze—common in the Cortez as well as the Pacific.

Equipment Sales and Rentals

If you're on your way to Baja by vehicle and need kayaking equipment or supplies, a convenient stop is **Southwind Kayak Center,** 17855-A Sky Park Circle, Irvine, CA 92614, tel. 949/261-0200 or 800/768-8494, info@southwindkayaks.com, www.southwindkayaks.com. They offer classes and rentals as well as sales.

In Baja, only **Baja Tropicales–EcoMundo** at Bahía Concepción near Mulegé offers reliable year-round equipment rental, though many mul-

surf kayaking, West Cape

© JOE CUMMINGS

tisport centers in Ensenada, Cabo San Lucas, and La Paz may carry a smaller number and variety of kayaks. See Vicinity of Mulegé in the Central Baja chapter for details.

Maps and Tide Tables

Nautical charts are of little use for kayak navigation. A better choice is 1:50,000-scale topo maps, available from Map Link, Map Centre, or Gerry Cruising Charts (see Boating, earlier on). Tide tables are also invaluable.

Organized Kayak Trips

A great way to learn sea kayaking in Baja is to join an organized trip led by experienced kayakers. Based in Loreto part of the year, **Paddling South,** P.O. Box 827, Calistoga, CA 94515, 707/942-4550 or 800/398-6200, fax 707/942-8017, info@tourbaja.com, website www.tourbaja.com, is a reputable Baja specialist. Paddling South organizes multiday paddle tours for US$995.

Whale-watching day-trip add-ons are available mid-January through mid-March. Seven-day paddle/mountain bike combination tours are also offered for US$795.

The venerable standby **Baja Expeditions,** 2625 Garnet Ave., San Diego, CA 92109, 858/581-3311 or 800/843-6967, fax 858/581-6542, travel@bajaex.com, www.bajaex.com, offers kayaking trips to Bahía Magdalena and to the Midriff Islands in the winter.

In Baja, reliable **Baja Tropicales–EcoMundo,** Apdo. Postal 60, Mulegé, BCS 23900, 615/153-0409, ecomundo@aol.com, is the only company offering year-round instruction and guided trips; prices are reasonable because it's headquartered in Mulegé. Itineraries vary from one-day and overnight Bahía Concepción tours to multiday paddles north and south along the Sea of Cortez coast from Mulegé. The company can also serve as an outfitter for custom-designed trips. For more information on Baja Tropicales programs, see Vicinity of Mulegé in the Central Baja chapter.

Outside Mexico, one of the most established outfitters is **Sea Trek,** P.O. Box 1987, Sausalito, CA 94966, 415/488-1000, paddle@seatrekkayak.com, www.seatrekkayak.com. Located on Schoonmaker Point in Sausalito, CA, Sea Trek specializes in one-week Sea of Cortez trips Dec.–May. The outfit also occasionally offers special Bahía Magdalena trips during gray whale migrations. Sea Trek will also design custom three- to 10-day Baja trips that include mountain biking, hiking, and kayaking.

Another good source of information on organized kayak trips and on Baja kayaking in general is **California Kayak Friends,** 2419 E. Harbor Blvd. #96, Ventura, CA 93001, www.ckf.org.

WINDSURFING

From November through March, the Sea of Cortez is a windsurfer's paradise, particularly from the central coast southward. Bahía de los Ángeles and Bahía Concepción are perfect for beginning and intermediate board-sailors, while the high winds of the East Cape will delight those in the advanced class. Any of the channels between the peninsula's east coast and the larger offshore islands—Canal de Cerralvo, Canal San José, Canal de Ballenas—usually offer good sideshore wind action, although sometimes with

ON THE ROAD

boardsailors on their way into the blue

strong currents. If you don't see other sailboards out, try to find someone who knows the currents before launching.

La Paz is also a very good area, even in summer, when a strong breeze called *el coromuel* comes in just about every afternoon. The best spots here lie along the mostly deserted beaches of the peninsula northeast of town—Punta Balandra to Punta Coyote. When nothing's blowing in the Bahía de la Paz vicinity, dedicated windsurfers can shuttle west across the peninsula to check out the action at Punta Márquez on the Pacific side, only 72 km (45 miles) away.

Los Barriles on Bahía de Palmas, along the East Cape, is one of the more accessible windsurfing areas in southern Baja. The wind blows a steady 18–30 knots all winter long, and wave-sailing is possible in some spots. During the season, uphauling (pulling mast and sail up from the water) is usually out of the question due to chop and high winds, so the ability to waterstart (mount and launch a sailboard from deep water) is a prerequisite for board-sailing in this area.

Los Barriles is also home to **Vela Windsurf Resorts,** U.S./Canada tel. 800/223-5443, www .velawindsurf.com, which offers highly rated instruction and package deals from mid-November through early March. Even if you're not a participant in one of its windsurfing vacations, you may be able to arrange for service and parts. Every January, Vela cosponsors the Vela–Neil Pryde Windsurfing Championships at Los Barriles.

The Pacific side of Baja generally demands a more experienced board-sailor. Those who can handle high surf and strong winds will love it. Novices and intermediate windsurfers will enjoy the larger bays of Bahía de San Quintín, Bahía Magdalena, and Bahía Almejas, all protected from major swells in all but the worst weather. Board-sailors with sturdy transport—four-wheel-drive or high-clearance trucks—can choose from dozens of smaller bays connected to Mexico Highway 1 by dirt roads of varying quality.

SURFING

Baja is one of the last refuges of "soul surfing," an experience that has all but disappeared from the crowded beaches of California and Hawaii. Instead of fighting for a wave, Baja surfers typically take turns, making sure everyone gets a ride now and then. Baja attracts a lot of older California surfers who are either fed up with the agro scene up north or are simply investigating new territory, or both. Also, since there are fewer surfers on Baja beaches, heated competition is less imperative. Perhaps the warmer waters also trigger a difference in attitude; you'll find the Pacific south to Punta Abreojos slightly warmer than in southern California, and south of Abreojos the water starts becoming noticeably warmer. Around the Cape Region you can wear shorties all year—or no wetsuit at all from May to October.

From the border all the way down to Cabo, most of the good surf areas lie below *puntas* (points) that offer right point breaks stoked by a northwest windswell all year-round and by a stronger west-northwest groundswell October to May. The latter usually comes without the heavy weather associated with the west-northwest groundswell in central and northern California, hence you can expect cleaner surf conditions in Baja than farther north. This time of year, even without any advance tips, a surfer need only drive down the Transpeninsular with a good road map in hand, turning west wherever the map shows a side road leading off to "Punta X." As with all other coastal recreation, more places are accessible to those with high-clearance vehicles or four-wheel drive, although many good surf spots lie within range of ordinary passenger cars as well.

In the summer the surf's mostly small to flat in northern Baja, except when a tropical storm comes up from the south. When this happens, there's usually high surf at the southern end of many offshore Pacific islands, the most notorious being Isla Natividad and Islas de Todos Santos. In southern Baja—particularly in the area curving around the Cape from Todos Santos (not the islands, the town) to San José del Cabo—a seasonal southeast-to-southwest groundswell forms good beach breaks Mar.–Nov. Stronger southwest-southeast hurricane swells usually arrive July–Nov. and can extend along the entire Pacific coast of Baja.

BAJA SURFING TOP 40

More than 80 named surf breaks can be found along the Pacific and lower Sea of Cortez coasts of Baja California and Baja California Sur, and there are probably at least that many unnamed breaks. The following is our summary of the 40 best, arranged from north to south down the Pacific side of the peninsula, then back north up the Sea of Cortez side.

Playa Rosarito—long beach break, NW
Baja Malibu—beach break, NW
"Rene's"—beach break, NW
Popotla—left reef break, SH
"Mushroom"—right reef break, NW
Calafia—right reef break, NW
Km 36.5—reef break, left or right, NW/SH
Km 39—right point, NW
Km 42—reef break, NW
Playa La Fonda—long beach break, NW
Salsipuedes—reef break, right or left, NW/SH
San Miguel—right point, NW
Punta San José—right point break and reef break, NW/SH
Erendira—reef break, right or left, NW/SH
Cabo Colonet—reef break, NW
Camalú—right point and reef break, NW/SH
Cabo San Quintín—beach, reef, and point breaks, NW/S/SH
Playa Santa María—beach break, SH
Punta Baja—reef break, NW/SH
Bahía Asunción—reef break, beach break, NW/SH
Punta Abreojos—right point, reef break, NW/SH
Isla Natividad—four right point breaks, two left point breaks, NW/S/SH

San Juanico—right point break, NW/S/SH
Punta Conejo—right and left point breaks, NW/S/SH
Punta Márquez—reef break, beach break, S/SH
La Bocana—beach break, S/SH
La Pastora—right sand point break, beach break, NW/SH
Punta Pescadero—reef break, S/SH
Playa Los Cerritos—beach break, reef break, NW/S/SH
Punta Gaspareno—right sand point break, NW
Bahía Migriño—beach break, NW/S/SH
Bahía Chileno—right reef break, S/SH
Playa Palmilla—right point break, reef break, S/SH
"Zippers" (Playa Costa Azul)—reef break, S/SH
Punta Gorda—right point break, reef break, S/SH
Boca del Salado (north of Gorda)—beach break, S/SH
Bahía Los Frailes—reef break, S/SH
Cabo Pulmo—reef break, SH
Punta Arena—right point break, SH
Punta Colorado—reef break, SH

Owing to ongoing natural climatic and geographic changes, surf locations and conditions may change from year to year. For further detail on these and other surfing locations in Baja and the rest of Mexico, visit www.surfline.com.

NW = northwest windswell and/or west-northwest groundswell
S = southeast-southwest groundswell
SH = southeast-southwest hurricane swell

Surf Locations

The number of surfers diminishes as you proceed south of Ensenada or north of Cabo San Lucas; any point between involves some serious road travel. In fact, even when the surf's really pumping in this middle zone, you stand a good chance of sharing monster breaks with only a handful of others—or even having them all to yourself—since there are no "surf hotlines" for central and southern Baja. This means serendipity is a major element in Baja surfing safaris—those who have the most time to scout the coastline will find the best wave action.

In the Ensenada area, the hot spot is San Miguel (also known as Rincón), a small bay just south of the last tollgate on the Tijuana–Ensenada

© JOE CUMMINGS

dawn patrol

toll road. A number of surfers live here year-round, and others make weekend trips from southern California, so at times it's a bit on the crowded side. The fast right point break here is usually reliable in the winter, pumping for weeks at a time. And when the surf's too small onshore, you can always climb in a *panga* and cruise 20 km (12 miles) out to Islas de Todos Santos, home of the biggest breaks on the entire west coast of North America. When San Miguel's nearly flat, Todos Santos waves may hit 3–4 meters (10–12 feet); when San Miguel's ripping at 2.5–3.5 meters (8–10 feet), the pros will be out at northern Todos on their nine-foot guns, tearing down 10-meter (30-foot) Waimea-style walls. The southern island of the twin Islas de Todos Santos produces a good left break during summer swells.

Several spots can also be found between Ensenada and the border in and around La Fonda, La Misión, and Rosarito, especially Punta Descanso, Punta Mesquite, and Punta Salsipuedes. South of Ensenada to the Cape are dozens of places with intermittent point breaks, but the most reputable for accessibility and steady surf are at Punta San José, Punta Baja, Punta Santa Rosalillita, Punta Abreojos, Punta El Conejo, and beaches in the vicinity of Todos Santos (the Baja California Sur town, not the islands).

Visit www.surfline.com for up-to-date info on conditions, and for additional reports on individual sites. Keep in mind that surf breaks do change over time due to erosion and other factors.

For important shark information relevant to surfers in Baja waters, see the sidebar Sharks: Myth vs. Fact.

Equipment

Surfing is a low-tech sport, so the scarcity of surf shops in Baja is not a major problem. For any extended trip down the coast, carry both a short and a long board—or a gun for the northwest shores of Isla Natividad or Islas de Todos Santos in winter. Besides wax and a cooler, about the only other items you need bring are a fiberglass-patching kit for bad dings and a first-aid kit for routine surf injuries. Most surf spots are far from medical assistance—don't forget butterfly bandages. Boards can be repaired at just about any boatyard on the coast, since most Mexican *pangas* are made of fiberglass and require a lot of patching.

Small surf shops in San José del Cabo and Cabo San Lucas sell boards, surfwear, and accessories. The best is San José's **Killer Hook.** You can buy Mexican-made boards—San Miguel and Cactus brands—for about US$50–75 less than what they cost north of the border, about US$100 less than retail for a comparable American or Japanese board.

Tide charts come in handy for predicting low and high tides; a pocket-size tide calendar available from **Tidelines,** P.O. Box 230431, Encinitas, CA 92023-0431, 760/753-1747 or 800/345-8524, surf@tidelines.com, charts daily tide changes from Crescent City, California, to Manzanillo, Mexico, with +/- corrections from a Los Angeles baseline.

Organized Trips

Baja Surf Adventures (BSA), P.O. Box 1381, Vista, CA 92085, 800/428-7873, fax 760/744-5921, bajabill51@aol.com, www.bajasurfadventures.com, maintains a "surf resort" in northern Baja that accepts novice as well as experienced surfers. BSA has asked us not to mention the exact location of its Pacific camp, but note that the beach features a long right point break, and that six other prime breaks lie within driving distance. The resort offers four separate sleeping quarters, men's and women's bathrooms, hot showers, a raised sundeck, three palapas with hammocks, a kitchen and mess hall, and on-demand electricity. Leisure activities other than surfing include fishing, kayaking, snorkeling, diving, horseshoes, darts, ping-pong, beach volleyball, basketball, and mountain biking. Two nights/three days at the resort costs US$325 per person, while six nights/ seven days is US$645. Prices include all meals plus transport to and from San Diego. A special instruction package for beginners goes for US$475/925 (three days/seven days) and includes two hours of training each day.

BSA also operates surf trips to central and southern Baja for advanced surfers only. Surfers aren't usually big on organized travel, but for one destination in Baja, Isla Natividad, some make an exception. Getting to Natividad ordinarily involves driving to Punta Eugenia on the Vizcaíno Peninsula, an ordeal in itself, and then chartering a boat to the island. BSA offers a special concession for the famous "Open Doors" break at Isla Natividad. It leads three- to five-day package surf trips to the island July–Sept.—peak time for the south swell—that include round-trip airfare from Ensenada, lodging on Natividad, and two meals per day. Tours are limited to 12 people.

© JOE CUMMINGS

pangas

Mag Bay Tours, 1835 Newport Blvd. A 109-242, Costa Mesa, CA 92627, 949/650-2775 or 800/599-8676, www.magbaytours.com, operates two surf camps at opposite ends of Bahía Santa María, part of the Bahía de Magdalena (Mag Bay in gringo-speak) on the Pacific coast of southern Baja. From June to mid-October, during the southern swell, the camp at the north end of the bay is open; during the Nov.–Apr. northern swell, the fun switches to the southern camp. Capacity is limited to just 10 surfers. Eight-day trips at Mag Bay start at US$1,040, not including airfare.

SNORKELING AND SCUBA DIVING

The semitropical Sea of Cortez coral reefs at the southern tip of the Cape Region are among the most well-known dive locations in Baja, simply because they're so close to shore. But many spots of interest along much of the coastline are accessible to divers with good boat transportation and the necessary diving skills. For the most part, Pacific diving is for experienced offshore scuba divers only, while the Cortez coast and islands are excellent for inshore novice divers as well as snorkelers.

Marinelife in Baja is concentrated among three types of environments: kelp fields, reefs (both rock and hard coral), and shipwrecks. The wrecks develop into artificial reefs with time and are particularly plentiful in Baja waters. Some of the sunken vessels available for exploration are Liberty ships, junks, steamers, tuna clippers, submarines, yachts, ferryboats, tugs, and full-rigged barques.

Pacific Diving

The most popular diving areas are those in the northwest—Islas Todos Santos and Islas Coronados—accessible to day-tripping southern Californians. As at most of Baja's Pacific islands, the west and southwest sides tend to offer the greatest proliferation of sea life, including kelp beds, rock reefs, and encrusted sea pinnacles amid scenic sandflats. Both the Todos Santos and Coronado Islands are popular among spearfishing enthusiasts because of the large yellowtail populations that feed in the vicinity (but remember that use of spears or spearguns while wearing scuba equipment is illegal). Halibut, various seabasses, and bonito are also common, as is lobster. The cold, fast-running currents mean visibility is usually good in offshore areas.

Farther south at Bahía del Rosario, off the coast near the town of El Rosario, are large kelp beds and the Arrecife Sacramento (Sacramento Reef). Along with an abundance of marinelife, this four-km-long reef features so many shipwrecks it's dubbed the "Graveyard of the Pacific." The reef—named for the paddlewheeler *Sacramento,* which ran aground here in 1872—is also home to a population of large lobsters referred to locally as *burros* (donkeys) or *caballos* (horses). Isla San Gerónimo, 2.5 km northwest of the reef, is known as an excellent spearfishing location.

The next diving area south lies off the tip of the Vizcaíno Peninsula at Isla Cedros, Isla Natividad, and Islas San Benito. These islands feature kelp beds, sea pinnacles, shoals, and rock reefs. Bahía Magdalena, much farther south, is of interest for its shallows teeming with sea life, including sea turtles, sharks, manta rays, seals, and whales. Heavy swells and surging along the Pacific coast mean that it should only be tackled by experienced scuba divers or with an experienced underwater guide. Ensenada has three dive shops; southward along the Pacific coast there are none before Cabo San Lucas.

Sea of Cortez Diving

The Sea of Cortez offers one of the world's richest marine ecosystems, and the underwater scenery is especially vivid and varied. Sea lions, numerous whale and dolphin varieties, colorful tropical species, manta rays, and schooling hammerhead sharks are all part of a thick food chain stimulated by cold-water upwellings amid the more than 100 islands and islets that dot the Cortez. The largest proportion of Cortez sea life consists of species of tropical Pan-American origins that have found their way north from Central and South American waters.

The northern Cortez is avoided by many divers because of strong tidal surges, speedy currents, and overall lack of underwater marine variety

SHARKS: MYTH VS. FACT

The word "shark" often evokes fear or loathing. Such a reaction is irrational, considering that of the 360 identified shark species, only four—bull, tiger, white, and ocean whitetip—attack humans. Around 60 shark species swim the Pacific and Sea of Cortez waters of Baja California, and of these the most common are smooth hammerhead, common thresher, bonito, sand, blue, and blacktip.

The shark's killer image is based on its natural prowess as a predator—sharks may, in fact, have been the world's first predators, having first appeared about 400 million years ago, 200 million years before the dinosaurs. Sharks can hear the sounds of other fish in the water from up to a mile away; they can smell blood from a similar distance and sense faint electrical fields transmitted by other animals that indicate whether the creature is in distress. A special lens in the shark's eye intensifies light so it can see prey in almost total darkness. All these attributes combine for quick, silent surprise attacks.

Most sharks feed on small fish, although the largest shark of all—the whale shark—feeds on tiny plankton. This leviathan reaches up to 18 meters (60 feet) long and may weigh as much as four tons. It's occasionally seen in the Sea of Cortez.

As animals at or near the top of the marine food chain, sharks play a role in the sea similar to that of lions or wolves on land; they help maintain an ecological balance by weeding out sick or feeble fish that can spread disease or bad genes. As with lions, sharks' greatest natural enemy is man, whose appetite for shark meat is fast depleting shark populations around the world—especially in the Pacific.

About 100 million sharks a year—about the same quantity as tuna—are taken by hook or net, a number marine biologists believe is 9,000 tons more than the shark population can endure. As a result, many shark species are on the brink of endangered status. This trend doesn't bode well for the marine ecosystem, as other species are affected by the shark's important place in the food web.

Shark Attacks

Most sharks are under two meters (seven feet) long and more likely to flee from a swimmer or diver than to attack. The most dangerous is the great white shark, which can reach over six meters (20 feet) long and weigh up to 2.5 tons; it's also the fastest and most powerful shark. Its sharp, serrated teeth are set in jaws that hinge widely for the largest possible bite. Although not common, they occasionally cruise the deeper waters of the Pacific and account for most fatal attacks on humans.

Surfers are usually at greater risk than swimmers or divers because the great white is more likely to confuse the profile of a surfer's dangling limbs with relatively small fish. When a shark can see the entire body of a swimmer, it's more likely to consider the prey too large to attack. Murky waters diminish general visibility and can add to potential confusion; hence, many shark attacks on humans occur in murky waters, often caused by abrupt changes in weather conditions. In an area known for the presence of large sharks (tiburónes), it's best for surfers to avoid unclear waters, especially at offshore breaks.

Searching the water's surface for shark fins is a relatively useless activity since a shark will pinpoint your location long before you become aware of it. Surfers with open wounds should stay out of the water since blood may attract sharks.

relative to the central and southern Cortez. In general, the northernmost diving area is Bahía de los Ángeles, where tidal conditions and visibility are suitable for recreational diving. The offshore islands are the main attractions here; a few small hotels service divers and arrange guided trips.

Next south are the Midriff Islands, which require long-range boats and an experienced appraisal of local currents and tidal changes. Rock reefs are abundant throughout these islands. Below the Midriffs, tidal conditions calm down considerably, and the water is generally warmer. Marinelife is plentiful and varied, and spearfishing is excellent in many areas.

In the central Cortez, Cortez Explorers (formerly Mulegé Divers) is one of the better dive shops in Baja. Many of the nearby islands, bays, and points are suitable for snorkeling as well as scuba diving; Isla San Marcos, Punta Chivato, Islas Santa Inés, and Bahía Concepción are among the best-known areas. Loreto, a bit farther south, also offers a dive shop and several popular nearby diving areas, including Isla Coronado, Punta Coyote, Isla del Carmen, and Isla Danzante; rock reefs, boulders, volcanic ridges, and sandflats are common throughout. Farther east in the Cortez lie vast submarine canyons as well as more remote volcanic and continental islands best left to experienced scuba divers.

From La Paz south, onshore water temperatures usually hover between 21°C (70°F) and 29°C (85°F) year-round, making the southern Cortez the most popular diving destination on this side of Baja. The area is known for Pulmo Reef, the only hard-coral reef in the Sea of Cortez and the northernmost tropical reef in the Americas. Water visibility is best July–October, when it exceeds 30 meters (100 feet); this is also when the air temperature is warmest, often reaching well over 32°C (90°F).

La Paz has several dive shops; popular local dive sites are numerous and include Playa Balandra (mostly snorkeling), Roca Suwanee, Isla Espíritu Santo, Isla Partida, the *Salvatierra* shipwreck, El Bajito Reef, Los Islotes, and the El Bajo Seamount. El Bajo is famous for its summer population of giant manta rays, who seem unusually disposed toward allowing divers to hitch

rides on their *allas* (pectoral fins). Schooling hammerhead sharks are also common in summer—when swimming in schools they're rarely aggressive toward divers, so El Bajo is an excellent observation area.

The Cabo Pulmo and Los Cabos areas are served by several small dive operations in Cabo San Lucas. The aforementioned Pulmo Reef in Bahía Pulmo consists of eight volcanic ridges inhabited by profuse coral life. The coral attracts a wide variety of fish of all sizes and colors; other, smaller reefs as well as shipwrecks lie in the general vicinity. Because most underwater attractions are close to shore, this area is good for diving from small boats or open-cockpit kayaks.

Several coves along the coast toward Cabo San Lucas make good snorkeling sites. Bahía Cabo San Lucas itself is a protected marine park; the rocks and points along the bayshore are suitable for snorkelers and novice scuba divers while the deep submarine canyon just 45 meters offshore attracts experienced thrill-seekers. This canyon is known for its intriguing "sandfalls," streams of falling sand channeled between rocks along the canyon walls. Nearby Playa Santa María and Playa Chileno, on the way east toward San José del Cabo, are popular snorkeling areas with soft corals at either end of a large cove.

Equipment

Except in the Cape Region, divers shouldn't count on finding the equipment they need in Baja, even in resort areas. Since most equipment sold or rented in Baja dive shops is imported from the United States, stocks vary from season to season. Purchase prices are also generally higher in Mexico than north of the border.

For Pacific diving south to Punta Abreojos, a full quarter-inch wetsuit is recommended year-round; from Punta Abreojos south lighter suits are sufficient in the summer. At Cabo San Lucas and around the Cape as far north as the central Cortez, a light suit may be necessary from late November through April; shorties or ordinary swimsuits will suffice the rest of the year. From the Midriff Islands north in the Sea of Cortez, heavier suits are necessary December through early April. In summer, many Sea of Cortez divers wear Lycra skins to protect against jellyfish stings.

Because divers and anglers occasionally frequent the same areas, a good diving knife is essential for dealing with wayward fishing line. Bring two knives so you'll have a spare. Include extra CO2 cartridges (for flotation vests), O-rings, and a wetsuit patching kit.

Air

Dependable air for scuba tanks is usually available in Ensenada, Mulegé, Loreto, La Paz, Cabo Pulmo, and Cabo San Lucas. Always check the compressor first, however, to make sure it's well maintained and running clean. Divers with extensive Baja experience usually carry a portable compressor not only to avoid contaminated air but to use in areas where tank refills aren't available.

Recompression Chambers

Servicios de Seguridad Subacuática (Underwater Safety Services), 624/143-3666, operates a hyperbaric decompression chamber in Cabo San Lucas at Plaza Marina (next to Plaza Las Glorias). The facility is equipped with two compressors, an oxygen analyzer, closed-circuit TV, and a hotline to Divers Alert Network (DAN). In the north, the nearest full-time, dependable recompression facility is the **Hyperbaric Medicine Center** at the University of California Medical Center in San Diego, 619/543-6222. The HMC is open Mon.–Fri. 7:30 A.M.–4:30 P.M. and for emergencies. For emergency air transportation to the facility contact one of the air-evacuation organizations servicing Baja (see Emergency Evacuation, later in this chapter).

Several commercial diving facilities on the Baja Pacific coast feature recompression chambers, but they're often marred by disuse and disrepair.

Organized Diving Trips

Divers will find skilled guides in Ensenada, Bahía de los Ángeles, Mulegé, Loreto, La Paz, Cabo Pulmo, and Cabo San Lucas. Most of the Baja dive outfits also offer instruction and scuba certification at reasonable rates.

Booking outside of Mexico you'll usually pay considerably more. One of the more reputable international companies offering prebooked dive trips along the Pacific coast is **Horizon Charters,** 4178 Lochlomond St., San Diego, CA 92111, 858/277-7823, divesd@horizoncharters.com, www.horizoncharters.com. Day trips visit the Coronados at a cost of around US$120 per person, while seven- to 10-day live-aboard dives make stops at the Coronados, Isla San Martín, Isla Gerónimo, Arrecife Sacramento (Sacramento Reef), and remote Isla Guadalupe for around US$150 per person per day. All meals are included; trips begin and end in San Diego. Horizon Charters is also happy to arrange custom charters to the dive sites of your choice. Over on the Sea of Cortez side, **Baja Expeditions,** 2625 Garnet Ave., San Diego, CA 92109, 858/581-3311 or 800/943-6967, fax 858/581-6542, www.bajaex.com, leads both day and live-aboard scuba diving excursions in the La Paz area.

RACE AND SPORTS BETTING

During the U.S. Prohibition era of the 1920s, casinos were a major part of Baja high life in Tijuana, Mexicali, the Coronado Islands, and Ensenada. Although the Mexican government outlawed casino gambling in the 1930s, it allows race and sports books in both states of Baja California—a significant source of revenue for the state, from betting locals as well as foreigners.

The heir to Tijuana's lavish El Casino de Agua Caliente is the **Caliente Race and Sports Book,** with locations at the famed Caliente Greyhound Track in Tijuana as well as in Los Algodones, Ensenada, Rosarito, Tecate, Mexicali, San Felipe, La Paz, and Cabo San Lucas. The Caliente Greyhound Track hosts weekly greyhound racing, and at all Caliente Race and Sports Book locations you can bet on basketball, football, baseball, and other sports. For more information on Caliente betting, as well as a directory of locations, log onto www.caliente.com.mx. The Caliente betting lounges also feature bars and restaurants; betting is not required if patrons just want a drink or a meal while watching sports events on multiple screens. The Caliente in Cabo San Lucas even shows free American movies.

Entertainment

Most visitors to Baja California come for the beaches, mountains, deserts, fishing, or water sports, not for what would normally be considered "entertainment." Nonetheless, it's not necessarily bedtime when the sun goes down, except in the most remote areas. The larger cities—Tijuana, Mexicali, Rosarito, Ensenada, La Paz, and Cabo San Lucas—offer museums, theaters, cinemas, concert halls, bars, and discos. For specific recommendations regarding these types of entertainment venues, see the destination sections of this book.

MUSIC

When most Americans think of Mexican music they think of brass-and-violins mariachi music, a style from the state of Jalisco on the Mexican mainland. In Baja, mariachi music is generally reserved for weddings and tourists, as is the music of the so-called Baja Marimba Band. (Marimba music also hails from elsewhere in Mexico.) The most commonly heard music on the peninsula is *la música norteña,* a style that's representative of ranchero life yet has a wide appeal throughout Northern Mexico and beyond, including as far north as Chicago and as far south as Colombia and Venezuela. Everyone from urban truckers in Tijuana to *pescadores* in Bahía Agua Verde plays *norteña* tapes on their boom boxes.

Norteña and Grupera

Norteña music shares common roots with Tex-Mex *(tejano)* or *conjunto* music enjoyed in Texas and New Mexico and made famous by Flaco Jiménez, Ramón Ayala, Los Tigres del Norte, Los Lobos, and the Grammy-winning Texas Tornados. It's typically played by an ensemble led by an accordion and *bajo sexto,* a large Mexican 12-string guitar. Originally, these two instruments were supported by a string bass and sometimes a trap drum set; later, electric bass and guitar were occasionally added, along with alto sax and keyboards. Still, most *norteña* bands maintain the traditional accordion, *bajo sexto,* and acoustic bass

lineup. The music itself encompasses an exciting mix of Latinized polkas and waltzes, *rancheras* (similar to American country and western), and *corridos* (Mexican ballads), as well as modern Latin forms like *cumbias* and salsa.

In Mexico, *norteña* has evolved into a more popular subgenre known as *grupera,* because it's almost always performed by groups rather than solo artists. *Grupera* blends the *ranchera*-and-polka *música norteña* with Sinaloan *perrada* or *tambora sinaloense.* The most popular *grupera* bands among *bajacalifornianos* are Los Tigres del Norte and Banda El Recodo, both bands with *superestrella* (superstar) status throughout Mexico. The lyrics of *norteña/grupera* reflect the daily lives and sentiments of Northern Mexican peasants, often with a political edge. In Mexico, *norteña* lyrics often chronicle the tragedies and triumphs of *mota* (marijuana) smugglers and other *narcotraficantes* on the run from law enforcement. Some of the songs recorded by Los Tigres and other *norteña* groups are banned by the Mexican government and can only be heard on bootleg tapes that circulate at cantinas or local fiestas. A Los Tigres album, *Jefe de Jefes,* contains two overtly political *corridos* (ballads), one chronicling the short career of Mexico's former antinarcotics czar, General Jesús Gutiérrez Rebollo, arrested in 1997 for allegedly taking bribes from Sinaloa drug kingpin Amado Carillo, and another about the 1994 assassination of presidential candidate Luis Donaldo Colosio.

Borrowing from the *antillana* or Afro-Caribbean songbook, many *grupera* tunes nowadays are based on *cumbia* rhythms.

Live *norteña* music is often heard at fiestas throughout Baja and in Mexican bars and cantinas in larger towns and cities. Strolling *trovadores,* for example, wander most evenings from bar to bar playing *norteña* music along Calle Ruiz in Ensenada. It's not the nicest area of town, but it's a place for the musically curious to hear the local sounds.

In more upscale *norteña* clubs in Tijuana, Ensenada, and Mexicali, you can still see the biggest dance craze to sweep Baja and Northern Mexico in the 1990s: the *caballito* (little horse). Danced to up-tempo *rancheras,* the dance utilizes a set of fancy equestrian-type maneuvers, including a step in which the female dancer briefly mounts the upper leg of the male dancer. *Bajacalifornianos* have developed their own variation of this dance called the *quebradita* (little break), which adds a steep bobbing of the head from side to side. Spearheaded by the popularity of Selena, the late Texan singing sensation, *tejano* (an updated, urbanized version of Tex-Mex music) has made serious inroads into the Mexican music scene in certain cities, including Tijuana.

Banda

Also *muy popular* in Baja is brassy *banda,* a style that originated in late-19th-century Sinaloa and is currently undergoing a big resurgence throughout Mexico. *Banda* ensembles consist mostly of brass instruments and drums that play loud in-strumental march music against the familiar two-step or waltz rhythms found in *norteña* music. La Banda Sinaloense carries the banner for this style (lots of bands manage to work "Sinaloa" or "Sinaloense" into their names). A permutation known as *tecnobanda* adds or substitutes electronic keyboards and may add vocals as well.

Rock en Español/ La Nueva Onda/Guacarock

Although lyrically descended from Latin American *nuevo canto* folk/rock music, *rock en español* (rock in Spanish, i.e., rock music with Spanish lyrics) takes its major musical inspiration from Anglo-American rock and Anglo-Jamaican ska. Starting with Mexico City the premier center for the movement, this international genre has spread all over Latin America, particularly to Argentina and Brazil. Also known as La Nueva Onda (The New Wave), the music began reaching critical popular mass in the mid-1980s. In the late 1980s, Botellita de Jeréz (Little Bottle of Sherry) and Maldita Vecindad (Cursed Neighborhood) began blending ska, punk, rock, jazz, and traditional Mexican elements as part of a movement within La Onda Nueva known by the descriptive *guacarock,* a reference to the mix of influences that are blended together like the ingredients in the Mexican avocado dip, guacamole. Maldita Vecindad's first major hit was "Mojado" ("Wetback"), a tribute to transborder Mexican workers. Botellita has since disbanded, but Maldita Vecindad still flourishes at the center of the *guacarock* movement.

Also popular are rock fusion/art groups Los Jaguares and Café Tacuba, bands that mix alternative rock sounds with some Amerindian instrumentation and wild live performances very much in the *guacarock* tradition. Santa Sabina adds a hint of Latin jazz improvisation to the mix. All the major groups working in this medium come from D.F. or the state of México except for ¡Tijuana No!, possibly the most political of all the current bands (the name signifies a plea not to flee Tijuana for the United States).

Other seminal groups working in this genre include La CuCa, Maná (with a lead vocalist who sounds exactly like Sting), Acido Verde, Plexo

© JOE CUMMINGS

La Banda Sinaloense, Ensenada

ON THE ROAD

Solar, La Castañeda, La Barranca, El Sr. Gonzalez, Garigoles, Caifanes, La Lupita, El Tri, Amantes de Lola, and Fobia. You may also come across bands who sing in Spanish but cleave more closely to Anglo styles, such as the glam/metal/goth Víctimas del Doctor Cerebro and Plastilina Mosh, or the punk/metal/rap sounds of Mauricio Garces. None of these bands was the first in Mexico to play rock music; Los Apson and Los Locos del Ritmo created Spanish versions of Chuck Berry and Bill Haley in the 1950s, and 1960s indie garage rock produced sufficient output to fill two current CD compilations available in the United States, *Mexican Rock and Roll Rumble* and *Psych-Out South of the Border.*

To get an idea of what young Mexicans are listening to, watch MTV Latino (formerly MTV Internacional), the Spanish version of America's MTV music channel available via cable or satellite throughout Mexico and in selected markets throughout the Americas, including the United States. The selections present a balance of English-language performances by groups from the United States or the U.K., Mexican performances in Spanish, and a good dose of Spanish-language videos from Spain and Latin America.

BULLFIGHTS

One type of entertainment you won't find north of the border is the bullfight. Variously called *la corrida de toros* (the running of bulls), *la fiesta brava* (the brave festival), *la lidia de toros* (the fighting of bulls), and *sombra y sol* (shade and sun), the bullfight can be perceived as sport, art, or gory spectacle, depending on the social conditioning of the observer.

To the aficionado, the *lidia* is a ritual drama that rolls courage, fate, pathos, and death together into a symbolic event. No matter how one may feel toward the bullfight, it is undeniably an integral part of Mexican history and culture. Every town of any size has at least one *plaza de toros* or bullring; in Baja California you'll find one major stadium in Mexicali and two in Tijuana, including the second-largest ring in the world. Occasionally, a small bullring is improvised for a rural fiesta.

History

Ritualistic encounters with bulls have been traced as far back as 3000 B.C., when the Minoans on the Greek island of Crete performed ritual dives over the horns of attacking wild bulls. A closer antecedent developed around 2000 B.C. on the Iberian peninsula, where a breed of fierce, wild bulls roamed the plains. Iberian hunters—ancestors of the Spanish and Portuguese—figured out how to evade the dangerous bull at close quarters while delivering a fatal blow with an axe or spear. When the Romans heard about this practice they began importing wild Spanish bulls and accomplished bullfighters for their coliseum games—possibly the first public bullfights.

During the Middle Ages, bullfighting became a royal sport practiced on horseback by both the Spanish and the occupying Moors, who used lances to dispatch the wild bulls. As the *toreros* (bullfighters) began dismounting and confronting the bulls on the ground, the game eventually evolved into the current *corrida* as performed in Spain, Portugal, Mexico, and throughout much of Latin America.

In the early years the only payment the *torero* received was the bull's carcass. Nowadays bullfighters receive performance fees that vary according to their status within the profession.

El Toro

The bulls used in the ring, *toros de lidia* (fighting bulls), are descendants of wild Iberian bulls that have been specially bred for over four centuries for their combative spirit. They're not trained in any way for the ring, nor goaded into viciousness, but as a breed are naturally quick to anger. The fighting bull's neck muscles are much larger than those of any other cattle breed, making the animal capable of tossing a *torero* and his horse into the air with one upward sweep.

Bulls who show an acceptable degree of bravery by the age of two are let loose in huge pastures—averaging 10,000 acres per animal—to live as wild beasts until they reach four years, the age of combat. By the time *el toro* enters the ring, he stands around 125 cm (four feet) high at the withers and weighs 450 kg (a half ton) or more.

The carcass of a bull killed in the ring does

© JOE CUMMINGS

not go to waste, at least not from a meat eater's perspective. Immediately after it's taken from the ring, it's butchered and dressed, and the meat is sold to the public.

El Torero

The bullfighter is rated by his agility, control, and compassion. The *torero* who teases a bull or who is unable to kill it quickly when the moment of truth arrives is considered a cruel brute. To be judged a worthy competitor by the spectators, *el torero* must excel in three areas: *parar,* or standing still as the bull charges, with only the cape and the torero's upper body moving; *templar,* or timing and grace, the movements smooth, well timed, and of the right proportion; and *mandar,* or command, the degree to which the *torero* masters the entire *lidia* through his bravery, technique, and understanding of the bull, neither intimidating the animal nor being intimidated by it.

Standard equipment for the torero is the *capote de brega,* the large cape used in the first two-thirds of the *lidia;* the *muleta,* a smaller cape used during the final third; the *estoque* or matador's sword; and the *traje de luces* (suit of lights), the colorful torero's costume originally designed by the Spanish artist Goya.

Although it's usually the bull who dies in a *lidia, toreros* are also at great risk. Over half of all professional matadors on record worldwide during the last 250 years have been gored to death in the ring.

La Lidia

The regulated procedures *(suertes)* followed in a bullfight date from 18th-century Spain. Anywhere from four to eight bulls (typically six) may appear in a *corrida,* with one *torero* on hand for every two bulls scheduled. The order of appearance for the *toreros* is based on seniority. *Toreros* who've proven their skills in several bullfighting seasons as *novilleros* (novice fighters) are called *matadores de toros* (bull killers). Ordinarily each *torero* fights two bulls; if one is gored or otherwise put out of action, another *torero* takes his place, even if it means facing more than his allotment of bulls.

Each *lidia* is divided into *tercios* (thirds). In *el tercio de varas,* the bull enters the ring and the matador performs *capeos* (cape maneuvers that don't expose the matador's body to the bull's horns, meant to test the bull or lead it to another spot in the ring) and *lances* (cape maneuvers that expose the matador's body to the horns and bring the bull closer to him). Meanwhile, two horsemen receive the bull's charge with eight-foot *varas* or lances. The *varas* have short, pyramid-shaped points, which are aimed at the bull's neck muscle and do not penetrate deeply on contact.

The purpose of the encounter is to force the bull to lower his horns and to give him the confidence of meeting something solid so he won't be frustrated by the emptiness of the cape as the *lidia* proceeds. Usually only two *vara* blows are administered, but more are permitted if necessary to produce the intended effect: the lowering of the head. The crowd protests, however, when more than two are applied, as they want the matador to face a strong bull.

In *el tercio de banderillas,* the bull's shoulders receive the *banderillas,* 26-inch wooden sticks decorated with colored paper frills, each tipped with a small, sharp, iron barb. They can be placed by the matador himself or more often by hired assistant *toreros,* called *banderilleros* when performing this function. The purpose of *banderilla* placement is to "correct" the bull's posture; the added punishment also makes the bull craftier in his charges. Placed in pairs, up to six *banderillas* may be applied to the bull, varying in number and position according to the reactions of the individual animal.

At the end of the *tercio de banderillas,* signaled by a bugle fanfare, the matador takes up his *muleta* and sword and walks before the box of the *juez* (judge) presiding over the *lidia.* He looks to the *juez* for permission to proceed with the killing of the bull and, after receiving a nod, offers his *brindis* (dedication). The *brindis* may go to an individual spectator, a section of the plaza, or the entire audience. If the dedication is to an individual, he presents his *montera* (matador's hat) to that person, who will return it, with a present inside, to the matador after the *lidia.* Otherwise, he waves his hat at the crowd and then tosses it onto the sand; he remains hatless for the final *tercio,* a gesture of respect for the bull.

The final round of the *lidia* is called *el tercio de muerte* (the third of death). The main activity of this *tercio* is *la faena* (literally, "the work") involving cape and sword, during which a special set of passes leads to the killing of the bull. The first two *tercios* have no time limit; for the last, however, the matador has only 15 minutes to kill the bull, or else he is considered defeated and the bull is led from the ring, where it is killed immediately by the plaza butcher.

In a good *faena,* a matador tempts fate over and over again, bringing the bull's horns close to his own heart. The time for the kill arrives when the bull is so tired from the *faena* that he stands still, forelegs squared as if ready to receive the sword. Then, with his cape, the matador must draw the bull into a final charge while he himself moves forward, bringing the sword out from under the cape, sighting down the blade, and driving the blade over the horns and between the animal's shoulders. A perfect swordthrust severs the aorta, resulting in instant death. If the thrust is off, the matador must try again until the bull dies from one of the thrusts.

It is not necessary to kill the bull in one stroke, which is quite an extraordinary accomplishment; the matador's honor is preserved as long as he goes in over the horns, thus risking his own life, every time. If the bull falls to his knees but isn't dead, another *torero* immediately comes forward and thrusts a dagger *(puntilla)* behind the base of the skull to sever the spinal cord and put the beast out of his misery. When the bull is dead, the *lidia* is over. If the matador has shown bravery and artistry, the crowd rewards him with applause; an unusually dramatic performance results in hats and flowers thrown into the ring. In cases of outstanding technique or bravado, the *juez* awards the bull's ears or tail to the matador.

Practicalities

It's usually a good idea to buy tickets for a *corrida* in advance; it's not unusual for an event to sell out. Check with the local tourist office to determine if any seats are available. In the event of a sellout, you may still be able to buy a ticket—at a higher price—from a scalper or *revendedor.* In a large stadium, the spectator sections are divided into *sol* (sunny side) and *sombra* (shaded side), then subdivided according to how close the seats are to the bullring itself. Since the *corrida* doesn't usually begin until around 4 P.M., the *sol* tickets aren't bad, as long as you bring a hat, sunglasses, and sunscreen, plus plenty of pesos to buy beverages. Tequila and beer are usually available, along with soft drinks.

CHARREADAS

Decreed the national sport of Mexico in a 1933 presidential edict, the *charreada,* or Mexican-style rodeo, can be seen in Baja only in Tijuana, Rosarito, and Mexicali. *Charreadas* are held in skillet-shaped *lienzos charros* or *charro* rings by private *charro* associations. Much like its U.S. counterpart (which was inspired by the Mexican version), *charreada* is a contest of equestrian and ranching skills. Though open to everyone, *charrería* (the *charro* art) is an expensive pastime requiring the maintenance of trained horses and elaborate clothing—somewhat analogous to polo in the Anglo world.

Unlike in American and Canadian rodeo, *charros* and *charras* (gentleman and lady riders) compete for team, not individual, awards. Each team fields six to eight persons, who singly or in combination perform a series of nine *suertes* (maneuvers or events); upon completion of all *suertes,* the team with the most points wins. Another difference is that *charreada* points are usually scored for style rather than speed. Live mariachi music adds drama and romance to the events.

One of the more thrilling *suertes* is the *paso de la muerte,* in which a *charro* leaps from the back of a horse onto the back of an unbroken mare—while both horses are at full gallop! In the *coleadero,* a *charro* leans down from his horse and throws a steer by catching its tail with his leg. For a *terna en el ruedo,* three mounted *charros* rope a wild bull and bring it to the ground within 10 minutes or three casts of *la reata* (origin of the English word "lariat"); points are scored for the complexity and style of the rope work, not speed.

Also striking is the *escaramuza charra,* a women's event featuring rapid, precision-timed, and carefully choreographed and executed equestrian moves by a group of 6–10 riders. This extremely colorful and popular event owes its name to the Italian *scaramuccia,* a 16th-century cavalry maneuver.

In the bull-riding event, or *jinete de toro,* the rider must stay atop the bull until it stops bucking, then dismount with the cinch in hand, landing on both feet simultaneously. By

© JOE CUMMINGS

charreada

ON THE ROAD

contrast, the American rodeo counterpart to this event requires a cowboy to stay mounted for only eight seconds.

A serious *charreada* regular maintains four *charro* suits: the *traje de faena* or plain working outfit; the *traje de media gala,* a semiformal suit with embroidery; and two *trajes de gala*—the silver-buttoned *traje de etiqueta* (dress suit) and the *traje de ceremonia,* an elegant tuxedo outfit for special ceremonies. Each *traje* consists of a broad-brimmed sombrero, tight-fitting trousers of cloth or leather, a short-waisted jacket, boots, and—when the *charro* is mounted—deerskin *chaparreras* (chaps). *Charras* generally dress in *coronela* or *china poblana* outfits, late 19th-century styles featuring full, embroidered blouses and long, billowing, brightly colored skirts with layers of lace and petticoats.

Holidays, Festivals, and Events

Mexicans love a fiesta, and *bajacalifornianos* are no exception. Any occasion will suffice as an excuse to hold a celebration, from a birthday to a lobster harvest. Add to all the civic possibilities the vast number of Mexican Catholic religious holidays, and there's potential for some kind of public fiesta at least every week of the year, if not all 365 days. Besides the national religious holidays, Mexico has feast days for 115 Catholic saints per year, nine or 10 each month. Any town, pueblo, *ejido,* or *colonia* named for a saint will usually hold a fiesta on the feast day of its namesake. Individuals named for saints often host parties on their *día de santo* (saint's day), too.

The primary requisites of a fiesta are plenty of food (especially tamales, considered a festive dish), beer and liquor, music, and dancing. More elaborate celebrations include parades, exhibitions, *charreadas* (Mexican rodeos), and occasional fireworks.

Some of the more memorable yearly events and public holidays observed throughout Baja are highlighted below by month. Smaller festivals and events held locally are mentioned later in the text. Actual dates can vary from year to year, so be sure to check with the appropriate tourist office in advance.

Government offices and some businesses close on national holidays. These closings are not always mentioned in the text; you may want to call ahead to find out.

January
New Year's Day, January 1, is an official holiday.

Día de los Santos Reyes is January 6. See Las Posadas under December.

February
Constitution Day, February 5, is an official holiday.

The pre-Lenten Carnaval festival is held in late February or early March as a last celebration of the carnal pleasures Catholics must forgo during the 40-day Lent season preceding Easter. The fiesta's name derives from the Italian *carne vale,* "flesh taken away." In Mexico, Carnaval is traditionally observed only in port towns; in Baja, the festival is celebrated most grandly in La Paz and Ensenada. Like New Orleans's Mardi Gras, Carnaval features lots of music, dancing, costumes, parades, and high-spirited revelry. See Ensenada for more information.

Flag Day, February 24, is an official holiday.

March
Birthday of Benito Juárez, March 21, is an official holiday.

Spring Break is not a Mexican holiday at all, but an annual ritual for American college and university students—mostly southern Californians and Arizonans—who go on the rampage in Rosarito, Ensenada, San Felipe, and Los Cabos. The spring break season usually straddles late March and early April. Unless you're one of the revelers, these towns should be avoided during the period.

April
Semana Santa: "Holy Week," or Easter Week (the third week in April), is second only to

Christmas as the most important holiday period of the year. One of the most prominent Semana Santa customs is breaking *cascarones,* colored eggs stuffed with confetti, over the heads of friends and family. Besides attending mass on Good Friday and Easter Sunday, many Mexicans take this opportunity to go on vacations. Baja resorts—particularly Rosarito, Ensenada, San Felipe, and Los Cabos—can be overcrowded this week because the peninsula receives a large influx of both Mexican mainlanders and gringos.

The **Rosarito-Ensenada 50-Mile Bicycle Ride** takes place on a Saturday in April and attracts as many as 10,000 participants, making it one of the world's largest cycling events. The route follows the coast, with an elevation differential of around 300 meters (1,000 feet). The same ride is repeated in fall. Sponsored by **Bicycling West,** P.O. Box 15128, San Diego, CA 92175-5128, 619/424-6084. To register online go to www.rosaritoensenada.com.

The **Newport-Ensenada Yacht Race,** reportedly the world's largest international yachting regatta, this event is held the last weekend in April. Boats race from Newport Beach, California, to Ensenada. Sponsored by the Newport Ocean Sailing Association, 949/644-1023, fax 413/254-8160, nosa@juno.com, www.nosa.org.

May

International Workers' Day, May 1, is an official holiday.

Cinco de Mayo: Held on May 5, this festival commemorates the defeat of an attempted French invasion at Puebla de los Ángeles, on Mexico's Gulf of Mexico coast, in 1862. Features music, dance, food, and other cultural events.

Mother's Day (Día de las Madres) is observed on May 10.

Fiesta de Corpus Christi: A religious holiday celebrated 60 days after Easter to honor the Body of Christ and the Eucharist. Corn-husk figurines and miniature mules are displayed in stores and homes.

June

Navy Day, June 1, is an official holiday.

September

Día de Nuestra Señora de Loreto is held in Loreto on September 8 to commemorate the founding of the first mission in the Californias. Special masses, processions, music, dancing, and food.

Mexican Independence Day (Fiesta Patria de la Independencia), also called Diez y Seis, since it falls on September 16, celebrates the country's independence from Spain, as announced in 1821 in the town of Dolores. Festivities begin on the 15th and last two days. The biggest celebrations are centered in Mexicali and La Paz and include fireworks, parades, *charreadas,* music, and folk-dance performances.

The **Rosarito-Ensenada 50-Mile Bicycle Ride** is held on the last Saturday in September; see description under April.

October

Día de la Raza, celebrated as Columbus Day north of the border, October 12 in Mexico commemorates the founding of the Mexican race as heralded by the arrival of Columbus in the New World.

November

Día de los Muertos: The "Day of the Dead" is Mexico's third most important holiday, corresponding to Europe's All Saints Day except that it's celebrated November 1 and 2 instead of only November 1. Some of the festivities are held in cemeteries where children clean the headstones and crucifixes of their deceased relatives *(los difuntos)* and play games unique to this fiesta. Roadside shrines throughout Baja are laid with fresh flowers and other tributes to the dead. Offerings of *pan de los muertos* (bread of the dead) and food and liquor are placed before family altars on behalf of deceased family members, along with papier-mâché skulls and skeletons.

In the second or third week of November, North America's most famous desert race, the **Baja Mil,** draws a dedicated crowd of off-road fanatics and automotive manufacturers hoping to gain advertising copy like "Baja 1000 Winner" or at least "Baja 1000-Tested." These days the course follows established auto trails to avoid further damage to Baja's fragile desert lands; the

© JOE CUMMINGS

Day of the Dead

course alternates from year to year between a full 1,000-mile (1,600-km) race between Ensenada and La Paz and a 1,000-km race that loops through the northern state only. The race runs in several classes from dirt bikes to four-wheel-drive trucks; about 300 drivers (approximately 120 motorcycle and 180 car/truck entries) compete. Sponsored by SCORE International, 23961 Craftsman Rd., Calabasas, CA 91302, 818/225-8402, www.score-international.com.

Anniversary of the 1910 Revolution, November 20, is an official holiday.

December

Día de Nuestra Señora de Guadalupe, the feast day of the Virgin of Guadalupe, Mexico's patron saint, is December 12; special masses are held that day throughout Mexico. The nearest Sunday to the 12th also features special events such as mariachi masses, food booths, and games. The celebrations at the border town of Tecate are particularly well attended.

Beginning on December 16, Mexicans hold nightly *posadas*—candlelight processions terminating at elaborate, community-built nativity scenes—in commemoration of the Holy Family's search for lodging. The processions continue for nine consecutive nights. Other activities include piñata parties where children shatter hanging papier-mâché figures filled with small gifts and candy. Churches large and small hold continuous Christmas masses beginning at midnight on the 25th (Día de la Navidad).

Las Posadas culminates on January 6, which is Día de los Santos Reyes—literally, Day of the King-Saints, referring to the story of the Three Wise Men. On this day Mexican children receive their Christmas gifts, and family and friends gather to eat a wreath-shaped fruitcake called *rosca de reyes* (wreath of the kings), baked especially for this occasion. Hidden inside each *rosca* is a small clay figurine *(muñeco)* that represents the infant Jesus. While sharing the *rosca* on this day, the person whose slice contains the *muñeco* is obliged to host a *candelaria,* or Candlemas party, on February 2 for everyone present.

At the *candelaria*—which commemorates the day the newborn Jesus was first presented at the Temple in Jerusalem—the host traditionally displays a larger Christ-infant figure and serves tamales and *atole,* a thick, hot grain drink flavored with fruit or chocolate.

Accommodations and Camping

Places to stay in Baja run the gamut from free campgrounds to plush resort hotels. Camping spots are more numerous than hotels or motels, so visitors who bring along camping gear have a greater range of options at any given location. Larger cities—Tijuana, Ensenada, Mexicali, La Paz, and Cabo San Lucas—have dozens of hotels to choose from.

HOTELS AND MOTELS

Rates

At many hotels and motels, midweek rates are lower than weekend rates. In northern Baja, some places charge high-season rates May–Oct. In southern Baja, it's generally the opposite; i.e., winter rates are highest. To save money on accommodations, try traveling in the off-season for each region; except for the inland deserts, most of the peninsula is livable year-round. Summer temperatures of 38°C/100°F on the Cortez coast are usually mitigated by sea breezes and relatively low humidity except in August and September, when high temperatures and high humidity are the norm all along the Cortez coast.

Whatever the rack rate (the main listed room rate), you can usually get the price down by bargaining, except during peak periods, e.g., Christmas, spring break, and Easter. When checking in, be sure to clarify whether the room rate includes meals—occasionally it does. Asking for a room without meals (*sin comidas*) is an easy way to bring the rate down, or simply ask if there's anything cheaper (*¿Hay algo más barato?*).

Large tourist hotels may add a 12 percent hotel tax to quoted rates. Some also add a 10 percent service charge. When quoted a room rate, be sure to ask whether it includes tax and service to avoid a 22 percent surprise over posted rates when you check out.

In this book, we're using the following price categories for accommodations:

Under US$25
US$25–50
US$50–100

US$100–150
US$150–250
US$250 and up

Unless otherwise specified, the price ranges quoted are based on double-occupancy, high-season rates. Single-occupancy prices may be lower, and suites may be available at higher rates. All rates are per room, per night.

While hotels and motels in Baja tend to be less expensive than their counterparts in the United States, Canada, or Europe, they're also usually more expensive than equivalent accommodations in mainland Mexico.

Under US$25

Lodging under US$25 per night is rare unless you stay at a youth hostel, *casa de huéspedes,* or *pensión,* where bathrooms are usually shared. The term *baño colectivo* indicates shared bathroom facilities.

For under US$25 you can sometimes find a simple but clean room with private bath and double bed (though you might have to pay up to US$35 for the same type of room in Tijuana, Ensenada, Mexicali, or Cabo San Lucas). Soap, towels, toilet paper, and purified drinking water are usually provided; in some places you may have to ask. Rooms in this price range don't offer air conditioners or heaters. In northern Baja you can often obtain a *calentador* or space heater on request for especially cool nights.

US$25–50

The largest number of hotels and motels in Baja fall into the US$25–50 range. Some are older Mexican-style hotels just a bit larger than those in the budget range, while others are American-style motels; most everything in this price range comes with heating and air-conditioning.

US$50–100

In this range is the **Hotel La Pinta** chain, a joint venture between the Mexican government and Del Prado Inns. In Baja you'll find La Pinta locations in Ensenada, San Quintín, Cataviña, San Ignacio, and Loreto.

Hotel Finisterra, Cabo San Lucas

La Pinta hotels are very similar in appearance and facilities; the Las Cazuelas restaurant at each features the same menu, though the food quality varies according to the talents of the local kitchen staff. Room rates are similar throughout the chain, around US$65 s/d (as low as US$40 midweek in Ensenada, US$77 anytime in Cataviña), not including 12 percent tax. La Pinta hotels in Loreto and Ensenada fall at the lower end of this rate spectrum but are also the least well maintained. These prices assume you're paying in pesos—if you pay in dollars, the low exchange rate will cost you extra.

Like most hotel or motel chains, the most you can say for La Pinta is that there are few surprises. Between Ensenada and Loreto these are virtually the only hotels that accept credit cards for room and meal charges.

Members of the Discover Baja Travel Club receive a card entitling the bearer to a 20 percent discount on all La Pinta stays. If you stay at two or more branches of La Pinta during a single Baja visit, your Discover Baja membership will have paid for itself.

Reservations for any La Pinta hotel can be made by calling tel. 800/800-9632 in the United States and Canada, or at www.lapintahotels.com.

US$100–150

Higher-end places are found in or near Tijuana, Rosarito, Ensenada, San Felipe, La Paz, San José del Cabo, and Cabo San Lucas. Prices in Baja for "international-class accommodations" average around US$100–150. Some of these places are good values, while others are definitely overpriced. When in doubt, stick to the less-expensive hotels. Or ask about "specials." The Grand Hotel Tijuana in Tijuana, for example, has advertised rooms that normally cost around US$165 for just US$100.

US$150–250

The most luxurious hotels in all of Baja—indeed among the best in all of Mexico—are found along the coast between San José del Cabo and Cabo San Lucas, in an area known as The Corridor. Beach frontage, huge pools, spas, world-class restaurants, and golf course privileges are all part of the experience at these resorts.

US$250 and Up

A few Cape resorts charge US$250 or more for particular rooms or suites. Las Ventanas al Paraíso, one of the latest and greatest of the Corridor palaces, starts at around US$575 for a junior suite and tops out at US$4,000 a night for a three-bedroom presidential suite.

Hotel Reservation Services

Most of the hotels and motels mentioned in this guidebook take advance reservations directly by phone, mail, or website. Some visitors may find it more convenient to use one of the following reservation services offered in the United States: **MainTour,** www.maintour.com; **Baja California Tours,** 858/454-7166 or 800/336-5454, baja-tours@aol.com, www.bajaspecials.com; or **Mexico Travel Net,** tel. 800/511-4848, www.mexico travelnet.com. Occasionally these agencies can arrange lower room rates or special packages not offered directly by the hotels themselves. Note that the lives of these kinds of booking agencies tend to be very short—Baja California Tours is in fact the only hotel reservation agency specializing in Baja that has lasted three editions of this guidebook. Your local travel agent may also be able to book lodging in Baja.

ALTERNATIVES TO HOTELS AND MOTELS

Casas de Huéspedes and Pensiones

Aside from free or very basic campgrounds, *casas de huéspedes* (guesthouses) and *pensiones* (boardinghouses) are the cheapest places to stay in Baja. Unfortunately for budgeteers they aren't very plentiful. They're most numerous in Baja California Sur towns, especially Mulegé and La Paz. The typical *casa de huéspedes* offers rooms with shared bath *(baño colectivo)* for US$7–11; US$11–15 with private bath. A *pensión* costs about the same but may include meals. At either, most lodgers are staying for a week or more, but the proprietors are usually happy to accept guests by the night.

The main difference between these and budget hotels/motels—besides rates—is that they're usually in old houses or other buildings (e.g., convents) that have been converted for guesthouse use. Soap, towels, toilet paper, and drinking water are usually provided, but you may have to ask.

Youth Hostels

Baja has one youth hostel *(villa deportiva juvenil,* or youth sports villa) each in Mexicali, La Paz, Punta Colonet, Rosarito, and El Sauzal. They feature shared dormitory-style rooms where each guest is assigned a bed and a locker. Bathing facilities are always communal, and guests must supply their own soap and towels. Rates are US$10–15 per night.

Staying at these hostels is a great way to meet young Mexicans and improve your Spanish; English is rarely spoken. About the only drawback is that some hostels are inconveniently located some distance from the center of town, so transportation can be a problem. For the fitness-oriented, they're ideal; sports facilities usually include a gym, swimming pool, and courts for basketball, volleyball, and tennis.

House Rentals and House-Sitting

For long-term stays of a month or more—and occasionally for stays of as short as a week—house rental may be significantly less expensive and more convenient than staying at a hotel or motel. Rents vary wildly according to facilities, neighborhood, and general location in Baja. The most expensive rentals are those in beach areas along the Tijuana–Ensenada corridor, followed by those in Los Cabos. Expect to pay a minimum of US$500 a month in these beach areas (in some instances you could easily pay that for a weekend), more typically US$1,000–1,500 a month for something quite simple.

Some of the best deals on beach houses can be found in Los Barriles, Buena Vista, and Todos Santos, all in Baja California Sur. At any of these places you can rent a furnished one- or two-bedroom with kitchen starting at around US$350–500 a month. In the Tijuana–Ensenada corridor of Baja California Norte, expect to pay about twice that. Property management services and real estate companies in these areas can help locate something in your price range— see the appropriate destination chapters for contact information.

In smaller Baja towns you'll be hard-pressed to find any real estate or property-management companies, so the best thing to do is just ask the locals. In interior towns like San Ignacio, even San Quintín, livable houses can be rented for as low as US$200 a month. Farther off the beaten track in such relatively remote oases as La Purísima, Comondú, or San Javier, rents may be even lower—if you can find someone with a place to rent.

Some of the same companies that manage rentals may be able to offer house-sitting opportunities in homes whose seasonal residents want someone to take care of their property while they're away. Living rent-free in Baja may sound wonderful, but keep in mind that many homeowners have a list of chores they want carried out on a regular basis, such as tending plants, feeding and exercising pets, and so on.

CAMPING

Both states of Baja California boast more campgrounds, RV parks, and wilderness camping areas than any other state in Mexico. Because the peninsula's population density is so dramatically low, it's easy to find hidden campsites offering idyllic settings and precious solitude, often for free. For travelers who like the outdoors, camping is also an excellent way to slash accommodations

costs. A recent tourist survey found that over half of Baja's foreign overnight visitors camp rather than stay in hotels.

Campgrounds and RV Parks
The Baja peninsula offers roughly 100 campgrounds—perhaps 125 if you count Sea of Cortez fish camps—that charge fees ranging from around US$3 for a place with virtually zero facilities to as high as US$28 for a developed RV park with full water, electrical, and sewage hookups plus recreation facilities. Most campgrounds charge around US$5–8 for tent camping, US$10–15 for full hookups. A few RV parks in the Rosarito area actually get away with charging US$28–35 a night—the same price you might pay for a modest hotel room in some Baja towns.

If you can forgo permanent toilet and bathing facilities you won't have to pay anything to camp, since there's a virtually limitless selection of free camping spots, from beaches to deserts to mountain slopes. You won't necessarily need four-wheel drive to reach these potential campsites, as plenty of turnouts and graded dirt *ramales* (branch roads) off the main highways can be negotiated by just about any type of vehicle.

Food and Drink

Much of what *bajacalifornianos* eat can be considered Northern Mexican cuisine. Because Northern Mexico is generally better suited to ranching than farming, ranch-style cooking tends to prevail in rural areas, which means that ranch products—beef, poultry, and dairy foods—are highly favored.

Unlike the northern mainland, however, just about any point in Baja is only a couple of hours' drive from the seashore, so seafood predominates here more than anywhere else in Mexico. In most places on the peninsula, seafood is more common than meat or poultry. If there's anything unique about Baja cuisine, it's the blending of ranch cooking with coastal culture, which has resulted in such distinctive Baja creations as the *taco de pescado* (fish taco).

WHERE TO EAT

Your selection of eating venues in Baja depends largely on where you are on the peninsula at any given moment. The most populated areas lie at either end of the peninsula, where you'll find the greatest range of places to eat. Baja's larger towns and cities—Tijuana, Mexicali, Ensenada, La Paz, and Cabo San Lucas—offer everything from humble sidewalk taco stands to *gran turismo* hotel restaurants.

Between Ensenada and La Paz the choices are fewer and more basic. Along certain lengthy stretches of the Transpeninsular Highway in central Baja, about the only places to eat are ranchos that serve whatever's on the stone hearth that day. Usually, ranchos that take paying diners

ON THE ROAD

© JOE CUMMINGS

quesadillas and coffee at a ranch

hang a sign out front or post an arrow along the highway that says Lonchería, Café, Comedor, Comida, Eat, or Food. A few post no signs and are known only by word of mouth.

Small towns might have only two or three restaurants *(restaurantes)* serving basic Mexican dishes or, if near the coast, *mariscos* (seafood). Most hotels in Baja have restaurants; in small towns they may be among the best choices. While the Hotel La Pinta chain's restaurants are not known for their culinary excellence, in the desert pit stop of Cataviña, the La Pinta is about the only place you can get a full meal. Sometimes the best meals on the road come from what you improvise yourself after a visit to a local *tienda de abarrotes* (grocery store).

Back in the city, one of the main nonrestaurant choices is the *taquería*, a small, inexpensive diner where tacos are assembled before your eyes— sort of the Mexican equivalent of the old-fashioned American hamburger stand. *Taquerías* tend to be in areas with lots of foot traffic—near bus terminals, for example. The good ones are packed with taco-eaters in the early evening.

Another economical choice is anything called a *lonchería*, which is a small, café-style place that usually serves *almuerzo* (late breakfast/early lunch) and *comida* (the main, midday meal). *Lonchería* hours are typically 11 A.M.–5 P.M. Municipal markets in Baja often feature rows of *loncherías* serving inexpensive basic meals and *antojitos* (snacks or one-plate dishes). Some *loncherías* offer *comida corrida,* a daily fixed-price meal that includes a beverage, an entrée or two, side dishes, and possibly dessert.

A *comedor* is a more basic version of a *lonchería;* they aren't as common in Baja as on the mainland but are seen occasionally. Cafés or *cafeterías* are similar to *loncherías* except that they may open earlier and serve *desayuno* (breakfast) in addition to other meals.

A *cenaduría* is yet another simple, café-style restaurant, this time concentrating on *la cena,* the evening meal. Often the menu will be similar to that of a *lonchería*—mostly *antojitos*—but the hours are later, typically 5–10 P.M.

Ordering and Paying

You really don't need much Spanish to get by in a restaurant. Stating what you want, plus *por favor* (please), will usually do the trick (e.g., *"dos cervezas, por favor,"* "two beers, please"). Don't forget to

COOKING STYLES

Entrées, whether meat, poultry, or seafood, are most commonly prepared in one of the following styles:

al adobo, adobada—marinated or stewed in a sauce of vinegar, chilies, and spices
albóndigas—meatballs
a la parrilla—broiled or grilled
a la veracruzana—seafood, often *al carbón*—charcoal-grilled
al mojo de ajo—in a garlic sauce
al pastor—slowly roasted on a vertical spit
al vapor—steamed
asado/asada—grilled
barbacoa—pit-roasted
con arroz—steamed with rice
empanizada—breaded
encebollado—cooked with onions
entomado—cooked with tomatoes
frito—fried
guisado—in a spicy stew
machaca—dried and shredded

say *"gracias"* ("thank you"). The menu is called *el menú* or, much less commonly in Baja, *la carta*.

La cuenta is the bill. A tip *(la propina)* of 10–15 percent is expected at any restaurant with table service; look to see if it's already been added to the bill before placing a tip on the table.

Costs

In this guidebook, we've tried to give some guidance as to the approximate meal cost at most sit-down restaurants. At "inexpensive" places, you can count on spending less than US$7 for an entrée (or for a *comida corrida*, where available—see Comida futher on), while a "moderate" meal will cost up to US$15, and an "expensive" one more than US$15.

WHAT TO EAT

Breakfasts

Menus at tourist restaurants are often confusing because some of the same "breakfast" dishes may

end up on more than one section of the menu. Mexicans have two kinds of breakfasts, an early one called *desayuno*, eaten shortly after rising, and a second called *almuerzo* that's usually taken around 11 A.M. To further confuse the issue, Spanish-English dictionaries usually translate *almuerzo* as "lunch," while bilingual menus often read "breakfast."

The most common Baja *desayuno* is simply *pan dulce* (sweet pastry) or *bolillos* (torpedo-shaped, European-style rolls) with coffee or milk. Cereal is also sometimes eaten for *desayuno*; e.g., *avena* (oatmeal), *crema de trigo* (cream of wheat), or *hojuelas de maíz* (corn flakes).

The heavier eggs-and-frijoles dishes known widely as "Mexican breakfasts" in the United States and Canada are usually taken as *almuerzo*, the late breakfast, which is most typically reserved for weekends and holidays. Eggs come in a variety of ways, including *huevos revueltos* (scrambled eggs), *huevos duros* (hard-boiled eggs), *huevos escafaldos* (soft-boiled eggs), *huevos estrel-*

lados (eggs fried sunny side up), *huevos a la mexicana* (also *huevos mexicanos,* eggs scrambled with chopped tomato, onion, and chilies), *huevos rancheros* (fried eggs served on a tortilla), and *huevos divorciados,* two *huevos estrellados* separated by beans, each egg usually topped with a different salsa.

Eggs also come *con chorizo* (with ground sausage), *con machaca* (with dried, shredded meat), *con tocino* (with bacon), or *con jamón* (with ham). All egg dishes usually come with frijoles and tortillas. The biggest *almuerzo* package on the menu is typically called *almuerzo albañil* (brickmason's *almuerzo*) or *huevos albañil* (brickmason's eggs); this means eggs with one or more varieties of meat on the side.

One of the cheapest and tastiest *almuerzos* is *chilaquiles,* tortilla chips in a chili gravy with crumbled cheese on top. Eggs and/or chicken can be added to *chilaquiles.* Another economical choice is *molletes,* which consists of a split *bolillo* spread with mashed beans and melted cheese, served with salsa on the side.

Comida

Bajacalifornianos typically eat the main meal of the day, *comida,* sometime between 2 and 5 P.M. While *desayuno* (breakfast) may consist of nothing more than a roll and coffee, and *cena* (the evening meal) not much more, *comida* is where Mexicans pack on most of the calories they take in during a day's eating. Whether eaten at home or in a *lonchería,* restaurant, or bar, this meal usually consists of several different dishes, including rice, soup, and a *plato fuerte* (main dish).

Many restaurants offer a *comida corrida* or *comida del día,* a special fixed-price, multicourse menu costing US$2.50–5. The typical *comida corrida* includes soup, a plate of flavored rice (served as an appetizer), a main dish, one or two side dishes, dessert, and a nonalcoholic beverage (often an *agua fresca*).

Cena

The large afternoon *comida* sustains most Mexicans till at least 8 P.M. or so, when it's time for *cena,* a light evening meal usually consisting of *pan dulce* (Mexican pastries) with herb tea or coffee. A larger repast taken in a restaurant may be called *merienda.*

Tortillas

A Mexican meal is not a meal without tortillas, the round, flat, pancakelike disks eaten with nearly any nondessert dish, including salads, meats, seafood, beans, and vegetables. Both wheat-flour and cornmeal tortillas are commonly consumed throughout Baja, although flour tortillas *(tortillas de harina)* are the clear favorite. Corn tortillas *(tortillas de maíz)* are more common in Southern Mexico, where Amerindian populations (the first corn cultivators) are larger, while flour tortillas are more popular in the ranching areas of Northern Mexico. Among Northern Mexicans, it is said that meat and poultry dishes taste best with flour tortillas while vegetable dishes go best with corn. Most restaurants offer a choice. If you order tortillas without specifying, you may get *"¿de harina o de maíz?"* as a response.

Although prepackaged tortillas are available in *supermercados* (supermarkets), most *bajacalifornianos* buy them fresh from neighborhood *tortillerías* or make them at home. Many restaurants and cafés in Baja, and virtually all *loncherías* and *taquerías,* serve fresh tortillas.

Incidentally, a tortilla has two sides, an inside and an outside, that dictate which direction the tortilla is best folded when wrapping it around food. The side with the thinner layer—sometimes called the *pancita,* or belly—should face the inside when folding the tortilla. If you notice the outside of your tortilla cracking, with pieces peeling off onto the table, you've probably folded it with the *pancita* outside instead of inside.

Antojitos and Main Dishes

Antojitos literally means "little whims," thus implying snacks to many people. However, the word also refers to any food that can be ordered, served, and eaten quickly—in other words, Mexican fast food. Typical *antojitos* include tamales, enchiladas, burritos, *flautas, chiles rellenos, chalupas, picadillo,* quesadillas, *tortas,* and tacos.

Visitors who identify these terms with dishes at Mexican restaurants in their home countries are sometimes confused by the different shapes and

ANTOJITOS

birria—stew made from beef, lamb, or goat in a sauce spiced with cinnamon, cloves, cumin, and oregano

burrito—a flour tortilla rolled around meat, beans, or seafood fillings; Baja's lobster burritos are legendary

chalupa—a crisp, whole tortilla topped with beans, meat, etc. (also known as a tostada)

chile relleno—a mild poblano chili stuffed with cheese (or occasionally ground beef), deep-fried in egg batter, and served with a ranchero sauce (tomatoes, onions, and chilies)

chiles de árbol, oregano, and fresh chopped onion; reputedly a sure hangover cure

enchilada—a corn tortilla dipped in chili sauce then folded or rolled around a filling of meat, chicken, seafood, or cheese and baked in an oven

enfrijolada—same as enchilada except dipped in a sauce of thinned refried beans instead of chili sauce

entomatada—same as enchilada except dipped in a tomato sauce instead of chili sauce

flauta—a small corn-tortilla roll, usually stuffed with beef or chicken and deep-fried

gordita—a small, thick, corn tortilla stuffed with a spicy meat mixture

huarache—literally, "sandal;" a large, flat, thick, oval-shaped tortilla topped with fried meat and chilies

menudo—a thick soup made with cows' feet and stomachs (and less commonly, intestines) and seasoned with **pozole**—hominy stew made with pork or chicken and garnished with radishes, oregano, onions, chili powder, salt, and lime

picadillo—a spicy salad of chopped or ground meat with chilies and onions (also known as **salpicón**)

quesadilla—a flour tortilla folded over sliced cheese and grilled; ask the cook to add **chiles rajas** (pepper strips) for extra flavor

sope—a small, thick, round corn cake with dimpled edges, topped with a spicy meat mixture and crumbled cheese

taco—a corn tortilla folded or rolled around anything and eaten with the hands; **tacos de pescado,** or fish tacos, are a Baja specialty

tamal—plural **tamales;** cornmeal (masa) dough wrapped in a corn husk and steamed; sometimes stuffed with corn, olives, pork, or turkey

torta—a sandwich made with a Mexican-style roll (**bolillo/birote** or the larger **pan telera**); one of the most popular is the **torta de milanesa,** made with breaded, deep-fried veal or pork

BOB RACE

forms they may take in Mexico. Tacos can be rolled as well as folded, and enchiladas can be folded or stacked as well as rolled; shape is irrelevant. An enchilada (literally "chilied") is any *antojito* made with a tortilla dipped or cooked in a chili sauce; an *entomada* (or *entomatada*) is the equivalent made with tomatoes, while the *enfrijolada* is the same made with a thin bean sauce.

A taco is any type of plain tortilla surrounding other ingredients. In some eateries you can order tacos either *suave*—heated, soft tortillas stuffed with meat and vegetable fillings—or *dorado* (golden)—thin corn tortillas stuffed tightly with meat, then deep-fried whole and served with lettuce and grated cheese.

The main dish, or *el plato fuerte,* of any meal can be a grander version of an *antojito,* a regional specialty (*mole poblano,* for example), or something the *cocineros* (cooks) dream up themselves. Typical entrées are centered around meats, seafood, or poultry.

Meats

Common meats include *carne de res* (beef), *puerco* (pork), and *cabrito* (kid goat). *Jamón* (ham), chorizo (sausage), and *tocino* (bacon) are usually reserved for *almuerzo.* Steak may appear on menus as *bistec, bistek, biftec,* or "steak." *Venado* (deer meat or venison) and *conejo* (rabbit) are commonly served on ranchos. Poultry dishes include *pollo* (chicken), *pavo* (turkey), and, less frequently, *pato* (duck) and *codorniz* (quail).

Carnitas

This dish from the state of Michoacán belongs in a category all its own and is usually sold only at butcher shops or at restaurants specializing in it. The usual method for producing *carnitas* is to slowly braise an entire pig in a huge cauldron, along with a variety of flavorings that are a closely guarded secret among *carnitas* purveyors. The results are chopped into thin slices and eaten with stacks of tortillas, pickled vegetables and chilies, guacamole, and various salsas.

Carnitas are almost always sold by weight. You can order by the *kilo* (one kilogram, about 2.2 pounds), *medio* (half kilo), *cuarto* (quarter kilo), or sometimes in 100-gram increments *(cien gramos)*. Figure on a quarter kilo (about a half pound) per hungry person and you won't have much left over. One of the best places to eat *carnitas* in all Baja is La Flor de Michoacán in Rosarito.

Seafood

Pescado (fish) entrées on the menu are often seasonal or dependent on the "catch of the day." Often just the word *pescado* and the method of cooking will appear (e.g., *pescado al mojo de ajo*). If you need to know exactly what kind of fish, just ask *"¿Hay qué tipo de pescado?"*—although in some cases the only response you get is something generic, like *"pescado blanco"* ("white fish"). For specific fish names, see the sidebar Fish Translators.

Baja's number-one seafood specialty is the *taco de pescado* (fish taco). If you've never tried one, you're most likely wondering "What's the big deal—a fish taco?" Eat one, though, and you're hooked for life. Short, tender, fresh fish fillets are dipped in batter and fried quickly, then folded into a steaming corn tortilla with a variety of condiments, including *salsa fresca* (chopped tomatoes, onions, chilies, and lime juice), marinated cabbage (similar to coleslaw in the United States), guacamole (a savory avocado paste), and sometimes a squirt of mayonnaise or *crema* (fresh Mexican cream). *¡La última!* Any kind of white-fleshed fish can be used—the best fish tacos are those made from yellowtail *(jurel)*, halibut *(lenguado)*, or mahimahi *(dorado)*.

Shellfish dishes *(mariscos)* popular on Baja menus include: *ostiones* (oysters), *almejas* (clams), *callos* (scallops), *jaibas* (small crabs), *cangrejos* (large crabs), *camarones* (shrimp), *langosta* (lobster), *langostina* (crayfish, also called *cucarachas*), and *abulón* (abalone). They can be ordered as *cocteles* (cocktails—steamed or boiled and served with lime and salsa), *en sus conchas* (in the shell), or in many other ways.

Beans

The beans *(frijoles)* preferred in Baja, as on the northern mainland, are pinto beans, usually dried beans boiled until soft, then mashed and fried with lard or vegetable oil (usually the former). Often this preparation is called *frijoles refritos* (refried beans), although they're not really refried except when reheated. Sometimes the beans are served whole, in their own broth, as *frijoles de olla* (boiled beans), or with bits of roast pork as *frijoles a la charra* (ranch-style beans). Frijoles can be served with any meal of the day, including breakfast.

Cheese

Even the most remote rancho usually has some cheese *(queso)* around, so if your appetite isn't stimulated by the *iguana guisada* simmering on the hearth, you can usually ask for *chiles rellenos* (mild poblano chilies stuffed with cheese and fried in an egg batter) or quesadillas (cheese melted in folded flour tortillas). A meal of beans, tortillas, and cheese provides a complete source of protein for travelers who choose to avoid meat, poultry, or seafood for health, economic, or moral reasons.

Among the most commonly used are *queso cotijo* (also called *queso añejo*), *queso chihuahuense* (called *queso menonita* in the state of Chihuahua), *queso manchego, queso oaxaqueño*, and *queso asadero*.

Queso menonita or *queso chihuahuense* (Mennonite or Chihuahuan cheese) is a mild, white cheddar produced in wheels by Mennonite colonists in Chihuahua and Durango. Spanish import (though also made in Mexico) *queso manchego* is similar but usually softer. *Queso asadero* (griller cheese) is a braided cheese somewhat similar to Armenian string cheese, made by combining sour milk with fresh milk. *Chihuahuense* is a common ingredient in dishes stuffed with cheese, such as enchiladas or *chiles rellenos,* which won't receive high, direct heat. *Asadero* melts well at high temperatures, without burning or separating, and as such is well suited to *chile con queso* (hot, blended chili-cheese dip), *queso fundido* (hot melted cheese topped with *chorizo* or mushrooms), and other dishes in which the cheese is directly exposed to high heat. *Queso oaxaqueño,* also called *quesillo,* is a lump-style cheese similar to *asadero* but a little softer—close to mozzarella. It's popular in *tortas* or Mexican-style sandwiches.

Cotijo or *añejo* is a crumbly aged cheese that resists melting and is commonly used as a topping for enchiladas and beans; the flavor and texture is somewhat like a cross between feta and Parmesan.

Many ranchos produce their own *queso fresco* (fresh cheese) from raw cow's, goat's, or sheep's milk. To make *queso fresco,* the rancheros first cure the milk with homemade rennet (from a calf's fourth stomach) until the milk separates, then press the curds with weights (sometimes under flat rocks lined with cloth) to remove excess moisture. In more elaborate operations, the initial pressing is then ground up and repressed into small round cakes. If you want to buy some *queso fresco,* look for Hay Queso signs as you pass ranchos. If you're very fortunate, you might even come across *panela,* an extra-rich cheese made from heavy cream.

Vegetables and Vegetarian Food

Although vegetables are sometimes served as side dishes with *comidas corridas,* with restaurant entrées, or in salads *(ensaladas),* they're seldom listed separately on the menu. When they do appear on menus, it's usually at restaurants in towns near farming areas in northern Baja or else in the La Paz–Los Cabos area, where many vegetables come over by boat from the mainland. The best place to add vegetables to your diet is at a market or grocery store.

It's difficult but not impossible to practice a vegetarian regime in Baja. Vegetarians can eat quesadillas (ask for corn tortillas, which unlike most flour tortillas do not contain lard) or *enchiladas de queso* (cheese enchiladas). With some luck, you'll stumble across restaurants that can prepare a variety of interesting cheese dishes, including *queso fundido con champiñones* (melted cheese with mushrooms, eaten with tortillas) and quesadillas made with *flor de calabaza* (squash flower). Some places make beans without lard *(sin manteca),* but you'll have to ask to find out. Many larger towns have at least one vegetarian/health food store (usually called *tienda naturista*) with a small dining section as well as bulk foods.

Vegans, for the most part, will do best to prepare their own food. Look for shops with signs reading *semillas* (seeds) to pin down a good selection of nuts and dried beans. You'll find plenty of fresh fruits and vegetables in markets and grocery stores.

Soup

The general menu term for soup is *sopa,* although a thick soup with lots of ingredients is usually a *caldo* or *caldillo. Menudo* is a soup of hominy *(nixtamal)* and cow's feet and stomach (or, less commonly, intestine) in a savory, reddish-brown broth, served with chopped onions, chilies, and crumbled oregano. It's seen throughout Mexico and is highly prized as a hangover remedy. *Pozole* is a similar soup with a much lighter-colored broth; some varieties of *pozole* are made with chicken instead of tripe.

Other tasty soups include *sopa de tortillas, sopa azteca,* and *sopa tlapeño,* all variations of artfully seasoned chicken broth garnished with *totopos* (tortilla wedges) and sliced avocado.

Bread and Pan Dulce

Bread *(pan)* arrived in Mexico not with the Spanish but during the brief era of French rule in the late 19th century. The most common bread is the *bolillo* (little ball), a small torpedo-shaped roll, usually rather hard on the outside. *Pan telera* ("scissor bread," so named for the two clefts on top) rolls resemble *bolillos* but are larger and flatter; they're mainly used for making *tortas,* the ubiquitous Mexican sandwich. *Pan de barra,*

American-style sliced bread, is also occasionally available but never measures up to crusty *bolillos* or *teleras*.

Sweetened breads or pastries are known as *pan dulce* (sweet bread). Common *pan dulce* varieties include *buñuelos* (crisp, round, flat pastries fried and coated with cinnamon sugar), *campechanas* (flaky, sugar-glazed puff pastries), *canastas* (thick, round, fruit-filled cookies), *capirotada* (bread pudding), *cortadillos* (cake squares topped with jelly and finely shredded coconut), *cuernitos* (small crescent rolls rolled in cinnamon sugar), *galletas* (cookies), *palmitas* (flat, fan-shaped, crispy pastries), *pan de huevos* (spongy yeast bread with patterned sugar toppings), and *polvorones* (small shortbread cookies).

> *On a hot day, nothing satisfies like* **helados** *(ice cream),* **paletas,** *(popsicles), or* **nieve,** *(grated ice), all of which come in more flavors than you can think of.*

Salsas and Condiments

Any restaurant, café, *lonchería, taquería,* or *comedor* offers a variety of salsas. Sometimes only certain salsas are served with certain dishes, while at other times one, two, or even three salsas are stationed on every table. Often each place has its own unique salsa recipes—canned or bottled salsas are rarely used. The one ingredient common to all salsas is chili peppers, though these vary in heat from mild to incendiary.

There are as many types of salsas as there are Mexican dishes—red, green, yellow, brown, hot, mild, salty, sweet, thick, thin, blended, and chunky. The most typical is the *salsa casera* (house salsa), a simple, fresh concoction of chopped chilies, onions, and tomatoes mixed with salt, lime juice, and cilantro. This is what you usually get with the complimentary basket of *totopos* (tortilla chips) served at the beginning of every Mexican meal. Another common offering is *salsa verde* (green sauce), made with a base of tomatillos (small, tart, green, tomato-like vegetables). Some salsas are *picante,* or spicy hot (also *picosa*), so it's always a good idea to test a bit before pouring the stuff over everything on your plate.

Whole pickled chilies are sometimes served on the side as a condiment, especially with tacos

and *carnitas.* Salt *(sal)* is usually on the table, although it's rarely needed since Mexican dishes tend to be prepared with plenty of it. Black pepper is *pimiento negro,* and if it's not on the table it's normally available for the asking. Butter is *mantequilla,* sometimes served with flour tortillas.

In *taquerías,* guacamole (mashed avocado blended with onions, chilies, salt, and sometimes other ingredients) is always served as a condiment. In restaurants it may be served as a salad or with tortilla chips.

Desserts and Sweets

The most popular of Mexican desserts, or *postres,* is a delicious egg custard called flan. It's listed on virtually every tourist restaurant menu, along with *helado* (ice cream). Other sweet alternatives include pastries found in *panaderías* (bakeries) and the frosty offerings at the ubiquitous *paleterías.* Strictly speaking, a *paletería* serves only *paletas,* flavored ice on sticks (like American popsicles but with a much wider range of flavors), but many also serve *nieve,* literally "snow," which is flavored grated ice served like ice cream in bowls or cones.

Another common street vendor food is *churros,* sweet fried pastries something like donut sticks sprinkled with sugar. One of the best places to sample *churros* is at La Bufadora at Punta Banda, just south of Ensenada. Nowhere else in Baja will you find so many *churro* vendors in one place.

Dulcerías, or candy shops, sell a huge variety of sticky Mexican sweets, usually wrapped individually. Often brightly decorated, *dulcerías* are oriented toward children and sometimes carry inexpensive toys as well as sweets. The larger ones sell piñatas, colorful papier-mâché figures filled with candy and small gifts and hung at parties (where children are allowed to break them with sticks, releasing all the goodies inside). Traditionally, piñatas are crafted to resemble common animals, but these days you'll see all kinds of shapes, including Pokémon, Santa Claus, and Batman.

ON THE ROAD

fruit vendor

Fruits

A large variety of delicious fruits are available in local markets and grocery stores. Most common are mango *(mango)*, banana *(plátano)*, guava *(guayaba)*, papaya *(papaya)*, grapes *(uvas)*, pineapple *(piña)*, and apple *(manzana)*, but you may occasionally see more exotic fruits from the mainland.

BUYING GROCERIES

The cheapest way to feed yourself while traveling in Baja is the same way you save money at home: buy groceries at the store and prepare meals on your own. Even the smallest towns in Baja have a little grocery store or corner market. A ripe avocado, a chunk of *queso fresco,* and a couple of *bolillos* can make a fine, easy-to-fix meal.

The humblest type of store is the small family-owned *tienda de abarrotes,* usually recognizable by the single word *abarrotes* (groceries) printed somewhere on the outside (*tienda* means "store"). These stock the basics—tortillas, dried beans, flour, herbs and spices, bottled water, a few vegetables, possibly *bolillos* and *queso fresco*—as well as limited household goods like soap and laundry detergent. As at convenience stores back home,

the food at the average *tienda de abarrotes* is not particularly inexpensive. Cheaper, when you can find them, are government-sponsored Diconsa (Distribuidora Conasupo), *tienda rural,* and ISSSTE (Instituto de Seguridad y Servicios Sociales para Trabajadores del Estado) markets.

Privately run supermarkets are found in larger towns. Like their American counterparts, they're usually well stocked with a wide variety of meats, baked goods, vegetables, household goods, and beer and liquor. Supermarket prices are often lower than those of smaller grocery stores.

Several towns and cities in Baja feature *mercados municipales* (municipal markets), large warehouse-type structures where meat, fruit, and vegetable producers sell their goods directly to the public. Prices are often very good at these markets, but it helps if you know how to bargain.

Another common *tienda* is the *ultramarinos,* which is primarily a place to buy beer and liquor, along with a few food items.

Panaderías

Although you can often buy a few bakery items at the aforementioned stores, the best place to buy them is at their source—a *panadería* (literally, "breadery," i.e., bakery). Many of the *panaderías* in Baja still use wood-fired *hornos* (ovens), which make the *bolillos* (Mexican rolls), *pasteles* (cakes), and *pan dulce* (cookies and sweet pastries) especially tasty. *Pan de barra*, American-style sliced bread, is also occasionally available. To select bakery items from the shelves of a *panadería*, simply imitate the other customers—pick up a pair of tongs and a tray from the counter near the cash register and help yourself, cafeteria-style.

Tortillerías

Unless you make them yourself, the best tortillas are found where they make them fresh every day. The automated process at a *tortillería* uses giant electric grinders and conveyor belts to transform whole corn into fresh tortillas, which you purchase by weight, not number. A kilo yields about 40 average, 12-cm (five-inch) tortillas; you may be able to order by the *cuarto* or *medio* (quarter or half kilo). The government-subsidized prices are low. Restaurants, *tiendas*, and home cooks purchase tortillas from the local *tortillería* to avoid spending hours at a *metate* (grinder) and *comal* (griddle).

NONALCOHOLIC BEVERAGES

Water

Bottled drinking water is usually available at every *tienda de abarrotes* or supermarket throughout Baja. If you're car camping, renting a house, or staying in one place for a long time, it may be more convenient to use the 20-liter (roughly five-gallon) reusable plastic containers called *garafónes* available in most Mexican towns. These typically cost around US$6 for the first bottle of water and bottle deposit, then US$1.60 for each 20-liter refill. This is much cheaper than buying individual liter or half-liter bottles, which can cost as much as US$2 apiece, and you won't be throwing away so much plastic. The water will be easier to dispense if you also buy a *sifón* (siphon) designed for that purpose. These are available for around US$2.50 at many grocery stores.

The water and ice served in restaurants in Baja is always purified—it's not necessary to order *agua mineral* (mineral water) unless you need the minerals. Likewise, the water used as an in-gredient in "handmade" drinks, e.g., *licuados* or *aguas frescas*, also comes from purified sources.

Soft Drinks

Licuados are similar to American "smoothies"—fruit blended with water, ice, honey or sugar, and sometimes milk or raw eggs to produce something like a fruit shake. In Baja, *tuna* (not the fish but the fruit of the prickly pear cactus) *licuados* are particularly delicious. Any place that makes *licuados* will also make orange juice *(jugo de naranja)*. Orange juice is very popular in Baja; you'll often see street vendors who sell nothing but fresh-squeezed OJ.

Aguas frescas are colorful beverages sold from huge glass jars on the streets of larger cities or at carnivals, usually during warm weather. They're made by boiling the pulp of various fruits, grains, or seeds with water, then straining it and adding sugar and large chunks of ice. *Arroz* (rice) and *horchata* (melon-seed), both usually spiced with cinnamon and vanilla, are two of the tastiest *aguas*.

American soft drinks *(refrescos)* such as 7UP, Coke, and Pepsi are common; their Mexican equivalents are just as good. An apple-flavored soft drink called Manzanita is popular.

Hot Drinks

Coffee is served in a variety of ways. The best, when you can find it, is traditional Mexican-style coffee (ranchos sometimes serve it), which is made by filtering near-boiling water through fine-ground coffee in a slender cloth sack. Instant coffee *(nescafé)* is often served at small restaurants and cafés; a jar of instant coffee may be sitting on the table for you to add to hot water. When there's a choice, a request for *café de olla* (pot coffee) should bring you real brewed coffee. When you order coffee in a Mexican restaurant, some servers will ask *"¿de grano o de agua?"* (literally "grain or water?"), meaning "brewed or instant?" One of the better Mexican brands found in supermarkets is Café Combate. If you'd like a darker roast than normally available, buy a bag of green coffee beans (available at most supermarkets) and roast your own in a dry iron skillet.

THE LIQUID HEART OF MEXICO

Tequila is a pallid flame that passes through walls and soars over tile roofs to allay despair.

Álvaro Mútis, Tequila: Panegyric and Emblem

Mexico's national drink has been in production, in prototypical form, since at least the time of the Aztecs. The Aztecs, in fact, called themselves Mexicas in direct reference to the special spiritual role mescal—tequila's forerunner—played in their culture via Mextli, the god of agave (the desert plant from which *pulque,* mescal, and tequila are derived). These names, as interpreted by the Spanish, eventually yielded "Mexico."

The Spaniards levied a tax on tequila as early as 1608, and in 1795, King Carlos IV granted the first legal concession to produce tequila to Don José María Guadalupe Cuervo. The liquor's name was taken from the Ticuila Amerindians of Jalisco, who mastered baking the heart of the *Agave tequiliana weber,* or blue agave, and extracting its juice, a process employed by tequila distilleries today. Native to Jalisco, this succulent is the only agave that produces true tequila as certified by the Mexican government. Contrary to the myth that all true tequila must come from Tequila, Jalisco, Mexican law enumerates specific districts in five Mexican states where tequila may be legally produced, including as far away as Tamaulipas on the United States–Mexico border.

All liquors labeled "tequila" must contain at least 51 percent blue agave distillates. Sugarcane juice or extracts from other agaves usually make up the rest. Many tequila aficionados will caution you to look for the initials NOM—for Norma Oficial Mexicana—on the label to be sure it's "real" tequila, but we've never seen a bottle of tequila sold in Mexico that didn't bear those letters.

Despite the fact that tequila sales are booming today, much of the tequila-making process is still carried out *a mano* (by hand). In the traditional method, the mature heart of the tequila agave, which looks like a huge pineapple and weighs 18–56 kg (50–150 pounds), is roasted in pits for 24 hours, then shredded and ground by mule- or horse-powered mills. After the juice is extracted from the pulp and fermented in ceramic pots, it's distilled in copper stills to produce the basic tequila, which is always clear and colorless, with an alcohol content of 38–40 percent.

True "gold" tequilas are produced by aging the tequila in imported oak barrels to achieve a slightly mellowed flavor. The *reposado* or "rested" type is oak-aged for at least two months, while *añejo* or "aged" tequila must stay in barrels at least a year. Inferior "gold" tequilas may be nothing more than the silver stuff mixed with caramel coloring—always look for *reposado* or *añejo* on the label if you want the true gold.

José Cuervo, Sauza, and Herradura are well-established, inexpensive to medium-priced tequila labels with international notoriety. Of these three, Herradura is said to employ the most traditional methods; tequila connoisseurs generally prefer it over the other two. In 1983 Chinaco, based in the state of Tamaulipas, became the first label to produce a tequila made from 100 percent blue agave, a formula now considered standard for all high-end tequilas. Many tasters claim a label called Reserva del Patrón (sold simply as "Patrón" north of the Mexican border) is the finest and smoothest tequila tipple of them all. Other very fine *tequilas reposadas* include Don Eduardo, Ecuario Gonzales, La Perseverancia, Don Felipe, and our personal favorite for flavor and price, Las Trancas. To emphasize the limited production nature of these private reserve distillations, these brands are usually sold in numbered bottles with fancy labels. Less expensive but also very good are the Jimador, Centenario, and Orendain labels. As with wine, it's all a matter of personal preference; try a few *probaditos* ("little tastes" or shots) for yourself to determine which brand best tickles your palate. The fancier tequilas may be served in brandy snifters instead of the traditional tall, narrow shot glass *(caballito)*.

Mescal and the Worm

The distillate of other agave plants—also known as magueys or century plants—is called mescal (sometimes spelled "mezcal"), not to be confused with the nondistilled mescal—*pulque*—prepared in pre-Hispanic Mexico. The same roasting and distilling process is used for today's mescal as for tequila. Actually, tequila is a mescal, but no drinker calls it that, just as no one in a United States bar orders "whiskey" when they mean to specify scotch or bourbon. Although many states in Mexico produce mescal, the best is often said to come from the state of Oaxaca.

The caterpillar-like grub or *gusano de maguey* (maguey worm) floating at the bottom of a bottle of mescal lives on the maguey plant itself. They're safe to eat—just about anything pickled in mescal would be—but not particularly appetizing. By the time you hit the bottom of the bottle, though, who cares? Maguey worms are often fried and eaten with fresh corn tortillas and salsa—a delicious appetizer.

Tequila Drinks

The usual way to drink tequila is straight up, followed by a water or beer chaser. Licking a few grains of salt before taking a shot and sucking a lime wedge afterward make it go down smoother. The salt raises a protective coating of saliva on the tongue while the lime juice scours the tongue of salt and tequila residues.

Tequila con sangrita, in which a shot of tequila is chased with a shot of *sangrita* (not to be confused with *sangría,* the wine-and-fruit punch), is a slightly more elegant method of consumption. *Sangrita* is a bright red mix of orange juice, lime juice, grenadine, red chile powder, and salt.

An old tequila standby is the much-abused margarita, a tart Tex-Mex cocktail made with tequila, lime juice, and Cointreau (usually "Controy" or triple sec in Mexico) served in a salt-rimmed glass. A true margarita is shaken and served on the rocks (crushed or blended ice tends to kill the flavor) or strained, but just about every other gringo in Baja seems to drink "frozen" margaritas, in which the ice is mixed in a blender with the other ingredients.

If you detect a noticeable difference between the taste of margaritas north or south of the border, it may be because bartenders in the United States and Canada tend to use bigger and less flavorful Persian limes *(Citrus latifolia),* while in Mexico they use the smaller, sweeter key or Mexican lime *(Citrus aurantifolia swingle).* A "Baja margarita" substitutes Baja's own damiana liqueur for the triple sec. The damiana herb is said to be an aphrodisiac.

ON THE ROAD

Café con leche is the Mexican version of *café au lait*, i.e., coffee and hot milk mixed in near-equal proportions. *Café con crema* (coffee with cream) is not as available; when it is, it usually means a cup of coffee with a packet of nondairy creamer on the side.

Hot chocolate *(chocolate)* is fairly common on Baja menus. It's usually served very sweet and may contain cinnamon, ground almonds, and other flavorings. A thicker version made with cornmeal—almost a chocolate pudding—is called *champurrado* or *atole*.

Black tea *(té negro)* is not popular among *bajacalifornianos*, although you may see it on tourist menus. Ask for *té helado* or *té frío* if you want iced tea. At home many Mexicans drink *té de manzanilla* (chamomile tea), *té de yerba buena* (mint tea), or *té de canela* (cinnamon tea) in the evenings.

ALCOHOLIC BEVERAGES

Drinking laws in Mexico are quite minimal. The legal drinking age in Mexico is 18 years. It's illegal to carry open containers of alcoholic beverages in a vehicle. Booze of every kind is widely available in bars, restaurants, grocery stores, and *licorerías* (liquor stores). *Borracho* means both "drunk" (as an adjective) and "drunkard."

Cerveza

The most popular and available beer brand in northern Baja is Tecate, brewed in Tecate, while in the south it's Pacífico, from Mazatlán, just across the Sea of Cortez from Cabo San Lucas. Both are good-tasting, light- to medium-weight brews, with Tecate holding a slight edge (more hops) over Pacífico. You can't compare either of these with their export equivalents in the United States, because Mexican breweries produce separate brews for American consumption that are lighter in taste and lower in alcohol content. It's always better in Mexico.

Other major Mexican brands such as Corona Extra (the number-one-selling beer in mainland Mexico and number-one imported beer in the United States), Dos Equis (XX), Superior, Carta Blanca, Bohemia, and Negra Modelo are available

in tourist restaurants, but you'll notice the locals stick pretty much to Tecate and Pacífico, perhaps out of regional loyalty.

The cheapest sources for beer are the brewery's agents or distributors (look for signs saying Agencia, Subagencia, Cervecería, or Depósito), where you can return deposit bottles for cash or credit. You can buy beer by the bottle *(envase)*, can *(bote)*, six-pack *(canastilla)*, or 20-bottle case *(cartón)*. A *cartón* of Pacífico or Tecate costs US$11.50, not counting the refundable bottle deposit. Most Pacífico *agencias* also sell Corona Extra for the same price. Large, liter-size bottles are called *ballenas* (whales) or *caguamas* (sea turtles) and are quite popular. When buying beer at an *agencia* or *depósito*, specify *fría* if you want cold beer, otherwise you'll get beer *al tiempo* (at room temperature). Many *depósitos* offer free ice with the purchase of a case of beer.

Wine

Baja is one of Mexico's major wine-production areas, and Baja wines are commonly served in restaurants. A broad selection of varietals is available, including cabernet sauvignon, chardonnay, chenin blanc, pinot noir, barbera, zinfandel, nebbiolo, and tempranillo. These and other grapes are also blended to produce cheaper *vino tinto* (red wine) and *vino blanco* (white wine). Better vintages may be labeled *reserva privada* (private reserve). When ordering wine in Spanish at a bar, you may want to specify *vino de uva* (grape wine), as *vino* alone can refer to distilled liquors as well as wine. *Vino blanco*, in fact, can be interpreted as cheap tequila.

Two of the more reliable and reasonably priced labels are L.A. Cetto and Santo Tomás, both produced in northern Baja. Domecq also produces a good medium-priced series of wines under the Domecq XA label. Better but more expensive—and hard to find—are Baja California's Monte Xanic and Château Camou. Monte Xanic's Cabernet y Merlot is considered one of the finest wines ever produced in Mexico. Camou makes an excellent *coupage* of cabernet franc, cabernet sauvignon, and merlot, labeled Gran Vino de Château Camou.

Liquor

Tequila is Mexico's national drink and also the most popular distilled liquor in Baja. The second most popular is brandy, followed closely by *ron* (rum), both produced in Mexico for export as well as domestic consumption. A favorite rum drink in Baja is the *cuba libre* (free Cuba), called *cuba* for short—a mix of rum, Coke, and lime juice over ice. Similar is the *cuba de uva*, which substitutes brandy for rum. Other hard liquors—gin, vodka, scotch—may be available only at hotel bars and tourist restaurants.

CANTINAS AND BARS

Traditionally, a cantina is a Mexican-style drinking venue for males only, but in modern urban Mexico the distinction between a bar and a cantina is becoming increasingly blurred. Is Hussong's Cantina in Ensenada a true cantina? Plenty of women are present each evening holding their own with the best of the machos, yet among locals it still has the reputation of a place where "nice" Mexican girls don't go. On the other hand, La Cañada del Diablo in Todos Santos is a perfect example of a *cantina familiar* (family cantina), where everyone is welcome.

A more typical Baja cantina is the kind of place you'll occasionally stumble upon in a small town—usually on the outskirts—where blinking Christmas lights festoon a palapa roof and palm-thatch or ocotillo walls. Inside are a few tables and chairs and a handful of *borrachos;* if any women are present, they're either serving the booze or serving as hired "dates." Unlike their counterparts in mainland Mexican cities, most Baja cantinas do not serve food. The only drink

choices will be beer, Mexican brandy, and cheap tequila or *aguardiente*—moonshine. Often when you order tequila in a place like this, you'll be served a large glass of *aguardiente,* considered an acceptable substitute.

Bars, on the other hand, are found only in hotels and in the larger cities or resort areas, i.e., Tijuana, Mexicali, Ensenada, San Felipe, La Paz, San José del Cabo, and Cabo San Lucas. They've developed largely as social venues for tourists or for a younger generation of Mexicans for whom the cantina is passé. A bar, in contrast to a cantina, offers a variety of beer, wine, and distilled liquor. By Mexican standards, bars are considered very upmarket places to hang out, so they aren't extremely popular—many young Mexicans would rather drink at a disco where they can dance, too.

Incidentally, a sign outside a bar reading Ladies Bar almost always means the bar provides ladies for male entertainment, not that it admits women, although it may.

BAR LINGO

botanas—snacks
cantinero/cantinera—bartender
casco—empty bottle
cerveza—beer
con hielo—with ice
envase, botella—bottle
la cruda—hangover
sin hielo—without ice
una copita, uno tragito—a drink
una fría—a cold one
vaso, copa—glass

Health and Safety

ON THE ROAD

By and large, Baja California is a healthy place. Sanitation standards are relatively high compared to many other parts of Mexico, and the tap water quality in some areas is superior to that of many places in California. The visitor's main health concerns are not food or water sources but avoiding mishaps while driving, boating, diving, surfing, or otherwise enjoying Baja's great outdoor life. Health issues directly concerned with these activities are covered under the relevant sections in this book.

FOOD AND WATER

Visitors who use common sense will probably never come down with food- or water-related illnesses while traveling in Baja. The first rule is not to overdo it during the first few days of your trip—eat and drink in moderation. Shoveling down huge amounts of tasty, often heavy Mexican foods along with pitchers of margaritas or strong Mexican beer is liable to make anyone sick from pure overindulgence. If you're not used to the spices and different ways of cooking, it's best to ingest small amounts at first.

Second, take it easy with foods offered by street vendors, since this is where you're most likely to suffer from unsanitary conditions. Eat only foods that have been thoroughly cooked and are served either stove-hot or refrigerator-cold. Many gringos eat street food without any problems whatsoever, but it pays to be cautious, especially if it's your first time in Mexico. Concerned with the risk of cholera, the Baja California Sur state government in July 1992 banned the sale of ice cream and ceviche (raw seafood salad) by street vendors.

Doctors usually recommend you avoid eating peeled, raw fruits and vegetables in Baja. Once the peel has been removed, it is virtually impossible to disinfect produce. Unpeeled fruits and vegetables washed in purified water and dried with a clean cloth are usually okay. After all, plenty of Mexican fruit is consumed daily in Canada and the United States.

Hotels and restaurants serve only purified drinking water and ice, so there's no need to ask for mineral water or refuse ice. Tap water, however, should not be consumed except in hotels where the water system is purified (look for a notice over the washbasin in your room). Most grocery stores sell bottled purified water. Water purification tablets, iodine crystals, water filters, and the like aren't necessary for Baja travel unless you plan on backpacking.

Turista

People who've never traveled to a foreign country may undergo a period of adjustment to the new gastrointestinal flora that comes with new territory. There's really no way to avoid the differences wrought by sheer distance. Unfortunately, the adjustment is sometimes unpleasant.

Mexican doctors call gastrointestinal upset of this sort *turista,* because it affects tourists but not the local population. The usual symptoms of *turista*—also known by the gringo tags "Montezuma's Revenge" and "the Aztec Two-Step"— are nausea and diarrhea, sometimes with stomach cramps and a low fever. Again, eating and drinking only in moderation will help prevent the worst of the symptoms, which rarely persist more than a day or two. And if it's any consolation, Mexicans often get sick the first time they go to the United States or Canada.

Many Mexico travelers swear by a **preventive regimen** of Pepto-Bismol begun the day before arrival in country. Opinions vary as to how much of the pink stuff is necessary to ward off or tame the foreign flora, but a person probably shouldn't exceed the recommended daily dose. Taper off after four days or so until you stop using it altogether.

Another regimen that seems to be effective is a daily tablet of 100-milligram doxycycline (sold as Vibramycin in the United States), a low-grade antibiotic that requires a prescription in most countries. It works by killing all the bacteria in your intestinal tract—including the ones that reside there naturally and help protect your bowels. It's available without a prescription in Mexican *farmacias,* but you should check with your doctor first to make sure you're not sensitive to it—some people have problems with sunlight while taking doxycycline. Consume with plenty of food and water. Some physicians believe when you stop taking the drug you're particularly susceptible to intestinal upset because there are no protective bacteria left to fight off infections.

Neither Pepto nor Vibramycin is recommended for travelers planning trips of three weeks or longer.

If you come down with a case of *turista,* the best thing to do is drink plenty of fluids. Adults should drink at least three liters a day, a child under 37 kg (80 pounds) at least a liter a day. Lay off tea, coffee, milk, fruit juices, and booze. Eat only bland foods—nothing spicy, fatty, or fried—and take it easy. Pepto-Bismol or similar pectin-based remedies usually help. Some people like to mask the symptoms with a strong over-the-counter medication like Imodium AD (loperamide is the active ingredient), but though this can be very effective, it isn't a cure. Only time will cure traveler's diarrhea.

If the symptoms are unusually severe (especially if there's blood in the stools or a high fever) or persist more than one or two days, see a doctor. Most hotels can arrange a doctor's visit, or you can contact a Mexican tourist office, U.S. consulate, or Canadian consulate for recommendations.

SUNBURN AND DEHYDRATION

Sunburn probably afflicts more Baja visitors than all other illnesses and injuries combined. The sunlight in Baja can be exceptionally strong, especially in the center of the peninsula and along the Sea of Cortez coast. For outdoor forays, sun protection is a must, whatever the activity. The longer you're in the sun, the more protection you'll need.

A hat, sunglasses, and plenty of sunscreen or sunblock make a good start. Bring along a sunscreen with a sun protection factor (SPF) of at least 25, even if you don't plan on using it all the time. Apply it to *all* exposed parts of your body—don't forget the hands, top of the feet,

and neck. Men should remember to cover thinned-out or bald areas on the scalp. Sunscreen must be reapplied after swimming or after periods of heavy perspiration.

If you're going boating, don't leave shore with just a bathing suit. Bring along an opaque shirt—preferably with long sleeves—and a pair of long pants. Since you can never know for certain whether your boat might get stranded or lost at sea for a period of time (if, for example, the motor conks out and you get caught in an offshore current), you shouldn't be without extra clothing for emergencies.

It's also important to drink plenty of water or nonalcoholic, noncaffeinated fluids to avoid dehydration. Alcohol and caffeine—including the caffeine in iced tea and cola—increase your potential for dehydration. Symptoms of dehydration include darker-than-usual urine or inability to urinate, flushed face, profuse sweating or an unusual lack thereof, and sometimes headache, dizziness, and general feeling of malaise. Extreme cases of dehydration can lead to heat exhaustion or even heatstroke, in which the victim may become delirious or convulse. If either condition is suspected, get the victim out of the sun immediately, cover with a wet sheet or towel, and administer a rehydration fluid that replaces lost water and salts. If you can get the victim to a doctor, all the better—heatstroke can be serious.

If Gatorade or a similar **rehydration fluid** isn't available, you can mix your own by combining the following ingredients: one liter purified water or diluted fruit juice; two tablespoons sugar or honey; one-quarter teaspoon salt; and one-quarter teaspoon baking soda. If soda isn't available, use another quarter teaspoon salt. The victim should drink this mixture at regular intervals until symptoms subside substantially. Four or more liters may be necessary in moderate cases, more in severe cases.

MOTION SICKNESS

Visitors with little or no boating experience who join fishing cruises in Baja, especially on the Pacific side, sometimes experience motion sickness

SNAKEBITE PREVENTION AND TREATMENT

The overall risk of being bitten by a rattlesnake while hiking in Baja California is quite low, mainly because the snake avoids contact with all large mammals, including humans. Most of the unfortunate few who are bitten by snakes in Baja are local ranchers who spend a great deal of time in snake habitats, or small children who may not know to retreat from a coiled rattler.

Nonetheless, anyone spending time in the Baja outback, including campers and hikers, should follow a few simple precautions.

Prevention
First of all, use caution when placing hands or feet in areas where snakes may lie. These include rocky ledges, holes, and fallen logs. Always look first, and if you must move a rock or log, use a long stick or other instrument. Wear sturdy footwear when walking in possible snake habitat; high-top leather shoes or boots are best. Rancheros wear thick leather leggings called *polainas* when working in known snake territory; these are sometimes sold at *zapaterías* (shoe stores) or leather and saddle shops.

Most snakes strike only when threatened. Naturally, if you step on or next to a snake, it's likely to strike. If you see or hear a rattlesnake, remain still until the snake moves away. If it doesn't leave, simply back away slowly and cautiously. Sudden movements may cause a snake to strike; rattlers rarely strike a stationary target. A rattler can't strike a target that is farther away than three-fourths of its body length; use this rough measure to judge when it may be safe to move away. Leave plenty of room for error. Don't attempt to kill a rattler unless you have a genuine need to use it as food. As nasty as they may seem, snakes are as important to the desert ecosystem as the most beautiful flowering cactus.

BOB RACE

Treatment
When bitten by a rattler or other poisonous snake, it's important to remain calm in order to slow the spread of venom, and to follow the necessary steps for treatment in a cool-headed manner. Don't panic—remember that few rattlesnake bites are fatal, even when untreated.

First, immediately following the bite, try to

caused by the movement of a boat over ocean swells. The repeated pitching and rolling affects a person's sense of equilibrium to the point of nausea. *Mareo* (seasickness) can be a very unpleasant experience not only for those green at the gills but for fellow passengers anxious lest the victim spew on them.

The best way to prevent motion sickness is to take one of the preventives commonly available from a pharmacist: promethazine (sold as Phenergan in the United States), dimenhydrinate (Dramamine), or scopolamine (Transderm Scop). The latter is available as an adhesive patch worn behind the ear—the time-release action is allegedly more effective than tablets. These med-

ications should be consumed *before* boarding the vessel, not after the onset of symptoms. It's also not a good idea to eat a large meal before getting on a boat.

If you start to feel seasick while out on the bounding main, certain actions can lessen the likelihood that it will get worse. First, do not lie down. Often the first symptom of motion sickness is drowsiness, and if you give in to the impulse you'll almost certainly guarantee a worsening of the condition. Second, stay in the open air rather than belowdecks—fresh air usually helps. Finally, fix your gaze on the horizon; this helps steady your disturbed inner ear, the proximate cause of motion sickness.

identify the snake. At the very least, memorize the markings and physical characteristics so a physician can administer the most appropriate antivenin. If you can kill the snake and bring it to the nearest treatment center, do it. Just remember that this could expose you or your fellow hikers to the risk of another bite.

Second, examine the bite for teeth marks. A successful bite by a poisonous pit viper will leave one or two large fang punctures in addition to smaller teeth marks; a bite by a nonpoisonous snake will not feature fang punctures. In general, nonpoisonous bites cause relatively small, shallow marks or scratches.

If you suspect the snake inflicting the bite was poisonous, immobilize the affected limb and wrap it tightly in an elastic bandage. This slows the spread of venom through the lymph system and mitigates swelling. Be careful that the bandage isn't wrapped so tightly that it cuts off circulation—you should be able to insert a finger under it without difficulty. Keep the limb below the level of the heart. Avoid all physical activity, since increased circulation accelerates the absorption of the venom. For this same reason, avoid aspirin, sedatives, and alcohol. Do not apply cold therapy—ice packs, cold compresses, and so on—to the bite area or to any other part of the victim's body. The old "slice and suck" method of snakebite treatment has likewise been discredited.

Get the victim to a hospital or physician if possible. Where feasible, carry the victim to restrict physical exertion. Even when wrapping the limb appears successful in preventing symptoms, the bite needs medical attention, and a physician may decide antivenin treatment is necessary. The general all-inclusive Spanish term for snake is *serpiente* or *culebra*. A rattlesnake is *un serpiente de cascabel* or simply *un cascabel.*

It's possible for a poisonous snake to bite without injecting any venom; up to 20 percent of all reported bites are "dry bites."

Snakebite victims who require antivenin treatment usually receive the broad-spectrum North American Antisnakebite Serum for pit viper poisoning, which is available only in larger cities like Tijuana, Mexicali, La Paz, and Cabo San Lucas. Your home physician may be able to provide a prescription for the serum in advance of your trip if convinced you'll visit areas where antivenin is unavailable or medical treatment inaccessible.

In cases where it's been determined a bite is venomous and serum unavailable, the best you can do is follow the treatment outlined above and keep the victim immobile and cool until the symptoms—pain in the affected limb, abdominal cramps, headache—have subsided. For some bites, wrapping the limb in an elastic bandage will avoid all or most of the worst symptoms. The victim should drink plenty of water.

BITES AND STINGS

Mosquitoes and Jejenes

Mosquitoes breed in standing water. Since standing water isn't that common in arid Baja, neither are mosquitoes. Exceptions include palm oases, estuaries, and marshes when there isn't a strong breeze around to keep mosquitoes at bay. The easiest way to avoid mosquito bites is to apply insect repellent to exposed areas of the skin and clothing whenever the mossies are out and biting. For most species, this means between dusk and dawn.

The most effective repellents are those containing a high concentration of DEET (N,N-diethyl-metatoluamide). People with an aversion to applying synthetics to the skin can try citronella (lemongrass oil), which is also effective but requires more frequent application.

More common in Baja than mosquitoes are *jejenes,* tiny flying insects known as "no-see-ums" among Americans—you almost never see them while they're biting. The same repellents effective for mosquitoes usually do the trick with *jejenes.*

For relief from the itchiness of mosquito bites, try rubbing a bit of hand soap on the affected areas. For some people this works, for others it doesn't do a thing. Andantol, available in many Mexican pharmacies, is a German-made cream that relieves itchy insect bites. *Jejene* bites usually stop itching in less than 10 minutes if you refrain from scratching them. Excessive scratching of either type of bite can lead to infection, so be mindful of what your fingers are up to.

In spite of the presence of the occasional mosquito, the U.S. Centers for Disease Control has declared all of Baja California malaria-free.

Wasps, Bees, and Hornets

Although stings from these flying insects can be very painful, they aren't of mortal danger to most people. If you're allergic to such stings and plan to travel in remote areas of Baja, consider obtaining antiallergy medication from your doctor before leaving home. At the very least, carry a supply of Benadryl or similar over-the-counter antihistamine. Dramamine (dimenhydrinate) also usually helps mitigate allergic reactions.

For relief from a wasp/bee/hornet sting, apply a paste of baking soda and water to the affected area. Liquids containing ammonia, including urine, also help relieve pain. If a stinger is visible, remove it—by scraping if possible, or with tweezers—before applying any remedies. If a stung limb becomes unusually swollen or if the victim exhibits symptoms of a severe allergic reaction—difficulty breathing, agitation, hives—seek medical assistance.

Ticks

If you find a tick embedded in your skin, don't try to pull it out—this may leave the head and pincers under your skin and lead to infection. Covering the tick with petroleum jelly, mineral oil, gasoline, kerosene, or alcohol usually causes the tick to release its hold to avoid suffocation.

Burning the tick with a cigarette butt or hot match usually succeeds only in killing it—when you pull it out, the head and pincers may not come with it. Stick with the suffocation method, and if the beast still doesn't come out, use tweezers.

Scorpions

The venom of the scorpion *(alacrán)* varies in strength from individual to individual and species to species, but the sting is rarely dangerous to adults. It can be very painful, however, resulting in partial numbness and swelling that lasts

scorpion

BOB RACE

several days. In Baja, the small yellow scorpions inflict more-painful stings than the larger, dark-colored ones.

The best treatment begins with persuading the victim to lie down and relax to slow the spread of the venom. Keep the affected area below the level of the heart. Ice packs on the sting may relieve pain and mitigate swelling; aspirin also helps.

Children who weigh less than about 13 kg (30 pounds) should receive medical attention if stung by a scorpion. Doctors in Baja usually have ready access to scorpion antivenin *(anti-alacrán),* but it should be administered only under qualified medical supervision.

Scorpions prefer damp, dark, warm places—dead brush, rock piles, fallen logs—so exercise particular caution when placing your hands in or near such areas. Hands are the scorpion's most common target on the human body; campers should wear gloves when handling firewood in Baja.

Other favorite spots for scorpions are crumpled clothing and bedding. In desert areas of Baja, always check your bed sheets or sleeping bag for scorpions before climbing in. In the same environments, shake out your shoes and clothing before putting them on. Lots of palm trees around a house or hotel mean there's a good chance scorpions will find their way to your room—they're nonaggressive creatures, so just keep an eye out for them.

Poisonous Sea Creatures

Various marine animals can inflict painful stings on humans. In Baja, such creatures include jellyfish, Portuguese men-of-war, cone shells, stingrays, sea urchins, and various fish with poisonous spines.

The best way to avoid jellyfish and Portuguese men-of-war is to scope out the water and the beach before going in—if you see any nasties floating around or washed up on the sand, try another beach. You can avoid stingrays by shuffling your feet in the sand as you walk in shallow surf, which usually causes rays resting in the sand to swim away.

To avoid cone shell and sea urchin stings, wear shoes in the water; several sport shoe manufacturers now produce specialized water shoes, e.g., Nike's Aqua Socks. You can also often spot cones and urchins in clear water, especially when wearing a diving mask. Anglers should take care when handling landed fish to avoid poisonous spines.

The treatment for stings from all of the above is the same: remove all tentacles, barbs, or spines from the affected area; wash the area with rubbing alcohol or diluted ammonia (urine will do in a pinch) to remove as much venom as possible; and wrap the area in cloth to reduce the flow of oxygen to the wound until pain subsides. If an acute allergic reaction occurs, get the victim to a doctor or clinic as quickly as possible.

Painful stingray wounds may require the famous hot-water treatment. If pain persists after thoroughly cleaning the wound, soak the affected limb in the hottest water the victim can stand. Continue soaking till the pain subsides—this can sometimes take up to an hour. The local folk remedy in Baja is to treat the wound with the sap of the *garambullo* cactus, often available from *botánicas* if not from a nearby patch of desert. Some stingray wounds may require medical treatment, even stitches.

MEDICAL ASSISTANCE

The quality of basic medical treatment, including dentistry, is relatively high in Baja's cities and larger towns; ask at a tourist office or at your consulate for recommendations. Hospitals can be found in Tijuana, Mexicali, Ensenada, Guerrero Negro, Ciudad Constitución, San José del Cabo, and La Paz; there are public IMSS clinics or Red Cross (Cruz Roja) stations in nearly every other town. In many areas the Red Cross can be reached by dialing 066 (toll-free) from any pay phone.

Emergency Evacuation

Over the years, several American companies have offered emergency 24-hour airlift service (accompanied by licensed physicians and nurses) from anywhere in Mexico to U.S. hospitals. Few have lasted more than a year or two. One of the longer-running operations is **Aeromedevac,** 4420 Rainier Ave. Suite 200, San Diego, CA 92120, 619/284-7910, U.S. tel. 800/462-0911, Mexico tel. 800/832-5087, fax 619/284-7918, www.aeromedevac.com. Aeromedevac accepts collect calls. Payment for the service can be made with a credit card or through your health insurance company.

Other companies with similar services include **Air Evac Services, Inc.,** 2630 Sky Harbor Blvd., Phoenix, AZ 85034, tel. 602/273-9348 or 800/421-6111 in the United States and Canada, fax 602/302-6721, www.airevac.com, and **Advanced Aeromedical Air Ambulance Service,** P.O. Box 5726, Virginia Beach, VA 23471, 757/481-1590, U.S./Canada tel. 800/346-3556, fax 757/481-2874, skip@aeromedic .com, www.aeromedic.com.

For information on other air evacuation services, contact the **Association of Air Medical Services,** 526 King St. #415, Alexandria, VA 22314-3143, 703/836-8732, fax 703/836-8920, information@aams.org, www.aams.org.

SAFETY

Statistics clearly show that violent crime is overall less common in Mexico than anywhere in the United States. In Baja California, crime statistics are many times lower than the United States national average. Yet Americans seem to be the most paranoid of all visitors to Mexico.

Historical reasons, to a large degree, account for this paranoia. Chief among them is the general border lawlessness that was the norm in the early 20th century—an era of border disputes and common banditry on both sides of the border. Americans living in these areas came to fear *bandidos* who stole livestock and occasionally robbed the Anglo ranchers themselves, while the Mexicans in turn feared American cattle rustlers, horse thieves, gunslingers, and the infamous Texas Rangers, a private militia whose conduct at the time fell somewhere between that of the Hell's Angels motorcycle gang and the Los Angeles Police Department.

Soon after this era had begun to wane, as politics on both sides of the border stabilized, the U.S. Prohibition experiment sent millions of Americans scrambling into Mexican border towns for booze. In the illicit atmosphere, boozers were soon rubbing elbows with gamblers and pimps, and it wasn't long before Mexican border towns gained an even more unsavory reputation.

Once Prohibition was lifted, Americans no longer had reason to come to Mexico solely for drinking, and the border towns began cleaning up their acts. Among the uninformed and inexperienced, however, the border-town image remains, sadly mixing with the equally outdated *bandido* tales to prevent many Americans from enjoying the pleasures of life south of the border.

Precautions

Neither the author nor anyone of the author's personal acquaintance has ever been robbed in Baja—or, for that matter, anywhere in Mexico. One morning, however, I left behind two shirts and a pair of slacks in a hotel closet in Loreto, BCS, and didn't remember them until arriving in La Paz that evening. A phone call that night and a visit to the hotel a week later were unsuccessful in retrieving the clothes—the management

claimed they were never turned in by the cleaning staff. The moral of the story: Try not to leave things behind in hotel rooms.

Visitors to Baja should take the same precautions they would when traveling anywhere in their own countries or abroad. Keep money and valuables secured, either in a hotel safe or safety deposit box, or in a money belt or other hard-to-reach place on your person. Keep an eye on cameras, purses, and wallets to make sure you don't leave them behind in restaurants, hotels, or campgrounds. At night, lock the doors to your hotel room and vehicle.

Private campgrounds usually have some kind of security, if only a night watchman, to keep out intruders. Secluded beach campsites seem to be safe due to their isolation—in Baja, it's rare for crime to occur in such areas. Nonetheless, don't leave items of value lying around outside your tent, camper, or RV at night.

Over the last five years or so, we've heard tales of campers getting robbed at certain beaches in northern Baja. The places with the worst reputations appear to be the beaches at or near Baja Malibu (between Tijuana and Rosarito) and at San Quintín. If you plan to camp at or near either of the latter, you'd be much safer to pay to camp at a private campground rather than to "boondock" for free. South of San Quintín we've never heard of a beach robbery, whether on a "free" beach or at a pay campground. Compared to the number of crimes reported along beaches in the United States' California, the risk appears to be low indeed.

SECTUR (the State Secretary of Tourism) maintains a 24-hour travelers' aid hotline for emergencies of all kinds: 55/5250-0123 or 01-800-903-9200.

Visas and Officialdom

ENTRY REGULATIONS

Tourist Permits

Citizens of the United States or Canada (or of 42 other designated countries in Europe and Latin America, plus Singapore) visiting Mexico solely for tourism are not required to obtain a visa. Instead they must carry validated "tourist cards" (*formas migratorias turistas* or FMTs), which aren't actually cards but slips of paper. These are available free at any Mexican consulate or Mexican tourist office, from many travel agencies, on flights to Mexico, or at the border. The tourist card is valid for stays of up to 180 days and must be used within 90 days of issue. Your card becomes invalid once you exit the country—you're supposed to surrender it at the border—even if your 180 days hasn't expired. If you'll be entering and leaving Mexico more than once during your trip, you should request a multiple-entry tourist card, available from Mexican consulates only.

To obtain the FMT you need proof of citizenship—a birth certificate (or certified copy), voter's registration card, certificate of naturalization, or passport. A driver's license doesn't qualify.

Once you cross the border (or land at an airport on an international flight), your tourist card must be **validated** by a Mexican immigration officer. You can arrange this at any *migración* office in Baja (many *municipio* seats have them), but it's accomplished most conveniently at the border crossing itself or at the immigration office in Ensenada (right around the corner from the tourist information booth on Boulevard Costero). Note: FMTs are also inspected at the army checkpoint at the north end of Guerrero Negro, so you'd best have your papers in order before entering Baja California Sur.

At airports you pass through immigration, where an officer stamps your paperwork with the date of entry and the number of days you're permitted to stay in Mexico.

Make sure you receive enough days to cover your visit. Some immigration officers, especially those at airports near tourist resorts, may fill in your FMT for 30 days, figuring that's sufficient for most holidays. If you want more than 30 days, it's best to mention it to the officer in advance.

In mid-1999, the Mexican government began collecting a tourist fee (currently 185 pesos, around US$18 at the most recent dollar–peso exchange rate) from all tourists entering the country. If you fly in, this fee is tacked on to your airfare. If you arrive by land, you can pay this fee at any bank in Mexico. The bank will issue a receipt, which you must show when you leave the country. *If you're going no farther south than Ensenada or San Felipe, you do not have to pay this fee.*

The fee is reasonable when you consider that Mexicans visiting the United States must pay US$45 for a tourist visa, even if their visa application is denied. Of course, comparing Mexican immigration into the United States with U.S. immigration into Mexico—legal or otherwise—is comparing apples to oranges, as relatively few Americans visit Mexico with the intention of sending Mexican pesos back home.

Before 1991, Mexican regulations required **children under the age of 18** crossing the border without one or both parents to carry a notarized letter granting permission from the absent parent, or both parents if both were absent. This regulation is no longer in effect, but we've heard that some Mexican border officers, as well as airline check-in crews, are still asking for the letter, apparently unaware the regulation has been rescinded. Hence, unaccompanied minors or minors traveling with only one parent should be prepared for all situations with notarized letters. In cases of divorce, separation, or death, the minor should carry notarized papers documenting the situation.

In reality, minors with tourist cards are rarely asked for these documents. Children under 15 may be included on their parents' tourist card, but this means that neither the child nor the parents can legally exit Mexico without the other.

ON THE ROAD

BUYING OR LEASING PROPERTY IN BAJA

With certain restrictions, the Mexican government allows both resident and nonresident foreigners to own Mexican real estate—both land and buildings. Under the Constitution of 1857, foreign ownership of land by direct title is permitted only in areas more than 100 km (62 miles) from any international border and 50 km (31 miles) from any seacoast. In Baja California, this limits prospective buyers to areas in the interior of the peninsula, where services—water, electricity, sewage, telephone—are often nonexistent.

However, since 1973 the Mexican government has offered a way for foreigners to acquire lots—including coastal property—that fall outside the geographic limits. The Ministry of Foreign Affairs issues permits to foreigners allowing them to create limited real estate trusts, administered by Mexican banks, with themselves as beneficiaries. Originally, these trusts were valid for 30-year nonrenewable terms only. In 1989 the government further liberalized real estate regulations so that the trusts (called *fideicomisos*) could be renewed at the end of each 30-year term for an additional 30-year term, with no limit on the number of renewals. *Fideicomisos* can be bought and sold among foreigners, at market rates, just like fee-simple property. In December 1993, the basic term for bank trusts was lengthened to 50 years, a period long enough to begin attracting U.S. housing lenders. Until recently, U.S. lenders had remained aloof about the *fideicomiso* market; mortgages are now available for financing up to 70 percent of appraised property values with terms of 15–20 years. Lending rates run around 3 percent higher than in the United States, and closing costs for a mortgage deal are high.

Needless to say, Baja real estate prices increased substantially as a result of these policy changes. An estimated 40,000 foreigners now reside in Baja California Norte alone, some of them Americans who commute to San Diego for work. The priciest coastal properties are those near the United States–Mexico border and on The Cape, but prices are still substantially below what's available in coastal California.

Lots large enough for a two- or three-bedroom home in the La Paz area are available for US$15,000 and up. Survivalist types can find beach hideaways with no services for even less; in remote areas, land can be had for US$1,000 per acre, sometimes less. With a desalinator, generator or solar cells, propane stove and refrigerator, and perhaps an airplane to get in and out, you can live in considerable style.

Precautions

Before you rush off to grab Baja land, you should be aware that a lot of people get burned in Mexican real estate deals. It's best to deal through an established, reputable real estate agent. The American company Century 21 has opened a Baja franchise, and although it generally represents only the more expensive properties, Century 21 people can be helpful with information on real estate trusts. Mexican tourist offices in Baja often carry information on residential property. And it's wise to talk to current owner-residents about which real estate companies have the best and worst reputations.

In condominium and subdivision situations a master *fideicomiso* is created. Only as the units are sold does the trust pass to the buyer, and then only if proper procedures are followed—which they often aren't. If you buy a condo or subdivision unit, you should receive a document naming you as beneficiary, thus transferring property from the master trust holder to the buyer. If you don't, you'll have to get the master trust holder's signature before you can sell or otherwise transfer the property to someone else.

Many sellers ask that the full purchase price be paid up front. Because a large number of gringos buy land in Mexico with cash, some Mexicans assume this is customary for all Americans and Canadians. Paying up front is not the typical procedure for Mexicans themselves, who usually make down payments and then send in monthly time payments; mortgage terms similar to those found in Canada and the United States are available in Mexico, though they are difficult for nonresidents to obtain. Even if you have the cash, don't hand over more than half the full amount until you have the *fideicomiso* papers in hand.

Once again, investigate the realtor thoroughly before signing on the dotted line. Mexico doesn't require salespersons or brokers to obtain any sort of real estate license, hence many Americans and Canadians who couldn't make the grade in the United States or Canada now work in Mexico.

Time Shares

Until recently, time-share salespeople were the scourge of Baja resort areas, especially San José del Cabo and Cabo San Lucas, where they hung out on street corners and in hotel lobbies, hounding every tourist who passed by. These hustlers, who were sometimes gringos, would try almost anything to convince you to sign on the dotted line, on the spot—including denying that what they were selling were time shares (one euphemism: "vacation club"). Fortunately, the situation has improved greatly in the last few years, and the aggressive time-share touts seem to be a thing of the past.

It pays to hold off on any decision until you've made inquiries among current time-share residents at the development and checked with your consulate to see if there have been any complaints. Time-share developments typically begin selling when construction has just begun—sometimes they don't get finished, or when they do they don't shape up as promised. Also, because time-share owners aren't year-round residents, they usually lack both a sense of community and a sense of responsibility toward the local environment. For the developer, time shares mean huge profits, as the same space is sold repeatedly in one-week segments. Because land in Baja is relatively inexpensive, considering the charming scenery and climate, it seems to attract get-rich-quick developers who show a decided lack of respect for the fragile Baja environment. Finally, keep in mind that from an investment perspective, time shares don't appreciate in value as much as single-owner properties—if they appreciate at all (not very likely).

This is not to say there aren't any good time-share opportunities in Baja. But as with any real estate deal, it pays to proceed cautiously. Don't buy without considering all the options.

Tourist Visas

Tourists from countries other than the 45 countries for which no visa is necessary must obtain tourist visas before arriving in Mexico. You must apply for your visa in person at a Mexican consulate; you usually can obtain a tourist visa within two weeks of filing an application. The Mexican Consulate General in San Diego can usually issue tourist visas on the day of application. Requirements include a valid passport, valid U.S. visa for multiple entries, form I-94, proof of economic solvency (such as an international credit card), a round-trip air ticket to Mexico, and a visa fee of around US$40.

Foreign visitors who are legal permanent residents of the United States do not need visas to visit Mexico for tourism. A free tourist card can be obtained by presenting your passport and U.S. residence card to any travel agency or at the airport or border crossing.

Business Travel

Citizens of Mexico's NAFTA (North American Free Trade Agreement) partners, the United States and Canada, are not required to obtain a visa to visit Mexico for business purposes. Instead you receive a free NAFTA business permit (*forma migratoria nafta* or FMN), similar to a tourist card, at the point of entry (border crossing or airport); it's valid for 30 days. At the port of entry you must present proof of nationality (valid passport or original birth certificate plus a photo identification or voter's registration card) and proof that you are traveling for "international business activities," usually interpreted to mean a letter from the company you represent, even if it's your own enterprise.

Those who arrive with the FMN and wish to stay over the authorized period of 30 days must replace their FMN with an FM-3 form at an immigration office in Mexico. The FM-3 is valid for up to one year, for multiple entries, and may be extended. Note that the FMN is not valid for persons who will be earning a salary during their stay in Mexico.

Citizens of other countries visiting for business purposes must obtain an FM-3 visa endorsed for business travel, which is valid for one year.

Overstays

If you overstay your visa and are caught, the usual penalty is a fine of around US$45 for overstays up to a month. After that the penalties become more severe. It's rare that a Mexican border official asks to see your FMT or visa when you're leaving the country. Your main risk comes if you get into trouble with the police somewhere in Mexico and they ask to see your immigration documents. Having expired papers only complicates your situation, so the best policy is to stay up-to-date in spite of the apparent laxity of enforcement.

Pets

Dogs and cats may be brought into Mexico if each is accompanied by a **vaccination certificate** that proves the animal has been vaccinated or treated for rabies, hepatitis, pip, and leptospirosis. You'll also need a **health certificate** issued no more than 72 hours before entry and signed by a registered veterinarian.

Since 1992 the requirement that the health certificate be stamped with a visa at a port of entry or at a Mexican consulate has been repealed. The certificate is still necessary; the visa isn't.

Upon recrossing the border into the United States, the U.S. Customs Service will ask to see the vaccination certificate.

Visitante Rentista and Inmigrante Rentista Visas

FM-3 visas may be issued to foreigners who choose to live in Mexico on a "permanent income" basis. This most often applies to foreigners who decide to retire in Mexico, though it is also used by artists, writers, and other self-employed foreign residents. With this visa you're allowed to import one motor vehicle as well as your household belongings into Mexico tax-free.

The basic requirements for this visa are that applicants must forgo any kind of employment while living in Mexico and must show proof (bank statements) that they have a regular source of foreign-earned income amounting to at least US$1,000 per month (plus half that for each dependent over the age of 15, e.g., US$1,500 for a couple). A pile of paperwork, including a "letter of good conduct" from the applicant's local police department, must accompany the initial application, along with an immigration tax payment and various application fees totaling about US$135.

The visa must be renewed annually, but the renewal can be accomplished at any immigration office in Mexico. After five years in Mexico, you have to start over or move up to the FM-2 or *inmigrante rentista* visa, which has higher income requirements and signifies an intent to stay longer. After five years on an FM-2, an *inmigrante rentista* is eligible to apply for *inmigrado* status, which confers all the rights of citizenship (including employment in Mexico), save the rights to vote and hold public office.

Many foreigners who have retired in Mexico manage to do so on the regular 180-day tourist visa; every six months they dash across the border and return with a new tourist card (issued at the border) on the same day. This method bypasses all the red tape and income requirements of the retirement visa. If you own a home in Baja, however, some local immigration officials may interpret the law to mean that you must have an FM-2 or FM-3 visa—not an FMT or tourist visa—to be able to stay in that home for any period of time whatsoever. Although it's clear from a straight reading that Mexico's immigration laws do not require any special visas for home ownership (just as you don't need a particular visa to own property in the United States or Canada), each immigration district behaves like an individual fiefdom at the mercy of the local immigration chief.

Monthly income requirements for both *rentista* visas are keyed to the Mexican daily minimum wage (400 times minimum wage for the FM-2, 250 times for the FM-3), hence figures may vary according to the current dollar– peso exchange rate.

Reentering the United States

Overseas visitors need a passport and visa to enter the United States. Except for diplomats, students, or refugees, this means a nonimmigrant visitor's visa, which must be obtained in advance at a U.S. consulate or embassy abroad. Residents of Western European and Commonwealth coun-tries are usually issued these readily; residents of other countries may have to provide the consulate with proof of "sufficient personal funds" before the visa is issued.

Upon arrival in the United States, an immigration inspector decides how long the visa will be valid—the maximum for a temporary visitor's visa (B-1 or B-2) is six months. If you visit Mexico from California (or from anywhere else in the United States) for stays of 30 days or less, you can reenter the United States with the same visa, provided the visa is still valid, by presenting your stamped arrival/departure card (INS form I-94) and passport to a U.S. immigration inspector. If your U.S. visa has expired, you can still enter the country for a stay of 29 days or less on a transit visa—issued at the border—but you may be required to show proof of onward travel, such as an air ticket or ship travel voucher.

BORDER CROSSINGS

Baja California's United States–Mexico border has five official border crossings: Tijuana (open 24 hours a day), Otay (open 6 A.M.–10 P.M.), Tecate (6 A.M.– midnight), Mexicali (24 hours), and Los Algodones (6 A.M.–10 P.M.). Tijuana is the largest and also the most heavily used, connecting Baja with United States Interstate 5, which extends all the way up the U.S. west coast to the Canadian border. For several years now, border officials have been considering longer hours for the nearby Otay crossing to ease congestion at Tijuana.

At any of the border crossings, you'll find the shortest waits (15–30 minutes at Tijuana) are between 10 A.M. and 3:30 P.M. or after 7 or 8 P.M. on weekdays. Weekends are the worst days in either direction, except late at night or before dawn, when traffic is light. If you're on your way out of Baja and find yourself near the border during rush hours, it might be best to find a restaurant and wait it out. A Saturday or Sunday morning wait at the Tijuana crossing can be as long as two hours in either direction; it's always longer going north.

If you're on foot, crossing is usually a breeze. Public and chartered buses also get through more quickly, utilizing special traffic lanes.

ON THE ROAD

© LANDIS BENNETT

Almost there, stay on target.

Mexican Consulate in San Diego

San Diego's Mexican Consulate General, 1549 India St., San Diego, CA 92101, 619/231-8414, fax 619/231-4802, www.consulmexsd.org, is relatively close to the Tijuana border crossing, about 30–45 minutes by car. The staff can assist with visas, immigration problems, special-import permits, and questions concerning Mexican customs regulations. The consulate's hours are Mon.–Fri. 8 A.M.–1:30 P.M.

CUSTOMS

Entering Mexico

Officially, tourists are supposed to bring only those items into Mexico that will be of use during their trip. This means you can bring in practically anything as long as it doesn't appear in large enough quantities to qualify for resale. Firearms and ammunition, as well as boats, require special permits (see Sports and Recreation).

Technically speaking, you're allowed to import one still camera and one video camera, up to 12 rolls of unused film or blank videocassettes for each, and used or developed film. Anything more is supposed to require permission from a Mexican consulate. In everyday practice, however, Mexican customs officials rarely blink at more film or an extra camera or two. Professional photographers and others who would like to bring more cameras and film into Mexico can apply for dispensation through a Mexican consulate abroad. Regarding audio equipment, you're limited to one CD player and one audiocassette player (or combo), five laser discs, five DVDs, and up to 20 CDs or recording cassettes. Other per-person limitations include one typewriter, a cellular phone and a pager, a new or used laptop computer, a musical instrument, two used personal sports gear items, one tent and accompanying camping gear, one set of fishing gear, a pair of skis, a pair of binoculars, two tennis rackets, five "toys," and one sailboard.

Other limits include three liters of liquor, beer, or wine and two cartons (20 packs) of cigarettes or 25 cigars or 200 grams of tobacco.

Other than the above, you're permitted to bring in no more than US$300 worth of other articles if arriving by air, US$50 if you arriving by land. You will be subject to duty on personal possessions worth more than US$300 (or

US$50), to a maximum of US$1,000 (except for new computer equipment, which is exempt up to US$4,000).

Foreign-registered motor vehicles—cars, trucks, RVs, motorcycles, etc.—do not require permits for travel anywhere on the Baja California peninsula. However, if you plan to take a vehicle registered outside Mexico onto one of the vehicle ferries that sail from Baja to the mainland, or if you plan to drive farther east than San Luis Río Colorado in Sonora, you must obtain an auto permit. These are available from any Mexican consulate abroad, or at the border, or from the ferry office in La Paz.

If you're bringing a vehicle across the border, you need Mexican auto insurance. For further information on vehicle permits and insurance, see the Getting There and Getting Around sections.

Returning to the United States

Visitors returning to the United States from Mexico may have their luggage inspected by U.S. Customs officials. The hassle can be minimized by giving brief, straight answers to their questions (e.g., "How long have you been in Mexico?" "Do you have anything to declare?") and by cooperating with their requests to open your luggage, vehicle storage compartments, and anything else they want opened. Sometimes the officers use dogs to sniff luggage and/or vehicles for contraband and illegal aliens.

Nearly 3,000 items—including all handicrafts—made in Mexico are exempt from any U.S. Customs duties. Adults over 21 are allowed one liter (33.8 fluid ounces) of alcoholic beverages and 200 cigarettes (or 100 cigars) per person. Note that Cuban cigars may not be imported into the United States and will be confiscated at the border if discovered. Since an estimated nine out of 10 cigars sold as Cubans in Mexico are reportedly fake, it's not worth the hassle, especially since a good hand-rolled cigar from Veracruz can challenge most Cubans. All other purchases or gifts up to a total value of US$400 within any 31-day period can be brought into the United States duty-free.

The following **fruits and vegetables** cannot be brought into the United States from Mexico: or-

anges, grapefruits, mangoes, avocados (unless the pit is removed), and potatoes (including yams and sweet potatoes). All other fruits are permitted (including bananas, dates, pineapples, cactus fruits, grapes, and berries of all types).

Other prohibited plant materials are straw (including packing materials and items stuffed with straw), hay, unprocessed cotton, sugarcane, and any plants in soil (this includes houseplants).

Animals and animal products that cannot be imported include wild and domesticated birds (including poultry, unless cooked), pork or pork products (including sausage, ham, and other cured pork), and eggs. Beef, mutton, venison, and other meats are permitted at up to 23 kg (50 pounds) per person.

Customs regulations can change at any time, so if you want to verify the regulations on a purchase before risking duties or confiscation at the border, check with a U.S. consulate in Baja before crossing.

Returning to Canada

Duty-frees include 200 cigarettes (or 50 cigars or 200 grams of tobacco) and one bottle (1.1 liters) of booze or wine, 24 cans or bottles (355 ml) of beer or ale, and gifts to the value of C$60 per gift (other than alcohol or tobacco). Exemptions run from C$50 to C$750 depending on how long you've been outside Canada. To reach the maximum exemption of C$750 you must be gone at least one week. Because Canada is also signatory to NAFTA, customs legalities will change over the next decade.

LEGAL MATTERS

All foreign visitors in Mexico are subject to Mexican legal codes, which are based on Roman and Napoleonic law updated with U.S. constitutional theory and civil law. The most distinctive features of the Mexican judiciary system, compared to Anglo–American systems, are that the system doesn't provide for trials by jury (the judge decides) nor writs of habeas corpus (though you must be charged within 72 hours of incarceration or else released). Furthermore, bail is rarely granted to an arrested foreigner—for

ON THE ROAD

many offenses, not even Mexican nationals are allowed bail. Hence, once arrested and jailed for a serious offense, it can be very difficult to arrange release. The lesson here is: Don't get involved in matters that might result in your arrest. This primarily means anything having to do with drugs or guns.

The oft-repeated saw that in Mexico an arrested person is considered guilty until proven innocent is no more true south of the border than north. As in Canada, the United States, or western Europe, an arrested person is considered a criminal *suspect* until the courts confirm or deny guilt. You have the right to notify your consulate if detained.

Mexican federal police *(federales* and *judiciales),* as well as the Mexican army, mostly under pressure from the United States, occasionally set up roadblocks to conduct searches for drugs and for arms. Such roadblocks used to be rare in Baja but have recently increased in number. On recent transpeninsular drives we've been stopped at six or seven different military checkpoints *(puestos de control)* between Tijuana and Cabo San Lucas. In each case, the soldiers were courteous and the vehicle searches were brief and cursory. If your vehicle is stopped at a *puesto de control,* be as cooperative as possible. If there are any irregularities or if you object to the way in which the procedure is carried out, make note of the incident, including whatever badge numbers, names, or license numbers you can obtain discreetly, and later file a report with the Mexican Attorney General for Tourist Protection. So far I've not heard of any problems encountered by foreign visitors, although a couple of Americans were arrested for carrying unregistered firearms—a serious federal offense in Mexico—in 1996.

La Mordida

In the past, Mexican police had a reputation for hassling foreigners, especially those who drove their own vehicles in Mexico. Tales of the legendary *mordida* (literally, "bite"), or minor bribe, supposedly a necessary part of navigating one's way around Mexico, swelled way out of proportion to reality but were nonetheless based on real incidents.

For several years now, the Mexican police have for the most part ceased singling out foreigners for arrest, partly as a result of anticorruption efforts by the federal government but more importantly because of a conscious effort to attract more tourists. Most foreign visitors who drive in Baja these days complete their trips without any police hassles. (See Getting Around for tips on traffic laws and dealing with traffic police.)

Military

In recent years the Mexican government has replaced many federal police officers around the country with active-duty army officers in an effort to clean up corruption among nonmilitary law enforcement agencies. In Baja all 84 *judiciales* involved in antidrug operations were replaced with army officers in 1996. Opinions are sharply divided as to whether this is having a net positive or negative effect on law enforcement, but it's a fact that you can see more military around the country than at any time in Mexico's history since 1920. Roadblock inspection points or *puestos de control* along major and minor highways have become increasingly common. All manner of vehicles—buses, trucks, private autos—may be stopped and searched at such inspection points; if you get stopped at one the best thing to do is simply be patient till it's over, usually in five minutes or less. For the most part, soldiers stationed at these checkpoints perform their duties in a serious but respectful manner. Typically they speak very little English; this usually works in favor of the non-Spanish-speaking foreign visitor because it means they can't ask very many questions.

In Case of Arrest

If you get into trouble with Mexican law, for whatever reason, you should try to contact your nearest consulate in Baja. Embassies and consulates for each town are listed under the respective destination chapters. You can also contact the local state tourism offices—see the sections on each town for phone numbers and addresses. These agencies routinely handle emergency legal matters involving visiting foreigners; you stand a much better chance of resolving legal difficulties with their assistance.

Money, Measurements, and Communications

CURRENCY

The unit of exchange in Mexico is the **peso,** which comes in paper denominations of N$20, N$50, N$100, N$200, and N$500. Coins come in denominations of five, 10, 20, and 50 centavos, and N$1, N$2, N$5, N$10, N$20, and N$100.

Prices

The N$ symbol (standing for "new pesos" to differentiate from pre-1993 "old pesos") is often used for indicating peso prices. Occasionally you may also encounter the $ symbol for pesos. While it's highly unlikely you'll ever confuse dollar and peso prices because of the differing values, you should ask when in doubt. Sometimes the abbreviation m.n. will appear next to a price—this means *moneda nacional* (national money) and also refers to pesos.

Coins smaller than one peso are scarce, so payments often must be rounded off to the nearest peso or at least to the nearest 50 centavos. For a marked price of N$8.55, for example, you have to pay only N$8.50; for a N$8.75 price, you may have to pay N$9.

Dollars vs. Pesos

Most places in Baja will take U.S. dollars as well as pesos. Paying with pesos usually means a better deal when the price is fixed in pesos; if you pay in dollars, the vendor can determine the exchange rate. If a can of motor oil, for example, is marked at N$18, and the bank rate is N$10 per dollar, you'll pay US$1.80 for the oil with pesos changed at the bank. However, if you ask to pay in dollars, the vendor may charge US$2.50, since vendors have the right—by custom rather than law—to charge whatever exchange rate they wish.

Some stores in smaller towns prefer not to take dollars since this means keeping track of two currencies and makes banking more complicated. Pemex stations (which are government-owned) sometimes refuse dollars—attendants are usually too busy to stop and calculate rates.

For anything larger than a N$100 note, getting

ON THE ROAD

Mexican pesos

change can sometimes be a problem in small towns, so try to carry plenty of notes and coins in denominations of N$50 or smaller. Small change is commonly called *morraya*.

CHANGING MONEY

Banks

Banks offer the best exchange rate for buying pesos, and they all offer the same rate, set by the Bank of Mexico. This rate is usually posted behind the counter where foreign exchange is handled. Banks also accept a wide range of foreign currencies, including Swiss francs, German marks, British pounds, Japanese yen, and Canadian dollars. Cash and traveler's checks are accepted. The main drawbacks with banks are the long lines and relatively short hours (Mon.–Fri. or Sat. 9 or 10 A.M.–1:30 or 3 P.M.); the foreign-exchange service usually closes at noon or 12:30 P.M.

Money-Changing

The second-best rate, generally speaking, is found at the *casa de cambio* or private money-changing office. The *casa de cambio* (also called *servicio de cambio*) either knocks a few centavos off the going bank rate or charges a percentage commission. It pays to shop around for the best *casa de cambio* rates since some places charge considerably more than others. Rates are usually posted; *compra*, always the lower figure, refers to the buying rate for US$ (how many pesos you'll receive per dollar), while *vende* is the selling rate (how many pesos you must pay to receive a dollar).

Money changers are usually open much later than banks; some even work evening hours, which makes them immeasurably more convenient than banks. American dollars are generally preferred, though many *casas* also accept Canadian dollars. However, Canadians should keep a reserve supply of U.S. dollars for instances when Canadian currency isn't accepted. Money changers usually accept traveler's checks; some border-town *casas*, however, take only cash. The latter often offer the best exchange rates.

Only the larger towns and tourist centers offer money-changing offices. In smaller towns you'll have to resort to a bank or local merchant. Many storekeepers are happy to buy dollars at a highly variable and sometimes negotiable rate. Few take traveler's checks, however, unless you make a purchase.

Money changers at Baja airports offer notoriously low rates. Try to buy pesos in advance if arriving by air, or pay with dollars until you can get to a bank or *casa de cambio*.

Hotels

Hotels, motels, *pensiones*, and other lodgings generally offer the lowest exchange rates. If you're trying to save money, avoid changing currency where you stay. Pay for your room in pesos if possible, since the same low rate often applies to room charges paid in dollars.

Credit Cards

Visa and MasterCard are widely accepted in Baja at large hotels, at restaurants catering to tourists or businesspeople, at car rental agencies (you can't rent a car without a credit card), and at shops in tourist centers or large cities. If in doubt, flash your card and ask *"¿Se aceptan tarjetas de crédito?"* A reply containing *"solo efectivo"* means "only cash."

It's important to keep in mind that many shops and some hotels add a 3–6 percent surcharge to bills paid with a credit card. Credit cards are not accepted at Pemex stations in Baja.

Cash advances on credit card accounts—a very useful service for emergencies—are available at many Mexican banks.

Debit Cards and ATM Cards

Most Mexican ATMs (automatic teller machines) accept MasterCard or Visa debit cards as well as ATM cards on the Plus or Cirrus systems. Using an ATM card to obtain pesos from ATMs in Mexico is much more convenient than cashing traveler's checks. Most Mexican banks now charge nominal fees for withdrawing cash from their ATMs with cards from other banks. ATMs are called *cajeros automáticos* (automatic cashiers) in Mexico.

At this time the most reliable machines seem to be those operated by **Banamex, Bancomer, HSBC, Banorte,** and **Banca Serfín,** whose

ATMs accept cards coded for the Visa, Master-Card, Cirrus, and Plus systems.

MONEY MANAGEMENT

Estimating Costs

Inflation in Mexico runs high. This means that when estimating travel costs based on prices quoted in this book, some allowance must be made for inflation.

Because of fluctuations in the peso–dollar ratio, and in an effort to keep prices up-to-date, all prices in this book are quoted in dollars. This doesn't mean, however, that there won't be any increase in prices by the time you arrive. A couple of phone calls to hotels for price quotes should give you an idea of how much rates have increased, if at all; this difference can be applied as a percentage to all other prices to get a rough estimate of costs.

Tipping

A tip of 10–15 percent is customary at restaurants with table service unless a service charge is added to the bill. Luggage handling at hotels or airports warrants a tip of US$.50 per bag. A few hotels maintain a no-tipping policy; details will be posted in your room. The tipping of chambermaids is optional—some guests tip and some don't. Remember that these folks typically earn minimum wage; even a small tip may mean a lot to them.

You don't need to tip Pemex station attendants unless they wash your windows, check the oil, or perform other extra services beyond pumping gas. The equivalent of US$.25–.50 in pesos is sufficient. When the change due on a gasoline purchase is less than N$1 it's customary to let the attendant keep the change.

Taxes

The Mexican government collects an *impuesta al valor agregado* (IVA) or "value added tax" (VAT) of 10 percent on all goods and services in Baja, including hotel and restaurant bills and international phone calls. On the mainland, the same tax is 15 percent, so Baja is a bargain in this area. Although by American standards this may seem high, this tax hike brings Mexico more in line with other countries that employ value-added taxes, such as France, where the VAT runs over 20 percent.

Hotels add a further two percent lodging tax. Most hotel rate quotes include taxes, but to make sure you might ask *"¿Se incluyen los impuestos?"*

MEASUREMENTS AND STANDARDS

Weights and Measures

Mexico uses the metric system as the official system of weights and measures. This means the distance between Maneadero and San Quintín is measured in kilometers, cheese is weighed in grams or kilograms, a hot day in San Felipe is 32°C, gasoline is sold by the liter, and a big fish is two meters long. A chart at the end of this book converts pounds, gallons, and miles to kilograms, liters, and kilometers.

Bajacalifornianos used to dealing with American tourists often use the Anglo-American and metric systems interchangeably. Even rancheros in remote areas occasionally use *millas* (miles) as a measure.

In this book, distances are rendered in kilometers, often followed by miles in parentheses. All road markers in Baja employ the metric system. Dimensions and weights are usually quoted using the metric system, but boat lengths and fishing line tests are quoted in feet and pounds (due to the influence of American boaters and anglers).

Time

Baja California Norte lies in the Pacific time zone, Baja California Sur in the mountain time zone. This means you should set your timepieces an hour ahead when crossing the BCS state line going south and back an hour when crossing north. Like the United States, Baja observes daylight saving time from the first Sunday in April the last Sunday in October.

Time in Mexico is often expressed according to the 24-hour clock, from 0001 to 2359 (one minute past midnight to 11:59 P.M.). A restaurant posting hours of 1100–2200, for example, is open 11 A.M.–10 P.M.

Electricity

Mexico's electrical system is the same as that in the United States and Canada: 110 volts, 60 cycles, alternating current (AC). Electrical outlets are of the North American type, designed to work with appliances that have standard double-bladed plugs.

TELEPHONE SERVICES

The national telephone company, **TelMex,** privatized in 1990 and has improved its services considerably over the last decade or so. In Baja California Norte, a regional company called **Tel-Nor** supplements the national system. Local phone calls are relatively cheap—a two-peso coin pays for a phone-booth call—as are long-distance calls *within* Mexico. If you can find a working phone (many public phones seem permanently out of order) connections are usually good, though you may have to wait a while to get through to the operator during busy periods like Sundays and holidays.

If you don't want to use a phone booth or a hotel phone (hotels usually add their own surcharges to both local and long-distance calls), you can make a call during business hours from a TelMex office. Only large towns offer TelMex offices with public telecommunications facilities; a small town may offer a private telephone office (usually called *caseta de teléfono* or *caseta de larga distancia*), often set up in the corner of a local shop, where you can make calls. Like hotels, private telephone offices add surcharges to calls, but rates are usually reasonable.

A public pay phone service called **Ladatel** (acronym for Larga Distancia Teléfono) offers phone booths where you can pay for local or long-distance calls with a *tarjeta de teléfono* (phone card) issued by TelMex or by TelNor. You can purchase debit cards in denominations of N$20, N$30, N$50, and N$100 at many pharmacies, convenience stores, supermarkets, bus terminals, and airports.

On the long stretch between Ensenada and Mulegé, few towns or villages have telephone service, much less a telephone office. Thus, some residents maintain their own two-way radio stations for communication with the outside world. Mulegé has only two public phone booths; visitors line up on Sundays to phone home.

Long-Distance Domestic Calls

To make a long-distance call within Mexico, dial 01 plus the area code and number.

If you have a calling card number for Sprint, AT&T, MCI, Bell Canada, or British Telecom, you can use it to make long-distance calls. Each has its own access code for direct dialing.

International Calls

To direct-dial an international call to the United States or Canada via TelMex, dial 001 plus area code and number for a station-to-station call. For international calls to other countries, dial 00 plus the country code, area code, and number. For operator-assisted calls, dial 09 plus the country code, area code, and number. Long-distance international calls are heavily taxed and cost more than equivalent international calls from the United States or Canada.

To reach toll-free 800 numbers in Mexico, dial 01 first. Dial 001 first for numbers in the United States, or 091 for Canada.

See the Telephone Codes chart for access numbers that will connect you with operators from AT&T, MCI, Sprint, Bell Canada, or AT&T Canada for calling card or credit card calls. For BT Direct dial *791.

The appropriate long-distance operator can then place a collect call on your behalf or charge the call to your account if you have a calling card for that service. If you try these numbers from a hotel phone, be sure the hotel operator realizes the call is toll-free; some hotel operators use their own timers to assess phone charges.

Warning: Since the deregulation of Mexican telephone service, several unscrupulous United States–based long-distance phone companies have set up shop in Mexico to take advantage of undiscerning tourists. The English-language signs next to the phone usually read "Call the U.S. or Canada Collect or With a Credit Card" or "Just Dial Zero to Reach the U.S. or Canada." Another clue is that the name of the

TELEPHONE CODES

Long-distance operator (national): 020

Time: 030

Directory assistance (local): 040

Mexico City area code: 55

Police, Red Cross, fire: 060

Emergency response: 066

Spanish-English emergency information: 07

International operator: 090

Long-distance direct dialing from Mexico via TelMex:

- station to station (in Mexico): 01 + area code + number
- person to person (in Mexico): 02 + area code + number
- station to station (United States and Canada): 00 + 1 + area code + number
- person to person (United States and Canada): 09 + 1 + area code + number
- station to station (other international): 00 + area code + number
- person to person (other international): 09 + area code + number

Other long-distance companies:

AT&T: 001-800/462-4240

MCI WorldPhone: 001-800/674-7000

Sprint: 001-800/877-8000

Bell Canada: 001-800/010-1990

AT&T Canada: 001-800/123-0201

TelMex: 01-800/728-4647 (800-SAVINGS)

Baja California Area Codes

Ciudad Constitución/Puerto San Carlos: 613

Ensenada: 646

Guerrero Negro/San Ignacio/Mulegé: 615

Loreto: 613

La Paz/Todos Santos: 612

Mexicali: 686

Rosarito: 661

San Felipe: 686

San José del Cabo/Cabo San Lucas: 624

San Quintín/El Rosario: 616

Tecate: 665

Tijuana: 664

Calling Mexico from Abroad

Mexico country code: 52

To call Mexico direct from outside the country, dial your international access code + 52 + area code + number. Example: To call the number 684-0461 in Tijuana from the United States, dial 011 (international access code) + 52 (Mexico country code) + 664 (Tijuana area code) + 684-0461.

company is not posted on the sign. If you try asking the operators on the line who they represent, you'll find the same company often operates under several different corporate names in the same area, charging at least 50 percent more per international call than TelMex, AT&T, MCI, or Sprint—or even many times more, as much as US$10–20 for the first minute, plus US$4 each additional minute, even on weekends. A percentage of these charges usually goes to the hotel or private phone office offering the service. At most private phone offices it's cheaper to use TelMex, even if you have to pay a service charge on top of TelMex rates, than to use these price-gouging U.S. companies. Or use MCI, Sprint, AT&T, or one of the other more well-known international companies. Unless you're independently wealthy, always ask which company is being used before you arrange an international call through a hotel or private phone office. Some Mexican hotels are now cooperating with these cutthroat American companies—the tip-off is a card next to the phone that says you can use credit cards to make a call to the United States or Canada.

Collect Calls

For international service, calling collect often saves hassles. In Spanish the magic words are *por cobrar* (collect), prefaced by the name of the place you're calling (e.g., *"a los Estados Unidos, por favor—por cobrar"*). This connects you to an English-speaking international operator. For best results, speak slowly and clearly. You may reach an English-speaking international operator directly by dialing 090.

Area Codes and Local Numbers

All area codes in Mexico now have three digits, except for Mexico City (area code 55). You may occasionally see phone numbers written using older numbering systems. The number 612/142-4274 in La Paz, for example, appeared as 1/142-4274 in 2000, and as 114/2-4274 prior to that year.

As of November 2001, all telephone numbers in both states of Baja California and most phone numbers elsewhere in Mexico consist of seven digits. This means if you are in La Paz and intend to call what would formerly have been written as 114/2-4274 or 1/142-4274 under one of the earlier systems, you must now dial 612/142-4274.

There's no standard way of hyphenating the numbers in Mexico. You may see the number in our La Paz example written as 1424274, 14-24274, 14-24-274, and so on.

Email and Internet Access

If you're bringing computer and modem to Mexico with hopes of staying on the infobahn, be aware that online options are limited to a handful of local Internet service providers and a few international ones.

CompuServe Interactive, Prodigy, America Online, and IBM Global are the only "international" providers so far that include local-access phone numbers in Mexico. Prodigy, which is owned by TelMex, Mexico's national phone company, now has the largest market share and the best networking infrastructure, and is thus the most reliable by far. Prodigy has many local-access phone numbers in Baja, and if you have a Prodigy account in the United States, you can use these numbers to access the Internet.

RJ11 phone jacks are the standard in newer hotels, but in older hotels, motels, and *casas de huéspedes* the phones may still be hard-wired. Most phone offices will let you plug your laptop into their system if you're polite and explain what you're up to. If the office telephone is hard-wired, ask if they have a fax machine, since all fax units use standard RJ11 jacks.

Cybercafés, where you can use public terminals to send and receive email or browse the Web, are multiplying slowly in Tijuana, Mexicali, Ensenada, La Paz, San José del Cabo, Cabo San Lucas, and Todos Santos.

POSTAL SERVICES

The Mexican postal service, though reliable, is relatively slow. Average delivery time between Mexico and the United States or Canada is about 10 days, while to Europe you must figure two weeks. Mail sent to Mexico from outside the country generally reaches its destination more quickly.

Most towns in Baja have a post office *(correo)* where you can receive general-delivery mail. Have correspondents address mail in your name (last name in all capital letters), followed by a/c Lista de Correos, Correo Central, the town name, the state, and the country, e.g., Joe CUMMINGS, a/c Lista de Correos, Correo Central, La Paz, Baja California Sur, Mexico. Mail sent this way is usually held 10 days. If you want your mail held up to 30 days, substitute the words "Poste Restante" for Lista de Correos in the address. If you have the postal code for the town or city, insert it just after the state name. Since delivery time is highly variable, it's best to use poste restante just to be safe.

Many foreigners who are seasonal Baja residents have their mail sent in care of a hotel or RV park. You can rent boxes at larger Mexican post offices, but the initial application process often takes several weeks. Tijuana, Tecate, Mexicali, San José del Cabo, and Cabo San Lucas have private mail companies that also rent boxes with minimal red tape.

Another option is **Direct Express,** www.directexpress.com, an authorized mail-receiving agency for the United States Postal Service. They offer their subscribers a mailbox address in San

Diego, with express forwarding four days weekly to several locations in Baja's cape region.

The Mexican post office offers an express mail service (EMS) called Mexpost. International rates are relatively high. Mexpost claims to deliver almost anywhere in Mexico within 48 hours, to major cities around the world within 72 hours.

UPS, Airborne Express, DHL, FedEx, and other courier services operate in Tijuana, Mexicali, La Paz, and Cabo San Lucas. So far DHL and UPS seem to offer the lowest prices and best services. Local companies such as Estafeta and Aeroflash are also available, but reliability does not appear to match the international services.

Services and Information

BUSINESS HOURS

The typical small business is open Mon.–Fri. 9 A.M.–2 P.M., closed until 4 or 5 P.M., then open again until 7 or 8 P.M. Retail businesses are usually open on Saturday as well. Official government offices typically maintain an 8:30 A.M.–3:30 P.M. schedule, although Secretary of Tourism offices usually open again 5–7 P.M.

Bank hours vary. Most are open Mon.–Fri. 8:30 A.M.–3 P.M., though some banks in larger towns are open on Saturday. The foreign exchange service usually closes around noon— probably to lock in the exchange rate before afternoon adjustments.

TRAVEL SERVICES

Online Information

See the Internet Resources section at the back of this book.

Tourist Information

Mexico's federal tourist bureau, the Secretaría de Turismo (SECTUR), staffs state offices in Mexicali and La Paz. These in turn maintain branch offices in Tijuana, Ensenada, Tecate, Rosarito, San Felipe, San Quintín, and Loreto. These offices usually stock free brochures, maps, hotel and restaurant lists, and information on local activities, but some offices are better staffed to handle visitor queries than others. Tijuana, Ensenada, Mexicali, and La Paz offer convention and visitors bureaus in addition to state offices and are particularly well stocked with useful information. The addresses, phone numbers, and hours of each office are listed under the appropriate destination sections of the book.

To contact the national office directly, call or write the **Secretaría de Turismo de México,** Presidente Mazaryk 172, 11587 México, D.F., 55/3002-6300. In the United States, SECTUR maintains a toll-free information number (tel. 800/482-9832). In Mexico, its toll-free information number is 800/903-9200, and its website is www.sectur.gob.mx/wb2.

Outside Mexico SECTUR operates Mexican Tourism Board (www.visitmexico.com) offices to handle requests for tourist information; several are in the United States.

Travel Clubs

Over the years Baja's popularity as a boating and RV destination has spawned several California-based travel clubs that specialize in recreational travel on the peninsula. Membership benefits include discounts (usually 10–20 percent) at various hotels, restaurants, and other tourist-oriented establishments in Mexico; discounted group auto and boat insurance; the opportunity to participate in such club events as tours and fiestas; and subscriptions to newsletters containing tips from other club members, short travel features, and the latest information on road conditions and Mexican tourism policy. The clubs can also arrange tourist cards, boat permits, and fishing licenses by mail.

Such clubs come and go, some lasting only a year or two. **Discover Baja Travel Club,** currently the largest and most successful club of this nature, invites members or potential members to visit its San Diego–area office on the way to Baja for up-to-date road and weather information. DB publishes a monthly newsletter packed with information on road travel, sightseeing, and new developments in Baja travel. Contact Discover Baja at 3089 Claremont Dr., San Diego, CA 92117, 619/275-1836 or 800/727-BAJA, ask@ discoverbaja.com, www.discoverbaja.com.

MEDIA

Newspapers

Several Spanish-language newspapers are published in Baja; *El Mexicano*, published daily in Tijuana, has the highest circulation, closely followed by Mexicali's *La Voz de la Frontera* (Voice of the Border). Also of considerable interest is the progressive *Zeta* (Z), in Tijuana. *El Sudcaliforniano*, out of La Paz, covers Baja California Sur news but is not a very good newspaper overall.

A few English-language newspapers are published monthly in Baja, all heavily oriented toward tourists. Although not exactly pillars of journalism, they nonetheless contain much information of value to the visitor, including up-to-date sketch maps. Typical features include restaurant reviews, cultural primers on upcoming festivals, Spanish language lessons, seasonal fishing recommendations, and the occasional editorial on national or local tourism policies. The content of each is oriented toward the town in which it is published.

The *Ensenada Baja News-Gazette,* available online only at www.gazette.ensenada.net.mx, covers tourism news in northern Baja. It's not very up-to-date these days, but the site contains lots of usable travel info nonetheless.

In southern Baja, several papers focusing on Los Cabos have come and gone over the years. *Gringo Gazette* contains the most useful information overall, even if the paper's reporting on Mexican affairs on occasion reveals a seemingly intentional lack of cultural comprehension. *El Calendario de Todos Santos,* based in Todos Santos, does a wonderful job of covering the West Cape.

In tourist hotels you'll often see day-old copies of *The San Diego Union-Tribune, Los Angeles Times,* or *USA Today.*

Radio and Television

In the border area of northern Baja, radios and TVs pick up a mix of broadcasts from Tijuana and San Diego. Farther south the San Diego stations first begin to fade, then the Tijuana stations. South of Ensenada you need shortwave radio to receive anything until you arrive in La Paz or Los Cabos, where TV and radio reception begin again.

Because of the lack of TV and radio reception in most of Baja, it would be pointless to pack an AM/FM radio or portable TV. An audiocassette or portable CD player makes more sense. Many towns in Baja have shops selling tapes and CDs, for prices generally less expensive than in the United States or Canada. American, Canadian, and European releases—in addition to Latino recordings—often appear on Mexican labels.

MAPS

Among the many Baja California maps available to visitors, three are particularly well suited to general-purpose Baja road travel. One is published by the Automobile Club of Southern California and is available from most AAA offices; maps are free to AAA members. This map is easy to read, accurate, and detailed enough for any border-to-Cape auto trip. Its clear graphics include topographic shading.

On the AAA map longer distances are marked in miles and kilometers (one inch = 12.4 miles or 20 km), but smaller distances are marked only in miles, which makes it convenient for anyone driving a vehicle purchased in the United States but frustrating for drivers of vehicles acquired anywhere else in the world. Even for American-market vehicles, it can be confusing trying to match map mileage with the Mexican roadside kilometer markers. The AAA map features a distance table with entries in both miles and kilometers, but this is of little use when trying to figure out distances between points not listed on the table.

The AAA map is accurate along Mexico 1 but inaccurate or out of date for many places on other highways or on smaller, unpaved roads. Even on or near Mexico 1, "dead" ranches that dried up 10–15 years ago haven't been removed. At the same time, thriving ranches like La Garita on Mexico 19, for example, may not be marked on the map. Remote coastal areas are particularly spotty. Still, it's useful for ordinary Tijuana-to-Cabo highway navigation.

International Travel Map Productions (ITM) publishes a well-researched map that's a bit harder to find, especially in the United States. Map and travel stores may carry it, or it can be ordered from ITM, 345 West Broadway, Vancouver, BC V5Y 1P8, Canada. In spite of its smaller scale (one inch = 15.78 miles or 25.4 km), the ITM map is far more detailed than the AAA map, and all distances are entered in kilometers as well as miles. Many dirt roads, trails, and destinations unmarked on the AAA map appear on the ITM map. In addition, the map features contour lines in 200-meter intervals and is annotated with useful historical and sightseeing information. The main drawback is that it's so detailed it's difficult to read. In addition, the map's graphics scheme uses far too much red, a color particularly difficult to read in low light (e.g., under a car dome light).

Baja California Almanac (see Hiking & Backpacking earlier in this chapter) also publishes an excellent one-sheet folding map, based on its popular book-form Baja atlas, for US$5.95.

Topographical Maps

Because differences in elevation often determine backcountry route selection, hikers, kayakers, mountain bikers, and off-road drivers should consider obtaining Mexican INEGI topographical maps before arriving in Baja. For information on what's available and where to get it, see Hiking and Backpacking in the Sports and Recreation section of this chapter.

Getting There

BY AIR

International Flights

Baja's most commonly used air gateway for flights from the United States (the only country with direct international flights to Baja) is Los Cabos (SJD), a modern airport about 15 km (nine miles) north of San José del Cabo. Daily direct flights to Los Cabos originate in Atlanta, Chicago, Dallas, Denver, Houston, Los Angeles, New York, Oakland, Phoenix, San Diego, San Francisco, and San Jose. Many other cities in the United States post flights to Los Cabos with one or more stopovers along the way, usually Mexico City or Monterrey. Los Cabos is well connected by air with mainland Mexico.

International flights to La Paz (LAP) arrive from El Paso, Los Angeles, Phoenix, San Antonio, and Tucson—all but Los Angeles flights require stops along the way. La Paz is very well connected with mainland Mexico, however.

Loreto (LTO) also fields regularly scheduled flights from the United States, but via Los Angeles only. Nondirect, connecting flights from Tucson and San Diego are also available. Aerolitoral provides service from mainland Mexico.

The small airport at San Felipe has received on-and-off service from various airlines based in Los Angeles or San Diego, but at the moment all services have been discontinued.

Tijuana International Airport (TIJ) fields one direct flight weekly from Los Angeles and is well linked with La Paz, Los Cabos, and the Mexican mainland. Depending on the travel season and the dollar–peso exchange rate, it may be less expensive to fly from Tijuana to Los Cabos than from San Diego to Los Cabos. When this is the case, Cabo-bound San Diego residents counting pennies should consider taking a bus or taxi across the border to Tijuana and using Mexican air services.

Santa Rosalía has an airport reportedly equipped to handle international service, but so far the only way to fly there is by chartered plane.

Air/Hotel Packages

Airlines serving Baja often offer package deals that include airfare, hotel, and airport transfers at money-saving prices. A typical package includes three nights' hotel accommodations, airfare, and airport transfers for about the same as airfare alone. Contact the airlines directly to inquire

ON THE ROAD

AIRLINES SERVING BAJA

Note: All routes are subject to change; call the airlines for the latest information.

Aero California, tel. 800/237-6225
- **to La Paz:** nonstop flights from Chihuahua, Culiacán, Guadalajara, Hermosillo, Los Mochis, Mazatlán, Monterrey, and Tijuana; connecting flights from Los Angeles and Mexico City
- **to Loreto:** nonstop flights from Los Angeles and La Paz
- **to Los Cabos:** flights from Los Angeles, Guadalajara, and Monterrey
- **to Tijuana:** flights from Aguascalientes, Culiacán, Durango, Guadalajara, Hermosillo, La Paz, Los Mochis, Mazatlán, Monterrey, Tepic, and Torreón

Aviacsa, tel. 888/528-4227, Mexico 800/711-6733
- **to Tijuana:** flights from Guadalajara, Hermosillo, Mexico City, and Monterrey

Aerolitoral, tel. 800/237-6639
- **to La Paz:** nonstop flights from Ciudad Obregón, Hermosillo, Loreto, Los Mochis, and Mazatlán; connecting flights from Chihuahua and Monterrey
- **to Loreto:** flights to San Diego, Ciudad Obregón and La Paz

Aeroméxico, tel. 800/237-6639
- **to La Paz:** nonstop flights from Culiacán, Mexico City, and Tijuana; connecting flights from Guadalajara and Phoenix
- **to Los Cabos:** direct flights from Mexico City and San Diego
- **to Tijuana:** nonstop flights from Guadalajara, Mexico City, Monterrey, and Tepic

Alaska Airlines, tel. 800/426-0333
- **to Los Cabos:** nonstop flights from Phoenix, San Diego, San Francisco, San Jose, and Los Angeles; connecting flight from Seattle

American Airlines, tel. 800/433-7300
- **to Los Cabos:** daily flights from Dallas/Ft. Worth and Chicago

America West, tel. 800/235-9292
- **to Los Cabos:** nonstop flights from Denver and Phoenix; connecting flights from many U.S. cities

Continental, tel. 800/523-3273
- **to Los Cabos:** nonstop flights from Houston; connecting flights from many U.S. cities

Delta Airlines, tel. 800/241-4141
- **to Los Cabos:** nonstop flights from Atlanta

Mexicana Airlines, tel. 800/531-7921
- **to Los Cabos:** nonstop flights from Guadalajara and Los Angeles.
- **to Tijuana:** nonstop flights from Los Angeles, Guadalajara, and Mexico City; connecting flights from many Mexican cities

about such packages, or check with a good travel agent. Newspaper travel sections often carry advertisements for air/hotel deals in Los Cabos.

Suntrips, 800/SUNTRIPS, www.suntrips.com, combines round-trip air between Oakland and Los Cabos with three nights' hotel accommodations beginning at US$379. Considering that round-trip airfare alone to Los Cabos can cost US$400 or more, these are bargain rates. Fares are subject to change, of course; these are only examples.

Private Planes

Baja is a popular destination among North American light-aircraft pilots. Entry procedures are minimal, air traffic over the peninsula light, and nearly 200 airstrips take pilots and their passengers in a matter of hours to corners of Baja usually accessible only by days of driving. Most of these airstrips are unpaved and unstaffed—a significant attraction for those who consider themselves bush pilots.

Private aircraft weighing less than 12,500 kg (27,500 pounds) and carrying fewer than 14 passengers are subject to the same customs procedures as automobiles and light trucks. In cases where the plane's owner doesn't accompany the aircraft, flights are further restricted to single-engine craft with five or fewer passengers. Cargo is restricted to the personal belongings of pilots and passengers.

Flight plans must be filed in advance with the Mexican airport nearest the point of entry. Southbound, pilots must clear immigration and customs at the Mexican airport of entry; northbound, a stop on either side of the border is required for pilots and passengers to satisfy both Mexican and U.S. border formalities. Mandatory paperwork includes your aircraft registration, pilot's license, medical certificate, Mexican liability aircraft insurance, and proof of citizenship (see Visas and Officialdom).

Fees and taxes for flying private aircraft into Mexico currently total around US$45 per craft along with the usual US$18 per person tourist fee. Other landing fees and taxes may be charged locally, typically US$8 for single-engined craft, US$12 for twins. Many airports in Baja are un-dergoing privatization, which means that new fees and policies may come into effect in the future.

For further information on flying regulations in Baja, contact a Mexican consulate or **Baja Bush Pilots,** 149 W. Boston, Chandler, AZ 85225, 480/730-3250, fax 480/730-3251, jack@bajabushpilots.com, www.bajabushpilots.com. For more information on flying conditions in Baja, see Getting Around.

BY BUS

To San Diego (or Los Angeles)

Whether they reach the United States–Baja California border by train, bus, or trolley, most visitors using public transportation first pass through San Diego. From there they can choose from several options for traveling to Tijuana or Mexicali. San Diego is connected to other points in the United States by frequent long-distance bus and rail service. From both Los Angeles and San Diego there are frequent buses to Tijuana and Mexicali.

Intercity buses generally depart more frequently and are less expensive than trains. Greyhound Bus Lines is the major carrier into San Diego. If you're busing a long distance to San Diego, a bus pass may be more economical than single-journey tickets. A **Greyhound Ameripass** (International Ameripass for non-U.S. citizens and a Domestic Ameripass for U.S. citizens) allows unlimited bus travel within the United States and including cross-border bus trips to Tijuana. It's valid between specified dates and may be purchased directly from Greyhound or from a travel agent. Students enrolled in a college or university may receive 15 percent discounts on all walk-up fares with a Student Advantage card. Call 888/GLI-PASS in the United States for Ameripass information or 800/231-2222 for other Greyhound fare and schedule information. For information on the Student Advantage card, call 800/333-2920 or visit www.studentadvantage.com/greyhound.

San Diego to Tijuana

Greyhound Bus Lines, 619/239-3266 in San Diego, operates around 17 buses a day from the San Diego bus terminal to Tijuana's downtown bus terminal for US$5 one-way or US$8 round-trip. Greyhound also runs a number of buses daily to Tijuana's Central de Autobuses—where you'll find the greatest selection of buses heading to Baja California Sur—for about the same fare. San Diego's bus terminal is at 120 W. Broadway.

The cheapest bus transportation to the border from San Diego is the Metropolitan Transit System's city bus no. 932 (also known as the Border Shuttle), which travels from the downtown area (Centre City) to San Ysidro every 30 minutes from around 5:40 A.M. to 10:52 P.M. (6:12 A.M.–10:52 P.M. weekends and holidays) for just US$2.25. Because it makes several stops along the way, the city bus takes 80 minutes to reach San Ysidro. For schedule information, call 619/233-3004.

Bright red, comfortable **Mexicoach** buses, 619/428-9517 in San Diego or 664/685-1470 in Tijuana, leave every 15 minutes 9 A.M.–9 P.M. from the San Ysidro border gateway for the Terminal Turística Tijuana on Avenida Revolución between Calles 6 and 7, in the middle of the tourist district. Drivers will also stop at the Tijuana Cultural Center on request. The fare is US$1.25 each way.

Three or four other shuttle bus lines operate from the border at any one time, each charging about US$1.25 each way. It's best to buy a one-way ticket so that you can use any bus on the way back. Most stop at Revolución and Calle 3, the most popular embarkation point for Tijuana residents commuting between the United States and Tijuana.

All of the border shuttles, including Mexicoach, leave from a spot in San Ysidro next to the Tijuana Trolley terminus, so a connection between the two is easy.

The San Diego Metropolitan Transit System's trolley line to San Ysidro, nicknamed the **"Tijuana Trolley,"** is probably the easiest form of public transportation to the border. San Ysidro–bound trains leave every 15 minutes 5 A.M.–1 A.M. from downtown San Diego (plus Saturday morning "night owl" service 2–5 A.M.). Tickets cost US$1–2.50, depending on the distance traveled (or $1 for seniors and disabled passengers, free for children under five, no matter the distance). You can buy a packet of 11 tokens for US$20, which reduces the price of each ticket to US$1.80. Like the city bus, the trolley makes numerous stops along the way to San Ysidro—figure on about an hour from downtown. Bicycles may be taken on the trolley. Call 619/685-4900 for general MTS information and 619/233-3004 for information on scheduling and stops.

Los Angeles to Tijuana

Greyhound Bus Lines, 1716 E. 7th St., 213/629-8401 in Los Angeles, operates more than 15 buses a day, nearly round the clock, from Los Angeles to Tijuana's downtown terminal. The fare is US$18 one-way or US$28 round-trip from L.A. Buses leave from the downtown Greyhound terminal in L.A. and arrive at Tijuana's downtown terminal at Calle Comercio and Avenida Madero. Travel time is around four hours, depending on traffic in L.A. and at the border. Mexican Customs doesn't make everyone get off the bus at the border; U.S. Customs does. Boxed bicycles may accompany paying passengers at no extra charge.

Buses to Mexicali and Calexico

Greyhound, along with its Mexican partner Crucero, operates several buses daily to Mexicali from Los Angeles (US$30) and San Diego (US$26). The company also runs buses to Calexico, California (opposite Mexicali), from Tucson (US$53), Yuma (US$16.75), Phoenix (US$43.50), and El Paso (US$86). The Calexico Greyhound terminal is on 1st Street; from there it's a short walk through the immigration and customs checkpoint into downtown Mexicali.

Buses from Mainland Mexico

Transportes Norte de Sonora (TNS) and **Autotransportes Estrellas del Pacífico** operate long-distance express buses to Mexicali and Tijuana from various towns in Guanajuato, Nayarit, Sonora, Chihuahua, Michoacán, Jalisco, Sinaloa, Zacatecas, Querétaro, and Mexico City.

Green Tortoise

To those who have never traveled by Green Tortoise, it's difficult to describe the experience. Imagine a sort of youth hostel on wheels, with a bit of a '60s spirit, and you'll begin to get the idea. The buses are refurbished Greyhounds with convertible beds and tables, comfortable but a bit of a tight squeeze at night when everyone's lying down. That's also when the bus travels. Great way to meet people.

Green Tortoise operates nine-day (from US$419), 15-day (US$549), and 17-day (US$599) trips Nov.–Apr. that begin in San Francisco (pickups in L.A. and San Diego are possible) and range as far south as La Paz. Prices are very reasonable and include transportation and lodging on the bus, plus guided hikes and side trips to remote Baja beaches. The food fund adds another US$9–10 per day to the trip; communal meals cover about 70 percent of the meals—some meals are left to the participants. The trips include an optional windsurfing and sailing program available for an additional fee. All things considered, it's a travel bargain and a novel introduction to Baja.

For further information, contact Green Tortoise Adventure Travel, 494 Broadway, San Francisco, CA 94133, 415/956-7500 or 800/867-8647, tortoise@greentortoise.com, www.greentortoise.com.

BY TRAIN

Getting to San Diego

The only long-distance passenger rail line to San Diego is Amtrak's San Diegan, which rolls between Los Angeles and San Diego 10 times daily. Other Amtrak lines serve Los Angeles from points north and east. Amtrak offers special one-way, round-trip, or excursion fares on occasion; always ask before booking.

Outside the United States, some travel agencies sell a **USA Railpass** allowing unlimited rail travel within specified dates. For schedule information or bookings inside the United States, call 800/872-7245 (800/USA-RAIL) or visit www.amtrak.com. A rail pass called **All Aboard America** is sold in the United States at slightly higher prices.

Mexican Railways

Mexico's national rail service has its westernmost terminus in Mexicali. The Mexicali line connects with the Mexico City–Nogales line at Benjamin Hill, hence it was until fairly recently an alternative way to get to Baja from Nogales or Mexico City, or anywhere in between. At the moment all passenger services to Mexicali have been discontinued.

BY CAR

Driving into Baja

The red tape for driving into Baja is minimal. No vehicle permits of any kind are required, no matter how long you stay in Baja, unless you plan to cross to the mainland by road (via San Luis Río Colorado) or ferry (Santa Rosalía or La Paz). For stays of less than 72 hours no farther south than Ensenada, United States and Canadian citizens don't even need a tourist permit, just identification.

More people drive private vehicles across the United States–Mexico border at Tijuana than at any other point along its 1,600-km (1,000-mile) length—nearly 20 million per year on average. If you find the traffic daunting, you can avoid Tijuana altogether by choosing any of four other Baja border crossings.

Insurance

Before driving into Baja, drivers should arrange for Mexican vehicle insurance. No matter what your own insurance company may tell you, Mexican authorities don't recognize foreign insurance policies for private vehicles in Mexico.

Vehicle insurance isn't required by law in Mexico, but it's a good idea to carry a Mexican liability policy anyway; without it, a minor traffic accident can turn into a nightmare. Short-term insurance—as little as one day's worth—can be arranged at any of several agencies found in nearly every border town between the Pacific Ocean and the Gulf of Mexico. One reliable insurance program is offered by Discover Baja Travel Club, tel. 800/727-BAJA. DB offers liability insurance for only US$68 per year, including legal defense with up to US$30,000 for attorney fees, bail bonds, and court costs (if your accident involves legal problems). It also includes emergency medical transportation to the nearest town where appropriate medical treatment can be found. Full coverage based on the value of the vehicle begins at only US$125 per year.

Another good source of Mexican insurance is **International Gateway Insurance Brokers,** 800/423-2646, where rates for liability or full coverage are similar. Gateway also offers optional legal assistance coverage for US$2 a day.

Those in a hurry might prefer **Instant Mexico Insurance Services.** IMIS sits at the last exit before the San Ysidro/Tijuana border crossing at 223 Via de San Ysidro, tel. 619/428-4714 or 800/345-4701, fax 619/690-6533, www.instant-mex-auto-insur.com. It's open 24 hours, and in addition to insurance IMIS offers tourist cards, fishing and boating permits, maps, guidebooks, and other Baja requisites.

Several agencies in Tijuana and Ensenada offer annual policies that charge you only for those days you're actually in Mexico. Of course, this requires a trip south of the border to obtain such a policy, so you'll need a day's worth of border insurance beforehand. One agency north of the border that can arrange Mexican liability insurance on a per-use basis is **Anserv Insurance Services,** 3900 Harney St. #250, San Diego, 619/296-4706. Rates are as low as US$67 based on 60 days' maximum use (any 60 days in a year) per policy year.

The Discover Baja and Vagabundos del Mar travel clubs (see Services and Information for addresses and phone numbers) offer lower group insurance rates for members only—check with each for the latest deals. These group policies are offered on a yearly basis only; they can't be purchased by the day, week, or month.

Some insurance companies try to justify higher premiums by claiming their policies cover repairs performed in the United States or Canada, pointing out that less-expensive insurance is valid only for repairs in Mexico. In most cases, such an argument is irrelevant; the primary reason you need Mexican insurance is to protect yourself against liability in the event of an accident. In cases where your vehicle is disabled, repairs have

to be performed in Mexico anyway. Even if you obtain a policy that covers U.S./Canada repairs, chances are it won't cover transportation of a disabled vehicle to the border. However, visitors driving vehicles with difficult-to-obtain parts might want to consider a policy valid for U.S./Canada repairs.

Whichever policy you choose, always make photocopies of it and keep originals and copies in separate, safe places. It's also a good idea to carry a photocopy of the first page—the "declaration" or "renewal of declaration" sheet—of your home country policy because Mexican law requires that you cross the border with at least six months' worth of home country insurance.

Temporary Vehicle Import Permits

If you're only driving in the states of Baja California and Baja California Sur, you won't need one of these. However, if you plan to take a vehicle aboard a ferry bound for the mainland from Santa Rosalía or La Paz, you need a temporary vehicle import permit before you'll be allowed to book a ferry ticket. To receive this permit, simply drive your vehicle to a Mexican customs office (this can be done at any official border crossing or in La Paz) and present the following: a valid state registration for the vehicle (or similar document certifying legal ownership), a driver's license, and a credit card (Visa, MasterCard, American Express, or Diner's Club) issued outside Mexico.

If you are leasing or renting the vehicle, you'll also have to present a leasing or rental contract made out to the person bringing the vehicle into Mexico. If the vehicle belongs to someone else (e.g., a friend or relative), you must present a notarized letter from the owner giving you permission to take the vehicle to Mexico. Contrary to rumor, you aren't required to present the "pink slip" or ownership certificate unless the state registration certificate is for some reason unavailable.

Once Mexican customs officials have approved your documents, you'll proceed to a Banjército (Banco del Ejército or Military Bank) office attached to the customs facilities, and your credit card account will be charged US$17 for the permit fee. This fee must be paid by credit card;

cash is not accepted. If you don't have a credit card, you'll have to post a bond (1–2 percent of the vehicle's blue-book value) issued by an authorized Mexican bond company, a very time-consuming and expensive procedure. Banjército is the bank used for all Mexican customs charges; the operating hours for each module are the same as for the border crossing at which it's located.

Once the fee has been charged to your credit card, the permit is issued, with a validity period equal to that shown on your tourist card or visa. You may drive back and forth across the border—at any crossing—as many times as you wish during the permit's validity. You are supposed to surrender the permit at the border when your trip is over, however.

In the United States, further information on temporary vehicle importation can be obtained by calling 800/922-8228. Under an agreement between the American Automobile Association (AAA) and the Mexican government, U.S. motorists with credit cards are able to obtain both tourist cards and auto permits from AAA offices in Texas, New Mexico, Arizona, and California. In reality, all AAA does is fill out the papers for you—you still have to stop at the border, walk into the customs office, and get the papers validated. When we tried doing this with AAA forms, Mexican customs rejected them because AAA had translated some of the forms into English, and this was deemed unacceptable. In addition, the AAA office we used in California filled the forms in incorrectly, writing in the section marked "For Official Use Only." We had to start from scratch, so the trip to AAA was wasted time.

If you're renting a car with Mexican license tags, none of the above is necessary, of course.

Parking in San Ysidro

Another alternative is to drive to San Ysidro, park your vehicle in one of the guarded fee lots, and walk across the border at Tijuana or take a Mexicoach bus. San Ysidro parking lots charge US$6–10 per day or any portion thereof. To use one these lots, take the exit off I-5 reading Last U.S. Exit. **Five-Star Parking** is a good choice if you want to shuttle across the border; Mexicoach stops there.

BY FERRY FROM MAINLAND MEXICO

Until recently, three passenger ferry services ran to southern Baja from the Mexican mainland—two to La Paz and one to Santa Rosalía. As we went to press, two of the services had just been suspended. The Toppolobampo–La Paz route is now used only for cargo, and the Guaymas–Santa Rosalía route has been discontinued. It may run again in the near future, but at press time, the SEMATUR office said it didn't know when or if it might be resumed. The only remaining ferry service currently runs between Mazatlán and La Paz. With this passenger/vehicle ferry anyone driving on the mainland in the Mazatlán area can reach southern Baja without a time-consuming U-turn at the top of the peninsula. Many drivers from the American west coast use Baja ferry services as an alternative way of reaching the mainland, since it allows them to avoid traffic-heavy Mexico 15 on the way to Mazatlán and points farther south.

We've found the ferries to be comfortable and efficient in all classes. In heavy seas you may want to consider taking motion sickness tablets before boarding.

Fares and Classes

Over a decade ago the vehicle ferry system was privatized under the directorship of Grupo SEMATUR (Servicios Marítimos y Turísticos) de California, S.A., and now that fares are market-priced rather than subsidized, they've risen substantially each year. The fares listed here were valid as of 2004; allow for average inflation, roughly 18 percent per year, when making ferry plans.

Passenger fares are based on class: *salón* (bus-style reclining seats in various general-seating areas), *turista* (shared bunk rooms with washbasins), and *cabina* (small, private cabins with two single berths and toilet facilities). Some ferryboats also feature an additional *especial* class with large, deluxe cabins. Fares for children under 12 are 50 percent of adult fares.

Vehicle fares are based on the length of the vehicle—the longer the rig, the higher the fare. All fares must be paid in pesos. Passenger and vehicle fares are separate.

You must drive the vehicle into the cargo hold yourself; this is usually the most unpleasant part of the journey, as most of the vehicles crossing are Mexican 18-wheeled trucks; the diesel fumes that accumulate in the hold while everyone gets in position (as directed by the ferry crew) can be intense. Soldiers or federal police are present on the piers at both ends of the journey, searching for arms and illegal drugs with the help of trained dogs.

Note: Signs at the vehicle ferry ticket offices in La Paz warn that passenger tickets will not be issued to pregnant women.

Reservations

Whether it was the fare increases or the reorganization of management under private auspices, ferry reservations are now much easier to make than before ferry privatization. Generally, if you show up at the ferry terminal one day in advance of your desired voyage, you should be able to get passenger tickets; vehicle passage is a little more difficult to arrange. To book vehicle passage, you must hold a valid temporary vehicle import permit (see previous mention).

Salón seats are sold on a first-come, first-served basis; *turista* can be reserved three days or more in advance; a *cabina* or *especial* can be reserved a month or more in advance. During holiday periods—especially Semana Santa (the weeks before Easter Sunday) and Christmas week, when you might want to avoid ferry service altogether—you should try to pick up your tickets at least a week or two in advance. Reservations must be confirmed by 2 P.M. the day before departure.

SEMATUR operates ticket offices at its ferry piers for advance as well as day-of-departure sales. A number of Mexican travel agencies are authorized to handle ticket reservations and sales. In Ciudad Constitución: Viajes Pedrín, 613/132-1012. In La Paz: Viajes Ahome (SEMATUR office), 612/125-2366 or 612/125-2346; Viajes Transpeninsulares, 612/122-0399; Viajes Perla, 612/125-8666; and Viajes Cabo Falso, 612/125-2393. In Mazatlán: Turismo Coral, 669/981-3290. In Mexico City: Festival Tours, 55/5682-7043.

SEMATUR's toll-free information and reservation number in Mexico is 800/696-9600; this number can be dialed from the United States and Canada with the prefix 011-52. Ferry schedules and fares are posted online, though they're not always kept up-to-date; visit www.ferrysematur.com.mx (Spanish only) or www.baja-web.com/ferrysch.htm (for information in English).

Baja Ferries

A new private company, **Baja Ferries,** operates a faster ferry that completes the Topolobampo-La Paz crossing (or vice versa) in just five hours. The ferry boasts a cafeteria, night club, restaurant, bar, and space for 1,000 passengers, including a choice of seats or cabins with two to four berths and attached bath. A seat on the ferry costs US$58. If you want a cabin berth, add US$71 to this fare. You can take a car or pickup truck along for US$87. A round-trip ticket for two passengers and one car goes for US$140. For information or reservations you can call the Pichilinque Terminal at tel. 612/125-7444. If you're starting from Topolobampo, the numbers are tel. 668/862-1003 or 800/718-2796, fax 668/862-1005. Or check www.bajaferries.com.

Mazatlán–La Paz

At the moment this is the only passenger-vehicle ferry available between Baja and the mainland. All three of the craft that regularly ply this route offer a restaurant/bar, disco, small video lounge, deck bar, and cafeteria. The most popular place to hang out, in good weather, is the stern deck bar, where there's a view, a well-stocked bar, and a CD jukebox.

Ferries depart each port daily at 3 P.M., arriving on the other side around 9 A.M. Fares run US$51 *salón,* US$115 *turista,* US$141 *cabina,* and US$166 *especial.*

Vehicle tariffs are: autos under five meters (15 feet) US$389; motorhomes US$672; motorcycles US$95; trailer rigs US$720–1,329.

Getting Around

Many visitors to Baja travel the peninsula with their own vehicles—cars, trucks, campers, RVs, or motorcycles. Alternative transportation includes domestic airlines, rented cars, public buses, bicycles, and hitchhiking.

BY AIR

Domestic air travel in Baja is generally less expensive than international flights of comparable distances from the United States to Baja. It's cheaper to fly from Tijuana to La Paz or Los Cabos than from San Diego to La Paz or Los Cabos, for example. Hence, especially for San Diego residents, the minor inconvenience of flying out of Tijuana could result in a considerable savings—if your destination is either La Paz or Los Cabos.

Local Airlines

Several small airlines in Baja specialize in short flights ("puddle-jumpers") to destinations—usually Pacific islands—inaccessible by land transportation. **Aero Cedros** (formerly Aerolíneas California Pacíficos) flies between Guerrero Negro and Isla Cedros. **Sociedad Cooperativa de Producción Pesquera** (nicknamed Cannery Airlines by resident Americans) schedules flights from Ensenada's El Ciprés airfield to Isla Cedros and Bahía Tortugas. If enough passengers are on hand to make it profitable—or one passenger is very generous—this company will also fly to Isla Natividad.

Charter Flights

Companies that can arrange small-plane charters to almost any legally open airfield in Baja from southern California include: AeroCargo in Los Angeles, 800/428-2163; California Jet LLC, 8721 Santa Monica Blvd. #150, Los Angeles, CA 90069, 302/744-9273, www.californiajetcharter.com; Lundy Air Charter, 1860 Joe Crosson Dr., El Cajon, CA 92020, 858/505-5650 or 800/293-3941, www.lundyair.com; and West Coast Charters, 19711 Campus Dr. Suite 200, Santa Ana, CA 92707, 800/352-6153, www.westcoastcharters.com.

In Baja, charter flights may be arranged through **Aero Calafía,** 624/143-4255 or 624/143-4302, www.aerocalafia.com, in Cabo San Lucas.

Private Flights

With a pilot's license and a plane, you can fly to any of Baja's nearly 200 airstrips. Air traffic over Baja is light, and the paperwork for crossing the border is minimal. At the moment aviation fuel is more expensive in Mexico than in the United States—ranging from US$3.20 per gallon in Tijuana to US$5 per gallon in Guerrero Negro—so most pilots stop at Brown Field, Calexico, or Nogales to top off before crossing the border. Another reason to take on fuel at the border is that it's available at or near only a fraction of the bush strips; careful planning is required. See Private Planes under Getting There for a summary of landing taxes and fees charged to foreign pilots flying into Mexico.

Note that it is illegal to fly at any height over two bays in the Vizcaíno Biosphere Reserve—Laguna de Ojo de Liebre (Scammon's Lagoon) and Laguna San Ignacio—during the period between January 1 and June 30 every year. This law has been enacted, and is strictly enforced, to protect the large numbers of gray whales calving in the lagoons in the winter and the thousands of migratory birds feeding and nesting on the islands and along the shores of these lagoons throughout the winter and extending into the summer months.

A San Diego—area outfit calling itself **Baja Bush Pilots** publishes a 384-page guide, *Airports of Baja and Northwest Mexico,* by Arnold Senterfitt. Now in its 20th edition, the book contains aerial photos, sketch maps, and descriptions of virtually every landing strip in Baja. Few pilots fly to Baja without this book, which is available through pilot supply sources for around US$70, or you can order the book directly from Baja Bush Pilots, 149 W. Boston, Chandler, AZ 85225, 480/730-3250, fax 480/730-3251,

ON THE ROAD

jack@bajabushpilots.com, www.bajabushpilots.com. BBP also maintains a membership organization of the same name. For an annual US$39 membership fee, you'll receive quarterly updates to the Senterfitt guide, the quarterly *Baja Bush Pilots Journal,* discounts at Baja hotels and resorts, and discounted Mexican insurance rates.

A two-volume video series entitled *Fun Flying Baja,* available via Amazon.com or www2.4dcomm.com/flybaja.temporary.disabled/press.htm, takes the viewer on videographic trips through 37 airfields in Baja and reveals various tips for would-be pilots, such as how to use gasoline when aviation fuel isn't available. Video one covers the Pacific side, video two the Cortez side. Each video is around an hour and a half long and costs US$49.95.

Planes that fly into Mexico are required to carry Mexican liability insurance. Baja Bush Pilots offers inexpensive annual **aircraft insurance** policies. Current rates are posted at www.bajabushpilots.com. Every pilot must show a valid insurance policy at the border to clear customs. In addition, U.S. Customs requires an annual inspection for planes flying into the United States, whether American- or foreign-owned.

BY BUS

Intercity Bus Service

Baja's reliable intercity bus transportation covers the peninsula from Tijuana to Cabo San Lucas. The longest direct ride available is the Tijuana–Cabo San Lucas route (about 30–32 hours), operated once daily by **Autotransportes águila.** Many people break up the bus trip with an overnight stop in La Paz (25–28 hours from Tijuana) and change to one of the many La Paz–Cabo San Lucas buses the following day.

Transportes Norte de Sonora (TNS) operates buses between Tijuana, Tecate, Mexicali, and points farther west, including destinations on the Mexican mainland as far away as Mexico City.

Special express buses with hostess service and air-conditioning are used on long-distance trips. Shorter trips may or may not have air-conditioning, but the buses are always tolerably com-

bus travel in Baja

© JOE CUMMINGS

fortable. Schedules aren't always scrupulously kept, but even smaller bus terminals may feature public phones, restrooms, and cafés. The infamous "chicken buses" of southern Mexico and Central America don't exist in Baja.

Bus fares are moderate. A Tijuana–La Paz ticket on a *primera* or first-class bus, for example, costs about US$90. Second class costs about half that (although to travel second class all the way from Tijuana to La Paz would necessitate changing buses along the way). Reservations for bus travel aren't usually necessary and for shorter distances aren't accepted. On longer trips, such as Tijuana–La Paz or Mexicali–Guerrero Negro, buses may depart only once daily, so it's a good idea to drop by the terminal a day in advance to ensure seat availability.

All the Spanish you need for riding a bus is *boleto* (ticket), the name of your destination (have a map handy just in case), and a reasonable command of spoken Spanish numbers for quoted fares (although the fare is always posted somewhere on the ticket office wall).

City Buses and Colectivos

Tijuana, Ensenada, Mexicali, San Quintín, and La Paz offer comprehensive city bus systems with fares averaging US$.25–.40, payable in pesos only. City buses come in a variety of sizes and shapes, from 12-passenger vans called *colectivos* to huge modern vessels with automatic doors. In Mexicali, painted school buses are the norm. The destination or general route—typically a street name—is usually painted somewhere on the front of the bus or displayed on a marquee over the front windshield.

Printed bus schedules are either hard to come by or nonexistent. If you can't figure out which bus to take by comparing the destination sign with a map, just ask other waiting bus passengers or, if your Spanish isn't up to that, make inquiries at the tourist office.

TAXIS

Route Taxis

Tijuana, Rosarito, Ensenada, and Mexicali feature *taxis de ruta,* specially licensed cars that follow set routes similar to and often paralleling the bus routes. These vehicles are usually large American station wagons that hold up to 12 passengers. Unlike city buses, you can flag them down anywhere along the route. The destination is usually painted in whitewash on the windshield, but locals often distinguish the route by the taxis' two-tone color scheme. A *roja y crema* may run from the central bus station to a market on the outskirts of town while a *negro y azul* may travel from the cathedral to the main shopping district. Other than the terminating points of the route at either end, there are no predetermined taxi stops; passengers must let the driver know where they want off. As on city buses, route taxi fares are the same no matter where you disembark. Usually they're only a bit higher than bus fares.

Hire Taxis

Regular-hire taxis congregate at hotels and designated taxi stands in most towns of any size. Sometimes fares are posted at the hotel or taxi stand, but often you must ask for a fare quote. If possible, try to find out the fare from hotel staff or a friendly resident before approaching a taxi driver—you'll feel more secure about not getting ripped off. If the quoted fare doesn't match what you've been told in advance, you can negotiate or try another driver. Fortunately, most *bajacaliforniano* city taxi drivers quote the correct fare immediately.

In smaller towns with no buses or route taxis you may sometimes find a few regular-hire taxis hanging out by the town plaza. They're generally used for reaching out-of-town destinations, since any place in Baja without a city bus system is small enough to wander around on foot. Although the locals pay a set fare based on distance, gringos are sometimes quoted a much higher fare. Dig in and negotiate until it's reasonable. Even if you can afford the higher fare, you owe it to other foreign visitors not to encourage price-gouging.

CYCLING

Among cyclists, Baja is the most popular area in all of Mexico. Traffic is relatively light, the scenery is striking, and cyclists can pull over and camp just about anywhere.

Touring or mountain bike? If you're only heading straight down the peninsula and back on the Transpeninsular, or doing the northern loop on Mexico 2, 3, and 5, a touring bike would be the best choice, as it's lighter and faster than a mountain bike. On the other hand, the Baja peninsula offers so many great off-road rides that anyone who really wants to see Baja—and has the time—should consider a mountain bike. Off-road riding requires a stronger frame, higher clearance, and wider tires.

Many interesting trail rides lie within 95 km (60 miles) of the United States–Mexico border. Parque Nacional Constitución de 1857—less than 80 km (50 miles) southwest of Mexicali—has been called "fat-tire heaven" by cycling editors at *Outside* magazine, offering rides through startling pine forests and subalpine meadows. The Cataviña Boulder Field in the Central Desert also features some excellent trails; don't forget the antipuncture booting on that one. For coastal routes Baja's best overall rides are in Baja California Sur, particularly the unpaved Camino

Rural Costero between San José del Cabo and Cabo Pulmo and the unnamed, unpaved road between Los Barriles and Bahía de los Muertos. The unpaved road network along the coast between San José and La Paz will astound even the most jaded dirt bikers as it takes them past deserted white-sand coves with coral reefs, over jagged desert peaks, and then down into lush San Juan de los Planes.

Popular paved touring routes include Tecate to Ensenada (116 km/72 miles) and Ensenada to San Felipe (236 km/146 miles), both on scenic Mexico 3, as well as the Cape loop on Mexico 1 and Mexico 19 (La Paz–Cabo San Lucas–Todos Santos–La Paz).

Because the sun can be particularly strong when you're on paved surfaces, which both reflect and radiate heat, you may find an 11 A.M.–3 P.M. siesta necessary no matter what time of year you ride. Don't forget to bring sunglasses and plenty of high-SPF sunscreen.

Equipment and Repairs

Whether you're riding a mountain or touring bike, you'll need the same basic essentials to han-

pedaling down Mexico

© JOE CUMMINGS

dle long-distance Baja riding. If you plan to camp along the way, you'll need the usual camping and first-aid gear, selected to fit your panniers. Camping is often your only choice, even on transpeninsular trips, because some cyclists simply can't make the mileage from hotel to hotel in central Baja.

Helmets are particularly important; a head injury is even more serious when you're in the middle of nowhere. A helmet also keeps direct sun off the top of your skull. A rearview mirror is a must for keeping an eye on motorists coming from behind on narrow roads. A locking cable is preferable to a clunky U-lock for long-distance trips because it weighs less, although bicycle theft isn't much of a problem in Baja. The only other security you might need is a removable handlebar bag for carrying your camera and valuables; you can take the bag with you when stopping at restaurants or *tiendas* and fill it with snacks for eating on the fly.

Water is the uppermost consideration on overnight trips. No matter what the time of year, cyclists should carry four one-liter bottles of water per day. The one-liter bottles used for cycling are more puncture-resistant than water containers designed for camping. Punctures are always a concern in Baja because of all the trees and plants bearing spines.

The puncture threat means you should outfit your bike with heavy-duty tires and tubes. Bring along two or three spare tubes, one spare tire, a tire gauge, and a complete tire repair kit. You should also carry duct tape and moleskin—or commercial plastic booting—to use as booting material against sidewall cuts caused by sharp rocks or cactus.

Check the nuts and bolts on your rack daily and retighten as necessary. Applying Locktite should lessen the need for retightening—carry a small supply along with extra nuts and bolts. Baling wire can be used for improvised repairs; carry two or three meters along with wirecutters.

Bike shops operate in Tijuana, Ensenada, San Quintín, Ciudad Constitución, La Paz, and Cabo San Lucas. Although the Mexicans who run these shops can sometimes perform miraculous repairs using nothing resembling a bike's original parts, it's safer to come prepared with spares, especially for parts that aren't easily jury-rigged. At a minimum, carry a spare freewheel, a rear derailleur, and all the wrenches and screwdrivers necessary to work on your bike. If in addition you bring along several extra spokes, cables, and a spare chain, you'll be ready for just about any repair scenario.

Bicycle Transportation

You can take bikes on the **Tijuana Trolley** to San Ysidro and then walk over the border. Until recently it was necessary to obtain a bike pass, but this is no longer a requirement. For more information about riding a bus or trolley with your bike, call 619/233-3004. To reserve a bike locker, call 619/237-POOL (see Getting There for further trolley details).

Mexicoach and **Greyhound** will transport bikes of paying passengers in bus luggage compartments for no additional cost, but bikes should be boxed. For return trips from Baja, you should be able to pick up a box from bicycle shops in Tijuana or Ensenada or build your own from discarded cardboard boxes.

Guided Bicycle Trips

If you're unsure of your off-road cycling skills, you might want to tackle Baja with an experienced cycle guide. Several tour operators now run cycling programs in Baja.

One of our favorites is **Pedaling South,** P.O. Box 827, Calistoga, CA 94515, 707/942-4550 or 800/398-6200, fax 707/942-8017, info@ tourbaja.com, www.tourbaja.com, which specializes in southern Baja cycling and offers a wide variety of programs from tour biking to mountain biking and kayaking combos at very reasonable rates relative to most tour packages. A seven-day mountain biking/kayaking vacation out of Loreto, for example, goes for US$795, including accommodations, vehicle support, camping, meals, bikes, and kayaks. For cycling purists, Pedaling South offers six different mountain bike itineraries starting at US$695. A US$95 discount is offered to those who bring their own bikes. Prices, of course, are subject to change.

DRIVING IN BAJA

The most heroic procedure for anyone who has decided to get a general idea of what the whole peninsula is like would be to set out from San Diego in a four-wheel-drive truck well loaded with food, water, camping equipment, and reserve gasoline to carry him over the long stretches between the border and the Cape, where nothing is available. He should allow a minimum of ten days of hard driving (it may well take more) to cover the thousand road miles to the tip, and he must be prepared to assume all responsibilities for himself and his car.

Famous naturalist Joseph Wood Krutch wrote the above in his classic *The Forgotten Peninsula* as an introduction to a chapter entitled "Seeing Baja the Easy Way." It's obvious that not only was this written in a time (1961) when literary license allowed a writer to use masculine pronouns exclusively when speaking of heroic endeavors, but that it was well before the construction of La Carretera Transpeninsular Benito Juárez, otherwise known as the Transpeninsular Highway or Mexico 1.

Skeletons of cars, vans, and trucks that didn't make it, rusting among the ocotillo and *cardón* alongside Baja's highways, are visible reminders of this era. If you look closely, you'll notice that some of those decaying hulks are post-1973 models, testifying that a certain challenge remains in spite of the long strip of tarmac winding down the peninsula.

For the most part, however, the 1973 completion of the Transpeninsular opened Baja travel to ordinary folks driving ordinary passenger cars, as long as they employ a little ordinary common sense. For the adventurer, there remain miles of unpaved roads that will take you as far from civilization as anyone would care to go. Such off-highway digressions are perfect for those who might agree with another of Krutch's fiats:

Baja California is a wonderful example of how much bad roads can do for a country.

Bad roads act as filters. They separate those who are sufficiently appreciative of what lies beyond the blacktop to be willing to undergo mild inconvenience from that much larger number of travelers which is not willing. The rougher the road, the finer the filter.

Baja Highways

A 1980s *Car and Driver* magazine story stated that driving in Baja compared with driving in America "like hiking in the Rocky Mountains compares with walking on Madison Avenue"— a more than slight exaggeration even then. In terms of how it feels to drive in Baja, however, there's more than a small element of truth in this comparison—people who *really* like to drive will love driving in Baja.

In less romantic terms, driving the Transpeninsular Highway is somewhat akin to two-lane driving in some of the less populated areas of the American Southwest, with two main differences. The road conditions vary more (sometimes a lot) from one section of highway to another, and once you're well into the center of the peninsula you're farther from any significant population centers than on any comparable section of American highway—hence accidents or errors of judgment can have serious ramifications. Drivers from western Canada may feel more at home than Americans on desolate sections of Baja highway—except that the terrain is completely different from anything in Canada.

Six paved national highways grace the Baja California peninsula: Mexico 1 (the Transpeninsular, from Tijuana to Cabo San Lucas), Mexico 2 (from Tijuana to Sonora), Mexico 3 (Tecate to El Sauzal, near Ensenada, and east to Crucero La Trinidad at Mexico 5), Mexico 5 (Mexicali to San Felipe), Mexico 19 (between Cabo San Lucas and San Pedro, via Todos Santos), and Mexico 22 (Ciudad Constitución to San Carlos). The only state highways are a small cluster of relatively short blacktops in the northeast corner above the Sea of Cortez (BCN 1, 2, 3, 4, and 8, which link farm communities in the Valle de Mexicali with Mexicali and the state of Sonora), BCN 23 (linking Mexico 1 with Punta

on the road

The best unpaved roads are probably those that have evolved more or less naturally, with little or no grading. When the weather's dry, some of these roads ride better than the Transpeninsular. Of course, unpaved roads may sometimes start out nicely but get increasingly worse with each passing mile, to the point where even the most intrepid explorers are forced to turn around. At other times, a road will suddenly improve after a long stretch of cavernous potholes and caved-in sides. Weather is a big determining factor; even the best ungraded, unpaved roads are often impassable during or following a hard rain.

How do you know when to turn around? There's always an element of risk when driving down a dirt road for the first—or even the hundredth—time, but it helps to ask around before embarking on a road that doesn't see much traffic. A good road map can also assist with such decisions. The AAA map (see Services and Information) classifies unpaved roads into four categories: gravel, graded, dirt, and poor. The annotated ITM map uses a similar but more specific fourfold system: gravel, graded, unimproved dirt, and vehicular track. Although neither of these maps is entirely up-to-date nor 100 percent accurate, using one or both in conjunction with local input will greatly improve your decision-making. A topographical map could be of considerable value to a four-wheel-drive navigator as well, since sometimes it's the steep canyon grades that spell defeat.

Even with the best planning there's always the possibility of getting stuck in muddy or sandy areas. Anyone engaging in serious off-highway driving should carry along a sturdy shovel for digging out mired wheels. The folding trench shovels sold at army surplus stores pack well and may even fit beneath the passenger seat in some vehicles. Some four-wheelers carry lengths of heavy rippled plastic—the kind used for "hall runners" to protect carpet in tacky home decor—to place between the front and back wheels when mired in soft sand; these can easily be rolled up and stored when not needed. Another handy trick for negotiating soft ground is to let the air out of your tires to a pressure of around 12–15 psi. This really works, but you should also carry

Banda), and the solitary BCS 286 in the south between La Paz and San Juan de los Planes.

In addition, Mexico 1 features two alternate routings, a four-lane toll road between Tijuana and Ensenada and a two-lane digression to Bahía de los Ángeles on the Sea of Cortez coast. All other roads in Baja are gravel, dirt, or some combination thereof.

Off-Highway Travel

Like the highways, Baja's unpaved roads vary considerably, from rutted jeep tracks to elevated, graded, gravel boulevards. The trouble with the graded unpaved roads is that they tend to degenerate quickly between gradings into washboard surfaces impossible to drive at anything but very low speeds (8–16 kph/5–10 mph)—unless you want to risk crushed vertebrae and a dropped transmission.

The effect of these unpaved roads on you and your vehicle depends a lot on what you're driving. Some off-highway Baja navigators drive pickups with customized shocks and suspension that enable a driver to float over the worst washboard surfaces. Other drivers—like many of the local residents, who can't afford heavy-duty, customized rigs—learn to drive slowly and appreciate the scenery.

HOW MUCH FARTHER?

Distances from Tijuana, along the Transpeninsular Highway, using the Tijuana-Ensenada toll road:

Ensenada:	109 km (68 miles)
San Quintín:	301 km (187 miles)
El Rosario:	359 km (226 miles)
Cataviña:	481 km (298 miles)
Punta Prieta:	599 km (371 miles)
Bahía de los Ángeles:	654 km (405 miles)
Guerrero Negro:	714 km (443 miles)
San Ignacio:	856 km (531 miles)
Santa Rosalía:	928 km (575 miles)
Mulegé:	990 km (614 miles)
Loreto:	1,125 km (698 miles)
Ciudad Constitución:	1,268 km (786 miles)
La Paz:	1,483 km (919 miles)
Cabo San Lucas:	1,704 km (1,056 miles)

along a 12-volt air compressor, one that will plug into the cigarette lighter, for pumping the tires back up after you're on firm ground again.

A nylon web towing strap—rather than chains, rope, or steel cable—is the best towing medium. **Ecological 4-Wheeling Adventures,** P.O. Box 12137, Costa Mesa, CA 92627, 949/645-7733, fax 949/645-7738, info@eco4wd.com, organizes off-highway trips in Baja, including a six-day trip from San Ysidro, California (opposite Tijuana), to Misión San Borja for US$835 per vehicle (and two people), and a four-day trip to San Felipe and Laguna Hansen for US$655. Dedicated to safe and ecological off-highway driving, the trips are led by recognized expert Harry "Silver Coyote" Lewellyn.

Driving Precautions

The first rule of Baja driving, no matter what kind of road you're on, is *never* take the road for granted. Any highway in Baja, including the Transpeninsular, can serve up 100 meters of smooth, seamless blacktop followed immediately by 100 meters of contiguous potholes or large patches of missing asphalt. A cow, horse, or burro could be right around the next curve, or a large dog could leap out in front of your vehicle just as you fasten your eyes on a turkey vulture drying its wings on top of a tall *cardón*.

The speed limits set by the Mexican government—80 kph (48 mph) on most highways, 110 kph (66 mph) on the Ensenada toll road—are very reasonable for Baja's highway conditions. Obey them and you'll be much safer than if you try to keep the speedometer needle in the spot you're accustomed to. Wandering livestock, relatively narrow highways widths (6–8 meters/19–25 feet max), and inconsistent highway maintenance mean you simply can't drive at U.S./Canada speeds.

Most Baja roadways also suffer from a conspicuous lack of shoulders. This doesn't mean you won't find any places to pull off, as some Baja writers have implied—gravel turnouts appear fairly regularly, and in many areas you can drive directly onto the roadside from the highway. It just means you can't count on a safe margin in an emergency situation. At the very least, an emergency turnout will raise a lot of rocks and dirt—small dangers in themselves—and in some spots, like the sierras on Mexico 3, leaving the highway can launch you and your vehicle into a thousand-foot freefall. Guardrails are often flimsy or nonexistent.

Yet another reason not to take the road for granted is the high frequency of sometimes unmarked blind curves and blind hilltops. Never assume a clear path around a curve or over a hilltop—potential obstructions include an oblivious 18-wheeler or bus passing in the opposite direction, wandering livestock, rock slides, or road washouts. To be on the safe side, keep toward the outside edge of your own lane. Commercial truck drivers in Baja roar down the road as if they're exempt from all speed limits, almost always flying at least 40 kph over the posted limit.

Rule number two: Never drive the highways at night. Except along portions of the Ensenada toll road and along the Corridor Highway that runs between San José del Cabo and Cabo San

Lucas, Baja highways have no lighting. In addition, reflectors and even painted lines are absent from many highway sections; even if no other vehicles besides your own were on the road at night, you could easily overshoot an unexpected curve. Add to this the fact that many poorly maintained local vehicles have nonfunctioning headlights, taillights, or brakelights, and it should be obvious that trying to make highway miles after sundown is crazy. Some *bajacalifornianos* may do it, but they're used to local conditions and know the roads relatively well. A high proportion of car accidents in Baja—around 80 percent according to insurance companies—occur at night.

When you see road signs marked **Vado** or **Zona de Vados,** slow down. The word *vado* is most often translated as "dip," but in Baja it usually means more than a slight depression in the road—it's any place where the road intersects an arroyo, or dry stream wash. The danger lies not only in the sudden grade drop but in the potential for running into a recently accumulated body of water. Some *vados* feature measuring sticks marked in meters; when water is present, you'll know roughly how deep it is. If you come to a *vado* full of water with no measuring stick, get out of your vehicle and measure the depth yourself using an ocotillo branch or other suitable object.

Vados aren't always signposted, so stay alert—they appear even on relatively flat terrain. Some *vados* are relatively mild road dips, while others are particularly treacherous, even in dry weather. The *vados* south of San Felipe on the road to Puertecitos are deadly—crossing them at a high rate of speed can severely damage the undercarriage of a passenger car.

Also watch out for sand drifts, which often aren't visible until it's almost too late to avoid them. They're most common in the San Felipe area but can occur anywhere in Baja where a road runs through sandy terrain.

In cities, *pueblos, ejidos,* or anywhere else people live in Baja, you'll encounter *topes* (speed bumps). Often unpainted and unsignposted, they can really sneak up on you. Some *topes* are real industrial-strength tire-poppers, so always take it very slow when traversing them.

Highway Signs

One of the pleasures of driving in Baja is the relative absence of signs cluttering the roadside. Billboards, in fact, are virtually nonexistent in most areas. The Mexican government does have a system of highway signs, however, based on common international sign conventions followed throughout most of the world; these can be very helpful as long as you know what they mean. Most display self-explanatory symbols (e.g., a silhouette of a person holding a shovel means "road crew working").

Along the Transpeninsular Highway as well as on many secondary roads, you can measure driving progress with the assistance of regularly spaced kilometer markers, usually black lettering on a reflective white background. In northern Baja these markers start at zero (K0) in Tijuana and ascend in number as you proceed southward. Starting at *paralelo* 28, the state borderline between Baja California Norte and Baja California Sur (BCN and BCS) the markers descend as you

© JOE CUMMINGS

Slow down!

ROAD SIGNS

move southward, beginning with K220 in Guerrero Negro. These contrary directions can be traced to the original construction of the Transpeninsular, which started at either end of the peninsula and met in the middle. To further add to the confusion, sometimes the numbers run only as far as the next town, then start over. Still, the markers can be a significant navigational aid, especially when you want to take note of a remote off-highway spot for a future trip.

Cautionary sign captions are especially helpful, including *Curva Peligrosa* (Dangerous Curve), *Despacio* (Slow), and *Zona de Vados* (Dip Zone). Other common highway signs include *Desviación* (Detour), *No Tire Basura* (Don't Throw Trash), *Conserve Su Derecha* (Keep to the Right), *Conceda Cambio de Luces* (Dim Your

Lights), *No Rebase* (No Passing), and *No Hay Paso* (Road Closed).

If you're having tire trouble, look for homemade signs reading Llantera, Desponchadora, or Vulcanizadora, all of which indicate tire repair shops. Our favorite Mexican traffic sign is No Maltrate las Señales—Don't Mistreat the Signs.

Traffic Offenses

Although Mexican traffic police don't go out of their way to persecute foreign drivers, it may seem that way when you're the foreigner who's stopped. The more cautiously you drive, the less likely you'll inadvertently transgress local traffic codes. This would seem like obvious advice, but for some reason many visiting motorists in Baja drive as if they think there are no traffic laws in

Mexico. Most of these people seem to have California plates.

If you're stopped by a *tránsito* (traffic cop), the first rule is to behave in a patient, civil manner. The officer might then let you off with just a warning. If the officer decides to make a case of it, you'll be asked to proceed to the nearest police post or station, where a fine will be assessed and collected. This is a perfectly legal request. But if the cop suggests or even hints at being paid on the spot, you're being hit up for *la mordida,* the minor bribe.

In Baja, requests for *mordida* from foreigners—for traffic offenses, at least—have become increasingly rare, and the government is making admirable progress toward stamping out the practice altogether. If confronted with such a situation, you have two choices. Mexico's Attorney General for the Protection of Tourists recommends you insist on going to the nearest station to pay the fine, and that as you pay you request a receipt. Such a request may result in all charges being dropped. If you don't feel like taking the time for a trip to the station, you can choose to negotiate the "fine" on the spot. Doing so, however, won't contribute to the shrinking of the *mordida* phenomenon.

Along Mexico 1-D, the toll highway between Tijuana and Ensenada, the federal highway police claim to be using radar speed detectors nowadays. Fines are assessed at a day's Mexican minimum wage (currently about US$5) for each kilometer over the speed limit. The fine is the same for foreigners as for Mexican nationals. The offender's driving license is attached to the citation and delivered to the nearest Baja *tránsito* station, or to another Baja station chosen by the offender, where the license is returned upon payment of the assessed fine. If you're cited just outside Tijuana, for example, you can elect to settle your citation in Ensenada.

Aside from speeding on Mexico 1-D, driving the wrong direction on one-way streets and running stop signs are the two most common traffic violations among foreign drivers in Baja. In Ensenada, for example, the stop (Alto) signs seem almost intentionally hidden in places; also, several intersections display no vertical signs at all, only broad stripes painted on the pavement indicating where vehicles are supposed to stop. The best practice is to assume you're supposed to stop at every single intersection in the city, which is pretty close to the truth. This can be generalized to include most other urban areas on the peninsula.

In Mulegé only two streets in town are open to two-way traffic; all the others are supposed to be one-way, although they're not signposted at every intersection. Always look carefully at the cars driving or parked on a street to determine which direction is legal before turning.

Note to patriotic visitors: In Mexico it's illegal to display any foreign national flag except over an embassy or consulate. A miniature flag flying from a vehicle's radio antenna provides Mexican police with a valid excuse to pull you over. It may also invite vandalism—Mexicans are extremely nationalistic. This is rarely a problem, but don't say you weren't warned.

Insurance

It's very important to carry a Mexican liability insurance policy on your vehicle while driving in Baja. In case of an accident, such a policy could keep you from going to jail. For details on Mexican insurance, see Driving into Baja under Getting There.

Fuel

The only automotive fuel commercially available in Mexico is sold at government-owned Pemex stations. The total number of Pemex stations in Baja varies from year to year, but they're always scarce outside the large cities. It's best to top off your tank whenever it reaches the half-empty mark and there's a Pemex station at hand.

Three kinds of fuel are available: an unleaded fuel with an octane rating of 87 (Magna Sin); a high-test unleaded rated at 89 (Premium), and diesel. All three are priced by Pemex according to standard rates and shouldn't vary from station to station. Because Pemex is government-owned, you don't see the week-to-week price fluctuations common in countries where oil companies are privately owned and rates influenced by small changes in international oil prices. All are roughly equivalent in price to their U.S. or Canadian

AUTOMOTIVE EQUIPMENT

Although plenty of visitors drive the length of the Baja peninsula and back without so much as a spare tire, anyone driving long distances in Baja should consider bringing the following extras, regardless of the type of vehicle:

- air filters
- battery cables
- brake, clutch, steering, and transmission fluids
- 8-meter (25-foot) tow rope
- emergency flares
- fan belts
- fire extinguisher
- fuel filters
- fuses
- lug wrench and jack
- one five-gallon water container
- one or two five-gallon gas cans
- radiator hoses
- spare tire
- spark plugs
- tire gauge
- tube-repair kit (if appropriate)
- 12-volt air compressor
- water filters

counterparts. The price should always be marked in pesos on the pump. Nearly all Pemex pumps in Baja now give readouts calibrated for the new peso, and they zero out automatically when the fuel nozzle is lifted from the pump.

Make sure the pump is zeroed before the attendant starts pumping your gasoline/diesel. If the nozzle hasn't been returned to the pump since the last sale, you could find your fuel total added to the previous customer's. This seems to be less of a problem than in previous years; stations in the border towns are still the most likely places to overcharge. It helps to get out of your vehicle to keep an eye on the pumping procedures. If you're confused by the pump readout, currency conversion, or price per liter, carry a handheld calculator to make sure it all

adds up; a calculator held in clear view deters most potential cheaters. As more new pumps are added they will be calibrated to read in new pesos to conform to the currency. This should make calculations considerably easier. A new scam (to us) for gas overcharging at modern, auto-zeroing pumps is to use a gas hose that comes from an open pump on the opposite side, so you can't see whether the readout starts at zero.

Fuel must be paid for in cash, so be sure to carry plenty of pesos for fuel purchases. Mexican currency is the overwhelming preference of most Pemex stations; some stations near the United States–Mexico border take U.S. dollars, but the rate is always rounded down.

Rumors about the quality of Pemex fuels sometimes suggest an extra fuel filter or additive are necessary. This may have been the case 15 or more years ago, but nowadays Pemex fuel seems to perform well with all types of vehicles.

The main problem with Pemex fuel remains its availability, although in recent years the situation has improved. Long lines at small-town stations—the lines at the Mulegé Pemex are legendary—and the occasional selling out of all types of fuel at a particular station are not uncommon. To notify customers, the hose is usually draped over the top of a pump when it's empty. Major culprits for pump sell-outs are American RV caravans; if 10 or 15 RVs fuel up at a Pemex station when it's between deliveries, the station may have to shut down until the next Pemex tanker arrives.

Liquefied petroleum gas (LPG) is available in Baja. The price per liter is about the same as for Magna Sin when bought for vehicular purposes. LPG sold for heating and cooking is subsidized and costs less than in the United States or Canada. The difficulty is finding it. Look for signs reading Butano.

Oil

Motor oil is widely available at *tiendas* and Pemex stations throughout Baja. If your vehicle takes anything lower (thinner) than 30-weight, however, you'd better bring along your own; most places stock only 30- or 40-weight oil.

Parts and Repairs

Good auto shops and mechanics are available in Tijuana, Mexicali, Ensenada, La Paz, San José del Cabo, and, to a lesser extent, San Quintín, El Rosario, Mulegé, Loreto, and Cabo San Lucas. Elsewhere in Baja, if you have a breakdown, it's either do it yourself or rely on the mercy of passing drivers. In areas where you can find a mechanic, the following makes can usually be serviced: Chevrolet, Dodge, Ford, Nissan, Toyota, and Volkswagen. For anything else, you should carry spare filters, plugs, points, hoses, belts, and gaskets—even for the shortest of trips.

Green Angels (Roadside Assistance)

The Secretaría de Turismo operates a fleet of green trucks called **Ángeles Verdes (Green Angels)** that patrol Baja's highways and offer professional assistance to anyone with automotive problems. Founded in 1960, this is the only such highway-assistance program in the world.

Each truck carries a first-aid kit, a shortwave radio, gasoline, and a variety of common auto parts. They're usually staffed by two uniformed employees, one of whom may speak some English. The drivers will perform minor repairs for the cost of the parts and can provide towing for distances up to 24 km (15 miles). If they can't remedy the problem or tow your vehicle to a nearby mechanic, they'll give you a lift or arrange for other assistance. They can also radio for emergency medical assistance if necessary.

The trucks supposedly patrol assigned highway sections at least twice a day; the author's experience is that the Green Angels are much more commonly seen south of Santa Rosalía, where they're most needed due to the longer distances between towns.

Mexico's federal highway department maintains 29 **roadside call boxes** at approximate three-km intervals along the Tijuana-Ensenada toll road. Calls are free and bilingual operators are on duty 24 hours a day to help arrange emergency medical or automotive assistance.

Trailers and RVs

Baja is a popular destination for RVers. Not only are there plenty of RV parks with services, but you can pull off the road and camp just about anywhere outside the cities, with few restrictions. The restrictions are largely physical; numerous

automotive angels

© JOE CUMMINGS

places simply can't accommodate a wide trailer or motorhome because of narrow roadways, steep grades, or sharp curves. Even the Transpeninsular is tight in some places. In fact, you shouldn't even attempt a Baja trip in any rig wider than three meters (10 feet).

Caravans: An RV caravan, in which a number of individual RV owners travel as an organized group with a caravan leader, is one way to accomplish an RV trip to Baja. Average costs run about US$100 a day, not including food and gasoline. In theory, RV caravans are a great introduction to Baja for RVers apprehensive about going it alone. The reality, however, is that everyone else on the road will hate an RV caravan if its members cause traffic jams—especially on winding, mountainous roads—or suck the Pemex stations dry. Those traveling to Baja in RV caravans must therefore carefully monitor their own behavior to ensure they do not become a menace or trial to others on the road. Caravans limited to no more than two or three vehicles are probably best. Keep in mind, though, that it's much cheaper to do it on your own—for US$100 a day you could be driving a more manageable sedan and staying in hotels.

The type of rig most suited to Baja travel is probably a well-equipped camper or van. With a bed, two 20-liter (five-gallon) water containers, a small propane stove and refrigerator, and a portable toilet, you can travel just as independently as someone driving a 12-meter (40-foot) motorhome. Add a deep-cycle RV battery under the hood and you can run a variety of electrical appliances for at least a week without turning over your engine. For extra power, mount a solar panel on top of the cab or camper.

When tricking out your rig, consider oversize tires for more traction and road clearance, overload shocks to protect your vehicle and its contents on rough roads, and a rollbar over the front seats. Whether or not you have high clearance, skid plates under your fuel tank, engine, and transmission are a good idea if you plan any off-highway driving.

What's the perfect Baja rig? Such a beast doesn't really exist, of course, because we all have individual needs. (How about a kayak with wings?)

Probably a near-perfect rig would combine features of the self-sufficient camper as described above with those of a rugged four-wheel-drive vehicle featuring a turning circle of six meters (20 feet) or less. Ambitious Baja hands have successfully tried everything from jeeps to three-ton diesel cabs as bases for custom-built campers. **Callen Camper,** 619/442-3305, in El Cajon, California, specializes in custom-outfitting Baja camper rigs.

For four-wheel-drive truckers expecting to travel off-highway, **Four Wheel Pop-Up Camper,** 1460 Churchill Downs Ave., Woodland, CA 95776, 800/242-1442, fwc@fourwheelcampers.com, offers a compact, stable solution. The camper's low-profile design produces less wind drag than conventional cabover campers and helps maintain a lower center of gravity. The roof lifts to provide a stand-up camper when parked.

Car Rental

You can rent cars in Tijuana, Rosarito, Mexicali, Ensenada, Loreto, La Paz, San José del Cabo, and Cabo San Lucas. In general, Tijuana, Cabo San Lucas, and San José del Cabo offer the least-expensive rentals, while Ensenada and Loreto agencies are the most expensive. At many agencies, various Volkswagen models are all that's available; most rental places charge daily rates of around US$40–45 for a VW Bug or Chevy Pop, US$50–55 for a VW Golf or Nissan Tsuru II (Sentra), US$65–70 for a Jeep Wrangler, and US$50–75 for a VW *combi* (van), plus per-kilometer fees ranging US$.20–.45 per kilometer. Often a little negotiating will get these same daily rates without any kilometer charges. Rates include Mexican liability insurance but not collision damage. For added collision coverage, figure an extra US$18–25 a day.

If you're planning on driving long distances, you can save money by arranging a flat rate with no kilometer costs. If you can rent by the week, the savings increase considerably. Typical long-distance deals in Baja might include a made-in-Mexico Chevy Pop (no a/c or radio) for US$150 per week, with unlimited free kilometers. One of the better companies for advance booking—

often less expensive than on-the-spot rentals—is **Avis International,** U.S./Canada tel. 800/331-1212, Mexico 800/712-1112, www.avis.com. It's worth checking in advance to see what kind of specials they may be running.

Rentals out of San Diego are sometimes a bit cheaper, but most agencies that allow their cars into Mexico won't allow them any farther south than Guerrero Negro. They often add mandatory collision damage waivers to the cost as well.

One company that specializes in vehicle rentals for all-Baja driving is **California Baja Rent-A-Car,** 9245 Jamacha Blvd., Spring Valley, CA 91977, 619/470-7368, U.S./Canada tel. 888/470-7368, fax 619/479-2004, info@cabaja.com or reservations@cabaja.com, www.cabaja.com. California Baja offers Jeep Cherokees, Jeep Wranglers, GMC Suburbans, Ford Explorers, Ford 4x4 pickups, plus various passenger cars, vans and convertibles. Internet discount rates start at US$36 a day plus US$.32 per mile beyond 100 miles per day (the first 100 miles driven each day are free) for a subcompact. A Wrangler rents for US$89 a day plus US$.32 per mile (100 free miles per day), while a Land Rover Discovery II 4x4 costs US$109 daily plus US$.35 per mile (100 free miles per day). Mexican insurance is not included in these discounted rates. Drop-offs in Cabo San Lucas can be arranged for an extra charge. The company also rents GPS units for US$9 a day, and Iridum satellite phones for US$10 per day plus online time.

Motorcycles

Much of Baja is excellent motorcycle country. The winding sierra roads are especially challenging, and since traffic is generally light you can really let it rip. Another advantage of motorcycle travel in Baja is that if your bike gets mired in soft ground, you can almost always extricate it without assistance.

As with automotive travel in Baja, pre-depar-

ture planning is important. You should be able to carry enough gear in two panniers and a backpack (tied down on the rear) for a trip all the way down the peninsula.

Motorcycle mechanics in Baja are few and far between—you must be entirely self-reliant to make this trip safely and successfully. Besides the usual camping and first-aid gear, bikers should carry all tools needed for routine maintenance, spare brake shoes, a tire repair kit, spare levers, an extra battery, a clutch cable, spare light bulbs, a four-liter reserve gas can, and a spare helmet visor.

For a transpeninsular trip, any bike smaller than 600cc is too small. A four-stroke gets better mileage than a two-stroke, an important consideration given the Baja gas station situation. Experienced Baja bikers replace standard fuel tanks with larger 20-liter tanks to extend their fuel range.

The same driving precautions that apply to four-wheel driving should be followed by bikers as well. Special care should be taken when negotiating blind curves because buses and trucks in Baja aren't used to seeing motorcycles on the highway. As with bicycle touring, motorcyclists may find that an 11 A.M.–3 P.M. siesta is necessary to avoid the sun's worst rays.

Several small tour operators have tried to offer motorcycling programs in Baja, but so far only two have lasted more than a couple of years. **Chris Haines Motorcycle Adventure,** P.O. Box 966, Trabuco Canyon, CA 92678, 866/262-8635, fax 949/888-1569, hainestours@aol.com, www.bajaoffroadtours.com, operates four-day rides from Ensenada to Mike's Sky Ranch for US$1,500–1,900 (depending on dates) and seven-day rides from Ensenada to Cabo San Lucas for US$4,500, inclusive of all equipment and road support. Custom itineraries are also available. The company uses Honda XR series off-road bikes, ranging from 200cc–650cc. **Baja Off-Road Adventures,** www.bajaoffroad.com, is similar.

Northern Baja

Tijuana and Vicinity

With a population well over a million, Tijuana is the seventh-largest city in Mexico. It's also one of Mexico's youngest cities, established as a line of defense against American freebooters like William Walker (see the Introduction chapter) following the Treaty of Guadalupe Hidalgo in 1848. During the U.S. Prohibition era, when Americans flocked south to the city's casinos, cantinas, and bordellos, Tijuana developed a bawdy, rough-and-tumble reputation. That image persists in the minds of many gringos, though the city has long since changed.

Today's Tijuana is a rapidly modernizing, bi-cultural city, where skyscrapers and shopping malls have replaced yesterday's shantytowns, and discos outnumber cantinas. A nearby industrial zone supports more than 500 *maquiladoras* or in-bond plants where international companies such as Sony, Kodak, and Mattel manufacture export products. Tijuana's colleges and universities (Colegio de la Frontera Norte, Iberoamericana University, Universidad Autónoma de Baja California) attract students from all over the peninsula as well as northwestern Mexico.

For some visitors "TJ" is merely a gateway to Baja, while for others—especially San Diegans—it's a destination in its own right. Like the rest of

ELANDA.R.M

© KIT KALAMARAS

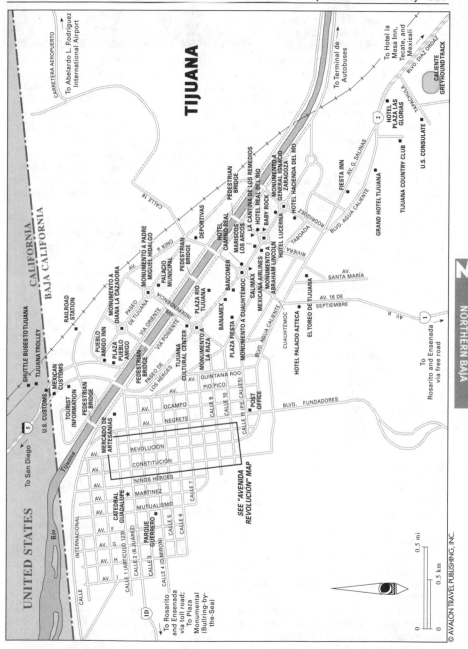

Baja, Tijuana enjoys duty-free status, and hence one of its main attractions is shopping—everything from Casas Grandes pottery to Tequila Sauza to Louis Vuitton luggage is available at discount prices. Avenida Revolución, once the city's booze-and-gambling center, is now lined with restaurants, cafés, and boutiques. Bullfights are no longer the only cultural attraction; the Tijuana Cultural Center and other city venues host symphonies, theater, art exhibits, and other events, thus firmly establishing Tijuana as northern Baja's cultural heart.

And yes, you can still don a glittering sombrero and have your photo taken sitting atop a zebra-striped burro, in front of a cloth canvas painted with famous Aztec royals.

CLIMATE

As in nearby San Diego, the climate in Tijuana is moderate year-round. Nov.–Mar., temperatures average 16°C (60°F) during the day, 12°C (53°F) at night. Rain is more likely this time of year but shouldn't deter a visit; the city generally receives less than 25 cm (10 inches) per annum. June–Sept., temperatures average 22–29°C (72–85°F) during the day and 18–21°C (65–70°F) at night. It rarely rains in summer; on still days, however, a thin layer of smog (originating in Los Angeles) may collect over the city. In fall and spring, daytime temperatures hover in the low 20s C (70s F).

HISTORY

The Frontier

Before the end of the Mexican-American War in 1848, when the Río Tijuana was designated as the westernmost portion of the United States–Mexico border, no town as such existed in the shallow river valley. Until the postwar border agreement, the border between Alta and Baja California lay about 20 miles farther south near El Descanso.

San Dieguito and Yumano Amerindian cultures intermittently occupied the area before the Spanish came in the late 17th century; the Yumano called the valley Ti-wan, meaning "Near

NORTHERN BAJA HIGHLIGHTS

Tijuana: This bustling gateway to Baja has stripped away its booze-and-gambling shroud to expose a culturally rich, shopping-heavy city of over one million residents (page 159).

Fox Studios Baja: Visit Estudios de la Playa in Popotla to get a behind-the-scenes glimpse at what movie-making is like (page 197).

La Bufadora: Twenty-five km from Ensenada, this blowhole spumes up to 30 meters at high tide, cooling off onlookers on the lower viewing platform who get caught in its spray (page 230).

Valle de Guadalupe: Taste Mexico's finest vintages at the renowned wineries in this fertile valley along Mexico 3 between Tecate and Ensenada (page 262).

Mike's Sky Ranch: Relive the ranching life of old Baja in the Sierra San Pedro Mártir (page 233).

Ejido Eréndira: Surfing, fishing, and camping are the draws at this out-of-the-way Pacific beach (page 236).

Tecate: "Mexico's Cleanest Window" on the United States–Mexico border is also famed for its many *taquerías* and the town's namesake *cerveza* (page 253).

Cañon de Guadalupe: A collection of turquoise-hued hot springs perched above the desert plains of northeastern Baja rewards those willing to tackle washboard roads from Mexicali (page 280).

Laguna Hanson: Camp and hike along the pine-studded banks of this natural lake high in the Sierra de Juárez (page 282).

San Felipe: When the weather's too cool for a dip along Northern Baja's Pacific coast, the mild Sea of Cortez waters at San Felipe are always inviting (page 290).

the Sea." Early 19th-century maps refer to today's Río Tijuana as Arroyo de Tijuan, obviously a Spanish rendering of the Yumano name. A local Mexican ranch in existence as early as 1809 was called Rancho Tia Juana—"Tijuan" had no Spanish meaning and "Tia Juana" (Aunt Jane) was easier to pronounce. Anglo settlers in California somehow latched onto this name, and today many Americans persist in calling the city "Tiawana." The pronunciation might have remained a southern California colloquialism if it hadn't been for the Kingston Trio's 1959 international hit "The Tia Juana Jail."

In the 1870s the Mexican government established a small customs house at the border, but Tijuana would probably have remained nothing more than a ranching area if it hadn't been for the development of San Diego across the border. In 1887 a savvy developer built the sprawling Hotel del Coronado, which advertised the locale's favorable year-round climate and quickly became a famous resort. A minor gold rush in the El Alamo area of northern Baja in 1888 brought additional American attention to the border area.

The Mexicans, knowing that wherever Americans congregated there was a danger of losing real estate, created the "Pueblo de Tijuana" or Town of Tijuana in 1889 and promoted the local hot mineral springs, Pozo de Agua Caliente. A small bathing resort established at the springs extolled the virtues of the water for treatment of rheumatism and arthritis, attracting visitors from across the border. During the Spanish-American War in 1898, San Diego grew further with the establishment of a U.S. naval base, and following the war many Navy men and their families chose to remain in the San Diego area. By the turn of the century, local entrepreneurs had opened several small resort hotels in Tijuana to compete with those in San Diego. Visitors made the 64-km (40-mile) trip between San Diego and Tijuana by horse or stagecoach; since there was no bridge in those days it was necessary to ford the Río Tijuana.

U.S. attention focused on Tijuana during a local revolution in the early 20th century. Following the 1910 Mexican Revolution, a group of Industrial Workers of the World (Wobblies), affiliated with the Mexican Liberal Party and under the leadership of Ricardo Magón, briefly took control of the town. Hundreds of San Diegans watched from the U.S. side of the border as Mexican federal troops entered Tijuana on June 22, 1911, to rout the Magonistas, killing 31 rebels.

This was the first time many Americans had heard of Tijuana.

Prohibition and Tourism

The town's frontier image was further enhanced in 1915 when the Tijuana Fair proffered bullfights, horse racing, boxing, cockfighting, and casino gambling. Curious San Diegans came in droves for the event, but Tijuana returned to its sleepy state once the fair was over. The city boomed practically overnight, however, when the San Diego city government banned cabaret dancing in 1917; as Tijuana's casinos and cabarets multiplied, the city began drawing visitors from Hollywood—only a three-hour drive away.

The 1920 grand opening of Tijuana's magnificent El Casino de Agua Caliente coincided with the announcement of the 18th Amendment to the U.S. Constitution, which prohibited the sale, manufacture, and consumption of alcoholic beverages. Well-heeled U.S. residents flocked to the plush new casino, which had no peer anywhere in the Americas. The lavish interior blended art deco, Spanish colonial, Moorish, and French provincial designs; Hollywood glitterati such as Douglas Fairbanks, Jean Harlow, Rita Hayworth, Clark Gable, Dolores del Rio, and the Aga Khan danced on its Italian marble floors beneath Louis XV chandeliers.

As the Tijuana high life boomed, rich American and Mexican investors poured millions of dollars into developing more racetracks, casinos, hotels, restaurants, and high-class bordellos. Mexicans from the interior of Mexico, hearing that the gutters of Tijuana ran with money (literally true inasmuch as drunk Americans were notorious for dropping change and greenbacks as they stumbled in and out of taxis), rushed to Tijuana as well.

Post–World War II Tijuana

Tijuana's golden days of sin lasted until the repeal of Prohibition in 1933. The ensuing slump became a crash when President Lázaro Cárdenas outlawed casino gambling in 1938 and expropriated all the resorts and lands around Agua Caliente, including those owned by Mexicans. Baja—and the rest of Mexico—

LA FRONTERA

We often think of international borders as thin lines separating entirely different worlds—geopolitical reference points that symbolize a great gulf between cultures. But the reality along the United States–Mexico border is that this jagged line—extending 3,326 km (2,062 miles) from the Gulf of Mexico in the east to the Pacific Ocean in the west—acts more as a glue binding cultures together.

Here First World meets Third World, and northern-European Protestant capitalism meets southern-European Catholic feudalism, forming a third, hybrid culture that's neither American nor Mexican. This newer world has its own name, "La Frontera"—the frontier—and its own culture, *fronteriza*. White Anglo-Saxons dine on fish tacos and breakfast burritos regularly and celebrate the availability of inexpensive, handmade leather boots, while mestizos (Mexicans of mixed Spanish and Amerindian ancestry) patronize Pizza Hut and use installment plans to purchase Japanese-made washing machines at Wal-Mart—all without ever crossing the border.

As a cultural region, La Frontera extends as far as 100 miles north and south of the border.

Despite the fact that Mexico ranks as America's second-largest trading partner, this wide swath contains some of the poorest areas in either country. The burgeoning twin-plant *(maquila* or *maquiladora)* industry along the Mexican side of the border, in which American—and increasingly, Canadian, European, and Japanese—technology and management exploits cheap Mexican labor, was supposed to be the hope of the future for the borderland. Goods produced at these plants are granted special trade status because they're established in "export processing zones" using U.S. capital. But the *maquilas* have been heavily criticized in recent years for their contribution to regional air and water pollution as well as worker exploitation.

As the number of *maquilas* increases, more unemployed Mexicans migrate to Northern Mexico in hopes of landing steady though low-paying jobs. Once on the border there's the attraction of higher-paying work just over the river, so labor tends to flow back and forth according to supply-and-demand forces in the border labor market. Many Mexicans work on the U.S. side during the day and sleep at home in Mexico at night.

was able to reverse its precipitous economic decline only after the outbreak of World War II. To alleviate unemployment in the border area, and to provide needed labor for the wartime U.S. economy, the United States and Mexico created the Bracero Program in 1942; this program gave Mexican workers the temporary right to work for American agricultural concerns in California. Another action that prevented Tijuana from becoming a ghost town was the declaration of Baja California as a duty-free zone.

The expansion of San Diego's military presence during World War II brought a new prosperity to the San Diego–Tijuana area, and shopping gradually replaced boozing and gambling as the main Tijuana attraction. Many Californians crossed the border regularly to purchase items rationed in the United States during the war—stockings, butter, meat, gasoline. Eventually, Tijuana began

to grow even faster than San Diego; between 1950 and 1970 the city's population grew 600 percent. This growth severely taxed the city's infrastructure as Tijuana became ringed by shantytowns practically overnight.

The situation of too many people and too few jobs created problems on both sides of the border. Although the United States discontinued the Bracero Program in the early 1960s, the flow of migrant labor to California continued. Improper sewage and garbage disposal on both sides of the border threatened to turn the San Diego–Tijuana area into an environmental disaster. Periodic flooding of the Río Tijuana was a bane to communities on either side as unchecked development came ever closer to the river.

Because there was simply no alternative, United States–Mexico cooperation over the last 25 years has begun to deal successfully with these problems. The arrival of the *maquiladoras* in the 1970s and

Human Smuggling

The westernmost 27 km of the border—between the Otay Mountains and the Pacific Ocean—is commonly called *la tierra de nadie* (no man's land) and is the busiest area of illegal human traffic in the world. Ninety percent of all illegal entries into the U.S. state of California occur here. Visitors driving south just north of the Tijuana international gateway often see Mexicans running alongside the freeway as they make their way into or out of Mexico—part of the daily commute. Made from surplus Gulf War materials, the corrugated metal fence running along the border has had an arguable effect on migration patterns but has not stopped the flow. The fence has become a canvas for graffiti artists on the Mexico side. Slogans scrawled on the metal compare the fence to the Berlin Wall; whether to call it a "fence" or a "wall" has become very much a political choice on both sides of the line.

For more permanent immigration, and to better avoid the U.S. Border Patrol, "coyotes" or *polleros* regularly smuggle groups of 7–10 *pollos* ("chickens," undocumented immigrants) across the border, delivering them to Los Angeles for fees of US$300–400 per Mexican, US$400–500 per Central American.

Portions of these fees are used to pay safe houses and drivers along the way. Once they've arrived, the immigrants easily blend into the huge, ever-growing Hispanic population in southern California.

Every empirical study on the economics of migrant labor, including one sponsored by the conservative Rand Corporation, has concluded that Mexican immigration, illegal or otherwise, does not pose an economic or political crisis for the United States. The evidence, in fact, clearly indicates that the influx of Mexican labor provides strong economic benefits for Southwestern states that greatly outweigh the undocumented immigrants' use of public facilities and services.

Border migration can be viewed as a systematic, rational labor-to-capital flow that meets a demand for lower-paid jobs in the United States that no one else is filling, creating an economically efficient pattern that, overall, benefits both the United States and Mexico. A UCLA study recently demonstrated that if California's notorious Proposition 187 had actually resulted in the removal of all undocumented aliens from California, it would have created the worst economic crisis in that state since the 1930s.

'80s alleviated unemployment to some degree, and stricter law enforcement is halting much of the environmental damage caused by uncontrolled waste disposal. Channelization of the Río Tijuana at the border, under the auspices of the International Boundaries and Water Commission (IBWC), solved the flood problem.

More recent economic reform at the national level allowed Tijuana a wider selection of resources, including foreign investment, with which to develop a livable city. Visitors who haven't been to Tijuana for some time may be surprised to find the city has made great strides during the last decade or so and now enjoys one of the highest standards of living of any city in Mexico. Conditions have improved to such a degree that many United States citizens who work in San Diego now reside in Tijuana, where living costs are at least a third lower than those north of the border.

SIGHTS

Centro Cultural Tijuana

One of the city's most distinctive monuments, this huge, government-built complex at the intersection of Paseo de los Héroes and Avenida Independencia, tel. 664/684-1111, was designed by Pedro Ramírez Vásquez—the same architect responsible for Mexico City's Museum of Anthropology. Its centerpiece is the spherical **Space Theater,** meant to resemble the Earth emerging from a broken shell.

The center's **Museum of Mexican Identities** features historical, anthropological, and archaeological displays focusing on various Mexican ethnic groups. The exhibits pack a lot of information into a relatively compact area negotiated by an ascending ramp—a pleasant change from the angular stairways found in most museums. The museum is open daily 10 A.M.–7 P.M.; guided

© JOE CUMMINGS

Centro Cultural Tijuana

English-language tours are offered at 1 P.M. Museum admission is US$2.20.

Other cultural center facilities include a 1,000-seat performing-arts theater where the National Symphony and Ballet Folklórico perform regularly, exhibit halls with rotating art exhibits, a cafeteria serving *platillos típicos,* a bookstore specializing in materials on Baja California, a shopping arcade with shops selling Mexican arts and crafts, and an outdoor area where cultural performances take place in summer. The cafeteria, bookstore, shops, and ticket windows are open daily 10 A.M.–7 P.M.

Tijuana Wax Museum

Opened in 1992, the wax museum, Calle 1 8281 (at Av. Madero), tel. 664/688-2478, presents a collection of Mexican and international celebrities (Marilyn Monroe, Elvis, John Lennon, Lola Beltrán), horror faves (Jack the Ripper, the Wolfman), and Mexican historical figures (Pancho Villa, Miguel Hidalgo y Costilla). This is a good place to kill time if you're waiting for a bus at the nearby downtown terminal. Admission is US$2 adults; open daily 10 A.M.–7 P.M.

Catedral Nuestra Señora de Guadalupe

At Calle 2 and Avenida Constitución, this large, urban cathedral is worth a visit only if you're Catholic or you've never seen a Mexican cathedral. The interior is perhaps more impressive than the exterior. Vendors on the adjacent sidewalks sell Catholic ritual objects.

Parque Teniente Vicente Guerrero

Tijuana doesn't have a *zócalo* or public square, but four blocks west of Avenida Revolución off Calle 3 is a park where late-afternoon strollers may tarry for a few minutes or hours. It's dedicated to the heroes of the 1911 Tijuana battle against the Magonistas; the park's namesake, Lieutenant Guerrero, led the federal troops who quashed the rebellion.

Art Exhibits

Tijuana attracts artists from all over the country and in recent years has become known as an arts center for Northern Mexico. The Tijuana Cultural Center is the main showcase for traveling exhibitions, but modern artists' works can also be seen at a few private galleries in the **Plaza**

JUAN SOLDADO Y LOS MIGRANTES

In Tijuana's oldest cemetery, **Panteón No. 1** (in Colonia Castillo on Avenida Carranza, near the intersection of Avenida Juárez), a small covered grave has become one of the city's most visited non-Catholic shrines. Lying beneath the humble shelter-altar is the corpse of "Juan Soldado," literally "John Soldier," a term with connotations similar to the English "Unknown Soldier." During daylight hours usually three or four visitors can be found kneeling or standing at the shrine, praying and lighting candles. Blurry photos in cheap gold-painted plastic frames, propped up among multicolored puddles of melted candlewax, depict a diminutive soldier in a 1940s-style Mexican army uniform standing poker-straight and looking slightly bewildered.

Several different accounts relate how Juan Soldado met his fate and came to be buried here. The consensus among the vendors selling Juan Soldado photos, prayer cards, candles, and rosaries in front of the cemetery is that the short but poignant tale began in 1938, when a ruthless army captain raped and killed a girl at a nearby army camp. The captain wrapped the girl's body in a cloth bundle and ordered the first soldier who came along to dispose of it. After blood from the bundled corpse stained the soldier's clothes, he was accosted by passersby, charged with the rape/murder, and turned over to the military for trial. The captain, realizing he couldn't allow the soldier to go to court, told the soldier he would let him escape if he ran. As Juan Soldado fled up the hill in back of the cemetery, the captain shot him dead and quickly had him buried in an unmarked grave in the middle of the graveyard.

The local people eventually figured out what had happened and began leaving offerings at his gravesite in sympathy. When *milagros* or miracles reportedly came to those who had left the offerings, the legend of Juan Soldado grew. Eventually his grave became the focal point for Mexicans who were heading north over the U.S. border illegally. Although not all visitors to his shrine come for this reason, it is believed Juan Soldado's spirit is able to protect *migrantes* who pray in earnest at his grave-shrine—perhaps in sympathy for a subculture that believes itself to be treated unjustly by the U.S. Border Patrol or by Grupo Beta, a special squadron of Mexican undercover police who patrol the Mexican side of the border.

Fiesta center on Paseo de los Héroes, diagonally opposite the cultural center.

Popular Mexican mural art is found throughout the city; the **Palacio Municipal** (County Hall) on Paseo de Tijuana features several examples. On the third-floor wall a mural depicts the history of Mexico, while on the second floor hangs a *Rebirth of Baja California* mural; other floors have murals as well.

ACCOMMODATIONS

Since most leisure visitors to Tijuana are coming only for the day—or are passing through on their way south—not many foreign tourists spend the night in the city. Most hotels and motels cater either to foreign and domestic business travelers or to impecunious transients.

Under US$25

Tijuana has one *villa juvenil* or youth hostel, just north of the river between Vía Oriente and Avenida Padre Kino near the Cuauhtémoc Bridge, tel. 664/684-7510. For the rock-bottom rate you get a bed and locker in a dorm-style room. From the border, you can reach the hostel by taking any bus marked Central Camionera; from the downtown area, take a blue-and-white bus south on Avenida Niños Héroes. The hostel is part of a large sports facility (look for the sign Deportivas) off Avenida Padre Kino.

Other than the hostel, the only places to stay for under US$15 a night are a handful of short-time hotels in the Zona Norte, a grubby district catering to the brothel trade, just northwest of the Avenida Revolución tourist zone. We've had a look at several of the hotels in this price category and unfortunately can't recommend any of them due to safety and sanitation concerns. Best to push on to Ensenada if you need something really cheap but don't want to stay at the hostel.

US$25–50

La Reforma district, in the vicinity of Avenida Revolución, boasts several decent hotels around US$25. One of the best deals is **Hotel Lafayette**, Av. Revolución 926 (between Calles 3 and 4), tel. 664/685-3940, a surprisingly quiet and very clean place offering simple rooms with private baths, phone, and TV.

The pink, five-story **Hotel Nelson**, Av. Revolución 151, tel. 664/685-4302, fax 664/685-4304, is a historic place that imparts some of the flavor of early Tijuana at reasonable rates (though some rooms now cost as much as US$60). The hotel features 92 worn but clean and comfortable rooms, all with heat, satellite TV, and telephone. A popular, inexpensive coffee shop and a barber shop are attached to the hotel.

Hotel Paris, Calle 5 (Emiliano Zapata) 8181, tel. 664/685-3023, is a five-story art deco place offering good rooms with air-conditioning, TV, and phone. Similarly priced but not as good, **Hotel Lorena**, tel. 664/688-3833, is squeezed into a cluster of shops around the corner at Avenida Revolución 910 (between Calles 3 and 4), tel. 664/688-3833.

Hotel Caesar, Av. Revolución 1079 at Calle 5, tel. 664/685-1606, is an also-ran if you can't get a room at the Nelson but want that "old Tijuana" feel. And of course attached to it is the world-famous Caesar's bar/restaurant where the Caesar salad and shrimp cocktails are first-rate.

If you're driving, one of your best choices in the upper end of this rate category is **Hotel La Villa de Zaragoza**, Av. Madero 1120 (between Calles 7 and 8), tel. 664/685-1832, fax 664/685-1837, www.hotellavilla.biz. Clean rooms have heat and air-conditioning, TV, and telephone. A parking lot and laundry room are also on the premises. The hotel offers nonsmoking and handicapped-accessible rooms. Kitchenette suites are available.

The city offers a number of good middle-class business hotels, all with parking. Modern, four-story **Motel León**, Calle 7 (Galeana) 1939, just west of Revolución, tel. 664/685-6320, is a friendly place with comfortable rooms.

US$50–100

In the Zona Río, **Hotel Real del Río**, Calle J.M. Velazco 1409, tel. 664/634-3100, fax 664/634-5053, realrio@telnor.net, features very nice rooms with heat and air-conditioning; amenities include a business center, bar, coffee shop, snack bar, parking, and car rental agency. Suites are available.

Northwest of El Toreo del Tijuana off Boulevard Agua Caliente, **Hotel Palacio Azteca**, Av. 16 de Septiembre (Blvd. Cuauhtémoc Sur) 213, tel. 664/681-8100, fax 664/681-8160, www.hotelpalacioazteca.com, has okay rooms with heat and air-conditioning; amenities include a laundry room, coffee shop, pool, parking lot, and car rental.

Several places in the area around Boulevard Agua Caliente provide easy road access. The **Baja Inn Hotel Country Club**, Calle Tapachula 1 (at Blvd. Agua Caliente), tel. 664/681-7733 or 800/026-6999, U.S./Canada tel. 800/303-2684, fax 664/681-7692, www.bajainn.com, offers 104 first-class rooms and 31 deluxe suites each with heat, air-conditioning, cable TV, a private safety deposit box, and courtesy coffee and newspaper. Other amenities include a restaurant, bar, pool, hot tub, sauna, and parking.

Farther southeast on the way out of town toward Tecate (follow Boulevard Agua Caliente southeast till it becomes Boulevard Díaz Ordaz), **Hotel La Mesa Inn**, Blvd. Díaz Ordaz 50 (at Gardenias), tel. 664/681-6522, fax 664/681-2871, U.S./Canada tel. 800/303-2684, www.bajainn.com, is another business-oriented hotel featuring comfortable rooms with air-conditioning, heat, direct-dial phone, satellite TV, and courtesy coffee and newspaper. Among the facilities are a couple of restaurants, a bar, coffee shop, pool, and parking lot.

In the Zona Río, **Hotel Lucerna**, Av. Paseo de los Héroes 10902, tel. 664/633-3900, fax 664/634-2000, U.S./Canada tel. 800/LUCERNA (800/582-3762), www.hotel-lucerna.com.mx, is a large, modern place with a laundry room, restaurants, a piano bar, two pools, gardens, a car rental desk, and a gym. The 175 rooms and suites come with all the amenities expected in an international-class hotel.

Hotel Hacienda del Río, Blvd. Sánchez Taboada 10606, tel. 664/684-8644, fax 664/684-8620, U.S. reservations tel. 800/303-2684, www.bajainn.com, caters to business travelers with a restaurant/bar, heated pool, parking, gym, copier and fax service, and courtesy coffee and newspaper. The 131 large, clean rooms and suites come with satellite TV, direct-dial phones, air-conditioning, and heat.

US$100–150

In this price range is one of the city's best hotels, the landmark **Grand Hotel Tijuana,** Blvd. Agua Caliente 4500, tel. 664/681-7000, U.S./Canada tel. 800/GRANDTJ (800/472-6385), www.grandhoteltijuana.com, completed in 1986 as one of Plaza Agua Caliente's glittering glass-and-steel twin towers—the city's first skyscrapers. The 22-floor, 422-room, five-star hotel features several restaurants and discos, a race-and-sports betting lounge, and penthouse suites accommodating visiting celebrities and politicos. Other facilities include a pool, tennis courts, a fitness center with sauna and hot tub, a car rental office, shopping gallery, and cinema. Complimentary airport transportation is available.

Several blocks southeast along the same road, **Hotel Plaza Las Glorias,** Blvd. Agua Caliente 11553, tel. 664/622-6600, fax 664/622-6602, has rooms with all the usual amenities, plus a couple of restaurants, a pool, hot tub, sauna, and car rental.

US$150–250

The 140-room **Fiesta Inn,** Av. Paseo de los Héroes 18818, tel. 664/636-6000, fax 664/636-0000, U.S./Canada tel. 800/HOLIDAY (800/465-4329), www.fiestainn.com, displays Spanish-Moorish architecture similar to that of the Frontón Jai Alai and is said to be a modernized replica of the original Casino de Agua Caliente, which once stood nearby. Very comfortable rooms and junior suites contain wet bars, refrigerators, and phones with data ports. Handicapped-accessible and nonsmoking

rooms are available, and continental breakfast is complimentary.

Hotel Pueblo Amigo Inn, Vía Oriente 9211, tel. 664/683-5030 or 800/026-6386, U.S. tel. 800/386-6985, fax 664/683-5032, reservaciones@hotelpuebloamigo.com, www.hotel puebloamigo.com, stands next to Plaza Pueblo Amigo shopping/entertainment center near the border and offers 108 rooms with posh standard amenities, plus a swimming pool. Because of its proximity to the Pueblo Amigo night scene, the hotel is popular with business travelers and conventioneers.

In the heart of the Zona Río, the grand **Hotel Camino Real,** Paseo de los Héroes 10305 and Cuauhtémoc, tel. 664/633-4000, U.S. tel. 800/7-CAMINO (800/722-6466), fax 664/633-4001, www.caminoreal.com, offers 250 deluxe rooms and suites in a branch of one of the finest Mexican-owned hotel chains. Amenities include two elegant restaurants, two bars, a delicatessen, car rental, travel agency, gift shop, and indoor parking.

Campgrounds and RV Parks

The nearest camping/RV facilities are on the coast between San Antonio del Mar and Rosarito, some 20–25 km south of Tijuana via Mexico 1-D. See Rosarito.

FOOD

Some of Baja's best food is found in Tijuana; it's worth a stopover just for a meal or two. Menus in the La Reforma (Avenida Revolución) district list prices in both N$ and US$ or US$ only, but if you pay in pesos you'll almost always save a little money. Virtually all the restaurants described below serve at least beer; most offer full bars as well.

Avenida Revolución & Vicinity

Caesar's Sports Bar & Grill, in front of the Hotel Caesar, Calle 5 at Avenida Revolución, tel. 664/685-1664, is a wood-paneled bar/restaurant famous for Caesar salad, invented here by Alex and Caesar Cardini in 1924. The original Caesar's recipe is prepared at tableside, using coddled eggs—eggs boiled for one

making *huaraches*

minute—in the dressing rather than the customary raw egg yolks used in America. Shrimp cocktails, which come with huge grilled shrimp, spicy salsa, avocado and lime, are among the best in Tijuana. Moderately priced. Open daily for lunch and dinner.

Café La Especial, Av. Revolución 718, is in the long vendor and shopping mall behind the Hotel Lafayette, between Calles 3 and 4. Very popular with Mexicans as well as tourists, this convivial middle-class spot offers all kinds of standard Mexican dishes, served to the musical *alegría* of wandering *trovadores*. Inexpensive to moderate. Open daily 9 A.M.–9 P.M.

Huaraches—flat, thick, football-shaped tortillas topped with a savory mix of minced meat, cheese, chilies, and onions—are a Tijuana specialty seldom seen elsewhere in Baja. The little pedestrian street that runs diagonally between the southwest corner of Calle 1 and Avenida Revolución and the northeast corner of Calle 2 and Avenida Constitución downtown holds several working-class mariachi bars and three humble places serving *huaraches*. The most popular continues to be **Boy'z Huaraches,** which in addition to *huaraches* serves *menudo, pozole, bir-*

ria, flautas, and *sopes*. Equally good are **La Fuente Mexican Restaurant** (which also serves breakfast) and **Restaurant D.F.**

Tacos María Candelaria, Av. Revolución between Calles 2 and 3, is a small but very nice taco restaurant serving *tacos de carne asada al pastor, carnitas,* and *birria,* as well as a full line of burritos, *tortas,* and quesadillas. Open daily 10 A.M.–11 P.M.

Restaurant La Costa, Calle 7 opposite the México Lindo nightclub in all its faux-nautical splendor, is one of the more reliable local seafood places in Tijuana. The *cabrilla* (sea bass) is particularly good. Moderately priced. Open daily 10 A.M.–11 P.M. **Restaurant El Farolito,** next door to La Costa, is smaller and less expensive.

Restaurant Nelson, Av. Revolución 100, tel. 664/685-7750, is a nondescript coffee shop on the ground floor of the Hotel Nelson. It's one of the cheaper sit-down places to eat in La Reforma district, especially for breakfast. Open daily for breakfast, lunch, and dinner.

Sanborns, Av. Revolución at Calle 8, tel. 664/668-1462, is one block south of the Frontón Jai Alai. Not related to Sanborns insurance or any other American company, this is part of a

RENDER UNTO CAESAR

Late one 4th of July in 1924, a crowd of San Diego and Hollywood socialites entered the dining room of Tijuana's Hotel Caesar seeking a light meal to top off a night of drinking. Whether by virtue of necessity or inspiration (probably both), Italian immigrant chef **Caesar Cardini** (1896–1956) gathered together romaine lettuce, a few eggs, anchovies, garlic-infused olive oil, lemon juice, bread crusts, and seasonings, and then assembled them with a flourish next to the tables where the salads were served. The flavorful salad impressed the picky diners. Word spread throughout southern California, and it soon became almost mandatory to sample a "Caesar salad" when visiting Tijuana.

In 1948 the Cardini family moved to Los Angeles, where they introduced the salad to such venerable eating establishments as Chasen's and Romanoff's, and soon began bottling the dressing under a self-named label. In 1953 the Society of Epicures of Paris declared that the Caesar salad was "the greatest recipe to originate from the Americas in 50 years."

Purists hold that the original Caesar salad contained no crushed garlic and no puréed anchovies. Garlic-infused olive oil is preferred, and anchovies should be placed whole atop the salad. Some chefs prefer to mix a little anchovy paste, along with dry mustard powder, into the salad. Here is the classic Caesar salad recipe.

3 medium heads romaine lettuce, washed, dried, and chilled

½ cup olive oil in which six cloves of sliced garlic have marinated for at least one day

1 cup French-bread croutons (best made by baking bread cubes with a little garlic oil)

½ cup grated parmesan cheese

2 tablespoons wine vinegar

juice of one lemon

1 coddled egg (an egg boiled for one minute, then cooled immediately under cold water)

½ teaspoon salt

½ teaspoon freshly ground black pepper

¼ teaspoon Worcestershire sauce

18 whole anchovies

Tear romaine leaves into pieces and place in a large salad bowl. Remove the yolk from the coddled egg and mash against the side of the bowl. Sprinkle the wine vinegar and lemon over the leaves, followed by the olive oil. Add salt, pepper, Worcestershire sauce, and grated parmesan. Toss the salad thoroughly. Divide into six servings, and top each serving of salad with croutons and three anchovies.

NORTHERN BAJA

Mexican department-store chain well known in Mexico for its *cafeterías*. The food is of high quality, prices are reasonable, and the menu runs the gamut from original-recipe Mexican standards to steaks, seafood, salads, sandwiches, and soups. Breakfasts are particularly memorable. Inexpensive to moderate. Open daily for breakfast, lunch, and dinner. Other branches are on Avenida Revolución between Calles 3 and 4; Avenida Revolución 737; and at Plaza Río.

Tia Juana Tilly's, Calle 7 at Av. Revolución, tel. 664/685-6024, is part of the Frontón Jai Alai. Tilly's started out as Café de Jai Alai in 1945, later became an elegant restaurant called La Puenta, and in the '70s settled into its current casual-but-polished image. Historic Tijuana photos line the walls, and TV screens to one side of the restaurant broadcast live sports and racing events, so bettors from the adjacent booking lounge can follow their fates. Although basically a tourist scene, the food at Tilly's—Mexican, steak, and seafood—is good, especially the *caldos,* served with *chipotle* salsa. The service is fine, too. Moderate to expensive. Open noon–midnight, Fri. and Sat. until 3 A.M. Another branch called **Tilly's 5th Ave** can be found at the southwest corner of Calle 5 and Revolución.

Tilly's features a more inexpensive outdoor section called **La Terraza,** serving good Mexican food and open June–Sept. noon–midnight, Oct.–May noon–7 P.M. For both restaurants, validated parking is available (three-hour limit) in the Frontón Jai Alai lot.

Farther north and around the corner on Calle 8, **Restaurant Cenaduría (Tacos, Menudos y Tupido's),** Calle 8 1941, between Av. Revolución and Av. Madero, tel. 664/688-0035, is a spotlessly clean, medium-priced *cocina tijuanense* with Mexican decor and a long list of Mexican breakfasts and other meals. It's very popular with locals who come for the unequalled *tacos guisados, menudo, pozole,* and enchiladas. Open daily 8 A.M.–9 P.M.

Restaurant Tortas Ricardo's, Av. Madero 1410 at Calle 7, tel. 664/685-4031, has been famous for its *tortas* since 1965. Besides the signature *tortas,* you'll find plenty of belt-busting Mexican standards on the menu. It's clean and air-conditioned, and only a 50-meter walk from Hotel La Villa de Zaragoza. Inexpensive to moderate. Open daily 7:30 A.M.–11 P.M.

Birrieria Guadalajara Pues, Calle 1 and Av. Constitución, tel. 664/685-0025, has been serving heaping plates of *birria de chivo* (spicy goat stew) since 1960 and is today one of the most famous and popular restaurants in the city. Prices are inexpensive; a complete order of *birria de chivo* for four people, with all the fixings (tortillas, salsa, onions, cilantro, and limes), costs only US$28. Coldest beer in town. Open daily 9 A.M.–7 P.M.

Zona Río

Cien Años, Calle José María Velazco 1407, next to the Hotel Real del Río, tel. 664/634-3039, is a tastefully decorated restaurant focusing on rich, authentic *alta cocina* recipes such as Oaxacan *mole* and *pollo en salsa cien años* (tender chicken in a

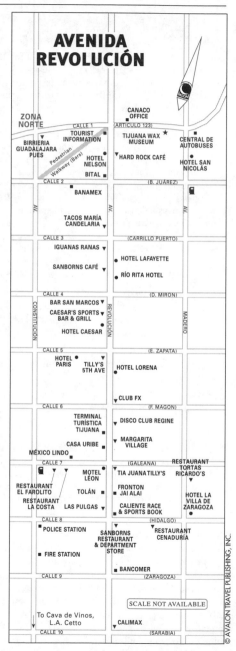

AVENIDA REVOLUCIÓN

light *chipotle* sauce). Also recommended are salads made with watercress *(berros)* and a similar plant called *verdolaga.* The adventurous can sample the crispy *chinicuiles* (fried maguey worms), served fresh from the skillet with tortillas, guacamole, and salsa. The bar is stocked with over 35 tequilas and a full range of *bajacaliforniano* wines. Moderate to expensive. Open daily 1 P.M.–midnight.

La Cantina de los Remedios, Calle Diego de Rivera 19, tel. 664/634-3065, opposite Baby Rock disco at the corner of Paseo de los Héroes and Diego Rivera, is a branch of a Guadalajara restaurant of the same name. Housed in a large, neo-Republican-style building with Tapatío-style decor, the kitchen offers mainland specialties *chalupas, pipián verde* (green mole), *albóndigas caseras* (home-made Mexican meatballs), and *chiles rellenos* stuffed with *picadillo* (spicy ground beef) and cheese. Roaming mariachis, moderate prices. Open daily 1:30 P.M.–2 A.M.

The popular and reasonably priced **Mariscos Los Arcos,** Blvd. Sánchez Taboada, near the Diego Rivera intersection, tel. 664/686-4757, dishes up Mazatlán-style *pescado zarandeado*— whole fish spread with a secret blend of spices, slashed to let the flavors in, and broiled to perfection. Other recommended menu items include ceviche, *sopa de mariscos* (seafood soup), and smoked marlin tacos. Open daily 8 A.M.– 10 P.M., Thurs.–Sat. till midnight.

Pleasantly decorated with lots of Mexican pottery and live plants, **La Casa de Mole Poblano,** Blvd. Paseo de los Héroes 1501, tel. 664/634-6920, serves delicious and authentic Mexican dishes at bargain prices. The *mixiote de pollo* (chicken baked in maguey leaves) is particularly good, as is the house *mole.* Live mariachi music. Inexpensive. Open daily 10 A.M.–11 P.M. The second (actually the original) branch can be found at Calle Serdán 543, Col. Libertad, tel. 664/682-9074.

Gypsy's, a tiny tapas bar in the Plaza Pueblo Amigo shopping center near the border, tel. 664/634-2766, is a great spot for light dishes such as *bacalao a la Vizcaína* (cured codfish with olives and tomatoes). The *paella,* an Arab-influenced dish of seasoned rice baked with seafood, is also quite good. The owner has covered the walls,

ceiling, and floor with art from his native Spain, and the sound system plays Spanish music. Open Tues.–Sun. 12:30 P.M.–2 A.M.

Restaurant Las Carnes, Paseo de los Héroes 10471, tel. 664/634-2721, is famous for steak, *carne asada, machaca, salsa verde,* fresh handmade tortillas, and other *cocina norteña.* Expensive. Open Tues.–Sun. 1 P.M.–midnight.

Vips Restaurant Cafetería, Blvd. Sánchez Taboada 10750, tel. 664/634-6196, is a well-managed branch of one of Mexico's largest coffee shop chains, with a long menu of breakfasts, Mexican standards, sandwiches, salads, and soups. Inexpensive. Open daily 7 A.M.–10 P.M.

Chan's Cuisine, Blvd. Sánchez Taboada 10880, tel. 664/634-2766, serves the best Chinese food in the city in a clean, almost elegant setting. Try the *pato pekín* (Peking duck) for US$12, enough for four people. Moderate. Open daily noon–midnight.

Agua Caliente

Carnitas Uruapán, Blvd. Díaz Ordaz 550 (opposite Plaza Patria), tel. 664/681-6181, is a classic *carnitas* joint where the pig is cooked on-site and sold by the kilo along with rice, beans, salsa, and guacamole. Other Mexican specialties and steak are also on the menu. Breakfasts are good, too. Moderately priced. Open 22 hours daily (closed 5–7 A.M.).

Café La Libanesa, Calle Tapachula 10-4, Col. Hipódromo (next to the U.S. consulate), tel. 664/686-3520, is an authentic Lebanese deli with out-of-this-world date/custard pie, baklava, cheese and spinach empanadas, and Lebanese flatbread. The proprietress will do coffee-grounds readings (for women only) for US$35 per session. This is a nice place to enjoy a cup of the café's signature sweet, black coffee, or a glass of beer or wine. Open Mon.–Sat. 9 A.M.–11 P.M.

In south Tijuana, **Mariscos Don Pepe,** Blvd. Fundadores 688 (about three km south of Blvd. Agua Caliente), tel. 664/684-8866, offers the city's best and most extensive seafood menu, including shellfish, freshwater fish, and saltwater fish prepared in a variety of Mexican, American, and continental styles. Don Pedro's *postres* (desserts), including his renowned flan and cheesecake, are made on the premises and sold at other Tijuana restaurants. All diners are offered a complimentary ice cream drink drenched in Kahlua and topped with nutmeg. Moderate to expensive. Open daily 11 A.M.–11 P.M.

At **Vallarta Natural Restaurant Vegetariano,** Blvd. Agua Caliente 1252 (corner of Río Yaqui, across from the bullring), tel. 664/686-1560, the totally vegetarian menu (some dishes use dairy products) features an extensive selection of classic Mexican dishes, along with sandwiches, soy burgers, salads, *licuados, aguas frescas,* and *lassis* (yogurt smoothies). The clean, simple, but very Mexican dining room, appointed with a Saltillo tile floor and rustic wooden furniture, is 100 percent nonsmoking. Inexpensive. Open daily 8 A.M.–8 P.M.

Loncherías and Cafés

Loncherías are often the least expensive and most colorful sit-down meal spots in Mexico, and Tijuana is full of them. Several are scattered along Avenidas Constitución and Madero, often wedged between larger shops. The diagonal bar strip between Avenidas Revolución and Constitución also sports a couple of diners. Public markets usually harbor a few—try the **Mercado Hidalgo** opposite the cultural center. Tacos, *tortas,* and other *antojitos* are the usual offerings—sometimes a *comida corrida* is available.

Head for Plaza Fiesta, on Paseo de los Héroes in the Zona Río, if you seek a wide selection of Mexican dishes at reasonable prices. Here **Restaurant Lupita, Alcatraz Café,** and Punto Café are open for breakfast, lunch, and early dinner—preparing their clientele for the night's bar crawl in the same complex.

Groceries

The northern Baja **Calimax** supermarket chain has several outlets in Tijuana. Food prices at Calimax are often lower than at smaller stores and the selection is huge. Probably the most accessible Calimax for those driving through the city is the one on the south side of Paseo de los Héroes just east of Boulevard Cuauhtémoc. The huge **Ley** supermarket/department store at Plaza Pueblo Amigo shopping center near the border has a tremendous selection, including lots of takeout

Mexican food. A good supermarket within walking distance of the Av. Revolución tourist strip is **Gigante** on Juárez between Calles 2 and 3.

For *bolillos, pan dulce,* and other Mexican bakery items, your best choice is **Panificadora Suzette,** in Plaza Río Tijuana. Although Mexican bakeries don't usually stock tortillas (they're made and sold at *tortillerías*), Suzette's does. For decent European-style pastries and baked goods, stop by **La Baguette** (open at 7:30 A.M.) at Plaza Fiesta or on Boulevard Agua Caliente southeast of El Toreo bullring. **Panadería Integral la Sonrisa** in Plaza Fiesta sells whole-wheat baked goods including *pan dulce,* empanadas, muffins, and rolls—all with no preservatives or chemicals.

Wineries

Two of Baja's more reputable winemakers maintain *bodegas* (storehouses) and offices in Tijuana. **Casa Domecq,** Av. Eusebio Kino s/n, Fracc. Garita de Otay, tel. 664/623-2171, www.domecq.com.mx, was founded in the Valle de Guadalupe by the daughter of the famous sherry and brandy producer of the same name in Jerez, Spain. **Cava de Vinos L.A. Cetto,** Calle Cañon Johnson 2108 (at Av. Constitución Sur), Col. Hidalgo, tel. 664/685-3031, www.lacetto.com.mx, was established by Italian immigrant Don Angelo Cetto in the same valley in 1936. Visitors are welcome by appointment Monday–Friday 10 A.M.– 5:30 P.M., Saturday 10 A.M.–4 P.M. Tours cost US$2, or US$5 with souvenir glass.

SPORTS AND RECREATION

Galgódromo Caliente (Caliente Greyhound Track)

Tijuana's first racetrack opened in 1916 just 400 meters south of the current border crossing, in response to a 1909 ban on pari-mutuel betting in California. Business was good right from the start, and when Prohibition sent even greater numbers of Californians south of the border, a larger track was needed. The Hipódromo Agua Caliente (Agua Caliente Horse-Racing Track) was constructed in 1929 following the highly successful 1928 opening of Tijuana's El Casino del Agua Caliente.

In 1931 Caliente became the first track in North America to become a "Hundred Grander," that is, to award US$100,000 in winnings. The track remained in operation even after the casino closed, and after the re-legalization of pari-mutuel betting in California in 1933, Caliente became an important training ground for young U.S.-owned thoroughbreds. A number of famous horses— Phar Lap (1932), Seabiscuit (1938), and Round Table (1958)—ran at Caliente.

Today, the *cupula* entrance to the Caliente Greyhound Track, a vestige of Tijuana's Prohibition-era splendor, preserves the 1920s' Moorish style that is the epitome of San Diego–Ensenada architecture. After renovations in the 1980s, the refurbished—and renamed, dropping "Agua"— facilities cover 160 acres and feature three racetracks, three restaurants (Restaurant J.R., Restaurant Casa de Alba, and the Jockey Club), two Caliente foreign book lounges (see Race and Sports Book), and several bars and snack bars.

Caliente is 12 km (eight miles) south of the international border on Boulevard Agua Caliente, just east of the Plaza Agua Caliente twin towers. Red-and-black route taxis marked La Mesa pass in front of the entrance, as do green-and-cream city buses.

Horses no longer pound the turf at Caliente— thoroughbred racing has been discontinued— but greyhounds run nightly at 8 P.M., with 2 P.M. matinees on Saturday and Sunday. Grandstand seating is free.

Pari-mutuel wagers include daily doubles, quinielas, trifectas, exactas, pick-six (invented at this track), win, place, and show. Caliente claims to collect the lowest take of any racetrack in North America; the racetrack pays all taxes, so figures shown on the tote board are the actual win amounts. U.S. winners are expected to voluntarily submit the appropriate portion of their winnings to the IRS, unless they spend at least 11 months of the year outside the United States. Bets are accepted in U.S. currency as well as pesos.

Race and Sports Book

Sporting folk don't have to go all the way out to Caliente Greyhound Track to make a wager, as Tijuana offers several venues for sports and off-track betting closer to the border. These legal betting lounges feature plush bars and restaurants, plus banks of closed-circuit TV monitors so you can keep up with your wagers or just watch for fun. Sports bets are based on line odds direct from Las Vegas, and all wagers and payoffs are in U.S dollars. Taxes are paid by the booking establishments, so what you see on the tote board represents your take-home winnings.

Caliente Race and Sports Book occupies locations at the Plaza Pueblo Amigo (Paseo de Tijuana, Zona Río), the Grand Hotel Tijuana, the Caliente Greyhound Track, and at Avenida Revolución and Calle 8. All book lounges keep the same hours: Mon.–Fri. 9 A.M.–1 A.M., Sat. and Sun. 8 A.M.–1 A.M.

Caliente operates a free minivan shuttle between the border and each of its racing and sports-book locations. The shuttle runs every half hour daily 9 A.M.–1 A.M.

Bullfights

The bullfight season in Tijuana runs May–Nov.— usually two *corridas* in May, one in June, and twice monthly thereafter through October. The city supports two permanent bullrings. **El Toreo de Tijuana,** Agua Caliente Blvd. 100, tel. 664/686-1510, is the oldest, with more atmosphere; it's close to city center. During the bullfight season, tickets are sold Wed.–Sun. 10 A.M.–2 P.M. and 4–6 P.M. The **Plaza Monumental,** Paseo Monumental, tel. 664/680-1808, is approximately 10 km (six miles) west of the city, in the Playas district next to the Pacific Ocean. Dubbed the "Bullring-by-the-Sea," this huge, stadiumlike edifice is reportedly the world's second-largest bullring; when the world's top matadors visit Tijuana, they always perform at the Plaza Monumental. El Toreo is often used for concerts, circuses, and other non-bullfighting events.

The *corridas* take place on Sunday beginning at 4 P.M. Current schedule and ticket information is available in Tijuana by calling 664/685-2210 or 664/686-1510. Depending on the seat and the matador lineup, prices range from US$10 general admission on the sunny side *(sol)* to US$65 for a box seat *(palco)* on the shady side *(sombra)*. Most midrange seats cost US$22–29. If you buy your

NORTHERN BAJA

tickets from Mexicoach, you'll pay a US$7 service charge on top of the ticket price.

Ticket reservations, often necessary, are obtained by calling the same number. Tickets usually go on sale the Thursday before the scheduled event. You can purchase tickets at Ticketron (Ticketmaster) outlets in San Diego, tel. 619/220-8497, and Los Angeles, tel. 213/480-3232; San Diego's Santa Fe Depot, tel. 619/239-9021; Mexicoach, tel. 619/428-9517, in San Diego or Tijuana; the bullfight information booth on Avenida Revolución, in front of the Hotel Lafayette between Calles 3 and 4; or at the bullrings themselves.

Charreadas

Although the *charreada* (Mexican rodeo) inspired the development of American and Canadian rodeo, it differs in many significant ways. Competition is generally based on the *charro's* (cowboy's) performance style, rather than on timed events, and the atmosphere is considerably more festive, featuring elaborate costumes and music. In Tijuana, occasional *charreadas* are held May–Sept. Saturday or Sunday at *lienzos charros* (*charro* rings) throughout the city, including the **Lienzo Charro La Misión,** Av. Braulio Maldonado, Zona Misión, tel. 664/680-4185. Easier to find are the **Cortijo San José** and **Lienzo Charro Misión del Sol,** both in the Playas Tijuana district near the Plaza Monumental bullring.

Smaller Tijuana *lienzos* arrange occasional rodeo events during fiestas. For the latest information on *charreada* schedules, call Tijuana's tourist information number, tel. 664/688-0555, or contact the Charro Association secretary at 664/681-3401 or 664/681-2611.

Jai Alai

Looming over the intersection of Avenida Revolución and Calle 7, the Frontón Palacio Jai Alai de Tijuana is a landmark Spanish-style structure in the city center and was once one of the San Diego–Tijuana area's major attractions. Until the mid-1990s the building hosted regular *jai alai* (pronounced "HAI-lai," a Basque term meaning "merry festival") matches. Known as "the fastest ball game in the world," jai alai descended from

© JOE CUMMINGS

Frontón Palacio Jai Alai de Tijuana

pelota, a 200-year-old Basque game that is also the forerunner of handball, squash, and racquetball. The *pelotaris* (jai alai players), who mostly hailed from France, Spain, and Mexico, would hurl and catch the *pelota* with a *cesta*—an elongated wicker basket imported from Spain—strapped to the playing hand. Using the curvature of the *cesta* and a skilled throwing technique, the *pelotari* could launch the *pelota* against the *frontis, rebote,* and *ayuda* (the front, back, and "helper" or side walls) as if shot from a cannon. Ball speeds could reach a blistering 290 km per hour.

Unfortunately, the Tijuana *frontón* closed its doors following a strike organized several years ago by employees of the Mexico City *frontón,* an act that has brought all professional jai alai in Mexico to a halt. However, you may usually tour the courts during the daytime. Facilities include the *frontón* itself (a three-walled court with hardwood floors and seating for 1,500 spectators) and a separate bar, both of which are frequently rented out for city events.

El Béisbol

Tijuana claims its own pro baseball team, Los Potros (The Colts), who play other ball clubs in the Mexican-Pacific League as well as the occasional visiting team from the U.S. or Central America. Games are played at the exemplary 15,000-seat **Estadio de los Potros,** off Blvd. Los Insurgentes near the Otay border crossing, tel. 664/625-1056. The Mexican baseball season runs from about the end of the American World Series through late January. Game admission costs around US$5.

Golf

The **Club Campestre Tijuana,** or Tijuana Country Club, tel. 664/681-7855, off Boulevard Agua Caliente near the Caliente Greyhound Track, offers a decent 6,500-yard, par-72, 18-hole course. The Mexican Open is played here on occasion.

ENTERTAINMENT

Although Tijuana is considerably tamer now than during Prohibition, it still has some nightlife—albeit of a more polished sort. For the most part, the entertainment center has shifted from the La Reforma district round Avenida Revolución to the Zona Río along Paseo de los Héroes.

Dance Clubs

San Diegans mix with a mostly local crowd at several high-tech discos, most of which are in the Zona Río. Plaza Pueblo Amigo is one of the most happening dance spots in Tijuana on weekends. Any night of the week, don't expect any action before midnight. Dance clubs tend to stay open till around 5 A.M.

Club Balak, Plaza Pueblo Amigo, Vía Oriente, tel. 664/682-9222, is the latest and greatest, with US$35 million worth of sound and lighting gear designed by the impresarios who created the famous Paladium Acapulco. Ricky Martín showed up for the dance club's 2003 inauguration. The cover charge runs a stiff US$18 during the week, US$20 on weekends. This is the one dance stop in Tijuana where you're most likely to hear the newest home-grown DJ form, Nortec (a blend of electronica/techno and norteña music).

Rodeo Santa Fe, Plaza Pueblo Amigo, Vía Oriente, tel. 664/682-4967, attracts the boots-and-hat crowd with the latest *norteña* and *tejano* music, along with a mechanical bull. Plaza Pueblo Amigo also harbors **Señor Frog's,** popular with young Mexicans despite the name's associations with the gringo tourist crowd farther south in Mexico. Dress for both of these clubs is much more casual than at Balak. Next door, **Zoo'll Bar-Galería** is more upscale again, with rotating DJs, open Friday and Saturday only (no cover charge on Friday).

Baby Rock, Calle Diego Rivera 1482, tel. 664/684-9438, looks like it escaped from the set of the *The Flintstones* but is a long-time favorite with a good house mix. Expect a cover charge and dress code prohibiting jeans or sneakers.

Oriented toward young San Diegans, more-casual dance clubs along Avenida Revolución—known locally as "La Revo"—include **Animale** (the most popular when we last visited), **Club FX, Señor Maguey, Iguanas Ranas, Las Pulgas, Tilly's,** and **Margarita Village.**

México Lindo, on the north side of Calle 7 (Galeana), west of Avenida Revolución, is a large *norteña* dance hall rarely visited by foreigners. **Nuevo Rancho Grande,** on the west side of La Revo between Calles 5 and 6, is similar but more reminiscent of a traditional cantina.

Mike's Disco, on the east side of Revolución at Calle 6, is a long-running gay and lesbian dance club that features drag shows on weekends. On nearby Calle 7, **Los Equipales** is another G&L-oriented disco.

Extasis, in Plaza Viva Tijuana just across the border, is a popular gay dance club open Thursday–Sunday nights only. Thursday night is designated "Lesbian Night," but on other nights visitors of all sexual orientations are welcome.

Tijuana's internationally renowned Nortec Collective occasionally organizes Nortec raves at the **Jai Alai Bar,** in the Frontón Jai Alai on Avenida Revolución. Stop by the Frontón lobby, where posters advertise coming events.

Bars

For those who prefer sitting and drinking to dancing, Avenida Revolución offers a string of bars and dance halls, from sleazy to posh, attracting an eclectic mix of *cholos,* punks, tourists, and the occasional American sailor. What was once the longest bar in the world, the Mexicali Beer Bar (also known as La Ballena), ran the entire length of the block between Calles 2 and 3 under a tent until the early 20th century. Beer cost five cents a glass. Now the strip consists of a succession of similar-looking discos and a few curtained go-go bars; in the cheaper places beer costs US$1 a bottle.

Locals patronize a boisterous collection of small bars along a diagonal pedestrian alley that cuts between the southwest corner of Calle 1 and Avenida Revolución and the northeast corner of Calle 2 and Avenida Constitución. Guitar-bass-accordion ensembles wander from bar to bar playing a repertoire of *norteña* and Mexican standards. Drinks in these bars cost around US$1, while a song from one of the *trovadores* typically costs US$3–5. **Bar Ballena,** one of the oldest of the half dozen on this alley, is a pretty safe bet. **El Ranchero** and **Villa García** along this strip attract a mostly gay clientele (Villa Garcia also has a lesbian following). At the northern end of this diagonal street is **Plaza Santa Cecilia,** a tree-planted, brick-paved square named for Mexico's patron saint of musicians. Mariachi ensembles wait here for pickup gigs—local Mexicans organizing a party may drive by and hire them on the spot.

Bar San Marcos, attached to Caesar's, tel. 664/688-2794, is a classic leftover from Tijuana's pre–World War II boom. In the old days a 10-piece mariachi band performed on a semicircular platform over a glistening bar done up in '40s–50s decor, like a set from a Ricky Ricardo show. The mariachi stand has since shrunk and is dwarfed by all the paraphernalia for sale around it. The clientele consists of day tourists from San Diego and local businesspeople. The sign on the outside of the building reads Le Drugstore Tijuana.

Planet G, on the east side of Revolución between Calles 9 and 10, is a music video and art bar catering to a mostly gay clientele.

Riding the line between bar and restaurant is Tijuana's own **Hard Rock Café,** Av. Revolución at Calle 2, tel. 664/685-0206. The decor consists of HRC's trademark rock memorabilia, and the music is modern and loud, though not too loud for conversation. A more elegant drinking establishment is the bar at **No Que No,** at the corner of Av. Sánchez Taboada and Calle Antonio Caso in the Zona Río. Attached to a large restaurant, No Que No features live marimba music in a classy, subdued atmosphere.

A popular local spot for middle-class bar-goers is Plaza Fiesta on Paseo de los Héroes in the Zona Río. Mixed in with various shops and taco bars you'll find **The Berlin Bar, The Ranas Bar, Mi Barra, Batacas Bar, Delfín Bar,** and **Bar Monte Picacho.** These are casual, relatively inexpensive, safe places to sit, enjoy a drink, and meet local residents.

Exercise caution if you decide to visit the notorious **Zona Norte** (also known as "La Coahuila"), a district of around 10 square blocks that extends north from Calle 1 downtown, not far from the border. Drug dealing and prostitution (which is legal in Tijuana) are two of the main income-generating activities in this area, and the local bars can be on the rough side. On the tamer side, several of the bars offer "taxi dancing," where customers pay to dance with female staff. If you must venture into the "zone," it's best to do so in a group. **Adelita's,** on Calle 1 and Av. Constitución, and **Chicago Club,** on Av. Constitución just north of Calle 1, are said to be the safest and best-run of all the Zona Norte "dance halls."

Cultural Performances

Highbrow evening entertainment takes place at the **Centro Cultural Tijuana.** Mexico's National Symphony performs at the center on a regular basis, as do the Ballet Folklórico and other performing-arts groups from around the country.

SHOPPING

For most visitors, shopping is perhaps Tijuana's number-one attraction. Although both Baja California states are designated duty-free zones, Tijuana offers the widest variety of merchandise—everything from Mexican-Amerindian handicrafts to pharmaceuticals to top-of-the-line European clothing.

Nearly everything is cheaper in Tijuana than it is north of the border. Some of the better bargains are found in leather goods, cosmetics, drugs (prescriptions aren't usually required, even for drugs dispensed by prescription in the United States), high-tag import items (e.g., designer fashions), cooking spices (vanilla costs a fraction of the U.S. price), handicrafts (especially blankets, rugs, basketry, and ceramics), and liquor.

Except at department stores, pharmacies, and liquor stores, bargaining for a lower price than marked or quoted is acceptable. U.S. currency is accepted anywhere in the city; some shops take credit cards. Most of the sales staffs in Avenida Revolución stores employ at least one person who can speak some English.

Avenida Revolución

For individual shops and boutiques, Avenida Revolución between Calle 2 and Calle 9 is one of the best window-shopping areas. **Sanborns,** at the corner of Avenida Revolución and Calle 8, is a favorite department store among day-tripping San Diegans. Although not large, it's divided into book, arts-and-crafts, pharmacy, liquor, and restaurant sections.

For high-quality Mexican handicrafts, **Tolan,** 1111 Av. Revolución, tel. 664/688-3637, has one of the best reputations in the city but is a bit pricey. In the same vicinity, **Casa Uribe,** Av. Revolución 1309, tel. 664/685-8332, has a tasteful selection of Mexican interior-design accessories, including colorful tablecloths and napkins, charming children's furniture, *alebrijes,* perforated tin mirror frames, and woodcarvings—all at reasonable prices. **La Fuente,** Av. Revolución 921-10, offers arts and crafts of similar quality, including masks, woodcarvings, *retablos* (altarpieces), and life-size papier-mâché Day of the Dead skeletons. **Irene's,** Av. Revolución 921, is a good spot for embroidered dresses at moderate prices.

Farther north along Av. Revolución, at Calle 2, is **Plaza Revolución,** a two-story mall with around 65 shops purveying arts and crafts, leather goods, jewelry, and other items. At the **Old Curio Market** on the east side of Revolución, quality isn't usually very high, but then neither are the prices. The huge hangarlike structure brings together a large number of different *artesanías* proffering everything from useful hammocks and blankets to black-velvet paintings—which in Tijuana have finally moved forward from bad renditions of Elvis Presley to bad renditions of Jimi Hendrix and Jim Morrison.

Avenida Constitución

Few visitors seem to know it, but one block west of Avenida Revolución is the town's major downtown shopping area. This is where the locals go. Especially for shoes and boots, liquor, and pharmaceuticals, shops on Avenida Constitución almost always beat the prices of their counterparts on Avenida Revolución. And unlike at some shops on Revolución, bargaining—or Spanish language mastery—isn't necessary because prices are always marked and fixed.

Shopping Centers

Tijuana was the first city in Mexico to erect American-style shopping malls; at last count, the city boasted over a dozen major *centros comerciales* (shopping centers), with more undoubtedly on the way.

The most praised is **Plaza Río Tijuana,** on Paseo de los Héroes between Via Poniente and Boulevard Cuauhtémoc in the Zona Río. Here you'll find over a hundred businesses, including department stores, pharmacies, optometrists, banks, jewelry and gift stores, music shops, clothing stores, a bakery, a florist, a cinema, photo shops, travel agencies, bookstores, sporting-goods stores, and even a chapel, all surrounded by a large parking lot.

Opposite Plaza Río is **Plaza del Zapato** (Shoe Plaza). This is one of Tijuana's best bargain centers, with over 35 *zapaterías* (shoe stores) in one location. In addition to footwear you'll find leather jackets, handbags, wallets, and other leather items, all usually costing less than half of what they would north of the border. Next to Plaza del Zapato is **Plaza Fiesta,** a mall featuring pseudo-old, Guanajuato-style architecture. Most of the businesses here are restaurants, bars, or cafés, interspersed with a few specialty shops. **La Herradura de Oro** in Plaza Fiesta sells Mexican, Western, and English riding equipment—chaps, sombreros,

NORTHERN BAJA

rebozos (a kind of shawl), saddles—and can also produce custom leather work.

The **Centro Cultural Tijuana,** Paseo de los Héroes at Av. Independencia, offers a shopping area with several stores specializing in regional arts and crafts, including textiles, ceramics, jewelry, paintings, sculptures, and handcrafted silver, gold, copper, and brass.

Other Tijuana shopping centers of note include **Plaza Patria** (Blvd. Díaz Ordaz, east of Caliente Greyhound Track), Plaza Pueblo Amigo (Av. Vía Oriente, near the border crossing), and Plaza Agua Caliente (Av. Agua Caliente, adjacent to the Grand Hotel Tijuana).

Californians who don't want to venture far from home can shop at **Viva Tijuana,** a big indoor-outdoor mall about 150 meters from the border gate. In fact, all pedestrians entering or exiting the country are forced to walk through this mall. Neither the restaurants nor the shops at Viva Tijuana offer anything special—it's strictly a place to pick up last-minute souvenirs.

Markets

For a more Mexican shopping experience, seek out Tijuana's public markets. The large **Mercado de Artesanías** at the intersection of Avenida Ocampo and Calle 2 offers thousands of pottery items at low prices. Much of what's stacked up in row after row is junk, but you can uncover worthwhile pieces with some diligent searching.

Opposite the Tijuana Cultural Center at Paseo de los Héroes and Avenida Independencia is the more atmospheric **Mercado Hidalgo.** This outdoor municipal market features dozens of vendor stalls arranged in a large square. Items for sale vary from year to year but generally include fresh fruits and vegetables, spices, and various other grocery items. A couple of *loncherías* and crafts shops make the market more than just a grocery stop.

The **Mercado de Todos** (Market of Everything) is on the 1800 block of Boulevard Agua Caliente/Díaz Ordaz, about four km east of the racetrack. Vendors here offer bargains on clothing, housewares, electronics, and just about anything else you might need to set up house on the peninsula. This market doesn't really get rolling until around 10 A.M. on weekdays, or 9 A.M. weekends; it stays open until dark.

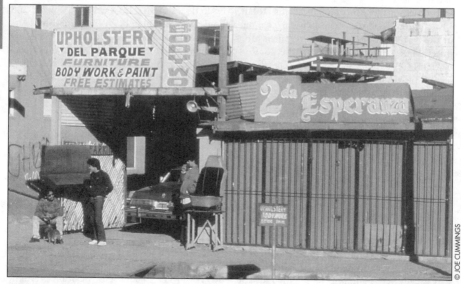

upholstery shop

"TIJUANA BIBLES":
NOT YOUR AVERAGE COMIC BOOKS

From the 1930s through the 1950s, a series of bawdy, eight- and 16-page underground comic books printed in U.S. basements and distributed in Tijuana to both Mexican and North American tourists achieved a legendary status before being shut out of the market by glossier publications like *Playboy* and *Cavalier*. Anonymously written and widely circulated north of the border, the pornographic comics came to be known as "Tijuana Bibles" not only because they were sometimes handed out on street corners in Tijuana, like bibles, but because in post-Depression America, the city was associated with practically anything sexually risqué. Most Tijuana Bibles were written in English, although a few appeared in Spanish.

Almost no famous figure from the American iconic realm, whether politician, comic-book hero, Hollywood idol, or nursery rhyme character, was spared the withering gaze and lewd irreverence of these booklets. Clark Gable, Popeye, Al Capone, Mahatma Gandhi, and the Fuller Brush Man were all burlesqued with equal relish. The gonzo crudeness of the stories, along with the energetic line art itself, served as a substantial inspiration for such later underground comic creators as Robert Crumb and Art Spiegelman. In their mix of sexual and political satire, they also bring to mind the later work of stand-up comic Lenny Bruce.

Today, Tijuana Bibles are hoarded by scholars of folk art, comic aficionados, and collectors of erotica. A hundred of them were selected for inclusion in *Tijuana Bibles: Art and Wit in America's Forbidden Funnies, 1930s–1950s*, (1997), a thorough history and critique of the ribald comics; written by Bob Adelman, Richard Merkin, and Art Spiegelman.

Books

Sanborns on Avenida Revolución at Calle 8 is the place to go for English-language books and magazines. For Spanish-language media, especially anything with a cultural bent, try *Librería El Día*, which has two storefronts: Boulevard Sánchez Toboada 10050-A, Zona Río, and Calle 6 1908, next to Cine Roble.

Auto Upholstery and Body Work

Tijuana is as legendary for auto work as Hong Kong is for tailoring. As in Hong Kong, patience in arranging for custom work and waiting for completion always pays off. The Tijuana Convention and Visitors Bureau, tel. 664/684-0537, maintains a list of reputable upholsterers and body shops—check this list first if you don't already possess a recommendation from someone you know.

The better upholstery shops offer tuck-and-roll, diamonds, plaids, squares, and just about any other style in leather, vinyl, or fabric. Prices are half, or less, of what a U.S. auto upholsterer would charge; a complete auto interior starts at around US$200 and requires a full day. Check the quality of the upholstery fill in advance—less reputable shops may use low-quality materials, like newspaper in place of foam. You'll find several other upholstery shops along Calle 3 between Avenidas Ocampo and Pío Pico. Prices quoted verbally are usually negotiable.

Body shops, or *carrocerías*, are mostly located along Ocampo between Calles 1 and 4. *Carrocerías* excel at banging out dents and applying primer, but if you need a fender or door painted, you can usually match the paint better at American auto dealers.

Furniture and Tile

Mexican-made furniture—of wood or wrought iron—and tile are considerably less expensive in Tijuana than in the United States or Canada. Most of the larger tile and furniture stores are on Boulevard Agua Caliente between Avenida Revolución and the Caliente Greyhound Track. A few stores specialize in high-quality handmade wood furniture, but generally the wrought-iron pieces are a better bargain.

Bazar de México, added on to the end of Tia

Juana Tilly's, at the corner of Avenida Revolución and Calle 7, displays a decent selection of Mexican housewares and furniture, including wrought-iron furniture (one of Mexico's best bargains). Another commendable aspect of this *artesanía* center is that, so far, the salespeople aren't as aggressive as in many shops along this street. Validated parking for three hours is available in the Frontón Jai Alai lot.

One of the widest wall and floor tile selections, including imported tiles from Europe, Brazil, and Japan, is at **Tile Express**, Av. Salinas at Aviación, tel. 664/681-8287 or 664/681-8305.

Be sure to check the latest United States Customs regulations before buying huge amounts of furniture or tile for U.S. import.

INFORMATION AND SERVICES

Tourist Assistance

The **Tourist Information Booth** on Av. Revolución at Calle 1, tel. 664/688-0555, distributes maps and useful information brochures on Tijuana and northern Baja; the bilingual staff also handle simple inquiries about where to go and what to see. The booth is open Mon.–Fri. 8 A.M.–8 P.M., Sat. and Sun. 10 A.M.–3 P.M. Similar booths can be found at the Tijuana border crossing and Tijuana International Airport. Any questions about Tijuana these people can't answer should be referred to the **Tijuana Tourism and Convention Bureau,** at the intersection of Calle Mina and Paseo de los Héroes in the Zona Río, tel. 664/684-0537 or 664/684-0538. This office is open Mon.–Fri. 9 A.M.–2 P.M. and 4–7 P.M. A private consortium also operates the friendly **Tijuana Tourism Board,** Blvd. Agua Caliente 4558-1108, tel. 664/686-1103, 664/686-1345, U.S./Canada tel. 888/775-2417, www.seetijuana.com.

The **Cámara Nacional de Comercio, Servicios y Turismo de Tijuana** (CANACO), opposite the State Secretary of Tourism (SECTUR) booth on Av. Revolución at Calle 1, tel. 664/684-0537, fax 664/684-7782, www.seetijuana.com, dispenses tourist information, stamps, and envelopes; it also offers restrooms and a public telephone. Open weekdays 9 A.M.–7 P.M.

For more tourist information on Baja California Norte, contact the **State Secretary of Tourism,** Plaza Patria, 3rd floor, Blvd. Díaz Ordaz, tel. 664/688-0555. Legal problems should also be referred to this office.

Money-Changing

The best place to exchange foreign currency for pesos is at one of the many *casas de cambio* along the pedestrian route from the border to about halfway down Avenida Revolución. You'll also find a couple of *casas de cambio* next to the Calimax supermarket on Paseo de los Héroes in the Zona Río.

The banks in Tijuana aren't accustomed to changing small amounts of foreign currency since just about everyone uses *casas de cambio* exclusively. If you want to cash traveler's checks, the banks will give you dollars, not pesos. As usual in Mexico, hotels offer low exchange rates but fast service. The Banamex just southeast of Plaza Fiesta and Plaza Zapato on Paseo de los Héroes has an ATM.

Public buses and government offices excepted, every business and service in Tijuana accepts U.S. currency.

Post and Telephone

The main post office is on Calle 11 (P.E. Calles) at Av. Negrete; open Mon.–Fri. 8 A.M.–7 P.M. The CANACO office on Calle 1 at Av. Revolución sells stamps and envelopes. The long-distance telephone and telegraph office is on

Calle 10 at Av. Pío Pico; open Mon.–Fri. 8 A.M.–2 P.M. and 4–7 P.M.

Internet Access

As with most of the larger towns in Mexico, Tijuana has no shortage of Internet cafés, far too many to list. The highest concentration can be found along the northern end of Avenida Revolución, on just about every other corner.

Immigration and Customs

Immigration and customs matters are handled at the Tijuana border crossing. These offices are open 24 hours a day. For specific information on visas and tourist permits, see Visas and Officialdom in the On the Road chapter.

Foreign Consulates

The **U.S.** consulate, Calle Tapachula 96, Col. Hipódromo, tel. 664/622-7400, can assist with lost or expired U.S. passports or American visa problems. It's open Monday–Friday 8 A.M.–4 P.M., except American and Mexican holidays. The **Canadian** consulate, Calle Germán Gedovius 10411-101, Condominio del Parque, Zona Río, tel. 664/684-0461, offers similar services for Canadians and is open Monday–Friday 9 A.M.–1 P.M.

The **French** consulate is located at Av. Revolución 1651, 3rd floor, tel. 664/685-7172, btdmex@telnor.net. The **German** consulate is at Av. Mérida 221, Col. Hipódromo, tel. 664/680-2515. The **United Kingdom** consulate, Blvd. Salinas 1500, Col. Aviación, La Mesa, tel. 664/686-5320, fax 664/681-8402, serves citizens of Australia and Belize.

Green Angels

The Green Angels automotive assistance service is headquartered in the Garita Federal Building (Edificio Federal Garita) at the Otay Mesa border crossing. For assistance or information in Tijuana, call 664/624-3479.

GETTING THERE

By Air

Abelardo L. Rodríguez International Airport (TIJ), tel. 664/607-8200, is in Mesa de Otay,

---

AIRLINE OFFICES IN TIJUANA

Aero California: Plaza Río Tijuana C-20, Paseo de los Héroes, tel. 664/684-2876, U.S. tel. 800/237-6225

Aeroexo/Aviacsa: Tijuana International Airport, tel. 664/683-8202 or 800/735-5396

Aeroméxico: Plaza Río Tijuana A12-1, Paseo de los Héroes, tel. 664/684-8444; Av. Revolución 1236, tel. 664/685-4401, U.S. tel. 800/237-6639

Mexicana de Aviación: Edificio Fontana, Diego Rivera 1511 (at Paseo de los Héroes), tel. 664/634-6566, U.S. tel. 800/531-7921, Canada tel. 800/531-7923

---

about 10 km northeast of Tijuana's city center. The following airlines fly to and from Tijuana: **Aeroméxico,** Plaza Río Tijuana 12-A1, Paseo de los Héroes, tel. 664/638-8444 or 800/021-4010, U.S. tel. 800/237-6639, fields flights to/from Guadalajara, Mexico City, Monterrey, and Tepic, while **Mexicana,** Edificio Fontana, Diego Rivera 1511 (at Av. Paseo de los Héroes), tel. 664/634-6566, airport tel. 664/682-4184 or 800/509-8960, U.S./Canada tel. 800/531-7921, offers direct daily flights to/from Mexico City, Guadalajara, and Los Angeles.

Aero California, Plaza Río Tijuana C-20, Paseo de los Héroes, tel. 664/684-2876, U.S. tel. 800/237-6225, flies to Aguascalientes, Culiacán, Durango, Guadalajara, Hermosillo, La Paz, Los Mochis, Mazatlán, Monterrey, Tepic, and Torreón. Monterrey-based **Aviacsa,** Blvd. Sánchez Taboada 4499, Plaza Guadalupe #6, tel. 664/622-5024; airport tel. 664/683-8202 or 800/711-6733, U.S.tel. 888/528-4227, services Monterrey, Mexico City, Guadalajara, and Oaxaca.

The airport has plenty of little gift shops, a restaurant/bar, snack bar, bookstore, taxis, a Serfín ATM, and a three-story parking garage with no elevator.

Foreign pilots may use this airport as an official port of entry. Fuel is available; the tower frequency is 122.8.

Airport Transportation: The airport is about

eight km east of the city; taxis to and from anywhere in the city cost a flat US$12 for up to five passengers. A taxi between the airport and the Central de Autobuses costs US$10. Public buses to downtown Tijuana are marked Centro and leave regularly from in front of the airport; fare is about US$.60 per passenger.

By Bus

Several intercity bus lines operate out of Tijuana. The main terminal for Mexico-based lines is the **Central de Autobuses de Tijuana** (also known as the Central Camionera), on Lázaro Cárdenas at Blvd. Arroyo Alamar, tel. 664/621-2982, about five km east of the city. The modern structure contains a restaurant, *lonchería,* telephone office, immigration office, and money changer. **Transportes Norte de Sonora** (TNS) and **Autotransportes de Baja California** (ABC) run buses eastward to Mexicali (US$9–12, nine times daily) and to various points on the Mexican mainland. **Transportes de Pacífico** and **Chihuahuenses** offer more extensive services to the mainland.

ABC, tel. 664/621-2668, runs a deluxe *ejecutivo* bus with air-conditioning, movies, and beverage service to Ensenada every half hour 6 A.M.–midnight for US$13 from the second Central de Autobuses, at the intersection of Avenida Madero and Calle 1 downtown. ABC also offers regular non-air-conditioned buses departing for Ensenada every half hour 6 A.M.–10 P.M. (US$8) from the small **Plaza Viva** bus station at the border, near the United States Customs/immigration post. Another ABC *ejecutivo* goes to San Felipe (US$22, twice daily). There are also regular non-air-conditioned ABC buses to San Felipe (US$18, twice daily).

Southward, **Autotransportes Águila** runs buses to El Rosario (US$21, twice daily), Santa Rosalía (US$48, four times daily), and La Paz (US$77, four times daily).

Taxis from the Central de Autobuses to the downtown area cost a flat US$6 pp; public bus fare is around US$.60. A taxi between the border and the Central de Autobuses costs US$10; the *taxi de ruta* rate is US$.70 pp.

The U.S.-based **Greyhound** buses from San Diego and Los Angeles terminate at the downtown Tres Estrellas de Oro terminal at Av. México and Av. Madero, tel. 664/688-0082; they run many times daily, and one-way tickets cost US$5 and US$18 respectively. Call 800/231-2222 in the U.S. for more information. This same terminal also serves Mexican ABC buses running every 20 minutes between Tijuana and Tecate (US$4.25).

Mexicoach (from San Ysidro) occupies its own depot called Terminal Turística Tijuana on Avenida Revolución between Calles 6 and 7. See Getting There in the On the Road chapter for more details.

By Taxi

A taxi from the United States–Mexico border crossing to anywhere in central Tijuana costs a flat US$5. You can charter a Tijuana taxi all the way to Rosarito for US$35 (one-way) or to Ensenada for US$100.

By Car

See Driving into Baja in the On the Road chapter for specifics on driving to Tijuana.

On Foot

A large number of tourists who visit Tijuana reach the city on foot from San Ysidro, the small California town on the immediate U.S. side of the border, after having parked their vehicles in one of the San Ysidro lots or after taking the Tijuana Trolley from San Diego.

The sidewalks that lead to the border crossing, then through Mexican immigration and customs and all the way to Avenida Revolución, are clearly marked. Along the way you'll pass rows of handicraft booths and money changers. A leisurely stroll from the border crossing to Avenida Revolución in the heart of downtown Tijuana takes 15–20 minutes.

GETTING AROUND

You can see much of downtown Tijuana on foot—Avenidas Revolución and Constitución, the cathedral, the jai alai palace, the Mercado Artesanías. You can reach outlying attractions like the Zona Río and the racetrack by city bus, taxi, or your own car.

Buses

City buses or *urbanos* in Tijuana come in several colors, shapes, and sizes. The route destination—usually the name of a district (e.g., Centro or La Mesa)—is displayed on a sign over the windshield or whitewashed directly on it. Fares are around US$.50, payable only in pesos. Most *urbanos* in and out of the downtown area *(centro)* can be caught along Avenida Constitución.

Two of the most useful bus lines are the "green and cream" *(verde y crema),* which operates between the city center and La Mesa district, east of Caliente Greyhound Track, and the "blue and white" *(azul y blanco),* running between the city center and the Playas district (Plaza Monumen-

tal). The "Baja P" is the bus to take for jaunts to Zona Río attractions, including the Tijuana Cultural Center, Plaza Fiesta, and Plaza Río Tijuana.

Taxis

Most trips by hired taxi within the *centro* cost US$4–5. From the city center to the Grand Hotel Tijuana/racetrack area costs as much as US$10; to the airport or Central de Autobuses expect to pay up to US$15 (although in the reverse direction it's only US$12). Taxis hired from hotels generally cost more than taxis hired on the street; rates are usually posted. If in doubt about a fare, inquire at the tourist information booths at the border or on Avenida Revolución at Calle 1. Drivers are happy to accept U.S. currency.

Bargaining usually isn't necessary—drivers generally quote the standard price immediately, with the exception of the yellow border taxis. You shouldn't have to pay more than US$8 from the border taxi stand to Avenida Revolución, but drivers often ask gringos for more. A better deal involves taking one of the several shuttle bus services that run from the Tijuana Trolley terminal in San Ysidro on the U.S. side of the border directly to Avenida Revolución; each costs only US$1 pp.

Route taxis *(taxis de ruta)* in Tijuana are large American-made station wagons holding up to 12 passengers. These taxis operate along set routes, much like city buses, but stop wherever they're flagged down. Fares are US$.60 pp, only a tad higher than city bus fares; as on buses, only pesos are accepted. Route taxis are one of the best ways to get around Tijuana cheaply, since you can tell the drivers exactly where you want off along their route—better than waiting for a bus stop to come along.

Like the city buses, route taxis are painted according to their routes. Red-and-black taxis operate between Calle 2 (between Avenidas Revolución and Constitución) and La Mesa, along Boulevard Agua Caliente; brown-and-white route taxis run to the Zona Río and Otay Mesa.

TIJUANA CAR RENTAL AGENCIES

Avis: Tijuana International Airport, tel. 664/683-2310; Blvd. Agua Caliente 3310, opposite Hotel Paraíso Radisson, tel. 664/686-3718, 664/686-1507, or 664/686-2075

Budget: Tijuana International Airport, tel. 664/683-2905; Paseo de los Héroes 77, Zona Río, tel. 664/684-3304

Central: Paseo de los Héroes 104, Zona Río, tel. 664/684-2257 or 664/684-2268

Dollar: Tijuana International Airport, tel. 664/683-1861; Blvd. Sánchez Taboada 10285, Zona Río, tel. 664/681-8484

Elite: 1495 Blvd. Agua Caliente, tel. 664/686-3854

Hertz: Tijuana International Airport, tel. 664/683-2080; Hotel Palacio Azteca, Av. 16 de Septiembre (Blvd. Cuauhtémoc Sur) 213, tel. 664/686-1725; Grand Hotel Tijuana, Blvd. Agua Caliente 4500, tel. 664/681-7000; Blvd. Agua Caliente 3402, tel. 664/681-7220

National: Tijuana International Airport, tel. 664/682-4436; Blvd. Agua Caliente 10598, tel. 664/686-2103

Thrifty: Tijuana International Airport, tel. 664/683-8130

Rental Cars

Tijuana has several different car rental operations, such as Avis, Budget, Central, Dollar, Hertz, and National. All offer day, weekend, and weekly deals either with per-kilometer charges added in (best rates for local driving only) or as flat rates only (most economical if you plan to drive long distances in Baja). Car rentals are less expensive in Tijuana than anywhere else on the peninsula. Especially for auto tours of northern Baja, you'll enjoy considerable savings if you rent a car here rather than in Ensenada or Mexicali.

Advance reservations are a good idea as most agencies don't maintain large fleets of cars. With or without reservations, a credit card is a prerequisite for car rental.

Driving

The traffic in Tijuana is fairly stiff all day long, so it's not one of the most pleasant cities in Baja to drive in. On the other hand, lots of visitors do manage to drive themselves around the city— all it takes is a good map and plenty of patience. Generally speaking, streets in the downtown area are well-marked; the biggest difficulty comes in trying to navigate out of the city to Rosarito, Mexicali, or beyond.

Another problem is parking, although the situation is not nearly as bad as in most larger cities in the United States. In the Avenida Revolución area, street parking is hard to come by; it's best to choose one of the fee parking lots. One of the less expensive ones is a parking garage called **Estacionamiento Leyva**, Av. Revolución 1026 (between Calles 6 and 7). The 24-hour open lot behind the Frontón Jai Alai costs US$5–6 a day, but if you patronize any of the restaurants or shops in the *frontón* complex, including the Bazar de México, you can receive three hours free parking with validation of the parking ticket.

If you've crossed the border into Tijuana without acquiring Mexican vehicle insurance, you'll have another chance at the **Allen W. Lloyd Insurance** office, in a small shopping center on the right immediately after you cross the border by road.

LEAVING TIJUANA

To the United States

To get back across the border, simply drive north on Avenida Revolución and follow signs to San Diego. When traffic is stiff, especially on Sunday, you can avoid much of the traffic by circling around to Avenida Padre Kino on the north side of town to approach the border crossing from the east lanes. The west lanes are almost always busiest. A carpool lane for vehicles with three or more occupants has been added on the far right side.

South to Rosarito and Ensenada

The drive from Tijuana to Ensenada or any points between is fairly straightforward, even for drivers who would never consider navigating the Transpeninsular all the way to the Cape. You can choose between two roadways: a modern, four-lane toll expressway (Mexico 1-D, also called the Carretera Cuota or "Toll Highway") and a slightly more challenging two-lane highway (the original Mexico 1, called along this stretch the Carretera Libre or "Free Highway"). Both are scenic drives of around 100 km (60 miles).

Mexico 1-D, the toll highway, parallels the coast the entire distance from Tijuana to Ensenada and offers generally better coastal views than the free road. On the negative side, there are limited opportunities for stopovers since highway exits can be as far as 18 km apart. To get on the toll road, take Calle 3 west and follow the signs for Ensenada; traffic is often very slow until you reach the toll-road entrance near Playas. Tolls are collected at three tollgates (*casetas de cobro*) along Mexico 1-D: at Playas de Tijuana, Rosarito, and San Miguel. At each gate, the toll is approximately US$3 for passenger cars, a bit more for cars with trailers, motorhomes, or large trucks. From Tijuana to Ensenada the total runs US$6, or US$10–15 for larger vehicles. Both U.S. and Mexican currencies are accepted at the tollgates; change is given in pesos, dollars, or a mixture of the two.

Mexico 1, the free road, begins just south of Tijuana and winds through a mountainous area for 18 km before reaching the coast at Rosarito. From Rosarito it hugs the narrow coastal plain for the next 50 km—providing plenty of opportunities for beach stopovers—then turns inland again at La Misión. The final 31 km threads through the mountains before joining Mexico

1-D just north of Ensenada at San Miguel. Getting onto the free road in Tijuana is a challenge; some visitors say they gave up looking for it and settled for the toll road. There's only one sign indicating the way; if you drive south along Avenida Revolución until it curves east into Boulevard Agua Caliente, you'll soon see a sign reading A Rosarito (To Rosarito) with an arrow pointing to the right; watch for a large Calimax store on the right. The next right-hand turn, Boulevard Cuauhtémoc, is the correct turnoff. You can also connect with Boulevard Cuauhtémoc by driving east on Paseo de los Héroes; look for the statue of an Aztec—that's Cuauhtémoc. Once on Boulevard Cuauhtémoc, make no other turns, wade through a seemingly endless succession of stoplights and stop signs, and eventually you'll find yourself on Mexico 1.

East to Tecate and Mexicali

For Tecate, Mexicali, and other points east via the free road, simply follow Boulevard Agua Caliente southeast out of town until it turns into Boulevard Díaz Ordaz and, finally, Mexico 2. If you want to take the toll road to Tecate, follow the signs for the airport rather than signs for Tecate, which are misleading.

Once you're beyond the eastern city limits, the scenery along Mexico 2—toll and free versions—mostly consists of boulders, rolling hills, and the occasional rancho. At Km 166, the highway crosses over the impressive **Presa Rodríguez** (Rodriguez Dam), usually called simply La Presa, "The Dam"), constructed in 1937. In the vicinity of **El Florido,** a small farm community near Km 158, are several dairy farms; look for Hay Queso signs if you'd like to buy some fresh cheese.

A few kilometers east of El Florido, a scenic unpaved road dating from the Spanish colonial period heads north to Valle Redondo. On the south side of Mexico 2, another road leads to Presa El Carrizo, a dam with a sizable lake. This gravel road continues south, past a couple of ranchos, to connect with Mexico 3 at Valle de las Palmas.

Just before the border town of Tecate, between Km 136 and 135, is the turnoff for **Rancho La Puerta,** one of the world's most highly rated health resorts. Mexico 2 then becomes Avenida Juárez, the main west-east thoroughfare through Tecate. Once through Tecate, the highway resumes its eastward direction toward Mexicali and the state of Sonora.

For complete information on Tecate, see Tecate and Vicinity later in this chapter.

ISLAS LOS CORONADOS

The four Los Coronados islands lie only 11 km west of San Antonio del Mar, a mostly American residential area 12 km south of Tijuana. The Spanish explorer Juan Cabrillo passed by in 1542 and called them Las Islas Desiertas (Desert Islands) because of the apparent lack of vegetation; in 1602 Vizcaíno renamed them Los Cuatros Coronados (The Four Coronados) after four brothers who died as Christian martyrs during the era of the Roman Empire.

Too steep and rugged for permanent habitation, the islands were briefly used as a pirate hideaway and later as a rendezvous for smugglers bringing rum and Chinese immigrants into the United States. In 1931 a short-lived hotel and casino called the Coronado Islands Yacht Club rose at the edge of a cove on the largest island, Coronado del Sur. The establishment closed in 1933 with the repeal of Prohibition, and little remains of the decaying three-story building. A few Mexican navy personnel live on the island to protect it from intruders.

Geography and Natural History

All four of Los Coronados are the tips of undersea mountain ridges. The largest island, Coronado del Sur, is about three km long and reaches an elevation of 204 meters at its highest point; California sea lions and northern elephant seals reside in a cliff-lined cove on the island's windward side. The second largest, Coronado del Norte, is about a kilometer long and a steep 142 meters high. The remaining two, Roca Media (Middle Rock) and Coronado del Medio (Middle Coronado), lie between the larger islands and are little more than rock outcroppings. Seagoing birds favor the middle islands as nesting grounds.

NORTHERN BAJA

The islands and the surrounding immediate area are protected by the Mexican government; commercial fishing, with the exception of a few lobster and sea urchin concessions, isn't permitted, nor can visitors land on any of the islands without government permission. As a result, the islands have become one of the most important brown pelican rookeries on the Pacific coast; over 160 other bird species have been identified as well. Along the west side of Coronado del Norte is a large sea lion colony; harbor seals are common along the same shoreline, with elephant seals occasionally seen. Island plant varieties number around 100, mostly cacti, mimosas, and other species suited to arid climates.

Fishing

Yellowtail fishing is usually excellent in the vicinity of the Coronados, with peak season running Apr.–Oct. Rock cod, bonito, halibut, barracuda, calico bass, and white sea bass are also frequently taken. Favorite fishing spots lie just north of Roca Media, at the southeast tip of Coronado del Sur, and inshore along the western side of the same island.

Diving

Los Coronados is the most heavily dived area in Baja waters. Many San Diego novices make their first open-water dives here, and spearfishers have long extolled the abundance of underwater game (but remember that spearfishing is illegal if you're wearing anything more than mask, snorkel, and fins). In some places the moray eels are so accustomed to handouts they immediately approach any diver who happens along.

Good sites for divers of all levels include "The Slot," an area of rich marinelife between the two middle islands; a rocky cove on the northeastern coast of Coronado del Norte called the "Lobster Shack" for an old shack onshore used by lobstermen; the large kelp bed just south of the southern tip of Coronado del Sur; and the rock reef at the northern end of Coronado del Sur. Advanced, open-ocean divers can tackle "Eighty-five-foot Reef," named for the depth at which much of the reef begins. The shallowest portion is about 18 meters (60 feet) below the ocean surface.

Transportation and Tours

No regular boat service to Islas Los Coronados exists—most visitors navigate their own craft—although you might find charters in San Antonio del Mar if you ask around.

Several San Diego fishing outfitters offer fishing tours of the islands. **Horizon Charters,** 4178 Lochlomond St., San Diego, CA 92111, tel. 858/277-7823, divesd@aol.com, www.horizoncharters.com, operates regular diving trips out of San Diego.

Rosarito

Rosarito's multiple personalities—ranchtown, beachtown, and boomtown rolled into one—reflect a short but varied history. During the mission era, the area was virtually uninhabited—out of the reach of Dominican missions to the south and Franciscan missions to the north. Although the Camino Real (Royal Road) passed nearby, it wasn't until a parallel road began snaking southward along the coast from Tijuana that anyone but ranchers developed an interest in the area. Early Baja travelers discovered the huge beach at Rosarito (one of the widest and longest on Baja's Pacific coast) in the 1920s, and it has become more popular with each passing decade.

A new side to Rosarito development arrived with the establishment of a massive American film set at nearby Popotla for the production of *Titanic* in 1996. Before the film had completed shooting, the city council granted permission for Fox Studios Baja to become a permanent production facility. The intermittent Hollywood presence is bringing a new style to the town, one that some residents and visitors love while others abhor.

Summer months see the highest tourist numbers in Rosarito, both Mexicans and foreigners. Winter—except Thanksgiving and Christmas/New Year's—is slow, and room rates hit their lowest. Between Semana Santa and U.S.

college/university spring break, March and April can be busy—avoid Rosarito during those times unless you like crowds. September, October, and May are splendid months for enjoying the town at its best.

History

In 1827, as Mexico was gaining its independence from Spain, Juan Machado received a land grant of 407,000 acres in the Rosarito area, then called El Rosario. The Machado family raised cattle and sheep on the property and leased land to other ranchers. In 1914 the family sold 14,000 coastal acres to a land development corporation, which in turn sold them to a New York attorney in 1920.

In 1924 the attorney opened El Rosario Resort and Country Club next to the beach. Initially the resort was little more than a rustic hunting cabin. A dirt road between Tijuana and Ensenada passed El Rosario, however, and it became a popular stopover for Americans sampling the casinos at either end of the road. The free camping allowed on the property probably didn't hurt its success.

Manuel Barbachano bought the property around 1930 and built the Rosarito Beach Hotel, a 10-room hotel with a small lobby, one bathroom, and a casino to take advantage of the Prohibition boom in gambling. Apparently no record exists as to why Barbachano changed the name from El Rosario to Rosarito—perhaps because "Rosarito" is easier for gringos to pronounce. Another theory claims that he named the hotel after Lee J. Rose, developer of one of Tijuana's first racetracks.

For most of the next 40 years, all development in Rosarito focused around the Rosarito Beach Hotel. After Prohibition ended and the Mexican government banned casino gambling, Barbachano closed the casino but enlarged the hotel, employing a Belgian architect and Mexican muralist to turn it into a major attraction. During the 1940s and '50s, Rosarito became a favorite haunt of Hollywood celebrities, Latin American presidents, and well-heeled international travelers.

The completion of a four-lane toll road to

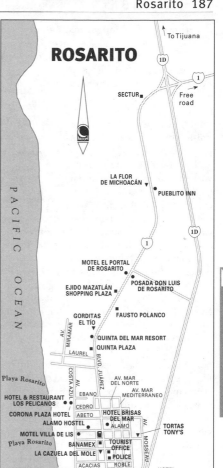

Rosarito in 1967 brought many more Californians into town and modified the exclusive nature of the resort. Other hotels were built and, although the Rosarito Beach Hotel remained the beach centerpiece for some time, the town expanded from a weekend resort to a large residential community of retirees and self-employed expatriates.

> *Rosarito's main draw is its eight-kilometer-long sandy beach, where you can swim, snorkel, surf, and spread out a beach towel.*

Today a four-lane roadway with bike lanes and lighted traffic islands passes through the center of Rosarito, lined with shopping plazas, neon-lit restaurants, high-rise hotels, and condominiums. Vacation and retirement homes, an estimated 10,000 owned by Americans and Canadians, stretch along the ocean for miles in either direction. During the last few years city officials have given some 40,000 trees to local citizens for planting throughout the city. Yet only about half the town's residents have running water.

Rosarito was once part of the *municipio* of Tijuana, and its relative prosperity provided a large portion of Tijuana's annual budget. Rosarito residents argued that if the town could secede from municipal Tijuana, more money could go toward local urban improvements. A 15-year battle to separate from Tijuana ended in June 1995, when Rosarito became BCN's fifth *municipio*. Locals estimate the population at just over 100,000, although the most recent official census counts only 46,000.

One outcome of Rosarito's new independence from Tijuana was the quick decision to allow the movie *Titanic* to set up production facilities nearby in 1996. As a result, Rosarito was the only *municipio* in the state to post a budget surplus that year. Several more blockbusters have been made here, including the Russel Crowe heroism-at-sea vehicle, *Master and Commander*.

Many residents voice the hope that zoning restrictions will come with increased wealth. However, high-rise buildings continue to race toward the Rosarito skyline, crowding the once-peaceful beach town closer and closer toward a Miami Beach fate. The controversial Hotel Festival Plaza, a bright yellow-and-green high-rise on the main drag, is meant to look like an amusement park with its roller-coaster facade and working Ferris wheel—a Coney Island touch hated by some, loved by others. The latest addition has been a 500-meter cruise ship and sportfishing pier attached to the Rosarito Beach Hotel. So far the cruises haven't been scheduled, and the pier is closed most of the time. Slow-growth advocates maintain that cruise ship traffic will spoil Rosarito's central attraction, the beach, while local merchants are delighted that cruise passengers will soon be wandering the town boulevard, their pockets bulging with dollars.

SIGHTS

The Beach

Rosarito's main draw is its eight-km-long sandy beach. Several beachwear and surf shops in town offer swimming, snorkeling, floating, and surfing equipment for rent or purchase.

The Rosarito Beach Hotel

An attraction in itself, this hotel was the only place to stay in Rosarito for nearly 75 years; for many repeat visitors it's still the first choice. Originally built in 1926 with only 12 rooms, during its heyday in the 1940s and '50s, the hotel gained a reputation among the Hollywood set as a romantic retreat. Frequent guests included Victor Mature, Mickey Rooney, Joan Bennett, Lana Turner, Orson Welles, Rita Hayworth, Debbie Reynolds, Robert Stack, Gregory Peck, Robert Preston, Spencer Tracy, Jack Palance, and Vincent Price. International playboy Ali Khan and actress Gene Tierney, along with an entourage of 24, took over the entire hotel for several weeks in 1955; Kim Novak and Dominican Republic president Rafael Leonidas Trujillo trysted here during the same era. Not all Hollywood rendezvous at the Rosarito were of the illicit variety; Burgess Meredith and Paulette Goddard married here.

The original owner's nephew, Hugo Torres, acquired the property in 1974. Following his uncle's example, Torres continues to expand the facilities and currently offers 280 rooms. Although no longer a celebrity hideaway, a tour of the Belgian-designed architecture, the Matía Santoyo murals, and the seaward-facing Beachcomber Bar is on the itinerary of nearly every Rosarito visitor.

A 500-meter sportfishing pier was added to the rear of the hotel in 2003. When it's open (when we last visited it was closed, with no explanation as to why), admission onto the pier costs US$1.10 for adults, free for hotel guests and children under 12. If you bring a rod or line, you'll pay US$4.50 per person to fish. Open daily 10 A.M.–6 P.M.

Museo Wa-Kuatay

This tiny museum attached to the Rosarito Beach Hotel (next to the pharmacy) houses a collection of historic photos of early ranchers, Hollywood celebrities, and politicos. One display features artifacts left by the Wakutais, the original inhabitants of the Rosarito area. The museum is open Thurs.–Sun. 10 A.M.–4 P.M.; admission is free.

ACCOMMODATIONS

Most of Rosarito's hotels are strung out along Boulevard Juárez, the main thoroughfare. Considering the proximity to the U.S. border, room rates are reasonable: from US$28 s, US$32 d at the cheapest motels to around US$95 at the most expensive hotels or over US$100 for a suite, condo, or townhouse. These rates are high for Mexico but a bargain for most southern Californians. Rates are usually discounted 30–50 percent during the low season (Nov.–Apr.) and on Sun.–Thurs. nights. During high season (July–Aug.), rates leap up, especially on weekends. Reservations are highly recommended. Hotels on the beach cost more than those on the opposite side of Boulevard Benito Juárez.

Time-share condos and vacation homes are also available at the various complexes around town and are often good bargains for four or more people. The tourist office (see Information and Services, farther on) can provide a list of agencies representing rental houses and condos.

Under US$25

German-run **Alamo Hostel,** Calle Alamo 15, tel. 661/613-1179, www.alamo-hostel.com, offers bunk beds in clean, shared rooms for US$15 per person per night. Calle Alamo is opposite Hotel Brisas del Mar, between the Rosarito Beach Hotel and the Corona Plaza.

US$25–50

The lowest prices we found were at **Motel Sonia,** on the east side of Boulevard Juárez (next door to Panadería La Espiga), tel. 661/612-1260, where the rooms are basic but clean and the showers are hot.

A real find in this range is **Motel Paraíso Ortiz** (P.O. Box 435349, San Ysidro, CA 92143-5349), tel. 661/612-1020, an old-fashioned beach cottage court well off the road and close to the beach at Rosarito's south end. To find the place, proceed south along Boulevard Juárez past the Rosarito Beach Hotel and associated beach home development, and look for Rene's Sports Bar Restaurant; Paraíso Ortiz is right next door. The tidy rooms all have wall heaters, and some face the ocean. The staff is friendly and parking seems secure.

In the same general vicinity but on the east (non-beach) side of the road, **Motel Quinta Chica,** Km 25 Rosarito-Ensenada Highway, tel. 661/612-2991, offers decent rooms in a modern, three-story brick building.

In the main commercial strip near Hotel Festival Plaza and opposite Restaurant El Nido, **Hotel California,** Blvd. Juárez 32, tel. 661/612-2552, is a two-story place offering clean rooms with cable TV. Although it's on the wrong side of the road for instant beach access, the Hotel California is convenient to restaurants and shopping.

Motel Villa de Lis, Calle Alamo at Av. Costa Azul, tel. 661/612-2320, occupies a modest building in a quiet downtown location with Rosarito Beach frontage. Although it's nothing special in terms of atmosphere or amenities, the motel appears to be clean and well run.

In the north-central part of town, on the west side of the main drag but not on the beach, 24-room **Motel El Portal de Rosarito,** Blvd. Juárez at Via de las Olas, tel. 661/612-0050, offers clean rooms with TV in a two-story pink building with off-street parking. In the same vicinity but on the other side of the street, the older **Motel Don Luis de Rosarito,** Blvd. Juárez 272, tel. 661/612-1166, offers good-sized rooms in a motel court at similar rates.

Hotel Los Pelicanos, Calle Ebano 113, tel. 661/612-0445, info@los-pelicanos.com, www.los-pelicanos.com, is well off the main drag, quiet, and on the beach. The place doesn't look like much on the outside, but the 39 rooms are spacious and well-kept, and all contain heaters and TVs.

US$50–100

At the north end of town on the west side of the main avenue (right next to the towering Quinta del Mar Resort condo complex), **Hotel Quinta Terranova,** Blvd. Juárez 25500, tel./fax 661/612-1650, www.hotelquintaterranova.iwarp.com, features 84 fresh, clean rooms, each with coffeemaker and TV. Well-behaved dogs are welcome here.

Now that we're used to seeing its slightly bizarre, multicolored profile, we've grown to like the **Hotel Festival Plaza,** Blvd. Juárez north of the Rosarito Beach Hotel, tel. 661/612-2950, U.S. reservations tel. 888/295-9669, www.festivalplazahotel.com. For the young and the young at heart, this is the coolest place to stay in Rosarito—except during the annual U.S. college spring break, when it transforms into Animal House. The unique all-in-one complex surrounds a plaza loaded with a Ferris wheel, tequila museum/bar, café, two restaurants, two dance clubs, a heated free-form pool, and a hot tub. The 114-room hotel section appears to be well managed. Suites and more expensive "villas," each with two bedrooms and a fully equipped kitchen, are available. And on the hotel's back side toward the beach are even more expensive town-houselike *casitas,* each containing one queen bed, a living room with a sofabed, a miniature hot tub, and your own private garage. There's a two-night minimum.

Back on the east side of Juárez away from the beach, **Hotel Brisas del Mar,** Blvd. Juárez 22, tel./fax 661/612-2547, U.S./Canada tel. 888/871-3605, features 71 well-appointed rooms and facilities including a restaurant, coffee shop, hot tub, volleyball and basketball courts, and secure parking.

At the north end of town the **Pueblito Inn** Blvd. Juárez 286, tel. 661/612-2516, www.rosaritobeach.net/pacifico_hotel, features 47 air-conditioned rooms with cable TV and phone; most rooms contain two double beds. The hotel is clean and comfortable but a bit sterile-feeling. Amenities include a restaurant, pool, and ATM.

The venerable **Rosarito Beach Hotel, Pier & Spa,** south end of Blvd. Juárez (P.O. Box 430145, San Diego, CA 92143-0145), tel. 661/612-1111 or 661/612-0144, U.S. tel. 800/343-8582, reservations@pacnet.com.mx, www.rosaritobeachhotel.com, has grown into a sprawling complex with several different varieties of rooms. Rooms in the oldest wing are atmospheric but in need of refurbishing. Facilities include restaurants, pools, tennis and racquetball courts, a fitness course, gym, and sauna. On the adjacent hotel grounds, Casa La Playa offers European-style spa treatments. Special hotel packages that include meals are often available, but all of the ones we've seen were either based on separate per person (double occupancy) rates—resulting in little or no savings over regular room rates if you didn't eat in the hotel—or provided one meal only, necessitating the purchase of another meal for couples. Spa packages may be a better deal.

Corona Plaza Hotel, U.S./Canada tel. 800/511-4848, is a monstrously tall, 325-room hotel with very undistinguished facilities and the feel of a cheap L.A. apartment building. One plus is the huge parking lot.

Condos

Quinta del Mar Resort, tel. 661/612-1145, 661/612-2826, qdelmar@telnor.net, www.quintadelmar.com, is a multistory condominium/

time-share complex with plenty of units for rent. Even the one-bedroom units are spacious and come with kitchen utensils. In the units we inspected, the electric stoves needed repair and the overall furnishings were worn. Mid-September to mid-March, rates are inexpensive, but after March 15 prices double, reaching the US$100–150 price range. A two-night minimum stay is required.

Out of Town

US$25–50: Hotel Calafia, at Km 35.5 on the free road, tel. 661/612-1581, fax 661/612-0296, U.S./Canada tel. 877/700-2093, www.hotelcalafia.com, is a rambling collection of tile-roofed buildings along a cliff on the water's edge, all done in mission kitsch. On the premises are two restaurants and a bar, plus a few historical exhibits chronicling the Misión del Descanso (which once stood nearby) and the missionization of the Californias.

US$50–100: Castillos del Mar, Km 36.5 (P.O. Box 1772, San Ysidro, CA 92073), tel. 661/612-1088, U.S. tel. 800/511-4848, www.rosaritobeach.net/castillos, offers small cottages on expansive grounds overlooking the ocean.

Las Rocas Resort and Spa (P.O. Box 189003, Coronado, CA 92178), tel. 661/614-0354, U.S./Canada tel. 888/527-7622, www.lasrocas.com, is an isolated resort hotel 9.5 km south of Rosarito at Km 37.5 on the free road. The cubelike concrete structures aren't particularly attractive on the outside, but cozy Mexican rustic interiors feature ocean views, fireplaces, and kitchenettes. Other facilities include secured parking, cable TV, restaurant, pool, hot tub, and tennis courts. The hotel also has a spa featuring massages, facials, hydrotherapy, full salon treatments, and a steam room.

US$100–150: About two km north of Rosarito at Km 25 lies the deluxe **Oasis Beach Resort and Convention Center** (P.O. Box 158, Imperial Beach, CA 91933), tel. 661/631-3250, U.S. tel. 888/709-9985, fax 661/633-3252. The resort has a "Las Vegas" look; its pseudo-Arabic architecture, along with a large sculpture of an Arab drinking water on top of a camel, has to be seen to be believed. Oasis offers 100 suites that sleep up to four adults—each with an ocean view, refrigerator, and microwave. Amenities include two restaurants, tennis courts, a gym, a sauna, two pools plus a kids' pool, two hot tubs, a minimarket, minigolf, Laundromat, and a fully equipped convention center. The beach here is impressive, and the park places an emphasis on family-oriented recreational activities. Oasis also offers RV sites (see the following section).

Camping and RV Parks

Chuy's Trailer Park, Av. Costa Azul 175 downtown, tel. 661/612-1608, features around 30 beachfront sites with full hookups for US$22 a night; it's often full. Also on Costa Azul, near the Motel Villa de Lis, **Alamo Trailer Park** (opposite Alamo Hostel), tel. 661/613-1179, has a few basic spaces with electricity and water for US$25 a night; weekly and monthly rates are also available.

The most expensive RV facility anywhere in Mexico, **Oasis Beach Resort and Convention Center** (see contact information under Out of Town) has 55 full-hookup RV spots, each with individual barbecue pits, satellite cable TV connections, and the use of all resort facilities. Beachfront sites for up to four adults cost US$50 and up. The resort also offers 22 mobile homes for rent for US$100 per day and up. Add 12 percent tax to all rates.

About three km south of Rosarito is **Campo Alegre,** with full hookups for US$20 per night. In the same vicinity is **Popotla Trailer Park,** tel. 661/612-1502, where most of the slots are occupied by long-term residents; when vacant, a space costs US$20–25 a night, while tent sites are US$17. Permanently sited trailers are sometimes available for rent for US$25–30 a night. **Campo Martha,** tel. 661/614-1022, near Hotel Las Rocas at Km 37.5 on the way to Ensenada, usually has full-hookup spots in the US$15 range. **Club Paradise,** a large trailer park between Km 47 and 48 on the toll road, offers full hookups in a basic dirt lot for US$15–20 per night.

FOOD

Rosarito's Boulevard Juárez is jammed with restaurants of every description. Every block seems to contain at least one taco stand and one seafood restaurant. Some of the better choices are listed below.

Antojitos, Tacos, Tortas

Los Arcos, on Blvd. Juárez next to the Rosarito Beach Hotel gate, tel. 661/612-0491, is an overgrown taco stand serving tasty and inexpensive *flautas,* tacos, burritos, *queso fundido* (melted cheese), *gorditas* (thick corn tortillas stuffed with meat), and Mexican breakfasts for around US$2. Open daily 8 A.M.–10 P.M.

In one corner of the Hotel Festival Plaza, **Rock and Roll Taco** offers moderately priced fish, chicken, and *carne asada* tacos. At night it's more of a bar than an eatery.

Romero's Tamale Inn, on the west side of Juárez opposite Hotel Brisas del Mar, is a gringo favorite. Its main strength is that it serves breakfast all day. Other specialties include burgers, sandwiches, tamales, and *taquitos.* Inexpensive to moderate; open daily except Tuesday, 7 A.M.–3 P.M.

Tacos El Yaqui is an upscale-looking outdoor taco place (there's even a little building with bathrooms, very unusual) specializing in *tacos de carne asada* made with top sirloin. Plenty of condiments. It's on the south side of Calle de la Palma, a block east of Boulevard Juárez not far from Hotel Festival Plaza and the Rosarito Beach Hotel. Inexpensive; open daily 10 A.M.–midnight.

Tortas Tony's, on the north side of Calle de Ciprés four blocks east of Boulevard Juárez, is another good and relatively inexpensive side-street place of some local fame. Despite the name, Tony's offers much more than *tortas,* the torpedo-shaped Mexican sandwich; try the *menudo, sopes, caldo de res, tostados, pozole,* burritos, and *barbacoa.* To find Calle de Ciprés, turn east off Boulevard Juárez directly opposite the Pemex station in the middle of town. Open daily 8 A.M.–8 P.M.

Gorditas El Tío, at the northwest corner of Cárdenas and Juárez, is worth a stop for their nicely spiced roast meats wrapped in thick corn tortillas. Open daily 10 A.M.–9 P.M.

Full Meals

High marks go to **La Cazuela del Mole,** on the west side of Blvd. Juárez, just south of Banamex and Calle René Ortiz, more or less opposite the police station. As the name suggests, the house specialty is *mole,* an extremely rich sauce made with chocolate, chilies, ground sesame seeds, and many other ingredients and usually served over chicken or turkey. Especially recommended are the *pollo en mole poblano* (Puebla-style chicken *mole*), *molotes* (chicken and cheese wrapped in cornflour dough and fried, somewhat like piroshkis), *pollo en mixiote* (roast chicken in a spicy, orange-colored sauce reminiscent of some curries), *sopes* (thick fried cornmeal cakes topped with chopped meat, onions, and chilies), and *tamales de dulce* (sweet tamales, here made with pineapple). The food is good, the service is very good, and the prices are low—the average entrée costs just US$3. Open daily except Tuesday noon–8 P.M.

At **La Flor de Michoacán,** Blvd. Juárez 291, tel. 661/612-1858, the Ochoa family has been making the best *carnitas* in town since 1950. Besides *carnitas* by the half kilo (US$14) or kilo (US$23–25—beans, guacamole, salsa, and tortillas are included in the price), the menu offers tacos, *tortas, burritos de carnitas* (US$3.50), and quesadillas (US$2), all served with bowls of fiery salsa, lime sections, and pickled chilies and vegetables. All breakfasts cost US$4 (except *bistek ranchero* and *machaca con huevo,* which are about US$6). Menudo is available on Saturday and Sunday. The service is excellent; some nights a roving group of *músicos* performs *norteña* music on request. Open daily 8 A.M.–10 P.M. Breakfast is served till noon.

Restaurant La Leña de Rosarito, Quinta Plaza shopping center, Blvd. Juárez, tel. 661/612-0826, is a branch of the well-known Tijuana steak house, specializing in Sonoran-style, mesquite-grilled meats. Most meals come with an appetizer of *machaca* (dried, shredded beef). Moderately priced. Open daily noon–10 P.M.

In the upper courtyard of the Hotel Festival Plaza, **El Patio Restaurant,** tel. 661/612-2950, proffers indoor/outdoor dining amid a vibrant Mexican decor. The extensive (and somewhat expensive) menu includes *carne asada tampiqueña,* Puerto Nuevo–style lobster, fish tacos, smoked marlin tacos, combo tacos, and several Mexican dishes you won't find elsewhere in town, such as *pollo pibil* (Yucatán-style barbecued chicken) and vegetarian tacos. It's open daily 8 A.M.–1 A.M. Also inside the hotel plaza is **Pepe and Penelope's Poolside Café,** a good spot for breakfast and light meals; open 7 A.M.–10 P.M.

Seafood

Despite the corny name, **La Casa de la Langosta,** in the Quinta Plaza shopping center next to La Leña, tel. 661/612-0924, really is the best spot in town for lobster, offered in several different styles. Puerto Nuevo–style is best; the creatures are split lengthwise, dropped briefly into spiced hot oil, grilled a few minutes, then served with frijoles, rice, and tortillas for around US$15. There's no better way to eat lobster. Moderate prices. Open daily 8 A.M.–10 P.M.

The Ortega family, owner of **Ortega's Place,** Blvd. Juárez 200, tel. 661/612-0022, started out serving lobster dinners to tourists at their home in nearby Puerto Nuevo in 1945. The house specialty is Puerto Nuevo–style lobster, but the massive buffet of other dishes has overtaken lobster among most of their clientele. Open daily for breakfast, lunch, and dinner. Their champagne brunch draws a hungry crowd every Sunday.

Yet another eatery in Rosarito's most unique hotel, **Portofino** (formerly Puerto Langosta), on the second floor of the Hotel Festival Plaza, tel. 661/612-2950, most matches the hotel's overall sense of whimsy. Reached via an "underwater" staircase, the darkened restaurant is lit by neon stars, the floor is thickly covered in sand, and the tables are set beneath individual palapa roofs. The menu focuses on seafood, of course, and it's not bad if a little on the pricey side. Tailor-made fun for spring-breakers. Open daily 1–11 P.M., Fri. and Sat. till midnight.

Los Pelicanos, Calle Ebano at Av. Costa Azul, tel. 661/612-1737, part of the hotel of the same name, is one of the few restaurants in town that's on the beach, offering a full ocean view. Good seafood and quail; upscale ambience. Open daily noon–midnight.

North of Rosarito in an area optimistically called Baja Malibu, **Mariscos La Costa Restaurant,** at Km 22 on the Tijuana-Rosarito toll road, San Antonio exit, tel. 661/613-3202, also looks toward the sea, if only over the roofs of local beach homes. The long menu encompasses all sorts of dishes created with fresh *frutas del mar,* from seafood cocktails and seafood soups to shellfish and finfish entrées served grilled, broiled, fried, raw, or marinated. The funky nautical decor hits the right note. Come hungry; complimentary appetizers and an after-dinner drink come with every meal. Open Mon.–Fri. noon– midnight, Sat. and Sun. 8 A.M.–midnight.

Other Eateries

The coffee shop at the **Rosarito Beach Hotel** serves a huge, reasonably priced Sunday brunch (7:30 A.M.–2 P.M.) that includes ceviche, *chilaquiles,* tamales, seafood, Mexican egg dishes, and fresh fruit. Upstairs, the **Azteca** offers more expensive lunch, seafood, and Mexican fare.

Chabert's, housed in the restored Barbachano mansion next to the Rosarito Beach Hotel (and under the same ownership), is a vanity restaurant serving upscale French and Continental cuisine. The elegant decor includes a Tiffany chandelier, Italian baroque tables, Louis XIV chairs, and mirrors framed in expensive dragon-carved teak. The pricey international menu covers all the bases, from chateaubriand to chicken Kiev. An attached ballroom hosts live music on occasion. Open Fri.–Sun. 5 P.M.–midnight in the low season, daily in high season. The restaurant is occasionally reserved for local events—probably the main source of profit for a place that appears to be rather high-priced for Rosarito.

El Canaveral Frutería, next to the Banamex on Blvd. Juárez, sells fresh fruit *licuados* (smoothies). For Mexican pastries your best bet is **Panaficadora La Espiga,** across Boulevard Juárez from Hotel Festival Plaza. Espiga also occupies two other locations: one at the north end of town opposite Ejido Mazatlán shopping plaza and a tortillería and one opposite Ortega's Place. For a superb cappuccino try **Cappuchino's Coffee and Pastry House,** diagonally across the street from Hotel Festival Plaza.

SPORTS AND RECREATION

Surfing

During the winter, intermittent surf—usually nothing huge, but still surfable—may appear at either end of the beach. Better breaks are usually found south of Rosarito, starting at Km 33, from Punta Descanso to Punta Mesquite. **Inner Reef Surf Shop,** Km 34.5 Mexico 1 (free road), tel. 661/615-0841, sells and rents surfboards and other surf gear. Inner Reef also builds custom surfboards for US$240–385 depending on size and finish.

Horseback Riding

Riding on the beach is a favorite tourist activity. Local wranglers wait for customers on the beach near the Rosarito Beach Hotel and at the north end of Boulevard Juárez. Rates start at around US$8 per hour but are negotiable when business is slow.

Wagering

Gamblers can indulge in off-track betting and sports book at **Caliente Race and Sports Book,** Quinta Plaza shopping center.

Charreadas

Small *charro* rings near town occasionally host *charreadas*—check with the tourist office on Boulevard Juárez for the latest schedule. Once a year, during the summer, a *gran charreada* takes place at Lienzo Charro Ejido Mazatlán—this is the one to see.

ENTERTAINMENT AND EVENTS

Bars and Nightclubs

On weekend nights and any night in July or August, Rosarito throbs with a disco beat. Several clubs are concentrated just north of the Rosarito Beach Hotel, on the beach side of Boulevard Juárez. **Papas and Beer,** at the beach end of Calle Nogal, features multilevel indoor and outdoor bar areas, plus a sand volleyball court; it's packed on warm summer nights, all but deserted in winter.

The Hotel Festival Plaza features four bars/dance clubs designed to attract night owls young and old. **Rock and Roll Taco** has a Boulevard Juárez entrance as well as a poolside area. The hotel's **El Museo Sal y Limón Cantina** also opens onto Juárez and claims the world's largest tequila collection. Other pluses are its semiau-

horseback riding on the beach

© JOE CUMMINGS

thentic Mexican cantina feel, good jukebox, and pool table. On the hotel's second floor, **Cha Cha Cha Barefoot Bar** attempts to imitate a Latin Caribbean beach club, including the appropriate music—canned during the week, live on Fri. and Sat. nights.

Rene's Sports Bar, right next to Paraíso Ortiz at the southern outskirts of town, maintains a few pool tables and a bank of TVs tuned to sports channels. It's very much a gringo hangout, but a comfortable one. The attached dining room, which serves seafood, steak, and quail, is mostly empty except in the highest of high seasons, when strolling *trovadores* offer *música romántica.*

Salón de Calamar, across from Quinta Mar Resort, hosts live Mexican music, including occasional *banda* ensembles, Thurs.–Sun. nights. It's attached to Vince's Grill Bar El Calamar.

El Mexicano in the Rosarito Beach Hotel features live Latin and international dance music on weekend nights. The hotel also hosts a "Fiesta Mexicana" every Friday evening 7–10 P.M. in one of the ground-floor lounges. For US$12 guests receive a full Mexican buffet and credible performances of folk dancing, mariachis, and *charro* rope tricks. The hotel's **Beachcomber Bar** overlooks the beach and is a good place for a quiet sunset drink.

Events

Twice yearly in April and September, Rosarito kicks off the **Rosarito-Ensenada 50-Mile Bicycle Ride.** It is reportedly the third-largest biking event in the world, with close to 10,000 cyclists. For more information, call Bicycling West in San Diego, tel. 619/424-6084, or register online at www.rosaritoensenada.com.

The **Feria Rosarito** or Rosarito Fair, held in July, brings all kinds of food and entertainment onto the streets and into the hotels and restaurants. For details, contact COTUCO, tel. 661/612-0396, U.S. tel. 800/962-2252.

Bajacaliforniano food fans won't want to miss the **Festival del Vino y la Langosta** (Festival of Wine and Lobster), held mid- to late-October; call CANIRAC (Cámara Nacional de la Industria Restaurantera—a restaurant-industry consortium), tel. 661/612-0700, for information.

For up-to-date information on Rosarito's ongoing schedule of events, call 661/612-0396 or 800/962-BAJA (800/962-2252).

SHOPPING

Rosarito offers a representative sampling of the same kinds of retail outlets found in Tijuana—liquor stores, pharmacies, curio shops, furniture outlets, leather shops, art galleries, and boutiques, most catering to American tastes. **Tile Express,** Blvd. Juárez 54A, tel. 661/612-1913, for example, is a branch of the larger Tijuana store. An even larger selection of handmade tiles is available at **Artesanías Hacienda,** Blvd. Juárez 2500-C, tel. 661/612-2435.

Custom-made Mexican rustic-style furniture is available at **La Casa de la Carreta,** Km 29 on the old (free) Rosarito-Ensenada road. **Pancho's,** on Boulevard Juárez toward the north end of Rosarito, offers cheaper curios, pottery, and the ever-present *equipales* (from the Nahuatl *icpalli,* meaning "chair"—the barrel-shaped leather-and-wood chairs seen all over southern California these days).

For high-end, hacienda-style Mexican furniture, have a look at **Fausto Polanco,** Blvd. Juárez 2400, tel. 661/612 2271, www.faustopolanco .com.mx. You'll find a second branch just out of town at Km 35 on the toll road to Ensenada (and another in Los Angeles).

Among the better art collections in town are **Del Mar** (south end of the Rosarito Beach Hotel complex) and **Pabel's** (a block north of the Rosarito Beach Hotel on the opposite side of Juárez).

On the west side of Boulevard Juárez, about midway between the Quinta del Mar and Rosarito Beach hotels, is the **Mercado de Artesanías,** a crafts market with around 200 vendors selling ceramics, textiles, wood carving, sculpture, and other handmade items. Just south of town is a string of vendor stalls where handicraft prices tend to be a bit lower. Bargaining is expected; most vendors are open 9 A.M.–6 P.M.

Many shops are grouped in shopping plazas, e.g., Plaza Ejido Mazatlán, Quinta Plaza, and the arcade attached to the Rosarito Beach Hotel.

INFORMATION AND SERVICES

Tourist Assistance

SECTUR, tel./fax 661/612-0200, is at the north end of town, north of the Tecate beer dealer and across from a Pemex station on Boulevard Benito Juárez. The helpful staff distributes Rosarito area and Baja California tourist information; English is spoken. Open Mon.–Fri. 9 A.M.–7 P.M., weekends 10 A.M.–4 P.M.

Money–Changing

Banamex and Serfín, both on the west side of Boulevard Juárez north of Hotel Festival Plaza, offer ATMs and can cash traveler's checks.

Transportation

No regular buses run between Tijuana and Rosarito. Instead yellow-and-white station wagon *taxis de ruta* ply the half-hour stretch between Tijuana and Rosarito from early in the morning until late at night for US$1.80 pp. These taxis can take you as far as La Mesa in Tijuana, depending on the route (five in all). The trip takes about 40 minutes or less, depending on traffic. You can catch these taxis anywhere along Boulevard Juárez, though the main *sitio* (taxi stand) seems to be at the southern end of the avenue near the Hotel Festival Plaza and Rosarito Beach Hotel. The white-and-red taxis offer only local service.

Route taxis also go to La Misión and Puerto Nuevo, both coastal towns south of Rosarito, for US$2. The main *sitio* for the latter is along Calle Villa Alamo, just south of Hotel Brisas del Mar and east of Boulevard Juárez.

Mexicoach (see "San Diego to Tijuana" in the On the Road chapter) operates between Tijuana and Rosarito for US$10 per person during regular operating hours.

From Tijuana to Rosarito it's 31 km via the toll road, 27 km via the free road. Mexico 1-D, the toll road, is much faster, with four lanes in each direction, no traffic lights, and a maximum speed limit of 110 km per hour (about 65 mph). The toll-road entrance in Tijuana is just south of the Río Tijuana.

To take the free road (Mexico 1) from Tijuana you'll need to find Boulevard Cuauhtémoc by driving east on either Paseo de los Héroes or Boulevard Agua Caliente, then turn south on Cuauhtémoc. Coming from San Diego, you can avoid Tijuana altogether by crossing the border at Otay Mesa east of Tijuana, then following signs for Tecate. Instead of taking the turnoff for Mexico 2 to Tecate, continue straight on Boulevard Lázaro Cárdenas—which becomes Boulevard Independencia or "Libramiento-Oriente"—until the road intersects with Mexico 1. Follow signs reading Ensenada Libre.

If you're driving north out of Rosarito, note that the highway signs are misleading—the sign for Tijuana actually puts you onto the highway south to Ensenada. For Tijuana, follow the sign reading San Diego.

Rosarito has two Pemex stations; the one near the Hotel Quinta del Mar is open 24 hours.

Small buses called *calafias* transport people up and down Boulevard Juárez for a few pesos.

South from Rosarito

The coast south of Rosarito holds a string of beaches, *ejidos* (see the glossary), and residential communities: Popotla, Las Gaviotas, Puerto Nuevo, Cantamar, El Descanso, La Fonda, La Misión, La Salina, Bajamar, and San Miguel. Real estate developers call this the "Gold Coast," but only the coves and beaches are particularly attractive.

From Bahía Descanso (especially Km 33–38, Km 48, and Km 56 on the free road) to as far south as La Misión, several surfing spots offer decent reef or beach breaks. An area of sand dunes near Km 54 south of Cantamar is frequented by hang-gliding enthusiasts.

POPOTLA

Roughly 6.5 km (four miles) south of Rosarito via the free road, near Km 33, is a turnoff leading through a large cement arch to Popotla. The village attracts a strong following of seafood aficionados.

Around 30 seafood stands and rustic cafés crowd onto a point at one end of a small bay. Each draws its menu choices from the catch of the day, hauled directly from local boats and stuffed into plastic coolers. The food is delicious and inexpensive relative to prices in Rosarito and Puerto Nuevo, but not necessarily as cheap as places farther south, such as the seafood market in Ensenada or fish camps along the Baja California Sur coast. Popotla's vendors open around 11 A.M.

In the recent past when Popotla was just a sleepy fishing village, not all visitors found the standards of sanitation acceptable. But all that has changed now that Fox Studios Baja is well established—today Popotla has electricity, cold beer, better sanitation, and lots of tourists.

Estudios de la Playa (Fox Studios Baja)

Twentieth Century Fox built this huge indoor/outdoor studio complex for the 1996 filming of the Academy Award–winning blockbuster *Titanic*. A 95 percent scale replica of the original ship was constructed on the lot and floated in a giant seawater tank near the beach, allowing camera angles that blended the tank's water surface with that of the Pacific Ocean. After production on *Titanic* ended, Fox decided to maintain the US$25 million studios as a permanent production facility and to lease it out to other filmmakers. Other films that have used the 15 hectare (35-acre) compound include *Tomorrow Never Dies, In Dreams, Deep Blue Sea, The Weight of Water, Pearl Harbor, Kung POW!—Enter the Fist,* and *Master and Commander.* Television commercials, made-for-television movies, and music videos are produced here as well.

FSB is the only coastal studio on the entire Pacific seaboard. In the United States the only other such facilities are found in Louisiana, Florida, and Mississippi. Unobstructed views of the ocean, a combined tank volume of over 76 million liters (20 million gallons), and a modern filtration plant capable of delivering 34,000 liters (9,000 gallons) of filtered seawater per minute, however, make FSB the world's premiere facility for water-related filmmaking. The studio complex also features over 840 square meters (9,000 square feet) of permanent office space, 6,500 square meters (70,000 square feet) of enclosed stage space, and more than 8,400 square meters (90,000 square feet) of construction workshops, storage areas, and physical plant facilities.

The latest addition to this growing complex is **Foxploration,** a sort of Fox Studios theme park that was conceived to allow the public to go behind the scenes at a working movie studio, learning firsthand about the production process in an entertaining and interactive way. Some of the attractions include: "Canal Street, New York,"

> **At Foxploration, go behind the scenes at a working movie studio and learn firsthand about the production process; don't miss seeing the sets, costumes, and props from the 1996 movie Titanic, which was filmed here.**

NORTHERN BAJA

an actual movie set re-creating a vintage Manhattan street; "Cinemágico," interactive exhibits involving sound effects, optical illusions, and animatronics; and "Titanic Expo," a guided tour through the actual sets, costumes, and props from the movie of the same name, including a replica of the White Star Southampton Pier and the following sets from the ship's interior: first-class smoking room, dining salon, and corridor; Palm Court Cafe; boiler room; and stateroom. Also on display are various pieces of furniture, suitcases, teacups, mailbags, signs, posters, toys, lifeboats, lifesavers, lifejackets, oars, and miscellaneous ship parts used in the movie. A video showing the actual Titanic wreckage is also screened. Another attraction is "Fox/JVC Presents," an exhibition of behind-the-scenes footage of recent Fox films, new Fox film previews, and "making of" footage from productions filmed at the studio. If you get hungry after all this excitement, there's a restaurant (serving sandwiches, pizza, and ice cream) conveniently located next to the souvenir shop. Admission is adults US$12, seniors US$9, children 3–11 US$9, children under three free. Visa and MasterCard are accepted. Foxploration is open Wednesday, Thursday, and Friday 9 A.M.–5:30 P.M., Sat. and Sun. 10 A.M.–6:30 P.M. Call 661/614-9444, U.S. tel. 866/FOX-BAJA (800/369-2252), or visit www.foxploration.com for further information.

Fox Studios Baja, known locally as Estudios de la Playa (Beach Studios), is about five km (three miles) south of Rosarito, just off the free road between Mexico 1-D and the ocean. Exit the toll road at the La Paloma, Popotla, Calafia exit, and look for the studio complex entrance at Km 32.8 on the free road, just before the big white arch advertising Popotla.

Along the dirt road that leads to Popotla, a cement wall separating the village from Fox Studios Baja is adorned with multimedia art created by local children.

PUERTO NUEVO

The tiny seaside town of Puerto Nuevo, 19 km (12 miles) south of Rosarito via Mexico 1, is known as Baja's lobster capital. Although the ac-

tual lobster harvest in the area isn't what it once was—the lobster served in Puerto Nuevo is mostly harvested in areas off the coast of Baja California Sur and distributed through San Diego—lobster restaurants are more plentiful than ever. When Baja travelers first discovered Puerto Nuevo in the 1950s, they dined in the houses of two or three local families. Now the village offers nearly 30 side-by-side seafood restaurants, some quite modern. An entire village devoted to eating.

The **Festival del Vino y la Langosta** (Festival of Wine and Lobster) occurs in Puerto Nuevo's restaurant zone in mid-October. For around US$15 pp participants are welcome to sample all the Baja lobster and wine they can consume.

Accommodations

A couple of places offer rooms at prices that fluctuate so much that they can't be neatly fit into one our price range categories. The **Hotel New Port Baja,** tel. 661/614-1188, U.S. tel.800/582-1018, Canada tel. 800/942-4244, info@newportbeachhotel.com, www.newportbeachhotel.com, offers deluxe ocean-view rooms, a pool, hot tub, volleyball court, tennis courts, and coffee shop. Rates: US$80–150 Sunday–Thursday, US$130–240 Friday, Saturday, and holidays. The **Grand Baja Resort,** just south of Puerto Nuevo at Km 44.5 on the free road, tel. 661/614-1493 or 661/614-1488, U.S. tel. 877/315-1002, www .grandbaja.com, features one-, two-, and three-bedroom condos on a bluff overlooking the Pacific. Rates: US$69–265, depending on the day of the week and the season.

Just south of Puerto Nuevo at Km 38 on the free road, a small RV park called **Surfpoint Camping** is sandwiched between a couple of moldy-looking condo developments—it's easy to miss. Expect to pay around US$15–20 a night if space is available, less by the week or month. Look also for **Cantama,** at Cantamar Beach, and **Rancho Reynosa** about 2.5 km north of the Cantamar toll road exit on the free road.

Food

The typical Puerto Nuevo–style lobster platter includes lobster, beans, rice, and tortillas. The lob-

BAJA CALIFORNIA LOBSTERS

Of the several species of lobster scooting about in Baja seas, the most numerous are *Panulirus interruptus* (known as red lobster or *langosta roja*), found as far south as the 25th parallel on both the Pacific and Sea of Cortez sides, and *P. inflatus* (blue lobster or *langosta azul*), found in the Pacific and lower Cortez as far south as Tehuantepec, Oaxaca. None of the lobsters found in Baja waters are related to the cold-water type (genus *Homarus*) found off the coast of the northeastern United States and southeastern Canada. Baja's warm-water lobsters are sometimes referred to as "spiny lobsters" because their shells bear spiny projections (the *Homarus* shell is smooth). Spiny lobsters also feature smaller pincers than the cold-water varieties.

BOB RACE

Adult spiny lobsters reach up to 61 cm (24 inches) in length and weigh as much as six kg (13 pounds). Most varieties are nocturnal and tend to frequent depths of 5–30 meters. During the day they stay beneath or between rocks, hiding from natural enemies like sharks, octopuses, rays, and a few larger finfish. Their diet consists mostly of crustaceans, mollusks, and other small sea organisms.

Lobstering is a major part of the fishing industry in Mexico, the world's eighth-largest harvester of lobster. The official lobstering seasons are March 16 to September 30 for red lobster and June 1 to September 15 for blue lobster. Most of the lobsters taken in Baja come from coastal waters off Baja California Sur, which now accounts for 55 percent of the total Mexican harvest.

It's illegal for foreigners to capture *any* lobster; only Mexican members of registered *cooperativas de pesca* (fishing cooperatives) may take lobsters.

ster is usually lightly fried in spiced oil and then briefly grilled before serving, but in some restaurants it is also prepared in a *ranchera* (tomato and chili) sauce or boiled New England–style.

The very first true restaurant to serve lobster here was **Restaurant Puerto Nuevo,** and judging from the crowds this is still the local favorite. The original Restaurant Puerto Nuevo serves only lobster, shrimp, and fish-fillet platters, and only cash is accepted. The fancier **Restaurant Puerto Nuevo II** next door features a more extensive menu and accepts credit cards; most of the clientele are visiting gringos. Other family-run favorites include **Miramar, Chela's, La Escondida, El Galeón,** and **La Perlita.** Smaller lobsters with rice, beans, and tortillas cost US$12, medium-sized crustaceans run US$14–16, and a half-kilo (1.5-pound) lobster costs US$16–18 or more. A few places

offer weekday specials as low as US$9 including a complimentary beer or margarita. As you walk or drive through town, men in front of the restaurants hold up hand-lettered signs advertising their restaurant's lobster dinners and prices; just remember, cheaper doesn't always mean better!

Transportation

Red-and-white route taxis operate between Rosarito and Puerto Nuevo for US$2 pp. In Rosarito they leave from in front of the Hotel Festival Plaza. In Puerto Nuevo you must stand at the side of the highway opposite the village entrance and flag one down; these taxis actually ply a Rosarito–La Misión route. For evening excursions it's safer to hire a *taxi de ruta* to Puerto Nuevo from Rosarito than to drive it yourself— these drivers know the road very well.

LA FONDA AND LA MISIÓN

To reach this area, approximately 60 km (37 miles) south of the border, take the La Misión–Alisitos exit from the toll road at Km 59. Here you'll find the best beaches between Tijuana and south of Ensenada. At one time the valley surrounding La Misión sheltered Misión San Miguel Arcángel de la Frontera, founded by Dominican Padre Luis Salles in 1788 and secularized in 1833. The only remains of the mission are two adobe walls standing in a schoolyard on the east side of the free road as it passes through the village.

Beaches

Playa La Misión is the better of the two gently curving beaches. A large public parking lot just off the highway makes it more accessible than most. Also here are rental horses, bathrooms, cement picnic tables, and trash barrels. **La Salina,** a few kilometers south of La Misión, is an up-and-coming beach area as well. A small marina has recently been constructed.

Near Km 55, a local surf spot known as Campo López features a consistent beach break that comes up best during a southwest swell.

Hotels

US$25–50: Overlooking the broad beach at La Misión, **Hotel La Misión,** tel. 615/155-0205, has 10 clean and large rooms, all with ocean view and fireplace. Suites with private hot tub and refrigerator are available, and the hotel has a decent restaurant and small grocery store.

US$50–100: In addition to its standard rooms, **Hotel La Fonda,** tel. 615/628-7352, offers oceanfront apartments—each with kitchen and fireplace—that accommodate up to four persons. La Fonda's restaurant serves good seafood with an ocean view.

La Salina Restaurant Bar and Hotel, six km south of La Misión, follows the example of the Hotel La Fonda and Hotel La Misión in providing good food and comfortable rooms near the beach at reasonable rates.

Beach condos are available at **Plaza del Mar,** at Km 58, about three km (two miles) north of La Misión, Tijuana tel. 664/685-9152, U.S. tel.

800/868-0248. The premises boast a pool, hot tub, basketball and tennis courts, gardens, and a small archaeological museum.

RV Parks

Alisitos Trailer Park Ejidal, a little north of Hotel La Misión, charges just US$7 per 24 hours whether you have a tent or a motorhome. There are no facilities as such, so you must be self-contained, but given the quality of the beach this is a steal.

Baja Seasons, Km 72, tel. 646/155-4015, U.S. tel. 800/754-4190, www.bajaseasons.com, offers reasonably priced motel rooms and RV sites with concrete pads, some shaded, on grassy grounds at the north end of La Salina. The park is accessible only from southbound Mexico 1-D, so if you're coming from Ensenada you'll have to make a U-turn at some point farther north.

Food

La Palapa de San José, just north of Hotel La Fonda on the west side of the free road at Km 58, is a simple café with indoor-outdoor seating for breakfast, lunch, and dinner. On weekends the café usually hosts live music. **Medio Camino** is a decent-looking restaurant right off the free road between Km 59 and 60 on the toll road.

SALSIPUEDES AND SALDAMANDO

At around Km 88 on Mexico 1-D, a steep, winding dirt road leads down to **Rancho Salsipuedes,** a secluded campground next to windswept cliffs and beach. Other than the low-key campground, this area is development-free and a good spot for hiking, fishing, and bouldering. Salsipuedes means "Leave If You Can" in Spanish, probably a reference to the steep half-mile descent from the highway. A guard kiosk at the hilltop gate isn't usually occupied, so keep driving past an olive grove till you come to the campground. Fairly well-kept campsites offer running water but no electricity and cost US$10 per night. If you're staying only for the day you must pay US$5. Simple cabins with private bath are available for US$35 per night. There is no phone service. Rumors say a housing or resort development may soon swallow this campground whole.

North of Salsipuedes between Km 84 and 85, brightly painted **El Mirador** offers a scenic view over the sea along with food and bar service.

South of Salsipuedes, an exit for **Playa Saldamando** leaves Mexico 1-D between Km 94 and Km 95 and leads to a similarly steep ride down to a similar camping setup. Tent/camper sites (water only) cost US$10 per night per vehicle (up to four people), while trailer sites go for US$13. Trailers with beds, shower, toilet, sink, stove, and a kerosene lantern are also available for US$30–40. You can use El Mirador de Ballenas (Whale Lookout), a lookout next to the exit, as a landmark. If you reach the third highway tollgate, you'll have gone about 4.5 km (three miles) too far.

SAN MIGUEL AND EL SAUZAL

A unique cross between retirement-oriented trailer park and surf camp, San Miguel is the legacy of a Polish-Mexican-American family, the Robertsons, who've lived in Northern Mexico and southern California for most of this century. The late Tomás Robertson, who founded the Villa de San Miguel residential community in the 1950s, was a mission historian and an active member of the Comité por Conservación de Misiónes de Baja California. His family now manages the trailer park, bar, and restaurant. Technically San Miguel belongs to the pueblo of El Sauzal.

The bay formed by Punta San Miguel is the most popular surfing locale in Baja. Mexico's first surfboard manufacturer—San Miguel—is named after the point. A few hardcore surfers live in San Miguel on a semipermanent basis, and during the winter a small legion takes up residence on the beach or in rented trailers to ride the bay's fast right point break. On winter evenings, those who aren't partying in Ensenada or exhausted by the day's surfing hang out in the San Miguel Restaurant bar swapping war stories about the three-story waves at Islas de Todos Santos.

Accommodations
Under US$25: In El Sauzal, **Hostel Sauzal,** Av. L 344, tel. 646/174-6381, http://hostelsauzal.tripod.com, offers dormitory-style accommodations—four beds to a dorm—all with an ocean view. Amenities include pillows and blankets, storage lockers for backpacks, hot showers with an ocean view, free continental breakfast, storage for bikes and surfboards, writing desks, and a library of Baja books, maps, and magazines. If you're driving south, El Sauzal begins about two miles after the San Miguel toll booth. To find the hostel, pass under the footbridge, then turn left after the Pemex station. Go two blocks, turn right, then go one block, turn left up a dirt road, and the hostel is in the third house on the right.

US$25–50: Ramona Beach RV, Km 104 opposite the big Pemex facility, tel. 646/174-6045, offers 30 simple motel rooms in little whitewashed buildings.

In El Sauzal, the 28-room **Motel Sausalito,** Km 102 on Mexico 1, tel. 646/174-6188, has no beach or scenic views, but is comfortable enough and has a pool and restaurant.

Motel Puesta del Sol, just opposite the Km 105 marker, tel. 646/174-4520, has well-kept rooms.

Camping
Camping is permitted on the beach at San Miguel for US$4–10 per night; full-hookup trailer sites are US$12–15. Facilities include a dump station, bar, restaurant, reasonably well-kept bathrooms, and hot showers. Trailers on the hill above the beach can sometimes be rented for US$25– 30 a night. Inquire at the restaurant, tel. 646/174-6225, or write San Miguel Village, Apdo. Postal 55, El Sauzal, BCN. Check to see if the water supply is working before accepting an offer; the water pressure in the trailers near the top of the hill is sometimes low or even absent. For permanent trailers with their own water storage tanks, this isn't a problem. Occasionally a trailer slot on the hill opens up.

Ramona Beach RV, Km 104 opposite the big Pemex facility, tel. 646/174-6045, offers 50 simple RV spaces with full hookups near the beach—many are permanently occupied but we've seen a few open ones. RV storage is available. Rates: US$15. **Motel Puesta del Sol** (see earlier mention) also offers RV spaces.

Food

The **San Miguel Restaurant** serves Northern Mexican dishes (including excellent *chiles rellenos*), steak, seafood, and frog legs. A fireplace adds to the cozy atmosphere on chilly winter evenings. Several inexpensive taco and *torta* stands can be found on the side of the highway in El Sauzal, including the well-patronized *Tortería y Taquería Los Faroles.*

Events

Surf competitions are held in San Miguel from time to time, though the names seem to change every other year. The **Tecate Mexican Surf Fiesta** brings together the best surfers from California and the Mexican Pacific coast in October and features surfing competitions, food, live bands, and bikini contests. Look also for the **Winter Surf Classic,** which is held when the promoters can get it together, mostly in December.

The village celebrates **San Miguel's feast day** on the weekend nearest to September 29; sometimes Paipai Amerindians from San Miguel Valley join the festivities. Another big party is held in late October at San Miguel in honor of **Oktoberfest;** the restaurant opens an all-you-can-eat, all-you-can-drink bar and buffet.

Getting There

San Miguel can be difficult to locate, especially if you're driving south from Rosarito or Tijuana as the exit is poorly marked. Driving south on the toll road, take the Tijuana Libre exit just past the tollgate at Km 99, then follow the road west across the toll road until it curves south and begins to merge with the toll road a half km farther. Instead of returning to the highway, follow the short, paved loop to the right and you'll come to San Miguel Village. If you're arriving via the free road, remember to take this road almost immediately before merging with the four-lane highway.

From Ensenada, take the exit marked San Miguel just before the first tollgate heading north. To get here by public transportation from Ensenada, take the yellow-and-white Brisa minibus.

ISLAS DE TODOS SANTOS

These twin islands about 20 km (12 miles) southwest of San Miguel—or west of Ensenada the same distance—offer a variety of recreational opportunities. Fishing is good along the western shores of both islands, especially for yellowtail, halibut, and sea bass. For longer visits, boats can safely anchor in three coves along the eastern shore of the southern island; the middle cove offers the best shelter overall. Local anglers stay at seasonal fish camps at the southern ends of both islands.

For hikers, the southern island offers the most interesting terrain, with cliffs along the perimeter and a hilly interior. The highest elevation, just below the island's midpoint, is approximately 100 meters. Near the northern end of this island are several caves; at the southern tip are a few tidal pools worth exploring. The northern island is mostly flat, with a radio tower and two lighthouses—one abandoned, one in use. Both islands are nesting grounds for brown pelicans, cormorants, blue herons, ospreys, and various other bird species.

Surfing

Islas de Todos Santos is perhaps best known as the site of the Pacific coast's biggest, baddest surf. As *Surf Guide* magazine wrote, "The waves here laugh at your 8'2". November through Febru-

ISLAS DE TODOS SANTOS

RADIO TOWER & LIGHTHOUSE

Isla Norte

FISH CAMP

PACIFIC

Isla Sur

100m/313ft

FISH CAMP

OCEAN

SCALE NOT AVAILABLE

LIGHTHOUSE

ary, a deep-water northwest swell sweeps the skinny northwestern point (partially submerged at high tide) of Isla Norte to produce powerful, eight- to 10-meter (25–30 foot) waves. Dubbed "Killer's," this is a break best attempted only by experienced gunners—unless it's running small. Todos surfers estimate that whatever height the surf at San Miguel is running, waves at Isla Norte will be double plus 2.5 meters (eight feet).

The northwest corner of the southern island also offers an excellent winter break. When the northwest swell is rolling hard, the channel between the two islands conjures up a monumental, long-riding right called Thor's Hammer, formed by the confluence of direct swell movement toward this point and refracted swell as it wraps eastward around the north island, then bounces off the south island and into the channel. This same channel pumps a grinding left break during the summer southwest swell, making the islands a year-round surf destination. Surfers sometimes camp on the flat northern island, but most boat in for the day from San Miguel or Ensenada.

Getting There

All-day *panga rápida* (fast *panga*—an open, motorized fiberglass skiff) charters to the islands can be arranged for US$150 at **Juanito's Boats,** in Ensenada behind the Plaza Marina on the waterfront, tel. 646/174-0953, U.S. tel. 800/569-1254. The trip takes around 30 minutes each way; one boat can take up to six surfers. You can also charter boats at fish camps in Punta Banda south of Ensenada, or sometimes in San Miguel. San Miguel surfers with their own boats will usually take along a passenger or two if the guests agree to buy gas for the trip and beer for the survivors.

Ensenada and Vicinity

Ensenada sees far more visitors than any other nonborder town on the peninsula. Every summer an estimated four million people—most of them Americans—pass through. Yet as a busy trade center for northern peninsula fishing and agriculture, the city retains a *bajacaliforniano* identity in spite of the tourists.

Ensenada is the capital of the Municipio de Ensenada, Mexico's largest *municipio* (roughly equivalent to the Anglo-American county), which extends all the way to the BCS border, comprises 52,511 square km, and covers two-thirds of Baja California Norte. The *municipio* has a population of around half a million; estimates for the city itself vary from 250,000 to 350,000. It's difficult to keep an exact count because so many semipermanent residents—including 40,000 or more gringos—live in the Ensenada area.

Baja California's third-largest city is also the peninsula's largest seaport due to its position on the wide Bahía de Todos Santos. The main industries in the area, aside from tourism, are fishing, fish processing, and agriculture, all relying on the bay as a shipping point for sending products to mainland Mexico, the United States, Canada, and Asia. Olives and grapes are the principal crops produced in the Ensenada area; the huge Oliveres Mexicanos plantation (48 km northeast of Ensenada, near Guadalupe) is the world's largest single olive producer, with over 120,000 trees under cultivation.

A portion of the grape harvest is used by a half dozen wineries based in Ensenada to produce wines for both domestic and international markets. Yellowtail and halibut are the top fish harvests, followed by various bottom fishes, lobster and other shellfish, and anchovies. Light manufacturing has also taken root in a warehouse area in the southern part of the city, where Fender Musical Instruments has a small plant.

During recent years Ensenada has expanded efforts to attract visitors. Cruise ships from Los Angeles and San Diego bring large groups of daytrippers who are gone at night. A first-class sailing facility, Marina Coral, can be found at the north end of the bay. The revenue generated from cruise ship and yacht tourism has been used to beautify the waterfront. A *malecón* or waterfront promenade has been added, along with Ensenada Cruiseport Village, a cruise-ship facility boasting

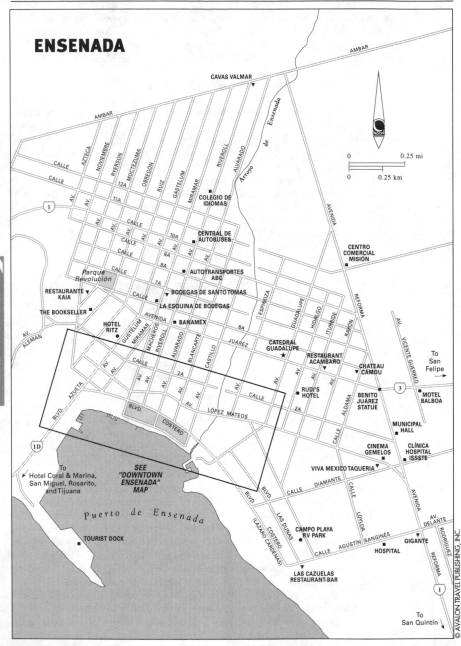

ENSENADA

AMBAR

CAVAS VALMAR

AMBAR

Arroyo de Ensenada

CALLE

CALLE

AZTECA
NOVIEMBRE
RYERSON
MOCTEZUMA
OBREGÓN
RUIZ
GASTELUM
MIRAMAR
RIVEROLL
ALVARADO

12A

11A

COLEGIO DE IDIOMAS

AVENIDA

CENTRO COMERCIAL MISIÓN

CALLE

10A

CENTRAL DE AUTOBUSES

CALLE

9A

CALLE

8A

AUTOTRANSPORTES ABC

Parque Revolución

CALLE

7A

REFORMA

BODEGAS DE SANTO TOMAS

RESTAURANTE KAIA

LA ESQUINA DE BODEGAS

THE BOOKSELLER

AVENIDA

BANAMEX

HOTEL RITZ

ESPINOZA
GUADALUPE
HIDALGO
ITURBIDE
RAMÓN

6A

AV. ALEMÁN

GUSTELUM
MIRAMAR
MACHEROS
RIVEROLL
ALVARADO
BLANCARTE
CASTILLO

JUÁREZ

CATEDRAL GUADALUPE

RESTAURANT ACAMBARO

AV. VICENTE GUERRERO

To San Felipe

CALLE

2A

CHATEAU CAMOU

CALLE

RUDI'S HOTEL

3

MOTEL BALBOA

BLVD. AZUETA

BLVD.

AV.

CALLE

BENITO JUÁREZ STATUE

ALDAMA

2A

COSTERO

LÓPEZ MATEOS

MUNICIPAL HALL

CALLE

1D

CINEMA GEMELOS

CLÍNICA HOSPITAL ISSSTE

To Hotel Coral & Marina, San Miguel, Rosarito, and Tijuana

SEE "DOWNTOWN ENSENADA" MAP

VIVA MEXICO TAQUERIA

BLVD.

CALLE

DIAMANTE

CALLE

AVENIDA

AV. DELANTE

Puerto de Ensenada

LAS DUNAS

COSTERO (LÁZARO CÁRDENAS)

CAMPO PLAYA RV PARK

LOYLOA

GIGANTE

RODRIGUEZ

TOURIST DOCK

AGUSTÍN SANGINÉS

CALLE

HOSPITAL

REFORMA

LAS CAZUELAS RESTAURANT-BAR

1

To San Quintín

0   0.25 mi

0   0.25 km

three state-of-the-art cruise ship berths, a 200-slip marina, retail shops, restaurants, crafts market, and small businesses offering sportfishing, diving, and sightseeing tours. A long section of Avenida López Mateos between Calles Ryerson and Castillo, a traditional focus of tourist shopping and dining, has received a face-lift comprising brick paving, wider sidewalks, wrought-iron street signs, street lighting, and the underground relocation of power and telephone lines. This section is now called Paseo Calle Primera.

Although some old Baja hands buzz right past Ensenada in a rush to get to the "real Baja" farther south, for many repeat visitors a Baja trip simply doesn't get off to a good start without a ritual *cerveza* at Hussong's or a couple of *tacos de pescado* from the harbor fish market. Is Ensenada Americanized? Though it's undeniably a hybrid culture, Mexican tourists prefer the town to San Felipe or Cabo San Lucas; once you escape the waterfront area, you'll find neighborhood *panaderías,* quiet residential streets, and few tourists of any nationality.

CLIMATE AND TOURIST SEASONS

Ensenada's climate is similar to San Diego's. Yearly rainfall amounts to about 25 cm (10 inches), most of which falls Oct.–May. Temperatures are mild year-round, averaging 7–18°C (45–64°F) in January and 17–24°C (63–75°F) in August.

The high tourist season is June–Aug., when the weather is warm and rain is rare. The Christmas/New Year's holidays and spring break in March through early April are also peak periods. To avoid the crowds, consider visiting Ensenada Oct.–Nov. or Apr.–May.

HISTORY

In pre-Hispanic times, nomadic Yumano Amerindian tribes occasionally stopped at Bahía de Todos Santos to fish and gather clams, but no permanent Amerindian settlements existed in the area when the Spanish missionaries arrived in the 18th century. The first Spaniard to lay eyes on the bay was explorer Juan Cabrillo, who in 1542 named it San Mateo. Sebastián Viz-

caíno's voyage of 1602 lent a different name to this piece of California coastal geography—Ensenada de Todos Santos, or "All Saint's Cove." Most likely this referred to a smaller cross-section of the bay (possibly the estuary where the Río San Carlos empties into the bay's south end), but eventually the entire bay came to be known as Bahía de Todos Santos.

Following a Spanish land grant to José Manuel Ruiz in 1804, several small farms and ranches were established in the hills east of the bay, including Ruiz's own Rancho Ensenada. A Spanish sergeant, Francisco Gastelum, bought and expanded the ranch in 1824. Following Mexican independence, the discovery of gold at nearby Real del Castillo in 1870 brought miners to the area; the miners needed supplies, and Ensenada, named for Gastelum's ranch, bloomed into a port practically overnight.

In 1882 Ensenada became the capital of the Territory of Baja California. The town continued to attract miners, farmers, and entrepreneurs who came to take advantage of the town's increasing prosperity. The boom lasted until the early 20th century, when few significant gold deposits remained and the political situation in the border area was becoming increasingly unstable. To counter growing Anglo-American influence along the border, the territorial capital was moved to Mexicali in 1915.

Ensenada faded into a farming and fishing village until U.S. Prohibition revived the economy. In the late 1920s, heavyweight boxer Jack Dempsey and a number of other Americans opened the Playa Ensenada Hotel and Casino, a grand Spanish-style structure overlooking the bay. Along with Tijuana and Mexicali, Ensenada became a favorite destination for the American drinking-and-gambling set until Prohibition's repeal in 1933 and Mexico's casino closure of 1938. The Playa Ensenada casino-hotel was converted to a resort hotel under a new name, the Riviera del Pacífico, but, unable to attract guests in sufficient numbers, it soon closed. About this same time, following the government's agrarian reforms, Valle de Mexicali agriculture expanded rapidly, and Ensenada's port facilities were steadily upgraded.

Throughout the 1940s and '50s the Ensenada area became a favorite destination for sportfishers and earned its title as "Yellowtail Capital of the World." Although increased commercial fishing and shipping decreased the bay's value as a sportfishing destination, overall economic development has fostered a cosmopolitan atmosphere, and Ensenada continues to cultivate its split personality as both tourist center and seaport.

SIGHTS

Ensenada's dual character—half resort, half commercial center—is split into two grids by Avenida Juárez in the center of the city. The portion of the city south of Juárez, toward the bay, is mostly given over to tourist-oriented businesses, while the portion to the north consists of local businesses like those found in any Mexican city. Most of the city's hotels, restaurants, and gift shops are found along Boulevard Costero and Avenida López Mateos, two parallel streets close to the waterfront.

Many of Ensenada's visual attractions lie out of town—at Estero Beach, Punta Banda, and La Bufadora—but a number of places of interest in the city are accessible by foot.

Riviera del Pacífico

Ensenada's most impressive edifice opened in 1929 as the Playa Ensenada Hotel and Casino, owned and operated by Jack Dempsey and his financial backers; Al Capone was allegedly a silent partner. The opening act in the hotel ballroom was Bing Crosby, backed by the Xavier Cugat Orchestra; the orchestra included a singer named Margarita Carmen Cansino, a Baja native later known as Rita Hayworth. Facing the bay, the hotel's massive white-walled, red-roofed, palm-encircled exterior became a prime symbol of the city's prosperity.

Like Tijuana's El Casino del Agua Caliente and Rosarito's Rosarito Beach Hotel, Playa Ensenada was a big hit with the Hollywood crowd until the U.S. repeal of Prohibition in 1933. Casino management converted it into the Hotel Riviera del Pacífico, but, deprived of its gambling clientele and suffering the effects of 1930s Depression, the hotel closed and fell into disrepair shortly thereafter.

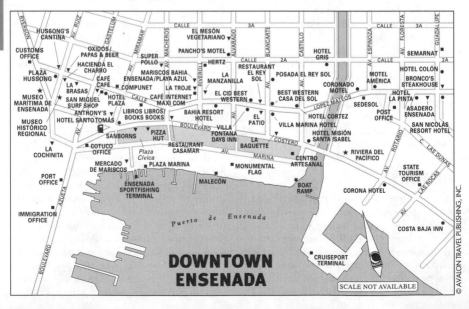

© JOE CUMMINGS

Riviera del Pacífico

In 1977 the city decided to restore the structure and turn it into the **Centro Social Cívico y Cultural Riviera** (Social, Civic, and Cultural Center of Ensenada). The various ballrooms and halls of the former hotel are now hired out for civic events, conventions, weddings, art exhibits, and other public and private occasions. One wing houses several municipal agencies; another contains a small Casa de la Cultura with a public library. Open Mon.–Fri. 8 A.M.–7:30 P.M.

On one of the upper floors at the northwest end of the building is the **Museo de Historia de Ensenada,** tel. 646/177-0594, a small historical museum with six permanent exhibition rooms dedicated to different historical periods, plus a gallery for traveling exhibits and a gift shop. One of the permanent exhibits focuses on Baja California's Amerindian heritage with displays of artifacts, pottery, weaponry and photographs (most captioned in Spanish and English), which are further enhanced by recordings of native chants. A unique "rupestrian pathway" reveals the four styles of rock art found in northern Baja while winding upward to the next exhibition level. Another exhibit examines early European seafarers and their routes, and the role

of Catholic missionaries on the peninsula. The museum is open Mon.–Sat. 9:30 A.M.–2 P.M. and 3–5 P.M., Sunday 10 A.M.–5 P.M.; admission is US$1.

Much of the Riviera del Pacífico's original interior tilework, murals, and painted ceilings remain intact. The **Bar Andaluz,** on the ground floor of the rear portion of the building, near the large parking lot, features a long, polished wooden bar and a mural by Alfredo Ramos Martínez (1871–1946), one of the original Mexican muralists and founder of Las Escuelas de Pintura al Aire Libre (Schools of Painting in the Open Air) in Mexico City. Visitors are welcome to tour the premises daily 9 A.M.–5 P.M. The bar is an excellent place for a quiet drink during these hours. The Riviera del Pacífico is at the corner of Avenidas Costero and Riviera—hard to miss since it's the largest structure along Boulevard Costero.

Museo Histórico Regional

Ensenada's Museum of Regional History, on Av. Gastelum near Av. López Mateos downtown, tel. 646/178-2531, is housed in a former military garrison dating to 1886 (and thus probably the oldest building in Ensenada) and contains a permanent display of artifacts pertaining to Amerindian culture in northern Baja, as well as temporary exhibits on various historical themes. Entry is by donation; the museum is open Tues.–Sun. 10 A.M.–5 P.M.

Museo Ex-Aduana Marítima de Ensenada

American-owned International Land Company of Mexico constructed this building in 1887, and for a while it was used by the British-owned Mexican Land and Colonization Company. Mexico's Aduana Marítima (Maritime Customs) gained control of the warehouselike structure in 1922, and in 1992 the Instituto Nacional de Antropología e Historia (INAH) renovated the building at Avenida Ryerson and Calle Uribe downtown and turned it into a museum, tel. 646/178-2531. INAH manages the rotating exhibits, most of which focus on Mexican cultural themes. Open Tues.–Sun. 10 A.M.–5 P.M. Donations are appreciated.

Waterfront

A *malecón* or waterfront promenade, inaugurated by President Ernesto Zedillo in 1997, affords views of the Bahía de Todos Santos from the **Parque Ventana al Mar** (Window to the Sea Park). A huge Mexican flag waves from the park's 106-meter (350-foot) flagpole. On clear days you should be able to see as far as Punta Banda and Islas de Todos Santos.

Along Boulevard Costero, near Plaza Marina and the cruise ship pier, the elliptical **Plaza Cívica** contains three huge busts of national heroes Benito Juárez (Mexico's first president), Miguel Hidalgo (the Catholic priest who initiated the Mexican Revolution), and Venustiano Carranza (Mexico's first post-Revolution president). Locally the plaza is more commonly called Plaza de las Tres Cabezas (Plaza of the Three Heads). The sportfishing piers and **Mercado de Mariscos** (Seafood Market) toward the north end of the waterfront continue to be the focus of most activity.

Catedral Nuestra Señora de Guadalupe

This cathedral at Avenida Floresta and Calle 6 exhibits standard-issue, Mexican colonial-style architecture, though the stained-glass windows are well executed. The best times to visit the cathedral

Catedral Nuestra Señora de Guadalupe

are during the Fiesta Guadalupano (Día de Nuestra Señora de Guadalupe, December 12 and 13) or Las Posadas (December 16–25), when the interior is filled with candles and worshippers.

El Mirador

The Chapultepec Hills rise along the city's west side and afford a city and bay view. To find El Mirador (The Viewpoint), follow Calle 2 west until it terminates at Avenida Alemán, then turn right and follow the road to the top.

Wineries

Ensenada's wine legacy continues to grow, and seven wineries now maintain offices in the city. Only one winery in town is open to the public on a regularly scheduled basis. **Bodegas de Santo Tomás,** Av. Miramar 666, tel. 646/178-3333, bstwines@hotmail.com, is Mexico's largest winery, the oldest winery on the peninsula, and a direct descendant of the Dominicans' first Valle de Santo Tomás harvest of 1791. The winery sold its first wine to the public, by the barrel, in 1888. In 1934, Bodegas moved its winemaking operation to Ensenada, although some operations have recently been transferred back to Santo Tomás. The grapes are still grown in the Santo Tomás area as well as in other northern Baja valleys.

Facilities in downtown Ensenada cover one and a half city blocks and produce over a half million cases of wine annually. Master vintners employ around 30 different varietals to produce wine, sherry, port, brandy, and champagne-style sparkling wine. Public tours of the winery, in English, are offered daily at 11 A.M., 1 P.M., and 3 P.M. The tours last about an hour and cost US$2 for the basic tour (with tastings of six table wines) or US$5 for the special tour (with tastings of a dozen table and premium wines plus a souvenir glass). Bread and cheese are served along with the wines. You can purchase bottles of Santo Tomás wine in the tasting room. Three-hour guided tours of the facilities in Valle de Santo Tomás are also available by appointment (made at least three days in advance) for groups of 12 or more. To make an appointment, call 646/178-3333.

As Santo Tomás has moved some of its operations out of this neighborhood, it is using the warehouse space to expand its culinary ventures, which so far include La Esquina de Bodegas and La Embotelladora Vieja, both exemplars of Ensenada cuisine (see Food later in this section for details).

The other five Ensenada wineries may open their doors by prior arrangement. The staff at **Cavas Valmar,** Av. Riveroll 1950 and Calle Ambar (at the northern edge of town), tel. 646/178-6405, valmar@telnor.net, www.cavasvalmar.com, is happy to provide tasting tours by appointment. Although Valmar's history and range of wines can't compare with those of Bodegas de Santo Tomás, its products are worth investigating; this was the second Mexican winery to export to the United States and Europe. If you can find a bottle of "Martain's 1992 Cabernet Sauvignon," buy it.

Monte Xanic, a highly rated boutique winery with just 200 acres of vineyards under cultivation in the Valle de Guadalupe, maintains a *bodega* and office at Av. Marina 10, tel. 646/174-6155, www.montexanic.com. Monte Xanic is winning awards and accolades from many quarters. The winery is open for tastings, tours, and sales Monday–Friday 9 A.M.–4 P.M. by appointment only, and may be arranged by calling the office. Tour fee is US$4.

Chateau Camou, Almada 599-2A, Col. Obrera, tel. 646/177-2221, contacto@chateau-camou.com.mx, www.chateaucamou.com.mx, is right behind Monte Xanic in its keenness to produce wine perfection. The winery offers three tours. The Claret Tour costs US$5 and includes a 25–30 tour of the winery, followed by a tasting featuring four wines, while the Bordeaux Tour (US$10) is the same with two additional wines featured. The Magnum Tour (US$40) is for parties of 10 or more by appointment only, and consists of a tour of the vineyards and winery with the winemaker and/or owner, a comprehensive tasting of their wines (including a barrel tasting), and lunch with a choice of paella, quail, ostrich or *carne asada*.

Mogor Badan, Isla de Cedros 437, tel. 646/177-1484, released its first wine in 1994. Reportedly a one-man owned-and-operated enterprise, production is small but is said to show promise. Try calling for an appointment. Tastings

BAJACALIFORNIANO WINE

Ensenada is the unofficial capital of Mexico's finest winemaking region, northwestern Baja California. Most Canadians and Americans are unaware of the quality of Mexican wines and assume beer and tequila are all the country has to offer. On the contrary, *bajacaliforniano* wines are shipped all over Mexico and western Europe, but because of U.S. and Canadian trade policies, they weren't exported north of the border until very recently. They're still difficult to find in Canada and the United States, even though *American Wine* magazine now runs a regular report on Mexican wines. This may change as NAFTA reaches full implementation in 2009. In the meantime, if you want to taste wines produced in northern Baja, you can always go to the source.

History

Hernán Cortés brought vinifera cuttings from Spain to Mexico in the early 16th century, and the *criolla* (creole) and *misión* (mission) grapes grown today in Baja are direct descendants of those cuttings. Jesuit padres founded the first winery in the Western Hemisphere in 1597 outside Parras de la Fuente (in today's Mexican state of Coahuila), and the tradition reached Baja California in 1697 when Padre Juan Ugarte transplanted vinifera at Misión San Javier. As the missionaries moved northward it became clear that the best areas for viticulture were the temperate valleys of northern Baja. In 1791, Dominican Padre José Lorieto founded Misión Santo Tomás de Aquino, planting the first Spanish vinifera in the Valle de Santo Tomás 45 km south of Ensenada. The product, a variety simply called *misión,* was used mainly for sacramental purposes but was highly regarded by padres throughout the mission system. Cuttings continued migrating north with the padres into Alta California and were eventually planted in some of the now-famous Northern California wine-producing valleys.

Following secularization of Misión Santo Tomás, an Italian miner named Francisco Andronequi took over the mission vineyards and founded Baja's first commercial winery, Bodegas de Santo Tomás, in 1888. Andronequi enjoyed some success selling wine by the barrel in booming late-19th-century Ensenada. In 1906, some 500 Russian immigrants settled the Valle de Guadalupe and cultivated extensive vineyards. Wine grapes thrived in the sandy soil and Mediterranean climate of northern Baja, and other winemakers, including the Italian family of oenologist Angel Cetto, followed the success of the Santo Tomás and Guadalupe operations with viticulture in valleys near Tecate, San Vicente, Guadalupe, Mexicali, and Ensenada.

Around this same time former Mexican Revolution general Abelardo Lujan Rodríguez bought Bodegas de Santo Tomás and, following a term as Mexico's president, moved the winery to Ensenada in 1939. At this point *criollo* and *misión* were still the only varieties under production. In the early 1960s Rodríguez hired an American oenologist from the school for viticulture and oenology at the University of California at Davis. This wine expert ushered in a new era for wine culture in Mexico, introducing grape varieties such as chenin blanc, chardonnay, and reisling, as well as cold fermentation and other modern techniques.

Spanish brandy-maker Pedro Domecq established a winery in Valle de Guadalupe in 1972, attracting international attention to the wine-producing valleys of northern Baja for the first time. Newer boutique labels like Monte Xanic and Chateau de Camou (Viñas de Camou) have raised the quality of Baja wines to a world-class level, and today many local vintages hold their own against wines from the United States, France, Australia, Spain, Chile, and South Africa. Today approximately 90 percent of all wine produced in Mexico comes from Baja California.

Wines and Winemakers
Today some two dozen viticulturists and labels compete in northern Baja, among them Bacco, Calafia, Casa de Piedra, Cavas Valmar, L. A. Cetto, Champbrulé, Chateau Camou, Casa Domecq, Don Miguel, Mogor Badan, Monte Xanic, Santo Tomás, San Antonio, Sol de España, and Viña Real. The highest-producing valleys, in descending order, are Ensenada, Guadalupe, San Vicente, Santo Tomás, Mexicali, Tijuana, and Tecate. Smaller *ejido* operations exist in El Porvenir, Ajusco, and Chapultepec.

Among the varietals produced in Baja are mission, zinfandel, cabernet sauvignon, sauvignon blanc, ruby cabernet, barbera, valdepeñas, cariñana, grenache, petite sirah, merlot, pinot noir, gamay, chenin blanc, fumé blanc, blanc de blanc, nebbiolo, palomino, colombard, muscatel, tempranillo, white riesling, and pinot blanc. The best *bajacaliforniano* wines are made from grapes cultivated in the Guadalupe and San Vicente valleys, where red varietals predominate.

To learn more about Baja wines and to sample some vintages, join one of the daily tours offered at Bodegas de Santo Tomás in Ensenada or call for an appointment at one of the other five wineries in that city or the two in Tijuana. A more ambitious outing would take you to the Valle de Guadalupe, where the Pedro Domecq and L. A. Cetto wineries are open to the public for tours and tastings. Smaller wineries in the valley may be open by appointment; inquire at their *bodegas* (warehouses) in Tijuana and Ensenada, listed under the respective city sections in this book. Two excellent Baja wine bars—where you can sample a wide variety of labels and vintages—are **La Esquina de Bodegas,** Av. Miramar 666 in Ensenada, and **Sancho Panza,** Plaza Las Glorias in Cabo San Lucas.

Fiesta de la Vendimía Bajacaliforniana
Every year in August or September, Baja wineries collaborate on a 10-day winemaking festival in Ensenada and the Valle de Guadalupe that includes winetasting, paella cook-offs, culinary exhibitions, fireworks, music, dancing, and other bacchanalian activities. Sponsored by the Asociación de Vinicultores de Ensenada (Ensenada Viniculturists Association), the festival offers a wonderful opportunity to taste wines not easily found in Baja restaurants and to sample dishes not normally seen in Ensenada restaurants (e.g., tuna chateaubriand and wonton stuffed with crab). On Saturday a panel of judges gathers for the Concurso Internacional, a blind tasting of wines from Mexico and abroad. For information on upcoming festivals, contact Bodegas de Santo Tomás in Ensenada, tel. 646/178-3333.

usually take place at Rancho El Mogor in Valle de Guadalupe, but you may be able to arrange a tasting in Ensenada.

Bodegas San Antonio, Calle 2 364, tel. 646/178-3939 or 646/174-0078, has its main winemaking operation in San Antonio de las Minas, in the southwest corner of the Valle de Guadalupe. This is a contrarian location since most of the valley's better wines are said to come out of vineyards in the valley's northeast sector. The company is only a few years old, but reports say the wine is good. You won't be able to taste any wines at San Antonio's Ensenada location, but you can buy them here, by prior appointment.

DOWNTOWN ACCOMMODATIONS

Most of Ensenada's hotels are on or just off Avenida López Mateos and Boulevard Costero. For most of the year except July and Aug., Carnaval, and U.S. college spring break, the supply of hotel rooms outstrips the demand; hence room rates are often negotiable. At any given moment several hotels may stock one or both tourist offices with promotional flyers advertising room specials.

Rates are highest May–Sept. Any time of year weekday rates may be lower than weekend and holiday rates. Add 12 percent hotel tax to all rates (some hotels may charge an additional 10 percent service charge).

US$25–50

Pancho's Motel, Calle Alvarado 711, tel. 646/178-2344, features 28 small, dank rooms in a single-story wooden building set around a parking court. Conditions are tolerable, and noise usually isn't a problem because the rooms are set back from the street. But overall this is a place only for those who really need to stretch pesos.

A similarly old-fashioned motel court, 20-room **Motel América,** Av. López Mateos 1309 (at Espinosa), tel. 646/176-1333, is in better shape. Some rooms have kitchenettes, and the woman in charge speaks some English.

Another motel court close by, two-story **Coro-nado Motel,** Av. López Mateos 1275, tel. 646/176-1416, offers 22 rooms and courtyard parking.

For more choice, try 44-room **Rudi's Hotel,** in a middle-class residential neighborhood at Avenida Hidalgo 450 (between Calles 4 and 5), tel. 646/176-3245. Rudi's has a loyal following of both Mexican and foreign travelers; arrive early (late morning is best) as rooms—particularly the cheaper ones—fill up fast. Rooms are available with one or two double beds, with or without TV. Under the same management, **Hotel Gris,** Calle 2 1180, tel. 646/178-2051, is a smaller place with similar rates and amenities.

One of our favorite Ensenada hotels in this price range is the three-story **Hotel Ritz,** Av. Ruiz at Calle 4, tel. 646/174-0501, fax 646/178-3262. If you don't need a parking lot (the Ritz has none) and would like to stay off the Avenida López Mateos tourist strip—but only three blocks north of Hussong's Cantina—you may find this hotel to your liking. Rooms are spacious and clean; the staff is friendly. Ask for a corner room if you want a view of bustling Avenida Ruiz below.

Seemingly taking up almost an entire downtown block, three-story **Hotel Plaza,** Av. López Mateos 540 (between Gastelum and Miramar), tel. 646/178-2715, fax 646/178-1590, offers 24 small and dark carpeted rooms. The bottom floor is entirely occupied by shops and the inexpensive hotel coffee shop. The hotel's best feature is its rosy terra-cotta exterior punctuated with dark green, arched windows. Rooms are available with one or two double beds.

Costa Baja Inn, Blvd. Costero 1536, tel. 646/177-2255 or 800/025-5215, U.S. tel. 877/666-0706, fax 646/177-2257, is a charmless, breeze-block highway hotel featuring 51 rooms with air-conditioning, heat, phone, and satellite TV; other amenities include a swimming pool and covered parking lot. This one's overpriced in our opinion.

Other nothing-special motels of acceptable quality in this range include **Motel Balboa,** Av. Vicente Guerrero 172, tel. 646/176-1077; **Hotel Colón,** Calle Guadalupe 134, between Cadrillo and López Mateos, tel. 646/176-1910; and **Motel (Bungalows) Playa,** northwest corner of

NORTHERN BAJA

Av. López Mateos and Av. Guadalupe, almost opposite the Colón, tel. 646/176-1430.

US$50–100

Bahía Resort Hotel, Av. López Mateos between Riveroll and Alvarado, tel. 646/178-2101, fax 646/178-1455, U.S. reservations tel. 888/308-9048, www.hotelbahia.com.mx, is a rambling, 64-room, two-story wooden hotel in the center of the tourist zone. The clean, comfortable rooms and suites all have tiled bathrooms, queen-size beds, spacious closets, cable TV, and direct-dial phones. Some rooms on the upper floor have bay views. On the premises are a restaurant, bar, pool, and secure parking lot. Both bar and hotel are favorites with southern California motorcycle clubs. Continental breakfast is included in the rate.

The well-run **Hotel Cortez,** Av. López Mateos 1089, tel. 646/178-2307 or 800/026-6999, U.S. tel. 800/303-2684, fax 646/178-3904, www.bajainn.com, is housed in a two-story mission-style building with a very nice lobby. All 75 rooms and suites come with air-conditioning, heat, direct-dial phones, carpet, cable TV, and courtesy newspaper and coffee. Nonsmoking rooms are available. On the premises are a heated pool, restaurant/bar, and parking lot.

Baja Inn Hotel Santo Tomás, Blvd. Costero 609, tel. 646/178-1503, fax 646/178-1504, Mexico reservations tel. 800/026-6999, U.S. reservations tel. 800/303-2684, www.bajainn.com, is a modern three-story place dominating the corner of Costero and Avenida Miramar. The staff seems exceptionally friendly and efficient, and the hotel's 80 well-maintained and comfortable rooms come with air-conditioning, heat, and satellite TV. Nonsmoking rooms are available. Other amenities include a coffee shop, restaurant, and secure parking lot. A large suite with three beds is available for US$100—a bargain.

The five-story, 93-room **Corona Hotel,** Blvd. Costero 1442, tel. 646/176-0901, fax 646/176-4023, www.hotelcorona.com.mx, is the closest hotel to the bay and offers rooms with bay views, balconies, satellite TV, air-conditioning, and heat. The **El Cid Best Western,** Av. López Mateos 993, tel. 646/178-2401, fax 646/178-3671, info@hotelelcid.com.mx, www.hotelelcid.com.mx, is

built in the mission style and offers 52 comfortable rooms, a Spanish tapas restaurant, coffee shop, pool, and parking. Rooms come with one or two beds, and a suite with a hot tub is available for US$100. Weekend prices are at least 30 percent higher than weekday rates.

Hotel La Pinta, Av. Floresta at Bucaneros, tel. 646/176-2601, fax 646/176-3688, U.S./Canada tel. 800/346-3942, www.lapintahotels.com, features 52 rooms with air-conditioning, heat, TV, and phone in a three-story, semimodern, Spanish-style building. Amenities include a restaurant and pool. This is the headquarters for Baja's La Pinta chain, and is relatively friendly and atmospheric. Although the hotel has no parking lot as such, a guard keeps an eye on the small streetside parking area out front. Midweek rates usually drop below US$50.

San Nicolás Resort Hotel, Av. López Mateos at Guadalupe, tel. 646/176-1901, fax 646/176-4930, www.sannicolas.com.mx, offers 150 good-sized rooms each with air-conditioning, heat, carpet, wet bar, direct-dial phone, and satellite TV; many rooms also have bay views. The hotel features indoor and outdoor pools, a hot tub, colorful tiled lobby, restaurant, disco, and betting (race and sports book) parlor. A master suite with hot tub is available for US$270.

Days Inn Villa Fontana, Av. López Mateos 1050, tel. 646/178-3434, fax 646/178-3837, reservations tel. 800/DAYS-INN, www.villafontana.com.mx, is a rambling wooden place opposite El Cid. Each of the hotel's 66 rooms and suites has air-conditioning, heat, phone, satellite TV, and bay-view balcony. Amenities include a coffee shop, bar, liquor store, courtyard parking, pool, hot tub, and sundeck. Complimentary coffee and Mexican pastries are available every morning in the tidy lobby. Midday rates occasionally drop below US$50.

Hotel Misión Santa Isabel, Blvd. Costero 1119, tel. 646/178-3616, fax 646/178-3345, takes up an entire block along Avenida Castillo stretching from Avenida López Mateos south to Costero. One of the more impressive mission-style Ensenada hotels with its big arched gate, tall domed tower, and tiled roof, the Santa Isabel features 57 small- to medium-size rooms with

Spanish-inspired furnishings, air-conditioning, heat, TVs, and phones. On the grounds are a restaurant and bar, parking lot, gift shop, and a small but well-designed courtyard pool. Rates go up Friday and Saturday nights and holidays.

Villa Marina Hotel, Av. López Mateos 1094, tel. 646/178-3321, fax 646/178-3351, U.S. fax 619/454-2703, is a high-rise with 130 rooms and suites, all with air-conditioning, heat, TVs, and phones. Other features include a coffee shop, pool, and parking lot.

Best Western Casa del Sol, Av. López Mateos 1001, tel. 646/178-1570, U.S. tel. 877/316-1684, fax 646/178-2025, www.casadelsol.com, is yet another place that capitalizes on Spanish mission-style architecture with plenty of arched windows, white stucco, and a terra-cotta tile roof. Each of the 48 well-worn but good-sized rooms comes with air-conditioning, cable TV, phone, carpet, and Mexican-tiled bathroom. The Casa del Sol also boasts a well-maintained swimming pool—the only hotel pool in Ensenada suitable for lap swimming. Other amenities include a restaurant, secure parking lot, and courtesy coffee every morning.

Posada El Rey Sol, Av. Blancarte 130, tel. 646/178-1601, U.S. tel. 888/315-2378, fax 646/174-0005, www.posadaelreysol.com, is as charming and elegant as its celebrated restaurant across the street. The recently refurbished hotel offers a heated pool, spa, restaurant, bar, and enclosed parking. The 52 spacious, meticulously decorated rooms come with climate control, direct-dial phone, in-room Internet connection, satellite TV, safe, and service bar. Each suite features a private hot tub. Children under 18 stay free.

US$100–150

Just northwest of town off Mexico 1 at Km 103 is Ensenada's top hotel, the **Hotel Coral & Marina,** tel. 646/175-0000, Mexico/U.S./Canada tel. 800/862-9020, fax 646/175-0005, www .hotelcoral.com. Take the Ensenada Centro exit off the highway to get here. The Coral combines modern, international-class accommodations with a full-service marina and European-style spa. Large, nicely decorated suites with separate sitting areas feature satellite TVs, international di-

rect-dial phones, coffeemakers, refrigerators, and balconies overlooking the marina. Other facilities include an *alta cocina* restaurant, lobby bar, nightclub, heated indoor and outdoor pools, a hot tub, sauna, lighted tennis courts, and parking garage. Suites run US$150–600, plus tax.

OUT-OF-TOWN ACCOMMODATIONS
US$25–50

About eight km south of town on Mexico 1 at Km 12.5, opposite Ciprés airfield in Ejido Chapultepec, **Joker Hotel and Trailer Park,** tel. 646/176-7201, fax 646/177-4460, U.S./Canada tel. 800/2-JOKER-2, looks like a pseudo-Bavarian castle that could have come from Disneyland, with a few Aztec statues thrown in for full incongruency. Its 40 rooms are spread out around landscaped grounds and feature satellite TV, direct-dial phones, air-conditioning, and private balconies. Facilities include a hot tub, restaurant, bar, pool, and several features oriented toward RVers staying at the adjacent trailer park.

Quintas Papagayo, tel. 646/174-4575 or 800/346-3942, fax 646/174-4155, stands behind a forbidding set of high walls about three km north of town off Mexico 1. Facilities include a restaurant, pool, hot tub, and tennis courts. Available accommodations include studios and one- and two-bedroom apartments.

US$50–100

Five km north of town at Km 106 off Mexico 1, on a point jutting into the Pacific, **Punta Morro Hotel and Suites,** tel. 646/178-3507, fax 646/174-4490, U.S./Canada tel. 800/526-6676, reservas@punta-morro,com, www .punta-morro.com, offers studios and one-, two-, and three-bedroom apartments. All units come with kitchens (with utensils) and terraces overlooking the ocean and pool area. This location is quiet and next door to a branch of the Universidad Autónoma de Baja California. Choose from studio apartments, one-bedroom suites, or two-story apartments with two or three bedrooms.

US$100–150

Las Rosas Hotel and Spa, six km north of town on Mexico 1, tel. 646/174-4310, fax 646/174-4595, www.lasrosas.com, offers 68 deluxe suites with ocean view. On the premises are a restaurant, seaside pool, hot tub, sauna, exercise center, and racquetball court.

CAMPING AND RV PARKS

The only RV park within the Ensenada city limits is **Campo Playa RV Park,** at Calles Las Dunas and Sanginés, tel. 646/176-2918. Shady spots with hookups are available for US$20, campsites without hookups go for US$18. Hot showers are available.

Joker Hotel and Trailer Park, across the highway from Ciprés airfield in Ejido Chapultepec, tel. 646/176-7201, fax 646/177-4460, U.S./Canada tel. 800/2-JOKER-2 (800/256-5372), has a dozen full-hookup sites shaded by olive trees entwined with bougainvillea for US$17 a night. Cable TV hookups are available at extra cost. Other facilities include hot showers, flush toilets, a restaurant, brick barbecue grills, and a ping-pong table; RVers are permitted to use the hotel's pool and hot tub.

See Salsipuedes and Saldamando as well as San Miguel and El Sauzal, earlier in this chapter, for details on campgrounds in these areas just a few kilometers north of Ensenada. Also see the Ensenada and Vicinity section for information on campgrounds and trailer parks at Estero Beach, La Jolla, and Punta Banda, all south of Ensenada.

FOOD

Ensenada features just about every kind of restaurant imaginable, but seafood and Northern Mexican ranchero-style food are the city's culinary strong suits. *Tacos de pescado* (fish tacos) are an Ensenada specialty, usually made from fresh yellowtail or halibut fillets cut in strips, deep-fried in a light batter, and served in folded corn tortillas with salsa, guacamole, and a touch of mayonnaise or *crema* (a less sour Mexican version of sour cream).

Seafood stands are scattered throughout the city, many of them selling *cocteles* (spicy shellfish cocktails) and ceviche (a lime-marinated seafood salad). Clams *(almejas),* abalone *(abulón),* shrimp *(camarones),* and oysters *(ostiones)* make the most popular cocktails. The healthiest stands use purified water—usually clearly displayed in large bottles—to wash ingredients and utensils before preparing each dish. One of the best places to sample fish tacos and seafood cocktails is the **Mercado de Mariscos,** next to and a little bit behind the huge Plaza Marina on the waterfront. You can also buy fresh fish to take away and cook elsewhere.

Speaking of cocktails, the *clamato,* a beverage made from clam, tomato and lime juices, Mexican spices, and vodka, was probably invented in Ensenada. *Clamatos* here are nothing like the pale imitations served north of the border—a good one comes half-filled with fresh clams.

If you don't like seafood on your plate or in your glass, try other Ensenada specialties like *tacos de carne asada* (grilled-beef tacos), Sinaloa-style grilled or roasted chicken, or one of the many varieties of burritos available. Several restaurants also specialize in American and Continental cuisines.

American and Pizza

Alfonso's, Av. Macheros 4-5 (at Blvd. Costero), tel. 646/174-0570, offers good pizza, seafood, and Mexican breakfasts at reasonable prices. Open daily for breakfast, lunch, and dinner. **Pizza Hut,** Centro Comercial Plaza Palmira (next to Plaza Marina), Blvd. Costero, tel. 646/178-1888, offers the American standby pizza pie, and delivers. Moderate to expensive. Open 11 A.M.–11 P.M. daily.

Asian

La Cochinita Japanese Food Factory, Paseo Hidalgo next to Maritime Customs, tel. 646/178-3443, is an indoor-outdoor place popular with local residents for its low prices, fast service, and Mexican-style Japanese food. The seafood can be overcooked, at least by Japanese standards; better are the chicken, tofu, or vegetable dishes. In addition to teriyaki, sushi, sukiyaki, and soups, the menu features such Mexican dishes as *cochinita*

NORTHERN BAJA

pibil (Yucatán-style marinated pork) and *tortas de pollo asado* (barbecued chicken sandwiches). A few vegetarian dishes are available, too. This is the original La Cochinita; there are now 12 more locations in Ensenada. Other links in this popular chain can be found in Mexicali, Tijuana, and La Paz.

Cafés

El Faro Café, next to Gordo's Sportfishing, behind Plaza Marina on the waterfront, offers breakfast only, from 4:30 A.M. It's oriented toward early-rising anglers, both sporting and commercial. Inexpensive.

Pueblo Café Deli, Av. Ruiz 96, tel. 646/178-8055, boasts its status as "Ensenada's first full espresso bar." It also serves breakfast, traditional Mexican foods, salads, pastries, wine, and beer. Friendly service. Open daily 8 A.M.–midnight.

Sanborns Café, Plaza Marina, Blvd. Costero, tel. 646/174-0971, offers a reliable range of soups, salads, sandwiches, breakfasts, and Mexican dishes. Moderately priced. Open daily 7:30 A.M.–10 P.M.

Tomas Café in Plaza Hussong is probably the best place in town for a caffeine fix. The menu runs the gamut of espresso drinks—from steaming cappuccinos to frosty, frothy concoctions—and offers a mouthwatering selection of pastries. Open daily 8 A.M.–10 P.M.

Café Café, Av. López Mateos 496, tel. 646/178-8209, provides a relaxed environment where you can sip espresso while admiring an array of artwork, some of which the owner has created, and all of which is for sale. On some nights the café doubles as a venue for cultural and artistic events such as performances of acid jazz, poetry, Latino rock, experimental performance art, and avant-garde cinema. Opens daily at 9 A.M.

European

For fine French cuisine, head to **El Rey Sol,** Av. López Mateos 1000 (at Av. Blancarte), tel. 646/178-1733. The renowned Doña Pepita, a native of southern Baja's French-influenced town of Santa Rosalía, opened this elegant French restaurant in 1947 after spending 16 years in France (where she studied at the famous Cordon Bleu cooking school). The kitchen prepares seafood, poultry, and meat dishes served with herbs and vegetables grown on the family's farm in Santo Tomás. One of the house specialties is a rabbit-quail-chicken pâté. The menu also includes a few Mexican dishes. In front of the restaurant is a sidewalk seating area where morning coffee and pastry can be enjoyed. Expensive. Open daily 7:30 A.M.–10:30 P.M.

La Embotelladora Vieja, Bodegas de Santo Tomás building, Av. Miramar at Calle 7, tel. 646/174-0807, offers gourmet Mediterranean cuisine with a Mexican flair, served in a wine-cellar ambience. At least 20 different wines from Mexico, the United States, France, and Italy are available each month by the glass. Expensive. This was the first phase of the expanding Centro Cultural Santo Tomás. Open Monday and Wednesday noon–10 P.M., Thurs.–Sat. noon–11 P.M., and Sunday noon–5 P.M. Closed Tuesday.

La Esquina de Bodegas, Av. Miramar 666 (between Calles 6 and 7), tel. 646/178-3557, is a bistro and wine bar in the back of a Soho-style renovated warehouse decorated in industrial chic. It's also part of the Centro Cultural Santo Tomás but is considerably more casual than La Embotelladora. The menu offers changing entrées and fixed-price meals, usually very good. On your way in you can browse the wine shop, bookstore, and art gallery. Moderate to expensive. Open Mon.–Thurs. 8 A.M.–10 P.M., Fri. and Sat. 8 A.M.–midnight.

Restaurante Kaia, Calle Moctezuma 479, tel. 646/178-2238, serves Basque cuisine, including paella, in a small house. Open Tues.–Sun. 1–11 P.M.

Mexican

Acambaro (El Refugio Ensenadense), Av. Iturbide 528 (off Av. Juárez between Calles 5 and 6), tel. 646/176-5235, offers traditional Mexican dishes—*pozole, mole, birria, chilaquiles, chiles rellenos,* enchiladas, and *nopales* (prickly-pear cactus)—freshly prepared and served with bowls of limes, oregano, and salsas. Also try the delicious breakfasts and the Mexican *postres* (desserts), which include homemade flan, *arroz con leche* (rice pudding), *capirotada* (Mexican-style bread pudding), and *pay de manzana* (apple pie).

© BRENT MADISON

at El Taco de Huitzilopochtli

Champurrado (thick hot chocolate) is served in winter. The wood-and-brick decor is rustic but tasteful. Inexpensive to moderate. Open daily for breakfast, lunch, and dinner.

Las Brasas, Av. López Mateos 486 (between Av. Gastelum and Ruiz), tel. 646/178-1195, specializes in Sinaloa-style, marinated, and mesquite-grilled chicken, and also serves steak, seafood, and Mexican platters, all at reasonable prices. Open daily except Tuesday for lunch and dinner.

Popular with locals and tourists alike, **Hacienda del Charro,** Av. López Mateos 454, tel. 646/178-2114, serves tasty roast chicken, homemade chicken tamales, *pollo pipián* (chicken cooked in a pumpkin-seed *mole*), grilled seafood, burritos, tacos (three large ones for US$4 with rice and beans), chicken *pozole,* and *botanas* of all kinds. Fresh tortillas are handmade on the spot. Beverages include *jamaica,* a refreshing Mexican drink made from crushed hibiscus seeds. Inexpensive. Open daily for lunch and dinner till 11:30 P.M.

Pollo Feliz, Av. Macheros at Calle 2, tel. 646/178-3111, is a fast-food place that cranks out Sinaloa-style roast chickens—whole or half— for eating on the premises or *para llevar* (to go).

Served with tortillas, beans, and salsa. Inexpensive. Open daily 10 A.M.–10 P.M.

A local favorite is **La Troje,** Riveroll 143-8R, tel. 646/178-8747, which offers traditional Mexican dishes such as *nopalitos navegantes* (delicate cactus strips with eggs). Prices are moderate. Open daily 8 A.M.–10 P.M.

Las Cazuelas Restaurant Bar, Calle Sanginés 6 (near Blvd. Costero), tel. 646/176-1044, is an old standby serving border-style cuisine, including *codorniz* (quail), seafood, steaks, ribs, and hearty Mexican breakfasts. Inexpensive to moderate. Open daily 7 A.M.–11 P.M.

Sofia y Alma, Av. de los Mangos 194 (at Av. Delante), one traffic light east of the Gigante supermarket, is a good all-around spot for *antojitos,* including tacos, burritos, *pozole,* and *chiles rellenos,* as well as *desayuno, almuerzo, comida corrida,* and Sunday buffets. Inexpensive. Open daily 7:30 A.M.–9 P.M.

Despite its cowboy name, **Bronco's Steakhouse,** near the Hotel Colón at Av. López Mateos and Av. Guadalupe, tel. 646/176-4900, serves a large variety of traditional Mexican platters. Hearty breakfasts cost US$4–7 and include *crepas de huitlacoche* (crepes made with a mushroomlike corn fungus), *cazuela de huevos puntas de filete al chipotle* (terra-cotta dish filled with eggs and beef tips in a spicy *chipotle* sauce), *nopal asado* (grilled prickly pear cactus), *chilaquiles toluqueños* (Toluca-style *chilaquiles*), and *enchihuevos* (egg enchiladas). Weekend breakfast buffets (Sat. and Sun. 9 A.M.– 1 P.M.) cost US$10 per adult or half that for children and offer a wide range of fresh fruit, Mexican breakfast dishes, and made-to-order omelettes. Lunch and dinner offerings are equally large: USDA rib-eye steaks and ribs, *parilladas* (grill platters), *tripitas asadas* (grilled tripe), *chiles rellenos,* and more, for prices ranging US$6–20 per entrée. Open daily 8 A.M.– 10:30 P.M.

Viva México Restaurant, Av. López Mateos 2184, tel. 646/177-2151, offers great *tacos de carne asada* and *tacos al pastor* in clean surroundings with sharp service. Also fish tacos, quesadillas, *quesaburros* (cheese burritos), and *conos de frijól* (bean cones). Inexpensive. Open daily 11:30 A.M.–11:30 P.M.

Our favorite *tacos de carne asada* come from

Asadero Ensenada, a very small and humble shop on the south side of López Mateos right around the corner from Hotel La Pinta (heading towards the San Nicolas Resort). Whatever they do to the beef here, it stands head and shoulders above the rest. Open daily 9 A.M.–2:30 P.M.

Farther from the center of town, **El Taco de Huitzilopochtli,** Av. de las Rosas 5, Col. Valle Verde, tel. 646/174-2381, is named for the Aztec god of the sun and of war. The hard-to-find, hard-to-pronounce spot is open only on weekends but is well worth the trouble it takes to plan a visit. Food preparation begins five days in advance; many of the ingredients are grown in back of the restaurant by the family owner-operators, who moved to Ensenada about 25 years ago from Texcoco in the state of Mexico. Quite simply, no other restaurant in Ensenada serves more authentic central Mexican food. House specialties include *mixiote* (lamb wrapped in maguey and baked in a mesquite-fired oven), *barbacoa, chancla* (thick corn tortillas with beef fillet and grilled nopal), *romeritos* (nopal, potato, and shrimp fritters in *mole*), *huauzontle* (a green pepperlike vegetable filled with cheese and cooked like a *chile relleno*), *tlacoyos* (thick corn tortillas filled with beans and served with grated cheese and *chile verde*), and *huitlacoche* (corn fungus) cooked with *rajas poblanas* (chili strips). It's a good place for lacto-vegetarians because many dishes feature solely vegetable (and dairy) ingredients. Unique beverages include *licuado de nopal* (a prickly-pear-cactus smoothie) and *pulque* (slightly fermented maguey juice); the latter is rather difficult to find outside central Mexico, so it's a real treat for the many Mexico fans who have read about *pulque* but have never tasted it. An English-language menu is available. At least four or five salsas are brought to the table, along with sliced limes, chopped onions, and cilantro. The modest decor consists of little more than a few Mexican calendars, ceramics, and serapes. Tapes of *música tropical* from Texcoco, including tunes by the well-known *cumbia* group ángeles Azules, are played in the background.

To find the restaurant, follow Avenida Reforma north from the Benito Juárez statue about 2.5 km (1.6 miles) to the second small bridge,

and turn right (east) onto Calle Ambar just before the bridge. This intersection is six traffic lights from the traffic circle with the statue of Benito Juárez. Look for Farmacia San Marín de Porres on the northeast corner of the intersection. Follow Ambar to its end, then turn left and continue two blocks; make another left and you'll see the brightly painted restaurant on the left side of the street. Inexpensive. Open Sat. and Sun. 9 A.M.–5 P.M. only.

Seafood

Las Conchas Oyster Bar and Restaurant, tel. 646/175-7375, in Plaza Hussong, serves perfectly prepared oysters, along with other seafood selections. This chic little restaurant is very popular; be prepared to wait (at the bar if you like) for a table. Moderate to expensive. Open daily for lunch and dinner.

The intimate, dimly lit **La Manzanilla,** Riveroll 122, tel. 646/175-7073, specializes in abalone and boasts a rare selection of *mezcal.* Dishes are unique and delicious. Expensive. Open Wed.– Sun. 1–11 P.M.

Mariscos Bahía Ensenada, Av. Riveroll at López Mateos, tel. 646/178-1015, is a local favorite for moderately priced seafood, with everything from *pulpo* (octopus) to *pargo*. Next door, **Restaurant Playa Azul,** tel. 646/174-0622, is also good. Both are open daily for lunch and dinner.

Mercado de Mariscos (Seafood Market), Blvd. Costero at Av. Miramar, on the harbor, is a real fish market, not a restaurant; vendors serve fresh shrimp, octopus, squid, clams, lobster, tuna, abalone, halibut, and yellowtail. This is the best and cheapest place in town for fish tacos. Open daily from late morning until early evening.

Restaurant Casamar, Blvd. Costero 987, tel. 646/174-0417, offers a wide selection of reasonably priced, freshly prepared seafood in a tourist-oriented atmosphere. Open daily for lunch and dinner.

Restaurant Haliotis, Calle Delante 179, tel. 646/176-3720, sounds Greek, but Haliotis is actually the Latin genus term for abalone, the house specialty. Other seafood here is consistent as well; the family owners frequently fly fresh fish in from Isla Cedros, where they run another restaurant. Moderately priced. Open daily 12:30 P.M.–10 P.M.

Vegetarian

Señor Salud, Calle Espinoza and Calle 9, tel. 646/176-4415, is a combination health food shop and restaurant. Open Mon.–Sat. 8:15 A.M.–5:30 P.M. **El Mesón Vegetariano,** Calle Alvarado 377, is a newer spot with veggie Mexican dishes served for lunch and early dinner.

Groceries

The **Gigante** at Avs. Reforma and Delante is a huge supermarket with just about anything you might need for picnics, camping, or an epic transpeninsular road trip. There are eight other Gigantes in town.

Scattered along Avenida Diamante are inexpensive *panaderías, tortillerías,* and *dulcerías.* For European-style baked items, investigate **La Baguette,** on Blvd. Costero near Av. Blancarte, tel. 646/178-2814. Prices at La Baguette are about double what you'd pay in an Avenida Diamante bakery; if you're pinching pesos, stick with the latter.

On Mexico 1, a few kilometers south of town between Estero Beach and La Bufadora, is a row of vendors selling fresh tamales stuffed with pineapple *(piña),* corn *(elote),* olives *(aceitunas),* chicken, beef, or red chilies. Vendors along this road also sell jars of olives, chilies, and honey.

La Milpa, Calle Espinoza 246, tel. 646/177-2092, is a health-oriented store carrying natural foods, nonalcoholic wine and beer, herbs, dried fruits, baked goods, and natural remedies.

SPORTS AND RECREATION

Fishing

Although commercial fishing (both local and foreign) has depleted the overall supply of game fish in the Ensenada area, sportfishing here can still be rewarding, especially from June through mid-September when several species make coastal runs from the south. Bahía de Todos Santos catches include lingcod, rockfish, calico bass, sand bass, barracuda, bonito, and occasional yellowtail. Though this was once known as the "yellowtail capital of the world," yellowtail catches now are generally rare and rather puny.

Long-range fishing trips from Ensenada—to

© JOE CUMMINGS

Marina Coral

Punta Colonet, Isla San Gerónimo, or Isla San Martín—yield bluefin, yellowfin, and albacore tuna; skipjack; white sea bass; salmon grouper; and the occasional dorado.

Several companies operate sportfishing trips from the Ensenada Sportfishing Terminal, off Boulevard Costero near the end of Avenida Macheros. **Sergio's Sportfishing Center** (write c/o 2630 E. Beyer Blvd. Ste. 676, San Ysidro, CA 92143-9011), tel./fax 646/178-2185, U.S. tel. 800/336-5454, www.sergio-sportfishing.com, runs day trips for US$50 pp, or overnights and multiday, long-range trips by charter. Rates for local trips (day and overnight) include license, tackle, and live bait when available; added services, like fish cleaning and filleting, cost extra. On the same pier, **Gordo's Sportfishing,** tel. 646/178-3515 or 646/178-2377, fax 646/174-0481, and **Juanito's Boats,** tel. 646/174-0953, 800/569-1254 offer similar services, and are also recommended. Gordo's also operates its own smokehouse.

See Punta Banda and La Bufadora for information on fishing trips arranged by Dale's La Bufadora Dive Shop.

Sergio's, Juanito's, and Gordo's each offer **tackle rental and sales** at the sportfishing pier.

Boating

A concrete launch ramp off the *malecón* accommodates boats up to 10 meters (32 feet) in length. Ensenada's **Marina Coral** (radio VHF 71), the first marina along northern Baja's west coast, has 373 slips available up to 150 feet in length; eventually, says marina management, there will be 600 slips. Services include electricity, water, restrooms, showers, lockers, telephones, cable TV, fuel, ramp, tennis court, two pools, a hot tub, spa, restaurant, and nightclub. Short-term slip rates for boats are US$1.25 per foot per day, with discounts for long-term stays. This includes electricity (110–220 V), cable TV, and use of facilities at the adjacent Hotel Coral. For further information or slip reservations, contact the Hotel Coral and Marina, tel. 646/175-0000, Mexico/U.S./Canada tel. 800/862-9020, fax 646/175-0005, www.hotelcoral.com.

Ensenada Cruiseport Village Marina, tel. 646/173-4141 or fax 173-4151, U.S. tel. 877/219-5822, toll free from Mexico 800/027-3678, www.ecpvmarina.com offers similar facilities and similar rates.

Juanito's Boats, tel. 646/174-0953, 800/569-1254, a boatyard at the old marina in back of Plaza Marina, offers a few slips and accepts foreign boats for servicing or repair, as does **Baja Naval** in the same area. Service rates are lower than for comparable work done in the United States. Fuel is also available here.

As Ensenada is an official Mexican port of entry, arriving boaters must check in with the COTP on Boulevard Azueta. See Sports and Recreation in the On the Road chapter for details on check-in procedures.

For outboard-motor repairs, inquire at **Motores de Baja California Norte,** Calle 6 1990, tel. 646/176-3025, which specializes in sales and service of American-made motors.

Surfing

The nearest consistent surfing areas are at Punta San Miguel, several kilometers north of Ensenada off Mexico 1, and Islas de Todos Santos, 20 km west by boat. (For details see San Miguel and El Sauzal and Islas de Todos Santos, respectively.) Playa La Jolla, approximately 16 km south of town via Mexico 1 and BCN 23, occasionally benefits from the winter northwest swell.

You can purchase surf gear, including Ensenada-made San Miguel boards, at **San Miguel Surf Shop,** Av. López Mateos 350, tel. 646/178-2475. San Miguel short boards run around US$220–250, long boards US$300–340. Locally made, full-length wetsuits cost a reasonable US$125–150.

Diving

The best local diving spots are the rocky shorelines and sandy coves around Punta Banda and Islas de Todos Santos, and the seamount of El Bajo de San Miguel, about midway between San Miguel and Islas de Todos Santos.

Ensenada's only dive shop is **Almar,** Av. Macheros 149, tel. 646/178-3013.

See Punta Banda and La Bufadora for infor-

© JOE CUMMINGS

San Miguel's surfboard factory

mation on dive trips arranged by Dale's La Bufadora Dive Shop.

Whale-Watching

Sergio's Sportfishing Center (see Fishing earlier on) offers four- to five-hour whale-watching trips from late December through late March for US$25 pp (US$15 for age 11 and under). Sergio's needs a minimum of 15 people to run a trip—usually not a problem on weekends. **Gordo's** (next door) offers similar trips at similar rates.

Spa

Spa Cirse at the Hotel Coral & Marina offers a full line of spa treatments, including facials and massage, as well as a hot tub, sauna, steam room, weight-lifting equipment, heated indoor pool, and two lighted tennis courts. Spa hours are Monday–Thursday 7 A.M.–6 P.M., Friday and Saturday 7 A.M.–8 P.M., Sunday 8 A.M.–4 P.M. See Accommodations for contact information.

Race and Sports Book

Caliente Race and Sports Book maintains an outlet at the Hotel San Nicolás, Avenida López Mateos at Blancarte, as well as one in Plaza Marina.

Cruises

As part of a multiday cruise along Mexico's Pacific coast from Los Angeles, Royal Caribbean's *Monarch of the Seas,* U.S. tel. 800/327-6700, www.royalcarribean.com, stops over in Ensenada.

Bay Cruises: As the name suggests, **We Hook 'Em,** tel. 949/650-4735, U.S. tel. 866/934-6653, wehookem@aol.com, specializes in sportfishing charters, but the company also offers a wide range of professional boating services, including whale-watching tours and sunset cruises. We Hook 'Em operates out of the Hotel Coral and Marina.

Other companies in the vicinity run similar trips.

ENTERTAINMENT

Bars and Discos

Many of the hotels and motels in the main tourist district, along Avenida López Mateos and Boulevard Costero between Calle Sanginés and Avenida Macheros, feature bars or lounges with occasional live music—usually *trovadores* (troubadours) or mariachis playing Mexican standards. **Ibis,** Blvd. Costero at Av. Alvarado, tel. 646/176-1440, offers dancing to recorded music and light

© JOE CUMMINGS

the fabled Hussong's Cantina

shows—not on a par with Tijuana's high-tech discos but good enough. Look for this place to be open during American holidays—Labor Day, Memorial Day, and July 4.

West of Avenida Macheros, the city leaves behind the middle-class tourist zone and revels in cheap seafood joints, bars, and dance halls with a slightly seedy air. In this area is one of Baja's most famous landmarks, **Hussong's Cantina,** Av. Ruiz 113, tel. 646/178-3210, quite justifiably advertised as "the bar that built a town." This could be amended to "the bar that built a shopping center" now that the neighborhood is studded with Hussong's souvenir shops.

At the same location since Johan Hussong, a German immigrant, opened shop in 1892, and still owned by his grandson, the clapboard structure has hardly changed in a hundred years but for the addition of electricity. A massive eland head mounted high on the wall at the back surveys the one-room cantina from above, while the resident shoeshine man takes in the view from the sawdust-covered floor. Hussong's carries three kinds of beer only—Tecate, Bohemia, and XX, plus its own brand of tequila (quite good). On any given night tourists are outnumbered two to one by regulars, a mixture of expats and *bajacalifornianos.* Unamplified *norteña* ensembles sometimes play polkas and *rancheras* as *gritos* (shouts) pierce the smoky air. Come in the late afternoon if you hope to claim a table, as it's always crowded. Open daily 10 A.M.–1 A.M.

Across the street from Hussong's is **Papas and Beer,** a slightly more sedate two-story bar with recorded music and a collegiate atmosphere. It lacks character but is a reasonable alternative for folks who find Hussong's too rowdy. Next door to Papas is **Oxidos,** a bar/restaurant that has the flavor of Soho high-tech, with lounge chairs and tables, long bar, and dance floor.

A wander north along Avenida Ruiz or especially Avenida Gastelum will turn up a number of Mexican-oriented bars and cantinas, many of the red-light sort. Out on Boulevard Costero at Avenida Miramar, **Anthony's** is a classic in this category, with a large bar/dance hall with a bawdy, boy's-town reputation. Look for the big gorilla head over the door. Beyond the curtained entrance revolves a merry-go-round of ranchers, surfers, painted ladies, and other lost—at least for the night—souls. **Coyote Club,** Blvd. Costero 1000, tel. 646/177-7369, is a predominantly gay video disco playing both Latin and Anglo-American pop.

El Gran Chaparral, a dance hall on the east side of Avenida Reforma just north of Avenida Delante, is occasionally open for live *norteña* music and dancing.

El Patio, López Mateos 1088, is a tastefully designed bar set in a charming garden patio—a nice change from the raucous sports bar, stuffy hotel lounge, or trendy club.

Cinema

Ensenada now has a quality movie multiplex, **CinemaStar,** next to Sanborns in the Plaza Marina.

EVENTS

Partly as a result of its mild climate, Ensenada hosts more events—many of them sports-oriented—than any other city in Baja.

February

Carnaval: Ensenada has observed the pre-Lenten festival since 1918, and the celebration seems to get bigger every year—over 300,000 visitors in an average season. Usually held for six days before Ash Wednesday, the second week in February, festivities start with the Quema de Mal Humor (Burning of Bad Humor), in which an effigy is hanged and burned. The victim is usually modeled after an unpopular politician.

Throughout the week, a nightly street fair stretches for 12 downtown blocks, offering food vendors, carnival rides, live music, and a steady flow of Mexican beer, brandy, and tequila. Carnaval parades, consisting of flowered floats and legions of costumed dancers, wind through the streets every afternoon amid clouds of confetti. The best streets for viewing the three main parades—held from around 2:30 P.M. until around 4:30 P.M. on Saturday, Sunday, and Tuesday—are Boulevard Costero, Avenida López Mateos, and Avenida Ruiz.

One Carnaval event with a local flavor is the *juegos florales* contest, in which poets compete to see who can compose the best "flowery verse"; Spanish students shouldn't miss this one. Another local highlight is the selection of the Reina de Carnaval (Carnaval Queen) and El Rey Feo (Ugly King) at a midfestival coronation ball on Saturday night. The Monday following this weekend is El Día del Marido Oprimido (The Day of the Oppressed Husband), during which married men are allowed 23 and a half hours of symbolic freedom to do whatever they wish.

Carnaval's grand finale is a masquerade ball held on the Tuesday night before Ash Wednesday. Prizes are awarded for best costumes as well as for other attainments over the course of the week—best float, best dance troupe, etc.

So many leather-clad motorcyclists—including show-biz celebs like Peter Fonda and Jay Leno—come down from southern California for Carnaval nowadays that city officials allow them to participate in at least one of the parades.

For specific information on Carnaval scheduling and venues for individual events, pick up a copy of the *California Sun* or contact the tourist office on Boulevard Costero.

April

The **Rosarito-Ensenada 50-Mile Bicycle Ride** takes place on a Saturday in April and attracts as many as 10,000 participants, making it one of the world's largest cycling events. The route follows the coast, with an elevation differential of around 300 meters (1,000 feet). Sponsored by **Bicycling West,** P.O. Box 15128, San Diego, CA 92175-5128, tel. 619/424-6084.

Tommy Bahama Newport-Ensenada Race is mother of all west-coast regattas, in which over 600 sailors leave Newport Beach at noon on the last Friday in April and see who reaches Ensenada first. For more information visit www.nosa.org.

May

The mid-May **Lifeguard Triathlon** based at the Hotel Coral & Marina consists of two events: the speed triathlon (750-meter swim, 20-km cycle, five-km run) and the Olympic triathlon (1.4-km swim, 40-km cycle, 10-km run).

June

Baja 500, a 500-mile off-road race out of Ensenada, is held in early June and sponsored by

NORTHERN BAJA

BAJA 1000

Every November, desert rats from around the globe gather in Ensenada for the grueling Baja 1000 (Baja Mil), the world's most prestigious off-road race. The first organized contest took place in October 1967, though dirtbikers had informally raced from Ensenada to La Paz since the '50s. In 1962, Dave Ekins and Bill Robertson Jr. were the first to record their efforts when they raced two Honda 250 motorcycles the length of the peninsula, establishing their times by stamping sheets of paper at telegraph offices in Tijuana and La Paz. Ekins pulled into La Paz after 39 hours, 54 minutes; Robertson made it an hour later.

From 1967 to the present, the event has occurred yearly except in 1974, when the National Off Road Racing Association lost Mexican permission to operate the race. Since 1975, SCORE International has organized the race, most recently with the sponsorship of Tecate beer. Participants can enter in one of 24 categories—16 car-and-truck, six motorcycle, and two ATV classes. The course alternates year to year between a straight 1,000-mile Ensenada–La Paz run and a shorter 1,000-km loop beginning and ending in Ensenada; the latter course offers more spectator opportunities and pit stops.

SCORE also sponsors a separate Baja 1000 Endurance Safari on a course parallel to, but rougher than, the usual 1,000-mile Ensenada–La Paz route. A rally rather than a race, in this event contestants aren't rated on their time achievements but rather on endurance—a quality of obvious interest to automotive manufacturers and marketers seeking the imprimatur "Baja-proven." Shorter races include the Baja 500 (out of Ensenada, in June) and the San Felipe 250 (from San Felipe, in February or March). For further information check www.score-international.com.

SCORE International and Tecate beer. See the November entry for the **Baja 1000.**

Ensenada Grand Prix is the only race of its kind in Mexico, a NASCAR-style rally through the streets of Ensenada. Held in mid-June.

July

In the **Baja Volleyball Open,** held in late July at Playa El Faro, local teams compete against teams from the U.S. for cash trophies. Call Ensenada Sports Promotions, tel. 646/177-6688, for details. Another Baja Open is held in August.

August

At **Fiesta de la Vendimia Bajacaliforniana (Bajacalifornian Wine Harvest Festival),** wineries in Ensenada, Tijuana, and Valle de Guadalupe cosponsor 10 days of winetasting, music, vineyard tours, and gourmet cooking at various venues; usually commences the second or third week of the month. Most events have admission prices; a winetasting at the Riviera del Pacífico, for example, costs US$20 for all the hors d'oeuvres and wines you can sample. On the final Saturday of the festival, a panel of judges conducts a blind tasting of wines from Mexico and abroad during the Concurso Internacional. Call 646/174-0170 for information.

The **Corona Cup Regatta** is a multilap yacht race held in the bay. For information contact the state or city tourist offices.

September

Feria Internacional del Pescado y el Marisco (International Seafood Fair), usually held the first weekend of the month, is one of the city's best-attended fiestas. Many local restaurants participate, as well as chefs from Tijuana, Rosarito, and southern California. A ticket entitles the holder to four dishes and four beverages. Sponsored by CANIRAC, tel. 646/174-0448 or 646/174-0435, canirac@infosel.net.mx.

J. D. Hussong Baja International Chili Cookoff & Salsa Contest a cookoff sanctioned by the International Chili Society (ICS) and one of Ensenada's biggest events, is usually held the third weekend in September at Quintas Papagayo Resort. The cookoff winner is eligible to compete in the annual ICS World Championship Chili Cookoff in Nevada. In addition to chili-cooking competitions for individuals, clubs, and local restaurants, the day's activities typically include chili-pepper-eating and tequila "shoot-and-holler" contests, live music and dancing, and the selection of Ms. Chile Pepper and Mr. Hot Sauce. You can extinguish the fire with beverages provided by Cervecería Cuauhtémoc Moctezuma, brewers of Tecate, Carta Blanca, Dos Equis (XX), and several other popular Mexican beers; tequila purveyors Viuda de Romero; and winemakers Bodegas de Santo Tomás. A US$10 admission fee is charged; part of the proceeds go to charity. For current information on scheduling and venue, contact Juan Hussong, tel. 646/174-4575, fax 646/174-4155, papagayo@telnor.net, www.hussongs.com.

October

Watch top surfers from the Pacific coast of Mexico and California ride the waves at the two-day **Mexican Surf Fiesta** at Playa de San Miguel (tel. 858/586-9173, surfiesta@yahoo.com).

November

SCORE-Tecate Baja 1000, the granddaddy of all off-road races takes place over a four-day period during the first or second week of the month. Call SCORE International in the U.S., tel. 818/225-8402, for complete information. On even-numbered years, the race is run as far south as La Paz. For a race schedule, consult the Ensenada tourist office, pick up a current issue of the *California Sun,* or visit SCORE's website at www.score-international.com.

SHOPPING

You'll find the usual assortment of tourist-oriented souvenir and beachwear shops along Avenida López Mateos and Boulevard Costero. The **Centro Artesanal** on Boulevard Costero caters mostly to cruise-ship passengers in town for a few hours but is worth a look for Oaxacan folk art and neo–Casas Grandes pottery from Chihuahua's Valle de Casas Grandes. **Plaza Marina** and the adjacent **Plaza Palmira** were developed as shopping venues for cruise passengers, but so far they offer very little in the way of unique

purchases—just the usual gift and clothing shops you'd find along Avenida López Mateos.

Possibly the most interesting *artesanías* shop in town, **Galería de Pérez Meillon,** in the Centro Artesanal, carries a high-quality selection of Paipai and Casas Grandes pottery, Kumyai basketry, and contemporary art by up-and-coming Latin American artists. **Bazar Pa'todos,** on Av. López Mateos between Miramar and Gastelum, also sells high-quality, unique pieces, including Mexican colonial-style paintings and wood carvings.

Another interesting find is **Bazar Casa Ramírez,** Av. López Mateos 496-3, a family-owned *artesanías* shop with two floors of arts and crafts from all parts of Mexico. Upscale items include good-quality *alebrijes* (carved animal sculptures), a vast collection of handmade Mexican crosses with religious icons attached, black clay pottery from Oaxaca, and handcarved-and-painted mirrors from the state of Michoacán.

A large flea market called **Los Globos,** on Calle 9 three blocks east of Av. Reforma, features vendor stalls selling everything from housewares to sandals. It's open daily 9 A.M.–6 P.M. A similar market at Calle 6 and Avenida Riveroll is open only on weekends.

The best bargains for everyday items are found deeper in the downtown area, away from Boulevard Costero and Avenida López Mateos. The locals do much of their shopping in the vicinity of the Avenidas Juárez and Ruiz intersection, where bookstores, record shops, and *zapaterías* are particularly numerous. Ensenada's *zapaterías* specialize in boots made from "exotic" skins like lizard or ostrich—don't buy anything prohibited by United States Customs if you plan on taking it across the United States–Mexico border.

Nuevo México Lindo, Av. López Mateos 688, tel. 646/178-1381, is a *talabartería* where you can buy handcrafted saddles, riding tack, handbags, and other leather goods.

Wine

The wine shop within **La Esquina de Bodegas,** Av. Miramar 666 (between Calles 6 and 7), tel. 646/178-3557, carries a very good assortment of California and Baja California labels, plus wine accessories and assorted wine-associated gifts. Santo Tomás wines can be purchased by the case across the street at **Bodegas de Santo Tomás.**

Books

Libros Libros/Books Books, López Mateos 690, tel. 646/178-8448, sells videos, CDs, magazines, cards, and of course books. The selection is impressive—from classic literature to children's stories, art history to science journals. As the name implies, about half the publications are in English. Open daily 9 A.M.–5 P.M. Another good source for material in English is **The Bookseller,** Calle 4 240, tel. 646/178-8964, which sells and trades used books and magazines. Open Mon.–Sat. 10 A.M.–5 P.M.

Shopping Centers

Ensenada has several large *centros comerciales* or shopping centers, the largest of which is **Centro Comercial Misión** on the northeast corner of Calle 11 and Av. Reforma. Among the businesses are Gigante supermarket, Banamex (with an ATM), Lavamática Express, Smart and Final, and Cinema Gemelos.

INFORMATION AND SERVICES

Tourist Assistance

The Delegación de Turismo del Estado (State Tourism Delegation) office at Blvd. Costero and Calle Las Rocas, tel. 646/172-3022, fax 646/172-3081, dispenses information on Ensenada events, dining, and hotels, as well as on BCN travel. The English-speaking staff is competent and helpful. Open Mon.–Fri. 8 A.M.–5 P.M., Sat. and Sun. 10 A.M.–3 P.M.

The city-sponsored COTUCO is at Blvd. Costero 540, opposite the Pemex station at the north entrance to town, tel. 646/178-2411, cotucoe@telnor.net. It distributes much of the same information as the state tourist office. Open Mon.–Fri. 9 A.M.–7 P.M., Saturday 10 A.M.–6 P.M., Sunday 11 A.M.–3 P.M.

The Tourism Trust (Fondo Mixto), Mexico tel. 800/025-3991, U.S. tel. 800/310-9687, info@

> ## USEFUL ENSENADA TELEPHONE NUMBERS
>
> Ensenada area code: 646
> Customs: 174-0897
> Fire Department: 068
> Green Angels: 176-4675
> Highway Patrol: 176-1311
> Immigration: 174-0164
> IMSS Hospital: 172-4500
> ISSSTE Hospital: 176-5276
> Police: 060
> Red Cross: 066
> State Police: 061
> State Tourism Office: 172-3022
> Tourist Assistance: 078

enjoyensenada.com, offers information about hotels, restaurants, and attractions in Ensenada.

Ensenada has an active chamber of commerce (CANACO), Av. López Mateos 693, tel. 646/178-2322, canaco@telnor.net, and a restaurant association (CANIRAC) with many American members, Calle 3 451, tel. 646/174-0448, fax 646/174-0435, canirac2@infosel.net.mx.

Money-Changing

Most banks in Ensenada refer visitors to a *casa de cambio* for foreign-exchange services. Several shopping centers along Avenida Juárez and Avenida Reforma feature money-changing booths or storefronts. ATMs are available at several Banamex branches, including one at Av. Juárez and Riveroll, and at Banca Serfín, Av. Ruiz 290.

Post and Telephone

The most convenient post office for visitors staying near the waterfront sits at the corner of Avenidas López Mateos and Rotario (Riviera), opposite Hotel La Pinta. Open Mon.–Fri. 8 A.M.–6 P.M., Saturday 9 A.M.–1 P.M.

Ensenada has a number of public telephones in the downtown area. For both local and long-distance calls, these are less expensive than hotel phones. If you need a phone line installed, pay a visit to the municipal telephone office at the intersection of Boulevard Ramírez Mendez and Avenida Reforma, near the Limón Bahía shopping center.

Internet Access

CompuNet, part of CompuClub at Riveroll 143, offers email services and Internet access. If you're going to be around awhile, monthly and annual accounts are available. Open daily 9 A.M.–9 P.M.

Café Internet Maxi Com, Av. López Mateos 582, upstairs in Plaza Miramar, is a big space full of fast machines, and unlike many Internet cafés, this one actually serves coffee. Open daily 10 A.M.–9 P.M. Libros Libros/Books Books bookshop (see Shopping) also offers Internet service.

Immigration

The Ensenada immigration office, tel. 646/174-0164, is next to the port captain's office (COTP) on Av. Azueta near the waterfront at the northern entrance into town. If you plan to travel farther south than Maneadero and haven't validated your tourist card yet, this is the place to do it. The office is open daily 9 A.M.–5 P.M. Parking in the vicinity can be problematic—the office has no public lot, and most of the curbs nearby are painted red. You may have to park elsewhere in town and walk to the office.

Note: We once stopped here to have our Mexican visas validated, and the officer on duty refused to do the job, saying we had to return to Tijuana and have them validated at the border immigration office. We also heard from other foreigners who had similar experiences, although this unofficial "moratorium" lasted only a short while. If you have any trouble with your paperwork at the immigration office in Ensenada, go straight to the state tourism office at Blvd. Costero and Calle Las Rocas, tel. 646/172-3022; ask for the SECTUR *delegado,* who should be able to straighten things out.

Language Schools

Colegio de Idiomas de Baja California (Baja California Language College), Av. Riveroll 1287, tel. 646/174-1741, U.S. tel. 619/758-9711, U.S./Canada tel. 877/444-2252, college@bajacal.com, www.bajacal.com, offers 30-hour small-group week-long Spanish classes at a cost of US$245. Private classes run US$495. Homestays with Mexican families can be arranged for US$22–27 a day including three daily meals. The school's U.S. mailing address is Baja California Language College, P.O. Box 7556, San Diego, CA 92167. Online registration is available.

The **Center of Languages and Latin American Studies,** Calle San Carlos 242, Fracc. Buenaventura near Av. Reforma and Calle Diamante, Calle Felipe ángeles 15, tel. 646/178-7600, U.S. tel./fax 760/476-9730 or 800/834-2256, www.mexonline.com/cllas.htm, operates a similar program but offers one hour less of classroom instruction per day. Tuition is US$270–295 per week depending on the time of year (US$180–210 per week for four or more weeks), plus US$35 for materials and US$22–30 daily (depending on length of stay)for private homestay and meals (US$19–25 in a shared room), and US$125 registration. The center's U.S. mailing address is P.O Box 130715, Carlsbad, CA 92013. Online registration is available.

UCSD Extension Travel Study Programs, 9500 Gilman Drive, 0170-A, La Jolla, CA 92093-0170, tel. 858/964-1050, fax 858/964-1099, travelstudy@ucsd.edu, arranges weekend and week-long Spanish study courses in Ensenada most of the year.

Real Estate

Bienes Raices Roca, Av. Riveroll 143, tel. 646/174-0053, www.ensenada.net/roca, offers various real estate services, including sale and purchase of existing houses, vacation rentals, and property management. **Century 21,** Calle 9 1701, tel. 646/177-2777, can also provide information on houses, condos, and lots for sale in the Ensenada area.

Media

The *Ensenada Baja News-Gazette* is a very informative web magazine at www.baja-web.com /ensenada/gazette. Although the listings reach far beyond Ensenada, the Ensenada info is the most complete and up to date. The gazette aims to update the site monthly.

Mini Detalles Liquor Store in the Limón Bahía shopping center, Av. Delante at Av. Reforma, carries the *San Diego Union-Tribune* and the *Los Angeles Times* on a regular basis.

Emergencies

The **Clínica Hospital ISSSTE,** Calle Sanginés and Av. Pedro Loyola, tel. 646/176-5276, has 24-hour emergency services. For ambulance service, call **Cruz Roja,** tel. 066. For medical problems requiring emergency treatment at San Diego medical facilities, contact **Transmedic,** Av. Obregón at Calle 11, tel. 646/178-1400, a 24-hour ambulance service providing either air or surface transportation to San Diego.

GETTING THERE

By Air

No regularly scheduled flights currently serve Ensenada. **Aeropuerto El Ciprés,** just south of town off Mexico 1, tel. 646/177-4503, is an official Mexican airport of entry with a paved airstrip suitable for small-plane arrivals and departures (Unicom 119.75). An air service operated by the **Sociedad Cooperativa de Producción Pesquera** (nicknamed Cannery Airlines by resident Americans), tel. 646/176-6076, flies small planes between this airfield and Isla Cedros near the tip of the Vizcaíno Peninsula farther south. See Isla Cedros in the Central Baja chapter for information.

Baja Helicopters, Obregón 527-6 (at Calle 4), tel./fax 646/178-8826, offers chopper charters in the region or to just about anywhere in Baja California.

By Bus

Intercity bus services to and from Ensenada are operated by **Autotransportes de Baja California** (ABC). Most air-conditioned buses use the Central de Autobuses terminal at Avenida Riveroll and Calle 11, tel. 646/178-6680, while non-air-conditioned departures use a smaller terminal at Avenida Riveroll and Calle 8, tel. 646/177-0909. The Central de Autobuses has a snack bar and a telephone office. ABC's *servicio plus* offers deluxe buses to Tijuana (US$13) five times daily

7:15 A.M.–7:15 P.M., and to Mexicali (US$16) twice daily. ABC's regular non-air-conditioned buses leave for Tijuana every hour 5 A.M.–9 P.M. (US$8). Buses to/from San Felipe also use this terminal—see the San Felipe section for details.

From the larger ABC terminal, you'll also find twice-daily departures for points south, including San Quintín (US$15, four hours), Guerrero Negro (US$30, eight hours), Santa Rosalía (US$50, 12 hours), Loreto (US$63, 15 hours), and La Paz (US$74, 20 hours).

Transportes Norte de Sonora (TNS), Elite, and **Estrellas de Oro** operate services to Guaymas, Los Mochis, Mazatlán, Guadalajara, and Mexico City on the Mexican mainland.

By Car

Ensenada is the southern terminus of Mexico 1-D, the four-lane toll road from Tijuana. Beyond Ensenada, Mexico 1 is, for the most part, a two-lane highway with road conditions varying from kilometer to kilometer.

Mexico 3 from Tecate also terminates in Ensenada, then reappears east of town winding across the Sierra Juárez to join Mexico 5 for San Felipe. Finding Mexico 3 east out of Ensenada can be difficult, as the route is not well signposted in the city. The simplest way to get there is to follow Avenida Juárez until it meets Avenida Reforma at the Benito Juárez statue. The street directly across Avenida Reforma is Calzada Cortés; after crossing Avenida Reforma, follow Calzada Cortés until it curves to the left and feeds into Mexico 3.

GETTING AROUND

Buses

Several varieties of buses and vans ply the city's main avenues (e.g., López Mateos, Juárez, Ruiz, Diamante, Delante, Reforma, and Calle 9). The route—designated by street name—is usually whitewashed on the vehicle's windshield or printed on a marquee over it. Fares are roughly US$.50, depending on the size of the vehicle; bigger is cheaper. Buses to outlying districts like Ejido Chapultepec leave from Avenida Juárez.

Bus Tours: Cali-Baja Tours, Plaza Marina,

Local G-3, tel./fax 646/178-1045, offers reasonably priced Ensenada city tours.

Taxis

Most of the city's taxis park along López Mateos or Juárez, or near the bus depot at Calle 11 and Av. Riveroll. Fares are negotiable; most trips in the city cost around US$3–7. A taxi to La Bufadora costs US$8–12.

Rental Cars and Motor-Scooters

Ensenada is an expensive place to rent a car compared to Tijuana or Los Cabos. The most reasonable rates are charged by **Fiesta Rent-A-Car,** Blvd. Costero 1442 (in the lobby of Hotel Corona), tel. 646/176-3344. Rates at this agency for a Nissan Sentra or something similar run around US$50 per 24 hours, including 100 free kilometers; there is a US$.10 charge for each additional kilometer. Two- to four-day rentals come down less than 10 percent.

Hertz, in the Bahía shopping center at Calle 2 and Av. Riveroll, tel. 646/178-3776, U.S. tel. 800/654-3001, has considerably higher rates.

A vendor at the south end of the Plaza Cívica (Plaza de las Tres Cabezas) on Blvd. Costero, **Chavo's Sport Rentals,** rents Yamaha motor scooters for US$18 per hour.

Driving

Driving in Ensenada is fairly straightforward as long as you're prepared to stop at *every* intersection. Even when you don't see a stop sign, chances are a stop is required. The Ensenada traffic police don't go out of their way to hassle visitors, but fines are stiff for speeding, running stop signs, and drinking while driving. Fines must be paid in cash at the municipal police station, Calle 9 at Av. Espinoza.

ESTERO BEACH

This huge, estuarial beach at the junction of Bahía de Todos Santos and Río San Carlos lies about 12 km south of the center of Ensenada via Mexico 1, behind Ejido Chapultepec. Not everyone will find the beach—which tends toward mudflats at low tide—to their tastes, but the area is quiet and nice for beach-walking, surf-casting, and birdwatching. Opinions differ as to just how clean the water here is, but plenty of folks swim here without any complaints.

The turnoff from Mexico 1 is 7.5 km (4.7 miles) south of the Gigante at Avs. Reforma and Delante. Except during July and August, the beach is surprisingly uncrowded. Ejido Chapultepec itself is a mostly uninspiring neighborhood of unfinished concrete-block houses and graffiti-covered walls, with a few nicer houses mixed in.

The **Estero Beach Museum,** part of the Estero Beach Resort complex, offers natural-history exhibits and a display of Mexican folk art. Nominal admission fee; open daily 9 A.M.–5 P.M.

Accommodations

Under US$25: From the highway turnoff for the Estero Beach Resort Hotel you can also reach several cheaper motels near a sandy bay beach known as Playa Hermosa. These are basic lodgings that cater to Mexican vacationers and other visitors on a budget. Finding them necessitates driving along a grid of unsigned, often unpaved and sandy roads off Mexico 1. On Playa Hermosa near El Faro Beach Motel and Trailer Park is **Mona Lisa RV Park and Motel** (no phone—turn right just before the road leading to El Faro). It offers simple rooms with kitchens.

US$25–50: Motel Costa Mar, Calle Veracruz 319 (1.5 km south of town), tel. 646/176-6425, is small and cheap. **Motel Hacienda Don Juan,** on the road to Estero Beach and within walking distance of the beach, offers rooms with kitchenettes and TVs.

Three-story **Hotel Joya Mar,** Calle Veracruz 360, tel./fax 646/176-7430, stands about a block away from Cueva de los Tigres, still a few blocks from Playa Hermosa, and offers 61 standard rooms. Facilities include a restaurant, small pool, and enclosed parking.

Along Playa Hermosa itself are several motels attached to trailer parks. **El Faro Beach Motel and Trailer Park,** tel. 646/177-4625, fax 646/177-4620, offers 23 basic rooms with kitchens in a two-story brick-and-stucco motel. To find El Faro, follow signs for Estero Beach off Mexico 1 at around Km 14, then continue straight ahead on this road (ignoring further signs for Estero Beach) until it dead-ends at El Faro. **La Villa Real Motel,** in the same vicinity as Mona Lisa, features larger palapas and grills. A rustic but atmospheric restaurant overlooks the bay.

US$50–100: **Estero Beach Resort Hotel,** Km 14, Carretera Transpeninsular, tel. 646/176-6225 or 646/176-6230, fax 646/176-6925, www.hotelesterobeach.com, is a Spanish mission-style complex scattered over much acreage landscaped with palms and grass. The 104 rooms and suites all enjoy beach views. Amenities include tennis courts, a boat ramp, boat rentals, horseback riding, a pool, playground, clubhouse, restaurant, bar, store, and museum. An adjacent RV park offers 60 RV spaces with full hookups and grassy camping areas. To make reservations from the United States, visit the website.

Camping and RV Parks

The deluxe **Estero Beach Trailer Park,** tel. 646/176-6265, is adjacent to the Estero Beach Resort Hotel. RVers can use all the hotel facilities, including boat ramp, tennis courts, and clubhouse. Full-hookup sites are US$25.

On Playa Hermosa, **El Faro Beach Motel and Trailer Park,** tel. 646/177-4625, fax 646/177-4620, maintains 20 full-hookup sites, many of them permanently rented, plus bathrooms and hot water showers, right on the beach. Rates are US$8–12 a night. You may park for the day (7 A.M.–7 P.M.) at El Faro for just US$3, a fee that includes use of showers and restrooms.

Several other motel/trailer parks at Playa Hermosa offer similar setups. Friendly **Mona Lisa RV Park and Motel** has 17 concrete pads with full hookups, as well as restrooms, hot showers, a small store, tiny beach *palapas,* barbecue grills, and a restaurant. **Corona Beach Hotel** (no phone), north of the Mona Lisa, has 60 pull-through RV sites with electricity and water in a big open sand area for US$10 a night. Facilities include flush toilets and cold showers; tent camping is permitted. **La Villa Real Motel,** in the same vicinity, has better RV sites (US$10), although all of the beachfront sites appear to be permanently occupied. Some sites have palapa tables.

Frequent buses, marked Chapultepec, ply between downtown Ensenada and this neighborhood.

PUNTA BANDA AND LA BUFADORA

The rocky Punta Banda peninsula juts into the Pacific at the south end of Bahía de Todos Santos and is largely undeveloped except for a few campgrounds and small residential communities. Hikers can explore the peninsula's windswept spine on unmarked trails leading from turnouts along the only paved road, BCN 23. From lookout points on Punta Banda, you can often see spouting gray whales as they pass by during their annual Jan.–Mar. migration.

La Bufadora

One of the Ensenada area's prime tourist sites, the scenic La Bufadora blowhole at the tip of Punta Banda is about 25 km (16 miles) from the city via Mexico 1 and BCN 23. During incoming

La Bufadora

tides, waves rush into an underground cavern and force spumes as high as 25–30 meters (80–100 feet) through a hole in the top of the cavern. "La Bufadora" means "The Snorter," referring to the sound created as water spews from the blowhole. A visitors center contains toilets and an interpretive display. Outside the center is a small desert garden in which the plants are accurately labeled.

A favorite weekend excursion among local Ensenadenses as well as foreign visitors, La Bufadora has taken on a look of prosperity since our last visit. Vendors selling snacks and souvenirs still line the road from the parking lot to the blowhole, but the storefront shacks have been replaced with more substantial buildings, all connected with wooden and red-tile roofs that arch over the walkway. This spot could be nicknamed "Baja *churro* capital" since there are probably more *churro* vendors here than anywhere else on the peninsula. Besides the vendor stalls, there are a few restaurants to choose from. One of the more popular seafood places is **Mariscos Alicia.** Also good are **Celia's Restaurante Bar** and **Restaurant Bar Los Gordos.** For the best bay view there is also **Los Panchos.**

A couple of pay lots at La Bufadora offer parking for US$5 per vehicle. Below the blowhole is Bahía Papalote (a bay) and small residential/recreational community Rancho La Bufadora.

Fishing

Dale's La Bufadora Dive Shop, tel. 646/154-2092, divebc@telnor.net, www.labufadora.com/dales/dales.htm, arranges half-day fishing trips for US$25–37.50 per person, depending on the number of signups (two minimum). Dale's overlooks Bahía Papalote at Rancho La Bufadora and is open on weekends or by appointment.

Scuba Diving

Detached rocks, underwater pinnacles, sea caves, and kelp beds below the cliffs on Punta Banda's south shore are popular among scuba divers, and accessible by boat or from the shore. Easiest access is at Bahía Papalote, the bay below La Bufadora; it's sheltered enough for intermediate divers or supervised novices; an underwater

hot springs at a depth of 25–30 meters warms the bottom of the bay.

Off the northwest tip of Punta Banda lies an underwater ridge—accessible by boat only—topped by a 2.4-km chain of small islands. The ridge is dotted with underwater cliffs, caves, rock reefs, and kelp beds. Cold-water upwellings along the ridge stimulate marinelife and help maintain good visibility. Because of swells and currents in the area, only divers with open-ocean experience should consider diving here unless accompanied by someone who knows local diving conditions well.

At Bahía Papalote, **Dale's La Bufadora Dive Shop,** (see Fishing) offers half-day guided dive trips for US$25–37.50 per person, depending on the number of signups (two minimum). Dale's also rents diving and snorkeling gear. Dive shops in Ensenada can also arrange guided trips to any Punta Banda dive spot, and there are also a couple of dive shops along the Punta Banda road (BCN 23).

Kayaking

Challenging sea kayak routes include following the peninsular shore from La Jolla around to La Bufadora, or crossing over to the Isla Sur of the Islas Todos Santos. The latter is a fairly straightforward 6.4-km (four-mile) paddle from Punta Banda. At Rancho La Bufadora near the blowhole, **Dale's La Bufadora Dive Shop,** (see Fishing) rents kayaks for US$20 per half day, US$30 per full day (US$30 and US$40 respectively for double kayaks).

Camping and RV Parks

A short distance along the road to La Bufadora (BCN 23), in the American retirement enclave of La Jolla, is the large, secure, and well-kept **La Jolla Beach Camp,** tel. 646/154-2005, fax 646/154-2004, facing Bahía de Todos Santos. Electric/water hookups or tent sites cost US$10 for two people, plus US$2 for each additional person. Other facilities include hot showers, a boat ramp, tennis court, disposal station, market, and restaurant.

The adjacent **Villarino RV Park (Campamento Turístico Villarino),** U.S. reservations

P.O. Box 2746, Chula Vista, CA 91912-2746, tel. 646/176-4246, Ensenada tel. 646/154-2045, fax 646/154-2044, offers 35 tent/camper sites with electricity for US$10, full hookups for US$15, two persons, each extra person US$5. Other facilities include clean bathrooms, hot showers, picnic tables, a boat ramp, boat rentals, restaurant, and market. The office is open daily 9 A.M.–noon and 1–5 P.M.

A couple of *ejido*-operated campgrounds with minimal facilities (toilets and water only) are available farther up on Punta Banda. **Ejido Coronel Esteban Cantú,** on the west side of Punta Banda, about a half mile off the dirt road that forms the final approach to La Bufadora, is a quiet spot ideal for self-contained campers with an interest in nearby fishing or diving; it costs US$5 a night.

Nearby **Campo No. 3,** part of the same *ejido,* is similar. **Campo Turístico Ejidal No. 5** offers no facilities other than parking space and a fence for security; you can camp here for just US$4 a night or park during the day only for US$2.

Rancho La Bufadora, overlooking Bahía Papalote, tel. 646/178-7172, offers ocean-view dry campsites (flush toilets available) with 24-hour security and is within walking distance of La Bufadora, Dale's La Bufadora Dive Shop, a boat ramp, restaurants and bars, and a minimarket. Rates run US$5–10, depending on the number of campers. **Dale's La Bufadora Dive Shop** also offers beds in a bunkhouse sleeping up to 15 persons for US$10 per person; there's a US$200 minimum per weekend for use of the bunkhouse. On weekdays you may be able to get a discount.

Getting There

To drive to Punta Banda from Ensenada, take Mexico 1 south to BCN 23 (just north of Maneadero), then follow this road west through olive orchards and the La Jolla community onto the peninsula. After La Jolla, the road begins to climb, winding its way toward La Bufadora and ending at a parking lot for the blowhole. You can hire a taxi from the city to La Bufadora for US$10–12.

East from Ensenada

Mexico 3 stretches southeast 198 km (123 miles) from Ensenada to San Felipe on the Sea of Cortez. The road is often in dire need of repair, with irritating potholes much of the way to San Felipe. What normally would be a three-hour drive can last up to six, depending on the state of repairs. The first two-thirds of the highway traverses high chaparral along the gradually ascending western slopes of the Sierra Juárez. Just past Km 39 is a short paved road leading north into **Ojos Negros,** a small farming center with a Pemex station (which more often than not pumps gas from a can), as well as several markets, an auto parts dealer, and a pharmacy. **Country Café** serves up hearty *chorizo* and egg dishes. A network of dirt roads out of Valle Ojos Negros leads to farms, the old mining settlement of Real del Castillo, and a longer road to Parque Nacional Constitución de 1857.

A natural spring flows from a steep hillside on the east side of the highway between Km 73 and 74—a good place to stock up on drinking water.

PARQUE NACIONAL CONSTITUCIÓN DE 1857

The most commonly used road to this national park branches northeast off Mexico 3 at Km 55 near Ojos Negros. Although ungraded much of the way, the 43-km (26-mile) dirt road is usually traversable, if caution is taken, by ordinary passenger car all the way to the park entrance. As the road climbs, passing a number of ranchos, the chaparral gradually gives way to conifer forests and the temperature drops.

Most of the 5,000-hectare park encompasses a subalpine plateau at the center of the Sierra Juárez with an average elevation of around 1,200 meters (3,950 feet); several granite peaks reach over 1,500 meters (5,000 feet). Containing several different species of pines, some exclusive to the region, the forests here form one of the most important woodland areas in Baja California—a virtual oasis surrounded by the rest of the state's aridity.

© JOE CUMMINGS

Mexico 3

Two natural lakes, Laguna La Chica and Laguna Juárez, surrounded by granite boulders, low hills, and Ponderosa pines, add to the oasis effect and generate scenes of great beauty during occasional winter snowfalls. Laguna Juárez—more commonly known as Laguna Hanson after an American settler who disappeared here in 1880 (legend has it he was cooked in a cauldron by a friend)—is for all intents the center of the park.

In years when rainfall is plentiful, the scenic lake is filled with bass and catfish; in the fall, ducks are common. Fishing is permitted; hunting isn't. A campground at the lake features raked grounds and neat firepits, some furnished with firewood and grills. Except for a 10-km path around the lake, there are no established hiking trails in the park. Smaller Laguna La Chica is less visited; in dry years it may not contain any water at all.

After you have chosen a campsite, a ranger or the park caretaker will drop by, place a trash container at the spot, and collect US$5 per night per vehicle. A fine for littering will be imposed if

garbage is discarded anywhere but in the trash can. Most of the year the park receives few visitors. This changes at Easter, when enough jeepsters arrive to dispel all peace and quiet. If you visit in winter, come prepared for cold weather and possible snow. The latter may make park roads temporarily impassable.

The road from Mexico 3 continues northeastward through the park and ends at Mexico 2—60 km (36 miles) from Laguna Hanson—near La Rumorosa. See Vicinity of Mexicali for details on the northern approach to Laguna Hanson.

INDEPENDENCIA

This pueblo of around 500 *ejidatarios,* at Km 92 on Mexico 3, is part of Ejido Héroes de la Independencia. It makes a good rest spot if you're driving Mexico 3 straight through, as it's roughly halfway between Ensenada and the Mexico 5 junction. Among the scattered buildings, some abandoned, are a *tienda rural,* a Pemex station (one pump with no diesel), a church, an auto shop, and a couple of handicraft shops. The latter sell pottery and other crafts made by the Paipai who live in nearby **Santa Catarina,** a former mission settlement eight km (five miles) east of Independencia via a graded dirt road. The adobe ruins—foundations only—of Misión Santa Catarina de los Paipais, founded by Dominican padres in 1797 and destroyed by Yumanos in 1840, are still visible in the village. The Paipai, who call themselves Akwa'ala and may be related to the Yavapai and Walapai of Arizona, make rustic coil pots prized by collectors for the orange-and-black swirls or "fire clouding" created during the firing process.

VALLE DE LA TRINIDAD AND MIKE'S SKY RANCH

A paved road to Valle de la Trinidad branches south from Mexico 5 at Km 121. This farming community of around 5,000 offers a Pemex station, a bank, several markets, cafés, and auto shops. Southwest of Valle de la Trinidad, a dirt road suitable only for sturdy, high-clearance vehicles continues southward some 48 km (30

NORTHERN BAJA

miles) past a few ranchos to the northern boundary of Parque Nacional Sierra San Pedro Mártir.

Just beyond Km 138, a dirt road leads 35.5 km (22 miles) south to Mike's Sky Ranch, a remote resort at the northwestern edge of Parque Nacional Sierra San Pedro Mártir (elevation: 1,200 meters/3,950 feet). Named for its late founder, Mike Leon, the ranch has long served as a checkpoint for the Baja 500 and Baja 1000 off-road races; nearby are hiking trails to year-round waterfalls and Río San Rafael. Ranch accommodations include 27 cabins for US$50 pp per night (includes all meals and swimming pool access) and campsites for US$8 a night (water and shower privileges only). Guests eat family-style meals together (campers pay US$12 for dinner and US$7 for breakfast and lunch). For information or reservations write Mike's Sky Ranch, 607 Twining Ave., San Diego, CA 92154, or call Mike's number in Mexico (664/681-5514).

The road to Mike's is rough in spots, though drivers with passenger cars and RVs can make it with patience. Beyond the ranch, this road continues southwestward to join the better, graded road between Mexico 1 and the national park. For more information on this route and Parque Nacional Sierra San Pedro Mártir, see South from Ensenada.

SAN MATÍAS PASS TO CRUCERO LA TRINIDAD

Southeast of Valle de la Trinidad, Mexico 3 climbs through 900-meter (2,950-foot) San Matías Pass. As the road descends the eastern escarpment of the Sierra de San Pedro Mártir, the scenery shifts from chaparral to desert. Between Km 160 and 170, ocotillos increase rapidly in number and size.

At Km 164, a dirt road leads southeast toward Rancho Villa del Sol, then south through the dry Laguna Diablo to the eastern approach to Picacho del Diablo, via Cañon del Diablo. This road also connects with a dirt track east to San Felipe.

Mexico 3 meets Mexico 5 at Crucero La Trinidad (Pemex, café); from here it's 109 km (65 miles) north to Mexicali, 48 km (29 miles) south to San Felipe.

South from Ensenada

MANEADERO TO COLONIA VICENTE GUERRERO

Maneadero

This farming community 20 km (12 miles) south of Ensenada is unremarkable except for the fact that it's the southernmost limit of Baja's "free zones." Beyond Km 23, every visitor is supposed to possess a valid tourist permit or visa. The immigration checkpoint at Km 23 has been closed for several years now, so be sure to validate your tourist card in Ensenada. A military *puesto de control* may be in operation to check for drugs and weapons.

Restaurants, small grocery stores, auto parts shops, and other small businesses line Mexico 1 in the middle of Maneadero. Locally grown olives—along with tamales—are sold in great abundance at roadside stands. A car wash on the east side of the highway performs an excellent exterior and interior cleaning for around US$5, something to consider if you're on the way north after extensive off-highway driving in the interior.

Just south of Maneadero at Km 30 is **Balneario Las Cañaditas,** a campground with a restaurant, pool, and barbecue pit. Rates: US$15 pp per night.

The highway through Maneadero is famous for its prodigious *topes* or speed bumps. Drive slowly.

Ejido Uruapán

Just south of Km 41 (19 km south of Maneadero) is the turnoff for Ejido Uruapán, a farming village set in a deep valley. During quail season, Nov.–Feb., Uruapán is frequented by American hunters, most of whom stay at a hunting lodge operated by the regional wildlife inspector, Billy Cruz. During the rest of the year, nonhunting visitors may stay here as well. Guests can explore the Valle de Uruapán, visit nearby vineyards and dairy farms, or make day trips to beaches at Punta Santo Tomás, 31 km west of the village.

Uruapán itself offers little to see. A stream on the valley floor is linked to a hot springs where *ejidatarios* bathe and wash clothes at a cement structure built for this purpose. The *ejido* also operates a sea-urchin processing plant; established with Japanese assistance, the plant prepares the tiny marine creatures for export to Japan, where they're a popular sushi ingredient.

Cruz's simple, red-brick **Uruapán Lodge (Rancho Cinegetico),** centers around a courtyard; guests dine in front of a huge fireplace. Open only during hunting season, the lodge rents spartan rooms for US$145 a day, which includes a hunting guide, transportation to hunt sites, and a large evening meal. For further information on staying at the lodge, contact the state tourist office in Ensenada (646/172-3022). For information on hunting, contact the **Mexican Hunting Association,** 6840 El Salvador St., Long Beach, CA 90815, tel. 310/430-3256.

At the junction of Mexico 1 and the turnoff for the village is a campground with well-shaded tent/camper sites and a few fire pits. Campers can bathe at the village hot springs.

La Bocana and Puerto Santo Tomás

Off Mexico 1 at Km 48, an unpaved graded road follows the Río Santo Tomás 29 km (18 miles) west to the seaside fishing villages of La Bocana and Puerto Santo Tomás, both on the south side of Punta Santo Tomás. The Río Santo Tomás drains into the Pacific at La Bocana (The Mouth); during the Dominican era, Puerto Santo Tomás served as a supply port for nearby Misión Santo Tomás.

The scenic coastal topography along Punta Santo Tomás and the coves to the south have attracted a small gringo settlement, but for the most part you'll have the beach all to yourself. Camping is free; you can rent rustic cabins at either village. The villagers also rent fishing *pangas.*

The shoreline in front of La Bocana offers occasional beach and reef breaks. Determined surfers can brave an ungraded dirt road that runs south off the graded road from Mexico 1—the

roadside tamale stand

turnoff is approximately 20.5 km (12.7 miles) west of the highway—and straggles 11 km (seven miles) southwest to Punta San José, where there are often good reef and point breaks.

Santo Tomás

The Valle de Santo Tomás, left by the Río Santo Tomás, is one of Baja's prime agricultural regions and a visual highlight of any transpeninsular journey. Winding up, down, and around olive-green hills, the highway repeatedly suspends drivers over vignettes of tidy olive groves, vineyards, fields of flowers, and the occasional herd of goats. For some visitors, a day's stopover turns into weeks, perhaps because Santo Tomás offers the ambience of California's Sonoma or Napa Valley without the tourists and high prices. The valley community of around 1,500 is friendly and welcoming.

The valley was originally settled in 1790 by Dominican missionaries as an intermediate point between Misión San Miguel to the north and San Vicente to the south. In 1791 the Dominican padres established **Misión Santo Tomás de Aquino,** which by 1800 boasted over 3,000 cattle, sheep, and goats, plus an estimated 200 acres of grapes, corn, and wheat. The mission wine produced at Santo Tomás was famous throughout the California mission system and is now one of several wines produced by Ensenada's Bodegas de Santo Tomás. The Santo Tomás mission was secularized in 1849.

The **Mission Ruins** lie in two locations. The original site is on a low mesa off the unpaved road to La Bocana and Puerto Santo Tomás; the second site, where the mission was moved in 1794, is just off the east side of Mexico 1 in the village of Santo Tomás, north of El Palomar Trailer Park. At both sites, the only remains are a few ruined adobe walls and a foundation.

Although grapes grown in this region may end up squeezed into the wines of several *bajacaliforniano* wineries, **Bodegas de Santo Tomás,** a descendant of the original Santo Tomás mission winery, still presides over the valley. For much of the 20th century, the winery's main operations took place in Ensenada, but in recent years the owners have been moving the company back

to the valley. Wine-tasting tours for groups of 12 or more are now available at the bodega's new eco-tech, gravity-fed winery overlooking the valley, by appointment only; tel. 646/177-0836, bstwines@hotmail.com.

The inexpensive family-owned **El Palomar,** at Km 154 on Mexico 1 in Santo Tomás (Apdo. Postal 595, Santo Tomás, BCN), tel. 646/178-2355, began as a restaurant in 1948 but now includes a motel, a trailer park with 101 spaces, a Pemex station, and even a small zoo. Rooms at the motel are comfortable and heated, and fall into the US$25 –50 range. Full-hookup RV sites in the trailer park cost US$12 a night for two people. El Palomar's dining room offers a full list of *bajacaliforniano* wines and home-cooked meals starting at US$7. The two swimming pools at El Palomar are a treat during the summer months.

Ejido Eréndira and Puerto San Isidro

At Km 78, a paved road leads west off Mexico 1 to the fishing and farming community of Ejido Eréndira. Although the village is far from attractive, the beaches north of town offer plenty of opportunities for camping and surf or boat fishing. The road to Puerto Isidro (two km north of Ejido Eréndira) and beyond is unpaved, ungraded, sandy, and potholed—a passenger car can manage it, but very slowly. Surfers will find six different point and reef breaks in the vicinity of Puerto Isidro. River's Mouth and Barny's Cove are closest to the *ejido,* while Half Moon Bay, Sunset Beach, Lighthouse, and Cuatro Casas are a bit farther away.

Twenty-four km from Mexico 1, **Hostel Coyote Cal's,** is a gringo-run surf camp with shared rooms for US$15 per person, private rooms for US$35 per couple, and tent/RV sites for US$10 per person. Room (but not camping) rates include breakfast, and discounted weekly and monthly rates are available for all accommodations. For enjoying the surrounding coast and hills, Cal's rents out mountain bikes, mask/snorkel/fins, surfboards, and boogie boards.

Castro's Place near Puerto Isidro (Apdo. Postal 974, Ensenada, BCN), tel. 646/176-2897, is a fish camp with simple cabins that sleep up to six people in bunk beds for around US$25–28 a night. Camping is permitted at Castro's for a nominal fee. The owner, Fernando Castro Ríos, leads guided fishing trips in the vicinity for US$140 per day for four persons, plus US$30 for each additional person. Reservations may be necessary on weekends.

A few kilometers north are plenty of free camping spots. Ejido Eréndira has one hotel, **Eréndira,** with 12 very rustic rooms in the US$25–50 range. There is a small grocery store, but the Pemex station is abandoned. The nearest working pumps are in Santo Tomás and San Vicente.

San Vicente

The scenic Valle de San Vicente and adjacent Llano Colorado (Reddish Plain), like the Río Santo Tomás valley, are heavily cultivated with olives, grapes, wheat, and corn.

Just south of the Km 88 marker, a dirt road leads west off Mexico 1 to the ruins of **Misión San Vicente Ferrer,** a Dominican mission in use 1780–1833. During its half-century tenure, the mission came under repeated attacks by Yumano warriors living in the Sierra Juárez. On a small mesa near the adobe walls of the mission is a mission-established cemetery—still in use—and the remains of a Spanish presidio. The mission area is fenced off and appears to be under private control at the moment. To enter you must pay an admission fee at a new visitors center out front. The center was closed when we stopped by, and there were no posted hours.

Along Mexico 1 in the small town of San Vicente sit a sprinkling of cafés, markets, an ABC bus terminal, a Pemex station, and three hotels with basic accommodations for under US$25: **Mary's Little Hotel & Restaurant,** a new cement-block place called **Hotel La Palma,** and old standby **Motel El Camino.**

San Antonio del Mar

At Km 126, just north of Colonet, an unpaved graded road leads 12.5 km (eight miles) northwest to this seaside settlement, little more than a collection of trailers, rustic beach houses, and a couple of beach camps that charge US$5–10 a night for tents or campers. The beach at San An- tonio del Mar, wedged into a large gap between high cliffs created by a tidal estuary, is wide, windy, and backed by sand dunes. If you can stand the wind, you can camp for free on the beach. Surfcasting and clamming are usually excellent here; the estuary is an added attraction.

The main road in from Mexico 1 becomes softer as it gets closer to the beach. Unless you have four-wheel drive, stick to the most well-worn, hardened tracks.

Colonet

Like San Vicente, Colonet is a small farming center with a Pemex station and a couple of cafés and markets. Travelers spending time at San Antonio del Mar, Rancho Meling, or Parque Nacional Sierra San Pedro Mártir often use the town as a supply depot.

A graded dirt road leads southwest out of town 14 km to a fish camp on Bahía Colonet. Cabo Colonet, at the north end of the bay, offers a point break during winter northwest swells. The town, bay, and cape are reputedly named for Captain James Colnett, a British sea captain who explored this section of the Pacific coast in the late 18th century. At **Cuatro Casas,** about 4.5 km south of Cabo Colonet on the bay, campsites are available for US$4–5 a day. Surfcasters will find plenty of barred surfperch, halibut, and bass.

Practicalities: Small two-story **Motel Sonora,** on the highway between Km 122 and Km 123 in Colonet, offers basic lodging for under US$25. In the center of town is **Yoanna's Pizza. Magui's Restaurant,** at the south end of town, is also a decent place for a meal. The usual taco stands can be found on the west side of the highway.

San Telmo and Rancho Meling

Between Km 140 and Km 141, an unpaved graded road branches east to San Telmo, Rancho Meling, and **Parque Nacional Sierra San Pedro Mártir.** San Telmo, six km (3.5 miles) east of Mexico 1, is a small farming and ranching settlement with little of interest to the traveler; supplies for extended trips into the interior should be procured in Colonet or Camalú on Mexico 1. There's a Pemex station with Premium fuel just north of San Telmo.

Rancho Meling, also known as Rancho San José, lies 42 km (26 miles) farther southeast along the road, at an elevation of 670 meters (2,200 feet). Founded in 1893 by Danish immigrant and Texas miner Harry Johnson as a base for his gold-mining operations in the western Sierra de San Pedro Mártir, the ranch was destroyed by Magonistas during the 1911 border rebellion. A Norwegian family, the Melings, helped rebuild the ranch shortly thereafter, turning it into a 10,000-acre cattle ranch.

Today, in addition to raising cattle, the ranch takes in paying guests who want to experience Baja's high country. Visitors are accommodated in a comfortable one-story, 12-room stone lodge for US$75 s, US$145 d (US$45 for children under 12) per day, including three family-style meals. Optional activities include swimming in a spring-fed pool, horseback riding, quail and dove hunting, and excursions into the Sierra de San Pedro Mártir—an excellent opportunity to see the national park with experienced guides. Guests with their own planes may use the 1,064-meter (3,500-foot) airstrip. For reservations or further information, call Duane Meling at 646/179-4106, or visit www.meling.com. You can also write to Meling Guest Ranch, P.O. Box 189003, PMB 120, Coronado, CA 92178.

Another recreational spot run by the Meling family is **Rancho La Ciénega,** at Km 73 on the observatory road about four hours from Ensenada and 51.5 km (32 miles) from Mexico 1. The main activity occurs on weekends in late summer and early fall, when Andy Meling fires up a deep-pit barbecue for a Saturday afternoon feast. Guests generally arrive Friday afternoon to camp overnight; facilities are limited to toilets and hot-water showers. For information, contact Rancho Meling.

Punta San Jacinto and Camalú

Between Km 149 and Km 150, a dirt track suitable in good weather for ordinary passenger vehicles proceeds west nine km (5.5 miles) to a sandy beach at Punta San Jacinto. A somewhat popular point break, known as Freighters because of the nearby wreck of the huge freighter *Isla del Carmen,* led to the establishment of the rustic **Punta de San Jacinto Campgrounds,** also known as El Parador Surf Camp. The camp offers few facilities—water, sometimes, and a couple of firepits. You can camp for free among the dunes behind the beach.

Camalú, beginning at Km 157, offers markets, pharmacies, and cafés, a mechanic's shop, and a Pemex station (diesel fuel is available). Just south of the Pemex is **Dragón de Oro** (Golden Dragon) Chinese restaurant, tel. 616/165-4405; open 11 A.M.–9 P.M. South of that is **Lonchería Anita's,** an okay place for a quick bite. An unpaved side road leads west to Camalú Via la Mar, a fish camp, and areas suitable for overnight camping. Reef and point breaks at Punta Camalú to the north attract surfers; an on-again, off-again surf camp provides minimal facilities.

Misión Santo Domingo and Colonia Vicente Guerrero

Colonia Vicente Guerrero is a growing agricultural center with a post office, market, motel, two banks (including a Banamex with ATM), restaurants, a police station, *panadería,* 24-hour Pemex station, *butano* (butane/propane) plant, clinic, ABC bus terminal, and two trailer parks. The surrounding fields produce a variety of vegetables and fruit.

The ruins of Misión Santo Domingo, named for the founder of the Dominican Order, lie north of town, eight km (five miles) east of Mexico 1, in a canyon formed by Arroyo de Santo Domingo. An earlier mission, established in 1775, lay eight km farther east along the arroyo. Moved to the current site in 1782, the mission closed in 1839 after most of the Amerindians in the area either died in battle or succumbed to smallpox. The meter-thick adobe walls at Santo Domingo are more extensive than those at Santo Tomás or San Vicente; the outline of the mission quadrangle and several rooms are clearly visible.

The mission road parallels Arroyo de Santo Domingo for several kilometers beyond the ruins, offering a scenic, if rough, drive past two ranchos. Originating in the high reaches of the Sierra de San Pedro Mártir, this arroyo is said to carry the largest volume of water of any stream on the peninsula and is stocked with an abundance of trout in season.

Motel Sánchez, in the middle of town on the west side of Mexico 1, offers basic rooms for under US$25. At the south end of town, on the west side of the highway next to the butane facility, is the nicely landscaped **Mesón de Don Pepe RV Park,** tel. 616/166-2216. Tent sites, on green grass—a Baja rarity—are US$6 a night; full-hookup sites cost US$10 for two people (US$2 for each additional person); rates may vary according to the time of year, and discounts are readily granted for long-term stays. Don Pepe's restaurant serves Mexican standards and seafood.

Follow the same turnoff to Don Pepe's farther west, toward the beach, and you'll come to the quiet **Posada Don Diego Trailer Park** (Apdo. Postal 126, Vicente Guerrero, BCN), tel. 616/166-2181, fax 616/166-2248, info@posada dondiego.com, www.posadadondiego.com. Full hookups are US$10–15 a night, tent space US$6–9, with discounts for long-term stays. The 100-site park also has a few small trailers for rent (US$25), in case you didn't bring your own. A restaurant in the park specializes in Mexican seafood dishes. If you dig up your own pismo clams on the beach, ask Señora Martínez, who operates the park with her husband José, to steam them for you. The park also features laundry facilities, clean bathrooms, a fully-stocked bar, and a playground.

Camping on the beach among the dunes is a possibility, but the sandy track gets a bit dodgy once you pass Posada Don Diego. Passenger cars can make it, but RVs—except those with four-wheel drive—risk getting stuck.

At the north end of town, on the west side of the highway, **El Vaquero Steak** serves steak and Mexican dishes. Farther south on the east side of the road is **Pollo Chilo,** featuring Sinaloa-style chicken.

A state tourist office at Km 178.3 in San Vicente, tel. 646/166-2728, is open Mon.–Sat. 8 A.M.–3 P.M. and 4–7 P.M. Look for a modern white building on the west side of the highway. Here you'll find a good collection of maps and brochures focused on San Quintín and Parque Nacional Sierra San Pedro Mártir. Thomas Guerrero, who runs the office, also offers 24-hour radio emergency service, tel. 646/166-2034.

The Banamex at the north end of town has an ATM.

PARQUE NACIONAL SIERRA SAN PEDRO MÁRTIR

Founded in 1947, this 170,000-acre national park is centered on the Sierra de San Pedro Mártir—the highest mountain range in the peninsular cordillera. Like other northern Baja sierras, the San Pedro Mártir tips toward the west, with its highest peaks thrusting out along the precipitous eastern escarpment. The peninsula's highest peak, Picacho del Diablo (Devil's Peak)—also known as Cerro de la Encantada (Enchanted Mountain) and La Providencia (Providence)—looms over the San Felipe Desert at 3,095 meters (10,154 feet). It's a challenging Class 3–5 climb.

Three prominent canyons radiate eastward from the base of the mountain—Cañon del Diablo, Cañon Providencia, and Cañon Teledo, providing magnificent bouldering and scrambling opportunities, sheer cliffs, waterfalls, fan palms, Amerindian petroglyphs, and several approaches to Diablo's twin granitic summits. Hikers interested in these eastern canyons, which lie just outside the park boundaries, usually approach them from Mexico 3 to the northeast.

Within the park, hikers and backpackers can choose from a network of trails and campsites on a pine- and juniper-forested plateau—approximately 70 km by 15 km—at the heart of the range. Because much of the park exceeds 1,800 meters (6,000 feet) in elevation, annual precipitation averages 60 cm (24 inches); thus water sources are abundant and shady conifers predominate. Only a few hundred people visit San Pedro Mártir each year, making it one of the most undervisited national parks in Mexico and an extraordinary opportunity for wilderness solitude. The mountain hiking conditions enjoyed here are similar to those in California's Sierra Nevada, but the park attracts far fewer people.

National Observatory

Because the air is exceptionally clear and potential sources of light pollution are remote, the Mexican government selected the San Pedro Mártir Plateau in 1967 as the site for its Observatorio Astronómico Nacional. The observatory facilities are at the end of the park access road (20 km past the park entrance), atop Cerro de la Cúpula at an elevation of 2,830 meters (9,286 feet). A locked gate just before the observatory means visitors must park and walk two km to reach the domed buildings. Several telescopes are in use at the observatory, including Mexico's largest, a 2.11-meter (83-inch) reflector.

Schedules for observatory tours vary greatly depending on time of year. For more information contact the Observatorio Astronómico Nacional in Ensenada, tel. 646/174-4580, contacto@astrosen.unam.mx. A viewpoint nearby offers an inspiring glimpse of the eastern escarpment and canyons. At night, stars appear over the plateau like a sea of diamonds—who needs a telescope?

Climate

Temperatures on the plateau, 1,800 meters above sea level, average 26°C (80°F) in July and August during the daytime, down to 4.5°C (40°F) at night. From December through March, temperatures run from 4.5°C (40°F) down to -12°C (10°F). Freezing nights sometimes occur in the spring and fall, with daytime temperatures in the 15–21°C (60–70°F) range.

Snowfall is common above 2,000 meters during the winter; Picacho del Diablo is often snow-capped Nov.–Apr. While occasional heavy rains fall in late summer, it's usually dry in spring, early summer, and fall.

The best hiking seasons are mid-April through mid-June (good for wildflowers) and late September through early November (when quaking aspens put on a show). For backpackers, the Apr.–June season is optimal because water sources from the snowmelt are most abundant. Late summer rains can cause hazardous flash floods in the arroyos.

Flora and Fauna

About 53 km east of Rancho Meling the San Telmo road begins ascending rapidly, the terrain changing from arid coastal plains to scrubby high chaparral. At 900–1,500 meters (3,000–5,000 feet), stands of pine, oak, and juniper appear, mixed with a dwindling number of desert and chaparral species—sagebrush, verbena, yucca, and fan palm. Above 1,500 meters, thickly forested glens leave the Baja desert mythos behind. Here you'll find piñon and Jeffrey pine, incense cedar, white fir, sugar pine, and at least three species not found elsewhere in Baja—quak-

MOUNTAIN OF MANY NAMES

Devil's Peak, Enchanted Mountain, Providence, and Mt. San Pedro Mártir are a few of the map designations given Baja's highest peak over the last four centuries. Whether the Yumano or Cochimí Amerindians had a name for the soaring peak isn't known, but they must have been acquainted with its serrated profile, visible from 160 km away on the Mexican mainland.

The first recorded mention of the jagged, sparsely vegetated, twin-summited mountain dates from 16th-century Spanish explorations of the Sea of Cortez. As the Spanish sailed into the thirsty upper reaches of the Cortez in late spring, the snowcapped peak hanging over the searing San Felipe Desert to the west must have seemed a mirage, a gift from God. Hence they called it La Providencia, a name sustained through the early 20th century.

La Providencia's semantically opposite name, El Picacho del Diablo (Devil's Peak), surfaced during the missionary period, probably in reference to the peak's formidable appearance when viewed from the west; Misión San Pedro Mártir, perhaps the most remote mission on the peninsula, was established some 25 km to the southwest. Another possible semantic explanation suggests the mountain was revered by local Amerindians; to divert spiritual attention from the peak and toward the mission, the San Pedro Mártir padres may have consigned it to the Devil.

The padres called a large, open meadow between the mission and the mountain La Encantada (The Enchanted), perhaps because it appears in the midst of heavy pine and juniper forests as if cleared by supernatural forces. The meadow appeared on Spanish maps thereafter, and Mexican cartographers in the 1920s, whether by mistake or intention, applied the name to the mountain.

Other names have made brief appearances this century, including El Picacho Blanco, a reference to both the peak's mostly white coloring and its snowbound condition in the winter. But El Picacho del Diablo is the most common term used among Sierra de San Pedro Mártir residents and mountaineers; it's also the most common name found on English-language maps of Baja. The official Mexican government name, however, remains Cerro de la Encantada.

The Climbers

In 1910, author A.W. North called El Picacho del Diablo "the unchallenged retreat of lions and mountain sheep, the unscaled lookout of eagles and mighty condors." The following year, American cartographer Donald McLain successfully attained the summit. The next recorded climb was made in 1932 by a U.S. Sierra Club group, which was forced to spend the night in Cañon del Diablo after struggling with the mountain's west face.

The peak was ascended by another American climber (Randall Henderson, editor of *Desert* magazine) in 1937, and by several more in the '50s. By the early 1970s, over 50 people a year (both Mexicans and foreigners) were scaling the heights—with as many attempting the climb and turning back short of the summit. Today the Class 3 Slot Wash approach is a straightforward but challenging ascent for experienced climbers, while the other six proven approaches encompass some of the toughest climbing in Mexico.

N

NORTHERN BAJA

ing aspen, lodgepole pine, and the endemic San Pedro Mártir cypress.

Streams in the sierra's western canyons carry an endemic trout species, the Nelson rainbow trout (*Salmo nelsonii,* named for E.W. Nelson, who discovered the fish in 1905). In the early 1980s, a group of Mexico City naturalists transplanted Nelson rainbows to several other canyon streams in the park. Today, fishing without a license is permitted. Mule deer, mountain lions, wildcats, coyotes, and the rare *borregón* (bighorn sheep) inhabit some of the canyons.

Domestic animals—cattle and sheep—are often seen in the park, especially along the east side where two ranches lie within park boundaries. Unfortunately, overgrazing is destroying much of the vegetation in this portion of the park, with the full consent of the Mexican government. On the positive side, the Mexican park service forbids logging in all national parks.

BOB RACE

mountain lion

Park Facilities and Regulations

The park entrance is 78 km (47 miles) from Mexico 1 via an unpaved but graded roadway; follow signs marked Observatorio. In winter, the occasional snowstorm may force temporary road closure, but during most of the year the road is passable by passenger car. The entrance station, at a forested meadow called La Corona de Abajo (Lower Crown), is open daily 7 A.M.–7 P.M.; the entry fee is US$7.50 per vehicle.

Established campsites and trails are minimally maintained by park staff. Overall, the park is most suited to wilderness hiking and camping. Although no facilities exist for car or trailer camping, it's safe to leave a vehicle parked anywhere within the park boundaries.

Neither hunting nor the possession of firearms (even with a Mexican permit) is permitted within park boundaries. When the occasional sanctioned deer hunt is held in adjacent Cañon del Diablo, the canyon may be closed to hiking and backpacking. Off-road driving is banned at all times. Fires, using fallen deadwood, are permitted only within established fire rings at a few campsites on the plateau; backpackers should carry portable camp stoves. Before leaving on an overnight hike, let park rangers know where you're going and how long you intend to be gone.

Preparations and Precautions

Park trails are not well marked; don't consider even a day hike without carrying a compass or GPS. The observatory road bisects the park east to west and makes a useful mental landmark. When embarking on a hike, note whether you're heading north or south of the road. If you get lost anywhere west of the eastern escarpment, simply head directly north (or south) from your current location and you should intercept the roadway.

Canyon hiking along the eastern escarpment is rugged and should be attempted only by experienced climbers or those in the company of someone who knows the terrain. You may be able to arrange for a guide through Rancho Meling (Apdo. Postal 1326, Ensenada, BCN).

The Mexican government publishes two topographic **maps** (20-meter contour)—*San Rafael H11B45* and *Santa Cruz H11B55*—that cover an area that includes the park. They're available by mail from **Map Centre,** 3191 Sports Arena Blvd., Ste. F, San Diego, CA 92110, 619/291-3830 or 888/849-6277, fax 619/291-3840, maps@mapworld.com, www.mapcentre.com, or at the offices of the Instituto Nacional de Estadística, Geografía e Informática (INEGI) in Tijuana and Mexicali (see Hiking and Backpacking in the On the Road chapter for INEGI addresses).

More up-to-date and easier to use is a 1988 topo map published by Centra Publications, 4705 Laurel St., San Diego, CA 92105, and titled *Parque Nacional San Pedro Mártir: Topographic Map and Visitor's Guide to Baja's Highest Mountains.* This well-designed, readable map is based on the Mexican topos but adds many physical features never mapped before. Also printed on the map are brief descriptions of 17 different hiking trails, including seven Picacho del Diablo climbing routes. This map/guide may be available through Map Center, at the INEGI offices, or at bookstores in Ensenada.

Except during midsummer, streams are abundant on the plateau and are generally considered clean enough to drink from. In the eastern arroyos and canyons, **water** is usually available year-round, though it may be contaminated by livestock. Whether on the plateau or in the canyonlands, always treat local water, just to be sure. Wherever you go in the San Pedro Mártir, carry extra water and a water-purification system—filter, iodine, or halazone.

Trails

The park is honeycombed with footpaths and hiking trails, particularly in the vicinity of Picacho del Diablo at the edge of the eastern escarpment. Longer, more isolated trails connect the large meadow areas of Vallecitos, Los Llanitos, La Encantada, La Grulla, and Rancho Viejo in a 50-km (31-mile) loop. The three trails described in this section, on the park's scenic northeastern edge, are well traveled and thus relatively easy to follow. For a more complete inventory, obtain Centra Publications' detailed topo map of the park.

Vallecitos–Blue Bottle Peak (9.5 km/5.9 miles): Vallecitos (Little Valleys) is the name given to a complex of little flats southeast of the observatory road, reached via a dirt track that begins 16.5 km (10 miles) from the park entrance. About 3.5 km (two miles) from the observatory road, a footpath branches left (east) up an arroyo for 1.7 km (one mile), then into an aspen-studded meadow. A smaller path leads north from the meadow to an excellent escarpment-edge view of Cañon del Diablo.

Two km (1.2 miles) farther southeast on the

SIERRA SAN PEDRO MÁRTIR TRAILS

VIEWPOINT

NATIONAL OBSERVATORY

GATE

RESIDENCES

VIEWPOINT

Aspen Groves

Cañon Diablito

Vehicle Track
Established Trail
Obscure Cross-Country Trail or Climbing Route

Vallecitos

Cañon del Diablo

Cañon Providencia

(3,095m/ 10,154ft)

Picacho del Diablo

Aspen Groves

VIEWPOINT

Scout Peak

CAMPO NOCHE

Slot Wash   (3,094m/10,152ft)

Night Wash

Cerro Botello Azul

Cañon Teledo

Los Llanitos

VIEWPOINT

0   1 mi
0   1 km

NORTHERN BAJA

main trail is a north-branching path that leads to Scout Peak (2,850 meters, 9,350 feet), where you'll find primitive campsites and an unobstructed view of Picacho del Diablo's western face. From this point, climbers can scramble down the side of the Cañon del Diablo to Campo Noche below and continue on to Cerro Botella Azul (Blue Bottle Peak) via the arroyos at the southern end of the canyon.

Meanwhile, the main trail below Scout Peak continues south and then east a couple of kilometers to a point just northwest of Blue Bottle Peak; a smaller trail ascends the peak itself. At 2,950 meters (9,680 feet), Blue Bottle is the highest point on the plateau and a reasonable alternative to Picacho del Diablo for the less adventurous. On a clear day—perhaps 85 percent of the time—you can see both the Pacific and the Sea of Cortez.

Observatory–Cañon del Diablo (5.3 km/3.3 miles): Just below the observatory gate, a trail branches east from the main road and leads into Cañon del Diablo, the deepest and longest canyon in the Sierra de San Pedro Mártir. Along the way, this trail passes through a scenic aspen meadow where a short path branches north to a rocky viewpoint over the canyon. Beyond the meadow, the trail becomes a demanding Class 3–4 descent that requires hikers to negotiate brush and boulders along an arroyo intersecting with the larger canyon. Water is available at several streams and waterfalls in the canyon.

Near the bottom of the canyon this trail joins the Cañon del Diablo–Campo Noche Trail, the beginning of one of the eastern approaches to Picacho del Diablo. This latter trail, though rated Class 2–3, involves a four-day hike in desert conditions and is best undertaken with a guide who knows the terrain.

The **Slot Wash Ascent of Picacho del Diablo** is the easiest—Class 3—of the seven routes used to climb Baja's highest mountain. To reach Slot Wash, an arroyo that descends Diablo's west face, follow the Vallecitos–Blue Bottle Peak Trail until you've passed the saddle northwest of Blue Bottle, then continue along the peak's north flank until the trail narrows and descends into Cañon del Diablo.

Near the bottom of the canyon, on the east side, is Campo Noche, a large campsite with a fire ring and nearby pools. The ascent to Slot Wash begins at a shallow arroyo, next to Campo Noche, called Arroyo Noche or "Night Wash," which segues into Slot Wash at an elevation of 2,240 meters (7,350 feet). The way is well marked with ducks (stone trail markers). At about 2,500 meters (9,840 feet) the route forks. The little-used southern branch leads out of Slot Wash, through a brushy side ravine, to the lower of Diablo's twin peaks (3,094 meters, 10,150 feet). The northern route, which most climbers take, continues through Slot Wash and over large stone slabs, until ducks point out a sharp left (north) up a rocky slope. This leads to a steep-walled arroyo nicknamed Wall Street, which in turn proceeds directly to the higher of the peaks (3,095 meters, 10,154 feet). If you continue straight up Slot Wash instead of taking the north branch, you'll come to a saddle between the two summits.

Starting at Blue Bottle Peak on the plateau, the trip to Picacho del Diablo and back usually takes three days—one night at Campo Noche in each direction, plus one night in the vicinity of the summit. Fit hikers with good orienteering skills can make it to Campo Noche in less than a day, but you really should spend the night for a fresh morning start on the peak.

Approaching Picacho del Diablo from Mexico 3

You can approach the network of trails below Picacho del Diablo from Mexico 3 (the section between Ensenada and Crucero La Trinidad), to the northeast of the park, via Cañon del Diablo. The road to the canyon area is 164 km (102 miles) southeast of Ensenada (or 34 km, 21 miles northwest of Crucero La Trinidad, if you're driving from Mexicali or San Felipe), south off Mexico 3. The road is graded as far as Rancho Villa del Sol, about eight km (five miles) south of the Mexico 3 junction, then joins vehicle tracks southeast across the salt flat Laguna Diablo.

Approximately 24 km (15 miles) south of Mexico 3, another set of tracks branches straight west toward Rancho Santa Clara. At Rancho Santa Clara, a dirt track passes just south of the ranch and leads nine km (5.5 miles) west until it ends at Cañon Diablito. You can park here, but don't leave valuables in the vehicle.

From Diablito, a three-km (1.9 mile) trail heads northeast to the mouth of Cañon del Diablo. Perhaps the greatest obstacle in the canyon is only about 800 meters into the mouth—a sizable waterfall tumbling down smooth granite walls. A cable bolted to the wall allows hikers to scramble up one side; sometimes accumulated sand creates a temporary platform high enough for you to surmount the wall without the assistance of the cable. The canyon itself is mostly a Class 2 hike with a few Class 3 bouldering exercises along the way; there are plenty of year-round pools and waterfalls to cool off in along the way.

Campo Noche lies 11 km (seven miles) into the canyon, at an elevation of 1,915 meters (6,300 feet). A round-trip hike at a comfortable pace from the end of the vehicle track to Picacho del Diablo usually takes four days, including stops at Campo Noche each way. See Slot Wash Ascent of Picacho del Diablo for a description of the usual route from Campo Noche.

VALLE DE SAN QUINTÍN AND BAHÍA DE SAN QUINTÍN

The Valle de San Quintín, actually more a coastal plain than a valley, is a broad flat between a row of seven extinct volcano cones to the west—six on the peninsula, one on Isla San Martín just offshore—and the Sierra San Miguel to the east. Two small rivers, Río San Miguel and Río Santa María, bisect the flat east to west and feed an irrigation system that makes the valley an important vegetable-farming center. Many Amerindians from the interior of Mexico, especially Oaxaca and Chiapas, work on the farms and live in shacks on the outskirts of San Quintín.

For visitors, San Quintín's main attraction is a complex coastal environment, the chief features of which are three large, interconnecting bays: Bahía San Quintín, Bahía Falsa, and Bahía Santa María. The innermost bay, surrounded by tidal flats and saltmarshes, is referred to as both Bahía San Quintín and Puerto San Quintín. The outermost bay, facing the Pacific, is called Bahía

Santa María as far south as the tip of Cabo San Quintín; beyond it's usually referred to as Bahía San Quintín.

The town of **San Quintín** itself is little more than a collection of shops, motels, restaurants, and other businesses clustered along Mexico 1. Useful services include a long-distance telephone booth, 24-hour medical clinic, travel agency, a couple of Internet cafés, and one bank, Bital. Five km (three miles) south of San Quintín is another town of similar size, **Lázaro Cárdenas,** consisting of Mexico's 67th Infantry battalion camp, the intercity bus terminal, a few shops and restaurants, and two motels.

Many people pass San Quintín by simply because the twin towns—as seen from the highway—don't appear to be very engaging. Traditionally most visitors staying more than one night in the area are sportfishers or hunters. But the pristine beaches and mild year-round climate also attract a number of folks content with long beach walks, birdwatching, and less active pursuits.

Climate

While most of northwestern coastal Baja features a climate similar to San Diego's, San Francisco is a better comparison for Valle de San Quintín. As in the San Francisco area, Pacific influences combine with the insulating effect of a large bay—in this case, three bays—to keep average temperatures within a narrow year-round range: from 12°C (54°F) Dec.–Jan. to 20°C (68°F) Aug.–Sept.

Annual precipitation averages 31 cm (12 inches); December usually records the most rainfall (average six cm), with Feb.–Mar. second (four to five cm); summer months are usually rain-free, with occasional coastal fog.

History

In the 1880s, British-owned Mexican Land and Colonization Company purchased much of the San Quintín area from the U.S.-based International Land Company (ILC), with plans to create a wheat empire. At the time, the ILC owned most of northern Baja. In response to promises of agricultural wealth, around a hundred English

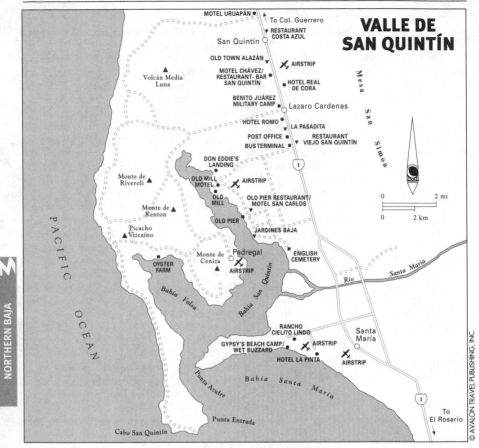

VALLE DE SAN QUINTÍN

MOTEL URUAPÁN
To Col. Guerrero
San Quintín
RESTAURANT COSTA AZUL
OLD TOWN ALAZÁN
AIRSTRIP
Volcán Media Luna
MOTEL CHÁVEZ/ RESTAURANT- BAR SAN QUINTÍN
HOTEL REAL DE CORA
BENITO JUÁREZ MILITARY CAMP
Lazaro Cardenas
Mesa San Simon
HOTEL ROMO
LA PASADITA
POST OFFICE
RESTAURANT VIEJO SAN QUINTÍN
BUS TERMINAL
DON EDDIE'S LANDING
Monte de Riveroli
OLD MILL MOTEL
AIRSTRIP
OLD MILL
OLD PIER RESTAURANT/ MOTEL SAN CARLOS
Monte de Kenton
OLD PIER
Picacho Vizcaíno
JARDINES BAJA
PACIFIC
Monte de Ceniza
Pedregal
ENGLISH CEMETERY
OYSTER FARM
AIRSTRIP
Bahía Falsa
Bahía San Quintín
Río
Santa Maria
OCEAN
RANCHO CIELITO LINDO
Santa María
GYPSY'S BEACH CAMP/ WET BUZZARD
AIRSTRIP
HOTEL LA PINTA
AIRSTRIP
Punta Azufre
Bahía Santa María
To El Rosario
Punta Entrada
Cabo San Quintín

0   2 mi
0   2 km

© AVALON TRAVEL PUBLISHING, INC.

colonists purchased subdivided land tracts from the parent company, planted wheat, and constructed a grist mill. For flour transportation, the English built a pier on inner Bahía San Quintín and began constructing a railway to link up with the Southern Pacific tracks in California. Thirty km of track were laid—including a rail causeway from the west bank of inner Bahía San Quintín—before the colony failed. A 17-ton, six-wheeled locomotive still lies underwater at the mouth of the bay, the remains of a loading accident for the aborted railway.

A drought devastated one of the first wheat harvests, and by 1900 all colonists had abandoned San Quintín. Although individual farmers were economically ruined, the U.S. and British land companies walked away all the richer, a pattern that would recur several times in northern Baja. Remains of the grist mill, railroad causeway, pier, and English cemetery still stand along the perimeter of the inner bay. The English names on the cemetery's heavily weathered wooden crosses have faded from sight, and more-recent Mexican graves are crowding out their neglected English counterparts.

In recent decades a small community of gringo retirees has moved into the area, leasing bayfront property and building homes. The most concentrated area is Pedregal, where some houses are built of volcanic rock. Around San Quintín you'll see many lots posted "for sale"; actually these are available only through lease or *fideicomiso* (bank trust) arrangements.

Beach and Bay Access

Several dirt roads south of Lázaro Cárdenas lead directly west from Mexico 1 to the inner bay; follow signs to the Old Mill Motel and Old Pier Restaurant. You can launch cartopped or trailered boats either here or from a boat launch on the bay's west shore. To reach the latter site, drive west out of Lázaro Cárdenas on a gravel road that leaves Mexico 1 between the Pemex station and a military camp; a sign here reads Bahía Falsa. This is a long, rough ride. Fourteen km (8.5 miles) from Mexico 1, just past Monte de Kenton with a cinder cone immediately to the west, a lesser dirt road forks left and leads to Pedregal, a bayside settlement suitable for boat launching. The marshes and tidal flats at the north end of Bahía Falsa make an excellent birding venue.

If, instead of turning south to Pedregal, you continue west along the road from Lázaro Cárdenas, you'll pass an oyster farm on Bahía Falsa (about 14.5 km, nine miles from the Bahía Falsa highway turnoff), where fresh oysters may be purchased by the dozen, then reach the road's end at a fish camp on the Pacific.

To reach Bahía Santa María or the larger, Pacific-facing Bahía San Quintín, drive 16 km (10 miles) south of Lázaro Cárdenas and turn right (west) on the paved road to Santa María. The turn is marked by signs advertising Hotel La Pinta and Rancho Cielito Lindo. Follow the signs along this pine-tree-lined road to Hotel La Pinta; Playa Santa María, the area's largest, longest, and most beautiful beach, lies behind the hotel. Sunsets can be superb at this beach.

Accommodations

Under US$25: In Lázaro Cárdenas, near the military camp, **Motel Las Hadas** and **Hotel Romo** both offer basic, nondescript rooms. The Romo is the better of the two.

US$25–50: In San Quintín, **Motel Chávez,** next to a highway bridge toward the south end of town (Apdo. Postal 32, San Quintín, BCN),

tel. 616/165-2005, offers clean, well-maintained rooms, some with kitchenettes; weekly and monthly rates available. Also in San Quintín, **Motel Uruapán,** Km 190, tel. 616/165-2050, has similar rates but is a poor second choice. The relatively new **Hotel Real de Cora** shows more promise.

Southwest of Lázaro Cárdenas, on the inner bay next to the Old Pier Restaurant, is **Motel San Carlos** (Apdo. Postal 11, Valle de San Quintín, BCN), tel. 616/163-4206, where the simple, quiet rooms all have bay views.

At the northeast end of the inner bay, **Don Eddie's Landing** (formerly Ernesto's Motel), tel. 616/162-2722, offers spacious, comfortable rooms. Fishing packages are available and include lodging, boat, and food. Good seafood dinners are available at Don Eddie's restaurant for around US$12.

Just south of Don Eddie's Landing, **Old Mill Motel,** tel. 616/165-3376 or 800/025-5141, U.S. tel. 619/428-2779 or 800/479-7962, lies on the site of a former grist mill and next to the main public boat launch. It's a longtime favorite among hunters and anglers; fishing and hunting trips can be arranged. Note that the din from partying anglers—especially on weekends—means nights here are anything but tranquil. Accommodations at the Old Mill—including some newly renovated brick cottages—are comfortable and well maintained. An RV park and campground are attached. The electricity is usually turned off midnight–5:30 A.M. The wide range of accommodations here includes basic rooms with private bath, rooms with kitchenette or full kitchen, a rustic "sleeping room" with four twin beds and private bath, rooms with fireplaces, and a two-bedroom suite.

Next to Bahía Santa María, **Rancho Cielito Lindo,** U.S. reservations 619/593-BAJA (619/593-2252), cielitolindo@bajasi.com, is mainly a restaurant and bar, but large, plain rooms are also available for rent. A short airstrip is adjacent, while out on the beach is Gypsy's Beach Camp (see Camping and RV Parks further on).

US$50–100: On Bahía Santa María is **Hotel La Pinta,** tel. 616/165-9008, U.S./Canada tel. 800/800-9632, www.lapintahotels.com. All of its spacious heated rooms have sea views and terraces. Hotel facilities include a restaurant, bar, tennis court, and private airstrip. Upkeep at La Pinta, unfortunately, has been neglected the past few years, and if it weren't for the adjacent beach we'd have to say it was overpriced.

Camping and RV Parks

Primitive beach camping is available at a number of spots in the San Quintín area, including Playa Santa María south of Hotel La Pinta—probably not the safest spot—and out at Bahía Falsa. More secluded cobble beaches are south of Santa María from Km 18 onward—a good number of dirt tracks lead west from the highway almost all the way to El Rosario.

If you're planning to stay awhile, you can check the west side of inner Bahía San Quintín at Pedregal or the Pacific shore (Playa Médano) below the cinder cone Picacho Vizcaíno. The latter area can be cold and damp, and the road there is long and rough; this is a place best enjoyed by hardcore Robinson Crusoes. The clams here are huge and plentiful.

Gypsy's Beach Camp, www.bajasi.com, offers shaded sites for self-contained tent or trailer camping for US$5 per night. Also on the premises are a clean restrooms, a restaurant called Wet Buzzard, and an RV dump. A night watchman patrols the area 9 P.M.–5 A.M.

At the **Old Pier/Motel San Carlos,** tel. 616/163-4206, self-contained camping costs only US$5 pp. Facilities include fire rings, toilet, and showers. RVs can park nearby for no charge. Farther north along this same shore, beyond the Old Mill, Campo Lorenzo has sites with full hookups, but they all seem to be permanently occupied by retirees. Tent/camper sites on the beach, with no hookups, may be available for US$5 a night.

A more remote choice, **El Pabellón RV Campground,** lies on a secluded beach 15 km (nine miles) south of Lázaro Cárdenas and 1.6 km (one mile) west of Mexico 1 (the turnoff is near Km 16). Sites with water and sewage, but no electricity, cost US$5 per night for tents or RVs. Other facilities include hot showers and flush toilets. The road to El Pabellón—two rutted tracks—could be a bit much for some rigs.

Food

Although at first glance it may seem that the San Quintín area may not offer much in the way of places to chow down, in fact the choices are numerous and varied. The highway through Lázaro Cárdenas and San Quintín is lined with taco and *mariscos* stands. Clam cocktails are usually superb. One of the best spots for *tacos de pescado* is **La Pasadita,** a modest stand on the plaza in Lázaro Cárdenas; it opens between 8 A.M. and 9 A.M. and usually closes by 4 P.M.

Pollos Lalos, on the west side of the highway in San Quintín, offers good *pollos al carbon* daily 10 A.M.–10 P.M. Nearby **Tuco's Pizza** will take care of pizza cravings; open daily 3–10 P.M.

The clean, efficient, and friendly **Restaurant Viejo San Quintín,** between two pharmacies (Farmacia del Parque and Super Farmacia San Diego), directly opposite the post office in Lázaro Cárdenas, is still the area's best Mexican eatery. Menu offerings include *machaca, chilies rellenos, carne asada,* enchiladas, *flautas,* fish fillets, steak, burritos, quesadillas, *sincronizadas,* and beer served in frosted mugs. Most entrées cost US$5–7. Open daily for breakfast, lunch, and dinner.

The tourist-oriented **Restaurant-Bar Quintín,** tel. 616/165-2005, next door to Motel Chávez, serves good Mexican dishes and seafood for US$9–14 per meal. The hearty breakfasts served here are tasty and reasonably priced at US$3–5.

Also in the town of San Quintín is **Costa Azul,** which offers fresh seafood in Continental and Mexican styles. Credit cards are accepted, and it's open for breakfast, lunch, and dinner, except on Sunday evenings, when the restaurant becomes a disco. Like the Restaurant-Bar Quintín, Costa Azul is a little pricier than average.

Restaurant Misión Santa Isabel, at Km 190 toward the north end of San Quintín, tel. 616/165-2309, specializes in *carne tampiqueña* and *machaca.* This is also a popular breakfast stop. Major credit cards accepted. Nearby **Palapa de Mariscos El Paraíso** is often touted as the best spot in town for fresh seafood; open daily for lunch and dinner.

The Old Mill has a large restaurant and bar called **Gaston's Cannery** that serves very good seafood and Mexican meals, including home-raised chicken and goat. Prices are relatively high, but portions are large.

The well-known **Old Pier (Muelle Viejo)**, next to Motel San Carlos on the inner bay, offers pricey—for Mexico—seafood, from clam dinners for around US$15 to abalone or lobster for US$20–22.

If you're driving to either the Old Mill Motel or the Old Pier Restaurant/Motel San Carlos in the afternoon with plans for an evening meal, be sure to note each turn along the way so you can find your way back. At night it's easy to become lost in the maze of sandy roads.

For long, leisurely meals in a quiet garden setting, brave the washboard road out to **Jardínes Baja.** An oasis seemingly plunked down in the middle of nowhere, this family-owned restaurant offers a long menu of Mexican and American dishes and is open Tues.–Sun., noon–10 P.M. The bar stays till midnight, and there's usually live music on Fri. and Saturday. To reach Jardines Baja, look for the sign on Mexico 1, then drive around 900m along a dirt road till you see the cluster of trees surrounding the restaurant, which stands a little south of the second turnoff for Old Mill.

The seafood at the **Rancho Cielito Lindo** restaurant can be as good as any in San Quintín, and prices are reasonable. Fishburgers and tasty crab claws in paprika are house specialties. They have been known to serve complimentary meals on Mexican or American holidays. Open for dinner only. **Wet Buzzard,** at adjacent Gypsy's Beach Camp, does big breakfasts plus tacos and burritos for lunch.

Las Cazuelas, the restaurant at Hotel La Pinta, features the usual La Pinta menu for breakfast, lunch, and dinner.

You'll find a number of *tiendas de abarrotes* in San Quintín, but the best are in Lázaro Cárdenas, including **Avigal, Alejandra,** and **Adelita.** San Quintín features a couple of *panaderías* while Lázaro Cárdenas has a *tortillería.*

Fishing

The unusually varied marine environment, created by the intersection of the Pacific and the three bays, makes the San Quintín coast an excellent area for surf casting and inshore fishing. Because the entrance to the two inner bays, Bahía Falsa and Bahía San Quintín (Puerto San Quintín), is blocked by steady surf year-round, the bays are inaccessible to commercial fishing fleets. This means more game fish available for casual anglers, who can launch small boats from inside or from the Pacific shore.

In general, San Quintín attracts the same fish species found north to Ensenada—except they're more highly concentrated. Flatfish are common in the shallows of the inner bays, bottomfish in the deeper sections. The channel near the bay entrance is reportedly good for large halibut; live mackerel is the recommended bait. Perch and croaker run along the Pacific beaches. According to several sources, nowhere in their range are croakers as large as the ones typically caught along San Quintín's beaches. **El Socorro,** 27 km (17 miles) south of Lázaro Cárdenas, is known for surf fishing and has attracted a small group of devoted gringo anglers who maintain homes there.

Farther out in the Pacific, particularly near the south end of volcanic Isla San Martín and at the tip of Cabo San Quintín, yellowtail, yellowfin, white and black sea bass, rock cod, and lingcod are common—in season, of course, and to properly equipped anglers. Tuna and dorado are occasionally caught. Isla San Martín features a fish camp and mussel farm; sheltered anchorages are possible in two coves, one at either side of a rocky cape at the southeast end of the island. If you plan to camp on the island, bring all the supplies and fresh water needed for your stay. Sturdy hiking shoes are necessary if you plan to explore San Martín; volcanic rock and cactus thorns will destroy the average pair of sneakers.

San Quintín Sportfishing (Rancho Cielito Lindo, tel. 616/165-9229), **Pedro's Pangas** (tel. 888/568-2252), **Tiburon's Pangas Sportfishing** (near The Old Mill, U.S. tel. 619/428-2779), **The Old Pier, Don Eddie's Landing,** or **Campo Lorenzo** can arrange guided fishing trips for around US$150–250 per *panga,* depending on the season. You can rent light fishing tackle at the Hotel La Pinta.

Clamming

All three bays are well endowed with clams and mussels. The easiest and most scenic spot for digging up large pismo clams is Playa Santa María, behind Hotel La Pinta. If you come at low tide, you'll most likely join a legion of local clamdiggers. A turnoff at Km 182 leads to Playa San Ramón (four-wheel drive recommended), another excellent clamming and surf-fishing spot. You can use your fingers to dig the huge clams out of the sand or bring along a mesh bag and pitchfork—available in Lázaro Cárdenas—as the locals do. A pro threshes the sand at the surf line with a pitchfork, tossing the clams into a bag tied around the waist. A mesh bag works best because it holds the clams but allows water and sand to drain away. Remember not to take more clams than you can eat that day, and don't take clams smaller than your hand.

Boat Rentals

San Quintín Sportfishing, Apdo. Postal 7, Cielito Lindo, San Quintín, BCN, tel. 616/165-9229, book4fish@aol.com, www.sanquintin-sportfishing.com, rents boats for bay fishing and offers guided sportfishing trips. Aluminum *pan-gas* go for US$20–28 a day and carry 3–5 people, depending on the length. You can charter a 22-foot, outfitted fishing cruiser for around US$225 a day. Special packages that include three nights lodging at Rancho Cielito Lindo, two days guided fishing, and lunches cost US$114–150 pp per day, depending on the size of the boat. Anglers can purchase ice to preserve their catch at the **ice factory** next to Bloques y Maderas hardware store, Km 194 in Lázaro Cárdenas.

Hunting

The tidal flats and marshlands around the inner bays attract migrating duck and Pacific brant (a small, black goose) during the winter and quail most of the year. The Old Mill and Cielito Lindo hotels organize local hunting trips.

Scuba Diving

Johnston's Seamount, nine km (5.5 miles) south-west of Cabo San Quintín, is a renowned site for underwater photography and spearfishing. Sixteen km northwest of Cabo San Quintín, Isla San Martín is surrounded by kelp beds, several rock reefs, and underwater pinnacles. Roca Ben, five km south of the island, rises within three

clam digger, Playa Santa María

© JOE CUMMINGS

meters of the surface, with intermediate depths of 30 meters (100 feet). Encrusted with hydrocoral formations, the rock is a habitat for abundant abalone, scallops, lobsters, and other shellfish. Due to cold-water upwellings, visibility ranges 15–25 meters (50–80 feet).

Surfing

Valle de San Quintín's Pacific coast offers at least two decent surfing spots. Both require tackling the long and bumpy coastal road from Lázaro Cárdenas to Bahía Falsa, then continuing to the coast on a lesser road. Follow the main road around Bahía San Quintín as far as Chapalita and the oyster farm, then continue west to the coast until the road forks south toward Cabo San Quintín. At the top of the cape a strong northwest swell produces a good beach break, while at the tip of the cape a couple of *puntas* catch both northwest and southern swells for long-riding point breaks. The beach along the west side of the cape, known as Playa Médano (or Playa Oeste Médano), is suitable for camping. Just be sure you're well supplied, as it's a relatively long haul back to civilization.

Information and Services

The nearest state tourist office is between Colonia Vicente Guerrero and San Quintín at Km 178. The office is open 8 A.M.–5 P.M. weekdays, and 10 A.M.–3 P.M. weekends.

For medical emergencies there is one 24-hour clinic in San Quintín, Clínica Santa María, tel. 616/165-2653.

Transportation

Two Pemex stations—one each in San Quintín and Lázaro Cárdenas—offer Magna Sin and Premium gas. Diesel is available at the San Quintín station only. Intercity buses arrive and depart from a bus depot in Lázaro Cárdenas, on the west side of Mexico 1. The San Quintín area is not a suitable destination for travelers arriving without their own vehicles, however, since everything is spread out and there is virtually no public transportation to the bayshores and beaches. **ABC** runs a *servicio plus* bus, with air-condi-

tioning and toilets, between Tijuana and Lázaro Cárdenas for US$18.

Bush pilots can land at a 1,200-meter (3,900-foot) hard-sand airstrip at Rancho Magaña, which lies about 400 meters east of Mexico 1, about 10 km (six miles) north of San Quintín near Km 183. Call Veronica Magaña at 616/165-2249 to clear landings. A restroom and telephone at the adjacent office are open to the public, but neither taxis nor aviation gas is available. Airstrips at Cielito Lindo (see Accommodations) and Pedregal are also usually open, though the latter is reportedly less friendly to nonresidents.

EL ROSARIO AND VICINITY

Near the mouth of a deep valley formed by Río del Rosario lies the town of El Rosario, a market center for valley farms and ranches as well as fish camps along the nearby Pacific coast. Although the valley has been continuously inhabited for at least 300 years, El Rosario today is little more than a cluster of modest homes, a rustic baseball field, a hospital, a school, a town hall, several markets, two motels, two Pemex stations, and a few *taquerías* and cafés. It is, however, the largest town for 356 km (221 miles) southward, and as such it's an important supply point for anyone exploring north-central Baja.

El Rosario actually consists of two communities: the larger El Rosario de Arriba, along the highway in the upper part of the valley, and the smaller El Rosario de Abajo, south of the highway and the Río del Rosario, toward the coast.

History

Little is known about the Cochimí who lived here when the Spanish arrived except that they subsisted mostly on Pacific shellfish and wild desert plants and called their valley community Viñadaco. In 1774, the Dominican Order established its first and southernmost California mission, **Nuestra Señora del Rosario,** on the east side of the valley facing the Pacific; the mission was moved downstream in 1802 to take advantage of a better water supply. The adobe ruins of the newer mission site can be found by turning right—west—at the supermarket, where Mexico 1 curves east, then left at the first road. After crossing the riverbed to El Rosario de Abajo, the minimal ruins lie on the right.

The valley was perfectly suited for agriculture, and at first the mission community thrived, producing the most abundant crops of any northern Baja mission. As elsewhere in the Californias, the Amerindians eventually succumbed to diseases brought by the missionaries, and, left without converts or laborers, the mission closed in 1832.

A Spanish land grant in the 1840s brought Carlos Espinosa to the valley, where he and his family became successful ranchers and farmers. Italian copper miner Eduardo Grosso arrived at the end of the 19th century. The union of the two families has been a prime source of El Rosario history ever since.

In the 1960s, El Rosario became a checkpoint for the Baja 1000 off-road race and the first landing for the Flying Samaritans, a group of American doctors who provide volunteer medical service by plane to several northern Baja settlements. El Rosario's Doña Anita Grosso de Espinosa, proprietor of Espinosa's Place café, helped assure the initial success of both endeavors by acting as a liaison between Americans and the local community.

In its disfavor, El Rosario has straddled its roads with an annoying number of speed bumps in recent years.

Punta Baja and Agua Blanca

Sixteen km (10 miles) southwest of El Rosario de Arriba, via an unpaved but all-vehicle road, is Punta Baja, a fish camp and headland at the north end of Bahía del Rosario. You can rent *pangas* here, or launch your own; the perch and rock cod fishing is good year-round. Farther offshore, tuna, croaker, bonito, and yellowtail are abundant. During northwest swells, the surfing off Punta Baja is excellent.

Agua Blanca is another fish camp, eight km (five miles) south of Punta Baja toward the middle of the bay. Between Punta Baja and Agua Blanca you may notice piles of sea urchin shells at the roadside. The harvesting of sea urchins constitutes the bulk of the local fishing industry; 90 percent of the catch is exported to Japan, mostly for sushi. The orange-colored "roe" consumed by the Japanese isn't the sea urchin's eggs, as is commonly believed, but the sex organs.

Agua Blanca is also a launching point for scuba excursions to **Isla San Gerónimo** (sometimes spelled Jerónimo) and Sacramento Reef. The latter lies about an hour's boat ride from Punta Baja, where you can launch your boat or hire a local *panga*. **Horizon Charters,** 4178 Lochlomond St., San Diego, CA 92111, tel. 858/277-7823, fax 858/560-6811, divesd@aol.com, operates seven- to 10-day live-aboard dive trips that focus on Sacramento Reef.

Accommodations and Food

El Rosario has two motels. In the US$25–50 category, the 10-room **Motel El Rosario** is on the east side of the highway as you enter town from the north. **Motel Sinai** is around the bend in the highway to the east. Both offer adequate rooms. One drawback of Motel El Rosario is its location at the bottom of a grade leading into town (and next to a Pemex station); decelerating truckers make quite a roar as they pass, even more when they stop for fuel.

Yet Motel El Rosario is but a short walk from the legendary **Espinosa's Place (Mama Espinosa's Lobster Burritos).** This restaurant, operated by the family of Doña Anita Grosso de Espinosa, has hosted Baja 1000 drivers, Flying Samaritans, and thousands of other Baja travelers since before the completion of the Transpeninsular. The burritos—from beans to lobster—are as tasty as ever. A plate of lobster burritos along with rice, beans, potatoes, tortillas, and salad—enough food for two—costs US$13. Profits from the restaurant help support a local orphanage. Doña Espinosa is also happy to accept donations of food staples and clothing for distribution among the community's poor. Six guest rooms, each with attached bath, one double bed, one twin bed, and a small sitting area, can be found behind the restaurant.

More or less in the center of town and along the highway right next to the bus station, the standard-issue **Restaurant Grullenses** specializes in fresh seafood. **Restaurant Los Portales,** just around the bend as Mexico 1 twists temporarily from north-south to west-east, specializes in fish tacos and standard Mexican food.

Around the bend toward Motel Sinai is **Restaurant Yiyo's,** a popular local hangout serving a variety of egg dishes, fish, lobster, beef *machaca,* breaded shrimp, and steak. Prices at these restaurants set the standard for just about every café and rancho between El Rosario and Guerrero Negro: US$3 for breakfast, US$4–8 for lunch or dinner.

Opposite Motel Sinai, **Restaurant Bocana Beach** serves *carne asada,* fish tacos, and breakfast.

At the southern edge of town, a house converted into **Baja's Best Café** serves light meals and fresh-brewed coffee, allegedly made with beans from the United States–based Starbucks chain.

Beach camping is free along Bahía del Rosario. The Motel Sinai charges US$16 a night for RV parking with electricity and water hookups.

Supplies

Several *tiendas* offer fresh vegetables, baked goods, and a variety of automotive and household items. **Mercado Hermanos Jaramillo,** a supermarket at the first bend in the highway, near Espinosa's Place, has the largest selection, including vaquero hats. The Pemex station at the town's northern entrance stays open 24 hours.

Tecate and Vicinity

During his 1964 presidential campaign, Gustavo Díaz Ordaz referred to Tecate as *la ventana mas limpia de México,* "the cleanest window of Mexico." He may have been fishing for the Tecate vote (which he didn't get; Díaz was unpopular in northern Baja), but as Mexican border towns go, this one is easily the most inviting.

Set in a bowl-shaped valley in the lower Sierra Juárez—known as the Laguna Mountains on the California side—Tecate is insulated from industrial Tijuana and Mexicali to the west and east. The fresh, unpolluted air in the valley lured the developers of North America's first and longest-running health spa, Rancho La Puerta. Tecate's other claim to fame is its namesake *cerveza,* brewed here from spring water since the 1940s.

NORTHERN BAJA

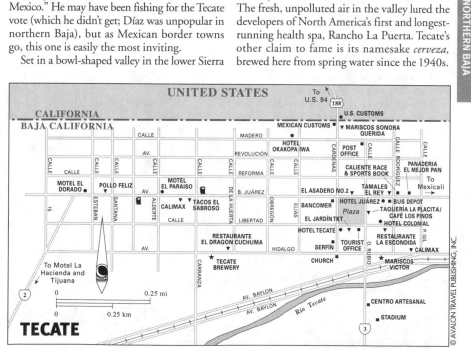

© AVALON TRAVEL PUBLISHING, INC.

The border crossing, four blocks north of town at the end of Calle Lázaro Cárdenas, is one of Baja's most relaxed. Savvy Californians use this crossing instead of Tijuana's when returning from an Ensenada holiday; the wait is much shorter, and the drive along Mexico 3 between Ensenada and Tecate provides an alternative to Mexico 1's coastal scenery. The town on the U.S. side of the border is also called Tecate.

Town life centers around **Parque Hidalgo,** a shady plaza at the intersection of Avenida Juárez and Calle Lázaro Cárdenas, Tecate's main thoroughfares. At the southeast corner of the park stands a statue of Miguel Hidalgo, the Dolores priest who issued the call for Mexican independence in 1810. In the vicinity of the small plaza are a number of restaurants, taco stands, *paleterías y neverías* (popsicle and ice-cream stands), craft shops, and the tourist office.

Tecate's general ambience is more that of a provincial Mexican town than a border town. Yet in spite of the many pleasantries Tecate has to offer, the area receives very few tourists compared with Tijuana, Mexicali, Rosarito, or Ensenada.

Note: Sights along Mexico 3 between Tecate and Ensenada are covered at the end of this Tecate section. Sights along Mexico 2 between Tecate and Mexicali are covered in the Vicinity of Mexicali section. Sights along Mexico 2 between Tecate and Tijuana are covered under Leaving Tijuana in the Tijuana and Vicinity section.

CLIMATE

Tecate is famous for its mild summers, thanks to an elevation of 514 meters (1,690 feet) and distance from both cold Pacific breezes and the high temperatures of the San Felipe Desert. The average temperature in the warmest months (July and Aug.) is 22°C (72°F); on a particularly hot afternoon, temperatures may approach 38°C (100°F), but by nightfall temperatures drop to the low 20s C (70s F).

In winter, Tecate records lower temperatures than either Tijuana or Mexicali; during the coolest months (Dec.–Feb.), the average temperature is 10°C (50°F), with an occasional frost. Average annual precipitation in the Valle de Tecate is 49 cm (19 inches). Typically, more than half the rainfall occurs Dec.–Feb.

HISTORY

Tecate is the oldest border town in Baja, though in terms of peninsular history it's still relatively young. In the early 19th century, a few mestizo farmers began working the valley lands. As word got around that the valley was fertile and water—supplied by the Tecate and Las Palmas Rivers—was abundant, more followed. In 1831 Peruvian Juan Bandini received a land grant of 4,500 hectares from the Mexican government and two years later laid out a town to serve the budding farming community.

Long before Bandini's arrival, the valley surrounding Tecate had been sporadically inhabited by Yuma Amerindians, who called it Zacate. The Yumas revered 1,520-meter (5,000-foot) Monte Cuchumá, the valley's most outstanding geographic feature, which today straddles the United States–Mexico border. Surviving Kumyais, a sub-

Yumanos, circa 1850s

WILLIAM EMORY/REPORT ON THE UNITED STATES AND MEXICAN BOUNDARY SURVEY

tribe of the Yumas, still revere the mountain, and in 1982 they successfully obtained a U.S. agreement to dismantle radio towers on Cuchumá's California side.

Most likely the name Tecate developed from a Spanish corruption of the Amerindian name for the valley, Zacate. Another theory, rather unlikely, has it that Tecate comes from the English "to cut," since Anglos to the north often came to the valley to cut wood in the late 19th century—though the vegetation in the valley has always consisted mostly of treeless chaparral. The settlement became the capital of a new Mexican municipality in 1892, following completion of a railroad built to connect Tijuana, Tecate, and Mexicali with the national rail system.

Tecate became a household word in Mexico after the founding of the Tecate Brewery in 1943. Aside from the brewery and a growing number of *maquiladoras* east of the city on Mexico 2, the town remains primarily dependent on agriculture. Tourism, though relatively limited, is also a source of local revenue.

© JOE CUMMINGS

Tecate truck

TECATE BREWERY

Tecate beer, the only beer in Mexico named for a town, was first brewed by Tecate entrepreneur Alberto Aldrete in 1943. Aldrete started the brewery as a sideline to his *maltería* (malt factory). The first bottles distributed to the public carried a label that read "Rubio Tecate" over a silhouette of Monte Cuchumá. Although the beer sold well locally and was even exported to San Diego, Los Angeles, and San Francisco via train (a Tecate–San Diego rail link existed for a short while in the early 20th century), Aldrete went bankrupt after 10 years. In 1954 Eugenio Garza Sada from Monterrey bought the brewery and added it to Cervecería Cuauhtémoc (later called Cervecería Cuauhtémoc Moctezuma), brewers of Carta Blanca and Bohemia, two other well-known Mexican beers.

Today, Cuauhtémoc Moctezuma operates breweries in six other Mexican cities and has added the Chihuahua, Indio, Superior, and Noche Buena labels to its output, with Dos Equis

and Sol as subsidiaries. The Tecate brand, however, is brewed only in Tecate and Monterrey. The Monterrey brewery produces canned Tecate—in the red-and-silver can familiar to many Americans—much of it for export; the Tecate plant produces only bottles and kegs. Mexican beer drinkers mostly consume Tecate in long-necked deposit bottles or liter-size *caguamas* (sea turtles). On both cans and bottles, every label still carries the profile of Cuchumá, the Kumyais' sacred mountain.

Beer aficionados claim the best Tecate comes from Tecate; the water used at the brewery there, tapped directly from local springs, is considered the purest in Mexico. According to Cuauhtémoc brewers, Tecate is brewed as a lager, with an alcohol content of 3.6 percent and sufficient hops to rate a 20 on the international bitterness scale. Tecate exported to the United States is reduced to 3.2 percent alcohol—a major reason the brand tastes so different north of the border (along with the fact that United States-consumed Tecate is usually canned product from Monterrey). The hops level for export Tecate is also reduced to produce the smoother, blander beer taste preferred by mainstream America.

Carta Blanca, the only other label produced at the Tecate brewery, is a lighter pilsner with a bitterness grade of 16 and an alcohol content of 3.5 percent. *Bajacalifornianos* overwhelmingly prefer Tecate to Carta Blanca, partially out of loyalty to Baja California—Carta Blanca originated in Monterrey—but also because they believe the latter a bland brew. Incidentally, the custom of drinking Tecate with salt and a squeeze of lime, now part of Cuauhtémoc's Tecate advertising campaign, was probably introduced by gringo Baja hands—who squeeze lime over everything they consume in Mexico—concerned with killing bacteria on the top of the can. Lime juice also tends to neutralize the "can" taste. Follow the *mexicano* example and drink bottled Tecate; it's cheaper (if you return the bottles for a deposit refund), better-tasting, and more ecologically responsible.

Tours

Brewery tours are on and off depending on the year. For awhile tours were offered only on Saturday morning and only for groups of 20 or more, but on our last visit the brewery had reinstated daily tours. To be sure you can join a tour, contact the state tourist office on the plaza or call the brewery, tel. 665/654-1111. The usual tour takes around 45 minutes and includes a look at all stages of the brewing and bottling process. A few facts, in case you miss the tour: The present brewery complex stands on the same site as Aldrete's original keg brewery; high-tech German equipment is used to produce 390,000 hectoliters per month (about 10.3 million U.S. gallons); and the brewery employs around a thousand people, who have their own recreational and cultural center south of town, paid for by the brewery.

ACCOMMODATIONS

Hotels and Motels

Under US$25: Hotel Colonial, Callejón Libertad Ote. 285, tel. 665/654-1504, occupies a long brick building around back of the bus station, almost opposite La Escondida Restaurant. Small, basic but adequate rooms with one double bed or two twin beds, private hot-water showers, TV, and phone surround a narrow courtyard.

Off-street parking isn't available. Cheaper yet are the very simple rooms at **Hotel Juárez,** just west of the bus terminal.

Around the corner and upstairs from the El Jardín TKT restaurant, **Hotel Tecate,** tel. 665/654-1116, features 12 basic rooms, some with TV. Ask for a room overlooking the plaza—the rooms without a view are rather dark.

US$25–50: Close to the center of town, **Motel El Paraíso,** Calle Aldrete 83 (at Av. Juárez), tel. 665/654-1716, offers basic but clean rooms with air-conditioning (old window units) and attached hot showers. In winter, if necessary, you can ask for a space heater *(calentador)*. Guests can park in the garage beneath the hotel.

Just west of town on the north side of Mexico 2, the two-story, pink **Motel La Hacienda,** Av. Juárez 861, tel. 665/654-1250, offers clean rooms with TV and air-conditioning. The interior courtyard is decorated with potted tropical plants and features off-street parking.

US$50–100: Two blocks west of the Paraíso, **Motel El Dorado,** Av. Juárez 160, tel. 665/654-1084, fax 665/654-1333, is a two-story wood-and-stucco motel court near the western entrance to Tecate at Av. Juárez and Calle Esteban. Spacious, well-kept rooms come with air-conditioning, heat, TV, and phones. Off-street parking available.

Hotel Okakopa Iwa, Madero 141, tel. 665/654-1144, offers clean, large rooms with hot showers, air-conditioning, heat, TV, and phones.

Ranch Resorts

US$50–100: The luxurious **Rancho Tecate Resort Country Club,** 9.5 km (six miles) southeast of Tecate off Mexico 3, tel. 665/654-0011, fax 665/654-0241, www.ranchotecateresort.com, is a sprawling ranch resort constructed in the typical Tecate hacienda style. Amenities include a nine-hole golf course, tennis courts, a swimming pool, and a lake stocked with freshwater game fish. Suites (each one unique) with kitchens are available.

Hacienda Santa Veronica, tel. 665/681-7428, is a ranch resort off Mexico 2, about 30 km east of Tecate near Km 106 on the free road or Km 94 on the toll road. You must exit from the free road as there is no exit from the toll road. Guest rooms, in mission-style condos, come with fireplaces and patios. Meal plans available. On the premises are six tennis courts, off-road racetracks for motorcycles and four-wheelers, equestrian trails, a swimming pool, volleyball court, and basketball court. Originally a *ganadería,* or breeding ranch for fighting bulls *(ganados bravos),* the Hacienda also offers elementary bullfighting lessons for ranch guests. Other facilities include a restaurant/bar decorated with bullfighting memorabilia and a campground/RV park open to the public.

Rancho La Puerta

One of the most famous spas in North America, La Puerta (The Door) is not open to the public as simple lodgings; the prices, in fact, tend to limit the clientele to CEOs and celebrity guests who have included Madonna, Steven Seagal, Jodie Foster, Oprah Winfrey, and Monaco's Princess Stephanie. Enrollees participate in an all-inclusive, week-long health regime designed for physical and spiritual rejuvenation. The regimen includes mountain hiking, low-impact aerobics, yoga and tai chi, swimming, weight training, and organic cuisine. The site was chosen for its location in one of the Californias' last "safe zones" for the environmentally sensitive and for its proximity to Monte Cuchumá, viewed by the spa's founders as a source of spiritual power.

Hungarian Edmond Szekely and his wife Deborah opened the Essence School of Life here in 1940, with guests paying US$17.50 a week to pitch their own tents, talk philosophy, climb Monte Cuchumá, receive massages, and eat organic food. In the '50s, the spa inspired Michael Murphy to found Big Sur's Esalen Institute. Today Szekely's son Alex oversees the ranch, which has been transformed into a beautifully landscaped, 300-acre health resort. Alex Szekeley also runs its sister spa, the Golden Door, in Escondido, California.

The hacienda-style architecture includes cottages and suites for a maximum 150 guests. Most units have fireplaces, and each has its own garden. A dining hall serves organic fruits and vegetables grown at the subsidiary Rancho Tres Estrellas, along with occasional fresh fish. State-of-the-art recreational facilities include 10 aerobic gyms

with sliding glass walls, a weight-training gym with fitness machines, a mind-body gym (for yoga and meditation), three heated swimming pools, five whirlpools, three saunas, four lighted tennis courts, volleyball and basketball courts, and gender-separated centers for massage, herbal wraps, and private sauna-steam baths. Nine cottages are set aside exclusively for women's use.

All-inclusive prices for the daily health program, meals, and accommodations range from US$2,850 per week for a studio with bath to US$3,550 for a two-bedroom villa suite. In other words, it costs about the same as a deluxe seven-day cruise but is probably a good deal healthier. Summer rates—late June to early September—are lower. If flying into San Diego, a ranch shuttle can be arranged to pick you up at the airport. For reservations or more information, contact Rancho La Puerta, P.O. Box 463057, Escondido, CA 92046, tel. 760/744-4222 or 800/443-7565, fax 760/744-5007, www.rancholapuerta.com.

Camping and RV Parks

Tecate KOA, also known as **Rancho Ojai RV Park,** tel. 665/655-3014, fax 665/655-3015, rojai@telnor.net, www.koakampgrounds.com/where/mexico, lies 21 km (13 miles) east of Tecate on Mexico 2. If you're on the toll road, exit at El Hongo and drive west on Mexico 2 for eight km (five miles) till you see the Rancho Ojai gates. Part of a working ranch, the Tecate KOA offers 41 oak-shaded sites with full hookups, surrounded by 16 hectares of boulder-studded rolling hills and chaparral. Tent sites for two people cost US$20–40 a night, RV sites with full hookups go for US$25–35, while Kamping Kabins cost US$50 for a one-room cabin, US$80 for two rooms. On the premises are a swimming pool, gender-separated restrooms and showers, a restaurant, camp store, club house, dump station, Laundromat, and open-air grills. Available activities include horseback riding and wagon and hay rides.

Costa RV Park at Rancho Santa Veronica (30 km east of Tecate at Km 98, Mexico 2) features full-hookup slots for US$30, tent spaces for only US$3. Guests have access to all the ranch recreational facilities.

NORTHERN BAJA

FOOD

For its size, Tecate offers an unusually high number of places to eat. Among the most renowned culinary attractions are the long-established *taquerías* surrounding Parque Hidalgo, which serve better-than-average tacos, burritos, and tostadas. Each *taquería* has its unique way of assembling the basic ingredients, but you can hardly go wrong if you choose one of the following: **El Asadero No. 2** (facing the north side of the plaza on Avenida Juárez), **Taquería la Placita** (east side of the plaza on Calle Rubio), **Super Taquería Tecate** (a half block east of the plaza on Avenida Juárez, near the bus terminal), or **Tacos El Secre** (same as previous). West of the plaza, a few blocks, near Motel El Paraíso, **Tacos El Sabroso** is the place to go for fish and shrimp tacos. The *taquerías* are typically open from late morning till late evening.

If chicken's your thing, head for **Pollo Feliz** at the northwest corner of Santana and Juárez. You can order take-away outside, or eat in the large air-conditioned dining room inside.

La Escondida, on Callejón Libertad east of the plaza near Hotel Colonial, has a more complete menu of *antojitos* and Mexican breakfasts and is open daily 7 A.M.–5 P.M.

For quick, inexpensive, sit-down meals, try the **El Jardín TKT (Tecate)**. This tiny diner on the south side of the plaza, a few doors west of the tourist office, offers Mexican standards at reasonable prices for lunch and dinner, plus a large variety of breakfasts. During warm weather, the Jardín places a few tables outside and instantly becomes the only sidewalk café in Tecate, complete with wandering *trovadores*. A Mexican combo plate costs US$4, fish tacos just US$1. All prices are posted in dollars. Open daily 6 A.M.–noon.

Just north of Taquería la Placita facing the plaza, tiny **Café Los Pinos** features perhaps the least expensive antojitos menu in town. Open daily 7 A.M.–7 P.M.

Mariscos Victor, Av. Hidalgo 284, serves reasonably priced Mexican-style seafood, including ceviche tostadas, fish tacos, seafood cocktails, and shrimp, as well as ranchero standards like *burritos de machaca, gorditas,* quesadillas, and *bistek* (steak).

A choice of nine different full breakfasts is available, starting at 7 A.M., for US$3–5. Open for breakfast, lunch, and dinner.

Moderately priced **Pollo Veloz,** at Av. Hidalgo 303 near the church, tel. 665/654-4028, has better-than-average Mexican dishes; its chicken tacos are a favorite. Open daily for lunch and dinner.

Attached to Motel El Dorado is the moderately priced restaurant/bar **El Tucán,** specializing in Mexican and Continental fare; open daily for breakfast, lunch, and dinner.

Noodle addicts can check out **El Dragón Cuchumá,** Av. Hidalgo at Calle Obregón, opposite the brewery. The Cantonese cuisine won't win any awards, but portions are huge and the table sauce is hotter than most Mexican salsas by several degrees. Open daily for lunch and dinner.

Los Cabos, at Km 4 on Mexico 3, tel. 665/654-3943, serves fresh fish and shrimp platters worth stopping for. Open for lunch and dinner. Just west of town on Mexico 2 in front of the Plaza Cuchumá shopping center, **La Misión,** Av. Juárez 1100, tel. 665/654-2105, offers steaks, seafood, and Mexican dishes. Open daily for lunch and dinner.

Groceries: *Tiendas* on Avenida Juárez and Avenida Hidalgo sell basic foodstuffs; there's also a medium-size **Calimax** supermarket on Avenida Juárez near the Calle Carranza intersection. For excellent *pan dulce, bolillos,* and other Mexican bakery items, grab tray and tongs at **Panadería El Mejor Pan,** on the north side of Avenida Juárez between Calles Rodríguez and Portes Gil. Some folks claim it's the best Mexican bakery in all of Baja; it's certainly a contender, and it's open 24 hours. Coffee is dispensed free.

Opposite Caliente Race and Sports Book at Calle Rodríguez and Avenida Juárez, **Tamales El Rey** sells ready-to-go tamales of chicken, pork, corn, and pineapple.

ENTERTAINMENT AND EVENTS

Tecate is not big on nightlife; the main source of evening entertainment seems to be promenading back and forth along Avenida Juárez until around 9 P.M., when the streets become practically de-

© JOE CUMMINGS

downtown Tecate

serted. Perhaps the healthy air sends everyone to bed early.

El Tucán restaurant has an attached bar that is usually open after dinner depending on the crowd.

Although it almost seems out of place in this low-key town, **Caliente Race and Sports Book,** at the northeast corner of Calle Rodríguez and Av. Juárez, offers the usual betting lounge, restaurant, and bar; it's open Wed.–Sun. 9 A.M.–11 P.M., Tuesday 9 A.M.–8:30 P.M.

The Santa Veronica Offroad Park and Roadway, a series of dirt racetracks at Hacienda Santa Veronica, 30 km (19 miles) east of Tecate off Mexico 2, is the site of several racing events throughout the year. The biggest is the three-day **Gran Carrera de Tecate,** held in late May and sponsored by Baja Promotions, P.O. Box 8938, Calabasas, CA 91302. Several classes of four-wheelers, as well as motorcycles and ATVs, participate in a series of multilap races scheduled over the three-day interval. Most of the entrants are from California or Arizona. The Tecate Brewery also sponsors smaller off-road races at

Santa Veronica in March, July, and October; contact Baja Promotions for information.

More popular among *bajacalifornianos* is Santa Veronica's **Gran Carrera de Caballos,** also sponsored by Baja Promotions, which takes place the last weekend in March. The 80-km horse race features mounts (horse with rider) entered by weight in heavy, medium, and light classes; riding tack must be either *charro* or *texana* (Mexican or Western) style. A fiesta is held at Hacienda Santa Veronica on the Saturday evening following the race.

The **SCORE Tecate Baja 500** occurs in June and early November. Call SCORE International in the United States at 818/225-8402; see Ensenada for information on SCORE activities.

During the second week of October, local residents celebrate the **Fiesta de la Fundación de Tecate,** honoring the founding of the city with parades, music, dancing, and fireworks.

SHOPPING

A few *alfarerías* (pottery and tile works) and *vidrierías* (glassworks) sell products in local stores. Visitors crossing into Baja at Tecate can't miss the highly visible **Patio del Sol** on the east side of Calle Lázaro Cárdenas, two blocks south of the gateway. The outdoor display features a large selection of unglazed pottery, plus a smaller number of decorative sculptures.

As in Tijuana and Rosarito, several shops in town depend on sales to U.S. residents crossing the border for bargains on tile and other building materials. **Baja-Mex-Tile,** Av. Juárez, tel. 665/654-0204, specializes in Mexican pavers, Mexican brick, handmade roof tile, Saltillo tile, Lincoln tile, flagstone, and ceramic tile.

The government-sponsored **Centro Artesanal,** south of the railway and Río Tecate on Mexico 3 (about 1.5 km south of Av. Juárez), houses two shops: **Tecate Handicraft Center** and **Artesanías Mexicanas.** Besides glasswork and pottery, the vendors offer blankets, rugs, folk art, and other crafts from elsewhere in Northern Mexico. **Rosita's Curios,** west of Calle Lázaro Cárdenas on the south side of Avenida Juárez, is a private shop with an interesting collection of handicrafts.

NORTHERN BAJA

faux fruits and vegetables

INFORMATION

Tourist Assistance

The state tourist office, tel. 665/654-1095, faces the south side of Parque Hidalgo and is open Mon.–Fri. 9 A.M.–7 P.M., Saturday 9 A.M.–3 P.M., Sunday 10 A.M.–2 P.M. The police station is next door. There is also a tourist information booth near the border crossing at Calle Lázaro Cárdenas and Calle Madero.

Money-Changing

U.S. dollars are accepted at most shops, hotels, and restaurants. If you want to change to pesos before crossing into Mexico, you'll find a money changing service in Tecate, California, in the same strip center with the U.S. post office, Home Office, and Western Union office.

A Banamex on Avenida Juárez and a Serfín on Calle Cárdenas each offer foreign exchange services and ATMs. There's also a private *casa de cambio* opposite the northwest corner of the plaza.

Post and Telephone

Tecate's post office is on the corner of Calles Madero and Ortiz Rubio. Probably the best place to make a long-distance call is from the staffed *caseta* at the bus depot.

Immigration and Customs

Immigration and customs offices at the border gateway in Tecate are open daily 6 A.M.–midnight.

TRANSPORTATION

The railway that passes through Tecate now carries freight trains exclusively. Most visitors arrive by bus or private vehicle.

By Bus

Tecate's bus depot is on Avenida Juárez at Calle Rodríguez; on the premises are a snack bar and long-distance telephone service. Departures include **ABC** buses to Mexicali (every hour or so, 7 A.M.–10 P.M., US$9 ordinary, US$14 *primero*), Tijuana (every half hour 5 A.M.–9 P.M., US$3 ordinary, US$4 express), and Ensenada (every 90 minutes 5:30 A.M.–7 P.M., US$7).

By Car

To drive to Tecate from San Diego, take U.S. 805

to U.S. 94 east 66 km (41 miles) to the Tecate turnoff near the border. From Arizona and points east, take I-8 west to the U.S. 94 junction at Jacumba, then follow U.S. 94 west to the Tecate turnoff. The Tecate border gate is open 6 A.M.–midnight.

A branch of **Oscar Padilla's Mexican Insurance,** tel. 800/258-8600, can be found in a small shopping center on the American side.

If you're on your way to mainland Mexico and need a temporary vehicle import permit, note that permits are issued only Monday–Saturday, 8 A.M.–4 P.M. at the customs office. Of course, if you're planning to drive in Baja only, you don't need an import permit and can cross any day of the week.

Tecate lies at the intersection of Mexico 2 (to Tijuana or Mexicali) and Mexico 3 (to Ensenada). The toll road between Tijuana and Tecate, Mexico 2-D, parallels the border closely; the toll is US$5.

If desired, you can park on the American side of the border and walk over to Tecate; parking lot operators charge US$3 for autos and pickups, US$5 or vans and trucks, US$12 for trailers and equipment.

MEXICO 3 TO ENSENADA

The two-lane highway between Tecate and Ensenada winds through the rolling, boulder-studded western slopes of the Sierra Juárez. Traffic is generally light, and the boulders offer plenty of opportunities to view modern rock art, including political slogans, evangelical exclamations—*"¡Cristo viene pronto!"* ("Christ is coming soon!")—declarations of love, and Catholic iconographs.

Except for the occasional valley, the terrain along Mexico 3 is mostly uninhabited chaparral. Valle de las Palmas, a small farming community at Km 27–28, features a café and a Pemex station. Roll up the windows at Km 32, location of a large, smoldering trash dump.

The next settlement of note is historic Guadalupe (Km 77), centered in a large valley created by the Río Guadalupe. Dominican padres established the last and shortest-lived of the Baja California missionary efforts, **Misión Guadalupe,** west of the current village in 1834. In 1836 the mission was successfully defended against an attack by 400 Yumanos; four years later a much smaller force, led by a Neji Amerindian baptized at the mission, chased away the last Dominican padre. The remains of the mission were incorporated into other buildings and are now difficult to identify.

The Russian Colony

A small Russian cemetery and around 25 Russian-style homes occupy a part of Guadalupe known as Colonia Rusa. The original Russian immigrants were Molokans (the word means "milk-drinkers," presumably in reference to the sect's abstinence from alcohol), a straitlaced Christian sect that broke from the Russian Orthodox Church. Around 105 Russian families (approximately 500 individuals) migrated to Guadalupe in 1905, fleeing religious persecution in czarist Russia.

The group purchased 13,000 acres of valley land from the Mexican government. There they planted grapes and wheat, raised geese, kept honeybees, and built whitewashed adobe and wood homes, complete with thatched roofs and glass windows. As in their Russian homeland, the Molokans built their houses along a main street with the front doors facing away from the street. The simple chapel contained no religious decorations or icons, but the Molokans worshipped with such fervor that to the local Mexicans they were known as the Spirit Jumpers.

In 1938, following President Cárdenas's seizure of all foreign-owned lands, the community was engulfed by 3,000 Mexican squatters and renamed Francisco Zarco. Many of the Russians left the valley. Of those that stayed on, most ended up marrying Mexicans; today only four families of pure Russian lineage remain. In almost every respect they've become ordinary Mexican citizens; Russian is the first language only among a few elders.

Physical, if not cultural, evidence of the Russian colony remains. Around 25 of the original Molokan houses are intact. In the cemetery, the older tombstones at the back are engraved

NORTHERN BAJA

in Russian, while later stones toward the front show a combination of Russian and Mexican names—e.g., Juan Samarin, Pedro Pavloff. Two small museums about 25 meters apart—**Museo Comunitario del Valle de Guadalupe** and **Museo Histórico del Valle de Guadalupe**—contain exhibits of Russian memorabilia from the former colony, including clothing, old photos, and tools. The exhibits in the latter are better labeled, and the curator there emphasizes the overall history of the valley, with some emphasis on Spanish and Amerindian influences, while the former focuses only on Russian history in the valley. To find the cemetery and museum, take the turnoff for Francisco Zarco (near Km 77 on Mexico 3) and follow the paved road to its end, then turn right and drive about 150 meters; the cemetery should appear on your left, opposite Monte Xanic. The Museo Comunitario is open Tues.– Sun. 10 A.M.– 6 P.M., while the Museo Histórico is open Tues.–Sun. 10 A.M.–5 P.M. Donations accepted at both. For information on the Museo Comunitario, call 646/174-0170.

Vineyards and Wineries

Although a variety of grains, fruits, and vegetables are grown in the Valle de Guadalupe, grapes have been the major crop ever since a colony of Russian immigrants established the valley's first vineyards early this century. Guadalupe vineyards cultivate grapes for wineries and fruit distributors throughout northern Baja. The northeast section of the Valle de Guadalupe devoted to viniculture is sometimes called **Valle de Calafia.**

Regular winetastings and tours are offered by: **Casa Domecq,** tel. 646/155-2249 (open Mon.– Fri. 9 A.M.–3 P.M., Saturday 9 A.M.–1 P.M.; US$2 for tour and tasting; no reservations necessary), and **L.A. Cetto,** tel. 646/685-3031 (open Mon.– Fri. 10 A.M.–5:30 P.M., Saturday 10 A.M.–4 P.M.; free; no reservations necessary).

Guadalupe's most acclaimed winery, **Monte Xanic,** has its headquarters just beyond the Museo Comunitario. Tours (US$4 pp) can be scheduled by appointment during regular working hours, Monday–Friday 9 A.M.–4 P.M. To arrange an appointment, call Monte Xanic's Ensenada office at 646/174-6155. For more information, check out www.montexanic.com.

Accommodations

US$100–150: So far the only place to stay in the main wine-producing area of the valley is the luxurious **Adobe Guadalupe,** U.S. tel. 949/733-2744, Mexico tel. 646/155-2094, fax 646/155-2093, adobegpe@telnor.net. The 60-acre winery offers six guest rooms in a rambling adobe-walled, hacienda-style complex. Rates include a complete breakfast served at a common table in the huge kitchen. Other meals may be arranged per cost.

To find Adobe Guadalupe, follow the road through Francisco Zarco past the two museums—where the road turns to dirt—and for about four miles, past the Monte Xanic and Chateau Camou wineries. When you reach a stop sign (adjacent to the Unidad Médica Familiar building), turn right and continue another half mile.

RV Park

Rancho Sordo Mudo Trailer Park, at Km 75 on Mexico 3, www.ranchosordomudo.org, offers full hookups for US$15 a night. Proceeds from the park aid a school for deaf children near Ensenada; the nightly fee is tax deductible.

Food

The valley has a couple of well-known restaurants, both of them well outside Francisco Zarco on Mexico 3. Around 22 km (14 miles) northeast of Ensenada, perched on a hill just north of the small community of San Antonio de las Minas, **Restaurant Mustafa** serves mostly Mexican food, along with a short list of Moroccan-influenced dishes, including lamb shish-kebab and chicken breast stuffed with spinach and cheese. In San Antonio itself, **El Mesón** is popular for breakfast and lunch stops; it's closed on Thursday. The owner is an admirer of British aviation artist Robert Taylor and displays Taylor's work on the restaurant walls.

Restaurant LAJA, about 50 meters off Mexico 3 via a washboard road, is housed in a private home with white walls and a red tile roof.

We've heard good things about this restaurant, which allegedly serves Mexican fusion cuisine. When we stopped by at 12.30 P.M. on a Wednesday afternoon, it was closed and there were no hours posted.

Francisco Zarco itself has a couple of small eateries worth trying. **Doña Chuy's** offers a very economic Mexican alternative to the other restaurants in the valley, which tend to be a bit on the expensive side, while small, clean **Restaurante La Cabaña** specializes in northern Mexican food, including fresh quail.

You can pick up travel supplies at **Mercado La Chica** or **Abarrotes C.R.**, both in Francisco Zarco. Abarrotes C.R. has its own *panadería* and *tortillería*.

West of Guadalupe

At Km 96 a gravel road leads west to the Valle San Marcos, a scenic area of cattle ranches and small farms. This gravel road meets paved Mexico 1, the free road, after 12 km (7.5 miles). Mexico 3 links with Mexico 1-D, the toll road, at El Sauzal (Km 105), a tiny coastal community supported by a fish cannery. No toll is charged for the final nine km south to Ensenada.

Mexicali

Driving or walking into Mexicali from Calexico, a visitor's first impression of the city focuses on the congested downtown area—the "old" Mexicali. Like other large Mexican border districts, it's chockablock with street vendors, souvenir shops, and *casas de cambio* (money changers). But a few blocks away from the border in any direction are broad, palm-lined boulevards and tidy residential areas reminiscent of San Diego or Phoenix. Definitely not Tijuana or Ciudad Juárez.

The only Mexican border town that's also a state capital, Mexicali boasts Baja's second-largest population; 700,000 is the official count. City promoters make much of the fact that the city is considerably less tourism-dependent than Tijuana; you won't find any zebra-painted burros on Mexicali streetcorners, or any place resembling Tijuana's Avenida Revolución. As a matter of fact, Mexicali is much cleaner and more orderly city than either Ensenada or Tijuana.

As citizens of Baja California Norte's capital, Mexicalienses view themselves as a step closer to Mexico City, while at the same time true *cachanillas*. Like the *cachanilla,* a sturdy desert plant that flowers in arid, saline soil, Mexicali has flourished at the edge of the harsh San Felipe and Sonora Deserts and bloomed as one of Mexico's most prosperous communities. Today, any northern *bajacaliforniano* can claim to be a *cachanilla,* but as the verse from Antonio Váldez's famous *corrido* "El Cachanilla" says, *"Mexicali, fue mi cuna"* (Mexicali was my cradle).

THE LAND

The nearly flat Valle de Mexicali extends westward from the Río Colorado delta to the Sierra de Cucapá. Millennia ago the entire area was covered by a northern extension of the Sea of Cortez; California's Salton Sea and Baja California Norte's Laguna Salada are vestiges of the Cortez trapped by the gradual silting of the Colorado delta. The city of Mexicali, in fact, is a foot below sea level.

South of the valley lies the San Felipe Desert, an extension of the Sonora Desert. The valley itself can be classified as desert since it averages less than 25 cm (10 inches) of rainfall a year. Unlike many deserts, centuries of river silting have made the soil here nutrient-rich; earth that once filled the Grand Canyon was carried into the delta at a rate of 160 million tons per year. Yet the region's overall lack of water sources meant that agriculture outside the Colorado floodplain was almost impossible before U.S. land companies established a canal system early this century to irrigate California's Imperial Valley and the Valle de Mexicali.

Before the damming of the Colorado River in the United States, the floodplain was enormous. The tidal bore at the mouth of the river,

NORTHERN BAJA

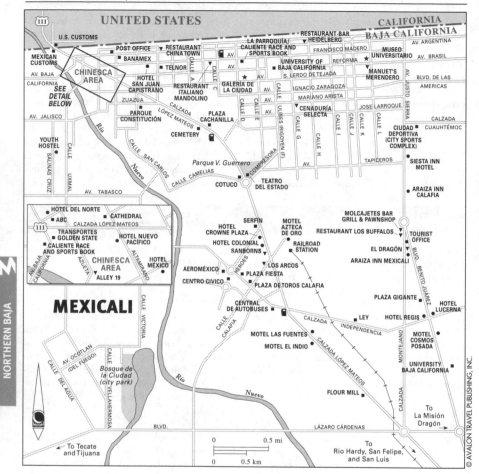

where it fed into the Cortez, was strong enough to sink ships. The outflow slowed with the U.S. dams and was then reduced to a trickle by the 1950 construction of Mexico's Morelos Dam near Los Algodones, which diverts water into the Valle de Mexicali to supplement the American-built canal system.

With irrigation, a 2.5-km-thick layer of river silt, and an abundance of sunshine, most of the valley today is under intensive cultivation, producing cotton, wheat, grapefruit, lemons, oranges, carrots, corn, asparagus, onions, broccoli, potatoes, lettuce, cauliflower, and grapes.

CLIMATE

During December and January, Mexicali's coolest months, temperatures average 12°C (54°F). In July, temperatures reach 35–38°C (95–100°F) in the daytime (occasionally as high as 48°C, 120°F), dropping to around 24°C (75°F) at night. The lack of humidity means that perceived temperatures in the summer are significantly lower, and since the Mexicali area is primarily agricultural, air pollution is not an appreciable problem. Still, summers are hot by any measure. Rainfall averages a scant 12 cm (4.7 inches) a year.

The best overall months for a Mexicali visit are Sept. and Oct., when the temperature averages 23°C (73°F) and desert plants are usually in bloom. Spring is also pleasant. Peak periods for visitors from the north are Nov.–Feb., especially for those on their way to San Felipe. July and August are the least hospitable months, as soaring temperatures bring the city to a standstill.

HISTORY

Pre-Hispanic Amerindian Cultures

In pre-Cortesian times, the Río Colorado delta—which, at the time, included the Valle de Mexicali—was inhabited by a centuries-long succession of Yumano tribes. When the Spanish first stumbled upon the delta after traversing, with great difficulty, the Sonora Desert's Camino del Diablo (Devil's Road), a sophisticated Río Colorado culture was cultivating squash, melons, peas, and five colors of corn: yellow, blue, white, red, and blue-white. The Amerindians also possessed an impressive knowledge of medicinal herbs and employed desert plants like mesquite and agave in a wide variety of uses.

Among the major Yumano groups in the region were the Cucapá, who navigated the difficult Río Colorado on reed rafts. Like their neighbors the Kiliwa, the Cucapá's numbers were greatly reduced by Spanish missionization in northwest Mexico. Today, Cucapá descendants inhabit a small government-protected corner of the delta near the junction of the Hardy and Colorado Rivers, an area marked by names like Colonia Indígena, Colonia Cucapá El Mayor, Terrenos Indios, and Mestizos. The Cucapá call themselves Ko Ipat, meaning "Those Who Go and Return," a reference to their migratory ways. The women can often be recognized by their colorful, billowing, floral-print dresses. For the most part, they work on agricultural *ejidos* or fish the rivers, although many have migrated to Mexicali. Few indigenous customs survived both the Spanish and Mexican eras; both the Kiliwa and the Cucapá continued to practice cremation rituals, for example, until they were banned by the Mexican government in the early 20th century.

The Building of an Agricultural Empire

After the Jesuits left, the Spanish and later the Mexicans had little to do with northeastern Baja, perceiving it as an untamable, flood-prone desert delta. Around the time of the American Civil War, a Yale geologist, while surveying a route for the Southern Pacific Railroad, wandered into the delta and discovered what the dwindling population of Yumanos had known for centuries: the 2.5-km-thick sediment was prime farming soil. The sediments extended far to the west of the river itself, accumulating in a shallow basin below the Sierra de Cucapá. All it needed was the addition of water to become an overnight agricultural miracle.

In 1900 the U.S.-based California Development Company received permission from the Porfirio Díaz government to cut a canal through the delta's Arroyo Alamo, thus linking the dry basin with the Colorado River. To attract farmers to the area, the developers named the basin the Imperial Valley. In March 1903, the first 500 farmers arrived; by late 1904, 100,000 valley acres were irrigated, with 10,000 people settled on the land and harvesting cotton, fruits, and vegetables. A collection of huts and ramadas that straddled the border was named Calexico on the U.S. side, Mexicali on the Mexican side.

Seeing that the equally fertile Valle de Mexicali lay undeveloped, another American land syndicate, the Colorado River Land Company, moved in. Led by Harry Chandler, then publisher of the *Los Angeles Times,* the syndicate controlled some 800,000 acres of northern Baja and in 1905 began constructing a Valle de Mexicali irrigation system. Instead of using Mexican labor, as the Imperial Valley developers had, Chandler imported thousands of Chinese coolies. After a major 1905 rainfall, the channel dug from Arroyo Alamo ended up diverting the entire outflow of the Colorado River into the Imperial Valley, taking Mexicali with it—unknowingly, the syndicate had tapped into one of the river's original routes. The Salton Sink, a dried-up remainder of the Sea of Cortez, became the Salton Sea virtually overnight.

Neither the U.S. nor Mexico wanted to take

MEXICALI CHINESE

Mexicali has one of the highest concentrations of Chinese residents in Mexico. Today around 5,000 (or roughly 6 percent) of the city's 850,000 residents are of Chinese ancestry. But early in the 20th century, Mexicali was more Chinese than Mexican.

Early Chinese Settlement

The first Chinese to arrive in the area came as laborers for the Colorado River Land Company, which designed and built an extensive irrigation system in the Valle de Mexicali. Some immigrants arrived overland from the United States, fleeing officially sanctioned anti-Chinese policies; others sailed directly from China via the Pacific Ocean and the Sea of Cortez. As in Alta California, thousands of Chinese coolies were lured to the area by the promise of high wages that never materialized.

A 200-meter desert peak near Crucero La Trinidad is named El Chinero in memory of a group of 160 Chinese laborers who perished while crossing the San Felipe Desert in search of work in the valley. The desert itself was known for a time as El Desierto de los Chinos, "Desert of the Chinese." An unscrupulous Mexican boatman landed the group at a fork in the Río Colorado, telling them Mexicali was only a short distance away; actually 65 km of burning desert lay between them and their goal, which they never reached.

Many of the Chinese laborers who survived the building of the irrigation system stayed on after it was finished, congregating in an area of downtown Mexicali known as Chinesca (Chinatown). During the Prohibition years, Chinesca housed many of the city's casinos and bars; an underground tunnel system led to bordellos and opium dens and under the border to Calexico. The latter route was used by bootleggers. By 1920 Mexicali's *chinos* outnumbered the *mexicanos* by a ratio of 14:1. A group of 5,000 single Chinese males started the Asociación China, a Mexicali social organization at least partly devoted to the procurement of Chinese wives from overseas. This association still exists in Mexicali, functioning as the social center of Chinesca.

The Anti-Chinese Movement and Overseas Refugees

In 1927 a series of Tong wars in Northern Mex-

---

responsibility for the growing "New River" created by Chandler's mistake. As both valleys became increasingly inundated, the Southern Pacific Railroad stepped in and, to protect its tracks, dumped a sufficient amount of rock into the river to head the Colorado back into the Cortez, leaving a canal to the Valle de Mexicali. From then on, both valleys became highly productive agricultural centers.

A New Capital, Prohibition, and the Postwar Boom

In 1911, both Mexicali and Tijuana were briefly occupied by American and Mexican *filibusteros* (see Tijuana). To defend the border from similar threats, the Mexican government moved the Baja California Norte territorial capital from Ensenada to Mexicali. That same year, the U.S. government passed Prohibition, forbidding the manufacture, sale, and consumption of alcohol; although Mexicali received fewer of the Hollywood high-rollers than did Tijuana, Americans nonetheless developed a romance with the city, as embodied in the popular song of the time, "Mexicali Rose."

Many of the Prohibition-era businesses were operated by *chinos,* Chinese laborers and farmers who moved into the city and spent their hard-earned savings to open bars, restaurants, and hotels. With people from both sides of the border drawn to the burgeoning town, Mexicali's urbanization accelerated. In the 1920s Mexicali experienced an influx of Punjabis from India, who in many cases took over Chinese farming enterprises.

Like Tijuana, Mexicali suffered an economic recession with the repeal of Prohibition in 1933 and the Mexican ban on casino gambling in 1938. But with a flourishing agricultural base and a federal presence, Mexicali bounced back sooner than Tijuana did. The 1947 establishment of the Ferrocarril Sonora-Baja California, a

ico erupted over control of gambling and prostitution rings. Mexican alarm over the Chinese control of organized crime led to the government-encouraged Movimiento Anti-Chino in the late 1920s. The wave of anti-Chinese sentiment that swept the country led to the torture and murder of hundreds of Chinese in Northern Mexico—a tragic echo of what happened on a larger scale in Alta California in the 1880s. To Mexico's credit, the government never enacted an equivalent to the U.S. Chinese Exclusion Act, which prevented all persons of Chinese heritage from holding U.S. citizenship.

Mexicali quickly became a refuge for Chinese fleeing the violence, since in that city *chinos* predominated. As the anti-Chinese movement faded away, still more Chinese arrived in Mexicali, where it became the Mexican headquarters for the Kuomintang, Sun Yat-sen's nationalist Chinese party. During World War II, the nationalists were pushed out of China first by the Japanese and then by the Communists; the Mexican government loosened its immigration policies to allow a large number of refugees into Mexico.

Hybridization

Postwar Mexicali featured two cinemas; both showed Chinese movies almost exclusively. But as the city recovered from the post-Prohibition recession, a steady influx of Mexicans diluted the local population until the Chinese became a minority. Mexicali still boasts more Chinese restaurants per capita than anywhere else in Mexico, and Chinesca survives downtown around the intersection of Juárez and Altamirano. Local Chinese associations struggle to preserve the arts and culture of the homeland through the sponsorship of Chinese festivals, calligraphy clubs, and language classes. The city even has a sister city in China (Nanjing).

But in most aspects, Chinese cultural life has blended with local traditions to create a unique, hybrid culture. Only in Mexicali will you find banners of the Virgin of Guadalupe hanging side by side with Chinese paper lamps, or a café where Chinese elders kibitz over hamburgers and green tea, speaking a mixture of Cantonese and Spanish. Surfers, note: Mexicali is probably the only place in the world where you can enjoy the revenge of eating shark-fin tacos.

railroad link between Mexicali and the main Nogales–Mexico City trunk line, further boosted the local economy. After Baja California Norte attained statehood in 1952, the capital began receiving a steady rotation of *chilangos* (Mexico City residents), some of whom stayed on and started new businesses after completing their terms of office. Although local residents might hesitate to admit it, part of Mexicali's postwar success in shedding its border-town image should probably be credited to the influx of outsiders—from the coming of the Chinese in the early 20th century to the postwar arrival of the *chilangos*.

Mexicali Today

Today the main source of Mexicali income remains agriculture, primarily cotton, wheat, alfalfa, and vegetables. Another moneymaker is geothermal power; the string of geothermal plants at nearby Cerro Prieto constitutes the world's third-largest producer of such power. The elec-

tricity it generates powers most of northeastern Baja and is even sold north of the border. A third major industry is the growing complex of in-bond plants, or *maquiladoras*, which currently number over 200 in 11 different industrial parks. Major multinational firms with Mexicali in-bond plants include Rockwell International, Daewoo, Hughes Aircraft, Emerson Electric, ITT, Goldstar, Nestle's, and Sony. From all appearances, Mexicali's *maquilas* seem to be among the cleanest and best managed along the entire United States–Mexico border.

The economic symbiosis evident all along the United States–Mexico border is especially visible in the Mexicali–Los Algodones area. Laborers work alternately at Imperial Valley or Valle de Mexicali farms on either side of the border. And, like Tijuana, Mexicali is a free-trade zone. Television and radio stations in El Centro (California) and Yuma (Arizona) broadcast ads for pharmacies in Mexicali and Los Algodones,

NORTHERN BAJA

where generic equivalents for American drugs are available without prescription at prices several times lower than those in the United States. In return, the small California town of Calexico (pop. 15,000) serves as a convenience mart for Mexicalienses shopping for discounted American-made apparel and housewares.

Mexicali serves as an important educational center for all of Baja. Reflecting the city's international orientation, the Universidad Autónoma de Baja California administers a reputable foreign-languages department offering instruction in teaching, translating, and interpreting English, French, German, and Japanese. See Sights, further on.

The current ruling party in the *municipio* of Mexicali is the National Action Party (PAN), a factor many believe explains why the city is cleaner—politically as well as physically—than Tijuana, a longtime bastion of the Institutional Revolutionary Party (PRI).

Tourism is important to Mexicali but is for the most part limited to short American shopping trips or brief stopovers by San Felipe–bound visitors. Most visitors—international and domestic—spending the night in Mexicali are business travelers. Less than a third of overnight hotel guests hail from the United States; about 70 percent come from Mexico, with the rest a mix of visitors from Japan, Central and South America, and Europe.

SIGHTS

Mexicali is not a city with a long list of tourist attractions, nor is it a particularly festive city by Mexican standards. It seems to focus on creating an amenable environment for government- and business-oriented activities, while trying to make the community as comfortable a place to live as possible. There are, however, a few modern cultural venues of interest.

The city has two hearts. First is the old downtown area, pushed up against the border and featuring early-20th-century architecture. A prime example is the Hotel Del Norte, almost Texan or New Mexican in appearance. Then there's the newer **Centro Cívico-Comercial de Mexicali**

(Mexicali Civic-Commercial Center), southeast of downtown along Calzada Independencia. Ambitiously dubbed the Zona Rosa after Mexico City's chic business-entertainment district, the center is a renovated warehouse district containing offices, restaurants, bars, and utilitarian shops selling paint, furniture, stationery, and office supplies. Although it's near the bullring and the bus and train stations, the Centro Cívico has become more of an attraction for Mexicali residents than for foreign visitors.

Linking the various city sectors is a system of wide avenues and *glorietas* (traffic circles), many encircling statues of Mexican national heroes.

Museo Universitario

This Universidad Autónoma de Baja California–sponsored museum of anthropology and natural history is unequaled on the peninsula. In spite of the museum's compact size, the exhibits manage to pack in a wealth of information on northern Baja's pre- and post-Cortesian history as well as the flora and fauna unique to the region. Exhibits are labeled in Spanish only; if you're familiar with the language, you can learn much about northern Baja ethnology, especially regarding the Yumano and San Dieguito cultures.

Temporary exhibitions are of equally high quality, such as the recent hosting of an exquisite and well-curated collection of indigenous textiles from the region, from the woven grass garments of the early Cucapá to the colorful silk saris of more recent Indian immigrants to Mexicali.

The museum is away from the main UABC campus, at Av. Reforma and Calle L. Hours are Mon.–Fri. 9 A.M.–6 P.M., Sat. and Sun. 9 A.M.–2 P.M. Admission is US$1. For more information, call 686/554-1977.

Museo Sol del Niño

On Boulevard López Mateos near the Hotel Crowne Plaza, this museum is oriented toward children, with an emphasis on science and technology. Open Mon.–Fri. 9 A.M.–7 P.M., Sat. and Sun. 10 A.M.–2 P.M.; admission is free. Call 686/554-9494 or 686/554-5579 for further information.

Galería de la Ciudad (City Gallery)

This privately owned gallery, Av. Obregón 1209 (between Calles D and E), tel. 686/553-5044, ext. 23, exhibits works by painters, sculptors, photographers, and other artists from the region and around Mexico. Open Mon.–Fri. 9 A.M.–8 P.M., Sat. and Sun. 9 A.M.–1 P.M.; admission is free.

Chinesca

Mexicali's Chinatown, known locally as Chinesca, is the only identifiably Chinese urban district anywhere in Mexico—unless you count one short street in Mexico City. It centers around the intersection of Calle Benito Juárez (don't confuse this street with the much larger and newer Boulevard Benito Juárez in the southeast sector of town) and Calle Altamirano. This intersection is just southwest of the traffic circle nearest the border crossing; if you're coming across the border by car or on foot, turn right immediately on Altamirano, which leads into Chinesca.

Although the neighborhood is anything but fancy, the first thing you may notice is the lineup of gold shops (casas de oro) selling gold chains and other jewelry—very much like Chinatowns throughout the world. Also obvious are the unusually numerous Chinese restaurants; in fact, every block in this area features at least three Chinese eateries. Even the Mexican restaurants here may bear Chinese names, as at Taquería de Chungui. Several Chinese associations and clan houses can be found tucked away in the neighborhood, including the Asociación Chung Shan de Baja California and Asociación China, both on Calle Juárez.

Another hallmark of the city's Chinese heritage is a Chinese pavilion standing on Plaza de Amistad near the border crossing (not in Chinesca, but nearby). Made entirely with Chinese materials by Chinese artisans, and inaugurated during Chinese New Year 1994, the pavilion is one of only two such structures in the Americas. A couple of downtown shopping centers nearby, such as Plaza Mandarín, feature modern architecture adorned with curving tile roofs and other Chinese motifs.

Parks

Bosque de la Ciudad, an oasis of green in a dry city, offers picnic areas, a playground, a botanical museum, and a zoo. It's in southwest Mexicali at Av. Ocotlán and Calle Alvarado; open Tues.–Sun. 9 A.M.–5 P.M. The smaller **Parque Vicente Guerrero,** wedged between Calzada López Mateos and Calle Compresora southeast of downtown Mexicali, is similar except that it's always open.

Colleges and Universities

Mexicali has four institutes of higher learning, including the respected **Universidad Autónoma de Baja California,** or UABC (University of Baja California). UABC's main campus is off Boulevard Juárez between Calzada Independencia and Boulevard Lázaro Cárdenas. The university rectory and administrative offices, tel. 686/551-8200, are housed in the former governor's palace, in an older section of the city between Avenida Reforma and Calle Lerdo de Tejada, off Calle Irigoyen. Anthropology, architecture, and foreign languages are among the university's stronger disciplines.

Tertiary institutions include the **Instituto Tecnológico Regional,** Blvd. Lázaro Cárdenas, tel. 686/561-8522, a federal institute specializing in engineering studies, and the **Centro de Enseñanza Técnica y Superior (CETYS),** Calz. Compuertas, tel. 686/565-0116, a private school that combines upper high school and college levels.

ACCOMMODATIONS

Room rates for Mexicali hotels and motels are very reasonable, and overall it's less expensive to spend the night here than in Tijuana, Ensenada, or San Felipe. Add 12 percent tax to all rates quoted here unless otherwise noted.

Under US$25

In this category Mexicali beats all other Baja California Norte towns. The **Instituto de la Juventud y el Deporte,** Calle Coahuila 2050 (at Av. Salinas Cruz) in the western part of the city (Parcela 36), tel. 686/557-6182, offers dorm beds. Unlike most government-sponsored youth hostels, the Mexicali facility has no cafeteria. You can take a blue-and-white No. 3a or 11 local bus to reach the hostel.

Aside from the hostel, your lowest-priced selections are found in Mexicali's Chinatown, about three blocks from the United States–Mexico border gate. **Hotel Nuevo Pacífico,** Calle Juárez 95 (just west of Calle Altamirano), tel. 686/552-9430, rents simple but adequate rooms with private baths, some with air-conditioning. The **Hotel 16 de Septiembre,** on Altamirano south of Juárez, tel. 686/552-6070, and the **Hotel Altamirano,** Calle Altamirano 378, tel. 686/552-8394, are similarly priced, but Nuevo Pacífico is the best of the three; none offers off-street parking.

US$25–50

East of Chinatown in the main downtown area, aging **Hotel México,** Av. Lerdo de Tejada 476 (just west of Morelos), tel. 686/554-0669, has decent if spartan rooms. No off-street parking. **Motel Las Fuentes,** Calz. López Mateos 1655, tel. 686/557-1525, is a modern motel with an enclosed parking lot and decent rooms. Its location between a busy boulevard and the railway might be a problem for light sleepers.

Diagonally opposite the train station, 57-room **Motel Azteca de Oro,** Calle de la Industria 600, tel. 686/557-1433, is a two-story place with rooms surrounding a courtyard. The main bus station is only 10 minutes away on foot.

In the downtown area, not far from the border, **Hotel San Juan Capistrano,** Av. Reforma 646, tel. 686/552-4104, is an older Spanish mission– style hotel offering worn but well-kept rooms with air-conditioning and heat. A popular coffee shop is downstairs. Off-street parking can be arranged.

Motel Cosmos Posada, Calz. Juárez 4257, tel. 686/568-1156, has standard motel rooms surrounding a parking lot. It's near the Universidad Autónoma de Baja California and close to highway access. All rooms have air-conditioning, heat, TV, and phone.

Over on Calzada López Mateos, near the Civic Center and main intercity bus terminal, is a cluster of inexpensive places to overnight. **Motel El Indio,** Calz. López Mateos 101 at Av. Fresnillo, almost opposite Las Fuentes, tel. 686/557-2277, features two stories with 50 decent rooms around a totally enclosed courtyard.

Hotel Regis, Calz. Juárez 2150, tel. 686/566-8801, fax 686/566-3435, www.hotel-regis.com, is a relatively new and efficient place to stay, with clean and comfortable rooms.

Hotel del Norte

US$50–100

Out in the eastern part of the city and more convenient to people driving their own vehicles onward to Mexico 2 or Mexico 5, the friendly and efficient **Siesta Inn Motel,** Calz. Justo Sierra 899, tel. 686/568-2001, U.S. tel. 800/426-5093, offers well-maintained rooms with air-conditioning, TV, and phone. On the premises are a swimming pool, restaurant, and parking lot. Farther southeast and closer yet to the highways, two-story **Motel Regis,** Blvd. Juárez 2150 (near Plaza Gigante and almost opposite Hotel Lucerna), tel. 686/566-8801, offers similar rates and conditions.

Hotel Del Norte, Calle Melgar at Av. Madero, tel. 686/554-0024, is a downtown Mex-Deco classic within easy walking distance of the border gate. Rooms come in three sizes; all have air-conditioning, phone, and TV. Facilities include an inexpensive coffee shop, a bar, and parking.

Araiza Inn Calafía, Calz. Justo Sierra 1495, tel. 686/568-3311 or 800/026-5444, U.S. reservations 877/7-ARAIZA (877/727-2492), fax 686/556-9717, www.araizainn.com.mx, is a well-managed four-story motel with 170 rooms containing all the usual amenities. Facilities include a swimming pool, Calafía Steakhouse restaurant, 24-hour coffee shop, bar, and security parking.

South of the turnoff for San Luis Río Colorado, the **Motel Liz,** Mexico 2, Km 1.5, tel. 686/561-8330, consists of a nicely kept, sprawling courtyard setup with 57 rooms, all with phones, air-conditioning, heat, and TV. Secured parking is available.

US$100–150

South of Araiza Inn Calafía along the same boulevard (which changes names en route) is the 170-room **Araiza Inn Mexicali,** Calz. Juárez 2220, tel. 686/564-1100 or 800/686-5444, U.S. tel. 877/7-ARAIZA (877/727-2492), www.araizainn .com.mx. On the premises are a pool, restaurant, coffee shop, bar, and disco.

Hotel Lucerna, Calz. Juárez 2151, tel. 686/564-7000, fax 686/566-4706, www.hotel-lucerna.com.mx, is a multistory Mexicali original. Its 190 well-appointed rooms feature climate control, servibars, satellite TV, and direct-dial phones. Facilities include two pools, a fitness center, the Restaurant Mezzosole, a coffee shop, piano bar, and disco.

Hotel Colonial, Blvd. López Mateos and Calle Calafía, tel. 686/556-1312, U.S./Canada tel. 800/437-2438, www.hotelescolonial.com.mx, is a well-run, two-story American-style hotel with 145 rooms next to Sanborns restaurant.

US$150–250

Hotel Crowne Plaza, Blvd. López Mateos at Av. de los Héroes, tel. 686/557-3600, fax 686/557-0035, U.S./Canada tel. 800/227-6963, www.crowneplaza.com, has all the features you'd expect of the Crowne Plaza line, including a pool, spa, restaurant, business center, and travel agency. A recently added sports bar contains pool tables and a wide-screen TV for sporting events. The hotel's 158 rooms come with climate control, satellite TV, and direct-dial phones. Nonsmoking rooms available.

Calexico

If you can't find a room to your liking in Mexicali, cross the border to Calexico and check out the **Don Juan Motel, Motel Villa Sur,** and **Border Motel,** all of which are on 4th Street; rates are in the US$25–50 range.

Camping and RV Parks

The nearest camping area is a cluster of rustic hunting and fishing camps 30–35 km (18–21 miles) south of the city, off Mexico 5 in the Río Hardy area. Tent/camper sites usually go for about US$5–7 a night; no hookups.

FOOD

Although not ordinarily thought of as a tourist town, Mexicali has more restaurants in the state-proclaimed *turística* category—125 out of over 550 total—than any other city in Baja. The older downtown area near the border offers the least expensive, most authentic Northern Mexican food, with vendors and cafés every other block or so. Another good area for cheap eats is opposite the bus station on Calzada Independencia, where taco and *torta* stands vie for the patronage of arriving and departing passengers.

Chinese

Mexicali has more Chinese restaurants per capita than any other city in Mexico—well over a hundred at last count. Chinese food is so much a part of the scene that the Baja California state tourist office recognizes Chinese cuisine as the city's most typical food.

Cantonese cooking predominates, but with few exceptions it's not the sort you'd recognize from Canton or Hong Kong—or Vancouver or San Francisco, for that matter. As in many Chinese restaurants outside of China, Hong Kong, Singapore, and Taiwan, immigrant cooks have adapted their native cuisine to local tastes. Almost every Chinese restaurant in Mexicali, for example, serves each dish with a small bowl of what tastes like generic steak sauce or ketchup, a distinctly *norteño* touch. Still, the city's Chinese restaurants are among the most economical places to eat and are worth visiting for their interior decor alone—some represent the ultimate in Chinese restaurant kitsch.

In Chinesca itself most of the Chinese places fall into the "hole in the wall" category. Two of the more popular Chinese cafés in this neighborhood include the **Nueva Asia** on Altamirano near the Hotel Nuevo Pacífico and **Restaurant Ho Yong** on Juárez. In operation since 1928, **Alley 19,** Av. Juárez at Calle Azueta, is the oldest restaurant in Chinesca, perhaps in all Mexicali. **China Town,** Av. Madero 701, tel. 686/554-0212, is also a good choice if you're touring Chinesca. Inexpensive. Open daily for lunch and dinner.

Several good bets are found in other neighborhoods. **Restaurant El Dragón,** Blvd. Juárez 1830, tel. 686/566-2020, is in a small shopping center just north of the Araiza Inn Mexicali and features one of the most elaborate Chinese interiors in town. Large portions and fresh ingredients make it one of Mexicali's most popular restaurants; the huge menu features several regional styles. Moderate prices. Open daily 11 A.M.–11 P.M. **La Misión Dragón,** Blvd. Lázaro Cárdenas 555, tel. 686/566-4320, offers more of the same, with the Chinese-style gardens and fountains a bonus. Moderate prices. Open daily 10 A.M.– midnight.

Other International

Restaurant-Bar Heidelberg, Av. Madero at Calle H, tel. 686/554-2022, offers German and Continental dishes; close to downtown. Moderate prices. Open Mon.–Sat. noon–1 A.M. **Restaurant Italiano Mandolino,** Av. Reforma 1070, tel. 686/552-9544, is the place to go for Italian food in Mexicali. Piano bar attached. Moderate prices. Open daily for lunch and dinner. **Sakura Restaurant Bar Japonés,** Blvd. Lázaro Cárdenas 2004 (at Calz. Montejano), tel. 686/566-4848, offers teppanyaki, tempura, sushi, and the like. Moderate prices. Open daily for lunch and dinner.

Mexican

Cenaduría Selecta, Calle G 1510 (at Av. Arista), tel. 686/552-4047, lies in a slightly less congested downtown area. The renowned Selecta has crowded them in since 1945 for some of the best tacos and burritos in town. Inexpensive to moderate. Open daily 8 A.M.–11 P.M.

Merendero Manuet's, Calle L at Av. Pino Suárez, tel. 686/552-5694, occupies a large, semicircular pink building resembling a 1950s American drive-in. The moderately priced menu focuses on *antojitos*. There's also a full bar. Popular with UABC staff. Inexpensive to moderate. Open daily 10 A.M.–1 A.M.

Molcajetes Bar-Grill & Pawnshop on Calz. Montejano across from the state tourism office, tel. 686/557-0600, specializes in fajitas, including chicken, shrimp, and fish versions or a combination of all three. "Pawnshop" refers to a business that previously occupied the space. On Friday and Saturday after 11 P.M. the tables are moved to create a dance floor, and a live band rocks until 4 A.M. Open for lunch and dinner Mon.–Sat. 1 P.M.–2 A.M.

La Parroquía, Av. Reforma at Calle D, tel. 686/554-2313, is a large restaurant oriented toward visiting gringos—a branch of Caliente Race and Sports Book is attached—and the prices are a bit high, but the all-Mexican menu is dependable. Open daily for breakfast, lunch, and dinner.

Restaurant Del Norte, Hotel Del Norte, corner of Av. Madero and Calle Melgar, is wedged onto a downtown corner near the border crossing. It's popular with tourists and locals alike for its large *platillos típicos*. Prices are very reasonable. Open daily 7 A.M.–10 P.M.

Sanborns, northwest corner of Av. Calafía and Av. López Mateos, tel. 686/557-0212, is conveniently located next to the Hotel Colonial. This is a typical Sanborns—good Mexican breakfasts and other meals, decent coffee, and moderate prices. Open daily 24 hours.

Sara's Restaurant, Blvd. Benito Juárez, Centro Comercial 19 (across from UABC), tel. 686/566-2455, offers good basic *comida mexicana,* including inexpensive breakfasts and *comida corrida.* Open daily 7 A.M.–10:30 P.M.

Seafood
In the Centro Cívico district, decorated with fishnets and vibrant Mexican colors, **Los Arcos Restaurant/Bar,** Calafía 454, tel. 686/556-0886, is the best place in town for fresh seafood. Its "seafood fiesta"—a stew consisting of fresh squid, octopus, shredded fish, marlin, and shrimp in a tomato-basil sauce—is the local favorite. A trio of Mexican singers provides entertainment on weekends. Moderately priced. Open Mon.–Thurs. 11 A.M.–10 P.M., Fri.–Sun. 11 A.M.–11 P.M.

Steak and Carne Asada
Along the Boulevard Juárez hotel strip, steak and *carne asada* are the clear favorites and are usually served in pseudo-rustic, ranch-style surroundings. **Restaurant Los Buffalos,** Blvd. Juárez 1990, tel. 686/566-3116 or 686/566-8338, is typical of the genre, offering highly rated steak platters, along with a few seafood and less meat-oriented Mexican dishes. Moderate to expensive. Open daily for lunch and dinner.

Vegetarian
El Mesón Vegetariano, Arcade Chapala 1096 (Centro Cívico), tel. 686/557-1219, is one of the few vegetarian restaurants in Baja specializing in Mexican dishes. Inexpensive. Open Mon.–Sat. 8 A.M.–6 P.M. **El Oasis,** Calz. Justo Sierra 1495, tel. 686/568-3311, serves international vegetarian cuisine. Inexpensive. Open daily for breakfast, lunch, and dinner.

Groceries
The city's best supermarkets include a **Gigante** at Plaza Gigante on Blvd. Juárez, almost opposite the Hotel Lucerna, and a 24-hour **Ley** on Independencia. Plaza Fiesta on Calzada López Mateos also features Ley.

SPORTS AND RECREATION
Bullfights
In Baja, Mexicali's **Plaza de Toros Calafía,** tel. 686/557-3864, is second in size only to the Plaza Monumental in Playas de Tijuana. At Boulevard de los Héroes and Calle Calafía near the Centro Cívico, the stadium hosts *corridas* two or three Sundays a month, Sept.–Nov. (especially during Fiesta del Sol in October). Current schedule information is available from the city tourist office. Ticket prices range from US$6 in general admission to US$26 for a first row seat on the shady side *(sombra);* most tickets cost US$14 –20. This is considerably less expensive than in Tijuana.

Charreadas
Mexicali has two *charro* rings: **Lienzo Charro de Mexicali,** tel. 686/566-5545, six km east of Calzada Justo Sierra on Calle Compuertas (the airport highway), and **Lienzo Charro Zaragoza,** west of Mexicali on Mexico 2. Regular *charreadas* are scheduled about once a month Sept.–Apr. but may also be held during a fiesta any time of year. Contact the city tourist office for the latest *charreada* schedules.

Baseball
Mexicali has its own baseball team, Las Águilas (The Eagles), and its local stadium is known as El Nido de las Águilas (Eagles' Nest). The stadium, in the **Ciudad Deportiva** (City Sports Complex) on Calz. Cuauhtémoc east of Calz. Justo Sierra, periodically hosts other teams in the Mexican Pacific League, as well as the occasional visiting team from the United States or Central America. The season lasts from the end of the American World Series November through late January. Seats cost around US$6–10; to find out when home games are played during the season, contact

the city tourist office or call the stadium, tel. 686/567-5129; www.aguilasdemexicali.com.mx

Sports Centers

Several sports centers in the city feature tennis courts and swimming pools open to public use for nominal day fees. **Casino de Mexicali,** Av. J.M. Suárez at Calle L, tel. 686/552-5893, is open Mon.–Fri. 6 A.M.–10 P.M., Sat. and Sun. 7 A.M.–7 P.M., while **Club Raqueta Britania,** Blvd. Anahuac and Calle Mar Baltico, tel. 686/557-1307, is open daily 6 A.M.–10 P.M. The latter also offers a restaurant, gym, sauna, and steam room. The **Mexicali Country Club** also has a pool and tennis courts.

The city-sponsored **Ciudad Deportiva,** Blvd. Cuauhtémoc, tel. 686/568-3025, features tennis courts, a swimming pool, jogging track, and a baseball stadium. The **Instituto de la Juventud y El Deporte,** Av. Salinas Cruz at Coahuila, tel. 686/557-6192, also has public tennis courts, basketball courts, and a pool. It's open 7 A.M.–11 P.M.

Golf

The **Club Social y Deportivo Campestre,** or Mexicali Country Club, at Km 11.5 on Mexico 5, Fracc. Laguna Campestre, tel. 686/563-6171, is an 18-hole, par-72, 6,628-yard golf course open to the public Tues.–Sun. 5 A.M.–7 P.M. Greens fees are considerably lower than in Tijuana.

Race and Sports Book

The ubiquitous **Caliente Race and Sports Book** has two branches in Mexicali: at Calle Melgar 116 (downtown near the border crossing) and nextdoor to Restaurant La Parroquía, Av. Reforma at Calle D. Hours for each: daily 9 A.M.–midnight.

Hunting

The Río Hardy area south of Mexicali has long been popular among visiting hunters for dove and waterfowl (see Vicinity of Mexicali), although recent regulations have made it relatively difficult to arrange for permits. Mexicali has one of only three stores on the peninsula authorized to sell ammunition to the public (the other two are in Tijuana and La Paz): **Tienda Alcampo Aceves,** Av. Zuazua 515, tel. 686/552-2782.

ENTERTAINMENT AND EVENTS

Live Music

Bars at the Lucerna, Hotel Crowne Plaza, Araiza Inn Mexicali, and Araiza Inn Calafía are popular local meeting spots where you can usually count on a *botanas* layout most weekdays around 6 P.M., with live music—*norteña,* Latin pop, international—later on in the evening.

Every Sunday afternoon during warmer weather, mariachi groups play outdoors at **Parque Constitución,** a small downtown park bordered by Avenida Zuazua, Avenida Hidalgo, Calle Mina, and Calle México.

Also see Molcajetes Bar-Grill & Pawnshop, under Food.

Discos & Bars

With nightlife in short supply in Mexicali try **Forum,** Av. Reforma and Calz. Justo Sierra, tel. 686/552-4091. Expect to pay a cover charge of US$6–7 Thurs.–Sun.

El Taurino, Calle Zuazua 480 at Calle José María Morelos, is a popular gay and lesbian bar.

Teatro del Estado (State Theater)

A variety of local and visiting theatrical, dance, and musical performances are held year-round at this modern, 1,100-seat building at Calz. López Mateos and Av. Castellanos. Ticket prices vary according to the performance but are usually quite reasonable. For information on the latest theater schedule, call 686/554-6418 or contact the city tourist office at 888/COTUCO-2.

Radio

Mexicali broadcast media receive a wide variety of transmissions from Mexican, Arizonan, and Californian stations. Two of the better local radio stations are XED (1050 AM), which mostly broadcasts Mexican folk music, and Pulsar (90.7 FM), a bilingual station that broadcasts everything from jazz to techno, banda to rock.

Events

In early February, the three-day **Salada 200** rally brings off-road racers to nearby Laguna Salada.

For information call Cachanillas Off-Road Promotions, tel. 686/552-5928.

Centered at Parque Vicente Guerrero in October, **Fiesta del Sol** celebrates the 1904 founding of Mexicali with the crowning of a festival queen, industrial/agricultural expositions, various cultural performances around town, art shows, horse races, and cockfights.

In mid-November the Chamber of Restaurants (CANIRAC) sponsors the **Muestra Gastronómica,** a food fair featuring Mexican, seafood, and Chinese cuisines. Call CANIRAC at 686/554-2666 for scheduling and venues.

SHOPPING

Mexicali features the usual border-town assortment of souvenir shops, many clustered along Calle Melgar in the downtown area, near the border crossing. **El Sarape** and **Mario's Curios,** both in the 100 block of Calle Melgar, carry a broad selection of Mexican handicrafts. As the name suggests, **Curiosidades Taxco** also on Calle Melgar, offers silverwork from the Valle de Mexico.

El Armario, Calz. Justo Sierra 1700 (Plaza Azteca, at the junction with Blvd. Juárez), tel. 686/568-1906, stocks a selection of rustic furniture, glassware, ceramics, sculpture, and other handicrafts.

Something you might not expect to find in Mexicali is a shop specializing in *guayaberas,* the pleated men's shirt characteristic of Mexico's Yucatán Peninsula. **Guayaberas Yucatecas,** in the 700 block of Av. Madero near the post office, does a good business selling these shirts to locals and visitors during Mexicali's furnacelike summers. In Mexico, the light, short-sleeved *guayabera* is considered appropriate apparel for any occasion, even in place of coat and tie.

A bit farther from downtown, **Arte Mexicano,** Calz. Independencia 3301, carries a higher quality selection of Mexican arts and crafts than most of the downtown places.

Mexicali's main *mercado municipal* is housed in a large green building on the west side of Calle Ramírez between Obregón and Lerdo de Tejada. As Mexican markets go, however, it's not a particularly interesting one.

Department Stores

Plaza Cachanilla, on Calz. López Mateos northwest of Parque Vicente Guerrero, contains over 300 stores of all types, including **Dorian's** and **Coppel,** both middle-class department stores. **Plaza Fiesta,** at the intersection of Calz. Independencia and Av. de los Héroes, has over 190 stores, including **Sanborns Department Store.** As usual, Sanborns carries a decent selection of books, magazines, and handicrafts.

INFORMATION AND SERVICES

Tourist Assistance

The Mexicali Tourism and Convention Bureau (COTUCO) maintains an office on Blvd. López Mateos at Calle Camelias (U.S. mailing address: P.O. Box 7901, Calexico, CA 92231), tel. 686/557-2561 or 888/COTUCO-2. The information counter—with a helpful, English-speaking staff—is open Mon.–Fri. 8 A.M.–7 P.M.

The SECTUR office is at Blvd. Benito Juárez 1 and Calzada Montejano, tel. 686/566-1161 or 686/558-1000. SECTUR's legal assistance department (Attorney for Tourist Protection) is headquartered here; tel./fax 686/566-1116. SECTUR is open Mon.– Fri. 8 A.M.–5 P.M., Sat. and Sun. 10 A.M.–3 P.M.

Money-Changing

Banamex, Bancomer, Banco Internacional, Serfín, and several other large Mexican banks maintain branches in Mexicali; as in most Mexican cities, the foreign-currency exchange service closes around noon each day. For better hours, shorter lines, and competitive rates, use any of the several *casas de cambio* in the vicinity of the Hotel Del Norte downtown, particularly along Madero near Azueta. The Bancomer on the northwest corner of Madero and Azueta features a 24-hour ATM.

South of downtown, Servi Cambios Mexicali in Plaza Cachanilla offers good exchange rates. As in most border towns, the best rates are given for cash rather than traveler's checks.

Downtown Calexico, near the border crossing, also features several small money changers. The dollar-to-peso rate is sometimes a bit higher here than in Mexicali, but check to see whether there's a commission before exchanging currencies.

Post and Telephone

Mexicali's main post office, at the corner of Calz. Independencia and Calle Pioneros downtown, is open Mon.–Fri. 8 A.M.–3 P.M., Saturday 9 A.M.– 1 P.M. Mail to the U.S. will move more quickly if deposited at a post office in Calexico; the main post office there is at Birch St. and George Ave., four blocks west of Imperial Avenue. A Western Union office can be found in the Mexicali post office, open Mon.–Fri. 8 A.M.–4 P.M., Saturday 8 A.M.–1 P.M. Long-distance Ladatel phones can be found throughout Mexicali; however, be sure that you know the rate before making any international call.

Mexican Consulate in Calexico

The Mexican government maintains a conveniently located consular office in Calexico, just across the border at 331 W. 2nd St., tel. 760/357-3863, fax 760/357-6284. If you're entering Mexico via Mexicali, you can save a stop in San Diego for information on tourist cards, visas, and other Mexican immigration or customs information. The consulate is open Monday–Friday 8 A.M.–3 P.M.

Border Crossing

The Mexicali border gateway is open 24 hours. Although the crossing here is less congested than Tijuana's, it's still wise to avoid morning and afternoon commute hours. If you're planning to drive east into the state of Sonora or to other points east of Baja and don't already possess a temporary vehicle import permit, obtain one from the Mexican customs office at the border. Sun.–Fri. the permits can be issued any time of day, but on Saturday issuance is restricted to the hours of 10 A.M.–2 P.M.

A second crossing east of the city links Calexico East with Mexicali's main industrial park and is open daily 6 A.M.–10 P.M.

GETTING THERE

By Air

Mexicali's **Aeropuerto Internacional General**

USEFUL MEXICALI TELEPHONE NUMBERS

Mexicali area code: 686
Central de Autobuses (Bus Depot): 557-2450
Chamber of Commerce (CANACO): 557-0005
Department of Fishing: 552-4987
Fire: 068
Green Angels: 554-0443
Highway Patrol: 552-2688
Immigration: 552-9050
IMSS Hospital: 555-5150
ISSSTE Hospital: 557-2240
Mexicali International Airport: 553-5158
Municipal Police: 060
Red Cross: 066
State Secretary of Tourism: 566-1116
Tourist Assistance: 078
U.S. Customs: 760/357-3863

Rodolfo Sánchez Taboada (MXL) lies 20 km (12 miles) east of the city via Blvd. de las Américas. **Aeroméxico,** Pasaje Alamos 1008-D, Centro Cívico Comercial, tel. 686/557-2551, and **Mexicana,** Av. Obregón, tel. 686/553-5401, each serve Mexicali from Hermosillo, Sonora, on the mainland. Mexicana also fields flights to/from Guadalajara, Monterrey, and Mexico City. The Aeroméxico flights connect with service to/from Tucson and Phoenix.

Taxi service between Mexicali and the airport costs US$15 per vehicle.

By Bus

Mexicali's intercity bus depot, Central de Autobuses, tel. 686/557-2410 or 686/557-2450, on the south side of Calz. Independencia, between Calz. López Mateos and Centro Cívico, contains a snack bar, money changer, and left-luggage service. Buses bound for northern Baja destinations are operated by **Autotransportes de Baja California (ABC)** and leave at least once a day for Tijuana (US$9–12), Ensenada (US$16–20), Tecate (US$9), and San Felipe (US$14). Southbound buses go at least once a day to La Paz

(US$105) via Santa Rosalía (US$62), Mulegé (US$70), and Loreto (US$87). **Transportes Norte de Sonora (TNS), Transportes del Pacífico,** and **Elite** handle services to these mainland destinations: Hermosillo (US$36), Guaymas (US$70), Mazatlán (US$80), Chihuahua (US$80), and Mexico City (US$120–130). To reach the bus terminal, board a bus marked Calle 6 from anywhere along Calzada López Mateos.

ABC also has a small downtown terminal on López Mateos between Azueta and Madero where you can catch buses every hour 6:30 A.M.–9:30 P.M. for Tijuana (US$10), four times a day to Ensenada (US$16), or three times a day to Tecate (US$9).

The Greyhound station in **Calexico**, tel. 760/357-1895, a few steps from the pedestrian border crossing on 1st St., offers frequent daily bus service to/from Los Angeles (US$30), San Diego (US$20), Tucson (US$46), Yuma (US$16), Phoenix (US$38), and El Paso (US$75). Greyhound also operates direct buses into Mexicali from Los Angeles for US$30 one-way.

By Train
Passenger service on the Ferrocarril Sonora-Baja California was suspended in the 1990s and is unlikely to resume in the near future.

GETTING AROUND
Buses
Mexicali's city buses are large converted school buses; the final destination is marked on the bus marquee (e.g., Centro Cívico for the civic center/zona rosa area, Justo Sierra for Calzada Justo Sierra). Many city buses start from Calle Altamirano downtown, just two blocks from the border crossing. Fares are around US$.50.

Taxis
Large *taxis de ruta* (route taxis) compete with city buses along popular routes and cost just a few pesos more. A private hired taxi costs US$3–5 within the downtown area, US$6–8 to the Centro Cívico area or the Boulevard Juárez hotel strip

from the border crossing. Taxis are most concentrated near the pedestrian border crossing and at the Lucerna, Calafía, and Crowne Plaza hotels. **Radio Taxis Cervantes,** tel. 686/568-3718, and **Ecotaxi,** tel. 686/562-6565, offer radio-dispatched, 24-hour taxi service.

Driving
Except for the congested downtown area near the border, the traffic in Mexicali moves fairly easily. Parking is sometimes a problem near the border but elsewhere in the city it is plentiful. The *glorietas* (traffic circles) are a bane for timid visiting drivers; lanes within the circles aren't generally marked, and drivers jockey for position according to where they plan to exit the circle. It's important to stay alert while maneuvering around the circle, always counterclockwise, so that when the desired spoke approaches you're in a position to take it.

To get onto Mexico 5 south for San Felipe, drive southeast on Calzada López Mateos until it meets Boulevard Juárez; follow the signs to the right (south). Just south of this intersection, Mexico 5 crosses Mexico 2, the highway west for Tecate and Tijuana or east to Sonora.

The city has plenty of Pemex stations, and most stock Premium. The Pemex opposite Plaza Cachanilla sells Premium and is open 24 hours.

Oscar Padilla Mexican Insurance, 747 Imperial Ave. in Calexico, tel. 760/357-4883, is a reliable source for auto and boat policies.

MEXICALI CAR RENTAL AGENCIES

Budget: Airport, tel. 686/552-3550; Crowne Plaza, Blvd. López Mateos at Av. de los Héroes, tel. 686/556-0888

Eco Rent: Blvd. Benito Juárez 2210, tel. 686/566-1222

Hertz: Blvd. Juárez 1223, tel. 686/568-1973

Price Rental: Blvd. Benito Juárez 1014, tel. 686/565-6363

NORTHERN BAJA

Vicinity of Mexicali

Southeast of Mexicali lies the agricultural Valle de Mexicali and Río Colorado delta area. Before the Mexican government's expropriation of foreign-owned lands in the 1930s, much of the delta belonged to the U.S.-based Colorado River Land Company. Since then, it's been divided among *ejidos*, many named for mainland Mexican states and cities. A network of two-lane state highways connects the *ejidos* with the small farm towns of Nuevo León, Murguia, Victoria, Ledón, Coahuila, Ciudad Morelos, and Los Algodones.

The state border between Baja California Norte and Sonora runs along the Río Colorado as far south as Coahuila. Mexico 2 east enters Sonora at the town of San Luis; once you cross the state line eastward, a temporary import permit is required for any vehicle not bearing Mexican license plates (this doesn't apply if you drive south from Nogales, Arizona, into Sonora, where a special no-permit program for the state of Sonora is available). Auto permits are available at the Mexican customs office at the Mexicali border crossing; in Baja, no permit is necessary. Remember to set your watch an hour ahead when crossing the Colorado—Sonora is on mountain time.

One of the more interesting *ejido* towns in the delta, if only because it straddles the BCN–Sonora line, is **Coahuila.** At the southeast end of BCN 4, past a toll bridge spanning the Colorado, this Baja outpost sits smack in the middle of the delta; the bumpy streets are paved with clay blocks. The popular **Restaurante India Bonita,** renowned for *milanesa* and *carne asada,* is almost reason enough to make the trip. The only other reason is to say you've crossed the Colorado River in Mexico; in Coahuila, when you stroll over the state line you pay a visit to Sonora.

Southeast of Coahuila, about 69 km (43 miles) into Sonora via SON 40, is **El Golfo de Santa Clara,** the northernmost town on the Sea of Cortez. This small fishing town has a couple of cafés, markets, a church, motel (Nuevo Motel del Golfo, US$32), Pemex station, and three campground/RV parks (US$5 tents/campers,

US$12–18 full hookups). A sandy road to the southeast leads into an area of dunes popular with ATV riders. At high tide, dunes become sandy beaches; low tide exposes broad mudflats where large clams are plentiful. Anyone bringing a boat to El Golfo should also possess a current set of Cortez tide tables, as the tidal range is extensive. From May through mid-September, summer heat turns the desert delta into an inferno.

LOS ALGODONES

This tidy, friendly *poblado* of around 12,000 inhabitants in the northeast corner of Baja California Norte, eight km (five miles) west of Yuma, Arizona, is named for the main cash crop in the region—cotton—brought by settlers from Sonora in the mid-19th century. Prickly pear cactus farms are also common in this area. West of town off BCN 8 are several roadside workshops where you can see bricks—both air-dried (adobe) and fired—being made.

In the town itself, however, the biggest business is dentistry for Americans; fees for dental services run 30–50 percent less than in the United States. Two or three dental clinics appear on virtually every commercial block.

The most common Baja gateway for Arizona residents, Los Algodones also receives a steady stream of day visitors from Yuma County, one of the top three "snowbird" counties in the United States (where retired Americans choose to spend their winters).

Sights

The southern tip of the huge **Algodones Dunes** complex straddles the United States–Mexico border just west of town. To reach it, drive west along Mariano Ma. Lee until it ends about eight blocks from the border crossing. Formed at the northeast banks of an extinct Pleistocene sea, the 650-square-km Algodones Dunes area is the driest spot in North America save for Death Valley and the Mojave Desert. Iron-bearing minerals lend a reddish tinge to some of the dunes.

Presa Morelos (Morelos Dam), constructed in 1950 as part of the Valle de Mexicali irrigation system, lies about 6.5 km (four miles) south of town via Calle 6. This is Mexico's only dam on the Río Colorado, which runs roughly 160 km (100 miles) south of the border before emptying into the Sea of Cortez. Considering the All-American Canal System and the 10 major dams on the U.S. side, it's a wonder any water is left in the river by the time it crosses the border—a sore spot in United States–Mexico relations since the early 20th century. The U.S. government is considering cementing the bottom of the All-American Canal to stop underground seepage—an action that would further decrease Mexico's supply of Río Colorado runoff.

Food

A popular restaurant in town among day visitors is **Pueblo Viejo,** tel. 658/514-7890, a combination Mexican restaurant, souvenir shop, and bar right on the border at Calle 2 and Mariano Ma. Lee. On Calle 1, the similar **El Paraíso,** tel. 658/517-7956, has been in business since 1953, serving Mexican dishes at reasonable prices; open daily 8 A.M.–10 P.M. Nearby **Asadero Los Pioneros de Algodones,** an outdoor taco place popular with locals, is also recommended. Other good spots in the tourist zone include **Rincón Tapatillo, Tucán, El Rancherito, El Mesón de Don Alfonso,** and **Restaurant Bar Olímpico.**

Shopping and Entertainment

Los Algodones pharmacies and liquor stores, concentrated along Calle 1 and several square blocks directly opposite the border crossing, do a booming business serving Yuma snowbirds. The **Mercado de Artesanías,** at the Parque de la Ciudad at Calle 4 and Av. B, offers a variety of Mexican handicrafts.

On the main tourist strip, **Caliente Race and Sports Book** offers a venue for betting on all manner of televised sports events taking place in and out of Mexico.

Information and Services

A Mexican insurance company at Calle 1 and Mariano Ma. Lee distributes tourist information on Los Algodones and northern Baja. It can also recommend dental clinics. The city has it's own website at www.losalgodones.com

You can change money at a *casa de cambio* on Av. B between Calles 2 and 3 (near the church and telegraph office). The post office is on Calle 5 at Av. D.

NORTHERN BAJA

SAND FOOD AND SIDEWINDERS

In spite of the fact that the Algodónes Dunes average less than 7.5 cm (three inches) of rainfall a year, the dunes aren't entirely barren. Evening primrose, sand verbena, desert lily, creosote bush, and other long-rooted plants grow in the hollows between the dunes, lending shape and structure to the landscape. Even during long rainless periods, extensive root systems enable these plants to survive by tapping into pockets of moisture deep below the sandy surface.

Living in symbiosis with these plants is the hidden sand food *(Ammobroma sonorae),* a root unique to the Sonoran Desert. It grows beneath the dunes, tapping moisture and sugar from the other vegetation through a network of root hairs barely touching the host plants. It is not quite a parasite, for in times when the host plants lack moisture, they receive nourishment from the sand food. The Sonoran Papago Amerindians depended on the sand-colored, melon-flavored root as part of their desert diet, and it was known to early European desert travelers as well— hence its odd English name.

Animate life in the dunes includes the common desert iguana; the sidewinder *(Crotalus cerastes),* a rattlesnake whose means of locomotion—tossing its body in side-to-side loops—is uniquely suited to sandy environments; and the rare fringe-toed lizard, the only reptile species totally limited to sand dunes.

Border Crossing

The border crossing, along with offices of Mexican immigration, tel. 658/517-7721, and customs, tel. 658/517-7733, is open 6 A.M.–10 P.M.

Transportation

A bus depot at Av. A and Calle 2 serves buses west to Mexicali (US$10) and Tijuana (US$18). Yuma, Arizona, eight km (five miles) east of Los Algodones, offers a Greyhound station and a regional airport.

A Pemex station at the corner of Av. B and Calle 5 pumps diesel, Magna Sin (unleaded regular), and Premium gasoline.

If you don't plan to drive into Algodones, you can park at a large security lot on the American side for US$4 a day or in a free dirt lot across the road.

MEXICO 2 TO TECATE

West of Mexicali, Mexico 2 skirts the northern edge of the Sierra de los Cucapá and flattens out along the top of **Laguna Salada,** a huge dry salt lake extending southward nearly 100 km (60 miles). At Km 24, an unpaved, ungraded road leads south to the northern shore of the lake, where a small fish camp survives on accumulated runoff from the Río Colorado delta; visitors are permitted to camp overnight. A Pemex station near this junction offers a chance to gas up before proceeding farther along Mexico 2 or south along Laguna Salada. The next gas station is 53 km (33 miles) west, in La Rumorosa.

Between Mexicali and Tecate on Mexico 2-D there are two tolls of US$2.50.

Palm Canyons

Several steep-walled palm canyons cutting deeply into the eastern escarpment of the Sierra Juárez have become prime destinations for a generation of adventurous visitors to northeastern Baja's desert extremes. The larger Tajo, El Carrizo, Guadalupe, and El Palomar canyons contain year-round streams and *tinajas* (springs) and are highly desirable hiking and backpacking destinations from November through mid-April. From late April to October, temperatures often exceed 37°C (100°F)—not the best of conditions for desert hiking. For all overnight hikes, come prepared for wilderness camping.

At Km 28 off Mexico 2-D, a graded and unpaved road to the south threads between the western edge of Laguna Salada and the eastern escarpment of the Sierra Juárez. Because of the way the toll highway (Mexico 2-D) is constructed—there is no free road along this stretch—you cannot take this turnoff directly if you're coming from Mexicali; a concrete barrier along the highway blocks access from the highway's north lanes, so you have to continue toward Tecate until you find a place to make a U-turn.

Although washboard surfaces much of the way mean progress is slow, the road to the canyon areas is adequate for ordinary passenger vehicles as far south as the turnoff for Cañon de Guadalupe; beyond that a four-wheel-drive vehicle is usually necessary.

Cañon Tajo, the most spectacular of the palm canyons, is reached by an unmarked sand road that branches west off the Laguna Salada road 34.5 km (21.5 miles) south of Mexico 2. From this point, most vehicles can only make it 2.5 km (1.5 miles) or so before the track contours become too extreme and the sand too deep; after that it's 5.5 km (3.5 miles) of hard slogging across sandflats to the mouth of the canyon. If you're concerned about security, you might be able to leave your vehicle at tiny **Rancho los Laureles del Desierto,** about a mile west of the Tajo turnoff, before hiking in.

Your hike will be rewarded by a wide canyon studded with thousands of fan palms and adorned with freshwater pools below 450-meter (1,500-foot) granite walls. It's 6.5 km (four miles) to the head of the canyon, where an old Amerindian trail leads north; you can see—but not touch—a number of petroglyphs and Amerindian relics along the way. *Borregón* (desert bighorn sheep) and deer occasionally wander into the canyon.

The signed turnoff west to **Cañon de Guadalupe** comes along nine km (5.6 miles) south of the Tajo turnoff, or about 44 km (27.5 miles) south of Mexico 2. Unlike the approach to

Tajo, this side road is passable by car or truck all the way to the mouth of the canyon (12 km/7.5 miles), where you'll find a public campground and hot mineral springs. Average driving time is 45 minutes. About five km (3.2 miles) from the main road, the road to Guadalupe jogs left—ignore the lesser fork that goes straight. Shortly thereafter the road narrows considerably, and at 9.6 km (six miles) the road surface contains many exposed boulders and large rocks that could pose problems for vehicles with lower-than-normal clearance. This is a pretty road, with lots of paloverde, cholla, ocotillo, and other Baja desert flora along the way.

Although not as large as Tajo, Cañon de Guadalupe is impressive, with tiered waterfalls, pools, and plenty of blue fan palms. The main stream through the canyon leads to the "Pool of the Virgin," surrounded by white granite walls and fringed with ferns, cottonwoods, and willows. As in Cañon Tajo, there are signs of an ear-lier Amerindian presence. Both canyons were used by the Cucapá and Paipai during seasonal pilgrimages to collect piñon nuts on the Sierra Juárez plateau.

At around 12 km (7.5 miles) from the main road a fence marks off **Guadalupe Canyon Hot Springs and Campground,** divided into three separate sections—Campo 1, Campo 2, and Campo 3. Campsites start at US$20/night for one auto on weekends during low season (June 2–Oct. 14). During peak season (Oct. 15–June 1) on weekdays the cost is US$25–40 per night for one auto. There's a two-night minuimum on weekends (US$60–200 for two nights), and a three-night minimum on holidays (US$200–400 for three nights); rates depend on the campsite and number of vehicles. Each of the 20 campsites comes with its own cement hot tub linked to the main hot springs, which pump out 120,000 gallons a day at temperatures of 41.5°C (107°F). Some sites are better than others, so take your time making a choice.

Outhouses and showers are available, and a small market sells burritos, tacos, egg dishes, and soft drinks. Firewood is also available. The campgrounds are open year-round but are most popular during the cooler winter months. Weekends and holidays can be crowded—you'll do much better to visit during the week. For information, write Rob's Baja Tours, P.O. Box 4003, Balboa, CA 92661, call 949/673-2670, email canyonmanrob@earthlink.net, or visit www.guadalupe-canyon.com.

An **alternate route** to reach the Cañon de Guadalupe turnoff from Mexico 2-D is usually quicker and smoother than the more well-known road described at the top of this section. Leaving the highway between Km 23 and 24 (accessible only when driving east from Tecate), opposite a Pemex station, this track goes right through the middle of Laguna Salada. It's only one lane wide, so you may have to pull over for other vehicles along the way, but the road is usually considerably smoother and less washboard-prone. Along the expansive salt flats in the middle, you can often drive much faster than on the main road. Some sections of the road feature soft sand, so you must be adept at sand driving—during the odd rain the road may be temporarily impassable.

© JOE CUMMINGS

Cañon de Guadalupe

The main problem with this road is that at its southern end, near the turnoff for Cañon de Guadalupe, it intersects a maze of connecting roads running in all directions, making it rather difficult to find the canyon access road. For this reason, we recommend using the main road coming south, then returning to the highway via the Laguna Salada road—you can ask for directions from the campground proprietors and at the same time inquire about road conditions.

La Rumorosa

At around Km 44, Mexico 2-D begins climbing the Juárez escarpment along the steep Cantú grade (also called Cuesta de la Rumorosa). The town of La Rumorosa, topping the grade at Km 68, is named for the constant murmuring of winds through the 1,275-meter (4,200-foot) mountain pass. Many Tijuana and Mexicali residents own summer homes in the vicinity, and the town holds a couple of cafés (**Restaurant Sonorita** is recommended), bakeries, grocery stores, a Red Cross, and a self-serve Pemex station.

Descending along the more gradual western slope of the Sierra Juárez, the environment changes rapidly from the arid, scrubby vegetation east of the mountains to piñon stands and chaparral. The toll between Mexicali and Rumorosa is US$.65; there is no longer a free road along this stretch.

La Rumorosa to Laguna Hanson

West of La Rumorosa at Km 73 is a dirt road that leads 63 km (39 miles) south to Laguna Hanson (also known as Laguna Juárez), part of the Parque Nacional Constitución de 1857. The road is graded for the first 37 km (23 miles) or so but rapidly deteriorates as it approaches the national park's northern boundary. High-clearance vehicles, preferably with four-wheel drive, are recommended for this route.

The more popular and easier route into the national park is via Mexico 3, southeast of Ensenada. For information on this road, and on the national park itself, see East from Ensenada.

El Condor to Tecate

At El Condor (Km 83), 14.5 km (nine miles) west of La Rumorosa, another unpaved road

heads south to Laguna Hanson, passing the ranchos of Cisneros, Jacaranda, El Encanto, Tres Pozos, and others. Although this route proves slower going than the La Rumorosa road, there's more to see, including several abandoned mines. Just beyond Rancho Jesayo and Mina Margarita (Margarita Mine), about 30 km from Mexico 2, the road joins the La Rumorosa–Laguna Hanson road. Basic services—food and gas—are available in El Condor.

The *ejido* settlement of **El Hongo** appears off Mexico 2 at Km 99, where a paved road leads southwest toward Hacienda Santa Veronica and a network of unpaved roads and vehicle tracks in the western foothills of the Sierra Juárez. The largest is an 83.5-km (52-mile) road, mostly ungraded, that winds southward to join the Mexico 3–Laguna Hanson road near Rancho El Coyote. Along the way are several ranchos and abandoned mines, including **La Rosa de Castilla,** a former gold-mining center that served as the territorial capital (1870–82) before Ensenada. This road is suitable for high-clearance vehicles only.

Beyond El Hongo, Mexico 2 dips through rolling dairy farms and olive groves, a relatively uneventful ride until you arrive in Tecate at Km 130. You may be able to camp at one of the *ejidos* between El Hongo and Tecate for US$5–10 a night.

MEXICO 5 TO SAN FELIPE

Mexico 5, the paved, mostly two-lane highway (some parts have four lanes) between Mexicali and San Felipe, is flat all the way and features one of the more durable roadbeds in Baja. Gringo rumor says the road was originally built by the U.S. Army Corps of Engineers following World War II to provide access to a radar station at Bahía de San Felipe's south end; local authorities insist it was 100 percent Mexican-built.

The first 45 km (27 miles) of the highway is flanked by *ejido* lands with irrigated vegetable farms and dairy farms. You'll find several nopal (prickly pear cactus) farms along the highway around Km 15; fresh and pickled cactus is sold from roadside stands.

Just south of the town of **La Puerta,** at Km 38,

BCN 4 branches east to the town of Coahuila and the Sonoran state border. La Puerta offers a Pemex station, a market, and a café. At about Km 48, the pastureland gives way abruptly to desert as you reach the southern limit of the delta irrigation system.

Río Hardy

Beginning at around Km 50 off Mexico 5, the marshy Río Hardy is easily accessed by a number of dirt tracks heading east off the highway. Several rustic *campos,* mostly catering to hunters and anglers, lie along the river to its junction with the Río Colorado (about 15 km southeast).

The Río Hardy attracts migrating bird species, including pintails, green-wing teals, egrets, pelicans, coots, cranes, and a dozen or more duck species. The main quarry for visiting hunters are quail and white-wing and mourning doves. Dove-hunting season generally runs Sept.–Dec.

Local Cucapá Amerindians fish the river for carp, flathead catfish, largemouth and striped bass, and, more recently, *mojarra* (tilapia), a prolific African species that has come down into the Río Hardy through locks in Colorado River dams. Reportedly, the best fishing is at the junction of the Hardy and Colorado Rivers, near Campo Los Amigos. This area is accessible by vehicle track from Río El Mayor (Km 55) or San Miguel, about 12 km farther south, just before the causeway over Laguna Salada.

Just south of **Cucapá el Mayor** (also called El Mayor Indígena), around Km 57, the tiny **Museo Cucapá** stands alongside a police station. Exhibits inside include historical photographs and artifacts, while outside the center are models of traditional willow-and-arrow weed thatched homes. An area is also set aside for the display and sale of traditional handmade Cucapá crafts, such as beaded collars and willow-and-cottonwood bark skirts. The museum is open daily 10 A.M.–1 P.M.

Camps in the Río Hardy area open and close from year to year depending on river conditions. They include Sonora, Las Cabañas, Mosqueda, Río Hardy, Club BBB, El Mayor, Muñoz, and Los Amigos. **Sonora, Las Cabañas, Mosqueda, Río Hardy,** and **El Mayor** are usually open and can accommodate RVs; rates are around US$10–12 a night. Las Cabañas also offers rustic cabins for rent.

La Ventana to San Felipe

Kilometer 105 marks the one-café town of La Ventana—sneeze and you'll miss it. The Pemex station at La Ventana is no longer open for business, so if you need to gas up you'd best stop earlier in Ejido Nayarit, at Km 31—coming from Mexicali, this is the last Pemex station before San Felipe. Farther south at Km 122 is an unpaved, graded road leading west to the Sierra Las Pintas and three abandoned mines: La Fortuna, Buena Vista, and La Escondida. A fourth, Jueves Santo, is still a working gold mine.

South of this turnoff, the highway crosses **Llano El Chinero** (Chinese Plain), where a large group of Chinese immigrants died of heat and thirst while trying to reach Mexicali on foot in the early 20th century. The lone peak east of the highway is 200-meter **Cerro El Chinero.**

Mexico 5 intersects with Mexico 3, the highway to Ensenada, at **Crucero La Trinidad** (Km 140). Just south of the junction is a Pemex station. A string of signs for beach camps on the east side of the highway, beginning at around Km 172, marks the final approach to San Felipe, reached at Km 189.

San Felipe and Vicinity

This unlikely beach community (pop. 11,000) squeezed between the San Felipe Desert and the Sea of Cortez received its name from Jesuit Padre Fernando Consag, who briefly landed four canoes here in 1746 and named the gently curving bay San Felipe de Jesús. In 1797, a padre from Misión San Pedro Mártir de Verona established a supply port at Bahía San Felipe; both the port and mission failed in 1806. In the late 19th and early 20th centuries, virtually the only people who knew of San Felipe's existence were nomadic fishermen working the Sea of Cortez coast.

The post–World War II construction of a paved road to a radar station at the south end of the bay finally linked San Felipe with the outside world. In the late 1940s and '50s, American anglers came in droves to land *totuava,* a strong-fighting, copper-silver-gray croaker with a weight range of 16–115 kg (35–254 pounds). Old-timers say it's one of the tastiest fish in the Cortez, but since they fished the species onto the endangered species list, most of us will never get a taste. Mexican law now forbids the taking of totuava.

The bay is protected from north-northeast winds by Punta San Felipe, a jutting headland topped by 240-meter Cerro El Machorro at the bay's north end. The summit offers a good view of the bay and bears a shrine dedicated to the Virgin of Guadalupe. Below the headland are an estuary and boatyard. At the bay's south end, an artificial harbor shelters the local commercial shrimp fleet—one of five such fleets licensed to net shrimp along Mexico's entire west coast. The tidal range in the northern Cortez is

extreme, so only the harbor's outer section is suitable for larger craft.

San Felipe today is a beach playground for Californians and Arizonans who camp or park their RVs on the many golden-hued beaches extending north and south of the bay. The nearby dunes attract dune-buggy and ATV enthusiasts who scream up and down the sloping sands with Cerro Juan (1,025 meters/3,369 feet) and Cerro

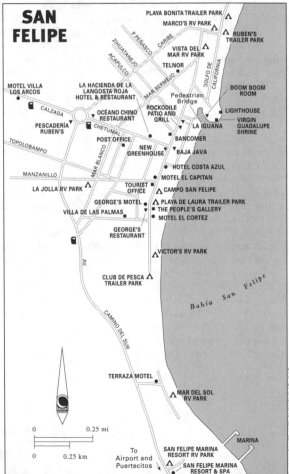

Kino (1,304 meters/4,290 feet) to the west as a backdrop. A number of Americans have retired in San Felipe, but most gringos come for a cheap beach or fishing vacation within two to three hours' drive of the U.S. border.

Visitors going no farther than San Felipe are not required to pay the US$15 tourist fee if staying less than 72 hours.

Climate and Tourist Season

Peak tourist season in the San Felipe area is Nov.–Apr., when temperatures are mild. Note, though, that Dec.–Feb. the northern Cortez may be a bit chilly for most swimmers. May–Oct., daytime air temperatures frequently break 38°C (100°F), but it doesn't get quite as hot as Mexicali. In summer, many gringos residing in San Felipe go elsewhere—usually to the Pacific coast—to cool off. Rainfall at any time of year is virtually nil.

ACCOMMODATIONS

Because San Felipe is so popular and so close to the U.S. border, hotel and motel rates tend to be a bit on the high side, at least for Baja. Rate categories below correspond to peak-season (Nov.–Apr.) prices. Off-season rates drop as much as 30 percent. Add 12 percent hotel tax to all rates unless otherwise specified; some hotels may charge an additional 10 percent service charge.

During the last two weeks of March, San Felipe is filled with hundreds of Arizona and California college and university students celebrating spring break. Needless to say, this is a bad time to look for a room.

US$25–50

Near the marina at the south edge of town, **Terraza Motel,** Av. Misión de Loreto 103, tel./fax 686/577-1844, offers a cluster of 12 separate, prefabricated cabins built on a hillside near the marina and beach. Each cabin has TV and a hot-water shower. Out by the entrance to town coming from Mexicali, near the arches monument, **Motel Villa Los Arcos,** Calz. Chetumal s/n, tel. 686/577-1588, contains 11 comfortable rooms in duplex whitewashed, red-tiled cabins, each with its own parking spaces. All units come with air-

conditioning, TV, and kitchenettes. A small pool area in back offers palapa-shaded chairs. Villa Los Arcos is not within easy walking distance of the beach.

Near the waterfront in the center of town, aging **Motel Chapala,** Av. Mar de Cortés, is the cheapest sleep in town. Despite its worn look, it's clean and safe. On the opposite side of the street, farther south, **Motel El Capitán,** Av. Mar de Cortés 298 (P.O. Box 1916, Calexico, CA 92231), tel./fax 686/577-1303, bsf@telnor.net, is a well-run, two-story place with 45 rooms built around a large parking lot and small pool. Rooms are clean and each has air-conditioning, TV, and a large private bathroom. The waterfront is a short walk away. El Capitán is popular with Mexican business travelers. Weekend rates are considerably higher than midweek rates.

Hotel La Hacienda de la Langosta Roja, Calz. Chetumal 125, tel. 686/577-0483, is a large two-story place attached to the Hacienda de la Langosta Roja restaurant, off the main avenue coming into town. All 24 rooms have air-conditioning and satellite TV that receives only two channels.

US$50–100

A few older hotels farther south in town are struggling for business but are perfectly acceptable. Inland a short walk from the beach, **Villa de las Palmas,** Av. Mar Báltico 1101, tel. 686/577-1333, is a rambling complex with tennis and volleyball courts, a pool, restaurant, and bar. At one time this was San Felipe's best hotel. It's quiet, and rooms are large; all have air-conditioning.

George's Motel, next door to George's Restaurant at Av. Mar de Cortés 336, tel. 686/577-1970, georges@sanfelipe.com.mx, has 12 good-sized, very clean, air-conditioned rooms with satellite TV.

Motel El Cortez, east of the Palmas on Av. Mar de Cortés, tel. 686/577-1055, fax 686/577-1056, cortezno@telnor.net, is a long building right on the beach with a pool, boat launch, laundry, beach *palapas,* and a restaurant. The 109 rooms have air-conditioning, TV, and phone.

Costa Azul Hotel, Av. Mar de Cortés at Calle Ensenada, tel. 686/577-1548, fax 686/577-1549, a sprawling three-story hotel with a swimming pool, coffee shop, restaurant, bar, and parking lot, offers 140 spacious but very bland rooms with air-conditioning, satellite TV, and phone. Room rates are high, even for San Felipe, and the hotel doesn't seem to get much business.

San Felipe Marina Resort and Spa, farther south off Av. Camino del Sur, tel. 686/577-1455 or 800/025-6925, U.S. tel. 800/291-5397, fax 686/577-1566, www.sanfelipe.com.mx, snmarina@telnor.net, offers nicely furnished accommodations. Rates vary tremendously according to the day of the week and the size of the unit. Rooms have fully equipped kitchens, satellite TV, and phones. Other amenities include a pool, tennis courts, a restaurant and bar, snack bar, indoor heated pool, outdoor pool with panoramic view, lighted tennis courts, a clubhouse, gym, sauna, massage room, minimarket, and laundry. Construction of a 243-slip marina has been halted, with no plans in sight for completion. The beach, a short walk away, is not San Felipe's best because of its proximity to the marina.

Condominiums

The San Felipe area has a rising number of "condotels" and resort villas—often part time-share, part hotel, and part year-round condo complex. Ask at the tourist office about renting local condos or apartments by the night; in some cases they're a better deal than the local hotels and motels. A typical place with two bedrooms and two bathrooms goes for US$50 per day Sun.–Thurs., US$100 per day Fri. and Sat., or US$300 per week.

US$50–100: The following is a list of condominiums between San Felipe and El Faro beach: **Suites Josefinas,** tel. 686/577-1673, 11 suites, ocean view with kitchenette; **Condominiums Playa Bonita,** tel. 686/577-1215, U.S. tel. 626/967-8977, www.sanfelipebeachcondos.com, eight full-service condo units on the beach with campgrounds available; and **Condominiums Careyes del Golfo,** tel. 686/577-1346, on the beach with 16 full-service units, kitchenettes, and two baths.

El Dorado Ranch, tel. 686/576-0402, U.S./Canada tel. 303/790-1749 or 800/404-2599, www.eldoradoranch.com, is a large gated community north of town with vacation and retirement homes for rent and for sale. Facilities include a tennis club, restaurant, bar, campground, car rental, recreational equipment rentals, *palapas,* heated pool, and whirlpool tub. Rates vary; call for information.

Camping and RV Parks

Over two dozen beachfront operations, both right in San Felipe and to the north and south of town, tout themselves as campgrounds or RV parks. Some—mostly those out of town—offer few facilities beyond a graded road between the highway and beach. Others come with full RV hookups, restaurants, bars, hot showers, and flush toilets.

Those in town generally cost US$20–30 nightly per site for two people, plus US$3–5 for each additional person. Long-term stays generally cost US$100 per week or US$350 per month. The beach camps farther north and south of town typically run US$5–10 for two per site, depending on the facilities, plus US$2 for each additional person; long-term stays of seven days or more earn 10–20 percent discounts.

The most popular campgrounds among the RV crowd are those along the beach just north of Punta San Felipe, on the outskirts of town. This area generally receives a good sea breeze and is thus cooler than parks on the bay itself. If you don't like the first one you try, you can always move to another. **Playa Bonita RV Park,** tel. 686/577-1215, U.S. tel. 626/967-4250, www.sanfelipebeachcondos.com (US$25 for full hookups), and **Ruben's RV Trailer Park,** Av. Golfo de California 703, tel. 686/577-2021 (US$15 a night, full hookups only), are particularly popular for their large deck-topped *palapas.* Ruben's caters to a younger crowd these days, and some people might complain about the sound level of the music emanating from the Coco Loco House Restaurant and Bar. Playa Bonita takes phone reservations; Ruben's doesn't.

Cheaper spots in this area include **Marco's,** tel. 686/577-1872, and **Vista del Mar,** tel. 686/577-1252, both back from the beach with rates of US$10–14 per vehicle.

On the beach toward the south end of town

trailer park, San Felipe

but still within easy walking distance of shopping and restaurants is a cluster of places that have been around a long time. All offer hot showers and flush toilets. Almost across from Motel El Capitán, **Campo San Felipe,** Av. Mar de Cortés, tel. 686/577-1012, charges US$15–20 for RVs depending on proximity to the beach. Next south along this stretch is **Playa de Laura RV Park,** tel. 686/577-1128, where simple spots with picnic tables and ramadas cost US$10 for tents, US$16–30 for RVs, depending on proximity to the beach. **Club de Pesca RV and Trailer Park,** tel. 686/577-1180, fax 686/577-1888, sits at the southern end of Av. Mar de Cortés; many of the sites are permanent, but a few places are usually available toward the beachfront—for US$25 a night—if you call in advance. Nearby **Victor's RV Park,** tel. 686/577-1055, is similar.

South of town is San Felipe's top trailer park, 84-site **Mar del Sol,** tel. 686/657-1280, U.S. tel. 800/336-5454. The management doesn't allow motorcycles, ATVs, or dune buggies, so it's one of the quietest trailer parks in San Felipe. Facilities include hot showers, flush toilets, pool, tennis courts, restaurant, *palapas,* boat launch, coin laundry, and groceries. RV sites are expensive by Baja standards: US$27 beachfront, US$23 back row, US$12 tent site. Discounts are given for Good Sam members and long-term stays.

Farther south on the bay, the **San Felipe Marina Resort RV Park,** tel. 686/577-1455 or 800/025-6925, U.S. tel. 800/291-5397, fax 686/577-1566, offers 143 large spaces overlooking a marine diesel storage facility, a marina, and the Sea of Cortez. Sites (US$20) have full hookups, including satellite cable TV, and unshaded concrete patios big enough to park an extra vehicle on. Facilities include a clubhouse, coin laundry, showers and restrooms, heated swimming pools, a well-stocked minimarket, and 24-hour security. The park is part of a 50-acre development that includes a 60-unit hotel (San Felipe Marina Resort and Spa, mentioned previously); all hotel facilities are available for the use of RV guests (there are separate entrances for the RV park and hotel).

Well away from the beach is **La Jolla RV Park,** Av. Manzanillo at Mar Bermejo, tel. 686/577-1222, where palapa-shaded spaces cost US$15 a night, less for long-term stays. La Jolla takes phone reservations.

Residence Faro Beach Trailer Park, at Punta Estrella 16 km south of town, offers full hookups (including 24-hour electricity), hot showers, tennis courts, a pool, and a bar, but no restaurant and no telephone. Cost: US$15 per night.

FOOD

Seafood is what San Felipe restaurants do best. Vendors sell fresh seafood cocktails and fish tacos along the *malecón* (waterfront) toward the south end of Paseo de Cortés. Some sell platters with two fish tacos, rice, and beans for only US$1.50. One of the better seafood joints along the waterfront, **Mariscos Conchita's,** specializes in steamed clams and oysters on the half shell, along with the usual fish tacos. **Plaza Maritaco,** in the same vicinity, brings together a collection of fish taco stalls.

A block and a half west of the *malecón* is **La Hacienda de la Langosta Roja,** Calz. Chetumal 121, tel. 686/577-1571, the only restaurant in town with a patio receiving full sun all day during the winter. Seafood entrées are moderately priced; the ceviche tostadas are delicious, and beer is served in chilled mugs. Open for breakfast, lunch, and dinner.

George's Restaurant Bar, Av. Mar de Cortés 336, tel. 686/577-1057, is a favorite among gringo regulars who come for the dependable seafood dinners and American breakfasts; hours are 7 A.M.–10 P.M.

Wherever you find a heavy concentration of gringos in Baja, you can be sure there's an **El Nido** steakhouse nearby, complete with wagon wheels and stone facade. San Felipe's is at Av. Mar de Cortés 348, tel. 686/577-1028, in the same area as George's. The menu features the usual steak and ranchero standards; dependable, but not particularly inspiring. Open Thurs.–Tues. 2–10 P.M.

Good Mexican breakfasts can be found at **Las Chabelas** on Mar Jónico Sur just off Chetumal. Look for a vintage 1928 Ford truck out front. Seating is in an outdoor patio that resembles a museum with antique artifacts, such as an old cast-iron stove and a horse-drawn buggy. Moderately priced. Open daily 8 A.M.–noon.

New Greenhouse, 132 Av. Mar de Cortés, is one of the only places to enjoy a not-too-greasy breakfast. For lunch and dinner it serves tasty seafood entrées. The fish tacos are especially good, and inexpensive. Open daily 7 A.M.–10 P.M.; closed in September. You can also enjoy café latte and fresh baked goods, sandwiches, bagels, or a light breakfast at **Baja Java,** upstairs on the corner of on Av. Mar de Cortés and Calz. Chetumal. It has a sunny patio with a view of Bahía de San Felipe.

Restaurant Bar Los Mandliles (also known as La Esquina de Luis), diagonally opposite Baja Java, is one of the oldest restaurants in town. With its bar and pool table, it's more of a local hangout but the Mexican menu, mostly *antojitos,* is fine, and the sidewalk tables are a plus. **Océano Chino Restaurant,** on Calz. Chetumal, presents another alternative.

To the north of Calzada Chetumal on Avenida Mar de Cortés are several small, inexpensive cafés, including **Petunia's Café** at the corner of Calle Puerto de Acapulco and Avenida Mar de Cortés. The main draw: tacos and burritos, along with Mexican and American breakfasts. **Lonchería El Club,** near Rockodile on the *malecón,* is very popular for Mexican breakfasts, including *chilaquiles,* one of Mexico's best hangover remedies.

Rockodile Patio and Grill, on the *malecón,* tel. 686/577-1219, serves tasty fish tacos along with a tray of six different condiments. It also has burgers, fries, and huge beef tacos, called "tacodiles." Food is served from around noon till midnight. **International Rosita,** at the north end of the *malecón,* is a friendly, nautical-kitsch-decorated spot with good Mexican standards and seafood. Open daily 9 A.M.–10 P.M.

Groceries: Several *tiendas* along Calz. Chetumal, on the way into San Felipe, sell fresh vegetables, ice, canned goods, and camping/household supplies. **Panaficadora Singapur,** on Av. Mar de Cortés, has the town's widest selection of baked items.

To buy fresh, locally harvested finfish and shellfish, pay a visit to one of the *pescaderías* off Av. Mar de Cortés just north of Punta Santa Felipe. Run by local fishing co-ops, they are usually open daily 7 A.M.–7 P.M. Look for **Pescadería**

Pepito and **Pescadería San Felo** or, on Calzada Chetumal at the traffic circle as you enter town, **Pescadería Rubén.**

SPORTS AND RECREATION

Fishing

Although the San Felipe fishery is not what it used to be, with the magnificent totuava now a protected species and many other varieties in the northern Cortez also becoming scarce, sportfishing is still one of the primary local tourist activities. The high fishing season is Mar.–June, when white sea bass runs are common. Croakers are available year-round, corvinas late March through November. Cabrilla, yellowtail, sierra, and grouper are plentiful May–Oct.; in the fall you can catch pompano.

Generally, the best onshore fishing area runs from Punta San Felipe north, while inshore fishing is good from Punta Estrella south. The best offshore fishing and the best overall is found around Roca Consag, 27 km (17 miles) east of Punta San Felipe. This is a particularly good area for croaker and white sea bass. For those with time to spare, multiday live-aboard trips reach the Midriff Islands 400 km (250 miles) to the south, where sportfishing is excellent.

A sportfishing service at the north end of the *malecón,* **Tommy Sport Fishing,** tel. 686/577-0446, offers guided fishing trips aboard eight-meter (24-foot) *pangas.* A 7 A.M.–noon bay fishing trip costs US$40 pp or US$35 pp for three or more people; bay angling usually nets calico bass, small croaker, sierra, or triggerfish. An all-day trip to Roca Consag (45 minutes away by boat) costs US$150 for two anglers or US$160 for three. Out at Roca Consag you may bag sierra, yellowtail, large croakers, and corvina. Bait, tackle, and poles are provided. Bring your own beer and sandwiches.

Down at the new marina, **Minimarket Las Americas** also offers sportfishing services. In the same vicinity, **Tony Reyes Fishing Tours,** Av. Mar Bermejo 130, tel. 686/577-1120, operates an 86-foot live-aboard sportfishing cruiser called *José Andres* with a capacity for 18 anglers. The craft features a large walk-in freezer and ice hold,

© JOE CUMMINGS

city beach, San Felipe

two live bait tanks, a modern galley, three heads, two showers, and staterooms with open-air bunks for those who want to enjoy the beautiful evenings at sea. Six *pangas* ride piggyback on the back deck so that anglers can go out three at a time once the Midriff Islands are reached. The boat sails from San Felipe to the Midriff Islands Mar.–Nov. for six days at a time. Typical catches include giant black sea bass, white sea bass, cabrilla, giant squid, red snapper, pargo, yellowtail, grouper, and, later in the season, roosterfish, sailfish, marlin, amberjack, and more yellowtail. Call for rates. The company can also be reached c/o Longfin Tackle Store, 2730 E. Chapman Ave., Orange, CA 92669, tel. 714/538-9300, fax 714/538-1368, longfin123@aol.com.

You can purchase fishing tackle at **Proveedora de Equipos de Pesca,** on Av. Mar de Cortés near the commercial marina south of town. Minimarket Las Americas also sells hooks and sinkers, and you can buy live bait from the shrimpers at the marina. As elsewhere in Mexico, every person in every boat that carries fishing tackle needs a valid fishing license. You can legally fish from shore without a license.

If you have your own small boat, you can launch at ramps at the Motel El Cortez, Ruben's Trailer Park, and the San Felipe Marina. All charge fees of around US$4 per launch.

Windsurfing

Sailboards can be rented at the Motel El Cortez or San Felipe Marina Resort. Spring is the best wind season on the bay, but there are breezes year-round. The shoreline north of Punta San Felipe receives the best wind.

Boating

Experienced, self-sufficient small-boaters and kayakers can put in at San Felipe for the 258-km (160-mile) coastal cruise to Bahía de los Ángeles. Although there are plenty of coves along the way, only a few places—Puertecitos, Punta Bufeo, and Bahía San Luis Gonzaga—offer limited supplies. It's best to do this route with someone who's done it before.

The *capitanía del puerto,* or captain of the port (COTP), can be found at the marina.

ENTERTAINMENT AND EVENTS

Entertainment

At night, the young and not-so-young shake it at **Rockodile** or **Beachcomber,** both large dance clubs on the *malecón.* Weekdays are usually on the dead side, while the weekends are packed. Rockodile has a sand volleyball court, while Beachcomber features a state-of-the-art laser light system. Both places offer happy hours from noon till around 5 P.M.

La Iguana, with entrances on both the *malecón* and Avenida Mar de Cortés, just north of Acapulco, is a lively sports bar and nightclub. Pool tables here are only US$.50 a game, beers US$2. On the hill just below Guadalupe's watchful eye, the three-story **Boom Boom Room** dwarfs all other clubs in town (and the lighthouse itself for that matter) and boasts multitiered, indoor/outdoor dance floors, a giant sound system, and impressive balcony views. Open evenings from 9 P.M. on.

For something more local in flavor, check out the **Club Miramar** toward the north end of the *malecón.* Open since 1948, it's basically just a bar with pool tables, though on occasion it may host wandering *trovadores.*

Events

Most of San Felipe's yearly events calendar revolves around desert or Sea of Cortez racing. The **Gran Carrera de San Felipe,** a 250-mile off-road race, is held in March and usually runs northwest around the Sierra San Felipe, south through Laguna Diablo and Arroyo Chanate, and east around the Sierra Santa Rosa.

Late February or March winds bring the **Hobie Cat Regatta,** a catamaran race on Bahía de San Felipe. The **San Felipe 250,** another off-highway race, also occurs around this time (and again in November).

Late February or early March is also time for **Carnaval,** which in San Felipe is celebrated in a much more macho fashion than in Mazatlán or La Paz, with amateur boxing, *palenque* (cockfighting), chili-eating contests, and greased-pole climbing.

California and Arizona college students invade the town the third week of March for their annual **spring break,** while Oregon and Washington students tend to arrive the fourth week of March. Either way, the last two weeks of March can be considered a total writeoff (unless, of course, you're one of the spring-breakers).

Navy Day (Día de la Marina), observed on June 1, is celebrated in San Felipe with a street festival, music, and dancing. Also in June is an all-terrain cycling race between San Felipe and Puertecitos; contact the tourist office in San Felipe or Mexicali for information on this new sporting event.

SHOPPING

If you're looking for fine art, you won't find it at **The People's Gallery,** but you will find a unique and fun collection of paintings, jewelry, and crafts made by locals and local expatriates. The gallery, at Av. Mar de Cortés 5, is open daily 10 A.M.–5 P.M.

INFORMATION AND SERVICES

Tourist Assistance

The state tourist office, Av. Mar de Cortés at Calle Manzanillo, tel. 686/577-1155, is open Mon.–Fri. 8 A.M.–7 P.M., Saturday 9 A.M.–3 P.M., Sunday 10 A.M.–1 P.M. In addition to handing out the usual hotel brochures and city maps, the staff can help with suggestions on how to spend your time in the area.

Money-Changing

On Avenida Mar de Cortés, **Bancomer,** San Felipe's only bank, has an ATM that may or may not be operational depending on maintenance. There are several *casas de cambio* in town, one at the end of Calzada Chetumal, across the street from the Beachcomber disco.

Post and Telephone

San Felipe's post office is on Mar Blanco, a block south of Calzada Chetumal. Hours are Mon.–Fri. 8 A.M.–1 P.M. and 2–6 P.M. Yet Mail Etc., Av. Mar de Cortés 75, tel. 686/577-1255, offers P.O. boxes for U.S. mail delivery, as well as photocopy, fax, and message services.

Internet Service

For staying in touch electronically, **The Net** at Plaza Canela on Mar de Cortés, tel. 686/577-1600, charges US$4 per hour. Open Mon.–Sat. 9 A.M.–4 P.M. Centrally located, less expensive (US$3 an hour), and bigger, is **Conexiones,** just south of Océano Chino Restaurant on Av. Mar de Cortés. Open daily 10 A.M.–9 P.M.

Miscellaneous

On Calle Puerto de Acapulco, just off the *malecón,* are a couple of small public *baños* (bathhouses). A hot shower costs US$.75 to $1.

San Felipe's sunny clime generates much residential electricity locally. **Solar Electric Systems,** on Calz. Chetumal (between a Pemex station and the arches monument), tel. 686/577-2475, solarex@sanfelipe.com.mx, stocks solar power panels, solar water pumps, digital meters, inverters, Trojan batteries, and RV supplies. The shop can also repair propane refrigerators.

TRANSPORTATION

By Air

Currently there are no commercial airline flights to San Felipe.

Aeropuerto Internacional de San Felipe, tel. 686/577-1368, lies 9.2 km (5.7 miles) southeast of the town center. For pilots flying private planes to Baja, San Felipe is a good place to clear customs and fill up on aviation fuel. Depending on your plane, a stop here could give you an extra hour or two of fuel for a southbound journey. The airport offers jet fuel and aviation gas, a control tower (118.5 Mhz), and a lighted, paved runway (1,618 meters/5,307 feet long, 35 meters/115 feet wide).

By Bus

San Felipe's bus depot is on Avenida Mar Caribe, south of Calzada Chetumal. **ABC** operates buses to and from Mexicali (US$14, twice daily), Ensenada (US$14, twice daily). Buses to/from San Felipe also use this terminal—see the San Felipe section for details—and Tijuana (US$22, first class, three times daily). Bus tickets go on sale an hour before departure.

By Taxi

Local taxis wait for the occasional fare on Calzada Chetumal just west of Restaurant Bar Los Mandiles. You can order a taxi by dialing 686/577-1293. Fares in central San Felipe should run US$3–5.

SOUTH TO MEXICO 1

This route offers hardy drivers the opportunity to see a side of Baja that can't be experienced from Mexico 1—a world of unpaved roads, subsistence ranches, fish camps, and desert coast wilderness.

To Puertecitos

The road from San Felipe to Puertecitos (85 km/53 miles), though paved, is in a fairly constant state of disrepair, especially south of the turnoff for Residence Faro Beach Trailer Park. In many places, a sand track parallels the paved road and provides a smoother ride for vehicles that can handle sandy surfaces. In some places, giant chunks of the road are missing, or there's heavy washboarding. Still, the road is passable by ordinary passenger vehicles—slowly. The *vados,* or places where dry culverts intersect the road, bear mention, as they're some of the most treacherous in all Baja. Road signs are mostly in English, as only Anglos seem interested in driving this desert road.

Indications of human habitation grow increasingly sparse the farther south you proceed. Three km south of San Felipe lie a handful of condo developments. Just past the Residence Faro turnoff is a huge, unsightly trash dump right off the highway, used by Faro and other beach-camp owners. Around this point begins an enchanting desert landscape of mesquite, ocotillo, cholla, elephant trees, cenizo, and sage. **Punta Estrella,** a good beach for clamming, is 6–7 km south of El Faro.

All the way to Puertecitos, every so often a beach camp is signed on the left. The going rate to park on the beach is around US$5, with facilities usually limited to drinking water and outdoor toilets. Numbers are multiplying year by year, and there's hardly a stretch of beach left that isn't affiliated with one camp or another.

Chelo's Café, at Km 35, makes a nice breakfast stop if you've started early. There's an adjacent curios shop, and resident Dr. José López offers medical assistance to travelers.

Campo García, 37.5 km (23.3 miles) north of Puertecitos, is one of the better beach camps toward the north end. Between Km 38 and 40 is **Playa Mexico,** a more elaborate one with restaurant, airstrip, and lots for sale. At around Km 42 you'll start seeing isolated beach homes, some of them loosely associated with Mexican property management companies. At the same time, beach camps in this middle stretch tend to be primitive—perfect for self-contained rigs, not so good if you need hookups of any kind.

Closer to Puertecitos—beginning at around Km 54—the camps become more elaborate again. **Campo Playa Cristina, Campo Alejandra, Campo Turisto Vallarta,** and **Campo Los Pulpos** all appear to be fairly well run.

Just north of Puertecitos, **Playa Escondida**

Puertecitos

RV Trailer Park fronts a broad, north-facing cove with white sand, brick grills, *palapas,* picnic tables, and two-way hookups for US$10 a day. Around a small headland toward San Felipe, the smaller **Campo Las Chivas** charges US$5 a day for palapa-shaded sites ensconced between a rocky hill and some sand dunes.

Puertecitos is a large cluster of small wooden, stone, or breeze-block homes built around a shallow cove with a small beach at one end. At one time probably a beautiful spot, today it's a jumble of mismatched shelters, rusting trailers, and discarded auto parts only a dune-buggy or fishing fanatic could love. An unnamed gated **tourist complex** offers a boat ramp, restaurant, airstrip, *tienda de abarrotes,* hot springs, camping (US$7), and beach *palapas.* The restaurant is open only Thurs.–Sun. 8 A.M.–2 P.M. Gasoline is available from a Pemex station with inoperative pumps; fuel is dispensed from large plastic bottles next to the pumps. A mechanic's shop called Taller Panama can help with vehicle repair.

South of Puertecitos

South of Puertecitos the road is appropriate only for vehicles with sturdy tires and shocks. **Bahía Cristina,** roughly five km (three miles) south of Puertecitos, offers a few palapas on a large, reddish sand beach; you can camp here or at other tiny rock coves nearby for a fee of around US$2 a night, collected by local *ejidos.* Just south of Bahía Cristina, **Campo La Costilla** is a small gated trailer community where most sites are permanently occupied. The coastline around Cristina and La Costilla is rocky but suitable for hiking and fishing.

About 29 km (18 miles) south along the coast are two small beach camp/retirement communities—**El Huerfanito** and **Nacho's Camp**—with minimal facilities for nonresidents. **San Juan del Mar,** another kilometer or so south, is a cluster of retirement/vacation homes similar to those farther south at Bahía San Luis Gonzaga. **Campo Tavo's,** just south of San Juan del Mar, offers primitive camping along a pretty bay. **Isla Miramar,** a few kilometers offshore, is a prime fishing destination for El Huerfanito, San Juan del Mar, and Campo Tavo's.

After another 30 km (19 miles) several more fish camps appear, with cabins for rent, at **Punta Bufeo.** The onshore fishing here and at the nearby **Islas Encantadas**—five islands and several islets close to shore—is reputedly good for yellowtail, croaker, corvina, and sierra. Several of the Encantadas—San Luis, Pomo, Encantada, Lobos—are of volcanic origin, displaying pumice and lava deposits. The islands make a good kayaking destination, although offshore winds can blow forcefully in winter. **Campo Punta Bufeo** charges US$3 to camp on the beach; the premises hold a restaurant, outhouses, showers, an airstrip, and a long rock motel with basic rooms for US$18. It's a better deal than Alfonsina's farther south. Other reputable camps along the coast on or just north of Punta Bufeo include **Campo Los Delfines, Campo Islas,** and **Campo Las Encantadas.** Each offers campgrounds (typically US$5 a night) as well as boat transport out to the islands.

Punta Willard and Bahía San Luis Gonzaga

About 12 km (seven miles) south of Punta Bufeo is Punta Willard, home of **Papa Fernández Resort,** a campground with secluded palapa beach sites (US$5), outhouses (but no showers), gas, meals, and fishing *pangas* for rent. Just north of the Papa Fernández Resort, **Campo El Faro** offers similar facilities. Just a few kilometers below Punta Willard, at the south end of Bahía Willard on a sandspit connected to Isla San Luis Gonzaga during low tide, is **Alfonsina's,** Tijuana tel. 664/648-1951, the main supply point for visitors and residents enjoying large, pristine Bahía San Luis Gonzaga, the next bay south. The flat, gray-sand beach is very clean and backed by clapboard beach houses, some of which are elaborate two-story affairs while others are little more than small trailer shelters. Many are prefab structures that have been trailered down from the United States. Airplanes, boats, and dune buggies are parked alongside. Many visitors and residents are pilots; along the main unpaved road, airplanes have the right of way over cars and trucks. Next to Alfonsina's is an unpaved 700-meter (2,300-foot) airstrip; during monthly high tides it may be partially submerged, so if you plan to stay overnight, taxi your plane up onto one of the inclined ramps just above the high tide line. Nearby, next to Rancho Grande, are two newer 1,220-meter (4,000-foot) runways that don't receive tidal inundation.

Climb Punta Final (actually a small cape with five points and a small lagoon) at the south end of Gonzaga for a good bay view. Fishing *pangas* are available for rent at Alfonsina's. Rooms cost US$40. Alfonsina's restaurant is also rather upmarket, with the cheapest dinner for two with one beer each costing around US$15. Alfonsina's was once famous for its annual Memorial Day bash, which drew visitors from all over the peninsula.

Rancho Grande, a campground facing Bahía San Luis Gonzaga just south of the main strip of beach homes, offers palapas on the beach for US$5 a night. Facilities include showers, a minimarket, and several outhouses.

The entire 72.5-km (45-mile) trip from Puertecitos to Alfonsina's takes 5–6 hours by car.

Bahía San Luis Gonzaga to Mexico 1 (Chapala)

From Bahía San Luis Gonzaga, a mostly graded but unpaved road leads southwest 64.5 km (40 miles) to meet Mexico 1 at Km 229/230; the drive generally takes about 90 minutes—this stretch is usually in much better condition than the road north to Puertecitos. About 38 km (24 miles) from Bahía San Luis Gonzaga, near Rancho Las Arrastras, the same road intersects an unpaved, partially graded road east to **Bahía de Calamajué,** another nearly untouched bay. You must pass through gated *ejido* property to reach the bay—you may have to search for someone to unlock the gate (ask at Coco's Corner). Rancho Las Arrastras offers some mechanical services and sells cold beer and sodas.

Coco's Corner, roughly halfway between Gonzaga and Mexico 1, consists of a small open-air café creatively decorated with beer cans and other discarded junk as well as desert plants. Owner Coco sells cold beer, soft drinks, and burritos. You can also camp here for US$5 a night—a primitive toilet and shower are available. A former Ensenada resident, Coco has lived alone in the middle of the desert here since 1990, following a 1989 accident in which he lost one leg. He speaks some English and is happy to dispense information on the area, including Calamajué, Gonzaga, and the road to San Felipe. Sign his guest book, to which he will add a color sketch of your vehicle.

Reportedly, the Mexican government has plans to extend the paved road from San Felipe all the way to Bahía San Luis Gonzaga and eventually to Mexico 1. This would provide an alternative route to Baja California Sur, along the east coast via Mexicali, for drivers of ordinary, low-clearance vehicles.

Central Baja

Into the Interior

SOUTH OF EL ROSARIO

After El Rosario, the Transpeninsular Highway drifts southeast, toward the center of the peninsula. For many Baja aficionados, this is where the "real" Baja begins. The population thins out rapidly, revealing 200 km (120 miles) of the peninsula's most classic desert scenery.

Once across the Arroyo del Rosario (Km 62), spindly *cirios* or "boojums" begin appearing, gradually increasing in number as you move farther inland. *Cardón* cacti are also prolific, along with barrel cactus, yucca, and a whole pantheon of Baja desert plants.

A graded road leaves the highway at Km 78, traveling 56 km (35 miles) southwest to **Bahía San Carlos,** a well-known spot among Baja windsurfers and surf anglers.

Misión San Fernando Velicatá

A dirt road at Km 114 leads west off the highway to the ruins of the only mission built by the Franciscans in Baja. The secluded site was first discovered in 1766 by Jesuit Padre Link, but the Jesuits were expelled before they could found a mission. Father Junípero Serra, on his way north, established San Fernando in 1769. Due to its location at a midpoint between the Gulf and Pacific coasts, it became an important way station on the Camino Real; at its peak 1,500 native devotees lived here. Dominicans took over the

CENTRAL BAJA HIGHLIGHTS

Cataviña: Surrounded by huge boulders, towering *cardón* cactus, elephant trees and *cirios,* Cataviña offers perhaps the most spectacular desert scenery in Baja (page 297).

Bahía de los Ángeles: Sail, swim, or kayak the calm blue waters of this island-filled bay, hike into the Sierra San Borja to abandoned silver mines, or kick back and eat fresh *dorado* (page 299).

Misión San Borja: Brave the rocky roads to this 18th-century Spanish church to view one of the peninsula's most atmospheric palm oasis mission settlements (page 306).

Laguna Ojo de Liebre: Every winter over 20,000 Pacific gray whales visit this bay system for frolicking and calving. Join a local whale-watching tour to watch the fun (page 309).

Vizcaíno Peninsula: Fans of the Baja outback will enjoy this remote, off-the-beaten-track "horn" jutting deep into the Pacific Ocean. Home to the rare *berrendo* or desert pronghorn antelope, much of the peninsula has been declared a UNESCO biosphere reserve (page 315).

San Ignacio: Baja's most well-preserved and pic-turesque mission town lies in a palm canyon conveniently close to Mexico 1 (page 321).

Sierra de San Francisco: Marvel at the extensive rock-art murals found on the walls and ledges of large palm canyons deep in this mountain range. Getting there via mule caravan is more than half the fun (page 325).

Laguna San Ignacio: Reach out and touch migrating Pacific grey whales, which for reasons not yet fully understood, solicit the touch of human visitors only in this bay (page 330).

Mulegé: Base yourself in this historic mission town where the Río Mulegé meets the Sea of Cortez for kayaking and snorkeling in the pristine Bahía de Concepción, hiking to painted caves and petroglyph sites, and trolling some of Baja's funkiest bars (page 338).

Comondú: Adventure into the twin palm valleys of San José and San Miguel in the Comondú, where the pace of life has changed little since the 19th century (page 353).

Bahía de Loreto: One of Baja's most treasured bays, now a national marine park, offers some of the best boating, fishing and diving in Mexico (page 357).

mission in 1772, but the entire community was wiped out by a 1777–80 epidemic.

Although the adobe ruins themselves aren't much, the arroyo setting is dramatic, and the short side trip (eight km/five miles) affords an opportunity for desert solitude and a chance to get closer to the regional flora and fauna. Two families operate *ranchitos* at the site, living off the slim bounty of the arroyo and making use of the original Spanish *acequias* (irrigation channels) built of stone block. Rock cliffs near the arroyo bear petroglyphs and pictographs, some created by the Cochimí in the 17th and 18th centuries, others possibly older. About eight km (five miles) farther toward the coast on this road you can view a couple of abandoned copper mines and the rusting ruins of a smelter.

Just south of the mission road, at Km 116, is **Rancho El Progreso,** the first of many ranchos along the Transpeninsular Highway that offer food to truckers and other passing motorists. The menu includes whatever's on the stove that day, usually simple ranchero fare like enchiladas, *chiles rellenos,* frijoles, and rice.

El Mármol

This abandoned onyx quarry, accessible via a 15-km (nine-mile) graded dirt road branching east off Mexico 1 at Km 143, makes another interesting side trip. *Mármol* means "marble" in Spanish, and for the first half of the 20th century, onyx—a brown-and-red-veined calcite or tufa that can be polished to a high gloss—was a popular marble substitute. A San Diego mining company began the El Mármol operation in the early 1900s; by the late '50s, when it closed due to the advent of cheaper synthetics, many of the world's onyx inkstands, bathroom fixtures, floor and wall panels, statues, and other decorative objects had come from this site. Onyx's peak was the art deco period, when celebrities like actress Theda Bara ordered custom-made onyx bathtubs.

The onyx at El Mármol is easy to quarry, since layers of it sit right on the desert surface. The problem lies in transporting the stone from this isolated site; onyx slabs had to be trucked to Puerto Catarina (80 km west on the Pacific coast), loaded through the surf one by one, and shipped north to San Diego by boat.

Banded onyx blocks remain strewn about the old quarry site. The ruins of a schoolhouse built entirely of thick onyx blocks sit to one side of the quarry. About midway between the highway and the old quarry a huge mesquite tree stands next to a well and an antique Aermotor windmill, a scene right out of West Texas.

Off the El Mármol road, between the highway and the quarry, **Rancho Tres Enriques** offers meals and rustic accommodations. **Rancho (Lonchería) Sonora,** between Km 144 and 145 on Mexico 1, also serves food.

CATAVIÑA

This Mexico 1 way station at Km 174 lies in the middle of possibly the most spectacular desert scenery on the peninsula. Protected by **Parque Natural del Desierto Central,** it's a vast area of car-sized boulders, *cardón* cacti, elephant trees, *cirios,* and a hundred other desert oddities.

Cataviña Boulder Field

At the north end of the Desierto Central, this area is honeycombed with trails and is an excellent area for hiking—except in summer when the heat is deadly.

Cueva Pintada

Just a short hike from the highway, a rock-art cave lies above Arroyo Cataviña (also known as Arroyo El Palmarito because of the fan palms growing here). From the Hotel La Pinta, walk or drive three km (two miles) north along the highway to the second dirt track past a prominent *vado* where the arroyo crosses the highway, near the Km 171 marker. Proceed down the dirt road to the edge of the arroyo, which is usually dry at this point. If

© JOE CUMMINGS

onyx schoolhouse, El Mármol

CENTRAL BAJA

driving, park here. Before hiking across the arroyo, look for a white wooden sign on the other side, high up on a bouldered bluff a bit south of your position at the edge of the arroyo. This marks the way to the nearby cave. If you can't locate the sign, start hiking in the described direction and *maybe* you'll stumble on it. It's much easier to spot from the west side of the arroyo.

No one knows who painted the geometric patterns and humanoid figures on the rock face, though the Cochimí have been suggested due to the presence of equestrian images.

During times of rain you might find enough water in the arroyo for a refreshing swim.

Mission Ruins

A very tough vehicle track—experienced dirt bikers or four-wheelers only—leads 23 km (14 miles) east of Rancho Santa Inés, just south of Cataviña, to the adobe ruins of **Misión Santa María de los Ángeles,** the last New World mission (1767–69) founded by the Jesuits. The site was known among the Cochimí as Cabujakamaang, "Place Where Spirits Dwell," when the Franciscans arrived in Baja. Though Father Junípero Serra refused to close the nonproductive mission simply because he found himself "addicted to the place," the mission was totally depopulated by 1800. The original roofs were palm thatch, so only portions of the adobe walls stand today. (Though touted today as a building aesthetic, the truth is adobe melts when exposed to rain.) A *palma azul* oasis near the ruins is almost worth the ordeal of negotiating steep grades, switchbacks, and melon-sized rocks—definitely a destination best reserved for obsessed historians or off-roaders.

Pacific-Coast Detour

Just north of Cataviña a dirt road signed "Faro San José 90km" leads to a lighthouse on the Pacific coast. From that point you can head north to **Punta Canoas** or south to **Punta Blanca,** both renowned surf spots.

Accommodations

Under US$25: Cabañas Linda, a pink low-rise motel on the left-hand side of Mexico 1 as you come into town, offers plainly furnished rooms.

A kilometer south of Cataviña is a turnoff east to **Rancho Santa Inés,** where ranchero food, hot showers, and bunkhouse accommodations are available. Self-contained campers/RVers can also park here for US$5 a night. The ranch was originally founded by a Spanish mission soldier stationed at the now-ruined Misión Santa María farther inland.

US$50–100: Hotel La Pinta, Ensenada tel. 646/176-2601, U.S. tel. 800/800-9632, www.lapintahotels.com. Large, clean guest rooms surround a small pool.

Food

Antojitos Mexicanos, a tiny café at the north end of Cataviña on the east side of the highway, serves Mexican food and coffee. **Café La Enramada,** in front of the defunct highway Pemex station opposite La Pinta, is similar but also stocks a few groceries. The newer **Café Oasis,** just north of La Pinta on the same side of the highway, is okay.

Driving

The stretch of highway between El Rosario and either Bahía de los Ángeles or Villa Jesús María presents the most challenging fuel situation along the entire length of Mexico 1. It's best to top off your tank in El Rosario before heading south toward Cataviña. If you know your tank won't bring you as far as Cataviña, be sure to carry a spare can of fuel.

Opposite La Pinta is a defunct Pemex station that closed several years ago. Making matters worse, of late the Pemex pump at La Pinta has been open only in the late afternoon, from 4 P.M. till dark. Even if you seem to have plenty of fuel left when you reach Cataviña, be sure to top off again here before heading farther south. Occasionally the pump at La Pinta runs dry. If that happens you'll be stuck in Cataviña till more gas is delivered the next day.

SOUTH TO PARADOR PUNTA PRIETA

About 30 km (19 miles) south of Cataviña, off the west side of the highway between Km 207 and

208, is **El Pedregoso,** a massive natural rock formation 610 meters (2,000 feet) high that looks as if it were constructed from a pile of boulders.

Rancho (Lonchería) San Ignacito, at Km 187, is yet another rancho food stop. A nearby plaque commemorating the completion of Mexico 1 marks the spot where road crews from the north and south finally met. At Km 191, a *lonchería* at **Rancho San Martín** is less inviting.

Between Km 229 and 230, a graded road heads northeast to Bahía San Luis Gonzaga and Bahía de Calamajué on the Sea of Cortez coast.

(See San Felipe and Vicinity in the Northern Baja chapter for details on this rewarding off-highway trip.) At this junction, **Rancho Nuevo Chapala** offers traveler's meals. The *cirio, cardón,* yucca, and cholla in the area are often exemplary specimens.

Parador Punta Prieta is a defunct rest stop at Km 280. Mexico 1 splits here, with the east fork leading southeast 68 km (42 miles) to Bahía de los Ángeles. Opposite the old *parador,* **Restaurant Los Dos Hermanos** serves inexpensive Mexican dishes daily 6 A.M.–10 P.M.

Bahía de los Ángeles

The highway to Bahía de los Ángeles passes thick stands of *copalquín* (elephant tree) as it winds through the Sierra de la Asamblea. While this is still a paved highway, be alert to the various potholes along the way. At Km 44 a four-wheel-drive-only track leads southwest 35 km (21 miles) to the restored Misión San Borja; a better road of similar distance is accessible from Rosarito, off the west branch of Mexico 1. The final descent to the bay from the sierra affords an inspiring view of the island-studded blue waters. The bay probably got its name because the white islands resembled someone's vision of angels floating in heaven.

Beginning in the late 1940s, American sportfishing enthusiasts began flying private planes into Bahía de los Ángeles; a few hardy souls even drove down here from San Diego and points north. Old Baja hands say in those days the village was nothing more than thatched-roof huts. But novelist John Steinbeck, who sailed into the bay in early 1940 with marine biologist Ed Ricketts, described his feeling of resentment at finding "new buildings, screened and modern, and on a tiny airfield a plane. . . ." Even then, Steinbeck wrote, there were Americans in Bahía de los Ángeles.

The town really hasn't grown much since the pre-Transpeninsular days; telephone service has become available only recently (A **TelNor** office on the main road offers the only long-distance phone service in Bahía de los Ángeles, open daily 9 A.M.–7 P.M.). Modern concessions to tourism include a small power plant, two trailer parks, a

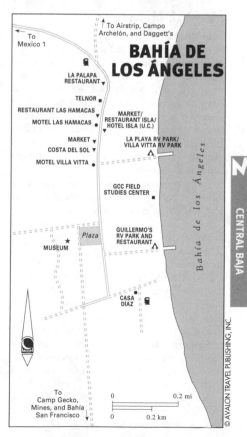

few motels, some cafés, two areas at the north and south ends of town for barrel gas only, a museum, and a small park. The major leisure activity remains fishing.

Behind the park is the small but well-curated **Museo de Naturaleza y Cultura** (hours daily 9 A.M.–noon and 2–4 P.M.), displaying gold- and silver-mining exhibits, shells and fossils, two whale skeletons, ranch life re-creations, and a collection of Seri and Cochimí artifacts. The toy-like locomotive in front of the museum once ran on the San Juan mine railway, 17.5 km (11 miles) south of the current town. The museum is staffed by volunteers. Postcards, books, and monographs on Baja are available for sale.

MARINE LIFE
Mammals
A variety of whales—including Bryde's, minke, gray, finback, blue, sperm, humpback, orca, and pilot—as well as common and bottlenose dolphins ply the **Canal de Ballenas** between Isla Ángel de la Guarda and the peninsula. Bryde's (summer) and finback (winter) are the most common whales here, although every one of the aforementioned species is spotted year after year by visiting marine biologists. Dolphins are most numerous in summer and early fall.

Along island shores the California sea lion is common year-round; during spring, northern elephant seals are occasionally seen.

Sea Turtles
The Sea of Cortez and lower Pacific coast are prime breeding areas for sea turtles, specifically the Pacific varieties of the green, loggerhead, hawksbill, and leatherback. At one time Bahía de los Ángeles was one of Mexico's principal turtle fisheries, but overharvesting in the 1960s and '70s placed every species under threat of extinction.

Programa Tortuga Marina, a sea turtle conservation and research station in operation since 1979, lies along the north shore of the bay behind Brisa Marina; cooperative local fishermen bring in sea turtles in hopes their chances of survival will increase and that someday there will again be a viable turtle fishery.

A loggerhead released from here in 1994 after several years in captivity was found in Japanese waters in 1995. Loggerheads nest in Japan, Australia, and Baja only, swimming with the Northern Pacific and Northern Equatorial currents. You can view sea turtles—both loggerheads and greens—in tanks at the facility.

ACCOMMODATIONS
Hotels and Motels
Note that the local power plant shuts down at 10 P.M. each night, plunging most hotels and motels into darkness. This means that hotels advertising air-conditioning may only be able to keep you cool during the day. Ask beforehand if this matters to you.

US$25–50: Motel Las Hamacas, just south of the restaurant of the same name, offers 10 good-sized rooms with drinking water supplied and attached hot-water showers.

At the south end of town, the long-established **Casa Díaz** offers large, funky, bayfront rooms. Long-term discounts are available. The Díaz family operates a fishing and bird-watching guide service to the bay islands, as well as a small market and a usually operative Pemex pump.

The 40-room **Motel Villa Vitta** (no phone) is a modern low-rise motel in the center of town. Facilities include a swimming pool, a restaurant/bar, a boat ramp, and ample parking. Room rates vary widely according to the occupancy rate and season—sometimes a fine value, other times overpriced. Water heaters are electric, so there's no hot water after 10 P.M.

US$50–100: Costa del Sol, U.S./Canada tel. 562/803-8873 or Mexico City tel. 555/151-4195, just north of motel Villa Vitta, has six rooms—five double rooms and one single. Somewhat out of place in this rustic fishing village, the small hotel resembles a Mexican-style Holiday Inn with peach-colored stucco and a red-tile roof. Rooms are spacious and clean with hot showers, air-conditioning, and 24-hour electricity (the only hotel in town for which this is the case). The hotel's small restaurant/bar serves breakfast, lunch, and dinner. The hotel also rents kayaks.

Three km north of town, just north of

Daggetts, **Raquel and Larry's,** U.S. tel. 619/429-7935, raquelnlarry@hotmail.com, is a family-run motel featuring seven spacious air-conditioned rooms with three more units under construction. A fully furnished three-bedroom house on the beach is also available for rent. The house has air-conditioning, ceiling fans in all bedrooms, a fully equipped kitchen, and a large covered veranda overlooking the bay. There's a small restaurant on the premises, as well as a boat ramp and a rental shop offering everything from snorkeling gear to kayaks. Scuba tank rentals and airfills are also available.

Guillermo's RV Park and Restaurant rents

five rooms, each with two king-size beds and one double bed. Air-conditioning is available all night during the summer.

Campgrounds and RV Parks

Across the street from Motel Villa Vitta on the bay, 30 unshaded tent/RV sites with morning and evening electricity (plus 20 spaces without hookups), showers, flush toilets, dump station, and a boat launch are available at **Villa Vitta RV Park and Campgrounds** for US$12. Adjacent **La Playa RV Park** offers 30 sites with full hookups, flush toilets, and a boat ramp for US$10.

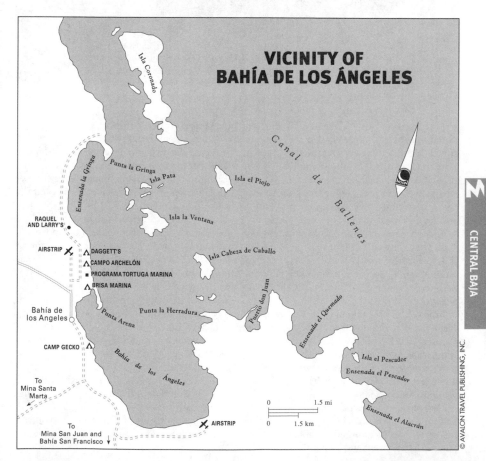

VICINITY OF
BAHÍA DE LOS ÁNGELES

Isla Coronado

Canal de Ballenas

Ensenada la Gringa

Punta la Gringa

Isla Pata

Isla el Piojo

Isla la Ventana

RAQUEL AND LARRY'S

AIRSTRIP

DAGGETT'S
CAMPO ARCHELÓN
PROGRAMA TORTUGA MARINA
BRISA MARINA

Isla Cabeza de Caballo

Puerto don Juan

Ensenada el Quemado

Bahía de los Angeles

Punta Arena

Punta la Herradura

CAMP GECKO

Bahía de los Ángeles

Isla el Pescador

Ensenada el Pescador

To
Mina Santa Marta

0   1.5 mi
0   1.5 km

To
Mina San Juan and
Bahía San Francisco

AIRSTRIP

Ensenada el Alacrán

CENTRAL BAJA

© JOE CUMMINGS

Campo Archelón

Just south of Villa Vitta and La Playa is **Guillermo's,** a fairly well-run trailer park, motel, and restaurant operation with *palapas,* tent sites, and full hookups for US$12 per night. Facilities include a boat launch (fee for nonguests), showers, toilets (sometimes they flush, sometimes they don't; no seats), and a small market/gift shop.

Nine RV sites with full hookups are available at **Casa Díaz** for US$5 a night.

Just north of town, near the paved airstrip, **Brisa Marina,** formally a full-hookup RV park, has closed. Camping is still permitted, though no facilities are available.

North of Brisa Marina and just north of the sea turtle project, rustic and ecologically oriented **Campo Archelón** offers semicircular rock shelters with palapa roofs (some with old chairs in them), three outhouses, and a wood-fired *baño,* all within a few feet of the bay. The shelters cost US$10 for up to four people.

Daggett's, a well-kept campground about a half mile north of Archelón, boasts wooden ramadas with grills alongside sizable campsites, plus separate showers and outhouses, for US$10.

Daggett's also offers fishing trips and diving trips, as well as lots for lease.

A graded road continues along the bayshore as far as **Punta La Gringa,** the end of the bay and a fish camp/retirement community. Along the way are a number of open campsites where camping is free.

In the opposite direction, about eight km (five miles) south of town, lies secluded **Camp Gecko,** www.campgecko.com, a unique spot featuring huts with rock walls and palapa roofs as well as simple open-sided palapas. The huts cost US$15, tent/camper sites are US$5, with an additional US$5 for each additional vehicle whether you stay in a hut or on the beach. Larger, more substantial cabins with kitchens go for US$25. During the summer you can probably negotiate rates of US$10 and US$3, respectively. The offshore breeze is refreshing, and the beach is kept exceptionally clean. Ramón, the man who runs the camp, leads fishing and whale/porpoise-watching trips aboard *pangas.*

Farther southeast of Camp Gecko you can find a number of bayshore areas suitable for camping.

FOOD

Ostensibly because of Bahía de los Ángeles's relative isolation, food—whether bought in local markets or at restaurants—is pricier here than in many places in Baja. A breakfast of two oatmeals and two hot chocolates, for example, costs US$6 at the cheapest place in town—high for both Baja and mainland Mexico. If pinching pennies, stock up in Guerrero Negro before coming.

Guillermo's nicely appointed restaurant/bar offers breakfasts for around US$4, dinner US$8, beer US$2. Specialties include fresh fish, shrimp, and lobster; the palapas out front are a nice spot for a margarita.

Restaurant Las Hamacas serves seafood and ranchero dishes for breakfast, lunch, and dinner; meals are in the US$5–12 range, with beer US$1.50. The restaurant also sells used paperbacks; proceeds reportedly go to the town museum.

La Palapa Restaurant, toward the north end of town on the west side of the main road, specializes in Mexican seafood, including fish tacos. Inexpensive. **Tacos La Reyna,** in front of the town plaza, has cheap and filling tacos.

A couple of small *tiendas* in town sell canned food, beer, and staples. On Thursday you can buy fresh vegetables from a vendor at the north end of the main road through town on the east side.

SPORTS AND RECREATION

Hiking

Arroyos west of the bay lead into the Sierra San Borja; for a good day hike, pick out a dry wash and follow it. As long as you keep the bay in sight, it's impossible to get lost.

Mina Santa Marta, a nearby abandoned mine, makes an interesting hike. Along with the more successful Mina San Juan farther south, Santa Marta operated during the 1890s using a cable-and-bucket system to transfer gold and silver ore (mostly the latter) from steep hillsides to a miniature railway below. Access to Mina Santa Marta begins about 3.5 km (two miles) south of Casa Díaz next to the town dump. Once you've located the dump alongside the graded road south, walk west until you come across the remains of the railway grade, then follow the grade west to the remains of the mine itself. The round-trip hike can be completed in one day, though many hikers spend a night at the mine.

The San Juan (also known as Las Flores) mine is reached by following the same road 17.5 km (11 miles) southwest of the bay to Valle Las Flores. You'll see the remains of a smelter and boiler along the west side of the road. This road can be followed farther south into the Sierra San Borja, where there are several major Amerindian rock-art sites; inquire at local ranches for trail guides. The graded road continues southward through the sierra all the way to **Bahía San Francisquito,** approximately 132 km (81 miles) south of Bahía de los Ángeles.

Fishing

Due to heavy local gillnetting, Bahía de los Ángeles fishing is not what it once was, although recent years have seen improved catches compared with a decade ago. The best bets are onshore angling for sand bass, guitarfish, and triggerfish, or spring fishing at Punta La Gringa for croaker and halibut. Farther out at nearby islands—especially near **Isla La Ventana, Isla Cabeza de Caballo,** and **Isla Coronado**—you can try for yellowtail, white and black sea bass, dorado, tuna, and grouper. Most of the offshore fish run in the summer months, though yellowtail runs are sometimes seen January–March.

Any of the hotels or campgrounds in town can arrange rental *pangas* for either sportfishing or scuba diving trips. Daggett's, Guillermo's, Camp Gecko, and Casa Díaz can arrange guided fishing trips to the islands for around US$100–120 a day. Bring your own tackle; it's scarce in Bahía de los Ángeles. Larry and Raquel's offers airfills and rents scuba and snorkel equipment.

Boating and Kayaking

Guillermo's, La Playa, Villa Vitta, and Casa Díaz each maintain boat launches; they also rent *pangas.* The bay is protected by the 68-km-long (42-mile-long) **Isla Ángel de la Guarda,** but strong northeasterlies set up a nasty chop on occasion.

Make local weather inquiries before venturing any considerable distance from shore.

Bahía de los Ángeles is popular among kayakers, who paddle to the nearby coves and islands. **Isla Coronado** (also known as Isla Smith) is three km (two miles) northeast of Punta La Gringa, while the southern tip of Isla Ángel de la Guarda is 19 km (12 miles) away. Landings for day-trippers are usually easiest on the west side of the islands.

Most anchorages on Isla Ángel de la Guarda, the second-largest island in the Sea of Cortez after Tiburón, are a day's sail from Bahía de los Ángeles. **Puerto Refugio**, at the island's northern tip (64 km/40 miles from Bahía de los Ángeles), provides all-weather protection along with several coves and beaches, hence it's the most popular landing. Also good are **Caleta Pulpito** on the mideastern shore and **Este Ton** on the southwestern shore. The latter is the closest safe anchorage from the mainland. Explorations on Ángel de la Guarda can take in *cirio* stands, 1,200-meter (4,000-foot) peaks, and beaches with basking sea lions. The best sand beaches are along the island's southeastern reach. The common rorqual or fin whale occasionally visits the island's coastal waters, especially Canal de Ballenas to the west. This cetacean measures up to 24 meters (78 feet) long—only the blue whale is larger—and can be recognized by its small dorsal fin and long, flat, V-shaped head.

An easier two- to three-day kayaking circuit involves paddling from the bay to Isla Coronado and back, stopping at smaller islands Ventana, Pata, and Cabeza de Caballo along the way.

East and south of Bahía de los Ángeles are several coves worth visiting. Those with beaches and camping areas include **Puerto Don Juan, Ensenada del Quemado,** and **Ensenada del Pescador.**

It's possible to complete a "stepping stones" kayak route from Bahía de los Ángeles (or from farther south at Bahía San Francisquito) to Isla Tiburón and Bahía Kino on the Mexican mainland. The usual route, once followed by Seri Amerindians in reed canoes, is Partida–San Lorenzo–San Esteban–Tiburón–Kino, but navigating the currents requires advanced kayaking abilities and knowledge of local geography. The University of Arizona Sports and Recreation Department, probably your best source of information on the route, sponsors a yearly Bahía de los Ángeles to Bahía Kino crossing by kayak.

Because many novice kayakers have experienced problems in the Bahía de los Ángeles area, a Californian kayaking club called San Diego Sea Kayakers has printed a set of Bahía de los Ángeles kayaking guidelines, distributed free at Guillermo's Restaurant, the mayor's office, and the museum.

Although Bahía de los Ángeles is a prime kayaking destination, only Raquel and Larry's (see Accommodations) is in the business of renting kayaking equipment.

> *A variety of whales—including Bryde's, minke, gray, finback, blue, sperm, humpback, orca, and pilot—ply the Canal de Ballenas between Isla Ángel de la Guarda and the peninsula.*

Windsurfing

Bahía de los Ángeles is a good bay for novice board-sailors because of the lack of large swells. Prevailing northeasterlies are strongest in the northern parts of the bay. A 10- to 12-km (six- to seven-mile) downwind run through the small islands west of Isla La Ventana, then all the way to the town waterfront, can be accomplished from Punta La Gringa.

Diving

Daggett's campground (see Campgrounds and RV Parks) can arrange dive trips in the bay through local resident Francisco, who maintains an air compressor and rents scuba equipment. For US$85 a day he will take a small group out on a 17-foot aluminum skiff to a rock reef at La Ventana; price includes unlimited airfills. If you're going out on your own, you can buy air from Francisco.

Bird-Watching

The shores of Bahía de los Ángeles and the bay islands host a wide variety of bird life, including terns, pelicans, gulls, egrets, herons, cormorants, petrels, boobies, and ospreys. The most renowned local marine bird rookeries are **Isla Partida** and **Isla Raza.** The latter, a tiny, guano-covered, sparsely vegetated island of 250 acres, is the site for annual territorial wars between approximately 100,000 Heermann's gulls and 200,000 elegant terns, who battle for nesting grounds on the small island. The conflict—including "war formations" and egg-smashing—takes place in April; Casa Díaz can arrange special boat trips to view the annual event.

A number of rare royal terns and tropic birds also inhabit Isla Raza, declared a national wildlife sanctuary in 1964 to stop egg-hunters from destroying the bird populations. It's possible the gull-tern wars are related to the elimination of egg-hunting, which local Amerindians had practiced—albeit at a slower pace than their Mexican successors—for centuries.

Baja California Field Studies Program

For over 20 years, California's **Glendale Community College** has sponsored a special field-studies program every summer at Bahía de los Ángeles. Courses include Introduction to Marine Biology, Natural History Field Studies, and Introduction to Marine Vertebrates, plus Basic Spanish Conversation. Students stay in the Field Studies Center, a building at the center of town on the bay. The typical four-unit course costs around US$685. For information, contact Dr. José Mercade, GCC, 1500 N. Verdugo Rd., Glendale, CA 91209, tel. 818/240-1000, ext. 5718, jmercade@glendale.edu/baja, www.glendale.edu/baja.

TRANSPORTATION

A paved, 1,460-meter (4,800-foot) airstrip serves small planes; buzz the town once for taxi service. The local Unicom frequency is 122.8.

Bus service to Bahía de los Ángeles is nonexistent; to get here you need your own wheels, boat, or plane, or you must hitch from the Parador Punta Prieta junction. Once you've arrived, all of Bahía de los Ángeles is accessible on foot. For trips to the Punta La Gringa airfield, or farther afield, you can hire a taxi at Restaurant Las Hamacas.

Gas is available from private barrel pumps at a couple of local *tiendas,* costing roughly 25 percent more than at government Pemex pumps. Behind Casa Díaz is an auto mechanic's shop offering minor repair services, air for tires, and gas. The Pemex station at the Parador Punta Prieta highway junction has been closed since January 1996.

South of Punta Prieta

Southwest of the Bahía de los Ángeles junction, the main section of Mexico 1 is marked by a new kilometer sequence beginning at Km 0. The ranch community of **Punta Prieta** is at Km 13; between Km 38 and 39 a graded gravel road heads west 13 km (eight miles) to **Santa Rosalillita,** a fish camp below Punta Santa Rosalillita.

The Santa Rosalillita area is a well-known surfing destination; in a northwest swell, the point break at the north end of the bay reportedly offers Baja's longest ride (much depends on current bottom conditions). Windsurfers also enjoy the breaks and the bay's steady breeze. At the bay's south end, **Punta Rosarito** produces decent reef breaks in swells from any direction. If the waves aren't tipping right at either of these spots, breaks at **Punta Negra, Punta María,** and **Punta Cono**—all positioned perfectly to catch winter swells—can be reached by following the dirt road north out of Santa Rosalillita for 24–30 km (14–18 miles).

The wreck of the double-masted schooner *Jennie Thelin* (built in 1869, stranded in 1912) lies buried in the sand dunes along Bahía Santa María. The schooner and her captain, Alexander McLean, were the inspiration for the infamous ship *Ghost* and skipper Wolf Larson in Jack London's novel *The Sea Wolf.* The ship was reputedly often used to transport illegal immigrants and untaxed merchandise between the United States and Mexico.

Rosarito

Rosarito, a small ranching center, appears on the east side of Mexico 1 at Km 52. The café **Mauricio** at the northeast end of town on the highway is a favorite stop for passing truckers. The ranchero food is good and reasonably priced, but best of all is the real coffee, filtered through a cloth strainer in the old Mexican style. There are other cafés in town as well.

San Borja

This small ex-mission farm settlement in the foothills of the Sierra San Borja is well worth visiting if you have the time and if you and your vehicle are capable of driving rough roads. **Misión San Francisco Borja de Adác** was founded here by Jesuit padres in 1759 (or 1762 according to some chronicles), then handed over to the Franciscans in 1767 along with large numbers of sheep, goats, cattle, horses, and mules. In 1773, the Dominicans took charge of the mission property and the 1,600 Amerindian parishioners in the Adác (the original Cochimí name for the site) community. Although the mission was officially secularized in 1818, it is undergoing restoration and offers occasional services for local residents. Ruined adobe walls of the original Jesuit mission—the last to have been built anywhere on the peninsula—have been preserved. A stone spiral staircase in the *campanario* or bell tower of the later Dominican mission is impressive.

The fig, pomegranate, olive, guava, mango, and date orchards planted by the missionaries continue to provide a livelihood for mission caretaker José Ángel Gerardo Monteón, a fourth-generation Cochimí, and his family of seven. The mission is open daily 8 A.M.–6 P.M. José's children are happy to take visitors on a half-hour walk through the orchards to a small, clean hot springs. A longer, 1.5 hour tour to see local rock art—using the visitor's own vehicle—can also be arranged. The family doesn't ask any set fee for such tours, although a donation is much appreciated.

Two unpaved roads, each about 36 km (22 miles) long, lead to San Borja. The faster and better-signed road, suitable for any sturdy, high-clearance vehicle, heads east from Rosarito on

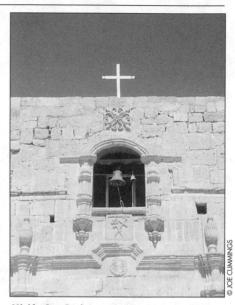

Misión San Borja

© JOE CUMMINGS

Mexico 1. Count on reaching the mission in about 45 minutes, an hour tops.

A considerably rougher track provides access from Km 44 on the road that links Bahía de los Ángeles with Mexico 1. Although this road was recently graded, there are still two or three spots where four-wheel drive is advisable due to the steep, slippery grades, deep *vados,* and stretches where you must drive 10 meters or more over basketball-size boulders. Coming from Bahía de los Ángeles, be sure to take the first fork to the left, then stay right. Just before reaching the mission area, roughly 34 km (21 miles), from the road entry, you'll come to a three-way fork; the left-most tong leads to San Borja. Along the way you'll pass thick stands of *cirio* and elephant trees. Coming in this way takes about an hour and half. Assuming your vehicle is suitable, you could make a partial loop by entering via one road and leaving via the other.

Rock Art

Northeast of San Borja are at least two major Amerindian rock-art sites; **Las Tinajitas** and

Montevideo are well known. Las Tinajitas can be difficult to find—inquire in San Borja for a guide. Montevideo can be reached by high-clearance vehicle, preferably four-wheel drive for safe traverse across sections of deep sand.

The road between the Transpeninsular Highway and Bahía de los Ángeles provides the quickest access for Montevideo, a rock-art site of interest mainly because the journey there traverses superb desert scenery. Take the turnoff signed for Misión San Borja at Km 44 and head west into the desert. This graded gravel road is in fair condition for several miles. Turn left (south) after 3.5 km (2.2 miles) onto a less-traveled road. After another 3.2 km (two miles) you should pass a small corral on your right. At this point the desert flora becomes thick and beautiful, with lush stands of *cardón*, ocotillo, and *cirio*. After another four miles you'll come to a large tree almost in the middle of the road, with a canyon wall on your right. Park here; you'll find the rock paintings—several *monos* (stylized human figures) and many more geometric designs—along the canyon wall. This spot would make a good campsite. As always, bring plenty of drinking water; assistance is very scarce in this area.

Villa Jesús María and Puerto Santo Domingo

The town of Villa Jesús María, at Km 94–95 on Mexico 1, has a Pemex station and a couple of cafés, including the dependable **Restaurant Ejidal**. In front of the Pemex station a cluster of old vans sell cold Cokes, tacos, *tortas*, and tamales. A paved road runs northwest from town to Ejido Morelos, connecting with a graded dirt road southwest to **Laguna Manuela,** a fish camp on the bay of Puerto Santo Domingo.

The occasional point break off volcanic **Morro Santo Domingo,** at the north end of Puerto Santo Domingo, draws a few surfers. A solar-powered lighthouse stands at the end of the point. Fishing is said to be good in the bay—corvina, croaker, and halibut inshore, and grouper, yellowtail, and white seabass offshore. You can easily launch trailered or cartopped boats on the beach, or rent *pangas* at Laguna Manuela. The laguna itself can be difficult to navigate due to high winds and unpredictable tidal surges. About 2.8 km (1.7 miles) northwest of the fish camp is a long sandy beach known locally as Playa Arcos.

Paralelo 28

The northern border of Baja California Sur, at 28° N latitude, is reached at Km 128. A 43-meter-high (140-foot-high) steel monument—a stylized eagle that looks more like a giant tuning fork—marks the border and the change from Pacific to Mountain time. South of the 28th parallel, kilometer markers on the Transpeninsular Highway begin at Km 220 and descend toward Km 0 (at Santa Rosalía). Mexico's First Cavalry maintains a military base around the perimeter of the eagle monument; a *puesto de control* often stops vehicles in either direction for a quick check. Be prepared to show your tourist card or visa.

Between the border and the town of **Guerrero Negro** (seven km south of the state border) is an immigration checkpoint and agricultural inspection station. Stops are now mandatory for all vehicles. In addition to checking your immigration papers, officials will spray insecticide under your vehicle (for which you may be charged about US$1).

Guerrero Negro and Vicinity

This town of around 10,000 took its name from the *Black Warrior,* a Hawaii-ported whaling barque that foundered in Laguna Guerrero Negro in 1858. Too overloaded with whale oil to leave the lagoon under its own power, the barque sank while being towed out to sea. This was just a year after Charles Melville Scammon "discovered" the Baja lagoons where migrating gray whales came to calve.

Within 20 years, tens of thousands of gray whales had been slaughtered and the whalers moved on to other Pacific hunting areas. But the gray made a remarkable comeback from the brink of extinction and currently numbers over 20,000. Once again the whales of Laguna Ojo de Liebre are attracting visitors, only this time the visitors are shooting photos instead of harpoons.

Today a huge sea-salt-extraction facility, jointly owned by the Mexican government (51 percent) and Japan's Mitsubishi Corporation (49 percent),

is Guerrero Negro's largest employer—see Saltworks further on for a description.

Note: After you cross the state line into Baja California Sur, don't forget to move your timepieces forward one hour; BCS follows the United States' Mountain Time.

CLIMATE

Temperatures in Guerrero Negro remain fairly steady year-round, due to the overall Pacific influence and the insulating effect of bays and lagoons to the west. Daytime highs are 21–24°C (70–75°F) in summer, 15–18°C (59–65°F) in winter. Rainfall is scarce, but an almost-constant fog keeps the air moist in summer.

WHALE-WATCHING AT LAGUNA OJO DE LIEBRE

During the season, January–March, Laguna Ojo de Liebre (also known as **Scammon's Lagoon**) offers several whale-watching options. Local tour operators take small groups of up to 10 people for US$40 pp (US$30 for children under 11), which often includes a box lunch. One of the most popular tour organizers is **Malarrimo Eco-Tours,** tel./fax 615/157-0100, malarimo@telnor.net, www.malarrimo.com. Prospective participants should book at the tour office next to Malarrimo Restaurant at least a day in advance. During the height of the season, vans leave daily from the restaurant at 8 A.M. and 11 A.M. and drive, via salt-company roads, to a shore of the lagoon, where a *panga* takes participants out on the water for about two hours. Passengers must arrive at the patio of the restaurant a half hour before departure time to sign the passenger list. Lunch, included in the tour fee, is eaten on Isla Arena, a large sandbar island covered in dunes.

You can book a similar tour at the same price through **Mario's Tours,** at Restaurant Mario's (no phone, see Food). Also well-established is **Laguna Tours** on Blvd. Zapata next to Motel San Ignacio, tel. 615/157-0050. Like Malarrimo's, these tours cost US$40 pp and leave twice every morning during the gray whale season.

A less expensive alternative is to drive on your

© JOE CUMMINGS

close encounters of the big and barnacled kind

own to the shore of the lagoon and deal directly with the *pangeros*. To do this, take Mexico 1 south of town nine km (5.5 miles) to the turnoff marked **Parque Natural de la Ballena Gris** and turn right (southwest). This 24-km (15-mile) road alternates between washboard and sandy surfaces that sometimes require slow driving. After about six km (3.5 miles), the road reaches a salt company checkpoint where you must usually wait for an attendant to open the gate. After the checkpoint, the road runs between two salt-evaporation flats; the drying salt looks like packed snow. The road ends at the edge of the lagoon, where a US$3 parking fee is collected. If you don't have your own wheels, hire a cab from in front of the bus depot in Guerrero Negro out to the *panga* piers at Laguna Ojo de Liebre for US$5; one cab can take up to five passengers.

Once you're at the shore, you can watch the whales from land or sign on with a boat tour.

CENTRAL BAJA

A VICTORY FOR VIZCAÍNO

Proposals to establish a large solar saltworks along Laguna San Ignacio—similar to the salt-production facilities near Guerrero Negro—ignited a fierce debate as to whether the Mexican government should allow the plan to proceed. At the heart of the debate was whether the saltworks would negatively affect the bay as a marine nursery for the Pacific gray whale, although there were many other issues at stake as well.

Exportadora Sal, S.A. (ESSA), a joint venture between the Mexican government (51 percent ownership) and Mitsubishi International (49 percent ownership), claimed the proposed saltworks would have no effect on the whales. This position was refuted by the International Fund for Animal Welfare, the National Resources Defense Council, and Mexico's Grupo de los Cien, all of whom had actively campaigned against the salt factory since 1997.

The proposed saltworks were supposed to lie squarely inside the buffer zone of El Vizcaíno Biosphere Reserve, a UNESCO designation recognizing the area's immense value to global ecology, particularly the diversity of marine and desert flora and fauna. The reserve protects not only the gray whale but also the pronghorn, the desert bighorn sheep, waterfowl, mangroves, salt-flat vegetation, and many other life forms. Opponents of the saltworks maintained the proposal contravened the UNESCO biosphere status, which the Mexican government endorses through current environmental legislation, and was thus illegal. Meanwhile, ESSA, using independent researchers, had complied with all Mexican government guidelines with regard to conducting an environmental impact assessment as well as a socioeconomic assessment.

About 38,000 people reside within the boundaries of the biosphere reserve. If established, the saltworks would have created only about 200 jobs in the San Ignacio area. Local opponents asked, What would the saltworks do for the other 37,800 residents?

Many residents, however, strongly favored the ESSA proposal and were resentful that outsiders—particularly Americans—opposed the saltworks. One local opinion:

Actually we don't really know what moves these [opponents]; so many people are so arrogant and still want to see us with our backs against the cactus, with a big sombrero and the donkey at our side, presuming Mexicans are not qualified to care for the environment and resources. But I ask you, who closed the lagoons to protect the whales? Who stops the fishing when the whales are here? Who remembers [us] when the whales are not here? What have the people received for this sacrifice to protect something in the name of humanity?

With a good pair of binoculars you can see the whales from shore, but you get much closer to them on the water and can hear them blowing. January–March, two or three boats are usually on hand at the park for charters. The going rate is US$25 per adult, US$15 per child; boats leave 9 A.M.–3 P.M. only and stay out about an hour and a half. After 3 P.M., the wind comes up, fog comes in, and whale-watching conditions are poor.

Private boats, kayaks, sailboards, inflatable rafts, and other floatables aren't permitted anywhere in Laguna Ojo de Liebre during the whale season. The *pangeros* who take tourists out to see

the whales are granted seasonal permits to do so. They're also very skilled at running the *pangas* so as not to frighten or threaten the whales, most of whom are mothers and babies. The males, for the most part, cavort near the entrance of the lagoon, farther from shore.

OTHER SIGHTS
Saltworks

More important to the local economy than whale-watching tourists is the local saltworks, a large solar-evaporative operation producing

Living here is not easy, our families have to fight against the weather, the distances, the desert, sea, mountains. I ask people behind their desks to camp and fish in the wind, to sleep in the cold, to have water one day and save some for the next day or two, what do they know about this and many other things? I agree we need to save the whales from danger, but who will save the people and their families from hunger? Who gives these people a better way to live?

Why does the USA not move its nuclear marine base from San Diego? Is it not there where the gray whale starts to mate? Do not some marine biologists say that they found gray whale food routes along the Washington and Oregon coast, where hundreds of fishing trawlers work from San Francisco to Washington? Doesn't the USA have oil towers in the sea in Alaska, the same place that provides food to many kind of whales, not just grays? Why they don't fight that? No food, no mating; no mating, no calf. It's a chain but they want to punish the weak link.

UNESCO representatives toured the El Vizcaíno Biosphere in August 1999 and issued a report that contained only a rather mild statement that ESSA's proposed saltworks would result in a transformation that could compromise the integrity of the reserve. No examples were offered.

Opponents pointed out that waste products from the existing Guerrero Negro saltworks have negatively impacted local fisheries and that the same would occur in San Ignacio. In addition to habitat and watershed-flow alterations, the introduction of ship traffic and noise, contamination of water, air, and soil, and the huge industrial footprint (in a nominally protected area), could damage both protected species such as the whale, and food fish harvested by local fishing communities. One specific concern related to plans to build the San Ignacio saltworks pier in a prime lobster- and abalone-harvesting area. They also pointed out that the main economic benefit would go to Japan rather than Mexico, through value-added processing of raw salt.

In March 2000, the Zedillo administration, concluding that the ecological/economic trade-off wasn't worth it, decided to halt the proposed Laguna de San Ignacio ESSA project.

around six million tons of salt a year. Exportadora Sal, S.A. (ESSA) maintains a 182-square-km (70-square-mile) system of diked ponds southwest of town that take in seawater from the lagoons and impound it, at a depth of about one meter, until the fierce Vizcaíno Desert sun turns it into thick layers of salt. The salt is then scooped into trucks and driven to Puerto El Chaparrito at the north end of Laguna Ojo de Liebre, where it's loaded onto barges and shipped 80 km northwest to Isla Cedros. From Isla Cedros the salt is shipped by freighter to the Mexican mainland, the United States, Canada, and Japan.

Dunes

About 9.5 km (six miles) from town or four km (2.5 miles) from Mexico 1 near Paralelo 28 are the **Dunas de Soledad,** a large system of coastal sand dunes up to eight meters (26 feet) tall. Along the other side of the dunes facing the Pacific is **Playa Don Miguelito,** a pristine beach named for the man considered the father of Guerrero Negro. In 1926 fisherman Don Miguelito came to the lagoon by burro all the way from Sonora and stayed in the area till his death in 1992 at age 96. You can reach the dunes by taking the wide sand/salt road off Mexico 1 near the Paralelo 28 monument.

ACCOMMODATIONS

Hotels and Motels

Except for La Pinta, all of Guerrero Negro's hotels and motels are on or just off Boulevard Zapata, the main street through town, west of Mexico 1.

Under US$25: The cheapest digs in town are at **Motel Gamez,** west toward the ESSA buildings, tel. 615/157-0370; rooms are very basic, and the hot-water supply is inconsistent. In this same general vicinity are the **Motel Salparaíso** (turn right at Frutería Loma Bonita) and **Motel Brisa Salina,** tel. 615/157-0115, both with adequate rooms. Farther southeast along Boulevard Zapata is the cheap but noisier **Dunas Motel,** tel. 615/157-0057.

Behind Motel El Morro on Calle Victoria, the quiet **Motel Las Ballenas,** tel. 615/157-0116, offers 14 simple rooms with TV and private bath.

Motel San José, tel. 615/157-1420, across from the bus station, has simple, clean rooms with hot showers and color TV.

US$25–50: East of the Dunas Motel on Blvd. Zapata, toward Malarrimo Restaurant, the two-story **Motel San Ignacio,** tel. 615/157-0270, offers simple but cozy rooms. Next to the Malarrimo Restaurant, **Cabañas Don Miguelito,** tel./fax 615/157-0100, malarimo@telnor.net, www.malarrimo.com, rents detached trailer-style units, all with carpet, a single bed and a queen-size bed, hot water, and cable TV. More recent additions are the four family rooms, done in colorful Mexican decor with loft bunks for the kids.

Next door to the Motel San Ignacio, the **Motel El Morro,** tel. 615/157-0414, offers 34 spacious rooms with ceiling fans and TVs.

Motel Don Gus, in the center of town on Blvd. Zapata, tel. 615/159-1115, has 10 carpeted rooms with double beds, spacious bathrooms, and TV with HBO. The restaurant serves good Mexican seafood dishes.

US$50–100: Just south of the state border and west of the Paralelo 28 monument off Mexico 1, the **Hotel La Pinta,** tel. 615/157-1300 or 615/157-1303, fax 615/157-1306, Ensenada tel. 646/176-2601, U.S. tel. 800/800-9632, www.lapintahotels.com, offers 27 large, comfortable rooms at the usual higher-than-average La Pinta rates. It's conveniently situated for getting on and off the highway but is a bit overpriced for what you get. It's also a seven-km (four-mile) drive into town; if you plan to spend a few days exploring Guerrero Negro, you might look for something in the town itself.

Camping and RV Parks

Coastal areas around Guerrero Negro offer plenty of free camping spots, but few are accessible by ordinary passenger vehicle. Camping is permitted along the lagoon in the Parque Natural de la Ballena Gris; a daily parking fee of US$5 is usually collected during whale-watching season, January–March. A few RVers have set up camp at a dirt lot near the old salt wharf, about 10 km (six miles) northwest of town via a graded road that meets Boulevard Zapata just past the Banamex.

In town next to Malarrimo Restaurant, **Cabañas Don Miguelito RV Park,** tel./fax 615/157-0100, offers 45 sites with electricity/water hookups and dump stations for US$12 d up to 35 feet, US$15 d over 35 feet, or US$10 d for campers and vans. Additional persons are US$5 per adult, US$2 per child age 4–12. Tent camping costs US$5 per person. Use of restrooms with hot showers is included in the rates.

Benito Juárez RV Park (formerly The Dunes), just south of Hotel La Pinta next to the state border off Mexico 1, has 18 electricity/water hookups (no shade) plus toilet and shower facilities for US$7–9 d, US$2 for each additional person.

FOOD

Guerrero Negro has several places to eat and a couple of supermarkets that supply residents as far away as Bahía de los Ángeles and San Francisquito. Like the hotels and motels, most are spread out along Guerrero Negro's main avenue, Boulevard Zapata.

The most popular restaurant in town, especially for gringos, is **Malarrimo Restaurant,** on the north side of Blvd. Zapata just as you enter Guerrero Negro, tel. 615/157-0100. The pismo clams, deep-sea scallops, lobster, and other fresh seafood are always good; breakfasts are another highlight, including lobster omelettes, home-made chorizo and eggs, and other diet-busters, served with beans, *chilaquiles,* and tortillas. It's open daily 7 A.M.–11 P.M.; prices are higher than average. Near the edge of town, **Puerto Viejo** offers a similar menu at lower prices; open daily 7 A.M.–11 P.M. Outside of town on Mexico 1 just south of the 28th parallel checkpoint, **Restaurant Mario's** also specializes in seafood. Mario's is open 7 A.M.–11 P.M. and prices are moderate.

Another restaurant on Boulevard Zapata competing for the tourist business is **La Vieja Hacienda,** specializing in steaks and Mexican food.

For something more local in price and ambience, try the **Cocina Económica Lety,** a small eatery on the east side of Blvd. Zapata next to the Secretaría de Pesca trailer. Simple homestyle meals run US$4–5, about half the average price at tourist restaurants here; in addition to regular menu items for breakfast, lunch, and dinner, Lety offers a daily *comida corrida.* No alcohol is served, but the banana *licuados* are excellent. **Cocina Económica Sinaloa,** next to the small intercity bus terminal on Blvd. Zapata, is similar.

Northwest of Lety's, across from the Pemex, is **Mariscos La Palapa,** a basic little seafood place. Good mesquite-grilled *tacos de carne asada* can be found at **Tacos Asadero,** on Blvd. Zapata in the center of town—US$1 per taco.

The long-established **El Figón de Sal** on Blvd. Zapata still serves moderately priced Mexican and seafood *platillos* for lunch and dinner.

China Express, opposite El Moro hotel, is a decent Chinese fast-food spot, open daily 11 A.M.–9 P.M.

Groceries

Guerrero Negro has the only supermarkets south of Ensenada and north of Santa Rosalía. **La Ballena** is the largest and most popular of the pair on Boulevard Zapata and is the only store in town that accepts traveler's checks. It stocks an amazing variety of things, including full picnic supplies.

Just northwest of Cocina Económica Lety on the north side of the road is the government-subsidized **Tienda ISSSTE,** which carries basic grocery items at discounted prices. There's also the similar **Tienda ESSA,** right across from the

main entrance to the salt plant, around the corner from Banamex.

Panadería Hermanos Águilar, on the south side of Blvd. Zapata west of Malarrimo Restaurant, offers a variety of Mexican pastries, including fresh *bolillos,* daily.

Panadería La Popular, near Motel Gamez and next door to the Red Cross, bakes fresh bread, along with various pastries and cakes, daily. Buy fresh corn tortillas at **Tortillería Mayma.** Directly across the street from the *tortillería* is a daily open-air fruit and vegetable market; it usually receives fresh produce every Wednesday.

INFORMATION AND SERVICES

Tourst Assistance

The tourist office (tel. 615/157-0100) in front of Malarrimo Restaurant has information on Guerrero Negro and the surrounding areas; open daily 10 A.M.–2 P.M. and 4–7 P.M.

Money-Changing

A **Banamex** near the ESSA buildings, near the end of Blvd. Zapata, offers a currency exchange service Mon.–Fri. 8:30 A.M.–3 P.M. Banamex also has an ATM, very convenient for travelers with cash cards.

Telephone

Except for the **TelNor** office in Bahía de los Ángeles, Guerrero Negro has the only public telephone service in a 200-km (120-mile) radius. Several privately operated phone offices in town add service charges to the cost of any call. Collect calls can be made at the public phone booth in front of Malarrimo Restaurant for no charge.

Laundry

Opposite Motel Las Ballenas, **Lavamática Express** offers coin-operated washers and dryers.

GETTING THERE

By Air to/from Isla Cedros

Aero Cedros, tel. 615/157-1626, operates flights to and from Isla Cedros daily at 10 A.M. The flight lasts about 40 minutes, and one-way tickets cost US$55; the airline office, next to the police station on Blvd. Zapata, is open Mon.–Sat. 9 A.M.–4 P.M.

Guerrero Negro's airfield is north of town near Paralelo 28, a few hundred meters off Mexico 1; the turnoff occurs between Km 125 and 126.

By Bus

Transportes de Águila and **ABC** use a small depot on the west side of Blvd. Zapata (between Malarrimo Restaurant and Motel San Ignacio). Five first-class buses head north daily to Punta Prieta (US$10), San Quintín (US$20), Ensenada (US$30), and Tijuana (US$37), and south to Vizcaíno (US$5), San Ignacio (US$7), Santa Rosalía (US$15), Mulegé (US$17), Loreto (US$27), Ciudad Constitución (US$30), and La Paz (US$40).

GETTING AROUND

Yellow *urbanos* or city buses, marked **Infonavit-Centro,** run frequently between the Paralelo 28 monument and the old town via Boulevard Zapata and Calle Madero; the fare is US$.40. You can hire taxis at the bus depot; a cab ride to anywhere in town costs US$3.

SIDE TRIP TO SAN FRANCISQUITO

A side trip east out to the Sea of Cortez passes through good desert mountain scenery and terminates in the small, secluded fish camp of San Francisquito on Bahía Santa Teresa. The turnoff for San Francisquito (signed for El Arco) occurs about 27 km (16.5 miles) south of the Guerrero Negro junction. From the highway, the 121-km (75-mile) road to the bay takes 3–4 hours, including the steep downgrade known as Cuesta de la Ley (Slope of the Law), which comes along approximately 29 km (18 miles) before San Francisquito. The grade has been lessened and is not quite as challenging as it once was. Modest supplies may be available along the way in El Arco, 34 km (21 miles) east of Mexico 1. Many roads join the main one east of El Arco, and you may have to ask directions along the way to ensure you're on a direct course for San Francisquito.

You can also reach San Francisquito by road from Bahía de los Ángeles in about the same amount of time. Count on lots of washboard along either road; be sure to gas up first in Bahía de los Ángeles, Guerrero Negro, or Vizcaíno. Both roads meet near Rancho El Progreso, approximately 21 km (13 miles) east of Bahía San Francisquito. The network of roads surrounding the ranch can be a trifle confusing; take the branch heading due east to reach the bay (a southeasterly branch goes to the fish camp of El Barril).

Accommodations and Camping

San Francisquito Resort, U.S. tel. 619/690-1000, maintains five simple, thatched-roof cabañas right on the beach. The resort charges US$15 pp for accommodations only, or US$30 with breakfast and dinner. *Pangas* are available for hire starting at US$80/day. Dive trips out to Isla San Lorenzo, Isla San Esteban, and other nearby islands can also be arranged. Rental tanks are available, but you must bring your own regulators. Camping on the grounds is permitted for US$5 pp, which includes use of hot-water showers and restrooms.

Alberto and Deborah Lucero, Apdo. Postal 7, San Ignacio, BCS 23930, allow visitors to camp on their bayside property for only US$2.50 pp per night. Deborah cooks wonderful meals and can arrange guided mule trips into the coastal mountain range as well as Sea of Cortez fishing trips. You can also purchase fuel and food supplies from them for your own explorations of the area.

Vizcaíno Peninsula

Jutting northwest into the Pacific, the coast of this huge desert peninsula is renowned among beachcombers, anglers, surfers, and scuba divers for the abundant opportunities to participate in their favorite recreational activities far from "civilization." The isolation and long distances involved in navigating the peninsula's interior deter the casual visitor, despite the fact that the roads aren't really all that bad. The greatest distance between Pemex stations on the Vizcaíno Peninsula (Península Vizcaíno in Spanish) is 166 km (100 miles). More critical is the lack of automotive and medical assistance along lengthy stretches of road.

> The coast of this huge desert peninsula is renowned for beachcombing, fishing, surfing, and scuba diving far from "civilization."

Although most visitors head straight for the peninsular shores, a leisurely drive through the interior affords close, uninterrupted views of the Vizcaíno Desert. Rainfall is scant, and the desert vegetation mostly survives on Pacific fog; yucca trees *(datilillos)* are particularly abundant. Several of the cactus and succulent species chosen for Biosphere II—an experimental dome environment in Arizona—were borrowed from this desert.

Fuel, food, and other supplies are available at four cannery towns along the southwest coast of the peninsula and, to a much lesser extent, from a handful of fish camps and ranchos between these settlements. A comprehensive loop trip involves driving west from Vizcaíno (Mexico 1, Km 144) to Bahía Tortugas or Bahía Asunción, then southeast to Punta Abreojos and back to Mexico 1 at Km 98. Beach camping is possible at numerous spots between Bahía Asunción and Punta Abreojos, and rustic rooms are available in Bahía Tortugas.

The best onshore/inshore fishing areas are generally between Bahía Asunción and Punta Abreojos. Typical catches include halibut, corvina, croaker, and sand, calico, and pinto bass.

Reserva de la Biósfera del Vizcaíno

Since 1988 much of the peninsula has belonged to the Reserva de la Biósfera del Vizcaíno, the largest such reserve in Mexico and one of the largest in the world at over 2.5 million hectares (77 percent of the Mulegé *municipio*). In 1993, Vizcaíno was added to UNESCO's list of "Man and the Biosphere" reserves. Sixteen different core zones, where human activity is heavily restricted, comprise 363,438 hectares; the remainder are buffer zones where limited activity is permitted. In addition to peninsular areas, the reserve boundaries take in all or parts of the islands of Isla Delgadito, Islotes Delgadito, Isla Pelicano, Isla Malcob, Isla San Ignacio, Isla San Roque, Isla Asunción, and Isla Natividad. Coastal waters along the peninsula harbor at least 66 percent of all marine mammal species in Mexico, including eight dolphin and 15 whale varieties.

Recent aerial surveys have confirmed that around 200 rare *berrendo* (desert pronghorn) survive on the peninsula—not 100 as previously estimated—although this number still makes them a very endangered species. The only antelope in the world that doesn't need to drink water, the *berrendo* satisfies all its moisture needs through the ingestion of plants, which are in turn nourished on Pacific fog. Other rare fauna include the *borrego cimarrón* (desert bighorn sheep), fishing eagle, white pelican, peregrine falcon, loggerhead sea turtle, and elephant seal.

Vizcaíno

Also known as Fundolegal and on American maps as Vizcaíno Junction, this small town on Mexico 1 is the easiest starting point for any peninsula trip, not least because supplies are available here. The bulk of the pueblo (pop. 2,340) lies west of the highway on the road leading into the peninsula interior, but several services of use to the traveler can be found along Mexico 1 itself. A huge packing plant processes local produce, so the junction is often lined with parked 18-wheelers.

Both of the motels in Vizcaíno are under US$25. **Kadekamán Motel and RV Park,** Mexico 1, Km 143, tel. 615/154-0270, fax 615/154-0127, offers small, clean, charming rooms. RV sites with water and electricity cost US$6 for two people. A café on the premises serves very good Mexican food at moderate prices; the *caldo de callos* (scallop soup) is particularly tasty.

Motel Olivia, tel. 615/154-0024, fax 615/154-0304, more or less across from the Pemex station, is a long, low building holding nondescript rooms with TV and air-conditioning. The attached restaurant specializes in *carnes* and *mariscos.* **Restaurant Marthita,** on the east side of the highway just south of the Pemex, is popular with truckers. **Restaurant Bar Nancy,** at the south end of town, is more popular in the evenings.

Vizcaíno has several small markets. Groceries are best purchased at **Supermercado California,** next to Motel Olivia.

Driving the Vizcaíno Road

The first 35 km (22 miles) of the 166-km Vizcaíno road are paved, after which, depending on how recently it has been graded, the unpaved surface tends toward heavy washboard. At some points along the way, parallel sand roads may provide smoother passage. In other places salt flats offer several hundred meters of flat surfaces. About eight km (five miles) south of the Bahía Asunción junction is an attractive area of *bolsones* or salt-flat wetlands.

Those with four-wheel drive vehicles can make a side journey to **Playa Malarrimo** via a challenging track that branches north off the Vizcaíno–Bahía Tortugas road 116 km (72 miles) from Mexico 1, near Rancho San José de Castro. It then winds through arroyos and around mesas for 44 km (27 miles) before fading out at the dunes behind the beach. Malarrimo receives the brunt of northwest Pacific currents and is therefore a beachcomber's paradise. It takes a hardened beachcomber to appreciate the beach, however, since much of the flotsam washed ashore consists of the dregs of civilization—Styrofoam, plastic, and garbage jettisoned from ships throughout the North Pacific.

BAHÍA ASUNCIÓN AND PUNTA ABREOJOS

Bahía Asunción

Bahía Asunción (pop. 1,200) lies 42 km (26 miles) southwest of the Vizcaíno–Bahía Tortugas road via a fair unpaved branch road. You can also reach Asunción via a second, longer road that leaves the Vizcaíno road farther northwest near Rancho San José del Castro. The latter makes a perfect entrée for motorcyclists, as it's a sand road with lots of mogullike hills; the northern section of this road passes through a low mountain range as well.

The town consists of clusters of ramshackle homes, trailers, small businesses, and sand streets around a pretty, sharply curving bay. Services include an unsigned Pemex station, SEMARNAT office (SEMARNAT is the government entity responsible for issuing permits for island visits), airstrip, marine products processing plant, clinic, and a few markets and cafés. Just north of town is a small beach.

Restaurant El Mayico, on the main strip through town, is a clean and friendly spot serving seafood, eggs, quesadillas, coffee, and cold beer. **Restaurant Goanda,** a windowless place near the main pier, is not as good.

Estero de Coyote

South of Bahía Asunción, this complex of lagoons and saltmarshes a few kilometers east of Punta Abreojos is well known as fishing grounds for bass (spotted bay and barred), corvina, and halibut. Grouper and sierra can also be taken at the mouth of the estuary, where it drains into the Bahía de Ballenas. You can camp on the beach near the mouth of the estuary.

Services are minimal in La Bocana and Punta Abreojos—the two nearest towns—though barrel gas is usually available in both.

BAHÍA TORTUGAS

The largest Vizcaíno town lies 166 km (100 miles) from Vizcaíno junction on Mexico 1 and boasts a population of 2,640. Aside from a cannery and Pemex station, the town offers several

© JOE CUMMINGS

Bahía Tortugas

markets and cafés, a clinic, a post office, modest motels, and an airfield. Most of the buildings—brightly painted in pinks, blues, and oranges—are constructed of wood that arrived by boat from the American Northwest. The dry hills around Tortugas bear almost no vegetation, and the little town swirls with dust and sand.

A gray sand beach not far from the town's long wooden pier looks fairly inviting, but with all the shipping and boating in the area it's doubtful the water is particularly clean. Toward the southeast end of the bay are some longer sand beaches. Bahía Tortugas's harbor is the best between Ensenada and Bahía Magdalena in terms of all-weather protection.

North of Bahía Tortugas, 26.5 km (16.5 miles) by graded dirt road, is **Punta Eugenia,** a small fishing village and jumping-off place for boat trips to Islas Natividad, Cedros, and San Benito.

Accommodations

Under US$25: Motel Nancy, tel. 615/158-0100, housed in a bright blue, U-shaped building around a small parking lot, offers modest rooms with private hot-water showers. The motel office is in Novedades Lupita next door. On the southwest side of town, **Motel Rendón** is a two-story breeze-block place with similarly priced rooms.

Food

Right near the entrance to town via the Vizcaíno road, **Taquería El Muro** sells tacos and *antojitos.* **Restaurant El Moroco,** near Motel Rendón, has a more complete menu that includes fresh seafood.

Services and Transportation

You can cash traveler's checks at a **Banamex,** just up the street from Motel Nancy. A *farmacia* on the same street (Av. Juárez) offers long-distance phone and fax services. You can also make calls from a **Telecomm** office in town and from the Motel Vera Cruz.

Aero Cedros (formerly Aerolíneas California Pacíficos) no longer flies to Bahía Tortugas from Guerrero Negro, but service could resume at any time. Sociedad Cooperativa de Producción Pesquera (Cannery Airlines) still flies from Ensenada.

ISLA CEDROS

Baja's largest Pacific coast island not of oceanic origin is 20 km (12 miles) north of the tip of the Vizcaíno Peninsula, or about 72 km (43 miles) northwest of Guerrero Negro. The two main industries on the 24-km-long (14.5-mile-long) island are fishing and off-loading salt from Guerrero Negro's saltworks for long-distance shipping. Because of the salt business, Cedros ranks as Mexico's third-largest port after Veracruz and Tampico, carrying over 9 percent of all offshore cargo. It is also the sixth most populated island in Mexico; according to INEGI, 2,732 people make the island their home—about two percent of all islanders in Mexico. This figure may be low; some Cedros residents claim as many as 5,000 persons inhabit the island, though for some residence is only seasonal.

Note: Isla Cedros lies in the same time zone as Baja California Norte; i.e., an hour behind Guerrero Negro.

CENTRAL BAJA

Flora and Fauna

Among naturalists, Isla Cedros is known for its small stands of scrub juniper and pine in the center of the island between its tallest peaks, Pico Gill (1,063 meters/3,488 feet) toward the north end and Cerro de Cedros (1,200 meters/3,950 feet) toward the south. Like cedars, the island's mistaken namesake, junipers belong to the cypress family. Even more impressive are the Cedros Island oak *(Quercus cedrosensis)* and Cedros Island pine *(Pinus radiata* var. *cedrosensis),* both endemic to this island. A rare variety of mule deer reportedly inhabits the island's center. Date palms stand along the northeast coast; no one remembers who planted them.

Cerro de Cedros

The hike from town to the island's high point takes around three hours and is rewarded by very good views. To reach Cerro de Cedros, follow the road northwest out of town till it ends at a trail that follows a water pipe most of the way up the hill. Keep an eye on the summit's radio towers and you'll have no problem following the trail.

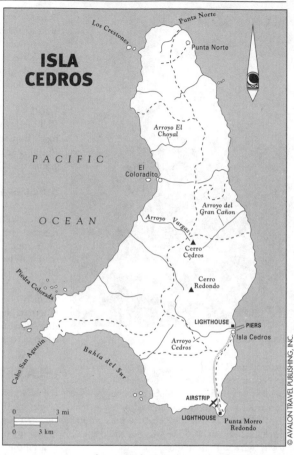

Around the Island

From the town and airport, the nearest good beach is at **Punta Prieta,** at the southwest end of the island; locally this beach is referred to as Playón. Taxis cost a standard US$10 for the 10-km (six-mile) trip from town, though some drivers will go as low as US$8. After Punta Prieta the vehicle road ends, but a rough track continues along the coast. You can also reach Playón by traversing the island via Cerro de Cedros, but this requires an overnight at the beach—carry plenty of water. Surfing is possible at **Playa Elefante,** an empty stretch of sand north of Cabo San Agustín; the only way to get there is by *panga* from town or from one of the fish camps. The going rate for a complete coastal circuit by *panga* is US$80–100. A *panga* to nearby Isla Natividad also costs US$80–100; these boats take up to five passengers.

Fish camps are at **Cabo San Agustín,** on the southwest corner of the island, and at **Punta Norte** to the north. The largest settlement on the island, **Cedros,** is a village of around 2,500 on the southeast coast facing the peninsula. Along the main street leading from the harbor are a COTP office, CONASUPO, fish cannery, post office, church, bank (traveler's checks cannot be cashed here), school, a couple of cafés, and a sizable residential area. South of the village along the same coast are the docks where salt from Guerrero Negro is off-loaded.

Accommodations and Camping

Basic lodgings in *casas de huéspedes* (guesthouses) in town can be arranged for US$10–15; the best of the two or three in operation is **Casa Elsa García.** If it's full, ask a taxi driver for other recommendations or look along the main street for signs reading "Se Rentan Cuartos." Primitive camping on a rocky beach north of town is also an option.

Food

La Pacenita, a block south of the main drag and two blocks inland from the harbor, offers a good, basic menu of Mexican fish, chicken, and beef dishes daily 6 A.M.–8 P.M. The nearby **Restaurant El Marino,** on the north side of the main street three blocks from the harbor, has more expensive—though not necessarily tastier—Mexican dishes and seafood.

Transportation

Aside from sailing over in your own boat, the easiest way to reach the island is by plane. Aero Cedros flies from Guerrero Negro daily at 10 A.M. for US$55 each way; the flight takes around 40 minutes. The return trip leaves straightaway, and you need to be at the airfield early in the morning to be sure of securing a seat. Sociedad Cooperativa

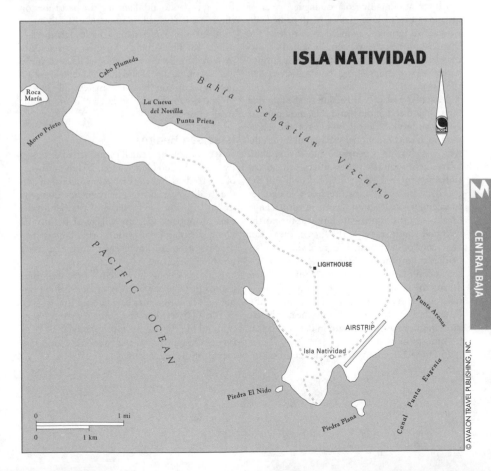

ISLA NATIVIDAD

CENTRAL BAJA

de Producción Pesquera (Cannery Airlines) also flies periodically from Ensenada. The island's paved airstrip lies south of Cedros village at Punta Morro Redondo. It's sometimes possible to charter a boat to the island from either Bahía Tortugas or Punta Eugenia.

A taxi from the airfield into town costs US$5 per car. Up to five passengers can split the fare.

OTHER ISLANDS

Isla Natividad

During the Spanish missionary period, a Cochimí subtribe lived on this arid island 10 km (six miles) northwest of Punta Eugenia, calling it Afegua, or "Island of Birds." Eventually a Jesuit padre from Misión San Ignacio convinced them to leave the island and live at the mission. Renamed Christmas Island, today it's one of the most famous surfing destinations along the Pacific coast of the Americas.

Most of the island's surf action can be found at the southern end of the island. The most popular Natividad break, "Open Doors," is off the southwest tip; it catches summer swells from the southwest—peak time is generally July–September. Waves here typically run 4–6 feet, with occasional sets up to 15 feet. "Frijole Bowl," off the southeastern tip (Punta Arenas), also catches southern or southwestern swells. In winter, large breaks—for pros only—are found at the northwest and southwest tips; the former break can be reached only by boat. The small village of Isla Natividad, on the southeast shore of the 22.5-square-km island, houses around 200 fishermen during the summer. In winter many visit relatives on the peninsula or work on farms in the Ensenada area. Thus boats out to the northwest shore break should be arranged in Punta Eugenia. Or bring your own.

In Punta Eugenia you can charter a boat to Isla Natividad for US$15 one-way; the best time to find a boat is the early morning, when local fishermen are heading out to sea. Likewise afternoons 2–3 P.M. are best for boat rides back to Punta Eugenia. Boat transportation to and from Isla Natividad can be difficult in the winter, when the island is mostly deserted.

In summer, and when there are enough passengers, Sociedad Cooperativa de Producción Pesquera flies to the island from Ensenada via Isla Cedros. The airstrip is less than a half kilometer from the village of Isla Natividad.

What else is there to do on the island besides surf? According to BSA, the surf and inshore fishing is good, and if surfing the best tubes on the coast isn't thrilling enough, cliff diving—from 10- to 15-meter-high ocean precipices—might be. Then there's "surging," an activity invented by bored surfers in which you jump into a deep tidal pool and then allow the wave action to pump your body 6–9 meters (20–30 feet) up and down. The island has a clinic to handle small injuries.

Islas San Benito

This group of three small islands (Isla Benito del Este, Centro, and Oeste), about 25 km northwest of Isla Cedros, has the best yellowtail fishing on the Pacific coast. Boats usually anchor along the leeward (southeastern) shore of Isla Benito del Oeste, opposite the tiny village of Benito del Oeste. Elephant seals, the world's largest pinnipeds, often sun themselves along the coves north of the village.

Rock reefs along the western shores of all three islands provide the best diving and fishing opportunities. Divers may be interested in the wreck of the U.S. tanker *Swift Eagle,* which went aground in 1934 off the north shore of Isla Benito del Oeste; parts of the wreck lie within two meters of the ocean surface.

San Ignacio and Vicinity

SAN IGNACIO

In pre-mission days, the local Cochimí called the sheltered arroyo formed by the Río San Ignacio Kadakaamán or "Creek of Reeds." Fed by an underground stream, this fertile palm oasis on the southeastern edge of the Vizcaíno Desert has supported mission crops of wheat, figs, grapes, pomegranates, oranges, corn, and dates for over 200 years. The sleepy town of San Ignacio (pop. 4,000) is a cluster of stuccoed, pastel-colored, colonial-style buildings and small *rancherías* centered around **Misión San Ignacio Kadakaamán** and the adjacent *plazuela*. Hemmed in on all sides by mesas, the town's palm-oasis ambience and ongoing resistance to change have made it a favorite among Baja travelers for decades.

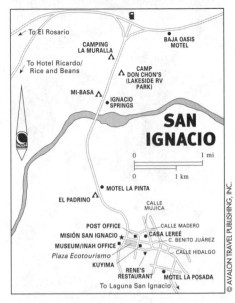

Climate

San Ignacio is very pleasant in the winter months, when daytime temperatures are 18–21°C (65–70°F), nights a bit cooler. In summer, the surrounding desert sizzles as high as 40°C (105°F), although the valley floor may be a few degrees cooler. Rainfall is nearly nil year-round.

Misión San Ignacio Kadakaamán

Jesuit records indicate the Cochimí of Kadakaamán sent several requests for mission assistance to Italian Jesuit Padre Píccolo of Misión Santa Rosalía de Mulegé in the early 18th century. Píccolo first visited the area in 1716 and stayed in a brush cabaña for a month, apparently converting and baptizing a willing Amerindian population. In 1728 Jesuit Padre Juan Bautista Loyando constructed a church and mission house on the present site, then proceeded to build a number of visiting chapels at nearby *rancherías*. He was succeeded by Padre Sigismundo Taraval, who brought Amerindians from the Pacific islands off the tip of the Vizcaíno Peninsula into the mission community. Eventually the San Ignacio mission became the largest and most successful in Baja California, with a parish of over 5,000 Amerindians.

After the Jesuits were expelled from New Spain, Dominican Friar Juan Crisóstomo Gómez took charge of the mission, building a grander church on the original site in 1786. The walls, 1.2 meters (four feet) thick, were constructed of local volcanic stone without the use of mortar. The lumber for the wooden beams was transported from Misión Guadalupe in the high sierra; the carved doors at the front of the church were brought from the Mexican mainland. According to Jesuit records, the queen of Spain paid 1.5 million pesos for the church's construction.

Today the venerable church stands largely in its original condition, thanks to a 1976 restoration, and is used by the local community for masses, weddings, funerals, and daily worship. The church's elaborate facade, with its engraved stone plaques and plaster ornamentation, makes it one of the most impressive of all Baja's mission churches. The plaque to the left of the main doors, above the lower left window, is emblazoned with two crowned lions (symbol of the Kingdom of León in Spain), two castles (for

CENTRAL BAJA

© JOE CUMMINGS

Misión San Ignacio

the Kingdom of Castile), and the crown of Spain. To the right of the portal, over the corresponding lower window, is a simpler plaque with two overlapping globes (representing the Old and New Worlds), flanked by the twin Hercules pillars of Spain and North Africa; the pillars are topped by the crowns of Spain and Portugal, while the globe motif features a hybrid crown combining aspects of both the Portuguese and Spanish crowns.

Inside the church, the statue at the center of the main viceregal-style altar is of the mission's patron saint, St. Ignacius Loyola. Surrounding the statue are paintings of St. Joseph and the infant Jesus (upper left), St. Bernard (lower left), Vírgen de Pilar (above the statue), St. John the Baptist (upper right), and St. Dominic (lower right). The two side altars, while not as impressive, also date from the mission period.

A sign in the church foyer requests that visitors dress with respect and refrain from chewing gum.

Museo Local de San Ignacio

Next to the church, a small museum operated by the Instituto Nacional de Antropología e História (INAH) contains color photos and mock mural exhibits dedicated to regional history, with a primary focus on the rock art of the nearby Sierra de San Francisco. The displays are heavily captioned in Spanish only. Open Mon.–Sat. 8 A.M.–6 P.M.; entry is free.

Next to the museum, a small **Unidad de Información y Manejo,** tel. 615/154-0222, serves as an INAH office that handles information about and registration for visits to Sierra de San Francisco rock-art sites. You're required to register here and obtain an INAH permit before visiting any of the sites.

Accommodations

US$25–50: Baja Oasis Motel, less than one km south of San Ignacio on the west side of Mexico 1, is a white stucco building with five clean rooms, some with king beds, others with queen and single beds, all with portable fans, pure drinking water, and hot showers.

Motel La Posada (Posada San Ignacio), tel. 615/154-0313, offers rooms in two small brick buildings; each room has two beds, dressers, a hot-water shower, and a fan. La Posada can be difficult to find: walk or drive away from the church along Avenida Hidalgo with the *plazuela* on your left, turn right at Callejón Ciprés, and then, after 200 meters, turn left; after passing a street to the right, you'll come to La Posada on the right-hand side of the road.

Casa Lereé, tel. 615/154-0158, fax 615/125-5750, janebames@prodigy.net.mx, is housed in a historical one-story building with thick adobe walls and a shady garden patio. Thought to be more than 100 years old, the restored structure has served as an inn or *pensión* off and on since the beginning of the 20th century. In its latest incarnation, the guesthouse offers two small patio rooms with shared bath plus a larger suite in the main house with private bath and anteroom. Parking is available.

Eight hundred meters north of the Pemex station, just off the highway next to Rice and Beans Restaurant Bar, is **Hotel Ricardo,** tel./fax

THE DÁTILES OF SAN IGNACIO

The lush, feathery date palm of Arroyo de San Ignacio, a welcome sight to those who've driven the Transpeninsular Highway south across Baja's Central and Vizcaíno Deserts, has multiplied considerably since its introduction to the valley by Spanish missionaries over 200 years ago. At last count, Baja holds some 100,000 of them.

First cultivated in Mesopotamia around 1000 B.C., *dátiles* (dates) were originally brought to Spain during the Moorish occupation of the Iberian peninsula. The Middle East is the second-greatest date producer after the United States; Mexico is a distant third.

Although mature date palms are easy to maintain, palm shoots must be planted near the mother tree for several years before they can be separated. If moved too soon, they'll perish.

From germination, it takes an average of 12 years for a date palm to mature and begin to produce commercially. It can then yield fruit for 85 years. Dates are rich in potassium and protein—the protein content of two dates equals that of one egg.

The annual date harvest is celebrated in San Ignacio on July 31, which also happens to be the feast day for the town's patron saint, San Ignacio Loyola. During the fiesta, all manner of date products are displayed in the town plaza, La Reina del Dátil (The Date Queen) is crowned, and music and dancing keep things lively well into the night.

BOB RACE

615/154-0283. The plain but modern hotel features one- and two-bed rooms, all with air-conditioning and satellite TV. The hotel also leads one-day whale-watching and cave-painting tours, including lunch, for US$65 pp.

Ignacio Springs Bed & Breakfast, tel. 646/173-4141 or 800/027-3678, U.S. tel. 877/219-5822, fax 173-4151, tdmarcer@hotmail.com, next to the oasis coming into town, offers one multibed yurt for rent to budget travelers.

US$50–100: About 3.5 km (two miles) off Mexico 1 on the edge of town, **Hotel La Pinta,** tel./fax 615/154-0300, Ensenada tel. 646/176-2601, U.S. tel. 800/800-9632, www.lapintahotels.com, offers 28 clean, spacious air-conditioned rooms, a restaurant, pool, and a billiards room. This is one of the better-kept La Pinta properties, although we've found the hot-water supply to be unreliable. During the whale-watching season, room rates zoom up to US$90 per night.

Ignacio Springs rents out comfortable canvas-sided yurts of varying sizes. Rates include a full home-cooked breakfast. Kayaks are available for rent and the Canadian owners can also arrange horseback trips in the surrounding mesas.

Camping and RV Parks: Four small campgrounds on the outskirts of town lie in palm groves on the Río de San Ignacio. **Camping La**

Muralla,** near the entrance to town between the highway and the river, has rustic, shaded sites for US$3 a day. No hookups, although the campground now has bathrooms and a barbecue pit.

Almost immediately on the left side of the same road comes **Camp Don Chon's,** also known as Lakeside RV Park, in a palm grove alongside the dammed portion of the river. Rates here run US$5, and there are no facilities other than a few *palapas.* A bit farther down on the right, on the other side of the road and next to the river on the other side of the dam, **Mi-Basa** (formerly Palapa Asadero La Presa) is similar.

Almost opposite Hotel La Pinta, **El Padrino RV Park,** tel./fax 615/154-0089, has much more in the way of facilities, beginning with close to 100 well-kept camper sites, about 20 of which have full hookups. These sites go for US$15 a night. Tent camping is US$8 per night. Also on the premises are a dump station, bar, and restaurant. El Padrino can arrange whale-watching and rock-art tours.

At all four of these campgrounds, mosquitoes and/or *jejenes* (no-see-ums) are sometimes a problem.

Rice and Beans (see Food) offers 30 RV spaces with full hookups and hot showers for US$15; US$5 without hookups. Tentsites are also available for US$10, including the use of toilets and hot showers. The owners even advertise a "Bike Rider's Campground Special": all campground facilities including hot showers and a "special healthy meal" for only US$6.50.

Food

Rene's, a palapa hut just east of the plaza next to an irrigation pond built by the Spanish, has tasty and reasonably priced seafood and *antojitos* served in a congenial atmosphere. An outside seating area under brick arches is a pleasant spot to dine. Victor, who usually works as a waiter in the evenings, speaks good English. Rene's is open Mon.–Sat. from around 8 A.M. till 9 or 10 P.M., on Sunday for dinner only.

Restaurant La Muralla, on the grounds of Camping La Muralla, serves straightforward Mexican and seafood meals in a clean, outdoor setting. Open daily 7 A.M.–10 P.M.

Hotel La Pinta's restaurant, **Las Cazuelas,** offers the standard La Pinta menu. As with the general condition of the hotel, the dining room here serves as one of the chain's best examples.

Rice and Beans Restaurant Bar sits at the edge of an arroyo northwest of town, off the highway, and has a pleasant atmosphere. Traditional Mexican and seafood dishes are cooked using vegetable oil only. Dinners cost US$5–15, breakfast US$5–15. Open daily 7 A.M.–11 P.M.

Out on Mexico 1, about three km (two miles) northwest of town, **Restaurant Quichule** has a very good menu of breakfasts, *antojitos,* and seafood. The meat, milk, and cheese served at Quichule comes from the owners' Rancho El Carricito (often cited as "the cleanest ranch in Baja"). Locally, Quichule is well known for its seafood cocktails and for the house specialty *tortas de almejas,* delicious clam cakes made with egg and chilies and served with lettuce, tomatoes, mayonnaise, and french fries. It's open daily 8 A.M.–11 P.M.

Also on Mexico 1, in nearby Ejido Alfredo V. Bonfil (Km 53, 21 km/12 miles southeast of San Ignacio), are the **Café Tuxpan** and **Restaurant El Sinaloense,** serving mainly *antojitos* and beer to passing truckers. The latter has a small budget hotel attached. Farther south at Km 39, **Ran-cho El Mesquitál** serves whatever's on the wood-fired stove that day; if the family's had hunting luck, it might be *venado guisado* (deer stew).

Groceries: A couple of small *tiendas* and *miscelanéas* in town supply the basics. **Mercados Mayoral López** has the best selection of groceries. **Tortillería La Misión,** just up from Rene's on the way toward the lagoon, makes and sells flour tortillas. As might be suspected, dates are plentiful, typically costing around US$2 per kilogram. Vendors near the plaza sell ripe dates as well as tasty *pay de dátil* or "date pie" (actually more of a cake).

Mercadito Rovi, on Mexico 1 next to the turnoff for Rice and Beans, is small but has a decent selection of groceries, as does the **Diconsa** next to the Pemex.

San Zacarías, about 21 km (13 miles) south of San Ignacio on the road to Laguna San Ignacio, is a small farm and ranch settlement with a tiny vineyard. A sweet, sherrylike wine can sometimes be purchased here in recycled gallon milk jugs for around US$4 each.

Recreation

Servicios Ecoturísticos Kuyimá (Ecoturismo Kuyimá), tel. 615/154-0070, kuyima@prodigy .net.mx, www.kuyima.com, has an office facing the plaza in the old Bancomer building. Kuyimá specializes in whale-watching tours at nearby Laguna San Ignacio but can also arrange guided trips into the Sierra de San Francisco to view prehistoric rock-art sites. Kuyimá guides can speak Spanish, English, and French.

Entertainment

Discoteque La Pila, next to Rene's, is a small but well-equipped dance club open Fri. and Sat. nights only. Count on a steady bill of *norteña* and *banda.*

Transportation

Águila and **ABC** buses traveling north and south stop in front of the *tienda* next to the Pemex station on the highway. As there is no bus depot or ticket office in town, you can't make reservations or buy tickets in advance; when the bus arrives (usually twice daily), you buy your ticket inside the *tienda.* Seats are usually available except during Holy Week in April.

If you're driving south, it's a good idea to fill up at Guerrero Negro as the Pemex station on the highway opposite the turnoff for San Ignacio often runs out of fuel.

SIERRA DE SAN FRANCISCO ROCK ART

San Ignacio sits in the middle of what Amerindian cave painting expert Harry Crosby has termed the Great Mural Region of Baja California. The most extensive and numerous pictograph and petroglyph sites are found in caves and arroyos north of San Ignacio in the Sierra de San Francisco, an area added to UNESCO's prestigious World Heritage list in 1993. Among the prehistoric archaeological sites found in this sierra are iron and stone tool

© JOE CUMMINGS

a mule train in Cañon Santa Teresa

workshops, camps, sleeping circles, petroglyphs (carved rock art), pictographs (painted rock art), ceremonial sites, cremation sites, and funeral caves. Only the pictograph sites are expressly open to visitors, although many of the other sites are associated with major pictograph areas and hence may be visited en route— guides usually point them out along the way.

Viewing these rock-art sites requires the services of a guide, not only because of the difficulties involved in finding the sites, but because the Mexican government requires it to prevent potential vandalism or pilfering. Registration with the Instituto de Antropología e História (INAH) is also required; arrangements can be made in San Ignacio or La Paz. This means traveling to one or the other *before* you head into the sierra; San Ignacio is obviously the most convenient stop if you're coming from the north. See Registration and Guides later in this chapter.

Each site is classified into one of four different levels *(niveles)* of permissible access according to its perceived importance or sensitivity to human visitation. The most accessible sites are those found in the canyons of San Pablo (also known as Santa Teresa), San Gregorio, El Batequí, and Santa Marta. For the first-time visitor, the most thorough introduction to the Great Mural Region would be obtained by concentrating on Arroyo de San Pablo, in which five different painted caves can be seen: Cueva del Ratón, Cueva La Pintada, Cueva de las Flechas, Cueva de la Música (Los Músicos), and Boca de San Julio. All of these sites fall into Level 2, which means anyone may visit them with the proper permit and in the company of a guide. Cueva del Ratón lies only 20 minutes on foot from the village of San Francisco de la Sierra. The other four sites are all deep in Arroyo de San Pablo (which our guide called Cañon de Santa Teresa; we have heard it called other names as well), requiring a good six-hour hike or mule ride from San Francisco de la Sierra and an overnight stay.

Cueva del Ratón

"Cave of the Rat" is the easiest of the sites to access. Visitors with campers or very small RVs can park in a wide space in the road near the

THE PREHISTORIC MURALS OF BAJA CALIFORNIA

In hidden palm oases and remote canyons throughout the sierras of Baja California, far from the Transpeninsular Highway and most of the peninsula's larger towns, the artistic heritage of a lost Amerindian culture arcs across rock walls. Dubbed the Painters by Baja rock-art expert Harry Crosby, these anonymous artists painted thousands of figures in hundreds of murals that rival the cave paintings of Lascaux and Altamira in Europe.

© JOE CUMMINGS

Most are concentrated in the central peninsular sierras of San Francisco, San Borja, San Juan, and Guadalupe. Paleolithic paintings are also found in northern Baja at San José de Tecate, Palmas de Cantú, Pilitas, and Arroyo Grande, and in the south at Sierra de Cacachillas and Miraflores.

The Paintings

Though largely unknown outside Mexico, central Baja's prehistoric murals are actually larger and more numerous than those found at Lascaux, France, and Altamira, Spain. Between Bahía de los Ángeles and Comondú alone are over 400 mural sites. Most paintings are placed high—as high as 10 meters (33 feet)—on the walls or ceilings of arroyos, canyons, and rock overhangs. Scaffolds, probably made of *cardón* ribs or palm trunks, were used to reach these heights. Styles were codified to such an extent that all human figures feature arms extended upwards, all four-legged animals are depicted running or leaping, fish are always shown from a dorsal view, and birds are in flight as seen from below, with their heads turned in profile.

Ritual purposes are implied by the fact that only the outlines of painted figures are representational, while interiors contain conventionalized abstractions. In some areas of the sierras, human figures are occasionally bicolored, with the left half of the body painted red and the right half painted black. Figures may also wear headdresses or top-knotted hair. Rock-art experts have discerned several different schools within the Great Mural Region of central Baja: in the Sierra San Borja, *monos* are painted in red; Sierra de San Francisco paintings show red-black bicolors; the Sierra de Guadalupe features monochrome, bicolor, and checkerboard color schemes, along with *monos* filled in with vertical lines.

One of the more awe-inspiring examples of prehistoric rock art is a 166-meter (500-foot) by 10-meter (33-foot) mural at Cueva Pintada in the Cañon de Santa Teresa (Sierra de San Francisco); the mural holds overlapping images of men and women, deer, bighorn sheep, rabbits, and birds. At Arroyo de San Gregorio a four-meter (12-foot) whale is painted onto a rock overhang.

The Painters

Little is known about the Painters except that they belonged to the only culture, in a succession of central peninsula cultures, to leave behind artifacts borne not of economic necessity but from the realms of art and ritual. Ancillary evidence discovered at the rock-art sites—*metates* (grinding plates), *manos* (grindstones), bows and arrows, choppers, scrapers, carved bone, woven fibers, and firepits—identify the Painters as Paleolithic. The artwork itself, ritualistic paintings of human and animal figures, correlates with art styles found in Paleolithic sites the world over.

Eighteenth-century missionary documents from Baja refer to a few mural sites, but the Cochimí living in the central peninsula at the coming of the Spanish padres had no knowledge of the significance of the symbols or motifs in the paintings, nor of the techniques of painting; they themselves didn't paint. Cochimí legends said the paintings were the work of a race of giants who inhabited the region well before the time of their ancestors. The Painters must have been giants, according to the Cochimí, because many of the paintings appear on rock walls up to 10 meters above the ground.

Because archaeological and anthropological research in Baja has been so scant, scholars haven't a clue whether the Painters were a separate cultural group that migrated from the north or an early phase of the Cochimí culture. That the Painters were migratory—like all early Amerindian cultures in Baja—is certain since they left behind no permanent dwellings or pottery. The desert conditions of central Baja meant they had to move with the migrations of game and the seasonal changes in surface water. Such a culture required highly portable materials made mostly of wood, hide, and fibers. The minerals used for painting, as well as materials for building the scaffolds, could be gathered on-site.

Rock-Art Research

Although the Spanish missionaries of the 18th and 19th centuries were aware of the murals, the first systematic study of the paintings was conducted by Leon Diguet, a French naturalist working at El Boleo copper-mining company in Santa Rosalía. Diguet visited several mural sites in 1893–94 and published his findings in a few French journals; he missed the Painters' most extensive sites in San Francisco.

The next person to delve into the mysteries of the murals was American mystery writer Erle Stanley Gardner, of Perry Mason fame. Gardner began traveling to Baja in the 1940s and was first led to El Batequí and other Sierra de San Francisco sites in 1962 by local ranchers. Realizing he'd viewed sites of great archaeological significance, Gardner devoted a considerable part of his income to the study of the murals and wrote about them for *Life* magazine and in his book *The Hidden Heart of Baja*.

In 1972, Baja historian Harry Crosby succeeded Gardner in the search for undiscovered sites, making extensive forays into the San Borja, San Francisco, San Juan, and Guadalupe mountain ranges. Crosby printed the results of his explorations in *National Geographic*, as well as in his excellent 1984 book, *The Cave Paintings of Baja California*, the most authoritative general reference work on Baja rock art.

Based on an assortment of facts and artifacts—including what appears to be a mural rendering of the supernova birth of the Crab Nebula in A.D. 1054—Crosby speculates that the Painters' artistic output extended over a thousand-year period around A.D. 500–1500. More recent studies by Mexico's Instituto de Antropología e Historia (INAH) have expanded the mural era considerably, finding evidence of Great Mural Region rock art dating from 3000 B.C. to A.D. 1650. If the latter date is correct, it means the Cochimí must have contributed to at least some of the paintings; it's very possible they denied involvement when queried by the Spanish to avoid persecution for their belief systems. To verify or refute these datings, more research is needed in the fields of archaeology, anthropology, geology, and meteorology.

UNESCO has designated Baja's Great Mural Region a World-Class Rock Art Site, an honor that allows mural researchers to apply for UNESCO grants.

CENTRAL BAJA

stairs that lead up to the cave, but take care not to block the road, and be sure to register and engage the services of a guide at the village first.

Follow the path up the stone stairs, across a wooden bridge, and through a cleft in a lower ridge of Cerro de la Laguna to reach the rock overhang that served as a minor ("small but choice" in Harry Crosby's words—see Cueva La Pintada) canvas for the Painters. Game animals—deer, rabbit, and bighorn sheep—form the main theme, along with a few *mono* or humanlike figures and the namesake rat, which may actually be a representation of a mountain lion.

Cueva de las Flechas

A large rock overhang high up the canyon wall, "Cave of the Arrows" is most notable for a cluster of three red-and-black *monos* or human figures wearing prominent headdresses. Two of the figures are pierced with multiple arrows and lances; projectile points depicted in the central figure are similar to types found in the area. The meaning of the arrows invites much conjecture, the most common theory being that the scene represents some sort of intertribal war. Such conflicts have been documented among the Cochimí, and it may be that the pictographs in this cave marked territorial limits between rival clans. Another hypothesis suggests the human figures represent Amerindian shamans and that the arrows serve as a metaphor for death and dying, thus symbolizing a shamanic passage into the supernatural realm.

Cueva La Pintada

Across the canyon from Las Flechas and north a few hundred meters is the "Painted Cave," also known as Gardner's Cave because of its associations with the late mystery writer Erle Stanley Gardner (creator of Perry Mason and a Baja rock art fanatic who "discovered" this cave in 1962).

In his unparalleled book *The Cave Paintings of Baja California,* Harry Crosby wrote that Cueva La Pintada "may be considered the focus of the Great Murals" and that "it is the most painted place in the most painted part of the entire range in which these giant realistic artworks are found." The 150-meter (500-foot) rock overhang "cave"

is jammed with figures of all kinds, many of them superimposed on one another in ways that imply they were executed in feverish bouts of artistic creativity; over three times as many clearly visible figures can be seen here as in any other comparable cave site in Baja. La Pintada is also unique because the paintings here are unusually well preserved compared to those of other caves in the region, in large part as a result of the intrinsic durability—the geological "freshness"—of these particular rock faces.

Various shades of black and red are the only colors employed, but the sheer number of figures and homogeneity of style suggest a highly systematic output. Whales, deer, *monos,* fish, rabbits, and an unusually numerous and impressive-looking collection of birds—they're all here, dancing to the rhythm of a long-gone muse who inspired the mysterious group of tribal artists we now call the Painters.

Planning Your Trip

On a one-night, two-day trip you can take in Cueva de las Flechas and Cueva La Pintada. The usual itinerary involves descending to the canyon floor by midday, making camp, spending the remainder of the day visiting the caves, and then ascending the canyon trail the following morning. As you descend over 365 meters (1,200 feet) to the canyon bottom, you'll enjoy unparalleled canyon vistas, passing startling red rock pillars and sheer rock walls. On the floor of the canyon you'll find profuse stands of sky-high palms, clear-running streams, large boulders, and cool *tinajas.* Camping is permitted in the canyon at selected sites.

By adding more days to your itinerary, you can take in Cueva La Soledad (in a branch canyon off Arroyo de San Pablo, not far from Cueva La Pintada), Cueva La Música (a small site farther down Arroyo de San Pablo), and Boca de San Julio (a beautiful site in a branch canyon almost opposite La Música).

Visits to other pictograph sites in the arroyos of San Gregorio, El Batequí, and Santa Marta can also be staged out of San Francisco de la Sierra. Those in Arroyo Santa Marta include Cuesta El Palmarito and the famous Cueva Serpiente of Arroyo del Parral, with its eight-meter-long (26-foot) deer-headed serpent and bicolored, rabbit-eared *monos*. These Santa Marta sites can also be reached via **Rancho Santa Marta,** the turnoff for which lies 40 km south of San Ignacio via Mexico 1. As always, check with the INAH office in San Ignacio first— it may regulate this choice.

Registration and Guides

All prospective visitors to Sierra de San Francisco rock-art sites must first register with the INAH in either San Ignacio (INAH Unidad de Información y Manejo, next to the mission church, tel./fax 615/154-0222) or La Paz (Centro Regional INAH, Calle Aquiles Serdán 1070, tel. 612/123-0399, fax 612/122-7389). Upon registration and payment of a US$3 registration fee, the INAH office will contact the appropriate INAH custodian in the area you want to visit (either San Francisco de la Sierra or Santa Marta) and give you a copy of the *Rules of the Archaeological Zone of Sierra de San Francisco* with the name of the custodian handwritten on the front, along with the number of days, number of people, and destinations approved.

Your next stop is the house of the local INAH custodian *(costudio de bienes patrimoniales)* in the appropriate town; in San Francisco de la Sierra, visitors check in with custodian Enrique Arce. Señor Arce will register your arrival, obtain your signature on a waiver (saying INAH isn't responsible for any accidents, injuries, or delays), assign you a local guide, and, if necessary, arrange pack animals and riding stock.

All visits must be conducted by an authorized INAH guide, to whom you will pay daily guide fees set by INAH; these currently run around US$10 per day. Arce and his Santa Marta counterpart coordinate each visit and call up each guide according to a rotation schedule.

You are responsible for your own food, plus food for the guide "in accordance with regional customs and preferences." In everyday practice, guides will bring a thick stack of tortillas, cans of tuna, instant noodles, and other food because they fear relying solely on your food selection. They will, however, eat just about anything you have to offer! You can also substitute money for food, at a mutually agreed rate.

LEVELS OF ACCESS TO ROCK ART IN THE SIERRA DE SAN FRANCISCO

Level 1: All may enter with permit and guide; accessible by road. Examples: Cueva del Ratón, Cuesta Palmarito.

Level 2: All may enter with permit and guide; accessible only by foot or on saddle stock, and pack animals are required. Examples: Arroyo de San Pablo (Cañon de Santa Teresa), Arroyo del Parral.

Level 3: Only for those who have already visited Level 2 sites, with guide and permit, and in the company of an INAH custodian; must apply for permits at least three months in advance. Examples: Cañon de San Gregorio, Arroyo de San Gregorito, Arroyo del Batequi.

Level 4: Only for academic purposes; all research must be approved well in advance by INAH or SEMARNAT. Site names and locations not available to the general public.

For overnight treks, you are also required to hire one pack animal—usually a burro or mule—for every 60 kg of luggage and equipment. The standard rate as of this writing is US$10 per animal. Riding animals—usually mules—are optional and cost the same. Note that there is a maximum weight limit of 110 kg (242 pounds) pp, regardless of whether you ride a mule or not. Anyone weighing more won't be accepted to participate in a trek, ostensibly because pack animals can't carry weights greater than this on canyon ascents. Guides must guarantee they can pack someone out by mule in case of emergency.

All trip fees are to be paid after completion of the trip, not before.

If you arrive too late in the day to set out for the caves, Señor Arce has a small campsite (with an outhouse toilet) near his house where you may camp. The village itself also has some primitive campsites; if you're taking a canyon trip the following day, there's no charge.

Once out on the trail, visitors and guides are

M

CENTRAL BAJA

supposed to stick to established campsites in the canyons; in reality guides sometimes bend the rules in favor of common sense owing to weather and other considerations. All trash must be packed out, no open fires are permitted, and you're not supposed to bathe in canyon streams. Water may be taken from the streams for drinking and cooking only.

Tours

You need to speak Spanish to negotiate all of this on your own. If your Spanish skills aren't up to it, you may want to book a tour out of San Ignacio through **Motel La Posada,** tel. 615/154-0313, or **Servicios Ecoturísticos Kuyimá,** tel. 615/154-0070, kuyima@prodigy.net.mx, www.kuyima.com, either of which can provide—for an extra charge—an English-speaking guide along with the local guide required by law.

Getting There

The well-signed turnoff for San Francisco lies 36 km (22 miles) northwest of San Ignacio. This road ascends gradually into the sierra and winds its way along mesa ridges into the interior of the range, passing splendid scenery along the way. A very rocky road surface, prone to heavy washboard, ensures slow vehicle speeds, all the better for enjoying the view. Sand tracks paralleling the road much of the way can be much smoother and faster.

Around 10.5 km (6.5 miles) from the highway the road begins climbing and soon provides views of the Valle del Vizcaíno below. At about 14.5 km (nine miles) from the highway, much of the cacti are draped with moss, proof that moist Pacific air travels far and high. Los Crestones, a goat ranch, appears after 21.4 km (13.3 miles), and at about 26 km (16 miles) you'll begin seeing *cirios* or boojum trees, an unusual sight this far south. After another two km or so you'll come to a fork; don't take the left branch, which goes to Rancho Santa Ana. Another small rancho appears on the left 31.5 km (19.5 miles) from the highway, and after another couple of kilometers the road starts winding along the edge of a deep canyon. The steps to Cueva del Ratón appear on the right at 35.5 km (22.1 miles). You'll reach the settlement of San Francisco de la Sierra at 37.8 km (23.5 miles).

LAGUNA SAN IGNACIO

Southeast of San Ignacio on the Pacific coast lies a large bay used by calving gray whales January–March every year. The grays are closer to shore here than at Laguna Ojo de Liebre to the north or at Bahía de Magdalena to the south and seem to exhibit friendlier behavior here than at other calving lagoons. Many mothers and calves at Laguna San Ignacio actively seek out tactile encounters, i.e., petting and scratching. They also like to play hide-and-seek with the boats, sometimes blowing bursts of bubbles into the bow, then spyhopping (extending the head vertically above the sea surface) to see the effect their shenanigans may have on the passengers.

During the calving season, only boats with whale-watching permits are allowed on the bay. Around a half-dozen camps along the sand road that parallels the bay offer the services of licensed *pangeros,* who will take visitors out to meet the whales for US$40 pp with a general minimum of four persons. **Campo La Fridera** is particularly friendly and efficient. The typical tour lasts 3–4 hours; you should be at the camp by around 9 A.M. to get on one of the boats. Since the 59-km (35-mile) drive from San Ignacio takes 90 minutes to two hours due to road conditions (most passenger vehicles can make it—slowly), you must leave town early in the morning or spend the previous night at one of the camps. If you don't have your own vehicle, taxi transportation to the bay can be arranged in San Ignacio for around US$50—inquire at the taxi stand on the main plaza in front of the church.

The farther south you go along the bayshore by car, the less time you'll spend on boat transit to the prime whale-watching area near the mouth of the bay. One of the last camps on the bay, **Ecoturismo Kuyimá,** Morelos 23, San Ignacio, BCS 23930, tel. 615/154-0070, kuyima@prodigy.net.mx, www.kuyima.com, has a fully equipped campground with hot-water showers, ecologically sound outhouses, and a tented dining room. Along with the 20 tent sites there are also 10 rustic cabins. It costs US$10 a night to pitch your own four-person tent, or for US$40, Kuyimá will provide a two-person tent, sleeping bags, and flashlights. Food, depending on the menu of the day, runs US$7–10 per meal. A four day/three night adventure package costs US$165 pp per day, and includes lodging in a cabin, all meals, and daily whale-watching tours, as well as the use of bicycles, kayaks, a library and video services, a trip to the salt fields, and access to naturalist guides. Travel from San Ignacio to the camp is not included in the package rate, but van transportation is available to/from San Ignacio for US$130 for up to 10 people. Kuyimá charges a little more for whale-watching *panga* tours than other camps on the bay, US$40 pp with a minimum of four. Kuyimá is far enough south that you can see whales spouting and spyhopping from shore in season.

Punta Piedra

Farther south toward the mouth of the bay lies Punta Piedra, also known as Punta Peñasco, a peninsula jutting out into the bay near the main calving grounds. **Baja Discovery,** U.S. tel. 619/262-0700 or 800/829-2252, www.bajadiscovery.com, maintains a well-equipped camp on Rocky Point where whales can be seen just yards offshore, but you must book a tour package (US$1,825 pp for five days) to make use of it. The package is all-inclusive and covers round-

trip charter airfare out of San Diego. **Baja Expeditions,** 2625 Garnet Ave., San Diego, CA 92109, tel. 858/581-3311 or 800/843-6967, fax 858/581-6542, travel@bajaex.com, www.bajaex.com, also has a camp here; five-day packages cost US$1,925 pp, including round-trip air from San Diego. Both companies run their tours from late January through late March.

You should be able to camp elsewhere on the point on your own; no one can legally block access to the tideline, which is a federal zone. High-clearance vehicles can reach Punta Piedra by road—a stream must be crossed along the way—or you can arrange to be dropped off by boat from one of the camps farther north. The road to Punta Piedra continues south all the way to Bahía San Juanico but is recommended only for four-wheel drive vehicles.

Isla de Pelicanos

This island in the northern section of the bay serves as nesting grounds for a large number of ospreys and a variety of other birds. Also known as Isla Garza and Isla de Ballenas, the island is closed to visitors during the whale season, but you can visit by boat the remainder of the year. Inquire at the fish camps along the bay's eastern shore for *panga* hire. In the case of Isla de Pelicanos, those camps farthest north along the bayshore—such as **Chema's** or **Maldo's**—provide the quickest access to the island. Figure on US$30 pp for a group of four.

Santa Rosalía

At Santa Rosalía (pop. 10,400), the Transpeninsular Highway completes its 215-km (129-mile) journey from Pacific coast to Cortez coast. As in San Ignacio, the town is wedged into a deep arroyo between mesas, but the similarity between the two towns ends there. Whereas San Ignacio's architecture is strongly Spanish-flavored due to the mission influence, the buildings along Santa Rosalía's narrow streets—many of them wood-frame houses fronted by long verandas in the French colonial style—were designed by a French mining company in the 19th century.

Other Gallic touches include a French bak-

ery and the only Eiffel-designed church in Mexico (see Iglesia Santa Bárbara de Santa Rosalía futher on). One of the most impressive French-built structures in town, the Palacio Municipal, was once a school. Although many of the town's current residents certainly appear as if they could be of French or part-French ancestry, the locals claim most French citizens left town when the mines closed in 1954.

A *malecón* (waterfront promenade) with benches, cement sidewalk, and street lamps runs along the bayfront near the Pemex station and bus depot, south of the ferry pier. Though not

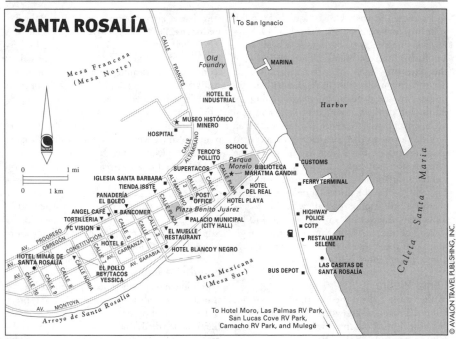

SANTA ROSALÍA

To San Ignacio

CALLE FRANCES

Mesa Francesa (Mesa Norte)

Old Foundry

MARINA

Harbor

HOTEL EL INDUSTRIAL

MUSEO HISTÓRICO MINERO

HOSPITAL

CALLE ALTAMIRANO

SCHOOL

TERCO'S POLLITO

CUSTOMS

Santa Maria

SUPERTACOS

Parque Morelo

BIBLIOTECA MAHATMA GANDHI

IGLESIA SANTA BARBARA

CALLE 1

HOTEL DEL REAL

FERRY TERMINAL

TIENDA ISSTE

CALLE 2

POST OFFICE

CALLE PLAZA

HOTEL PLAYA

PANADERÍA EL BOLEO

ANGEL CAFÉ

BANCOMER

Plaza Benito Juárez

HIGHWAY POLICE

TORTILLERÍA

PALACIO MUNICIPAL (CITY HALL)

COTP

PC VISION

CALLE 5

CALLE 3

EL MUELLE RESTAURANT

AV. PROGRESO

AV. OBREGÓN

CONSTITUCIÓN

HOTEL 6

CALLE 4

RESTAURANT SELENE

HOTEL MINAS DE SANTA ROSALÍA

AV. CARRANZA

HOTEL BLANCO Y NEGRO

Caleta Santa Maria

CALLE NORIA

AV. SARABIA

EL POLLO REY/TACOS YESSICA

Mesa Mexicana (Mesa Sur)

BUS DEPOT

LAS CASITAS DE SANTA ROSALÍA

CALLE 9

CALLE 10

AV. MONTOYA

Arroyo de Santa Rosalía

To Hotel Moro, Las Palmas RV Park, San Lucas Cove RV Park, Camacho RV Park, and Mulegé

0   1 mi
0   1 km

© AVALON TRAVEL PUBLISHING, INC.

particularly scenic, this is a good spot to catch a refreshing offshore breeze.

Santa Rosalía is the capital of the Municipio de Mulegé, and, before ferry service was suspended, Santa Rosalía was a terminus for the SEMATUR ferry to Guaymas, eight hours across the Sea of Cortez. The weather can be stiflingly hot June–October.

History

Copper-bearing deposits, in blue-green globules called *boleos,* were discovered near here in 1868, and in 1885 a French mining company calling itself El Boleo acquired mineral rights to the area for 99 years. To help build over 600 km (375 miles) of mine tunnels, a large copper-smelting foundry (imported by ship from Europe), a pier, and a 30-km (18-mile) mine railway, the French brought in Yaqui Amerindians from Sonora; fresh water was piped in from the Santa Agueda oasis, 16 km (10 miles) west. Two thousand Chinese and Japanese laborers, told they would be able to plant rice, also came to work at El Boleo.

When they found that rice wouldn't grow in central Baja, almost all of them left; many ended up in Sinaloa across the Cortez.

After smelting, the copper ore was shipped to Tacoma, Washington, for refining. Instead of returning empty, copper-transport ships brought lumber from the Pacific Northwest to Santa Rosalía, and, as the town grew, the French filled the arroyo and mesas on either side with wooden buildings to house workers, company officials, and Mexican soldiers. During El Boleo's heyday in the 1940s, a sooty cloud issued constantly from the foundry's smokestack, hanging over the town. Eventually the ore began to run out, and in 1954 the French company sold its mining facilities back to the Mexican government. Copper ore from the Mexican mainland is smelted in Santa Rosalía on occasion, but the mines closed in 1985.

Without the mines in operation, Santa Rosalía is probably a far more pleasant place to live than ever before. Today it serves as a government, transportation, and market center for central Baja. It's also an important tourist crossroads for visitors stocking up on supplies for further peninsular explorations.

The **Mahatma Gandhi Public Library** in Parque Morelos, at the east end of town near the harbor, features an exhibit of historic photos from Santa Rosalía's mining days.

SIGHTS

Iglesia Santa Bárbara de Santa Rosalía

A novelty in Baja—or anywhere for that matter—is this prefabricated, iron-walled church designed by famous French architect Alexandre Gustave Eiffel in 1884.

Eiffel, who earned his reputation by designing locks for the Panama Canal and the frame for the United States's Statue of Liberty, originally constructed this church in France in 1887; it was intended as a prototype for missionary churches built to withstand the climate in France's equa-

© JOE CUMMINGS

Iglesia Santa Bárbara

torial colonies. Two years later it was exhibited in Paris, together with the Eiffel Tower, at the 1889 Paris World Exposition. Eiffel took first prize for the church's modular, tropics-proof design.

When a French official at Compañía El Boleo later heard the church had been warehoused in Brussels, he purchased it and had it shipped in sections to Santa Rosalía, where it was reassembled in 1897. The exterior is modern, even minimalist, in tone, while the interior resembles that of any Catholic church. Except for two side wings added locally, the entire structure is made of galvanized iron. The church is still very much in use, with an Italian priest in residence.

Mesa Francesa (Mesa Norte)

Some of the best examples of French colonial-style architecture in town can be seen on the mesa along the north side of town, known locally as Mesa Francesa ("French Mesa"). Several of the homes in this neighborhood—large wooden affairs with wraparound verandas and pitched roofs—are being restored with help from INAH.

The **Hotel Frances** is one of the best preserved of the old French structures on the mesa—see Accommodations, later, for more information. Various examples of rolling stock and locomotives from El Boleo's short-line railway are displayed in front of the hotel.

Another of the French buildings on the mesa houses the **Museo Histórico Minero de Santa Rosalía,** which focuses on the town's mining history. Exhibits on display include miniature models of historic buildings in the area, historical photos, handwritten accounting ledgers used by El Boleo, old office furniture, a walk-in bank vault, various minerals of local provenance, miners' equipment, and a ship's wheel from the *Argyle,* an English barque originally launched in 1892. A small snack bar in the back of the building is occasionally open, as is a counter selling books on Mexican history. Open Mon.–Sat. 8 A.M.–2 P.M. and 5–7 P.M.; admission costs US$1.30.

You can reach Mesa Francesa via a steep and decrepit set of stairs that starts near the Iglesia Santa Bárbara, or by following curving Calle Altamirano.

ACCOMMODATIONS AND CAMPING

Hotels

Under US$25: In an old wooden French building, the **Hotel Blanco y Negro,** Av. Sarabia at Calle 3, tel. 615/152-0080, offers relatively clean if ramshackle rooms, some with private baths, and friendly proprietors. Rooms with shared bath or private bath are available. The most expensive room has a TV, and they offer one single room with private bath upstairs. To reach this hotel through the town's one-way street system, head southwest on Avenida Obregón, turn left at Calle 4 (in front of Panadería El Boleo), and follow Calle 4 until it ends at Avenida Sarabia; turn left at Avenida Sarabia, and after two short blocks you'll find the Hotel Blanco y Negro on your right.

Hotel Playa, Calle Playa at Av. Montoya, tel. 615/152-0267, is similarly priced but more exposed to dust and noise. On Av. Montoya, the spruced-up **Hotel del Real,** tel. 615/152-0068, offers 13 small air-conditioned rooms; ask for one in back *(detrás)* for more quiet and less road dust.

The two-story **Hotel Minas de Santa Rosalía,** on Av. Constitución between Calles 9 and 10, tel. 615/152-1060, offers good value with large rooms, each with two double beds, air-conditioning, ceiling fan, and private bath.

US$25–50: Perched on a cliff overlooking the bay, and conveniently located just off Mexico 1, **Las Casitas De Santa Rosalía,** tel. 615/152-3023, mariahsantarosalia@hotmail.com has a number of clean, comfortable cottages built in modern Mexican style. On the premises are a whirlpool tub and a terrace where guests may relax and enjoy a drink while watching boats come in and out of the harbor.

Adjacent to the abandoned copper smelting plant on Mexico 1 is the attractive **Hotel El Industrial** tel. 615/152-1078. This old French colonial-style hotel offers 14 small but clean rooms, seven of which face the harbor and allow glimpses of the bay; all have private baths, double beds, air-conditioning, and TV. Off-street parking is available.

The tourist-oriented **Hotel Moro,** tel./fax 615/152-0414, overlooking the Sea of Cortez about 1.5 km south of town on Mexico 1 (between Km 194 and 195), features 39 large air-conditioned rooms with TV, plus a restaurant, bar, and swimming pool.

US$50–100: Overlooking the copper smelter on Mesa Norte is the venerable **Hotel Frances,** Calle Jean M. Cousteau 15, tel./fax 615/152-2052. The restored 1886 French colonial-style building features 17 rooms with high ceilings, TV, and air-conditioning. The hotel courtyard holds a small pool and the Museo Pierre Escalle—a small outdoor display of historical objects pertaining to the town's French mining era.

Camping and RV Parks

Just south of Santa Rosalía off Mexico 1, **Las Palmas RV Park** offers 30 spaces (some with full hookups), hot showers, and a dump station; US$12 per vehicle per night. Tent sites rent for US$6 per site.

Fifteen km (nine miles) south of town off Mexico 1, on the pretty bay of Caleta San Lucas and accessible via a bumpy sand road, is the secluded and well-kept **San Lucas Cove RV Park** (Apdo. Postal 131, Santa Rosalía, BCS). Tent/ camper sites (no hookups) cost US$6 per vehicle. Facilities include hot showers, disposal station, and boat ramp. Caleta San Lucas is somewhat protected from winter northerlies, so it's generally a calm, warm place to camp. Only small boats can moor here since the *caleta* entrance is very shallow. Nearby, the newer **Camacho RV Park** is similar, with hot showers and flush toilets for US$5.

FOOD

Most of the town's restaurants and cafés are spread out along Avenida Obregón. **Restaurant Terco's Pollito,** Av. Obregón at Calle Playa (opposite Parque Morelos), tel. 615/152-0075, specializes in mouthwatering barbecued chicken as well as a wide variety of moderately priced breakfasts, seafood, soups, and Mexican standards. You'll find a pleasant palapa eating area off the main air-conditioned dining room. Open daily 8 A.M.–10 P.M.

Just south of the ferry terminal overlooking the harbor is **Restaurant Selene,** tel. 615/152-0685, a nice spot to enjoy the occasional sea breeze and savor moderately priced seafood

© JOE CUMMINGS

Panadería El Boleo

dishes. When available, the breaded garlic do-rado and seafood combination soup make good choices. The chef will be happy to discuss the catch of the day and how she might prepare it. Also serving breakfast, the restaurant is open daily 8 A.M.–10 P.M.

The restaurant at **Hotel Frances** serves very good breakfasts and is open daily 6–1:30 A.M.

Pepe's, a cart vendor usually parked along the north side of Parque Morelos on Avenida Obregón, makes delicious fish and shrimp tacos, triggerfish ceviche, and shrimp cocktails. **Supertacos,** on the south side of Obregón right before Calle 1, is a popular spot for beef tacos. The corner of Calle Noria and Calle Constitución is also a fine place to get fed quickly, as you'll find both **Tacos Yessica** and **El Pollo Rey** here.

El Muelle Restaurant Bar, tel. 615/152-0931, housed in an old wooden building, serves break-fasts, seafood, and pizza daily 8 A.M.–11 P.M. The outdoor patio at El Muelle is a pleasant dining spot during the cooler months.

Groceries

The **ISSSTE Tienda,** Av. Obregón at Calle 3, purveys a wide selection of foodstuffs and house-hold supplies at government-subsidized prices.

Just west of this store, on the same side of the street, is the famous **Panadería El Boleo,** which typically draws a long line out front when it opens at 10 A.M. The baguettes or *pan birote* here are legendary. The bakery also offers a good va-riety of other Mexican- and French-style baked goods, including delicious *kakita de zanahoria*—carrot muffins.

For fresh flour tortillas, visit the **Tortillería Santa Agueda** on Av. Obregón near Calle 6, just west of the Bancomer. If corn tortillas are your preference, try the **Tortillería Ranchería** toward the west end of Obregón where it merges with a two-way street.

SPORTS AND RECREATION

Boating

Marina Santa Rosalía, tel./fax 615/152-0011, in the breakwater-protected harbor, has 20 moorings for rent with fuel available. As Santa Rosalía is an official port of entry, the harbor boasts COTP, immigration, and customs offices.

Fishing

Corvina, pompano, grouper, and snapper are usually plentiful at **Caleta San Lucas,** 15 km (nine miles) south of town. You can launch small boats here at low tide. Farther offshore in the Canal San Marcos (between Caleta San Lucas and Isla San Marcos), sierra is available, especially in the winter months.

Events

Santa Rosalía's biggest festival is **Carnaval,** a pre-Lenten celebration held six days before Ash Wednesday, usually in mid-February. The **Fiesta de Santa Rosalía,** held annually around September 4, brings concerts, food fairs, and fishing tournaments to town, all in honor of patron saint Santa Rosalía. A **founder's day celebration** takes place the second week of October.

SERVICES AND TRANSPORTATION

You can exchange foreign traveler's checks or cash for pesos at the Bancomer and Banamex branches, both on Av. Obregón and open Mon.–Fri. 8:30 A.M.–3 P.M. Both also have ATMs.

The post office is east of the plaza at Calle 2 and Av. Constitución. On the south side of the plaza is a public telephone available for local and long-distance calls. Plenty of TelMex Ladatel card phones are scattered around town, especially on Avenida Obregón. The bus depot contains a *caseta de larga distancia.*

PC Vision, on the corner of Av. Obregón and Calle 6, has a few relatively fast Internet connections. Open daily 10 A.M.–10 P.M.

Santa Rosalía has an **airfield** outside of town, but so far no regularly scheduled commercial flights are offered. **Taxis Aereos Santa María** (no phone) offers chartered flights out of Santa Rosalía and maintains an office a little southwest of Terco's Pollito on Avenida Obregón.

Santa Rosalía's **intercity bus depot** lies on the west side of Mexico 1, just south of the ferry terminal. Two or three first-class buses a day travel north to San Ignacio (US$8), Guerrero Negro (US$15), San Quintín (US$33), Ensenada (US$42), Mexicali (US$60), and Tijuana (US$48), as well as south to Mulegé (US$10), Loreto (US$13), and La Paz (US$28). Less expensive second-class buses are also sometimes

available to San Ignacio, Guerrero Negro, Mulegé, and La Paz.

The Pemex station, near the ferry terminal on Mexico 1, is infamous for overcharging and or short-changing tourists. Most locals recommend you not fill up in Santa Rosalía if you can help it. Instead get gas in San Ignacio to the north or Mulegé to the south.

VICINITY OF SANTA ROSALÍA

South of Santa Rosalía, on the way to Mulegé via Mexico 1, two side roads suitable for high-clearance vehicles lead into the Sierra de Guadalupe. At Km 188, just beyond the state prison, a graded road branches 12 km (7.5 miles) west to **Santa Agueda** and beyond to several ranchos. Local ranchers may be willing to act as guides to Amerindian murals at La Candelaria, San Antonio, or Los Gatos. The Guadalupe "school" of Amerindian rock art shows more variation than the paintings found farther north in the Sierra de San Francisco, and known sites are more numerous. According to author Harry Crosby, more sites are found in the Guadalupe than in any of Baja's other sierras. Murals here are typically smaller than those in the San Francisco area, however.

An even more scenic side road leaves Mexico 1 at Km 169, about 20 km (12 miles) south of the Santa Agueda turnoff, and heads 14 km (8.5 miles) west to the isolated farming community of **San José de Magdalena.** The winding, rocky road climbs several steep grades with inspiring views of palm-studded canyons, healthy stands of *cardón,* mesquite, and ocotillo, and picturesque rock outcroppings—you almost expect to see the Lone Ranger and Tonto around the next bend. San José de Magdalena is known as Baja's garlic capital, and many visitors purchase long *ristras* (strands) of linked garlic bulbs here.

Beyond San José, the road continues another 48 km (30 miles) to several ranchos. A number of Amerindian mural sites are accessible in this area, assuming you can find a guide at one of the ranchos. You can also reach the adobe ruins of **Misión Señora de Guadalupe de Guasinapi** (1720–95), one of the peninsula's most remote mission sites, about three hours' hard drive from San José. Only parts of the stone-block foundation and adobe walls remain, so this side trip is best reserved for hard-core mission buffs.

San Bruno, a small fishing community before the turnoff to San José de Magdalena, has a Pemex station, bus stop, school, church, and *tienda rural.* A small encampment of RVers and shack dwellers here used to be operated as a public trailer park and campground, but since a 1993 storm blew several spaces away it has been full with semipermanent residents. The turnoff for the town is just north of Km 173. The village ambience is enhanced by wandering cows and chickens, along with fishing nets hanging out to dry or awaiting mending. If you take a liking to the village, ask around for places where you can camp. **Restaurant Las Palmas,** near Km 171 south of the San Bruno exit, is a small place with a limited menu.

See Vicinity of Mulegé for information on Punta Chivato and Bahía Santa Inés.

Isla San Marcos

A few kilometers off the coast of San Bruno, 32-square-km (12-square-mile) Isla San Marcos holds a settlement of 600–700 people at its southwestern tip and is the only permanently inhabited island in the Sea of Cortez—all other contenders have seasonal populations. A gypsum mine near the main village supports the population. The island even has its own baseball team, the San Marcos Stars, who host games at a stadium complete with bleachers and outfield wall.

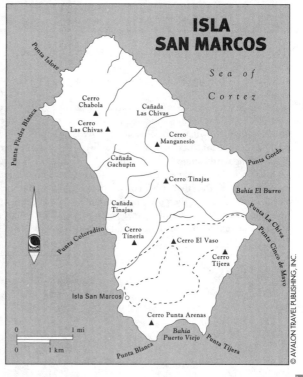

Hiking the interior of the dry, hilly, and relatively barren island might be interesting; there is one main cross-island trail about a third of the way up from the south and several minor ones elsewhere. Diving and snorkeling are best at Punta Piedra Blanca (at the northwest end of the island) and at two points—Punta Gorda and Punta La Chiva—at either end of Bahía El Burro along the eastern shore.

Boats to San Marcos can be chartered from the fishing community in San Bruno on the mainland. You may also be able to hitch a ride on one of the infrequent supply boats from Santa Rosalía.

CENTRAL BAJA

Mulegé

The town of Mulegé (pop. 3,100) straddles a wide arroyo formed by the Río Santa Rosalía (also called Río Mulegé), an estuarial river that feeds into the Sea of Cortez. The abundance of water made it a desirable mission location in the early 1700s, and today the agricultural legacy of the Jesuit padres—dates, figs, bananas, olives, and oranges—comprises most of the local livelihood, along with fishing and tourism.

Steinbeck and the crew of the *Sea of Cortez* passed up Mulegé on their 1941 coastal journey because they'd heard "the port charges are mischievous and ruinous" and "there may be malaria there." The quaint mission-style buildings, nar-

row streets, and riverside palms, however, have made Mulegé a favorite stopover among modern transpeninsular travelers. The local facilities, including a first-class dive shop, Laundromat, four or five auto mechanics, a couple of auto parts stores, markets, restaurants, hotels, and campgrounds, provide all the necessities and amenities for a long-term bivouac. Mulegé offers enough activities to occupy visitors for at least a couple of weeks, including hikes to nearby Amerindian cave paintings, snorkeling, scuba diving, fishing, clamming, birding, and kayaking.

Although it's well above the Tropic of Cancer, Mulegé is the first point south along the

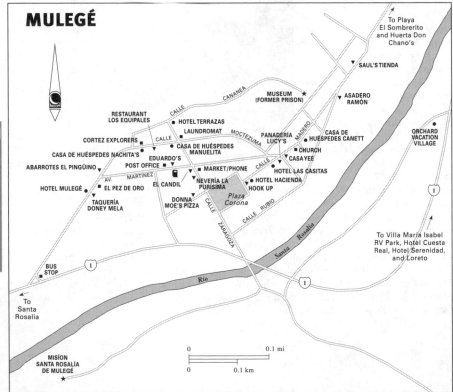

© AVALON TRAVEL PUBLISHING, INC.

peninsular coast where the climate and ambience begin to feel tropical. Winters are mild, summers are hot and humid, and mosquitoes appear along the river when the wind is still.

Climate

Weather conditions along the coast from Mulegé to Loreto are subtropical. December–March, daytime temperatures average 15–21°C (60–70°F); April–July, daytime temperatures run 26–35°C (80–95°F); and August–November the thermometer ranges 32–43°C (90–110°F). Annual rainfall averages 10 cm (four inches), with much of the precipitation occurring in late summer and early fall. These weather patterns mean that, for most prospective visitors (divers and anglers excepted), August–November is low tourist season.

SIGHTS

Misión Santa Rosalía de Mulegé

Mulegé's original mission was founded on the riverbanks in 1705. In 1770, a flood destroyed most community structures, and shortly thereafter the church was rebuilt at its current site, on a bluff overlooking the river. Although not one of Baja's most striking mission churches (compared to the missions at San Ignacio and San Javier), it's worth a visit just for the unobstructed views of the town and palm-lined river below. The church is usually locked except when services are held.

The church is best approached by following Calle Zaragoza southwest beneath the highway bridge, then west (right) until the road climbs the bluff by the church, about three km (1.8 miles) from the bridge.

Museum

The prison on the hill overlooking town functioned as a criminal detention facility 1907–75. During much of that time the prison operated on an honor system; trustee prisoners were permitted to walk into town from 6 A.M. each day as long as they returned when the conch shell blew at 6 P.M.

The walled facility stood empty until a few

Mulegé jail, now a community museum

years ago, when a local historian and a group of volunteers established a small museum inside. In addition to the old cells, visitors can view a collection of local historical artifacts—many marine-related—and a desk used by mystery writer Erle Stanley Gardner while researching central Baja's prehistoric murals.

Although hours are supposed to be daily 9 A.M.–1 P.M., in reality the museum is open only sporadically. If you're intent on seeing the museum and find it closed, look up curator Homero Yee at Casa Yee market. Admission is by donation.

ACCOMMODATIONS AND CAMPING

Hotels

US$25–50: On Mexico 1 just before the entrance to town, coming from the north, stands **Hotel La Noria,** a relatively new, modern, basic two-story hostelry popular with truckers. The similar but nicer **Hotel Mulegé,** Calle Moctezuma, tel. 615/153-0090, fax 615/153-0416, on the main access road into town and

CENTRAL BAJA

opposite Taquería Doney Mela, offers 10 American-style motel rooms with reliable air-conditioning and hot water—one of the better bargains in town even if the place lacks ambience.

Popular **Hotel Las Casitas,** Calle Madero 50 (on the town's main east-west street), tel. 615/153-0019, fax 615/153-0190, was once the home of Mexican poet Vicente Gorosave. The eight-room establishment features modest air-conditioned accommodations and a very nice patio restaurant and bar. Like most hotels in town, Las Casitas offers no off-street parking.

A bit farther west, the rambling, colonial-style **Hotel Hacienda,** Calle Madero 3, tel./fax 615/153-0021, hotelhacienda_mulege@hotmail.com, has 24 small to medium-size rooms, all with air-conditioning, surrounding a flagstone courtyard. The courtyard is planted with banana, citrus, and palm and features a small pool; a small restaurant/bar lies to one side. Off-street parking is available in the rear of the building.

Hotel Terrazas, at the north end of Calle Zaragoza, tel. 615/153-0009, has seen better days but is one of the quietest places to stay in town. Each of the good-size, clean rooms has two double beds, a fan, air-conditioning, and private bath. Hot-water showers are on-again, off-again, but the rooms are still a bargain. Free coffee is provided every morning; take it on the palapa terrace on the second floor with pastries purchased in town, and you'll have breakfast with a view for pennies. Guests also have free use of a small kitchen. The hotel has a small parking lot across the street plus three off-street slots in front of the hotel itself.

Two km east of town off Mexico 1 is the well-maintained **Hotel Cuesta Real,** tel./fax 615/153-0321, with 12 air-conditioned rooms. Look for the archway that marks the hotel's entrance off Mexico 1 at Km 132. The hotel has a tiny swimming pool, a restaurant/bar, and a Laundromat. The hotel also offers mountain bike rentals for the short ride into town via the old road along the river.

Hotel Brisa del Mar, Camino al Puerto, tel. 615/153-0574, fax 153-0089, perches on a high hill above the road out to Playa El Sombrerito. Its slightly isolated location means it's very quiet.

Sweeping views of the river and sea are another plus. Fourteen clean, comfortable, air-conditioned rooms are arranged in a three-story, U-shaped, salmon-stuccoed building adjacent to secure courtyard parking.

US$50–100: Four km (2.5 miles) east of town off Mexico 1 is Mulegé's largest inn, the 50-room **Hotel Serenidad,** Apdo. Postal 9, Mulegé 23900, tel. 615/153-0530, fax 615/153-0311, hotelserenidad@prodigy.net.mx. The Serenidad operates its own paved, 1,200-meter (4,000-foot) airstrip, officially referred to as El Gallito (Unicom 122.8); it's a favorite among *yanqui* pilots, many of whom fly in for the Saturday night all-you-can-eat pig roast. The spacious hotel grounds, which include a pool, tennis court, boat ramp, restaurant, and bar, are impressive. Each year the kitchen closes for the month of September, while the bar and hotel remain open. Besides the standard rooms, Serenidad offers two-bedroom air-conditioned cottages with a fireplace and parking space.

US$100–150: Orchard Vacation Village (Huerta Saucedo), Apdo. Postal 24, Mulegé, tel./fax 615/153-0300, orchardvv@prodigy.net.mx, on the river about a kilometer east of town off Mexico 1, is a trailer park that also offers two-story, thatched-roof villas for those who don't want to rough it (in fact for those who want to royally pamper themselves). Each villa features palm beams, a tiled Roman tub, a fireplace, a spacious kitchen, and access to a resort-style swimming pool—complete with swim-up bar. Eight-hour maid/cook service is also included in the rates.

Casas de Huéspedes

Mulegé supports three *casas de huéspedes,* or guesthouses, all with accommodations under US$25. **Casa de Huéspedes Cannett,** tel. 615/153-0272, on Calle Madero opposite a church, is the most livable of the three; the rooms are clean, and some have a private bath. A minor (or major, depending on your sensibilities) drawback is that the church bells across the street ring most mornings at around 6 A.M.

Casa de Huéspedes Nachita's, on Moctezuma, tel. 615/153-0140, the least expensive of the three, tends to send gringos across the street to the Hotel Terrazas, but when they're taking guests, they provide very basic rooms and hot showers. **Casa de Huéspedes Manuelita,** opposite Restaurant Los Equipales on Calle Moctezuma, tel. 615/153-0175, is a fair second choice, with hot showers and a parking lot. Manuelita also has a few budget-priced air-conditioned rooms.

Camping and RV Parks

A couple of well-run trailer parks down on the river serve Mulegé's campers and RVers. Long popular is the attractively landscaped **Orchard Vacation Village** (Huerta Saucedo, see Hotels, previously), which has riverfront tent sites on the grass that cost US$5 for two persons, full hookups US$17 for two, plus US$1.50 for each additional person. Monthly RV rates range US$200– 245 depending on the number of consecutive months.

Facilities at the park include a boat launch, canoe rentals, monthly storage, free fruit (mangoes, dates, oranges, limes, figs), picnic areas, an *asador* (Mexican-style grill), hot showers, toilets, and a dump station. Many spaces are now permanently occupied.

In the same vicinity, also along the river, **Villa María Isabel RV Park,** tel. 615/153-0246, features 30 pull-through RV spaces with full hookups for US$15 d (add US$2 for each additional person), shaded tent camping sites for US$6.50 pp, hot showers, a swimming pool, boat ramps, a good bakery, and a Laundromat. Discount rates are generally granted travel club members and long-term stays. As at the Orchard, many spots are permanently rented.

On the opposite side of the river off the dirt road to Playa El Sombrerito, Huerta Don Chano's offers RV and tent sites at similar rates.

The **Hotel Serenidad,** tel. 615/153-0530, fax 615/153-0311, serenidad@bajaquest.com, has an RV park with 15 full-hookup slots; it's a partly shaded lot next to the hotel, with none of the ambience of the riverfront parks. Use of a boat ramp, dump station, showers, flush toilets, tennis court, and pool is included in the price. Rates: US$12 d, plus US$2 for each additional person. Many camping visitors to Mulegé end up camping south of town at Bahía Concepción (see Vicinity of Mulegé, further on, for details) because of the shortage of places on the river— and because of the mosquitoes.

Free Camping: Playa El Sombrerito, the beach between the estuary and the Sea of Cortez, is a fine place to spend a few nights. Just take care not to pitch a tent too far toward the lagoon side, which cars and trucks use as a road to the fishing marina.

FOOD

Mulegé boasts several good restaurants; like the town's hotels, they're generally less expensive than those in most other Baja resort towns. During the off season (anytime outside November–February), they look rather empty, but this doesn't mean they're not good—it's typical outside "the season."

The tastefully decorated **Los Equipales** (named for the style of leather-and-wood chair featured prominently in the restaurant's decor), Calle Moctezuma, tel. 615/153-0330, has a second-floor dining room overlooking Calle Moctezuma next to Casa de Huéspedes Nachita's. Though a bit on the pricey side, this restaurant features the best Mexican specialties and seafood in town; it's worth every peso.

The service at **Restaurant El Candil,** on Calle Zaragoza opposite Plaza Corona since 1961, is slow, as everything is made from scratch. But the food is generally worth the wait and the prices are reasonable. House specialties include fresh seafood and the *combinación mexicana,* a huge plate of *taquitos,* enchiladas, *chiles rellenos,* beans, rice, and tortillas.

Mulegé has several very good taco stands. Next to the now-defunct El Nido Restaurant on Calle Romero Rubio, **Asadero Ramón** specializes in *tacos de carne asada* and quesadillas; open Mon.– Sat. 8 A.M.–8 P.M. This is also a good spot for brewed coffee in the mornings. On Saturdays the cook whips up a batch of mouthwatering *carnitas,* which can be purchased as tacos or by the kilo.

Taquería Doney Mela, on the road in from Santa Rosalía, has good *tacos de carne asada, pollo asado,* quesadillas, fish and shrimp tacos, and tostadas (here called *mulitas*). Also on the menu are *frijoles charros* and *horchata*. Doney is open from midmorning to midevening. Great fish tacos are available from **Taquitos Mulegé**, a taco vendor on Plaza Corona, usually open 9 A.M.– 1 P.M. or until the fish supply runs out.

Eduardo's on Calle Moctezuma bakes pizza from 7 P.M.–10 P.M. during the week but on Sunday makes a total departure to serve family-style Chinese food. Corona beer is available on tap.

Excellent *nieve* (Mexican-style, no-milk ice cream) is available from **Nevería La Purísima** near Restaurant El Candil.

Restaurant Profe. Angelina offers the best Mexican food in Mulegé, next to the Pemex station outside town.

The restaurants at the **Las Casitas** and **Serenidad** hotels are popular among the tourist crowd and serve decent, moderately priced Mexican fare. The garden patio at Las Casitas offers the best all-around ambience in town, and the delicious daiquiris—especially the "bango" banana/mango concoction—are legendary. Las Casitas hosts live *norteña* music on Fridays and mariachis on Saturdays. The Serenidad puts on a pig roast with mariachis every Saturday night.

Groceries

Several *tiendas* stock fresh, locally produced meats, poultry, fruits, and vegetables, along with smaller supplies of canned goods. Generally the best stocked are **Casa Yee** (Calle Madero 46 near Las Casitas), **Abarrotes El Pingüino** (on the road in from the highway, near Hotel Mulegé), and **Saul's Tienda** (on Calle Madero where it becomes Calle Playa). Saul's caters to the gringo market; owner Saul Davis speaks English and can get just about anything grocery-related— Thanksgiving turkeys, for example—if given enough advance notice.

Block ice and purified water are available from the **Hielera Mulegé** on "Ice House Road," the road signed San Estanislao just north of town west off the highway. It's open 24 hours. You can also get free drinking water from the spigot at the small plaza opposite Las Casitas. Purified water is available in gallon jugs from local grocery stores.

Panadería Lucy's, opposite Casa Yee, has the usual Mexican baked goods.

Villa María Isabel RV Park on the river operates a small bakery with reasonably priced *bolillos* and cookies.

SPORTS AND RECREATION

Fishing

The Hacienda, Las Casitas, Serenidad, and Vista Hermosa hotels can arrange guided fishing trips to Punta Chivato, Bahía Concepción, and nearby islands. Onshore fishing near the estuary—the south side is best—sometimes lands winter catches of yellowtail, roosterfish, sierra, and pargo; farther offshore are summer runs of dorado, yellowfin, and various billfish. Typical rates are US$120 per day in a *panga* for up to three persons, US$180 in a small cruiser that holds four anglers, or US$200 per day for a five-person diesel cruiser.

Diving and Snorkeling

The marinelife in the Sea of Cortez off the coast of Mulegé and Santa Rosalía is more prolific and colorful than in the upper Cortez. Many of the tropical or Pan-American species appear in reef areas, including the green moray eel (much less shy than its Pacific counterpart), angelfish, damselfish, parrotfish, triggerfish, flag cabrilla, several wrasses, and three varieties of lobster (red, spiny Cortez, and slipper). Generally, the best diving season is June–November, when visibility extends up to 30 meters (100 feet) and water temperatures near the surface are in the mid-20s C (mid-80s F). Full wetsuits are necessary in winter; in summer a Lycra skin is good protection against jellyfish.

Islas Santa Inés, three small islands in the northern part of Bahía Santa Inés, offer good snorkeling along their eastern shores, where rock reefs with soft corals lie at depths of around 4.5–12 meters (15–39 feet). There's also a sea lion colony here. Reefs and rock pinnacles extending from the north end of these islands are excellent scuba diving spots, with depths of 6–25 meters (20–85 feet). Scuba diving is also good at a reef at the north end of the bay, about a kilometer northeast of **Punta Chivato.** Other possibilities, farther north toward Santa Rosalía, include **Caleta San Lucas** and **Isla San Marcos.** The islands and reefs of **Bahía Concepción,** south of Mulegé, provide plenty of diving and snorkeling opportunities, including **Pelican Reef, Isla Santispac, Isla Guapa, Isla Requesón,** and **Roca Frijole.**

In Mulegé, **Cortez Explorers,** Calle Moctezuma 75A, tel./fax 615/153-0500, info@cortez-explorer.com, offers just about everything scuba and free divers need, including air, equipment, and boat charters. Guided dive trips start at US$60 if you supply the equipment, US$70 with weight belt and two tanks, US$80 for all equipment except wetsuit.

For those requiring scuba instruction, Cortez Explorers offers a four-hour basic resort course for US$90, including all equipment and transportation. Equipment rentals are very reasonable, from US$3 a day for a weight belt to US$8 for a regulator or power-inflated buoyancy compensator; airfills are available for US$3–4 (2,250– 3,000 psi). You can rent snorkeling equipment as well, and arrange guided snorkeling trips for US$35, including mask, snorkel, and fins, or US$30 if you supply your own gear. Credit cards are accepted for all services. The shopfront in Mulegé is open Mon.–Sat. 10 A.M.–1 P.M. and 4–7 P.M.

Snorkeling equipment can also be rented from EcoMundo–Baja Tropicales (Mulegé Kayaks)—see Kayaking.

Kayaking

You can launch kayaks at the estuary for excursions into Bahía Santa Inés to the north or Bahía Concepción to the south. Most kayakers intending to paddle in Bahía Concepción launch farther south—see Vicinity of Mulegé.

Experienced kayakers enjoy the well-known Mulegé-Loreto coastal trip, a 135-km (84-mile), five- to seven-day paddle. Because shore campsites are few and far between, you should attempt this route only in the company of someone who's made the trip before.

EcoMundo–Baja Tropicales (Mulegé Kayaks), tel./fax 615/153-0320, ecomundo@aol.com, operates half-day trips on easy-to-paddle, open-cockpit kayaks, in the estuary area and

at Bahía Concepción—see Vicinity of Mulegé for details. Baja Tropicales also rents kayaks to experienced kayakers for US$25–45 a day (depending on whether the craft chosen is open-deck or closed-deck, single or tandem), less for overnight or long-term rentals.

Mountain Biking and Off-Roading

Cortez Explorers (see Diving and Snorkeling) rents mountain bikes for US$15 on the first day, US$10 for each of the second through fourth days, US$8 for each day afterward. You can also rent a mountain bike and snorkel set (snorkel, mask, fins, and map) for a bargain US$20 per day. Cortez Explorers also rents Honda 300cc ATVs for US$20 an hour, US$65 for six hours, and US$80 for nine hours.

Bird-Watching

The small lagoon where the river meets the sea is a good bird-watching site. For a view of the lagoon, river, fishing marina, and town, climb to the top of **El Sombrerito,** the hat-shaped hill topped with a cross at the south end of Mulegé's beach. Mornings are best for photography.

Baja Adventure Tours, Calle Rubio 27, tel./fax 615/153-0481, cirocuesta@yahoo.com, leads small-group tours of the Mulegé area for visitors interested in cave paintings, bird-watching, petroglyphs or fishing.

ENTERTAINMENT

The plainly named **Disco Bar,** an upstairs place at the southwest corner of Calle Moctezuma and Zaragoza, packs a crowd on the weekends. Usually the music is live *norteña* or *banda,* though occasionally the management resorts to recorded sounds in true disco fashion. Sometimes the whole place will be hired for a private function.

Hook Up, next door to Hotel Hacienda, is a big, high-ceilinged sports bar, with a homier feeling than most big-screen beer venues. It occasionally features live music and dancing on weekends. It's a nice place to hang out in the early evening. The later it gets the louder it is. Open daily 11 A.M.–11 P.M.

SERVICES

Money-Changing

Mulegé has no bank. You can cash traveler's checks at **El Pez de Oro,** Moctezuma 17, a *casa de cambio* (money changer) just about opposite the Hotel Mulegé (open 9 A.M.–1 P.M. and 3–7 P.M.), and also at Hotel Las Casitas. Neither place will change pesos back to dollars, only dollars to pesos. The nearest banks are in Santa Rosalía, 61 km (38 miles) north.

Post and Telephone

The post office on Av. Martínez, opposite the Pemex station, tel. 615/153-0205, is open Mon.–Fri. 8 A.M.–3 P.M. A public phone with local and long-distance service can be found on the plaza off Calle Zaragoza. More reliable is a small, private long-distance telephone office in the Minisuper Padilla, tel./fax 615/153-0190, at the corner of Calle Zaragoza and Av. Martínez. As usual, a service charge is added to the phone charges.

Laundry

Lavamática Claudia, one of the cleanest Laundromats you'll ever see in Mexico, is at the corner of Calles Zaragoza and Moctezuma; open Mon.–Sat. 8 A.M.–8 P.M.

TRANSPORTATION

Getting There

The nearest commercial **airport** is Loreto, where Aero California fields daily nonstop flights from Los Angeles and La Paz. Next to the Hotel Serenidad is a well-used 1,200-meter (4,000-foot) dirt airstrip (Unicom 122.8); aviation fuel is usually available.

ABC and **Águila buses** stop at the town entrance on Mexico 1 on the way north and south. Although they follow no strict schedules, two southbound buses usually arrive every day, one in the late morning and one in midafternoon, while northbound buses arrive one in the midafternoon and one each in the early and late evening. The schedule is highly variable from year to year. As there are no bus depot or ticket offices in town, you can't make reservations or buy tickets

in advance. When the bus arrives, buy your ticket on board. Tickets to La Paz cost US$25, Santa Rosalía US$10, Tijuana US$52.

Getting Around

You can easily reach every point in town on foot, even from the riverfront RV parks. For a bit more reach, rent a **mountain bike** at Cortez Explorers.

Downtown Mulegé's system of narrow one-way streets might seem a bit confusing at first but is pretty easy to figure out. Some streets are marked with arrows; some aren't. A policeman usually stands at the main intersection of Avenida Gral. Martínez and Calle Zaragoza to make sure motorists drive in the correct direction. They're easygoing fellows who are there to direct traffic, not catch and fine foreigners. Still, a flagrant traffic violation can result in a trip down to the station; drive carefully.

The Pemex station in town, on Avenida Martínez, sometimes has vehicles waiting for gas backed up all the way to the end of the block. A quicker alternative—in spite of the drive—is the **Mulegé Pemex Centro** on Mexico 1, about 15 minutes south of Mulegé by car. This station offers four self-service pumps (reduced from 13 when it first opened), and there's rarely a long wait. The locals all claim the pumps at this highway station are rigged to give you 10 percent less fuel than what the pumps read out. A small café and a minimarket with ice are attached to the station.

Vicinity of Mulegé

SIERRA DE GUADALUPE CAVE PAINTINGS

The Sierra de Guadalupe, west of Mulegé, contains the largest number of known prehistoric mural sites in Baja California. Several hotels in Mulegé can arrange excursions to the more accessible sites for US$25–35 pp.

La Trinidad

One of the best rock-art hikes is to a canyon near Rancho La Trinidad, about 29 km (18 miles) west of Mulegé. As with other sites encompassed by central Baja's Great Mural tradition, those at La Trinidad are federally protected, and you must visit with a licensed guide. Viewing the major sites at La Trinidad means a challenging canyon hike of around 6.5 km (four miles) that includes several river crossings—at least two and sometimes three usually require swimming. Although the hike isn't particularly difficult or dangerous, it requires good overall fitness, the ability to swim up to a hundred meters (300 feet) through calm waters, the strength to hoist oneself out of the water onto stone riverbanks up to a meter high, and a fair sense of balance for walking along narrow paths.

You should also carry at least two liters (roughly a half gallon) of drinking water per person, preferably in canteens or other containers slung over the shoulder. You can float a limited amount of camera gear up the river on small, impromptu rafts made of inflated inner tubes and any flat, sturdy material used as a platform over the tube. Everything else you bring along, including shoes (Teva-style sports sandals are the perfect footwear for this trip), should be submersible. Count on a half day to complete the canyon hike itself, although some visitors prefer to spend an entire day in the canyon. Others may want to spend some time at the various ranchos along the way.

The trip begins with a scenic desert drive to Rancho La Trinidad, a large goat and cattle ranch at the foot of the mountains. Some guides stop at other ranches along the way to allow visitors to observe leather tanning, cheese-making, and other ranch crafts. After you arrive at Rancho La Trinidad, you hike about 800 meters (a half mile) to a four-meter (12-foot) stone dam. These are reportedly the headwaters of the Río Mulegé, though the river drops underground before resurfacing near town. Once inside the mouth of the canyon, you make one river crossing before reaching the first and largest group of murals. Among the many red and black animal representations on the canyon walls is a large ocher deer silhouette, considered one of the best prehistoric deer paintings in Baja; others throughout the peninsula are often compared to the "Trinidad deer." Among humanoid representations in this group is a shamanistic figure sometimes referred to as a

swimming in Cañon La Trinidad

CENTRAL BAJA

© JOE CUMMINGS

"*cardón* man," though there's no real evidence to suggest the image is linked to local legends about *cardón* cacti coming to life at night. Arrows pierce the figure's neck, chest, and groin. There are also a couple of vulva drawings and a painting of a fish skeleton, thought to be the only such work in Baja; other fish paintings in Baja appear to represent whole fish.

To reach the second group of murals you must ford the river several more times. Depending on river height, at least one crossing requires a swim of up to 100 meters through a narrow stone gorge. For many people this is the high point of the trip. The water is safe to swim in but should be boiled or treated before drinking. Some years a swim isn't necessary, but hurricanes in some years fill the canyon. The canyon scenery is spectacular, with cactus and wild fig trees clinging to the sides of high tuff (volcanic ash) cliffs.

The final site is reached by ascending a sloped canyon wall affording long views of the canyon, which splits in two here. The paintings at this site are neither as numerous nor as impressive as the first, but the hike/swim through the canyon makes it a worthwhile objective.

Two of the most experienced guides in Mulegé authorized by INAH to lead this trip are: Salvador Castro, tel. 615/153-0232, and Ciro Cuesta, tel. 615/153-0021. Any hotel in town can arrange for one of the guides. The usual price is US$35 pp, less if there are four or more persons or you drive your own vehicle rather than using those belonging to the guides. High road clearance is required, and a cache of spare parts is suggested. The fee usually includes a simple burrito lunch at the ranch, sodas, and beer. Overnight Trinidad trips cost US$50 per person if a guide is available. Most tours include an interesting stop in the desert to learn about medicinal plants. At the ranch itself you'll be required to sign an INAH register.

You can also drive to Rancho La Trinidad and arrange for someone at the ranch to take you to see the murals. Although this is much less expensive—no more than US$10 pp—the drive to the ranch involves several unsigned turns. Ask at one of the hotels for detailed directions. The turnoff for the main road from Mexico 1, known

locally as Ice House Road for the ice factory alongside it, is just a few miles north of Mulegé; it's signed San Estanislao. Continue following signs to San Estanislao until you see a sign for La Trinidad.

San Borjitas

Another area of prehistoric rock art, the San Borjitas site has been known to local residents since mission times; Leon Diguet visited San Borjitas in the 1890s, Erle Stanley Gardner in the 1960s, Harry Crosby in the 1970s. To get there from Mulegé, drive north on Mexico 1 to the Km 157 marker near Palo Verde at the turnoff for Punta Chivato, then take the dirt road west into the sierra. This route is appropriate for high-clearance vehicles only and takes around two hours each way. Be sure to bring plenty of drinking water, as this area tends to be warm even in winter.

Keep left at all forks, pass two abandoned ranchos (when you reach a gate, go through it and close it after you), and continue until you arrive at Rancho Las Tinajas (also known as Rancho Cerro Gordo, approximately 27 km/17 miles from the highway), where you should be able to hire a guide. Until recently you had to arrange a two-hour mule ride and hike to reach Cueva San Borjitas from here. A new road allows you to drive to within just a mile of the cave. At Rancho Las Tinajas you must register and obtain keys for two locked gates that must be entered between here and the cave; a fee of around US$4 in pesos is collected. With the first key, unlock the gate next to the ranch and continue driving northwest 2.1 km (1.3 miles) till you reach yet another fork (this will be the third fork coming from the highway), then pass through an unlocked metal gate and drive another mile till you reach a T-intersection. Turn left and pass through another locked gate (using your second key), continue another mile, pass through an unlocked gate, and at 35.7 km (22.2 miles) from the highway you can park at **Rancho San Baltasar.** From here it's a one-mile walk to the cave along a trail that begins at the far end of a small corral, follows the left (south) side of an arroyo, then cuts into the canyon wall and leads to the main cave.

The paintings at San Borjitas are unique among Baja rock-art schools in several respects: at least a dozen of the more than 50 large *monos* (human figures) in the rock shelter are apparently transfixed with arrows; some exhibit male genitalia; and about a dozen are filled in with longitudinal stripes. Colors employed at San Borjitas include black, red, ocher, gray, white, and combinations of all five, painted in monocolor, bicolor, and checkerboard patterns. Along the tuff side walls of the cave is a collection of petroglyphs (rock carvings) depicting female genitalia; the fire-blackened back wall shows fish and deer.

BAHÍA SANTA INÉS AND PUNTA CHIVATO

Large, gently curving Bahía Santa Inés, just north of Mulegé, bears very little coastal development and is a great site for beachcombing and beach-walking. The bay is rimmed almost its entire length by sandy **Playa Santa Inés,** which can be reached via a long sand road that turns off Mexico 1 near Km 151. This road branches frequently, but if you always take the trunk most traveled and ignore any small branches you'll eventually come to the beach. The road is soft and hilly in places. At five km (three miles) from the highway you'll come to a relatively major fork; take the right fork to run parallel to the shoreline and then choose any of several very sandy turnoffs to the left leading directly to the beach.

The wide, white-sand beach is backed by low dunes topped with cholla and other thorny plants. Driving beyond the crest of the dune-line isn't recommended as you're likely to become mired in deep, soft sand unless you're driving on sand tires or using chains. Self-contained camping is certainly possible anywhere along the beach; we didn't see a single soul all day long on a recent visit. Toward the center of the beach are a couple of trash barrels; whoever collects the trash may want to collect a couple of dollars from campers for hauling garbage away.

Accommodations US$100–150: At the north end of Bahía Santa Inés, 44 km (30 miles) northeast of Mulegé (24 km north via Mexico 1, then another 20 km (13 miles) east on a graded, unpaved road), is the secluded **Posada de las Flores** (formerly Hotel Punta Chivato), tel./fax 615/153-

0188, U.S. tel. 877/245-2860, has its own 1,220-meter (4,000-foot) airstrip (Unicom 122.8; US$10 landing fee), boat ramp, small desert golf course, pool, sea kayaks, and lovely nearby beaches. The hotel sits on Punta Mezquitito, part of the larger cape known as Punta Chivato. Large, attractive rooms feature air-conditioning, private baths, fireplaces, and semiprivate garden patios.

The resort previously maintained a campground with approximately 40 RV sites along a sandy cove a bit north of the hotel, but the new owners closed the campground permanently. Isla Santa Inés lies just southeast of the point; fishing and diving excursions can be arranged.

BAHÍA CONCEPCIÓN

From this point south to the Cape Region, the Sea of Cortez and its many bays begin matching the tourist-brochure description of a "desert Polynesia." This huge bay, open to the north and sheltered on the east, has a string of sandy beaches along its west side and a number of small islands anchored in the middle—a perfect setting for anglers, small-boaters, windsurfers, divers, and especially kayakers.

The entire bay, now a national marine preserve, is reportedly one of the cleanest marine bay systems in the world. It's home to an amazing variety of marinelife, from blue-footed boobies and magnificent frigates to whales, porpoises, and abundant shellfish. Commercial fishing is prohibited within the bay—if you spot any fishing boats working in Concepción and feel like doing something about it, report your sighting to Mulegé authorities immediately. If you plan to sail a yacht into the bay, please refrain from dumping the head until north of Punta Concepción.

Mexico 1 parallels the west bayshore, providing inspiring views of the blue-green bay and conical, flat-topped islands to the east and Sierra Coyote peaks to the west, as well as access to several beaches and coves along the way. Most of the beaches are *ejido* lands where the local *ejidatarios* collect camping fees of US$3–5, regardless of whether you're parking a motorhome or sleeping on the sand.

CENTRAL BAJA

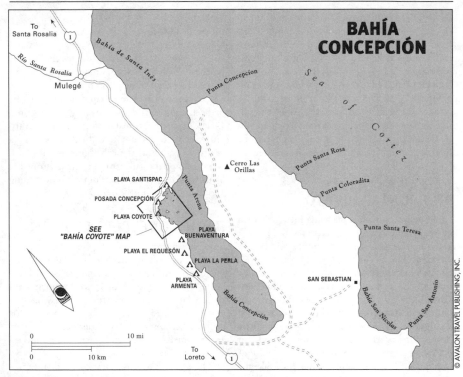

BAHÍA CONCEPCIÓN

Bahía Concepción attracts a loyal following of Canadians, Mexicans, Americans, and Europeans who return year after year to the beaches—staying in tents, palapa huts, and motorhomes—for intervals ranging from two weeks to six months. So far only one permanent settlement, Posada Concepción, has developed along the bayshore. Now that the bay is a national preserve, perhaps it will be the last.

For the most part Concepción's sandiest beaches are concentrated along the northwest shore in a bay subsystem sometimes called Bahía Coyote (not to be confused with Playa Coyote, near Bahía Coyote's south end).

Punta Arena

At the top of the bay's western shore, a signed, four-km (2.5-mile) road leads to Punta Arena, a sandy, windy point with a string of palapas and palapa huts—many of them permanent homes—

for US$8 a night. This area offers the best wind-surfing along the bay's west shore; the winds also make this one of the more comfortable camping beaches in the summertime. The turnoff for Punta Arena is 13.2 km (8.2 miles) from the Motel Serenidad turnoff from Mexico 1.

Playa Santispac

Farther south (entrance between Km 115 and 114) is the largest and most popular beach, Playa Santispac (Km 118), where tent and trailer camping next to shade palapas is available. The fee here is about US$6 per vehicle whether you camp or not. This is the most developed camping beach along the bay, and many sites are occupied year-round by motorhomes. Satellite dishes and solar batteries are common. Facilities include toilets, showers, and the famous **Ana's Restaurant Bar,** where fresh-baked goods, meals, *licuados,* and beer are available daily 7 A.M.–10 P.M. **Ray's Place** is a small, bright and airy palapa-roofed restaurant near the back of the beach in the middle of the property. Ray serves up some original tasty seafood dishes. One of his specialties is *papagallos,* shrimp and scallops fried in a beer batter and wrapped in bacon and Monterey Jack. Expensive. Open daily noon–11 P.M.

This is a popular put-in point for kayakers. You can reach several nearby islands by small boat or kayak, including **San Ramón, Liebre, Pitahaya** (Luz), and **Blanca.** Between Liebre and Pitahaya is a reef known as **Arrecife Pelicanos,** or Pelican Reef. On the point at the south end of Santispac are a couple of thermal springs.

Posada Concepción

Accessed at Km 113, this congested development of houses and trailer homes along Playa Concepción offers a market and tennis courts. Full-hookup slots, when vacant, cost US$10 for two persons, including flush toilets and showers. Electricity is available 10 A.M.–10 P.M. You can sometimes rent houses on **Punta Tordillo,** a steep, rocky point southeast of the beach community; inquire at Posada Concepción.

Playa Escondida

About 50 meters south of the Posada Concepción entrance, at Km 111, an 800-meter (half-mile) bumpy, narrow road unsuitable for larger RVs parallels the highway and provides access to other beaches. Follow the road over some hills to Playa Escondida, a scenic, uncrowded beach with a few palapa campsites for US$5 a day. The beach is rather shelly, confirming the fact that the clamming is very good here.

EcoMundo–Baja Tropicales

Exit at the same Km 111 road used for Playa Escondida to reach EcoMundo, tel./fax 615/153-0320, ecomundo@aol.com, just southwest of Posada Concepción. EcoMundo is a relatively new project with intentions of becoming a prototype for ecological beachfront development.

Already it's an excellent model for the kind of environmentally friendly, in-touch-with-nature beach resorts many in Baja would like to see.

With help from a San Diego State University professor who specializes in tropical architecture, as well as lots of local energy, the three-hectare (7.5-acre) facility has established several structures using straw-bale construction. When we last visited, 11 camping palapas with hammocks and solar-powered lights were available for US$12 per night. Similarly equipped, but enclosed, the palapa-roofed cabins go for US$20. The complex makes use of waterless toilets, showers with gray-water recovery, recycling and composting bins, and solar generators. Camping is permitted for US$6 in designated areas on the grounds—no RVs or generators permitted—and kayaking and snorkeling equipment is available for rent. EcoMundo's restaurant serves salads, smoothies, and healthy meals.

The entire bay, now a national marine preserve, is reportedly one of the cleanest in the world. It's home to an amazing variety of marinelife, from blue-footed boobies and frigates to whales, porpoises, and shellfish.

Playa Los Cocos

Slightly north of Km 111 lies Playa Los Cocos, one of the prettiest beaches along this section of Bahía Concepción; the limestone in the surrounding cliffs lends a turquoise hue to the bay. Camping is permitted here for US$5; the only facilities are a few two- and three-sided, well-spaced palapas and pit toilets. Behind the beach is a small, pristine lagoon lined with mangrove.

Playa El Burro and Playa Coyote

Two kilometers farther along the shore is Playa El Burro, a public beach with palapas and trash barrels next to a scrappy-looking residential section; it costs US$6 per day to camp there. Separated by Punta Cola de Ballena (Whale's Tail Point) is the adjacent Playa Coyote, with a campground/RV park (pit toilets, well-spaced *palapas,* showers, drinking water) that charges US$6 per vehicle for camping, RV, or day use with a palapa, US$3 for camping on the beach, and US$2 for day use without a palapa. The

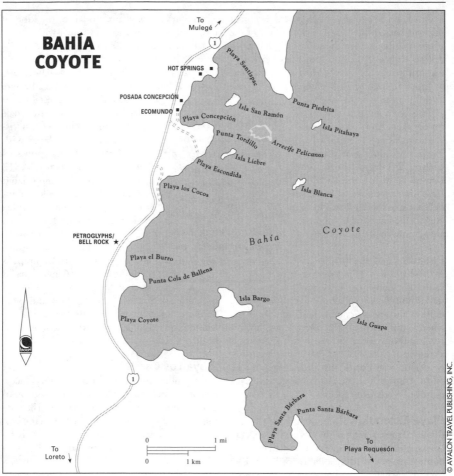

BAHÍA COYOTE

To Mulegé

HOT SPRINGS

Playa Santispac

POSADA CONCEPCIÓN

ECOMUNDO

Playa Concepción

Isla San Ramón

Punta Piedrita

Isla Pitahaya

Punta Tordillo

Arrecife Pelicanos

Isla Liebre

Playa Escondida

Playa los Cocos

Isla Blanca

Bahía   Coyote

PETROGLYPHS/
BELL ROCK ★

Playa el Burro

Punta Cola de Ballena

Isla Bargo

Playa Coyote

Isla Guapa

Playa Santa Bárbara

Punta Santa Bárbara

To
Loreto

To
Playa Requesón

0   1 mi

0   1 km

© AVALON TRAVEL PUBLISHING, INC.

Restaurant Estrella del Mar, opposite Playa Coyote, serves breakfast, lunch, and dinner. **Restaurant Bertha's** serves good, simple Mexican meals at Playa Coyote itself.

On the opposite (north) side of the highway from Playa El Burro is an arroyo containing hundreds of prehistoric **petroglyphs.** This site may have been sacred to Amerindians in the area because of a large, horizontal "bell rock" lying in the arroyo; when struck with a stone or hard stick, the rock resonates with a bell-like tone. A few hundred meters east of Playa Coyote is **Isla Bargo** (Coyote Island), an elbow-

shaped island with a sandy beach suitable for camping in the "elbow."

Playa Santa Bárbara

Around 2.4 nautical km (1.5 nautical miles) southeast of Playa Coyote is the idyllic **Playa Santa Bárbara,** also known as Honeymoon Cove. This sandy, palm-fringed inlet is accessible only by boat and makes an excellent kayak camp for those paddling the bay circuit.

Playa Buenaventura

After El Coyote, Mexico 1 veers away from the

coast for a short distance, returning at Km 94.5 to Playa Buenaventura.

Accommodations US$50–100: This half-sand, half-rock beach holds **Hotel San Buenaventura**, tel. 615/153-0408, a small resort with a modern motel, a a campground, a market, and a restaurant/sports bar. The motel features well-maintained rooms with air-conditioning and ceiling fans surrounding a courtyard. Palapa-shaded campsites go for US$20; toilets and hot showers are available. The beach at Buenaventura has coarse sand but is kept very clean. **George's Olé Sports Bar and Grill** serves food and drinks daily 8 A.M.–10 P.M.; chess boards and a paperback library are available.

Playa El Requesón and Playa La Perla

A kilometer or so farther south is the nicer Playa El Requesón. Tent and RV camping (pit toilets, *palapas,* no drinking water) is permitted along the broad, sandy beach here for US$3–5 per vehicle, depending on the season. At the north end a sandbar connects the shore with Isla El Requesón, forming sheltered coves on either side.

South of Requesón the bayshore becomes a bit rocky and swampy. Accessible by the same road that leads to Playa Requesón, Playa La Perla lies just 400 meters south and offers several palapa campsites at similar rates.

Playa Armenta

The last road-accessible beach on Bahía Concepción, Playa Armenta can be reached via a signed dirt/sand road off Mexico 1 between Km 90 and 91. This road cuts south and runs parallel to the highway, passing a little *ranchito* before hitting the beach after about 800 meters. It's a pretty beach facing northwest, so it can get pretty breezy in the winter on some days. A few substantial palapa campsites and a couple of outhouses are available; when anyone bothers to collect, camping costs US$5 a day.

Península Concepción

The peninsula forming the east side of the bay is visited less than the western shore because access requires a sturdy, high-clearance vehicle, preferably with four-wheel drive. None of the numerous camping areas along the peninsula's usually deserted bayshore have toilet or water facilities. Branching off Mexico 1 at the south end of the bay, the 60-km (37-mile) road north along the far bayshore ends just southeast of Punta Concepción at an abandoned manganese mine. The road follows the left (west) side of the peninsula most of the way, then just before it reaches the end, it cuts across the mountains and terminates near the northeastern tip. At some points the road bisects the high-tide line, so during high-tide periods you must time it right to traverse the road all the way. The beaches and coves of Península Concepción are best visited by boat from Punta Arena, west across the bay.

Kayaking

Scalloped with sandy beaches, dotted with islands, and protected from winds on three sides, Concepción is the perfect Sea of Cortez kayaking destination. While many other Baja kayaking spots may be blown out several months per year, kayakers in Concepción typically lose less than a cumulative two weeks—spread out over a year—to high winds. **EcoMundo–Baja Tropicales,** at Km 111 (see previous mention), rents open- and closed-topped kayaks for US$25–45 per day; less for multiday rentals. EcoMundo can arrange self-guided, paddle-and-snorkel tours of Bahía Concepción that include basic kayaking instructions, no-roll, open-top kayaks, snorkeling equipment, a visit to at least one nearby island, informative descriptions of flora and fauna, a snorkeling stop, and a lunch of fresh clams and beer. The kayakers themselves gather the mollusks from the sandy bay bottom while snorkeling. Participants meet at EcoMundo at 8 A.M. and finish lunch by around 2:30 P.M. The fee for the trip is US$45 pp, plus 10 percent tax. Other kayaking programs offered include moonlight paddles and Río Mulegé explorations. EcoMundo–Baja Tropicales is the only Baja kayaking concession that runs year-round. You can make reservations at the EcoMundo office in front of Hotel Las Casitas in Mulegé or by writing, calling, or emailing EcoMundo, Apdo. Postal 60, Mulegé, BCS 23900, Mexico, tel./fax 615/153-0320, ecomundo@aol.com.

CENTRAL BAJA

open-top kayaks for rent in Bahía Concepción

© JOE CUMMINGS

SOUTHWEST OF MULEGÉ

Southwest of Mulegé lies a series of volcanic valleys, isolated from the rest of Baja California Sur by the rugged Sierra de la Gigante, that support the historic farm/ranch communities of San Isidro, La Purísima, and Comondú. Although a journey to this region is easiest via the paved and gravel roads heading north from Ciudad Insurgentes, the rugged trip from Mexico 1, from a point south of Bahía Concepción, is shorter and more scenic.

The turnoff for this rough byway into Old Baja branches west from Mexico 1 just below the Km 60 marker, 75 km (46 miles) south of Mulegé. The first 18 km (11 miles) is graded, threading through a series of steep-walled arroyos before meeting a four-way junction.

Left is an unpaved, ungraded, 40-km (25-mile) road southwest to San José de Comondú, the larger of the two villages comprising Comondú. The second half of the Comondú road is rough and features steep grades; except for four-wheel drive vehicles, a better approach would be from San Isidro to the northwest or La Poza Grande to the southwest.

The road to the right at the four-way junction is abandoned. Take the unpaved, ungraded road straight ahead to arrive, via a series of switchbacks, in Valle de la Purísima, at San Isidro (37 km/23 miles west of the junction).

San Isidro

San Isidro (pop. 1,000) offers a church, a rustic café, clinic, market, *télefono rural,* barrel gas, and drinking water, but most visitors continue another five km (three miles) west—past stands of date palm, *higuera,* mango, and citrus—to the slightly larger and more historic La Purísima.

Motel Nelva, behind the church, offers simple rooms with shared shower. On the south side of the main road through town, after the gas station, is a **no-name motel,** also offering very basic rooms with shared hot shower.

La Purísima

Amid ponds and orchards (date, citrus, and mango), surrounded by high volcanic cliffs, and backed by a sloped butte—Cerro El Pilón, considered an emblem of the region—La Purísima represents a fairly typical early Baja settlement of the interior. Originally established by Padre

Nicolás Tamaral as a mission community in 1717, the village was abandoned in 1822 and revived in the late 19th century by Mexican farmers. Splendid examples of purple bougainvillea cascade over crumbling walls here and there around town. The ruined foundation of Misión de la Purísima Concepción, incorporated into a private residence, lies several kilometers north of the village.

If a proposed second highway along the peninsula's east side becomes a reality, it will most likely pass just west of here. A small Mexican army post sits at the east end of town.

Facilities in La Purísima include barrel gasoline (look for a small sign reading Gasolina off the main road near the northeast end of town), a post office, market (with ice), auto parts store, drinking water, and medical clinic. **Abarrotes Neferik,** near the airstrip, offers cheap, simple fare such as burritos, *tortas,* hamburgers, and quesadillas. You can camp at a primitive campground—really no more than a cleared spot—just off the main road through town.

Following the late-summer rains, it's possible to canoe or kayak—with a few portages—all the way west down Arroyo de la Purísima to the Pacific Ocean at Punta San Gregorio. A 48-km (30-mile) graded road leads west and then north to Bahía San Juanico, a little-known surfing destination; from San Juanico another graded road heads northwest to Laguna San Ignacio.

BOB RACE

Cerro El Pilón, symbol of La Purísima

Comondú

To reach the twin communities of **San José de Comondú** and **San Miguel de Comondú** (known collectively as Comondú), take the road east out of San Isidro, following an old stone acequia (irrigation canal). You'll pass a picturesque lagoon and the tiny village of **Caramuche** before the road splits at 3.7 km (2.3 miles); bear right to continue on to Comondú. From San Isidro to San José de Comondú it's 36 km (22 miles), not 24.8 km (15.4 miles) as the AAA map says, of unpaved, ungraded—and often stony—road surfaces.

The descent from the desert plains into steep-sided, 11-km-long (seven-mile-long) Arroyo de Comondú is dramatic. Wedged between barren volcanic mesas, well-watered Comondú produces dates, figs, mangoes, bananas, citrus, corn, grapes, sugarcane, and vegetables; in fact there appear to be more date palms here than in either Mulegé or San Ignacio. A small plaza in San José is surrounded by stone and adobe buildings, including a surviving Jesuit missionary house from Misión San José de Comondú (1737–1827); the boxy stone structure is now used as a church. A church bell dating to 1708 is on display next to the edifice. A restoration of sorts is proceeding slowly.

San Miguel de Comondú, about three km (two miles) west of San José, was originally the site of a *capilla de visita* (visiting chapel). Architecturally it's the most impressive of the two towns; before the completion of Mexico 1, Todos Santos and San Ignacio must have resembled this place. Locally grown sugarcane is still processed in San Miguel using traditional donkey-powered presses. Although smaller than San José, the village offers more local services because it's on the road southwest to Ciudad Insurgentes. San Miguel has a post office, a restaurant, and a *tienda rural;* drinking water is available at either village. **Restaurant Oasis** is open all year 8 A.M.– 8 P.M. It serves regional dishes for US$5–10. The owner, Martina, is happy to give out help and information to any tourists who might happen by. She sells finely woven palm-leaf baskets as well. Along the 2.4-km (1.5-mile) road between San José and San Miguel, mango trees are abundant, and rock walls have been used to build terraced gardens.

CENTRAL BAJA

One of the best times of year for a Comondú visit is on the feast day for San Miguel (29 September), when tiny San Miguel de Comondú bursts with music and dancing.

You can complete a loop drive back to Mexico 1 by continuing southeast from San José to Loreto via the charming mission village of **San Javier.** This road is suitable only for sturdy, high-clearance vehicles. See Loreto and Vicinity, farther on, for details.

Alternate Route

Another way—in fact the easy way—to reach La Purísima, San Isidro, and Comondú is to use the paved road that runs north from Ciudad Insurgentes to within a few kilometers of La Purísima, joining the network of unpaved roads that link all three communities. If you don't have your own vehicle, catch one of the Águila buses traveling between Ciudad Insurgentes and La Purísima once a day. San Isidro lies within easy walking distance of La Purísima, and you may be able to hitch rides onward to Comondú, San Javier, and Loreto.

Bahía San Juanico

From La Purísima, an ungraded road leads northwest 48 km (30 miles) to Bahía San Juanico on the Pacific coast. Gas, a public phone, and limited supplies are available there. Punta Pequeña (Little Point) at the north end of the bay protects sailors from the predominant northwest winds and provides a good launching point for local fisherfolk. Fishing is in fact the main local livelihood, with low-key tourism a distant second.

Surfers, who know San Juanico as Scorpion Bay, can choose from six different point breaks here during summer swells, some of which reportedly hook up on occasion to provide epic two-point rides. Winter surfing isn't too shabby either. Counting from the north, the first point

is often too weak to ride, the second point is usually best for beginning surfers, and the third point puts out perfect 100-meter peelers in a southern swell. Pack your guns for the remaining breaks.

A few expat Americans and Canadians have begun building rustic homes and palapa trailer shelters along a low bluff over the ocean near the village.

Scorpion Bay, Destination Surf Resort, tel. 613/138-2850, U.S. tel. 619/239-1335, ruben@scorpionbay.net or scorpionbay2002@hotmail.com, www.scorpionbay.net, offers a quiet campground for tents, campers, and self-contained RVs. Two sites include three palapa shelters. Tent and camper sites near the beach cost US$5 pp (children under 8 free) per day, including the use of hot shower facilities. Palapa shelters with four padded cots and sleeping bags are US$30 per day for one or two persons, US$10 per day for each additional person, including hot showers and a private bath. The spacious shelters can accommodate up to eight people. Self-contained trailers and RVs may park for a bargain US$5 a night or US$50 a month, plus the camp fee. Scorpion Bay Resort boasts a restaurant-cantina open daily 7:30 A.M.–10 P.M. Grilled seafood is a specialty.

In addition to the resort restaurant, **Restaurant Gloria's,** Calle Rosalía (the road to San Ignacio), serves the usual seafood and Mexican dishes under a palapa roof. Open 8 A.M.–8 P.M.

The road continues north from San Juanico all the way to San Ignacio via Laguna San Ignacio. Portions of the road between San Juanico and Laguna San Ignacio require four-wheel drive vehicles and skilled driving—it's best to drive the road with someone who knows the way well because of the many intersecting turnoffs. Although San Juanico has a small unpaved airstrip, it has been closed for a few years.

Loreto and Vicinity

At first sight, it's difficult to believe this unassuming seaside town of 10,000 became the first European settlement in the Californias over 300 years ago and served as the Californias' secular and religious capital for 132 years. Superseded by La Paz following an 1829 hurricane, Loreto all but vanished for three-quarters of a century, until Mexican fishermen again began frequenting the area. As word of the prolific fisheries spread, a handful of American anglers started flying to Loreto fish camps in private planes.

Although Loreto never regained its former glory, the 1973 completion of the Transpeninsular Highway finally brought the area within range of the average tourist. Today Loreto is part of a 27-km (17-mile) coastal segment, including **Nopoló** and **Puerto Escondido,** long slated by the Mexican government for development as a major tourist resort. In the town itself, a restored cobblestone plaza adjoins the historic mission church and museum, and a *malecón* has transformed the old seawall into a picturesque promenade. One infrastructure demerit for Loreto is the badly engineered streets, which tend to flood in the slightest rain.

Offshore fishing remains a principal tourist attraction. Other major assets include an international airport, a world-class tennis center, and an 18-hole golf course at Nopoló. Smaller cruise ships, such as Holland America's 720-foot *MS Ryndam,* are beginning to moor at Loreto.

Not entirely reliant on tourism, Loreto also

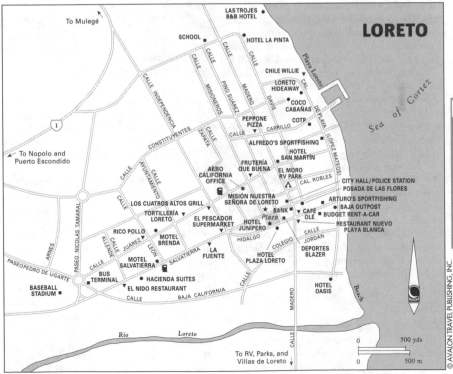

CENTRAL BAJA

benefits from the saltworks on **Isla del Carmen,** opposite the peninsular coast, where 40,000 tons of salt per year are harvested from a salt basin formed by an extinct volcano crater. Other important local sources of income include commercial fishing and agriculture.

In spite of Fonatur accomplishments, Loreto for the moment remains a sleepy seaside town when compared to Ensenada or Los Cabos. The expected tourist invasion has yet to appear—a bonus for Baja visitors looking to get away from the crowd.

History

After several unsuccessful attempts over a 167-year period to establish a permanent Spanish settlement on the peninsula, Jesuit Padre Juan María Salvatierra founded the first mission in the Californias at Loreto in 1697. As the Loreto colony grew, it served as a base for California exploration and for the expansion of the mission system throughout the peninsula. Franciscan Padre Junípero Serra started his journey north to California from here in 1769, eventually founding Alta California's first mission at San Diego Bay.

As the "mother of the California missions" and Spanish California capital, Loreto prospered until a hurricane destroyed much of the town in 1829. The mission church survived, but damage was so extensive, and fear of future hurricanes so high, the capital was moved from Loreto to La Paz the following year.

The town remained virtually deserted until the 1850s and '60s, when a small group of intrepid immigrants—some from England—resettled the area. A surprising number of Loreto residents today bear surnames such as Green, Davis, Cunningham, and Drew. Loreto remained a frontier backwater until after World War II, when it began developing a small commercial and sportfishing industry.

SIGHTS

Misión Nuestra Señora de Loreto

The first chapel at Loreto was a large tent erected at the mouth of Arroyo San Dionísio in October 1697. The building of the mission church proper

Misión Nuestra Señora de Loreto

© JOE CUMMINGS

proceeded in three stages, beginning in 1699 with a simple rectangular chapel with presidio near the current site. The foundations for a larger church, with a cruciform floor plan, were laid in 1704, and the church as it now appears attained its basic form in 1752.

After weathering the 1829 hurricane and several subsequent earthquakes, the church was restored in 1976 and is currently in use as a place of worship. A sign over the massive front doors reads Head and Mother of the Missions of Lower and Upper California. Despite its history, however, it's not a particularly impressive Spanish mission church. Nonetheless, the original Virgen de Loreto, brought ashore by Padre Kino in 1697, is nicely displayed, and the church contains a well-restored 18th-century gilded altar.

Museum

Of equal or greater interest is the adjoining **Museo de los Misiónes,** tel. 613/135-0441, a small but well-endowed historical and anthropological museum with exhibits on regional history and culture, Baja California mission history, and religious art. An anthropological library and small bookstore offer literature on Baja and Mexico history. The museum is open every day 9 A.M.–1 P.M. and 1:45–6 P.M. Admission costs around US$3.

Plaza Salvatierra

A plaza southwest of the church is dedicated to Padre Juan María de Salvatierra, the father of all California missions, whose likeness appears on a bust in the square's center.

On the first weekend of every September, the church and town cosponsor a Virgin of Loreto festival with plenty of feasting, music, and dancing. Another big fiesta is celebrated during the last week of October to commemorate the city's founding. Activities for both events are centered around the plaza.

Nopoló and Puerto Escondido

Loreto—along with Cancún, Huatulco, Ixtapa, and Los Cabos—was slated for tourist development on the recommendation of a computer study carried out by the Mexican government during the oil-rich 1970s. The prime criterion in Loreto's selection was the fact the area enjoys an average of 360 sunny days per year. Most of the completed and ongoing projects in the Loreto area have been entirely or partially funded by Fonatur, which has invited investors from around the world to participate in the area's future. Even gringos looking for an inexpensive vacation home in the Loreto area can receive Fonatur assistance in the form of low-interest, low-down-payment loans.

The focus of most ongoing local development is Nopoló, eight km (five miles) south of Loreto. Nopoló consists of a hotel zone, a recreation zone (tennis center and golf course), and a residential zone, linked by wide, palm-lined boulevards. What wasn't entered into the computer equation, or so it seems, is the lack of sandy beaches at Nopoló (Playa Notri and Playa Juncalito, both several kilometers south, fill the bill). One nice sand beach at Nopoló flanks the golf course, but since the course was built the beach is apparently inaccessible except by golfers! Another factor apparently not taken into consideration is the proximity of Loreto, already a destination in its own right. Most people choose to stay in Loreto, where there's more to do. Meanwhile Nopoló's complex of streets and sidewalks are sprouting grass, and only a few of the streetlamps actually light up at night.

Loreto Bay National Marine Park

In 1997 President Zedillo declared Loreto's entire offshore marine system, from **Isla Coronado** in the north to **Isla Catalán** in the south, a preserve called **Parque Marítimo Nacional Bahía de Loreto** (Loreto Bay National Marine Park). Part of the federal Sistema Nacional de Areas Protegidas (SINAP), the park forbids trawlers and commercial netters for a distance of 35–47 km offshore along the park's entire 60-km length. This decree has been a major boost to tourism in the Loreto area.

Primer Agua

The graded, unpaved road to Primer Agua, a Fonatur-owned palm oasis, begins near the San Javier turnoff at Km 114 on Mexico 1. A road sign is posted just south of a highly visible electric transformer station next to the highway. The Primer Agua road reaches the oasis after 6.5 km (four miles); ordinary passenger vehicles can make it in dry weather. This fenced-off section of arroyo, a branch of Arroyo de San Javier, serves as a nursery for propagating plants to be used at nearby Fonatur projects. A picnic area, complete with tables and barbecue grills, is near a natural pool at the bottom of the arroyo. If the gate to the facility is locked—and it sometimes is, even in the middle of the day—a hike into nonfenced sections of the arroyo, west of the orchards, is still worthwhile. The Fonatur office in Nopoló says that, if given a day's notice, it will provide a visit permit and ensure that the park is open.

ACCOMMODATIONS

Hotels

Under US$25: The cheapest sleep in town, **Motel Brenda,** is on the north side of Calle

Juárez between León and Ayuntamiento, tel./fax 613/135-0707. All rooms come with air-conditioning, TV, and hot showers.

US$25–50: Away from the waterfront is the slightly less basic **Motel Salvatierra,** Calle Salvatierra 125, tel. 613/135-0021. The Salvatierra features clean air-conditioned rooms with hot showers and TV but little else in the way of amenities. Rates vary according to occupancy.

The two-story, neocolonial-style **Hotel Plaza Loreto,** Paseo Hidalgo 2, tel. 613/135-0280, fax 613/135-0855, is a block from the mission church. It offers 29 clean, well-furnished rooms with hot water, air-conditioning, and cable TV; a small restaurant/bar is attached.

Hotel San Martín, Calle Juárez 14 (between Madero and Davis near the plaza), tel. 613/135-0442, offers eight spartan rooms with either two or three beds, plus floor fans and private bathrooms. Next door is the very small, very charming **Iguana Inn,** tel. 613/135-1627, www.iguanainn.com. The three spacious, spotless bungalows each have a small but very well-equipped kitchenette, two queen beds, and a fabulously oversized tile shower.

Hotel Junípero, tel. 613/135-0122, on Calle Hidalgo near the mission, has 12 clean rooms with ceiling fans, hot showers, and double beds; some rooms have TV. This is a good choice as the hotel is in the center of town. **Hotel Quinta San Francisco,** facing the malecón near the marina, boasts motel-like rooms with sliding glass door entries in a one-story, palapa-roofed building.

El Moro RV Park, on Calle Rosinda Robles just off Calle Davis (between the plaza and the malecón), tel. 613/135-0542, offers eight rooms with air-conditioning and cable TV. See Camping and RV Parks, further on, for details on camping at El Moro.

US$50–100: American-owned **Coco Cabañas,** tel. 613/135-1729, email barrett@coco-cabanas.com, off Calle Davis, is a relatively new collection of separate, well-constructed cottages that are perfect for travelers who want privacy and the capability to cook their own meals. Each cottage comes with air-conditioning, hot-water, and a full kitchenette. Inside the gated compound are a small swimming pool and BBQ area. It's a five-minute walk to the waterfront. Weekly rates are available.

Six long blocks north of the town plaza, **Las Trojes Bed & Breakfast Hotel,** Calle Davis Norte (Apdo. Postal 236, Loreto, BCS 23880), tel. 613/135-0277, fax 613/135-1207, lastrojes@prodigy.net.mx, www.loreto.com/costa2.htm, is a unique collection of eight cottages cobbled together from remodeled wooden Tarascan granaries *(trojes)* brought in from the Michoacán highlands. Each room is different, but all come with air-conditioning, ceiling fans, and private showers. A beach bar and pebbly beach are a short walk away through a cactus garden. Free use of bicycles and Internet access are available for guests. Rates include continenetal breakfast.

Facing the *malecón,* **Baja Outpost,** tel. 613/135-1134, U.S. tel. 888/649-5951, fax 613/135-1229, outpost@bajaoutpost.com, offers rustic cottages as well as four newer rooms, all with air-conditioning and double beds. The kitchen is open to guests—there's an honor system for beer and beverages. Rates include breakfast. A restaurant on the front patio overlooking the Sea of Cortez is planned for the future.

Hacienda Suites, Salvatierra 152, Mexico tel. 800/224-3632 U.S. tel. 866/207-8732, fax 613/135-0202, www.haciendasuites.com, is the newest hotel in town. Faux-hacienda courtyard rooms come with air-conditioning, direct-dial phone, cable TV, minibar, safety deposit box and coffeemaker kit. There's also a large pool, secure parking, and a minimarket. Rates include full breakfast. Every Saturday night the hotel hosts a "Mexican fiesta," replete with huge platters of Mexican food and live Mexican music.

North along the waterfront, on Calle Davis, the **Hotel La Pinta,** tel. 613/135-0025, U.S. tel. 800/800-9632, fax 613/135-0026, www.lapintahotels.com, offers spacious air-conditioned rooms with sea views and terraces. Facilities include a restaurant, bar, and pool. This is one of the more threadbare La Pinta properties.

Loreto Shores Villas and RV Park (see Camping and RV Parks) also has bungalows available in this price range.

A longtime favorite among anglers, the **Hotel Oasis,** at the south end of Calle de la Playa/Blvd.

López Mateos (Apdo. Postal 17, Loreto, BCS), tel. 613/135-0211, U.S. tel. 800/497-3923, fax 613/135-0795, loretooasis@prodigy.net.mx, www.hoteloasis.com, started as a fish camp many years ago but has since been transformed into a nicely landscaped, palapa-roofed hotel facing the Sea of Cortez. The hotel's 39 air-conditioned rooms are large, but they don't represent a great value in this price range. Facilities include a restaurant and bar, pool, tennis court, and the hotel's own sportfishing fleet.

US$150–250: Easily the most elegant hotel in Baja between Tijuana and Los Cabos, the **Hotel Posada de las Flores,** tel. 613/135-1162, U.S./Canada tel. 877/245-2860, fax 613/135-0199, www.posadadelasflores.com, occupies a heavily renovated colonial-style building adjacent to Plaza Salvatierra. A rooftop pool features a glass-block bottom through which sunlight shines into the antique-decorated lobby below. All 15 rooms and suites—each named for a flower—are tobacco-free and decorated with handcrafted furniture, pottery, tile, and wrought iron from the mainland. Modern amenities include air-conditioning, satellite TV, VCR, and telephone. The hotel has two upscale restaurants and a separate bar offering 250 different types of tequila, 50 types of mescal, and 15 types of brandy, along with cigars from Cuba, Honduras, Santo Domingo, and Mexico.

Houses

Several homes in Loreto—some of them owned by part-time residents or retirees—can be rented by the day, week, or month. If you use the kitchens provided with most of them, you can save considerably on eating out.

US$50–100: Loreto Hideaway, across from Playa Loreto, tel. 613/135-0212, offers well-furnished bungalows with barbecue grills, TV, VCRs, and air-conditioning. **Sukasa,** on the corner of Paseo López Mateos (the *malecón*) and Calle Jordán (Apdo. Postal 215, Loreto, BCS), tel. 613/135-0490, sukasa@prodigy.net.mx, is a duplex; each fully furnished unit sleeps four.

In Colonia Zaragoza just across the arroyo at the south edge of town is **Villas de Loreto,** Antonio Mijares at Playa Colonia Zaragoza, tel.

613/135-0586, fax 613/135-0355, info@villasdeloreto.com, www.villasdeloreto.com, a small, independent resort with 10 villas, all with private patios, air-conditioning, coffeemakers, and small refrigerators. Two units contain kitchens, some have a fireplace, and all units are smoke-free. A couple of the villas are in the US$100–150 range. On the grounds are laundry facilities and a swimming pool; bicycles are provided free of charge for the short ride to town. Kayaks can be rented (guests only), and the proprietor can arrange permits for beach camping on nearby islands.

Outlying Hotels

US$150–250: Eight km (five miles) south of Loreto in Nopoló, the **Camino Real Loreto Baja,** tel. 613/133-0010, U.S. tel. 800/873-7484, fax 613/133-0306, ltreserv@camino-real.com, rivals its Mexican chain mates in sheer scale and luxury, though not necessarily in charm. This expansive, modern, 156-room, five-restaurant resort features every imaginable amenity—from digital safety deposit boxes to private hot tubs. Fishing, kayaking, windsurfing, snorkeling, and scuba diving are all offered from the property's private beach. Bordering the grounds are Fonatur's 18-hole golf course and the Centro Tenístico de Loreto, both free for guests.

Camping and RV Parks

El Moro RV Park, on Calle Rosinda Robles just off Calle Davis (between the plaza and the *malecón*), tel. 613/135-0542, offers full hookups for US$12 and tent sites for US$5. You'll receive one night free for each week of your stay. Outsiders may use the hot showers for US$2. El Moro also offers fishing packages that include three nights' hotel accommodation and two days of fishing on a 22-foot *panga* with airport transfer, continental breakfast, box lunch, captain-guide, and fishing gear.

In Colonia Zaragoza just across the arroyo at the south edge of town, **Loreto Shores Villas and RV Park,** tel. 613/135-0629, fax 613/135-0711, offers 36 RV spaces with full hookups for US$15 per day; tent spaces cost US$5 pp, showers are US$3 pp. Every seventh day is free. Facilities include hot showers, laundry service, a boat launch, and palapas along the waterfront. Bungalows are also available (see Hotels, earlier).

Villas de Loreto, tel./fax 613/135-0586, www.villasdeloreto.com, rents RV spaces with full hookups for US$20 per night. Services include kayak rentals and laundry; bicyles are available to guests free of charge.

Although officially prohibited, many folks still camp at the south end of Playa Juncalito, 22.5 km (14 miles) south of town, a small, brown-sand cove backed by date and Washington palms. The north end is private, but some foreigners are able to rent spaces on a semipermanent basis. North of Juncalito, toward Nopoló, you should be able to camp on the beach for free.

The trailer park at **Tripui Resort** in Puerto Escondido, tel. 613/133-0818, U.S. tel. 512/749-6070, www.tripui.com, contains 120 "permanent" yearly spaces and only 31 overnight slots. A full-hookup slot costs US$17 a night for two people, plus US$5 for each additional person. Discounts for Good Sam members and Discover Baja Club members are available. Facilities include a boat launch, boat storage, a pool, a restaurant, laundry service, bar, and a well-stocked grocery store. For reservations, call one of the numbers above or write Tripui Resort, Apdo. Postal 100, Loreto, BCS (or P.O. Box 839, Port Aransas, TX 78373).

Beware the "Call the USA" pay phone at Tripui. Although rates listed on the phone claim a call to the United States will cost US$1 a minute, the real charges are more like US$7 per minute; thus a 15-minute call to the United States on this phone will cost over US$100.

Use of the facilities at Tripui for nonguests: swimming pool US$7 a day; launch ramp US$2; parking US$5.

FOOD

Breakfast, Tacos, and Fast Food

Café Olé, Calle Madero 14 (on the plaza), tel. 613/135-0495, serves inexpensive breakfasts and lunches, including seafood omelettes, *huevos con nopales* (eggs with cactus), tacos and other *antojitos,* plus burgers, ice cream, and milk shakes. It's open daily 7 A.M.–10 P.M. **La Fuente,** a small thatched-roof eatery on Calle Salvatierra southwest of El Pescador supermarket, serves *antojitos* and breakfasts.

Another good choice for quick, inexpensive snacks is **McLulu's,** a taco stand just west of Calle Colegio on Calle Salvatierra. Lulu's fish tacos are legendary (cabrilla or dorado in the summer, yellowtail or snapper the rest of the year); other offerings include *tacos de carne asada, tacos de guisado,* homemade chorizo, and *picadillo* (spicy meat-and-chili salad). Lulu doesn't mind if you buy beer at the nearby supermarket to drink while eating at her tables. Usually open 10 A.M.–7 P.M.

Next to McLulu's, **Lupita's** serves mesquite-broiled pork tacos, two for about US$1.50. It usually opens midmorning then closes midday and reopens toward late afternoon.

Rico Pollo, just west of Márquez de León on the north side of Juárez, serves good mesquite-grilled chicken at a few indoor tables. Open daily 8 A.M.–9 P.M. Another recommended vendor-style street restaurant is **El Rey del Taco,** two or three blocks up from the *malecón* on the south side of Juárez. *Carne* and *pescado* are available, both very good. **Taquería la Esquina,** on Calle Davis next to the fish market, is a local favorite for *tacos de carne asada.* Open 11 A.M.–1 P.M. and 4–8 P.M.

Mexican and Seafood

Nuevo Playa Blanca, Hidalgo at Madero, tel. 613/135-1126, is an old Loreto standby with an upstairs, open-air dining area decorated with whale vertebrae, lacquered turtle shells, and other marine memorabilia. You can order food in the downstairs Bar Playa Blanca as well. Prices are moderate; opens at noon.

Restaurant-Bar Pachamama, Calle Davis between Salvatierra and Magdalena, tel. 613/135-1655, is a cozy, rustic restaurant/bar that specializes in traditional Argentine fare such as *empanadas,* grilled sweet peppers, thick grilled steaks, and caramel-gilded desserts. Pachamama also serves a varied and delicious selection of wood-fired pizza, fresh salads, soup, and sandwiches. Moderately priced. Open daily for lunch and dinner.

CEVICHE

Ceviche (sometimes spelled "cebiche" or "sibiche") is a seafood appetizer in which fish or shell-fish is marinated in lime juice until "cooked." It's very popular throughout Baja, and there are as many recipes as there are cooks—it can be a wonderful experience in one restaurant and a bad excuse for getting rid of fish scraps in another.

Since it's easy to make even while camping on the beach (no fire necessary), ceviche offers an excellent alternative to the usual fried, baked, or grilled fish dishes. One of the best types of fish to use for ceviche is sierra, a common type of mackerel usually caught inshore/offshore; John Steinbeck, during his 1941 Sea of Cortez expedition, pronounced it "the most delicious fish of all." Other great candidates for ceviche are halibut, shark, shrimp, lobster, or just about any other fish whose flesh is not too dry. The oilier the better, since the lime juice counteracts the oil. Always use the freshest fish available.

Ceviche de Sierra
serves four

1 pound fresh sierra fillets, thinly sliced
½ cup fresh lime juice
1 ripe avocado, peeled and cut into half-inch cubes
8 ripe, red cherry tomatoes cut in half (or one large ripe tomato, cut into sixteenths)
1 serrano chili, minced (or more if you want it *really* hot)
2 tablespoons fresh cilantro leaves, minced
2 tablespoons olive oil
1 teaspoon salt or to taste (optional)

Put the sliced sierra in a large bowl, mix with the lime juice, and marinate in a cooler for a half hour. Drain, then gently toss the remaining ingredients. Best served with fresh tortilla chips and cold *cerveza*.

Restaurant Bar La Palapa, on Paseo Hidalgo about a half block up from the *malecón,* tel. 613/135-0284, serves moderately priced—and very good—seafood and Mexican dishes in an informal palm-roofed ambience. Open daily 1–11 P.M.

Restaurant Bar La Terraza, tel. 613/135-0496, sits above Café Olé, with an open-air terrace overlooking the plaza. Grilled steaks made with fresh Sonoran beef (US$10) are a house specialty. Open daily 1–10 P.M.

Los Cuatro Altos Grill Sports Bar—named in reference to the four stop signs at the intersection of Juárez and Independencia—is on the second floor of a brick building with a mini-market on the bottom floor. Decorated with cactus skeletons, plants, stuffed fish, and fishing nets in a desert/nautical theme, Los Cuatro Altos

offers two separate menus: a higher-priced seafood menu in English only and a Spanish menu with lower-priced *botanas,* burgers, sandwiches, and *antojitos.* Northerners may be handed a higher-priced seafood menu, in English, automatically, so ask for the *menú de antojitos* if that's what you're after. From either menu, the *almejas al horno con queso* (clams baked with cheese) are highly recommended. Against one wall is a full bar, and on the next floor up is a rooftop garden terrace. Open daily 1 P.M.–midnight.

Peppone Pizza, at the northwest corner of Calle Camarillo and Calle Madero, is dedicated to the flat round stuff, and they do a good job of it. Inexpensive. Open daily 2 P.M.–midnight.

Chile Willie, at the north end of Playa Loreto, tel. 613/135-0677, is a round palapa-roofed restaurant/bar with an eclectic menu of seafood,

Mexican, American, and Italian dishes, plus breakfasts. House specialties include *filete Guaycura*, which is fish served in a damiana liqueur sauce with *almejas de chocolate* (chocolate clams, so named for their color), and *chiles rellenos* served with crab in a basil tomato sauce. Homemade desserts, such as *profiterolles*, a puff pastry with ice cream smothered in hot chocolate, can be superb. This is also a good place for an afternoon happy-hour drink (two for the price of one) with views of the ocean and nearby islands. Open daily 7 A.M.–11 P.M. Next to the restaurant is a handy children's playground.

El Nido, Calle Salvatierra 154, tel. 613/135-0284, features the usual menu of mesquite-grilled steaks and seafood, but this restaurant is generally considered one of the better links in the small Baja chain. Open daily for breakfast, lunch, and dinner.

Fine Dining
Vecchia Roma Ristorante, tel. 613/135-1162, off the lobby of the Hotel Posada de las Flores, features fine Italian cuisine accompanied by imported wines and polished service. Recommended dishes include *ensalada de langosta* (chilled lobster in a citrus vinaigrette) and *medallones de filete al oporto* (medallions of filet mignon with a port sauce). Menu prices range US$7–30. Shorts and T-shirts are not allowed in this upscale restaurant. Open Tues.–Sun. 6–11 P.M. for dinner only.

Another restaurant, only slightly less formal, is appended to one side of the hotel facing the plaza. Aptly named **La Plaza,** the open-air restaurant focuses on *alta cocina*–style Mexican and seafood and is open daily for breakfast and dinner. The hotel also has a small open-air coffee shop in front, **Café con Leche,** serving breakfast and afternoon tea.

Groceries
El Pescador is the largest supermarket in town; there are two branches on Calle Salvatierra. **Tortillería Loreto,** on Calle Juárez between Ayuntamiento and Independencia, sells fresh tortillas as well as *bolillos* and Mexican pastries. **Panadería Kiz,** just east of Restaurant La Fuente on Calle Salvatierra, sells *pan dulce* and other Mexican pastries and breads. For fresh fruit and vegetables, amble down to the friendly, open-air **Frutería Que Buena** on Calle Juárez. Small *tiendas* and *ultramarinos* are scattered around town.

SPORTS AND RECREATION
Most visitors to Loreto come to enjoy the desert, the sea, the mountains—or all three. If you feel like taking an organized trip into any of these worlds, making arrangements is easy, and costs tend to be reasonable.

Fishing
Although commercial gillnetting has to some extent affected Loreto's coastal fisheries, this section of the Sea of Cortez is still considered one of Baja's hottest sportfishing destinations, and the Mexican government has taken steps to keep commercial operations out of the area. Offshore fishing is best east of Isla del Carmen, where you'll find yellowtail and sierra in winter, dorado, snapper, cabrilla, grouper, tuna, sailfish, and marlin in summer. Inshore fishing, between Loreto and Isla del Carmen (particularly at the north end of Carmen), nets smaller yellowtail, snapper, white seabass, and, in spring, roosterfish.

Fishing trips can be arranged at the Oasis, La Pinta, and Camino Real Loreto hotels, or at one of the sportfishing outfits in town. **Arturo's Sportfishing Fleet,** tel. 613/135-0766, fax 613/135-0022, www.arturosport.com, near restaurant Nuevo Playa Blanca on Calle Hidalgo, and **Alfredo's Sportfishing,** on the *malecón,* tel. 613/135-0132, fax 613/135-0590, are two of the oldest sportfishing fleets. The going rate for a *panga* trip is US$130 per day for up to three anglers. Super *pangas* run US$175 for three, and fishing cruisers run US$290 for up to four.

Boating
You can launch small boats at the north end of the *malecón,* at the Loreto Shores Villa and RV Park, or farther south at Playa Juncalito and Puerto Escondido. The *municipio* of Loreto boasts the highest percentage of Cortez islands of any *municipio* in Mexico. Jaunts to Isla del Carmen (18 km from Loreto, eight km from Puerto

© JOE CUMMINGS

Loreto marina

Escondido) are popular; the island has several good beaches, with the best anchorages at Puerto Balandra and Bahía Marquer on the island's west shore or at Bahía Salinas on the east.

Any of the hotels that organize fishing trips can arrange *pangas* by the day. You can also rent *pangas* at the harbor at the north end of Loreto's waterfront. Alfredo's Sportfishing offers four-hour *panga* tours of Isla Coronado for US$65 pp.

Hotel Posada de las Flores and some travel agencies in Loreto can organize picnic trips to Isla del Carmen and Isla Coronado beaches, as well as **whale-watching** excursions to spot blues, humpbacks, and fins.

Sea cruisers generally anchor at the sheltered, deep-water marina at Puerto Escondido. Both Loreto and Puerto Escondido have COTP offices. Loreto's COTP, tel. 613/133-0656, fax 613/133-0465, issues launch ramp permits for US$3. For safety reasons the Loreto COTP requests that kayakers file float plans in advance of any overnight paddling expedition. The COTP monitors VHF radio channel 16.

Kayakers can put in at Loreto for excursions to Isla Coronado or the north end of Isla Carmen. For the southern or eastern shores of Isla Car-

men, as well as for Isla Danzante and Los Candeleros, Puerto Escondido is the most convenient starting point. Setting out from Puerto Escondido, the ambitious, experienced sea kayaker can paddle out to Isla Monserrate or even Isla Santa Catalina. A logical run begins at Puerto Escondido, then continues south with the currents to Bahía Agua Verde (described below in South toward Ciudad Constitución) by way of Danzante (13 km/eight miles) and Monserrate (24 km/15 miles). You can rent open-top kayaks at **Deportes Blazer** and at **Baja Outpost** (see Diving). **Paddling South,** P.O. Box 827, Calistoga, CA 94515, tel. 707/942-4550 or 800/398-6200, fax 707/942-8017, info@tourbaja.com, www.tourbaja.com, leads highly regarded kayak tours out of Loreto. During the winter you can contact Paddling South at **Las Parras Tours** (see Guided Tours).

Diving

The islands off Loreto's coastline offer numerous diving opportunities, including rock reefs, seamounts, and underwater caves. The best local diving areas include the north end of Isla Coronado; the north and east shores of Isla del

Carmen; the 120-foot sunken freighter near del Carmen's Bahía Salinas; Playa Juncalito, with its wreckage of a small, twin-engine plane; and the smaller islands of Monserrate, Santa Catalina, and Danzante (northern and eastern shores). South of Isla Danzante is a string of granite islets called Los Candeleros; the vertical walls make an awesome underwater sight.

Guided excursions, scuba equipment rentals, and airfills are available through **Deportes Blazer,** Paseo Hidalgo, tel. 613/135-0911, and **Arturo's Sportfishing Fleet,** tel. 613/135-0766, www.arturosport.com. **Baja Outpost,** on the *malecón,* tel. 613/135-1134, U.S. tel. 888/649-5951, fax 613/135-1229, www.bajaoutpost.com, offers diving packages starting at US$241 pp for three nights' accommodation in Loreto, two days' diving, two tanks daily, weights and belt, and a few meals. More extensive packages include a seven-day trip to various Cortez islands with four day-dives per day, two night dives, and five nights' island camping for US$700. Baja Outpost also offers guided trips to view blue whales in February and March.

Horseback Riding

Saddling South, P.O. Box 827, Calistoga, CA 94515, U.S. tel. 707/942-4450 or 800/398-6200, fax 707/942-8017, info@tourbaja.com, www.tourbaja.com, the equestrian branch of Paddling South, sponsors seven-day (US$795) and nine-day (US$895–995) horseback trips into the peninsular interior. One 12-day trip is offered in January for US$1195. Each trip has a theme; in October the pack trip focuses on traditional plants, while in April the gang follows old mission trails. At the end of November a mixed group of riders heads for the annual San Javier festival. Saddling South provides two nights' hotel, ground transportation, meals on tour days, end-of-tour fiesta dinner, guides, mules, pack animals and related equipment, camping gear, tents, repair and first aid kits, saddlebags, and informational books.

Mountain Biking

Pedaling South, P.O. Box 827, Calistoga, CA 94515, U.S. tel. 707/942-4450 or 800/398-

6200, fax 707/942-8017, info@tourbaja.com, www.tourbaja.com, runs the following multiday cycling tours: Sierra Ridge Ride (nine days for US$795 pp), San Javier Singletrack (eight days, US$795), Oasis Bases (seven days or eight days, US$695), and Cross Baja/Whale Watch (nine days, US$995). Combo sea kayak/mountain bike trips are also available at US$795 for seven days. If you bring your own bike, Pedaling South deducts US$95 from the tour rates. Included in the price are accommodations, ground transport, meals on tour days, camping gear, tents, guides, tracking vehicles, and first aid.

Tennis

The **Nopoló Tennis Center (Centro Tenístico de Nopoló),** tel. 613/133-0129, has nine lighted courts, a clubhouse, bar, and pro shop. Resort guests may use the courts at no charge; nonguests pay very reasonable court fees.

Golf

The 18-hole **Campo de Golf Loreto** at Nopoló is probably the least crowded coastal golf course in North America. The back nine is harder than the front nine, and the 14th hole is particularly tough; US$40 for 18 holes, US$25 for nine holes; additional fees for carts and club rentals.

Guided Tours

Las Parras Tours, Calle Madero near Café Olé and the mission church, tel. 613/135-1010, fax 613/135-0900, lasparras@loretoweb.com.mx, www.tourbaja.com/tourbaja.html, can arrange whale-watching, cave art, kayaking, diving, hiking, and mountain-biking excursions. The popular Mission San Javier trip takes 6–7 hours and costs US$49 pp with two persons minimum, US$39 each for three or more. This trip can be expanded to include hiking and mule riding. Excursions to view cave paintings in the Sierra de Guadalupe run US$79–89 pp depending on the number of persons. Half-day *panga* trips to Isla Coronado are also available for US$22–29 pp depending on the number of people.

You can rent mountain bikes from Las Parras Tours for US$7.50 per hour, US$25 half day, or US$35 all day. Mountain bike tours run

US$20–40 a day. Kayak rentals are available for US$25 per half day, US$35 all day, or you can take a guided kayak tour for US$20 (2.5 hours), US$25 (4–5 hours), or US$40 (all day). Other Las Parras offerings include a 90-minute to two-hour walking tour of Loreto's historic district (US$5 pp) and a one-hour beach and desert horseback ride (US$10 pp for the first hour, US$5 per hour thereafter). All Las Parras tours include an English-speaking guide, transportation, and lunch or snacks.

Loretours, on Blvd. López Mateos next to the Hotel Misión, tel. 613/135-0088, offers some of these same services as well as car rentals, fishing excursions, and dive trips.

Hotel Posada de las Flores can arrange off-road humvee excursions into the mountains and desert.

INFORMATION AND SERVICES

Tourist Assistance
A SEMARNAT office, tel. 613/135-0477, is at the marina; it's open Mon.–Fri. 8 A.M.–3 P.M. Along with its many other functions, government agency SEMARNAT is responsible for issuing permits for island visits.

The tourist office (Departamento de Turismo Municipal), tel. 613/135-0411, is in the Palacio de Gobierno on the plaza at Calles Salvatierra and Madero. Open Mon.–Fri. 8 A.M.–3 P.M. Fonatur, tel. 613/135-0650, runs an office in Nopoló where you can pick up tourist information on the area.

Money-Changing
The **Bancomer** on the plaza offers exchange services Mon.–Fri. 8:30–11:30 A.M. only. The bank changes dollars to pesos but not pesos to dollars. It has an ATM. Hotels will exchange dollars for pesos at a low rate. We couldn't find anywhere in town that would change pesos to dollars.

Post and Telephone
On the plaza sit the post office and a Ladatel card phone with long-distance service. You'll also find a public phone with long-distance service inside Mercado El Pescador and a couple of private telephone offices toward the west end of Calle Salvatierra.

Internet Service
The conveniently located **Internet Café** is on Calle Madero, right next to Las Parras Tours. Another surf spot is the more uniquely named **Café Internet** on Calle Juarez near Independencia. Phones and fax service are also available. Open from 8 A.M.–9 P.M.

Travel Agencies
Viajes Pedrín, tel. 613/135-0204, a travel agency on Paseo Hidalgo next door to Hotel Plaza Loreto, can book air tickets, bus tickets, and hotel reservations.

TRANSPORTATION

By Air
Aero California, tel. 613/135-0500 or 613/135-0555, U.S. 800/237-6225, fax 613/135-0566, currently the only international airline with service to Loreto, schedules daily nonstop flights from Los Angeles and La Paz. The airline has an office in town at Calle Juárez and Zapata. **Aerolitoral,** tel. 613/135-0999, has daily flights to Ciudad Obregón and La Paz.

An official port of entry, the airport features a 2,200-meter (7,200-foot) paved runway (Unicom 118.4) and a stone-walled, palapa-roofed waiting hall. Aviation fuel is usually available. For private flight registration call 613/135-0565. The airport contains a small gift shop, a Budget car rental desk, and a bar.

By Bus
Loreto's bus terminal, one of the nicest and cleanest in Baja, sits at the junction of Paseo Ugarte, Calle Juárez, and Calle Salvatierra. ABC operates several first-class buses daily to Mulegé (US$8), Santa Rosalía (US$13), Guerrero Negro (US$27), San Quintín (US$51), Ensenada (US$63), Mexicali (US$87), La Paz (US$21), San José del Cabo (US$33), Cabo San Lucas (US$32), and Todos Santos (US$27). Departures change frequently, but there are usually six buses per day in either direction. The bus depot

CENTRAL BAJA

consists of a dirt parking lot with a small breeze-block building beside it. The attached **Restaurant La Posta** serves inexpensive seafood and *antojitos;* there are a couple of Ladatel phones right next to the station.

By Taxi

The main taxi stand sits at Madero and Hidalgo. Taxis between Loreto and Nopoló or the airport cost US$8, Loreto to Puerto Escondido costs US$25, and a trip to the airport from Puerto Escondido is US$12. In town you shouldn't pay more than US$3; walking is free and the town isn't very large.

By Rental Car

Budget Rent-A-Car has an office in town on Calle Hidalgo near López Mateos, tel. 613/135-1090; rates are anything but budget.

SAN JAVIER

This village of thatched-roof stone or adobe houses, 36 km (22 miles) southwest of Loreto, contains one of the peninsula's most well-preserved Jesuit mission churches. In a deep arroyo paralleling the road west of town, a small dam impounds water to irrigate the area's many farms via traditional acequias, narrow irrigation canals fashioned by the Spanish. The cultivation of citrus, onions, guavas, figs, papayas, grapes, corn, chilies, and dates supports a local farm population of around 150 people. Onions are the major crop; San Javier produces around 400 tons of onions per year.

A good time to visit is during the week leading to December 3, San Javier's patron-saint day. Pilgrims sometimes number in the hundreds. Another occasion for much *alegría* arrives on August 15, when an onion harvest dance is held at the large village community center.

Misión San Francisco Xavier de Viggé-Biaundó

This mission, nowadays simply called Misión San Javier, was originally founded by Italian padre Francisco Píccolo in 1699, two years after the establishment of the peninsula's first mission in Loreto. In 1701, Padre Juan de Ugarte arrived at Arroyo de San Javier from Mexico City,

© JOE CUMMINGS

Misión San Javier

bringing with him seeds and seedlings for the Californias' first cultivated fruit orchards. Many of the mission varieties of grapes, olives, figs, oranges, and lemons now grown throughout the Californias are descended from Ugarte's original San Javier plantings.

To make room for the orchards, the mission church was moved to its current site in 1720 and rebuilt by Padre Miguel del Barco between 1744 and 1758. Del Barco was a writer of some talent who brought an organ to the mission and, after his return to Italy, produced two notable books: *The Natural History of Baja California* and *Ethnology and Linguistics of Baja California*, both published in English by Dawson's Book Shop, Los Angeles (in 1980 and 1981, respectively).

The entire building, from the foundation to the fine vaulted roofs, was constructed using stone blocks quarried from nearby Arroyo de Santo Domingo. Although the church facade is not as ornate as that of Misión San Ignacio to the north, the side windows are splendid—no two are alike. The statuary and three gilded *retablos* inside the church were probably transported from Mexico City by boat and burro in the mid-18th century. The center altar bears a statue of San Javier, while the two side altars are devoted to San Ignacio and the Virgen de los Dolores. Two of the bells in the single church tower are dated 1761, the third 1803. A glass cabinet in the sacristy contains imported silk vestments worn by resident padres over 200 years ago.

A priest from Loreto says mass on the second Wednesday of every month. On other days the church is usually open 7 A.M.–6 P.M.; caretaker Francisca Arce de Bastida will gladly lead visitors on a short tour of the church in return for a small donation. If the church is closed, ask around the village for Señora Arce.

Accommodations

Under US$25: If you're on a budget and need to spend the night in San Javier, follow the footpath behind the church through the *huertas* (orchards) and ask at the farmhouse for Ramón. He rents a palapa-roofed, A-frame *casita* with three beds (one double, two twins). The *casita* has its own bathroom, but the toilet must be flushed

with a bucket of water and there is no electricity; a lantern is provided. The cabin is surrounded by a menagerie of peacocks, chickens, donkeys, dogs, and fighting cocks.

US$25–50: Casa Ana, at the east end of the cobblestone road that leads to the church entrance, offers nice little palapa-roofed cabañas, each with its own bathroom. For more information, contact Ana Gloria at Hotel Oasis in Loreto, tel. 613/135-0112, fax 613/135-0795.

Food

Ramón's brother runs the only restaurant in the village, **La Palapa San Javier Guillermos,** very near the church. The limited but tasty menu includes very simple quesadillas, beans, and fried potatoes. Open 8 A.M.–8 P.M. A couple of small *tiendas* sell beverages and limited foodstuffs.

Transportation

The road to San Javier, one of Baja's most scenic interior drives, is a section of the old Camino Real (Royal Road) used by Spanish missionaries and explorers. Access to the road is off Mexico 1 at Km 118, south of Loreto. Only drivers with sturdy, high-clearance vehicles should attempt the trip, as surfaces are stony, and, except in the driest years, it's necessary to ford a winding stream in several places. Following heavy rains, this road shouldn't be driven at all for a few days, unless you have a four-wheel drive vehicle and are skilled at driving through mud. Grades approach 15 percent in places; the average driving time is 90 minutes.

Along the way, the road winds around Cerro La Gigántica (1,490 meters/4,885 feet), passing several palm oases hidden away in narrow arroyos, *zalates* (wild fig trees) clinging to cliffs, and other rewarding vignettes. **Rancho Las Parras**—an oasis settlement consisting of a stone chapel, small dam, and orchards of dates, mangos, grapes, olives, figs, and citrus—appears about midway to the mission (20 km/12 miles from Mexico 1) in the Arroyo de las Parras. This arroyo provided water and a way into the Sierra de la Giganta for Amerindians and later missionaries; the vicinity holds old Amerindian trails and rock art.

About 9.2 km (six miles) beyond Las Parras, the San Javier road meets a lesser branch road

CENTRAL BAJA

leading 34 km (21 miles) northwest to San José de Comondú (not 26 miles as indicated on the AAA map). This route to Comondú is in poor condition, although it has been regraded in recent years so that road inclines aren't as steep as they once were. Any sturdy vehicle can make the trip nowadays, though high clearance helps, and if it rains all bets are off.

For those without their own vehicles, or without the right kind of vehicle, it's possible to arrange a car and driver from Loreto to San Javier for about US$38. Inquire at any Loreto hotel.

SOUTH TOWARD CIUDAD CONSTITUCIÓN

Ensenada Blanca and El Santuario

Around 40 km (25 miles) south of Loreto, behind the fishing village of Ligüi, lies an area of white-sand beaches, dunes and estuaries known as Ensenada Blanca. Near the latter is **El Santuario,** tel. 613/104-4254, U.S. tel. 805/541-7921, www.el-santuario.com, a collection of six environmentally friendly *casitas* designed to appeal to those seeking a quiet place to reflect and interact with the natural surroundings. Lights are solar powered and showers are solar heated, so don't bother bringing a hair dryer or boom box. Rates are US$65 single, US$95 double, inclusive of all meals. At times meditation- or yoga-oriented groups book all of the *casitas* for retreat purposes, so it's best to call ahead to make sure space is available.

To find Ensenada Blanca, keep an eye out for the the Ligüi turnoff between Km 83 and 84 (about 10 km/six miles south of the Tripui turnoff). Coming from Loreto, the Mini Super Ligüi will be on your left and you'll see a sign announcing the Parque Marino Nacional. Just after the market, turn into the first dirt road heading east. If you take a bus from Loreto or La Paz, ask to be let off in Ligüi and you'll end up at this same spot.

From this point it's around four km (2.5 miles) to Ensenada Blanca and El Santuario. Follow the dirt road toward the coast, and ignore lesser roads branching off. When the road forks, stay to the right. You'll cross a large *arroyo* (usually dry,

unless there's been a tropical storm) and the road will extend another kilometer or so before reaching the village of Ensenada Blanca. Drive or hike through Ensenada Blanca, past a collapsed church. Keep to the right of the church and follow the road behind the bay. On the left you'll see a small sign reading El Santuario Retreat.

Bahía Agua Verde (Puerto Agua Verde)

Between Km 64 and 63, where Mexico 1 veers inland from the Cortez coast, a part-graded, part-ungraded, gravel-and-dirt road heads southeast for 41 km (26 miles) to the fish camp of **Agua Verde.** The roadbed is steep and winding in places, not at all suitable for trailers or motorhomes. As the road approaches Agua Verde, it flattens out and divides into several tracks running to five small coves scalloped into the bayshore. The turquoise waters are framed

Bahía Agua Verde

© JOE CUMMINGS

by Islas Monserrate and Santa Catalina to the north and east, and hillsides of paloverde, palo blanco, *cardón*, palm, and mesquite to the west. Very picturesque.

Local residents make a living herding goats, fishing for small shark *(cazón)*, or servicing a steady trickle of outside visitors who brave the road in from Mexico 1. Near the first coastal contact the road makes, **Rancho El Carricalito**, a goat ranch 24 km (15 miles) from the highway, boards visitors for a few dollars a night and can also provide meals. As for groceries, you can buy tortillas and goat cheese from the restaurant, but that's about it. Rocky bayshore campsites with palapas cost US$3–5. Ask directions to the local hot springs. *Panga* fishing trips can be arranged for US$50–60 a day, and mule trips into the sierra are also available. **Isla San Cosme** and **Isla Damian,** opposite this bay, feature good snorkeling along their south shores.

A graded gravel-and-sand road continues parallel to the shoreline from this point. At a few places along the way you can drive down to the taupe-colored sand beaches. Self-contained camping is possible in several places.

About 34 km (21 miles) from the highway the road begins climbing into the hills again, and at 38 km (23 miles) you'll have a splendid view of rock formations, sandbars, and coves below. The steepest grade along the entire road comes upon the final approach to Bahía Agua Verde, more commonly known in these parts as Puerto Agua Verde. As the cove becomes visible you'll see how it got its name—reflections off

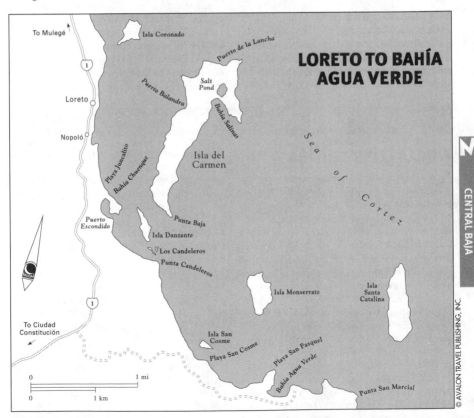

LORETO TO BAHÍA AGUA VERDE

To Mulegé

Isla Coronado

Puerto de la Lancha

Puerto Balandra

Salt Pond

Loreto

Bahía Salinas

Nopoló

Playa Juncalito

Bahía Chuenque

Isla del Carmen

Sea of Cortez

Puerto Escondido

Punta Baja

Isla Danzante

Los Candeleros

Punta Candeleros

Isla Monserrate

Isla Santa Catalina

To Ciudad Constitución

Isla San Cosme

Playa San Cosme

Playa San Pasquel

Bahía Agua Verde

Punta San Marcial

0   1 mi

0   1 km

the white-sand bottom give off a brilliant emerald-green hue similar to that seen at Bahía Concepción and many other places in the southern coastal reach of the Sea of Cortez. Puerto Agua Verde is a popular anchorage for pleasure boats as well as the occasional shrimp trawler. The road ends next to a beach at Puerto Agua Verde's west bight, which curves around to face south and thus provides some protection from north winds. This end of the bay is formed by a narrow neck of Punta San Pasquel; on the opposite side of the neck is another beach. You can camp on either side; someone from the local *ejido* will probably come along and collect a few dollars a day.

Limited supplies—including drinking water—are available at a little green-and-white *tienda* in the nearby settlement of Agua Verde.

Isla Montserrate and Isla Santa Catalina

Uninhabited Isla Montserrate lies around 13 km (eight miles) north of Puerto Agua Verde and is ringed by rock reefs with excellent snorkeling. The north end of the island features a long and pretty beach known to gringo yachties as Yellowstone Beach, considered a good summer anchorage.

Larger Isla Santa Catalina, 18 km (11 miles) east of Isla Monserrate, is known for its endemic "rattleless rattlesnake" *(Crotalus catalinensis)* and for the largest barrel cactus species in Baja, *Ferocactus diguettii,* named for French naturalist Leon Diguet. Individuals of this variety may reach four meters (13 feet) in height and a meter (more than three feet) in diameter. *Ferocactus diguettii* is also found on Islas Cerralvo, Monserrate, Danzante, and Del Carmen.

Ciudad Insurgentes

At Ciudad Insurgentes (pop. 8,500), the kilometer marker countdown from Santa Rosalía reaches Km 0 and starts over again at Km 236. The town itself has little to recommend it except as a fuel and food stop or as a transit point for the "easy" road north to La Purísima (102 km/61 miles) and Comondú (101 km/60.5 miles). The road is now paved to within a few kilometers of La Purísima, after which it is graded to San Isidro and San Miguel de Comondú.

Ciudad Constitución to La Paz

CIUDAD CONSTITUCIÓN

Even though it boasts more hotels than any other town between Santa Rosalía and La Paz, few Baja travelers stop over in Ciudad Constitución (pop. 45,000), the capital of Municipio de Comondú and the second-largest population center in Baja California Sur. Founded in the 1960s to serve as a market center for the irrigated Llano Magdalena (Magdalena Plain) agricultural basin, the town features two Pemex stations (a third one just north of town at Km 213 offers the use of bathrooms with hot showers), several banks, three bicycle shops, several supermarkets, a *mercado* (one block south of Hotel Conchita), a hospital, an Aero California office, *panaderías, tortillerías,* auto shops, and a number of other small businesses.

Boulevard Olachea, the main thoroughfare through town, is divided into two lanes in each direction, along with one-way frontage roads on either side, with stoplights every other block or so. None of the lights ever seem to work, and negotiating back and forth between the central lanes and frontage roads can be a daunting experience on one's first driving visit.

Accommodations

Under US$25: Of the nine hotels in town, the best value remains the clean and friendly 50-room **Hotel Conchita,** Blvd. Olachea 180 (at Hidalgo), tel. 613/132-0266, fax 613/132-0973, toward the north end of town. Rooms have air-conditioning, phones, and color TV.

The economical **Hotel Reforma,** Calle Obregón 125, tel. 613/132-0988, is a two-story place around a courtyard, a block east of the plaza.

US$25–50: The **Hotel Maribel,** Calle Victoria 156 at Blvd. Olachea (next to Banco Internacional), tel. 613/132-0155, offers 39 clean, basic rooms.

The clean, welcoming, three-story **Hotel Conquistador,** Calle Bravo 161, tel. 613/132-2745 or 613/132-1555, fax 613/132-1443, right around the corner from Restaurant Queretana going east off Olachea, offers 29 air-conditioned rooms and an attached coffee shop.

Manfred's Pull Thru RV Trailer Park (see Campgrounds and RV Parks) includes two motel-like rooms with air-conditioning and king-size beds.

Campgrounds and RV Parks

Manfred's Pull Thru RV Trailer Park, right on the east side of Blvd. Olachea at the north edge of town (Km 213, just north of the John Deere dealership), tel. 613/132-1103, has hookups that run US$17–20 a night. The premises contains a pool.

Spacious, palm-surrounded **Campestre La Pila RV Park,** tel. 613/132-0562, well off the highway south of town, has full hookups, a pool, hot showers, a picnic area, and dump station. Rates are US$10 for two people, plus US$5 for each additional person. The turnoff is on the west side of the highway next to a textile *maquiladora* called California Connection de México, near a power substation. There's not a lot of shade on the grounds, but the distance off the highway means it's quiet.

Palapa 206 (Mike & Bertha's) RV Park, at the south edge of town, tel. 613/132-3463, fax 613/132-5128, looks a bit nicer although many of the spots are unshaded. Full hookups US$12, water and electric US$10, dry camping US$6. Like La Pila, it's well off the highway. RV storage is available.

Food

The main boulevard—part of Mexico 1—through Ciudad Constitución is dotted with restaurants, *asaderos* (grills), and *taquerías.* In the northern part of town, before the turnoff for Mexico 22 west to San Carlos, good choices along the boulevard include the **Nuevo Dragón de Oro** (Chinese), **Estrella del Mar** (seafood), and **Super Pollo** (Sinaloa-style barbecued chicken).

At the southwest corner of Mexico 1 and the highway to San Carlos, **El Taste** is a branch of a La Paz restaurant of the same name. The menu is oriented toward tourists and wealthy Mexicans, with heavy Mexican *platillos* and steak. Open for lunch and dinner daily. At the northwest corner of the same intersection, **Gran Pollo** out-does Super Pollo for barbecued chicken.

Longtime personal favorite **Lonchería La Laguna,** north of the plaza on the main boulevard just north of Calle Olachea, serves very reliable *tortas,* tacos, *chilaquiles, carne asada, mole* and a decent cup of *café de olla.* Open Mon.–Sat. 8 A.M.–5 P.M.

The Maribel, Conchita, and Conquistador hotels each contain decent restaurants open for breakfast, lunch, and dinner. The best supermarkets, both on Boulevard Olachea, are **Super**

CENTRAL BAJA

Ley and **La Americana**. The town also offers several *tiendas de abarrotes* and *ultramarinos*.

Misión San Luis Gonzaga

Ciudad Constitución is a convenient departure point for an excursion to this surviving mission settlement 42 km (26 miles) southeast of Mexico 1. The best of two secondary roads leading from Mexico 1 starts at Km 195, where a sign reads La Presa Iguajil. Founded in 1737 and rebuilt in 1751, the simple mission church is well maintained by local ranchers and farmers. The surrounding arroyo is planted in figs, dates, pomegranates, citrus, grapes, and olives.

BAHÍA MAGDALENA

This unique marine environment is only a 45-minute drive from Ciudad Constitución, yet many transpeninsular voyagers pass it by. Where the flat Llano Magdalena has sunk lower than the Pacific, the ocean has intruded and created a string of barrier islands over 209 km (130 miles) long, separated from the peninsula by a series of shallow bays with an average depth of less than 18 meters (60 feet). Arroyos that sank under the Pacific have become *bocas* or "mouths" that let the sea in; these *bocas* now form channels between the barrier islands.

Starting at Boca de las Ánimas in the north, the most prominent barrier islands are **Isla Santo Domingo, Isla Magdalena, Isla Santa Margarita**, and **Isla Creciente**. The largest of the bays between the islands and peninsula, Bahía Magdalena and Bahía Almejas, are linked by Canal Gaviota to form a vast, protected waterway—the best on Baja's Pacific coast for kayaking and windsurfing. Naturalists could spend a lifetime exploring the mangroves and estuaries along the eastern bayshores, which support an astounding variety of marinelife and bird life.

History

Because of the proximity of Bahía Magdalena's natural harbor to the fertile Llano Magdalena, several groups of colonists attempted to settle the coastal plains here. In 1879 the Chartered Company of Lower California, an American land syndicate, settled 5,000 Americans along the bayshore. For a time the colony made money harvesting orchilla, a lichen used in commercial dye. The introduction of synthetic dyes killed the orchilla industry and the colony along with it.

The shore remained unpopulated throughout the first half of the 20th century except for the occasional visit by *bajacaliforniano* anglers and a few unplanned visits by passing mariners. Several ships foundered on the barrier islands, including the famous steamer *Independence* in 1853. Of the 400 passengers aboard, 150 perished in fires on the ship or by drowning after jumping into the breakers.

In 1920, the U.S. submarine *H-1* ran aground on Isla Santa Margarita. What the sub was doing in Mexican waters—at a time when relations between the two countries were tense—has never come to light. Although all but four of the crew were rescued by a passing ship, the sub was mysteriously looted of all logs and other classified material before U.S. Navy rescue ships could approach it; the Navy scuttled the sub at a depth of nine fathoms just off the island coast and erased virtually all records of its existence. More submarine lore: During World War II, Japanese submarines used Bahía Magdalena as a hiding place. Max Miller, author of *Land Where Time Stands Still*, spotted a Japanese sub in the bay when he made an overland journey to the edge of the Llano Magdalena in 1941.

In the 1960s, after Mexico recovered full ownership of the Llano Magdalena basin from foreign investors, the valley was irrigated and farmers began moving in. The harbor settlement of **Puerto San Carlos** soon developed as a relay point for the shipping of agricultural products, principally cotton and alfalfa, from the plains to mainland Mexico and abroad.

PUERTO SAN CARLOS

From Ciudad Constitución, paved highway Mexico 22 leads west 57 km (34 miles), then crosses a causeway onto a small hooked peninsula. Mangroves fringe the peninsula; a long wharf stretches from the western shore to the only other deepwater port besides Ensenada on

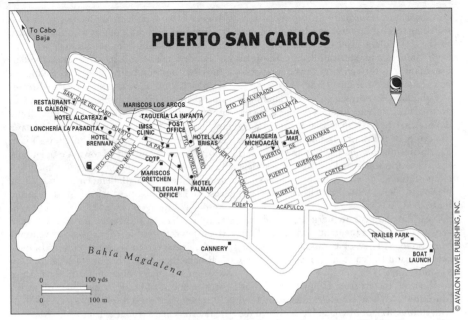

PUERTO SAN CARLOS

To Cabo
Baja

RESTAURANT
EL GALEÓN
HOTEL ALCATRAZ
LONCHERÍA LA PASADITA
HOTEL
BRENNAN

SAN JOSE DEL CABO
MARISCOS LOS ARCOS
TAQUERÍA LA INFANTA
IMSS
CLINIC
POST
OFFICE
HOTEL LAS
BRISAS
PANADERÍA
MICHOACÁN
BAJA
MAR
PTO. DE ALVARADO
PUERTO VALLARTA
GUAYMAS
PUERTO DE
PTO. CHAMELA
PTO. MEXICO
LA PAZ
COTP
PTO. MADERO
PUERTO
MORELOS
PUERTO GUERRERO
NEGRO
MARISCOS
GRETCHEN
MOTEL
PALMAR
TELEGRAPH
OFFICE
ESCONDIDO
PUERTO CORTEZ
PUERTO
PUERTO
PUERTO ACAPULCO

TRAILER PARK

Bahía Magdalena
CANNERY
BOAT
LAUNCH

0   100 yds
0   100 m

© AVALON TRAVEL PUBLISHING, INC.

the Pacific coast. Often simply called San Carlos, this small port town of 3,200 residents comprises a motley collection of prefab or breeze-block buildings lining sandy roads. Facilities include a Pemex station, *tiendas,* a café, several hotels and restaurants, a cannery, and COTP, customs, immigration, telegram/telegraph, and fishery offices. The cannery can be smelled throughout town at times, but particularly toward the southwest end of the peninsula.

Accommodations and Camping
US$25–50: Hotel Las Brisas, Puerto Madero at La Paz, tel. 613/136-0152, and **Motel Palmar,** Puerto Acapulco at Morelos, tel. 613/136-0035, offer basic rooms. A better deal is the friendly **Hotel Baja Mar,** a few blocks east on Puerto de Guaymas, a very clean motel with hot-water bathrooms.

US$50–100: Hotel Brennan y Suites, Calle Puerto Acapulco, tel. 613/136-0288, fax 613/136-0019, turismo@balandra.uabcs.mx, www.hotelbrennan.com.mx, has the best rooms in town. Suites here feature ceiling fans, air-conditioning, kitchenettes, and satellite TV. A restau-

rant/bar is on the premises. The hotel can arrange fishing trips and tours oriented toward whale-watching, natural history, and kayaking.

Hotel Alcatraz, Calle Puerto La Paz, tel. 613/136-0017, fax 613/136-0086, on the main road through town and thus easy to find, features decent rooms around a courtyard. Each room comes with TV, hot shower, and minibar. Many whale-watching and kayaking tour groups stay here. **Molly's Suites,** next door on Calle Puerto La Paz, tel. 613/136-0131, is similar.

Camping: Camping and RV parking at the northwest and southeast ends of the small peninsula costs around US$5 per vehicle. The most developed is the southeastern camp.

Food
Restaurant El Galeón, a seafood place not far from Hotel Alcatraz, Molly's Suites, Motel Palmar, and Hotel Brennan, features the largest dining room in town. In addition to lots of fresh seafood, including a delicious clam dip served free with *totopos,* the restaurant offers *carnes* and chicken.

El Patio, at Hotel Alcatraz, offers courtyard dining—nothing special but it's usually a convivial spot, especially during the whale-watching season. **Restaurant China Mex,** next to the town plaza, lives up to its name with both Chinese and Mexican dishes. **Taquería La Infanta,** in the center of town, appears to be the most popular taco stand.

Cabo Baja, an open-air palapa restaurant just north of town, offers several ways of preparing the day's catch, which is displayed in a refrigerator in the center of the dining room. On Calle Juan Padrín (formerly Calle La Paz), the main dirt road in town, **Mariscos Los Arcos** serves delicious seafood, *antojitos,* and hearty Mexican breakfasts. The *ceviche de callos* (scallops ceviche) is excellent.

Near the plaza is **Lonchería La Pasadita,** a very small seafood restaurant, with tasty, cheap Mexican food. They serve some really tasty *pozole* here, and the coffee is quite good. Opens around 7 A.M.

About 20 meters from the plaza you'll find **Mariscos Gretchen,** which features tacos filled with shrimp, fish, or machaca. Open early in the morning. You'll also find **taco stands** on Calle Puerto La Paz.

Panadería Michoacán is a bakery near Hotel Baja Mar.

Puerto López Mateos and Puerto Chale

Trailered or cartopped boats can be launched from a concrete boat ramp in San Carlos; you can easily launch *pangas* from the beach. Other launching points for small boats or kayaks are Puerto López Mateos to the north (reached via Ciudad Insurgentes), Puerto Cancún to the south (accessible from Mexico 1 at Km 173), and Puerto Chale (via Santa Rita, Km 157, Mexico 1).

Puerto López Mateos is a small town with a cannery, post office, barrel gas, tiendas, a *farmacia,* three hotels, and a few seafood restaurants.

Hotel Posada La Pasadita, tel. 613/131-5032, has four rooms—only one of which has a private bath. **Hotel Posada Tornavuelta,** Abelardo L. Rodríguez, tel. 613/131-5106, offers basic rooms with private bath. Check in at the *farmacia* next door. Open year-round.

Posada La Belleza López, Abelardo L. Ro-dríguez 219 (no phone), features one room with private bath and three others with shared bath. Showers are available for nonguests.

Food: The town boasts a few seafood restaurants. **El Camarón Feliz,** Abelardo L. Rodríguez, tel. 613/131-5032, serves good fish tacos. **Restaurant Ballena Gris,** on the right as you come into town, features fish, shrimp, and lobster dishes in the US$6.50–11 range. Restaurant **Cabaña Briza,** one block west of the church, is similar. Most of the restaurants in town are open only January–April during the whale-watching season. The **Festival de Ballena Gris** (Gray Whale Festival) takes place at the *embarcadero* in the west end of town every weekend from mid-February to the end of March. It's like the usual small-town festival in Mexico—food vendors, music, *artesanías,* and balloon vendors. In mid-February they have a big one-day celebration with entertainment, disco music, regional dance performances, and singers, all topped off with a 30-minute fireworks display.

Puerto Chale is marked on some Mexican maps as Puerto Charley. Puerto Chale is basically a fish camp on a beautiful bay system. The settlement offers a minisuper with all the basics, a church, a school, and several clean outhouses. There are good camping spots here along the inland waterway. Hotel Brennan in San Carlos rents kayaking equipment. Bay destinations of interest include the populated islands of Isla Santa Margarita (pop. 549) and Isla Magdalena (pop. 275).

During the peak January–March whale-watching season, kayaking and other boating is restricted to areas north or south of Boca de Soledad, and even for these areas you must obtain a permit from SEMARNAT in La Paz first.

Fishing

The bay fisheries provide steady sportfishing due to the relative lack of commercial fishing interests. Onshore catches, near the mangroves, include halibut, occasional yellowtail, red bass (mangrove snapper), corvina, and snook. Farther out in the bay, anglers take grouper, black bass, and yellowtail; offshore, beyond the 100-fathom line, are sailfish, marlin, dorado, wahoo, and giant

© JOE CUMMINGS

San Carlos fishermen

seabass. Although most of these game fish frequent the area year-round, July–November is generally the most productive fishing season. Best places to get live bait are the mackerel holes off Punta Entrada.

You can gather clams in the shallows of both bays, although Bahía Almejas lives up to its name with the most extensive clam grounds.

Windsurfing

Mag Bay, as gringo board-sailors usually refer to Bahía Magdalena, offers the best windsurfing on Baja California's Pacific coast. A strong year-round breeze, together with the relatively calm bay surface, creates perfect conditions for novice and intermediate windsurfers; experienced wave-sailors can experiment at or near the *bocas,* where breakers and stronger winds increase the challenge.

A protected run of 88 km (52 miles) begins at Puerto López Mateos and ends at Puerto Cancún; you can lengthen this run to 113 km (70 miles) by staying in until Puerto Chale.

Whale-Watching

During the annual gray whale migration, January– March, the canals, bays, and *bocas* of the Bahía Magdalena complex are practically filled with the whales' undulating forms. Puerto López Mateos and San Carlos are the usual centers for whale-watching activities. Often you can spot grays from shore at Puerto López Mateos as they come and go via Boca de Soledad to the north; a public parking and viewing area lies north of the port's fish-processing plant. *Pangeros* offer two-hour *panga* tours from this area for US$50 per *panga* if you can find six people; four people can go for US$55 pp. Ask at any hotel in San Carlos, or go talk to the *pangeros* directly at the embarcadero on the west side of town near the lighthouse. Local operators officially authorized to lead whale-watching tours include: **Viajes Mar y Arena,** tel. 613/136-0076, fax 613/136-0232; **Brennan's y Asociados,** tel. 613/136-0288, fax 613/136-0019, turismo@balandra.uabcs.mx; and **Unión de Lancheros y Servicios Turísticos de Puerto San Carlos (ULYSTOURS),** tel. 613/136-0310. Although limited numbers of *pangas* are allowed in the bay at any one time, early morning and late afternoon are best for avoiding crowds. Because the waters of San Carlos are deeper, you can usually see more whale acrobatics in this area than off López Mateos.

M

CENTRAL BAJA

While pregnant female grays venture into shallower parts of the bay for calving, males tend to loiter near bay entrances, where they cavort with other males and nonpregnant females, often breaching and spyhopping—but not "mating," as myth would have it. One of the best viewing spots is **Punta Entrada,** at the southern tip of Isla Magdalena, which forms the north end of the wide channel between Bahía Magdalena and the Pacific. The island is accessible only by boat, with the best anchorage on the southeast side of the point, or by small plane (a landing strip lies just north of Punta Entrada). You can camp at the fish camp near the tip or farther north near the village of **Puerto Magdalena.** A San Carlos *pangero* will drop you off on the island and pick you up the following day; the usual hourly rates apply.

You can book Bahía Magdalena whale-watching tours in La Paz through several travel agencies.

From late January to early March, **Baja Expeditions,** 2625 Garnet Ave., San Diego, CA 92109, tel. 858/581-3311 or 800/843-6967, fax 858/581-6542, travel@bajaex.com, www.bajaex.com, offers frequent seven-day kayaking/whale-watching trips in Bahía Magdalena for US$1,250 pp.

Transportation

The road to Puerto San Carlos (57 km/35 miles from Ciudad Constitución), one of Baja California Sur's only official state highways, is an easy drive of less than an hour. Buses ply the Ciudad Constitución–Puerto San Carlos route several times daily for about US$1 per passenger.

Buses from La Paz go back and forth to San Carlos twice a day for US$10 each direction. Check at the bus station for the latest schedule. Buses are more frequent during whale-watching season.

For finding roads along the coast of Bahía Magdalena and Bahía Almejas, the 1:250,000-scale INEGI La Paz map (G12-10-11) is invaluable.

EL CIEN AND PUNTA EL CONEJO

At Km 100, about midway between Ciudad Constitución and La Paz, lies the tiny roadside settlement of El Cien (One Hundred). As a pit stop, El Cien offers the **Lonchería El 100** (*machaca* and *carne asada* are the mainstays), a CONASUPO, and barrel gas, the only place for gas between Ciudad Constitución and La Paz. A nearby fossil reef reportedly contains whale vertebrae and other marine skeletons; inquire at the *lonchería* for a guide. A couple of similar *loncherías* can be found a little farther south between Km 97 and 98 (**Lonchería Lupita**), and at Km 96 (**Lonchería Tere's**).

At Km 80, a good dirt road branches west 19 km (12 miles) to Punta El Conejo. El Conejo (The Rabbit) is well known among surfers for steady point breaks in both northwest and southwest swells. Near the coast, the road to El Conejo intersects a lesser dirt road heading south 17 km (12.5 miles) to another surfing spot, **Punta Márquez.** This road continues southward along the coast all the way to Todos Santos (124 km/77 miles from El Conejo), passing a number of good beach breaks. Recommended for four-wheel drive vehicles only.

If you're driving south and need to eat something before Km 100, check out **Restaurant Las Brisas del Desierto,** between Km 172 and 173, **Restaurant Rosita** at Km 128, or **Restaurant Rossy** at Km 114.

Cape Region

La Paz and Vicinity

Ensconced along the largest bay on Baja's Sea of Cortez coast, La Paz is a city of 180,000 noted for its attractive *malecón* (waterfront walkway) backed by swaying palms and pastel-colored buildings, its splendid sunsets, easygoing pace, sunny climate, and its proximity to uncrowded beaches and pristine islands. Many Baja travelers—Mexicans and gringos alike—cite La Paz (Peace) as their favorite city on the Baja California peninsula, A few even go as far as to pronounce it their favorite in all of Mexico. Nowadays Cabo San Lucas, 221 km (137 miles) farther south, receives more attention than La Paz in the American press, which suits La Paz fans fine since it means fewer tourists.

Of all the cities in Baja, La Paz is steeped most profoundly in mainland Mexico's traditions; it was the first major European settlement on the peninsula and has long been a haven for Mexicans dissatisfied with life on the mainland. Many *paceños* (La Paz natives) are descendants of mainlanders who sailed to La Paz to avoid the political turmoil of the 19th and early 20th centuries. And it's not uncommon to meet more-recent Mexican émigrés who have resettled in La Paz

©KATA KLAMARAS

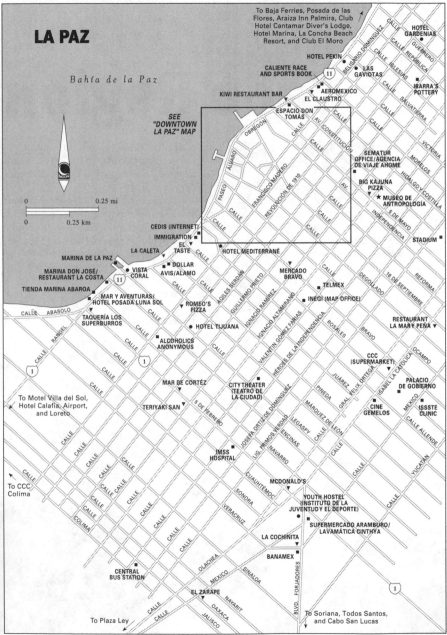

LA PAZ

Bahía de la Paz

To Baja Ferries, Posada de las
Flores, Araiza Inn Palmira, Club
Hotel Cantamar Diver's Lodge,
Hotel Marina, La Concha Beach
Resort, and Club El Moro

HOTEL PEKIN

CALIENTE RACE
AND SPORTS BOOK

KIWI RESTAURANT BAR

LAS
GAVIOTAS

AEROMEXICO
EL CLAUSTRO

ESPACIO DON
TOMÁS

HOTEL
GARDENIAS

IBARRA'S
POTTERY

SEE
"DOWNTOWN
LA PAZ" MAP

SEMATUR
OFFICE/AGENCIA
DE VIAJE AHOME

BIG KAJUNA
PIZZA

MUSEO DE
ANTROPOLOGÍA

STADIUM

0   0.25 mi

0   0.25 km

CEDIS (INTERNET)

IMMIGRATION

EL
TASTE

HOTEL MEDITERRANÉ

LA CALETA

MARINA DE LA PAZ

MARINA DON JOSÉ/
RESTAURANT LA COSTA

TIENDA MARINA ABAROA

VISTA
CORAL

DOLLAR
AVIS/ALAMO

MAR Y AVENTURAS/
HOTEL POSADA LUNA SOL

ROMEO'S
PIZZA

MERCADO
BRAVO

TELMEX

INEGI (MAP OFFICE)

RESTAURANT
LA MARY PEÑA

TAQUERÍA LOS
SUPERBURROS

HOTEL TIJUANA

ALCOHOLICS
ANONYMOUS

CCC
(SUPERMARKET)

PALACIO
DE GOBIERNO

To Motel Villa del Sol,
Hotel Calafia, Airport,
and Loreto

MAR DE CORTÉZ

CITY THEATER
(TEATRO DE
LA CIUDAD)

CINE
GEMELOS

ISSSTE
CLINIC

TERIYAKI SAN

5 DE FEBRERO

To CCC
Colima

IMSS
HOSPITAL

MCDONALD'S

YOUTH HOSTEL
(INSTITUTO DE LA
JUVENTUD Y EL DEPORTE)

SUPERMERCADO ARAMBURO/
LAVAMÁTICA CINTHYA

LA COCHINITA

BANAMEX

CENTRAL
BUS STATION

EL ZARAPE

To Plaza Ley

To Soriana, Todos Santos,
and Cabo San Lucas

© AVALON TRAVEL PUBLISHING, INC.

after becoming fed up with modern-day political machinations in Mexico City, Guadalajara, or Monterrey. *Paceños* are proud of the many ways in which their city lives up to its name.

The city offers a wide variety of accommodations and dining venues, well-stocked supermarkets, marine supply stores, and a ferry terminal with a daily departure for Mazatlán across the Sea of Cortez. Parking can be a bit tight, and minor traffic snarls are common in *el centro,* the city center, but can be avoided by using Boulevard Forjadores, a wide avenue skirting the southern section of the city. Along the bay, La Paz remains much as John Steinbeck described it in 1941:

> *La Paz grew in fascination as we approached. The square, iron-shuttered colonial houses stood up right in back of the beach with rows of beautiful trees in front of them. It is a lovely place. There is a broad promenade along the water lined with benches, named for dead residents of the city, where one may rest oneself. . . . [A] cloud of delight hangs over the distant city from the time when it was the great pearl center of the world. . . . Guaymas is busier, they say, and Mazatlán gayer, but La Paz is* antigua.

Climate and Travel Seasons

The most pleasant time of year to visit La Paz is mid-October through June, when days are balmy and evenings are cool. In January, maximum temperatures average 22°C (72°F), minimum temperatures 14°C (57°F). Temperatures for July average 35°C (96°F) maximum, 24°C (75°F) minimum, but daytime highs of over 38°C (100°F) aren't unusual. Hot summer afternoons are moderated by the daily arrival of the *coromuel,* a strong onshore breeze that bedevils yachties trying to escape the harbor but cools down the rest of the population.

La Paz and vicinity average only around 15 cm (six inches) of rainfall per year, over half generally falling during the Aug.–Sept. *chubasco* (tropical storm) season. Full-fledged *chubascos* with gale-force winds actually reach La Paz only every couple of years. Most of the time the area receives

CAPE-REGION HIGHLIGHTS

La Paz: Baja's most Mexican city throws together Sea of Cortez beaches, *sudbajacaliforniano* cultural events, inexpensive hotels, and duty-free shopping. If you visit in February, don't miss the annual Carnaval celebrations (page 377).

Isla Espíritu Santo: Dozens of immaculate coves and rocky islets ring this large, deserted island in the Sea of Cortez, perfect for kayaking, swimming, snorkeling and hiking undisturbed by tourism development (page 407).

Sierra de la Laguna: Hike the folded, granitic peaks of this sierra to La Laguna, a huge meadow teeming with both tropical and desert flora (page 421).

Bahía Pulmo: This quiet bay on the East Cape boasts deserted beaches and Mexico's northernmost coral reefs (page 432).

San José del Cabo: The Cape Region's most sophisticated town features well-preserved postcolonial architecture, fine restaurants, and some of the best *artesanías* (handicrafts) in Baja (page 436).

Playa del Amor (or Playa del Amante): Hop a water taxi to "Lover's Beach" from the harbor in Cabo San Lucas, and enjoy a day of swimming, snorkeling or picnicking on Mexico's most pristine municipal beach (page 469).

La Candelaria: Drive inland from Cabo San Lucas to this *bajacaliforniano* village famed for ranch pottery and *curanderos* (traditional healers) (page 495).

Playa Las Palmas: This "secret" beach near Todos Santos is tucked away between two stony headlands and backed by tall palms as well as a freshwater lagoon—perfect recipe for a day of relative solitude (page 500).

Todos Santos: Charming bed-and-breakfasts, artist-owned galleries, fresh seafood, and hidden surf spots attract everyone from Hollywood refugees to backpackers (page 502).

CAPE REGION

only the remote influences of storms centered along mainland Mexico's lower west coast.

February tends to be La Paz's peak tourist month. Even then you should be able to find a hotel room easily since the average occupancy rate runs around 50 percent all year-round.

HISTORY

Early Spanish Contact

When the Spanish first landed on the shores of Bahía de la Paz in the early 16th century, the area was inhabited by migrating bands of Guaicura and Pericú, who allegedly called their homeland Airapi. Hunters and gatherers, these Amerindian groups lived mostly on shellfish, small game, and wild plants. As artifacts on display at La Paz's Museum of Anthropology demonstrate, they were also skilled weavers and potters.

Into this peaceful scene entered the first European, a Basque mutineer named Fortún Jiménez who commandeered the Spanish ship *Concepción* on the Sea of Cortez in 1533. Originally under the command of Captain Diego Becerra, the *Concepción* had been sent to explore the sea on behalf of Spain's most famous conquistador, Hernán Cortés. After executing the captain, Jiménez landed at Bahía de la Paz in early 1534, where he and 22 of his crew were killed by Amerindians while filling their water casks at a spring. The survivors sailed the *Concepción* back to the mainland, where the ship was immediately captured by Cortés's New Spain rival, Nuño de Guzmán. At least one crew member managed to escape and returned to Cortés with descriptions of a huge, beautiful bay filled with pearl-oyster beds.

Cortés himself landed at the northeast end of the bay, probably at Pichilingue near the present ferry terminal, in May 1535 and named it Puerto de Santa Cruz. Cortés was able to effect a truce with local Amerindians, but his attempt at establishing a permanent Spanish colony lasted only through 1538, when the colonists were forced to abandon the peninsula due to supply problems.

The next Spaniard to visit the bay was famed explorer Sebastián Vizcaíno, who landed here in 1596 during his long voyage around the

Hernán Cortés

BOB RACE

peninsula's perimeter and north to California. Because he and his crew were treated so well by the Pericú, Vizcaíno named the bay Bahía de la Paz (Bay of Peace).

Pirates and Colonization

Baja California remained free of Spaniards another 100 years before the successful establishment of a mission colony at Loreto to the north. By this time, English and Dutch pirates were plundering New Spain's Manila galleons as they returned from the Orient weighted down with gold, silks, and spices. One of the freebooters' favorite staging areas was Bahía de la Paz, which contained numerous *ensenadas* (coves) and inlets perfect for concealing their swift corsairs. When Spanish crews put in for water, the pirates raided the galleons, often using their knowledge of strong afternoon winds to attack the ships when they were effectively pinned down.

Increased pirate activity in the late 17th and early 18th centuries created the need for a Spanish presence in the Cape Region. In 1719 Padre Juan de Ugarte, then President of the Missions, contracted a master shipbuilder to construct a

ENGLISH PIRATES ON THE SEA OF CORTEZ

Sir Francis Drake, Thomas Cavendish, William Dampier, Woodes Rogers, Thomas Dover, and other English privateers left behind a colorful Baja legacy. In spite of Spain's repeated attempts to colonize the peninsula, throughout the Spanish colonial period the pirates probably gained more wealth in the Californias than the Spanish themselves. For 250 years they plagued the Manila galleons off the coast of the Californias, finding the bays and lagoons of Baja's Cape Region perfect hiding places from which to launch attacks on treasure-laden ships.

In La Paz, using their knowledge of the strong breeze that blows into the harbor every summer afternoon, the pirates attacked Spanish galleons while the vessels were effectively trapped in the bay. Four centuries after the first Manila-Acapulco voyages, this afternoon wind is still known as *el coromuel,* named for the Puritan Cromwells—father and son—who ruled successively as Lord Protectors of England.

The Disappearance of the *Desire*
The most notorious of the Pacific privateers was Sir Thomas Cavendish, whose greatest feat of plunder occurred at Cabo San Lucas in 1587. There his two English vessels, *Desire* and *Content,* commandeered the Spanish galleon *Santa Ana* following a protracted sea battle. Cavendish set fire to the *Santa Ana* after looting its cargo holds and setting its crew and passengers ashore. The Spanish crew later retrieved the burned hulk and restored it for a return to Acapulco.

The plundered treasure, meanwhile, was divided between the *Desire* and the *Content.* The ships set sail for England immediately, but during the first night of their triumphant voyage the *Desire* disappeared. Cavendish reported in England that the captain and crew of the *Desire* must have scuttled the ship on a nearby island and disappeared with the loot. Neither the wreckage of the vessel nor the treasure was ever discovered; some historians speculate that at least part of the missing wealth remains buried near The Cape.

A Visit by Robinson Crusoe
In 1709, famed corsair Woodes Rogers landed in La Paz after rescuing a seaman who'd been marooned five years on a deserted island off Chile's coast. The rescued man was Alexander Selkirk, whose island sojourn became the inspiration for Daniel Defoe's *Robinson Crusoe,* published in 1719. Selkirk was aboard Rogers's *Dover* when the crew captured the Spanish galleon *Encarnación* off Cabo San Lucas in 1709; he served as sailing master on the ship's return voyage to England the following year.

ship for the specific purpose of exploring the Sea of Cortez coast and improving supply lines with the mainland. The barque *El Triunfo de la Cruz,* assembled of native Baja hardwood at the Mulegé estuary, made its first sailing to Bahía de la Paz in 1720 with Ugarte and Padre Jaime Bravo as passengers.

Ugarte and Bravo founded the mission community of Nuestra Señora del Pilar de la Paz at the current city site. The padres didn't find the Pericú to be as friendly this time around; the mission lasted only until 1749, when it was abandoned following a series of Amerindian rebellions.

By this time, another mission and a presidio had been founded farther south at San José del Cabo—a better location for monitoring pirate activity.

La Paz Reborn

Left with European diseases and without the support of the mission system, the local Pericú population dwindled quickly. By 1811, Mexican ranchers and *pescadores* who had settled along the Bahía de la Paz started their own town, which they named La Paz after the bay. After Loreto was severely damaged during a hurricane in 1829, the capital of Baja California Sur was

CAPE REGION

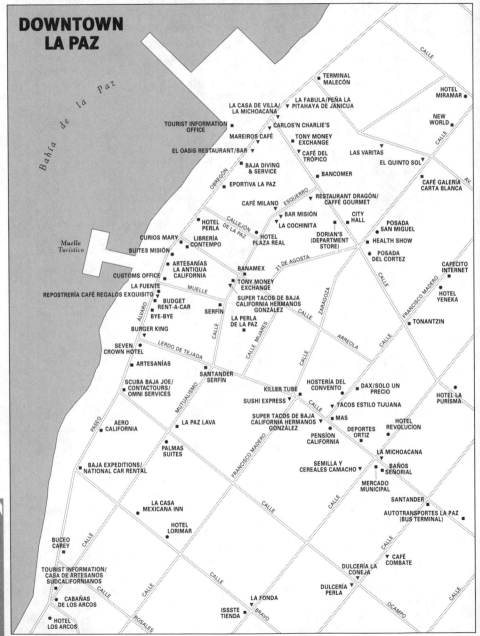

DOWNTOWN LA PAZ

Bahía de la Paz

Muelle Turístico

TERMINAL MALECÓN

HOTEL MIRAMAR

LA CASA DE VILLA/ LA MICHOACANA

LA FABULA/PEÑA LA PITAHAYA DE JANICUA

NEW WORLD

TOURIST INFORMATION OFFICE

CARLOS'N CHARLIE'S

MAREIROS CAFÉ

TONY MONEY EXCHANGE

EL OASIS RESTAURANT/BAR

CAFÉ DEL TRÓPICO

LAS VARITAS

EL QUINTO SOL

OBREGÓN

BAJA DIVING & SERVICE

BANCOMER

EPORTIVA LA PAZ

CAFÉ GALERÍA CARTA BLANCA

AV

CAFÉ MILANO

ESQUERRO

RESTAURANT DRAGÓN/ CAFÉ GOURMET

BAR MISIÓN

CITY HALL

POSADA SAN MIGUEL

HOTEL PERLA

CALLEJÓN DE LA PAZ

LA COCHINITA

CURIOS MARY

LIBRERÍA CONTEMPO

HOTEL PLAZA REAL

DORIAN'S (DEPARTMENT STORE)

HEALTH SHOW

SUITES MISIÓN

POSADA DEL CORTEZ

ARTESANÍAS LA ANTIGUA CALIFORNIA

CAFECITO INTERNET

CUSTOMS OFFICE

BANAMEX

21 DE AGOSTA

LA FUENTE

MUELLE

TONY MONEY EXCHANGE

HOTEL YENEKA

REPOSTRERÍA CAFÉ REGALOS EXQUISITO

ALVARO

BUDGET RENT-A-CAR

SUPER TACOS DE BAJA CALIFORNIA HERMANOS GONZÁLEZ

ZARAGOZA

TONANTZIN

SERFÍN

LA PERLA DE LA PAZ

BYE-BYE

BURGER KING

CALLE

CALLE MIJARES

CALLE

AREOLA

CALLE

SEVEN CROWN HOTEL

LERDO DE TEJADA

ARTESANÍAS

SANTANDER SERFÍN

SCUBA BAJA JOE/ CONTACTOURS/ OMNI SERVICES

KILLER TUBE

HOSTERÍA DEL CONVENTO

DAX/SOLO UN PRECIO

HOTEL LA PURÍSMA

SUSHI EXPRESS

TACOS ESTILO TIJUANA

MUTUALISMO

SUPER TACOS DE BAJA CALIFORNIA HERMANOS GONZÁLEZ

MAS

HOTEL REVOLUCIÓN

PASEO

AERO CALIFORNIA

LA PAZ LAVA

DEPORTES ORTIZ

PENSIÓN CALIFORNIA

LA MICHOACANA

PALMAS SUITES

FRANCISCO MADERO

SEMILLA Y CEREALES CAMACHO

BAÑOS SEÑORIAL

BAJA EXPEDITIONS/ NATIONAL CAR RENTAL

MERCADO MUNICIPAL

SANTANDER

CALLE

AUTOTRANSPORTES LA PAZ (BUS TERMINAL)

LA CASA MEXICANA INN

CALLE

HOTEL LORIMAR

CALLE

BUCEO CAREY

CALLE

CAFÉ COMBATE

TOURIST INFORMATION/ CASA DE ARTESANOS SUDCALIFORNIANOS

DULCERÍA LA CONEJA

DULCERÍA PERLA

CALLE

CABAÑAS DE LOS ARCOS

LA FONDA

CALLE

OCAMPO

HOTEL LOS ARCOS

ROSALES

ISSSTE TIENDA

BRAVO

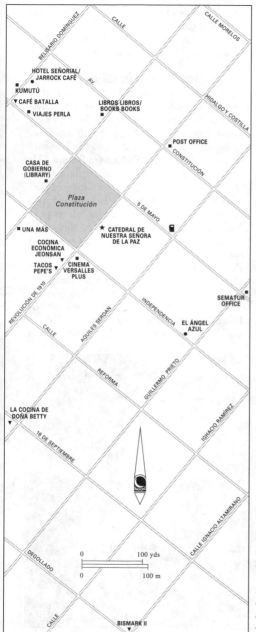

moved to burgeoning La Paz, where it has remained ever since.

During the Mexican-American War (1846–48), U.S. troops occupied the city; the soldiers left when the Californias were split by the 1848 Treaty of Hidalgo. But American general William Walker, dissatisfied with the treaty and hoping to add another slaveholder state to counter the growing U.S. abolitionist movement, formed his own army of New York Volunteers and retook La Paz in November 1853. Proclaiming himself President of the Republic of Sonora, Walker lasted only six months; he and his mercenaries fled upon hearing that the United States wouldn't back their claims, and that the Mexican army was on its way to La Paz from the mainland. Walker was tried in the United States for violation of neutrality laws, fined, and two years later was executed by the Nicaraguan army for attempting a similar takeover of Nicaragua.

La Paz remained a sleepy tropic seaport, known only for pearl harvesting, until it was declared a duty-free port following World War II. After an epizootic disease killed off the entire pearl-oyster population, the city's economic focus turned to farming and trade with the mainland. During Mexico's postwar economic boom, mainland Mexicans crossed the Sea of Cortez in droves to buy imported merchandise; enchanted by La Paz itself, many stayed on.

In the 1950s, La Paz became well known as a fishing resort and was visited by a succession of North American literati and Hollywood celebrities, thus initiating the city's reputation as an international vacation spot. But until the Transpeninsular Highway was completed in 1973, the city remained for the most part a tourist destination for mainland Mexicans.

Statehood was bestowed on the Territory of Baja California Sur in 1974, and La Paz was made state capital. Linked by air, ferry, and highway to mainland Mexico and the United States, the city has grown considerably yet manages to maintain its tropic port ambience. As a tourist destination, it remains more Mexican than foreign—of the 150,000 or so leisure visitors who visit La Paz annually, Mexican nationals typically outnumber foreigners three to one.

CAPE REGION

SIGHTS

Museo de Antropología

Baja California history buffs shouldn't miss this well-designed museum at Calles 5 de Mayo and Altamirano, tel. 612/125-6424, fax 612/122-0162. Three floors of exhibits cover Cape Region anthropology from prehistoric to colonial and modern times. On display are fossils, minerals, Amerindian artifacts, dioramas of Amerindian and colonial life, and maps of rock-painting sites throughout central and southern Baja. Labels are in Spanish only.

A small gift section offers Spanish-language books in the fields of anthropology, archaeology, and art history, including such hard-to-find volumes as the *Catálogo Nacional de los Monumentos Históricos Inmuebles de Baja California Sur,* an inventory of historical buildings in the *municipios* of San Antonio, San José del Cabo, Santiago, and Todos Santos.

Next to the museum is an older building that has served La Paz as a hospital, prison, and, more recently, the **Biblioteca Justo Sierra,** a children's library. Behind the library is an ethnobotanical garden dedicated to the exhibition of medicinal herbs and sculpture from the region.

The museum is open Mon.–Fri. 8 A.M.–6 P.M., Saturday 9 A.M.–2 P.M.; admission free.

Plaza Constitución (Jardín Velazco)

La Paz's tidy downtown *zócalo* is enclosed by Avenida Independencia and Calles 5 de Mayo, Revolución de 1910, and Madero. There's a kiosk in the center and wrought-iron benches to sit on. At the southwest side of the plaza is the post-missionary-style **Catedral de Nuestra Señora de la Paz,** which replaced La Paz's original mission church in 1861. Although the twin-towered brick edifice looms over the plaza, it lacks the charm of earlier Jesuit missions. Inside, only an image of Nuestra Señora del Pilar and a few theological books survive from the earlier 1720 mission. A couple of blocks southwest of the plaza, on Calle Zaragoza between Arrival and Lerdo de Tejada, a plaque commemorates the original mission site.

At the northwest side of Plaza Constitución, opposite the cathedral, is the **Biblioteca de História de las Californias** (Library of Californias' History). Housed in the 1880s-era former

Catedral de Nuestra Señora de La Paz

Casa de Gobierno (Government House), the library is filled with Spanish- and English-language volumes on Alta and Baja California history. The general public is welcome to use the library for research. Officially, the library hours are Mon.–Fri. 9 A.M.–6 P.M., Saturday 9 A.M.–3 P.M., though these are not always strictly adhered to. For library information, call 612/122-0162.

La Unidad Cultural Profesor Jesús Castro Agúndez

This cultural center at Calles Farías and Legaspy, in the Cuatro Molinos (Four Windmills) district, includes an art gallery, community art school, city archives, and the **Teatro de la Ciudad** (City Theater), tel. 612/125-0207, a 1,500-seat performing-arts facility that hosts musical, theatrical, and dance performances throughout the year. Next to the theater, four windmills pay tribute to a time when La Paz relied on wind power to pump water and generate electricity.

Also at the complex is **La Rotonda de los Sudcalifornianos Illustres,** a circle of sculpted figures representing Baja California Sur's most celebrated heroes—most of them teachers and soldiers.

Malecón

One of the city's major attractions is the pleasant five-km *malecón,* a seawall promenade along the northwest side of Paseo Alvaro Obregón extending from Calzada 5 de Febrero (Mexico 1 south) to the northeastern city limits. Palm-shaded benches are conveniently situated at intervals along the walkway for watching sailboats and yachts coming in and out of the bay. The best time of day for people-watching is around sunset, when the city begins cooling off, the sun dyes the waterfront orange, and *paceños* take to the *malecón* for an evening stroll or jog. Snacks and cold beverages are available at several palapa bars along the way.

A few years ago, the city transformed the former Muelle Fiscal into the Muelle Turístico (Tourist Pier) by adding an archway over the entry, cobblestone paving, potted plants, and well-lighted wrought-iron seating areas. Over the entrance to the pier, a sign reads Bienvenidos a La Paz, Puerto de Ilusión (Welcome to La Paz, Port of Dreams). Decorative paving has been

La Paz malecón

laid along the southern stretches of the *malecón* as well. With locals strolling and hanging out on the pier on warm evenings, the revitalized pier has taken on the feel of a traditional Mexican plaza.

Universities

As Baja California Sur's educational center, La Paz supports a large number of schools at the primary, secondary, and tertiary levels. The prominent **Universidad Autónoma de Baja California Sur** (University of Baja California South), on Boulevard Forjadores, has an enrollment of around 2,000 and reputable programs in agriculture, engineering, and business. The **Instituto Tecnológico de la Paz** (Technological Institute of La Paz), also on Boulevard Forjadores, enrolls approximately 3,000 students and is primarily known for its commercial-fishing department.

BEACHES

Bahía de la Paz is scalloped with 10 signed, public beaches. Most inviting are the seven beaches

© JOE CUMMINGS

CAPE REGION

strung out northeast of La Paz along Península de Pichilingue—they get better the farther you get from the city.

Playa Palmira, around four km (2.5 miles) east of downtown La Paz via the La Paz–Pichilingue Rd., has been taken over by the Araiza Inn Palmira and Club de Yates Palmira, leaving little remaining beachfront. A kilometer farther, the small but pleasant **Playa El Coromuel** offers restaurant/bar service, a waterslide, *palapas,* and toilets.

In front of La Concha Beach Resort near Km 5, **Playa Caimancito** (named for an offshore rock formation that resembles a small gator) features a rock reef within swimming distance of the grayish beach. Although it's close to the city and resort developments, you can see a surprising number of tropical fish here; incoming tide is the best time for swimming and snorkeling. The bus fare to these three beaches from the *malecón* bus terminal in downtown La Paz is US$1.50.

Playa del Tesoro, 14 km (8.5 miles) from the city, is another casual, semiurban beach with palapas and a sometimes-open, often-closed restaurant. The beach was purportedly named for a cache of silver coins unearthed by crews building a road to the Pichilingue ferry terminal near the beach. Just southwest of El Tesoro, a dirt road leads to hidden **Playa Punta Colorada,** a small, quiet cove surrounded by red-hued hills that protect it from the sights and sounds of the La Paz–Pichilingue Road. Buses from the malecón terminal cost US$2.50.

At Km 17, just beyond the SEMATUR ferry terminal, is **Playa Pichilingue,** the only public beach in the La Paz vicinity with restrooms available 24 hours for campers. The beach also has a modest palapa restaurant.

After Pichilingue the once-sandy track has been replaced by pavement as far as Playa Tecolote. The turnoff for **Playa Balandra** appears five km (three miles) beyond Pichilingue, then it's another 800 meters (half mile) to the parking area and beach. Several *palapas,* brick barbecue pits, and trash barrels have been installed by the city. Depending on the tide, the large, shallow bay of Puerto Balandra actually forms several beaches, some of them long sandbars. Ringed by cliffs

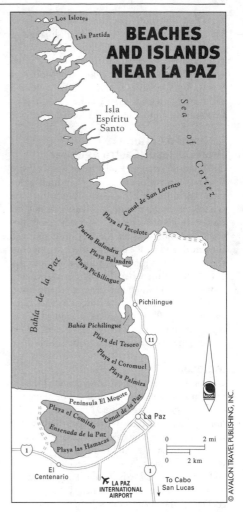

and steep hills, the bay is a beautiful and usually secluded spot, perfect for wading in the clear, warm waters. Clams are abundant, and a coral reef at the south end of the bay offers decent snorkeling. Climb the rock cliffs—carefully—for sweeping bay views. Camping is permitted at Balandra, but oftentimes a lack of breeze brings out the *jejenes* (no-see-ums), especially in the late summer and early fall. The beaches sometimes draw crowds on weekends.

About three km (1.5 miles) beyond the Playa

© JOE CUMMINGS

palapas on the bay in La Paz

Balandra turnoff is **Playa El Tecolote,** a wide, long, pretty beach backed by vegetated dunes. Because Tecolote is open to the stiff breezes of Canal de San Lorenzo, the camping here is usually insect-free. Two *palapa* restaurants, **El Tecolote,** tel. 612/127-9494, and **Palapa Azul,** tel. 612/122-1801, sell seafood and cold beverages and rent *pangas,* beach chairs and umbrellas, fishing gear, and plastic canoes. Both restaurants have pay showers. Free municipal *palapas,* barbecue grills, and trash barrels dot the beach north and south of the restaurants. At the opposite end of the beach from El Tecolote and Palapa Azul is the similar **La Concha Restaurant and Bar,** which charges US$10 for the use of tables, chairs, *palapas,* showers, and toilets if you bring your own food; no charge if you buy your food from the restaurant. If you visit during the week, the place is almost deserted. Only two buses per day, on weekends only, go as far as Tecolote and Balandra, departing the *malecón* terminal at noon and 2 P.M. and returning at 5:30 P.M.; the fare is US$2.50.

Isla Espíritu Santo, 6.5 km (four miles) away, is clearly visible in the distance; for around US$40–50 you can hire a *panga* from Palapa Azul to cross the channel (see Islands, farther on).

Farther Afield

From Tecolote the road returns to sand as it winds across the peninsula for about 13 km (eight miles) before ending at remote **Playa Coyote.** Along the way shorter roads branch off to rocky coves suitable for camping. Don't tackle this road expecting to find the perfect white-sand beach; the farther northeast from Tecolote you go, the stonier and browner the beaches become.

South of Playa Coyote you can navigate a network of sand roads to Puerto Mejia and **Las Cruces.** Named for three crosses topping a bluff near the cove where Cortés supposedly landed, Las Cruces served as a supply port for Isla Cerralvo pearl beds during the pearl era. It was abandoned in the 1930s after the pearl-bearing oysters died out. In 1949, Abelardo L. Rodríguez III, grandson of a former Mexican president, designed and built at Las Cruces a fly-in getaway resort for Hollywood celebrities, including Desi Arnaz and Bing Crosby. The 20,000-acre resort was incorporated as Club de Caza y Pesca Las Cruces (Las Cruces Hunting and Fishing Club) in 1961 and today remains a private association counting around 225 members. Although the resort's popularity

CAPE REGION

THE PEARLS OF LA PAZ

Pearls develop from sand grains or other small particles that manage to get between an oyster's mantle and its shell. The oyster secretes a substance that cushions it from the irritation of the particle—if the grain moves freely during the secretion buildup, the pearl is more or less spherical; if it stays in one place or is embedded in the shell, it becomes a "baroque" pearl. Even when an oyster doesn't contain a pearl, the interior of the shell is valued for its rainbow luster, known as mother-of-pearl. Only particular mollusk varieties within the family Pteridae, found only in certain coastal areas off East Asia, Panama, and Baja California, can form pearls.

Pearl-gathering in the New World goes back at least 7,000 years. When the Spanish found Amerindians along the Sea of Cortez coast wearing pearls and mother-of-pearl shells as hair ornaments in the early 16th century, they quickly added pearls to the list of exploitable resources in Mexico. Finding the source of the luminescent, milky-white spheres—oyster beds—became a priority of marine expeditions off Mexico's west coast.

After a Spanish mutineer reported the presence of pearls in Bahía de la Paz in 1533, harvesting them became one of Cortés's primary interests in exploring Baja's lower Sea of Cortez coast. Between 1535, when Cortés finally managed to establish a temporary settlement at Bahía de la Paz, and 1697, when Jesuit padres began missionizing the Baja peninsula, untold thousands of pearls were harvested. The Jesuits, however, strongly objected to any secular exploitation of the peninsula, preferring to keep Baja within the domain of the church. Hence during the mission period (1697–1768), pearling was restricted to sporadic illegal harvests; still, many pearls found their way to Europe, where they encrusted the robes of bishops and Spanish royalty.

In the mid-19th century, following the secularization of Baja missions, the Baja pearl industry was revived by *armadores* (entrepreneurs), who hired Yaqui divers from Sonora to scour the shallow bays, coves, and island shores between Mulegé and La Paz. The invention of diving suits in 1874 revolutionized pearling by allowing divers access to deeper waters. By 1889 the world pearling industry was dominated by Compañía Perlífera de Baja California, based in La Paz.

Intensive harvesting rapidly depleted the oyster beds, and between 1936 and 1941 most of the remaining pearl oysters were wiped out by an unknown disease. Many La Paz residents today believe the disease was somehow introduced by the Japanese to eliminate Mexican competition in the pearl industry, but it's more likely the disease simply took advantage of an already weakened population.

The mystique of La Paz pearls continued long after the industry's demise. John Steinbeck based his novella *The Pearl* on a famous pearl story he heard while visiting La Paz in 1941.

peaked in the 1950s and '60s, some of the fabulous beach villas are still occupied on occasion. The road's final approach is so difficult (intentionally so, according to rumors) that few people arrive by road; instead guests use the resort's private airstrip or arrive by yacht. Membership is conferred by invitation and sponsorship only.

Península El Mogote

This 11-km (seven-mile) thumb of land juts across the top of Ensenada de la Paz directly opposite the city. The southern shore of the peninsula is rimmed by mangroves, while the north side facing the open bay offers clean water and a long beach sullied only by everyday flotsam. It's not uncommon to see dolphins swimming by. Local myth says that if you eat the wild plums of the *ciruelo (Cryptocarpa edulis)* growing on El Mogote's sand dunes, you'll never want to leave La Paz.

Road access to El Mogote is problematic; the easiest way to reach the peninsula is by kayak from the Marina de la Paz area (see Kayaking, later in this chapter, for more information). Most kayakers land on the mangrove side facing Ensenada de la Paz then walk across the peninsula's narrow isthmus to reach the bay/ocean side.

HOTELS

La Paz offers the most varied and least expensive selection of places to stay of any city in Baja. Room rates are quite reasonable for a seaside area, with most rooms falling in the US$30–75 range. The tourist information office on the *malecón* is a good place to stop for updated rate information on most local hotels.

Under US$25

Accommodations in this price range come without air-conditioning—a significant inconvenience July–Oct. And since most of them are in the central commercial zone they can be a bit noisy.

As old as the city itself, **Pensión California,** Calle Degollado 209, tel. 612/122-2896, fax 612/123-3525, pensioncalifornia@prodigy.net.mx, is housed in a former 18th-century convent between Revolución de 1910 and Madero. The interior courtyard of this rambling Moorish-style building contains a tropical garden of sorts and a display of old and new paintings that lend a distinctly Bohemian feel to the atmosphere. Rooms are basic—little more than a few worn sticks of furniture, fan, and hot shower—but reasonably comfortable. Practically every backpacker on the Baja circuit turns up at the Pensión California at one time or another. Discounts are possible for long-term stays.

The same family operates **Hostería del Convento,** Calle Madero Sur 85, tel. 612/122-3508, fax 612/123-3525, misioner@prodigy.net.mx, in another former convent right around the corner. It has a similarly funky and faded feel, with a bit more greenery in the courtyard. Long-term discounts are available.

Posada San Miguel, Calle Domínguez 1510, tel. 612/122-1802, is a colonial-style inn built around a tiled courtyard. The 13 basic, almost bare rooms have fairly hard beds, but the ornate entryway—decorated with historical photos of La Paz—is a major plus. You may want to borrow a broom to sweep your room before settling in. Just around the corner is the similar-looking but slightly nicer **Posada Del Cortez,** tel. 612/122-8240, which recently received a fresh coat of paint.

Seemingly undiscovered by visiting budget travelers is the family-run **Hotel Señorial,** Calle Domínguez 254 (no phone), which offers a cozy front balcony sitting area and clean rooms with attached bath. The public areas aren't particularly charming, but the beds are comfortable, and Jarrock Café is right next door (see Food).

Hotel Revolución, Revolución 85 (between Degollado and 16 de Septiembre), tel. 612/125-1934, has basic rooms with private shower and toilet, and occupies the upper two stories of a three-story building.

La Paz has a youth hostel at the **Instituto de la Juventud y el Deporte** (Villa Juvenil La Paz), tel. 612/122-4615, a sports complex on Boulevard Forjadores (Km 3) near Calz. 5 de Febrero. Facilities include a pool, gym, cafeteria, and volleyball and basketball courts. Beds are single bunks in gender-segregated, four-person dorm rooms. The hostel is distant from the town center and about the same cost for two people as some of the more centrally located hotels, considering the cost per bed. But it's closer to the main bus terminal than the downtown lodgings. All ages welcome.

US$25–50

One of the better downtown lodgings in the lower end of this price category is the well-kept and efficient **Hotel La Purísima,** Calles 16 de Septiembre and Serdán, tel. 612/122-3444, fax 612/125-1142, which occupies a four-story, red-and-white building near the municipal market. All 110 rooms feature air-conditioning, fan, and TV, and service is excellent. Foreign travelers appear to be rare in this hotel, so it's a good choice for visitors looking to immerse themselves in urban Mexican hotel culture.

Another good choice is the similarly priced **Hotel Tijuana,** Legaspi 345, tel. 612/122-1504 or 612/122-0613. Three and a half blocks from the bay, this hotel offers simple clean room with one or two beds. Some rooms have TV, and air-conditioning is available in the summer. Shaded secure parking is a plus.

Although in name it's a hotel, **Posada Hotel Yeneka,** Calle Madero 1520 (between Calle 16 de Septiembre and Av. Independencia), tel./fax 612/125-4688, looks and operates much like a guesthouse. Long known on the backpacker circuit, the Yeneka is built around a courtyard filled with tropical vegetation, a rusting Model T, and an amazing collection of other items giving the appearance of an ongoing garage sale. The proprietors can arrange snorkeling, diving, fishing, boating, and horseback-riding excursions. A *lavandería* and car-rental agency are also on the premises. Rooms are very basic and a bit scruffy.

Around the corner from Hotel Los Arcos, the friendly **Hotel Lorimar,** Calle Bravo 110, tel. 612/125-3822, fax 612/125-6387, is a longtime budget favorite with European, Canadian, and American visitors. Its 20 air-conditioned rooms are clean and well-maintained. The proprietors speak English but are happy to let you practice your Spanish; they can also arrange kayaking and diving trips through local outfitters. The Lorimar is just a block off the *malecón;* guests often meet in the cozy upstairs dining area to exchange travel tips. Groups of three or four people can also be accommodated in some rooms.

Hotel Posada Luna Sol, tel. 612/123-0559, Calle Topete 564, on the premises of Mar y Aventura, is a very new building featuring spacious, clean rooms decorated in Mexican kitsch. Posada Luna is one of the few hotels in this price range where rooms have satellite TV.

The **Hotel Plaza Real,** Callejón de la Paz and Calle Esquerro, tel. 612/122-9333, fax 612/122-4424, a block off the *malecón* and right around the corner from the Hotel Perla, is a three-story, modern hotel popular with middle-class Mexican businesspeople. Rooms have air-conditioning and TV, and the downstairs coffee shop is a popular local spot for breakfast and Mexican food.

Also a block off Paseo Obregón, the three-story, apartment-style **Hotel Miramar,** Calles 5 de Mayo and Domínguez, tel. 612/122-8885, fax 612/122-0672, hmiramar@prodigy.net.mx, www.bajaproyectur.net/hoteles/miramar, features clean rooms with fan, air-conditioning, minibar, and TV with VCR. Some rooms come with balconies and bay views at no extra charge, so be sure to ask what's available. The parking lot is a plus. Credit cards are accepted here.

Hotel Pekin, Paseo Obregón at Calle Guadalupe Victoria, tel. 612/125-5335 or 612/125-0995, fax 612/122-8491, occupies a vaguely Asian two-story building facing the *malecón*. It offers clean rooms with air-conditioning and TV (some with bay views) and is attached to a Chinese restaurant of similar name (Nuevo Pekin).

In a residential neighborhood in the northwest part of the city, the friendly **Hotel Gardenias,** Calle Serdán Norte 520, tel. 612/122-3088, fax 612/125-0436, hotelgar@prodigy.net.mx, www.hotelgardenias.com.mx, is a large, modern, two-story hotel built around a pleasant courtyard and pool. Popular among Mexicans, the Gardenias offers 56 clean rooms with air-conditioning and TV. The attached restaurant is open for breakfast and lunch, and the hotel has a secure parking lot. Note: Although the hotel's street address reads Calle Serdán, the entrance is on Guerrero between Serdán and Guillermo Prieto.

Highway Hotels: If you're blazing through town on your way south to Los Cabos, two budget hotels along the highway here make convenient stops. Opposite Casa Blanca RV Park, **Motel Villa del Sol,** near Km 5 on Mexico 1, tel. 612/124-0298 or 612/124-0299, is a motel-style complex with rooms encircling a parking area. Rooms have air-conditioning, bath, and TV. Farther in toward the city at Km 3.5, well-kept **Hotel Calafía,** tel. 612/122-5811, fax 612/125-4900, has similarly arranged rooms, secure parking, and a pool. Rates include continental breakfast.

US$50–100

The venerable **Hotel Perla,** Paseo Obregón 1570, tel. 612/122-0777 or 800/716-8799, Calif./Ariz. tel. 888/242-3757, fax 612/125-5363, has long been one of the city's most popular hotels. In 1941, Max Miller, author of *Land Where Time Stands Still,* wrote:

> The Hotel Perla is the place to stay. For an American there's no other choice unless he wishes to rent a room with a Mexican family or live in a Mexican board-and-rooming house. . . . [T]he Mexicans themselves expect an American to stay at the Hotel Perla. If he doesn't stay there when he first arrives, then he's in La Paz for no good reason. He's under suspicion.

The two-story, tile-roofed hotel enjoys a prime location right at the center of the *malecón* and just a few steps away from the main shopping district. La Terraza, the hotel's downstairs, open-air restaurant, remains a favorite gathering place for La Paz residents and visitors alike, while the upstairs nightclub draws a mostly local crowd. The mezzanine floor features a small pool. The clean, plainly decorated rooms have high ceilings, air-conditioning, TVs, and telephones. Indoor parking is available on the ground floor. On the downside, La Perla has continued to raise its prices at a pace beyond that of normal inflation, and the hotel now seems rather overpriced by La Paz standards.

Another *malecón* standby around since the dawn of La Paz's tourist industry is **Cabañas de los Arcos,** Paseo Obregón 498, tel. 612/122-2744 or 800/716-8644, fax 612/125-4313, U.S. tel. 949/450-9000 or 800/347-2252, fax 949/450-9010, reservations@losarcos.com. Built in 1954, during La Paz's heyday as an exotic playground for Hollywood celebrities, *paceño*-owned Los Arcos became the city's first center for sportfishing trips. Today you can choose from among 52 air-conditioned rooms in the original *cabaña* section (fireplaces), junior suites behind the *cabaña* section (no fireplaces), and rooms and suites in the much larger **Hotel Los Arcos** section less than 100 meters down the street. Like the *cabañas,* rooms in the newer hotel section face the *malecón* and bay. Both the new and original sections have swimming pools; the new one also offers a coffee shop, restaurant, bar, gift shop, sauna rooms, massage service, and whale-watching, diving, and sportfishing tours. Considering the nicer rooms and additional hotel amenities, Los Arcos is a better value than La Perla.

Seven Crown Hotel, tel. 612/128-9090, at the corner of Obregón and Lerdo de Tejada facing the malecón, looks like an office building from the outside, with a lobby-cum-travel-agency one might mistake for an airlines office. Nonetheless, the rooms are quiet, clean, and well-equipped.

The three-story, blue-and-white stucco **Hotel Mediterrané,** Calle Allende 36, tel./fax 612/125-1195, mail@hotelmed.com, www.hotelmed .com, enjoys a good location, just a half block from the *malecón.* The small, well-managed hotel features large, airy, sparkling-clean rooms with air-conditioning, refrigerator, and TV/VCR; each room is named for a different Greek island. There's also a rooftop sundeck with lounge chairs. Kayaks and canoes are on hand for guests who would like to paddle in the bay. Bicycles are available for land-lovers. La Pazta restaurant is downstairs.

North of downtown, **Club El Moro** at Km 2, La Paz–Pichilingue Rd., tel./fax 612/122-4084, elmoro@prodigy.net.mx, www.clubelmoro.com, is a whitewashed, Moorish-style place on landscaped grounds. All rooms and kitchenette-equipped suites come with air-conditioning, satellite TV, and private terrace. Other amenities include a pool, restaurant, and bar. Buses heading downtown pass the hotel frequently during daylight hours; otherwise it's a two-km (1.2-mile) walk to the town center. Weekly and monthly rates available on request.

Club Hotel Cantamar Sports Lodge, P.O. Box 782, La Paz 23000, tel. 612/122-1826, 612/122-7010, or 612/122-1133, fax 612/122-8644, www.clubcantamar.com, is next to the Baja Ferries terminal in Bahía Pichilingue. The four-story lodge features 31 standard rooms, four suites, and a recently added unit housing four apartments, each with two bedrooms, two bathrooms, full kitchenette, dining room, living room, and private balcony. Other amenities include a 35-slip marina (US$8 per foot per month), swimming pool overlooking the ocean, bar, dockside restaurant, and swim-up bar. There's also a boat ramp, kayak rentals, private beach, fishing fleet, dive shop, scuba shop, and recompression chamber. Dive packages are available for 3–10 nights. Included are round-trip airport transfers and lunch on dive days. Discounted weekly rates are available.

At Km 2.5 on the La Paz–Pichilingue Rd., almost opposite Club de Yates Palmira, the palm-encircled **Araiza Inn Palmira,** tel. 612/122-400 or 800/026-5444 (reservations), U.S. tel. 877/727-2492, fax 612/122-3727, www.araizainn .com.mx, caters to conventioneers as well as vacationers with its large meeting rooms, banquet halls, and quiet garden rooms. Other facilities include a pool, tennis court, restaurant, bar, and disco.

South of the *malecón* and Marina de la Paz is **Hotel La Posada de Engelbert,** Calles Nuevo Reforma and Playa Sur (Apdo. Postal 152, La Paz, BCS or P.O. Box 397, Bonita, CA 91908), tel. 612/122-4011, tel./fax 612/122-0663, info@ laposadaengelbert.com, www.laposadaengelbert.com. Originally built by pop crooner Engelbert Humperdinck for the Hollywood set, the recently renovated Posada offers 25 large, Mexican colonial-style suites and fireplace-equipped *casitas*. All rooms have satellite TV, phone, and air-conditioning. A pool, tennis court, activities center, restaurant, and palapa bar fill out the compound. The quiet waterfront atmosphere is a plus.

You'll pay a bit more to stay right on the water rather than along the *malecón*. None of the bayfront hotels are within easy walking distance of the *malecón* or downtown La Paz, although taxis are always available.

Opposite the Araiza Inn Palmira (adjacent to the plush Club de Yates Palmira) at Km 2.5, La Paz–Pichilingue Rd., stands the **Hotel Marina,** tel. 612/121-6254 or 800/685-8800, U.S. tel. 800/250-3186 or 800/826-1138, fax 612/121-6177, www.hotelmarina.com.mx. Facilities include tennis courts, a large pool, and an outdoor bar; boat slips are available nearby for visiting yachties.

US$100–150

Coral-hued **Posada de las Flores,** Paseo Obregón 440 between Militar and Guerrero, tel./fax 612/125-5871, faces the malecón and is an eight-unit branch of the Italian-owned La Paz hotel of the same name. Well-tended landscaping and a small pool grace the entry. Rustic Mexican furniture and tile are used throughout, and the all-marble bathrooms each feature a large bathtub and extra-thick towels. Rooms are outfitted with air-conditioning and a small refrigerator; a TV (with local channels only) is available upon request. A larger *casa* is available next door. Rates include breakfast.

La Concha Beach Resort & Condos, tel. 612/121-6161, U.S. tel. 800/999-BAJA (800/

999-2252), U.S fax 619/294-7366, laconcha@ juno.com, sits on Playa Caimancito (near Km 5, La Paz–Pichilingue Rd.), the city's closest swimming beach. All of the 154 well-kept rooms have bay views. On the premises are two pools, tennis courts, an aquatic sports center, restaurant, bar, and gift shop. The swimming pool in La Concha's newer condo section (see Apartments, Condos, and Long-Term Rentals, further on) is nicer than the original hotel pool; both pools are open to hotel guests. The resort's Cortez Club offers water sports, including fishing, diving, kayaking, and windsurfing.

US$150–250

Southwest of town, at Km 5.5 on northbound Mexico 1 (it turns north eventually), the eight-story **Crowne Plaza Resort,** tel. 612/124-0830 or 800/009-9900 (reservations), fax 612/124-0837, info@crowneplazalapaz.com, offers 158 bayside Mediterranean-style suites. Amenities include nonsmoking rooms, three swimming pools, sauna baths, pool tables, a gym, squash court, hot tub, tennis facilities, massage room, restaurant/bar, and car-rental agency. The hotel stands opposite the state tourism office and next to the site of the long-awaited FIDEPAZ marina.

BED-AND-BREAKFAST INNS
US$25–50

Managed by a friendly, bilingual *paceña*, **Palmas Suites,** Calle Mutualismo 314, tel./fax 612/122-4623, www.laspalmasbb.com, offers seven large air-conditioned one- and two-bedroom apartments with kitchenettes, each available by the day, week, or month. Casually furnished, each apartment accommodates up to three people without additional charges. Breakfasts are served in an enclosed patio area out front of the apartments. Palmas Suites sits only a block off the *malecón* and is within convenient walking distance of shops and restaurants.

US$50–100

A half block off the *malecón*, **La Casa Mexicana Inn,** Calle Bravo 106 (between Madero and Mutualismo), tel./fax 612/125-2748, inn@casa mex.com, www.casamex.com, offers five well-decorated rooms in a Moorish/art deco–style inn. All rooms come with air conditioning, fans, VCRs, private baths, and bay views. Rates include a breakfast of delicious home-baked pastries.

US$100–150

El Ángel Azul, Independencia 518, tel./fax 612/125-5130, hotel@elangelazul.com, www .elangelazul.com, is housed in a historic building that once served as the La Paz courthouse. Carefully restored with INAH guidance, the hotel offers nine guest rooms and one suite around a large, landscaped courtyard. All rooms are air-conditioned and nonsmoking. The work of local artists is showcased throughout. Secure parking is available.

APARTMENTS, CONDOS, AND LONG-TERM RENTALS

US$50–100

Operated by La Concha Resort, **Las Gaviotas,** Belisario Domínguez at Salvatierra, tel. 612/123-3948, is a five-story apartment-style complex in a residential neighborhood downtown. Each huge, two-bedroom apartment features a bay view, air-conditioning, TV, phone, full-size kitchen, two bathrooms, and private patio. Security parking is available. Rates vary depending on whether or not the kitchen is used. You can also rent by the week. Electricity is billed separately.

Suites Misión, on Paseo Obregón between Arrival and Bañuelos, tel. 612/122-0014 or 800/826-1138, fax 612/122-6277, offers spacious two-bedroom furnished apartments for rent by the week or the month. All have air-conditioning, a small TV, and a kitchenette; linens are provided.

US$150–250

La Concha Beach Resort & Condos, tel. 612/121-6161 or 800/716-8603, U.S. tel. 619/260-0991 or 800/999-BAJA (800/999-2252), fax 612/121-6218, laconcha@juno.com, is on Playa Caimancito near Km 5 on La Paz–Pichilingue Road. La Concha rents large one- to three-bedroom condos each with air-conditioning, TV, and kitchenette, but without direct-dial telephone; you must go through the resort switchboard to dial out. Condo residents have full use of hotel facilities, including two pools, a beach, restaurant/bar, and water-sports center. Long-term discounts available.

Rental Agent

La Paz Realty, Obregón 460, tel./fax 125-1080, maintains a list of local house and apartment rentals, most of them available by the month.

CAMPING AND RV PARKS

Free beach camping is available north of the Pichilingue ferry terminal at Playa Pichilingue, Playa Balandra (Puerto Balandra), Playa El Tecolote, and Playa El Coyote. Except for El Tecolote, none of these beaches has fresh water; all supplies must be brought from La Paz. Two restaurants at El Tecolote supply food and beverages.

Several trailer parks spread west from city's edge out onto Mexico 1. Starting from the farthest away, just before Km 15 in El Centenario comes **Los Aripez (Oasis de Aripez) RV Park,** tel. 612/124-6090 or 612/125-6202, VHF channel 22. Popular among transpeninsular voyagers making short La Paz stopovers, 26 full-hookup slots here cost US$12–16 for two, plus US$2 per each additional person; facilities include hot showers, flush toilets, laundry, restaurant, bar, and boat access to Ensenada de la Paz. Tents are okay. Open year-round.

Five km (three miles) west of the city on Mexico 1, across from Motel Villa del Sol, is the well-maintained **Casa Blanca RV Park,** tel. 612/124-0009, fax 612/125-1142, where more than 46 full-hookup sites are US$16 a night for two persons plus US$2 for each additional guest. The facility includes showers, flush toilets, a pool, tennis courts, spa, laundry, restaurant, and a small market. Open Nov.–May.

A kilometer closer to the city center and surrounded by a high wall, **El Cardón Trailer Park,** at Km 4 (Apdo. Postal 104, La Paz, BCS), tel./fax 612/124-0078, elcardon@starmedia.com, features 80 shaded, well-tended palapa sites with full hookups for US$12–15 for two, depending on the size of your vehicle, plus US$2 each additional person. Tent camping is permitted, and fees vary from US$3 for people on foot to US$4 for those arriving on bicycles, and a little bit more for those coming in on motorcycles. El Cardón offers a pool, groceries, recently renovated bathrooms with flush toilets and hot showers, a children's play area, a dump station, and laundry. An Internet café in the park offers very good rates and is open daily 6 A.M.–8 P.M. The park is open year-round.

Off Avenida Abasolo (Mexico 1) not far from the bayshore is the upscale, 96-slot **La Paz RV Park,** Apdo. Postal 482, La Paz, BCS, tel. 612/122-4480 or 612/122-8787, fax 612/122-9938. Full hookups alongside concrete pads cost US$17 for two plus US$3 per additional guest. Tent sites on the ground go for US$14 for one or two people, plus US$7 per extra tent-dweller. Facilities include showers, flush toilets, potable tap water, a small but clean pool, hot tub, tennis court, laundry, restaurant, and bar. Weekly, monthly, and yearly rates are available. Credit cards and checks are not accepted here. To find this well-kept RV park, go east on Avenida Abasolo and turn left (toward the bay) just before the VW dealer, then turn left on Calle Brecha California just before Posada Engelbert and continue three or four blocks. Open year-round.

A bit farther east toward the city center, off Calle Nayarit on the bay, is the smallish, palm-planted **Aquamarina RV Park,** Calle Nayarit 10, Apdo. Postal 133, La Paz, BCS, tel. 612/122-3761. Though a bit run-down compared to La Paz RV Park, its shady spots are a favorite among boaters and divers, Aquamarina features its own marina, complete with boat ramp, storage facilities, and air for scuba tanks, plus showers, flush toilets, potable tap water, a pool, and laundry facilities. Nineteen full-hookup sites cost US$19 for two, plus US$2 per additional guest. Open Nov.–May only. The Aquamarina also offers three apartments for rent.

FOOD

La Paz offers dining venues for all tastes and budgets, and, as might be expected in a coastal city, the seafood selection is particularly good.

American

Visiting and resident yachties crowd **The Dock Café,** Marina de la Paz, at the corner of Topete and Legaspy, tel. 612/125-6626, a small, casual diner serving fried chicken, hamburgers, fish and chips, bagels, salads, steaks, American breakfasts, some Mexican dishes, and homemade apple pie. A blues trio occasionally performs in the evening. Moderately priced. Open daily 8 A.M.–10 P.M. (It's usually closed for two weeks at the end of August/beginning of September.)

La Fabula Pizza serves American-style pizza and Italian specialties at six locations: Paseo Obregón 15 (at Av. Independencia), tel. 612/122-4101; Ocampo 31 (between Revolución and Serdán), tel. 612/122-5603; Isabel La Católica at Allende, tel. 612/122-4153; Blvd. Kino 2590, tel. 612/122-8641; Fco. Mújica at Colima, tel. 612/125-7741; and Blvd. 5 de Febrero 535-B, tel. 612/122-0830. Moderately priced. Open daily for lunch and dinner.

A branch of the U.S. chain **Big Kahuna Pizza,** near the northwest corner of 5 de Mayo and Altamirano, tel. 612/125-6290, is another good choice for pizza. Moderate. Open daily for lunch and dinner till 11 P.M. Two relative newcomers to La Paz are **McDonald's,** at the corner of 5 de Febrero and Calle Ortega, and **Burger King,** on Obregón and Lerdo de Tejada.

Restaurant Grill Campestre, opposite the FIDEPAZ building on Mexico 1 north, near Km 55, tel. 612/124-0454, is popular with gringos and Mexicans alike for barbecued ribs, Cobb salad, and other American specialties. Moderately priced. Open daily for lunch and dinner.

Though mostly a takeout place, **Romeo's Pizza,** Calle Madero 830 (between León and Legaspy), tel. 612/125-9495 or 612/122-4550, offers a few tables on the sidewalk in front. Good standard pizza. Inexpensive to moderate. Open Tues.–Sun. 11 A.M.–10 P.M.

Antojitos

In the afternoons, the downtown area centered around the *malecón* and Calle 16 de Septiembre features street vendors serving fish tacos and *cócteles*. One of the best stands for fish, shrimp, clam tacos, and *aguas frescas* is the extremely popular **Super Tacos de Baja California Hermanos González.** On Calle Esquerro beneath a big tree, opposite the side entrance of La Perla department store, this famous stand is still packed around lunchtime. The fish tacos for US$1 are eminently worth the price, especially the smoked marlin. The condiments are outstanding, and the *horchata* delicious. A second location with slightly cheaper prices has opened on Degollado at Madero, next to Pensión California. Both now offer sidewalk tables.

Tacos Estilo Tijuana, near the Hostería del Convento on Calle Madero (no phone), is a clean, inexpensive diner serving tacos, *milanesa, flautas, sopes,* tostadas, *licuados,* and midday *comida corrida.* It also has a good, cheap breakfast special (under US$3). Open daily 7 A.M.–7 P.M.

Tacos Pepe's, south of the plaza on Revolución de 1910, offers good, inexpensive Mexican *antojitos* such as *huaraches* and tacos.

Taquería Los Superburros, over on Abasolo between 5 de Febrero and Navarro, serves hamburgers, tacos (US$.95), quesadillas (US$.89), *huaraches* (US$3.50), and *papas rellenas.* On the same street near Calle Sinaloa is the similar **Antojitos Mexicanos Super Burro.**

Right next to Hotel Señorial on Domínguez is **Jarrock Café,** a cute little *lonchería/artesanía* where you can get some coffee and a bite to eat. During the daytime, the cluster of *loncherías* in the **Mercado Municipal Francisco E. Madero,** Revolución and Degollado, serves as a very inexpensive grazing spot for *antojitos* and *comidas corridas.* **Mercado Bravo,** at the corner of Bravo and Guillermo Prieto, also holds a few *loncherías.*

Asian

La Cochinita, Forjadores and Veracruz, tel. 612/122-1600, is an extremely clean fast-food spot serving generous portions of Mexicanized Japanese dishes. It's a very popular lunch spot with the locals. Open daily 10 A.M.–10 P.M. A newer, smaller branch has opened on Calle Mutualismo, next to Bar El Misión.

Restaurant Dragón, 16 de Septiembre at Esquerro, tel. 612/122-1372 (upstairs over Caffé Gourmet), is generally considered the best of the five or six Chinese restaurants in La Paz's tiny Chinatown. It's also the most upscale (though not expensive) and is an important lunch spot for local *políticos.* The menu is basically Cantonese, with Mexican influences. Not the place to wear shorts and T-shirt. Open daily except Tuesday 1–9 P.M.

Sushi Express, Madero and Degollado, tel. 612/122-3425, specializes in fresh sushi, teppanyaki, and tempura. Free delivery. Inexpensive. Open Wed.–Mon. 1–11 P.M.

Teriyaki San, 5 de Febrero at Ramírez, tel. 612/122-1674, is a clean, efficient, air-conditioning fast-food joint with inexpensive Japanese food. Open daily except Monday noon–7 P.M.

Cocina Económica Jeonsan, south of the plaza on Revolución de 1910, is a little hole-in-the-wall place specializing in *comida china;* open noon–midnight.

Cafés

Over the last three or four years there has been a coffee shop boom in La Paz, with new places opening seemingly every other month. One nice spot to enjoy coffee and pastries in air-conditioned comfort is **Caffé Gourmet,** Esquerro and 16 de Septiembre, tel. 612/122-6037. The menu offers a long list of hot and cold coffee drinks, chai, smoothies, Italian sodas, pies, cookies, and pastries along with cigars and liquors. A cozy nonsmoking section can be found in the back. Open Mon.–Sat. 8 A.M.–10 P.M.

Mareiros Café, on Obregón north of Oasis, tel. 612/123-5439, is also air-conditioned, and the menu contains a whole page of coffee drinks, hot and cold, plus deli sandwiches, salads, snacks, and pastries. Mareiros has a few tables outside as well, and is attached to one of the best Internet cafes in the city. Open Mon.–Sat. 8 A.M.–11 P.M., Sun. 9 A.M.–5 P.M.

Repostrería Café Regalos Exquisito, on Obregón south of La Fuente, is another popular spot on the malecón with sidewalk tables. Open Mon.–Fri. 6:30 A.M.–11 P.M., Sat. and Sun. 8 A.M.–noon.

A tiny place with a couple of outdoor tables and a recently added air-conditioned area, **Café del Trópico,** Calle 16 de Septiembre, tel. 612/123-3000, a half block southeast of the *malecón,* serves Veracruz-style coffee (including decaffeinated) made from fresh-roasted and fresh-ground Veracruz coffee beans. It's open daily 8 A.M.–1:30 P.M. and 5:30–9 P.M.

International

Owned by a friendly Chinese/Italian couple, **Caffé Milano,** Calle Esquerro 15, between Callejón de la Paz and 16 de Septiembre, tel. 612/125-9981, boasts "original Italian cuisine." It's definitely one of the better dining options in La Paz. Open Tues.–Sun. 1 P.M. until late.

The Malecón de Vista Coral, also known as Plaza Vista Coral, is a good spot for those seeking eclectic dining alongside the harbor. **Bougainvillea Restaurant,** Malecón de Vista Coral 5, tel. 612/122-7744, is the more upmarket of the two eateries in the relatively new dining/entertainment area next to the Vista Coral development. The Bougainvillea offers sharp service and such culinary arcana as peppered tuna sashimi and grilled lobster in orange *chipotle* sauce. Unfortunately, the food quality here can be uneven. Moderate to expensive. Open daily noon–midnight. Credit cards are accepted.

At **Café Bar Capri,** Malecón de Vista Coral (Local 4), between Márquez de León and Topete, tel. 612/123-3737, you'll find crepes, baguettes, *antojitos,* cakes and desserts, exotic drinks, books, music, art, and a bay view. Colorful tables inside and out fill with locals who stop by for early-evening drinks. Inexpensive to moderate. Capri has live music on Friday and Saturday. Open Tues.–Sun. 7 A.M.–12:30 A.M.

Kiwi Restaurant Bar, on the *malecón* between 5 de Mayo and Constitución, tel. 612/123-3282, offers a good bay view and a varied menu of seafood, Mexican, and international recipes. On weekends the restaurant occasionally features live music. Moderately priced. Open daily 8 A.M.– midnight.

La Pazta, on Calle Allende adjacent to Hotel Mediterrané, tel. 612/125-1195, is simply decorated with works of art, pastel stucco, and exposed brick. The light and airy restaurant offers breakfast, lunch, and dinner. The evening menu features a long list of pastas, pizzas, fondues, and other Swiss and Italian specialties. The extensive wine list includes Italian, U.S., Chilean, and *bajacaliforniano* labels. Moderately priced. Open Wed.–Mon. 7 A.M.–11 P.M., Tuesday 7 A.M.–3 P.M.

The venerable **El Taste,** Paseo Obregón at Juárez, tel. 612/122-8121, features steaks, Mexican food, and seafood. It's patronized by a mostly tourist and expat clientele. Moderate to expensive. Open daily 8 A.M.–midnight.

Outdoors beneath the Hotel Perla, **La Terraza,** Paseo Obregón 1570, tel. 612/122-0777, features an extensive menu of seafood, Mexican, steak, and Italian dishes. A steady crowd of both tourists and locals comes for the best people-watching in town, as well as for the reasonably tasty, reasonably priced food.

Friendly **El Oasis Restaurant and Bar,** Paseo Obregón 115 (between 16 de Septiembre and Callejón de la Paz, next to Carlos'n Charlie's), tel. 612/125-7666, is a sidewalk patio restaurant with great service and a large menu of well-prepared seafood, steaks, and Mexican dishes. The food is moderately priced, and live music is featured in the evening. Open daily noon–midnight.

Mexican

A popular coffee-shop-style place, **Restaurant Plaza Real,** Hotel Plaza Real, Calle Esquerro at Callejón de la Paz, tel. 612/122-9333, offers moderate prices, efficient service, and good Mexican food. The fresh orange juice is quite refreshing on a hot day. Open daily 7 A.M.–3 P.M. Attached to the Terminal Malecón is **Ultra Marinos Chatos,** where a filling breakfast of eggs, beans, tortillas, and coffee costs only US$2.75.

Carlos'n Charlie's, Obregón at 16 de Septiembre, tel. 612/123-4547, is part of the same chain as El Squid Roe and Señor Frog's, but the atmosphere is much more low-key than the typical Grupo Anderson enterprise. The interior decor features old Mexican movie posters, while the menu emphasizes good Mexican fare, seafood (try the *ceviche paceño*), and steak dishes. Much of the clientele is Mexican. The terrace tables usually catch a breeze. Moderate to expensive. Open daily noon–1 A.M.

In a courtyard behind La Fabula on Obregón, **Peña La Pitahaya de Janicua,** Obregón 15, tel. 612/126-2234, is an almost hidden spot with a

"Carnaval bread" in La Paz

bohemian ambience and a Mexican menu. Artwork and Mexican crafts are on display throughout, and there's live Latin folk music nightly.

Super Pollo makes a good, economical choice for *pollo asado al carbón estilo Sinaloa* (Sinaloa-style grilled chicken), sold with tortillas and salsa. Eat in or take out at six locations: Calz. 5 de Febrero at Gómez Farías, tel. 612/122-5588; 5 de Mayo at Gómez Farías, tel. 612/122-0088; Blvd. Forjadores at Loreto, tel. 612/121-0637; Ocampo 145 (between Revolución and Madero), tel. 612/122-0137; Blvd. Colosio 390 (between Guillermo Prieto and Serdán), no phone; and Calz. Olachea 4915, no phone. Open daily 10 A.M.– 8 P.M.

La Fonda, on Revolución de 1910, between Bravo and Ocampo, opposite ISSSTE Tienda, is a friendly little place serving breakfast and home-style traditional Mexican dishes. A *comida corrida* is offered daily 1–7 P.M. for US$4. Breakfast prices run just US$1.60–3.50; the orange juice here is fresh-squeezed. You can eat inside or out in the recently added patio area. Inexpensive. Open daily 7 A.M.–10 P.M.

The simple but pretty restaurant/bar **El Zarape,** Av. México 3450 (between Oaxaca and Nayarit), tel. 612/122-2520, features a tiled entryway and a menu of traditional Mexican dishes. On Saturday evenings El Zarape hosts a *cazuelada,* i.e., a buffet of *cazuelas* (large, open clay pans) filled with *moles* and other specialties of Central and Southern Mexico. A popular breakfast buffet is offered Tues.–Sun.; on Sunday noon –6 P.M., a more modern Mexican buffet brings together recipes from all over the republic. Moderately priced. Open daily 7:30 A.M.–midnight.

Cafetería El Tucán, in the supermarket CCC (Centro Comercial California) on Isabel La Católica at Bravo, is a coffee shop serving Mexican dishes.

La Cocina de Doña Betty, opposite Hotel La Purísima on Calle 16 de Septiembre, is a clean little diner with inexpensive yet slightly unusual dishes such as *pozole de camarón* (shrimp and hominy stew) and *tacos de guisado* (beef stew tacos), along with economic breakfasts and *tortas.*

Seafood

Restaurant La Costa, at Navarro and Topete near La Marina Don José, is a simple palapa-roofed restaurant with some of the freshest seafood in La Paz. Moderately priced. Open daily 10 A.M.–11 P.M. Operated by local seafood wholesalers Mar y Peña, **Restaurant La Mar y Peña,** Calle 16 de Septiembre between Isabel la Católica and Albañez, tel. 612/122-9949, is a small air-conditioned place with a terrific menu that features practically everything that swims, including several *machaca* (dried and shredded) versions. The *sangría preparada* (homemade sangria) is also good. Credit cards accepted. Moderately priced to expensive. Open daily 9 A.M.–10 P.M.

The casual, family-run **Bismark II,** Degollado at Altamirano, tel. 612/122-4854, specializes in lobster, abalone, and *carne asada.* All meals start with the restaurant's unique *totopos*—instead of chips, they're fried whole tortillas, served with a smooth guacamole. The ceviche is also very good. Moderately priced. Open daily 8 A.M.–10 P.M.

One of the better hotel restaurants, **Restaurant Bermejo,** Los Arcos Hotel, Paseo Obregón, tel. 612/122-2744, overlooks the *malecón*—ask for a window table. The Italian chef prepares a varied menu of seafood, steaks, and pastas. If you've had a successful day fishing, the restaurant will prepare your catch for US$7.35 pp, including all the dinner accompaniments. Moderate to expensive; open Mon.–Sat. 7 A.M.–11 P.M., Sunday 2–11 P.M.

About a block south of Nuevo Pekin, the rustic **Mariscos El Carrito,** Alvaro Obregón and Morelos, serves basic but fresh seafood dishes. At this popular spot, the floor is sand, and the tables and chairs are plastic. The popular **Mariscos Moyeyo's** at the corner of Obregón and Calle Héroes de 47 is similar. The slightly less rustic **Mar de Cortéz,** 5 de Febrero and Prieto, tel. 612/122-7274, is also a clean, palapa-roofed place specializing in seafood.

Vegetarian

El Quinto Sol, Domínguez and Av. Independencia, tel. 612/122-1692, is a natural food/vegetarian store with a café section serving *tortas, comida corrida,* pastries, salads, granola, fruit and vegetable juices, and yogurt. The healthful breakfasts are particularly nice after an extended period of travel.

Groceries

The **Mercado Municipal Francisco E. Madero,** Revolución at Degollado, houses a collection of vendor stalls purveying fresh fish, meats, fruit, vegetables, and baked goods at nonsubsidized free-market prices. Since prices are usually posted, no bargaining is necessary. At the corner of Revolución and Bravo is a *tortillería.* Other traditional markets include **Mercado Bravo** (Bravo at Guillermo Prieto) and **Mercado Abastos** (on Blvd. Las Garzas).

The government-subsidized **ISSSTE Tienda,** Calle Revolución de 1910 at Bravo, has the city's best grocery prices, although the selection varies according to what ISSSTE purchased cheaply that week. The **Tienda Militar** (Military Store), on Calle 5 de Mayo at Padre Kino, offers a larger selection than ISSSTE Tienda and is almost as inexpensive.

La Paz supermarkets include two large **CCC** (Centro Comercial California) outlets—one on Av. Abasolo at Colima, the other on Isabel La Católica at Bravo. These carry American-brand packaged foods as well as Mexican products, but prices are about a third higher than what you'd usually pay elsewhere in town. Another good supermarket chain is **Supermercado Arámburo,** with three branches: 16 de Septiembre at Altamirano, Madero at Hidalgo y Costilla, and Durango 130 Sur (between Ocampo and Degollado).

The latest and greatest addition in this category is a branch of the **Soriana** chain. This store carries a huge selection of groceries as well as clothing, gardening supplies, appliances, housewares, and hardware, and boasts a food court and pharmacy. **Plaza Ley,** part of a Sinaloa-based chain on the eastern outskirts of town on Las Garzas at Teotihuacán, is similar.

Natural Foods

El Quinto Sol, Domínguez at Av. Independencia, offers natural juices, wheat gluten, soybean meat substitutes (including soybean *chorizo*), whole-wheat flour, herbs, yogurt, and ice cream, as well as a few ready-to-eat items like *tortas* and salads.

Semilla y Cereales Camacho, on the north

side of Calle Revolución de 1910 about a half block southwest of the Mercado Municipal Francisco E. Madero, stocks an intriguing selection of herbal medicines as well as cereals, dried fruits, jams, nuts, culinary herbs, dried chilies, and various beans. Similar shops can be found along the north side of Serdán between Ocampo and Degollado.

More herbal medicines can be found at **El Show de la Salud** (Health Show), on Domínguez at Calle 16 de Septiembre, and **Tonantzin,** Madero and Calle 16 de Septiembre. Open Mon.–Sat. 10 A.M.–8 P.M.

Ice Cream, Sweets, Coffee Beans

Downtown La Paz is packed with *tiendas* selling *nieves* (Mexican-style ice cream) and *paletas* (popsicles). **Paletería y Nevería La Michoacana** is a big one, with branches on Paseo Obregón and Calle Madero. A personal favorite is tiny **La Fuente,** on Paseo Obregón between Degollado and Muelle; though small, this place offers an amazing variety of flavors (including *capirotada,* a Mexican bread pudding), as well as *licuados, aguas frescas,* and all-fruit *paletas.* (The ones made from *pitahaya* are delicious!)

Two *dulcerías* (sweet shops) lie on two corners of the intersection of Calles Ocampo and Serdán. On a third corner is a large school, the obvious target market for these sweet shops. **Dulcería Perla** has a complete selection of traditional and modern Mexican sweets, while **Dulcería La Coneja** specializes in candy-filled piñatas, including a few in the shape of Pokémon characters. Nearby, opposite the Mercado Municipal, is **La Michoacana,** with cool drinks and delicious ice cream; it's a good place to slake your thirst on a sweltering summer day.

Fresh-roasted coffee beans can be purchased at the outlets of **Café Combate** (Serdán between Ocampo and Degollado, and on Bravo at the southeast entrance to Mercado Bravo), **Café Batalla** (Calle Gral. Felix Ortega 1645), and **Café Marino** (Jalisco at Yucatán). We'd give Café Batalla the edge, but better yet are the fresh-roasted Veracruz beans from **Café del Trópico** on Calle 16 de Septiembre (see Cafés, earlier).

SPORTS AND RECREATION

Fishing

Outer bay and offshore fishing in the La Paz area are very good; a boat is mandatory since onshore and surf-fishing opportunities are limited. The bay and canals west of the islands hold roosterfish, pargo, cabrilla, needlefish, bonito, amberjack, jack crevalle, yellowtail, sierra, and pompano. Beyond Isla Espíritu Santo are the larger game fish, including dorado, grouper, marlin, tuna, and sailfish. Yellowtail usually run in the area Jan.–Mar., while most other game fish reach peak numbers Apr.–Nov. Canal de Cerralvo, around the east side of Península de Pichilingue, provides excellent fishing for roosterfish and *pargo colorado* Jan.–July.

Any of the major La Paz hotels will arrange fishing trips; one of the oldest operations is **Jack Velez Sportfishing Charters,** Apdo. Postal 402, La Paz, BCS, tel. 612/122-2744, ext. 608, fax 612/125-5313. Another established outfit is **Fisherman's Fleet,** tel. 612/122-2744, ext. 628, also with a desk at Los Arcos. Both offer fully equipped boats with guides, tackle, ice, and fish-cleaning and -filleting service at daily rates ranging from US$200 (for a 22-foot *panga*) to US$375 (for a 30-foot cabin cruiser).

You can also arrange guides and boats at the pier just east of the Pichilingue ferry terminal. From here, *panga* fishing trips in the bay generally cost US$100 a day for two people, while trips beyond Isla Espíritu Santo or to Canal de Cerralvo cost around US$180. Long-range fishing cruises run US$275–380 a day and usually accommodate up to four anglers.

Anglers with a sturdy set of wheels and their own tackle can drive the desolate road north from El Centenario (west of La Paz on the way to Ciudad Constitución) to **Punta El Mechudo** and **San Evaristo** at the northernmost end of Bahía de la Paz, where the onshore and inshore fishing—for grouper, snapper, pargo, cabrilla, sierra, dorado, and yellowfin—is almost as good as in the Canal de Cerralvo. Most visiting anglers camp on either side of Punta El Mechudo. The road is paved for the first 40 km (25 miles) as far as the phosphate-mining town of San Juan de la Costa, then it becomes graded gravel interspersed with ungraded sand for the final 53 km (33 miles) to San Evaristo. This road is best traversed by high-clearance vehicles only.

Fishing tackle is available at **Deportiva La Paz,** Paseo Obregón 1680, tel. 612/122-7333.

Boating

With a huge, protected bay, one private and four public marinas, and several boatyards and marine supply stores, La Paz is Baja California's largest and best-equipped boating center.

At the west end of the *malecón* (Calle Topete at Legaspy) is **Marina de la Paz,** Apdo. Postal 290, La Paz, BCS, tel. 612/125-2112 or 612/122-1646, fax 612/125-5900, VHF 16, marinalapaz@bajavillas.com, www.marinadelapaz.com, owned by original *panga* designer Malcolm "Mac" Shroyer. Facilities include a launch ramp, fuel dock (diesel), market with groceries and marine supplies, café, water and electricity outlets, cable TV, laundry, showers, restrooms, a chandlery, and boat and vehicle storage. **Club Cruceros de La Paz,** cruceros@baja.com.mx, www.clubcruceros.org, is a local nonprofit association that maintains a clubhouse at the marina and offers incoming mail service. The 80 slips range 30–110 feet in length and are 16 feet deep. Daily rates range from US$17.65 for a 24-foot craft to US$55 for a 70-foot craft. The daily rate is discounted June–Oct.; monthly rates start at US$323. Showers cost US$1.30 daily. Cable TV is US$1 per day or US$15 per month. Parking for slip clients is US$1 daily or US$22 per month. Marina de la Paz is the most popular marina in the bay and is often full Nov.–May; call or write in advance to check for vacancies before sailing in.

Northeast of town, on the Canal de la Paz at Km 2.5, the well-planned **Club de Yates Palmira,** Apdo. Postal 34, La Paz, BCS, tel. 612/121-6175 or 612/6159, fax 612/121-6142, lupita@marinapalmira.com or mpalmira@prodigy.net.mx, www.marinapalmira.com, VHF 16, currently offers 140 electricity-supplied slips accommodating yachts up to 100 feet long and 12 feet deep, as well as dry-storage facilities, a market, laundry, water, showers, bathrooms, a

pool, hot tub, tennis court, two restaurants, a bar, 24-hour security, parking for one car per registered guest, a public phone, marine supplies, a fuel dock (diesel as well as gas), and boat launch. Crewed and bareboat yacht charters are available. Daily slip rates range US$15.75–60 depending on the size of the boat; monthly rates are US$11.75–15 per foot for slips of 60 and 80 feet, and US$17 per foot for slips of 100 feet, plus 10 percent tax. Electrical service costs extra. Condos and hotel rooms adjacent to the marina are available for rent by the day, week, or month.

La Marina Don José, at the end of Calle Encinas, one street south of Marina de la Paz, tel./fax 612/122-0848, offers mooring facilities for up to 25 boats but is usually full. Rates run US$8.80 per foot per month. The marina office is open Monday–Friday 8 A.M.–noon and 2–6 P.M., Saturday 8 A.M.–1 P.M. There are a couple of eateries behind the marina: **Restaurant la Costa** and **Los Angeles del Palmar,** with a pleasant patio seating area and good fish specials for lunch and dinner.

You can launch trailered and cartopped boats at Marina de la Paz, Club de Yates Palmira, La Marina Don José, Aquamarina RV Park, and Pichilingue. Smaller boats and kayaks can put in at any of the public beaches.

Parts and Repairs: Marina de la Paz is the best local source of information about boating needs; **Ferretería Marina SeaMar** (SeaMar Marine Chandlery), tel. 612/122-9696, www.agenciaseamar.com, a marine supply store opposite the marina entrance, stocks many everyday nautical items and is open Mon.–Fri. 8:30 A.M.–1:30 P.M. and 3–6 P.M., Saturday 8:30 A.M.–1:30 P.M. A booklet by Janet Calvert entitled *La Paz Boater's Guide to Goods and Services,* available at the marina, contains a thorough list of all boatyards, outboard-motor shops, and marine supply stores in La Paz. Boaters at the marina can also offer recommendations for the best places to obtain boat parts and repairs. Another marine supply store is the **López Marine Supply,** Vista Coral Plaza, tel. 612/125-4160. Open Mon.–Sat. 8 A.M.–5 P.M. It accepts Visa and MasterCard.

Buying a *panga*: La Paz is the *panga* capital

of Mexico. Until 1968, when American Mac Shroyer designed and built the first molded fiberglass *pangas,* many Sea of Cortez fishermen still used dugout canoes of Amerindian design; glass *pangas* made in La Paz are now sold all over Mexico. **Embarcaciones Arca,** tel. 612/122-0874, fax 612/122-0823, makes and sells *pangas* at a factory on Calle Guillermo Prieto between Juárez and Allende. The standard *panga* is sold in 16- to 26-foot lengths, but the factory can accommodate special orders as long as 36 feet. The standard *panga* outboard motor is a "cinco-cinco caballos," 55 horsepower. Prices run US$3,000–4,000 each, depending on whether canopy, stowage compartment, and other options are included.

Boat Charters

Baja Coast SeaFaris, tel. 612/125-9765, information@bajaseafaris.com, www.bajaseafaris.com, can organize customized charters aboard its *Irish Mist* 50-foot sailing yacht and *Tesoro del Mar,* a Beneteau 50 sailboat. Multiday trips include visits to Espíritu Santo, Isla Partida, and Los Islotes, with stops along the way for swimming with sea lions, scuba diving, kayaking, sailing, beachcombing, whale-watching, bird-watching, snorkeling, or fishing. The cost of this trip on either boat is US$200–395 pp per day; the more people aboard, the lower the rate per person. Rates include all onboard meals, snacks, and cocktails, lodging at Los Arcos Hotel on the last evening, and airport transfers. Scuba diving and rental gear are also available. Reservations should be made at least four months in advance for trips during the spring, fall, or major holidays.

Kayaking

Two local outfits operate excellent guided kayak trips in the region. **Baja Expeditions,** Nicolás Bravo and Obregón, tel. 612/125-3828, U.S. tel. 800/843-6967, travel@bajaex.com, www.bajaex.com, offers seven-day sea kayaking tours around Isla Espíritu Santo (Mar.–May and Oct.–Jan. only), seven-day kayaking/whale-watching trips in Magdalena Bay, eight-day whale-watching cruises around the tip of Baja, and 10-day coastal paddles between Loreto and La Paz. A more adventurous 10-day, open-water kayak trip hops

among the islands of Espíritu Santo, Los Islotes, San José, Santa Cruz, and Santa Catalina. These trips are available Oct.–Apr. only. Rates range from US$1,045 pp for the seven-day Espíritu Santo trip to US$1,995 pp for the whale-watching cruise (deluxe rooms). All rates based on double occupancy. The office is open Mon.–Fri. 8 A.M.–8 P.M., Saturday 8 A.M.–3 P.M. Baja Expeditions has one computer terminal available for Internet service.

Mar y Aventuras, Calle Topete 564 (between 5 de Febrero and Navarro, near La Marina Don José and Marina de la Paz), tel./fax 612/123-0559, U.S. tel. 406/522-7595 or 800/355-7140, fax 406/522-7596, www.kayakbaja.com, is geared toward kayak renters and day-trippers as well as persons interested in multiday guided tours. Three- to four-day tours cost US$495–650. Five-day expeditions around Isla Espíritu Santo (Oct.–Apr. only) cost US$700–800 depending on the number of participants. Other tours can last up to 10 days and cost upwards of US$1,250. Shorter excursions include a six-hour bay kayak tour to visit Península El Mogote's mangrove and beach areas (US$35 pp including lunch), an all-day paddling and snorkeling trip to Playa Balandra and Playa Tecolote (US$65 pp), and more ambitious all-day outings around the various hidden beaches and outlying islands of La Paz (US$65–95 pp). Custom-designed kayak trips of any length can be arranged.

Experienced kayakers can also rent kayaks from Mar y Aventuras for paddling to El Mogote or to the islands on their own. The company rents single kayaks for US$40 a day, including PFD (personal flotation device), paddle, bilge pump, and spray deck. Double kayaks go for US$55/day. Also available for rent are snorkeling gear, wetsuits, dry bags, tents, small stoves, and sleeping bags. Boat shuttles out to Isla Espíritu Santo (US$200–250 round-trip) as well as truck shuttles to Playa Tecolote for beach launches to Espíritu Santo (US$40 per vehicle one-way) can be arranged.

Baja Quest (see Diving) organizes three- to five-day kayaking/hiking/camping trips around Isla Espíritu Santo (March–May, and Oct.–Dec. only). The price is US$540–830 pp. Six- to eight-hour kayak tours start at US$90.

Another La Paz company offering kayaking trips to Isla Espíritu Santo is **Baja Outdoor Activities,** tel. 612/125-5636, www.kayakin-baja.com.

Diving

Carey Diving (Buceo Carey), tel. 612/128-4048, www.carey.com.mx, Paseo Obregón, one of the older and more-respected local dive centers, offers a large range of one-day and multiday dive trips to the *Salvatierra* wreck, Los Islotes, or other nearby sites for US$85 a day including guide, transportation, lunch, unlimited sodas and beer, weight belt, and two tanks. Dive trips to El Bajo and Isla Cerralvo cost US$95. In addition, Carey offers snorkeling trips for US$65 to Playa Encantada and the sea lion colony. Available rental equipment includes regulators, BCDs, wetsuits, masks, snorkels, fins, tanks, weight belts, booties, and portable air compressors. Carey prides itself in the fact that they offer their clients a choice of 15 different lunch menus. The company maintains a second office at Marina de la Paz.

The granddaddy of all dive outfits in La Paz is Fernando Águilar's **Baja Diving and Service,** Paseo Obregón 1665-2 or Independencia 107-B, tel. 612/122-1826 or 612/122-7010, fax 612/122-8644. In addition to a wide variety of dive trips and rental equipment, Baja Diving and Service operates the only recompression chamber available to sport divers in La Paz.

Baja Expeditions, on Bravo at Obregón, tel. 612/125-3828, offers day-long and live-aboard dive programs in the La Paz vicinity. Most of these—particularly the live-aboard trips on the air-conditioned, 86-foot *Don José*—are booked out of the U.S. office, 2625 Garnet Ave., San Diego, CA 92109, tel. 619/581-3311 or 800/843-6967, fax 619/581-6542, travel@bajaex.com, www.bajaex.com, but it's occasionally possible to sign up in La Paz when space is available. From May 28–Nov. 30 the company runs eight-day expeditions aboard the *Don José;* US$1,445 pp for standard rooms to US$1,645 pp for superior rooms (double occupancy). Three eight-day excursions specifically dedicated to viewing the magnificent whale shark are offered in May and June for US$1,495 pp for standard rooms to US$1,695 pp for superior rooms (double occupancy).

Day excursions aboard Baja Expeditions' 50-foot *Río Rita* dive boat can be booked in La Paz at a rate of US$125 per day, which covers three dives, breakfast, lunch, snacks, and happy hour. A rate of US$375 buys a three-day package complete with three nights of hotel accommodations (at Los Arcos) and two days of diving.

Operated by a Mexican-Japanese couple, **Baja Quest,** Rangel 10 (between Sonora and Sinaloa), tel. 612/123-5320, fax 612/123-5321, www.bajaquest.com.mx, offers four-night, three-day dive-trip packages May–Dec., including hotel and airport transfers, for US$1,085 depending on hotel and number of people. You can also sign up for more luxurious live-aboard dive packages (US$799–990) with stops at Isla Espíritu Santo, El Bajo, San Francisquito, Las Animas, and Isla Cerralvo. Accommodations are aboard the *Garota* for basic dive tours and the *Marco Polo* or *New Beginning* for luxury cruises. Longer cruises are also available. Baja Quest also organizes five-day dive/cruise/camping combinations (Apr.–Nov. only) for US$856–1,083 pp. Daily dive tours are offered Mar.–Dec.; a two- to three-tank tour costs US$110–125. Snorkeling tours (US$65) are also scheduled; playing with the sea lions is a blast. Whale-watching and camping tours cost US$650–1,050 for 3–5 days, including campsite with large kitchen, tents, cots, sleeping bags, sun showers, toilets, round-trip transportation, kayaking equipment and instruction, and *pangas* but not airfare, hotel, airport to hotel transfers, meals on arrival and departure dates, airport taxes or crew tips.

Two other dive operators in town include **Scuba Baja Joe,** Ocampo and Obregón 460, tel. 612/122-4006, fax 612/122-4000 and **Toto's Dive Shop and Service,** on Guerrero between Revolución de 1910 and Serdán, tel. 612/122-7154, fax 612/123-4521, totosdive@prodigy.net.mx, www.totosdive.com.

Diving equipment and airfills are sold at **Deportiva La Paz,** Paseo Obregón 1680, tel./fax 612/122-7333. The shop doesn't organize dive trips.

DIVING AND SNORKELING AROUND LA PAZ

Some of Baja's best dive sites lie in the vicinity of La Paz, but most are accessible only by boat. Along the western shores of **Isla Espíritu Santo** and **Isla Partida** lie several good diving reefs. Bahía San Gabriel, a large cove along Espíritu Santo's southwest shore, features a shallow boulder reef (San Rafaelito) at its northern end suitable for both scuba diving and snorkeling. Similar rock reefs—along with submarine caves—can be found farther north off Espíritu Santo's western shore near Caleta El Candelero, extending from the west side of **Isla Ballena.** The latter islet also features a black-coral forest and is protected from strong prevailing winds. All of these sites lie 1–2 hours from La Paz by boat.

One of the most colorful dive sites in the vicinity is **Los Islotes,** the tiny islet group off the north end of Isla Partida. Boulder reefs and underwater pinnacles off the north and northeast shores draw large marine species, including schools of hammerhead sharks, manta rays, and other pelagic (open-ocean) fish. A nearby cove is home to around 300 sea lions, who seem to enjoy swimming alongside divers and performing tricks for the camera. Late in the breeding season (January–May) is the best time to visit the colony, since this is when the adolescent pups are most playful. The south side of Los Islotes is well protected from prevailing winds virtually year-round.

To the southwest of Los Islotes lies **El Bajito,** a large rock reef that extends to within six meters (20 feet) of the sea's surface; the base of the reef meets a sandy bottom at about 24–28 meters (80–90 feet). The diverse marinelife frequenting the reef includes grouper, cabrilla, and an unusually large number of morays living among the many cracks and crevices in the reef; attached to the rocks are gorgonians, sea fans, and other invertebrates. Wind protection here is scant.

A group of three sea pinnacles called **El Bajo** (also known as Marisla Seamount), about 13 km (8.2 miles) northeast of Los Islotes, is renowned for the presence of large pelagics such as marlin, sharks (hammerhead, blacktip, tiger, and silvertip), dorado, corvina, and manta rays. Mantas frequent El Bajo from July to mid-October and here seem unusually friendly. Whale sharks, the largest fishes in the world, are occasionally seen near El Bajo during the same months, as are pilot whales. Depths range 18–43 meters (60–140 feet). Boats typically take 2–3 hours to reach El Bajo from La Paz.

Due to strong tidal currents and lack of wind protection, El Bajito and El Bajo are best left to experienced open-ocean divers.

The wreck of the *Salvatierra,* a 91-meter (300-foot) La Paz–Topolobampo ferry that went down in the Canal de San Lorenzo in 1976, presents one of the more challenging dives. The hull lies about 2.5 km (1.5 miles) southeast of the southern tip of Isla Espíritu Santo at a depth of approximately 10 fathoms (18 meters/60 feet). Encrusted with sponges, sea fans, mollusks, and gorgonians, the wreck attracts numerous varieties of tropical fish, including groupers, barracuda, angelfish, goatfish, parrotfish, moray eels, and rays.

Southeast of Península de Pichilingue, the somewhat more remote **Isla Cerralvo** offers several additional diving opportunities. **La Reinita,** a rock reef off the island's northern shore, attracts large pelagic fish. Even more remote—generally reached by live-aboard boat trips—are **Isla Santa Cruz** and **Islas Las Ánimas** to the north. The former is known for rock reefs at depths of around 17 meters (35 feet) with a profusion of sea horses, while the latter reportedly offers the greatest variety of diving experiences—caves, hammerheads, whale sharks, sea lions—of any site in the Sea of Cortez. Only Baja Expeditions leads Santa Cruz and Ánimas dives at the moment.

As elsewhere in the Sea of Cortez, the optimum diving months are May–August, when visibility reaches 30 meters (100 feet) or more and water temperatures run around 27°C (80°F). In September tropical storms are an obstacle, and during the late fall and winter months high winds and changing currents reduce visibility to 10–15 meters (35–50 feet). A light wetsuit is necessary any time except June–August.

Cycling

Katún, tel. 612/348-5649, info@katun-tours
.com, www.katun-tours.com, rents Trek 2004
mountain bikes with front suspension for US$7
an hour, US$10 for three hours, or US$15 per
day. The proprietors supply hand-drawn maps of
local bike trails with any rental on request.

Organized Tours

Contactours, Obregón 460, 2nd floor, tel.
612/123-2212, between Ocampo and Degollado, contactours@baja.com, www.contactin-
centives.com, organizes several package land
tours in the La Paz area. The "city tour" takes
you through the downtown area, stopping at a
pottery factory, a weaver, a couple of museums,
the cathedral, shops, and the public market.
The 10 A.M.–1 P.M. tour costs US$25. The com-
pany also organizes beach tours, whale-watching
tours, and snorkeling/diving tours.

ENTERTAINMENT

Bars

Bar Pelícanos, overlooking the *malecón* in Hotel
Los Arcos, is a large, sedate watering hole popular among tourists and old hands. It's worth at
least one visit to peruse the old photos along the
back wall; subjects include a motley array of unnamed vaqueros and revolutionaries, as well as
Pancho Villa, General Blackjack Pershing, President Dwight Eisenhower, Emiliano Zapata, and
Clark Gable, who poses with a marlin. The bar is
open daily 10 A.M.–1 A.M.

On Calle Esquerro near the Hotel Perla, the
slightly seedy **Bar Misión** features live *norteña*
bands nightly.

Tequilas Bar and Grill, in a rustic house next
to Palmas Suites on Calle Mutualismo, is an intimate bar with pool tables and a small private
room popular with local politicians.

El Claustro, Obregón near Calle Hidalgo y
Costilla, tel. 612/122-1609, is a rock 'n' roll bar
ensconced in a two-story pseudo-Italianate structure, complete with heavy faux-painted "marble"
pilasters around the doors and stained-glass windows, plus lots of ironwork. It's decorated inside
and out with an angel motif. Closed Monday.

Caliente Race & Sports Book, on Paseo
Obregón, has the usual array of satellite-linked
TV monitors for viewing international sports
events—and betting on them if the mood strikes
you. Open Mon.–Fri. 10 A.M.–midnight, Sat.
and Sun. 9 A.M.–midnight.

On the beach side of Paseo Obregón, three
blocks west of Hotel Los Arcos, is the casual and
sometimes lively palapa bar **La Caleta,** where the
clientele is predominantly local. Yachties from
the nearby Marina de la Paz occasionally arrive via
Zodiac rafts, which they park on the adjacent
beach. Drinks are reasonably priced, especially
during the 4–8 P.M. happy hour, and there's live
music Friday and Saturday 9 P.M.–3 A.M.

Discos and Nightclubs

Living up to its laid-back reputation, La Paz isn't
big on discos. A slightly older crowd packs **Las
Varitas,** Av. Independencia 111, tel. 612/123-
1590, downtown near El Quinto Sol natural
foods store and Plaza Constitución. The club offers dancing to recorded and live music and is
open till nearly dawn on weekends.

One block from Plaza Constitución is **New
World (Centro de Espectáculos),** Belisario
Domínguez between Independencia and 5 de
Mayo (the entrance is on Independencia), a big
disco that occasionally offers live music.

Carlos'n Charlie's, on Paseo Obregón, has
an attached dance club that experiences occasional waves of popularity, especially on Thursday evenings when women are admitted without
having to pay the usual cover charge. Over La
Michoacana nearby, also on Obregón, the
friendly **La Casa de Villa** boasts an open-air
bar overlooking the bay. This is a great spot to
watch the Carnaval parade. There are a few pool
tables inside.

Bahía Rock, next to the Crowne Plaza Resort at Km 5.5, draws a crowd Friday and Saturday nights.

Nightclub La Cabaña, at the Hotel Perla,
usually offers live *norteña* and *tecnobanda* music
and attracts a mostly local crowd.

Bullfights and Charreadas

The municipal stadium at Constitución and Verdad occasionally hosts *corridas de toros* in the late winter months, usually Feb.–Mar.

Paceños are more active in *charrería* than in bullfighting, and you can attend *charreadas* (Mexican-style rodeos) at **Lienzo Charro Guadalupano,** just south of the city on the west side of Mexico 1 south (heading toward San Pedro). For information on the latest schedules for *charreadas* and *corridas de toros,* contact the state tourism office between Km 6 and 5 on Mexico 1 (Av. Abasolo), opposite the FIDEPAZ marina, tel. 612/124-0199. A *gran charreada* is usually held to celebrate Cinco de Mayo (May 5).

Cinemas
La Paz has three movie theaters. **Cinema Versalles Plus,** Revolución de 1910, tel. 612/122-9555, south of the plaza, shows first-run movies on four screens. The two-screen **Cine Gemelos,** tel. 612/125-8055, can be found at Isabel La Católica 126, between Allende and Juárez. The third and newest movie house is a **Cine Gemelos** multiplex in the new Soriana shopping complex out on Boulevard Forjadores.

EVENTS

La Paz's biggest annual celebration is **Carnaval,** held for six days before Ash Wednesday in mid-February. Carnaval is also held in the Mexican cities of Mazatlán, Ensenada, and Veracruz, but Carnaval connoisseurs claim La Paz's is the best— perhaps because the city's *malecón* makes a perfect parade route.

As at all Mexican Carnavals, the festival begins with the Quema de Mal Humor, or "Burning of Bad Humor," in which an effigy representing an unpopular public figure is burned. Other events include the crowning of La Reina del Carnaval (Carnaval Queen) and El Rey Feo (Ugly King), colorful costumed parades, music, dancing, feasting, cockfights, and fireworks. The festival culminates in El Día del Marido Oprimido, or "Day of the Oppressed Husband" (23.5 hours of symbolic freedom for married men to do whatever they wish), followed by a masquerade ball on the Tuesday evening before Ash Wednesday.

Also prominent on the city's yearly events cal-

costumed Carnaval celebrants in La Paz

endar is the **Fiesta de la Paz** (officially known as Fiesta de la Fundación de la Ciudad de la Paz), held May 3, the anniversary of the city's founding. The state tourist office can provide up-to-date details on festival scheduling and venues.

SHOPPING

Before the city's duty-free status was recalled in 1989, imported merchandise could be purchased in La Paz free of import duties and sales tax. Nowadays sales tax is commensurate with the rest of Mexico's. But the city still offers some of Baja's best shopping in terms of value and variety, starting with the downtown department stores of **Dorian's** (Calle 16 de Septiembre at Esquerro) and **La Perla de la Paz** (Calle Arrival at Mutualismo). Dorian's resembles a typical middle-class, American-style department store; La Perla is more of a discount department store, featuring a good supply of coolers (ice chests), toiletries, housewares, liquors, and pharmaceuticals at low prices. A newer Dorian's can be found in the Soriana shopping complex on Boulevard Forjadores, at the southwestern edge of town.

Also in the discount-store category, **MAS,** at the corner of Madero and Degollado, is a three-story department store where good bargains are to be had. MAS stocks everything from clothing to luggage to housewares. Open daily 9 A.M.–9 P.M.

Next door on Madero, opposite Hostería del Convento, is **DAX,** an American-style pharmacy with many hard-to-find cosmetic and toiletry items. Open daily 9 A.M.–9 P.M. Next door is the popular **Solo Un Precio** (Only One Price), where everything in the store is only 11 pesos. You can find some great deals here. Open daily 8 A.M.–9 P.M.

Along Paseo Obregón in the vicinity of the Hotel Perla and Hotel Los Arcos are a number of souvenir and handicraft shops of varying quality. One of the better ones is **Artesanías La Antigua California,** Paseo Obregón 220, which sells quality folk arts and crafts from the mainland. There a few similar shops on Obregón between Degollado and Ocampo. **México Lindo,** next to Carlos'n Charlie's, is also good for *artesanías.* **Curios Mary,** Arreola 25 at Obregón, tel. 612/122-0815, specializes in Majorcan pearls.

Kumutú, Domínguez 1245 (between 5 de Mayo and Constitución, tel. 612/122-2471, marcam1224@yahoo.com, is a wonderful shop/ museum run by two anthropologists, Marta Inés López T. and her husband Aldo Piñeda. Kumutú is dedicated to Señor Piñeda's father, Cesar Piñeda Chacón, a well-known Baja anthropologist, artist, and poet. The shop features regional products from southern Baja, such as wine, candles, pearls, pottery, weaving, and other crafts. They carry a selection of books, maps, and music, all relating to the history of Baja California Sur, and are a good source of ecotourism information. A simple café inside offers coffee, herb teas, date pie, cakes, and tuna, meat, or chicken *empanadas.*

Casa de Artesanos Sudcalifornianos, a government-supported shop next door to the Tourist Information/Tourist Police office on Paseo Obregón, focuses on *artesanía* from Baja California Sur.

Attached to Palmas Suites, **Uguet's,** Mutualismo 314, tel. 612/122-4623, features decorative hand-painted Mexican tiles, as well as rustic bathroom and kitchen accessories and hardware.

Away from the city center, the **Centro de Arte Regional,** Calle Chiapas at Encinas, produces and sells pottery, as does **Ibarra's Pottery,** Prieto 625 between Iglesias and República, tel. 612/122-0404, where you can watch pottery being made Mon.–Sat. 8 A.M.–4 P.M.

Artesanía Cuauhtémoc, Av. Abasolo between Jalisco and Nayarit, weaves rugs, blankets, wallhangings, tablecloths, and other cotton and wool items. Custom orders are possible, and customers are welcome to watch the weavers at their looms in back of the shop.

Opposite Plaza Constitución at the corner of Madero and Independencia, **Una Más (Artesanías Colibri),** tel. 612/128-5833, carries a good selection of *artesanías,* rustic furniture, and decorating accessories. Open Mon.–Sat. 10 A.M.– 2 P.M. and 4–8:30 P.M.

For tourist-variety souvenirs, especially *playeras* (T-shirts), a good choice is **Bye-Bye,** on Paseo Obregón between Calle Degolado and Muelle. For bottom-dollar bargains on clothing, housewares, and leather, browse the **Mercado Municipal Francisco E. Madero,** Revolución de 1910 at Degollado. Inexpensive electronics, watches, and jewelry are available at a string of shops along Calles Domínguez and Madero between Avenida Independencia and Calle 16 de Septiembre, and along a pedestrian alley off Calle 16 de Septiembre near Dorian's department store.

Deportes Ortiz, Calle Degollado 260, almost opposite Pensión California, tel. 612/122-1209, carries a modest selection of camping, diving, and other sports equipment. Nearby on Degollado opposite Sushi Express, **Killer Tube** sells water sports apparel as well as skateboards. **Santander,** a large store at the corner of Serdán and Degollado, tel. 612/125-5962, stocks a wide variety of useful *artesanías,* including saddles, guitars, and *huaraches.*

ISLANDS

The large and small islands clustered just north of Península de Pichilingue offer an amazing variety of recreational possibilities both in and out of the water. The 22.5-km-long (14-mile-long) Isla Espíritu Santo and its smaller immediate neighbor to the north, Isla Partida, are excellent destinations for all manner of watercraft from sea kayaks to yachts. Sandy beaches and large coves along the western shores of both islands provide numerous opportunities for small-craft landings and camping. In full sun, the sand-bottom reflections of these bays create such a bright, translucent color that white seagulls flying over them are transformed into glowing blue-green UFOs.

Isla Espíritu Santo

Around Isla Espíritu Santo, rock reefs provide good **snorkeling** at: Punta Prieta, at the north

Caleta El Candelero, Isla Espíritu Santo

end of Bahía San Gabriel toward the island's southwestern tip; at the west end of Isla Ballena, an islet off the northwest coast of Espíritu Santo; at three islets in Caleta El Candelero, toward the island's northern end; and off Punta Bonanza on Espíritu Santo's southeast side.

Even if you don't snorkel, picturesque, sand-bottomed **Bahía San Gabriel** is worth a visit to see the ruined walls of a pearlery dating to the early 20th century. The low walls form an inner lagoon that fills and empties with the tides, creating little waterfalls along the edges of the bay.

Just north of Ensenada La Ballena (directly opposite Isla Ballena), near a spot where the Guaicura found year-round water, several small rock shelters known as **Las Cuevitas** bear petroglyphs. More caves formerly used by the Guaicura can be found in the dry arroyo behind Ensenada La Ballena.

Espíritu Santo's most interesting **hike** starts from the beach at Caleta Candelero and follows a deep, rocky arroyo inland into the 200-meter-high (650-foot-high) volcanic bluffs. The trail passes wild fig and wild plum trees clinging to the arroyo's rock sides; if you're lucky you might even spot a rare, endemic black jackrabbit.

Isla Partida

On the northern tip of Isla Partida you can hike to the top of a bluff called **El Embudo** for sweeping sea and island views. At the north and south ends of Isla Partida a couple of fish camps may have drinking water and food available, but don't count on it. Plenty of yachts frequent the area. A narrow sandbar almost bridges Partida and Espíritu Santo, leaving a tight channel for small-boat movement between the two islands.

Los Islotes

Just north of Isla Partida lie Los Islotes, a cluster of guano-covered volcanic rock islands popular among divers, anglers, birds, and sea lions. The sea lions and their pups often join divers and snorkelers for a swim. A lone adult male elephant seal has taken up residence at Los Islotes. While this animal may appear friendly, his great size, strength and large teeth have the potential to inflict serious injury; local dive operators advise

© JOE CUMMINGS

CAPE REGION

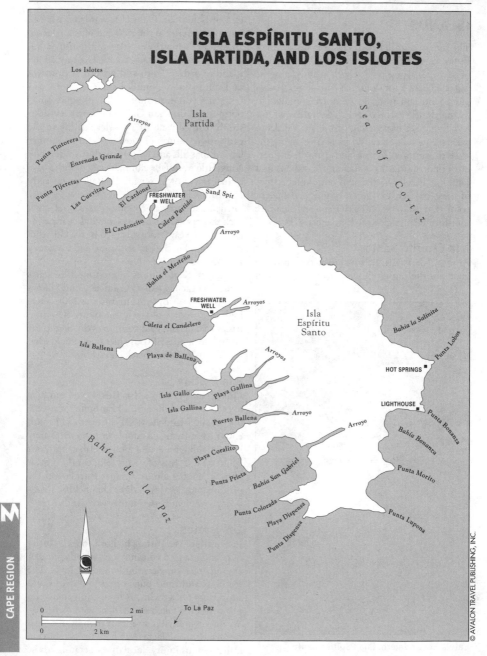

ISLA ESPÍRITU SANTO, ISLA PARTIDA, AND LOS ISLOTES

Los Islotes

Isla Partida

Arroyos

Punta Tintorera

Ensenada Grande

Punta Tijeretas

Las Cuevitas

El Cardonel

FRESHWATER WELL

Sand Spit

Caleta Partida

El Cardoncito

Arroyo

Bahía el Mesteño

FRESHWATER WELL

Arroyos

Caleta el Candelero

Isla Espíritu Santo

Bahía la Salinita

Punta Lobos

Isla Ballena

Playa de Ballena

Arroyos

HOT SPRINGS

Isla Gallo

Playa Gallina

LIGHTHOUSE

Punta Bonanza

Isla Gallina

Arroyo

Puerto Ballena

Arroyo

Bahía Bonanza

Playa Coralito

Punta Morito

Punta Prieta

Bahía San Gabriel

Bahía de la Paz

Punta Colorada

Playa Dispensa

Punta Lupona

Punta Dispensa

Sea of Cortez

0   2 mi

0   2 km

To La Paz

MOON

© AVALON TRAVEL PUBLISHING, INC.

that you not approach this animal or attempt to swim with him. For further details on scuba diving sites see Diving under Beaches and Activities, later in this chapter.

Isla San José

Other than day visits by the occasional Sea of Cortez cruising vessel, this 24-km-long (15-mile-long) island sees very few travelers, whether Mexican or foreign. It lies well to the north of Isla Partida and Los Islotes, a long boat trip from La Paz. To save travel time, most small-boaters heading to the island launch from either Punta Coyote or Punta Mechudo, both reached via a rough graded road from San Juan de la Costa (see Fishing, further on, for information on getting to San Juan). The 60-km (37-mile) road from San Juan de la Costa to Punta Coyote takes at least 90 minutes in good conditions, while Punta Mechudo is roughly another 11 km (seven miles).

The average skiff or *panga* can make **Isla San Francisco,** a small island off the southern tip of Isla San José, in about an hour, or all the way to Bahía La Amortajada at the larger island's south end in 90 minutes. Bahía La Amortajada makes a fair anchorage in winter, when northern winds prevail. A ridge in the center of the island crests at 500 meters, high enough to protect the southwestern coast from those cold winter winds, which means you can expect warmer temperatures here than on the mainland opposite.

Isla San José holds a couple of small settlements: Isla San José de la Palma, a village of fewer than 50 inhabitants toward the north end of the island, and a smaller fish camp on the rock-reef islet of Arrecife Coyote, northwest of Isla San Francisco. Limited supplies—water and gas—may be available from the Mexican fishermen at these camps, but don't count on it. The island can be miserably hot and buggy in summer.

ISLA SAN JOSÉ

© AVALON TRAVEL PUBLISHING, INC.

Camping

Caleta El Candelero and El Cardoncito, on the west sides of Isla Espíritu Santo and Isla Partida, respectively, are generally considered the best camping beaches because each has a freshwater well suitable for bathing. To be certain of hauling some water out, you should bring your own bucket and five meters (15 feet) of rope. For drinking purposes bring enough purified water for the duration of your stay. If you must drink from the well, treat the water with purification tablets/iodine or boil it for at least 10 minutes.

Because these islands are part of an ecological preserve, you must obtain permission from the La Paz SEMARNAT office, Calle Ocampo 1045 (between Profr. Marcelo Rubio and Lic. Primo Verdad), tel. 612/122-4414 or 612/125-4945, before setting up camp.

CAPE REGION

Getting to the Islands

Punta Lupona, on the southern tip of Espíritu Santo, lies within kayaking range—just 6.5 km (four miles)—from Península de Pichilingue. Once at Espíritu Santo, it's easy to explore Isla Partida by kayak; the shallow channel between the two islands is only a few hundred meters across. Playa Tecolote or the smaller beaches just to its east are good put-in points for kayak trips to the island. Because of winds and tidal currents, this isn't a trip for the novice paddler. Even experienced sea kayakers on a first voyage to the island should follow someone who knows the tricky interplay of currents, shoals, tides, and winds. Two outfitters in La Paz lead kayak trips to the islands with experienced guides; see Kayaking, later, for contact information.

Several travel agencies in La Paz arrange two-hour powerboat jaunts to Isla Espíritu Santo and Isla Partida for around US$140 per boat including lunch. At Palapa Azul (tel. 612/122-1801) on Playa Tecolote, you can arrange a four-hour trip around the west side of Espíritu Santo to a large island bay (Ensenada Grande) on Isla Partida and to the sea lion colony at Los Islotes; the cost for this trip, US$100 for up to six persons, includes lunch. A one-way shuttle out to the island costs US$60. **Mar y Aventuras,** Calle Topete 564 (between 5 de Febrero and Navarro, near La Marina Don José and Marina de la Paz), tel./fax 612/123-0559, U.S. tel. 406/522-7595 or 800/355-7140, fax 406/522-7596, www .kayakbaja.com, offers a *panga* trip to Espíritu Santo and Los Islotes for US$65 per person, with a minimum of three persons. **Baja Outdoor Adventures,** www.kayactivities.com, operates four- and seven-day kayaking/camping trips to Isla Espíritu Santo.

Whether booking with an agency in town or at the beach, remember to inquire about the quality and contents of the lunch. If the lunch situation sounds iffy or awful (one prominent La Paz company a few years ago served one lousy sandwich of white bread glued to two slices of processed American cheese), demand more food or carry your own lunch. Life preservers are another variable worth inquiring about; some boats don't carry them.

INFORMATION AND SERVICES

Tourist Assistance

Baja California Sur's **Coordinación Estatal de Turismo** office lies between Km 6 and 5 on Mexico 1 (Av. Abasolo) opposite the Crowne Plaza Resort, tel. 612/124-0100, 612/124-0103, or 612/124-0199, fax 612/124-0722, turismo@correro.gbcs.gob.mx. The friendly staff can assist with most tourist inquiries; the Attorney for the Protection of Tourists is also stationed here. The office maintains an information booth on the *malecón* near Calle 16 de Septiembre, where you can pick up maps and brochures. This is a good place to stop for lodging information, as they maintain a list of updated rates. The office on the highway is open Mon.–Fri. 8 A.M.–8 P.M., while the information booth on Obregón is open Mon.–Sat., same hours. You'll also find a city-supported **Tourist Information and Tourist Police** office on Paseo Obregón near Hotel Los Arcos.

Money-Changing

Several banks and money changers can be found on Calle 16 de Septiembre near the *malecón*. As elsewhere in Baja, the banks provide currency-exchange service only Mon.–Fri. before noon. Both Bancomer and Banamex have ATMs.

Money changers *(casas de cambio)* stay open till early evening and on Saturday but are closed on Sunday, when your only alternative is to change money at a hotel at lower rates. Pesos are a must for everyday purchases in La Paz; city merchants are not as receptive to U.S.-dollar transactions as their counterparts in Cabo San Lucas simply because they're not as used to them. The two branches of **Tony Money Exchange,** on Mutualismo near La Perla and nearby on Calle 16 de Septiembre near the *malecón,* have decent rates; hours are 9 A.M.–9 P.M.

The local American Express representative is **Viajes Perla,** ground floor of Seven Crown Hotel, Paseo Obregón, tel. 612/122-8666. Hours for AmEx service are Mon.–Fri. 9 A.M.–5 P.M.

Post and Telephone

The main post and telegraph office is at Revolución and Constitución, a block northeast of the

USEFUL LA PAZ TELEPHONE NUMBERS

La Paz area code: 612
COTP: 122-0243 or 122-4037
Fire Department: 068
Ferry Office (Pichilingue): 122-5005
Green Angels: 124-0100, 124-0199
Highway Patrol: 122-0369
Immigration: 124-6349
IMSS Hospital: 122-7377
Police: 060
Red Cross: 066
State Tourism Department: 124-0100
or 122-6799
Tourist Assistance: 078

cathedral; open Mon.–Fri. 8 A.M.–3 P.M., Saturday 9 A.M.–1 P.M.

DHL, Av. Abasolo at Nayarit, tel. 612/122-8282, is the most reliable courier service in the city. The company picks up packages at no extra charge. If you are sending goods out of the country via DHL, you must first stop at the nearby Mexican customs office to have the parcel opened and inspected. Your parcel will then be sealed and you'll receive an official customs form which you must subsequently show to DHL before they can accept the parcel for shipping.

Internet Access

Internet cafés can be found all over town, especially along the stretch of waterfront between Hotel Los Arcos and Posada de las Flores. The rates in La Paz are quite reasonable. Nearly adjacent to Hotel Yeneka is **Cafecito Internet,** while farther north, **Café Galería Carta Blanca,** Calle Belisario Domínguez between Independencia and Reforma, tel. 612/122-3199, also has reasonably priced Internet access, as well as fax and copy services.

The most atmospheric place in town to check email is **Espacio Don Tomás,** tel. 612/128-5508. In a beautiful historic building at the corner of Obregón and Constitución, Espacio Don Tomás holds a legitimate art gallery and a seven-terminal

Internet café. The gallery features works of fine art by Mexican artists. Fluent English-speaking staff are on hand to help. They also offer the use of a printer, scanner, and CD burner. The café features all kinds of coffee drinks, as well as croissants and sandwiches. The café is open 8 A.M.–10 P.M., while the terminals are available 7 A.M.–11 P.M.

Newspapers and Magazines

Two Spanish-language dailies are published in La Paz: *Diario Peninsular* and *El Sudcaliforniano.* Neither is any great shakes as Mexican newspapers go.

Librería Contempo, a bookstore on Calle Arrival at Paseo Obregón, carries Mexican newspapers as well as a few American magazines.

The La Paz branch of **Libros Libros/Books Books,** Calle Constitución at Madero, tel./fax 612/122-1410, has a good selection of American newspapers, magazines, and books.

Language Courses

If you'd like to study Spanish while you're in La Paz, **Centro de Idiomas, Cultura y Comunicación (CICC),** Calle Madero 2460 and Legaspy, tel. 612/125-7554, fax 612/125-7388, www.cicclapaz.com, offers classes at all levels, from beginner to advanced. The standard course costs US$910 and includes four weeks of intensive classes (25 hours per week); a homestay with a Mexican family can be arranged but is paid for separately. Longer or shorter courses are available; a one-week travel Spanish course, for example, costs US$99. Business-Spanish and medical-Spanish courses are now offered.

Se Habla La Paz, Calle Madero 540, tel./fax 612/122-7763, info@sehablalapaz.com, www.sehablalapaz.com, also offers Spanish classes.

Laundry

If you need to do some laundry, **La Paz Lava** at Ocampo Pte. and Mutualismo is a good choice. This clean, modern self-service Laundromat is within walking distance of the *malecón,* so you can stroll along the waterfront while waiting for your clothes. La Paz Lava also provides delivery service to home or hotel.

On Boulevard Forjadores adjacent to Supermercado Arámburo (opposite the youth hostel) is the enormous **Lavamática Cinthya;** you're sure to get a machine here.

Public Baths

Adjacent to the Mercado Municipal along Calle Degollado is **Baños Señoral,** a public bath with clean hot showers for US$1.50. Hours are Mon.–Sat. 8 A.M.–8:30 P.M., Sunday till 5 P.M.

Immigration

If you're planning to cross the Sea of Cortez by ferry and haven't yet validated your tourist card, stop by the immigration office on Paseo Obregón between Allende and Juárez, tel. 612/124-6349. It's usually open daily 8 A.M.–8:30 P.M. The immigration office at the airport is open seven days a week, while the one at the Pichilingue ferry terminal is open only an hour or so before each ferry departure.

GETTING THERE

By Air

Márquez de León International Airport (LAP) is 12 km south of the city; the airport access road leaves Mexico 1 at Km 9. Although it's a small airport, facilities include a couple of gift shops (one of which also offers snacks such as smoked tuna burritos and chicken sandwiches), two snack bars, rental car booths, Ladatel phones (cards available for purchase from the snack bar), an ATM machine, and a fax/telegraph service.

La Paz's principal air carrier, **Aero California,** on Obregón, between Bravo and Ocampo, tel. 612/125-1023, flies daily to and from Culiacán, Guadalajara, Hermosillo, Loreto, Los Mochis, Mazatlán, Monterrey, and Tijuana, along with connecting flights from Los Angeles, Tucson, and Mexico City.

Aeroméxico, Paseo Obregón between Hidalgo y Costilla and Morelos, tel. 612/124-6366, 612/124-6367 or 800/021-4000, www.aeromexico.com, and its subsidiary, **Aerolitoral,** offer daily nonstop flights to La Paz from Ciudad Obregón, Culiacán, Loreto, Los Mochis, Mazatlán, Mexico City, and Tijuana, as well as connecting flights from Guadalajara and Phoenix.

Airport Transportation: Transporte Terrestre operates yellow-and-white vans between the city and the airport. The standard fare is US$15 *colectivo* (shared), US$30 for private service *(especial),* and US$56 for a larger van. To Todos Santos the prices run US$200 *especial,* US$278 for a large van; to Los Cabos US$245/US$333; to San Carlos and López Mateos US$311/US$556. A regular taxi to the airport should cost around US$15. Some hotels operate airport vans that charge just US$3–4 pp.

By Bus

Intercity Bus: From the **Central Camionera,** Calle Jalisco at Av. Independencia, **Águila,** tel. 612/122-3063 or 612/122-4270, runs northbound buses to Ciudad Constitución (US$11.50, more or less hourly 7 A.M.–9 P.M.), Puerto San Carlos (US$12.50, twice daily), Puerto López Mateos (US$13, twice daily), Loreto (US$21, twice daily), Mulegé (US$29, several times daily), Santa Rosalía (US$34, several times daily), San Ignacio (US$39, several times daily), Vizcaíno Junction (US$40, twice daily), Guerrero Negro (US$43, several times daily), San Quintín (US$73, several times daily), Ensenada (US$85, four times daily), Tijuana (US$91, once daily), Tecate (US$97, once daily), and Mexicali (US$108, once daily).

Southbound, Águila buses depart from the **Terminal Malecón** (612/122-7898). Only one bus (5 P.M.) runs through the central Cape Region towns of El Triunfo (US$3.50), San Antonio (US$4), San Bartolo (US$4.50), Los Barriles, (US$5), Santiago (US$7), and Miraflores (US$8), terminating in La Ribera (US$10). Most run via Mexico 19 through Todos Santos (US$5.50), continuing on to Cabo San Lucas (US$11.25) and San José del Cabo (US$12); the 3 P.M. bus continues all the way to La Ribera.

If you're traveling southbound, you may find it more convenient to head to the centrally located terminal of **Autotransportes La Paz,** Calle Degollado at Calle Guillermo Prieto, tel. 612/122-2157, which has eight departures to Los Cabos via the West Cape (not via Los Barriles) 6:45 A.M.–7:50 P.M. daily; departures are roughly every other hour in the morning, increasing to every hour in the afternoon. Fares are Todos Santos US$5.50; Pescadero US$6; Cabo San Lucas US$9; San José del Cabo US$9.50.

By Boat

The ferry port at Pichilingue, 16 km (9.5 miles) northeast of downtown La Paz via Mexico 11, serves vehicle and passenger ferries between La Paz and Mazatlán. **SEMATUR** runs the ferries on this route.

You can book SEMATUR ferry tickets in advance at the ferry terminal, tel. 612/122-5005 or 800/718-9531, or the city ticket office (Agencia de Viajes Ahome), Calle 5 de Mayo at Guillermo Prieto, tel. 612/125-2366, tel./fax 612/125-2346.

For SEMATUR fares and schedules, see By Ferry from Mainland Mexico in the On the Road chapter.

A new private company, **Baja Ferries,** operates a faster ferry that completes the Topolobampo-La Paz crossing (or vice versa) in just five hours. The ferry boasts a cafeteria, night club, restaurant, bar, and space for 1,000 passengers, including a choice of seats or cabins with two to four berths and attached bath. A seat on the ferry costs US$58. If you want a cabin berth, add US$71 to this fare. You can take a car or pick-up truck along for US$87. A round-trip ticket for two passengers and one car goes for US$140. For information or reservations you can call the Pichilinque Terminal at tel. 612/123-0208 or 612/123-0508 (fax 612/123-0504O), or the La Paz city office at Calle Isabel la Católica and Navarro, tel. 612/125-7443, 612/128-6822, or 800/122-1414, fax 612/125-7444. If you're starting from Topolobampo, the local numbers are 668/862-1003, 668/862-1004, or 800/718-2796, fax 668/862-1005. Or check www.bajaferries.com.

A temporary **vehicle import permit** is necessary for vehicular travel on the Mexican mainland. These permits aren't needed for Baja California travel, but if you've driven down to La Paz and decide you'd like to take your wheels

on a mainland-bound ferry, you need to get one before buying a ticket. The whole process operates more smoothly in Tijuana, so if you anticipate using the ferry service, doing the paperwork in advance will save time and hassle.

If for whatever reason you decide to take the ferry and haven't done the paperwork in advance, you can obtain the proper permit in La Paz from the **Aduana Marítima** office at the north end of the Pichilingue ferry terminal; open 9 A.M.–1 P.M. and 5–7 P.M. To receive the permit, you need the original and three copies of your vehicle title or registration, a major credit card (in the vehicle owner's name), your driver's license, and your passport with valid Mexican visa. You can also try the Aduana Marítima office at Paseo Obregón and Ignacio Bañuelos, opposite the Muelle Turístico on the *malecón,* tel. 612/122-0730, but applying at this office is usually a more cumbersome procedure than applying at the ferry office. The permit can usually be processed on the spot, but budget a couple of days anyway, just in case all the right bureaucrats aren't in.

La Paz is an official Mexican **port of entry,** so the COTP office near Club de Yates Palmira has authority to clear yachts for movement throughout Mexican waters. Unless you plan to anchor outside, the easiest way to arrange this is to check in at Marina de la Paz or Club de Yates Palmira and let the marina staff process all port clearance papers. For Marina de la Paz clients, clear-in service is US$15. Only one clearance in and out is required for entering and exiting the country; between Mexican ports the same papers can be presented. See Sports and Recreation, earlier, for information on La Paz marinas.

GETTING AROUND

You can reach most points of interest downtown on foot. For outlying areas, you can choose city buses or taxis, or rent a car.

Buses

Regular city buses and *colectivos* radiate in all directions from the *zona comercial* surrounding the Mercado Municipal on Calle Degollado. Each bears the name of either the principal street along its run or the district where the route begins and ends. Any bus marked El Centro, for example, will end up near the Mercado Municipal at Revolución and Degollado. Bus fare anywhere in town is US$.40.

From Terminal Malecón, Paseo Obregón 125, **Transportes Águila** runs buses between La Paz and various points along Península de Pichilingue. Buses to Pichilingue leave seven times daily 7 A.M.– 2:30 P.M. and cost US$1.50. Buses to Playa Balandra and Playa Tecolote operate on weekends only, at noon and 2 P.M., for US$2.50. Call 612/122-7898 for more information.

Taxis

Taxis can be found throughout El Centro, the downtown area between Calles 5 de Mayo and Degollado (especially along the west end of Calle 16 de Septiembre in the shopping district), and in front of the tourist hotels. On the *malecón* (Paseo Obregón), the main taxi stands are in front of Hotel Los Arcos and Hotel Perla. The average taxi hire downtown costs around US$2–3, a bit more after dark. La Paz taxis don't have meters, so it's sometimes necessary to haggle to arrive at the correct fare.

Longer trips are more economical if you use a shared taxi van or *colectivo*. A *colectivo* from the Central Camionera to the center of town, for example, costs US$.60 pp; by private taxi it's as much as US$6.

Rental Cars

Several La Paz travel agencies can arrange auto rental, but rates are generally lower if you deal directly with a rental agency. Local agencies include: **Alamo,** on Obregón almost opposite Vista Coral, tel. 612/122-6262 or 800/849-8001, www.alamo-mexico.com.mx; **Baja California Autorentas,** Av. Obregón 826 (between Salvatierra and Victoria), tel. 612/125-7662; **Avis,** on Av. Obregón between Pineda and Márquez de León, tel./fax 612/122-2651; **Budget,** Av. Obregón 1775, tel. 612/123-1919 or 800/322-9975, www.budget.com.mx; **Dollar,** at the corner of Obregón and Pineda, tel. 612/122-6060 or 800/849-4922, dollar3@prodigy.net.mx; **Hertz,** Paseo Obregón 2130-D, tel. 612/122-0919 or

800/709-5000; **Local Car Rental,** Obregón 582-1, tel. 612/122-5140; **National,** Obregón and Bravo, tel. 612/125-6585, fax 612/125-6595; and **Thrifty,** Paseo Obregón and Lerdo de Tejada, tel. 612/125-9696 or 800/021-2277, www.thrifty .com.mx. Daily rental rates typically run higher than in Los Cabos, and companies tend to levy per-kilometer charges on top of the daily rate. All companies offer significant discounts for rentals of six days or more.

Alamo, Avis, Budget, Dollar, Local Car Rental, National, Thrifty, and Hertz operate service counters at La Paz International Airport.

La Paz has plenty of **Pemex stations,** all offering Magna Sin (unleaded), Premium, and diesel.

SOUTHEAST OF LA PAZ

State highway BCS 286 begins south of La Paz off Mexico 1 (at Km 211) and leads southeast 43 km (26 miles) to the agricultural center of San Juan de los Planes. Along the way this paved road climbs over the northeastern escarpment of the Sierra de la Laguna (here sometimes given its own name, Sierra de las Cacachilas), then descends toward the coastal plains, offering a panoramic view of aquamarine Bahía de la Ventana and Isla Cerralvo in the distance. At the crest of the ridge you'll pass stands of live oak, several ranches, and the village of **La Huerta** (Km 17 on BCS 286). When the weather in La Paz seems intolerably hot, a drive up into the Sierra de las Cacachilas is a good way to cool off.

Bahía de la Ventana

At Km 38 a paved road branches northeast off BCS 286 and leads eight km (five miles) and 11 km (6.8 miles), respectively, to the fish camps of La Ventana and El Sargento on Bahía de la Ventana. Along the way it passes a small saltworks. Windsurfing is very good at La Ventana due to the strong northeasterlies channeled through Canal de Cerralvo to the north. Onshore and inshore fishing is good all the way along the L-shaped bay; farther offshore in the Canal de Cerralvo, catches of marlin, skipjack, and dorado are common in the summer months. The gently sloped beach offers easy small-boat launching. If you don't fish, the bayshore still makes a worthwhile destination for blessedly secluded camping, swimming, and snorkeling, especially in the spring and fall (summers are hot). Isla Cerralvo (see below) lies about 16 km (10 miles) offshore.

La Ventana Campground, along the beach just north of the village of La Ventana, offers simple tent/camper sites, trash barrels, toilets, and showers for US$5 a night. Boats can easily be beach-launched here; Dec.–Mar. the campground is taken over by windsurfers. Many people are buying or leasing beach lots in the area and planting breeze-block cubes on them.

The **Ventana Bay Resort,** reservations@ventanabay.com, www.ventanabay.com, features bungalow-style guest rooms set around a clubhouse, along with private residences, restaurant, bar, and a full-service windsurfing, kiteboarding, and dive shop operated by Baja Adventures. The eco-resort also offers activities such as kayaking, Hobie Cat sailboating, mountain biking, sportfishing, and snorkeling. A seven-day package includes accommodations, two meals per day, and unlimited use of recreation equipment. Rates run US$545 for the "sports package," US$725 for the windsurfing package, and US$775 for the kiteboarding package. For further information about Baja Adventures, contact Mr. Bill at 612/128-4333, U.S. tel. 800/533-8452, or mrbill@ventanabay.com.

Basic supplies are available in El Sargento, which boasts a Centro de Salud (Public Health Clinic), baseball diamond, soccer field, and a place where you can buy barrel gas.

San Juan de los Planes

Los Planes, as it's usually called, has several markets, a café, and around 1,500 inhabitants supported by farming (cotton, tomatoes, beans, and corn) or by fishing at nearby bays.

Bahía de los Muertos

This pretty, curved bay with primitive beach

> *If you don't fish, Bahía de la Ventana still makes a worthwhile destination for blessedly secluded camping, swimming, and snorkeling— especially in the spring and fall.*

camping is reached by a graded road running east 21 km (13 miles) from San Juan de los Planes. Historians don't know why a 1777 Spanish map named this shore Bay of the Dead, but the name gained substance when a Chinese ship beached here in 1885. The ship had been refused entry at La Paz harbor because the crew was suffering from yellow fever; after putting in at this bay, all 18 crewmen died. Mexican fishermen buried the bodies above the tide line and marked their graves with wooden crosses, a few of which still stand. In the early 20th century, a community of American farmers tried unsuccessfully to cultivate the desert surrounding the bay; some died of thirst or hunger, adding to the bay's list of *muertos*.

You can pitch a tent or sleep under the stars anywhere along the north end of Bahía de los Muertos for no charge.

Ensenada de los Muertos, an abandoned port at the north end of the bay, was built in the 1920s for the shipping of ore from El Triunfo mines in the Sierra de la Laguna.

Punta Arenas de la Ventana

A lesser road branches northeast about four km before Los Muertos and leads eight km (five miles) to beautiful Punta Arenas de la Ventana. **Las Arenas Resort** has had a couple of different owners and is once again closed for business.

The waters off Punta Arenas reputedly offer Baja's best roosterfish angling; wahoo, amberjack, grouper, dorado, and billfish are also in abundant supply. Guided *panga* trips may be available from the beach next to the resort, where local *pangeros* moor their boats, for US$60–85 per day. A bit south of the resort, off **Punta Perico** (Parakeet Point), is a lively reef with varied depths of 3–25 meters (10–82 feet).

Alternate Routes

Bahía de los Muertos can be reached from the south via a 47-km (30-mile) dirt road between Los Barriles and San Juan de los Planes. The road is wide and flat from Los Barriles as far as Punta Pescadero and El Cardonal—13 km (8 miles) and 22 km (14 miles), respectively. North of El Cardonal, the road begins to rise along the Mesa Boca Alamo, eventually cutting inland and ascending steeply into the jagged, red Sierra El Carrizalito. Several kilometers of the road here wind around narrow, adrenaline-pumping curves with steep drop-offs. Contrary to popular belief, four-wheel drive is not a necessity for this section of road, but careful driving and good road clearance are. Twenty-four km (15 miles) from El Cardonal, the road leaves the mountains and meets the paved end of BCS 286.

San Juan de los Planes, La Ventana, Punta Arenas de la Ventana, and Bahía de los Muertos can also be reached from Mexico 1 via a graded, unpaved road from San Antonio. The road's east end begins on BCS 286 about 3.5 km (2.2 miles) south of the turnoff for La Ventana and El Sargento. See El Triunfo and San Antonio in the Central Cape section for details.

Isla Cerralvo

Across Bahía de la Ventana and Canal de Cerralvo lies Isla Cerralvo, one of the largest islands in the Sea of Cortez. At the time of early Spanish exploration, the island held large pearl-oyster beds and was inhabited by a small group of Pericú.

Later the rugged island reportedly became a favored final resting place for the *vagabundos del mar*, Amerindians who roamed the Sea of Cortez in dugout canoes until well into the 20th century.

Today Cerralvo remains one of the least visited of Baja's large coastal islands, simply due to its location on the far side of the Península de Pichilingue. Coral-encrusted **Roca Montaña,** off the southeastern tip of the island, is an excellent diving and fishing location, as is **Piedras Gordas,** marked by a navigation light at the southwestern tip. Depths at these sites range 3–15 meters (10–50 feet). Other good dive sites include the rock reefs off the northern end (average depth 18–21 meters/60–70 feet), which feature a good variety of reef fishes, sea turtles, and shipwrecks. One of the reefs, **Arrecife de la Foca,** features an unidentified shipwreck with Mazatlán marked on the hull. **La Reina,** another reef at the north end of the island, is the site of a large steel-hulled freighter that sank half a century ago. Barely a hundred meters off the island's west shore are two adjacent rock reefs known as **La Reinita.**

Access to Isla Cerralvo is easiest from Bahía de la Ventana or Punta Arenas, where beach launches are possible. From La Paz, it's a long haul around the Península de Pichilingue via Canal de San Lorenzo.

Central Cape

Along Mexico 1 between La Paz and San José del Cabo, a number of mining-turned-farming towns sport cobblestone streets and 19th-century stone-and-stucco architecture. Nestled among well-watered arroyos in the Sierra de la Laguna, these neglected settlements now support themselves growing citrus, avocado, mangoes, corn, and sugarcane, and, to a lesser extent, serving the needs of passing travelers. Many of the families living in the central Cape Region are descended from Spanish settlers of the 18th and early 19th centuries. Others are newcomers—including a few Americans and Canadians—drawn by the area's solitude and simplicity.

SAN PEDRO TO SAN BARTOLO

San Pedro

This town of only 377 inhabitants appears—and quickly disappears—just before the junction of Mexico 1 and Mexico 19. *Carnitas* connoisseurs swear by **El Paraíso** and **El Pin** (featuring *carnitas, chicharrones,* and hot dogs), two unassuming roadside cafés on the highway's west side. The junction itself is reached at Km 185; if Cabo San Lucas is your destination, you must decide whether to take Mexico 19 via Todos Santos or the Transpeninsular Highway (Mexico 1) via El Triunfo, San Antonio, San Bartolo, Santiago, and Miraflores.

Unless you're in a hurry to reach Cabo San Lucas, Mexico 1 is the most scenic choice for drivers of autos and light trucks. South of San Pedro, Mexico 1 winds through the Sierra de la Laguna and features a succession of dizzying curves and steep grades. Hence for trailers, RVs, and other wide or lengthy vehicles, Mexico 19 is the better choice since it runs along relatively flat terrain.

El Triunfo and San Antonio

During the Jesuit missionary period, this section along the lower northern slopes of the sierra was earmarked for cattle ranching. But mining concessions moved in following the discovery of silver in 1748, and San Antonio quickly grew into a town of 10,000 people, many of them Yaqui laborers. Then known as Real de Minas de Santa Ana, it was the first nonmission town founded in Baja. The Spanish crown took over the mines in 1769 and struggled to turn a profit from a relatively low quality of ore. When Loreto was heavily damaged by a hurricane in 1829, San Antonio briefly served as capital of the Californias before the capital was transferred to La Paz in 1830.

In 1862 better gold and silver deposits were uncovered at El Triunfo (Triumph), seven km (4.5 miles) north of San Antonio. By 1878 the large El Progreso mining concern had established seven gold and silver mines around the village, attracting a number of Mexican, French, English, Italian, German, and American immigrants. The company paid for the region's first post office and installed the first electrical and phone lines to La Paz.

Both San Antonio and El Triunfo bustled with frontier commerce through the end of the 19th century, when the ore began running out. Then a hurricane flooded the mines in 1918 and sounded the death knell; by 1925 both towns were virtually abandoned. Today El Triunfo has only around 400 residents, most of them involved in small-scale mining (extracting ore from leftover tailings) or the weaving of palm baskets. A few *artesanías* can be found on the main road through town. San Antonio, in a lushly planted valley that descends eastward all the way to the Sea of Cortez, has developed into a farming community with around 800 residents, a Pemex station, a post office, and a few markets.

© JOE CUMMINGS

El Triunfo

A number of historic adobe buildings in both towns have been restored, including El Triunfo's Casa Municipal and San Antonio's unusual 1825 church exhibiting train and paddlewheeler motifs. A fun time to visit San Antonio is June 13, the feast day of St. Anthony, when everyone from both San Antonio and El Triunfo turns out for music and dancing.

Baja travelers have also mentioned lots of old mines and mining paths throughout the region, often good for exploratory hikes. Hiring a guide is always a good idea; locals in El Triunfo and San Antonio know who's good.

Near San Antonio, between Km 156 and 157, a road heads north off Mexico 1 and leads 22 km (14 miles) to BCS 286, the highway to San Juan de los Planes and La Paz. This is the shortest way to reach Bahía de los Muertos and La Ventana from the central Cape. The road is signed for Los Planes coming from the south along Mexico 1, but not from the north. Although the road surface starts out with asphalt, it quickly becomes a wide, graded dirt road traversable by most vehicles. Once you hit BCS 286, turn left for La Paz, right for Los Planes and the Cortez coast.

While El Triunfo has no restaurants thus far, you'll find a modest selection of groceries in town at **Abarrotes La Escondida** (on Mexico 1) and the **Tienda Comunitaria** (off Mexico 1 in the center of town).

San Bartolo

Beginning just past Km 128, San Bartolo (pop. 550) is the greenest and lushest of the central Cape settings, thanks to a large spring gushing straight out of a mountainside into the arroyo. To complete the tropical picture, many homes sport thatched roofs. Mangoes, avocados, and other fresh fruits are available at roadside stands or in town. **Restaurant El Paso** and **Dulcería Daniela's** on the east side of the highway serve meals. **El Oasis** sells regional *dulces* made of fruit such as guava or mango, as well as homemade cheese, *empanadas, bistec ranchero,* quesadillas, and the coldest beer in town.

San Bartolo's patron saint day is June 19, conveniently close to San Antonio's.

From San Bartolo, a 26-km unpaved road follows an arroyo lined with huge *güeribos* to the tiny settlement of **San Antonio de la Sierra.** This arroyo in turn leads to the arroyo and ranch settlement of **Santo Domingo,** where rustic ranch furniture, leather, and fruit candy are produced.

The **Rancho Verde RV Haven,** between Km 143 and 142, Mexico 1, tel. 612/126-9103, offers 3,400 acres of mountain desert wilderness for camping, biking, or just taking time out during a transpeninsular road journey. Spaces cost US$11 with full hookups and hot showers, or US$7 if you're self-contained. This admits up to three persons per site; a fourth is charged US$2 per night, and children under 10 stay free. Food service isn't ordinarily available, but the friendly Mexican staff can prepare simple *antojitos* on request.

SANTIAGO

The largest of the central Cape Region towns, Santiago (pop. 2,500) was founded as Misión de Santiago el Apóstol in 1723 by Italian padre Ignacio María Nápoli. The mission was abandoned in the latter half of the 18th century following a series of Pericú rebellions, and only in relatively recent times has agriculture revived the arroyo community.

A two-km road flanked by vegetable plots, leafy fruit orchards, and blue fan palms leads west from Mexico 1 (Km 85) across the wide, flat Arroyo de Santiago, dividing the town into Loma Norte and Loma Sur (North and South Slopes). Santiago and environs serves the region as an important source of palm leaves for making palapa roofs. *Palmeros* claim the fan-shaped fronds are best cut during a full moon, as rising sap makes the palm leaves last longer. Properly dried and stored, 250 palm leaves equals one *carga* or load, for which the *palmeros* receive US$30–50 depending on leaf quality.

Various *tiendas* line the town plaza; the town also offers a Pemex station, hotel, supermarket stocked with local fruit and vegetables, post office, telegraph office, church, and the only zoo on the peninsula south of Mexicali.

The residents of the small but nicely landscaped **Parque Zoológico** include a peccary,

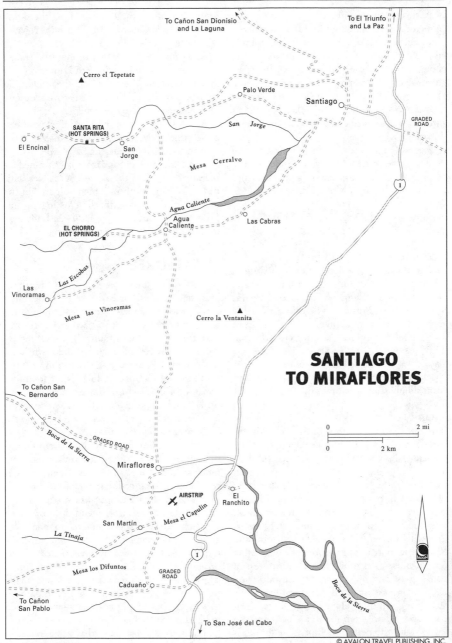

To Cañon San Dionisio
and La Laguna

To El Triunfo
and La Paz

▲ Cerro el Tepetate

Palo Verde

Santiago

GRADED
ROAD

SANTA RITA
(HOT SPRINGS)

San   Jorge

El Encinal

San
Jorge

Mesa   Cerralvo

Agua Caliente

EL CHORRO
(HOT SPRINGS)

Agua
Caliente

Las Cabras

Las Escobas

Las
Vinoramas

Mesa las Vinoramas

▲ Cerro la Ventanita

**SANTIAGO
TO MIRAFLORES**

0   2 mi

0   2 km

To Cañon San
Bernardo

Boca de la Sierra

GRADED ROAD

Miraflores

✈ AIRSTRIP

El
Ranchito

San Martín

Mesa el Capulín

La Tinaja

Mesa los Difuntos

GRADED
ROAD

Caduaño

Boca de la Sierra

To Cañon
San Pablo

To San José del Cabo

© AVALON TRAVEL PUBLISHING, INC.

CAPE REGION

bear, coyote, fox, monkey, parrots, and ducks. Some of the animals are Cape Region natives. The park is open daily 6 A.M.–6 P.M. in summer, till 5 P.M. the rest of the year. Admission is free, though donations are gladly accepted. To bypass the town center and proceed directly to the zoo, take the left fork just after crossing the dry arroyo near the town entrance, then take the next left fork onto a levee road that curves along the south end of town to the zoo.

A small, rustic museum adjacent to the church at the corner of Calzada Misioneros and Calle Victoria contains colonial artifacts and local fossils. It's open Mon.–Fri. 8 A.M.–1 P.M.; free admission.

Santiago celebrates its patron saint day, the feast day of St. James, on July 25.

Accommodations and Food

Under US$25: Casa de Huéspedes Palomar, tel. 612/122-0604, south of the plaza on the east side of Calzada Misioneros, offers six tidy rooms around a quiet courtyard. The Palomar's highly regarded restaurant, decorated with local fossils, serves seafood, enchiladas, and burgers Mon.–Sat. 11:30 A.M.–8 P.M. Entrées start at US$7; *pescado mojo de ajo,* fish cooked in garlic butter, is a house specialty. At last pass the only sign we saw out front simply read Restaurant Bar.

Vicinity of Santiago

The dirt road to the zoo continues southwest nine km (5.5 miles) to the village of **Agua Caliente** (also known as Los Manantiales), where a hot spring in a nearby canyon (about seven km, four miles west of the village) has been channeled into a concrete tub for recreational purposes. Camping is permitted in the canyon. Ask directions to two other hot springs in the area: **El Chorro** (west of Agua Caliente) and **Santa Rita** (north). The network of roads behind Santiago passes through dense thornforest in some spots, and it's easy to get lost unless you keep a compass on hand or a good fix on the sun. If you can bring along a copy of the Mexican topographic map for this area (Santiago 12B34), all the better; each of these locales is clearly marked. Do not attempt these roads at night. If you continue south along the sandy road past Agua Caliente, you'll reach the town of Miraflores after 8.7 km (5.4 miles).

At the north end of Santiago, another dirt road leads northwest to **Rancho San Dionísio** (23.5 km/14.5 miles), where the Cañon San Dionísio approach to Picacho La Laguna begins. See Sierra de la Laguna, later, for sierra hiking details.

At **Las Cuevas,** five km (three miles) northeast of Santiago on Mexico 1 (around Km 93), is the turnoff to La Ribera and the East Cape.

Three km south of Santiago, a large painted cement sphere marks the **Tropic of Cancer** (latitude 23.5°N), south of which you are "in the tropics." As if to sanctify the crossing, an impressive Guadalupe shrine has been built next to the rather unattractive marker.

MIRAFLORES

A 2.5-km (1.5-mile) paved road to Miraflores branches west off Mexico 1 at Km 71 next to a Pemex station. This ranching and farming community is known for leatherwork; **Curtiduría Miraflores** (Miraflores Tannery), just off the access road between the highway and town (look for a small sign reading Leather Shop on the north side of the road), sells handmade leather saddles, bridles, whips, horsehair lariats, and other ranching gear, as well as a few souvenir items such as leather hats, belts, and bags, and the occasional bleached cow skull.

Owned and operated by the Beltrán family, the tannery is particularly known for its rustic ranch saddles. One saddle may use up to eight cowhides, each tanned in the traditional *sudcaliforniano* manner with local palo blanco bark and powdered *quebrache,* a reddish-brown, tannin-rich extract from a type of dogbane tree grown on the mainland. Saddle frames are fashioned out of local woods—*ciruelo, copal*—or *cardón* skeletons. Custom orders are accepted. The *curtiduría* also sells engraved knives made from salvaged car springs—a source of particularly strong metal for knife blades—and sheathed in handtooled leather.

The town's **Casa de Cultura** has recently been completely renovated, and now contains a collection of modest displays chronicling local history.

Miraflores honors the Virgin of Guadalupe as its patron saint, so Fiesta Guadalupana (December 12), celebrated throughout Mexico, is especially fervent here.

Well past the tannery, after you've crossed an arroyo and are just getting into the center of Miraflores, a large hedge of bougainvillea nearly obscures the open-air, palapa-roofed **Restaurant Las Bugambilias,** to the left on a small side street off the main road. All manner of inexpensive, Bajacaliforniano-style *antojitos* are available here from morning till evening. **Restaurant Miraflores,** next to Mini Super El Nidito near the market and plaza, makes good tacos with shrimp, fish, or beef. Several *mercaditos* in town provide local produce and *machaca.*

Vicinity of Miraflores

A dirt road northwest of Miraflores leads to **Boca de la Sierra** (Mouth of the Sierra), a settlement at the mouth of Cañon San Bernardo—the second of the three canyons providing access deep into the Sierra de la Laguna. *Ejido* farms in the Boca de la Sierra area cultivate vegetables and herbs—especially sweet basil—for Cape Region supermarkets and restaurants as well as for export to the United States.

Another dirt road southwest of town leads to the mouth of Cañon San Pablo, a third Laguna hiking route. Inquire at the tannery about guided trips into the sierra to view Amerindian rock-art sites.

SIERRA DE LA LAGUNA

The mountainous heart of the Cape Region extends southward from the Llano de la Paz (the plains just south of La Paz) to Cabo San Lucas, a distance of around 135 km (81 miles). Originally called Sierra de la Victoria by the Spanish, the interior mountains were renamed Sierra de la Laguna in the early Mexican era. These peaks are unique among sierras in the southern half of Baja California in that they're granitic rather than volcanic. And unlike the sierras to the north, the entire Laguna range is tilted eastward instead of westward; i.e., its steepest slopes are on the west side of the escarpment rather than the east.

Picacho de la Laguna (elevation 2,161 meters/7,090 feet), roughly in the sierra's center, is usually cited as the highest peak in the range, although according to some sources **Cerro las Casitas**—approximately 6.5 km (four miles) southeast of Picacho de la Laguna and measuring 2,083 meters (6,835 feet) by most accounts—may be higher. Between these two peaks is a large, flat meadow called **La Laguna** (elevation 1,707 meters/5,600 feet). This depression held a mountain lake until around 1870, when Cañon San Dionísio became sufficiently eroded to drain away accumulated water.

The sierra flora has been little researched; the most recent detailed studies were undertaken in the 1890s by botanist T. S. Brandegee for the California Academy of Sciences. The foothills and mesas below 500 meters are covered with dry *matorral*—low-growing cacti, succulents, thornscrub, and abundant herbs. Common species include barrel cactus, cholla, *palo verde,* ironwood, damiana, and oregano. Canyon walls may be draped with *zalate* (wild fig). At elevations of 500–750 meters (1,640–2,460 feet), tropical-subtropical deciduous forest and columnar cacti are the dominant flora (e.g., *mauto,* palo blanco, prickly pear, *cardón, palo adán*). From 750 to 1,200 meters (2,460–3,940 feet), live-oak woodlands (encino, madrone) dominate, and above 1,200 meters a mix of live oak and piñon pine prevails. At its highest elevations, La Laguna qualifies as a cloud forest during the moist summer months, when the peaks are consistently shrouded in mist or rain.

Islands in the Sky

The range's highlands receive more annual precipitation—up to 89 cm (35 inches) per year in some microclimates—than any other place in Baja California. As a result, the meadow of La Laguna and other flats and high canyons in the sierra contain a number of "relic environments" preserving flora and fauna long ago lost on the arid plains below.

These "islands in the sky" support a mix of desert, tropical, and subalpine plant species that are found together nowhere else in North America. Among the unlikely combinations seen growing side by side: mosses and cacti, madrone and monkey flower, palm and willow. Of the 447 plant species known to grow in the sierra, at least 70 are reportedly indigenous. Undisturbed by human progress, deer, coyote, mountain lion, Pacific tree frog, and dozens of hummingbird species also thrive in the highland areas of the sierra.

For many years, naturalists and outdoor enthusiasts clamored for the upper sierra to be declared a national park or preserve, and in June 1994 the Mexican government finally granted the Sierra de la Laguna official recognition as a "bios-phere reserve." Such status prohibits development within the reserve's 32,519-hectare core zone; local ranchers are permitted to graze livestock in a buffer zone surrounding the protected core.

Hiking and Backpacking

The Sierra de la Laguna is a popular hiking area for Cape residents, as it offers the opportunity to leave behind the fig trees and palms of the arid-tropical environment for a walk among cottonwoods and subalpine meadows. Three lengthy east-west canyons—Cañon Dionísio, Cañon San Bernardo, and Cañon San Pablo—provide the principal access into the sierra. All three routes en-

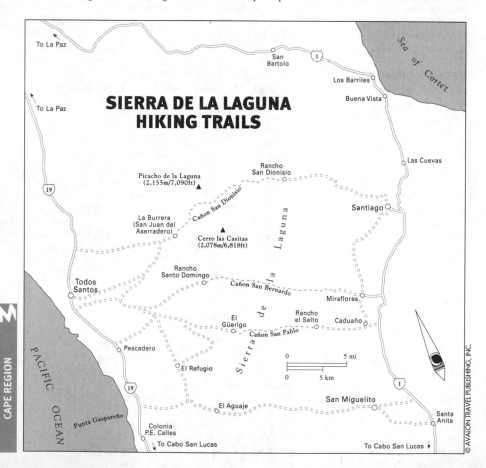

SIERRA DE LA LAGUNA HIKING TRAILS

To La Paz
San Bartolo
Los Barriles
Buena Vista
To La Paz
Las Cuevas
Rancho San Dionisio
Picacho de la Laguna (2,155m/7,090ft)
Cañon San Dionisio
Santiago
La Burrera (San Juan del Aserradero)
Cerro las Casitas (2,078m/6,818ft)
Rancho Santo Domingo
Todos Santos
Cañon San Bernardo
Miraflores
El Güerigo
Rancho el Salto
Caduaño
Cañon San Pablo
Pescadero
0   5 mi
0   5 km
El Refugio
San Miguelito
El Aguaje
Santa Anita
Punta Gaspareño
Colonia P.E. Calles
To Cabo San Lucas
To Cabo San Lucas
Sea of Cortez
PACIFIC OCEAN
Sierra de la Laguna

able hikers to cross the sierra's spine from east to west or vice versa. Primitive campsites are available along each of the three routes.

The northernmost and most popular route, via Cañon San Dionísio, leads directly to La Laguna, the range's largest and highest meadow. La Laguna lies at an altitude of just under 1,800 meters (6,000 feet), between Picacho de la Laguna and Cerro las Casitas, the sierra's tallest peaks. The scenery on this hike is impressive. A straight traverse of this route, starting from either side, is possible in three days, although this would allow little time for taking it easy. Add at least another day to allow some time to enjoy La Laguna once you've reached it.

Cañon San Dionísio: Western (Todos Santos) Approach

Most hikers ascend to La Laguna from the west side, which is a steeper but more straightforward hike (and about two km shorter) than from Rancho San Dionísio. Unlike the network of cattle trails on the east side—which are best negotiated with local guides—the western ascent can be easily accomplished without a guide. From the west side a round-trip can be completed in two days.

Near Todos Santos, the sandy road to La Burrera leaves Mexico 19 about 100 meters south of the Punta Lobos turnoff. Past an old water tower, take the first left and continue straight through several intersections till the road ends at a gate and parking area. From the gate, follow the dirt road till you reach La Burrera (about 25 minutes away), where a sign in English advises hikers to follow marked trails (ironic since we've never seen any marked trails in the sierra). Also known as San Juan del Aserradero, this village on the sierra's western slopes lies around 17.5 km (11 miles) northeast of Todos Santos. Continue along this road another 20 minutes or so till you see a clearing on the right that has been used for camping; look for a sign reading No Tire Basura (Don't Throw Trash). Just past this sign, the road ascends to a small rise, at the top of which the main trail begins. After 30 meters or so of easy grade, the trail begins its long, steady climb straight up the mountain. Following this wide,

established (rutted in places), 11-km (seven-mile) trail, you should reach La Laguna in 5–8 hours, depending on your pace. Along the way the vegetation changes quickly from desert and thornforest into lush piñon-oak woodlands; about 20 minutes before you reach La Laguna the forest canopy opens up to magnificent views of the sierra and Pacific Ocean.

Follow the arroyo that drains La Laguna at its southeast corner, near where the trail comes in from Rancho San Dionísio, to reach a 20-meter (66-foot) cascade with deep pools suitable for swimming.

The return descent along the same trail takes about four hours to reach La Burrera.

If you need a ride to La Burrera from Todos Santos, your best bet is to inquire at Siempre Vive (at the corner of Calles Juárez and Márquez de León) in the late morning, when ranchers from the western sierra sometimes turn up for supplies and gossip. Fees for such a ride are negotiable—some ranchers will give you a lift for gas money and a six-pack of Tecate, others ask up to US$30. You might also inquire at the Todos Santos taxi stand next to the town park.

Cañon San Dionísio: Eastern (Santiago) Approach

From the east side of the sierra, count on 3–4 days to La Laguna and back with time to explore the area. The eastern mouth of the main canyon is reached via a dirt road to Rancho San Dionísio from Santiago (19 km/12 miles). From there it's a 13-km (eight-mile) hike west through the canyon mouth, then into a side arroyo and finally along the southern rim of the canyon to La Laguna. Piñon pine and cape live oak began appearing about two-thirds of the way up. This trail is relatively difficult to follow and is intersected by potentially confusing animal paths; a guide, available at Rancho San Dionísio or in Santiago, is highly recommended. If you decide to go it alone, be sure to carry a topo map and compass, and watch out for cattle trails branching off the main trail in every direction. Scout ahead at questionable junctions, even if it means going slower. Once you're up on the ridgeline you should be able to spot La Laguna in the distance and then confidently follow any trail heading in that direction.

Those wishing to explore a bit can follow the canyon four km straight west of the ranch into a steep area of boulders; where the arroyo forks there's a 20-meter (66-foot) waterfall and deep pools suitable for swimming. Don't attempt to follow the canyon all the way to the meadow unless you're into some very serious bouldering and scrambling.

Near the northwest edge of the meadow itself are a couple of herder's shacks. Just past these the trail cuts into the forest and divides; the southern branch descends to La Burrera, while the north branch ascends Picacho de la Laguna, a 90-minute hike away. (A lesser third trail leads to an arroyo with fresh water.) Easy to climb, the peak is bare of trees and provides splendid views of the surrounding terrain. Closer to the meadow, a hill surmounted by radio towers also makes a good vantage point.

Those wishing to traverse the sierra can descend westward from La Laguna another 11 km (seven miles) to La Burrera; see Western (Todos Santos) Approach, above. About 20 minutes into the descent from the meadow, you'll come upon terrific views all the way to the Pacific Ocean. Roads from La Burrera meet Mexico 19 south and north of Todos Santos; the area east of these junctions is honeycombed with other dirt roads, but if you continue in a westerly direction you'll eventually come to the highway.

The **Asociación Nacional de Guías en Ecoturismo y Turismo de Aventura,** Calles Bravo and Rubio, La Paz, tel. 612/125-2277, fax 612/125-8599, offers a five-day camping trek across the sierra from Santiago via Cañon San Dionisio, with a side trip into scenic Cañon de las Zorras. The trip costs around US$850 pp, with a minimum of six participants; this does not include transportation to La Paz, and you must bring your own sleeping bag.

Cañon San Bernardo

The next route to the south, via **Cañon San Bernardo,** is a relatively easy (from east to west) hike that crests at around 900 meters (3,000 feet). The canyon trailhead is accessible via an eight-km (five-mile) dirt road from Miraflores to Boca de la Sierra, where the trail skirts a dam and follows the canyon to the crest, 16 km (10 miles) northwest. Several pools along the way provide fresh water year-round. From the 900-meter crest, the trail continues over the sierra to the village of Santo Domingo on the western side, for a total traverse of 22.5 km (14 miles). The Cañon San Bernardo crossing makes a good four- to five-day hike, although it's possible to make a quick overnight to the crest and back from the eastern approach.

Cañon San Pablo

Cañon San Pablo provides the southernmost route into the sierra, reaching an elevation of around 1,000 meters (3,300 feet). The canyon mouth is best approached by taking a 6.5-km (four-mile) dirt road west from Caduaño, a village four km (2.5 miles) south of Miraflores, to Rancho El Salto. From Rancho El Salto, it's approximately 10.5 km (6.5 miles) to the crest; the trail continues over the ridge and along a steeper 4.8-km (three-mile) westward descent to the village of El Güerigo on the other side, where a network of dirt roads leads west to Mexico 19. A leisurely El Salto–El Güerigo hike takes 4–5 days.

Seasons

The best backpacking season here is late fall, after the rainy season has passed and sierra streams and *tinajas* are full. Temperatures above 1,500 meters (5,000 feet) typically measure 12–22°C (54–72°F) during the day, 5–12°C (41–54°F) at night. In January and February, temperatures can dip below freezing at night, while daytime temps run around 10–20°C (50–68°F).

The warmest temperatures are usually encountered in May and June, when the mercury reaches around 25°C (77°F) during the day, 10–15°C (50–60°F) at night. Although the scenery isn't as spectacularly green this time of year, it's a fine time to beat the heat down on the coastal plains.

July–Oct. rains may wash out trails and flood the canyons. Rainfall peaks in August, averaging 7.5 cm (three inches) but sometimes reaching a drenching 20 cm (7.8 inches) for the month.

Supplies

A compass and good topographic map are musts for any trip into the Sierra de la Laguna. To cover all three routes, you should possess copies of Mexico's relevant 1:50,000-scale topos: El Rosario F12B23; Las Cuevas F12B24; Todos Santos F12B33; and Santiago F12B34. (See Hiking and Backpacking in the On the Road chapter for recommended map sources.) Bring warm clothing and sleeping bags for the summit; morning frost isn't uncommon even in fall and spring. Long pants and sturdy hiking shoes are recommended as a defense against the abundant cactus and nettles.

On the Cañon San Dionísio trail, bring all the water you'll need to reach La Laguna, as there are no dependable sources on the way up, even in wet weather. An arroyo at La Laguna itself carries water year-round. On the Cañon San Bernardo trail, pools of water can be found along the way year-round. Water may be available from ranchos along the Cañon San Pablo trail, but bring your own to be safe. Be sure to use a water-purification system of some kind on all water sources in the mountains; although the water is generally uncontaminated, the presence of livestock precludes absolute safety.

Guides

For eastern ascents into the sierra, those unsure of their backpacking and orientation skills should consider hiring a local guide, since trails across the eastern escarpment are often obscured and junctions not always obvious. A guide can also prepare simple camp meals and point out items of natural interest—Amerindian rock art, flora and fauna—that first-timers might otherwise miss. Guides are available in Santiago and Miraflores; simply ask around. For the Cañon San Dionísio route, you can sometimes arrange a guide at Rancho San Dionísio, just before the eastern trailhead.

The going rate for guides in Santiago is US$30–35 per day pp, plus an extra US$15 per day per pack animal. Rancho San Dionísio charges US$30 for a guide without mules, no matter how many people are hiking.

Many hikers make the western approach to Cañon San Dionísio from Todos Santos with-

out a guide; the main difficulty is finding your way (or arranging a ride) to the trailhead. If you decide to hire a guide, there are a couple of options in Todos Santos. Fernando Arteche is fluent in English and very knowledgeable about the Sierra de la Laguna. His guided trips usually take three days, and you can go on foot or by mule. Fernando can be reached via email at sierradela laguna@hotmail.com.

Another local guide, Juan "John" Sebastián López, offers three-day trips on horseback, with pack horses to carry the gear. He also leads two-day trips to the hot springs. You can contact Juan at onejohnone@hotmail.com or www.rental.baja retreats.com.

Todos Santos Eco Adventures, Juárez and Topete, tel./fax 612/145-0780, info@tosea.net, www.tosea.net, is a new company based in Todos Santos offering professionally guided tours of the sierra, as well as other eco-adventures.

Driving Across the Sierra

Visitors with sturdy, high-clearance vehicles may be able traverse the Sierra de la Laguna in dry weather via a road that leaves Mexico 1 about 16 km (10 miles) south of Miraflores (about eight km, five miles north of Santa Anita) near Km 55. Among gringo road hogs this route is often called the "Naranjas road"; the correct name is Ramal Los Naranjos (*naranjo* means "orange tree," a probable reference to the many small citrus farms in the area). Because parts of it may suffer from washouts, this is not a road to tackle during the rainy season (July–Sept.), and any time of year you should make inquiries to determine whether the road is clear all the way.

From the Mexico 1 turnoff the road leads west-northwest 42 km (26 miles) to the village of **El Aguaje,** past the *ranchitos* of San Miguelito, Cieneguita, San Pedro de la Soledad, and El Remudadero. The ungraded road passes a couple of 1,500- to 1,800-meter (5,000- to 6,000-foot) peaks before cresting at around 1,035 meters (3,400 feet) and descending into a challenging set of sharp curves and grades approaching 30 percent. At 27 km (17 miles) from Mexico 1 you get your first view of the Pacific Ocean, by which point the road begins hugging the edge of a rock mountain. Shortly thereafter the road may be washed out or blocked by rock slides and you may not be able to continue. The track eventually widens to a graded, gravel road near El Aguaje, then continues another 12.8 km (eight miles) before terminating at Mexico 19 near Playa Los Cerritos south of Todos Santos. Two INEGI topo maps, San José del Cabo F12B44 and La Candelaria F12B43, would make helpful—though not required—companions on this cross-sierra road trip.

East Cape

The Cabo del Este (East Cape) consists of a succession of scenic arid-tropical coves and beaches extending from the northern end of Bahía de Palmas south to San José del Cabo, at the tip of the Cape.

Beach camping is available along almost the entire length of the coast, although the area is developing gradually and some of the prettiest beaches now bear small-scale housing developments. Coastal development, in fact, is ongoing from Buena Vista all the way around the Cape to Cabo San Lucas, with land prices skyrocketing in recent years. Fortunately, a few choice spots remain where the fishing (some of the best in the world) and camping are free. The coastline north of Los Barriles as far as Bahía de los Muertos remains relatively untouched.

> *World-famous Tuna Canyon reaches depths of 50 fathoms and has a year-round population of sizable yellowfin tuna; rocks along Tuna Canyon's submerged walls tend to cut the lines of all but the most skilled sportfishers.*

BAHÍA DE PALMAS

The gently curving shore of Bahía de Palmas, stretching 32 km (20 miles) from Punta Pescadero south to Punta Arenas, began its commercial life in the 1960s as a fishing resort accessible only by yacht or private plane. Now that the Transpeninsular Highway swerves to within a couple of miles of the bay, it has become a full-fledged drive-in fishing and windsurfing mecca.

In many places along the bay, anglers can reach the 100-fathom line less than a mile from shore, especially toward Punta Pescadero (Fisherman's Point) at the north end. Billfish frequent the area June–Dec., yellowtail Jan.–June, and roosterfish, wahoo, tuna, and dorado year-round (best in summer, however). Inshore catches include pargo, cabrilla, grouper, amberjack, wahoo, and pompano, plus the occasional yellowtail or rooster. The world-famous "Tuna Canyon," about 6.5 km (four miles) directly south of Punta Pescadero, reaches depths of 50 fathoms and has a year-round population of sizable yellowfin tuna; rocks along Tuna Canyon's submerged walls tend to cut the lines of all but the most skilled sportfishers. Guided fishing trips can be arranged at any of the hotels along the bay; the cost is generally US$80–150 a day for a *panga,* US$200–325 a day aboard a fishing cruiser. You can launch trailered or cartopped boats off sandy beaches or at the boat ramp just north of the Hotel Buena Vista Beach Resort (see Buena Vista, later in this chapter).

Sailboarders flock to Los Barriles Nov.–Apr. when sideshore winds—collectively called El Norte and aided by thermals from the Sierra de la Laguna—blow 18–30 knots for weeks at a time. The rest of the year, you'll have to settle for around 12–14 knots—not too shabby. During the high-wind season, inshore water temperatures average 22–24°C (72–75°F), with air temperatures in the 25–29°C (78–85°F) range. The same basic conditions can be found all the way north to El Cardonal. Several hotels on the bay rent windsurfing equipment and provide basic instruction.

With such favorable recreational conditions, it's little wonder legions of *norteamericano* anglers, boaters, and sailboarders are buying up property along the bay to build vacation and retirement homes. The Barriles–Buena Vista area is starting to look like a San Diego suburb. Several roads branch east off Mexico 1 between Km 110 and 105 to hotels and trailer parks—most owned by foreigners—scattered along the central section of Bahía de Palmas. Because zoning regulations are virtually nonexistent, construction varies from flimsy palapa extensions to impressive beach homes. Construction trash is unfortunately a common sight; in some spots an unmistakable stench indicates improper installation of cesspools. Those seeking more solitude and less development can head north of Los Barriles to Punta Pescadero at the northern end of Bahía de Palmas or farther north to El Cardonal.

PUNTA PESCADERO AND EL CARDONAL

The sandy, washboard road to Punta Pescadero and El Cardonal heads north from Los Barriles—look for a turnoff from Mexico 1 signed El Cardonal. The road crosses a couple of arroyos that could be problematic in heavy rains.

Punta Pescadero

At the extreme north end of Bahía de Palmas (13.6 km/8.5 miles north of Los Barriles), **Hotel Punta Pescadero,** Apdo. Postal 362, La Paz, BCS 23000, tel. 612/141-0101, U.S. tel 800/426-BAJA (800/426-2252), U.S. fax 949/766-6677, www.punta-pescadero.com, is a small fishing resort on 125 palm-studded acres overlooking a sandy beach. Each room comes with a sea view, private veranda, air-conditioning, satellite TV, and refrigerator; some have fireplaces (quite nice on winter evenings). The resort features a restaurant and bar, dive shop with compressor, small pool, lighted tennis court, nine-hole golf course, landing strip (1,065 meters/3,500 feet, Unicom 122.8), and rental equipment for scuba and free diving, boating, and fishing. Petroglyphs are visible in nearby rock caves that once served as Amerindian burial sites. The unpaved side road out to the actual point is not recommended for RVs or trailers. A housing de-velopment is growing up around the resort, so the Punta Pescadero's once-secluded nature is changing. Hotel Punta Pescadero can also be contacted in the United States at 31 Calle Alamitos, Rancho Santa Margarita, CA 92688. Rates: US$175 s/d, additional adult $25. Add 12 percent tax and 15 percent gratuity. Baja Bush Pilot and AAA discounts are available.

A mile north of Punta Pescadero along this same road, the little-known **Restaurant Marimar** serves simple but well-prepared seafood.

El Cardonal

Past Punta Pescadero and technically at the south end of Bahía de los Muertos is El Cardonal (23 km/14 miles from Los Barriles). Inshore coral heads here provide worthwhile underwater scenery, while nearby prehistoric cave paintings reportedly depict marlin, turtles, and human figures.

Accommodations US$25–50: The Canadian-owned **El Cardonal's Hide-A-Way,** tel./fax 612/141-0040, elcardonaleddy@hotmail.com, www.elcardonal.net, offers six tidy suites for US$60/399 per night/week as well as spaces for RV and tent camping. Each of the large beach-front suites comes with two full-size beds, a sofa, a fully equipped kitchen, ironing board, and ceiling fan. Small campers and tent camping on large campsites costs US$10 d per day; sites with electricity and water only are US$12; full hookups cost US$13 d. A dump station is available, as are fishing boats (*pangas* and a 32-foot cruiser), hot-water showers, a 24-hour restaurant, Laundromat, a public telephone, horseshoe pit, badminton court, picnic tables, ice, and rental shop with equipment for fishing, windsurfing, diving, kayaking, and snorkeling. Discounts offered for long-term stays.

Beyond El Cardonal, the road continues northward along the coast, then west across the Sierra El Carrizalito to San Juan de los Planes (see Southeast of La Paz).

LOS BARRILES

During the high-wind season, Nov.–Mar., hotels in Los Barriles can arrange package deals that include windsurfing seminars, use of state-of-the-art equipment, air transportation, and accommodations. Keep in mind that although lessons are typically geared to your level, wind and surf conditions at Los Barriles are best enjoyed by experienced board-sailors rather than novices.

For five days during the second week of January, Vela Windsurf Resort and sailboard manufacturer Neil Pryde cohost the annual **Vela–Neil Pryde Baja Championships** sailboard race at Los Barriles. The week before the competition, the center offers a race clinic staffed by world-class instructors. Spectators are welcome to watch the event from shore and to join in on the beach barbecues and partying. For more information, contact Vela Windsurf Resort (see Accommodations).

Accommodations
US$50–100: Martin Verdugo's Beach Resort, Apdo. Postal 17, Los Barriles, BCS 23501, tel. 612/141-0054, www.martinverdugos.com, an extension of the trailer park of the same name, features around 29 well-kept rooms in a two-story hotel next to the beach. Facilities include a small pool and boat launch. Kitchenettes are available. Tax and service charges are not included in the rates.

Hotel Playa del Sol, P.O. Box 9016, Calabasas, CA 91372, U.S./Canada tel. 818/591-9463 or 800/368-4334, fax 818/591-1077, is an all-inclusive hotel with 26 air-conditioned rooms (many have recently been remodeled), an oceanfront pool, tennis and volleyball courts, an outdoor terrace restaurant, bar with satellite TV, rental gear (for fishing, kayaking, mountain biking, and windsurfing), charter boats for sportfishing, and a full-service Vela windsurfing center. Rates include meals; tax and service are extra. The hotel is closed in September.

US$100–150: Vela Windsurf Resort, U.S./Canada tel. 831/461-0820 or 800/223-5443, fax 831/461-0821, info@velawindsurf.com, www.velawindsurf.com, is based at the Hotel Playa del Sol. Seven-night packages start at US$973 and include all windsurfing equipment, instruction at every level except novice, accommodations, meals, tax, and service. Guests also have free

Los Barriles windsurfers

use of kayaks and mountain bikes; the staff provides good maps and descriptions of nearby kayaking/biking routes. Snorkeling, tennis, and volleyball are also available through the center at no cost to package guests. Scuba diving, kitesurfing lessons, and horseback riding can be arranged at additional cost.

Vela opens just before Thanksgiving and closes the first week in March. Outside the center's peak period (Dec. 20–Jan. 20), nonpackage guests at Hotel Playa del Sol may be able to rent sailboards, kayaks, and bikes.

About 300 meters south of Hotel Playa del Sol and just a half mile off the highway, the all-inclusive **Hotel Palmas de Cortez** (same contact information as the Playa del Sol) offers 50 standard air-conditioned rooms with sea views, plus higher-priced suites and 10 two-bedroom condos that sleep up to six. Rates include three meals daily. Facilities include a restaurant and bar, ping pong tables, an infinity-edge pool, tennis and racquetball courts, an 868-meter (2,850-foot) landing strip (Unicom 122.8), windsurfing gear, charter boats (US$220–350, not including fishing permits), and equipment for both fishing and hunting. Dove and quail hunting in the nearby Sierra de la Laguna is reportedly good.

East Cape Vacation Rentals, tel./fax 612/141-0381, handles rental properties in Los Barriles, Buena Vista, Punta Pescadero, and Los Frailes.

Camping and RV Parks

North of Hotel Playa del Sol are **Martin Verdugo's Beach Resort,** Apdo. Postal 17, Los Barriles, BCS 23501, tel. 612/141-0054, martinv@lapaz.cromwell.com.mx, a well-run and well-maintained park, and **Playa de Oro RV Resort,** 3106 Capa Dr., Hacienda Heights, CA 91745, U.S. tel. 818/336-7494. Both have beach frontage, dump stations, flush toilets, showers, boat ramps, laundry facilities, and full hookups for US$14 for two people, plus US$2 for each additional person. Tent sites cost US$11 a night at Verdugo's, US$10 at Playa de Oro. Verdugo's has a small pool and also operates a restaurant. It's a short walk from the beach. Playa de Oro is next to the beach and offers bonded boat storage.

Both parks can arrange fishing trips. Both tend to stay completely full during the windsurfing season, so be sure to arrange advance reservations Jan.–Mar.

On the west side of the dirt road heading north, the smaller **Juanito's Garden RV Park,** Apdo. Postal 50, Los Barriles, BCS 23501, tel./fax 612/141-0024, has trailer and RV spaces without hookups for US$8 a night and offers bonded storage. Camping spaces are also available.

North of these is **El Jardín,** tel. 612/141-0247, with 10 full hookups (no tents) for US$10 (two people).

Free primitive camping is available in the area north of these parks, usually referred to by gringos as the North Shore.

Food

Tío Pablo's, on the main north-south road through Los Barriles, tel. 612/142-1214, is a large, smartly designed palapa-style structure with ceiling fans, a well-stocked bar, sports TV, and a menu of salads, sandwiches, and burgers. It's open daily 11:30 A.M.–10 P.M. **Tío's Tienda** next door stocks grocery items as well as office supplies. **Supermercado Fayla,** just past Juanito's Garden RV Park, is more gringo-oriented.

Nearby **Restaurant and Cantina Otra Vez,** tel. 612/141-0249, occupies a long, low whitewashed building with a colorful arch out front. The restaurant features Thai and Chinese cuisine on Wednesday nights, Italian on Saturday nights, and a mix of American and Mexican the rest of the week.

In a strip mall just off Mexico 1 on the access road to Los Barriles, **The Bakery** serves gringo favorites like blueberry pancakes, omelettes, cinnamon rolls, and bagels; open daily 6 A.M.–2 P.M. **Buzzard Bay Sports Cantina,** in the same shopping center, offers a menu of burgers, sandwiches, appetizers, and Mexican food, and has both outdoor and indoor seating. Farther toward Los Barriles on this same access road, **Supermercado Chapito's** stocks basic food supplies. **Taquería Los Barriles,** at the junction with the beach road, is packed all afternoon and evening for the great seafood and *carne asada* tacos; the breakfasts are cheap.

BUENA VISTA

Accommodations

US$100–150: Old-timer **Rancho Buena Vista,** P.O. Box 1408, Santa Maria, CA 93456, reservations 805/928-1719 or 800/ 258-8200, fax 805/925-2990, info@rancho buenavista.com, www.ranchobuenavista.com, features a nice restaurant and bar facing the sea, as well as a pool, whirlpool, tennis and volleyball courts, a weight room, fitness programs, fishing tackle (including fly-fishing equipment), cruisers, windsurfing gear, a boat ramp, boat storage, unpaved airstrip, and 57 air-conditioned cottages. All meals are included; tax and service charges are not. It's easy to miss the entrance to Rancho Buena Vista if you're coming south on Mexico 1. The left turn comes just after a small mountain pass that obscures it; watch for a blue highway sign on the right that says Hotel.

Trailer Park: About two km south of Hotel Buenavista Beach Resort is the modest **La Capilla Trailer Park,** with flush toilets, showers, and full hookups for US$8 a day.

US$150–250 (All-inclusive): **Hotel Buenavista Beach Resort,** P.M.B. #86 2220 Otay Lakes, Chula Vista, CA 91915, direct resort tel. 624/141-0033 or 800/623-0710, U.S. tel. 800/752-3555 or 619/429-8079, fax 619/330-4539, info@hotelbuenavista.com, www.hotelbuenavista.com, offers 60 air-conditioned Mediterranean-style bungalows with private baths, sitting areas, and private terraces. Facilities include a garden, two pools, a swim-up bar, cocktail lounge, beachfront dining, water aerobics center, tennis courts, two whirlpool tub–powered hot springs mineral spas, spa services, kayaks, horseback riding, and equipment for diving, snorkeling, fishing, and hunting. The resort organizes various outings, such as tours of cave-paintings and waterfalls, as well as bird-watching, hiking, and snorkel tours. All meals, snacks, nonalcoholic beverages, beer, and domestic well drinks are included. Lower European plan rates are available. Tax and service extra. Fishing and diving packages are also offered.

The sportfishing fleet at the resort features a 23-foot *panga* (US$240), a 28-foot cruiser (US$350), a luxury 29-foot twin-engine cruiser (US$410), and a 31-foot twin-engine cruiser (US$450). Tax, tips, tackle, bait and fishing licenses are extra.

Round-trip or one-way transportation from the airport can be arranged in advance by the U.S. reservations office.

Food

Restaurant Calafia, on Mexico 1 near the Buena Vista police station, offers good shrimp tacos and tables with views of Bahía de Palmas. It's usually open for lunch and early dinner only. Popular **Flag's Sports Bar** opposite the Pemex isn't really a sports bar, but it has lots of libation options.

LA RIBERA

To reach the Coastal Road from the north, take the paved road signed La Ribera east at Km 93 off Mexico 1 (at Las Cuevas). This 20-km (12-mile) road passes through La Ribera (La Rivera), a small town of around 2,000 with a Pemex station, church, *tortillería,* cemetery, banana and mango trees, trailer shelters, and simple homes lining up along a network of sandy roads overlooking a sand beach. Worn palapa shelters at the south end of the beach can be used for camping when not occupied by fishermen. Several *mercaditos* in the village offer local produce and other supplies for long-term visitors.

Just north of La Ribera, in a large mango orchard near the beach, the tidy and well-run **La Ribera Trailer Park (Correcamino Trailer Park),** tel. 612/125-3900, CB channel 66, offers shady tent/camper/RV spaces with full hookups for US$12 per day. Facilities include hot showers, flush toilets, propane, bait, firewood, storage, and a boat ramp.

A sandy road just south of La Ribera Trailer Park leads .6 km (.4 miles) to a casuarina-shaded beach where you can camp for free. A point at the north end of the small bay (also accessible from La Ribera) creates a surf break during heavy southwest swells.

AROUND PUNTA COLORADA

Punta Colorada lies at the south end of the bay, 16 km (10 miles) east of Mexico 1 via the La Ribera road.

Accommodations

US$100–150 (All-inclusive): Hotel Punta Colorada, P.O. Box 9016, Calabasas, CA 91372, tel. 612/121-0044, U.S./Canada tel. 818/591-9463 or 800/368-4334, fax 818/591-1077, www.bajaresorts.com, is a favorite of roosterfish fanatics; the roosterfishing off nearby Punta Arena is usually the best in Baja. The hotel offers 29 large rooms and five newer suites with three meals daily included in the price. All tap water at the resort comes from a mountain well. The hotel also has an indoor/outdoor bar and its own airstrip (1,000 meters/3,300 feet, Unicom 122.8). Guided fishing trips are available starting at US$220 a day. The hotel is closed September and the first week of October.

US$150–250 (All-inclusive): South of Buena Vista, just north of Punta Colorada, lies the secluded **Rancho Leonero Resort,** Apdo. Postal 7, Buena Vista, BCS 23501, tel./fax 612/141-0216, or 1560 N. Coast Hwy., Levcadia, CA 92024, tel. 760/634-4336 or 800/646-2252, www.rancholeonero.com. Perched on a low promontory overlooking the sea, this comfortable, quiet, and rustic resort features 30 spacious rock-walled, palapa-roofed rooms, suites, and bungalows. All have sea views, but to emphasize Rancho Leonero's sense of seclusion and retreat, none of the rooms contain phones or TVs. The expansive grounds hold a restaurant and bar, pool, hot tub, fully equipped dive center, sportfishing fleet, and 20 miles of running/hiking trails. A rock reef in front of the hotel is suitable for snorkeling. Three meals a day are included in the room price. Fishing charters start at US$250 for a super *panga,* US$350 and up for cruisers. Snorkeling equipment is available for US$5 per day, and a snorkel tour costs US$25–50 pp. Horseback riding, kayaking, scuba, and hiking trips can also be arranged. Tax and service are not included in the rates; a US$25 discount is offered Aug.–Sept. and Nov.–Mar., excluding Dec. 20–Jan. 1.

Surfing

One of Baja's least-known surfing spots—simply because no one expects surf this far up

Punta Colorada

the Sea of Cortez—can be found at **Punta Arena,** just below Punta Colorada. A left point break can crop up here anytime during the Mar.–Nov. southwest swell, but the peak surf usually comes in late summer or early fall—*chubasco* season.

EL CAMINO RURAL COSTERO

La Ribera is the northern end of the notorious El Camino Rural Costero (The Rural Coastal Road), which runs all the way to Pueblo La Playa. About halfway along the route stands a brass plaque commemorating the road's May 1984 grading. For first-time drivers who have braved washouts and sandpits to read it, the sign never fails to elicit a few chuckles.

In general, driving conditions along the Coastal Road are suitable for passenger cars of average road clearance; even smaller RVs sometimes manage to make it all the way. Sand can be a problem in places, and shoulders are invariably soft. Weather plays an important role in day-to-day conditions; following late-summer or early-fall storms, parts of the Coastal Road can be impassable. Make inquiries before embarking on the trip and be prepared to turn back if necessary. The unpaved 77-km (48-mile) stretch between El Rincón and San José del Cabo can take up to four hours.

Eventually the Coastal Road is supposed to be paved all the way to San José del Cabo. Pavement is now slowly being laid along an interior track parallel to the current road, but not much progress has been made since the last edition of this book; rumor says it will one day hit the coast again at Bahía de los Frailes.

In spite of the rough access, certain areas along the route—e.g., Cabo Pulmo and Los Frailes—are filling up with small-scale housing/resort developments. Yet plenty of open space for beach camping is still available. Contrasting strongly with the budding resort developments toward the northern end of the route are several ranchos along the central and southern portions that raise cattle, goats, pigs, and sheep—mostly without fencing. If you substitute fiberglass *pangas* for dugout canoes, the ranchos today appear

much as they must have in 1941, when John Steinbeck described Cabo Pulmo:

> *On the shore behind the white beach was one of those lonely little rancherías we came to know later. Usually a palm or two are planted nearby, and by these trees sticking up out of the brush one can locate the houses. There is usually a small corral, a burro or two, a few pigs, and some scrawny chickens. The cattle range wide for food. A dugout canoe lies on the beach, for a good part of the food comes from the sea. Rarely do you see a light from the sea, for the people go to sleep at dusk and awaken with the first light.*

CABO PULMO

Heading south from La Ribera, the Coastal Road is paved for a short way, then turns to dirt. The unpaved portion of the 26.5-km (16.5-mile) stretch between La Ribera and Cabo Pulmo is usually in fair condition.

Bahía Pulmo

Noted for its reef-building corals, this tidy bay is bounded by Cabo Pulmo to the north and Corral de los Frailes to the south. Coarse white-sand beaches ring the bay, most of them readily accessible from the parallel Coastal Road. Baja California pearling once reached its southernmost point here.

A pristine, fine-sand beach known as **Playa La Sirenita** (Mermaid Beach, named for a rock formation whose silhouette resembles the head and bust of a female figure) lies against the north escarpment of Corral de los Frailes at the bay's southeastern tip. Best reached by small boat or kayak from the village of Cabo Pulmo, the beach's crystal waters are protected from southerly winds in the summer and early fall; rock reefs close by offer snorkeling opportunities. There's just enough room above the tideline for undisturbed overnight camping.

Farther south around the wide headland of **Corral de los Frailes** (named for a rock formation with a resemblance to hooded friars), a colony of sea lions lives among geometric boulder piles.

Take the first sand road north of Corral de los Frailes that isn't barbwired to reach **Playa Corral de los Frailes,** a secluded beach sheltered from most onshore winds.

Pulmo Reef System

The bay's reef system, the northernmost of only three coastal reefs in North America and the only coral reef in the Sea of Cortez, is rich with tropical marinelife and hence a favorite snorkeling and scuba diving destination. Its accessibility from shore adds to the attraction.

The only coral reef in the Sea of Cortez, Pulmo Reef is rich with tropical marinelife and hence a favorite snorkeling and scuba diving destination.

The reef consists of eight hard coral fingers scattered throughout the bay, from Cabo Pulmo at the north end to Corral de los Frailes at the southern end. Four finger reefs extend from the center of bayshore: two solid lengths called **Las Navajas;** an unnamed broken length used by (harmless) nurse sharks as a breeding zone; and a solid, kilometer-long finger known as **El Cantil.** Water depths along these four reefs range 4.5–10.5 meters (15–35 feet).

Farther offshore (up to 3.2 km, two miles), running more or less parallel to the bayshore, are the reef fingers of **La Esperanza** (at depths of around 18 meters/60 feet), **El Bajo de los Meros** (15 meters/50 feet), and **Outer Pulmo** (30 meters/100 feet).

Soft coral heads can be found at **El Islote**—a rock island near La Esperanza—and at **Las Casitas,** rock caves just off Corral de los Frailes at a depth of 13 meters (45 feet).

The reef system here is very delicate; reef corals can't tolerate temperatures lower than 21°C (70°F) and must have clear water since debris settling on their disks and tentacles will kill them. The reefs are important breeding grounds for several marine species, so if the corals die it will negatively impact all manner of fish in the area.

The Universidad de la Paz is currently surveying the bay for possible national-park status. Meanwhile, the Mexican government has declared Pulmo Reef an underwater nature preserve—no fishing or anchoring at the reef (or anywhere in Bahía Pulmo) is permitted. Shore development remains the reef's biggest ecological challenge, because the corals rely on unpolluted and unimpeded runoff. If resorts or housing developments further expand along Bahía Pulmo, the reef will probably perish.

Diving and Boating

Optimum visibility in the waters around Pulmo Reef occurs Mar.–Oct. Aside from the natural reefs cited above, directly off Cabo Pulmo (the cape itself) lies the wreck of *El Vencedor,* a tuna boat that sank in 1981 and now forms an excellent artificial reef. Pilot whales are commonly seen in the vicinity in April, large jack crevalles Aug. and Sept.

Ask for personable José Luis Murrieta in Cabo Pulmo if you're interested in a guided dive or boat service. His **Pepe's Dive Center,** Cabo Pulmo–La Ribera, BCS, tel. 877/733-2252, offers a complete diving service (including equipment rentals and airfills) to 14 dive sites in the area. Another small dive center—**Cabo Pulmo Divers,** cabopulmodivers@yahoo.com—also operates out of Cabo Pulmo. Rates at both run an economical US$55 pp for a one-tank dive tour, US$75 for a two-tank tour, US$30 for snorkeling tours, and US$55 for night dives (most tours don't include all gear in these prices). Pepe's English-speaking crew offers a PADI-approved scuba resort course for US$80 or full scuba certification for US$375. Rentals are available at US$10 per snorkel set, US$12 for a scuba tank, and US$10 per regulator or BCD. For US$50 a day you can rent full scuba gear and a kayak from Pepe's for self-guided beach diving.

The dive operators are also happy to arrange boat trips for nondivers interested in touring the bay, Playa La Sirenita, and the Corral de los Frailes seal colony.

Fishing

Neither sport nor commercial fishing is permitted in Bahía Pulmo, but inshore north of Cabo

Pulmo anglers can find giant seabass, snapper, pargo, ladyfish, and roosterfish. Offshore are grouper, sierra, skipjack, dorado, marlin, and tuna. The tuna are found closer in at Bahía de los Frailes farther south, but anywhere along this coastal stretch the heavyweights can come within three km (two miles) of the shoreline. Peak months for most varieties are May, June, October, and November.

Accommodations and Camping

US$50–100: In the midst of Cabo Pulmo village, **Cabo Pulmo Beach Resort,** P.O. Box 774, Ketchum, ID 83340, local tel./fax 612/141-0244, U.S. tel./fax 208/726-1306 or 888/99-PULMO (888/997-8566), www.cabopulmo.com, offers 25 palapa-roofed, solar-powered *cabañas* by the day, week, or month. The bay is just a short walk from each. The choice of accommodations here includes a beach house that accommodates 4–6 persons, *casitas,* and basic and deluxe bungalows; all come with kitchenettes or full kitchens, plus all bed and bath linens. Some feature patios, decks, or barbecue grills. Monthly rates available. In addition, the resort offers guided snorkeling (US$35—snorkel rental only is US$15); scuba diving (one-tank dive US$50, two tanks US$65), kayaking (US$35–50), tennis, fishing, hiking, and rock climbing.

US$250 and Up: Just north of Cabo Pulmo Beach Resort stands **Villa and Casa del Mar,** P.O. Box 226, Ketchum, ID 83340, tel. 208/726-4455 or 888/225-2786, fax 208/726-2529, info@bajaparadise.com, a large, deluxe beachfront house with a full kitchen, spacious living areas, shaded terraces, and a rooftop sundeck. All rooms come with fan and air-conditioning, which must be run sparingly since the house is solar-powered. The main part of the house rents for US$325 a night or US$2,250 per week in peak season. These rates apply for up to four guests. A smaller attached studio apartment costs US$145/night or US$995/week. A newer, self-contained cottage called El Nido goes for US$185/night or US$1,250/week and includes a fully equipped kitchen. During the Christmas and New Year's holidays, these rates increase a bit.

You can camp for free on the beach at the south end of Bahía Pulmo, or for US$2 per night at the north end.

Food

Nancy's Restaurant and Bar, a rustic collection of tables beneath a palapa shelter (adjacent to the resort and near the road), provides a changing menu of fish (the café's own or bring your catch), pizza, tacos, vegetable enchiladas, soups, homemade breads, cinnamon rolls, and other delights prepared by an American cook. Popular with divers during the dive season, the simple restaurant has an especially cozy ambience at night when illuminated by hurricane lamps. Nancy appreciates two hours' notice for a full-course dinner (US$12); drop in anytime for breakfast or lunch.

Tito's, a casual palapa restaurant on the opposite side of the road, provides simple fish meals, beer, and drinking water—when you can find the proprietors. **Restaurant El Caballero,** on the opposite side of the road near Nancy's, is similar.

Getting There

Most visitors drive themselves to Cabo Pulmo via El Camino Rural Costero. With advance notice, Cabo Pulmo Resort can arrange round-trip transportation from Los Cabos airport for a fee; a stop at a grocery store near the airport on the way up can be included.

BAHÍA DE LOS FRAILES

About eight km (five miles) south of Cabo Pulmo village is a sandy spur road east to gently curving, white-sand Bahía de los Frailes. With Bahía Pulmo just to the north serving as a protected nursery, onshore and inshore fishing is unusually good here. Surfcasters can land roosterfish, while boating anglers can hook yellowfin tuna, leopard grouper, skipjack, dorado, and marlin, all within a couple miles of shore.

The north end of the bay is protected from Nov.–Apr. northern winds by Cabo Los Frailes, but windsurfers will find a steady cross-shore breeze at the bay's south end. The bay plummets here as deep as 210 meters (688 feet).

According to the owner of Hotel Bahía Los Frailes, Amerindian rock art can be found inland nearby.

Accommodations and Camping
US$250 and Up (All-inclusive): Hotel Bahía Los Frailes, Apdo. Postal 230, San José del Cabo, BCS, tel. 624/145-1332, U.S. tel. 800/934-0295 (reservations), losfrailes@compuserve.com, www .losfrailes.com, offers well-constructed, nicely furnished cottages with high palapa roofs facing the south side of the bay. Three meals a day are included (beverages not included); suites are available. Deep-sea *panga* fishing, including boat and captain, runs US$195 per day (eight hours). Tackle is an additional US$15 per day, and there's an extra charge for bait when available. Add 12 percent tax and 15 percent gratuity to all rates.

Beach camping is permitted along the north end of the bay—a nominal fee of US$2–3 per site may be collected to pay for trash collection.

SOUTH TO SAN JOSÉ DEL CABO
South of Los Frailes, the Coastal Road deteriorates rapidly, but those with sturdy vehicles and steady nerves will be rewarded by secluded arroyo campsites and vignettes of disappearing ranch life. About 12.5 km (7.5 miles) south of Los Frailes is **Rancho Tule,** followed after 5.5 km (3.5 miles) by **Rancho Boca de la Vinorama.** The coastal desert scenery along this stretch can be particularly impressive, with lots of green cacti and *torotes* (elephant trees). A late-summer beach break sometimes hits at Boca del Tule, sending a few clued-in surfers scurrying across the landscape in this direction.

Just south of Vinorama, a graded dirt road heads west across the lower Sierra La Trinidad to the ranching settlement of **Palo Escopeta.** From there it continues on to meet Mexico 1 near San José Viejo, a distance of 34 km (22 miles). Although roughly the same distance as the remainder of the Coastal Road to San José, the Palo Escopeta road often rides more smoothly and quickly. Hence, unless you're heading for a specific spot along the coast between Pueblo La Playa and La Vinorama, it's normally faster to cut across the hills here to Mexico 1 rather than follow the coast.

From La Vinorama along the coast, it's another five km (three miles) and 1.5 km (one mile) southwest, respectively, to **Rancho San Luis** and **Rancho Santa Elena.** This section of road is often the most rugged along El Camino Rural Costero, with lots of soft spots and washouts. Following another 5.5-km (3.5-mile) section is the small dairy farm of **La Fortuna,** after which the road improves a bit for 24 km (15 miles) before terminating at **Pueblo La Playa,** a fishing village on the eastern outskirts of San José del Cabo.

Jutting from the coast about 10.3 km (6.4 miles) before Pueblo La Playa is **Punta Gorda,** known for good onshore/inshore fishing and, in a south or southwest swell, surfing. Surfers know the breaks here as Santa Cruz, the name of a small *ranchería* nearby (actually Santa Cruz de los Zacatitos). Beach campsites are free and plentiful in this area.

Around 10 km (six miles) offshore lie the world-famous **Gorda Banks,** a pair of seamounts that are a hot spot for marlin and wahoo fishing. *Pangeros* are sometimes available for guided fishing trips out to the banks, but it's easiest to hire someone at La Playita, the beach behind Pueblo La Playa farther on. If you have your own boat, beach launching is generally easier at La Playita. Guided scuba trips to the Gorda Banks can be arranged through dive outfitters in Cabo San Lucas.

The last couple of kilometers between Pueblo La Playa and San José del Cabo are more tropical than the entire East Cape, offering up mango trees, huge banyan trees, and wild sugarcane.

San José del Cabo

Although closer to Los Cabos International Airport, San José del Cabo is a quieter, more traditional resort than neighboring Cabo San Lucas. A somewhat older tourist crowd frequents San José (pop. 25,000), leaving Cabo San Lucas to partying singles and young couples.

The Jesuit padres who founded a mission community here in the 18th century situated San José on a mesa a couple of kilometers north of the beach. Century-old brick and adobe buildings, many of them proudly restored, line the main streets radiating from the plaza and church. These are interspersed with Indian laurel trees and other greenery, making San José one of the most pleasant pedestrian towns in the Cape Region.

The architecture thins out and becomes more modern as you descend toward the beach, culminating in a golf course, condos, resort homes, and

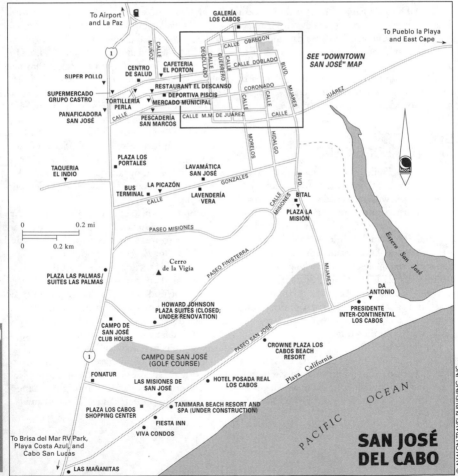

SAN JOSÉ DEL CABO

© AVALON TRAVEL PUBLISHING, INC.

the *zona hotelera*. Because of the town's mesa geography, the beachfront hotels thankfully don't obscure the view from town. Areas to the north and east of town are dotted with irrigated orchards producing mangoes, avocados, bananas, and citrus.

As the *cabecera* (roughly equivalent to "county seat") of the Municipio de San José del Cabo, the town enjoys well-maintained streets and city services. Employment in the public as well as private sector has lured a variety of talented *bajacalifornianos* to establish residence here. A number of foreigners also have retirement or vacation homes in the area, although the overall gringo presence, whether resident or visiting, is much smaller than in Cabo San Lucas.

CLIMATE

San José del Cabo's climate, influenced by the city's tropical latitude, estuarine environment, and proximity to both sea and desert, belongs in the classic tropical-arid category. Average maximum temperatures run 30°C (86°F) in January up to 40°C (104°F) in June, the warmest month. Average minimum temperatures in the winter are around 18°C (64°F), though rare readings as low as 3°C (37°F) have been recorded.

Average annual rainfall amounts to just 32 cm (12 inches). September is typically the wettest month, while virtually no rainfall is usually recorded Feb.–July. Even "wet" September usually has just three or four rainy days, with total rainfall for the month under 10 cm (four inches). Like much of the Cape Region, San José is subject to occasional tropical storms called *chubascos* Aug.–Oct. On rare occasions a storm may bring torrential downpours, as in 1993 and 2001 when *chubascos* caused serious flood damage to roads and beachside buildings.

HISTORY

The Pericú who frequented the San José area before the Spanish *entrada* called the area Añuiti, a name whose meaning has been lost. Spanish galleons first visited Estero San José—the mouth of the Río San José—to obtain fresh water near the end of their lengthy voyages from the Philip-

pines to Acapulco in the late 17th and early 18th centuries. During this period the estuary was known among seamen as Aguada Segura (Sure Waters) and, less commonly, San Bernabe, a name left behind by Sebastián Vizcaíno during his coastal navigations. As pirate raids along the coast between Cabo San Lucas and La Paz became a problem, the need for a permanent Spanish settlement at the tip of the Cape became increasingly urgent. The growing unrest among the Guaicura and Pericú south of Loreto also threatened to engulf mission communities to the north; the Spanish had to send armed troops to the Cape Region to quell Amerindian uprisings in 1723, 1725, and 1729.

In 1730 Jesuit padre Nicolás Tamaral traveled south from Misión La Purísima and founded Misión Estero de las Palmas de San José del Cabo Añuiti (or Misión San José del Cabo, for short) on a mesa overlooking the Río San José, some five km north of the current town site. Due to the overwhelming presence of mosquitoes at this site, Tamaral soon moved the mission to the mouth of the estuary, on a rise flanked by Cerro de la Vigía and Cerro de la Cruz. During the mission's first year, Jesuit records show the padre baptized 1,036 *salvajes* (savages), while at the same time establishing fruit orchards and irrigated farmlands.

Tamaral and the Pericú got along fine until he pronounced an injunction against polygamy, long a tradition in Pericú society. Wrote Tamaral about Pericú men:

> *It is highly difficult to induce them to leave the great number of women they have, because women are very numerous among them. Suffice it to say that the most ordinary men have at least two or three . . . because the larger the number of their women, the better served they are and better provided with everything necessary, as they lie in perpetual idleness in the shade of the trees, and their women work looking in the woods for wild roots and fruits to feed them with, and each one tries to bring her husband the best to be found in order to win his affection in preference to the others.*

JOHN O'BRIEN: LEGEND OF THE FLAME

A little-known episode featuring a shipwrecked Irishman footnotes San José's colorful history. Fleeing political strife in 18th-century Ireland, John O'Brien and several of his countrymen sailed to the New World—along the same route followed by Sir Francis Drake and earlier English explorers—only to become stranded at Estero San José in 1795. After marrying a local Pericú woman, O'Brien refused rescue when his father and the rest of the Irish crew were later picked up by a ship on its way back to the British Isles.

From this point in the story onward, facts merge with fable as O'Brien gained legendary status among the *bajacalifornianos* as "La Flama" (The Flame) for his red hair and fiery disposition. Also known as Juan Colorado (Red John), or more prosaically as Juan Obregón, the Irishman set out on a lifetime adventure throughout the Californias as far north as San Francisco, working as a cowboy and singing the nostalgia-tinted praises of San José del Cabo everywhere he went. For O'Brien, San José replaced the Emerald Isle as his homeland, and one imagines him crying in a shot of tequila instead of ale as he expresses his longing for "San José del Arroyo," as imagined in Walter Nordhoff's book *The Journey of the Flame:*

> On seeing our dear Valley of San José del Arroyo for the last time, with the cattle grazing everywhere, on both sides of the fertile land, on the hillsides, I remembered the violent stampedes of the wild bulls and the delicious sips of warm milk I stole, and I thought: If heaven is like this valley, I can only repeat after the Indians, "Father, lead us there!"
>
> How many times, in subsequent years, someone galloping by my side in the desert has asked me, "Where are you from, countryman?" And when I answered him "From San José!" something crept into his voice that no other place is capable of evoking when he asked: "Would that be San José del Arroyo?" Then the horses could scatter, the cattle begin a stampede, the water be a thousand burning leagues away, or death lie close by in ambush for us, and nevertheless we had to stop. Because when two who love this Arroyo Valley meet and know each other, everything else loses importance.

After Tamaral punished a Pericú shaman for violating the antipolygamy decree, the Amerindians rebelled and burned both the San José and Santiago missions in October 1734. Tamaral was killed in the attack. Shortly thereafter, the Spanish established a garrison to protect the community from insurgent natives and the estuary from English pirates.

By 1767, virtually all the Amerindians in the area had died either of European-borne diseases or in skirmishes with the Spanish. Surviving Pericú were moved to missions farther north, but San José del Cabo remained an important Spanish military outpost until the mid-19th century when the presidio was turned over to Mexican nationals.

During the Mexican-American War (1846–48), marines from the U.S. frigate *Portsmouth* briefly occupied the city. A bloody siege ensued, but the Mexicans prevailed under the leadership of Mexican naval officer José Antonio Mijares. Plaza Mijares, San José's town square, is named for him, as is Boulevard Mijares, the main avenue connecting town center and the hotel zone. As mining in the Cape Region gave out during the late 19th and early 20th centuries, the population of San José and the rest of the region decreased. A few sugarcane farmers, cattle ranchers, and fishermen began trickling into the San José area in the 1930s, and in 1940 the church was rebuilt.

San José remained largely an agricultural backwater known for its avocados, mangoes, citrus, and other fruits until the Cape began attracting sportfishers and later the sun-and-sand set in the 1960s and '70s. Since the late '70s, Fonatur (the Mexican tourist bureau) has sponsored several tourist and residential development projects along San José's shoreline. Fortunately, the development has done little to change San José's Spanish colonial character, and local residents take pride in restoring the town's 18th-century architecture and preserving its quiet, laid-back ambience.

SIGHTS

Plaza Mijares

The shady town plaza at the intersection of Boulevard Mijares and Calle Zaragoza—San José's two main streets—is a well-tended expanse of brick with benches and a gazebo. At the plaza's west end is the twin-towered **Iglesia San José,** built in 1940 on the site of the original 1730 Misión San José del Cabo. A mosaic over the main entrance depicts a scene from the infamous 1734 Pericú uprising, with Amerindians shown dragging Padre Tamaral toward a fire, presumably to be burned alive.

Most town festivals are centered at Plaza Mijares.

Estero San José

The freshwater Río San José meets the Pacific Ocean at this 50-hectare (125-acre) estuary just east of the Presidente Inter-Continental Los Cabos. A sandbar at the mouth of the river forms a scenic lagoon surrounded by tall palms and marsh grasses—habitat for over 200 species of birds, including brown pelicans, ring-necked ducks, common egrets, and herons. Bird connoisseurs should keep an eye peeled for Belding's yellowthroat, also commonly seen here. You can rent canoes at Tío Sports next to the Presidente for paddling around the lagoon.

A public footpath, **Paseo del Estero,** follows the estuary and river through scenic fan palms, river cane, and tule—a perfect place for birdwatching. The path begins at the Presidente and

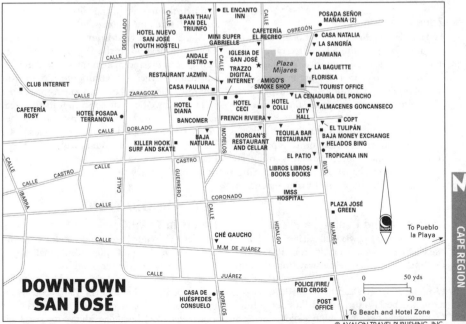

DOWNTOWN SAN JOSÉ

© AVALON TRAVEL PUBLISHING, INC.

© JOE CUMMINGS

Estero San José

comes out on Boulevard Mijares near a modern water-treatment plant.

Zona Hotelera

Fonatur has developed 4,000 shoreline acres adjacent to San José into a hotel/recreation zone. Thus far, the zone contains five resort hotels, an 18-hole Campo de Golf, a shopping center, and several condo and housing developments. Some of the nicest homes are along the north side of the golf course.

The wide, sandy beach here, known either as Playa Hotelera or Playa California, is perfect for sunbathing, but the undertow is very strong. For several years now, Fonatur has been discussing a proposal to develop a small marina along the shore here.

La Playita and Pueblo La Playa

Just east of San José via Calle Juárez, adjacent to the village of Pueblo La Playa, is La Playita (Little Beach). An ocean beach away from the hotel zone, La Playita offers *pangas* for rent and free camping. This area can be reached by walking along the beach northeast of Presidente Inter-Continental Los Cabos about a kilometer, or by walking a similar distance east along Calle Juárez from downtown. Continue along a dirt road through the middle of the village, past a radio tower, to reach the most secluded spots.

Along the dirt road from here to Pueblo La Playa and beyond to the East Cape are large banyan *(zalate)* and mango trees as well as wild sugarcane. Earlier this century much of the Río San José valley was planted in sugarcane.

Home development continues in the area. Fonatur has long been considering plans to develop a marina called Puerto Los Cabos at La Playita, a scheme that would involve building a huge semi-enclosed breakwater and completely dredging the beach to create a harbor.

ACCOMMODATIONS
Hotels in Town

Besides the major hotels and condotels in the *zona hotelera,* San José offers some smaller, reasonably priced inns in the town itself.

Under US$25: Casa de Huéspedes Consuelo, Calle Morelos s/n, just south of María de Juárez on the west side of the street, tel. 624/142-0643, is a long breeze-block building with two rows of about a dozen basic rooms. Although it's in a fairly quiet neighborhood, it's a 20-minute walk from the Zaragoza and Mijares restaurants. The rooms are nothing special, but all have attached toilets and showers, and some have air-conditioning.

The very basic but clean **Hotel Ceci,** Calle Zaragoza 22 (opposite the church), tel. 624/142-0051, contains 14 rooms with fans. At night, busy Calle Zaragoza might make this a noisy choice, but most of the noise subsides by 11 P.M. A little farther away from the heart of the tourist district but still very much downtown is **Hotel Nuevo San José (Youth Hostel),** on Calle Obregón between Degollado and Verde, tel. 624/140-0828, fax 624/142-1705. The two-story concrete building has 15 basic and slightly dank rooms with private baths. No frills, but it's decent and the staff are generally friendly. Many rooms have TV. Weekly and monthly rates available.

US$25–50: You'll find two **Posada Señor Mañana** lodging options in San José; more confusing, they sit side by side on Calle Obregón behind the plaza at the northeast edge of town, overlooking some *huertas.* A few years back, half of the original operation was bought out, including the name. The founder changed the orig-

inal name for a couple of years but has now reverted to the former appellation, thus the confusion. The original Posada Señor Mañana, tel./fax 624/142-0462, is a rambling affair; rooms are clean and a variety of group sizes can be accommodated. Just to the east sits the other Posada Señor Mañana, tel./fax 624/142-1372, www.sr-manana.net. A small pool and open palapa sitting areas with hammocks are a bonus, as is the common kitchen area with individual locked pantry cabinets. Rooms are fresh here; take a look at a few, as there is a variety. Rollaway beds are available for an extra US$10. Rates are approximately the same at both, depending on the room—some have views, sizes vary, and some are newer than others.

Friendly and economical **Hotel Colli,** on Calle Hidalgo between Zaragoza and Doblado, tel. 624/142-0725, offers 12 simple but clean and comfortable rooms in a family-run operation. This is the best deal in town under US$30. Some rooms have fans, others are air-conditioned, and all have a private bath. Similarly priced is **Hotel Diana,** at Calle Zaragoza 30, tel. 624/142-0490, a bit west of the Hotel Ceci, which has spartan rooms with air-conditioning, TV, and hot water.

US$50–100: Behind the Tropicana Bar and Grill, **Tropicana Inn,** Blvd. Mijares 30, tel. 624/142-0907, fax 624/142-1590, U.S. fax 510/939-2725, tropicana@1cabonet.com.mx, www.tropicanacabo.com, features 40 attractively decorated rooms around a tile-and-cobblestone fountain courtyard. Each room comes with air-conditioning, satellite TV, coffeemaker, minibar, and direct-dial telephone; other amenities include a swimming pool and complimentary transportation to La Playita and Playa Palmilla. Complimentary continental breakfast is served in a gardenlike pool area.

The hospitable **Hotel Posada Terranova,** on Calle Degollado just south of Zaragoza, tel. 624/142-0534, fax 624/142-0902, terranova@1cabonet.com.mx, www.hterranova.com.mx, offers good value in this range (and, during the week, rates may fall slightly below this range). It's a converted home that has been expanded to encompass 25 clean, air-conditioned rooms, each with satellite TV and two beds. Direct-dial

LA PLAYITA / PUEBLO LA PLAYA

To La Fonda del Mar B&B and Los Frailes

CALLE DELFÍN

EL DELFÍN BLANCO

LOS DOS RICARDOS

MOON

To San José del Cabo

BEER STORE

LONCHERÍA LA PASADITA

RESTAURANT/BAR EL GRINGO VIEJO

LA PLAYITA RESTAURANT

LA PLAYITA RESORT

SPORTFISHING PANGAS

0   100 yds
0   100 m

© AVALON TRAVEL PUBLISHING, INC.

Calle Zaragoza, San José del Cabo

phones are a plus (but make sure not to use the multiple-digit prefix option that allows use of a credit card, as this accesses one of the infamous price-gouging American phone companies). The inn also features a good Mexican restaurant (conveniently open 7 A.M.–10 P.M. daily) with an intimate dining room and an outdoor eating section, plus a bar.

The quiet, Mexican colonial–style **El Encanto Inn,** Morelos 133, tel. 624/142-0388, fax 624/142-4620, U.S. tel. 512/465-9751, www.elencantosuites.com, is an attractively landscaped oasis offering 19 clean, comfortable rooms, all with phones, air-conditioning, and satellite TV.

Suites Las Palmas, Mexico 1, Km 31, tel. 624/142-2131 or 800/714-2536, fax 624/142-4442, reservations@suiteslaspalmas.com, is in Plaza Las Palmas out on the highway through town. One- and two-bedroom suites come with fully equipped kitchens, air-conditioning, satellite TV, and direct-dial phones with Internet access. Guests may use the outdoor heated pool on the second floor. The surrounding plaza offers several restaurants, boutiques, shops, a minimarket, and a movie theater. Free daily beach shuttle service is available.

US$150–250: The posh **Casa Natalia,** Blvd. Mijares 4, tel. 624/142-5100 or 888/277-3814, fax 624/142-5110, casa.natalia@1cabonet.com.mx, www.casanatalia.com, is a contemporary Mexican-style hotel right off the plaza and consists of 14 deluxe rooms, two hot-tub suites, and two connecting rooms, all individually decorated with authentic artwork from San Miguel de Allende, Oaxaca, and Puebla. Besides the usual amenities found at accommodations in this price range, all rooms have private bougainvillea-covered terraces hung with hammocks. Other features include a heated pool, outdoor palapa bar, and in-room spa services. The attached Mi Cocina restaurant is open for breakfast, lunch, and dinner.

El Encanto Inn has recently opened the more upscale **El Encanto Suites** (see El Encanto Inn for contact information) diagonally across from the original. Designed in grand hacienda style, the V-shaped building wraps 14 large, elegant suites around a small swimming pool and fountain.

Beach Hotels

The hotels along Playa Hotelera are seldom full except in the peak months of December through mid-April. Friendly negotiation can often net a savings of as much as 40 percent off the usual rack rate. Rates given below do not include 12 percent tax and 10 percent service unless otherwise noted. **Tanimara Beach Resort and Spa** was under construction as this edition was being prepared. The Tanimara is reportedly going to have the largest pool in the Los Cabos area.

US$100–150: The well-maintained **Hotel Posada Real Los Cabos,** tel. 624/142-0155, fax 624/142-0460, U.S. tel. 800/528-1234, www.posadareal.com.mx, features 150 rooms and suites with air-conditioning, telephone, and satellite TV. Hotel facilities include a heated pool, swim-up pool bar, tennis courts, two seaside hot tubs, and restaurant. Most rooms offer ocean views.

Crowne Plaza Los Cabos Beach Resort, tel. 624/142-9292, U.S. tel. 866/365-6932, fax 142-9290, www.farodelcabo.com, is the newest and largest beach resort in San José, offering over 300 guest rooms as well as five restaurants, four bars, five swimming pools, two tennis courts and racquetball court. Rates are inclusive of all meals.

US$250 and Up (All-inclusive): The 153-room **Fiesta Inn,** tel. 624/142-0701, fax 624/142-0480, U.S. 800/FIESTA-1 (800/343-7821), offers a restaurant, a pool with swim-up bar, and remodeled rooms and suites with air-conditioning, TVs, and phones. Fiesta Inn offers its guests water sports, aerobics, Spanish lessons, and cooking classes. Meals are included in the room rates.

At the far northeastern end of the *zona hotelera* is the 400-room **Presidente Inter-Continental Los Cabos Resort,** tel. 624/142-0211, U.S./Canada tel. 888/567-8725, fax 624/142-0232, loscabos@interconti.com, www.loscabos.interconti.com, a well-designed resort next to the Estero San José. This resort recently completed a US$11 million expansion and renovation. Each spacious room comes with air-conditioning, satellite TV, minibar, and telephone. Amenities include three pools, two swim-up bars, three lighted tennis courts, hot tubs, a fitness center, kids' club, beach *palapas,* six restaurants, two snack bars, and auto/ATV rental. Rates cover standard accommodations, three meals a day (including buffets and à la carte dinners), open bar, service charges, free greens fees at a nearby nine-hole course, all entertainment and recreational activities, and two nighttime theme parties weekly. The resort also maintains a playground and offers special children's activities. Tío Sports next to the hotel rents ATVs and sit-on-top kayaks.

Condominiums and Condotels

Several condominium complexes in the golf course and beach area and on the hill west of Mexico 1 rent vacant units to visitors for anywhere from US$75 a night for a studio or one-bedroom unit to around US$450 for a deluxe two- or three-bedroom unit. Discounted weekly and monthly rates are usually available. Local companies that help arrange condo rentals include: **Baja Properties,** Doblado and Morelos, tel. 624/142-0988, www.bajaproperties.com; and **Dynasty Real Estate,** Paseo Finisterra 7, tel./fax 624/142-0523. Listed below are several complexes that take reservations directly.

US$100–150: Along the south edge of the Campo de Golf, **Las Misiones de San José,** tel./fax 624/142-1544, offers 82 one- and two-bedroom condos—with choice of ocean, pool, or golf-course views. All have air-conditioning, full kitchen, and private terrace.

Next to Playa Costa Azul, at Km 29, **La Jolla de los Cabos,** tel. 624/142-3000, fax 624/142-0546, U.S. tel. 800/524-5104, lajolla@1cabonet.com.mx, features 220 studios as well as one- and two-bedroom suites and condos, each with private living room, balcony with ocean view, air-conditioning, ceiling fans, satellite TV, phone, refrigerator, and coffeemaker. The one- and two-bedroom suites contain full kitchens, while studios feature wet bars. The premises hold four pools, a swim-up bar, a saltwater aquarium/lagoon, two tennis courts, a fitness center, sauna, minimarket, and restaurant/lounge.

US$150–250: At the southwestern end of the zone, a sprawling condo complex called **Las Mañanitas,** tel. 624/142-6300, U.S. tel. 877/GO2CABO (877/462-2226), fax 624/142-6222, has 42 one- to three-bedroom units, all with beach access. Amenities include a pool, barbecue grills, and hot tub; the complex features a self-contained water purification system.

US$250 and Up: Southwest of San José del Cabo proper, near Playa Costa Azul, **Mira Vista**

Beachfront Condos, tel. 624/144-5049, fax 624/142-4027, rents one-bedroom condos by the week (only).

Next door to La Jolla, white-and-blue Mediterranean-style **Mykonos Bay Resort,** tel. 624/142-0716, U.S. tel. 888/319-9070, fax 624/142-0270, rents 69 one- and two-bedroom condos, each with air-conditioning, satellite TV, full kitchen, and washer/dryer. Amenities include a snack bar, gym, and lighted tennis courts.

Bed-and-Breakfasts

US$50–100: Perched on a bluff overlooking Playa Costa Azul and the Sea of Cortez (but across the highway from the beach), **Casa Terra Cotta,** Km 29, Mexico 1, tel./fax 624/142-4250, info@terracotta-mex.com, boasts a collection of four small, private *casitas* and a trailer in a quiet garden setting. Each has a ceiling fan, private bath, and a hammock-slung veranda; from one of the cottages, Casita Azul, you can spot all three surf breaks—perfect for surfers who want to check conditions without taking a long, steep walk down to the beach. Breakfast is complimentary, and healthy à la carte meals are available for lunch and dinner. A fully equipped kitchen is available for guest use for a fee of US$10 per day.

US$100–150: Next to the public golf course, **Casa del Jardín,** Paseo Finisterra 107, tel. 624/142-1964, casa@casajardin.com, www.casajardin.com, offers four rooms in a renovated former residence. Each room is named and decorated according to a different nature theme. All room have ceiling fans, air-conditioning, and private balconies. The property is lushly planted with citrus trees, flowers, palms, and a large herb-and-vegetable garden. Guests have free run of the house (including an upstairs sitting room and downstairs living room, both equipped with TVs) as well as access to a telephone, fax, and computer. A full breakfast is served on a covered terrace overlooking the garden and swimming pool or in the formal dining room. Smoking is not permitted in the house. Weekly rates are available.

About three km north of San José, east of the hamlet of Santa Rosa and across the Arroyo del San José, lies secluded **Huerta Verde Bed and Breakfast Inn,** (U.S. mailing address 7674 Reed St., Arvada, CO 80003), tel./fax (cell) 044/1-148-0511, U.S. tel. 303/431-5162, U.S. fax 303/431-4455, www.lovemexico.com, an old ranch converted to a full-service bed-and-breakfast. Well-furnished suites are available in either a brick-and-tile building or separate cottages. Four of the suites overlook the pool and orchards. No two units are decorated the same. All have air-conditioning and ceiling fans; the separate cottage units also contain kitchenettes. Two large Mexican breakfasts are included with each unit, and light lunches and fixed-price dinners are available upon request. A small pool is on the premises. The proprietors are happy to arrange fishing, biking, or hiking trips. Call or write for directions.

La Playita

US$50–100: Northeast of San José in the village of La Playita, within walking distance of the beach in Pueblo La Playa itself, cozy **El Delfín Blanco,** Apdo. Postal 147, San José del Cabo, BCS 23400, tel. 624/142-1212, tel./fax 624/142-1199, eldelfin@prodigy.net.mx, offers quiet *cabañas* facing the beach. El Delfín Blanco also rents bicycles for US$10 per day.

La Fonda del Mar Bed and Breakfast, U.S. tel. 909/303-3918, oasis1396@msn.com (reservations), www.buzzardsbar.com, can be found three miles past La Playita toward the East Cape. Here you can choose among three simple palapa structures with comfortable beds and tile floors, all with shared bath. Breakfast for two at the adjacent Buzzards Bar & Grill (same owners) is included.

US$100–150: La Playita Inn, Apdo. Postal 437, San José, BCS 23400, tel./fax 624/142-4166, laplayitahotel@prodigy.net.mx, offers well-tended rooms each with air-conditioning, ceiling fan, TV, and large shower. The inn is just a short walk from the sportfishing *pangas* on the beach.

Camping and RV Parks

Brisa del Mar RV Park, 3.2 km (two miles) southwest of San José off Mexico 1 at Km 28 (Apdo. Postal 45, San José del Cabo, BCS), tel. 624/142-2935, brisarv@hotmail.com, is the only beachfront RV park in Los Cabos. As such, it's often full Dec.–Feb., the high snowbird season.

For two people/one vehicle, full-hookup RV slots range from US$18.50 for spaces in the back row up to US$30 for beachfront spots (US$25 Mar.–Nov.). Tent spaces cost US$12 when available (US$11 Mar.–Nov.), plus US$2 per additional guest. Weekly and monthly discounts are available. Facilities include flush toilets, showers, a laundry, pool, restaurant, and bar. Some full-timers have built studio apartments on the grounds, and these may occasionally become available as rentals. Brisa del Mar is easy to miss; watch carefully for the small sign.

You can camp free on the beach at La Playita between San José and Pueblo La Playa and between Brisa del Mar RV Park and the water.

FOOD

Most of San José's fashionable restaurants are along Boulevard Mijares and Calle Zaragoza near the plaza. These eateries are for the most part geared to Mexican diners as well as foreigners—so far the town harbors no equivalents to Cabo San Lucas's Giggling Marlin or El Squid Roe.

As a general rule, the closer a restaurant to the plaza, the more expensive the menu. To save money and experience local flavor, seek out the spots where San José residents eat—most are in the western part of town toward Mexico 1.

Alta Cocina

Restaurants specializing in Mexican foods prepared in the *alta cocina* ("high cuisine" or gourmet) style seem to have proliferated in the last few years in San José. **Tequila Bar Restaurante,** in a restored classic adobe just west of Boulevard Mijares on the south side of Doblado, tel. 624/142-1155, was the first of the high-class eateries to open. It looks small from the entryway but opens onto a sizable open-air, tree-shaded courtyard in back. The tasteful, low-key Mexican decor is enhanced by candlelight after sunset. In addition to a prime list of tequilas, the restaurant

> *The closer a restaurant to the plaza, the more expensive the menu. To save money and experience local flavor, seek out the spots where San José residents eat—in the western part of town toward Mexico 1.*

specializes in traditional Mexican dishes such as *chile en nogada* (a fancier version of the *chile relleno*) and tequila shrimp served with grilled plantain and black beans, as well as innovative Pacific Rim/Mediterranean cuisine, including seafood ravioli, Asian spring rolls with orange ginger sauce, grapefruit and avocado salad, cold linguine salad, grilled fish with mango and ginger sauce, and grilled chicken breast sautéed in peanut sauce. Moderate to expensive; open daily for dinner only. Tequila offers the occasion wine tasting, usually announced in a glass case in front of the restaurant a week or so in advance. A small attached deli serving baguette sandwiches is open Monday–Saturday 11 A.M.–4 P.M.

The upscale **Mi Cocina,** inside Casa Natalia, tel. 624/142-5100, serves nouvelle Mexican-Euro cuisine in a beautiful contemporary outdoor setting. Open daily 6–11 P.M.

The newest entry in this group is the modestly elegant **El Patio,** Plaza de Casa de Don Rodrigo along Blvd. Mijares, tel. 624/142-5508. As the name suggests, a courtyard filled with umbrellas allows for refreshing alfresco dining. The chef touts the kitchen's *"mexicanísimo"* food—*alta cocina* with a twist. In addition to standards like a good Caesar salad and bacon-wrapped filet mignon, creative Mexican dishes include barbecue-beef quesadillas with papaya salad and a memorable *"diablo"* sauce. The mushroom-and-squash-blossom soup has garnered a few kudos. Open daily for lunch and dinner.

Antojitos and Fast Food

At the west end of Calle Doblado are several inexpensive taco stands and *fruterías*. The **Mercado Municipal** features a section of side-by-side, clean *loncherías* open Monday–Saturday 6 A.M.–6 P.M., Sunday 6 A.M.–4 P.M.

Restaurant El Descanso, an outdoor palapa-roofed place on Calle Castro, diagonally opposite the Mercado Municipal, serves inexpensive *menudo, pozole, birria, barbacoa,* tamales, and

© JOE CUMMINGS

loncherías in the Mercado Municipal

other Mexican soul food 24 hours a day. Look for large vats on a wood fire. **Cafetería El Portón,** on the north side of Doblado east of Calle Muñoz, tel. 624/142-4115, offers good basic Mexican fare in clean surroundings. It's very inexpensive and very local; open Mon.–Sat. 8 A.M.–5:30 P.M.

Restaurant Las Hornillas, toward the west end of Calle Doblado, specializes in inexpensive mesquite-grilled chicken, steaks, and burgers for a mostly local clientele; open daily noon–9 P.M. **Super Tacos de Baja California Hermanos Gonzales,** on the north side of Calle Doblado, west of the Centro de Salud, is a branch of the famous taco stand of the same name in La Paz. Look for inexpensive fish, shrimp, and clam tacos, with a large selection of condiments.

Another good place for tacos is **Taquería Erika,** near Mexico 1 on the south side of the street. They serve *tacos de carne asada* and *tripa,* as well as quesadillas.

Taco stands come in and out of fashion. **Tacos El Indio,** off the west side of Mexico 1 on Calle Malvarrosa (one street north of Calle González) in the Colina de los Maestros neighborhood, is one of the stalwarts. El Indio offers very good corn on the cob *(elotes), tacos de carne asada,* que-sadillas, *frijoles charros, cebollas asadas,* and pota-toes *(papas),* with choice of shrimp, mushrooms, steak, or corn. Lots of fresh condiments. Inex-pensive; generally open 6 P.M.–midnight.

El Mesón del Ahorcado, on Calle Barlovento west of Mexico 1 almost across from Ferro Gases de los Cabos, is a funky, rustic outdoor place with a full selection of quesadillas (including *huitlacoche,* mushrooms, squash-flower, and cac-tus fillings), tacos, *frijoles charros, champurrado,* and *café de olla.* Despite the fancy name, the restaurant's design can best be described as "flea-market junk decor." Look for a stuffed scare-crowlike effigy hanging outside. Open 6–11 P.M.

La Picazón, tel. 624/147-3857, just east of the bus terminal on Calle González, serves good, basic *antojitos* at low prices in a pleasant outdoor palapa atmosphere. You can get *taquitos, tacones* (wraps), quesadillas, and even good burgers; more substantial fare includes chicken, lots of seafood, and steaks. It's popular with the locals; open Mon.–Sat. for lunch and dinner.

Cafetería Rosy, a small, humble Mexican café on Calle Zaragoza, is nicer on the inside than it looks on the outside. In addition to tacos (choice of beef, shrimp, fish, or chicken), the friendly family-run kitchen serves all sorts of well-prepared Mexican breakfasts, including *machaca, chilaquiles, molletes,* hotcakes, and French toast, along with fresh-brewed coffee. Inexpensive; open daily 8 A.M.–5 P.M.

Super Pollo, perched on a rise overlooking the west side of the highway just north of Supermercado Castro, is a branch of Mexico's widespread chicken chain. This one outdoes itself with tasty roast chicken and out-of-this-world roasted banana chilies. Inexpensive; open daily 10 A.M.–10 P.M.

Baja Natural, on the south side of Calle Doblado between Hidalgo and Morelos, tel. 624/142-3105, serves delicious fresh juices, malts, green salads, hot dogs, veggie burgers, *tortas,* fruit salads, and other fruit and vegetable concoctions with interesting names. The *"chupacabra"* is made with blended pineapple, oranges, carrots, beets, and celery; the one-liter servings cost about US$3. Open Mon.–Sat. 7 A.M.–8 P.M.

Good fish and shrimp tacos are available at **Cafetería El Recreo,** a small stand with a few tables just north of the church on the plaza. Open for breakfast at 7 A.M., then again in the middle of the day for tacos. Inexpensive to moderate. Open Wed.–Mon. 2–9 P.M.

International

Andale Bistro, on the west side of Calle Morelos between Zaragoza and Obregón, tel. 624/142-4114, is a little bistro offering Mediterranean-influenced creations with a nice array of economical specials nightly—often one lamb and one pasta dish. An overhanging balcony is a nice spot to eat alfresco. Open daily 11 A.M.–3 P.M. and 5–10 P.M.

El Tulipán (The Tulip Tree), on Manuel Doblado just off Mijares, tel. 624/146-9900, is a casual place open for lunch and dinner. The menu features such gringo favorites as hamburgers, rib-eye steak, veggie burgers, salads, stir-fries, and pastas.

Baan Thai, Calle Morelos between Obregón and Comonfort, tel. 624/142-3344, serves good, semiauthentic Thai cuisine as well as other Pacific Rim dishes. The dining areas are nicely appointed with Asian furniture, and the

food is light and tasty, a nice break from heavy Mexican fare. Moderate to expensive. Open Mon.–Sat. noon–10 P.M.

Corre Caminos Café and Bakery, tel. 624/142-3510, is a small air-conditioned place with a few outdoor tables attached to Plaza La Misión, the small shopping plaza with Banco Bital on Boulevard Mijares. The café offers sandwiches (smoked turkey on a croissant with jack cheese, Cabo garden sandwich), subs, coffee drinks, lemonade, iced tea, smoothies, pastries, and fresh-baked breads. Moderate. Open Mon.–Sat. 7 A.M.–8 P.M., Sunday 8 A.M.–3 P.M. In the same plaza, you'll also find **Health Naturally,** tel. 624/142-0035, a health food store and juice bar where you can also indulge in massage and reflexology.

Morgan's Restaurant and Cellar, Hidalgo and Doblado, tel. 624/143-3825, brings Mediterranean culinary influences to San José del Cabo. All breads and pastries are baked on the premises, and the wine list is stellar. The separate bar makes a favorite gathering place for residents and tourists alike. Open daily 6 P.M.–midnight (dinner served till 10 P.M. only). Closed the month of September each year.

In the Plaza Los Cabos shopping center in the *zona hotelera* is **Rusty Putter Bar and Grille,** a sports bar/restaurant with some outdoor tables—the palapa-covered area is a great spot to catch a nice ocean breeze. The shopping center is a bit decayed and forlorn, but don't let that stop you; this restaurant has some great food, and prices are reasonable considering the size of the portions. The bar features live music on weekends.

Right off the plaza, **Floriska,** Blvd. Mijares 16-1, tel. 624/142-4600, is an elegantly decorated place with three separate indoor eating areas and a patio dining area in the back. The ambience is upscale and the international menu is creative, with prices to match—US$17.50–28 for an entrée. Open 8 A.M.–10:30 P.M.

The upscale **Da Antonio,** on the Estero San José, tel. 624/142-0211 or 624/142-1001, next to the El Presidente Inter-Continental Los Cabos, claims to be an authentic Italian trattoria. The outdoor tables have a view of the scenic estuary. Expensive. Open Tues.–Sat. 1–10:30 P.M.

A half block west of the TelMex tower, **Ché Gaucho,** Margarita de Juárez, tel. 624/142-1244, is an Argentine steakhouse specializing in fresh pastas, barbecued meats, and grilled steaks. Open Tues.–Sun. 2–10 P.M.

Brisa Lighthouse, the simple restaurant/bar at Brisa del Mar RV Park, serves good, reasonably priced American and Mexican food for breakfast, lunch, and dinner.

Mexican

La Cenaduría del Poncho, opposite the plaza on the south side of Calle Zaragoza, tel. 624/145-5470, is a friendly eatery housed in an old thick-walled adobe. Inside are two colorful high-ceilinged dining rooms, while up on the roof a few more tables sit under a palapa. The varied menu covers a range of mainland-style *antojitos,* including tostadas, *gorditas, pozole, flautas,* enchiladas, quesadillas, tamales, tacos, *carne asada, pollo a la plaza,* and *pollo en mole.* Inexpensive to moderate; open daily 11 A.M.–9 P.M.

Restaurant Bar Jazmín, just off Zaragoza on Morelos, opposite the *nevería,* is a once-casual local eatery now gone air-conditioned and upscale. The menu offers fresh juices and *licuados,* Mexican breakfasts, French toast and pancakes, *chilaquiles,* burgers, tortilla soup, *tortas,* tacos, tostadas, fajitas, *carne asada,* and seafood. Moderately priced; open daily for breakfast, lunch, and dinner.

Damiana, on the plaza, tel. 624/142-0499, named for the Cape Region's legendary herbal aphrodisiac, is housed in a restored 18th-century townhouse and is one of the original romantic courtyard restaurants in Los Cabos. Rooms include a tastefully decorated bar, an indoor dining area, and a patio dining area—candlelit in the evening—surrounded by lush foliage. House specialties include cheese soup, shrimp, lobster, abalone, and steak. A complimentary taste of *damiana* liqueur is served to guests upon request. Expensive. Open daily 11 A.M.–10:30 P.M., serving *almuerzo,* lunch, and dinner.

Tropicana Bar and Grill, tel. 624/142-1580, is a large, touristy restaurant/bar with outdoor patio, big-screen sports TV, and live music and dancing at night. The menu is basic Tourist Mex/Fake Caribbean, but the drinks are strong. Moderately priced; open daily for lunch and dinner.

The family-run **Posada Terranova,** on Calle Degollado just south of Zaragoza, tel. 624/142-0534, features a small dining room and bar as well as outdoor seating. In addition to standard Mexican dishes, the menu offers a good variety of high-quality Mexican and American breakfasts. Inexpensive to moderate; open daily 7 A.M.–10 P.M.

La Playita and Pueblo La Playa

Just east of San José via Calle Juárez, **Los Dos Ricardos,** tel. 624/142-3068, is a typical but out-of-the-way open-air seafood palapa on the road through Pueblo La Playa. Inexpensive to moderate; open 9:30 A.M.–10:30 P.M. daily except Thursday.

Palapa-roofed **La Playita,** in Pueblo La Playa near the beach, has long held a good reputation for serving fresh seafood in a laid-back, beachy atmosphere. It changes management from time to time so it unfortunately lacks consistency, but it's worth a try in case it's going through a good phase. Open nightly for dinner only; occasional live music.

La Playita Ali's International Place, the second thatched-roof building on the right as you enter La Playita proper, does fish tacos a little differently. Instead of dunking the filets in batter and deep-frying them, the cooks stir-fry unbattered fish in an onion and pepper sauce, and serve it with large flour tortillas. Ali's will also be happy to cook (or smoke) any fish you may have caught.

Going inland, just up from La Playita is **Restaurant/Bar El Gringo Viejo,** a very rustic place, then right next to that is **Lonchería La Pasadita,** serving *antojitos,* tamales, *tortas,* and tostadas.

Playa Costa Azul

Surfers, surfer wannabes, and tourists head to **Zipper's,** a round, palapa-topped beach restaurant at the southwest end of Playa Costa Azul. The menu offers tasty mesquite-grilled hamburgers, fish burgers, teriyaki chicken sandwiches, chili, *chiles rellenos,* and quesadillas. Indoor seating areas feature air-conditioning, while the large outdoor patio offers a great ocean view. Moderately priced. Open daily 11 A.M.–10 P.M.; live music on weekends during the tourist season.

Groceries

The **Mercado Municipal,** between Calles Castro and Coronado in the west part of town, provides fresh fruits and vegetables, fish, meats, a *licuado* stand, and a cluster of *loncherías;* it's open daily from dawn to dusk. **Mini Super Gabrielle,** across from La Provence on Obregón, carries typical Mexican grocery items.

More-expensive canned and imported foods, plus beer and liquor, are available at decades-old **Almacénes Goncanseco,** Blvd. Mijares 14-18 (opposite city hall); this supermarket accepts credit cards. Near the Hotel Diana on Calle Zaragoza, the **Supermercado Zaragoza** carries canned and bottled goods but very little produce. A couple of smaller grocery stores lie along the west end of Calle Zaragoza. Across from Piso 1, **Arámburo** on Zaragoza at Degollado is a basic medium-size grocery store.

On the east side of Mexico 1, just north of the west end of Calle Doblado, **Supermercado Grupo Castro** is larger and more well-stocked than Almacénes Goncanseco. Better yet is the large and modern **Supermercado Plaza,** a half kilometer north of town on the east side of Mexico 1. Both of these supermarkets can supply just about any food/liquor/ice needs.

Mini Super, in Plaza Los Cabos opposite the Fiesta Inn, carries a few imported food items along with standard Mexican fare.

Toward the west end of Calle Zaragoza is **Pastelería y Panadería La Princesa,** with a good selection of Mexican cakes, pastries, and bread. Pricier European-style baked items are available at **La Baguette,** Blvd. Mijares 10, on the east side of the plaza. Open 8 A.M.–8 P.M.

Tortillería Perla, diagonally opposite the Centro de Salud health center on Calle Doblado, sells corn tortillas by the kilo Mon.–Sat. 6 A.M.–3 P.M., Sunday 6 A.M.–1 P.M. On the west side of Mexico 1, almost opposite the west end of Calle Doblado, **Tortillería de Harina** supplies flour tortillas during roughly the same hours. Along the same side of the highway, just south of

Calle Doblado, **Panaficadora San José** has the usual tongs-and-tray baked goods.

The most convenient place to buy fresh seafood in town is **Pescadería San Marcos,** a small fish market near the Mercado Municipal on Calle Coronado.

Cafés

A great place to enjoy coffee and pastries in air-conditioned comfort is **French Riviera,** at the corner of Hidalgo and Doblado. The menu offers a long list of hot and cold coffee drinks, chai, smoothies, Italian sodas, pies, cookies, and pastries along with cigars and liquors. Open daily 8:30 A.M.–10:30 P.M.

Sweets

For Mexican-style ice cream or fresh-fruit popsicles, try **Paletería y Nevería La Michoacana** on Calle Morelos near Zaragoza across from Restaurant Jazmín. The *paletas de mango* (mango popsicles) are quite refreshing. For American-style ice cream, **Helados Bing,** on the east side of Blvd. Mijares, has a good selection.

Dulcería Arco Iris, on the north side of Calle Doblado, west of Green, and **La Bonita del Señor San José,** on the south side of Doblado east of Morelos, both feature all types of Mexican candies.

SPORTS AND RECREATION

Fishing

All hotels in the *zona hotelera* can arrange guided fishing trips. Since San José has no harbor or marina, all trips are in *pangas.* One of the more reputable outfits is **Victor's Sportfishing,** headquartered at Hotel Posada Real, tel. 624/142-1092, U.S. tel. 800/521-2281, fax 624/142-1093, www.jigstop.com/fiesta.asp. A six-hour *panga* trip for 2 or 3 persons costs US$180; bring your own food and drinks. An eight-hour trip aboard a 28- to 32-foot cabin cruiser can accommodate up to six anglers for US$385. You can also hire *pangas* directly from the *pangeros* at the beach next to Pueblo La Playa. For example, **Gordo Banks Pangas,** tel./fax 624/142-1147, U.S. tel. 800/408-1199 (reservations), U.S. fax 619/447-4098, www.gordobanks.com, rents 22-foot *pangas* for US$180 (six hours, 1–3 anglers) or 23-foot super *pangas* for US$220 (six hours, 1–3 anglers). Whether using a guide arranged through one of the hotels or at La Playita, it's best to bring your own rods and tackle as the quality of local guide-supplied gear is low.

Onshore and inshore catches include cabrilla, grouper, roosterfish, sierra, snapper, jack crevalle, pompano, and the occasional yellowtail. Farther offshore you might catch tuna, dorado, and sailfish. One of Baja's best marlin and wahoo grounds is Bancos Gorda (Gorda Banks), two seamounts about 16 km (10 miles) southeast of San José. Striped marlin are seen year-round in Cape Region waters; angling for dorado, roosterfish, and sailfish is best in the late summer and early fall.

Killer Hook Surf and Skate, on Calle Guerrero in town, tel. 624/142-2430, rents rod-and-tackle sets for US$6 a day. **Deportiva Piscis,** on the south side of Calle Castro, tel. 624/142-0332, sells fishing tackle as well as bait. Open 9 A.M.– 7 P.M.

Golf and Tennis
Though not a world-class course, the **Campo de San José** (San José Country Club, also known simply as Campo de Golf) is an attractive, nine-hole, par-35, 3,330-yard course designed for intermediate and beginning golfers. Built and well maintained by Fonatur, it's surrounded by nicely landscaped residential properties and has a sea view. This is a popular course with the locals; it does not take reservations. There are plans to add another nine holes in the near future. Greens fees are reasonable here compared to fees at the larger and more glamorous courses in The Corridor, US$33–45 for nine holes, US$55–75 for 18 holes, depending on the time of year. Club rental costs US$16.50. Bottled water and other goods may be purchased at the caddy shack. The club also features tennis courts, a pool, clubhouse, pro shop, restaurants, and a bar. There's a putting green but no driving range. Call 624/142-0900 for more information.

Kayaking
Los Lobos del Mar Kayak Ventures, based at Brisa del Mar RV Park, tel. 624/142-2983, offers several different sea kayaking itineraries, including a US$55 sunset paddle that includes a beach picnic by lantern light. A full-day Cabo Pulmo trip costs US$104 pp, including kayak and snorkeling gear, breakfast, lunch, and round-trip transportation between San José and Cabo Pulmo.

Surfing
Nearby **Playa Costa Azul** (Blue Coast Beach) boasts two good summer breaks: a short fast inside known as Zippers and a middle right point break called The Rock. At the next little bay south, almost invisible from the highway, **Playa Acapulquito** (Little Acapulco Beach) gets an outside break that sometimes connects with the Costa Azul waves in larger summer swells.

Killer Hook Surf and Skate on Guerrero at Doblado, tel. 624/142-2430, rents surfboards with leash and wax for US$15 per 24 hours. Rentals of four days or more earn a discount. A bodyboard and fins can be rented for US$10 (or bodyboard alone for US$8).

Organized Tours
Nómadas de Baja, Calle Zaragoza near the Pemex, tel./fax 624/146-9642, adventure@nomadasdebaja.com, www.nomadasdebaja.com, organizes a full range of guided expeditions throughout southern Baja. You can choose from desert hot-springs walking tour (nine hours, US$65), historic walking tours, kayak adventures around Cabo Pulmo (nine hours, US$105), snorkeling and diving (nine hours, US$140), and mountain-bike tours (2.5–5 hours, US$20–35). Rates include a bilingual guide, all related gear, lunch and/or snacks, and beverages.

ENTERTAINMENT AND EVENTS
Bars and Nightclubs
While San José doesn't offer as much of a nighttime party scene as Cabo San Lucas, neither does the town close down at sunset—although in low season it may seem that way. On Mijares, the popular **Tropicana Bar and Grill,** tel. 624/142-1580, features lounge-lizard folk music in the

© HOWARD EKMAN

mariachis performing in San José del Cabo

front room and canned music in the back. Both bars host a two-drinks-for-the-price-of-one happy hour in the late afternoon.

Morgan's Restaurant and Cellar (see Food) often hosts live music, usually jazz, in the popular and comfy bar.

Havana Supper Club, perched on a rise overlooking Mexico 1 and Playa Costa Azul, hosts live jazz nightly. Nearby **Zipper's,** at Km 28.5 near Costa Azul (see Food), is a bar and grill with live "baby-boomer music" Friday and Saturday nights.

Cinema
In Plaza Las Palmas, on the west side of Mexico 1 at Km 31, is **Cinemas Los Cabos,** a two-screen theater showing first-run movies.

Miniature Golf
Near the Rusty Putter Bar and Grille in the Plaza Los Cabos shopping center is **Caddy Shak,** an 18-hole miniature golf course.

Events
On most Saturday evenings during the Dec.–Mar. high tourist season San José hosts a fiesta in Plaza Mijares. Although it's held mostly for the benefit of tourists, lots of locals attend as well. Typical events include folk dances, mariachi performances, cockfight demonstrations, and piñata-breaking. Numerous vendors sell arts and crafts

and food; profits from food and beverage sales go to local charities and service clubs.

San José's biggest annual festival is held March 19, the feast day of its patron saint. In addition to music, dancing, and food, celebratory activities include horse races and parades.

SHOPPING
Arts, Crafts, and Souvenirs
Near the intersection of Boulevard Mijares and the road to Pueblo La Playa, about halfway between the *zona hotelera* and the plaza, is a large open-air market selling inexpensive Mexican handicrafts; it's generally open 11 A.M.–9 P.M.

Higher-quality, higher-priced arts and crafts are offered in shops along the east end of Calle Zaragoza and the north end of Boulevard Mijares. These include **Antigua Los Cabos** (handmade furniture, antiques, rugs, folk art, and ceramics), **Bye-Bye** (T-shirts and souvenirs), **Sol Dorado** (*artesanías* and jewelry), **Veryka** (Mexican crafts), **Copal** (Mexican crafts), and **La Mina** (silver jewelry).

Cigars
Amigos Smoke Shop and Cigar Bar, Calle Hidalgo, tel. 624/142-1138, features a walk-in cigar humidor and offers good Italian espresso, premium wines, and spirits. Closed Sunday.

Interior Design
In recent years San José has amassed quite a collection of shops dealing in interior design products of all kinds. **Galería Los Cabos,** on Calle Hidalgo north of Obregón, sells a unique assortment of antique and rattan furniture, stoneware, crafts, decorator items, and locally made barrel-back chairs.

Casa Paulina, tel. 624/142-5555, more or less opposite Bancomer on Calle Zaragoza, sells high-quality, original home accessories and furniture—perfect for anyone looking to furnish a vacation home.

A shop offering really unique upscale home furnishings and accessories as well as design consultation is **Adobe Diseño,** Plaza Los Portales on Mexico 1, tel. 624/142-4281.

CAPE REGION

USEFUL SAN JOSÉ DEL CABO TELEPHONE NUMBERS

San José del Cabo area code: 624	Police: 060
Fire: 068	Red Cross: 066
General Hospital: 142-0013	Tourism Office: 142-2960
IMSS Hospital: 142-0180	Tourist Assistance: 078

Surf Shop

Killer Hook Surf and Skate, on the east side of Calle Guerrero at Doblado, tel. 624/142-2430, stocks surfing, snorkeling, and other water-sports equipment, as well as T-shirts and stickers. Killer Hook also has a branch opposite Playa Costa Azul, southwest of town, where you can rent surf gear.

Fishing Gear

Deportiva Piscis, on the south side of Calle Castro near the Mercado Municipal, tel. 624/142-0332, sells fishing tackle and bait *(carnada)*.

Clothing

Next to **Killer Hook Surf and Skate** on Calle Guerrero, **Clio** is a small boutique featuring fashions for young women. **La Sangría,** just north of Restaurant Damiana, specializes in women's clothing of original design.

Bookstores

Publicaciones May, on the north side of Calle Doblado near the street's west end, carries a large collection of books, magazines, and newspapers—though mostly in Spanish. A branch of **Libros Libros/Books Books,** tel. 624/142-4433, on the west side of Blvd. Mijares, just north of Plaza José Green, carries a good selection of English-language paperbacks, magazines, maps, books on Baja, children's books, and U.S. newspapers. Open daily 9 A.M.–9 P.M.

INFORMATION AND SERVICES

Money-Changing

Four banks in town offer foreign-currency exchange services Mon.–Fri. 8:30–11:30 A.M. The lines at Bancomer, one block west of the plaza at Calles Zaragoza and Morelos, are generally the longest; during high tourist season if you're not in line by 11 A.M., you might not make it to the foreign-exchange window before it closes.

Santander Serfín, two blocks west of Bancomer on Calle Zaragoza, usually has shorter lines, and its ATM cuts the queue even further. **HSBC,** in a small relatively new shopping center on Boulevard Mijares, just south of Calle Misiones, also offers exchange services. A **Banamex,** in Plaza José Green on Blvd. **Mijares,** south of Coronado, also has an ATM.

Baja Money Exchange, on the east side of Blvd. Mijares just north of Helados Bing, changes cash and traveler's checks at a low exchange rate. The major hotels also gladly take your dollars at a low exchange rate. Stick to the banks if you want the most pesos for your dollar.

Post and Telephone

San José's post and telegraph office, on Blvd. Mijares, is open Mon.–Fri. 8 A.M.–5 P.M. Next to the post office, the Telecomm office sends and receives Western Union telegrams.

Mail Boxes Etc. maintains an outlet at Plaza Las Palmas (Km 31 on Mexico 1), tel. 624/142-4355, fax 624/142-4360. MBE carries mailing supplies, postage stamps, and magazines and rents mailboxes.

The public telephone office on Calle Doblado, opposite the hospital, offers direct-dial long-distance phone service. Ladatel booths, the most convenient public phones for making international calls, can be found at Calles Doblado and Muñoz and on Calle Hidalgo between Obregón and Comonfort.

Internet Services

One of the best-operated Internet centers in

town, **Trazzo Digital Internet,** Zaragoza 24 between Hidalgo and Morelos, tel. 624/142-0303, fax 624/142-1220, info@trazzodigital.com, was also the fastest when we last checked. Trazzo also offers copies, printing, and scanning.

Laundry
Laundería Vera and **Lavamatica San José,** both on Calle Gonzáles east of the bus terminal, offer washing, drying, and folding services Mon.–Fri. 8 A.M.–8 P.M.

Canadian Consulate
The office of the Canadian consulate is on the second floor of Plaza José Green, Blvd. Mijares, tel. 624/142-4333, fax 624/142-4262, loscabos@canada.org.mx. Open Mon.–Fri. 9 A.M.–1 P.M.

RV Service and Supplies
Wahoo RV Center, near the CFE electric utility office in Colonia Chula Vista, off Mexico 1 (turn west between the Super Pollo and the turnoff for the Pemex station), tel./fax 624/142-3792, sells RV parts and accessories, does maintenance and repairs—including air-conditioning and refrigeration—for trailers and motorhomes, and offers the use of a dump station. It's open Mon.–Fri. 8 A.M.–1 P.M.

COTP
Although it's unlikely any international boaters will be needing a captain of the port since there are as yet no marinas or harbors in San José del Cabo, the town does have its own *capitanía del puerto,* tel. 624/142-0722. The office sits at the east end of Calle Doblado after it crosses Boulevard Mijares.

SEMARNAT
A *subdelegación* office of the Secretaría de Medio Ambiente y Recursos Naturales (SEMARNAT), the government organ responsible for ecological protection, can be found at the southwest corner of Calle Obregón at Morelos.

Storage
Los Cabos Mini and RV Storage, tel. 624/142-0976, cell 044/1-147-3117, U.S. tel. 310/924-5853, offers locked, garage-style storage units within a fenced and lighted complex with 24-hour security. One of the few services of its kind anywhere in southern Baja, the storage facility can be found at Km 37 on Mexico 1 (about five km south of Los Cabos International Airport).

TRANSPORTATION
By Air
Los Cabos International Airport (SJD), 12.8 km (eight miles) north of San José del Cabo via a speedy four-lane section of Mexico 1 at Km 44, tel. 624/142-5111, serves both San José and Cabo San Lucas. An official port of entry, Los Cabos's paved 2,195-meter (7,200-foot) runway is tower-controlled (Unicom 118.9) and can receive DC-10s and 747s. Aviation fuel is available.

Two terminals now serve this airport. The old terminal holds a few food kiosks (Dominos Express, Subway Sandwiches, Dunkin Donuts, and Carnation Ice Cream), two snack bars, souvenir shops, a money-exchange service, and an upstairs restaurant but has no seats in the waiting area for arriving flights—a minor inconvenience for those meeting incoming passengers. This terminal is served by eight airlines: Aero California, Aeroméxico, Aerolitoral, Allegro, American Airlines, America West, Continental, and Mexicana.

Aero California's offices are in the Centro Comercial Plaza and in Plaza Náutica in Cabo San Lucas. Mexicana and Aero California also have ticket counters at Los Cabos airport; Continental and most others handle ticket sales only at the airport.

Aero California, tel. 624/143-3700 or 800/685-5500, offers daily flights to Los Cabos from Los Angeles, Guadalajara, and Monterrey.

Mexicana, tel. 624/146-5001/2 (airport), U.S. tel. 800/366-5400, www.mexicana.com.mx, fields daily flights to Denver, Mexico City, Guadalajara, Mazatlán, and Los Angeles.

Aeroméxico, tel. 624/146-5097, 624/146-5098, or 800/021-4010, U.S. tel. 800/237-6639, www.aeromexico.com, has flights from San Diego, Ontario, Los Angeles, and Mexico City; its subsidiary **Aerolitoral** handles most connecting flights.

American Airlines, tel. 624/146-5300, U.S. tel. 800/433-7300, www.aa.com, flies from Dallas/Ft. Worth daily (with a direct flight to Chicago in high season), while **Continental,** tel. 624/146-5040 or 624/146-5050, U.S. tel. 800/231-0856, www.flycontinental.com, offers nonstops between Houston and Los Cabos daily, as well as weekly flights to/from Newark Dec.–Apr. **America West,** tel. 624/146-5380, U.S. tel. 800/235-9292, www.americawest.com, offers daily nonstop flights from Phoenix and connecting flights from Seattle and many other U.S. cities. **Allegro,** Mexico tel. 800/715-7640, U.S. tel. 877/443-7585, reservations@allegroair.com.mx, www.allegroair.net, offers flights between Los Cabos and Tijuana, Guadalajara, Mexico City, and other Mexican destinations. Operating out of the new terminal, **Alaska Airlines,** tel. 624/146-5210 or 624/146-5212, U.S. tel. 800/252-7522, www.alaskaairlines.com, schedules nonstop flights to Los Cabos from Los Angeles, San Francisco, San Jose, San Diego, Seattle/Tacoma and Phoenix, with connecting flights from Portland and other cities. Alaska sells tickets only in the Los Cabos area at the airport. **Delta,** Mexico tel. 800/902-2100, U.S. tel. 800/221-1212, www.delta.com, offers a daily direct flight to/from Atlanta.

There are no seats in the waiting area for arriving flights at the new terminal, except at the small bar. The second level of the new terminal—for departing passengers only—has a couple of snack bars, a restaurant, a bar, and several relatively upscale shops.

Airport Transportation: A *colectivo* (shared) van into the San José area runs US$12 pp, US$14 to the mid-corridor area, and US$15 to the Cabo San Lucas area. A private taxi from the airport to any destination in San José del Cabo costs US$35, or US$70 to Cabo San Lucas.

Auto rental agencies with airport booths include Budget, National, Avis, Hertz, Dollar, and Thrifty. National, Thrifty, and Budget rent their cars from offices opposite the old terminal. National has offices in downtown San José.

By Bus

From San José's main bus station on Calle González, tel. 624/142-1100, Águila/ABC runs

15 buses a day to La Paz (US$12), with four buses a day from 7 A.M. and 3 P.M. continuing to Pichilingue for the ferry and six buses to Cabo San Lucas (US$2.50). The last bus to Cabo San Lucas leaves around 7 P.M. There is also hourly bus service between Cabo San Lucas and San José via the Flecha Verde and Estrella de Oro bus lines. The blue-and-orange Subur Cabo buses run between the two towns for US$2.50. It's easy to pick them up anywhere along Mexico 1. Officially, they're supposed to run till around 10 P.M.

Each day at 4 P.M., a first-class bus also leaves for the 24-hour trip to Tijuana (US$125), with stops in Ciudad Constitución (US$25), Mulegé (US$35), Loreto (US$33), Guerrero Negro (US$57), and Ensenada (US$90). The bus station contains a small cafeteria and a *licuado* stand.

By Rental Car

Auto rental agencies with desks at Los Cabos International Airport as well as offices in or near town include: **Avis,** tel. 624/146-0201, U.S. tel. 800/331-2112, www.avis.com.mx; **Budget,** tel. 624/146-5333, U.S. tel. 800/527-0700, www.budget.com.mx; **Dollar,** tel. 624/142-0164, U.S. tel. 800/800-4000, www.dollar-rentacar.com; **Hertz,** tel. 624/143-1396, U.S. tel. 800/654-3131; **National,** tel. 624/143-1818, U.S. tel. 800/328-4567; **Advantage Rent-a-Car,** tel. 624/142-3990; and **Thrifty,** tel. 624/146-5030, U.S. tel. 800/367-2277.

Most agencies allow you to pay rental plus a per-kilometer charge, or pay a higher price with free kilometers. All the companies appear to charge roughly the same rates, from US$26 per day plus US$.20 per kilometer for a subcompact up to US$50 per day plus US$.30 per kilometer for a Jeep, or US$50 per day with free miles for the same subcompact up to US$85 a day with free miles for the Jeep. (Of course, lots of larger vehicles are available, whose prices rise in direct proportion to size.) Some companies also offer a "topless" or open-air VW bug or Chevy Pop for US$25 a day (US$150 per week), including unlimited free kilometers.

In town, Dollar has an office at the corner of Mexico 1 and González, and both National and Advantage Rent-a-Car have offices on Zaragoza along with offices along Mexico 1 and at many hotels in the *zona hotelera*. Thrifty has an office along Paseo San José (no. 2000-A), Payless has an office in Plaza Garufi along Paseo San José, while Avis has an outlet in the Hotel Meliá and numerous others in The Corridor. In general the best place to cut a deal on a rental car is at the airport booths, where you can look at price lists and compare one agency with another. Often you can negotiate the rental price downward.

By Taxi

Visitors staying in town or at the beach are able to see most of what San José has to offer on foot. If you tire of walking, cabs are available; typical taxi fares are US$3.50 from the *zona hotelera* to the plaza downtown, US$4–5 from downtown to Pueblo La Playa, US$33 from town to Los Cabos airport, and around US$35 all the way to Cabo San Lucas. Taxis congregate in front of the bus station, the beach hotels, and along Boulevard Mijares toward the plaza. A taxi stand signed Sitio San José can be found on Boulevard Mijares, just south of Plaza José Green.

The Corridor

The Transpeninsular Highway's 29-km (18-mile), four-lane stretch between San José del Cabo and Cabo San Lucas provides access to numerous beaches, coves, points, and tidal pools along the Pacific Ocean/Sea of Cortez. It's known officially as the Corredor Náutico (Nautical Corridor), or more commonly in English simply The Corridor. The whole strip is sometimes referred to as Costa Azul or "Blue Coast," although this is also the name of a single beach near San José.

This section of Mexico 1, four lanes all the way, represents one of Mexico's finest non-toll routes. However most of the roads branching south of the highway are unpaved. Almost all can be negotiated by ordinary passenger vehicles, though the overall number of public access roads continues to decline due to private development. Although it's illegal for any hotel or other private development to block all access to any beach along The Corridor, guarded gateways may dissuade all but the very bold. In some cases it's necessary to park along the highway or in a nearby hotel parking lot and walk down to the beach.

BEACHES AND ACTIVITIES

One after another, beautiful beaches and coves hug the coastline between San José and Cabo San Lucas. Some are hidden from highway view by bluffs, others are marked by resort development.

To find these beaches, follow the blue-and-white signs along Mexico 1, sometimes labeled Acceso a Playa but more often than not simply bearing a simple outline of a snorkel mask or swimmer. The accompanying key lists all beaches accessible from the highway.

Swimming

Not all of The Corridor's beaches are suitable for year-round swimming. Starting from the San José end, one of the best is **Playa Costa Azul**, where a long strip of sand next to the Mykonos and La Jolla condo developments is gently washed by low breakers (except during the *chubasco* season—see Surfing). A restaurant/bar called **Zipper's** serves food and booze.

Playa Palmilla at Km 26 is a decent swimming beach—local kids dive here for golf balls that have dropped into Neptune's realm from the Palmilla Golf Club Ocean Course links. **Restaurant-Bar Pepe's** at Km 27, tel. 624/144-5040, will cook your catch for a few dollars, or you can rely on the restaurant's own dependable source of seafood. **Victor's Sportfishing** can be booked at Pepe's as well.

Farther southwest, a new breakwater has tamed the waters along **Playa El Mirador,** a lengthy stretch of beach north of the Hotel Meliá Cabo Real and part of Bahía El Bledito. Look for an access road just north of Km 20. As the huge Cabo Real development expands, public access may change, though hopefully access won't be (illegally) denied.

A little more than halfway to Cabo San Lucas,

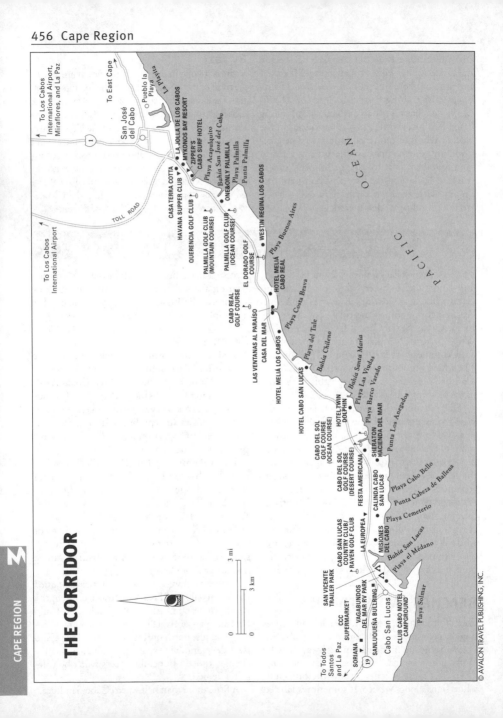

THE CORRIDOR

CAPE REGION

© AVALON TRAVEL PUBLISHING, INC.

BEACHES ALONG THE CORRIDOR

Beach	Marker	Meters West of Nearest Km Marker (in meters)
Costa Azul	29	500
Acapulquito	27	800
Playa Palmilla	26	400
Punta Bella	24	400
Buenos Aires	22	400
El Mirador	20	—
San Carlos	19	—
El Zalate	17	500
Costa Brava	17	100
Cantamar	16	700
Del Tule	15	400
Punta Chileno	14	—
Santa María	12	200
Las Viudas (Twin Dolphin)	12	500
Barco Varado (Shipwreck)	9–10	—
Cabo Bello	5–6	200
Cemeterio	4	—

the wide crescents of sand rimming Bahía Chileno and Bahía Santa María constitute two of The Corridor's most popular and accessible swimming beaches. **Playa Chileno** is larger and more well-endowed with public facilities. Visitors walk through a gate in the chain-link fence protecting the beach from vehicles and follow a path through a grove of fan palms to reach the beach itself. The palms provide natural shade, a component lacking at most other Corridor beaches. Free public restrooms and showers are available, while Cabo Acuadeportes rents water-sports equipment from a booth at the south end of the beach. Beneath the houses perched on headlands at either end of the bay are rocky areas with good snorkeling. Though very picturesque and suitable for swimming, **Playa Santa María** offers a smaller beach and is short on facilities and shade; it's a beach best enjoyed by snorkelers and divers rather than swimmers. Both Chileno and Santa María enjoy an extraordinary abundance of marinelife.

Playa Las Viudas (Widows Beach), more commonly known as Twin Dolphins Beach, is reached via a rough sand turnoff at Km 12 next to the private entrance to the Hotel Twin Dolphins. Vehicles with high road clearance will fare better than ordinary sedans. The tan-colored beach—actually several scalloped beaches separated by small rocky points—tends to be on the pebbly side, though the swimming is usually excellent.

Northeast of Cabo San Lucas at Km 4, little-known and uncrowded **Playa Cemeterio** offers calm swimming and white sands.

Just northeast of the Meliá Cabo Real at Km 19.5 is the upscale **La Concha Beach Club and Restaurant,** tel. 624/144-0102. This beautiful secluded spot consists of three small, curving,

© JOE CUMMINGS

Bahía Chileno

sand-fringed bays. The club offers a splash pool, showers, beach umbrellas, and beach chairs and rents towels and snorkeling equipment. The restaurant serves international cuisine and is open for lunch and dinner 11 A.M.–10 P.M. daily. Instead of an entrance fee, there's a reasonable food-and-drink minimum purchase requirement (easily achieved in the club's well-run open-air dining areas). It's forbidden to bring in pets, ice chests, or food from the outside. Open daily 10 A.M.–10 P.M.

Surfing

Although Los Cabos is less famous than Baja's northern and central Pacific coast for surf, the summer southwest swell brings consistent wave action to the tip of the peninsula, when most of the west coast points are flat. The surf reaches peak height during the *chubasco* season, late summer to early fall. The most dependable surfing area between San José and Cabo San Lucas is **Playa Costa Azul,** at Km 29–28, where a grinding shore-breaker called Zippers is sometimes backed by Hawaii-style outside breaks in heavy swell. See Surfing under the San José del Cabo section for further detail.

Punta Palmilla, below the One&Only

Palmilla at Km 28–27, whips out a sometimes large right point break, while the bay to the point's immediate north, **Playa Acapulquito,** between Costa Azul and Palmilla, offers a good reef break in heavy swell.

Reef breaks sometimes occur at **Playa Buenos Aires,** Km 22 (beware strong rips), and at **Playa Cabo Real,** Km 20; then there's a gap until **Playa Cantamar** at Km 16 and **Punta Chileno** at Km 14, both offering workable point breaks. To reach Cantamar—which is often confused with **Playa El Tule** (also known as Puente del Tule)—you need eagle eyes. Coming from Cabo San Lucas in your own vehicle (the turnoff is accessible only from this side of the highway), cross Arroyo El Tule and then immediately turn right off the highway as the road begins to rise toward the Solidaridad monument. Here look for a small dirt road through a gate in a barbed-wire fence (usually open), after which a sand road leads around to the northeast end of Puente El Tule, a good spot to park and camp.

In summer, a good-sized, well-shaped right point break sometimes forms off **Playa Barco Varado,** Km 9—access comes just northeast of the turnoff for the Cabo del Sol golf course/hotel complex. This site seems to have missed the attention of the Baja surf reports and west-coast surfing magazines.

Playa Cabo Bello, between Km 6 and 5 (near the Hotel Cabo San Lucas), is known for a consistent left point break nicknamed Monuments for the H-shaped concrete monument that used to stand next to the highway near here. This break is fueled by northwest swell refracted off Cabo San Lucas and is the easternmost break for winter surfing. During heavier swell it may be joined by an outer reef break.

Most of these beaches now feature some sort of condo or resort development in progress, but there's always a way to drive through or around them: it's illegal to restrict public beach access.

> *Even if you have no plans to spend upwards of $250 to stay in the area, hotel restaurants or bars are well worth a visit for a meal, drink, or simply the ocean view.*

Diving

Several beaches along The Corridor feature rock reefs suitable for snorkeling and scuba diving, particularly **Playa Santa María** (Km 12), **Playa Chileno** (Km 14), and **Playa Barco Varado** (Shipwreck Beach, Km 9–10). Santa María offers rock reefs at either end of a protected cove at depths of 13 meters (40 feet) or less. The north point displays sea fans and gorgonians, along with the usual assortment of tropical fish. The south end has sea caves, coral outcroppings, and large rocky areas inhabited by reef fish and lobster.

The remains of the Japanese tuna boat *Inari Maru No. 10,* stranded on rocky shoals in 1966, is the main diving destination at Shipwreck Beach. A local story says that when Cabo *pescadores* noticed the Japanese vessel fishing illegally, they extinguished the nearest lighthouse beacon and rigged a light of their own that lured the boat onto the shoals after nightfall. The hull and other wreckage lie 2–26 meters (6.5–85 feet) underwater, near scenic rock reefs. Tidal pools along Shipwreck Beach support starfish and sea urchins.

HOTELS

The priciest and best-situated hotels in Los Cabos grace the coast along The Corridor. De-

signed to appeal to the well-heeled hedonist seeking a degree of privacy and seclusion not found in Mexican beach resorts like Puerto Vallarta, Cancún, Mazatlán, or Acapulco (and avoiding the hot, rainy summers elsewhere in coastal Mexico), these resorts take full advantage of their desert remoteness. Don't forget to pack your irons and woods; golf is quickly becoming as big an attraction as beachgoing and fishing now that the area boasts six world-class golf courses, with more under construction. Major resort developments are so far centered around four courses: Cabo Real, El Dorado, Palmilla, and Cabo del Sol. Welcome to Palm Springs, Mexico.

All of the resorts listed below have rates of US$250 and up, unless otherwise noted. Twelve percent tax and 15 percent service are not included in the standard rates unless otherwise noted. Even if you have no plans to stay in the area, the hotel restaurants or bars are well worth a visit for a meal or drink and the ocean view.

Cabo Surf Hotel

Hidden away below Mexico 1, just two km southwest of San José at Km 28, Cabo Surf Hotel, tel. 624/142-2666, fax 624/142-2676, info@cabosurfhotel.com, offers a small cluster of 10 recently remodeled comfortable apartments and villas overlooking Playa Acapulquito. All units come with a minibar, coffeemaker, satellite color TV, and sea-view terraces. Kitchenettes and full kitchens are available. The grounds include a large barbecue area, a restaurant/bar, hot tub, swimming pool, and plunge pool. Rates range US$165–195

One&Only Palmilla

The former Hotel Palmilla Resort received an $80 million makeover and opened as the One&Only Palmilla in early 2004. Covering 384 hectares (950 acres) of Punta Palmilla near Km 27, the resort (Mexico tel. 624/146-7000, U.S. tel. 954/809-2726 or 866/829-2977 (reservations), fax 624/146-7001, www.one-andonlyresorts.com/oao/palmilla), was the Cape's first major resort; it was built in 1956 by "Rod" Rodríguez, son of former Mexican president Abelardo Luis Rodríguez. Coconut palms, clouds of hibiscus, and sweeping sea views dominate the grounds. Facilities at the resort's new incarnation include two infinity-edge pools and a children's pool; a fitness center, yoga garden, and spa with 13 private-treatment villas; two restaurants, and a bar; and a chapel used for weddings. All 172 rooms and suites feature flat-screen satellite TV with DVD and CD player with Bose surround-sound system, state-of-the-art voice and data lines, minibar, desk, and separate sitting area. All rooms and suites are provided with personal butler service, twice-daily maid service, daily fruit delivery, and an aromatherapy menu. The One&Only Palmilla maintains its own sportfishing fleet and offers *panga* fishing trips, scuba diving, and snorkeling.

Palmilla also boasts a world-class golf course (see Golf Courses, later in this chapter).

The resort's two new restaurants are **C** (created by Charlie Trotter of Chicago restaurant fame)

and the palapa-style **Aqua Restaurant** featuring Mediterranean cuisine and a view of the sea. If the hotel's restaurants seem beyond your budget, you might at least enjoy the beach below by stopping in at **Restaurant-Bar Pepe's** on Playa Palmilla, where the first drink is on Pepe; if he's not in attendance, the first *two* drinks are on the house.

Westin Regina Golf and Beach Resort Los Cabos

Hidden from the highway by brick-hued Cerro Colorado, just past Km 22 on the Transpeninsular Highway (10 minutes' drive from San José del Cabo), the *gran turismo*-class Westin Regina Golf and Beach Resort Los Cabos, tel. 624/142-9000, fax 624/142-9010, U.S. tel. 800/WESTIN-1 (800/937-8461) or 888/625-5144, westinregina@cabonet.com.mx, www.westin.com, opened in 1994 at a cost of US$200 million, making it the most expensive hotel ever built in Mexico. Renowned Mexican architect Javier Sordo Magdaleno endowed the bold curvilinear design with a bright palette of colors abstracted from the surrounding geological, floral, and marine environment. A Zen-like rock-and-

Westin Regina Golf and Beach Resort, Los Cabos

cactus garden on a hillside overlooks a dramatic seaside pool fed by a sophisticated water-recycling system. On the opposite hillside to the immediate north of the hotel stand numerous pastel-colored time-share and residential units managed by the hotel.

All 243 rooms and suites come with sea views, large marble bathrooms with telephone, ceiling fans, air-conditioning, in-room safes, refreshment bars, coffeemakers, hair dryers, furnished balconies, satellite TVs, and international direct-dial phones.

The resort's **Restaurant Arrecifes** commands a view of the wave-battered beach below and offers an eclectic menu emphasizing Mediterranean, sushi, and seafood. A restaurant on the ground floor, **La Cascada,** specializes in Mexican and seafood. Guests have golf privileges at the Cabo Real golf course, about 2.5 km southwest. The resort also features two lounges, two lighted tennis courts, seven pools, and a new state-of-the-art European spa and fitness center.

Cabo Real

A bit farther down the highway at Km 19.5, the Cabo Real complex presides over scenic Bahía El Bledito and comprises the Meliá Cabo Real Convention Center Beach and Golf Resort, Hotel Casa del Mar, and Casa del Mar Condos, as well as the renowned Cabo Real Golf Course and the Jack Nicklaus–designed El Dorado Golf Course (see Golf Courses).

Rated a *gran turismo* resort, the **Meliá Cabo Real,** tel. 624/144-0000, U.S. tel. 800/901-7100, fax 624/144-0101, melia.cabo.real@ solmelia.com, www.solmelia.com, offers 349 well-appointed rooms and suites—refurbished in 2000 and almost all with ocean views—laid out like a squared-off horseshoe around a huge glass-and-onyx, pyramid-topped open-air lobby. Guests can swim at the beach (tamed by the addition of a rock jetty) or in the hotel's free-form pool, which is billed as the largest in Los Cabos. A spa and shopping gallery are relatively recent additions to the list of amenities. On the beach, Tío Sports rents sports equipment and organizes scuba tours/instruction. Three restaurants, including the *alta cocina* Ailem and Cafetería El

Quetzal, offer complete food service in the high style required by Sol Meliá, a hotel-management group based in Spain.

The **Casa del Mar Golf Resort and Spa,** tel. 624/144-0030, fax 624/144-0034, U.S. tel. 800/221-8808, rescasamar@caboreal.com, www .casadelmarmexico.com, is a smaller place containing 24 ocean-view rooms plus 32 deluxe one-bedroom suites with spacious bathrooms, air-conditioning, complete kitchenettes, direct-dial phones, fax machines, minibars, and in-room safes. The premises also hold a full-service European-style spa, six pools, four tennis courts, the adjacent Cabo Real Golf Club, three bars, and a restaurant. *Conde Nast Traveler* named Casa del Mar one of the top 10 Mexican Golf Resorts for 2003 and Casa del Mar was designated Central and Latin America's Leading Golf Resort by World Travel Awards 2003.

The newest Meliá property in Cabo is the **Meliá Los Cabos All Suites Beach and Golf Resort,** tel. 624/144-0202, fax 624/144-0216, ventas.melia.los.cabos@solmelia.com, www.solmelia.com. Opened in 1998, it consists of 150 deluxe ocean-view suites with air-conditioning, phone, satellite TV, kitchenette, and minibar. Near the Robert Trent Jones II–designed Cabo Real Golf Course and the Jack Nicklaus–designed El Dorado Golf Course, the resort offers two restaurants, two bars, a gym with spa facilities, two tennis courts, and an outdoor swimming pool with a swim-up bar.

Las Ventanas al Paraíso

One of the most talked-about newer resorts in Los Cabos, if not all of Mexico, Las Ventanas, just northeast of Km 20 (Rosewood Hotels and Resorts, 500 Crescent Court, Suite 300, Dallas, TX 75201), tel. 624/144-0300, U.S. tel. 888/ 767-3966, fax 624/144-0301, lasventanas@rose-woodhotels.com, www.lasventanas.com, brings a new level of luxury and service to The Corridor's already distinguished market. Under the auspices of Rosewood Hotels and Resorts (which also manages the prestigious Mansion on Turtle Creek and Hotel Crescent Court in Dallas, The Lanesborough in London, and Little Dix Bay in the British Virgin Islands), Las Ventanas was designed using an innovative combination of Mexican-Mediterranean architecture and interior design. Unlike the bright primary colors favored by many Mexican beach resorts, here pastels and earth tones are emphasized. Underground tunnels hide many of the day-to-day guest service activities to keep aboveground architecture to a minimum, adding to the overall sense of intimacy.

Guest suites average 90 square meters (960 square feet), and each features custom-made furniture, inlaid stone-and-tile floors, an adobe fireplace, private furnished patio with individual splash pool/hot tub, computerized telescope aimed at the sea, dual telephone lines for modem/phone use, satellite TV/VCR, in-room CD/stereo equipment, freshly cut blooms, and a huge bathroom. Each room also comes with a complimentary bottle of high-end tequila.

Guests have free use of a full-service spa and fitness center. The beach in front of the resort, Playa Costa Brava, is a little too *brava* for most swimmers, but overlooking the beach is a large free-form horizon pool with swim-up bar. The resort's restaurant, simply called The Restaurant and managed by a chef with one of the most impressive culinary backgrounds in the region, offers one of the most adventurous cuisines in all of Baja. The menu changes seasonally, but past offerings have included such dishes as grilled shrimp hash with poached eggs, sliced tomatoes, and roast chili sauce for breakfast; Baja shellfish and fettuccine in saffron broth for lunch; and habanero- and merlot-glazed tuna mignon with pinto beans for dinner. The resort also offers a less formal restaurant and a tequila- and ceviche-tasting bar. Las Ventanas has a working agreement with airlines that allows them to cater your meal for the flight home!

The concierge can arrange play at any golf course in The Corridor.

Hotel Cabo San Lucas

Farther southwest between Km 15 and 14, the Hotel Cabo San Lucas, tel. 624/144-0017, fax 624/144-0015, U.S. tel. 323/512-3799 or 866/733-2226 (reservations), fax 323/512-3815, hotelcabo@earthlink.net, www.hotelcabo.com,

sits on Punta Chileno, facing Playa del Tule. Another heavy hitter in the colonial-luxury league, the Cabo San Lucas came along early in the game in 1958. Almost more Hawaiian than Mexican in style, the resort features 77 rooms, suites, and studios and eight beachfront villas, plus its own hunting ranch, sportfishing excursions, horseback riding, a three-level swimming pool, dive center, restaurant, bar, 1,200-meter (3,950-foot) airstrip, and Asian art gallery. The reef below the hotel, on the Playa Chileno side of the point, is suitable for snorkeling and surfing.

Hotel Twin Dolphin

One of The Corridor's original 1950s' triumvirate, the Twin Dolphin, at Km 11.5, tel. 624/145-8190, fax 624/145-8196, U.S. tel. 800/421-8925, U.S. fax 213/380-1302, www.twindolphin.com, offers splendid ocean views. Playa Santa María, to the immediate north, is one of Los Cabos' best snorkeling/diving beaches. The hotel has its own fishing fleet, 18-hole putting green, dive center, pool, tennis courts, horseback riding, restaurant, and quiet, wood-paneled bar reminiscent of Cabo's more macho past. Each of the 50 oceanfront rooms has a private terrace. American plan (three meals per day) rates are available.

Cabo del Sol

On the drawing board at Cabo del Sol are the usual housing sites, a tennis center, and exclusive hotels. One hotel already up and running on the beach side of Cabo del Sol is **Sheraton Hacienda del Mar,** tel. 624/145-8000 or 800/903-2500, U.S. tel. 888/672-7137, fax 624/145-8008, information@haciendadelmar.com, http://sheratonhaciendadelmar.com, a plush Mediterranean-style spot with 171 condo-style suites, all equipped with air-conditioning, satellite TV, and kitchenettes. Some rooms also contain hot tubs. Other amenities include a three-tier pool, two outdoor whirlpool tubs facing the ocean, a gym, spa, and tropical gardens.

The hotel boasts five bars and five restaurants, including **Pitahayas,** tel. 624/145-8010, a large open-air restaurant with an impressive underground wine cellar and an innovative menu of Pacific Rim cuisine focusing on fresh seafood and a mesquite grill. Pitahayas is open daily for breakfast, lunch, and dinner. Formal resort attire required.

The main access road for Cabo del Sol leaves Mexico 1 near Km 10.

Fiesta Americana Grand Los Cabos

Adjacent to the the Jack Nicklaus–designed Cabo del Sol Golf Course is the **Fiesta Americana Grand Los Cabos,** tel. 624/145-6200, fax 624/145-6202 (reservations), U.S. 800/FIESTA-1 (800/343-7821), resfalc@posadas.com, www.fiestaamericana.com. This relatively new US$70 million resort consists of 278 guest rooms and suites. All rooms feature a sea view and have air-conditioning, TV, minibar, safety deposit box, two telephones, and bathrobes. Facilities include three restaurants, two bars, pools, two championship tennis courts, shopping arcade, and a full-service spa.

Calinda Cabo San Lucas

Off Mexico 1 at Km 4.5, this is the nearest of The Corridor hotels to Cabo San Lucas and also one of the least expensive. **Calinda Cabo San Lucas,** tel. 624/145-8045 or 800/021-6840, U.S. tel. 887/441-9944, fax 624/145-8057, resercabo@calinda.com.mx, www.hotelescalinda.com.mx, features 125 rooms, each with a balcony and an ocean or garden view, all with air-conditioning, decorative fireplaces, sitting areas, phone, and satellite TV. The grounds encompass landscaped gardens, a restaurant, three bars, three pools, three hot tubs, a gymnasium, and two lighted tennis courts. Rooms are in the US$150–250 range.

Misiones del Cabo Resort

At Km 5.5 near Cabo San Lucas, Misiones del Cabo, tel. 624/145-8090, U.S. tel. 888/377-8762, fax 624/145-8097, misionesdelcabo@prodigy.net.mx, www.misionescabo.com, is a resort offering dramatic views, safe swimming beaches, lighted tennis courts, pool and swim-up bar, and a complimentary daily shuttle to/from Cabo San Lucas. The adjacent cliffside restaurant Da Georgio II affords breathtaking views of

Cabo San Lucas. The 214 one- and two-bedroom condominium suites have full kitchens, satellite TV, air-conditioning, and spacious private balconies.

GOLF COURSES

Golf is king in The Corridor, which is home to three Jack Nicklaus–designed golf courses (the 27-hole Palmilla, 18-hole El Dorado at Cabo Real, and 18-hole Cabo del Sol), the 18-hole Robert Trent Jones II–designed Cabo Real course, the Tom Fazio-designed 18-hole Querencia, and the 18-hole Tom Weiskopf addition to Cabo del Sol.

These courses boast landscapes and playing terrain comparable to that found in many Arizona and California desert courses, the main difference being the visual addition of the sparkling Sea of Cortez. Despite the professional status of the four main courses, which have attracted the PGA Grand Slam Tournament annually since 1995, all are eminently playable. As a local golf guide put it, "Low handicap players will find them challenging and will appreciate the genius and skill that went into their designs, while less experienced players will be rewarded with a good day's combat."

Querencia

Querencia, the first completely private course in Los Cabos, covers 341 hectares (840 acres) of hills between Palmilla and Costa Azul, near San José del Cabo. Querencia includes an 18-hole Tom Fazio–designed course (his first outside the United States), a nine-hole short course (also designed by Fazio), and a modern practice facility. The Querencia development also features home sites, villas, and condos. Call 624/145-6670 in Mexico or 888/346-6188 in the United States for more information, or email info@loscabosquerencia.com.

Palmilla

Opened in 1992, the Jack Nicklaus–designed 27-hole golf course at the Palmilla is divided into an arroyo course, a mountain course, and an ocean course, splendid by all accounts. Nearly every hole has a view of the Sea of Cortez in the distance. This course hosted the 1997 PGA Senior Slam, 1997 Taylor Made Pro-Am, and 1998 World Pro-Am tournaments. Nicklaus himself, though admitting his bias as the designer (this was his first course in Latin America), claims the 17th and 18th holes are the best finishing holes in the world. The course's signature hole is the 440-yard, par-4 "Mountain Five," which necessitates a long drive across two desert arroyos. Gray water irrigates the fairways and greens, easing the strain on the Los Cabos water supply. The public is charged a greens fee of US$125–195 per 18 holes, depending on the day of the week and time of year. Fees include golf cart, practice balls, bottled water, and use of the driving range. Clubs may be rented for US$50 plus tax. The golf course serves as the centerpiece of a 384-hectare (950-acre) development surrounding the original hotel with fairway homes, a network of paved roads, a clubhouse, and a tennis complex. Call 624/144-5250 for more information.

Cabo Real

The Cabo Real complex boasts two world-class golf courses. The 18-hole, par-72 **Cabo Real Golf Course** stretches over more than 7,000 yards of verdant landscape. The first six holes are in mountainous terrain, while others lie along the shore. The course is open to the general public for a greens fee of US$220 for 18 holes, including tax, golf cart, practice facilities, club service, and bottled water. There's a lower Twilight rate of US$154, including tax, or you can play nine holes anytime for this rate. Hotel guests staying at the Westin Regina Los Cabos, Meliá Cabo Real, and Casa del Mar receive a 10 percent discount. Club rentals are available for US$25. Call 624/144-0040 or 800/393-0400 in the United States, or email reservations@caboreal.com for course information.

The Jack Nicklaus–designed **El Dorado Golf Club** is the second championship course in the Cabo Real development. The 18-hole, par-72 course features six oceanfront holes; the rest are carved out of two picturesque canyons surrounded by trees, cacti, and rock formations. Six holes come into play beside four lakes. This 7,050-yard course has been called the finest course in Mexico and one of the best in the world. Greens fees run US$168–251, depending on the season, and include tax, shared golf cart, practice facilities, club service, and bottled water. The clubhouse and restaurant afford views of the Sea of Cortez and the ninth and 18th holes. Call 624/144-5450 for more information.

Cabo del Sol

Jack Nicklaus designed his second set of Mexican fairways on 730 hectares (1,800 acres) of land between Playa Barco Varado and Cabo Bello. This is Los Cabos's highest-rated golf course so far. *Golf Digest* has rated it as one of the top 10 public golf courses anywhere; Nicklaus himself insists that it includes some of the greatest ocean holes in the world. Seven of the course's holes feature dramatic oceanfront play along the shore of Bahía de Ballenas. The front nine is 3,597 yards, par 36, while the back nine extends 3,440 yards, also par 36. A newer Desert Course, a 7,100-yard, par-72 piece of eye candy designed by PGA great Tom Weiskopf (his first golf course in Mexico), spreads across 57 hectares (140 acres) of desert landscape. A third 18-hole course for Cabo del Sol is still in the planning stages.

The public is charged a greens fee of US$196–262 for 18 holes on the Ocean Course, or US$170–223 on the Desert Course (depending on time of year), which includes tax, a golf cart, practice facilities, club service, and bottled water. Hotel guests pay US$135–145. Callaway clubs can be rented for US$46. For information on the golf course, call 624/145-8200 or 800/386-2465 in the United States.

Raven Golf Club

Part of Cabo San Lucas Country Club, this Roy Dye–designed, 300-hectare (745-acre), 18-hole course lies just one km northeast of Cabo San Lucas, on sloping terrain facing the sea, with views of Land's End and Bahía San Lucas from each fairway and five tee-offs for each hole (back, championship, member, forward, and front). At 600 yards (par 5), the seventh hole is said to be the longest in Mexico. The front nine is 3,651 yards (par 36), the back nine is 3,569 yards (par

36). Greens fees are among the lowest outside of San José del Cabo, US$105–175 for 18 holes for nonmembers, including cart. Clubs may be rented for US$40 a set. To avoid drawing excessively from the Cape's precious aquifer, gray water from the resort spends a month cycling through a series of duckweed ponds until the fast-growing plant renders the water safe for irrigation. Along with fairway homes, the resort features tennis, swimming, and fitness clubs. Call 624/143-4653/4 or 888/328-8501 in the United States for further information or reservations.

Cabo San Lucas

Cabo San Lucas and San José del Cabo enjoy equal access to the great beaches along The Corridor between the two towns, but because the San Lucas harbor provides shelter for a sizable sportfishing and recreational fleet, the preponderance of the 300,000-plus yearly Los Cabos visitors station themselves here rather than in San José or along The Corridor. Several cruise lines also feature Cabo San Lucas on their itineraries. With a permanent population of only 30,000, many of them retirees, the city has a tourist-to-resident ratio higher than elsewhere in the Cape Region, especially during the peak Nov.–Mar. tourist season.

Yet in spite of all the tourists—most of whom confine themselves to the waterfront—Cabo manages to retain something of a funky, small-town feel. Away from Boulevard Marina, many of the unpaved, sand streets are lined with the *tortillerías,* hardware shops, and markets typically found in any small coastal Mexican town.

Named for the slender cape extending eastward from Baja California's southernmost tip, Cabo San Lucas is the only city in Mexico with a marine preserve within its city limits. Created in 1973, the protected 36-square-km (14-square-mile) patch of sea and shore designates special boat lanes, boating speed limits, and restricted fishing and recreation craft areas, all under the watchful eye of Grupo Ecológico de Cabo San Lucas. Nowhere else among Mexico's top-drawing seaside resorts will you find such pristine beaches within so short a distance (5–10 minutes by boat taxi) of the town center.

Outside this area, however, hotel and condo development marches ahead full steam. Pedregal—a fashionable hillside district to the west—the marina, and Playa El Médano to the east are all chockablock with condos and villas. Next to undergo development will probably be the large section of unused harborfront property near the inner harbor entrance, where an old cannery and ferry pier sit abandoned.

While yachting and sportfishing bring an older, early-to-bed crowd to Cabo, the town's nightlife attracts an energetic youth market, creating a more vibrant ambience than at relatively staid San José del Cabo, 29 km (18 miles) northeast. As the last stop on the 1,700-km (1,000-mile) transpeninsular Baja road trip, Cabo also acts as a receptacle for old Baja hands looking for a few days or weeks of R&R before beginning the long return drive across relatively unpopulated desert landscapes.

Thus, as residents and repeat visitors will point out, you never know who you'll run into in Cabo; yachties on their way to and from exotic South Pacific ports, cops on a fishing vacation, Baja road warriors, honeymoon couples, Mexico City denizens cleaning out their lead-filled lungs, rockers resting up after a continental tour, or Montana cowboys escaping the snow—they've all set themselves temporarily adrift in the Pacific, like the Cape itself as it inches westward from mainland Mexico.

CLIMATE

Cabo San Lucas lies below the Tropic of Cancer and is sunny and mild year-round. The town's location at the confluence of the Pacific Ocean and the Sea of Cortez means ocean currents and airstreams from both sides of the peninsula tend to moderate the general climatic influences of each; neither the cool Pacific nor the warm Cortez completely dominates in any

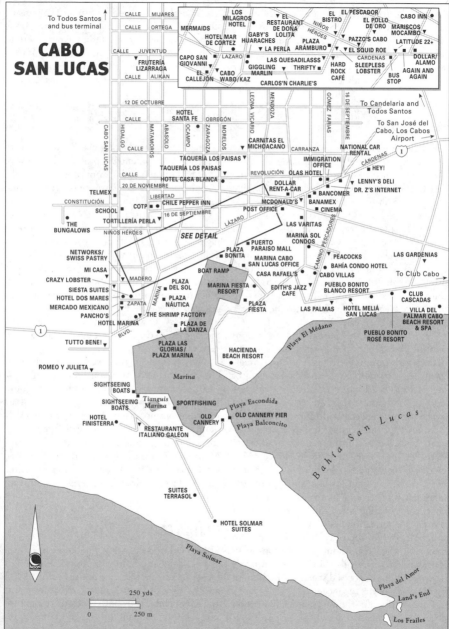

CABO SAN LUCAS

To Todos Santos and bus terminal

CALLE MIJARES
CALLE ORTEGA
CALLE JUVENTUD
CALLE ALIKAN

FRUTERÍA LIZARRAGA

12 DE OCTUBRE

HOTEL SANTA FE

CALLE
OBREGÓN

CARNITAS EL MICHOACANO
CARRANZA

TAQUERÍA LOS PAISAS
TAQUERÍA LOS PAISAS
HOTEL CASA BLANCA
20 DE NOVIEMBRE
REVOLUCIÓN
OLAS HOTEL
IMMIGRATION OFFICE
HEY!
NATIONAL CAR RENTAL

TELMEX
CONSTITUCIÓN
SCHOOL
COTP
TORTILLERÍA PERLA
THE BUNGALOWS
NIÑOS HÉROES

LIBERTAD
CHILE PEPPER INN
16 DE SEPTIEMBRE
LAZARO

DOLLAR RENT-A-CAR
BANCOMER
MCDONALD'S
BANAMEX
POST OFFICE
CINEMA
LAS VARITAS
LENNY'S DELI
DR. Z'S INTERNET

SEE DETAIL

NETWORKS/ SWISS PASTRY
MI CASA
CRAZY LOBSTER
SIESTA SUITES
HOTEL DOS MARES
MERCADO MEXICANO
PANCHO'S
HOTEL MARINA
MADERO
ZAPATA
BLVD.

PUERTO PARAISO MALL
PLAZA BONITA
MARINA CABO SAN LUCAS OFFICE
CASA RAFAEL'S
MARINA SOL CONDOS
PEACOCKS
BAHÍA CONDO HOTEL
CABO VILLAS
LAS GARDENIAS
To Club Cabo

BOAT RAMP
PLAZA DEL SOL
PLAZA NÁUTICA
THE SHRIMP FACTORY
MARINA FIESTA RESORT
EDITH'S JAZZ CAFE
PLAZA FIESTA
LAS PALMAS
PUEBLO BONITO BLANCO RESORT
HOTEL MELIÁ SAN LUCAS
CLUB CASCADAS
VILLA DEL PALMAR CABO BEACH RESORT & SPA

TUTTO BENE!
ROMEO Y JULIETA

PLAZA DE LA DANZA
PLAZA LAS GLORIAS/ PLAZA MARINA
HACIENDA BEACH RESORT
Playa El Médano
PUEBLO BONITO ROSÉ RESORT

Marina

SIGHTSEEING BOATS
SIGHTSEEING BOATS
HOTEL FINISTERRA
Tianguis Marina
SPORTFISHING
OLD CANNERY
RESTAURANTE ITALIANO GALEÓN
Playa Escondida
OLD CANNERY PIER
Playa Balconcito

Bahía San Lucas

SUITES TERRASOL
HOTEL SOLMAR SUITES

Playa Solmar

Playa del Amor
Land's End
Los Frailes

0 250 yds
0 250 m

To Candelaria and Todos Santos
To San José del Cabo, Los Cabos Airport

CALLE
HIDALGO
MATAMOROS
ABASOLO
OCAMPO
ZARAGOZA
MORELOS
LEONA VICARIO
MENDOZA
GÓMEZ FARÍAS
16 DE SEPTIEMBRE
CAMINO PESCADORES
CÁRDENAS

Detail inset:

LOS MILAGROS HOTEL
MERMAIDS
HOTEL MAR DE CORTEZ
CAPO SAN GIOVANNI
EL CALLEJÓN
CABO WABO/KAZ
EL RESTAURANT DE DOÑA LOLITA
GABY'S HUARACHES
LA PERLA
GIGGLING MARLIN
THRIFTY
CARLOS'N CHARLIE'S
EL BISTRO
NIÑOS HÉROES
PLAZA ARÁMBURO
LAS QUESADILASSS
HARD ROCK CAFE
EL PESCADOR
EL POLLO DE ORO
PAZZO'S CABO
EL SQUID ROE
CÁRDENAS
SLEEPLESS LOBSTER
BUS STOP
CABO INN
MARISCOS MOCAMBO
LATITUDE 22+
DOLLAR/ ALAMO
AGAIN AND AGAIN

© AVALON TRAVEL PUBLISHING, INC.

CAPE REGION

given season. Hence summers aren't as hot as in La Paz (220 km north on the Cortez side), and winters aren't as cool as in Todos Santos (72 km north on the Pacific).

The average temperature in August is 27°C (81°F); in January it's 18°C (64°F). Maximum temperatures rarely exceed 33°C (92°F), and minimum readings seldom fall below 13°C (56°F). Since Cabo is completely protected from prevailing north winds, winters here are warmer than anywhere else in Baja, a distinct attraction for the snowbird market.

Cabo San Lucas boasts an average of 360 days of sunshine a year. Annual rainfall averages a scant 19 cm (7.5 inches), most falling Aug.–Oct. Brief showers are sometimes encountered as late as November or early December.

HISTORY

The Pericú and the English

In pre-Cortesian times the only humans enjoying Cabo San Lucas were the Pericú, one of the nomadic Guaycura Amerindian groups that inhabited the Cape Region for hundreds if not thousands of years. Standard anthropology says that, like other Amerindians in North and South America, the Pericú were descendants of Asian groups who traversed the prehistoric land bridge between the Eurasian and American continents. One fringe theory, however, suggests the Pericú may have descended from Tahitian mariners blown off course on their way to Hawaii. English accounts from the 17th and early 18th centuries lend at least partial credence to this theory by pointing out how much the physical and social characteristics of the Pericú differed from that of other Amerindians of the same era.

Spaniard Juan Rodríguez Cabrillo made first contact with the Pericú here in 1542 while exploring the coastline. Sir Francis Drake stopped off in 1578, followed by privateer Thomas Cavendish in 1587. English pirating exploits inspired the Spanish to gain a stronger foothold on the Cape. Spanish explorer Sebastián Vizcaíno spent a week here in 1596, then returned in 1602 to map the region with cartographer Gerónimo Martín Palacios. Vizcaíno strongly recommended the establishment of a colony at Cabo San Lucas; Loreto, farther north on the Sea of Cortez, was selected instead, leaving Cabo to the English for another hundred years.

Until the mid-18th century, English pirates used the harbor as a hiding place for attacks on Manila galleons. Woodes Rogers anchored here in 1709, when he and his crew captured the Spanish galleon *Encarnación*. Another English corsair, George Shelcocke, landed in 1721 and carried out a regional survey that included extensive drawings of the Pericú. In his descriptions, Shelcocke wrote:

The men are tall, straight, and well formed; they have very large arms and black, thick, poorly cared for hair, which does not reach the thighs, as a previous sailor reported on his voyage [apparently a rebuke to Woodes Rogers's earlier descriptions], nor even barely to the shoulders. The women are smaller; their hair is longer than the men's and sometimes almost covers their faces. Some of both sexes have a good appearance, although of a darker color than other Indians I have seen in these seas, as they have a dark copper color. The reader may reasonably conclude that they cannot be more savage, but there is much difference between what one would think on first sight of them, and what they truly are: because from everything I could observe of their behavior with each other and us, they are endowed with all imaginable humanity, and might shame some other nations . . . because during our entire stay there, constantly among so many hundreds of them, we observed only perfect harmony; when one of us gave something edible to one of them in particular, he always divided it into as many parts as there were people around, and normally reserved the smallest part for himself.

The First Settlers

During the remainder of the Spanish colonial era, Cabo's natural harbor was periodically used by passing galleons, but since it offered no source of fresh water and scant protection from late-summer *chubascos* rolling in from the southeast, it was largely ignored in favor of San José del Cabo, where fresh water was abundant.

The Mexican independence movement largely bypassed San Lucas, although the Chilean ship *Independence* visited Cabo in 1822 in support of the Mexican struggle. The visit accomplished little as a military exercise because Mexico had gained independence from Spain the previous year, but it may have sparked renewed interest in San Lucas as a convenient harbor in this part of the world. By the end of the 19th century, an enterprising group of *bajacalifornianos* began processing and shipping bark from the local palo blanco tree, a key ingredient in leather tanning. The principal route for the bark trade ran between Cabo San Lucas and San Francisco. Shipping traffic gradually increased, and port authorities built the lighthouse now known as Faro Viejo at nearby Cabo Falso in 1890.

In 1917 an American company floated a tuna cannery from San Diego to San Lucas to take advantage of the abundance of tuna in the area. As San Lucas gathered a small population, a roadbed to San José del Cabo, the nearest federal government seat, was laid in the 1920s. By the 1930s, a cannery and a small fishing village inhabited by around 400 hardy souls occupied the north end of the Cabo San Lucas harbor. Fish-canning remained the backbone of the local economy until the cannery was heavily damaged by a hurricane in 1941. During World War II the area was all but abandoned as Japanese submarines cruised the Pacific coast; Cabo seemed destined for obscurity.

Marlin Alley and La Carretera Transpeninsular

Fortunately for *sanluqueños* (residents of San Lucas), post–World War II leisure travel brought fly-in anglers, who spread the word that Cabo was a game-fish paradise. The Cape sportfishing craze of the 1950s and '60s—when the waters off the peninsula's southern tip earned the nickname Marlin Alley—expanded the population to around 1,500 by the time the Transpeninsular Highway was completed in 1973. Following the

establishment of the highway link between the United States and Cabo San Lucas, the town was transformed from a fly-in/sail-in resort into an auto-and-RV destination.

When Baja California Sur received statehood in 1974, a ferry route from Puerto Vallarta on the mainland was established, thus opening the area to increased Mexican migration. The construction of Los Cabos International Airport near San José del Cabo in the '80s brought Cabo within reach of vacationers who didn't have the time for a six-day drive from border to Cape and back. The establishment of a water pipeline between San José and San Lucas further loosened the limits on development.

Today the local economy rests on the provision of tourism services—hotels, restaurants, fishing, diving, and other water sports—and on the construction industry, which supplies the growing need for leisure, residential, and business structures throughout the lower Cape Region. At the moment Cabo San Lucas's population is roughly equal to that of San José del Cabo, the *cabecera* or *municipio* seat—but the San Lucas population may soon exceed its older twin's. A vocal group of *sanluqueños* is campaigning for the Cabo area to separate from San José's jurisdiction and become the state's sixth *municipio*.

LAND'S END

A large cluster of granitic batholiths, carved by wind and sea into fantastic shapes, tumbles into the sea at the Cape's southernmost point. Forming the coccyx of a rocky spine that reaches northward all the way to Alaska's Aleutian Islands, the formations are collectively known as **Finisterra,** or Land's End.

El Arco, a rock outcropping at the tip of Land's End, has become Cabo San Lucas's most immediately recognizable symbol. During low tide you can walk along Playa del Amor to the 62-meter (200-foot) rock formation, which features an eroded passage through the middle. El Arco is also known as the Arch of Poseidon since it marks the "entrance" to a precipitous submarine canyon—the perfect throne room for the King of the Seas—just offshore. Running northwest from El Arco and Playa del Amor are several unnamed rock formations, including two large granite clusters as tall or taller than El Arco. These should be of interest to rock climbers.

Just offshore stand **Los Frailes** (The Friars), two rock islets shaped like clusters of hooded monks and frequented by sea lions. A smaller, bird-limed rock pinnacle off the northeast side of the Cape, **Roca Pelícanos** (Pelican Rock), serves as a crowded pelican roost. The base of the pinnacle, about six meters (20 feet) down, is richly endowed with marinelife, including coral, sea fans, gorgonians, sea urchins, and numerous tropical fish. Recent reports from divers say visibility at the rock is declining, however, due to discharge from cruise ships moored in the outer harbor.

Cerro La Vigía, rising 150 meters (500 feet) above the harbor, once served as lookout point for English pirates awaiting Manila galleons to plunder. Today it's still an excellent vantage point for viewing Land's End, the town, the marina, Playa Solmar (the beach next to the Hotel Solmar), and Cabo Falso. A steep trail begins just behind the old cannery on the harbor and leads to La Vigía's summit, which is marked by a crucifix.

BEACHES

Beachgoers can choose among five beaches close to the downtown area and a string of beaches and coves along the San José del Cabo to Cabo San Lucas Corridor.

Playa El Médano

The most popular and easily accessible local beach, Playa El Médano (Dune Beach) extends several kilometers along Bahía San Lucas northeast from the inner harbor's entrance channel. This is Baja's most heavily used beach—it's packed with swimmers and sunbathers during peak vacation periods—and is one of the few local beaches where swimming is safe year-round. Beach vendors rent *pangas,* jet skis, inflatable rafts, sailboards, snorkeling equipment, volleyball equipment, *palapas,* and beach furniture. Several palapa bars and restaurants scattered along the beach—Billygan's Island, The Office, El

Playa El Médano, Cabo San Lucas

Delfín, and Las Palmas—offer cold beverages and seafood.

Minor annoyances at Playa El Médano include the many vendors who plod up and down the beach hawking jewelry, rugs, hammocks, hand-painted plates, and the like (they won't persist if you show no interest) and the condo developments in the background that mar the view of the Sierra de la Laguna foothills.

Playa del Amor

Cabo's next most popular beach can be reached only by boat or by a difficult climb over two rock headlands along the ocean. Named one of Mexico's 10 best beaches by *Condé Nast Traveler* magazine, Playa del Amor (Love Beach), also known as Playa del Amante (Lover's Beach), lies near the tip of Cabo San Lucas—the cape itself, not the town—just northwest of the famous arch-shaped rock formation featured in virtually every Los Cabos advertisement. The wide, sandy,

© JOE CUMMINGS

Playa del Amor, Cabo San Lucas

pristine beach extends across the cape behind the arch to the other side, forming two beach-fronts—one on Bahía San Lucas and one on the Pacific. The latter is sometimes whimsically called Divorce Beach.

Only the beachfront facing the bay is generally safe for swimming. Bring along a cooler full of beverages, as the entire area is free of vendors and commercial enterprises. Unless you have a portable beach umbrella, go early in the day to command one of the shady rock overhangs. The southeast end of the bay features a series of coral-encrusted rocks suitable for snorkeling; a deep submarine canyon lying only 50 meters (164 feet) offshore is a popular scuba diving site.

You can reach Playa del Amor by water taxi from the marina, or take a Dos Mares glass-bottom boat tour (US$10 round-trip for both options) and arrange a drop-off at the beach. Any tour boat in the vicinity should give you a ride back to the marina upon presentation of your ticket stub; the last tour boat leaves the marina around 3 P.M. In calm seas, you can also rent a kayak on Playa El Médano and paddle across the inner harbor entrance to the beach.

Those skilled at bouldering can reach the south

side of the beach by climbing from the east end of Playa Solmar (in front of the Hotel Solmar) over two rocky points that separate the two beaches. The climb is best attempted during low tide, when the cove between the rock formations reveals a sandy beach useful as a midway rest stop. The second set of rocks, to the east, is more difficult than those to the west; turn back after the first set if you've reached the limit of your climbing skills.

Playa Solmar

This very wide, very long beach running along the southwestern edge of the Cape is accessible via the road to Hotel Solmar. The strong undertow and heavy surf make it suitable for sunbathing and wading only. Solmar's biggest advantage is its lack of people, even during peak tourist seasons.

Cannery Beaches

Next to the abandoned Planta Empacadora (the old tuna cannery on the south side of the inner harbor entrance) are two small public beaches virtually ignored by most Cabo visitors. The first, **Playa Escondida** (Hidden Beach), lies next to the cannery pier and is easily reached by walking along the west bank of the marina and alongside the main cannery building. The sand extends only around 50 meters (164 feet), less in high tide, but it's popular with local Mexican families because Dad can fish from the pier while the kids play in the calm water. I once watched a local resident haul in a 4.5-kg (10-pound) tuna with a handline here.

Playa Balconcito (Little Balcony Beach), a bit larger than Playa Escondida, lies beyond the pier on the other side of the cannery toward the sea. You must walk along a stone ledge—part of the cannery foundation—to get there.

Corridor Beaches

Northeast of Cabo San Lucas—on the way to San José del Cabo—a number of uncrowded, relatively pristine beaches are suitable for swimming, fishing, camping, snorkeling, and scuba diving. See the sidebar Beaches along The Corridor for names and locations.

ACCOMMODATIONS

Cabo San Lucas offers a greater number and variety of hotels than neighboring San José. Most are in the US$50–110 range although two hotels charge under US$35 a night and several cost well over US$110 in winter and early spring.

Unless otherwise noted, rate ranges quoted below are for double rooms, peak season, usually Nov.–May. Some hotels may offer a 15– 20 percent discount Mar.–Oct. Add 12 percent tax to all rates; some hotels may charge an additional 10–15 percent service charge.

Downtown Hotels

Although Cabo's beaches are the average visitor's preferred address, you can save considerably by staying downtown and walking or driving to the beach.

US$25–50: A bit off the beaten track, on Calle Revolución a half block east of Morelos (and close to the bus terminal), **Hotel Casa Blanca** (formerly Casa Blanca Inn), tel. 624/143-5360, offers 15 basic rooms with ceiling fans; you get what you pay for and this is about as spartan as it gets in this town. Although lacking in atmosphere, the Casa Blanca has the advantage of being relatively quiet. In the same vicinity as Hotel Casa Blanca, **Olas Hotel,** Calle Revolución at Gómez Farías, tel. 624/143-1780, fax 624/143-1380, has 28 rooms, each with TV, fan, and patio.

The two-story **Hotel Marina,** Blvd. Marina at Guerrero, tel. 624/143-3332, fax 624/143-0030, has 18 fairly clean and tidy air-conditioned rooms and one large air-conditioned suite with refrigerators and TVs. On the premises are a modest pool and hot tub. One drawback is that it can get a bit noisy during peak season (Dec.–Mar.), when the hotel is jam-packed and there's lots of pedestrian traffic on Boulevard Marina.

One of the best values downtown is the friendly and efficient **Siesta Suites Hotel,** Calle Zapata between Guerrero and Hidalgo, tel./fax 624/143-2773, U.S. tel. 602/331-1354, siesta@cabonet .net.mx, www.cabosiestasuites.com, near the better downtown restaurants and one block from the marina. All 15 suites and five hotel-style rooms are immaculate and quiet. The suites come with a full kitchen and separate bedroom. All rooms have air-conditioning, cable TV, and telephone (local calls are free). The hotel also features a sun deck, barbecue area, and secured parking. Because of price and location, Siesta Suites is a popular spot; advance reservations are recommended, even in summer (when fishing's high season lures droves of North American anglers).

Next door, the friendly **Hotel Dos Mares,** Calle Zapata s/n, tel. 624/143-0330, fax 624/143-4727, hoteldosmares@cabotel.com.mx, rents 37 quite adequate, air-conditioned rooms with TV and phone. A small pool is on the premises.

US$50–100: Cabo Inn Hotel, 20 de Noviembre between Leona Vicario and Mendoza, tel./fax

For scuba diving fanatics, submarine canyons featuring sandfalls are not to be missed. These streams of underwater sand tumble over a canyon rim and form sand rivers between rock outcroppings at depths of 98 feet.

CAPE REGION

624/143-0819, caboinn@cabotel.com.mx, is a cash-only place with nice courtyard areas downstairs and small, clean rooms with air-conditioning, ceiling fans, and tiny bathrooms. A shared TV is usually on in the downstairs lobby, though it's turned off at a reasonable hour. The roof patio has a seating area furnished with a sofa, chairs, and a cabinet full of books, as well as a "social pool." One palapa unit features a whirlpool and another unit can hold up to six people.

Three blocks back from the marina, old gringo standby **Hotel Mar de Cortez,** Blvd. Lázaro Cárdenas at Guerrero, tel. 624/143-0032, U.S./Canada tel. 800/347-8821, fax 624/143-0232, U.S. fax 831/663-1904, info@mardecortez .com, stays full virtually all season. Its clean air-conditioned rooms surround a small pool and patio area planted with date palms; some of the rooms have their own small patios attached. Facilities include a restaurant and outdoor bar area.

A large arched metal door leads to the attractive walled courtyard of the **Los Milagros Hotel,** Matamoros 116, tel. 624/143-4566, fax 624/143-5004, U.S. tel. 718/928-6647, fish@1cabonet.com.mex or info@losmilagros.com.mx. The 12 spacious rooms—some with kitchenettes—are well decorated and well maintained. An inviting splash pool/hot tub is available.

Another place in this price category is the friendly **Chile Pepper Inn,** on 16 de Septiembre, tel./fax 624/143-0510, next to the Capitanía del Puerto. The one-story mustard-colored building holds nicely furnished fair-sized rooms, all with air-conditioning, ceiling fans, telephones, and satellite TV.

Hotel Santa Fe, at the southwest corner of Zaragoza and Obregón, tel. 624/143-4401, fax 624/143-4403, U.S. tel. 866/448-4623, gerenciasantafe@prodigy.net.mx, www.hotelsantafeloscabos.com, is a tidy, Mexican-style compound containing 46 studios, each with kitchenette, air-conditioning, satellite TV, and phone. Amenities include off-street parking, 24-hour security, a restaurant, pool, and laundry.

US$100–150: One block off the marina on the second floor of Plaza de la Danza, **Viva Cabo Hotel and Cantina,** Blvd. Marina, tel./fax 624/143-5810, marycruz@vivaloscabos.com,

www.vivaloscabos.com, is a small luxury hotel featuring eight studios with fully equipped kitchens, air-conditioning, satellite TV, and sitting areas. Amenities include a restaurant and bar, with a pool and fitness center next door.

Playa El Médano Hotels

The preponderance of Cabo's beach hotels are along this long strip of sand southeast of the town center.

US$50–100: East along Playa El Médano, behind San Vicente and Vagabundos RV Parks, **Club Cabo Hotel and Campground Resort,** Apdo. Postal 463, Cabo San Lucas, BCS, tel./fax 624/143-3348, www.clubcaboinn.com, rents 10 one- and two-bedroom suites with TVs, verandas, and king-size beds, some with air-conditioning and full kitchens. Other amenities include laundry facilities, Internet access, table tennis, a trampoline, pool, hot tub, a large refrigerator for storing your catch, and a shuttle to town. English, Spanish, and Dutch are spoken. Special long-term rates are available. Club Cabo is also an RV park; see Camping and RV Parks for further information. It's a 15–20 minute walk from the park to the marina/downtown or a short walk to the beach, which is separated from the park by a dirt road and one of the last stands of natural thornforest in the Cabo area—a good birding site.

US$150–250: Not on the beach, but close to it, is the 10-room **Casa Rafael's,** tel. 624/143-0739, fax 624/143-1679, casarafa@cabonet.net.mx, www.allaboutcabo.com/casarafaels.htm, tastefully decorated in Mexican-colonial style. Rooms with handicapped access are available; some rooms have hot tubs and some have ocean views. The premises are generously planted in banana and papaya and feature exotic caged birds, a pool, hot tub, small gym, piano bar, cigar lounge, and a restaurant with a good wine collection.

Surrounded by coconut palms, the stately mission-style **Hacienda Beach Resort,** tel. 624/143-0663, U.S. tel. 800/733-2226, fax 624/143-0666, reserve@haciendacabo.com, www.hacienda-cabo.com, has presided over the south end of the beach since 1960. Some of its 115 spacious air-conditioned rooms have ocean views, and some are two-story affairs with sleeping lofts and full kitchens. The grounds contain a pool, tennis court, water-sports center, full-service dive shop, small-boat anchorage, and five restaurants and bars. The hotel provides free shuttle service to San José del Cabo.

Yet another Mediterranean-inspired structure, **Villa del Palmar Cabo Beach Resort & Spa,** Mexico 1, Km 0.5, tel. 624/145-7000, U.S. tel. 800/795-1809 (reservations), fax 624/143-2664, ventasvdp@cabotel.com.mx, www.villadelpalmarloscabos.com, stands along a more secluded area of El Médano and offers 458 suites, including junior suites and one- to three-bedroom ocean-view deluxe suites, all with full kitchens, marble bathrooms, and furnished balconies. Other amenities include two pools (one with poolside bar), two lighted tennis courts, a large European-style health spa, a fitness center, a water-sports facility, and rooftop and beach-side restaurants. Some units are only available by the week.

US$250 and Up: Moving northeast along the beach, next up after Hacienda Beach Resort is the **Hotel Meliá San Lucas,** tel. 624/143-4444, fax 624/143-0420, U.S. tel. 800/336-3542, ventas.melia.san.lucas@solmelia.com, www.solmelia.com, a multistory resort built in a horseshoe shape around a large pool and patio area. The first phase of a US$1 million renovation program has recently been completed. Facilities include international direct-dial telephones, air-conditioning, satellite TV, in-room safes, minibar, in-room coffeemakers, two heated pools, two lighted tennis courts, three restaurants, two bars, live nightly entertainment, a water-sports center, horseback riding, a shopping arcade, and a beauty salon. Most of the Meliá's 142 spacious rooms and suites have ocean views. More expensive deluxe suites are available.

A couple of hundred meters northeast along the beach is the striking **Pueblo Bonito Blanco Resort,** tel. 624/142-9797, fax 624/143-1995, U.S. tel. 800/990-8250, rquintero@pueblo bonito.com, www.pueblobonito.com, a white, five-story Mediterranean-style building topped by blue-tiled domes and arrayed in a horseshoe around gardens and a free-form pool with a waterfall. The 148 junior and luxury suites come

with international direct-dial telephones, satellite TV, fully equipped kitchenettes, and ocean views. The hotel offers two restaurants, two bars, and a full-service health spa and fitness center.

Farther northeast is the sister resort of the Pueblo Bonito Blanco, the **Pueblo Bonito Rosé Resort,** tel. 624/142-9898, fax 624/143-5523, U.S. tel. 800/990-8250, vescamilla@pueblo bonito.com, www.pueblobonito.com. The 260 suites are situated on 2.2 hectares (5.5 acres). Rooms feature private balconies, ocean views, hand-painted terra-cotta floors, full kitchens, and original artwork. One of the hotel's finest features is its lavish lobby, which is decorated with velvet draperies, a 17th-century Flemish tapestry, and fountains surrounded by 16th-century Italian baroque cherubs. Amenities include a fitness center, a free-form pool, a European health spa, and various sports activities.

Playa Solmar Hotels

Two of Cabo's most distinguished hotels are secluded from the rest of town by the rocky ridge leading to Land's End.

US$100–150: Impressively constructed high on the ridge itself, overlooking the beach and Pacific Ocean, is the 1971-vintage, 287-room **Hotel Finisterra,** tel. 624/143-3333, U.S. tel. 800/347-2252 (reservations), fax 624/143-0590, www.finisterra.com. A newer tower wing, known as the Palapa Beach Club, offers spacious suites with ocean views and extends from the beach below all the way to the original hotel and lobby area, to which it is connected by a bridge. A 1,040-square-meter (11,200-square-foot) swimming pool with whirlpools and swim-up bar sits on the beach at the foot of the Palapa Beach Club. Some of the rooms and suites in the original Finisterra section feature city, marina, or garden views rather than bay views. Amenities include lighted tennis courts, sauna, pool, massage service, a travel agency, Dollar rental-car office, wedding chapel, restaurant, and bar.

The sleek V-shaped **Hotel Solmar Suites,** tel. 624/143-3535, fax 624/143-0410, U.S. tel. 310/459-9861 or 800/344-3349, U.S. fax 310/454-1686, caboresort@aol.com, www.solmar.com, features 90 one-bedroom and two-bedroom suites built right on the beach, directly into the rocks that form Land's End, plus 35 time-share/condo units overlooking the beach. Some of the suites have a private hot tub on the terrace. The suites have ocean views and kitchenettes, and all rooms have air-conditioning, satellite TV, in-room safes, coffeemakers, and direct-dial phones. Down at the original beach wing are tennis courts, an aquatic center, an indoor-outdoor restaurant, and two heated pools with swim-up palapa bars and hot tubs. The Solmar is renowned for its fishing fleet; special all-inclusive fishing packages are popular during the late-summer fishing season. The hotel's dive boat, the *Solmar V,* is one of the finest in Baja.

Marina Hotels

US$50–100: Overlooking the east side of the marina, the **Marina Cabo Plaza,** tel. 624/143-1833, fax 624/143-2077, U.S. tel. 510/652-6051 or 800/524-5104, U.S. fax 510/652-9039, has a pool and is adjacent to a shopping center with restaurants, stores, and a private mail center. Playa El Médano is a 10-minute walk away. Kitchenettes available.

US$150–250: Next to Plaza Fiesta, near the Marina Cabo San Lucas office, stands **Marina Fiesta Resort & Hotel,** tel. 624/145-6020, fax 624/145-6021, U.S. tel. 877/243-4880, reservations@marinafiestaresort.com, www.marinafiestaresort.com. The hotel's well-designed, comfortable suites come with kitchenettes. Among the facilities are a sun deck and solarium (both with hot tubs), a massage and therapy room, 24-hour supermarket, drugstore, children's playground, and a free-form heated pool with a swim-up palapa bar.

Largest of the marina hotels is **Plaza Las Glorias,** tel. 624/143-1220 or 800/716-8770, U.S. tel. 800/342-2644, fax 624/143-1238, http://hotel.sidek.com.mx, a pseudo-Pueblo-style pink structure on the marina's west side. The sprawling, 287-room hotel is nicknamed Cabo Jail because it takes so long to walk from one end to the other. All rooms come with air-conditioning, telephones, refrigerators, and in-room safety box. Facilities include a pool, restaurants, bars, a shopping center, travel agency, and a beach club at Playa El Médano.

Condominiums, Time Shares, and Beach Homes

Some of the best deals for families or small groups

Plaza Las Glorias, Cabo San Lucas

© JOE CUMMINGS

are rental condos, which usually sleep up to four for US$75–180 per night. The following condo sites take reservations directly (rates do not include tax and service unless otherwise noted).

US$100–150: Well-managed, four-story **Bahía Condo Hotel,** just off Camino de los Pescadores above Playa El Médano, tel. 624/143-1888, fax 624/143-1891, U.S. tel. 408/776-1806 or 800/932-5599, U.S. fax 408/278-1513, grupobahio@aol.com, www.grupobahio.com, rents clean, comfortable air-conditioned units, some with ocean views, all with fully equipped kitchenettes, satellite TV, and direct-dial phones. Other amenities include laundry facilities, a good restaurant, and a pool with hot tub and swim-up palapa bar. Rates here include tax.

Close to downtown but also within easy walking distance of El Médano, **Marina Sol Condominiums,** Apdo. Postal 177, Cabo San Lucas, BCS 23410, tel. 624/143-3231, fax 624/143-6286, U.S. tel. 877/255-1721, info@marinasolresort.com, www.marinasolresort.com, features simple but good-size, well-kept one- and two-bedroom condos built around a garden courtyard with a pool. A handicapped-accessible room is also available. The complex also has a hot tub, swim-up bar, and a small gym. An independently operated grocery store and laundry service can be found in the lobby.

US$150–250: Club Cascadas, at the east end of El Médano next to Pueblo Bonito Resort, tel. 624/143-1882, fax 624/143-1881, U.S. tel. 800/365-6494, www.clubcascadasdebaja.com, is a nicely designed time-share complex with one- to three-bedroom interconnected villas, two pools, and tennis courts.

Near Casa Rafael's off Camino de los Pescadores, a short walk from Playa El Médano, stand the two round, whitewashed towers of **Cabo Villas,** tel.624/143-9166, fax 624/143-2558, cabovillasresort@prodigy.net.mx. One-bedroom, one-bath units and two-bedroom, two-bath units are available.

The **Hotel Solmar Suites** (see Playa Solmar Hotels, earlier) rents a number of time-share/condo units on the hill overlooking Playa Solmar.

Next door, the **Suites Terrasol,** tel. 624/143-2754, U.S. tel. 800/524-5104, fax 624/143-1804,

rents studios, one-bedroom units, and two-bedroom units, all with full kitchens and ocean views. On the premises are two pools, a sauna, health club, restaurant, and bar. You can walk to the beach from both the Solmar and Terrasol.

Many real estate and property-management companies rent units in condo complexes not mentioned above. Some of these companies also handle time-share and beach-home rentals.

Companies with a broad variety of rental units in the Los Cabos area include: **Earth, Sea, and Sky Tours,** U.S. tel. 800/745-2226, fax 831/662-8426, www.cabovillas.com; **A-1 Cabo Vacation Properties,** tel. 624/144-5089; **Cabo Villa Rentals,** U.S. tel. 877/944-CABO or 310/823-2367, www.cabovillarentals.com; **Real Easy Rentals,** tel./fax 624/143-6096, www.realeasyrentals.com.

Bed-and-Breakfasts

US$50–100: Off Calle Constitución in the residential western part of town, **The Bungalows Breakfast Inn,** tel./fax 624/143-5035, U.S. tel. 888/424-2226, thebungalows@earthlink.net, www.cabobungalows.com, offers eight well-decorated one-bedroom suites, each with ceiling fan, air-conditioning, fridge, stove, and TV; one larger, deluxe one-bedroom suite; one "honeymoon suite" with a private veranda and view of town; and six two-bedroom bungalows, each sleeping four to six guests. Smoking isn't permitted anywhere on the premises, inside or out. The small but well-landscaped grounds also contain a heated swimming pool, hot tub, and outdoor barbecue, plus a small gift shop selling many of the Mexican decor accessories seen in the guest rooms. A Mexican cook and pastry chef prepare the complimentary full breakfast.

Camping and RV Parks

In the northwestern section of town on the way to Todos Santos, shady and well-kept **El Faro Viejo Trailer Park,** Matamoros at Mijares, Apdo. Postal 64, Cabo San Lucas, BCS, tel. 624/143-0561, tel./fax 624/143-4211, hectormoraila@prodigy.net.mx, offers 20 spaces with full hookups for US$17 d. Facilities include flush toilets, showers, a Laundromat, public phone, security guard, and a reputable restaurant/bar.

Add US$4 for each additional person per site. Monthly rates of US$400 are available. This park tends to fill up Nov.–May but is more likely to have a spot than Vagabundos or San Vicente (see later mention).

Three km northeast of Cabo San Lucas off Mexico 1, the **Vagabundos del Mar RV Park,** tel. 624/143-0209, fax 624/143-0511, U.S. tel. 707/374-5511 or 800/474-2252, has 85 well-serviced slots with full hookups for US$18 for two plus US$4 per additional guest; discounts are available for members of the Vagabundos del Mar travel club. November–June this park is usually booked up for weeks or months at a time, so be sure to make contact well in advance if you want to park here. Caravans are not accepted. Facilities include a restaurant, bar, flush toilets, *palapas,* showers, a pool, and laundry.

The nearby **San Vicente Trailer Park,** Apdo. Postal 463, Cabo San Lucas, BCS, tel. 624/143-0712, is lushly planted, and all spots are ramada-shaded. Full hookups (when available) cost US$15–18, and amenities include hot showers, a recreation room, bar, and restaurant. This park is also fully occupied much of the time, as evidenced by the many semipermanent, nicely constructed RV shelters and bungalows within.

Behind San Vicente and Vagabundos RV Parks and Playa El Médano is tidy **Club Cabo Hotel and Campground Resort,** tel./fax 624/143-3348, www.clubcaboinn.com; to get there, turn east off Mexico 1 onto the road to Club Cascada, then turn onto the first dirt road on your left and follow the signs. This small campground offers 10 tent sites and 10 RV slots—some shaded, some not. Tent sites cost US$8 pp, RV spots US$18 for two persons. Facilities include well-kept toilets, hot showers, a hot tub, hammock lounge area, table tennis, trampoline, and pool. Club Cabo also rents eight suites with full kitchens for US$40–80 a night—see Playa El Médano Hotels, previously, for further information. Nowadays Club Cabo is more likely to have a vacancy than El Faro, Vagabundos, or San Vicente; it is also closer to the beach than the others. The proprietor, an accomplished pilot, can arrange ultralight flights and instruction in the area. Visiting pilots may receive discounts

on accommodations. Other activities that can be arranged through Club Cabo include kayaking, sailing, horseback riding, and mountain biking. The adjacent natural thornforest is a habitat for many resident and migratory bird species.

On a rise at Km 5.5 on Mexico 1, **El Arco Trailer Park,** tel. 624/143-0613 or 624/143-1686, commands a view of town and Bahía San Lucas even though it's on the north side of the highway. El Arco has many permanent shelters and few vacancies; when available, full hookups cost US$17, tent sites US$9. The park features flush toilets, a pool, and a large palapa restaurant with distant bay views.

You can camp on the beaches farther northeast along Mexico 1 (see The Corridor, earlier) or northwest along Mexico 19.

FOOD

Downtown Cabo San Lucas is riddled with restaurants and bars, most of open-air design. Menus typically attempt to cover the main bases demanded by any Mexican resort area—seafood, Italian, Mexican, and steak. Because Cabo is Baja's number-one resort town, prices are above what you'd find in La Paz, Ensenada, Tijuana, or other tourist areas. Quality is also generally high since Cabo attracts chefs from all over Mexico and beyond. One complaint: Cabo restaurants sometimes hold back on the chilies in Mexican dishes and table salsas, hence *picante*-lovers may be forced to request extra chilies or fresh *salsa cruda* to bring things up to the proper level of heat.

American and Eclectic

Latitude 22+, Blvd. Lázaro Cárdenas between Morelos and Leona Vicario, tel. 624/143-1516, opposite the boat ramp, serves American fare throughout the day, but it's more of a bar than a restaurant. Daily specials include roast chicken, prime rib, pork chops, chicken-fried steak, meat loaf, Croatian pastas, and roast beef. Inexpensive to moderate. Open Wed.–Mon. 8 A.M.–11 P.M.

At the back of the Plaza Las Glorias complex overlooking the marina is **Café Canela,** tel. 624/143-3435. The menu features sandwiches,

© JOE CUMMINGS

asadero, el Pollo de Oro

soups, salads, fresh-squeezed juices, and Mexican dishes with a twist, such as blue-cheese quesadillas with smoked tuna. Canela also offers box lunches. Prices run US$6–10. Open 6 A.M.–5 P.M.

Olé Olé, tel. 624/143-0633, faces the marina at Plaza Bonita. The large outdoor tapa bar features paella, brochettes, and tapas dinner combos such as *gazpacho andaluz, tortilla española,* and *jamón serrano* (Spanish-style cured ham). Try the *gambas a la ajo,* a plate of shrimp in garlic sauce, also available in an octopus version. Moderate to expensive. Open daily 11 A.M.–11 P.M.; paella is served only on Sunday from 1 P.M. (and sometimes on Friday).

Cozy **Sancho Panza,** Locales D19-22, Plaza Las Glorias, tel. 624/143-3212, is one of the nicer restaurant/bars in town. To find it, walk under the pedestrian bridge that connects the wings of Plaza Las Glorias and look for it on your right, before Seafood Mama's. Aided by an artistic and colorful Miró-esque decor, the pro-

prietors have created a first-class wine bar that stocks such hard-to-find, top-of-the-line Baja labels as Monte Xanic and Chateau de Camou along with over 150 other wines. The short menu offers delicious "New World tapas" that mix New American, Mediterranean, and Latin American influences with positive results—try the mushroom-brie fondue, smoked salmon cakes, vegetarian lasagna, or Cuban sandwich. Best salads in town, also espresso and live jazz. Expensive. Open daily 4 P.M.–2 A.M.

Pazzo's Cabo, corner of Niños Héroes and Morelos, tel. 624/123-4313, is a Cabo branch of the Vail, Colorado, pizza place of the same name. Look for fresh pasta, pizza, calzones *mariscos,* and a TV tuned nonstop to sports channels. Live music is featured in the evening. The kitchen is open daily 11 A.M.–midnight; free pizza delivery. One block west of Pazzo's Cabo is the very eclectic **El Bistro,** tel. 624/143-8999, serving mostly Italian and French dishes, with other international cuisines thrown in for good measure. You'll find steaks and seafood too, along with interesting items such as a Thai shrimp dish. Moderate. Open Mon.–Sat. 5 P.M.–midnight.

Peacock's Restaurant and Bar, Camino de los Pescadores, tel. 624/143-1858, next to the driveway of Hotel Meliá San Lucas, boasts a Continental kitchen presided over by a German chef. The changing menu at this large, palapa-roofed, open-air restaurant is diverse and creative, and the wine list is extensive. Moderate to expensive. Open daily 6–10 P.M.

Ruth's Chris Steak House, tel. 624/3232, Puerto Paraíso, a branch of the U.S. chain of the same name, serves their trademark fresh broiled beef on an open-air patio with a marina view. Expensive. Open daily 1 P.M.–11:30 P.M.

Asian

Nick-San Restaurant, Plaza de la Danza, Blvd. Lázaro Cárdenas, is centrally located along the main strip and serves excellent sushi, seafood, and Japanese barbecue. In fact this is probably the most reliably high-quality restaurant in San Lucas, regardless of cuisine. Don't miss the sashimi salad. Moderately priced; open Tues.–Sun. 11:30 A.M.–10:30 P.M.

Kaz, a Japanese restaurant/sushi bar on Calle Guerrero just south of the Cabo Wabo entrance, tel. 624/143-2396, features a palapa-roofed eating area upstairs and an air-conditioned section below. The cooks will prepare your catch if you bring it to them in advance. Open daily 4–11 P.M.

Italian

Capo San Giovanni, Calle Guerrero at Madero, tel. 624/143-0593, just across the road and south of Cabo Wabo, is a restaurant/bar with a pleasant ambience, a spacious courtyard out back, and an inventive southern Italian menu. Open Tues.–Sun. 5–11 P.M. Closed Monday.

Da Giorgio's II, Km 5.5 on The Corridor, part of the Misiones del Cabo complex, tel. 624/145-8160, is a well-designed palapa restaurant with long-distance views of Land's End. Food quality varies; at times the pasta and seafood entrées upstage all the other local Italian venues, while at other times they can be disappointing. Very expensive. Open daily 8:30 A.M.–11 P.M.

Ristorante Italiano Galeón, Blvd. Marina just south of the Hotel Finisterra entrance, tel. 624/143-0443, is an elegant restaurant with harbor views. Specialties include Neapolitan cuisine and pizzas baked in wood-fired ovens. Live piano music nightly. Expensive. Open 4–11 P.M.

Romeo y Julieta, on Blvd. Marina near Hotel Finisterra, tel. 624/143-0225, offers an Italian menu featuring fresh pasta and wood-fired pizzas. Moderate to expensive. Open daily 4–11 P.M.

Mexican

Mi Casa, on Calle Cabo San Lucas opposite the plaza, tel. 624/143-1933, is often cited as the most authentic Mexican restaurant in Cabo. The tastefully designed, half-palapa, half-open-air dining room is encircled by pastel murals intended to look like a small Central Mexican village. The menu lists dishes from all over Mexico, including fajitas, *mole verde, mole poblano, pipián, carne asada a la tampiqueña, pollo borracho,* and *cochinita pibil.* The food is good but doesn't always match menu descriptions. Moderate to expensive. Open daily for dinner 5–10:30 P.M., open for lunch Mon.–Sat. noon–3 P.M.

Just to the northeast of Plaza Náutica, in Plaza

del Sol, **O Mole Mío Restaurant & Bar,** tel. 624/143-7577, features original Mexican recipes such as El Solo Mío (grilled red snapper seasoned with Cajun spices and served with mango salsa) or Camarones Frida y Omar (shrimp baked in a tequila sauce and topped with julienned potatoes). The interior, decorated with unusual custom-designed wicker-and-iron furniture, is as interesting as the menu. The bar section is a fun place for drinks and *botanas.* Moderate. Open daily 11:30 A.M.–11:30 P.M.

For authentic Mexican dishes that won't cost a lot, two places off the main tourist track can be recommended. **La Perla,** Blvd. Lázaro Cárdenas at Guerrero, is a simple Mexican eatery supported by a mainly local clientele. The menu features inexpensive *desayuno, tortas, molletes, tingas,* tacos, burritos, quesadillas, and *licuados;* the daily *comida del día* costs only US$3.20. Open Mon.–Sat. 7:30 A.M.–4:30 P.M. **El Restaurant de Doña Lolita,** opposite Pescadería El Dorado on Niños Héroes near Matamoros, serves inexpensive, authentic *antojitos mexicanos,* plus *champurrado* (hot chocolate made with cornstarch). Open daily 6:30 A.M.–4:30 P.M.

Another very good, non-tourist Mexican eatery is **Las Gardenias,** a family-owned spot on the road to Playa El Médano. It's divided into two sections, the right side serving tacos of various kinds and the left side a changing menu that includes dishes such as *chiles rellenos, cochinita pibil, nopales,* and *chicharrón.*

Back in gringolandia, **Pancho's,** Calle Hidalgo off Blvd. Marina, tel. 624/143-2891, serves huge Mexican platters at reasonable prices, good Mexican breakfasts, and over 190 varieties of tequila. All the waiters speak English. Mexican beer costs US$1 a bottle, cheap house tequila shots 30 cents. Pleasant outdoor seating. Open daily 7 A.M.–11 P.M.

Carlos'n Charlie's, Blvd. Marina, tel. 624/143-1280, functions primarily as a place for tourists to drink themselves silly. But this Grupo Anderson restaurant serves good Mexican food. Volleyball court on the premises. Moderately priced. Open daily 11 A.M.–midnight (or often beyond).

Casa Rafael's, tel. 624/143-0739, is a small

hotel with an elegant dining room specializing in *nacional novelle*, or nouvelle Mexican cuisine—served à la carte or as a seven-course, fixed-price meal. The changing menu also features international dishes and seafood. The wine list is impressive; live music is featured nightly. Expensive. Open Mon.–Sat. 6–10 P.M.; reservations suggested.

Cilantro's Bar & Grill, at the Pueblo Bonito Resort on Playa El Médano, tel. 624/142-9797, is one of Cabo's better hotel-oriented Mexican restaurants, featuring mesquite-grilled seafood and homemade tortillas. Moderate to expensive. Open daily 11 A.M.–11 P.M.

Seafood

El Pescador, Zaragoza at Niños Héroes, serves very good Baja-style seafood—oysters, shrimp, and red snapper are specialties—at low prices. The humble palapa restaurant is a piece of the old Cabo, still patronized by locals. Open daily 8 A.M.–9 P.M.

Mariscos Mocambo, at Calle Vicario and 20 de Noviembre, tel. 624/143-6070, is a very casual, local-style place with a huge seafood menu and low to moderate prices. Open daily noon–10 P.M.

Equally fresh but more creative and naturally more expensive, **Fish House,** tel. 624/144-4501, Plaza La Danza (upstairs from Nik-San and KFC), Blvd. Marina, specializes in fresh clams and oysters, salmon pasta, and live Maine lobster. Despite the name, steak also holds a place of honor here, and the wine selection is very good. Moderately priced; open daily 11 A.M.–11 P.M.

El Shrimp Bucket, in the Plaza Fiesta shopping center on the marina, near Marina Fiesta Resort, tel. 624/143-2598, is a transplant from Mazatlán and the best of the several restaurants in town with the word "shrimp" in the name. The pink crustaceans are served in every conceivable fashion, including the ever-popular fried shrimp served in a terra-cotta bucket. Breakfasts are also good here. Moderately priced. Open daily 6 A.M.–11 P.M.

The Shrimp Factory, Blvd. Marina at Guerrero, tel. 624/143-5066, serves shrimp only by the half kilo or kilo; each order comes with salad, bread, and crackers. It's a no-frills, open-air place. Inexpensive to moderate. Open daily noon–11 P.M.

Lobsters aren't to be ignored, however; nowadays there are an equal number of restaurants employing the word "lobster" in their name. Two of the most popular, under the same ownership, are the oddly named **Sleepless Lobster,** opposite Arámburo Plaza, tel. 624/143-1021, and **Crazy Lobster,** on Hidalgo a block and a half north of Blvd Marina, tel. 624/143-6535. The former is a favorite of the locals for cheap but good eats. Lots of tourists walk right past due to the rustic looks, but it's real-deal food here. Lobster combos start at around US$10, and there are plenty of other seafood specials as well. It's just as famous for the cheap *huevos rancheros* breakfasts: US$1.75 with free coffee. Open for breakfast, lunch, and dinner. Crazy Lobster has a variety of shrimp and lobster platters to choose from (from US$9); the scallop tacos are popular, and steaks are also on the menu. Open daily 8 A.M.–10 P.M.

Las Palmas, on Playa El Médano, tel. 624/143-0447, was the first palapa restaurant on Médano, and most residents agree it's still the best, in spite of the ugly concrete addition. The grilled seafood is always a good choice. Moderately priced. Open daily 10 A.M.–11 P.M.

El Squid Roe, Blvd. Lázaro Cárdenas at Zaragoza, tel. 624/143-0655, is one of the many Grupo Anderson restaurant/bars in Mexico that combine zany, tourist-on-the-loose fun with tried-and-true menus based on regional cuisine. House specialties at this one include seafood, barbecued ribs, and Mexican combos; the kitchen will cook fish you bring in. Moderately priced. Open daily noon–3 A.M.

Giggling Marlin, on Calle Matamoros near Blvd. Marina, tel. 624/143-0606, is better for appetizers and booze than entrées. Most tourists come here to snap photos of themselves hanging upside down—like landed marlins—from the restaurant's block-and-tackle rig. Others come for the big-screen satellite TV. Moderately priced. Open daily 8 A.M.–2 A.M.

Tacos and Fast Food

The local fast-food scene is concentrated along Calle Morelos, where a string of stands offer tacos,

M

CAPE REGION

carne asada, and *mariscos* at the lowest prices in town. The *taquerías* seem to change owners and names every other year or so but rarely close down completely. A cluster of inexpensive restaurants serve seafood cocktails, chicken, and *tortas* at the south end of Calle Ocampo where it meets Boulevard Lázaro Cárdenas.

From December to March a trolley cart at the corner of Boulevard Lázaro Cárdenas and Guerrero assembles delicious custom fruit salads for US$1 a cup, including your choice of sliced papaya, watermelon, cucumber, mango, orange, cantaloupe, and jicama, with a squeeze of lime. Salt and chili powder optional.

Six American fast-food chains have crept into Cabo: **KFC** and **Dairy Queen,** next to Plaza Las Glorias on Boulevard Marina; **Domino's Pizza** (complete with a fleet of delivery motorcycles), tel. 624/143-0592; **Baskin-Robbins,** at Plaza Náutica; **Burger King,** behind the Hard Rock Café; and the most recent import (it was only a matter of time), **McDonald's,** on Lázaro Cárdenas just east of the post office.

100% Natural, Puerto Paraíso, focuses on organic vegetarian dishes, fresh fruit shakes, soy burgers, salads, soups, pastas, and light Mexican. Inexpensive; open daily 7 A.M.–9 P.M.

Felix's, just up from Pancho's on Hidalgo, specializes in fresh fish tacos served with 19 handmade salsas. Note for the sanitation-oriented: here they keep their slaw and *crema* in the refrigerator. As Mexican fish taco places go it's not cheap—shrimp tacos cost US$1.60 each, fish tacos US$1.20 each—and the tacos are ordinary. The *licuados* are more like American smoothies, full of crushed ice. Only the tremendous salsas compel a return visit. Open daily 3–10 P.M.

Las Quesadillasss, opposite Arámburo Plaza on the corner of Blvd. Marina and Lázaro Cárdenas, is a little two-story outdoor spot under a palapa roof near the marina serving dependable tacos, quesadillas, grilled lobster, steak, French dessert crepes, coffee drinks, and beer. Inexpensive and good. Open daily 7 A.M.–3 A.M.

El Pollo de Oro, on Morelos just north of Niños Héroes, is a longtime favorite for Sinaloa-style barbecued chicken, as well as grilled shrimp,

lobster, *arracheras* (fajitas), and ribs. Good breakfasts. Inexpensive. Open daily 8 A.M.–8 P.M.

El Pollo Sinaloense, Calle Zaragoza at 20 de Noviembre, is similar to El Pollo de Oro. Open 11 A.M.–10 P.M.

Super Pollo, Morelos at Ortega, tel. 624/143-0788, is part of the Sinaloa-style chicken chain found throughout Baja. Very reliable and inexpensive. Open daily 7:30 A.M.–10 P.M.

There is a string of inexpensive Mexican restaurants along Calle Leona Vicario, north of Revolución. One is **Taquería los Paisas,** serving tacos and stuffed potatoes (with two other locations—another along Leona Vicario and one opposite Hotel Casa Blanca). A bit farther north past Carranza is **Carnitas El Michoacano.**

Wabo Grill, on Calle Guerrero between Madero and Lázaro Cárdenas, tel. 624/143-1188, is part of Cabo Wabo, the Sammy Hagar–owned nightclub. The menu offers such items as excellent tortilla soup, *ceviche,* lobster burritos, and breakfasts, served inside or out on the patio. Moderately priced. Open daily 7 A.M.–11 P.M.

Deli

Lenny's Deli, just east of Camino Pescadores and south off Lazaro Cardenas, tel. 624/143-8380, is a self-proclaimed "almost kosher deli," with fresh-baked breads, imported cheeses, cold cuts, and other deli items. Open daily 7 A.M.–4 P.M.

Groceries

Cabo's several supermarkets stock Mexican and U.S. foodstuffs—from fresh Mexican cheeses to Sara Lee frozen cheesecake—plus cooking and cleaning supplies, and even auto parts. Ranging from small to huge, they include **Almacénes Grupo Castro** (southwest corner of Calle Morelos and Revolución), **Supermercado Sánliz** (three locations: Blvd. Marina at Madero, Calle Ocampo at Matamoros, and Calle Leona Vicario at López Mateos), and **Supermercado Arámburo** (at Arámburo Plaza, Calle Lázaro Cárdenas at Zaragoza). Supermercado Arámburo stocks a large selection of both domestic and imported foods, as does the new CCC (Centro Comercial California) on the east side of Mexcio 19 just north of the junction with Mexico 1. Next door, **Soriana** carries a huge selection of groceries as well as clothing, gardening supplies, appliances, housewares, hardware, and more.

Pescadería El Dorado, on the south side of 5 de Febrero between Abasolo and Ocampo, stocks a large selection of fresh finfish and shellfish. The most convenient place to buy fresh tortillas is **Tortillería Perla,** on the west side of Calle Abasolo just south of Calle 16 de Septiembre, tel. 624/143-0121.

Panaficadora la Moderna, on Calle Leona Vicario across from Mariscos Mocambo, is a small bakery with a decent selection of Mexican baked goods.

La Baguette, on Blvd. Lázaro Cárdenas next to the entrance for Pedregal, carries European and American-style baked goods including pastries, bagels, and breads; it's open Mon.–Sat. 8:30 A.M.–7:30 P.M. **Swiss Pastry,** Hidalgo at Lázaro Cárdenas (across from the plaza), tel. 624/143-3494, serves chicken pot pie, sandwiches, fresh bagels, and other pastries as well as coffee. It's open Mon.–Sat. 7 A.M.–4 P.M. and has a few tables in front as well as inside.

Frutería Lizarraga, Calle Matamoros at Av. de la Juventud, tel. 624/143-1215, stocks a very good selection of fruits and vegetables; several local hotel and restaurant chefs shop here. **Frutas Selectas Santa Barbara,** on the south side of 20 de Noviembre a little bit west of Morelos, is also good.

Tutto Bene!, Blvd. Marina opposite Plaza Las Glorias, near the traffic circle, stocks an impressive selection of organic foods and imported wines. Open daily 9:30 A.M.–9 P.M.

The best shopping area for beer and liquor is the string of *subagencias* and *licores* along Calle Matamoros.

FISHING

Other than swimming and lying on the beach, sportfishing is Cabo's number-one outdoor activity. An average of 50,000 billfish a year—marlin, sailfish, and swordfish—are hooked off the Cape, more than anywhere else in the world. The biggest trophy of all, the *marlín azul* (blue marlin), can reach five meters (16 feet) in length and weigh close to a ton. In the Cape area, it's not

yellowfin tuna, Cabo San Lucas

© JOE CUMMINGS

unusual to hook 200- to 400-kg (440- to 880-pound) blues. A smaller species, the *marlín rayado* (striped marlin), grows to over 270 kg (600 pounds), while the *marlín negro* (black marlin) is almost as big as the blue.

To catch a glimpse of these huge game fish, stop by the sportfishing dock on the marina's west side around 3–4 P.M., when sportfishing boats return with their catches. Note the flags flown over the boats; a triangular blue flag means a billfish has been bagged, while a red flag with a T means one has been tagged and released. All Cabo sportfishing outfits request that anglers release billfish to fight another day; some even require it. Instead of skinning and mounting these beautiful fish, they recommend bringing a video camera along to record the catch from start to finish. Even where customers demand to keep a billfish, the Sportfishing Association of Los Cabos stipulates that only one billfish per boat may be killed (you can catch and release as many as you like).

Good marlin-fishing spots include **Banco San**

CAPE REGION

Jaime, 29 km (18 miles) southwest of Cabo Falso, and **Banco Golden Gate,** 31 km (19 miles) west of Cabo Falso. Dorado and wahoo are also common in those areas. Sportfishing cruisers—powerboats equipped with electronic fish-finders, sophisticated tackle, fighting chairs and harnesses, and wells for keeping live bait—are the angler's best chance for landing large game fish.

Almost unbelievably, marlin are also somewhat common just beyond the steep dropoffs between Los Frailes and Cabo Falso, an area easily reached by *panga* or skiff. Without the technology of a fishing cruiser, *panga* marlin-fishing becomes the most macho hook-and-line challenge of all—the resulting fish stories reach *Old Man and the Sea* proportions. For anglers with more humble ambitions, black seabass, cabrilla, sierra, and grouper are found in inshore waters; surfcasters can take corvina, ladyfish, sierra, and pargo.

Guided Sportfishing

Several outfitters arrange sportfishing trips aboard cruisers and pangas. Rates average US$300 a day (or around US$165 per half day) on a four-angler, 26-foot custom *panga;* US$465–500 a day for a six-person, 36-foot fishing cruiser; US$350–365 on a 28-foot cruiser; or US$200 per couple on a 31-foot party boat. Charter boats generally hold up to six anglers; rates usually include tax, license, gear, and ice. **Pisces Fleet,** Blvd. Marina at Madero (opposite Supermercado Sánliz), tel. 624/143-1288, fax 624/143-0588, www.piscessportfishing.com, is one of the more reliable independent outfitters; others can be found along the west side of the harbor.

Guided cruiser trips are also easy to arrange through any major Cabo hotel. Solmar, Finisterra, and Meliá Cabo Real each have their own fleets, while other hotels typically use local brokers.

Whomever you go with, be sure to get a breakdown of exactly what to expect on any guided trip. One reader wrote to us and complained he paid for eight hours of marlin fishing but got two hours of marlin fishing, three hours of bottom fishing, one hour waiting to buy bait, and two hours of idle boating. If you know that you're expected to provide your own bait, shop ahead.

And expect that the farther out you go, the more time you'll spend in transit to and from your intended fishing destination.

Panga Trips

The least expensive fishing trips of all are those arranged directly with local *pangeros,* the men who own and operate single fishing *pangas.* Such *pangas* are sometimes available in Cabo San Lucas, but most *panga* fishing trips operate out of La Playita near San José del Cabo. The typical *panga* trip costs US$150 in a three-person, 22-foot boat. Off Playa El Médano you can sometimes find *pangeros* willing to go out for just around US$85 a day. *Panga* rates usually don't include rental gear or fishing licenses. When inquiring about rates—*panga* or cruiser—ask whether the quote includes filleting of edible game fish. The better outfits include fish preparation and packing among their services at no extra charge.

Surfcasting

Cheaper yet is to forgo boating altogether and drop a line from the beach. The best surfcasting in the immediate area is at **Playa Solmar,** but watch the surf closely, as very large waves sometimes seem to arrive out of nowhere. You can also fish from the old pier extending from the abandoned tuna cannery at the entrance to the harbor, where the water is relatively calm. On **Playa El Médano,** you can fish only at the far northeastern end of the beach.

Bait, Tackle, and Fish Processing

Minerva's Baja Tackle, Blvd. Marina at Madero, next door to Pisces Fleet, tel. 624/143-1282, is well stocked with lures and other tackle designed specifically for Cabo sportfishing. Minerva's is also the area's official IGFA representative.

Fresh bait can be purchased at the San Lucas harbor docks for about US$2 cash. Locals here will also clean and fillet your catch on the spot for tips. You can arrange to have fish cleaned, processed, vacuum-packed, and frozen through **Gricelda's Smoke House,** in Plaza Las Glorias on the marina, tel. 624/143-7266, dale@dreammakercharter.com.

DIVING AND SNORKELING

Cabo is a unique diving destination because it's in the middle of a transition zone between tropical and temperate waters. Strikingly large fish like amberjack, hammerheads, and manta rays—which are partial to temperate waters—mix with the smaller, more colorful species typical of tropical waters.

It's also unique in that several snorkeling and scuba sites are only a 15- to 25-minute boat ride from the marina. Snorkelers find the base of the cliffs on each side of **Playa del Amor,** about three meters (10 feet) deep, worth exploring for coral and tropical fish. Nearby **Roca Pelícanos,** some six meters (20 feet) deep, is a bit more challenging. Strong divers, on calm days, can swim south around the arch to the seal colony at Los Frailes and frolic with the creatures.

Divers with experience below 30 meters (100 feet) can visit a vast **submarine canyon** that begins just 50 meters (164 feet) off Playa del Amor. Part of a national marine preserve, the canyon is famous for its "sandfalls"—streams of sand tumbling over the canyon rim at a depth of around 30 meters and forming sand rivers between rock outcroppings. At a depth of around 40 meters (130 feet), the outcroppings give way to sheer granite walls, where the sand rivers drop vertically for over two kilometers (to a depth of around 2,750 meters/9,000 feet). The size of the sandfalls and sand rivers depends to a large extent on climatic conditions; during long spells of very calm weather they may even come to a halt.

The phenomenon was first documented by a Scripps Institute of Oceanography expedition in 1960 and later made famous in one of Jacques Cousteau's television documentaries. The edges of the canyon walls are also layered with colorful coral, sea fans, and other marinelife. These in turn attract schools of tropical fish, including many open-ocean species not ordinarily seen this close to shore.

Several spots along The Corridor between San Lucas and San José feature good diving and snorkeling, including **Playa Chileno** and **Playa Santa María** (for details, see The Corridor, earlier on).

Dives farther afield to **Cabo Pulmo** (for details, see East Cape) and the **Gorda Banks** (sometimes incorrectly called Gordo Banks) can also be arranged from Cabo San Lucas. The Gorda seamounts, at a depth of around 41 meters (135 feet), are famous for sightings of whale sharks (the world's largest fish), huge tuna, amberjacks, groupers, and manta rays.

Dive/Snorkel Guides and Outfitters

As with sportfishing, many Cabo hotels can arrange guided dive trips and equipment rentals. Independent outfitters include: **Amigos del Mar,** next to Solmar Fleet on the west side of the harbor, tel. 624/143-0505, U.S./Canada tel. 800/344-3349, fax 624/143-0887; **Cabo Acuadeportes,** Playa El Médano or Playa Chileno, tel./fax 624/143-0117, VHF channel 82, www.cabowatersports.com; **Tío Watersports,** at the Meliá San Lucas, Meliá Cabo Real, and Marina Fiesta hotels, tel. 624/143-2986; **Underwater Diversions,** Plaza Marina, attached to Plaza Las Glorias facing the marina, tel. 624/143-4004, VHF radio 06, www.divecabo.com; **Pacific Coast Adventures,** tel. 624/143-1777; Andromeda Divers/CYAN Ecology Club, next to Billygan's on Playa Médano, tel. 624/143-8232, www.cabowatersports.com.

Typical rates run US$25–45 pp for snorkeling tours (the more expensive tours go to Playa Santa María), US$40–50 pp for a guided local, one-tank scuba dive, US$65–75 for a two-tank dive (to Shipwreck Beach or the sandfalls), US$125 for a Gorda Banks or Cabo Pulmo dive (including two tanks), US$400–450 for full PADI certification. Each of the foregoing outfitters also offers dive-equipment sales and rental. During the summer months, some dive operations offer certification courses for just US$200; since summer is the best time to dive in Baja with regard to underwater visibility, this is a real bargain.

Amigos del Mar (see previous mention) arranges luxury live-aboard dive trips to the Gorda Banks, Los Frailes, El Bajo, Cabo Pulmo, and other more-remote sites aboard the 112-foot *Solmar V.* The wood-and-brass-fitted boat features two onboard air compressors and a dive platform for easy exits. Prices run around US$2,000 for eight-day Sea of Cortez trips, including all land transfers, food and beverages (including wine and beer), accommodations in air-conditioned staterooms (each with

TV and VCR), and up to three guided dives per day. Longer nine-day trips to the remote Socorro Islands run around US$2,900.

The *Pez Gato,* tel. 624/143-3797, pezsail@ prodigy.net.mx, a large catamaran moored at Playa El Médano, offers a four-hour snorkeling tour to scenic Bahía Santa María along The Corridor, where divers will find rocky reefs, sea caves, coral outcroppings, and abundant tropical marinelife. The tour costs US$45 per adult (kids half price) and includes two hours of swimming and snorkeling at Santa María, plus ceviche, tuna salad, guacamole, salsa and chips, open bar, bottled water, sodas, and cold beer on the way back. The boat departs Sat.–Thurs. at 10 A.M. and returns around 2 P.M.; departure and return times are an hour later on Friday. Another cat, the *Sunrider,* tel. 624/143-2252, leaves from the pier near Plaza Las Glorias and does a Santa María snorkel-and-lunch for only US$38 (children US$19), daily 10 A.M.–1:30 P.M. In this case, the lunch consists of an open bar and full Mexican buffet.

Equipment

Divers seeking equipment rentals can expect the following daily rates only from outfitters in Cabo: wetsuit US$10; mask and snorkel US$10; fins US$3–5; weight belt and weights US$5; regulator US$10; tanks US$12 each; BCD US$10; underwater camera and film US$25; airfills US$4–5.

Cabo Sports Center in Plaza Náutica, tel. 624/143-4272, carries a limited selection of snorkeling gear. Some dive ops also dabble in sales.

Recompression

Buceo Médico Mexicano (BMM), tel. 624/ 143-3666, cabo@sssnetwork.com, maintains a hyperbaric recompression chamber at Plaza Las Glorias.

OTHER SPORTS AND RECREATION

ATV Trail Rides

The sandy beaches and dunes in the Cabo San Lucas area are open to ATVs (all-terrain vehi-

cles) as long as they're kept away from swimming areas (Playa El Médano) and turtle-nesting areas (Cabo Falso). Any of the hotels in town can arrange ATV tours for US$45–50 pp per half day (four hours), US$80 pp all day (six hours). The basic route visits sand dunes, the ruins of El Faro Viejo, and a 1912 shipwreck; the six-hour tour adds La Candelaria, an inland village known for its pottery and *curanderos* (traditional healers). On all-day trips rates include a box lunch and refreshments. Vendors along Boulevard Marina also book these trips.

Baja's ATVs & Watersports, with locations in many local hotels and beaches, tel. 624/143-2050, allows two riders per ATV at a discounted rate. A single rider to El Faro Viejo, for example, pays US$50, while two riders on the same machine pay US$70. For the Candelaria tour one rider pays US$90, two US$110.

Boat Cruises

Dos Mares, tel. 624/143-4339, operates a fleet of glass-bottom tour boats that depart frequently from the marina and from Playa El Médano between 9 A.M. and 4 P.M. each day (sometimes till 5 P.M. depending on the number of clients). The standard 45-minute tour costs US$10 pp and covers Roca Pelícanos (Pelican Rock), the famous Land's End arch, and the sea lion colony. For no extra charge, the crew will let passengers off at Playa del Amor near the arch; you can flag down any passing Dos Mares boat and catch a ride back to the marina later in the day. Simpler launches without glass bottoms will do the same trip, including beach dropoff and pickup, for slightly less.

Sunset cruises with all the beer and margaritas you can drink are also popular and usually last around two hours and 15 minutes. You can make reservations at the marina or at most hotels; tickets cost US$25–50 pp depending on whether dinner is included.

The 42-foot Hawaiian-style catamaran *Pez Gato,* tel. 624/143-3797, VHF channel 18, offers a US$35 pp sunset all-the-margaritas-you-can-drink cruise that leaves from the Hacienda Beach Resort dock at 6 P.M. and returns at 8 P.M. (the cruise can be booked through any hotel). **Jungle**

© JOE CUMMINGS

El Arco, Cabo San Lucas

Cruise, tel. 624/143-8150, does an adults-only catamaran cruise that leaves from the marina at 5 P.M. and returns at 7 P.M.; US$40 pp. A couple of similar boats operate sunset cruises from the west side of the harbor near Plaza Las Glorias. During high season these companies may offer sunset cruises on two separate boats simultaneously—a "romantic" cruise oriented toward couples, and a "booze cruise" for young singles.

Boating

With an average of 1,200 yacht arrivals per year, Cabo San Lucas is a major Baja California boating center. Even though harbor size and marine-repair facilities don't match those of La Paz, the greater variety of other services, nightlife, shopping, and dining venues more than compensates.

The outer harbor anchorages are mostly occupied by sportfishing cruisers; recreational boaters can moor off Playa El Médano to the northeast. Ringing the inner harbor, first dredged in the early 1970s, is **Marina Cabo San Lucas,** tel. 624/143-1251, fax 624/143-1253, U.S. tel. 310/541-3830, marina@cabomarina.com.mx, VHF 88A. Facilities include hot showers, restrooms, a pool, snack bar, laundry, dry storage

and personal storage facilities, a chandlery, fuel (both diesel and gas), water, and 390 slips complete with electricity, telephone hookups, and satellite TV. Also available are a 70-ton lift and full-service boatyard. The marina can accommodate boats up to 180 feet. Permanent and monthly renters at Marina Cabo San Lucas have priority over short-term visiting boaters; daily rentals are available on a first-come, first-serve basis. Guest boaters pay US$1.15–2.60 per foot per day, plus tax, minimum US$28.75 per day. Rates for permanent boaters start at US$266 per month for 20-foot boats; the slip rate for a 43-foot boat would be US$792 per month, US$2,562 for a 120-foot boat. Visiting boaters should call the marina 15 days before arrival to check on the availability of slips. The Marina Cabo San Lucas office is open Mon.–Sat. 9 A.M.–5 P.M., Sunday 10 A.M.–3 P.M. The marina's condos are occasionally available as rentals, and the adjacent Marina Fiesta Resort & Hotel usually has vacant rooms.

Also in the inner harbor are two boat ramps, one near the old ferry pier and one at the northeast end of the harbor near Plaza Las Glorias. A fuel dock is between the old ferry pier and the

CAPE REGION

abandoned cannery, just inside the entrance to the inner harbor. Cabo San Lucas is an official Mexican port of entry; the **COTP** office is on Calle Matamoros at 16 de Septiembre.

AMCSA Accesorios Marinos stocks basic marine supplies. It's next to Amigos del Mar and Solmar Fishing Fleet, on the west side of the harbor just past the turnoff for Solmar Suites.

Golf

Lining the highway between Cabo San Lucas and San José del Cabo are three world-class golf resorts: **Cabo del Sol,** U.S. tel. 624/145-8200 or 800/386-2465; **Palmilla Golf Club,** tel. 624/144-5250, U.S. tel. 800/637-2226; and **Cabo Real,** tel. 624/144-0040 or U.S. tel. 800/393-0400. A second Jack Nicklaus–designed 18-hole course—the **El Dorado,** tel. 624/144-5450—can be found at Cabo Real, and a new Tom Weiskopf–designed 18-hole course was recently completed at the Cabo del Sol resort. **Querencia,** tel. 624/145-6670 or U.S. tel. 888/346-6188, the only private golf course on The Corridor, opened recently near the Palmilla. For details on these courses, see The Corridor earlier in this chapter.

About one km north of the Cabo city limits, the 300-hectare (746-acre) **Cabo San Lucas Country Club,** tel. 624/143-4654, U.S. tel. 888/328-8501, offers The Raven, a Roy Dye–designed course with views of Land's End and Bahía San Lucas from each fairway. See the Raven Golf Club entry earlier for more information.

Gyms

Most of the larger hotels contain fitness centers with free weights, weight machines, and exercise equipment. **Club Fit,** upstairs in Plaza Náutica (also on Blvd. Marina near the marina), adds pool aerobics to the usual gym array. More oriented toward weight-training alone is **Rudo's Gym,** at the northwest corner of Cárdenas and Guerrero. Outside of the city center, the Marina Sol Resort and condo complex offers aerobics classes, a juice bar, and massages.

Horseback Riding

Red Rose (La Rosa) Riding Stables, at Km 4 on Mexico 1 (across from Cabo San Lucas Country Club), tel. 624/143-4826, appears to be the area's most serious saddle outfit. A choice of Western or English tack is offered. A one-hour ride along Playa El Médano costs US$30; a two-hour mountain ride is US$45. Custom horseback trips and riding lessons are available.

Reyes Collins, behind the Hotel Meliá San Lucas, tel. 624/143-3652, offers horseback riding either by the hour or on scheduled trail rides. The hourly rate is a relatively high US$20; better value is the 3.5-hour trail ride to dune-encircled El Faro Viejo (The Old Lighthouse), built in 1890 for US$60. Take this ride in the morning or at sunset for maximum scenic effect. A 90-minute beach ride is also available for US$30.

La Sanluqueña Bullring, at the junction of Mexico 1 and Mexico 19, tel. 624/147-8675, offers well-fed, well-trained horses for private trail rides or for rides along Playa El Médano. Horses are available for beginners as well as experts. A 75-minute ride runs US$30.

Paddling, Sailing, and Windsurfing

The onshore surf at Playa El Médano is mild enough for launching wind- and paddle-powered craft easily. You can rent kayaks, canoes, Hobie Cats, sailboards, and Sunfish sailboats from **Cabo Acuadeportes** at the Hacienda Beach Resort, tel./fax 624/143-0117, VHF radio 82.

In stormy conditions it's not a good idea to try paddling or sailing across the harbor entrance. Be sure to inform the vendors where you plan to take the craft; they'll know the conditions and advise accordingly. Watch out for powerboats, yachts, and cruise ships; larger craft have the de facto right of way. Novices should stick close to Playa El Médano no matter what the conditions.

Race and Sports Book

Casino Real Casino Sports Bar, tel. 624/143-1934, in Plaza Náutica near the marina, features a full-service bar and restaurant, and a bank of closed-circuit television screens tuned to various sporting events. Hours are daily 9 A.M.–11 P.M.

Also in Plaza Náutica next to Baskin-Robbins is **Caliente Race and Sports Book,** tel. 624/143-2866, where customers can place bets based on

Las Vegas odds. Satellite-linked TV monitors show thoroughbred and greyhound races, as well as American football, basketball, baseball, and other games.

Surfing

The nearest surfable waves occur well outside the city limits at **Playa Cabo Bello,** between Km 6 and 5, near the Hotel Cabo San Lucas. See The Corridor for details on this and other surf breaks northeast of town. Most good surf occurs here only during summer/early fall (Cabo Bello, recipient of a winter northwestern swell, is the one exception). If you need equipment or ding repair in Cabo San Lucas, try **Cadillac Surf and Skate,** on Zaragoza near 16 de Septiembre.

Whale-Watching

Whales pass within a few hundred meters of Cabo San Lucas throughout the year, but the most activity occurs during gray whale migration season, Jan.–Mar. The Dos Mares tour-boat fleet operates whale-watching trips from the marina during the migration season for US$35 pp. With binoculars you can also see passing whales from the Hotel Finisterra's Whale Watcher's Bar.

ENTERTAINMENT AND EVENTS

Bars

Nightlife in Cabo starts in the bars downtown near the marina and after midnight moves to the discos, which stay open till 3 or 4 A.M. Tourists bent on getting well-primed for the evening pack **Río Grill** (Blvd. Marina at Zapata), **Magnolia** (farther east along Blvd. Marina), or **Giggling Marlin** (Calle Matamoros at Blvd. Marina).

One of the oldest and funkiest bars in town is **Latitude 22+** ("Lat 22"), on Blvd. Lázaro Cárdenas between Morelos and Leona Vicario, opposite the boat ramp. This is a yachties' hangout with authentic marine decor assembled from salvaged boats. There's a pool table in back. Prices for drinks (very good Bloody Marys) and food are very reasonable; the bar is open Wed.–Mon. 7 A.M.–11 P.M. and offers a happy hour 4–6 P.M.

If wine is your beverage, head to **Sancho Panza,** in Plaza Las Glorias off Blvd. Marina, which offers the one of the best wine lists in southern Baja. Although there's no dress code, you'll fit into the artsy decor better if you wear something other than beachwear. This is the perfect place for a quiet drink, and the tapas menu is tops.

A beach band rocks the afternoon.

© JOE CUMMINGS

The **Whale Watcher Bar** at the Hotel Finisterra has a more sedate but well-attended 3:30–5:30 P.M. happy hour that features two drinks for the price of one. The bar hosts an excellent mariachi group Thurs.–Sun. and offers great Pacific views every day of the week.

The lively bar at **Hacienda Beach Resort,** south end of Playa El Médano, doubles as a weekend social center for older resident gringos. **Edith's,** near Playa El Médano, on the west side of the Camino de los Pescadores, tel. 624/143-0801, presents live and recorded jazz (mostly 1940s and '50s vintage) nightly 6 P.M.–1 A.M.; enjoy views of Bahía Cabo San Lucas and Land's End as long as the sun's up.

Hard Rock Café, Blvd. Marina, Plaza Bonito, tel. 624/143-3779, marked by a pink vintage Cadillac protruding from the front of the building at Plaza Bonita, is a lively place featuring sports-oriented TV rather than music videos, the entertainment staple of HRCs elsewhere. The Hard Rock hosts occasional live rock bands from La Paz and the mainland. Open 11 A.M.–2 A.M. **Jazz on the Rocks,** Niños Héroes at Zaragoza, tel. 624/143-8999, has international cuisine to go along with cool jazz that starts up nightly at 8 P.M. The music plays till 2 A.M. Closed Mondays.

Cabo has recently become a minor Mexican capital for "exotic dancing"—the international English euphemism for women dancing barebreasted or nude on a stage. The audience consists mostly of young American males, although there are plenty of Mexican voyeurs as well. Mexican laws forbidding topless dancing in nightclubs are strictly enforced these days in Tijuana and Juárez, yet the practice thrives in Cabo. In the local clubs' favor, it should be mentioned that they appear to be clean, well-run, and safe—possibly inspired by the growing crop of "gentlemen's clubs" in the United States. Major venues include **Lord Black,** tucked away behind Plaza Náutica and advertising "sushi and showgirls"; **Amnesia,** Plaza del Sol, 2nd floor, Blvd. Marina; and **Mermaids,** Guerrero at Lázaro Cárdenas.

Dance Clubs

Cabo's discos begin filling up around 11 P.M.,

but the crowd doesn't really break a sweat till around midnight or later. A perennial favorite is the two-story dance floor at **El Squid Roe,** Blvd. Lázaro Cárdenas at Zaragoza, where bleacher-balconies offer a bird's-eye view of the swirling masses below. The Squid may stay open as late as 3 A.M., depending on the crowd.

Californians are partial to **Cabo Wabo** on Calle Guerrero between Madero and Lázaro Cárdenas, tel. 624/143-1188, a dance club/restaurant owned by California rock 'n' roller Sammy Hagar. The music here alternates between a recorded mix (with video) and live bands. Cabo Wabo was built in 1989 and named for a Van Halen song describing the "wobble" exhibited by tourists walking around town after a night of club-hopping. Sammy and his band play at the club at least twice a year (on the club's April anniversary and again for the Red Rocker's birthday in October) and occasionally more often—Christmas or New Year's is a good bet. The atmosphere is loose, though not beachy.

If you're more adventurous than the average Cabo visitor, dip into **Hey!** a more sophisticated disco and salsa club on Boulevard Lázaro Cárdenas east of the Banamex. In keeping with Latin tastes, people dress a little more for this one.

Spy's, in the Plaza Las Glorias complex, on the corner facing Blvd. Marina, features live salsa music Thurs.–Sat. from 10:30 P.M.

For a true Latin disco experience, check out **Again and Again Discoteque,** on Blvd. Lázaro Cárdenas near Latitude 22+—a local favorite.

Cinema

On the second floor of Puerto Paraíso mall, **Cinema Paraíso** shows first-run Mexican, American and international films.

Charreada

Despite the name, **La Sanluqueña Bullring,** a small wooden stadium at the northeast corner of Mexico 19 and Mexico 1, actually hosts horseback-riding shows rather than bullfights. One of the performances, billed as "Ladies on Horseback Ballet"—is *escaramuza,* a female equestrian event from the traditional *charreada.* The facility also rents horses (see Other Sports and Recreation, later in this chapter). Call 624/147-8675 for reservations and information.

Events

Cabo San Lucas hosts several sportfishing tournaments throughout the year. The largest is the **Bisbee's Black and Blue Marlin Jackpot Tournament,** held for three days each October. The purse for the contest has exceeded US$850,000, making it the world's richest marlin tournament. Proceeds go to local charities. For information call the tournament organization, tel. 624/143-1622, or the Hotel Finisterra in Cabo San Lucas, tel. 624/143-0100, fax 624/143-0590, U.S. tel. 714/476-5555 or 800/347-2252.

Cabo Jazz Festival rolls around in July, and is held in various locations around town. In 2003 performers included Stanley Clarke, Ruben Blades, and George Duke. Check www.cabojazz.com for more information.

Another notable yearly event falls around the Festival of San Lucas on October 18; look for a week of music, dancing, and feasting in the Mexican tradition.

local pottery

SHOPPING

The streets of Cabo are filled with souvenir shops, street vendors, clothing boutiques, and galleries—probably more shops of this type per capita than anywhere else in Baja.

Arts, Crafts, and Souvenirs

For inexpensive handicrafts—rugs, blankets, baskets, leatherwork—from all over Mexico, try the outdoor **Mercado Mexicano** on Calle Hidalgo at Obregón; for the best prices you'll have to bargain. Another place where bargaining is useful is the **Tianguis Marina,** an outdoor souvenir market on the southwest side of the inner harbor toward the old ferry pier. Typical items here include "Baja-style" hooded cotton pullovers, wood sculptures, straw hats, T-shirts, and costume jewelry.

Among the more interesting craft shops in town are **Faces of Mexico,** Calle Hidalgo off Blvd. Marina (next door to Pancho's Restaurant), selling Mexican masks and other ethnic art; **Taxco Silver,** on Calle Hidalgo opposite Capitán Lucas

Restaurant, with the best selection of silver jewelry in town; and **Joyería Albert,** on Calle Matamoros between Niños Héroes and Lázaro Cárdenas, a branch of the reputable Puerto Vallarta jeweler.

For Mexican-made leather sandals, hop into **Gaby's Huaraches** at Lázaro Cárdenas and Matamoros.

The newer shopping centers are all along the marina side of Boulevard Marina. Modern **Plaza Bonita** faces the marina and holds shops offering tourist-oriented sportswear, jewelry, and souvenirs. Two of the more interesting shops are **Dos Lunas** (handpainted clothing) and **Cartes** (rustic colonial furniture, Talavera pottery, arts and crafts, and classy home-decor accessories).

The arrival of a **Sergio Bustamante** gallery several years ago in Plaza Bonita shows that Cabo San Lucas has attained a market rank similar to Cancún and Puerto Vallarta. People tend either to love or to hate Bustamante's whimsical but costly ceramic sculptures, with their angelic faces and otherworldly, Peter Max–like themes.

CAPE REGION

Mall

The first enclosed shopping mall in Los Cabos, the glitzy Puerto Paraíso is Cabo's newest and most upscale shopping and entertainment plaza. So far you'll find mostly international fashion franchises such as Quicksilver, Nautica, Mossimo, Guess, and Harley Davidson (apparel and gifts, no motorcycles!). When finished it will contain more pricey shops, a convention center, two hotels, condo units, and a spa. Restaurants and food outlets already open include Ruth's Chris Steak House, Häagen Dazs, Houlihan's, and Johnny Rocket's.

Bookstore

Libros Libros/Books Books, in Plaza de la Danza, tel. 624/143-3172, stocks an excellent selection of English-language paperbacks, magazines, maps, books on Baja, children's books, and U.S. newspapers. A second, larger branch recently opened on Boulevard Marina, near Carlos'n Charlie's. Open daily 9 A.M.–9 P.M.

Home Decor

El Callejón, on Calle Guerrero between Blvd. Lázaro Cárdenas and Blvd. Marina, tel. 624/143-1139, stocks a good collection of Talavera ceramics, religious art, pewter, wood and wrought-iron furniture.

Decor America Interiors, Mendoza and Obregón, tel./fax 624/143-0575, is a full-service interior design shop offering a wide selection of furniture, custom upholstery, and accessories. **Casa Maya,** Calle Morelos, tel. 624/143-3197, also offers design services and sells wood and wrought-iron furniture, quality fabrics, draperies, and upholstery. Open Mon.–Fri. 9 A.M.–9 P.M., Saturday 9 A.M.–5 P.M.

In Plaza Los Portales on Mexico 1 is a branch of **Adobe Diseño,** tel. 624/142-4281, with an assortment of well-designed and unusual rustic Mexican furniture and accessories.

Northeast of town, at Km 4 on Mexico 1, **Artesanos** is a large shop selling rustic furniture, hand-painted Mexican tiles, colorful ceramic sinks, terra-cotta wall sconces, glassware, pewter, and many other ceramic and iron decorating accessories, all at low prices (for Cabo). Open Mon.–

Fri. 10 A.M.–2 P.M. and 4–6 P.M., Sat. 10 A.M.–2 P.M., closed Sunday. Bring plenty of pesos, as credit cards aren't accepted here. Next door, **Mármol y Granito** stocks marble and granite materials for floors, kitchens, and bars.

Wine

Just outside of Cabo on The Corridor, directly opposite Santa Carmela, **La Europea** features a good selection of discounted wines, including some California labels, plus just about every other type of booze and upscale deli items such as balsamic vinegar, crackers, olives, cheeses, rose petal marmalade, and great baguettes. It also offers a decent array of cigars displayed in a walk-in humidor. Credit cards are accepted. Open Mon.–Thurs. 9 A.M.–8 P.M., Fri. and Sat. 9 A.M.–9 P.M., Sunday 10 A.M.–3 P.M.

Leather, Coffee, and Cigars

Plaza Marina, attached to the Hotel Plaza Las Glorias on the marina, contains a string of small shops; good buys in leather are available at **Navarro's,** tel. 624/143-4101.

Cuban cigars have really taken off in Cabo. One of the nicest Cuban cigar stores is **J & J Habanos** on Blvd. Marina near Madero. **Pazzo's Cigars,** at Morelos and Niños Héroes (next to Pazzo's Cabo), tel. 624/143-4313, has a walk-in humidor and sells Cuban cigars, tequilas, and liquors. You'll also find Cuban *puros* in several shops along Boulevard Marina. Be sure you know your *habanos*, as fakes aren't unheard of.

La Europea also carries a selection of cigars (see above).

Sporting Goods

Another shopping center near the marina, **Plaza Náutica,** contains the useful **Cabo Sports Center,** which sells beach supplies (coolers, umbrellas, etc.), sports sandals, and varied equipment for golf, swimming, surfing, snorkeling, boogie-boarding, and mountain-biking.

INFORMATION AND SERVICES
Tourist Assistance

Cabo San Lucas has no government tourism offices or information booths, although Fonatur maintains an office on the marina. Its representatives are always interested in speaking with potential investors, but they don't distribute general tourist information. Information on Los Cabos—maps and hotel lists—can be obtained from the state tourism office in La Paz, between Km 5 and 6 on Mexico 1, tel. 612/124-0100, 612/124-0103, or 612/124-0199, fax 612/124-0722, turismo@correro.gbcs.gob.mx.

Money-Changing

American dollars are readily accepted throughout Cabo, although in smaller shops and restaurants you'll save money if you pay in pesos. Foreign-currency exchange service is available 8:30 A.M.–noon at Bancomer, Hidalgo at Guerrero; Banamex, Hidalgo at Lázaro Cárdenas; and Santander Serfín, in Arámburo Plaza. All three banks now offer ATMs; the machine at Santander Serfín appears to be more reliable than the other two. Hotel cashiers also gladly change dollars for pesos, albeit at a lower rate than at the banks.

There's a full-service American Express office (tel. 624/143-5766, fax 624/143-5988) in town near the marina in Plaza Bonita. It offers emergency check-cashing, cardmember services, foreign exchange, and tours. Open Mon.–Fri. 9 A.M.–6 P.M., Saturday 9 A.M.–1 P.M.

Except in emergencies, stay away from Cabo's money changers, which charge high commissions or sell currency at low exchange rates. **Baja Money Exchange** (at Plaza Náutica and several other locations around town), for example, lists an exchange rate that's lower per U.S. dollar than the going bank rate, on top of which it charges five percent commission on personal checks and five percent plus bank fees for wire transfer or cash advances. Although this is expensive, many visiting foreigners—too timid to try a Mexican bank—line up for such services.

Post and Telephone

Cabo's post office, on Blvd. Lázaro Cárdenas, is open Mon.–Fri. 8 A.M.–4 P.M., Saturday 9 A.M.–noon. Public telephone booths are at various locations throughout town, including the main plaza and Arámburo Plaza.

Mail Boxes Etc., Blvd. Marina 39-F in the Plaza Fiesta shopping center (next to the marina and Marina Fiesta Resort), tel. 624/143-3033, fax 624/143-3031, carries mailing supplies, postage stamps, and magazines and rents mailboxes.

Cabo San Lucas has experienced the usual proliferation of Internet cafés; the following list is by no means exhaustive. Of all the spots to surf the Net, only a couple have been around since the last edition of this book. **Dr. Z's Internet Café and Bar** (NetZone), behind BajaTech on Blvd. Lázaro Cárdenas (across from the Pemex), tel. 624/143-5390, netzone@caboguide.com, www.caboguide.com, sells computer time for email and Web surfing in a very comfortable café/bar atmosphere. AOL and CompuServe access is available. Twenty minutes of terminal use runs US$4.50, 40 minutes about US$6.75, and an hour will cost US$8.25; if you use a laptop, those rates jump by about one-third. The small, air-conditioned facility features a full bar (advertising "fabulous martinis") and light food menu. Free parking.

Internet Access

Internet Café Cabomíl in Arámburo Plaza, tel. 624/143-7797, is another choice. Cozy booths are a plus here. Twenty minutes online costs US$2.25, and the terminals have Web cams. Laptop rates are US$5.50 per 15 minutes within Mexico, US$20 per 15 minutes to the United States or Canada, and a whopping US$33 per 15 minutes elsewhere. The scanning, color printing, photocopying, and CD-copying services here are reliable. Open 10 A.M.–9 P.M.

Networks, just off Blvd. Marina on Calle Hidalgo, advertises some very cheap rates—US$2 per 15 minutes at last check.

Magazines and Newspapers

The annual magazine *Los Cabos Guide* contains a number of features, ads, annotated lists, and announcements concerning hotels, restaurants, clubs, and recreational events as well as local social and business news. It's offered for sale at some local newsstands, but free copies can be collected at real estate offices. The local Spanish-language newspaper is *El Heraldo de los Cabos. Gringo Gazette,* a tourist newspaper written and edited locally but printed in the United States, carries whimsical local news stories and events listings. Another tourist rag, *Cabo Life,* contains less news and more ads.

USA Today and *The News* (from Mexico City) are usually available at **Supermercado Sánliz,** Blvd. Marina at Madero, as well as at other larger grocery stores catering to gringos. **Libros Libros/Books Books** in Plaza de la Danza carries *The News, USA Today,* and the *Los Angeles Times.*

Laundry

Lavamática Cristy, tel. 624/143-2959, and **Lavandería Evelyn,** both opposite El Faro Viejo Trailer Park on Calle Matamoros, offer banks of washing machines for self-service laundry; ask the attendants to start the machines for you. Or you can pay (by weight) to have the washing, drying, and ironing done by the staff—one-day service is the norm. Cristy is open Mon.–Sat. 7 A.M.–10 P.M., Sunday 7 A.M.–2 P.M., while Evelyn is open daily 7 A.M.–7 P.M. Several other *lavanderías* are scattered around town, including **Nela's Laundry** on the corner of Alikan and Zaragoza.

Immigration

Cabo's *migración* office is on Blvd. Lázaro Cárdenas between Gómez Farías and 16 de Septiembre.

U.S. Consular Agent

A U.S. consular agent in Cabo, under the auspices of the United States consul general in Tijuana, maintains a small office at Plaza Naútica, C-4, Blvd. Marina. The office, tel. 624/143-3566, usconsulcabo@hotmail.com, is open Mon.–Fri. 10 A.M.–1 P.M. The consular agent can assist U.S. citizens with lost or stolen passports and other emergency situations.

Travel Agencies

Cabo's major hotels—Solmar, Finisterra, Hacienda, Plaza Las Glorias—have their own travel agencies for making air reservations and flight changes or arranging local tours. In town, the most reliable and longest-running independent is **Los Delfines,** on Calle Morelos at Niños Héroes, tel. 624/143-1396 or 624/143-3096, fax 624/143-1397, www.delfintvl.com; it's open Mon.–Fri. 8:30 A.M.–6 P.M., Saturday 8:30 A.M.–3 P.M.

Medical Services

As always, dial 066 for emergency situations. For medical care, English-speaking doctors advertise in Los Cabos media and a couple of clinics specializing in gringo care can be found. **AmeriMed,** in the Pioneros Building along Lázaro Cárdenas, tel. 624/143-9670, is a 24-hour clinic with bilingual staff who specialize in urgent and emergency services, along with ob/gyn care, family practice, and more. Most insurance programs are accepted.

GETTING THERE

By Air

See the San José del Cabo Transportation section for details on domestic and international service to **Los Cabos International Airport.** The airport is 12.8 km (eight miles) north of San José del Cabo. **Mexicana** has a Cabo San Lucas office at Plaza Comercial Copán, tel. 624/143-5352 or 800/366-5400; **Aero California** is in Plaza Náutica, Blvd. Marina, tel. 624/143-3700.

Private pilots will find a 1,550-meter (5,100-foot) paved airstrip just north of town; fuel is not available.

By Sea

The SCT Cabo San Lucas–Puerto Vallarta ferry

service was discontinued in 1989; SEMATUR, the private corporation that took control of the formerly government-owned ferry line, has no plans to reinstate service. The nearest ferry service to the mainland operates between La Paz and Mazatlán (see the La Paz section).

Marina Cabo San Lucas is the main docking facility for transient recreational boats; bow-stern anchorages are also permitted in the outer bay. See Boating for details on services and rates.

By Land

Autotransportes Águila, tel. 624/143-7880, operates 17 buses a day to La Paz (US$11.25), a dozen via Todos Santos (US$5.60). This is the quickest route at 3.5 hours total; the rest go via San José del Cabo, Los Barriles, and the East Cape, totaling 4–4.5 hours. The first bus leaves Cabo San Lucas at 5:45 A.M.; the last leaves at 8:30 P.M. Buses that depart at 7:40 A.M., 9:40 A.M., and 12:30 P.M. continue on to Pichilingue for the ferry; if you miss these, take any La Paz bus and transfer to one of the hourly buses to Pichilingue from the La Paz bus station. Cabo's main intercity bus terminal is on Mexico 19, just north of the Mexico 1 junction, opposite the Pemex station.

Autotransportes La Paz also has buses to La Paz, usually slightly cheaper than the competition. The bus stop is on the opposite side of the road, just south of the same junction. Buses depart at 6, 7, 8:30, and 9:30 A.M., then roughly every 90 minutes thereafter. Buses to Todos Santos cost US$5.

A handful of Águila and Autotransportes La Paz buses to La Paz run along the highway outside **San José del Cabo,** and many stop at the downtown station; the trip takes 30–45 minutes and costs US$2 pp. Aside from the main depot, you can also catch comfy orange-and-blue local buses (US$2) to San José (you get off along the highway, from where it's a 15-minute walk to the town center) from a bus shelter on the south side of Boulevard Lázaro Cárdenas across from the Calle Leona Vicario intersection. This latter option is infinitely easier.

Águila operates one bus per day to **Loreto** (10:30 A.M., US$30) and **Tijuana** (4:40 P.M., US$101).

If you've driven down from the United States border, congratulations—you've reached "Land's End." If you've arrived via the La Paz ferry terminal and plan to drive north to the United States, count on three eight-hour days (Mulegé first night, Cataviña second night) or 2.5 dawn-to-dusk days (Santa Rosalía first night, San Quintín second night). If you stretch your itinerary to include a week's driving time, you'll have a safer trip and more of an opportunity to enjoy the sights along the way.

GETTING AROUND

Airport Transport

Taxis from Los Cabos International Airport cost US$65 per vehicle for up to four persons. In the reverse direction, from San Lucas to the airport, you can usually get a taxi for US$40 for up to four persons. The less expensive airport shuttle bus from Plaza Las Glorias, tel. 624/143-1220, is US$14 pp and departs from the hotel at 9 A.M. and 3 P.M., though this schedule changes often.

Taxis and Pedicabs

In Cabo itself, you can easily get around on foot, bicycle, or scooter, though car taxis are available for US$2–6 a trip.

Checker Cabo is a fleet of mountain bikes welded to two-wheeled carts to produce Asian-style pedicabs. A pedicab trip anywhere in Cabo costs around US$1.70 pp, maximum of two passengers per vehicle.

Water Taxi: You can hire harbor skiffs from the marina in front of Plaza Las Glorias to Playa El Médano (US$2.50 pp one-way) and Playa del Amor (US$10 round-trip only). In the reverse direction, skiffs are plentiful at El Médano, but for Playa del Amor, advance arrangements for a pickup are necessary.

Rental Cars

You can rent VW sedans, VW combis (vans), and Chevy Cavaliers at Los Cabos International Airport (see Transportation in the San José del Cabo section). In Cabo, they can also be rented—albeit more expensively than at the airport—at **Budget,** across from McDonald's, tel. 624/143-4190;

water taxi at Playa del Amor

Dollar, Blvd. Lázaro Cárdenas at Mendoza (or another in Plaza Las Glorias), tel. 624/143-1250 or 624/143-1260, airport 624/142-0100; **Avis,** downtown in Plaza Los Mariachis (near Cabo Wabo), tel. 624/143-4607; and **Thrifty,** Blvd. Marina, tel. 624/143-1666, among many, many, *many* others. Rates vary from around US$25 a day plus US$.33 per kilometer for a no-frills Chevy Pop or VW Bug to US$45/day plus US$.55/km for a VW Jetta. You can arrange kilometer-free rentals for these vehicles for higher day rates of around US$45 and US$78 per day, respectively. It's usually cheaper to rent at Los Cabos International Airport than in Cabo San Lucas, but it's always worth shopping around and, if necessary, bargaining.

Vendors along Boulevard Marina rent mopeds, ATVs, and—less often—motorcycles. These are hard to come by without going on a three-hour, US$50 tour of some sort, usually to the Old Lighthouse. If you can find them by the hour, typical prices are US$20 per hour, US$60 for a half day, US$80 for a full day.

Tours

Several local travel agencies and hotels offer land tours of the area, typically US$50 for the city and El Faro Viejo, US$90 for La Candelaria and Todos Santos.

For information on bay tours, see Other Sports and Recreation, previously.

West Cape

Although a paved, two-lane highway (Mexico 19) extends the full 76 km (47 miles) between Cabo San Lucas and Todos Santos (and beyond all the way to La Paz), this is still the least developed coastal stretch on the lower Cape. Some say it's only a matter of time before this area is dotted with resorts; housing developments are already slowly appearing along the southern end of the highway outside Cabo San Lucas. Local resistance to development—especially in the Todos Santos area—is growing, so perhaps the area farther north will remain preserved and relatively pristine.

Mexico 19 heads west out of Cabo San Lucas toward Cabo Falso before making a long lazy arc to the north. An alternate route heads due north out of San Lucas, following unpaved ranch roads to the picturesque foothills village of La Candelaria. From there, those with four-wheel drive can follow a sandy arroyo road west, rejoining Mexico 19 near Playa Migriño. Those without four-wheel drive will find a visit to La Candelaria worthwhile but will have to return to Cabo San Lucas the way they came, then head north up Mexico 19. Both routes are covered in detail later.

CABO FALSO TO PLAYA MIGRIÑO

About three km west of the Cabo San Lucas city limits is Cabo Falso, once incorrectly thought to be Baja California's southernmost point. Because the wide beach along Cabo Falso is protected as a nesting ground for sea turtles, visitors aren't permitted within 50 meters (165 feet) of the surf line. The dunes behind the beach, however, are a popular destination for rented ATVs from Cabo San Lucas. The abandoned lighthouse, **El Faro Viejo,** signaled ships from 1895 to 1961; the original lens is now installed in a newer lighthouse higher on the beach. Surrounded by loose sand for at least a half mile, the old lighthouse can be approached only on foot, ATV, or horse.

Past Cabo Falso the highway begins climbing over the southwestern foothills and coastal plateaus of the Sierra de la Laguna to reach the small ranching settlement of Migriño after about 21 km (13 miles). Playa Migriño, accessed at Km 94 or 97, is a long section of beach next to Estero Migriño, a small estuary linked with Río Candelaria. In winter, surfers can catch a point break at the north end of the beach. Different sections of Playa Migriño are accessible via a network of sandy roads; several spots are suitable for camping.

Simple **Restaurant Migriño,** on the sea side of Mexico 19, just south of Km 102, serves *antojitos* and cold beer.

LA CANDELARIA

Palapa-roofed adobe and block homes, a small church, a school, split-rail and *carrizal* fences, and saddled burros tethered to paloverde and mesquite trees set the scene at this small village in the foothills of the lower Sierra de la Laguna. A palm oasis in a shallow canyon on the northwest edge of the quiet village holds an underground stream, which has been dammed to irrigate mangoes, citrus, guavas, avocados, papayas, corn, and bamboo. Pigs wander in and out of the canyon, seeking cool mud around the pumphouse. Around 80 people live in the village full time; the population swells during school sessions when children from ranchos deeper in the sierra board here to attend the local school.

The area's hilly, tropical-arid thornforest makes for good hiking. Bring plenty of water, even in winter, as the sun bakes everything unprotected by shade. At the edge of town near an old cane mill is a hill surmounted by a cemetery that can be reached on foot. Look for the headstone of Rafael Salvatierra, whose engraved dates of birth and death indicate he lived to the age of 130; opinions are divided as to whether the dates are accurate, although several generations ago residents in this area often passed the century mark.

Curanderos

La Candelaria is known throughout the Cape Region for its *curanderos* (healers). Tourism flacks in Los Cabos call the *curandero* culture "white

CLAYWARE OF CANDELARIA

Candelaria is widely known in the Cape Region for its rustic clay pottery, known as *trastes de barro* locally or, among foreign collectors, as "ranchware." No one's sure how or when the pottery tradition arrived here, but one theory speculates that when the southern Baja missions were secularized in the 19th century, many mestizos who had worked for the mission system chose to establish ranches farther into the sierra, where water was more abundant and the land more fertile. They may have brought with them the simple pottery techniques that were eventually lost to the cities that grew up along the coast.

Earth for Candelaria ranchware is dug from local hillsides, traditionally during the two weeks

American expatriate Lorena Hankins has helped to create a revival of traditional pottery in Candelaria.

between the full and new moons (because of a belief that earth collected during this time makes better potting material). After grinding and sifting the earth by hand, potters add water and knead it into clay, which is then pinched, pulled, and punched into the desired pot shape. Some coiling techniques—rolling clay into ropelike lengths, then coiling them in layers along the rim—may be used near the tops of the vessels.

When the basic shape is finished, the potter smoothes the vessel's surfaces using a cow's rib, a thick piece of leather, or a dried corncob. The pot is left to dry for 12 hours, then polished by troweling the surface with stones and water. Cycles of dry-

ing and polishing continue until the artisan is satisfied with the overall aesthetic result, and then, after a final drying, the pots are taken out of the sun in late afternoon and warmed on a stove until they are too hot to touch. Pots are then placed on a grate and individually covered with "cowchips" (dried cow dung), which are carefully ignited.

The burning fuel functions as a natural kiln, firing the pots without benefit of an oven or other exterior structure. Potters tend the fire to make sure it burns evenly and steadily, all the while checking between layers of chips to see how the pot is progressing; when the entire pot glows red (usually this takes about one hour), it is fired. Pots created this way have a smooth, burnished terracotta appearance. Chips that touch the pot's surface during firing create blurred black "fire clouds," considered an error in the world of refined kiln techniques but valued by ranchware collectors.

Trastes de barro come in all shapes and sizes, from teacups to frijoles bowls to the rare *porrón,* a very large jar used for grain or water storage. The larger the piece, the more difficult it is to make and the more expensive it is to buy. *Tinajas,* medium-size water jars, are easier to find and very functional. The slightly porous surfaces allow a little water to leak out and evaporate, thus keeping the vessel and its contents cooler than the ambient air temperature—call it ranch refrigeration.

© JOE CUMMINGS

magic," but in reality the local villagers simply have a way with medicinal herbs, which grow in the sierra in some abundance. Considering Candelaria's relative remoteness from modern pharmacies and lack of economic resources, it's not surprising that some knowledge of herbal treatments has been preserved by necessity.

Arts and Crafts

Local artisans produce rustic ranchware pots, cane baskets, and *palo escopeta* chairs with palm-fiber bottoms. Look for a sign reading Pottery in the village if you're interested in purchasing these crafts. Candelaria resident Lorena Hankins sometimes leads pottery workshops; check with Lorena in La Candelaria, or ask around in Todos Santos.

Getting There

The quickest way to La Candelaria is via a 9.1-km (5.6-mile) sandy arroyo road that turns inland off Mexico 19 near **Playa Migriño** (just on the north side of Río Candelaria). The unsigned turnoff lies three km (1.9 miles) south of the Km 94 marker, or about a half kilometer (.3 miles) north of the main Playa Migriño turnoff. This road, suitable for four-wheel-drive vehicles only, parallels the deep, wide Río Candelaria arroyo. It's sandy and narrow in spots, so drivers must take care not to stray off the track into sand traps. And since the road runs across the bottom of the arroyo at one point, it would be risky during or after a hard rain. If you're two-wheeling it, stick to the San Lucas road both ways.

This route is longer and more scenic than the road from Playa Migriño. From downtown **Cabo San Lucas,** begin driving toward San José along Boulevard Lázaro Cárdenas, then turn left at a sign marked La Paz Via Corta directly opposite the entrance to Club Cascada. You are now heading northwest toward Todos Santos and La Paz. After passing a soccer field on the left, look for a power plant on your right and turn onto the wide dirt road near the plant (1.7 km/1.1 miles from the Via Corta intersection); this turnoff lies opposite the entrance to Minisuper Luly's and a *llantera* at Calle Morelos.

From this intersection, La Candelaria is 27.7 km (17.2 miles) away according to my odometer

(the highway sign says 23 km). Make another right 4.3 km (2.7 miles) from the highway at a road signed La Candelaria and Los Pozos; you'll pass through a fence and cattle guard here. A military checkpoint has on occasion been set up near this gate.

As you ascend the sierra foothills into relatively dense thornforest (very green in early fall) and stands of *cardón* and pitahaya, it's not unusual to see cattle or burros in the road, so drive slowly. The road forks about 12 km (7.5 miles) from the highway; don't take the right fork signed for San Felipe and El Sauzal but rather the left one, which leads to the charming *ranchitos* and adobe ruins of Los Pozos. Pass a small chapel at 14 km (8.9 miles) and follow signs for La Candelaria and La Trinidad. Stay with the main road and ignore any smaller forks from this point.

The road begins climbing, and 18.5 km (11.5 miles) from the highway you'll see the Pacific Ocean to the west. Around 21 km (13 miles) from the highway you pass a signed turnoff for Rancho San Ramón, and at 24 km (15 miles) you come to a relatively major fork. The right branch is more direct to La Candelaria, though the left curves around to a *ranchito* and eventually cuts back onto the same road. About 800 meters (half a mile) farther (following the right branch), the road crosses an arroyo that could be problematic in heavy rain. Ignore a right turn to La Trinidad at 26.4 km (16.4 miles). Less than 1.6 km (one mile) later you'll arrive at La Candelaria.

Note: Almost any type of vehicle can safely navigate the Cabo San Lucas–Candelaria road in dry weather. Low-lying Los Pozos—almost halfway to La Candelaria—may flood in heavy rains, so if it begins raining during the first half of the drive, turn back. Once you're past Los Pozos, keep going! Becoming stranded in La Candelaria would beat getting mired in Los Pozos.

PESCADERO AND VICINITY
Beaches South of Pescadero

Of the many deserted beaches strung out along the Pacific coast between Playa Migriño and Todos Santos, one of the easiest to reach is **Playa**

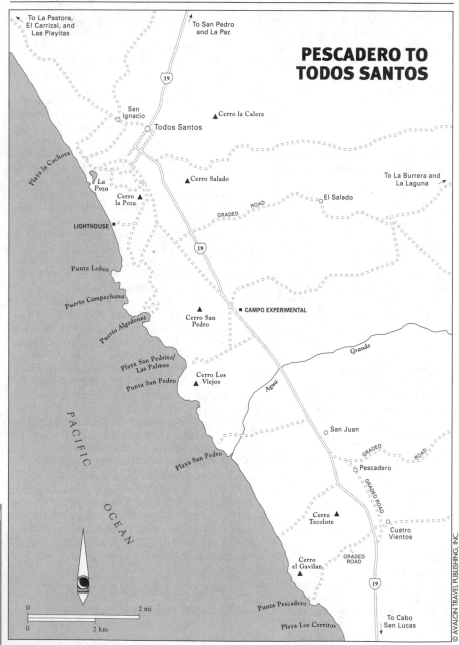

PESCADERO TO TODOS SANTOS

To La Pastora, El Carrizal, and Las Playitas

To San Pedro and La Paz

19

San Ignacio

▲ Cerro la Calera

Todos Santos

Playa la Cachora

La Poza

▲ Cerro Salado

To La Burrera and La Laguna

Cerro la Poza ▲

El Salado

GRADED ROAD

■ LIGHTHOUSE

19

Punta Lobos

Puerto Campechana

■ CAMPO EXPERIMENTAL

Puerto Algodones

▲ Cerro San Pedro

Grande

Playa San Pedrito/ Las Palmas

Cerro Los ▲ Viejos

Agua

Punta San Pedro

PACIFIC

San Juan

GRADED ROAD

Playa San Pedro

Pescadero

GRADED ROAD

OCEAN

Cerro ▲ Tecolote

Cuatro Vientos

GRADED ROAD

0   2 mi

0   2 km

MOON

Cerro el Gavilan ▲

19

To Cabo San Lucas

Punta Pescadero

Playa Los Cerritos

© AVALON TRAVEL PUBLISHING, INC.

Las Cabrillas, south of Pescadero (turnoff at Km 81). Flat and sandy, the beach was named for the plentiful seabass that can be caught from shore. Grass-tufted dunes provide partial windscreens for beach camping, which is free.

Other free beach campsites along this stretch of highway can be found at the ends of dirt roads branching off Mexico 19 at Km 89–90, Km 86, Km 75, and Km 70–71.

Surfer's Note: Punta Gspareño, around Km 73, catches a right point break.

Cuco's

A sandy road near Km 73 leads to a trailer homestead where La Paz native Cuco makes customfitted *bajacaliforniano*-style leather sandals with recycled tire-rubber soles; US$25 a pair. He can take your measurements one day and have the sandals ready the next. An amateur naturalist, Cuco can also arrange mule trips into the Sierra de la Laguna and is a good source of information about sierra flora. He'll need about a week to make the arrangements. Cuco helps Lorena Hankins with Candelaria pottery workshops from time to time as well. To find Cuco's place, follow the dirt road off Mexico 19 till it ends, then turn left and continue straight till you reach his gate; park outside the gate and walk in.

Pescadero

At Km 62, Pescadero (pop. 1,500) was, until recent years, little more than a plaza lined with *tiendas,* two *loncherías,* two restaurants, and a couple of small hotels and campgrounds, surrounded by farms and fishing shacks. But the town is growing little by little, and several new businesses (including a Pemex station) have opened up since the last edition. Several pristine beaches lie along this stretch of the Pacific coast, and the town makes a good jump-off point for explorations of the western Sierra de la Laguna.

Accommodations under US$25: Hotel Bungalows Ziranda, tel. 612/163-0241, sits on the northern edge of Pescadero on the east side of Mexico 19. The "bungalows" are actually four units in a cement-block building, painted white with green trim. Rooms are basic but clean, fea-

turing kitchenettes. Inquire about the rooms at Mini Super Los Arcos next door. A bit farther north on the opposite side of the road, **Hotel Las Auroras** has six basic rooms in two brick buildings. Though close in price to Hotel Bungalows Ziranda, the rooms are smaller and don't offer kitchenettes.

Pescadero Surf Camp, tel. 612/130-3032, www.pescaderosurf.com, is on the east side of the highway at Km 64. Besides tent and palapa camping, you can rent a *cabaña* that sleeps six and is equipped with kitchen and bath. Daily or weekly rates are available. Pescadero Surf Camp also offers campsites with shade palapas for US$8 pp per night. Amenities include water, electricity, bathrooms with hot showers, a pool with a swim-up bar, and a cooking area. The camp rents tents, as well as surfboards and boogie boards by the hour or by the day. Instruction is offered at all levels; guided "surfaris" are also available.

RV Park Baja Serena, cel. 612/130-3006, offers spaces with water and sewer hookups that can be rented by the day (US$10), week (US$49), or month (US$150). The entrance is just south of Mini Super Los Arcos, which is where you check in.

A dirt road west off of Mexico 19 between Hotel Las Auroras and Hotel Bungalows Ziranda leads to two places to stay right on the beach. The well-kept **Casa Cyrene,** tel. 612/145-0288, casacyrene.@email.com, http://todossantos.cc/cyrene.html, is a casual place offering three modern rooms in a two-story house. All rooms have stoves, toilets, attached bath with hot showers, and fans. In addition to the ground-floor *cabañas,* an upper "family floor" has two bedrooms, and goes for US$125 per night; bunkhouse lodging is offered for US$40. Full RV hookups as well as a camping area are also available. The spacious main palapa holds a satellite TV; weekly and monthly rates are available.

Right on the beach just south of Casa Cyrene, the new **Casa Simpática,** casasimpatica@yahoo.com, http://todossantos.cc/casasimpatica.html, features three clean *casitas,* each with queen bed and private bath; amenities include a communal outdoor cooking area and Internet access.

Lonchería Rosita, on the east side of Mexico 19, just north of the main Pescadero intersection, is a small palapa-roof place serving breakfast, lunch, and dinner. Specialties include *pescado empanizado, tamales de puerco,* quesadillas, enchiladas, chicken and *machaca* burritos, and soft drinks. BYOB. **Lonchería Choya,** nearby, is similar. A bit north is the very simple **Antojitos El Parador.**

Friendly **Cesar's Seafood Restaurant,** on the west side Mexico 19 near Km 63, is a simple open-air palapa restaurant serving tasty seafood dishes, *chiles rellenos,* Mexican combination plates, seafood soup, and tacos. Open afternoons and evenings till 9 P.M. Look for the giant cement octopus out front.

The new **Felipe's Restaurant** at Km 61 specializes in tasty Mexican dishes and seafood. Open for breakfast, lunch, and dinner; dishes run about US$4.

Mini Super Los Arcos is a *tienda* on Mexico 19 that carries a good selection of gringo items such as American cheese, nonfat milk, whole turkeys, yogurt, tofu, feta cheese, and balsamic vinegar. Special orders are welcomed.

For a good selection of fresh organic produce, go to **Sueño Tropical,** in a small *palo de arco* structure opposite Hotel Las Auroras on Mexico 19. Open Mon.–Sat. 9 A.M.–5 P.M. Closed June–Oct.

A string of *artesanías* selling such items as colorful Mexican blankets, hammocks, and pottery line the highway in the Pescadero area.

Playa Los Cerritos

Closer to Pescadero at Km 64 (12.8 km/eight miles south of Todos Santos), a good dirt road branches 2.7 km (1.7 miles) southwest to Playa Los Cerritos, another fine beach for camping and fishing. Because the beach is sheltered by Punta Pescadero at its north end, swimming is usually safe. During the winter the northwest swell tips a surfable point break and during the summer a mushy beach break sometimes occurs. Because wave size rarely intimidates, Cerritos is popular with novice surfers.

Los Cerritos Trailer Park is little more than a shell of what it once was, having ceased operations several years ago. You can still use the campground for tent- or car-camping, but there are no functioning facilities. Outside the park you may camp anywhere on the beach for US$4 a night in the winter or for free in the low season.

Playa San Pedro

Just south of Punta San Pedro begins the long Playa San Pedro (7.4 km/4.6 miles south of the Todos Santos town limits), which is stony at the north end but sandy for a long stretch south. The beach's south end, toward Punta Pescadero, is sometimes called Playa Pescadero. Surfing toward the north end can be good, and it's a lot easier to find than San Pedrito (see the following section); the 3.1-km (1.9-mile) access road west from Km 59 is clearly marked.

During the winter surfing season, the local *ejido* sometimes collects a nominal parking fee for vehicles parked in the small area at the end of the road near Punta San Pedro.

Though the highway sign still stands, the popular **San Pedrito RV Park,** was destroyed in 2003 by a hurricane. The owners have reopened the park for camping only, and eventually plan to rebuild.

Playa San Pedrito (Playa Las Palmas)

Just north of Pescadero between Km 56 and 57 is an unsigned, 2.5-km (1.5-mile) dirt road west to Playa San Pedrito, called Palm Beach or Playa Las Palmas by local *norteamericanos.* Stretched between two rocky points and backed by Mexican fan palms and a saltmarsh, this scenic beach offers good fishing and the occasional mushy beach break for surfing or body-boarding. For swimming, the middle 200 meters or so in the center of the cove is usually safest. Toward the north and south ends, the water looks deceptively shallow and inviting, but riptides have been known to carry swimmers out of the cove into open ocean or onto the rocks.

The best thing about Las Palmas/San Pedrito is that there is no easy vehicle access, so the sand isn't crisscrossed with vehicle tracks like many other beaches along the West Cape. However, the beach sand is often streaked with black volcanic sediments from Puerto Algodónes a little farther north. If you arrive expecting "the most beautiful beach on the Pacific coast" (as one guidebook described Las Palmas), you may be disappointed, although the secluded nature of the beach and its visual completeness—framed by rocky headlands at each end and palms to the rear—lend a definite charm.

Trails lead across the headlands at either end of the cove to beach vistas. In back of Punta San Pedro, the slopes of **Cerro Los Viejos** offer a rough but scenic hike.

This beach is sometimes incorrectly called Playa San Pedro. Mexican topographic surveys confirm its original name as Playa San Pedrito or "Little San Pedro Beach"—it's smaller than Playa San Pedro, immediately south of Punta San Pedro. Further proof can be found inside the Casa de la Cultura museum in Todos Santos, where a photo of this beach is clearly labeled Playa de San Pedrito. This same museum contains a historical photo of the Hacienda de San Pedrito—the hacienda now standing in ruins at the back of Playa San Pedrito. Nonetheless most gringos and some locals confuse the names, chiefly because a campground on Playa San Pedro calls itself San Pedrito.

Camping is no longer permitted in the palm grove or in the ruined hacienda behind it. Beach camping on the sand west of the palm grove is allowed, but don't leave any rubbish behind. The owner of the property behind the federal zone generously keeps the access road open so that people can visit the beach; if this privilege is abused by visitors who trash the beach, access could halt at any time. Water is available from a spring at the south end of the beach; treat before drinking.

Getting There: The more commonly used road to San Pedrito leaves Mexico 19 almost opposite the white buildings of the Campo Experimental on the east side of the highway between Km 56 and 57. A more direct road just a bit farther south is sometimes marked with a sign reading Road Closed; all the local residents use it anyway. Both roads intersect several other sandy tracks; when you see a ruined mansion just ahead, make sure you take the left fork that curves around to the south end of the palm orchard. If you head straight toward the middle or north end of the orchard you'll run into the saltmarsh and have to hike a couple of hundred yards through tall saltgrass and mud to reach the beach.

For information on beaches north of Playa San Pedrito, see Beaches in the Todos Santos section.

Exploring the Sierra

East of town, you can follow a network of dirt roads up into the sierra foothills to palm-filled arroyos, remote ranches, thick *cardonales* (*cardón* stands), and other delights whose existence most highway travelers aren't even slightly aware of. If you decide to explore the area, you should do so only in a high-clearance vehicle, preferably with four-wheel drive; better yet, park in the foothills and hike in. It's easy to become lost here, so you may be better off hiring a guide in Pescadero (the aforementioned Cuco may know someone willing to act as a guide) or in Todos Santos. Some of the best spots, such as **Cascada del Refugio,** a sparkling, palm-shaded waterfall, can be reached only by hiking across private land, for which you'll need permission—best arranged by someone local.

One road leading southeast from south of town near Playa Los Cerritos continues approximately 56 km (35 miles) across the Sierra de la Laguna to Mexico 1 between Santa Anita and Caduaño, about 16 km (10 miles) south of Miraflores; see Sierra de la Laguna in the Central Cape section for details. Parts of this road—properly called Ramal Los Naranjos but known by many Anglophone residents as the "Naranjas road"—are graded, but the middle section is passable only by sturdy four-wheel drive.

Todos Santos

One of the more lushly vegetated arroyo settlements in the Cape Region, Todos Santos (pop. 4,000) is a good midpoint stopover for travelers making their way between Cabo San Lucas and La Paz on Mexico 19. The town offers several restaurants, cafés, and taco stands; a few modest hotels, bed-and-breakfasts, RV parks, and a few up-scale accommodations; and a Pemex station. Long-term visitors can wander miles of virgin, as-yet-undeveloped beaches stretching north and south from Todos Santos along the Pacific, explore the steep western escarpment of the Sierra de la Laguna, or simply hang out and soak up the small-town ambience.

The town sits on a *meseta* (low plateau) buttressing the sierra foothills. Looming over Todos Santos to the east, the sierra provides an underground stream that irrigates dozens of orchards laden with mangoes, avocados, guavas, papayas, citrus, coconuts, and other fruits. Most of these are cultivated along wide Arroyo de la Reforma to the town's immediate north, in an area commonly known as **La Huerta** or "The Orchard." At the west end toward the beach is **La Poza**, a small freshwater lagoon favored by resident and migrating waterfowl. North of town, amid a dense palm grove, is another natural pool where local children go swimming.

Beneath the town's sleepy surface, behind the century-old brick and adobe facades, lives a small, year-round colony of artists, surfers, and organic farmers who have found Todos Santos the ideal place to follow their independent pursuits. A number of La Paz residents maintain homes here as temporary escapes from the Cortez coast's intense summer heat; these are complemented by a seasonal community of California refugees from the high-stress film and media worlds who make the town their winter retreat. Several small farms in the area specialize in organic produce for the North American market.

Writeups in *Travel And Leisure* (". . . a new Mexican Oz in the making, destined to become the Carmel of Baja") and later the *Los Angeles Times* briefly stimulated outside interest, much of it focusing on real estate—the town's streets are now tacked with For Sale signs. With each passing year the town seems to move a little closer toward becoming if not the next Carmel, then perhaps the next San José del Cabo.

CLIMATE

Straddling the Tropic of Cancer, Todos Santos has perhaps the coastal Cape Region's most comfortable climate. December through February nights are cool, days warm—warmer, in fact, than most areas along the Cortez coast, which is exposed to the prevailing north winds. Mulegé and Loreto, for example, can easily drop to 15°C (59°F) in Jan.–s while Todos Santos remains in the 20s C (70s F). In March and April the air around Todos Santos begins warming up, but the ocean reaches its coldest annual temperatures (still comfortable for swimming).

Increasing air temperatures in June interact with the cooler seas to bring a marine fog in the evenings; visitors are often surprised how cool the nights are during this month. Although the air is relatively dry most of the year, the months of July, August, and September can become humid enough that the heat index may reach uncomfortable levels on days when there is no rain or cloud cover. At the same time, because of its location on a *meseta* facing the Pacific, the town receives the ocean's overall cooling effect, and hence summer temperatures are always lower than in Cabo San Lucas, San José, or La Paz, all of which are heated to greater or lesser degrees by the warmer Sea of Cortez. When it's 38°C (100°F) in La Paz or Cabo, for example, Todos Santos will register just 32°C (90°F).

July through September are peak rainfall months, although the Sierra de la Laguna partially blocks the heavier storms coming from the Mexican mainland that affect Los Cabos. The November 1993 storm that inundated San José and Cabo San Lucas and caused millions of dollars of damage, for example, barely touched Todos Santos. In September 1996 and 2001, Todos Santos

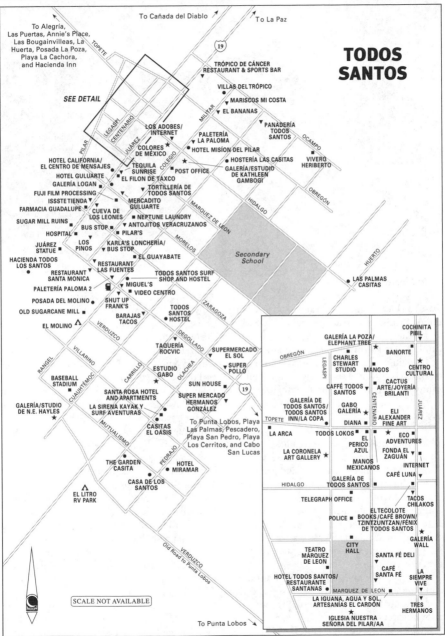

TODOS
SANTOS

SCALE NOT AVAILABLE

© AVALON TRAVEL PUBLISHING, INC.

CAPE REGION

© HOWARD EKMAN

Calle Topete, Todos Santos

wasn't so lucky; hurricanes came ashore causing floods, eroding dirt roads, knocking down trees, and taking down several roofs and utility poles. But few such storms ever reach the town.

The rain tapers off in October as temperatures descend a bit. November usually brings beautiful, sunny weather with an abundance of greenery.

HISTORY

The earliest traces of human habitation in the Todos Santos area date back 3,000 years to "Matancita Man," the defleshed and painted remains (thus indicating a second burial) of a tall male who lived to at least 75 years on a vegetable and animal-protein diet. The first Spaniard to sight the oasis, Jesuit padre Jaime Bravo, found nomadic Guaicura availing themselves of the inland water source and collecting shellfish along the coast.

Padre Bravo established a farm community and a *misión de visita* (visiting mission) called Todos Santos here in 1724, to supply the water-poor mission community at La Paz with fruits, vegetables, wine, and sugarcane. By 1731 Todos Santos was producing 200 burro-loads of *panocha*

(raw brown sugar) annually, along with figs, pomegranates, citrus, and grapes. Two years later, deeming the local Guaicura amenable to missionization, Padre Sigismundo Taraval founded Misión Santa Rosa de las Palmas at the upper end of the arroyo about two km inland from the Pacific. Taraval fled to Isla Espíritu Santo near La Paz following a 1734 native rebellion, and the mission returned to visiting-chapel status the following year.

The local Guaicura population was soon wiped out by smallpox, and Pericú were brought in to work the fields. Reinstated as a *misión de visita* in 1735, Todos Santos outgrew La Paz by the mid-18th century; from 1737 until 1748, Padre Bernardo Zumziel actually spent more time in Todos Santos than at the mission in La Paz. Renamed Nuestra Señora del Pilar de Todos Santos in 1749, the town served as Spanish military headquarters for La Escuadra del Sur, the southern detachment of the Loreto presidio. This enabled the community to weather the Pericú rebellions to the southwest in Santiago and San José del Cabo, although 49 Todos Santos inhabitants were killed defending the town in one related skirmish. Polish Jesuit padre Carlos

Neumayer presided over the mission from 1752 until his death in Todos Santos in 1764. Todos Santos remained an important mission settlement until secularization in 1840.

When Governor Luis del Castillo Negrete ordered the distribution of church lands to the local community in 1841, he was contested by Padre Gabriel González, a local priest and former president of the mission who had used mission property for his own farming and ranching, becoming a powerful local trader in the process. González's armed rebellion was put down in 1842; the priest and his followers fled to Mazatlán.

Anglo whalers visiting Todos Santos in 1849 praised the town as "an oasis" with "friendly and intelligent people." In the post-mission era, Todos Santos thrived as Baja's sugarcane capital, supporting eight sugar mills by the late 19th century. While carrying out a survey of Cape Region flora for the California Academy of Sciences in 1890,

© JOE CUMMINGS

remnants of a sugarcane mill

botanist T. S. Brandegee commented on the area's beauty and bounty. During this period handsome hotels, theaters, municipal offices, and homes for painters and sculptors were built.

Sugar prices dropped precipitously following World War II, and all but one mill closed when the most abundant freshwater spring dried up in 1950. The remaining mill closed in 1965, though smaller household operations continued into the early '70s. The town faded into near obscurity.

Around 1981 the spring came back to life, and the arroyo once again began producing a large variety and quantity of fruits and vegetables. Three years later, Mexico 19 was paved between San Pedro and Cabo San Lucas, opening Todos Santos to tourists and expatriates for the first time.

SIGHTS

Iglesia Nuestra Señora del Pilar

Although the structure itself is rather plain, this church facing the southwest edge of the main plaza contains an important orange-and-blue-garbed figure of the Virgin of Pilar, the focus of the town's biggest festival each year in October. In August the famous Virgin of Loreto—considered the "mother" of all Baja churches founded by the Jesuits—is brought to the church from Loreto.

Centro Cultural Profesor Nestor Agúndez Martínez

Housed in a restored U-shaped brick building on Av. Juárez at Obregón, the Centro Cultural displays a modest collection of artifacts evoking the anthropology, ethnography, history, and natural history of the region, along with small displays of modern art and handicrafts. Named in honor of a venerated local high school teacher, the museum's pottery collection includes classic local ranchware, as well as older ceramics produced by the now-extinct Pericú. Some rare painted Amerindian skulls are also on display. One of the five exhibit rooms contains paintings by local artists, including a set of pastels of historic structures in Zacatecas. Open Mon.–Fri. 8 A.M.–5 P.M., Sat. and Sun. 9 A.M.–1 P.M.; free admission.

© HOWARD EKMAN

Iglesia Nuestra Señora del Pilar on the plaza

Architecture

Although Todos Santos has been inhabited continually since 1731, the oldest standing structures date back only 100–150 years. The town's most historic buildings—a mixture of one- and two-story affairs, all with courtyards—can be seen along the streets nearest the plaza, particularly along Pilar, Centenario, Legaspi, Topete, and Obregón. Most are constructed of fired Mexican brick laid in double or sometimes triple courses (some walls are plastered, some not) topped by flat parapet roofs. A few feature palm-thatched roofs. Large windows and doors bounded by *pilastres* in the classic Andalusian style (favored in provincial Mexico from the time of the Spanish until the middle of the 20th century) predominate in this area. The large building housing **Café Santa Fé** on Calle Centenario, facing the plaza, is one of the only substantial adobe structures downtown. Many of the buildings in this small, semihistoric district are owned or occupied by foreigners.

On the hill overlooking town (off Mexico 19 on the way out of town toward La Paz) stand a few older adobe ruins. The newer eastern half of Todos Santos holds many small residences built of adobe brick or *chiname*—mud plastered over woven *palo de arco* (trumpetbush) branches. Brick ruins of several of the old sugar mills can be seen around town.

BEACHES

The pueblo of Todos Santos sits a couple of kilometers inland from the beach, a fact that has probably helped to maintain tourism growth in the area at a slow, even pace. Also, none of the roads leading from Todos Santos to the beach are paved or even marked, and so far there hasn't been a single hotel or condo development along the Pacific shoreline for at least 65 km in either direction.

To enjoy nearby beaches, then, you'll need good directions and a little patience for those inevitable moments when you realize you've taken a wrong turn and need to retrace your steps. The following list starts south of Todos Santos and proceeds north.

Punta Lobos

About two km (1.2 miles) south of the town limits via Mexico 19, a signed, unpaved access road suitable for most vehicles leads 2.4 km (1.5 miles) to Punta Lobos, a rocky point at the south end of a sandy cove. The point is named for a resident colony of sea lions. The surf here is usually okay for swimming, but take a good look at the currents before leaping in. This cove is used as a launching point for the local fishermen, so there's always a small fleet of *pangas* toward the point. The *pangas* usually bring the catch in after 3 P.M.; watching the pilots time the waves so that they can safely run the boats onto the beach is a treat. Sometimes fresh fish can be bought directly from the *pangeros*.

The ruins of an old stone-walled cannery lie at the side of the access road toward the beach; north along the beach stands a lighthouse. Swimming in the lighthouse area is not recommended due to strong currents. If you continue walking past the lighthouse you'll eventually reach Playa Las Pocitas and Playa La Cachora (see below).

A small spring-fed lagoon lies behind the south end of the beach, marked by a large Virgin shrine. A narrow trail leads up and over the 215-meter (700-foot) headland to a panoramic view of the beach and sea below. On the other side of the headland you can see sandy **Puerto Campechano** and, farther south, Puerto Algodónes.

Punta Lobos can be reached on foot from town by following Calle Pedrajo southwest past Hotel Miramar one long block till you meet a wide dirt road. Turn left and follow the road until you can see the lighthouse on the right; take the next wide dirt road heading in that direction till you reach Punta Lobos. This walk takes 20–30 minutes each way.

Hidden away two headlands south of Punta

WATER WARNINGS

While walking close to the surf line along any of the beaches north of Punta Lobos, watch out for **"sneaker"** waves that rise up seemingly out of nowhere to engulf the beach. Though rare, accidental drownings have occurred on these beaches.

Also beware—during the late *chubasco* season, especially September, small blue jellyfish called *aguas malas* are commonly encountered in inshore waters.

Lobos and almost surrounded by steep cliffs, the deep and secluded cove **Puerto Algodónes** can be reached via a very rough, winding, and sometimes steep dirt-and-stone road that runs southwest off the Punta Lobos access road. According to local history, Algodónes was used for the shipping of tomatoes, sugarcane, and canned fish from the 1930s through the '50s, when a stone-block road was laid between the cannery and the bay. How it got the name Algodónes (cotton) is a mystery; cotton was never cultivated in the Cape Region.

Along the north side of the U-shaped cove stands a tall pier made of rough-hewn stone blocks. The sure-footed can hike along a narrow trail at the bottom of a cliff and reach the rock pier—worth the effort for the view back into the bay. Smaller animal paths lead up a steep slope above the pier for more panoramic views. If you've got all day you could probably hike to Puerto Campechano and back from here.

A black-hued beach of rounded volcanic stones rims the middle reach of the bay, where the waves are sometimes suitable for bodysurfing. To reach the beach you can hike down a cliff or follow the old road. Snorkeling is good at the rocky headlands at each end of the bay, but currents and tidal surges can be too strong for some swimmers. Sea lions are sometimes seen along the rocks.

The old road to Algodónes starts just east of the cannery ruins near Punta Lobos and climbs along the eastern rim of a large arroyo. You can hike to the bay from the cannery area in about 45 minutes at a steady pace, an hour if you take it slow. Start in the early morning and plan to spend the day there so that you can hike back in late afternoon, thus avoiding the hottest part of the day. If you have a sturdy off-highway vehicle that can take soft sand, you can drive about a fourth or a third of the way before the road becomes too rocky for anything but tractor tires.

For information on beaches south of Punta Lobos and Puerto Algodónes, see Pescadero and Vicinity, in the West Cape section.

Playa La Cachora and Playa Las Pocitas

Playa La Cachora is a very broad swath of sand backed by verbena-trimmed dunes, a good spot for strolling and sunset-watching. From the Galería de Todos Santos, follow Calle Topete across the palm-filled arroyo known as La Huerta; the first sand road on the other side (turn left just before the low rock wall; if you start going uphill, you've gone too far) leads west to the beach after curving through a quiet residential section perched on a *meseta* above the northwest corner of the arroyo.

If you walk south along Playa La Cachora, you'll come to Las Pocitas, also known as La Poza de Lobos. Along the back edge of the beach is a freshwater lagoon (La Poza), and toward the south end a rocky ridge heads inland. It's possible to walk back to town via a trail running along the base of the north side (the Huerta side) of this ridge.

The undertow and shore break along La Cachora and Las Pocitas are usually too heavy for swimming, except during the summer when there are occasional long periods of relative calm.

Playa La Pastora

A wider network of sand roads crosses the arroyo and runs north parallel to the beach for some 26 km (16 miles). The roads pass small coconut and papaya orchards and larger farms at Las Playitas and El Carrizal, then head inland to join Mexico 19. Several sandy tracks branch west off this road to a lengthy succession of dune-lined beaches perfect for secluded sunbathing and beachcombing.

For much of the year the surfline here is too precipitous for swimming, though surfers can ride the waves at a break called La Pastora, named for a meadow some distance away. In winter La Pastora offers a right point break in a northwest swell; in summer you'll find an occasional beach break in a southern swell, or a point break in a southwestern swell.

La Pastora is about 5.6 km (3.5 miles) northwest of La Huerta via the only coastal road north; just past a wide arroyo that runs right up to the beach, look for a large, lone palapa next to a long, low stone wall.

Farther North

Beyond El Carrizal a rough dirt road snakes north along and away from the coast 57 km (36 miles) to a cluster of ranchos—Los Inocentes, El Rosario, El Tepetate, and El Tomate—where another dirt road leads northeast 29 km (18 miles) to meet Mexico 1. Sand beach lines the entire coastline

© HOWARD EKMAN

strolling on Playa La Pastora

here all the way north to **Punta Marqués** (about 24 km/15 miles north of Rancho El Tomate) and **Punta Conejo** (18 km/11 miles north of Punta Marqués). Both points offer excellent surfing and windsurfing in the winter and early spring. And surfable reef and point breaks can form in many other spots along the 58-km (36-mile) stretch of sand extending south of Punta Marqués; check out **La Bocana,** an arroyo mouth near Los Inocentes. Self-contained beach camping is permitted anywhere along the shore.

ACCOMMODATIONS

Hotels

The town's several hotels come in a variety of price ranges, but overall Todos Santos is the second least expensive place to overnight in all of Baja California Sur, after La Paz.

Under US$25: At Juárez and Morelos in the center of town, the two-story **Hotel Guluarte,** tel. 612/145-0006, has clean rooms with hot-water showers and a minifridge. Upstairs is a common balcony with chairs; downstairs is a small pool.

US$25–50: In this price category, **Santa Rosa Hotel and Apartments,** on Calle Olachea, tel. 612/145-0394, santa_rosa_baja@hotmail.com, santarosa2.tripod.com, near the south entrance to town, offers eight large, fairly well-maintained studio units with kitchenettes. Facilities include a good pool, laundry, and enclosed parking. Small discounts are available for long-term stays. The signed turnoff for the Santa Rosa is three blocks south of the Pemex station, after which it's another two blocks west to the hotel. Discounted monthly rates are available.

In a dusty but quiet neighborhood in the town's southwestern quarter stands **Hotel Miramar,** Mutualismo at Pedrajo, tel. 612/145-0341. The two-story L-shaped motel contains 10 clean, small rooms, each with two twin beds. On the premises are a pool, small restaurant, and laundry. It's about a 20-minute walk from the beach via the dirt road to Punta Lobos. Off-street parking is available.

The friendly **Hotel Misión del Pilar,** Colegio Militar at Hidalgo, tel. 612/145-0114, is a small,

two-story modern place attached to a small shopping center. The comfortable, nondescript rooms have air-conditioning or fans, hot water, and TV. Discounts are available for long-term stays.

US$50–100: Hotel Todos Santos, on the plaza, tel./fax 612/145-0009, U.S. fax 425/940-0446, reservations@hoteltodossantos.com, www .hoteltodossantos.com, offers four comfortable air-conditioned rooms in a historic building with original colonial Mexican furnishings and vaulted black-palm ceilings.

North of town in a former private residence is the **Alegría,** on the north side of the road leading to Playa La Cachora, tel. 612/145-0700, fax 612/145-0292, alegriats@prodigy.net.mx, www .mexonline.com/alegria.htm. This quiet, smoke-free inn features standard rooms with queen-size beds and suites with king-size beds. All rooms are decorated with hand-painted details and rustic Mexican furniture, and have private patios, telephones, and TVs. The suites also have refrigerators. Continental breakfast (fresh pastries, fruit, juices, coffee, and tea) is included in the rates, and a large kitchen is available for limited use.

Another choice in this price category is the nicely landscaped **Hacienda Inn Todos Santos,** on the road to La Pastora, tel./fax 612/145-0002, haciendainnts@msn.com, www.haciendainntodossantos.com. Far from the center of town, this multidomed hotel is a bit inconvenient for those without their own transportation. Amenities include a pool and a restaurant/bar. The 18 rooms and suites come with cable TV, air-conditioning, bath robes, hair dryer, minifridge and iron. Rates include continental breakfast.

US$100–150: Todos Santos Inn, Calle Legaspi 33 at Topete, tel./fax 612/145-0040, todossantosinn@yahoo.com, www.todossantos inn.com, occupies a well-restored, 1880-vintage brick building. The original owner was said to have thrown his cashbox down the hole of an outhouse to keep it from marauding revolutionaries in 1910. Since then the building has served as a school, cantina, and movie house; the faded mural in the foyer dates to the 1930s. Large rooms with high adobe-brick ceilings and private bath are simply but elegantly decorated with Mexican furniture, Saltillo tile, oriental rugs,

© HOWARD EKMAN

Todos Santos Inn

mosquito nets, and ceiling fans. Larger suites offer sitting areas, private patios, and air-conditioning. Recent additions to the inn include an inviting pool and cozy wine bar.

US$150–250: In this price range is the beautiful **Posada la Poza,** Apdo. Postal 10, Todos Santos, BCS 23305, tel. 612/145-0400, fax 612/145-0453, contact@lapoza.com, www.lapoza.com. Situated on the shore of La Poza, a small freshwater lagoon, and set in a tropical desert garden, Posada la Poza is a Swiss-owned place featuring four garden suites, two junior suites with private hot tubs, and one honeymoon suite. All the spacious rooms have ocean and lagoon views, air-conditioning, telephone, CD player, a safe, and binoculars, and they boast Swiss linens and hypoallergenic blankets and pillows. The honeymoon suite has a sitting area with fireplace and a large private terrace. Other amenities include a large saltwater swimming pool, whale-watching deck, outdoor workout area, the use of bicycles and fishing equipment, and Internet access. Rates include continental breakfast; guests of the honeymoon suite also receive a fruit basket and bottle of champagne. The elegant El Gusto! restaurant is also on the premises (see Food).

There are two ways to get to Posada la Poza; drive down Calle Topete and follow the blue-and-white signs, or turn southwest off of Degollado (Mexico 19) onto Calle Olachea or Calle Carrillo and follow the signs.

Before it closed in January 1999, the run-down, two-story, **Hotel California,** Av. Juárez between Morelos and Márquez de León, tel. 612/145-0525, hotelcaliforniareservations@hotmail.com, was the most popular place to stay in Todos Santos for first-time visitors, some of whom mistakenly believed the hotel had some connection with the Eagles' song of the same name. Reopened in 2003, the hotel has been beautifully renovated by the new owners and now features 11 luxurious suites, a pool and garden, restaurant/bar **La Coronela** (see Food), and **Emporio Hotel California** (see Shopping). A spa featuring an adobe sauna is on the drawing board. They also offer a few rooms in the US$100–150 range.

Bed-and-Breakfast Inns

US$50–100: Hostería Las Casitas, on Calle Rangel between Obregón and Hidalgo (Apdo. Postal 73, Todos Santos, BCS 23305), tel./fax 612/145-0255, wendy_faith@yahoo.ca or info@

CAPE REGION

lascasitasbandb.com, www.lascasitasbandb.com, offers a cluster of four charming, renovated *chiname* adobe cottages plus a newer *casita* built of various desert woods, amid lush landscaping. Some rooms have private baths, others shared facilities. Room rates include breakfast served on a shaded outdoor patio. Las Casitas also houses an art-glass studio specializing in architectural-quality art glass and kiln-worked dinnerware.

Guesthouses

Several homes in town, most of them owned by American or Canadian expatriates, offer lodgings in cottages adjacent to, in back of, or attached to the principal house. Often the owners are happy to supply information about things to see and do in Todos Santos and environs.

US$50–100: In a residential section of unpaved streets south of Mexico 19, **The Garden Casita,** at Olachea and Mutualismo, tel./fax 612/145-0129, gardencasita@todossantos-baja.com, www.todossantos-baja.com/gardencasita.htm, is an owner-designed palapa-roofed guesthouse with a living area, dining area, fully equipped kitchenette with coffeemaker, bedroom, and patio surrounded by an enclosed courtyard. Weekly and monthly rates are available. Long-term rates include weekly maid service.

In roughly the same neighborhood, **Casitas El Oasis,** (formerly Jane's Place),at Villarino and Olachea, tel. 612/145-0216, bigdawgt@aol.com, offers four clean and comfortable apartments on a large, landscaped lot surrounded by a security wall. Three units come with kitchenettes and full-size refrigerators. Pleasant indoor and outdoor sitting areas are found throughout. Long-term stays are welcome.

Three blocks from the center of town, north of Mexico 19, **Las Palmas Casitas,** at Hidalgo and Huerto, tel./fax 612/145-0213, janeLB3@yahoo.com, consists of two one-bedroom *casitas* and one two-bedroom, two-story *casita,* each with palapa roof. All *casitas* are smoke-free. All come with a kitchen, covered patio, tropical gardens, modern amenities, and secure parking. Discounted weekly rates are available.

Behind the Pemex, near the sugarcane mill ruins, is the new **Posada del Molino,** off Calle Rangel, tel. 612/145-0233, corado1@prodigy.net.mx, www.todossantos.cc/posadadelmolino.html, featuring four comfortable, air-conditioned studios facing an inviting swimming pool. Each studio sleeps two, and comes with satellite TV, CD player, and fully-equipped kitchenettes. Maid service is included, and there are coin-operated laundry facilities on the grounds.

North of town, on the north side of the road leading to Playa La Cachora, **Annie's Place,** tel. 612/145-0385, offers Casa de Arbol, a unique three-level "tree house" surrounded by coconut palms and mango trees. A perfect retreat for artists and writers, the tree house features a kitchen, sitting area, bathroom, and two patios on the first level. A light, airy bedroom fills the second level, while the third-level open deck boasts views of the ocean and mountains. Long-term stays are encouraged.

US$100–150: Behind wrought-iron gates in a palm oasis at the south end of Juárez is **Hacienda Todos Los Santos,** Juárez, tel. 612/145-0547, haciendadelossantos@prodigy.net.mx, www.mex-online.com/haciendatodoslossantos.htm. Operated as a hotel with daily housekeeping service, Hacienda Todos Los Santos features three beautifully appointed guesthouses, each with private terrace, fully equipped kitchen, and use of a swimming pool. Choose from Casa Santa Luz, with an air-conditioned bedroom with a queen-size bed, TV, VCR, dining/day room with fireplace, living room with fireplace, and spacious bathroom; Casa del Palmar, a studio suite surrounded by terraces, with a king-size bed, living area, spacious bathroom with shower and bathtub, and a TV/VCR; or Casita del Encanto, a studio suite with a queen-size bed, wet bar, seating area, two patios, and a large bathroom. Access to a kitchen is available when Casita del Encanto is rented together with Casa del Palmar.

In a residential area next to the Garden Casita is the new **Casa de Los Santos,** corner of Pedrajo and Mutualismo, tel. 612/145-0547, haciendadelossantos@prodigy.net.mx. Under the same management as Hacienda Todos Los Santos, this is a charming two-bedroom, two-bath brick house with palapa roof. The casita is surrounded by mature palms and flowering shrubs, and includes a fully equipped kitchen and a small sitting room for the second bedroom. The spacious living/dining room's large arched windows and wooden doors open to a stone terrace which is furnished with outdoor wrought-iron furniture and landscaped with flowering gardens. Off-street parking and weekly maid service are included. Contact Hacienda Todos Los Santos for information. Daily, weekly and monthly rates are available.

Across the wide arroyo north of town, on the south side of the road leading to Playa La Cachora, **Las Puertas,** tel./fax 612/145-0373; reservations@alaspuertas.com, www.alaspuertas.com, features a large two-bedroom, two-bath guesthouse with a fireplace; a smaller one-bedroom guesthouse; and an ocean-view suite with a fireplace, all with thick adobe walls, palapa roofs, sunny patios, and custom, Baja-style furniture. Surrounded by mango and other fruit trees, all units have gourmet kitchens; one guesthouse comes with a separate, full kitchen while the other two have attached kitchens. Daily maid service is a plus. The beach is a five-minute walk away.

Farther down toward the beach on the opposite side of the road, inside a lushly landscaped, walled compound, **Las Bougainvilleas,** tel./fax 612/145-0106, omommag@aol.com, offers two semiluxurious guesthouses, each with a fully equipped kitchen, living room, bathroom, and private patio. The tall profile of one of the cottages encloses a sleeping loft overlooking a sitting room and kitchen and affords a view of the beach and palms to the northwest, while the second *casita* features an unusual round floor plan with a high palapa roof. Guests may use a good-sized swimming pool and palapa-covered barbecue grill on the grounds.

In addition to the tree house at **Annie's Place,** tel 612/145-0385, anniesoups@yahoo.com, there is also Casa Amplia, a spacious two-bedroom palapa-roofed house with one and a half baths and a great room with fully equipped kitchen and a fireplace. Large covered patios extend the living space graciously into true indoor/outdoor living.

Apartments and Houses

Monthly rentals in town range from around US$350–450 a month for small, local-style cottages with few amenities to US$700–1,000 a month for larger, better-furnished houses.

Villas del Trópico, Calle Colegio Militar at Ocampo, tel. 612/145-0019, consists of six simple, furnished apartments inside a shady, walled complex for US$100–125 a week, US$300–500 per month. Nightly stays can probably be arranged in the off season, May–Oct., for US$30–40 a night. Outdoor washing machines may be used at no charge.

A number of part-time Todos Santos residents rent their houses by the day, week, or month. For other current listings and availability, check with **El Centro de Mensajes** (The Message Center), Hotel California, Av. Juárez (Apdo. Postal 48, Todos Santos, BCS 23305), tel. 612/145-0003, fax 612/145-0288, messagecenter1@yahoo.com; **Su Casa,** on Degollado between Pedrajo and Olachea, tel. 612/145-0657, sucasarentals@hotmail.com; or **Como El Sol,** 11 Hidalgo (in the back of Colores de México), tel./fax 612/145-0485, comoelsol@prodigy.net.mx. The office of Como El Sol is open Tuesday, Wednesday, and Saturday 10 A.M.–2 P.M.

Hostels

The **Todos Santos Surf Shop and Hostel** at Degollado (Mexico 19) and Rangel, tel. 044 612/108-0709, teampaty1@hotmail.com, www .todossantos.cc/ecosurfcamp.html, rents surfing equipment at Los Cerritos. While the surf shop is in town, the solar powered, hostel-style surf camp is out at the beach. The proprietors provide transportation from town and will take you around to local *tiendas* to buy food and other supplies before heading out to the hostel. Accommodations at the beach include an array of trailers and campers, a composting toilet, and solar-heated showers. Rates for the trailers are US$25 per night. In the future, they plan to offer guided desert hiking. Women's surf camps are offered Nov.–Aug. at Los Cerritos. The five-day camps include surfing instruction, yoga classes, all meals, and lodging.

Todos Santos Hostel at 69 Calle Degollado, one and a half blocks south of the Pemex station, tel. 612/145-0657 or 044 612/115-2474, www.rental.bajaretreats.com, is one of the least expensive accommodation options in town. The hostel offers five cots in a common room, tent space under shade trees (for those with their own tents), and hammocks under a palapa. All three options cost about US$5, and this rate includes the use of a hot shower and kitchen. Guided mountain treks and kayaking tours are offered by the owners.

Camping and RV Parks

Hostería Las Casitas (see Bed-and-Breakfast Inns, previously) has some space for tent campers at US$7 per person.

El Litro RV Park, a big dirt lot with 15 RV sites surrounded by palm trees, south of Mexico 19 at the end of Calle Olachea, tel. 612/145-0389, invites campers and RVers to park alongside full hookups for US$12 a night or US$250 a month—the use of hot showers and bathrooms is included. The park also has 30 tent sites (US$9 per night) in an orchard camping area. From El Litro, it's a 15-minute walk to the beach.

Three RV slots with palapa shelters and full hookups are available at **Villas del Trópico** (see Apartments and Houses, above) for US$14 per night.

El Molino Trailer Park, at the southeast edge of town off Mexico 19, tel. 612/145-0140, has become a permanent RV community that doesn't rent spaces by the day anymore. RVers interested in long-term leases can try their luck.

North of town a maze of sandy roads leads to a string of undeveloped beaches suitable for camping (see Beaches, earlier on). La Pastora is popular with surfers. Camping, both free and fee, is also available at several of the beaches south of Todos Santos; see Pescadero and Vicinity in the West Cape section.

FOOD

For a small, relatively undiscovered town, Todos Santos has a surprising number of places to eat, though some seem to flourish and die with each successive tourist season.

Taquerías and Fast Food

Several vendors in town offer inexpensive but tasty fish tacos—usually either shark or dorado—

and shrimp tacos. **Pilar's,** at the northeast corner of Colegio Militar and Zaragoza, is the most well known (open 11 A.M.–2 P.M.), but the **Tres Hermanos** vendor stand at the corner of Márquez de León and Juárez is even better. Tres Hermanos sells especially good fish, shrimp and clam tacos most days 8 A.M.–2 P.M., sometimes longer depending on the season.

On Calle Colegio Militar, north of Pilar's is the new, friendly **Antojitos Veracruzanos,** featuring Veracruz-style *antojitos* such as chicken or beef *empanadas* (turnovers), *sopes, gorditas,* and tamales.

Karla's Lonchería, on Calle Colegio Militar opposite the park, is a little outdoor place serving inexpensive, delicious Mexican breakfasts, *antojitos,* and good coffee.

Near the southwest corner of Juárez and Hidalgo in the center of town, **Tacos Chilakos** serves dependable *carne asada,* tacos, quesadillas, bean burritos, and coffee at a few outdoor tables on the sidewalk. *Papas rellenas* are available in the evening. Hours tend to fluctuate, but Tacos Chilakos is usually open Monday–Saturday 8:30 A.M.–9 P.M. **Cochinita Pibil,** diagonally across from the bank, serves *birria.*

On Degollado (Mexico 19) toward the south edge of town are several popular vendor stands, including **Barajas Tacos,** serving *carnitas* and *tacos de pescado y camarones* during the day and *tacos de carne asada* and *papas rellenas* (stuffed potatoes) at night (closed Tuesday); and **Taquería Rocvic,** featuring *tacos de carne asada,* quesadillas, and *champurrada* (a thick drink made from hot chocolate and cornmeal), open in the evening only. **Super Pollo,** on Mexico 19 at Olachea, tel. 612/145-0078, in the same small complex as Supermercado El Sol, is the only chain eatery in town. As usual Super Pollo serves inexpensive charbroiled chicken and fries, with lots of tortillas and salsa. It offers pizza, *carne asada,* hamburgers, and turkey burgers as well. Beans and macaroni salad are offered as sides, all available either to go or to eat at plastic tables on-site. Open 10 A.M.–10 P.M.

At the northern outskirts of town on Mexico 19, amid the string of highway vendors selling fruit pastries and honey, a couple of simple *loncherías* offer a limited selection of burritos, tacos, and other *antojitos*. Very inexpensive.

At least three or four hot dog vendor carts roll out in the evening—usually one each on Juárez, Colegio Militar, and Degollado. Most sell only turkey dogs—often wrapped in bacon (ask for *sin tocino* if you don't want the bacon wrap).

Inexpensive Restaurants

The friendly sand-floor **Mariscos Mi Costa,** Colegio Militar at Ocampo, is a casual seafood place. The *sopa de mariscos* and *camarón al ajo* are particularly recommended. Open daily 10 A.M.– 8 P.M.

Miguel's, at the corner of Degollado and Rangel, is a rustic outdoor place featuring basic Mexican cuisine such as nachos, *chiles rellenos,* enchiladas, and burritos. A good place for breakfast and tourist information. Open daily 8 A.M.–9 P.M.

Open since 1973, old standby **Restaurant Santa Monica,** tel. 612/145-0204, just north of the Pemex station on Mexico 19 (Calle Degollado), serves tasty shrimp, lobster, and *carne asada* dinners at reasonable prices. Service can be slow, but everything is made from scratch. One of the house specialties is *pollo estilo Santa Monica,* a quarter chicken braised in something akin to barbecue sauce. Open daily 8 A.M.–9 P.M.

Nearby in the park is **Los Pinos,** tel. 612/145-0353. It serves simple satisfying fare such as beef fajitas, fresh fish, hamburgers, nachos, sandwiches, *quesadillas,* burritos, *flautas,* and *licuados* The soda fountain has a selection of Carnation ice cream. Los Pinos also offers copy and fax service and film processing. Reasonably priced. Open Wed.–Mon. 10 A.M.–10 P.M.

Café Brown, in the back of the Hotel Misión del Pilar complex, serves a variety of breakfasts, including omelettes, enchiladas, *molletes,* sandwiches, lasagna, smoked marlin, salads, baked goods, cakes, croissants, muffins, herb teas, regular teas, soy milk, assorted espresso drinks, smoothies, wine, and beer. Open daily 7 A.M.–5 P.M. A second location on Av. Juárez and Hidalgo, in the Plaza de los Cardones commercial center, offers the same fare at outdoor tables, but is closed on Monday. Internet service is available here as well.

If you're heading to La Paz along Mexico 19

© HOWARD EKMAN

Miguel's Restaurant

and need a cup of java or a bite to eat, consider stopping off at **Lonchería La Garita** near Km 29, about 22.5 km (14 miles) northeast of Todos Santos. With its large palapa roof and open-front *carrizo* eating area, it looks much like any other Baja highway truck stop. But the family operating La Garita seems to have a special flair for preparing humble but high-quality fare. The fresh ranch cheese and the bean or *machaca* burritos with *panela* are superb here, as are *empanadas* filled with slightly sweet, cinnamon-spiced *frijolitos*. Yet another major draw is the coffee, made from fresh-roasted and fresh-ground Chiapas beans; many people buy bags of coffee beans from La Garita. Open daily 6 A.M.–6 P.M.

Moderate Restaurants

Popular among locals as well as visitors for fresh seafood, tasty Mexican dishes, and cold beer served in frosted mugs is **Restaurant Las Fuentes,** at Calles Degollado and Colegio Militar, tel. 612/145-0257. The house specialty is *pescado empapelado,* fish baked in paper with tomatoes, mild chilies, and various other condiments, and the *chiles rellenos* are the best. This restaurant also offers a full bar. You can dine in the well-lighted indoor seating area or out on the palapa-roofed patio, surrounded by three fountains, bougainvillea, and palms. Service is friendly and efficient. Open Tues.–Sun. 7:30 A.M.–9:30 P.M. Visa and MasterCard are accepted here.

If you're in the mood for some great gringo food served in a congenial atmosphere, **Restaurante Santanas,** in Hotel Todos Santos on the plaza, tel. 612/145-0009, is worth checking out. It specializes in delicious pizzas, calzones, sandwiches, Mexican dishes, and salads. Wednesday is all-you-can-eat pizza night and on Friday evening they feature live music. They offer free Internet service at the bar for customers. Open Wed.–Sun. 5–9 P.M. Visa and MasterCard are accepted.

Shut Up Frank's, on Degollado, tel. 612/145-0146, is a sports bar and grill offering decent American-style dinners such as steak and lobster and a variety of burgers (even veggie), as well as burritos and other Mexican fare. Open Mon.–Sat. 10 A.M.–10 P.M., Sunday 10 A.M.–8 P.M.

© HOWARD EKMAN

Fonda El Zaguán

Trópico de Cáncer Restaurant & Sports Bar, Juárez and Ocampo, tel. 612/145-0867, is open for breakfast, lunch, and dinner from 8 A.M.–10 P.M. Dishes include red snapper with rice and vegetables for about US$8, as well as other seafood choices, T-bone steak, sandwiches, burgers, pasta dishes, and traditional Mexican food. **Cañada del Diablo** (see Bars and Nightclubs) is a cantina offering cook-your-own T-bone-steak night with all the trimmings (US$14) on Thursday starting at 5 P.M., and fish-and-chips night (US$7) on Sunday, also starting at 5 P.M.

At the well-run **Caffé Todos Santos,** tel. 612/145-0300, housed in a historic building on Centenario between Topete and Obregón, you can choose between indoor seating on chairs painted by local artists, or outdoor dining either in the garden area out back or on the shaded veranda in front. The café offers excellent cappuccino and other coffee drinks, hot chocolate, fresh pastries, waffles, omelettes, deli sandwiches (smoked turkey is a specialty), vegetarian sandwiches, ice cream, bagels, granola, fruit shakes (made with produce from the owner's farm), fresh-baked bread, salads (try the Pacific Rim–inspired "Java salad"), and other snacks. Delicious cheesy pizzas are available on Friday only from 5–9 P.M. Prices are a little high by local standards, but so is the quality of the food, and portions are large. It's open Monday 7 A.M.–2 P.M., Tues.–Sun. 7 A.M.–9 P.M.

On Av. Juárez opposite Hotel California, **Tequila Sunrise Bar & Grill** is a colorfully decorated, tourist-oriented restaurant featuring home-style Mexican food. Open daily 10 A.M.–9 P.M.

Nestled in an alley on Juárez between Topete and Hidalgo is **Fonda El Zaguán,** a popular place specializing in fish tacos, vegetarian tacos, seafood soups, organic salads, and delicious Mexican seafood dishes. Daily specials are shown on a chalkboard out in front. The smoked marlin salad is popular. Closed Sunday.

The new **Santa Fé Deli,** on the plaza next to Café Santa Fé, tel./fax 612/145-0340, is open Wednesday–Monday 8 A.M.–4 P.M. for breakfast and lunch, with a deli/gourmet market open till 6 P.M.

Café Luna, Hidalgo and Juárez, offers a choice of secluded patio dining as well as indoor seating. The international menu lists tapas such as tomato-and-goat-cheese tarts, Aztec soup, and gazpacho. Entrées include seafood dishes, pasta, chicken stuffed with goat cheese and mushrooms, filet mignon, and beef medallions with peanut sauce. Open Thurs.–Tues. 11 A.M.–3 P.M. and 6–10 P.M.

Fine Dining

Housed in a 150-year-old *casona* with 46-cm-thick (18-inch-thick) adobe walls, the atmospheric **Café Santa Fé,** on Calle Centenario off Márquez de León facing the plaza, tel./fax 612/145-0340, is still *the* place to eat and be seen during the Dec.–Apr. high tourist season. The changing, mostly Italian menu emphasizes the use of fresh, local ingredients (including organic vegetables) to produce wood-fired pizza, ravioli (a shrimp-and-lobster version is the house specialty), *pasta primavera,* lasagna, fresh seafood, octopus salad, and the occasional rabbit. Complementing the menu are espresso drinks, a full wine list, tiramisu, and fresh fruits. Choose between interior tables or courtyard dining amid palm greenery. Prices match the café's aristocratic flair. The Santa Fé is open Wednesday–Mon-

day noon–9 P.M.; the restaurant often closes in October during the town fiesta.

About two blocks away from Fonda El Zaguán on Hidalgo is **Los Adobes,** Hidalgo between Juárez and Colegio Militar, tel. 612/145-0203, www.losadobesdetodossantos.com. On the back patio of a beautifully restored adobe house, this restaurant features upscale Mexican cuisine. Menu items include *sopa Azteca,* Caesar salad, chicken fajitas, Cornish game hens, *mole poblano,* fillets, and creative desserts such as pears in *salsa de café* (pears cooked in spiced coffee with a coffee sauce) and *crepas de cajeta* (goat milk caramel crepes). A full bar, soft drinks, and American coffee round out the menu. Open Mon.–Sat. 11:30 A.M.–9 P.M., Sunday 11:30 A.M.–5 P.M. Visa and MasterCard are accepted.

The beautiful Posada La Poza on Playa La Cachora features the elegant **El Gusto!** restaurant, tel. 612/145-0400. It specializes in Mexican gourmet cuisine. The changing menu features a selection of delicious vegetarian dishes, as well as creative meat and seafood choices; all the produce used is organic and locally grown. Seating is available inside or out, with breathtaking views of the lagoon and ocean. The bar terrace and whale-watching deck are great spots for a sunset cocktail, and service is attentive. Open Fri.–Wed. 11:30 A.M.–4 P.M. for lunch, and 6–9 P.M. for dinner. Tapas are available most days on the bar terrace.

Hotel California on Calle Juá boasts the atmospheric **La Coronela** restaurant/bar. Open daily 7 A.M.–1 A.M. The international menu includes a selection of delicious tapas including pear and gorgonzola pizza, as well as pastas, seafood, steak, and Mexican dishes. Visa and MasterCard are accepted.

Groceries

The usual assortment of staples can be bought at any of several markets in town, which include **Mercadito Guluarte** (next to Hotel Guluarte), **Tienda Disconsa** (Colegio Militar), **Super Mercado Hermanos González** (Calle Pedrajo), and **Supermercado El Sol** (Calle Degollado).

The friendly **Super Mercado Hermanos González,** off Mexico 19 at the south end of town on Calle Pedrajo, has the usual *tienda* items but also caters to the northern population by stocking such items as nonfat milk, bagels, yogurt, ricotta cheese, and balsamic vinegar, to name a few. Special orders are welcome. The larger **Supermercado El Sol** also stocks gringo items and is open until 10 P.M. A second location of El Sol is located on the road to Playa La Pastora one block west of Hacienda Inn Todos Santos.

La Siempre Vive, at Calles Juárez and Márquez de León, opens around 7 A.M., which is an hour or two earlier than the others. La Siempre Vive stocks household wares and a few ranch supplies as well as groceries; the meats, cheeses, produce, and honey sold here come from local farms and ranches.

The government-subsidized **ISSSTE Tienda** (Av. Juárez between Zaragoza and Morelos) offers a changing selection of inexpensive groceries and holds a fairly well-stocked pharmacy.

Panadería Todos Santos sells *bolillos, pan dulce, coyotes, arepas,* and other Mexican-style baked goods cooked in the wood-fired oven, as well as *pan salado,* an Italian-style loaf. Open in the afternoon 2–8 P.M. or until sold out, closed Sunday, the bakery operates from an unsigned two-story brick building at the north end of Calle Rangel near Ocampo.

You can buy fresh and inexpensive corn tortillas for about US$.50 per kilo at the **Tortillería de Todos Santos** on Calle Colegio Militar between Morelos and Márquez de León. Fresh seafood can often be purchased from the *pangeros* at Punta Lobos, south of town.

All the various *tiendas* mentioned above sell purified water in *garafónes,* 20-liter returnable containers, as well as the usual smaller-sized bottles. Beer is available from any market in town or from the *depósitos* on Calle Colegio Militar adjacent to the post office; on Calle Degollado near the gas station; and also on Calle Degollado next to Super Pollo. Ice is available at most *tiendas,* as well as at the ice plant on Mexico 19 on the southern outskirts of town, and at beer *depósitos.*

Fresh tropical fruits—mangoes, guavas, figs—are most abundantly available during the July–Sept. rainy season, although certain fruits, such as papaya, are available year-round. Fresh vegetables peak in January and February.

Homemade ice cream can be found at **Paletería la Paloma,** on Colegio Militar next to Hotel Misión del Pilar, along with refreshing fresh-fruit *paletas* (popsicles). It's usually open 8 A.M.–9 P.M. You may see pushcart vendors selling the *paletas* around town. They have a second location, **Paletería la Paloma 2,** opposite the Pemex. **Los Pinos,** in the park, tel. 612/145-0353, has a good selection of American-style ice cream and *paletas* and is open 10 A.M.–10 P.M. **Nevería Rocco,** a small shop in a pink house on Hidalgo between Centenario and Juárez, sells Carnation ice cream and *paletas.*

Just north of town on the way to La Paz, along the east side of Mexico 19, vendors sell candies and pastries made from local produce. Among the goodies available are tasty *empanadas* made from mango, guava, and *cajete* (goat milk caramel); *panocha* (brown-cane-sugar cakes); lemon peel and coconut candies; wild honey; and refreshing sugarcane juice.

SPORTS AND RECREATION

Much of the outdoor recreation enjoyed in the Todos Santos area—e.g., fishing, swimming, and surfing—focuses on the coast; see Beaches earlier in this section, and Pescadero and Vicinity in the West Cape section for beach descriptions.

Fishing

Many of the same game fish commonly found from Cabo San Lucas to La Paz can be caught offshore here. If you speak Spanish, you can go to Punta Lobos and ask the fishermen there about hiring *pangas* and fishing guides. The asking price is usually around US$30 per hour with a three-hour minimum.

Surfcasting, though possible at any of the Todos Santos area beaches, is safest and easiest at Playa San Pedrito (Palm Beach), Playa San Pedro, and Playa Los Cerritos (see Pescadero and Vicinity in the West Cape section).

Whether fishing onshore or inshore, you'll need to bring your own rods, tackle, and lures. Live bait can be purchased from the local fishermen at Punta Lobos.

Whale-Watching

Although you won't see as many whales close to shore here as farther north in Bahía Magdalena (an important calving bay for the Pacific gray whale), newborn calves and their mothers do swim by on their "trial run" to the Sea of Cortez before beginning the long migration back to the Arctic Circle. The best months for spotting grays are Dec.–Apr.

With a pair of binoculars and some luck, you can stand on any beach in the vicinity and spot grays (and other whales) spouting offshore. One of the best places to see them is near the rocky ridge at Playa Las Pocitas. For a much better view from shore, climb Punta Lobos (see Beaches, earlier). *Pangeros* at Punta Lobos will take up to five passengers out to see the whales for about US$25 an hour; inquire at the beach or at any of the hotels in town.

Surfing

Most of the Pacific breaks near Todos Santos hit their peak during the northwest swell, Dec.–Mar. See Beaches earlier in this section, and Pescadero and Vicinity in the West Cape section for beach locations. Experienced surfers who paddle around the larger points at Punta Lobos and Punta San Pedro during the late summer southern swell will sometimes turn up a nice break, although the usual summer custom is to head for The Corridor between Cabo San Lucas and San José del Cabo or to lesser-known spots around the east side of the Cape (see the East Cape section).

You may see auto window stickers bearing the label Todos Santos Surfboards, but don't go looking for them—it's a small made-in-California brand. The **Todos Santos Surf Shop & Hostel** at Degollado (Mexico 19) and Rangel rents surfing equipment at Los Cerritos. The new **La Sirena Kayak y Surf Aventuras** (Calle Olachea off Degollado, tel. 612/108-0578, lasirena_ts@ hotmail.com) in town also rents surfing equipment and supplies.

Baseball

Todos Santos fields its own baseball team at the stadium on Calles Rangel and Villarino.

ENTERTAINMENT AND EVENTS

Theater

The nicely restored **Teatro Márquez de León,** Calle Legaspi at Márquez de León, hosts musical and folkloric dance performances from time to time, especially during the annual October fiesta. Before the Teatro de la Ciudad in La Paz was built, this was the only proper theater in the state of Baja California Sur.

Simple outdoor cinemas—featuring grade-C Mexican films with the usual *ranchero/narcotraficante* themes—are sometimes set up next to the soccer field near La Huerta.

Bars and Nightclubs

The only real cantina in town is **Cañada del Diablo,** a large, round, palapa-roofed place a little out of town at the northeastern end of Calle Centenario. Cañada del Diablo offers a fully stocked bar, including a few choice tequilas and free popcorn. On occasion local residents will hire a live *norteña* ensemble to play for a party here. Women and families, as well as men, patronize this bar, whose management is good about not letting the rare *borracho* get out of hand.

Shut Up Frank's, on Degollado, is an expat bar featuring satellite broadcasts of sporting events. Happy hour is Mon.–Fri. 4–6 P.M. (see Food, earlier in this section).

Trópico de Cáncer Restaurant & Sports Bar, (see Food) is the newest sports bar in town. They have satellite TVs tuned exclusively to sports, plus free Internet access.

Disco Bar La Iguana, in a historic building on the corner of Zaragoza and Rangel, is a sports bar and disco with a few pool tables. It opens in the afternoon; hours vary.

The local **Cueva de los Leones** (Lion's Club) holds Saturday-evening dances at its hall opposite Hotel California. A small cover charge is collected at the door; there's an additional fee to sit at a table.

Restaurante Santanas, the popular restaurant behind Hotel Todos Santos on the plaza, often features live music on Friday evening, usually performed by local expats, and Latin jazz and salsa on Sunday night.

La Copa is a new upscale wine bar with a cozy romantic ambience. Located in the gardens of the Todos Santos Inn, the bar is open Tuesday –Saturday 5–9 P.M. The entrance is on Calle Topete.

The bar in Hotel California's uniquely decorated **La Coronela** is frequented by local expats as well as the hotel's guests, and is a fun place to have a few drinks. Live music is offered on Saturday evenings.

Events

Fiesta Todos Santos is held around the feast day of the town's patron saint, Virgen del Pilar, on October 12. For four days beginning the second Saturday of the month, residents enjoy dances, soccer and basketball games, fishing tournaments, cockfights, horse races, theater performances, amusement-park rides, and other merriment centered around the church and town plaza.

For 12 days beginning **Día de Guadalupe** (December 12), Todos Santos Catholics participate in nightly candlelight processions to the plaza church. The celebrations culminate in a midnight mass on **Christmas Eve.**

In February the **Todos Santos Fiesta del Arte** is held at various venues around town. Sponsored by local galleries, the show features sculptures, paintings, ceramics, and other visual works by local artists as well as a few out-of-towners. If the town can unite behind it, the Fiesta del Arte could become an important Cape event.

SHOPPING

Although Todos Santos hardly compares with Cabo San Lucas or San José del Cabo when it comes to variety and quantity, several interesting, high-quality shops have opened during the last few years. **Sun House,** on Calle Pedrajo just off Mexico 19, tel. 612/145-0355, sells unique home furnishings and gifts produced by local artists.

At Juárez and Hidalgo, in the Plaza de los Cardones commercial center, **El Tecolote Books/Libros,** tel. 612/145-0295, fax 612/145-0288, carries a good selection of foreign and Mexican magazines (including surf magazines), new and used paperbacks (trades welcome), maps, and a large number of hardcover and softcover books on Mexican arts, architecture, and culture, as well as over 150 books on tape for sale or rent. Movies rent for around US$2. The store also stocks art supplies such as paintbrushes and watercolor, acrylic, and oil paints. In a room in the back of El Tecolote is **Traditions,** a small shop featuring gifts, cards, and holiday decorations. In the same building, **Fénix de Todos Santos,** tel./fax 612/ 145-0666, specializes in hand-crafted Mexican art. Jewelry, rugs, leather bags, handwoven fabrics, *equipal* furniture, rugs, and decorative tinware are on display, as well as resortwear from Puerto Vallarta. In the same commercial center, **Tzintzuntzan,** (Place of the Hummingbirds) is a small shop featuring unusual handcrafted *artesanías* and ornaments from Michoacan.

Emporio Hotel California, attached to Hotel California, features an eclectic selection of decorative items, clothing, and jewelry.

In a refurbished historical building on Centenario opposite the Charles Stewart Galley is **Mangos,** tel. 612/145-0451, a beautiful gift shop featuring a nicely displayed assortment of Mexican folk art, ceramics, pewter ware, metal sculptures, silver jewelry, and beautiful Guatemalan textiles, rugs, and wood carvings. Open 10 A.M.– 5 P.M. Closed Sunday.

In the green building next to Mangos, **Arte Cactus,** Calle Centenario, tel. 612/145-0773, offers a good selection of Mexican folk art and jewelry. Next door, check out **Joyería Brilanti,** tel./fax 612/145-0726, www.brilanti.com, for good-quality silver jewelry. A second location can be found nearby on the same street, next to Perico Azul.

Nearby on Calle Topete at Centenario, opposite **Caffé Todos Santos, El Perico Azul,** tel. 612/145-0222, features women's and men's clothing made from the best of Mexican textiles, handwoven and minimally processed. The shop also offers a few clothing items from Bali and India, local crafts, jewelry, and some leather pieces. Open Mon.–Sat. 11 A.M.–5 P.M., Sunday 11 A.M.–4 P.M.

On the opposite side of Centenario, **Manos Mexicanas** carries rustic Mexican furniture and an interesting selection of decorative accessories and unique jewelry. **El Filon de Taxco,** opposite the Hotel California, features a large selection of quality silver jewelry.

Several shops in Todos Santos, all featuring typical Mexican art and crafts, seem to open in a new location with each successive season. Ones that have lasted longer than most are **La Iguana** and **Artesanías El Cardón,** palapa-roofed *artesanías* on the northwest corner of Márquez de León and Juárez opposite the church. They sell Mexican crafts, blankets, T-shirts, sterling silver, quartz, and onyx. Next door in a pink building on the corner is **Bazar Agua y Sol,** tel. 612/145-0537, featuring exclusive jewelry designs, sculptures, pottery, and paintings. Credit cards are accepted here.

> *Interested in art? The exhibit at Galería de Todos Santos features the work of artists who live in Baja California. The collection changes every six weeks or so.*

Beachwear and T-shirts, as well as imported perfumes, are sold at Sisy's Boutique on Calle Hidalgo and Colegio Militar.

If you're looking for tropical plants—bougainvillea, hibiscus, jasmine, oleander, and more—to decorate your local villa, sooner or later you'll end up at **Vivero Heriberto,** tel. 612/145-0643, a well-stocked plant nursery on Ocampo just southeast of Cuauhtémoc.

Artist Studios and Galleries

Todos Santos has a small but growing colony of expat artists, most of whom live in or near the town year-round. At last count 14 art galleries were in operation, remarkable for a town of less than 5,000 people. One of the first artist arrivals was Charles Stewart, who has a home gallery, the **Charles Stewart Gallery & Studio** (usually referred to as Stewart House) at Centenario and Obregón, tel./fax 612/145-0265, marichasart@yahoo.com, www.mexonline.com/stewart.htm. You can't miss this 1810-vintage, French-designed house smothered in foliage and enlivened by caged singing birds. Formerly of Taos, New Mexico, Stewart produces watercolor and oil paintings, wooden sculptures, and hand-carved doors; among his more recently conceived works are small *retablo*-style pieces that feature colorful

bajacaliforniano pictograph motifs on salvaged wood. His home studio is open to the public daily 10 A.M.–4 P.M.

Galería de Todos Santos, at Topete and Legaspi, tel. 612/145-0500, mplcope@prodigy .net.mx, www.galeriatodossantos.com, in the same building as the Todos Santos Inn, is owned by American artist Michael Cope and his wife Pat. The high-ceilinged gallery focuses on the work of artists who reside in Baja California. Look for pieces by Walker and Derek Buckner, Gloria Marie V., Carlos Uroz, Margaret Torres, Erick Ochoa, Anibal Angulo, Jack Smith, and Angelina Cimino. The works displayed are fine art and dimensional pieces, and the collection changes every six weeks or so. Michael and Pat have a second gallery at the site of a historic building at the corner of Centenario and Hidalgo that was formerly the town billiards hall; it once appeared in a Chris Isaak music video. This gallery features abstract pieces, while the original gallery displays more representational works of art.

La Coronela Art Gallery, in a yellow building on Legaspi between Topete and Hidalgo, features works by Mexican artists.

A brightly hued house at Juárez and Morelos contains **Galería Logan,** tel. 612/145-0151, jillogan2001@yahoo.com, www.jilllogan.com, focusing on the work of artist Jill Logan, who creates dramatically colored landscapes, still lifes, and portraits in oil and acrylic. Open Mon.–Sat. 10 A.M.–4 P.M., Sunday by appointment.

The new **Eli Alexander Fine Art,** 612/145-0274, ezra@ezrakatz.com, elialexanderfineart .com, is a gallery featuring several award-winning artists including Ezra Katz, Armand Cabrera, Lesley Rich, and John Comer. Open Tues.–Sat. 10 A.M.–6 P.M., Sunday morning by appointment. Closed in summer.

Galería/Estudio de Kathleen Gambogi, tel. 612/145-0460, Near Hotel Misión del Pilar, in a house on Hidalgo between Colegio Militar and Rangel, features colorful paintings

© HOWARD EKMAN

artist Michael Cope, Galería de Todos Santos

depicting Mexican scenes and still lifes by artist Kathleen Gambogi.

On the corner of Centenario and Obregón, **Galería La Poza,** tel. 612/145-0866, www.galerialapoza.com, displays the distinctive contemporary-style paintings of Libusche.

Galería/Studio de N. E. Hayles, Calle Cuauhtémoc, tel./fax 612/145-0183, www.mexonline.com/hayles.htm, displays unique paper-tile mosaics, multimedia art, and tables fashioned by the artist/owner. Open Mon.–Sat. 11 A.M.–4 P.M. or by appointment. **Galería Wall,** 4 Juárez, tel. 612/145-0527, catherine_wall@hotmail.com, shows Mexican-themed original oils by artist Catherine Wall. Open most afternoons.

Estudio Gabo, 7 Calle Verduzco between Olachea and Carrillo, tel. 612/145-0505, features paintings by La Paz native Gabo, whose work is inspired by Baja's colors and textures. His work can be found at Estudio Gabo and at the small **Gabo Galería** on Centenario near Topete.

Colores de México, 11 Hidalgo, tel. 612/145-0106, omommag@aol.com, opposite Los Adobes, is a photographic gallery featuring beautiful images by local residents Pat Gerhardt and Suzanne Hill. They specialize in photos of Mexico printed on watercolor paper in large format, suitable for framing.

INFORMATION AND SERVICES
Tourist Assistance
Although Todos Santos has no tourist office as such, you can usually find someone to answer your questions at El Tecolote Libros, El Centro de Mensajes, or Caffé Todos Santos. If you speak Spanish and seek information on the sierra backcountry, try La Siempre Vive at Calles Juárez and Márquez de León; this is where sierra ranchers traditionally come to supplement foods they produce at home.

The locally produced *El Calendario de Todos Santos,* issued monthly, is an excellent source of current events and short articles on regional culture; it's distributed free at El Centro de Mensajes, El Tecolote Libros, and many other establishments in town.

The Todos Santos Book, written by local residents Lee Moore and Janet Howe and available at El Tecolote Books, contains lots of information on things to see and do in the area.

M

CAPE REGION

A useful website full of up-to-date information can be found at www.todossantos-baja.com.

Money-Changing

BANORTE, Calles Juárez at Obregón, is open Monday–Friday 9 A.M.–2 P.M. To cash traveler's checks or exchange dollars here you need to show your passport. A 24-hour *cajero* (ATM) is available outside the bank. Instructions are in English and Spanish, but the machine only dispenses pesos.

Post and Telephone

The post office is on Colegio Militar (Mexico 19) between Hidalgo and Márquez de León. It's supposed to open Mon.–Fri. 8 A.M.–1 P.M. and 3–5 P.M., but the hours can be erratic.

Long-distance phone calls can be made from the rustic public telephone office at Pilar's, Colegio Militar at Zaragoza; it's open daily 7 A.M.– 7 P.M. Be wary of the private phone services that charge outrageous rates for international calls; the phone office at Pilar's is hooked into a ripoff system from the United States. Ask to use TelMex or, if you have an access number for your long-distance carrier at home, use that; of course there will be a surcharge, but that's usually cheaper than using the fly-by-night long-distance services that charge as much as US$14 a minute.

El Centro de Mensajes Todos Santos (The Message Center), Juárez in the lobby of Hotel California (Apdo. Postal 48, Todos Santos, BCS 23305), tel. 612/145-0033, fax 612/145-0288, messagecenter1@yahoo.com, can give you a quick and honest rate comparison between TelMex, AT&T, MCI, and other telephone companies. The office charges a reasonable surcharge over whichever long-distance service you choose. In addition to long-distance calling, this office offers fax, DHL courier, mail forwarding, reservations, travel agency, fax, and answering services. El Centro de Mensajes is open Mon.–Fri. 8 A.M.– 3 P.M., Saturday 8 A.M.–2 P.M.

Email and Internet Service

Two Internet cafés in town offer high-speed connections. **The Todos Santos Internet Café** at Milagro Real Estate on Juárez, tel. 612/ 145-0219, dale@milagro.cc (open Mon.–Sat.

9 A.M.–5 P.M.), has several computer stations as well as two laptop connections via Ethernet. The Internet café at Los Adobes restaurant on Hidalgo (open 9 A.M.–9 P.M.) offers laptop and Wi-Fi connections.

Laundry

The *lavandería*, tel. 612/145-0006, on Juárez in the Hotel Guluarte, offers wash-and-dry service for about US$4 per load; for US$.50 less you can do it yourself. Open daily 8 A.M.–6 P.M. Hot water and soap are available.

The new **Neptune Laundry** on Colegio Militar next to Antojitos Veracruzanos, is similar.

Film Processing

Fuji Film Processing, opposite Mercado Guluarte on Morelos, develops your film in one hour. Open Mon.–Sat. 9 A.M.–2 P.M. and 4–7 P.M., Sunday 9 A.M.–noon.

Los Pinos, in the park, also has a film-developing service, but it takes a couple of days because they send it to La Paz rather than processing it on site.

Language Schools

El Dharma de Todos Santos, info@eldharma .com, www.eldharma.com, offers dharma talks and *vipassana* meditation classes each Sunday 10–11:30 A.M. at the La Arca building on Topete. Donations are appreciated.

Ongoing one-hour **Spanish, English, and French lessons** are offered by Guillermo Bueron, g_bueron@yahoo.com, at the Centro Cultural. Guillermo uses the Berlitz total-immersion method of instruction. Group and individual classes are available at all levels.

Tai Chi Chuan instruction is available at the Centro Cultural Oct.–June, Monday and Friday for a fee of around US$6. Hours vary with the season. For more information, check the latest copy of *El Calendario*.

The Elephant Tree, on Calle Obregón between Centenario and Juárez, tel. 612/145-0299, bajaelephanttree.com, is an inner resource community center holding a variety of workshops including yoga, tarot, and writing. You can email them to request their monthly e-newsletter.

Pharmacies

Farmacia Guadalupe, tel. 612/145-0300, on Av. Juárez, can fill prescriptions any time of day or night. Other pharmacies in town include **Farmacia Hipocrates,** on Morelos opposite Mercado Guluarte, and **Farmacia Similares,** in the Hotel Misión de Pilar complex, which offers discounted generic versions of most prescriptions.

TRANSPORTATION

Seven **Águila buses** a day run between Todos Santos and La Paz to the north and Cabo San Lucas to the south. The buses to La Paz are scheduled to leave at 8 A.M., 8:30 A.M., 11:30 A.M., 1:30 P.M., 4:30 P.M., 5:30 P.M., and 7 P.M. Buses to Cabo San Lucas and San José del Cabo depart at 10 A.M., 3 P.M., 7 P.M. and 9 P.M.; three buses to Cabo San Lucas leave only at noon, 1 P.M., and 5 P.M. In everyday practice, of course, these times are never strictly adhered to. The La Paz and Cabo San Lucas bus trips take about two hours and cost about US$5 pp; a bus through to San José del Cabo costs US$7. Tickets are sold on the buses, which arrive at and depart from Colegio Militar and Zaragoza, opposite Pilar's fish taco stand/phone office (for San José del Cabo and Cabo San Lucas), or in front of Karla's Lonchería (for La Paz).

A small fleet of blue vans parked next to the park opposite Pilar's can provide **taxi service** around town for US$2 a trip. A van all the way to Los Cabos International Airport will cost around US$100; one van can hold 8–10 people with luggage. Call 612/145-0063 for more information.

CAPE REGION

Resources

Glossary

abarrotes—groceries

aduana—customs service

antojitos—literally "little whims," quick Mexican dishes like tacos and enchiladas

aparejo—burro saddle

bahía—bay

basura—trash or rubbish; a sign saying No Tire Basura means "Don't Throw Trash."

boca—literally "mouth," a geographic term describing a break in a barrier island or peninsula where sea meets lagoon

calle—street

callejón—alley or lane

cañon—canyon

cardón—*Pachycereus pringlei,* the world's tallest cactus

casa de huéspedes—guesthouse

cerro—mountain peak

cerveza—beer

charreada—Mexican-style rodeo

charro/charra—horseman/horsewoman

colectivo—van or taxi that picks up several passengers at a time for a standard per-person fare, much like a bus

correo—post office

corrida de toros—"running of the bulls" or bullfight

COTP—captain of the port, *capitanía del puerto* in Spanish

curandero—traditional healer

Diconsa—Distribuidora Conasupo, S.A., a government-subsidized food distributor

efectivo—cash payment

ejido—collectively owned agricultural lands

ensenada—cove or small bay

Fonatur—Fondo Nacional de Fomento del Turismo (National Foundation for Tourism Development)

Gral.—abbreviation for "General" (rank)

hostería—hostelry, inn

IMSS—Instituto Mexicano del Seguro Social (Mexican Social Security Institute)

INAH—Instituto Nacional de Antropología e Historia (National Institute of Anthropology and History)

indios—Mexicans of predominantly Amerindian descent; *indígenas* (indigenes) is the less common, but more politically correct, term

INEGI—Instituto Nacional de Estadística, Geografía e Informática (National Institute of Statistics, Geography, and Information)

ISSSTE—Instituto de Seguridad y Servicios Sociales para Trabajadores del Estado (Security and Social Services Institute for Government Workers)

laguna—lagoon, lake, or bay

llano—plains

lleno—full

malecón—waterfront promenade

maquiladora (maquila)—a "twin-bond" or "in-plant" manufacturing enterprise where foreign components may be imported and assembled, then exported to a foreign country, free of customs duties in each direction; now that NAFTA has been enacted, the *maquiladora* may become extinct

mariscos—literally "shellfish," but often used as a generic term for seafood

mercado—market

mochila—knapsack or backpack

mochilero—backpacker

nopalitos—strips of cooked or pickled prickly-pear cactus

palacio municipal—literally "municipal palace," equivalent to city or county hall in the United States

palapa—thatched, umbrellalike shade shelter or roof

PAN—Partido Acción Nacional

panadería—bakery

parrada—bus stop

Pemex—Petroleos Mexicanos (Mexican Petroleum)

pensión—boardinghouse

playa—beach

plazuela—smaller plaza

PRD—Partido Revolucionario Democrático

pre-Cortesian—a reference to Mexican history before the arrival of Spanish conquistador Hernán Cortés, i.e., before 1518; other terms with the same meaning include pre-Columbian (before Columbus's arrival) and pre-Hispanic (before the arrival of the Spanish)

PRI—Partido Revolucionario Institucional

punta—point

ramal—branch road

rancheria—a collection of small ranching households, most often inhabited by *indios*

ranchito—small ranch

SECTUR—Secretaría de Turismo (Secretariat of Tourism)

SEDESOL—Secretaría de Desarrollo Social (Secretariat of Social Development)

SEMARNAT—Secretaría de Medio Ambiente y Recursos Naturales (Secretariat of the Environment and Natural Resources)

tienda—store

tinaja—pool or spring

topes—speed bumps

ultramarinos—minimarket/delicatessen

Glossary

Abbreviations

a/c—air-conditioned, air conditioning
ATV—all-terrain vehicle
Av.—Avenida
BCN—the state of Baja California Norte, more properly called just Baja California
BCS—the state of Baja California Sur
BCD—buoyancy compensation device
Blvd.—Boulevard
C—Celsius
Calz.—Calzada
cm—centimeter(s)
Col.—Colonia (neighborhood)
COTP—captain of the port
d—double occupancy
F—Fahrenheit
hp—horsepower
kg—kilogram(s)

km—kilometer(s)
kph—kilometers per hour
mph—miles per hour
nte.—*norte* (north)
ote.—*oriente* (east)
PADI—Professional Association of Dive Instructors
pp—per person
pte.—*poniente* (west)
q—quadruple occupancy
RV—recreational vehicle
s—single occupancy
s/n—*sin número* ("without number," used for street addresses without building numbers)
t—triple occupancy
tel.—telephone number

Spanish Phrasebook

Your Mexico adventure will be more fun if you use a little Spanish. Mexican folks, although they may smile at your funny accent, will appreciate your halting efforts to break the ice and transform yourself from a foreigner to a potential friend.

Spanish commonly uses 30 letters—the familiar English 26, plus four straightforward additions: ch, ll, ñ, and rr, which are explained in "Consonants," below.

Pronunciation

Once you learn them, Spanish pronunciation rules—in contrast to English—don't change. Spanish vowels generally sound softer than in English. (Note: The capitalized syllables below receive stronger accents.)

Vowels

a — like ah, as in "hah": *agua* AH-gooah (water), *pan* PAHN (bread), and *casa* CAH-sah (house)

e — like ay, as in "may:" *mesa* MAY-sah (table), *tela* TAY-lah (cloth), and *de* DAY (of, from)

i — like ee, as in "need": *diez* dee-AYZ (ten), *comida* ko-MEE-dah (meal), and *fin* FEEN (end)

o — like oh, as in "go": *peso* PAY-soh (weight), *ocho* OH-choh (eight), and *poco* POH-koh (a bit)

u — like oo, as in "cool": *uno* OO-noh (one), *cuarto* KOOAHR-toh (room), and *usted* oos-TAYD (you); when it follows a "q" the **u** is silent; when it follows an "h" or has an umlaut, it's pronounced like "w"

Consonants

b, d, f, k, l, m, n, p, q, s, t, v, w, x, y, z, and **ch** — pronounced almost as in English; **h** occurs, but is silent—not pronounced at all.

c — like k as in "keep": *cuarto* KOOAR-toh (room), Tepic tay-PEEK (capital of Nayarit state); when it precedes "e" or "i," pronounce **c** like s, as in "sit": *cerveza* sayr-VAY-sah (beer), *encima* ayn-SEE-mah (atop).

g — like g as in "gift" when it precedes "a," "o," "u," or a consonant: *gato* GAH-toh (cat), *hago* AH-goh (I do, make); otherwise, pronounce **g** like h as in "hat": *giro* HEE-roh (money order), *gente* HAYN-tay (people)

j — like h, as in "has": *Jueves* HOOAY-vays (Thursday), *mejor* may-HOR (better)

ll — like y, as in "yes": *toalla* toh-AH-yah (towel), *ellos* AY-yohs (they, them)

ñ — like ny, as in "canyon": *año* AH-nyo (year), *señor* SAY-nyor (Mr., sir)

r — is lightly trilled, with tongue at the roof of your mouth like a very light English d, as in "ready": *pero* PAY-doh (but), *tres* TDAYS (three), *cuatro* KOOAH-tdoh (four).

rr — like a Spanish r, but with much more emphasis and trill. Let your tongue flap. Practice with *burro* (donkey), *carretera* (highway), and Carrillo (proper name), then really let go with *ferrocarril* (railroad).

Note: The single small but common exception to all of the above is the pronunciation of Spanish **y** when it's being used as the Spanish word for "and," as in "Ron y Kathy." In such case, pronounce it like the English ee, as in "keep": Ron "ee" Kathy (Ron and Kathy).

Accent

The rule for accent, the relative stress given to syllables within a given word, is straightforward. If a word ends in a vowel, an n, or an s, accent the next-to-last syllable; if not, accent the last syllable.

Pronounce *gracias* GRAH-seeahs (thank you), *orden* OHR-dayn (order), and *carretera* kah-ray-TAY-rah (highway) with stress on the next-to-last syllable.

Otherwise, accent the last syllable: *venir* vay-NEER (to come), *ferrocarril* fay-roh-cah-REEL (railroad), and *edad* ay-DAHD (age).

Exceptions to the accent rule are always marked with an accent sign: (á, é, í, ó, or ú), such as *teléfono* tay-LAY-foh-noh (telephone), *jabón* hah-BON (soap), and *rápido* RAH-pee-doh (rapid).

Basic and Courteous Expressions

Most Spanish-speaking people consider formalities important. Whenever approaching anyone for information or some other reason, do not forget the appropriate salutation—good morning, good evening, etc. Standing alone, the greeting *hola* (hello) can sound brusque.

Hello. — *Hola.*
Good morning. — *Buenos días.*
Good afternoon. — *Buenas tardes.*
Good evening. — *Buenas noches.*
How are you? — *¿Cómo está usted?*
Very well, thank you. — *Muy bien, gracias.*
Okay; good. — *Bien.*
Not okay; bad. — *Mal* or *feo.*
So-so. — *Más o menos.*
And you? — *¿Y usted?*
Thank you. — *Gracias.*
Thank you very much. — *Muchas gracias.*
You're very kind. — *Muy amable.*
You're welcome. — *De nada.*
Goodbye. — *Adios.*
See you later. — *Hasta luego.*
please — *por favor*
yes — *sí*
no — *no*
I don't know. — *No sé.*
Just a moment, please. — *Momentito, por favor.*
Excuse me, please (when you're trying to get attention). — *Disculpe* or *Con permiso.*
Excuse me (when you've made a boo-boo). — *Lo siento.*
Pleased to meet you. — *Mucho gusto.*
How do you say . . . in Spanish? — *¿Cómo se dice . . . en español?*
What is your name? — *¿Cómo se llama usted?*
Do you speak English? — *¿Habla usted inglés?*
Is English spoken here? (Does anyone here speak English?) — *¿Se habla inglés?*

I don't speak Spanish well. — *No hablo bien el español.*
I don't understand. — *No entiendo.*
How do you say . . . in Spanish? — *¿Cómo se dice . . . en español?*
My name is . . . — *Me llamo . . .*
Would you like . . . — *¿Quisiera usted . . .*
Let's go to . . . — *Vamos a . . .*

Terms of Address

When in doubt, use the formal *usted* (you) as a form of address.

I — *yo*
you (formal) — *usted*
you (familiar) — *tu*
he/him — *él*
she/her — *ella*
we/us — *nosotros*
you (plural) — *ustedes*
they/them — *ellos* (all males or mixed gender); *ellas* (all females)
Mr., sir — *señor*
Mrs., madam — *señora*
miss, young lady — *señorita*
wife — *esposa*
husband — *esposo*
friend — *amigo* (male); *amiga* (female)
sweetheart — *novio* (male); *novia* (female)
son; daughter — *hijo; hija*
brother; sister — *hermano; hermana*
father; mother — *padre; madre*
grandfather; grandmother — *abuelo; abuela*

Transportation

Where is . . . ? — *¿Dónde está . . . ?*
How far is it to . . . ? — *¿A cuánto está . . . ?*
from . . . to . . . — *de . . . a . . .*
How many blocks? — *¿Cuántas cuadras?*
Where (Which) is the way to . . . ? — *¿Dónde está el camino a . . . ?*
the bus station — *la terminal de autobuses*
the bus stop — *la parada de autobuses*
Where is this bus going? — *¿Adónde va este autobús?*

the taxi stand — *la parada de taxis*
the train station — *la estación de ferrocarril*
the boat — *el barco*
the launch — *lancha; tiburonera*
the dock — *el muelle*
the airport — *el aeropuerto*
I'd like a ticket to . . . — *Quisiera un boleto a . . .*
first (second) class — *primera (segunda) clase*
roundtrip — *ida y vuelta*
reservation — *reservación*
baggage — *equipaje*
Stop here, please. — *Pare aquí, por favor.*
the entrance — *la entrada*
the exit — *la salida*
the ticket office — *la oficina de boletos*
(very) near; far — *(muy) cerca; lejos*
to; toward — *a*
by; through — *por*
from — *de*
the right — *la derecha*
the left — *la izquierda*
straight ahead — *derecho; directo*
in front — *en frente*
beside — *al lado*
behind — *atrás*
the corner — *la esquina*
the stoplight — *la semáforo*
a turn — *una vuelta*
right here — *aquí*
somewhere around here — *por acá*
right there — *allí*
somewhere around there — *por allá*
road — *el camino*
street; boulevard — *calle; bulevar*
block — @GI>la cuadra@P>
highway — *carretera*
kilometer — *kilómetro*
bridge; toll — *puente; cuota*
address — *dirección*
north; south — *norte; sur*
east; west — *oriente (este); poniente (oeste)*

Accommodations

hotel — *hotel*
Is there a room? — *¿Hay cuarto?*
May I (may we) see it? — *¿Puedo (podemos) verlo?*

What is the rate? — *¿Cuál es el precio?*
Is that your best rate? — *¿Es su mejor precio?*
Is there something cheaper? — *¿Hay algo más económico?*
a single room — *un cuarto sencillo*
a double room — *un cuarto doble*
double bed — *cama matrimonial*
twin beds — *camas gemelas*
with private bath — *con baño*
hot water — *agua caliente*
shower — *ducha*
towels — *toallas*
soap — *jabón*
toilet paper — *papel higiénico*
blanket — *frazada; manta*
sheets — *sábanas*
air-conditioned — *aire acondicionado*
fan — *abanico; ventilador*
key — *llave*
manager — *gerente*

Food

I'm hungry — *Tengo hambre.*
I'm thirsty. — *Tengo sed.*
menu — *carta; menú*
order — *orden*
glass — *vaso*
fork — *tenedor*
knife — *cuchillo*
spoon — *cuchara*
napkin — *servilleta*
soft drink — *refresco*
coffee — *café*
tea — *té*
drinking water — *agua pura; agua potable*
bottled carbonated water — *agua mineral*
bottled uncarbonated water — *agua sin gas*
beer — *cerveza*
wine — *vino*
milk — *leche*
juice — *jugo*
cream — *crema*
sugar — *azúcar*
cheese — *queso*
snack — *antojo; botana*
breakfast — *desayuno*

lunch — *almuerzo*
daily lunch special — *comida corrida* (or *el menú del día* depending on region)
dinner — *comida* (often eaten in late afternoon); *cena* (a late-night snack)
the check — *la cuenta*
eggs — *huevos*
bread — *pan*
salad — *ensalada*
fruit — *fruta*
mango — *mango*
watermelon — *sandía*
papaya — *papaya*
banana — *plátano*
apple — *manzana*
orange — *naranja*
lime — *limón*
fish — *pescado*
shellfish — *mariscos*
shrimp — *camarones*
meat (without) — *(sin) carne*
chicken — *pollo*
pork — *puerco*
beef; steak — *res; bistec*
bacon; ham — *tocino; jamón*
fried — *frito*
roasted — *asada*
barbecue; barbecued — *barbacoa; al carbón*

Shopping

money — *dinero*
money-exchange bureau — *casa de cambio*
I would like to exchange traveler's checks. — *Quisiera cambiar cheques de viajero.*
What is the exchange rate? — *¿Cuál es el tipo de cambio?*
How much is the commission? — *¿Cuánto cuesta la comisión?*
Do you accept credit cards? — *¿Aceptan tarjetas de crédito?*
money order — *giro*
How much does it cost? — *¿Cuánto cuesta?*
What is your final price? — *¿Cuál es su último precio?*
expensive —*caro*
cheap — *barato; económico*

more — *más*
less — *menos*
a little — *un poco*
too much — *demasiado*

Health

Help me please. — *Ayúdeme por favor.*
I am ill. — *Estoy enfermo.*
Call a doctor. — *Llame un doctor.*
Take me to . . . — *Lléveme a . . .*
hospital — *hospital; sanatorio*
drugstore — *farmacia*
pain — *dolor*
fever — *fiebre*
headache — *dolor de cabeza*
stomach ache — *dolor de estómago*
burn — *quemadura*
cramp — *calambre*
nausea — *náusea*
vomiting — *vomitar*
medicine — *medicina*
antibiotic — *antibiótico*
pill; tablet — *pastilla*
aspirin — *aspirina*
ointment; cream — *pomada; crema*
bandage — *venda*
cotton — *algodón*
sanitary napkins — use brand name, e.g., Kotex
birth control pills — *pastillas anticonceptivas*
contraceptive foam — *espuma anticonceptiva*
condoms — *preservativos; condones*
toothbrush — *cepilla dental*
dental floss — *hilo dental*
toothpaste — *crema dental*
dentist — *dentista*
toothache — *dolor de muelas*

Post Office and Communications

long-distance telephone — *teléfono larga distancia*
I would like to call . . . — *Quisiera llamar a . . .*
collect — *por cobrar*
station to station — *a quien contesta*
person to person — *persona a persona*
credit card — *tarjeta de crédito*

post office — *correo*
general delivery — *lista de correo*
letter — *carta*
stamp — *estampilla, timbre*
postcard — *tarjeta*
aerogram — *aerograma*
air mail — *correo aereo*
registered — *registrado*
money order — *giro*
package; box — *paquete; caja*
string; tape — *cuerda; cinta*

At the Border

border — *frontera*
customs — *aduana*
immigration — *migración*
tourist card — *tarjeta de turista*
inspection — *inspección; revisión*
passport — *pasaporte*
profession — *profesión*
marital status — *estado civil*
single — *soltero*
married; divorced — *casado; divorciado*
widowed — *viudado*
insurance — *seguros*
title — *título*
driver's license — *licencia de manejar*

At the Gas Station

gas station — *gasolinera*
gasoline — *gasolina*
unleaded — *sin plomo*
full, please — *lleno, por favor*
tire — *llanta*
tire repair shop — *vulcanizadora*
air — *aire*
water — *agua*
oil (change) — *aceite (cambio)*
grease — *grasa*
My . . . doesn't work. — *Mi . . . no sirve.*
battery — *batería*
radiator — *radiador*
alternator — *alternador*
generator — *generador*
tow truck — *grúa*

repair shop — *taller mecánico*
tune-up — *afinación*
auto parts store — *refaccionería*

Verbs

Verbs are the key to getting along in Spanish. They employ mostly predictable forms and come in three classes, which end in *ar, er,* and *ir,* respectively:

to buy — *comprar*
I buy, you (he, she, it) buys — *compro, compra*
we buy, you (they) buy — *compramos, compran*

to eat — *comer*
I eat, you (he, she, it) eats — *como, come*
we eat, you (they) eat — *comemos, comen*

to climb — *subir*
I climb, you (he, she, it) climbs — *subo, sube*
we climb, you (they) climb — *subimos, suben*

Got the idea? Here are more (with irregularities marked in **bold**).

to do or make — *hacer*
I do or make, you (he she, it) does or makes — **hago,** *hace*
we do or make, you (they) do or make — *hacemos, hacen*

to go — *ir*
I go, you (he, she, it) goes — ***voy, va***
we go, you (they) go — ***vamos, van***

to go (walk) — *andar*
to love — *amar*
to work — *trabajar*
to want — *desear, querer*
to need — *necesitar*
to read — *leer*
to write — *escribir*
to repair — *reparar*
to stop — *parar*
to get off (the bus) — *bajar*
to arrive — *llegar*

to stay (remain) — *quedar*
to stay (lodge) — *hospedar*
to leave — *salir* (regular except for **salgo,** I leave)
to look at — *mirar*
to look for — *buscar*
to give — *dar* (regular except for **doy,** I give)
to carry — *llevar*
to have — *tener* (irregular but important: **tengo, tiene,** tenemos, **tienen**)
to come — *venir* (similarly irregular: **vengo, viene,** venimos, **vienen**)

Spanish has two forms of "to be." Use *estar* when speaking of location or a temporary state of being: "I am at home." "*Estoy en casa.*" "I'm sick." "*Estoy enfermo.*" Use *ser* for a permanent state of being: "I am a doctor." "*Soy doctora.*"

Estar is regular except for **estoy,** I am. *Ser* is very irregular:

to be — *ser*
I am, you (he, she, it) is — **soy, es**
we are, you (they) are — **somos, son**

Numbers

zero — *cero*
one — *uno*
two — *dos*
three — *tres*
four — *cuatro*
five — *cinco*
six — *seis*
seven — *siete*
eight — *ocho*
nine — *nueve*
10 — *diez*
11 — *once*
12 — *doce*
13 — *trece*
14 — *catorce*
15 — *quince*
16 — *dieciseis*
17 — *diecisiete*
18 — *dieciocho*
19 — *diecinueve*

20 — *veinte*
21 — *veinte y uno* or *veintiuno*
30 — *treinta*
40 — *cuarenta*
50 — *cincuenta*
60 — *sesenta*
70 — *setenta*
80 — *ochenta*
90 — *noventa*
100 — *ciento*
101 — *ciento y uno* or *cientiuno*
200 — *doscientos*
500 — *quinientos*
1,000 — *mil*
10,000 — *diez mil*
100,000 — *cien mil*
1,000,000 — *millón*
one half — *medio*
one third — *un tercio*
one fourth — *un cuarto*

Time

What time is it? — *¿Qué hora es?*
It's one o'clock. — *Es la una.*
It's three in the afternoon. — *Son las tres de la tarde.*
It's 4 A.M. — *Son las cuatro de la mañana.*
six-thirty — *seis y media*
a quarter till eleven — *un cuarto para las once*
a quarter past five — *las cinco y cuarto*
an hour — *una hora*

Days and Months

Monday — *lunes*
Tuesday — *martes*
Wednesday — *miércoles*
Thursday — *jueves*
Friday — *viernes*
Saturday — *sábado*
Sunday — *domingo*
today — *hoy*
tomorrow — *mañana*
yesterday — *ayer*
January — *enero*
February — *febrero*

March — *marzo*
April — *abril*
May — *mayo*
June — *junio*
July — *julio*
August — *agosto*
September — *septiembre*
October — *octubre*
November — *noviembre*

December — *diciembre*
a week — *una semana*
a month — *un mes*
after — *después*
before — *antes*

(Courtesy of Bruce Whipperman, author of
Moon Handbooks Pacific Mexico.)

Suggested Reading

For information on Spanish-English dictionaries and phrasebooks, see the Language section of the Introduction.

Description and Travel

Berger, Bruce. *Almost an Island: Travels in Baja California.* Tucson: University of Arizona Press, 1998. Berger, a pianist, poet, desert aficionado, and keen observer of human behavior, surveys Baja's social landscape, with a special focus on La Paz.

Burleson, Bob, and David H. Riskind. *Backcountry Mexico: A Traveler's Guide and Phrase Book.* Austin: University of Texas Press, 1986. Part guidebook, part anthropological study covering Northern Mexico, with some relevance to Baja California backcountry travel.

Cudahy, John. *Mañanaland: Adventuring with Camera and Rifle Through California in Mexico.* New York: Duffie and Co., 1928. Provides an interesting glimpse of pre–World War II Baja, but no outstanding revelations.

Mackintosh, Graham. *Into a Desert Place.* New York: W. W. Norton & Co., 1994. A thoroughly engaging report of Mackintosh's walk around the entire coastline of Baja California over the course of two years. A classic of gringo-in-Baja travel literature for its refreshingly honest style and insights into Baja fishcamp and village life.

Miller, Max. *Land Where Time Stands Still.* New York: Dodd, Mead, and Co., 1943. A classic travelogue that chronicles Baja life during World War II, when Mexicans alternately fell prey to German and American propaganda.

Salvadori, Clement. *Motorcycle Journeys Through Baja.* North Conway, NH: Whitehorse Press, 1997. The author, a senior editor for *American Rider* and *Rider,* does an admirable job of digesting the peninsula for other motorcyclists who might want to tackle the Holy Grail of North American road trips. Contains lots of invaluable tips.

Steinbeck, John. *The Log from the Sea of Cortez.* New York: Penguin USA, Viking, 1951. This chronicle of the author's Baja research voyage with marine biologist Ed Ricketts (the inspiration for *Cannery Row* protagonist Doc) reveals Steinbeck as a bit of a scientist himself. Annotated with Latin, the book is full of insights into Pacific and Sea of Cortez marinelife as well as coastal *bajacaliforniano* society. Sprinkled throughout are expositions of Steinbeck's personal philosophy, implicit in his novels but fully articulated here. Also reveals the source for his novella *The Pearl.*

History and Culture

Crosby, Harry. *Antigua California.* Albuquerque: University of New Mexico Press, 1996. This well-researched and detailed history covers the Jesuit period in Baja, from the mission-planning stages in Sonora and Sinaloa through the expulsion from New Spain.

Francez, James Donald. *The Lost Treasures of Baja California.* Chula Vista, CA: Black Forest Press, 1996. A slim, hardbound volume containing chronicles of 19 Jesuit missions, in Spanish and English. Notable for its identification of some of the more obscure saints and iconographic elements in the mission sanctuaries and the inclusion of photos of models constructed by the author depicting missions—such as Comondú—that no longer exist.

Paz, Octavio. *The Labyrinth of Solitude: Life and Thought in Mexico.* New York: Grove/Atlantic Inc., Grove Press, 1961. Paz has no peer when it comes to expositions of the Mexican psyche, and this is his best work.

Robertson, Tomás. *Baja California and Its Missions.* Glendale, CA: La Siesta Press, 1978. Robertson was the patriarch of an old Baja California–Sinaloa family of northern European extraction as well as a patron of Baja mission restoration. His useful amateur work synthesizes Baja mission history from several sources; like its sources, the book contains a few minor contradictions and muddy areas. Out of print.

Natural History

Case, T. J., and M. L. Cody, eds. *Island Biogeography in the Sea of Cortez.* Berkeley: University of California Press, 1983. A collection of essays on the geography and wildlife of various Cortez islands.

Edwards, Ernest Preston. *The Birds of Mexico and Adjacent Areas.* Austin: University of Texas Press, 1998. A field guide to birds of Mexico, Belize, Guatemala, and El Salvador, with excellent illustrations and detailed descriptions for easy identification of all of Mexico's regular species.

Krutch, Joseph Wood. *The Forgotten Peninsula: A Naturalist in Baja California.* Tucson: University of Arizona Press, 1986 (reprint from 1961). Combines natural history and a curmudgeonly travelogue style to paint a romantic portrait of pre–Transpeninsular Highway Baja.

Leatherwood, S., and R. R. Reeves. *The Sierra Club Handbook of Whales and Dolphins.* San Francisco: Sierra Club Books, 1983. A useful field guide for identifying cetaceans in Baja seas.

Nickerson, Roy. *The Friendly Whales: A Whalewatcher's Guide to the Gray Whales of Baja California.* San Francisco: Chronicle Books, 1987. A light study, with photographs, of the friendly-whale phenomenon in Laguna San Ignacio, where gray whales often initiate contact with humans.

Peterson, R. T., and E. L. Chaliff. *A Field Guide to Mexican Birds.* Boston: Houghton Mifflin Co., 1973. Although it may be a little weak on birds found in Baja, this is still one of the best handbooks for identifying Mexican bird life.

Roberts, Norman C. *Baja California Plant Field Guide.* Natural History Publishing Co., 1989. Contains concise descriptions of over 550 species of Baja flora, more than half illustrated by color photos.

Scammon, Charles Melville. *The Marine Mammals of the Northwestern Coast of America.* Mineola, NY: Dover Publications reprint, 1968. Originally published in the 19th century by the whaler who almost brought about the gray whale's complete demise, this is *the* classic, pioneering work on Pacific cetaceans, including the gray whale.

Wiggins, Ira L. *Flora of Baja California.* Stanford, CA: Stanford University Press, 1980. This weighty work, with listings of over 2,900 species, is a must for the serious botanist. But for the average layperson with an interest in Baja vegetation, Norman Roberts's *Baja California Plant Field Guide* (listed earlier) will more than suffice.

Zwinger, Ann Raymond. *A Desert Country Near the Sea.* New York: Penguin USA, Truman M. Talley Books, 1983. A poetic collection of essays centered around Baja natural history (including a rare passage on the Sierra de La Laguna), with sketches by the author and an appendix with Latin names for flora and fauna.

Sports and Recreation

Fons, Valerie. *Keep It Moving: Baja by Canoe.* Seattle: The Mountaineers, 1986. Well-written account of a canoe trip along the Baja California coastline; recommended reading for sea kayakers as well as canoeists.

Kelly, Neil, and Gene Kira. *The Baja Catch.* Valley Center, CA: Apples and Oranges, 1997. The latest version of this fishing guide pushes it firmly to the top of the heap. Contains extensive discussions of lures and tackle, expert fishing techniques, and detailed directions to productive fisheries, plus numerous maps.

Lehman, Charles. *Desert Survival Handbook.* Phoenix: Primer Publishers, 1990. A no-nonsense guide to desert-survival techniques; should be included in every pilot's or coastal navigator's kit.

Romano-Lax, Andromeda. *Sea Kayaking in Baja.* Berkeley, CA: Wilderness Press, 1993. This inspiring 153-page guide to Baja kayaking contains 15 one- to five-day paddling routes along the Baja coastline, plus many helpful hints on kayak camping. Each route is accompanied by a map; although these maps are too sketchy to be used for navigational purposes, a list of Mexican topographic map numbers is provided so that readers can go out and obtain more-accurate material.

Tsegeletos, George. *Under the Sea of Cortez (Early Underwater Exploration and Spearfishing).* Chapel Hill, NC: Professional Press, 1998. Early, in this case, means starting in 1962, and the accounts make for fascinating, if a bit sorrowful (knowing how much marinelife has been lost in just 40 years), reading.

Williams, Jack. *Baja Boater's Guide, Vols. I and II.* Sausalito, CA: H.J. Williams Publications, 1988 (Vol. I) and 1996 (Vol. II). These ambitious guides, one each on the Pacific Ocean and the Sea of Cortez, contain useful aerial photos and sketch maps of Baja's continental islands and coastline.

Wong, Bonnie. *Bicycling Baja.* El Cajon, CA: Sunbelt Publications, 1988. Written by an experienced leader of Baja cycling tours, this book includes helpful suggestions on trip preparation, equipment, and riding techniques, as well as road logs for 17 different cycling routes throughout the peninsula.

Wyatt, Mike. *The Basic Essentials of Sea Kayaking.* San Francisco: ICS Books, 1990. A good introduction to sea kayaking, with tips on buying gear, paddling techniques, safety, and kayak loading.

Real Estate

Combs-Ramirez, Ginger. *The Gringo's Investment Guide.* Monmex Publishing, 1994. Succinct but complete advice on buying and selling real estate in Mexico.

Peyton, Dennis John. *How to Buy Real Estate in Mexico.* San Diego: Law Mexico Publishing, 1994. The most thorough and in-depth reference available in English on buying Mexican property. Anyone considering real estate investments in Mexico should read this book before making any decisions.

Internet Resources

Baja.com
www.baja.com
This is arguably the best-looking and hippest Baja site on the Web.

Baja Nomad
www.bajanomad.com
Still the best all-around Baja site for hard information that doesn't appear to have been paid for, with more nitty-gritty information than any rival. Great links page, copious information on hotels and restaurants, plus continually updated Baja news and essays.

Baja Online
www.sandiego-online.com/baja
A well-designed and well-written section of *San Diego* magazine's website, for the most part devoted to dining, shopping, and entertainment in Tijuana, Rosarito, and Ensenada only.

Baja Travel Guide
www.bajatravel.com
A complete online travel guide covering all of Baja. It also features telephone listings, maps, a free Web-based translation service, and a calendar of events.

Baja-Web
www.baja-web.com
Lots of information on accommodations, transportation, and other practical detail in list form, but slanted toward larger cities

CNN Weather
cnn.com/WEATHER/cities/mexico.html
One of the fastest-loading and best all-round weather sites, with info listed by city.

Cruise the Sea of Cortez
www.cruisecortez.com
As the title indicates, this is a site for people who sail or who would like to sail the Cortez.

Although it was a year out of date when we last visited, the site nonetheless carries valuable info and links to other sailing-oriented sites.

Eco Travels in Latin America
www.planeta.com
A rich site with information on officially protected areas in Mexico and elsewhere in Latin America, as well as regularly updated files on ecologically related news.

Flying Samaritans
www.geocities.com/Heartland/Plains/1134
Flying Samaritans is a volunteer organization comprising doctors, dentists, nurses, translators, pilots, and support personnel who fly to clinics in Baja in private aircraft—all time and materials are donated.

Information Pages on Baja California, Mexico
math.ucr.edu/~ftm/baja.html
A homegrown, one-man website with decent Baja links. The road conditions section would be useful if your upcoming transpeninsular drive happens to coincide with one of the author's recent updates—reportedly every three or four months.

In Search of the Blue Agave
www.ianchadwick.com/tequila
An excellent website devoted to tequila connoisseurship.

Instituto Nacional de Estadística, Geografía e Informática
ags.inegi.gob.mx
This Mexican government agency publishes statistics on population and economics for all of Mexico, as well as complete topographical maps. The maps aren't available online yet, but many stats are.

Mexican Embassy in Washington, D.C.
207.224.13.65/english/
This is the place to come for the latest Mexican visa information.

Mexico Online
www.mexonline.com/baja.htm
Carries much general information on Mexico in many categories, plus hot links to other sites. Some Baja information as well.

Moon Handbooks
www.moon.com
Moon's website contains occasional excerpts from this book and other Moon titles, as well as ordering information.

Mr.News.Mx
www.mrnewsmx.com/default.asp
A news digest for Mexico news in English from many sources.

NaftaNet
www.nafta-sec-alena.org
Information pertinent to the North American Free Trade Agreement.

Olsen Currency Converter
www.oanda.com/converter/travel
For fast quotes on exchange rates for all international currencies, including the Mexican peso. Print out a "cheat sheet" to make easy conversions without having to do any math.

Quick Aid
www.quickaid.com
International airport information and flight schedules.

Rock en Español
www.rockeros.com
A compendium of links and commentary on *rock en español, la nueva onda, guacarock,* and other new rock movements in 13 countries in Latin America, plus the United States and Spain. MP3 downloads available.

Sanborns Mexican Insurance
www.sanbornsinsurance.com
Contains ample information on Mexican vehicle insurance plus tips on driving in Mexico.

Secretaría de Turismo (SECTUR)
www.mexico-travel.com
Home page for Mexico's Secretariat of Tourism, organized by region and state. Unfortunately there is very little information on Baja California—north or south—and Baja is not even mentioned in the regional chapters.

SEMARNAT
www.semarnat.gob.mx
Website for the Mexican government agency concerned with environmental matters.

SEMATUR
www.ferrysematur.com.mx/
Ferry schedules, passenger fares, and reservation information.

U.S. Embassy
www.usembassy-mexico.gov
Contains the home page for the U.S. Embassy in Mexico City, with information on consular services to U.S. citizens, as well as State Department warnings.

Internet Providers in Baja
Cabonet
www.cabonet.net.mx

Electrónica Cromwell
www.cromwell.com.mx

Prodigy
www.prodigy.net.mx

Index

Diving/Snorkeling

general discussion: 82–85
Bahía de los Ángeles: 304
Cabo Pulmo: 433
Cabo San Lucas: 483–484
The Corridor: 459
Ensenada: 220–221
Isla Espíritu Santo: 407
Islas Los Coronados: 186
La Paz: 402, 403
Loreto: 363–364
Mulegé: 342–343
San Quintín: 250–251

M

Index

Sportfishing

Acknowledgments

For their invaluable assistance with the update of *Moon Handbooks Baja,* I'd like to thank Jane Ames, Ken Bradley, California Baja Rent-A-Car, Celia DeVault, Coco Cabañas, Howard Ekman, E.S. Hanson, Hugh Kramer, Nigel & Shelly Matthews, and William Stawicki. Very special thanks to Lynne Cummings, who updated the West Cape section of the Cape Region chapter, helped with general research, and helped prepare the manuscript for editing.

U.S. ~ Metric Conversion

1 inch	=	2.54 centimeters (cm)
1 foot	=	.304 meters (m)
1 yard	=	0.914 meters
1 mile	=	1.6093 kilometers (km)
1 km	=	.6214 miles
1 fathom	=	1.8288 m
1 chain	=	20.1168 m
1 furlong	=	201.168 m
1 acre	=	.4047 hectares
1 sq km	=	100 hectares
1 sq mile	=	2.59 square km
1 ounce	=	28.35 grams
1 pound	=	.4536 kilograms
1 short ton	=	.90718 metric ton
1 short ton	=	2000 pounds
1 long ton	=	1.016 metric tons
1 long ton	=	2240 pounds
1 metric ton	=	1000 kilograms
1 quart	=	.94635 liters
1 US gallon	=	3.7854 liters
1 Imperial gallon	=	4.5459 liters
1 nautical mile	=	1.852 km

To compute Celsius temperatures, subtract 32 from Fahrenheit and divide by 1.8. To go the other way, multiply Celsius by 1.8 and add 32.

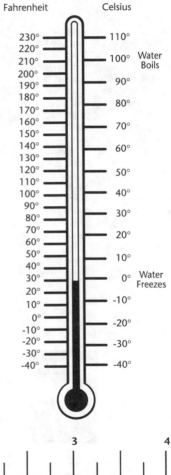

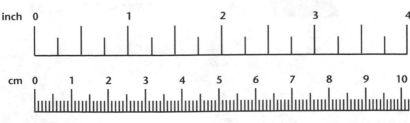

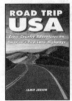

Keeping Current

Although we strive to produce the most up-to-date guidebook humanly possible, change is unavoidable. Between the time this book goes to print and the moment you read it, a handful of the businesses noted in these pages will undoubtedly change prices, move, or even close their doors forever. Other worthy attractions will open for the first time. If you have a favorite gem you'd like to see included in the next edition, or see anything that needs updating, clarification, or correction, please drop us a line. Send your comments via email to atpfeedback@avalonpub.com, or use the address below.

Moon Handbooks Baja
Avalon Travel Publishing
1400 65th Street, Suite 250
Emeryville, CA 94608, USA
www.moon.com

Editor: Marisa Solís, Christopher Jones
Series Manager: Kevin McLain
Acquisitions Editor: Rebecca K. Browning
Copy Editor: Candace English
Graphics Coordinator: Deb Dutcher
Production Coordinator: Darren Alessi
Cover Designer: Kari Gim
Interior Designers: Amber Pirker,
  Alvaro Villanueva, Kelly Pendragon
Map Editor: Naomi Adler Dancis
Cartographers: Kat Kalamaras,
  Mike Morgenfeld
Indexers: Peter Brigaitis and Marie S. Nuchols

ISBN: 1-56691-606-2
ISSN: 1098-6685

Printing History
1st Edition—1992
6th Edition—October 2004
5 4 3

Avalon Travel Publishing
An Imprint of
Avalon Publishing Group, Inc.

AVALON
publishing group incorporated

Some photos and illustrations are used by permission and are the property of the original copyright owners.

Front cover photo: Sea of Cortez, Mexico, © Steve Bly
Table of contents photos: © Joe Cummings

Printed in the United States by Worzalla